The New Penguin Dictionary of Computing

Dick Pountain was born in 1945 in Chesterfield, Derbyshire, and educated at Chesterfield Grammar School and Imperial College, London (BSc Hons Chemistry). He was a columnist and book/film/music reviewer for underground magazines *Frendz*, *Ink* and *Oz* from 1968 to 1972. Co-founder of Bunch Books (now Dennis Publishing) with Felix Dennis, he was Production Director at the company from 1972 to 1981. Since then he has worked on a number of leading computer magazines, including *Personal Computer World* (Managing Editor, 1981–3), *Soft* (1983) and *Byte* (Contributing Editor, 1983–98). He is currently Editor of *Real World* and columnist on *PC Pro* magazine, as well as non-executive director of Dennis Publishing. His previous books include *Object Oriented Forth* (1983), *A Tutorial Introduction to Concurrent Programming in Occam* (1987) and *Cool Rules: Anatomy of an Attitude* with David Robins (2000). Dick Pountain lives in Camden Town, London.

The New Penguin Dictionary of Computing

Dick Pountain

PENGUIN BOOKS

PENGUIN BOOKS

Penguin Books Ltd, 80 Strand, London WC2R ORL, England
Penguin Putnam Inc, 375 Hudson Street, New York, New York 10014, USA
Penguin Books Australia Ltd, 250 Camberwell Road, Camberwell, Victoria 3124, Australia
Penguin Books Canada Ltd, 10 Alcorn Avenue, Toronto, Ontario, Canada M4V 3B2
Penguin Books India (P) Ltd, 11, Community Centre, Panchsheel Park, New Delhi – 110 017, India
Penguin Books (NZ) Ltd, Cnr Rosedale and Airborne Roads, Albany, Auckland, New Zealand
Penguin Books (South Africa) (Pty) Ltd, 24 Sturdee Avenue, Rosebank 2196, South Africa

Penguin Books Ltd, Registered Offices: 80 Strand, London WC2R ORL, England
www.penguin.com

First published 2001
1

Typeset in TheAntiquaB and TheSans
Edited and typeset by Book Creation Services Ltd, London
Printed in England by Clays Ltd, St Ives plc

Contents

Acknowledgements

I would like to thank Jonathon Green and Nigel Wilcockson for encouraging me to undertake this dictionary in the first place, David Wilcockson for his indefatigable tailoring of the authoring software Librios to speed the task, and the editing team at Book Creation Services who rooted out most of my mistakes: the mistakes that remain are of course mine alone. I must also thank the following friends and colleagues who offered advice and assistance that in various ways advanced the compilation of the book: all my ex-colleagues at *Byte Magazine* (1983-98) whose combined knowledge provided an invaluable corpus; my current colleagues in the Real World section of *PC Pro* magazine, whose dispatches from the front help to keep me in touch; in particular Jon Honeyball, Paul Ockenden, Dave Jewell, Davey Winder, Steve Cassidy, DJ Walker-Morgan and Derek Cohen for unstintingly submitting to my brain-picking phone calls. Also my late friend and arbiter of programming taste, Nick Walsh.

Guide to the Dictionary

The text of the dictionary has been arranged so as to require a minimum of additional explanation. The structure of entries is as simple as possible, namely a headword in **bold-face** followed by the text of its definition. Many of the definitions are fuller than is usual in less specialist dictionaries, somewhere between a conventional dictionary and an encyclopedia in length: the principle adopted is that the most fundamental and general concepts are treated at greatest length, while highly technical or esoteric topics are dealt with more tersely and with a greater density of cross-reference.

Format

There is no special format for pronunciation, part of speech, derivation or usage in this dictionary, these matters being dealt with as appropriate in the main text. Cross-references are printed in SMALL CAPITALS and *italics* are used for emphasis.

Acronyms and abbreviations are listed in the dictionary itself and cross-referred to their expansions, or vice versa if the acronym is deemed to be much better known than its expansion: for instance Random Access Memory is defined under its ubiquitous acronym RAM, whereas SDLC is defined under Synchronous Data Link Control. 'See more under ...' means that a fuller definition is available under a different headword, whereas 'See also ...' refers the reader to related topics.

Collation order

The headwords are printed in alphabetical order, except that those that begin with numbers are sorted under the first letter of their spoken form: so for example 10baseT ('ten base tee') appears under 't', but 16-bit ('sixteen bit') appears under 's'.

Numbers

Unless otherwise stated all numbers in the text are decimal numbers. Hexadecimal numbers are marked by the suffix h, as in 23D1h. Binary numbers are accompanied by the word binary, as in 'binary 1011' or '1010 binary'.

Keystrokes

The names of special keys on the IBM PC-compatible keyboard are spelled in capital letters (e.g. HOME, END, PAGE UP). Two notations are employed for control sequences: when actual keystrokes typed by a user are meant the convention CTRL+B is used, whereas when the control code is meant the convention ^B is used. Sequences of typed keystrokes are surrounded by angle brackets, as in <ALT+A+L>.

Trademarks

Because of their frequent occurrence, trademarked product names are not marked with (TM) in this dictionary. Whenever a proper name such as Adobe Photoshop is mentioned, it should be assumed to be a registered trademark.

A20 gate A switch added to IBM-compatible PCs that used the 286 and later CPUs, to ensure compatibility with the original 8088 CPU of the IBM PC, which only had 20 address lines. Once Windows arrived the A20 gate created keyboard problems for some PCs, requiring a patch to the memory manager called an *A20 handler* to be installed. Modern PCs are not affected by the problem.

A20 handler See under A20 GATE.

AAL Abbreviation of ATM ADAPTATION LAYER.

abort To terminate a running computer program, or some function within a program.

ABR 1 Abbreviation of AVAILABLE BIT RATE.
2 Abbreviation of AUTOMATIC BAUD RATE DETECTION.

absolute addressing A simple ADDRESSING MODE in which the OPERAND is located at the stated memory address: e.g. ADD FF00h, FF04h might add the two numbers found at those two addresses.

abstract class In OBJECT-ORIENTED PROGRAM-MING, a class created for the sole purpose of inheriting from it, no instances of which are ever created.

abstract data type (ADT) A DATA STRUCTURE which is accompanied by a set of ACCESS FUNC-TIONS that must be employed to create objects of that type and access their contents, without the programmer being concerned with the internal layout of the data structure.

The CLASSES employed in OBJECT-ORIENTED PROGRAMMING are abstract data types whose concealment is actually enforced by the language syntax, but abstract data types may be created in conventional languages such as C, PASCAL and MODULA-2 too, where the concealment is voluntary.

The purpose of an abstract data type is INFORMATION HIDING – that is, to prevent programmers from writing programs that depend on intimate details of the type's implementation that might be changed in future and could cause such programs to cease working correctly. For example, an abstract data type that implements a STACK would hide from programmers the exact way the stack body is implemented (is it an array or is it a list?) thus preventing them from accessing it directly by making assumptions that may become invalid for future versions.

abstraction 1 The process of extracting common properties from particular examples. In programming, it typically means replacing the specific numbers and strings in a particular instance of a problem by variables and functions, so that the same program can solve many problems of the same kind.

2 A data structure or subprogram, derived by such a process of abstraction, that represents some aspect of a problem: for example a computer file can be a suitable abstraction for an accounts ledger.

Abstract Windowing Toolkit See AWT.

acc Abbreviation of ACCOUNT.

Accelerated Graphics Port (AGP) A high-speed expansion slot introduced by Intel to speed up 3D graphics operations in Pentium-based PCs. AGP provides a 32-bit wide POINT-TO-POINT data channel that enables a graphics card's processor to directly access the PC's system memory, bypassing the PCI system bus and the main CPU – bulky graphics data such as texture maps can be delivered straight to the GRAPHICS PROCESSOR at up to 533 megabits per second (Mbps). See also MMX.

accelerator 1 In the hardware world, a device that is designed to speed up the processing of a specific kind of data, for example a GRAPHICS ACCELERATOR or a FLOATING-POINT ACCELERATOR. See also COPROCESSOR.
2 In the software world, an alternative name for a KEYBOARD SHORTCUT that speeds the typing of some command sequence, especially one that is the initial letter of the corresponding menu item (such as <ALT+F+S> for Save file).

accelerator key A key stroke that acts as an abbreviation for a MENU selection, typically indicated in the menu by underlining the appropriate letter. For example under Microsoft Windows, 'F' is the accelerator key for the 'File' menu, and typing <Alt+F+O> has the same effect as selecting File|Open. So called because accelerator keys are quicker for a touch typist than leaving the keyboard to grasp the mouse. See also SHORTCUT.

Acceptable Use Policy A set of rules, for example to restrict commercial activities, often imposed by government-funded networks like ARPANET and the UK's JOINT ACADEMIC NETWORK.

acceptance test A final phase of testing for BESPOKE software, to determine whether the product satisfies its acceptance criteria, and so whether the customer will accept delivery.

Access The RELATIONAL DATABASE MANAGEMENT SYSTEM that forms part of the MICROSOFT OFFICE software suite. See more under MICROSOFT ACCESS.

access A generic term that encompasses both reading data from, and writing data to, any computer STORAGE medium or device. It is more economical to say 'when accessing...' than 'when reading, writing or verifying...' but the word is over-used and vague in computer documentation. See also ACCESS CONTROL, ACCESS PERMISSION.

access control The process or mechanism by which the use of a computing resource is restricted to a list of permitted users: see also ACCESS PERMISSION.

Access Control List A file that lists all the services available on a server, along with which users are permitted to use each service.

access function A function written to accompany an ABSTRACT DATA TYPE, whose purpose is to create INSTANCES of that type, and to inspect or change the data contained in such instances.

Accessibility Options A set of special features provided in the Microsoft Windows operating system's CONTROL PANEL, which modify the way the system works to make it easier for people with various disabilities. These features include STICKY-KEYS for those with hand injuries, keyboard sounds for those with impaired vision, visualized sound messages for those with impaired hearing, and a facility to use the numeric keypad in place of a mouse.

access permission An attribute that an operating system associates with a file to determine how that file may be used. The most commonly seen permissions are 'read-only', meaning that the file may not be modified; 'write' meaning the file may be modified; and 'execute' which means that a program file may be executed. The permissions for any file may appear differently to different users or groups of users (e.g. an administrator might be given write privileges while a casual user gets read-only access). See also PASSWORD, AUTHENTICATION.

access time The average time taken for a storage device (e.g. a hard disk or RAM chip) to read or write a piece of data, measured from its receipt of a request to delivery of the data. For a disk drive the access time includes both the head SEEK TIME and the LATENCY.

account See USER ACCOUNT.

accumulator A special REGISTER provided in most early computer and microprocessor architectures to temporarily hold the results of an arithmetic or logic operation and so avoid having to write it back into main memory. Modern processor architectures employ many general-purpose registers, any one of which can act as an accumulator, so the term has become archaic. See also REGISTER FILE, ARITHMETIC AND LOGIC UNIT.

accuracy The degree to which some measurement or computation approximates a standard or accepted value, often expressed as a percentage. It is to be distinguished from PRECISION, which states only the degree to which a value differs from similar values, without reference to any measured object.

ACID Atomic, Consistent, Isolated, Durable, the properties required of a computerized TRANSACTION system:

Atomic – either all the actions comprising the transaction are completed, or none are.
Consistent – the transaction as a whole creates a correct transformation of the database.
Isolated – each transaction runs as if there were no other transactions taking place.
Durable – once committed, the effects of a transaction survive any failure.

TRANSACTION MONITORS and TRANSACTION PROCESSING systems automatically provide these ACID semantics to programmers, by employing LOCKS, LOGS with ROLLBACK, TWO-PHASE COMMIT and other techniques.

ACK 1 In communications, a message returned by a receiver to indicate successful receipt of data. If the sender does not receive an ACK message within a certain time, or receives the NAK (Not Acknowledge) message, then it must resend the data.
2 The mnemonic for ASCII character 6, the control character 'Acknowledge'. This relates to meaning **1** as this character was used as the ACK message for early TELETYPE machines and terminals.

ACL Abbreviation of ACCESS CONTROL LIST.

ACM Abbreviation of ASSOCIATION FOR COMPUTING MACHINERY.

Acorn Computers A British computer firm founded in 1978 that started out making kit computers but rose to prominence after winning the contract to build the BBC MICROCOMPUTER in 1982.

In 1985 Acorn produced the world's first high-volume, low-cost RISC processor chip, the ARM, and used it in a family of personal computers called ARCHIMEDES, which featured a multitasking operating system and graphics performance that was ahead of its competitors in many ways. However, the Archimedes was not compatible with either the Intel PC or the Macintosh, and never achieved a sufficiently large software base to be commercially viable in the world market. The Archimedes was made PC compatible by adding an Intel CPU in the early 1990s, but Acorn ceased building computers in 1998.

The ARM chip manufacturing business was spun-off as a separate company ARM Ltd, which remains highly successful in the embedded processor sector.

Acorn RISC Machine See ARM.

acoustic coupler An early and obsolete type of MODEM that clipped onto a standard telephone handset, and used a small loudspeaker and microphone to send and receive data via sounds, rather than making a direct electrical connection to the phone line.

ACPI (Advanced Configuration and Power Interface) A power-management standard for PCs, developed jointly by Intel, Microsoft and Toshiba, and introduced with WINDOWS 98, which puts the operating system rather than the BIOS in control of the computer's power supply. ACPI allows the PC to appear to be turned off, but in fact be ready for immediate use when the power button is pressed; it also enables it to 'wake up' in response to events such as an incoming phone call or network message.

Acrobat Adobe's reader program for PORTABLE DOCUMENT FORMAT files.

acronym An abbreviation consisting of the initial letters of a phrase, as in RAM for Random Access Memory. The computer industry is reviled for employing thousands of ever-changing acronyms, but the reason for this proliferation is that computing constantly creates new concepts and devices that need to be uniquely named; no one objects to the use of acronyms in physics or chemistry, simply because these subjects impinge less on everyday life.

activation record In a programming language's RUN-TIME SYSTEM, a data structure that is dynamically created (usually on a STACK) to hold the variables of a process currently being executed. Also called a *stack frame*.

Active Desktop A feature introduced in Microsoft's WINDOWS 98 that allows the user to select a WEB PAGE to be displayed as their desktop WALLPAPER, which (given an open

INTERNET connection) will be continually updated. A typical application would be to have news bulletins or changing stock prices as wallpaper.

Active Directory The DIRECTORY SERVICE provided in Microsoft's WINDOWS 2000 operating system. Active Directory is a fully distributed service that includes a REPLICATION ability to automatically keep up to date the contents of directories dispersed throughout an organization. It can act as a METADIRECTORY, incorporating and synchronizing other directory services that are based on, for example, the LDAP protocol or Novell's NETWARE DIRECTORY SERVICE.

active-high A type of digital LOGIC in which a higher voltage (say 5 volts) signals that an event is occurring, while a low voltage (say 0 volts) represents the off or quiescent state. Contrast this with *active-low* logic in which the interpretation of the voltages is reversed. See also EDGE-TRIGGERED.

active-low See under ACTIVE-HIGH.

active matrix display A type of LIQUID CRYSTAL DISPLAY in which every pixel on the screen has its own electronic storage element (i.e. one or more transistors) printed as a thin film on the back of the glass. Compare this with a PASSIVE MATRIX DISPLAY (or dual scan display), where all the transistors are deployed along the edges of the screen and a grid of intersecting wires switches the pixels. Active matrix displays offer faster REFRESH RATES and sharper resolution, but are more costly to manufacture.

active object In an object-oriented program, an object that has been allocated its own THREAD, so that it can execute methods concurrently with other objects.

active port A PORT in a network SWITCH or HUB through which communication is currently taking place.

Active Server Pages (ASP) A web technology invented by Microsoft which enables program code and ACTIVEX objects to be embedded into web pages to achieve effects, such as pull-down lists or tables of database records, not possible in HTML alone. ASP works only with Microsoft's Internet Information Server, and permits scripts to be written in a variety of languages. When a request is made for the URL of their containing page, such scripts run on the server (rather than in the browser as Java applets do) and dynamically generate a page of ordinary HTML that is returned to the requesting client.

Microsoft's own WINDOWS SCRIPTING HOST and various third-party add-ons enable ASP scripts to be written in a wide variety of languages including VISUAL BASIC Script (VBScript), JScript, PERL and REXX. See also JAVA SERVER PAGES, SERVLET.

Active Template Library (ATL) A library of C++ TEMPLATES for creating ACTIVEX controls and other COM objects, supplied by Microsoft as an adjunct to the MICROSOFT FOUNDATION CLASSES library. ATL templates implement all the basic COM INTERFACES and handle REFERENCE COUNTING, while two Visual C++ WIZARDS, called the ATL COM AppWizard and the ATL Object Wizard, interactively generate the skeleton code for an object.

ActiveX A format developed by the Microsoft Corporation for implementing object-oriented software components. ActiveX controls are prefabricated components based on Microsoft's COM object model, which can be employed to create new applications with little or no programming, for example by simply dragging-and-dropping them into a document, or by downloading them into a browser from a web site.

The VISUAL BASIC programming language works by dragging different ActiveX controls onto a blank container, and then writing a minimal amount of code to connect them together. There is a large market in such prefabricated controls, many written by vendors other than Microsoft, with spreadsheets, text editors, picture viewers, sound players and many other functions available ready to run.

ActiveX Database Objects (ADO) A Microsoft OBJECT LIBRARY that provides extensible, object-oriented access to data held in a variety of formats. It is intended to supplant the firm's earlier database access libraries DATA ACCESS OBJECTS and RDO, and is employed by both MICROSOFT TRANSACTION SERVER and INTERNET INFORMATION SERVER as their main means of retrieving data from both local and remote databases. See also ODBC, UDA.

actual parameter A value supplied as a PARAMETER in a call to a subprogram, replacing one of the FORMAL PARAMETERS.

actuator An electrical device that turns an electrical current into motion, for example to close a door or turn a valve.

acyclic graph A GRAPH that contains no cycles; that is, whenever there is a path from A to B, there is no path back from B to A.

Ada A programming language developed on behalf of the US Department of Defense, whose use is mandatory for military programming projects. The language is named after Ada Lovelace, sister of Lord Byron, credited with being the first programmer for her work with Charles BABBAGE.

Ada is a block-structured language with many similarities to PASCAL. It includes facilities for real-time programming and concurrency, and supports run-time error handling which makes it suitable for programming embedded control systems such as missile guidance. Ada also emphasizes TYPE CHECKING, DATA ABSTRACTION and ENCAPSULATION to assist with large-scale cooperative software engineering projects.

ADABAS A RELATIONAL DATABASE system developed by the German company SOFTWARE AG for IBM mainframes, but now ported to Unix and other systems.

Ada Programming Support Environment A program development environment for the ADA language that includes text editors, debuggers, a version control system and a repository for storing and retrieving reusable PACKAGES.

adapter, adaptor A general term for any hardware device (typically built as a plug-in EXPANSION BOARD) that exists solely to alter the function of some other device, or to enable two other devices to communicate.

adapter card See EXPANSION BOARD.

Adaptive Pulse Code Modulation (ADPCM) A class of algorithms used for compressing digital audio data, which work by storing the differences between one SAMPLE and the next: for example with 16-bit samples, only a 4-bit difference might be stored, thus achieving 4:1 compression ratio. The popular WAV sound file format employs variants of the ADPCM scheme.

adaptive routing A network routing system that can automatically reconfigure itself when traffic patterns, or the network's TOPOLOGY, change.

ADC Abbreviation of ANALOGUE-TO-DIGITAL CONVERTER.

adder A logic circuit that adds pairs of numbers; employed in the ARITHMETIC AND LOGIC UNIT of all computers.

add-on, add-in Any hardware device or software module that can be installed by an ordinary user (rather than a programmer or engineer) to enhance a computer or application program.

address A unique identifier assigned to distinguish different devices on a network or the location of data in a computer's MEMORY. As in the everyday use of the word (e.g. the address of a house in a street), uniqueness is of the essence, and precautions are taken to avoid different objects sharing the same address (see ADDRESS SPACE).

Addresses are always ultimately represented as numbers, for ease of traversal and sorting, but they are often given an alternative textual form to make them more memorable to people, as for example with an EMAIL ADDRESS. Also used as a verb to mean the action of selecting a device or locating a piece of data by its address.

addressable Capable of being distinguished by a unique ADDRESS value. Used mostly of network devices, where it contrasts with the situation where one can only broadcast a command to all devices rather than address them individually.

address aging A parameter that controls how long a network switch or ROUTER will store learned IP addresses in its address table before discarding them for new ones.

address bus The BUS upon which a computer's CENTRAL PROCESSING UNIT issues addresses to the memory system in order to read or write a word of data. In some system architectures, the data word itself may be transported via a separate DATA BUS.

address generation An operation that calculates the address of the next instruction or piece of data required, performed within the CENTRAL PROCESSING UNIT of a computer.

addressing mode A particular method of specifying the OPERAND for a MACHINE CODE instruction for some computer processors.

The simplest possible addressing modes are: REGISTER ADDRESSING, in which the operand is actually present in the specified register; IMMEDIATE ADDRESSING, where the operand value is supplied as part of the instruction, and ABSOLUTE ADDRESSING, also called direct addressing, where the memory address of the operand is given as part of the instruction.

Other commonly supported modes are: REGISTER INDIRECT, where the operand is to be found at the address contained in a specified register; and INDEXED ADDRESSING, where the operand address is calculated by adding an offset to a BASE ADDRESS contained in a register. There are dozens, if not hundreds, of possible addressing modes, and different processors vary widely in the number and kind that they support.

address line One of the parallel conductors that make up a processor's address bus, and by extension the data bit that corresponds to that particular conductor: used as in 'we decode only the lower 17 address lines'.

address mapping The act of converting an ADDRESS from one ADDRESS SPACE into another, for example from a LOGICAL ADDRESS to a PHYSICAL ADDRESS.

address space 1 Most generally, the range of values within which an ADDRESS has meaning and can be guaranteed to be unique. In everyday life, for example, each street constitutes a separate address space so that the same number, 12, might be used to describe different houses in Acacia Avenue and Laburnum Grove.

2 The range of contiguous memory addresses allocated to a single TASK or PROCESS.

3 The full range of PHYSICAL addresses that a computer's processor can access, which is determined directly by the width of the processor's ADDRESS BUS: a 16-bit bus can address 65,536 words (2^{16}) while a 32-bit bus can address 4,294,967,296 words (2^{32}), which

would correspond to 4 gigabytes if the machine uses BYTE-ADDRESSING.

address translation The act of converting the ADDRESS of some resource in one ADDRESS SPACE into an equivalent address in a different address space. An example is the LOGICAL-TO-PHYSICAL TRANSLATION performed by a computer processor's MEMORY MANAGEMENT UNIT to convert virtual addresses into actual locations in RANDOM ACCESS MEMORY.

An example from a completely different sphere is the NAT scheme used to convert between the internal IP ADDRESSES used by devices in a LOCAL AREA NETWORK and external Internet addresses, to enable the LAN users to send email and browse the Web.

See also VIRTUAL MEMORY, TRANSLATION LOOK-ASIDE BUFFER, MAP.

administrator 1 The person in charge of a computer network or multi-user computer who has responsibility for granting accounts to new users, allocating shared resources such as disk space, and maintaining the software.

2 A software component whose purpose is to manage resources for other components.

ADO Abbreviation of ACTIVEX DATABASE OBJECTS.

Adobe Systems Inc. An American software company best-known for inventing the POSTSCRIPT page-description language and the PDF document format. Adobe also sells several widely-used graphics products including the PAGEMAKER and INDESIGN DESKTOP PUBLISHING packages, the Illustrator drawing program and Premier video editing program. The firm also produces its own family of type FONTS: see under ADOBE TYPE 1 FONT, ADOBE TYPE 3 FONT, ADOBE TYPE MANAGER.

Adobe Type 1 font The primary FONT format supported by Adobe's POSTSCRIPT page description language, often simply called a PostScript font.

Type 1 fonts are OUTLINE FONTS in which each character is described by an encoded PostScript routine that constructs each letter form from lines and BEZIER CURVES. They contain several levels of HINTING information to improve the appearance of letters at lower resolutions, including global hints that apply to all characters in a font or family of fonts, and hints for individual character shapes. This enables Type 1 fonts to generate smoother and more detailed letter forms than the alternative ADOBE TYPE 3 FONT format, and they are also typically smaller and faster to download to the printer.

Adobe itself sells only Type 1 fonts, though it has opened up this originally proprietary format to other typeface vendors. The ADOBE TYPE MANAGER program, which can be used on Macintosh and Windows systems, supports Type 1 but not Type 3 fonts.

See also TRUETYPE, OPENTYPE, GLYPH, BITMAPPED FONT, DESKTOP PUBLISHING.

Adobe Type 3 font A FONT format supported by Adobe's POSTSCRIPT page description language as an alternative to the ADOBE TYPE 1 FONT format. Type 3 fonts render each character as a graphic object using the standard PostScript drawing commands, and may therefore include features such as GREY SCALE shading and bitmap data that Type 1 fonts cannot.

A Type 3 font file consists of PostScript source code which can be edited, and may therefore be adapted by adding special user-defined symbols. Type 3 fonts therefore require the presence of a full PostScript interpreter, and so are not supported by ADOBE TYPE MANAGER – this means they cannot be automatically smoothed when scaled to different sizes, and they also lack HINTING information to improve letter appearance at small type sizes. For these reasons they are less used than Type 1 fonts.

See also OUTLINE FONT, BITMAPPED FONT, TRUETYPE, OPENTYPE, GLYPH, FONT RENDERING.

Adobe Type Manager (ATM) An add-on FONT rendering program that can be applied to both Apple Macintosh and Windows computers, to generate scalable screen and printer fonts from a single set of font outlines.

Since Microsoft built its own rival TRUETYPE font system into the operating system, ATM fonts are now encountered more often on Macintosh systems than on Windows machines. ATM employs a simplified subset of the POSTSCRIPT language to render its fonts, and incorporates a font substitution system that can automatically replace any fonts that are missing from a document with a serif or sans serif default font at the appropriate size and spacing.

See more under ADOBE TYPE 1 FONT, OUTLINE FONT, FONT RENDERING. See also BITMAPPED FONT, GLYPH, OPENTYPE.

ADPCM Abbreviation of ADAPTIVE PULSE CODE MODULATION.

ADSL (Asymmetric Digital Subscriber Line) A BROADBAND digital telecommunications technology that can operate over existing copper telephone lines, and is one of the technologies vying to replace ISDN. See more under DIGITAL SUBSCRIBER LINE.

ADT Abbreviation of ABSTRACT DATA TYPE.

Advanced Configuration and Power Interface See ACPI.

Advanced Data Connector See REMOTE DATA SERVICE.

Advanced Micro Devices See AMD.

Advanced Research Projects Agency See ARPA.

Advanced RISC Computing An outdated open specification for RISC-based computer systems based on POWERPC, MIPS and DEC ALPHA AXP microprocessors, launched in 1993 by a consortium of workstation manufacturers.

Advanced RISC Machines Ltd A UK company, founded in 1990 as a joint venture between ACORN COMPUTERS, APPLE COMPUTER INC. and VLSI Technology Inc. to design and market microprocessors of the ARM family. ARM Ltd now creates custom chips for many applications based on the ARM processor core, and is Britain's most successful microprocessor vendor, its low-power consumption chips being widely used in mobile telephones and handheld computers. See also STRONGARM.

Advanced Windowing Extensions (AWE) A Microsoft APPLICATION PROGRAMMING INTERFACE that enables software to make use of physical, non-paged, memory beyond the 4 gigabyte virtual address space on PENTIUM Pro and later processors that include the PHYSICAL ADDRESS EXTENSIONS.

adventure game See under GAME.

AFAIK Online shorthand for As Far As I Know.

affine transform A set of fundamental geometrical transformations – translation, rotation, scaling and reflection in an axis – that leave the intrinsic shape of a figure to which they are applied intact. Such transformations may be represented as a 3×3 MATRIX of multiplicative factors that transform one point into another, which can be applied to all the points composing a figure: therefore hardware for assisting 3D GRAPHICS operations is mostly designed to accelerate MATRIX ARITHMETIC.

AFP (AppleTalk Filing Protocol) A protocol that allows applications running on PC or Unix systems to use their own file system commands to manipulate files on a remote Apple Macintosh.

agent 1 A program that autonomously performs some service on behalf of its user. For example an agent might autonomously scan web sites searching for certain key words or phrases and gathering pages that relate to its owner's interests. It is frequently predicted that agents are the future of software, being used, say, to bid on the user's behalf for the lowest telephone charge for each call made. However, leaving technical issues aside, adequate control over and legal responsibility for such agents present enormous problems.
2 More narrowly, a component of a CLIENT/SERVER software system that gathers and prepares server data for the client.
3 An abstraction used in designing concurrent software systems to describe part of the system that performs a specific task.

aggregation In OBJECT-ORIENTED PROGRAMMING, the process of defining a new class of object by embedding an object of an existing class as one of its INSTANCE VARIABLES, rather than by inheriting from the existing class. Aggregation expresses the 'has a' relation (e.g. a car 'has a' steering wheel) whereas inheritance expresses the 'is a' relation (e.g. a car 'is a' motor vehicle). See also INHERITANCE.

AGP Abbreviation of ACCELERATED GRAPHICS PORT.

AI Abbreviation of ARTIFICIAL INTELLIGENCE.

AIFF Abbreviation of AUDIO INTERCHANGE FILE FORMAT.

airbrush A painting tool provided in most bit-mapped painting programs that simulates a fine spray of paint and is used for creating shadows, halos, fog, cloud and similar effects. The airbrush tool typically offers the user control over the size and shape of the spray and the transparency or density of the applied colour. See also BRUSH, FLOOD FILL, GRADIENT FILL.

air-cooled Any system that dissipates its excess heat directly into the atmosphere, either passively via cooling fins or actively using a fan-assisted air stream. All personal computers are air-cooled, as opposed to older mainframe computers which were liquid-cooled like car engines.

AIUI Online shorthand for As I Understand It.

AIX (Advanced Interactive eXecutive) IBM's own version of the UNIX operating system, adopted as the basis for the OSF Unix standard.

algebra 1 Informally, that branch of mathematics in which arithmetical operations and relationships are generalized – that is, turned into ABSTRACTIONS – by employing alphabetic symbols to stand for unknown or variable quantities.
2 More precisely, a formal system consisting of a SET of elements together with a number of operations that map some combinations of these elements onto another element of the set. Examples of algebras include: the set of whole numbers (or INTEGERS) together with the operations of addition, substraction, multiplication and remainder; the set of REAL NUMBERS with addition, substraction, multiplication and division, that corresponds to ordinary high school algebra; the two-membered set [True, False] together with the operations AND, OR and NOT that is called BOOLEAN ALGEBRA; the set of all sets together with the operations of INTERSECTION, UNION and COMPLEMENT.

In computing, algebras are associated with different DATA TYPES: a programming language must supply a set of operations appropriate to each type that it supports (e.g. integer, Boolean). In those languages that support user-defined types, the definition of the algebraic operations permitted on a new type constitutes its ABSTRACT DATA TYPE.

algebraic data type A concept supported in some FUNCTIONAL PROGRAMMING LANGUAGES that enables a new type of data structure to be defined merely by describing the set of CON-STRUCTOR functions needed to build it. For example a TREE structure might be defined by:

type Tree = Empty OR Leaf(Any) OR Node(Tree, Tree)

where Empty is the NULL value and Leaf and Node are the constructors in question. See also DECLARATIVE LANGUAGE, ALGEBRA, RECURSIVE FUNCTION, ABSTRACT DATA TYPE.

ALGOL (ALGOrithmic Language) The first BLOCK STRUCTURED programming language, defined in 1960 by a committee of the ASSOCIATION FOR COMPUTING MACHINERY and intended for scientific programming tasks.

The most widely used version, ALGOL 60, introduced many of the control constructs found in modern languages, such as IF–THEN–ELSE, a very general form of FOR loop, a SWITCH statement, and local variables for subroutines: however, it lacked data structures apart from the ARRAY. A later version, ALGOL 68, added many complex new features including concurrency and procedure parameters, but proved too complicated for efficient implementation and the language fell into disuse.

Algol had a strong influence on the development of all subsequent languages, most notably on the PASCAL and MODULA-2 family and to a lesser extent on C and VISUAL BASIC.

algorithm A well-defined set of instructions for solving a problem. The word is believed to be a corruption of the Arabic name of the medieval Persian mathematician al-Khuwarizmi, whose writings introduced algebra and the Arabic numeral system to Europe.

Algorithms may be expressed in more or less formal languages, ranging from everyday English (or French etc) to specially designed mathematical notations. For example a simple algorithm for finding a required item among an ordered set of items could be expressed in plain English as 'examine each item in turn', while a more sophisticated search algorithm might be stated as 'split the items into two halves; decide which half contains item; split this half, and repeat until found'.

An algorithm is more abstract than a computer program, avoiding any assumptions about the equipment to be used to solve the problem. However, most computer programs are based on algorithms, and choosing the appropriate algorithm, then implementing it in a PROGRAMMING LANGUAGE, forms the basis of computing. Different algorithms for solving the same problem may perform very differently in practice, and the analysis of their performance forms an important branch of computer science; for example the BINARY SEARCH described above will find one item among a million in no more than 20 steps, compared to an average of 500,000 steps for the simple LINEAR SEARCH.

An algorithm is said to be effective if it can solve a problem correctly in a finite number of steps. Except for the very simplest cases (e.g. the linear search), it is very difficult to formally prove that an algorithm is correct and solves the required problem: usually the best that can be achieved is to test an algorithm on many different examples of the problem (which still leaves the possibility that a rare failing case has been missed).

algorithmic complexity A measure of the amount of information encoded in some entity by the size of the shortest ALGORITHM that can generate or describe that entity. More formally, the algorithmic complexity of a string of symbols S is the length of P, the shortest program running on a Universal TURING MACHINE whose output is S. For example 1111111..., an infinitely long string of 1s, has only a low algorithmic complexity since a trivial program (keep copying 1) can generate it, while a string of random numbers has a high complexity because the only program that can generate it contains itself as a LITERAL. In between these extremes, a number such as pi can be generated to any number of places by running a modestly sized program for a long enough time. Since computers are in essence Turing Machines, this theoretical pursuit finds practical application in estimating the performance of algorithms in real life computing problems: see also COMPLEXITY ANALYSIS, COMPUTATIONAL COMPLEXITY, TIME COMPLEXITY.

alias 1 Under many operating systems, including Unix, MacOS and Netware, an alternative name (or icon) via which a program, file, device or other resource may be accessed. Often employed to conceal the absolute location of some resource from software, to simplify making changes to the configuration.

2 In Unix, a SHELL command that allows an alternative PATHNAME to be assigned to a file.

3 In microprocessors that use REGISTER RENAMING, a temporary identifier stored in an internal table that keeps track of the registers' contents.

4 In programming, a VARIABLE name that points to the same memory location already occupied by another variable.

aliasing   **1** The phenomenon by which a line drawn on a computer screen appears as a jagged sequence of steps (informally known as the *jaggies*) rather than as a smooth line. It can be ameliorated by the technique of ANTIALIASING.

2 The phenomenon by which a digitized sound sample may pick up unwanted spurious frequencies.

Both these phenomena result from sampling the data (see SAMPLE) at a frequency below its NYQUIST FREQUENCY: that is, displaying a line on a screen of too low a resolution, or sampling the sound at too low a frequency. In fact aliasing is a potential source of distortion when sampling any form of data, another example being the optical illusion that wheels are rotating backwards often seen when old movies are shown on television.

Alice   **1** A software tool for DATA MINING produced by the French firm Isoft.

2 An experimental parallel computer built as a collaboration between ICL and Imperial College in the late 1980s.

alkaline cell   Strictly, any battery technology that employs an alkaline electrolyte such as sodium or potassium hydroxide, rather than acid. Nickel/iron or NiFe cells were the first alkaline cells to be widely used. The term now refers almost exclusively to miniature disposable alkaline batteries, such as those made by Duracell, that are used to power cameras, personal stereos and PALMTOP computers.

Allen, Paul   (b. 1953) Co-founder of MICROSOFT and principal author, along with Bill GATES, of MICROSOFT BASIC.

allocation   The act of dispensing a portion of some resource from a central pool; for example allocating memory to a variable or a program, or allocating disk space for a file.

Alpha AXP   See DEC ALPHA.

alphabet   A set of symbols, arranged into a fixed order, that may be combined to produce different words. In those human languages that employ alphabets (for example English, which uses the Roman alphabet) each symbol or letter represents a different PHONEME in the spoken language. Computer languages, however, may employ alphabets that have no connection with speech. Each symbol in an alphabet is assigned one or more images called GLYPHS to visually represent it, but in a computing context such images must be clearly distinguished from the abstract and unique symbol itself (consider, for example, all the different possible glyphs that stand for the letter A). See also CHARACTER SET, FONT.

alpha/beta pruning   An OPTIMIZATION ALGORITHM employed by computer chess programs and other two-player games, which seeks the best counter-move to the opponent's last move without investigating too many alternatives. An improvement of the MINIMAX ALGORITHM, alpha/beta pruning shrinks the tree of possible moves by removing those branches not considered relevant, assigning a value to the player's position following each possible move (alpha) and the opponent's response (beta). The goal is to find the move with the largest alpha: on the assumption that the opponent is equally trying to minimize beta then, whenever beta is less than alpha, alternative opponent's moves can be safely ignored.

alphabetize   To sort into alphabetical order.

alpha blending   See under ALPHA CHANNEL.

alpha channel   An extra layer of information stored in a digital picture to describe transparency or opacity. For each pixel, the alpha channel stores an extra value called alpha, in addition to its red, blue and green values, which indicates the degree of transparency of that pixel. The display software then mixes the colour of this pixel with the background colour in proportion to its alpha value (so an alpha value of 0.5 would display half foreground and half background), a process called *alpha blending*. An alpha channel enables special effects such as blurring or tinting of the background as a transparent object passes across it, and fog or mist effects to suggest distance. Alpha blending is supported as a hardware function by advanced graphics accelerators (AGP).

alphanumeric Consisting of, or capable of displaying, both letters and numerals.

alpha release The first release of a software product outside of the development team: an alpha release is possibly unfinished, certainly contains BUGS and comes with no guarantees of correct functioning. See also ALPHA TESTING, BETA RELEASE, BETA TESTING, RELEASE CANDIDATE.

alpha testing One the earliest phases of software testing, which originally involved customers trying out the software on the developer's premises and equipment. Alpha software is now often released outside of the vendors premises, but with absolutely no guarantee that it will work and with disclaimers about responsibility. See also BETA TESTING.

Altair 8800 The first commercially successful PERSONAL COMPUTER, made by the US firm MITS in 1975 and sold as a home construction kit via mail-order. The Altair was based on the 8-bit Intel 8080 microprocessor and fitted with 256 bytes of memory. Its user interface was a FRONT-PANEL fitted with toggle switches and LEDs, and luxuries such as keyboard, display monitor or disk drives had to be purchased separately from different vendors. One of the first programs that MITS offered, only for Altairs expanded to 4 or 8 kilobytes of memory, was a version of Basic developed by Bill Gates and Paul Allen of the new company Microsoft.

Alta Vista A web site (www.altavista.com) that contains a powerful SEARCH ENGINE developed by DIGITAL EQUIPMENT CORPORATION. Alta Vista was among the first search engines to actively index the WORLD WIDE WEB by sending out an autonomous program called a SPIDER to visit millions of sites every day. In 1999, Alta Vista

required a cluster of 16 servers each fitted with 8 gigabytes of memory, and its 200 gigabyte index contained information on over 200 million web pages.

alternating current (AC) An electrical current that periodically reverses its direction. The electrical mains supply is an alternating current that varies in a sinusoidal fashion, reversing itself 50 times per second in the UK and Europe, and 60 times per second in the USA. Digital signals are SQUARE-WAVES that do not actually change direction, but switch between, for example 0 and 5 volts; in their electrical properties, however, they behave more like alternating currents than DIRECT CURRENTS. See also FREQUENCY, HERTZ, IMPEDANCE.

ALT key An alternative shift key, labelled 'Alt' or 'ALT', introduced as part of the original IBM PC keyboard and present on all subsequent compatible PCs. Pressing the ALT key simultaneously with another key generates a code that software may interpret as a command. For example Microsoft Windows uses many combinations that include ALT+F4 to close a window and ALT+TAB to switch tasks. The ALT key is sometimes pressed and followed by a three digit number to type ASCII characters that are not available on the keyboard: for example inside certain programs ALT+165 will type a £ sign.

ALU Abbreviation of ARITHMETIC AND LOGIC UNIT.

aluminium (*US* aluminum) A soft white metal, atomic number 13, melting point 660.37°C, that has until recently been used as the conductive layer in most semiconductor devices, such as memory chips and microprocessors. A thin aluminium layer is deposited onto the surface of the WAFER by evaporation in a high vacuum, to form the wires that connect the silicon transistors together.

The development by IBM of a technique for depositing copper onto wafers now threatens to displace aluminium from high performance applications.

Always On (AO) Any Internet service that is always connected, for example a LEASED LINE, ADSL or CABLE MODEM connection, as opposed to a DIAL-UP telephone line and modem connection that must be re-established before every session. Computers connected via an

Always On connection typically have a fixed IP ADDRESS and need to employ a FIREWALL to prevent unauthorized access. The distinction is as much financial as technical, since the viability of Always On connections depends on them using a charging model that is not based on connection time as domestic telephone charges are.

AMD (Advanced Micro Devices) A US manufacturer of Intel-compatible microprocessors, including the widely used K6 and Athlon PENTIUM-compatible chips.

Amdahl, Gene (b. 1922) An ex-IBM engineer who founded the Amdahl Corporation, a mainframe company that pioneered clustering and multi-processor computing. Best known for AMDAHL'S LAW.

Amdahl's Law A design principle for PARALLEL computers discovered by Gene Amdahl. Informally stated, it says that applying more processors to a computation will have no effect if the computation is inherently sequential. More formally, if the percentage of a program that is inherently sequential is S, then the best speed up you can hope for by running it on P processors is:

$$100/(S + (100-S)/P)$$

The practical consequence of the law is that designers of parallel computers must increase I/O BANDWIDTH in strict proportion to processing power.

American National Standard See ANS.

American National Standards Institute See ANSI.

American Standard Code for Information Interchange See ASCII.

America Online See AOL.

Amiga A range of personal computers made by COMMODORE BUSINESS MACHINES from 1985 to 1995 that had superior graphics performance thanks to their use of custom graphics and audio chips. The Amiga attracted a devoted band of users, including many video professionals, and for many years Amigas were used to create video special effects for TV title sequences.

Amoeba An experimental DISTRIBUTED OPERATING SYSTEM developed at the University of Amsterdam.

ampere (amp, A) The SI unit of electric current, defined as that constant current which produces a force of 2×10^{-7} newtons per metre if maintained between two parallel conductors of infinite length and negligible cross-section placed 1 metre apart in free space.

The ampere was formerly defined by the deposition of silver from a silver nitrate solution by electrolysis: 1 ampere deposits 0.001118 gram per second of silver. See also VOLT, OHM.

ampersand The & character, ASCII code 38, used in text as an abbreviation for 'and' and often used in programming as a prefix to identify particular data types.

amplifier An electronic circuit that increases the amplitude of its input signal and outputs the result. The most familiar type is the audio amplifier, as found in domestic hi fi or telephones, but amplifiers are to be found in every sort of device, including silicon chips: for example there is a microscopic amplifier in each of the thousands of cell rows on a RAM chip.

amplitude Size, magnitude, extent. When used of a WAVEFORM it refers to the height of the wave, measured from top to bottom of the following trough.

amplitude modulation The transmission of information by altering the magnitude of the successive cycles of a CARRIER wave, as opposed to FREQUENCY MODULATION where it is the spacing of successive cycles that encodes the information.

Amulet A complete implementation of the ARM processor architecture using ASYNCHRONOUS LOGIC, developed at Manchester University as part of an ESPRIT project.

anaglyph An old-fashioned technique for 3D picture display that involves the viewer wearing spectacles with red and green lenses.

analogue (US analog) **1** A physical object or quantity, for example a moving clock hand or an electrical voltage, that is used to measure or represent some other quantity, and is hence analogous to it.

2 A family of electronic devices that represent other physical quantities by continuously varying voltages rather than the two discrete voltage levels used in DIGITAL devices. For example the output voltage of an analogue microphone follows exactly the changes in sound pressure of a speaker's voice. All telephone, radio and television systems prior to the 1990s were based on analogue electronics.

The disadvantage of analogue devices compared to digital ones is that any physical effect that changes the voltage – such as non-linearity in the conductors, stray electrical or magnetic fields, power supply fluctuations – will corrupt the data. The advantage of analogue devices is that they may operate faster than digital devices, or store data more densely, since they avoid the overheads incurred in digitizing the data.

analogue computer (*US* analog computer) A computer that represents numbers by some continuously variable physical quantity, whose variations mimic the properties of some system being modelled. Analogue computers have been built using mechanical motion (such as rotation), pneumatic or hydraulic pressure, or electrical voltage as the requisite quantity. For example, an old-fashioned carburettor may be considered a simple analogue computer that computes a petrol/air mixture strength function given the inputs of throttle pedal position and engine airflow.

The military has used analogue computers for artillery range finding, and they are used to simulate car suspensions and similar elastic systems where real-time performance is valuable. However, in common with other analogue circuits, they lack digital logic's robustness against errors introduced by stray fluctuations.

analogue-to-digital converter (A/D converter, ADC) An important type of electronic circuit that inputs an ANALOGUE signal and outputs a stream of bits that reproduces that input signal in the digital domain. Conversion involves sampling the strength of the input signal at very short intervals and expressing the sampled value as a binary number. ADCs are widely employed in electronic equipment of many kinds, including digital cameras and camcorders, telephones and MODEMS, and the SOUND CARDS used in personal computers.

The two most important parameters in describing an ADC are the size (in bits) of the samples it takes, and how many samples it takes per second. For example to digitize an analogue microphone signal at CD quality requires an ADC capable of taking 44 million 16-bit samples per second.

analogue video A video signal that is captured, transmitted and stored as a continuously varying voltage, rather than as a stream of bits as in digital video. Up until the advent of digital TV in the late 1990s, television worked by transmitted analogue video signals, and older video tape recorders such as VHS, PAL, Betamax and Umatic all store analogue signals.

The disadvantage of analogue video is that it is prone to noise interference, while its advantage is its great density: a domestic 3-hour VHS cassette holds the equivalent of 16 gigabytes of digital data.

analyst A person whose job is to examine some kind of complex system. In the computing industry the term used alone usually refers to someone who performs either systems analysis or investment analysis.

anchor An area within a HYPERTEXT document, such as a WEB PAGE, that is either the source or the destination for a LINK. A source anchor is typically a word or phrase (usually highlighted by colour or underlining), a button or a picture, and clicking on it with the mouse causes the link to be followed and the corresponding destination anchor to be displayed; this may be a whole new page or a position within a page. Anchors are created in the HTML SOURCE CODE using the <A>..<A/> tag with an HREF that points to the destination anchor, as in:

```
<A HREF="about.htm">About
AltaVista</A>
```

AND A BOOLEAN operator that is true only if both of its two operands are true. See also OR, XOR.

ANDF Abbreviation of ARCHITECTURE NEUTRAL DISTRIBUTION FORMAT.

Andreesen, Marc (b. 1971) One of the authors of the NETSCAPE NAVIGATOR web browser and a founder of NETSCAPE COMMUNICATIONS CORPORATION.

angstrom (Å) A unit of length equal to 10^{-10} metres or one tenth of a NANOMETRE. Used principally to express the wavelengths of electromagnetic radiation in the visible and shorter regions of the spectrum.

animated GIF A GIF format picture file containing multiple images that, when viewed in a suitable WEB BROWSER, appear as an animated sequence.

animation The creation of an illusion of motion by displaying a rapid sequence of progressively changing images, which must succeed one another 20 times or more per second to deceive the human eye into perceiving a smooth motion. See also IN-BETWEENING, ANIMATED GIF, COLLISION-DETECTION, FLASH, SHOCKWAVE.

anisotropic Having different physical properties in different spatial directions, as for example with a material like wood: the converse of ISOTROPIC.

annealing, simulated See SIMULATED ANNEALING.

annotation The process of attaching a note or comment to a document. Most modern WORD PROCESSING and SPREADSHEET programs support the addition of such annotations, which may be read on screen but do not normally print as part of the document.

anode The positively charged ELECTRODE that attracts ELECTRONS within a current-consuming device such as an electrolytic cell, discharge tube or valve. In a current-producing BATTERY, the anode is the electrode that receives electrons internally and hence is connected to the external negative terminal.

anonymity The ability to send an EMAIL or visit a WEB SITE without revealing one's own email address or identity. Such anonymity is a service provided to Internet users by specially dedicated PROXY SERVERS such as www.anonymizer.com, which reroute all messages and delete all header information that would lead to them being traceable.

Anonymous services may be used by people with a legitimate concern about privacy, but also to cover criminal activities, and as such have been subject to legal action (so far unsuccessful) by various government agencies. Using an anonymous service makes it impossible to receive replies to emails. See also REMAILER.

anonymous FTP A service provided on many Internet servers that permits a casual visitor to download files using the FTP file transfer protocol without needing to possess a named account or password. The user merely logs in under the name 'anonymous' or 'ftp' and uses his/her email address as the PASSWORD, and is then granted access to a restricted set of directories that have been reserved for public access (and which are typically separated from those used by the local users).

ANS (American National Standard) A prefix attached to the name of documents that describe standards ratified by the American National Standards Institute (ANSI), e.g. ANS X3.215-1994, or to languages or software that conforms to such a standard, e.g. ANS FORTH.

ANSI (American National Standards Institute) The body responsible for promulgating software and hardware STANDARDS in the USA, and the US member of the ISO. ANSI is a private sector, non-profit membership organization and its standards are voluntary rather than statutory. It was founded in 1918 by the merger of five different engineering societies and three government agencies.

ANSI does not develop American National Standards (ANSs) itself but instead facilitates development by establishing consensus among qualified groups from industry and academia. Its standards are particularly influential in the field of programming languages: see ANSI C. See also IEEE, ANSI CHARACTER SET.

ANSI C The current standard version of the C language, subject of ANSI standard X3.159-1989. It added several important features to the language, including function prototypes, STRUCTURE passing and structure ASSIGNMENT.

ANSI character set Any CHARACTER SET adopted as an ANSI standard, which means either ANSI X3.4-1968, better known as the ASCII character set, or the set of 217 characters based on 8-bit EXTENDED ASCII adopted by Microsoft as the Windows ANSI character set

(ANSI 1252-1983) and supplied with versions of Windows up to and including Windows 95 and NT4. The lower 128 characters of Windows ANSI are identical to ASCII, but characters in the range 128–255 vary between Windows ANSI and other extended ASCII sets (for example that used by MS-DOS) which may result in Windows programs displaying a black or white square in place of some characters in documents that were created on a different operating system. Microsoft has since added the euro currency symbol to Windows ANSI, and Windows 2000 employs the new WGL4 character sets. See also UNICODE, ISO 8859, CODE PAGE.

ANSI terminal A CURSOR-ADDRESSABLE TERMINAL that employs the codes defined by the US ANSI standards body for cursor positioning. The ANSI codes were an attempt to impose standardization on the chaos of different terminal types that proliferated in the 1980s, and they were adopted by IBM for its PC displays under the character-based PC-DOS. The ANSI codes are complex strings beginning with the ESC character (see ESCAPE SEQUENCE), as for example:

ESC [# B moves the cursor down # lines.
ESC [#;# H moves the cursor to position #,#.
ESC [2J erases the screen and moves the cursor to top left.

Almost all communications software nowadays will include ANSI among its supported TERMINAL EMULATORS, and so the standardization effort has succeeded.

answerback A less frequently used term for CALLBACK.

antialiasing A technique employed in computer GRAPHICS to smooth the jagged appearance of text and lines (see ALIASING) by applying varying shades of colour. Consider a black diagonal line drawn on a white screen background: on a low RESOLUTION display it will appear stepped like a staircase because the positions of screen pixels will not coincide exactly with the desired path of the line. On a screen that can display shades of grey, antialiasing involves colouring each pixel black if it lies wholly within the line, white if it lies wholly outside the line, but otherwise a shade of grey proportional to the degree with which it overlaps the line.

The same principle works with any foreground and background colour combination, by exploiting a property of the human eye that expects the edges of objects to display some tonal gradation due to light and shadow. Antialiased text is a feature of most sophisticated text processing and design software.

antireflection coating A surface treatment applied to a VDU screen to prevent reflected ambient light from spoiling the contrast of the displayed image. Various techniques have been employed for this purpose, ranging from etching the glass surface itself, to applying chemical layers, embossed plastic film or fine textile meshes.

anti-twitter A technique that improves the readability of computer text displayed on ANALOGUE television screens, and hence is important for WEB TV applications. TWITTER is an artefact caused by the INTERLACED DISPLAY employed in television sets, which causes text to judder up and down. Anti-twitter software works by defeating interlacing; displaying half the lines of a frame as normal, but using digital filters or other interpolation techniques to invent the other half.

anti-virus software Software that can detect the presence of a computer VIRUS and remove it if found. Anti-virus programs are of two main types: those that scan a computer's whole hard disk on request, and those that work continuously as a BACKGROUND TASK, inspecting every file that is loaded onto the computer. Both kinds work by comparing every byte sequence they encounter against a large database containing the SIGNATURES of all currently known viruses, but since new viruses are being written all the time, this database has to be frequently updated in order to maintain effective protection. The invention of the MACRO VIRUS has necessitated new types of anti-virus software that vet the execution of all macro code.

AOL (America Online Inc.) The largest online PORTAL and ISP (Internet Service Provider) in the world, with more than 12 million subscribers in more than 70 countries around the world. Founded in 1985, AOL absorbed Compuserve, the previous largest network provider, in 1998. In 2000 it merged with the Time Warner media empire to form AOL Time Warner Inc.

In addition to providing its own proprietary content channels, AOL acts as a web portal, with a version of INTERNET EXPLORER built into its own access software. It was among the first Internet Service Providers to offer unmetered Internet access.

Apache A very popular WEB SERVER developed and distributed free of charge as OPEN SOURCE software by an Internet-based community of unpaid volunteers. Apache's great strengths lie in the availability of its source code and its well-defined interface for writing add-on modules: many large and profitable e-commerce sites run on modified versions of Apache. The name is a wince-making pun on the phrase 'a patchy server', bestowed because of the numerous software PATCHES released for it in its early days.

apartment threading The model for MULTI-THREADING employed by Microsoft COM systems such as WINDOWS NT and MICROSOFT TRANSACTION SERVER. An apartment is a process space in which one or more THREADS may run. A single-threaded apartment or STA contains a single thread of execution, and any objects that thread creates which may only execute their method code on that thread. A multithreaded apartment contains several threads of execution, which can execute method code in objects created by any thread in the apartment; however all such objects must be of the same class.

aperiodic Not occurring at regular intervals.

aperture grille One of the two main types of CATHODE RAY TUBE (CRT) technology employed in computer monitors, in which a large number of closely-spaced wires are arranged vertically just behind the inside face of the CRT, which steer the electron beams so that

they strike the proper phosphor areas. To lessen the chance of movement of the wires in the grille, two damper wires are threaded across them, and these can be seen as two faint, fine grey lines that run horizontally near the top third and bottom third of the screen. The most widely sold aperture grille tubes are the Trinitron range from Sony, the DiamondTron from Mitsubishi, and the SonicTron from ViewSonic. The other main competing tube technology is the SHADOW-MASK TUBE.

API Abbreviation of APPLICATION PROGRAMMING INTERFACE.

APL (A Programming Language) An INTERPRETED interactive programming language designed by Ken Iverson in 1960 at Harvard University for performing mathematical computations.

APL is notorious for its terse and cryptic commands, which enable it to express complex calculations in very short, often single-line, programs. There are so many of these commands that Greek and other symbols were employed in addition to the normal alphabetic characters to give short names to them; this created difficulties over keyboard layout, and restricted the spread of the language. APL was most widely used on IBM MAINFRAMES in the 1960s and 70s.

The principal data structure employed in APL programs is the ARRAY, and the language's many commands are mostly concerned with combining, transforming, reordering and otherwise manipulating arrays of numbers: in the hands of an expert user it may be used interactively, like a powerful calculator, to perform large statistical calculations in a very few operations.

Apollo A former US major manufacturer of GRAPHICS WORKSTATIONS.

append 1 To add new data to the end of some data structure, such as a file or array, rather than to insert it into the middle or to overwrite existing data. At the operating system level, appending to a file requires the allocation of new storage units (see for example CLUSTER, I-NODE) whereas inserting or overwriting may be performed by resizing the current allocations.

2 An MS-DOS command that permits programs to open data files stored in remote directories as if they were in the current directory. For example the command line:

```
c:> append d:\documents\letters
```

would allow a word processor running from the C: directory to open files in the letters directory without having to specify their full PATHNAME. When issued with the /x:on switch, append also causes the named directories to be searched for executable files as if they were on the current PATH. See also ASSIGN, SUBST.

Apple Computer Inc. One of the first successful PERSONAL COMPUTER manufacturers, created in Cupertino, California by Steve JOBS and Steve WOZNIAK in 1976.

The firm's first product, Apple I was a bare circuit board for home construction, but its second effort, APPLE II, was the first properly packaged personal computer and sold millions of units. It also created the mass software market when in 1979 the first spreadsheet program, VISICALC, was written for it.

In the early 1980s the success of the IBM PC destroyed sales of Apple II, but Apple fought back with the innovative but unsuccessful LISA, followed by the hugely successful MACINTOSH line which is still manufactured. These machines introduced the public to the concept of the GRAPHICAL USER INTERFACE using WINDOWS and a MOUSE, and so set the style for all future personal computers.

Apple II The first widely popular PERSONAL COMPUTER, launched in 1977 by Steve JOBS and Steve WOZNIAK. The Apple II came complete with a keyboard and a graphical display, and with the MICROSOFT BASIC programming language built in, making it much easier to program and use than most contemporary machines. The creation of VISICALC, the first electronic SPREADSHEET program, for Apple II in 1979 almost singlehandedly led to the acceptance of personal computers for business use. Production of Apple II variants continued into the late 1980s.

Technically the Apple II employed the 8-bit MOS Technology 6502 microprocessor, with 16 kilobytes of RAM and 16 kilobytes of ROM, plus eight EXPANSION SLOTS.

Apple Macintosh See MACINTOSH.

Apple Newton See NEWTON.

applet A small program that is temporarily loaded into and executed within a larger application program to add some extra function. A common example is the JAVA applet, a small section of Java code that is downloaded along with a web page and is executed when the page is viewed in a WEB BROWSER to produce, say, an animated graphic.

Microsoft employs applets in several of its Office applications to provide extra functions. For example MICROSOFT WORD employs a number of different applets that are loaded automatically when editing a graphic embedded within a document, to create fancy headline fonts, for example, or to lay out mathematical equations within a document. Applets cannot in general be executed outside of their intended host program.

AppleTalk A proprietary LAN protocol that is built into Apple's MACINTOSH computers. AppleTalk is independent of the underlying network transport, and is currently able to run over serial cable (LocalTalk) or over an ETHERNET network (EtherTalk).

application framework A set of pre-fabricated software components that may be combined and extended in various ways by a programmer to produce an APPLICATION PROGRAM, such as communications or database management, for a particular domain.

application layer The seventh layer of OSI REFERENCE MODEL protocols; those that govern interactions between application programs.

application program A computer program that performs useful work on behalf of the user of the computer (for example a word processing or accounting program) as opposed to the SYSTEM SOFTWARE which manages the running of the computer itself, or to the DEVELOPMENT software which is used by programmers to create other programs. An application program is typically self-contained, storing data within files of a special (often proprietary) format that it can create, open for editing and save to disk: this is in distinction to a UTILITY program, which typically performs simple operations on files created by other programs. See also PROGRAM, SOFTWARE.

Application Programming Interface (API) A standardized interface via which an application program can access services provided by the operating system or other subsystems. An API is usually defined by source code in a high-level programming language such as C or C++, and consists of a set of functions each of which invokes a particular service; programmers then call these functions from their own programs.

application server A network SERVER that enables users to run application programs such as word processors or spreadsheets on the server itself, rather than downloading the application's code and running it on their local workstation. Application servers are often used in conjunction with diskless workstations or so-called THIN CLIENTS. See also TERMINAL SERVER, WINFRAME, X WINDOW SYSTEM.

Application Service Provider (ASP) A company that rents out the use of software running on its own SERVERS to remote customers, who may use a THIN CLIENT technology such as CITRIX WINFRAME or a PC and a web-based connection to log on to the service: the viability of such services depends upon the availability of a BROADBAND connection from client to server.

A significant attraction of using an ASP is that it relieves its customers of the task of installing, configuring and maintaining their own software. A wide variety of application types is now available remotely from ASPs, including office applications such as word processing and spreadsheets; system utilities such as VIRUS SCANNING and FIREWALL protection and, increasingly, disk space for automatically scheduled off-site data BACKUPS. See also SERVICE LEVEL AGREEMENT.

application software Computer programs intended to perform user's tasks, as opposed to those used by the computer itself or by programmers writing further programs: see under APPLICATION PROGRAM.

Application Specific Integrated Circuit See ASIC.

applicative language See FUNCTIONAL LANGUAGE.

apply button An on-screen button presented by many MODELESS dialogues in Windows, which when pressed in preference to the OK BUTTON causes an action to be performed immediately but without closing the dialogue.

approximation algorithm An ALGORITHM that yields a good, though not always optimal, solution to a problem. Some approximation algorithms, such as Newton's Method for extracting square roots, produce better and better answers the longer they are run, while others produce an optimal solution most times but a sub-optimal one occasionally (with no way of predicting when). This latter class of algorithms is important for dealing with problems such as the TRAVELLING SALESMAN PROBLEM, for the exact solution of which only impractical EXPONENTIAL-TIME ALGORITHMS are known. See also HEURISTIC.

APSE Abbreviation of ADA PROGRAMMING SUPPORT ENVIRONMENT.

ARAMIS (Asynchronous Random Access MOS Image Sensor) A type of CMOS RAM chip that is sensitive to light and can be used as an image sensor as an alternative to a CHARGE-COUPLED DEVICE.

arbitrary precision The ability to perform mathematical calculations to any required degree of precision rather than some fixed number of decimal places, a feature provided in only a few advanced programming systems.

arbitration The process of deciding which of several competing devices shall have access to some shared resource such as a BUS, MEMORY or DISK DRIVE. There are many possible arbitration algorithms, from a simple 'first come, first served' to random allocation, the most desirable quality being fairness to ensure that no device is permanently excluded from access.

Arbitration is most often carried out by dedicated hardware – as a function within a CONTROLLER chip – but occasionally in software, as in some telephony software interfaces. Hardware arbitration typically takes place as a separate phase that must be completed before the actual work cycles (for example data transfers) can take place. See also CONTENTION, SEMAPHORE, PRIORITY.

arbitrationless architecture A class of BUS architectures that permit several disk drives to use the bus at the same time. See also ARBITRATION, BUS CONTENTION.

ARC 1 One of the first file compression utilities for MS-DOS files, which was later supplanted by the more popular PKZIP.
 2 ADVANCED RISC COMPUTING, a now obsolete specification for RISC-based workstations.

arcade game See under GAME.

Archie An Internet tool that automatically indexes FTP ARCHIVES, enabling a user who is running Archie CLIENT software to find files by name from anywhere on the Internet. Named after a character in a US cartoon strip. See also JUGHEAD, VERONICA.

Archimedes A range of powerful personal computers made by the UK firm ACORN COMPUTERS in the early 1990s, based on their ARM RISC processor. Its operating system RISC OS was in several respects more robust and capable than either WINDOWS or MACOS, offering superior multimedia performance and hardware-assisted memory management. However it could not run either IBM PC or Macintosh software, which made it an unattractive target for software vendors and restricted its market severely, though it was fairly widely used in British schools until the mid-90s. Later versions called RISC PC incorporated a separate Intel processor to enable Windows software to be run.

architecture The overall gross structure of a computing system, whether hardware or software, ignoring the precise working details of its various subsystems. For example, a system might employ a CLIENT/SERVER architecture.

Architecture Neutral Distribution Format (ANDF) A cross-platform binary file format that enables the same application to be run on different types of processor by translating an intermediate ANDF code file into NATIVE CODE before loading it into memory. ANDF was developed by the OSF as part of a European Community initiative and has so far been deployed only for Unix systems.

archive A collection of data files stored for the purpose of permanent preservation. Often such a collection will be bound together into a single file and compressed using an archiving

program such as PKZIP under Windows, STUFFIT on the Macintosh or TAR under Unix (see more under FILE COMPRESSION).

The term is also used as a verb, meaning to save files onto some removable storage medium such as tape, CD-ROM or Zip disk, for safe long-term storage. Archiving is normally performed only on historical data such as old accounts or original texts that will not be referred to very often, and so it requires different disciplines and storage media from day-to-day BACKUP.

On the Internet, an archive implies a special FTP SERVER containing many files (usually in TAR format) that are accessible for downloading by the public.

archive flag, archive bit A two-valued FLAG contained in the header of all files under most computer OPERATING SYSTEMS that may be used to mark the archival status of the file. Any program that changes the file's contents sets the flag to true, and BACKUP programs reset the flag to false again once the file has been copied: the flag therefore marks out just those files whose backup copy is out of date, and this can be exploited to perform an INCREMENTAL BACKUP or DIFFERENTIAL BACKUP.

ARCnet (Attached Resource Computing Network) One of the earliest networking technologies, introduced by Datapoint in 1977. ARCnet's advantages included robustness and its use of cheap 92 ohm COAXIAL CABLE. It was nevertheless displaced by ETHERNET, partly because it was four times slower at 2.5 megabits per second, but mostly because Datapoint kept it proprietary while Ethernet and TOKEN RING gained IEEE standard status.

area fill A function provided in computer painting and drawing programs which fills a whole region with a chosen colour: see also FLOOD FILL.

arg See ARGUMENT.

Argonne National Laboratory A US government research establishment near Chicago, which performs much work on high-performance computing.

argument 1 In mathematics, an element to which a function (or predicate or other operation) is applied; the independent variable of a function; a property of a COMPLEX NUMBER, defined as its angle from the real axis in an Argand diagram.

2 In programming, an alternative name for a PARAMETER passed into a procedure or function.

Arithmetic and Logic Unit (ALU) A subunit within a computer's CENTRAL PROCESSING UNIT that performs mathematical operations such as addition, and logical shifts on the values held in the processors REGISTERS or its ACCUMULATOR. It is the size of the word that the ALU can handle which, more than any other measure, determines the word-size of a processor: that is, a 32-bit processor is one with a 32-bit ALU.

The simplest sort of ALU performs only addition, BOOLEAN LOGIC (including the NOT or complement operation) and shifts a word one bit to the right or left, all other arithmetic operations being synthesized from sequences of these primitive operations. For example, subtraction is performed as complement-add, multiplication by a power of two by shifting, division by repeated substraction (see more under ONES COMPLEMENT, TWOS COMPLEMENT, ARITHMETIC SHIFT, LOGICAL SHIFT). However, there is an increasing tendency in modern processors to implement extra arithmetic functions in hardware, such as dedicated multiplier or divider units.

The ALU might once have been considered the very core of the computer in the sense that it alone actually performed calculations. However, in modern SUPERSCALAR processor architectures this is no longer true, as there are typically several different ALUs in each of several separate integer and floating-point units. An ALU may be required to perform not only those calculations required by a user program but also many internal calculations required by the processor itself, for example to derive addresses for instructions that employ different ADDRESSING MODES, say by adding an offset to a base address. Once again, however, in modern architectures there is a tendency to distribute this work into a separate load/store unit.

See also PIPELINE, REGISTER BYPASS, MULTIPLY-ACCUMULATE, MULTIPLY-ADD, MATHS-COPROCESSOR, FLOATING-POINT UNIT, BARREL SHIFTER.

arithmetic shift A type of PROCESSOR INSTRUCTION that moves all the BITS making up a binary WORD one or more places to the left or right: bits that move off the end of the word are discarded and zeroes are introduced to fill the vacated positions. However, unlike the otherwise similar LOGICAL SHIFT operations, arithmetic shifts preserve the sign of a number by propagating the value of its MOST SIGNIFICANT BIT. Hence they can be used in calculations, offering a fast way to perform multiplication and division by powers of two. See also ROTATE.

arity The number of arguments taken by a FUNCTION or PROCEDURE. For example Add(x, y) has an arity of two while Replace(oldtext, newtext, direction, matchcase) has an arity of four. The word was coined by abstracting the suffix from the sequence unary, binary, ternary, etc.

ARM (Acorn RISC Machine) The world's first commercially manufactured REDUCED INSTRUCTION SET COMPUTER, a microprocessor developed in 1985 by the UK personal computer firm Acorn, and designed to be small (and hence cheap to manufacture) and to consume little electrical power. Chips based on the ARM architecture are still manufactured by the separate firm ARM plc and are widely used as EMBEDDED processors in a variety of portable devices from mobile telephones to hand-held computers and games consoles.

ARPA (Advanced Research Projects Agency) The former name for the US military research organization now called DARPA. See also ARPANET.

ARPAnet The first extensive WAN set up by the US Department of Defense in 1968. It became the test bed on which the INTERNET protocols were developed, and formed the original backbone of today's Internet. For military applications ARPAnet has now been replaced by NSFNET. See also ARPA.

array A collection of data items of the same type, any one of which can be accessed by specifying its position in the array as a number, which is called an INDEX or ARRAY SUBSCRIPT. For example if A is an array containing the four numbers 119, 205, 346, 487, then A[2] is called an array REFERENCE where 2 is the index, and A[2] has the value 205. (This assumes that permitted index values start from 1, but in many programming languages array indices must start from 0, in which case the value of A[2] would be 346.) A is a one-dimensional array, but arrays may have many dimensions, each of which has its own index: for example B[2,3] would select the second item of the third row of a two-dimensional array B.

An array is the simplest and most efficient compound data structure because it almost directly mirrors the way that a computer retrieves values from its memory via a numerical address. In most programming languages the size of an array must be declared (that is, the array must be DIMENSIONED) at the start of a program, which enables the language compiler to set aside the appropriate amount of memory to store it.

In most compiled languages an array's size is therefore fixed once it has been dimensioned and cannot be subsequently altered: such an array is said to be STATIC. Some languages support dynamic arrays which may be redimensioned after declaration (see under DYNAMIC ALLOCATION) or even at runtime, examples include certain dialects of PASCAL, ADA and many interpreted languages including VISUAL BASIC. These are typically less efficient than static arrays, and impose a significant runtime overhead. See also ARRAY BOUNDS, BOUNDS CHECKING, ASSOCIATIVE ARRAY.

array bounds The largest and smallest permitted index values for accessing the elements of an ARRAY; the difference between the upper and lower bounds gives the allocated size of the array. Referring to an element whose index lies outside the array bounds is always an error condition, which may be reported at compile time or run time in different programming languages.

array index A number that describes the position of an element in an ARRAY. See also ARRAY BOUNDS.

array processor See under VECTOR PROCESSOR.

array subscript Another name for an ARRAY INDEX.

arrow keys See under CURSOR KEYS.

artefact A spurious effect created by small errors or inaccuracies in a data processing operation: a well-known example of a visual artefact is the appearance of moving coloured bands on brightly coloured garments in a television picture.

artificial intelligence (AI) A branch of computer science that was pursued with great optimism in the 1960s and 70s, in an attempt to make computers think more like human beings. Typical problems tackled in AI departments are COMPUTER VISION, NATURAL LANGUAGE understanding and advanced ROBOTICS. The meagre rate of progress led to a more realistic understanding that these problems are vastly more difficult than was then thought. The effort has, however, produced many powerful programming techniques and software tools, most of which have yet to be exploited commercially, though the military employs many in 'smart' weapons.

The programming languages LISP and PROLOG and techniques such as EXPERT SYSTEMS, NEURAL NETWORKS and case-based reasoning all emerged from university AI research. The term AI became rather unfashionable (especially with funding bodies) and tends to be replaced nowadays by less hubristic titles such as Knowledge Engineering. A similar tendency is to sneak elements of AI into ordinary software products so that the user is aware only of improved performance; for example a word processor that can generate an automatic summary of a document.

Artificial Life A branch of software research that simulates living systems by creating entities within the computer that can reproduce themselves, pass on genetic traits and consume resources. See also LIFE, GAME OF.

AS/400 A range of MINICOMPUTERS manufactured by IBM that are based on a proprietary CPU design and run IBM's own OS/400 operating system. They are typically sold complete with bundled application software into small and medium sized businesses. AS/400s are available in fault-tolerant, MULTIPROCESSOR and CLUSTERED SMP configurations for use as WEB SERVERS. Though the closed nature of its architecture prevents the AS/400 from running PC software, there is a whole industry devoted to porting data and making network connections between the AS/400 and PCs, Unix machines and the Macintosh.

ascender A vertical stroke in a typographical character that rises above the average height of the other characters (that is, the X-HEIGHT):

for example the uprights of b, d, f, h, k, l and t. See also DESCENDER.

ASCII (American Standard Code for Information Interchange) The most commonly used CHARACTER SET for computers, which employs the 128 possible 7-bit integers to encode the 52 uppercase and lowercase letters and 10 numeric digits of the Roman alphabet, plus punctuation characters and some other symbols. The ASCII codes below 32 encode invisible CONTROL CHARACTERS that can be embedded in texts but are not displayed or printed. Instead, they may be interpreted by software to cause some action, the most important being ASCII code 9, the TAB character, 10 the LINE FEED and 13, the CARRIAGE RETURN.

Unlike some earlier character encodings that used fewer than 7 bits, ASCII does have room for both the uppercase and lowercase letters and all normal punctuation characters but, as it was designed to encode American English it does not include the accented characters and ligatures required by many European languages (nor the UK pound sign £). These characters are provided in some 8-bit EXTENDED ASCII character sets, including ISO LATIN 1 or ANSI, but not all software can display 8-bit characters, and some serial communications channels still remove the eighth bit from each character. Despite its shortcomings, ASCII is still important as the 'lowest common denominator' for representing textual data, which almost any computer in the world can display.

The ASCII standard was certified by ANSI in 1977, and the ISO adopted an almost identical code as ISO 646.

ASCII art A peculiar skill, perfected in the pioneering days of computing before graphical displays became available, which creates pictures using nothing but ASCII characters. Some were serious attempts to create diagrams in a text-only document, as in :

but most were of Snoopy or the Starship Enterprise. This skill has been revived on a smaller scale by Internet users who add 'smileys' (such as ;-)) to embellish text-only email.

Ashton-Tate The now-defunct US software house once responsible for the popular DBASE II database.

ASIC (Application Specific Integrated Circuit) Also called a CUSTOM CHIP. An integrated circuit which is designed to perform a specific task, as an alternative to programming a general-purpose microprocessor to do the same task in software. An ASIC is significantly faster than a software solution for the same task, and is also cheaper to manufacture since all superfluous circuitry may be omitted which reduces the size of the chip.

However, the start-up costs of designing and making the MASKS for fabricating a new ASIC are very large, so they are cheaper than a software solution only for manufacturing volumes large enough to spread this cost. Hence they are mostly employed in mass market consumer electronic devices such as mobile telephones, personal stereos and electronic toys.

Many techniques have been devised to reduce the initial cost of designing an ASIC, by building up libraries of reusable partial circuit layouts: see STANDARD CELL, MACROCELL. For products whose manufacturing volume does not justify a full ASIC design, solutions using partly prefabricated GATE ARRAY or PROGRAMMABLE LOGIC ARRAY chips may be preferable.

ASP 1 Abbreviation of APPLICATION SERVICE PROVIDER.
2 Abbreviation of ACTIVE SERVER PAGES.

aspect ratio A measure of the proportions of an object, normally stated as the ratio of its width to its height – for example 4:3 for a computer screen. This measure is of special significance in the cinema (film formats) and in the design of VISUAL DISPLAY UNITS for computers, whose aspect ratio was originally chosen to coincide with that of the domestic television screen to take advantage of mass production. The aspect ratio of the screen determines the most efficient screen RESOLUTIONS and the most desirable shape for individual PIXELS, all of which may have to change upon the introduction of HIGH DEFINITION TELEVISION.

ASPI (Advanced SCSI Programming Interface) A programming interface for controlling SCSI disk drives. See also CAM.

assembler 1 Strictly, a program that translates ASSEMBLY LANGUAGE into machine code that can be executed by a computer processor.

2 Hence, a shorthand for the assembly language code itself, as in 'this program is entirely written in assembler'.

assembler mnemonic See INSTRUCTION MNEMONIC.

assembly The new name given to a LIBRARY of prefabricated components under Microsoft's COMMON LANGUAGE RUNTIME environment. See also MANAGED CODE, OBJECT LIBRARY, TYPE LIBRARY, CLASS LIBRARY, COMPONENT ARCHITECTURE, DYNAMIC BINDING.

assembly code See ASSEMBLY LANGUAGE.

assembly language The oldest and simplest class of programming language, invented in the 1950s soon after the manufacture of the first computers. An assembly language assigns a symbolic name or MNEMONIC to each of the binary numbers that encodes the instructions that a particular processor can execute, making programs easier for people to write and understand. A program called an assembler then translates the list of mnemonics into a list of MACHINE CODES that the computer can execute. In contrast to a HIGH-LEVEL PROGRAMMING LANGUAGE in which each statement may compile many machine instructions, in a typical assembly language each mnemonic produces precisely one machine instruction. The only CONTROL STRUCTURE offered by simple assembly languages is the ability to jump to a textual LABEL instead of a numeric ADDRESS.

assertion 1 A test inserted into the code of a program as a check on its SEMANTICS, that is, that it is running in the way that the programmer expected. For example the programmer might assert that the value of variable x must always be less than 100, and raise an error if it is not. Some advanced programming languages like EIFFEL and OBERON support assertions as part of the language (see under PRECONDITION, POSTCONDITION) but assertions can be programmed in any language by using an ordinary conditional statement of the form:

```
if not(x < 100) then exception(3);
```

2 In LOGIC PROGRAMMING, any fact or relation that is added to (that is, asserted in) the database.

asset management Part of the task of computer NETWORK MANAGEMENT that involves automatically determining and keeping track of devices connected to a network, and the software installed on all of them. An important part of the job of asset management software is the checking and distribution of SOFTWARE LICENCES.

assign 1 To store a new value into a program variable: see more under ASSIGNMENT.

2 An MS-DOS command that redirects requests for disk operations made to a particular disk drive to a different drive. For example, the command:

```
c:> assign a:=c:
```

makes all commands that try to access the A: drive look instead on the C: drive. Its principal use was to rescue very old, pre-hard disk era, software that had been written only to recognize the floppy drives A: and B:. See also SUBST.

assigned number One of the many unique identifiers used within the Internet's software and protocols to label its links, SOCKETS, PORTS and various other entities: for example the port used by the FTP file transfer program has the assigned number 21. An author of a new software product who requires such a number has to obtain it by applying to the Internet Assigned Numbers Authority (IANA). All the currently assigned numbers are listed in an RFC (STD 2) which is updated periodically.

assignment The action of changing the value of a VARIABLE in a high-level programming language, typically performed by a statement that looks like:

```
x := 8
```

which makes 8 the current value of x. Assignment in most languages is destructive, that is, the previous value of the variable is lost forever, reflecting the fact that the underlying code merely stores a new number at the memory location for which that variable is a name.

associate To create a linkage, whether permanent or temporary, between two data items. For example a particular FILENAME EXTENSION might be associated with an application that can open files of that type: see under FILE

ASSOCIATION. See also ASSOCIATIVE ARRAY, ASSOCIATIVE MEMORY.

Association for Computing Machinery (ACM) The oldest and largest association of computer professionals, founded in 1947, now officially called the Association for Computing but still abbreviated to ACM. It publishes the respected journal COMMUNICATIONS OF THE ACM.

associative 1 In arithmetic and logic, an operator whose meaning is not altered by the grouping of terms within an expression: for example ordinary multiplication is associative because $(2 \times 4) \times 3$ is the same as $2 \times (4 \times 3)$. See also COMMUTATIVE.

2 In computing, the term is used to mean the retrieval of a data item via some meaningful value that is associated with it, rather than via a simple numeric index, as in ASSOCIATIVE ARRAY or ASSOCIATIVE MEMORY. See also ASSOCIATIVE CACHE.

associative array A type of ARRAY whose elements may be accessed by matching a symbolic key value rather than a numeric INDEX. For example, given an associative array A that contains [dog:23, pig:45, cat:98], then A[pig] would return the value 45. Some scripting languages, such as AWK and PERL, support associative arrays to simplify the writing of text processing programs.

associative cache A type of CACHE designed to solve the problem of cache CONTENTION that plagues the DIRECT MAPPED CACHE. In a fully associative cache, a data block from any memory address may be stored into any CACHE LINE, and the whole address is used as the cache TAG: hence, when looking for a match, all the tags must be compared simultaneously with any requested address, which demands expensive extra hardware. However, contention is avoided completely, as no block need ever be flushed unless the whole cache is full, and then the least recently used may be chosen.

A *set-associative cache* is a compromise solution in which the cache lines are divided into sets, and the middle bits of its address determine which set a block will be stored in: within each set the cache remains fully associative. A cache that has two lines per set is called two-way set-associative and requires only two tag comparisons per access, which reduces the extra hardware required. A DIRECT

MAPPED CACHE can be thought of as being one-way set associative, while a fully associative cache is n-way associative where n is the total number of cache lines. Finding the right balance between associativity and total cache capacity for a particular processor is a fine art – various current CPUs employ 2-way, 4-way and 8-way designs.

associative memory A type of computer memory from which items may be retrieved by matching some part of their content, rather than by specifying their ADDRESS (hence also called a CONTENT-ADDRESSABLE memory.) Associative memory is much slower than RAM, and is rarely encountered in mainstream computer designs.

asterisk The * character, ASCII code 42, which is employed in almost all computer programming languages as the multiplication operator (e.g. $2 * 4 = 8$).

asymmetric 1 Lacking symmetry, behaving differently in different directions. Examples in computing include a communications PROTOCOL that employs a different data-rate in each direction (see for example ADSL) or a data compression technique in which compression is much slower than decompression.

2 When applied to a MULTIPROCESSOR computer, having each processor dedicated to a different kind of computing task: as opposed to a SYMMETRIC MULTIPROCESSOR.

3 In mathematics, any RELATION that holds between x and y if and only if it does not hold between y and x. For example $x > y$ ('greater than') is an asymmetric relation.

See also its opposite SYMMETRIC.

Asymmetric Digital Subscriber Line See ADSL.

asymmetric multiprocessor See under MULTIPROCESSOR.

asynchronous 1 Literally, not synchronized; that is, proceeding at its own pace.

2 In electronics, it describes circuits that do not operate in step with other devices controlled by a shared CLOCK SIGNAL. See also ASYNCHRONOUS LOGIC.

3 In communications, it refers to any communication PROTOCOL under which data transmission may start at any time – not just on a clock tick – and where the length of each data element is determined by markers (e.g. START

BITS and STOP BITS) embedded in the data stream itself, rather than by any external timing constraint. An example is the common RS-232 serial protocol.

4 In a communications context, the term is sometimes used metaphorically to refer to any method of communication that does not require both parties to a discussion to be online at the same time (e.g. email, newsgroups, dial-up conferencing services).

asynchronous logic A class of logic circuit that does not require any CLOCK SIGNAL to drive its operations. All events happen at their own pace, the individual circuit elements synchronizing with one another only when they need to exchange data. The advantages of asynchronous logic include its optimal use of energy (those circuits that have no work to do draw no current) and its speed, since it will operate as fast as the underlying physics will permit. The disadvantage is the great difficulty of debugging complex circuits whose instantaneous state is very difficult to determine.

A family of basic asynchronous circuits based around the Muller C element and the micropipeline has been developed, and even used to implement entire microprocessors: see for example AMULET.

Asynchronous Transfer Mode (ATM) Also called *cell relay*, a high-speed switched network technology developed by the telecommunications industry to implement the next, BROADBAND, generation of ISDN. ATM was designed for use in WANs such as the public telephone system and corporate data networks, though it has also been applied to create super-fast LANs. It can carry all kinds of traffic – voice, video and data – simultaneously at speeds up to 155 megabits per second.

ATM is a CONNECTION-ORIENTED scheme, in which switches create a VIRTUAL CIRCUIT between the sender and receiver of a call that persists for the duration of the call. It is a PACKET SWITCHING system, which breaks down messages into very small, fixed length packets called CELLS, generally 53 bytes in length (48 bytes of data plus a 5-byte header). The advantage conferred by such small cells is that they can be switched entirely in hardware, using custom chips, which makes ATM switches very fast (and potentially very cheap).

The ASYNCHRONOUS part of the name refers to the fact that although ATM transmits a continuous stream of cells, some cells may be left empty if no data is ready for them so that precise timings are not relevant. This is ATM's greatest strength, as it enables flexible management of the QUALITY OF SERVICE, so an operator can offer different guaranteed service levels (at different prices) to different customers even over the same line. This ability will enable companies to rent VIRTUAL PRIVATE NETWORKS based on ATM that behave like private leased lines but in reality share lines with other users.

ATA Abbreviation of AT ATTACHMENT.

AT&T (American Telephone and Telegraph Inc.) The former US telephone monopoly, which was forced to divest itself of its local telephone interests by the US government in 1983, leading to the creation of seven smaller independent telephone companies (see BABY BELL).

Still one of the world's largest phone companies, AT&T was incorporated in 1885 and traces its origins to Alexander Graham Bell's invention of the telephone in 1876. AT&T set up the famous BELL LABORATORIES at which so much of modern computing – including the transistor and the Unix operating system – was invented. See also LUCENT TECHNOLOGIES.

ATAPI (ATA Packet Interface) An interface standard used to connect CD-ROM drives to early IBM PC compatible personal computers. ATAPI is still in use though SCSI is more often used for the purpose nowadays. See also AT ATTACHMENT, EIDE.

Atari A US electronics firm that originally manufactured amusement arcade GAMES, including Pong, the first popular screen-based video game. Atari went on to produce a range of personal computers during the 1970s and 80s that proved very popular with game players. The Motorola 68000-based Atari 520ST was briefly a serious competitor to Apple's Macintosh in 1985, and as the first low-cost computer with a MIDI interface, it attained an important niche following in the music recording business for controlling mixing desks.

The Atari Jaguar and Lynx, hand-held competitors to Sony's GAME BOY, somewhat revived the firm's fortunes in 1993, but it effectively ceased to trade following a forced merger in 1994.

AT Attachment The name given by the ANSI standards body to the IDE disk drive interface for small computers. Its successor Enhanced Integrated Drive Electronics (EIDE) is standardized as ATA-2.

AT Command See under HAYES-COMPATIBLE.

Atlas An early British MAINFRAME computer made by Ferranti that pioneered the use of VIRTUAL MEMORY.

ATM **1** Abbreviation of ASYNCHRONOUS TRANSFER MODE.
2 Abbreviation of ADOBE TYPE MANAGER.
3 Abbreviation of AUTOMATED TELLER MACHINE.
4 Online shorthand for At The Moment.

ATM Adaptation Layer A software layer that accepts user data, such as digitized voice, video or computer data, and converts to and from cells for transmission over an ASYNCHRONOUS TRANSFER MODE network. AAL software mostly runs at the end-points of a connection, though in a few circumstances AAL software is run inside an ATM switch. AAL includes facilities to carry traffic that uses other network protocols, such as TCP/IP, over ATM.

atomic Any operation that must be allowed to proceed to completion without interruption. The term is most often used in connection with a computer TRANSACTION: see more under ACID.

Atomic, Consistent, Isolated, Durable See ACID.

atomicity The property of not being divisible or interruptible.

ATRAC (Adaptive Transform Acoustic Coding) Sony's proprietary audio compression system, as employed in its minidisc players and the memory stick Walkman portable music player. See also ADAPTIVE PULSE CODE MODULATION, WAV.

attachment See under BINARY ATTACHMENT.

attenuation A diminution in the strength of a signal due to the distance it has been transmitted and other factors.

ATX A standard specification for PC MOTHERBOARDS, created by Intel.

audio Having to do with the generation, reproduction and storage of sound. See more under AUDIO SAMPLING, DIGITAL AUDIO, SOUND CARD, SOUND.

audio-band Capable of handling the range of frequencies found in sound information, roughly from 5 to 50,000 Hz.

audio compression The application of FILE COMPRESSION algorithms to digital sound files to reduce their required storage space and hence their download time over low-bandwidth communication links such as the Internet. Lossless audio compression can be achieved using exactly the same algorithms as for any other kind of digital data (see more under COMPRESSION). However, as with visual images, compression is most effective when some quality is sacrificed (so-called LOSSY compression methods), and the most widely used compressed formats such as MP3 and REALAUDIO use such methods to achieve compression ratios on the order of 60:1 to 80:1. See also ADAPTIVE PULSE CODE MODULATION, ATRAC, WAV.

The easiest way to reduce the information content in a sound file is to lower the SAMPLING RATE and WORD SIZE below those required for CD-QUALITY music (44 kHz and 16-bit samples). To increase compression further, a variety of sophisticated algorithms have been invented, based on psycho-acoustical research into human sound perception. 'Perceptual noise shaping' devotes more bits to encoding those frequency components to which the ear is most sensitive, while other techniques discard altogether those sound frequencies to which the human ear is least sensitive: for example the very highest and lowest frequencies, and frequency components that are momentarily drowned out (so-called 'psycho-acoustical masking') by a louder sound at a more sensitive frequency. Those low frequencies that are retained may be combined into a single monoaural sound instead of stereo, since the ear lacks directionality at low frequencies.

Audio Interchange File Format (AIFF) A file format devised by Apple Computer to store high-quality sound samples and musical instrument data. AIFF is also employed on SILICON GRAPHICS workstations and by professional studio equipment manufacturers.

audio processor An INTEGRATED CIRCUIT specially designed for handling sound information, typically used as a principal component of a SOUND CARD. Tasks accelerated by such a processor may include compressing and decompressing sound streams (see for example MP3), digital music synthesis, sound effects such as echo, and some aspects of VOICE RECOGNITION. More advanced audio processors also handle WAVETABLE SYNTHESIS using sound samples stored in memory. An audio processor may be fitted to the MOTHERBOARD of some computers, particularly games consoles such as the Sony Playstation, but in the PC market they are more often provided on a separate plug-in card, along with memory and other peripheral chips.

audio sampling The process of SAMPLING an analogue sound signal generated by a microphone to turn it into a digital data stream, using an ANALOGUE-TO-DIGITAL CONVERTER chip. The SAMPLING RATES employed for this purpose range from the 8-bit samples at 22 kHz used in low quality PC sound cards, through 16-bit samples at 44.1 kHz used on compact discs, to 48 kHz with 20-bit samples used in professional recording studios.

Audio Video Interleave (AVI) A standard format for computer ANIMATION files, invented by Microsoft and specific to the Windows operating system.

audio-visual A jargon term used to describe presentations, whether computerized or otherwise, that employ both pictures and sound.

audit trail A continous record of all the transactions that have been carried out on a computing system.

AUP Abbreviation of ACCEPTABLE USE POLICY.

authentication The process of verifying the identity of a person or process by a computer, typically performed by examining some identifying information such as a PASSWORD, DIGITAL SIGNATURE, or CAPABILITY.

authoring system A class of software system used for constructing highly structured types of document such as MULTIMEDIA presentations, WEB SITES or interactive training courses. The term implies a software system that does not demand knowledge of a PROGRAMMING LANGUAGE, and whose user will be concerned mostly with combining and arranging textual and pictorial content created in other programs. Examples of widely used authoring systems include Macromedia's DIRECTOR for multimedia projects, Dreamweaver for web sites, or Click2Learn's Toolbook for training courses.

auto-answer The ability of a MODEM to answer incoming telephone calls without intervention from the user.

autobaud Shorthand for AUTOMATIC BAUD RATE DETECTION.

AutoCAD The leading COMPUTER AIDED DESIGN program for small computers, published by the US firm AUTODESK INC.

Autocode The name given to what would now be called symbolic ASSEMBLY LANGUAGE, developed for the earliest commercial computers in the 1950s.

AutoComplete A facility built into Microsoft applications, including Internet Explorer, EXCEL and WORD, that enables the user to type the first few letters of, for example, a date or a recently entered number and have the program complete the rest of the typing by picking from a menu of possibilities. See also COMMAND COMPLETION.

auto-correct A function of some WORD PROCESSORS – for example MICROSOFT WORD – in which the program detects common spelling mistakes as they occur and corrects them. See also INTELLISENSE.

Autodesk Inc. A US software firm whose best-known product is the PC-based draughting and design package AUTOCAD.

auto-detect The ability of a computer, peripheral device or program to sense the presence, identity and properties of other equipment to which it is connected. Common examples include: the auto-detect MODEM, which can establish the speed of the serial line to which it is connected; the auto-detect NETWORK INTERFACE CARD, which can determine the frame type of the network it is connected to; and many graphics programs that can auto-detect the screen type and resolution of the computer they are running on. There is a general trend toward putting auto-detect abilities into more and more devices to ease the problems of CONFIGURATION: see for example PLUG-AND-PLAY and JINI.

auto-dial The ability of a MODEM to initiate a call over the public telephone system using a number stored in computer memory.

AUTOEXEC.BAT A special file employed by MS-DOS (and hence the earlier versions of WINDOWS) containing commands that are automatically executed whenever the computer is first started up. The file was typically used to issue configuration and initialization commands to the operating system and PERIPHERAL devices such as CD-ROM drives and sound cards, a typical entry being:

```
path c:\dos, c:\myapps
```

which tells MS-DOS the default directories in which to look for executable files. In later versions of Windows, its function has been largely replaced by the REGISTRY.

AUTOEXEC.BAT must be stored in the ROOT DIRECTORY of the computer's BOOT DRIVE in order to be found and executed, and the commands it contains follow the same syntax as any other MS-DOS BATCH FILE, that is, a list of operating system commands exactly as they would be typed manually at the COMMAND PROMPT, plus certain control structures such as GOTO that cannot be deployed manually. See also CONFIG.SYS, BATCH PROCESSING.

auto-execute To execute without any direct command from the user: used especially to describe SCRIPTS and MACROS embedded into Microsoft Word documents that execute themselves whenever the document is opened.

auto-flow A facility provided in most DESKTOP PUBLISHING programs that automatically distributes a quantity of imported text throughout multiple columns and pages, where necessary running it around embedded pictures and box-outs.

auto-focus A facility provided in many types of modern optical equipment – such as digital cameras, camcorders and SCANNERS – whereby the lens system can focus itself on the region of interest using some form of remote distance sensor connected via a microprocessor to a SERVO-MOTOR that alters its focal length. The two most popular sensing media are ultrasound and infrared waves. Even the smallest compact cameras may nowadays contain sophisticated image processing functions in their auto-focus systems, that can discriminate to a greater or lesser degree between objects at different distances within a scene and focus on the appropriate one, an ability rendered possible by the availability of ever smaller and more powerful microprocessors.

auto-increment A class of processor instruction that employs some variety of INDEXED ADDRESSING and before or after performing the operation automatically advances the index value so that it points to the next item to be processed. See also PRE-INCREMENT and POST-INCREMENT.

auto-indent A feature offered by many TEXT EDITORS, particularly specialized PROGRAM EDITORS, whereby, once the user indents a line from the left margin, all subsequent lines automatically align themselves to this new margin.

AutoLISP A simple dialect of the LISP programming language that is built into Autodesk's AUTOCAD application, and may be used to write MACROS to automate repetitive tasks or to customize the user interface.

Automated Teller Machine (ATM) Also called a CASHPOINT, a combined computer terminal and cash dispensing machine connected via a WAN to a bank's central computers, that enables customers to make cash withdrawals and inspect account details from public sites such as streets, airports, shops and petrol stations. ATMs typically provide a small display screen that presents menus to the user, surrounded by a small number of buttons to make menu selections, and a numeric keypad for entering the customer's PIN number – the latter is checked against that stored on the customer's cash card, which must be inserted into a slot as a means of AUTHENTICATION.

ATMs are not DUMB TERMINALS, but self-contained computers with their own local processing power, which makes the worldwide ATM network perhaps the most successful and reliable example so far of DISTRIBUTED computing: it is possible to withdraw cash from one's home account in countries right across the world, often using ATMs belonging to a different bank.

Automatic Baud Rate detection A mechanism by which a receiving device, such as a modem or terminal adapter, can determine the speed, encoding and stop bits of an incoming data stream by examining its first character (a specially chosen sign-on character). Autobaud devices can connect to services operating at different speeds without the operator having to configure their data rate in advance.

Automation A proprietary term now employed by Microsoft to describe its COM-based system of communication between application programs (originally called OLE Automation). Applications that support the Automation interface – which includes all the components of MICROSOFT OFFICE – can exchange data and activate each other's functions via scripts written in VISUAL BASIC FOR APPLICATIONS that call the COM objects and methods exposed by each application.

automation 1 The introduction of machinery to replace human labour for a particular task.
2 Of computer software, the writing or recording of a SCRIPT or MACRO to automatically perform some repetitive task.
3 More particularly, the act of making one application program drive another, for example making Microsoft Word employ Excel to format a table of numbers: see more under AUTOMATION, OBJECT LINKING AND EMBEDDING.

automaton Any device that operates according to a precise sequence of pre-defined instructions – hence a computer is a type of automaton. A branch of computer science deals with the properties and capabilities of different classes of automata, for example FINITE STATE MACHINES and TURING MACHINES, and its findings are important for the design of programming languages (indeed for the study of language in general: see also CHOMSKY HIERARCHY).

autonomous Capable of operating under its own control. In a computing context, used of software AGENTS that can roam a network collecting information without central control, and of robots.

auto-numbering A feature of many WORD PROCESSORS and TEXT EDITORS that automatically labels successive lines or paragraphs with consecutive numbers.

AutoRecover A feature of MICROSOFT WORD that automatically reconstructs potentially damaged documents that were open when the system crashed.

auto-routing 1 The ability of a communications network to ROUTE messages without them needing to contain any explicit routing data.
2 The ability of a COMPUTER AIDED DESIGN program for PRINTED CIRCUIT BOARDS or INTEGRATED CIRCUITS to automatically choose the most space-efficient route for the conductors between one location and another. The term may also be applied to programs that find the best road route between two points on a map.

auto-save A feature of many application programs that saves the user's working data to disk at regular intervals without any explicit instruction from the user. Auto-save is a security feature, to prevent loss of data should the program crash, the power fail or any other unexpected happening force the computer to be REBOOTED.

However, auto-save can be a double-edged weapon – following some types of mishap (for example accidental deletion of part of a document) it might overwrite a good saved version with the new bad data. For this reason more sophisticated auto-save systems offer the facility to create one or more generations of duplicate BACKUP files by renaming the data file each time a save takes place.

auto-sensing The ability of a hardware device to detect what is connected to it without requiring a human operator to tell it by, for example, setting a switch or jumper. The most common examples currently are those ETHERNET interface cards that can detect whether they are connected to a 10 megabits per seconds (Mbps) or a 100 Mbps network, but others include graphics cards that can detect free interrupt channels and memory addresses, modems that detect serial port speed, and printers that detect which data format they have been sent.

AutoSignature A feature offered by, for example, MICROSOFT WORD and many EMAIL client programs, that automatically appends the sender's signature to new email messages.

autostereogram (Single Image Random Dot Stereogram, SIRDS) A method of encrypting a picture into a seemingly random array of dots that reveals a three-dimensional image when viewed with the eyes defocused – in other words, those annoying posters that purport to depict dinosaurs that everyone can see but you.

Autostereograms work by fooling the brain's binocular vision system, causing it to integrate patterns perceived among the random dots as if they were twin images from a three-dimensional scene. The viewer's eyes need to be focused at twice their distance from the picture surface, rather than on the surface itself. Autostereograms are created by using a computer program that processes the original image into the appropriate dot distribution.

AutoSummarize A feature of MICROSOFT WORD that can automatically create a summary of the contents of a document, working in a semi-intelligent manner that attempts to identify and preserve important words and phrases, rather than by merely cutting the length. AutoSummarize analyses each document by assigning a score to each sentence it contains, giving higher scores to sentences containing the words that occur most frequently in the document as a whole. The user is invited to choose what percentage of these highest-scoring sentences are displayed in the final summary.

AV 1 Abbreviation of AUDIO-VISUAL.
2 Abbreviation of ANTI-VIRUS SOFTWARE.

availability The proportion of the time for which a system is capable of performing its specified task, usually expressed as a percentage. See also UPTIME, DOWNTIME.

Available Bit Rate A low quality type of ASYNCHRONOUS TRANSFER MODE traffic that will accept whatever bandwidth is available. Typically used for email or other non-time critical data.

avatar An animated graphical figure used to represent a person within an online VIRTUAL COMMUNITY or a shared online game such as a MULTI-USER DUNGEON.

AV drive (Audio Visual drive) A type of HARD DISK drive that is certified for use in audio and video recording and editing applications, because it has been designed to deliver a smooth, uninterrupted data stream. Features incorporated into an AV drive include: a larger than normal DISK CACHE; ON-THE-FLY ERROR CORRECTION to avoid lengthy retry sessions; an intelligent THERMAL RECALIBRATION mechanism that does not launch itself during reads or writes, or when the cache is empty; and a HEAD DEGAUSSING mechanism to improve the SIGNAL-TO-NOISE RATIO and reduce error correction delays.

average seek time The SEEK TIME of a disk drive averaged over many different inter-track distances, which gives a good estimate of the typical time taken to locate a single piece of data. For a modern HARD DISK drive this time is under 10 milliseconds. See also TRACK-TO-TRACK SEEK TIME, FULL STROKE SEEK TIME.

AVI Abbreviation of AUDIO VIDEO INTERLEAVE.

avionics All the electronic equipment (radar, radio, computers etc) used in aircraft.

AWE Abbreviation of ADVANCED WINDOWING EXTENSIONS.

AWE32 (Advanced Wave Effect) The WAVETABLE SYNTHESIS sound synthesizer technology used in CREATIVE LABS popular SOUNDBLASTER cards: the original 32-bit version was called AWE32, but this is now supplanted by AWE64.

Awk An interpreted SCRIPTING LANGUAGE supplied with many versions of UNIX that is specially designed for manipulating text data. It employs a C-like syntax but supports higher-level data structures, such as ASSOCIATIVE ARRAYS, and powerful PATTERN MATCHING operations.

AWT (Abstract Windowing Toolkit) A platform-independent JAVA class library, containing components such as buttons and list boxes for building graphical user-interfaces. It was supplied with earlier versions of Sun's JAVA DEVELOPMENT KIT (JDK). In the latest JDK versions, AWT is superceded by SWING.

axiom In mathematics and logic, a fundamental assertion that is accepted as true without proof, and forms the basis for proofs of other assertions.

axiomatic semantics A scheme for ascribing meaning to computer programs by making assertions about how their properties will be affected following their execution.

An important part of such axiomatic semantics are PRECONDITIONS and POSTCONDITIONS for all the available program's operations, enabling the programmer to stipulate constraints on the values of the program's variables before and after executing that operation. For example, given a function that takes the square root of numbers, a precondition could be that its argument be a positive number, and a postcondition that its return value be also a number. See also OPERATIONAL SEMANTICS, DENOTATIONAL SEMANTICS.

axis 1 A real or imaginary line about which a shape or solid body may be rotated, or with respect to which the body displays symmetry.

2 In geometry, one of the lines used to represent each dimension when locating a point in space – hence also the lines used to convey the scale of a GRAPH.

3 In an optical system, such as a camera or telescope, the imaginary line of symmetry that passes perpendicularly through the centre of the lens system and that must be aligned with the target object. Hence the term 'off-axis', to refer to objects far removed from this line and therefore in the periphery of the system's vision.

AZERTY The typewriter and computer keyboard layout employed in French-speaking countries that exchanges the positions of the Q and A keys compared to the English QWERTY layout, hence the name.

azimuth 1 In general, for example in astronomy or surveying, the angular separation of two objects in the horizontal dimension, as opposed to *elevation*, which refers to vertical angular separation.

2 The alignment of the HEADS of a magnetic tape recorder with respect to the direction of tape movement.

B

B2B Short for business-to-business, a class of online business that specializes in selling to other businesses. An example might be an auction web site for procuring manufacturing components at the lowest price, established by a group of manufacturers. See also B2C.

B2C Short for business-to-consumer, a class of online business that sells directly to the public, for example Amazon.com.

Baan A Dutch software house that publishes a widely used suite of software for automating manufacturing and resource planning processes.

Babbage, Charles (1791–1871) An English mathematician and prolific inventor who from 1823 onward designed mechanical calculating machines that anticipated the modern computer. His Difference Engine was completed and used to generate tables of logarithms, but the more advanced programmable Analytical Engine (comparable with the ARITHMETIC AND LOGIC UNIT of a modern computer processor) was never finished. His many other significant inventions included the standard railroad gauge, uniform postal rates and the Greenwich time signals.

Baby Bell A widely used nickname for any of the seven US REGIONAL BELL OPERATING COMPANIES created by the breakup of AT&T in 1984.

backbone A fast, high-capacity long-distance network link that connects various smaller, slower local networks (as for example on the Internet).

back channel, backchannel, back-channel
See under UPLINK.

back door A loophole deliberately left in an ENCRYPTION algorithm to enable interested parties (e.g. security or police agencies) to decipher traffic encoded with it.

The term also applies to loopholes deliberately programmed into the access control of some computer programs (e.g. an operating system or application) by its authors so that they can gain future access – not always for legitimate purposes.

back-end The part of a distributed computer system furthest from the user, for example a FILE SERVER, or a MAINFRAME application. The converse of the FRONT-END or user interface.

background task A software PROCESS that continues to run without any user interaction or visible user interface while other programs are being run on the same computer. To run a task in the background requires a MULTITASKING operating system: typically, the operating system will grant the most CPU time to any foreground programs with which the user is currently interacting, and give the background task what time remains.

Background tasks are frequently employed for monitoring purposes – such as watching for the arrival of new email messages or for virus detection – and for lengthy HOUSEKEEPING operations such as disk defragmentation or file indexing that do not require any attention from the user and are not time critical as to their completion. See also DAEMON, TERMINATE AND STAY RESIDENT.

backing store An alternative but rather outdated term for MASS STORAGE: that is, any permanent, non-volatile data storage medium such as magnetic and optical disks and tape drives.

backlight A light source situated behind the LCD display of a portable computer to illuminate its screen. A true backlight – fitted to more expensive models – is an electroluminescent plastic panel that covers the full screen area and provides evenly spread light intensity. Lower cost machines often have a system more accurately described as edge lighting (see under EDGE-LIT) that uses fluorescent tubes arranged around the edges of the display.

back-of-envelope A rough calculation or design schema.

backplane A PRINTED CIRCUIT BOARD containing only a power supply and a BUS that connects together a series of sockets into which many smaller printed circuit boards may be plugged. Backplanes were more widely used in the days of the MINICOMPUTER, as a means of integrating all the computer's components: the economics of PC manufacture instead favour placing as many components as possible onto a single MOTHERBOARD, and using a fast LOCAL BUS to connect them. Backplanes are still employed in MULTIPROCESSOR servers and PARALLEL COMPUTERS to enable the plugging in of extra processing elements (each plug-in board contains a separate processor and memory) and in communications equipment cabinets to hold multiple plug-in modem or network cards.

back-propagation A technique employed for training NEURAL NETWORKS in which correct examples for a recognition problem are presented at the network's outputs, and adjustment of the connection weightings proceeds backward towards the inputs.

back quote The ` character, ASCII code 96, also called grave accent. Before the advent of graphical typography software it was used as a left quote mark to open quotations, which were then closed with character 39, the apostrophe '. These two characters are still often confused and used interchangeably. Modern type systems employ different characters for quotation marks, so this usage is obsolete (see more under SINGLE QUOTE, DOUBLE QUOTE).

backside bus A second PROCESSOR BUS built into high-performance microprocessors, such as the PENTIUM II and later, used to connect the processor to its LEVEL 2 CACHE memory so that the latter does not have to share the bandwidth of the ordinary I/O bus with main memory accesses. See also FRONTSIDE BUS, SOCKET 8, SLOT 1, SLOT 2.

backslash The \ character (ASCII code 92), employed by the MS-DOS operating system and Windows as the separator for file PATHNAMES, as in C:\My Documents\Dictionary.doc.

A rich source of confusion and error is that Unix, and hence also the Internet, employs forward slash for this purpose (say in a URL such as http://www.penguin.com/index.html/), reserving backslash as the symbol to introduce ESCAPE SEQUENCES such as \t for tab and \n for newline.

Some programming languages use backslash as the integer division or as the remainder operator (e.g. 14 \ 3) to distinguish these from ordinary division (e.g. 5.67 / 23.8).

backspace 1 A key fitted to all computer KEYBOARDS which when pressed deletes the last character typed and moves the cursor one space backward.
2 The CONTROL CHARACTER with ASCII code 8, which many programs and printers interpret as an instruction to move the cursor or printhead one space backward. In some programs it deletes the last character as well as moving the cursor.

backtrack When performing a search operation, the ability to undo recent refinements and retrace one's steps to some earlier, more general criterion. For example, if searching for Hotels/4Star/London/Vacancies uncovers no vacancies, then backtracking to Hotels/3Star and trying from there might find something.

More formally, in a programming context backtracking refers to the ability of an ALGORITHM that searches a tree-structured hierarchy to retreat to a node nearer the root of the tree in order to explore a different branch. Backtracking is an important mechanism in LOGIC PROGRAMMING (see under PROLOG) and in many scheduling and resource allocation algorithms. See also DEPTH-FIRST SEARCH, BREADTH-FIRST SEARCH, UNDO.

backup The copying of the data stored on a computer so that it can be restored should the original data be destroyed by whatever cause (mechanical or software failure, theft or disaster). Backup regimes vary in sophistication from the simple copying of a few crucial files onto floppy disk, to automatically scheduled backups onto a remote tape drive made across a network.

There are several distinct modes of backup procedure: a full backup copies all the data; an INCREMENTAL BACKUP copies only those files whose contents have changed since the last incremental backup, thus copying the minimum number of files, for the sake of speed; a DIFFERENTIAL BACKUP saves all files changed since the last full backup, hence preserving only the most recent version of any file that changes frequently.

A rigorous backup regime will employ frequent (e.g. daily) incremental or differential backups, interspersed with less frequent (e.g. weekly) full backups, using three or more different sets of backup media in rotation to enable a return to yesterday's or the day before's data status. It will also include storing some or all of these backup media on different premises to guard against the loss of all through fire or burglary.

backup domain controller See under PRIMARY DOMAIN CONTROLLER.

backup tape A cartridge or reel of magnetic recording tape used to make a copy of the contents of a computer's hard disk to preserve the data they contain in the event of their failure. See more under BACKUP.

Backus, John (b. 1924) Co-creator of FORTRAN and a pioneer of research into FUNCTIONAL PROGRAMMING LANGUAGES.

Backus-Naur Form (BNF) A notation for defining formal grammars, often employed to describe the SYNTAX when designing a new programming language. A BNF description consists of a set of equations that define each type of construct permitted by the grammar in terms of simpler ones, until finally the level of the uninterpreted atoms (the LEXEMES) of the language is reached. As an illustration, consider this BNF expression of a person's name:

```
<personal-name> ::= <marital-sta-
tus><names>
<names> ::= <individual-name><fam-
ily-name> | <family-name><individ-
ual-name>
```

```
<marital-status> ::= "Mr" | "Mrs" |
"Ms"
```

The | symbol denotes alternatives, so this simple grammar accepts either Western (Ms Aretha Franklin) or oriental (Mr Bartok Béla) name orders.

backward chaining A type of reasoning employed in some types of EXPERT SYSTEM and in LOGIC PROGRAMMING languages, where a desired proof is broken down into ever-smaller sub-proofs until only demonstrable facts (i.e. statements that are always true) remain.

For example this rule from a hypothetical expert system employs backward-chaining reasoning:

```
rule olderthan(X, Y)
if age_of(X) is A1 &
age_of(Y) is A2 &
(A1 > A2)
then olderthan(X, Y) is TRUE
else olderthan(X, Y) is FALSE
```

Also called goal-driven or inductive reasoning, backward chaining is most useful for solving diagnostic problems where all the possible answers are known in advance, and just one must be selected. The PROLOG logic programming language employs backward chaining logic to resolve queries from the facts stored in its internal database. See also FORWARD CHAINING, RULE-BASED SYSTEM.

backward compatible Of a new computer or operating system, capable of running the programs that ran on its predecessor. Of a new application program, capable of processing data files created by its predecessor.

bag A very general kind of DATA STRUCTURE that can hold any number of objects of any mixture of data types, in unsorted order and with duplicates allowed. In some OBJECT-ORIENTED languages, including SMALLTALK, bag is a primitive class from which more ordered classes such as SET and DICTIONARY are descendants.

balanced tree A variety of the BINARY TREE in which at each node there is an approximately equal number of items descending from either branch. Maintaining a tree as balanced minimizes the path length from any arbitrary leaf node to the root, and so optimizes search times. See also B-TREE, BTRIEVE.

ball grid array (BGA) A type of integrated circuit package similar in geometry to the PIN GRID ARRAY, but in which thin wire pins are replaced by tiny spheres of solder that when heated can be fused onto a grid of copper pads on the printed circuit board. See also PACKAGE, SURFACE MOUNT, QUAD FLAT PACK.

Balloon Help A system of pop-up help messages, in the shape of cartoon speech balloons (hence the name), that appear when the mouse pointer is moved over a button or an icon in Apple's MACOS. See also TOOLTIP.

bandwidth 1 In an ANALOGUE communication, the difference between the highest and lowest frequencies that a transmission channel can carry: that is the band of frequencies it can pass, hence the name.
2 In DIGITAL communication, the number of bits per second that can be transmitted through a communications channel.

With its reference to waves of various frequencies, the term properly belongs to the realm of analogue electronics (e.g. radio, TV, radar), but it has been adopted in a rather informal way by digital engineers to refer to signalling speed. However, these two usages are not incompatible, being connected by the concept of SAMPLING an analogue waveform to turn it into a stream of digital bits, the sampling interval needed to capture all the information being twice the wave frequency (see NYQUIST FREQUENCY). A computer engineer's measure of the bit rate of some channel might nevertheless differ considerably from a physicist's measure of its bandwidth, because the lower signalling layers of the communication PROTOCOL employed may consume some bandwidth in encoding and error-correction schemes.

bandwidth on demand The ability to automatically request extra BANDWIDTH as network traffic increases, supported by many FRAME RELAY and ASYNCHRONOUS TRANSFER MODE services.

bang path A hackers' jargon term for the UUCPNET address format as used in the early days of the INTERNET before the universal introduction of the modern DOMAIN NAME SYSTEM. Such addresses used the ! character as a separator, as in `bigserver!penguin!dickp`, hence the name.

bank A term often used in computing to describe a collection of objects, for example a bank of processor REGISTERS or a bank of memory chips: see more under MEMORY BANK, BANK SWITCHING.

bank switching A method of organizing computer memory to give faster access to more space than the ADDRESS length should permit – the total RAM complement is divided into two or more banks whose address lines are switched electrically to appear at the same starting address. Bank switching was once used to improve the performance of GRAPHICS CARDS, but modern RAM speeds and bus widths render it unnecessary and overcomplicated.

banner advert A paid advertisement, contained within a small rectangular window and often animated, that is displayed on a WEB PAGE.

Banyan US vendor of the widely used Vines NETWORK OPERATING SYSTEM.

bar chart See BAR GRAPH.

bar code A pattern of vertical black stripes, of variable width, printed on the packaging of merchandise sold in shops to enable automatic stock control and pricing: the stripe widths encode a number that identifies the item. A BAR CODE READER measures these stripes to calculate the number, which can then be looked up in a price database by software running in a POINT-OF-SALE TERMINAL.

bar code reader A computer input device that reads the BAR CODE printed on an article of merchandise and converts it to a number: such readers depend on the reflection of a low-powered laser beam to read the pattern of stripes. Bar code readers are available both as hand-held units for stocktaking, and built into tills or supermarket checkout stations.

bar graph Also called a *bar chart*. A type of graph in which a number of discrete items arranged along one axis are represented by bars whose length is proportional to each item's magnitude on the other axis. The advantage of the bar chart is that it assists in visually identifying maximum and minimum values and trends, and so it is much favoured in business for displaying quantities such as profits, costs and sales figures. Refinements of the basic bar graph idea include plotting several different data sets as different coloured bars on the same chart (e.g. this month's and last month's sales figures) using three-dimensional bars for emphasis, and stacking fractional component figures within the same bar so that its total length represents a total value: see STACKED BAR CHART.

barium ferrite A magnetic compound used in some tape and floppy disk STORAGE systems because its very high magnetic coercivity can support greater data densities than older systems based on iron and cobalt oxide mixtures. See also FERRITE, FERRIC OXIDE, FERROMAGNETISM.

barrel distortion A form of distortion seen on CATHODE RAY TUBE monitors, in which the edges of the image are slightly convex rather than straight. The opposite distortion (i.e. concave edges) is called *pincushioning*. See also diagram under PINCUSHIONING.

barrel shifter A type of hardware REGISTER circuit that can shift or rotate its contents to the left or right by any number of bits, as employed in the ARITHMETIC AND LOGIC UNIT of some microprocessor designs to assist the implementation of multiplication and division operations. Each place shifted to the left represents a binary multiplication by two:

101 = 5
1010 = 10

while similarly each shift to the right is a binary division by two. See also ARITHMETIC SHIFT, LOGICAL SHIFT, ROTATE.

barrier synchronization A class of algorithms for synchronizing multiple PARALLEL processes in which all the processes are halted at various intermediate stages of a calculation (the barriers) to allow the slower processes to catch up, in the manner of a cross-country race in which the runners meet up to make each river crossing. See also RENDEZVOUS.

base 1 The control ELECTRODE of a BIPOLAR TRANSISTOR, whose voltage determines the current that flows through the device.

2 The number that is raised to various powers to represent numeric quantities in a POSITIONAL NOTATION scheme. For binary numbers the base is 2; for DECIMAL numbers the base is 10.

base 10 Another term for ordinary DECIMAL NOTATION numbers.

base64, base 64 A method of encoding binary information so that it can be transmitted across text-only communications systems such as Internet EMAIL (which will pass only ASCII characters in the range 32 to 126 decimal). Base64 is used by the MIME protocol to encode binary attachments to email.

The method works by concatenating each three consecutive bytes into a single 24-bit quantity, splitting this into four 6-bit numbers, and using them as indices into the string

```
ABCDEFGHIJKLMNOPQRSTUVWXYZabcdefgh
ijklmnopqrstuvwxyz0123456789+/
```

the four corresponding characters being transmitted in place of the original three bytes. Quantities smaller than three bytes are padded out with = characters, which may sometimes be seen at the ends of lines when MIME-encoded email is viewed by older mail reader programs.

base address An ADDRESS that represents the start of a memory SEGMENT or DATA STRUCTURE.

baseband A communications medium over which signals are sent with no shifting of their frequency, so that only one signal can be carried at a time: the original ETHERNET and the ANALOGUE public phone system are both baseband media. The alternative is to alter the frequency and phase of signals to permit many to share one channel (see under MULTIPLEX, FREQUENCY DIVISION MULTIPLEXING, PHASE SHIFT KEYING, DIGITAL SUBSCRIBER LINE).

base class In an OBJECT-ORIENTED PROGRAMMING LANGUAGE, a class from which subclasses inherit. In some languages it is called a SUPERCLASS.

basename The shortest name of a file, that is, the part of its PATHNAME which identifies just that particular file rather than its location within the whole DIRECTORY structure. For example, in `c:\myfiles\letter.txt` the basename is `letter.txt`. Many files may share the same basename, but no two such files may exist in the same directory. See also PATH.

Basic A simple INTERPRETED PROGRAMMING LANGUAGE designed for teaching beginners that was invented in 1964 at Dartmouth University by John G Kemeny and Thomas E Kurtz. Basic was the first language made available for personal computers (Microsoft started its business selling a version) and in recent years it has returned to importance as VISUAL BASIC, though the latter bears little resemblance to earlier versions.

The original Basic employed line numbers and provided only the primitive GOTO `<linenumber>` and GOSUB `<linenumber>` for altering the control flow, which encouraged unstructured and unreadable programs. Modern dialects such as Visual Basic have proper control structures such as IF..THEN..ELSE and named subroutines, which makes them far more suitable for writing large programs.

basic block In COMPILER theory, a consecutive sequence of instructions that contains no halts or branches before its end: in other words, a section of code that is guaranteed to execute in its entirety, or not at all. Basic blocks are therefore the preferred unit for any type of COMPILER OPTIMIZATION that involves changing the ordering of instructions.

Basic Input/Output System See BIOS.

Basic Multilingual Plane See UNIVERSAL CHARACTER SET.

Basic Rate Interface (BRI) The lowest grade of ISDN line offered to home and small business users, capable of supporting two 64 kilobits per second connections. See also CHANNEL BONDING.

Basic Storage Microsoft's term for its older partition-table-based disk storage system, to distinguish it from the DYNAMIC STORAGE system employed in Windows 2000.

batch file A file containing a sequence of OPERATING SYSTEM commands that can be executed like a program to repeat some complex series of actions, such as copying, moving and renaming multiple files. On personal computers running MS-DOS, batch files are frequently employed to install new software products, automatically creating the correct directories and copying the necessary files into them.

MS-DOS batch files consist of the normal operating system commands (e.g. DIR, DEL, COPY and MKDIR) together with some extra commands such as IF, FOR, GOTO, SHIFT and PAUSE that provide conditional control of execution and enable PARAMETERS to be passed so that the same batch file can be used in many different contexts. Under UNIX, batch files are called SHELL SCRIPTS, and are written in a C-like scripting language.

batch processing The grouping together of several processing jobs to be executed one after another by a computer, without any user interaction. This is achieved by placing a list of the commands to start the required jobs into a BATCH FILE that can be executed as if it were a single program: hence batch processing is most often used in operating systems that have a COMMAND LINE user interface. Indeed, batch processing was the normal mode of working in the early days of mainframe computers, but modern personal computer applications typically require frequent user interaction, making them unsuitable for batch execution.

battery A portable device that harnesses a chemical reaction to store and distribute electricity. Batteries may be used to temporarily power portable computers when away from a source of mains electricity.

Disposable types of battery such as the ALKALINE CELL and ZINC–CARBON CELL must be discarded when exhausted, and are used only in hand-held and pocket computers. Other batteries types, such as the LITHIUM ION BATTERY, NICKEL-CADMIUM CELL and NICKEL METAL HYDRIDE CELL can be replenished from a recharger connected to a mains supply, and will typically drive a laptop or notebook computer for from 2 to 5 hours on a single charge. Most notebooks have removable battery packs, so a spare charged one can be carried to prolong mains-free operation.

battery-backed A computer MEMORY system that has its own battery to maintain its contents after the mains power is switched off. An example is the small CMOS memory built into IBM-compatible PCs that, between sessions, stores crucial BIOS parameters such as the hard disk type. Some early hand-held computers employed cards containing battery-backed SRAM chips as mass-storage devices but, for such applications, non-volatile FLASH MEMORY has now almost entirely replaced battery-backed RAM.

Baudot code A now-obsolete five-bit CHARACTER SET invented in 1880 (long before ASCII or EBCDIC) that was used in punched-tape teleprinter systems.

baud rate The rate at which a communications channel can transmit information, where one baud is defined as one symbol per second, a symbol being a unique state that the receiver can distinguish from others.

Baud rate is often used when specifying computer SERIAL communication systems (for example a MODEM connection) as if it were a synonym for BITS PER SECOND, which is not strictly accurate since the START BITS and STOP BITS do not contribute to signal information – it is better to quote bits per second, characters per second or bytes per second for such applications. The baud is named after the French engineer J M E Baudot who invented the TELETYPE.

BB Abbreviation of BULLETIN BOARD.

BBC Microcomputer, BBC Micro A low-cost PERSONAL COMPUTER commissioned in 1982 by the British Broadcasting Corporation to accompany an educational television series on computing. Manufactured by ACORN COMPUTERS and based on the MOS Technology 6502 processor, it held an important place in British schools and universities for almost a decade, but found little acceptance outside the UK.

The BBC computer had superior graphics capabilities to its competitors the APPLE II and Commodore PET, and its inbuilt BASIC language interpreter employed a more advanced, Pascal-like dialect. Limited memory expansion severely restricted the size of programs that could be written for the BBC, but such was its quality of construction that examples running scientific programs could still be encountered in laboratories in the mid-1990s

BBS Abbreviation of BULLETIN BOARD SYSTEM.

BCD Abbreviation of BINARY CODED DECIMAL.

BCPL A programming language invented in 1967 by Martin Richards at Cambridge University and designed for writing compilers.

BCS British Computer Society, an organization for computer professionals.

BDC Abbreviation of backup domain controller: see more under PRIMARY DOMAIN CONTROLLER.

beancounters Accountants and financial directors who control the purse-strings of programming projects.

bearer channel In telecommunications, a channel dedicated to a single user's data. There may be multiple bearer channels within a single connection.

BeBox See under BE INC.

beenz A form of virtual money, invented by Beenz.com Inc., which can be given as a bonus for visiting web sites and 'spent' online to buy access to information and services.

beep An informal name for the BELL character, ASCII code 7 or ^G (CTRL+G), and a literal description of the feeble noise emitted through the tiny sound generator on its motherboard by an IBM PC that is not fitted with a sound card.

Be Inc. A computer firm set up in 1986 by Jean-Louis Gassée, a former executive of Apple, to create a rival and successor to the MACINTOSH at a time when Apple was technically stagnating. The resulting BeBox featured twin POWERPC processors with an innovative operating system called BeOS that offered exceptional multimedia performance and direct support for OBJECT-ORIENTED applications. After cancellation of a mooted merger with Apple, the BeBox failed commercially, but BeOS was ported to the Macintosh and Intel platforms where it survives as a minority operating system for high-performance applications: it has recently been modified for use in portable devices.

bell The non-printable ASCII control character with code 7 or ^G (CTRL+G) which originally caused a bell to ring in the terminal when received. On a modern PC it produces an electronic beep from the loudspeaker.

Bellcore The abbreviated name for Bell Communications Research Inc., a research laboratory founded jointly by the seven US regional telephone companies (see REGIONAL BELL OPERATING COMPANY) as a replacement for the BELL LABORATORIES, which AT&T had retained for itself. In 1999 Bellcore changed its name to Telecordia Technologies following its acquisition by SAIC.

bell curve In statistics, the graphical representation of a Normal or GAUSSIAN DISTRIBUTION, resembling the outline of a bell with a hump around the mean value that tapers off toward the higher and lower values.

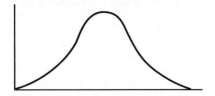

Bell Laboratories The prestigious research laboratory complex founded by the Bell Telephone Company (now AT&T) at Murray Hill, New Jersey, USA in 1947. A great deal of modern computing technology was invented at Bell Labs, including the TRANSISTOR, the UNIX operating system, the C and C++ programming languages and the TIME DIVISION MULTIPLEXING method used in all digital communications networks including the Internet. More recent developments include the Plan 9 and Inferno operating systems and a variety of optical computing and communication devices.

The laboratories are now owned by Lucent, the firm created by spinning-off AT&T's microelectronics division, and have branches in other countries such as the Netherlands that are developing the next generation of electronic and optical communication technologies.

bells and whistles Extra (by implication perhaps unwanted) features of a computer or program.

benchmark A test program used to measure the performance of some aspect of a computer system, such as the speed of its processor or disk drives. Well-known benchmark suites include: WHETSTONE, DHRYSTONE, LINPACK and SPECMARK for pure processor power; TPC for transaction processing; WINSTONE, WINBENCH and SYSMARK for Windows system performance.

There is controversy within the computer industry over the usefulness of benchmarks, with some people arguing that they are artificial and bear little resemblance to real-world tasks (see also BENCHMARK-OPTIMIZED): these proponents tend to advocate instead tests based on real applications running with standard test data sets. However, there is no question that separate component benchmarks have their place, especially for engineers and software developers who must measure directly the effect of a supposed enhancement to a component. What is perhaps controversial is the indiscriminate deployment of such figures in marketing literature.

benchmark-optimized A product whose design has been deliberately modified to yield the best results in some particularly influential BENCHMARK suite, possibly (though not always) to the detriment of its performance in real-world problems: a semi-sharp practice that is not unknown in the semiconductor and compiler businesses.

BeOS See under BE INC..

Berkeley System Distribution See BSD.

Berkeley Unix See under BSD.

Berners-Lee, Tim The English physicist who invented the WORLD WIDE WEB protocols (HTTP and HTML) while working at the Center for European Particle Research (CERN) in 1991, as a means to disseminate scientific papers across the Internet. Now Director of the WORLD WIDE WEB CONSORTIUM at MIT.

Bernoulli drive A class of DISK STORAGE device that employs a rapidly rotating flexible plastic medium (similar to that in a FLOPPY DISK) that is kept very close to – without touching – the recording heads by an aerodynamic suction effect known as the Bernoulli Effect.

The advantage of the Bernoulli drive mechanism over conventional HARD DISK drives is its great resistance to mechanical shock: the gap between head and flexible medium adjusts itself automatically following any accidental displacement, and an air cushion prevents destructive contact between head and medium (see more under HEAD CRASH). The disadvantage is that the less precise positioning limits disk capacity compared to the latest hard drives. Bernoulli-effect media are therefore most suitable for medium-capacity removable drives such as the ZIP DRIVE range of products from Iomega Corp., the most widely used examples of Bernoulli drive technology.

bespoke Software written especially for a particular customer, as opposed to OFF-THE-SHELF or SHRINK-WRAP, i.e. packaged commercial software.

best-effort traffic See under RESOURCE RESERVATION PROTOCOL.

beta release, beta A pre-production, functioning but potentially unreliable version of a program, that is released only to selected BETA TESTERS.

beta tester Someone who participates in the BETA TESTING of a program.

beta testing One the phases of software testing in which the program is made available to a few selected users to try on their own equipment and premises: such *beta testers* submit BUG REPORTS about any problems they encounter.

Bezier curve A class of cubic functions used to draw complex but smoothly curved lines and surfaces that are defined by a few (typically four) control points. In interactive drawing programs, a Bezier tool permits the user to drag several control handles that alter the curvature of a drawn line. Bezier curves are employed by the POSTSCRIPT language to describe curved lines, and by ADOBE TYPE MANAGER to define character outlines. They are named for their French inventor who developed them at the Renault car company in 1972 for modelling automobile surfaces. See also CUBIC SPLINE.

Bezier surface A smoothly curved surface defined as a mesh of BEZIER CURVES.

BFN Online shorthand for Bye For Now.

BGA Abbreviation of BALL GRID ARRAY.

BGP Abbreviation of BORDER GATEWAY PROTOCOL.

bias A small DC voltage applied across a semiconductor junction to cause it to conduct current: a reverse bias stops conduction.

BiCMOS (Bipolar-on-CMOS) A fabrication process for semiconductor devices that combines BIPOLAR TRANSISTORS and CMOS transistors on the same chip, to achieve a better balance between speed and power consumption. The process was adopted by Intel for early variants of the PENTIUM, to achieve the necessary density, though latest Pentiums are pure CMOS. See also TRANSISTOR, MOS, VLSI.

bicubic surface patch, bicubic patch Small, three-dimensionally curved tiles whose edges are defined by cubic curves rather than straight lines, used instead of linear POLYGONS to build up complex surfaces in photorealistic graphics applications where the greatest possible smoothness is required. The technique was invented in 1974 by Ed Catmull who later founded Pixar corporation.

Interpolating a curved surface using bicubic patches requires 16 pixels to be averaged for each patch as opposed to only 4 for linear polygons, significantly increasing the computational burden. Graphics applications such as PHOTOSHOP offer a bicubic option for highest quality output but, for real-time rendering applications such as games, the less precise GOURAUD or PHONG SHADING techniques are still generally employed. See also CUBIC SPLINE, BEZIER SURFACE.

bidirectional Capable of operating in two directions, applied for example to a printer that can print both from left to right and from right to left, or to a communications link that can transmit in both directions.

bidirectional printing The scheme whereby a PRINTER prints alternate lines from left to right, then right to left, to avoid wasting the time taken to return the print head to the left margin. Nearly all DOT-MATRIX and INK-JET-printers print bidirectionally. The term is not applicable to laser printers, which print whole pages rather than lines at each pass.

bi-endian A processor that can switch between BIG-ENDIAN and LITTLE-ENDIAN modes of addressing.

Big Blue The industry nickname for IBM, derived from the companies corporate colour scheme.

big-endian Said of any computer memory addressing scheme in which multi-byte data words are stored so that their most significant byte is stored at the lowest address: that is, data is stored 'big end' first. Most IBM mainframes, DEC's PDP-10 minicomputers, most RISC microprocessors including PowerPC and the Motorola 6800x family are big-endian. See also LITTLE-ENDIAN, ENDIANISM.

big iron A MAINFRAME or other large, powerful computer system.

Big Red Switch The power switch on the original IBM PC, turned off as the last resort after a program has HUNG the system. Hence by association, the act of turning off any PC to reboot it. See also THREE-FINGER SALUTE.

bilinear filtering, bilinear interpolation A sampling technique used in computer graphics systems to calculate the colour values of PIXELS, for example when warping a TEXTURE MAP to fit onto a 3D surface. The values of pixels are interpolated within a two dimensional square region (along two axes; hence bilinear) from the values of the pixels at each corner of the square, so each new pixel is the average of its four neighbours. The result is less realistic, but easier to compute, than the alternative TRILINEAR FILTERING. See also INTERPOLATE, BICUBIC SURFACE PATCH, TEXTURE MAPPING.

bimodal Capable of operating in two distinct modes.

binary 1 Capable of having one of two values, or displaying a bifurcate structure, as in BINARY TREE or BINARY SEARCH.
2 A shorthand for BINARY NOTATION, as in 'fifteen is 1111 in binary'.
3 In programming, a shorthand term for a BINARY FILE or for BINARY CODE, as in 'we'll need delivery of the binary by next week'.

binary attachment A file of data in some BINARY format – for example a word processor document, a picture or a spreadsheet – that is

attached to an EMAIL message to be sent over the INTERNET or other network. Most email systems to not permit such binary data to be included within the email itself, which is restricted to 7-bit ASCII text, and so such a file has to be encoded in a text format (see UUENCODE, MIME) and sent as an attachment, which is opened separately by the recipient to read its contents. However, the increasing use of HTML and XML based email formats such as MHTML is (slowly) rendering such attachments redundant.

binary chop Programmer's slang for the BINARY SEARCH algorithm.

binary code The sequence of instruction codes output by a programming language COMPILER or an ASSEMBLER that is directly executable by a computer: unlike the program's textual, human-readable SOURCE CODE form. See also BINARY COMPATIBILITY, BINARY IMAGE.

binary coded decimal (BCD) Also called *packed decimal*. A format for representing numbers supported by some programming languages in which, rather than convert the whole number to binary, each individual decimal digit is converted to a four-bit NIBBLE (the sign is contained in an extra nibble). BCD offers the advantage of avoiding decimal-to-binary conversion errors, and so is sometimes employed for storing sums of money. However, it is an inefficient format for performing calculations.

binary compatibility Two computers are said to be binary compatible if the same program can be run on either of them without first needing to be RECOMPILED. For example all PCs that use Intel (or AMD) microprocessors are binary compatible and can run the same copy of, say Microsoft Windows and Word. However, a UNIX workstation that employs a SPARC processor is not binary compatible with one that has a DEC Alpha processor, so a program that runs on one will need to be recompiled to run on the other. This lesser degree of compatibility is called SOURCE level compatibility.

binary file Any file that consists of arbitrary byte values (i.e. any values between 0 and 255), in contrast to a TEXT FILE, which contains only the printable ASCII characters 32 to 126 and carriage returns. Executable program files are normally binary files, as are most database, spreadsheet and word processor files. When viewed in a text editor, a binary file will appear to contain a random jumble of symbols; binary files are not as a rule portable, and make sense only to the program that created them.

binary format Any computer data format that consists of a sequence of values intended to be treated as pure binary numbers (for example an executable program file), in contrast to a text format where successive values are interpreted as characters from the ASCII character set.

The difference between the two formats is only superficial since ultimately the computer can recognize only binary numbers: the same value, say 65 decimal, might be treated as a number, a program instruction, or as the letter 'A' depending solely upon context and the software that is reading it. There is, however, a practical difference in that binary format files appear as meaningless jibberish if viewed as TEXT FILES, since they contain some values outside the range of printable ASCII characters and also numbers that will be wrongly interpreted as ASCII characters. Many application programs (for example word processors) store their in data in binary format files, which cannot therefore be easily read except by the application that created them.

binary image The sequence of bits in computer memory that represents a running computer program. A binary image is not in general the same as the BINARY FILE on disk that represents an executable program, whose layout is normally altered during the process of program loading. A binary image may be stored on disk to enable instant restarting of the program, as seen in the Suspend/Resume feature on many laptop computers.

Binary Large Object See BLOB.

binary notation A number system that employs the BASE two so that numbers expressed in it are represented by sequences of only two possible digits, 0 and 1. Computers represent numbers internally in a binary notation, because the electronic or magnetic switches they use to store data have just two positions, on and off, which are made to stand for the two digits.

Binary notation is a positional notation just as the ordinary DECIMAL NOTATION is, but instead of tens, hundreds, thousands each position represents twos, fours, eights, sixteens – that is, powers of two. For example the number of fingers on your hand is 5 in decimal notation, but 101 in binary notation because $5 = 1 \times 2^2 + 0 \times 2^1 + 1 \times 2^0$.

Programmers use binary notation explicitly only when the value of individual bits is considered important, for example when creating a BIT MASK to read the value of a FLAG, or when manipulating BITMAPPED graphics: most of the time HEXADECIMAL NOTATION is a more compact and convenient way to enter binary values into a program text. See also BINARY NUMBER, SIGN BIT, MOST SIGNIFICANT BIT.

binary number A number expressed in base two notation as a string of 0s and 1s. For example the decimal number 237 is 11101101 in binary notation: see more under BINARY NOTATION.

binary search A very efficient search algorithm that divides the data to be searched (which must be in sorted order) in two and decides which half the answer must lie in. This half is in turn divided in two, and so on until only one item remains. A binary search can find one item among 1 million by making only 20 decisions ($2^{20} = 1,048,576$)

binary synchronous An early serial communication PROTOCOL used to connect terminals to IBM's mainframe computers: the character-based protocol permitted several terminals to share the same data link. Though now replaced by newer protocols such as HDLC, the name (sometimes shortened to bisync) may still be encountered as an option when configuring communications software.

binary tree A data structure composed of NODES, each of which points to two further nodes. A binary tree provides a fast way to access data objects, and is employed in many indexing and memory allocation procedures in computing. Traversing such a tree is equivalent to performing a BINARY SEARCH.

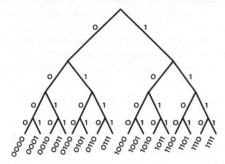

binder A kind of COMPOUND DOCUMENT introduced in MICROSOFT OFFICE 95 to contain various parts of a project created with different Office components, such as texts, spreadsheets and graphics. A binder is an ACTIVEX container and thus allows in-place editing of any of its contained parts using the appropriate application.

bindery A database incorporated into the NOVELL NETWARE network operating system from version 3.11 onwards, to store information about individual users, groups and WORKGROUPS. The bindery contains the PASSWORDS and PERMISSIONS for each user and group, and allows these to be administered from a single central location on the server.

The Novell bindery employs OBJECT-ORIENTED principles, storing objects that represent physical or logical entities in the network such as a user, a group of users or a file server: each object has properties such as access permissions, passwords or network addresses; the set of the values of each object's properties is a separately stored entity called a property data set.

binding The process of associating some configurable entity with a particular attribute or value, for example linking a program VARIABLE name with its contents or a NETWORK INTERFACE CARD with a particular network PROTOCOL. Also used as a noun to describe an instance of such association, as in 'have you checked the network binding'.

In programming languages, the concept of binding is central to the meaning or semantics of any program: in most languages, entities that are unbound, that is which have not had a value assigned to them, cannot be sensibly processed. The binding of a program's variables may be static (established prior to RUN TIME and unable to be changed) or dynamic (established at run time and capable of being changed according to the rules of the language). This distinction is also often referred to as EARLY BINDING versus LATE BINDING, particularly in OBJECT-ORIENTED programming. Another important property of any act of binding is its domain of validity: the binding of a particular name and value may be decreed to be valid only within a limited domain (see more under NAMESPACE and SCOPE).

BinHex A method of encoding BINARY ATTACHMENTS to EMAIL messages; used only by the APPLE MACINTOSH. See also MIME, UUENCODE.

biocomputing A generic term that describes various experimental uses of biological systems and compounds to construct computing machines: for example the use of proteins to build integrated circuits, rhodopsin pigment as a memory medium, or DNA replication as a computing mechanism. The last of these has been demonstrated experimentally by encoding text strings as synthetic DNA strands and then using the ability of DNA strands to bind to their complementary form to search for a particular string from among millions in parallel. However, there have not as yet been any commercial applications of biocomputing.

biometrics The measurement of parts of a person's body, for example fingerprints, voice timbre or unique patterns in the iris of the eye, to identify the person for security purposes. Computers can now process such data sufficiently fast for biometric methods to be used in real time as keys to gain access to a system. For example, when a finger is placed on a scanning pad, the print is immediately compared with one stored in a database of authorized persons.

Iris-recognition is touted as the biometric technology most likely to be used by banks in future CASHPOINT machines, because the iris pattern is difficult to fake and can be read without bodily contact by a digital camera installed above the display screen.

bionic Combining both biological and electronic elements: as, for example, in the implantation of sensors to restore damaged eyesight or hearing, or computers that detect nerve impulses to control a prosthetic limb.

BIOS (Basic Input/Output System) A set of crucial, low-level code routines that give access to the input and output hardware of an IBM PC compatible personal computer.

The BIOS routines are responsible for reading characters from the KEYBOARD and reading data from the DISK DRIVES, and therefore must be running before any commands can be issued by the user or an OPERATING SYSTEM can be loaded from disk. For this reason the BIOS is stored in a ROM chip and automatically executed whenever the power is switched on, whereupon it supervises the loading of the operating system from disk. Modern PCs employ FLASH MEMORY rather than ROM to store the BIOS routines so that they can be updated from a floppy disk whenever a new version is released, say to support some newly invented device (see FLASH-UPDATABLE).

The BIOS keeps a store of crucial parameters, such as the number and nature of disks present and the type of PROCESSOR fitted, in a small, separate writeable memory area called the CMOS – one of these settings determines on which disk to look for an operating system. The user can inspect and alter these CMOS settings by holding down certain combination of keys (e.g. function key F1 for some makes of PC) to interrupt the computer's BOOT-UP sequence.

bipolar See BIPOLAR TRANSISTOR.

bipolar-on-CMOS See BICMOS.

bipolar transistor The earliest form of TRANSISTOR, formed by sandwiching layers of P-TYPE and N-TYPE semiconductor materials in either an *npn* or *pnp* configuration. The middle layer is called the BASE and the outer layers are the EMITTER and COLLECTOR respectively: applying a voltage to the base changes the current flowing between emitter and collector, allowing the device to be used as an amplifier (e.g. in radios and hi-fi) or as a switch in computer circuits. Bipolar transistors switch very fast, but they consume power even when turned off, and so in modern chip designs have been displaced by the more power-efficient CMOS transistor.

BISDN Abbreviation of BROADBAND ISDN.

bistable An electronic device that can exist in two stable states, which it can be made to switch between by sending a control signal. The FLIP-FLOP is such a bistable device, and is used to implement computer memory chips by interpreting its two states as representing 0 and 1.

bisync Shorthand for BINARY SYNCHRONOUS.

bisynchronous A mistaken expansion of bisync, the abbreviation for BINARY SYNCHRONOUS.

bit One BINARY digit, the fundamental unit of information in computing, communications and physics. A single bit can have only one of two values, 0 or 1.

Inside digital devices, bits are represented by physical quantities: for example different voltages on a piece of wire (0 volts and 5 volts), or different orientations of a magnetic field in ferric oxide particles, or the presence or absence of a pit in the surface of a CD may be taken to represent 0 and 1.

bitblit Abbreviation of BIT BLOCK TRANSFER.

bit block transfer (bitblt, bitblit) An operation used in computer graphics programming that moves a block of bits en masse from one location in memory to another. If these bits represent display pixels, the effect is to move part of an image from one place to another, and so bitblt is much used in graphical user interface code to display WINDOWS, ICONS and FONT characters quickly. Because this operation is used so extensively, many modern microprocessors provide special instructions to speed it up (see MMX) and a hardware GRAPHICS ACCELERATOR usually contains a dedicated unit called a BLITTER that performs the operation as quickly as possible.

bitblt Abbreviation of BIT BLOCK TRANSFER.

bit bucket An imaginary receptacle for discarded data: a register or memory location whose content may be written to, but which is never read. Also used metaphorically for the act of discarding data, as in 'throw it in the bit bucket'. A commonly used example of a bit bucket is the NUL device in MS-DOS and Unix, which may be used to throw away unwanted text output from a command: mode > nul

bit error An error in a single BIT within a BYTE or WORD of data transmitted over a noisy channel: for example if the byte sent were 11111111 then a received value of 11111101 would represent a bit error in the second bit. There are well-known ERROR DETECTION AND CORRECTION algorithms that can correct one or more such bit errors, given some extra, redundant information, and these techniques are widely applied in the mechanisms of HARD DISK and CD-ROM drives, as well as in telecommunication systems. See more, for example, under REED-MULLER CODE and HAMMING DISTANCE.

bit field An arbitrary subdivision within a bit string that represents a BINARY NUMBER: for example, for the purposes of different programs, a 16-bit number might be treated as if it consisted of two 8-bit fields, or of four 4-bit fields. Bit fields are useful, for example, when storing graphical PIXEL data in a PACKED format. The C and C++ programming languages provide special operators for the easy extraction and manipulation of bit fields.

bitmap A table of digital BITS used to represent, for example, a picture or a text character, each bit in the table being interpreted as the presence or absence of a screen PIXEL or a printed dot. The principle can be illustrated by the following table, which represents the letter Z as a 6 × 6 table of bits:

```
1 1 1 1 1 1
0 0 0 0 1 0
0 0 0 1 0 0
0 0 1 0 0 0
0 1 0 0 0 0
1 1 1 1 1 1
```

bitmap editor The generic name for programs, such as Adobe's PHOTOSHOP, whose function is to create and manipulate BITMAPPED images: that is files in which pictures are stored as a collection of individual PIXELS rather than as geometric descriptions (see more of this distinction under GRAPHICS). A bitmap editor enables its user to change the colour of individual pixels or whole areas of pixels at once, using a variety of tools that mimic the effect of paintbrushes, pencils, spray cans and more. Typical bitmap editors also support a variety of graphics FILTER operations, such as EDGE ENHANCEMENT, that can be applied automatically to the whole image.

bitmapped Used to describe any hardware device or software data structure that employs a table of single BITS to represent its data objects, for example images on a monitor screen or on a printer. See more under BITMAP, BITMAPPED DISPLAY, BITMAPPED FONT.

bitmapped display Strictly, a display in which each PIXEL on the screen is represented by a BIT stored in VIDEO MEMORY, which would limit its applicability to black-and-white images only. More frequently used, however, to describe any display in which each pixel corresponds to a byte or word in video memory, which covers all contemporary computer colour displays. The term was coined in distinction to the now-obsolete VECTOR DISPLAY, which drew lines instead of pixels.

bitmapped font, bitmap font A character FONT in which each individual letter form is stored as a table of PIXELS (a picture), in contrast to an OUTLINE FONT where each character is stored as a set of lines or strokes (a description of how to draw the character). Bitmapped fonts are fast and easy to RENDER onto a screen or printer – by simply copying the bits for the character – and for this reason were preferred on older computer systems (up to and including MS-DOS PCs) that used CHARACTER-BASED displays.

Bitmapped fonts render correctly only at the size they were created: to enlarge or reduce their characters involves duplicating or removing pixels, which gives the letters an unattractive jaggy appearance. In contrast, outline fonts can be scaled to any size (above a minimum) with little loss of quality and hence they have almost entirely displaced bitmapped fonts, except for applications such as instruments and hand-held computers with small fixed-size displays. Examples of bitmapped fonts include the fixed-pitch Courier and MS Serif fonts supplied with Windows. See also GLYPH.

bitmapped graphics See under GRAPHICS.

bitmap texture In computer GRAPHICS, a 2-dimensional image projected onto the surface of a 3D object to give it a realistic appearance of, for example, wood, brick or stone. See more under TEXTURE MAPPING.

bit mask A sequence of bits used to read or set bits in other data words by applying bitwise logical operations. For example the bit mask value 4 (i.e. binary 100) may be used to detect whether the third bit is set in any word by calculating the value of `word AND mask`, the result 1 indicating that the third bit of `word` is set.

Bitnet A US academic and research network joining more than 3000 university computers, which offers FTP and email services and pioneered the use of LIST SERVERS. Bitnet runs over the Internet, using its own protocol on top of IP.

bit ordering The direction in which a computer's processor reads the bits in the words stored in its memory, which may be either from the higher to the lower or from the lower to the higher ADDRESSES. See also BYTE ORDERING, ENDIANISM.

bit-parallel Referring to a hardware device or operation that moves data in whole WORDS (that is, several BITS at once) along a parallel BUS. See also BIT-SERIAL.

bit pattern Any particular sequence of BITS such as 10101011. See also BIT FIELD, BITMAP, BIT MASK.

bit plane In computer GRAPHICS, an array of numbers (called a BITMAP) that contains the data for just the red, the green or the blue component of a whole picture. A complete picture is stored as three consecutive bit planes, one for each colour, which may be shown diagrammatically thus:

RRRRRRRRR...GGGGGGGG....BBBBBBB....

This is in contrast to various PACKED PIXEL storage formats in which the red, green and blue data for each pixel are stored consecutively, followed by those for the next pixel, and so on:

RGBRGBRGBRGB.....

bit-serial Any hardware device or operation that moves data one BIT at a time down a single conductor. See also BIT-PARALLEL.

bits per second A fundamental measure of digital communication speed. See also DATA RATE.

bitstream Any signal that consists of a continuous procession of digital BITS.

bit-twiddling Low-level programming in machine code.

bitwise An operation that is performed on individual BITS rather than on whole words. For example bitwise logic operators treat their operands as sets of individual bits rather than as the single logic values True (non-zero) and False (zero).

Consider for example the AND operation on the numbers 5 (binary 101) and 6 (binary 110). Logical 5 AND 6 gives the result True, since neither 5 nor 6 is False (i.e. 0) but *bitwise* 5 AND 6 gives 4 (binary 100), the result of ANDing each pair of bits individually:

101
110
100

The operations AND, OR, NOT and XOR can all be used in either a logical or a bitwise fashion, and most programming languages employ different symbols to distinguish them: for example in C, logical AND is & and bitwise AND is &&.

Biztalk Microsoft's APPLICATION FRAMEWORK for creating distributed business applications that exchange XML documents over the Internet using the SOAP protocol. See also .NET, DISTRIBUTED APPLICATION ARCHITECTURE.

BlackBerry A range of powerful radio-based pocket PAGERS, made by the Canadian firm RIM, that can receive both Internet EMAIL and SMS text messages.

blackboard A data structure employed in some ARTIFICIAL INTELLIGENCE programs to collect together significantly related concepts uncovered during the analysis of a problem.

black box Any subsystem, whether software or hardware, whose inner workings are deemed irrelevant at the current level of inquiry. When trying to understand any complex system, it is often useful to temporarily treat some subsystem as if it transforms its inputs into outputs by 'magic' – for example, when explaining how key strokes are interpreted by a word processing program, the workings of the circuitry inside the keyboard would be considered a black box that simply passes on key strokes to the computer. See also MODULE, ABSTRACTION.

black listing A software mechanism that forces an AUTO-DIAL MODEM to wait a certain period before redialling the same number, introduced as a legal requirement in many countries to prevent the nuisance caused by wrong numbers.

blanking interval During the scanning of a CATHODE RAY TUBE screen to produce an image, those periods during which the electron gun is turned off to allow the dot to return to the top or the left-hand edge without being seen (see more under FLYBACK, REFRESH RATE). There are two such intervals, the vertical blanking interval or VBI that occurs once per frame (e.g. 60 times per second on a typical computer VDU), and the horizontal blanking interval or HBI that occurs once per SCAN LINE (e.g. 480 times per frame for a VGA display). Computer system software often exploits the blanking intervals to manipulate data, for example to update the DISPLAY BUFFER without interfering with image quality, and broadcasters use the blanking intervals to transmit extra data such as TELETEXT to television sets (see also WEBCAST).

bleeding edge A cynical pun on 'leading edge' that highlights the potential cost of being too quick to adopt some new and unproven technology.

blend A painting tool provided in most BITMAPPED graphics programs that creates a smooth transition between two selected colours. See also GRADIENT FILL.

Bletchley Park A country house in Buckinghamshire, England that was requisitioned as a secret signals interception station (called Station X) before and during World War II. A team of engineers and mathematicians worked there in greatest secrecy to break the ciphers used by the Axis powers, and included the team lead by Alan TURING that cracked the Enigma code used by German forces. In the process of cracking the codes, the world's first practical electronic computers, the COLOSSUS machines, were built at Bletchley. See also CIPHER, ENIGMA MACHINE, BOMBE, LORENZ CIPHER, ENCRYPTION, CRYPTOGRAPHY.

blind packet forwarding A technique for reducing network PACKET OVERHEAD by avoiding the exchange of BROADCAST or MULTICAST messages. When packets that do not contain a local NETWORK LAYER address arrive at a router from some connected LAN, they are automatically forwarded on to a WAN, while packets

from the wide-area circuit are automatically forwarded to the attached LAN.

blink The action of an OFF-LINE READER program as it connects to a server, downloads mail or files, then automatically disconnects: the name is meant to suggest the short duration of this transaction.

blit Abbreviation of BIT BLOCK TRANSFER.

blitter A GRAPHICS PROCESSOR or accelerator that specifically speeds up the important BIT BLOCK TRANSFER operation (commonly abbreviated to Bit BLT, or Bit Blit, hence the name) which is heavily used in displaying windows and text characters by graphical operating systems such as Windows and MacOS.

blitting See BLITTER.

bloat The tendency of software systems to grow larger with each successive version.

bloatware Software that suffers from BLOAT.

BLOB (Binary Large Object) A large block of BINARY data, for example a digitized picture or sound file, that is stored in a field in a database. Since a BLOB has no internal record structure (hence the punning name) that could be queried, it is known to the database software only by its location and size, and must be labelled with an associated text field to enable it to be retrieved.

block The basic organizing unit of any BLOCK STRUCTURED programming language, a group of actions that has a marked beginning and end but does not have a name (unlike a PROCEDURE or FUNCTION). C, C++ and JAVA for example, delimit blocks with curly brackets, as in:

```
while ( cur && cur->fno == LISTFNO )
{
if ( cur->item==pItem )
if ( cur )
{
next=cur->next;
cur->next=list_GCreate();
return next;
}
cur=cur->next;
}
```

block copy A class of processor INSTRUCTION that copies the contents of a whole series of memory locations in a single operation, given only a source and a destination address and a block length as operands. See more under BLOCK MOVE.

block move A class of processor INSTRUCTION that moves the contents of a whole series of memory locations to a new location as a single operation, given only the source and destination addresses and the block length as operands. A block move instruction is typically more efficient than a loop containing single-word move instructions, because the processor's internal datapaths do not need to be reconfigured after each value is transferred, and the hardware can be designed, at minimal transistor cost, to automatically increment the source and destination addresses without affecting the general registers. An equivalent instruction that leaves the original data in place is called a BLOCK COPY. Block move operations assume a particular significance in computer GRAPHICS where they are continually employed to move BITMAPS from one place to another, and so a great deal of effort has been expended on optimizing their performance. See also BIT BLOCK TRANSFER.

block structured A PROGRAMMING LANGUAGE that supports the grouping of code statements into units called blocks, which may be wholly separate or wholly nested within one another, but may not overlap; variables may be declared local to a block, their SCOPE being confined to that block and any nested within it. Subprograms such as PROCEDURES and FUNCTIONS also behave as blocks.

A typical block-structured language is PASCAL, which indicates blocks by surrounding them with the keywords BEGIN...END and permits procedure declarations to be nested within one another. However, most modern languages incorporate some degree of block structuring – for example C, C++ and JAVA support blocks within functions, delimited by the braces { and }, but do not permit nested function definitions. Block-structured languages offer control structures such as IF..THEN..ELSE..ENDIF and REPEAT..UNTIL and WHILE..ENDWHILE in which control must flow through clearly delimited blocks, and discourage the use of unstructured jumps such as GOTO or BREAK.

Block structure makes it easier for humans to reason about the workings of a program, and allows a language COMPILER to manage memory economically by allocating local variables temporarily on a STACK.

blow Used as in to 'blow an EPROM': to program the contents of an eraseable read-only memory chip.

Blue Screen of Death The text-mode error message screen, showing white text on a blue background, that appears when any Microsoft Windows system encounters a FATAL ERROR condition; it signifies that Windows cannot run and the computer must be rebooted.

Bluetooth A short-range radio technology that enables portable devices such as personal organizers, mobile telephones and domestic equipment to connect to a computer network such as the INTERNET without the need for cables. Bluetooth is being developed by a consortium including 3Com, Ericsson, IBM, Intel, Lucent, Microsoft, Motorola, Nokia and Toshiba. The name comes from the nickname of a 10th-century Danish king Harald Bluetooth.

Bluetooth wireless transmitter/receiver chips can be built into many kinds of device: they operate in the 2.4 GHz (Industry, Science and Medicine) waveband, and the sending and receiving devices need not be within line of sight to establish a connection, but must be within the total range of 10–30 metres. Bluetooth supports both POINT-TO-POINT and MULTIPOINT types of connection, under which up to seven slave devices may be controlled from a single master: software controls and identity codes within each chip allow the owner to select which pieces of equipment will communicate.

Sample applications for Bluetooth technology include advanced cordless telephones, 'roving' connections to a company network within a building, Internet access from a hand-held computer, or automatic synchronization of a hand-held computer with a desktop computer whenever it comes within range. See also WI-FI, WIRELESS COMMUNICATIONS.

BMP, .BMP A bitmapped GRAPHICS FILE FORMAT invented by Microsoft for use in its Windows operating system that uses .BMP as its normal file extension. The original .BMP format used a 4- or 8-bit PALETTE stored in the file along with an array of index values representing the PIXELS, which was fast and efficient for storing flat-shaded Windows images for 8-bit displays. Later versions abandoned the palette to store 24-bit pixels in RGB format, and were far less efficient, with the result that other formats such as GIF, TIFF and JPEG have overtaken it in importance. See also DEVICE INDEPENDENT BITMAP.

BMP/DIB (Bitmap/Device Independent Bitmap) The principal bitmapped GRAPHICS FILE FORMAT supported by Microsoft Windows. See more under DEVICE INDEPENDENT BITMAP.

BNF Abbreviation of BACKUS-NAUR FORM.

body A term used to describe the main substance of some software object such as a message or a program definition, as opposed to its descriptive HEADER. See also FUNCTION BODY.

bogometer See BOGOSITY.

bogon See BOGOSITY.

bogosity An imaginary physical quantity attributed by programmers to ideas and projects of which they disapprove, especially the efforts of marketing departments. Bogosity is measured with a *bogometer* and its fundamental particle is the *bogon*.

boilerplate Standard paragraphs that may be assembled and edited using a WORD PROCESSOR to create routine business letters such as legal contracts.

Bolt, Beranek and Newman, Inc. A US software firm based in Cambridge, Massachusetts that performed much of the pioneering work that lead to the INTERNET, including installing the computers for the original ARPANET. See more under ARPA.

bomb In the context of software, to crash in a spectacular manner (e.g. with sound effects or screen disruption).

Bombe Electro-mechanical calculating machines used during World War II to assist in deciphering messages encrypted using the German ENIGMA MACHINE. The machines contained spinning rotors that mimicked those in the Enigma itself, and could rapidly try out millions of combinations, automatically stopping when a match was found: the name alluded to the ticking noise they made while running.

The first Bombes were developed by the Polish intelligence service in 1938 to attack the three-rotor Enigma code, but were rendered ineffective when the Germans added two more rotors in 1939. Further generations of Bombe were designed in England at BLETCHLEY PARK by a team lead by Alan TURING, and were successful in decoding German message traffic until the end of the war.

More than sixty Bombes were built at Bletchley, each capable of testing 20 rotor configurations per second, and they checked the half million configurations needed to decipher that day's messages in a few hours. Bombes performed only part of the decryption process (though the most difficult part) and much further manual work was required. Later in the war Turing visited BELL LABORATORIES and advised on the building of many more Bombes by the US Navy.

Unlike the COLOSSUS machines used to crack the LORENZ CIPHER, the Bombes were not modern digital computers, but a mechanical solution to a single, highly specialized cryptographic problem. See also CIPHER, ENCRYPTION, CRYPTOGRAPHY, ENIAC.

Booch method An OBJECT-ORIENTED DESIGN method set out by Grady Booch in his 1990 book *Object Design with Applications*.

bookmark 1 In a WORD PROCESSOR or TEXT EDITOR, a place marker used to permit a rapid return to the same place in a document. Some word processors employ anonymous symbols as bookmarks, which the user can visit in sequence by pressing a particular key, while more sophisticated ones allow the creation of meaningful names as bookmarks, presenting a menu of these names so that selecting one moves the cursor immediately to that location.
2 In NETSCAPE NAVIGATOR, the name for a stored URL used to revisit the same WEB SITE in future.

Boolean A simple data type that contains only two permitted values, the truth values True and False. Booleans are supported by all programming languages of the ALGOL family such as PASCAL and MODULA-2. See more under BOOLEAN LOGIC.

Boolean algebra A type of ALGEBRA devised by George BOOLE that consists of a set of two elements 0 and 1 (which may be interpreted as True and False) and three operations on these elements which are generally called AND, OR and NOT, sometimes denoted by the symbols ∩, ∪ and ~. These operations correspond quite closely with the normal meanings of the words, so that x AND y is 1 only if both x and y are 1, x OR y is 1 if either x or y is 1, and so on. These operations satisfy a set of laws that include idempotency, identity, distribution, commutation and association. The TRUTH TABLES for the three operations are as follows:

A	B	A and B
0	0	0
0	1	0
1	0	0
1	1	1

A	B	A or B
0	0	0
0	1	1
1	0	1
1	1	1

A	not A
1	0
0	1

Boolean algebra and the related BOOLEAN LOGIC are of paramount importance in computing, as the transistor switches from which digital computers are constructed embody Boolean functions in hardware, while most computer programming languages and many database query languages support Boolean calculations. Boolean algebra is also fundamental to switching theory, ALGORITHM design, program semantics and many other related fields.

Boole, George (1815–64) An Irish mathematician remembered chiefly for his formalization of symbolic logic as BOOLEAN ALGEBRA, though he also made important contributions in probability theory and differential equations.

Boolean logic A formal logic system derived from the BOOLEAN ALGEBRA by interpreting its two permissible values 0 and 1 as the TRUTH VALUES True and False. It is used in electronics to define the behaviour of all the kinds of LOGIC GATE from which computer processors are constructed, and in programming to define operators that work on truth-valued variables.

boot To start up a computer system by loading a fresh copy of the operating system: see BOOTSTRAP.

boot drive The disk drive of a computer system from which the operating system is loaded when the computer is first started up. Many operating systems allow the identity of this drive to be altered: for example on IBM-compatible PCs it is determined by a setting in the machine's BIOS parameter area. See also BOOTSTRAP, BOOT SECTOR, BOOT IMAGE.

boot image An exact bit-for-bit copy of a computer's OPERATING SYSTEM as it exists in memory immediately after the initial BOOT operation. Such an image may not be identical to the operating system executable file stored on disk, as it will probably have had various drivers and other configuration options applied during boot up. Boot images are sometimes stored on disk to speed up a lengthy start-up process. See also INITIAL PROGRAM LOADER.

boot record A set of crucial data written on the BOOT SECTOR of a HARD DISK or FLOPPY DISK that contains the information required by the INITIAL PROGRAM LOADER to locate a copy of the operating system on the disk and load it into memory. Damage to the boot record can prevent the computer from booting from that disk, and render the disk's other contents inaccessible; many disk repair utilities work by preserving and restoring backup copies of the boot record. Some types of VIRUS hide themselves within the boot record. See also MASTER BOOT RECORD, BOOT SECTOR VIRUS.

boot sector The first sector on a FLOPPY DISK or HARD DISK formatted for the MS-DOS operating system, which records the number of HEADS, CYLINDERS and SECTORS per cylinder used on that disk. This information is needed by the disk controller to access data on the drive, and the boot sector is located at head 0, cylinder 0, sector 0, so the controller can always find it regardless of how the drive is formatted. Other operating systems such as UNIX also reserve a special sector for such initialization information, but it is typically in a different form, so one operating system can rarely boot from another's disk. See also BOOT SECTOR VIRUS.

boot sector virus A computer VIRUS program that hides its code within the BOOT SECTOR of a FLOPPY DISK, so that the virus code is executed before the operating system itself has loaded, making countermeasures difficult to apply.

Once loaded into memory, such a virus infects the boot sectors of any other floppy disk that is placed in the drive, hence ensuring its spread. See also ANTI-VIRUS SOFTWARE.

bootstrap To start a computer by loading its OPERATING SYSTEM from disk storage into memory. The name alludes to the seeming absurdity of trying to lift oneself off the floor by pulling on one's own bootstraps – since it is the operating system that enables a computer to read disks, then loading itself from disk would seem to be a similar impossibility. This paradox is resolved by the presence of a small program called the BOOTSTRAP LOADER, which resides permanently in the computer (stored in a ROM chip) and contains just sufficient code to read the rest of the operating system from disk. This process is informally called 'booting' or 'booting up' the computer. See also REBOOT, BOOT DRIVE, BOOT SECTOR.

bootstrap loader More formally called an Initial Program Loader (IPL), a small section of executable code, permanently stored in a ROM chip within the computer, whose sole function is to load into memory from DISK just that small part of a computer's OPERATING SYSTEM needed to load the remainder of the operating system.

boot-up The time interval during which a computer is loading its OPERATING SYSTEM from disk. See BOOTSTRAP.

Border Gateway Protocol A PROTOCOL for routing between different DOMAINS in large networks that forms part of the TCP/IP suite and is defined in RFC 1267-8.

Borland International Inc. A software publisher, originally Danish but now based in California, best known for developing the TURBO PASCAL and DELPHI programming languages.

bot An abbreviation derived from ROBOT, but most often used in net jargon to mean a software agent rather than a hardware device. See, for example, HELPBOT.

bottom-up design Any design method in which the most primitive operations are specified first and the combined later into progressively larger units until the whole problem can be solved: the converse of TOP-DOWN DESIGN. For example, a communications program might be built by first writing a routine to fetch a single byte from the communications port and working up from that.

While top-down design is almost mandatory for large collaborative projects, bottom-up design can be highly effective for producing 'quick-and-dirty' solutions and rapid prototypes, most often by a single programmer using an interactive, interpreted language such as VISUAL BASIC, LISP or FORTH.

boule A roughly cylindrical or sausage-shaped ingot of pure SINGLE-CRYSTAL SILICON that is sliced up into thin circular WAFERS for the manufacture of INTEGRATED CIRCUITS. The shape of a boule arises from the way that the growing crystal is very slowly pulled upwards from a circular bath of molten silicon.

bounce To return an email to its sender because the recipient cannot be found (e.g. because of a mispelt address).

boundary condition Any mathematical relationship that holds only near to the extremities of some data set, and not in its interior.

bounded Any quantity whose upper and lower limits are known.

bounds checking A DEBUGGING procedure that works by adding extra code to a program that detects any attempt to access ARRAY elements beyond their declared ARRAY BOUNDS and raises an error condition. Many COMPILERS offer a bounds checking option, and it is also a function provided by some dedicated debugging utilities such as Purify.

bound variable A program VARIABLE whose value has been established.

Bourne shell The original command SHELL and SCRIPTING LANGUAGE supplied with the UNIX operating system, written by S R Bourne in 1978 at BELL LABORATORIES. It is still widely used for writing SHELL SCRIPTS, but has been superceded for most interactive users by the C SHELL.

Box-Jenkins A statistical method used in forecasting that extrapolates into the future correlations found between past data. See also EXPONENTIAL SMOOTHING.

bozo filter Popular term for KILL FILE.

BPR Abbreviation of BUSINESS PROCESS RE-ENGINEERING.

bps Abbreviation of BITS PER SECOND.

braces The punctuation symbols { and } with ASCII codes of 123 and 125 respectively, also called *curly brackets*.

bracket Either one of the two characters [and] with ASCII codes of 91 and 93 respectively, sometimes called *square brackets*. Brackets have a special application within most PROGRAMMING LANGUAGES, being almost universally employed to signify an ARRAY INDEX, thus my_array[100].

bracketed 1 Employing brackets or parentheses as delimiting characters: for example {Name: Pountain}{Age: 56}{Sex: Male} would be a bracketed data format.
　2 A desirable feature of the CONTROL STRUCTURES in a programming language that clearly marks both the beginning and the end of the code segment to which they apply. For example the construct:

IF test THEN dosomething ENDIF
is a fully bracketed construct, while
IF test THEN dosomething
is not.

brain dump Programmers' slang for a serious technical discussion. By analogy with a CORE DUMP where the raw contents of a computer's memory are printed out in order to trace an error.

branch A class of MACHINE CODE instruction, also called a *jump*, that causes program execution to transfer to a different address rather than automatically continuing at the next instruction. In a CONDITIONAL BRANCH, execution is either transferred or continues as normal, depending upon the result of a test that is stored in a FLAG REGISTER or FLAG BIT.
　Branches have important consequences for those modern processors that attempt to improve execution speed by 'reading ahead' in the program to anticipate future requirements – when a branch is taken, such anticipations may become invalid. (See more under BRANCH PREDICTION, SPECULATIVE EXECUTION, PIPELINE STALL.) For this reason, some recent designs try to do away with branches in favour of conditional execution, where every instruction contains a test flag and may execute or not according to its value.

branch delay slot An optimization employed in many RISC processor architectures, in which the instruction immediately following a CONDITIONAL BRANCH instruction is executed without waiting to see whether the branch will be taken: if the branch is not taken a PIPELINE BREAK is avoided but if it is taken, the delay slot instruction must be discarded. See also SPECULATIVE EXECUTION.

branch prediction An important optimization mechanism used in modern microprocessors that guesses the outcome of a CONDITIONAL BRANCH instruction (i.e. branch taken or not taken) so that the processor can continue by executing instructions from the predicted branch without waiting for the result, and thus avoid a PIPELINE STALL. If the prediction is wrong, all this work is wasted and a stall occurs anyway, but an efficient prediction algorithm (some are right 90% of the time) brings benefits that outweigh the penalties.
　Static branch prediction requires the program code to contain cues inserted by a language COMPILER concerning the probability of each branch. Dynamic branch prediction (as used for example in the PENTIUM) employs a BRANCH TARGET BUFFER to store previous predictions: a simple algorithm would be to guess every branch as not taken initially, and then to reverse any prediction that proves wrong, thus gambling that a branch will tend to go the same way when revisited (which is true, for example, for all but the last iteration of a LOOP.)

Branch Target Buffer A small on-chip CACHE reserved for the use of the BRANCH PREDICTION mechanism of many modern microprocessors (for example the Intel PENTIUM) which stores a history of previously predicted branch results and their target addresses. This allows repeating patterns such as loops to be recognized, and the target address to be re-used to save repeated address calculations.

breadboard A plastic board covered with a grid of small holes into which metal pins can be inserted, on which WIRE-WRAP prototypes of electronic circuits can be built by winding the connecting leads of discrete components around the pins.

breadth-first search A class of ALGORITHM for searching in a TREE-STRUCTURED graph, which operates by extending all the current branches by a single extra step, then repeating this process until all the nodes have been visited. Whether this is more efficient than a DEPTH-FIRST SEARCH depends on the structure of the tree.

breakpoint A point in a program's code where execution will be halted, for example to inspect the value of a certain variable. Breakpoints are an important feature of any interactive DEBUGGING tool.

Bressingham's Algorithm An efficient graphical ALGORITHM for drawing straight lines and circles on a RASTER DISPLAY, invented by the eponymous IBM researcher.

bridge A device that connects two or more data networks together in a passive way. A bridge lacks the built-in processing power of a ROUTER and merely passes packets unchanged from one network into another. See also HUB, GATEWAY.

broadband A communications medium that can carry a wide range of signal frequencies, typically from audio up to video frequencies. In telecommunications the significance of a broadband system is that it can carry television and videoconferencing data as well as voice calls. A broadband medium can be made to carry many signals at once by apportioning its total bandwidth into many independent channels, each of which carries only a specific range of frequencies. In contrast, a BASEBAND can carry only a single channel. ATM, ADSL and Cable TV are all broadband media, while standard ISDN barely qualifies.

Broadband ISDN (BISDN) The next-generation of ISDN technology, with promised bandwidths from 150 megabits per second upward, sufficient to carry video-phone calls and movies. BISDN will be carried over FIBRE-OPTIC cabling rather than wire, and the underlying transport protocol will be ASYNCHRONOUS TRANSFER MODE. Different implementations are planned in the USA, which will employ SYNCHRONOUS OPTICAL NETWORK, and Europe, which will use SYNCHRONOUS DIGITAL HIERARCHY.

broadcast Any form of communication in which a single sender transmits messages to many receivers at once, the most familiar examples being the television and public radio systems. The opposite of broadcast is POINT-TO-POINT or narrowcast communication, between just a single transmitter and a single receiver – a telephone conversation for example. When such a multiple connection is made via a network cable as opposed to wireless, such communication is often called MULTIPOINT, as opposed to a point-to-point or UNICAST.

browser 1 A program that is used to view the contents of a large collection of files or other software objects. It will typically present the user with a list of such objects, selecting one of which will open it for inspection.
2 More specifically, a program (such as Netscape Communicator or Microsoft Internet Explorer) used to view web pages downloaded from the WORLD WIDE WEB.

browser-specific Any feature of a WEB PAGE that will work only when viewed via a particular WEB BROWSER.

brush The most basic tool provided by all BIT-MAPPED painting programs that simply applies a foreground colour over the background colour. Most such programs allow the user to select from a variety of brush sizes and shapes, and many support the creation of customized brushes. The most advanced programs offer brushes that can vary colour density according to the pressure and velocity of application, and also vary across the width of the stroke to simulate the effect of bending bristles. See also AIRBRUSH, FLOOD FILL, GRADIENT FILL.

BSD (Berkeley System Distribution) A family of versions of the UNIX operating system developed at the University of California at Berkeley in the early 1980s. BSD Unix version 4.0 was released in 1980 for DEC's VAX and PDP-11 computers. BSD Unix introduced many technical enhancements that have now been universally adopted, such as paged VIRTUAL MEMORY and built-in TCP/IP networking. It formed the basis for several commercial Unix versions, including Sun's (prior to Solaris 2) and Hewlett Packard's ULTRIX.

BSD Unix See under BSD.

BSOD Abbreviation of BLUE SCREEN OF DEATH.

B-spline A variety of CUBIC SPLINE curve that is smoother than the alternative BEZIER CURVE, but is less useful than the latter for interactive drawing programs because it does not pass through its control points, which makes accurate manual control over the curve's shape more difficult.

BTB Abbreviation of BRANCH TARGET BUFFER.

B-tree An ambiguous term, sometimes referring to a BINARY TREE and sometimes to a BALANCED TREE.

Btrieve A once-popular ISAM (see under INDEXED SEQUENTIAL ACCESS METHOD) CLIENT/SERVER database engine proprietary to Btrieve Technologies Inc., whose indexed file format is still widely supported as an import and export format by database products.

BTW Online shorthand for By The Way.

bubble-jet printer A type of INKJET PRINTER that works by heating the capillary tubes containing the fluid ink, so that tiny droplets are ejected toward the paper by the pressure of the vapour bubbles formed.

bubble sort A very inefficient sorting ALGORITHM that is sometimes taught to (but more often rediscovered by) novice programmers. The program passes repeatedly over the data, exchanging each adjacent pair of items if they are out of order; when no exchanges are needed, the data is sorted. So called because items 'bubble up' toward their final destination one place at a time.

bucket A receptacle, such as an ARRAY element, into which diverse data items may be collected.

buffer 1 Any area of memory reserved for the temporary storage of data.
2 In particular, a memory area used as a reservoir to smooth out fluctuations in the flow of data from some communications channel. In such buffered communication, the receiving program reads its input data from the buffer rather than directly from the channel (rather as one might fill a bucket from a hosepipe rather than drink straight from the pipe).

buffered seek A mode of hard disk operation in which a sequence of commands to perform SEEK operations are collected and executed all together rather than one at time. This saves time compared to non-buffered modes in which one seek must be executed before the

next command can be accepted. All modern SCSI and ATA drives have buffered seeks built into their internal mechanism. See also ELEVATOR SEEK.

bug A mistake in, or unintended aspect of, a computer program's design or coding that causes it to behave incorrectly or to fail completely. Computer folklore has it that the term was first coined in 1947 by Admiral Grace HOPPER (the pioneering programmer who commissioned COBOL) in joking reference to an incident where a moth trapped in relay contacts caused an early computer to malfunction. However, it is reported to have been in use, meaning a defect, in the 19th century in the early days of the electrical telegraph, and it may simply derive from the ancient word 'bugbear'.

Regrettably, there is as yet no systematic way to ensure that a program is free from bugs, short of running it until the bugs have all manifested themselves, which may take years for a complex program. See also ERROR CONDITION, DEBUGGER, CRASH, HANG.

bug fix An interim release of a software product intended to remedy a list of known BUGS: see also BUG LIST.

bug-free A software product that contains no BUGS; encountered with about the same frequency as hen's teeth.

bug list A list of the bugs which are fixed by a new release of a software product. See also BUG FIX.

bug report A document (most often an email message) from a developer, BETA TESTER or user of a software product that reports to its manufacturer the discovery of a BUG in the program. Bug reports are expected to contain enough detail and context information for the failure to be reproduceable by the manufacturer, though for some intermittent bugs this may not be possible. See also BUG LIST, BUG FIX, KNOWLEDGE BASE.

build 1 *n.* One particular version of a program that is under development, compiled and linked from date-stamped versions of all the separate modules that make up the program. Individual builds are typically identified either by build number or by a date, and the management of the various modules involved is frequently partially automated by using a VER-SION CONTROL system.

2 v. To create the final version of a program by compiling all the SOURCE files from which it is composed and linking them with any LIBRARY files or other resources that it uses. Modern INTEGRATED DEVELOPMENT ENVIRON-MENTS typically offer a 'smart build' feature that fulfills the same role as a MAKE utility, recompiling only those components of the current project that have been changed since the last build.

build number An identifying number used internally by a software vendor to distinguish between the hundreds or thousands of different versions of a complex program that may be generated during its development and service lifetime. Each full VERSION of a program will typically go through many BUILDS, which change daily or even hourly.

build time The stage in the programming cycle when all the compiled modules that comprise a finished program are brought together into one or more executable files. See also COMPILE TIME and RUN TIME.

Business Highway British Telecom's brand name for its business-oriented ISDN service.

bulletin board A storage area on a computer system that is reserved for people to post messages for other users to read. This may take place within a local area network, on a dedicated dial-up BULLETIN BOARD SYSTEM server, or via the Internet in a NEWSGROUP or on a WEB SITE.

bulletin board system (BBS) A single computer running special communications software that allows remote users to dial in via a public telephone line to exchange messages and chat with one another. Before the wide availability of the INTERNET, thousands of separate BBSs provided the only gathering places for amateur net afficionados, and were also used by companies to provide technical support. The USENET now fulfills much the same role.

bump In programmers' slang, to increment (usually by one) the value stored in a REGISTER or VARIABLE.

bump mapping An extension of the technique of TEXTURE MAPPING to create more realistic 3D images, in which an additional BITMAP

(the bump map) applied to a surface contains not colour data but small displacements to be applied to the surface normals at each point. After the image is rendered, these displacements alter the angles of reflected rays in such a way as to convey the illusion of surface relief, even though the surface actually remains completely smooth.

bundle 1 To sell software along with computer hardware for an all-in price.

2 A combination of hardware and software sold in such a fashion.

bureau A company that provides some computing service to paying clients, the most common bureau services being general accounting, database storage, typesetting and graphics, and backup/disaster recovery.

burn 1 To record data onto a CD-R disk.

2 To store data into a PROM or EPROM chip.

3 Referring to a computer or Internet START-UP company, to consume one's first round of funding in the pursuit of market share, hence also 'burn rate'.

burn-in To set a computer running for hours (or days) before loading it with software and handing it over to its user. The intention is that any faulty components will reveal themselves by failing before any harm is done.

BURN-proof An enhanced mechanism for CD-R and CD-RW drives patented by Sanyo, which prevents Buffer Under Run errors (BURN errors) caused by data being supplied too slowly from the computer.

Burroughs One the earliest commercial computer companies, which later merged with Univac to form UNISYS CORPORATION.

burst-mode, burst-transfer mode A mode of data access supported by many devices – from DISK DRIVE controllers to RAM chips – in which, once the first of a sequence of desired data items has been located, the following items can be retrieved at a faster rate than usual by simply reading from consecutive locations.

bursty A data stream whose rate fluctuates widely, with busy peaks interspersed with quiet interludes. For example Ethernet LAN traffic, email (indeed most Internet traffic), and human speech are bursty data streams.

bus The electrically conducting path along which data is transmitted inside any digital electronic device. A bus consists of a set of parallel conductors, which may be conventional wires, copper tracks on a PRINTED CIRCUIT BOARD, or microscopic aluminium trails on the surface of a silicon chip. Each wire carries just one bit, so the number of wires determines the largest data WORD the bus can transmit: a bus with eight wires can carry only 8-bit data words, and hence defines the device as an 8-bit device. A bus normally has a single-word memory circuit called a LATCH attached to either end, which briefly stores the word being transmitted and ensures that each bit has settled to its intended state before its value is transmitted.

The speed at which its bus can transmit words, that is, its bus BANDWIDTH, crucially determines the speed of any digital device. One way to make a bus faster is to increase its width; for example a 16-bit bus can transmit two 8-bit words at once, 'side-by-side', and so carries 8-bit data twice as fast as an 8-bit bus can. A computer's CPU will typically contain several buses, often of differing widths, that connect its various subunits. It is common for modern CPUs to use on-chip buses that are wider than the bus they use to communicate with external devices such as memory, and the speed difference between on- and off-chip operations must then be bridged by keeping a reservoir of temporary data in a CACHE. For example many of the Pentium class of processors use 256 bits for their fastest on-chip buses, but only 64 bits for external links.

bus contention A loss of performance that can arise when two or more devices – for example computer PROCESSORS or disk controllers – try to transfer data simultaneously over the same BUS. For example hesitation may be introduced into a video or audio playback whenever the disk is being accessed. Contention is ameliorated by some kind of ARBITRATION scheme that regulates bus usage in a fair and orderly way, ensuring that all the contending devices are granted access for a reasonable duration and within a reasonable time. It can be avoided altogether by changing the hardware architecture so as to provide separate buses for each device – see for example ACCELERATED GRAPHICS PORT.

bus cycle The sequence of primitive operations for transferring each item of data over a computer's BUS, which are performed in time with the system CLOCK SIGNAL. Each bus cycle may take several clock cycles, and may be either a READ or WRITE cycle depending on the direction of data transfer. The steps for a read cycle might be:

1. Request control of the bus.
2. When granted, place target address on bus.
3. Receive data from bus.
4. Release bus.

Different bus PROTOCOLS employ variants and enhancements to this simple schema, for example possibly transferring more than one data item per cycle. See also BUS MASTER, DIRECT MEMORY ACCESS.

bus driver An INTEGRATED CIRCUIT chip that implements the SYSTEM BUS in a computer.

business-critical application A computerized business system upon whose correct functioning a company depends for its continuing operation; for example payroll, sales and ordering systems or, in the case of an E-COMMERCE company, its WEB SITE. The implication behind the use of the term is that such systems must have adequate BACKUP and DISASTER RECOVERY plans in place and, in the case of real-time systems such as airline or theatre ticket booking, they should be designed to be FAULT-TOLERANT. See also MISSION-CRITICAL, HIGH-AVAILABILITY.

business logic That collection of processing tasks, such as price computation and customer account management, that are common to a whole business and are needed by many users, and hence should be performed at SERVER rather than CLIENT level, but which are too specific to be usefully performed within a RELATIONAL DATABASE running on the company mainframe. The existence of such tasks is the rationale for interposing a 'third tier' server (see under THREE-TIER ARCHITECTURE) between the users and the BACK-END database.

business object A jargon term used by vendors of OBJECT-ORIENTED PROGRAMMING tools to describe ready-made object classes for processing business-related data.

business process re-engineering (BPR) A business jargon term meaning to examine the practices of a company with a view to streamlining them by using computers. See also SYSTEMS ANALYSIS, METHODOLOGY, COMPUTER AIDED SOFTWARE ENGINEERING.

business rule Part of a business software system that deals with conditions in the real world (e.g. sums of money, hours worked, goods ordered) rather than with the operation of the program itself (e.g. memory allocation, file input). The term gained currency with the advent of large applications that employ a THREE-TIER ARCHITECTURE: business rules are implemented as the middle tier, using COMPONENT SOFTWARE techniques, so they can be easily modified as business conditions change without alteration either to the user interface or BACK-END databases.

bus locking A type of BUS architecture in which some particularly bandwidth-hungry device, for example a GRAPHICS PROCESSOR, is permitted to keep control of a computer's bus for many successive cycles to the exclusion of other devices. It was employed in some early Apple MACINTOSH systems to improve graphics throughput, but would be frowned on in today's highly multitasking, multiprocessor environments.

bus master Any device within a computer that is capable of taking control of the BUS and initiating data transfers with the memory and PERIPHERALS (which are slave devices and can only respond passively to access attempts). In simple systems the CPU is the only bus master, but in others such as the PCI BUS, there may be multiple masters: for example it is common for a SCSI disk controller to be granted bus master status so that it can transfer data to and from memory without CPU involvement. See also DIRECT MEMORY ACCESS.

bus snooping A mechanism for maintaining CACHE COHERENCY in MULTIPROCESSOR computers, under which each CPU's cache-control logic watches the external memory bus, looking for reads or writes made by other processors (that is, it 'snoops' on their transactions). Whenever such a transaction is detected, the cache logic enquires whether a copy of the target address exists in its own cache, and if so either writes that line back to memory or declares it invalid. See also MESI PROTOCOL.

bus speed The rate at which a computer's PROCESSOR BUS can transmit data, which is a crucial determinant of its overall performance. The bus speed of most personal computers remained at 33 MHz for a decade, only recently being increased to 100 MHz, and technologies such as the two-level processor CACHE, DIRECT MEMORY ACCESS or the ACCELERATED GRAPHICS PORT can be seen as ways to surmount this restriction by bypassing the processor bus.

bus traffic The amount of data flowing across a computer's BUS, typically measured in megabytes per second.

busy wait A situation in which a computer is doing no useful work – because it is waiting for some external event to happen – but is nevertheless executing a loop of code (see under POLLING) and therefore potentially depriving other useful processes of CPU time. Busy waits are frowned upon, especially in portable systems where they waste battery power as well as CPU cycles: it is better to have the external event raise an INTERRUPT to notify when it has happened.

butterfly 1 A mathematical operation used in computing the FAST FOURIER TRANSFORM, which involves multiplying two complex numbers; when drawn as a diagram the cross-multiplication of their two halves suggests a butterfly's wings.
2 A type of folding computer KEYBOARD in which two wings open out laterally to give the full width, pioneered by IBM in its early THINKPAD models.

button 1 A small, sprung switch that closes when depressed with the finger, used, for example, for dialling a telephone or turning on the power supply of many appliances.
2 A small region on a computer screen that mimics the action of 1, sending an EVENT to its controlling program whenever the user clicks a MOUSE button with the pointer positioned over it.

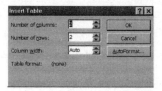

button-press A software EVENT raised whenever a user clicks the MOUSE with its pointer over an on-screen BUTTON.

buzzword A technical term that has been adopted by a marketing department and used to sell a product, often with consequent blurring (or even total loss) of meaning. AI, OBJECT-ORIENTED and E-COMMERCE are among the words that have suffered such a fate in the past.

byte A group of eight bits, which can represent any number in the range 00000000 to 11111111 binary, or 0 to 255 decimal. From the early days of digital computing, the byte became a fundamental unit, used to measure both memory size (kilobytes, megabytes) and data transfer speed (kilobytes per second). Even now that most processors handle data in 32, 64 or 128 bit chunks, it is still convenient for programmers to treat such quantitities as being composed of 4, 8 or 16 bytes. A byte is large enough to hold a single alphanumeric character encoded in the ASCII code. See also NIBBLE, BYTE ORDERING, BYTE-WIDE, BYTE-ADDRESSING, BINARY NUMBER.

byte-addressing Any memory addressing scheme in which the smallest value that can have its own unique address is a BYTE: in other words, each successive address identifies a different eight-bit quantity. This contrasts with various word-addressing schemes, where for example a 32-bit word might be the smallest addressable object. See also ENDIAN-ISM.

bytecode The intermediate code produced by certain semi-compiled programming languages, in particular SMALLTALK and JAVA, so called because each instruction is one byte long. Source programs are compiled into bytecode, which is then executed by a bytecode INTERPRETER or VIRTUAL MACHINE that forms part of the language RUN-TIME SYSTEM. In such languages, programs may be distributed either in SOURCE CODE or in bytecode form. See also PSEUDO-CODE, P-CODE, INTERMEDIATE LANGUAGE, JUST-IN-TIME, OBFUSCATION.

byte level The level at which some data structure (for instance a FILE or a disk DIRECTORY) is treated as pure binary data, a stream of BYTES, ignoring both its structure and function. If its FORMAT is well understood, data may be edited at byte level, using a DEBUGGER or a SECTOR EDITOR rather than the application that originally created it.

BYTE Magazine One of the earliest personal computer magazines, founded in 1975, and often described as the '*Scientific American* of computing' for its in-depth technical features. The paper magazine closed in 1998 and became an online publication.

byte ordering The direction in which a computer's PROCESSOR reads the BYTES that make up each WORD stored in its memory. Some machines are designed to read the byte at the lower address first, so that 0C 77 is read as 0C77h or 3191 decimal, while others read the higher address first, so that 0C 77 is read as 770Ch or 30476 decimal. A difference in byte ordering represents the greatest possible degree of incompatibility, since not only can two such computers not execute each other's programs, but they cannot even agree on the value of any particular instruction or data item. See more under ENDIANISM.

byte striping A technique for speeding up the retrieval of data stored on an ARRAY of hard disks (see more under RAID). The data stream is divided up into, say, 4-byte portions, and the bytes from each such portion are written to four different drives: this effectively quadruples the data rate since the four drives can be written to or read from simultaneously. Byte striping is covered by the RAID 4 and 5 specifications, and driver software to accomplish it is built into, for example, WINDOWS NT and WINDOWS 2000.

byte-wide A data item, or a PARALLEL data pathway, that is 8 bits wide.

C

C Probably the most popular PROGRAMMING LANGUAGE so far invented, created at BELL LABORATORIES in 1972 by Dennis RITCHIE for the purpose of writing the UNIX operating system and its utilities. C is a relatively low-level language that permits direct access to memory and so may be used to write DEVICE DRIVERS as easily as application programs. Its ubiquity is largely due to two factors: a C COMPILER is supplied with every Unix system, and it proved the language best able to cope with the awkward memory model of early Intel microprocessors, hence becoming the language of choice under MS-DOS and WINDOWS too.

C is only weakly typed (see TYPE CHECKING) and permits easy conversion of one type to another and the use of POINTERS to directly access any data object in memory. On the other hand, it supports structured data types through its STRUCT and UNION constructs, and encourages STRUCTURED PROGRAMMING techniques by program code organized into blocks delimited by curly brackets:

```
main()
{
printf("Hello world")
}
```

C's great strength lies in its ability to manipulate data at the individual bit level, which means that it can be used for many tasks that would otherwise require ASSEMBLY LANGUAGE programming. Nowadays it has been largely displaced as an application language by its OBJECT-ORIENTED descendant C++.

C++ An OBJECT-ORIENTED PROGRAMMING LANGUAGE derived from the C language by Bjarne Stroustrup at BELL LABORATORIES in 1986. C++ is now the most widely used object-oriented language, and perhaps the most important programming language.

C++ extends the C concept of a STRUCTURE into a CLASS, by allowing it to contain subprograms called MEMBER FUNCTIONS as well as variables called DATA MEMBERS, which correspond to the METHODS and INSTANCE VARIABLES of other object-oriented languages. C++ relaxes the strict ENCAPSULATION of some object-oriented languages, by allowing FRIEND FUNCTIONS of a class to access its private data without being members. C++ is a large and complex language, whose other features include MULTIPLE INHERITANCE, overloading of operators and STREAM I/O.

C# Pronounced C Sharp, a new SCRIPTING LANGUAGE introduced by Microsoft as part of its Internet-oriented .NET initiative, intended for writing both CLIENT-SIDE and SERVER-SIDE distributed applications and WEB SERVICES. C# is an OBJECT-ORIENTED language that shares several features with JAVA, namely that it is a SEMI-COMPILED language with a syntax based on that of C++, and it supports GARBAGE COLLECTION to make dynamic memory allocation less error-prone. Here is an example of C# code:

```
using System;
class GreetWorld
{
public static int Main(String[]
args)
{
Console.WriteLine("Hello World!");
return 0;
}
}
```

C# contains many features aimed at creating more secure and stable programs including hierarchical namespaces to control overriding of methods, STRUCTURED EXCEPTION HANDLING, restrictions on the use of POINTERS and TYPE CASTS and automatic array BOUNDS CHECKING. Pseudo-code compiled from a C# program runs within a runtime system (see COMMON LANGUAGE RUNTIME) that imposes all these safety features and is therefore called MANAGED CODE, though it can also make outside calls to code within traditional, unmanaged DYNAMIC-LINKED LIBRARIES. C# is intended to eventually replace VISUAL BASIC as the programming language for Microsoft's web development systems.

C1 security The lowest of the levels of computer security defined in the US Government's ORANGE BOOK, which requires that users should log on to the system, but permits groups of users to share the same password. See also C2 SECURITY.

C2 security A medium level of computer security as defined in the US Government's ORANGE BOOK, which requires that users should log on to a system with individual passwords, and that an audit record of who has logged in be maintained. See also C1 SECURITY.

CA Abbreviation of COMPUTER ASSOCIATES.

cable **1** A multi-core wire terminated with multi-pin plugs used to connect a piece of PERIPHERAL equipment to a computer.
2 Shorthand for 'cable television'.

cable modem A MODEM that allows computer DATA TRANSFERS and Internet access via cable TV connections. Cable TV services employ COAXIAL CABLING, so a cable modem can operate at much a higher maximum speed than a telephone modem, typically between 0.5 and 20 megabits per second. However, cable TV systems support only downstream traffic (i.e. from TV station to the home) so require a telephone modem to be used in parallel to carry upstream traffic. Also cable TV lines are shared by many households, so the BANDWIDTH achieved in practice may be highly variable and far below the maximum.

cable TV A communication technology that transmits television signals into the home over a local area network of optical or coaxial cable, rather than via radio-frequency broadcast or satellite transmission. Its significance for computing is that this relatively high-speed network may also be used for Internet access and other data transmissions by installing a CABLE MODEM.

cabling The physical conductors used to carry data around a NETWORK. The term is applied to both metal wire that conducts electrical signals and to OPTICAL FIBRE that conducts light signals, since the engineering problems of running either sort around a building are related. See also various cable types such as TWISTED-PAIR, UTP, COAXIAL CABLE, THICK ETHERNET and THIN ETHERNET.

cache A small region of fast MEMORY interposed between a data processing device and a larger slower memory to hold copies of the most frequently or recently used data so that they may be accessed more quickly. The same principle is at work in a library when someone takes several books they are consulting from the main shelves and places them on their desktop for easier access.

Caches are universally employed between the CPUs of modern computers and their main memory, reflecting the fact that the speed of processors has been enhanced far more rapidly than the speed of memory: a cache helps to bridge this growing discrepancy. Indeed the latest generations of PENTIUM and other processors employ two (or even three) levels of cacheing. A small, typically 32 to 64 kilobyte, cache on the chip itself acts as a cache for a larger off-chip cache which may be many megabytes in size, and which in turn caches the main memory accesses. (See more under L1 CACHE and L2 CACHE.)

The mechanics of deciding precisely how to arrange the data within a cache, how much to read at a time, and how to ensure consistency between the cache contents and main memory constitute a complex area of engineering: see more under CACHE LINE, CACHE HIT, CACHE COHERENCY, ASSOCIATIVE CACHE, DIRECT MAPPED CACHE, SET-ASSOCIATIVE CACHE, FULLY ASSOCIATIVE CACHE, UNIFIED CACHE, HARVARD ARCHITECTURE.

Caches may be employed in many other forms of communication, for example to enable WEB PAGES recently read to be read again more quickly, and between a computer's CPU and disk drives of various kinds (where the speed discrepancy is even greater than with memory): see for example DISK CACHE, WRITE-THROUGH CACHE, WRITE-BACK CACHE.

cacheable Capable of, or allowed to be, stored in a CACHE. Many operating systems permit certain regions of memory to be declared as NONCACHEABLE, particularly those used for I/O by MEMORY-MAPPED peripherals.

cache coherency A problem intrinsically associated with SHARED-MEMORY MULTIPROCESSOR computer systems. When multiple processors access the same memory, it is possible for a data item that currently resides in one processor's CACHE to be updated in main memory by a different processor, leaving the first processor unaware that it holds stale, out-of-date, data. To avoid this situation it is necessary to maintain cache coherency, and the most popular method is to implement the MESI PROTOCOL.

cache controller An INTEGRATED CIRCUIT that controls access to the BUS connecting a computer's CPU core to its CACHE memory, performing several functions that include locating a requested address in the cache, storing the TAGS for an ASSOCIATIVE CACHE and sorting memory accesses into line-order to economize on bus bandwidth.

All modern MICROPROCESSORS incorporate an on-chip or LEVEL 1 CACHE whose controller is part of the on-chip circuitry. However, some recent designs (for instance the POWERPC G3 and G4) also integrate a controller for an external or LEVEL 2 CACHE onto the chip, provided with its own bus to enable access to the L2 cache faster than the system bus would permit. Intel's PENTIUM family of CPUs employ an external L2 cache controller that is integrated instead into the SYSTEM CHIP SET. See also CACHE COHERENCY, BACKSIDE BUS, MESI PROTOCOL, BUS SNOOPING.

cache hit A request by a computer's processor to read or write a data item that finds its target in the processor's CACHE and therefore does not have to reach out over the bus to external memory to access it. Since the purpose of a cache is to keep traffic local to the processor

and reduce the traffic to external memory, a high ratio of cache hits to CACHE MISSES is a good thing.

cache line The unit of data that is stored within a processor CACHE. For example each line might be 64 bytes long, so that whenever a single byte in main memory is accessed, its surrounding 64 bytes are fetched into the cache too. See also ASSOCIATIVE CACHE, TAG.

cache memory A region of memory (whether on-chip, or external in the form of RAM chips) that is dedicated to use as a CACHE.

cache miss A request by a computer's processor to read or write a data item that does not find its target in the processor's CACHE and therefore must continue through into main memory to access the item. See also CACHE HIT.

CACM Abbreviation of COMMUNICATIONS OF THE ACM.

CAD Abbreviation of COMPUTER AIDED DESIGN.

CAD/CAM (Computer Aided Design/Computer Aided Manufacturing) The use of computers to assist in the complete manufacturing cycle of a product, from design to final delivery. The term implies a degree of integration between the design software, a parts database, ordering and stock control software for parts from outside suppliers, and software that controls the manufacturing process itself, so that information flows from one stage to the next. See more under COMPUTER AIDED DESIGN, COMPUTER AIDED MANUFACTURING, JUST-IN-TIME.

CADD Abbreviation of COMPUTER AIDED DESIGN AND DRAFTING.

caddy A shallow removable plastic tray with a hinged lid used by early CD-ROM drives: a disk was loaded into the caddy and the caddy inserted into the drive. Most modern drives use instead a retractable, lidless tray.

CAE Abbreviation of COMPUTER AIDED ENGINEERING.

CAI Abbreviation of COMPUTER AIDED INSTRUCTION.

Cairo The internal codename given by Microsoft to its unified, 32-bit OBJECT-ORIENTED version of WINDOWS that was under development throughout the 1990s, some components of which eventually came to fruition as WINDOWS NT4 and WINDOWS 2000.

CAL Abbreviation of Computer Assisted (or Aided) Learning. See COMPUTER AIDED INSTRUCTION.

calculator A simple computer designed to perform arithmetic operations. The earliest calculators were mechanical devices, operated by turning a handle that rotated spools bearing numbers. The quest for an electronic calculator drove much early innovation in microelectronics – Intel's 4004, the first MICROPROCESSOR, was designed in 1971 for a desktop calculator.

Now that many calculators are programmable they are becoming hard to distinguish from hand-held computers, but a calculator typically has a more prominent numeric than alphabetic keypad.

calculus **1** Loosely, any system of calculation involving the use of symbols. More strictly, in mathematical logic, an uninterpreted formal system: a set of rules for manipulating purely abstract symbols with no meanings ascribed to them. Examples include the PREDICATE CALCULUS and the PROPOSITIONAL CALCULUS in formal logic.

2 The branch of mathematics, invented by Isaac Newton and Baron Leibnitz, that deals with continuously varying quantitities by breaking their variation down into notional, infinitesimally-small steps. The Differential Calculus deals with rates of change (and changes of rate of change, etc) while its complement, the Integral Calculus, aggregates the effects of a variable rate of change over time. Digital computers can solve calculus problems only by substituting finite steps (see for example FINITE ELEMENT ANALYSIS and DISCRETE EVENT SIMULATION), though sophisticated SYMBOLIC MATHS programs such as MATHEMATICA permit the analytical solution of calculus problems. However, ANALOGUE COMPUTERS, whose hardware is based on continuously varying voltages, can solve sets of complex higher-order differential equations directly, and this is their principal application – for example simulating fluid flow or the ballistic trajectory of an artillery shell.

Calendar API See CAPI.

calendar service A type of WEB SERVICE that enables users to maintain their diary of daily appointments on a remote WEB SERVER that may be accessed from anywhere in the world with an Internet connection and WEB BROWSER: widely used examples are operated by YAHOO! and Anyday.com. Such services normally provide a GROUP CALENDAR facility so that the user's office can add new appointments and schedule meetings.

calibrate To determine or restore the accuracy of some device, for example a measuring instrument or a colour monitor. (Originally an artillery term meaning to measure the calibre of a gun.)

call A class of processor INSTRUCTION that causes program execution to transfer to a SUBROUTINE, rather than automatically continuing at the next instruction. Unlike a simple JUMP, a call saves the current program position on the STACK, allowing return from the subroutine to the next sequential instruction. See also CALL AND RETURN.

call and return To transfer program execution to a subroutine and, once that terminates, to continue the original program from the point where execution left off. The state of the calling program is preserved.

callback **1** An AUTHENTICATION scheme used by some DIAL-UP online services, whereby a user first dials in and enters a USER NAME and PASSWORD, then the host computer hangs up the connection and uses an AUTO-DIAL modem to call back to the telephone number on record for that user. This means that someone who steals a password will not only fail to gain access, but the callback will go to the authorized user and alert them to a breach of security.

2 A technique employed by some EVENT-DRIVEN software in which the program registers a callback HANDLER for a particular event. Whenever that event occurs, the handler is called – with arguments describing the nature of the event and without interrupting the main program.

call-by-name, call-by-reference, call-by-value See under PARAMETER PASSING CONVENTION.

call centre A building equipped with many telephone lines and operators, used by large companies to provide sales, technical support and other customer services. Specialized communications systems for equipping call centres now form a whole new market category. Such systems integrate computer-controlled branch exchange hardware with database software that allows the operators to look up a caller's account details, log the contents of each call, perform transactions on the database and route calls to other stations all from a single user interface.

caller A program that CALLS another, which is referred to as the *called* or *callee*.

Caller ID A feature of a public telephone service that enables the recipient of a call to identify the caller, whose phone number can be retrieved by dialling a special code after the call terminates or, if a suitably equipped handset is used, may be displayed during the call. Many of the latest MODEMS can exploit Caller ID to maintain a log of caller's numbers.

calling convention See under PARAMETER PASSING CONVENTION.

callout The caption that describes, and the line that points to, a part of a labelled illustration.

call sign A unique combination of letters and numbers used to identify a radio transmitting station, for example an amateur PACKET RADIO user.

Caltech The California Institute of Technology, a research-based institution in Pasadena that has pioneered the science of INTEGRATED CIRCUITS, having had Ivan SUTHERLAND and Carver MEAD on its faculty.

CAM **1** Abbreviation of COMPUTER AIDED MANUFACTURING.
2 Abbreviation of Common Access Method, a programming interface for controlling SCSI disk drives, which is now less used than the alternative ASPI.

camcorder Any small video camera, whether analogue or digital, that combines camera and recorder in the same unit; that is, which stores images onto an internal tape cartridge or RAM chip rather than sending them via a cable to a separate video recorder.

camera-ready A relic of the days of manual typesetting and design, when it meant artwork for a book or magazine that had all its text and pictures pasted down in their proper places, so that the printer could photograph it onto positive or negative film from which to make a litho plate for the press. Now that DESKTOP PUBLISHING software is used for most document design, the term refers to a finished layout even though no camera is involved and the POSTSCRIPT output files are printed directly onto film.

cancel button A standard BUTTON available within almost all DIALOGUE boxes under a GRAPHICAL USER INTERFACE such as Windows or MacOS, which causes the current action to be abandoned. It is typically located immediately to the right of a button that commits to the action, such as an OK or Save button.

capability A kind of software token employed by some operating systems (for example CHORUS) to manage access to resources. In order to use a particular resource, a PROCESS must first obtain a capability for it, which is a small packet of data encrypted to avoid forgery.

capacitance The ability of a CAPACITOR to store charge, measured in FARADS. All electrical circuits have some capacitance, just as they have RESISTANCE and INDUCTANCE, and it becomes an important factor when designing high-speed computer circuits. For example, the capacitance created between closely spaced tracks on a chip or printed circuit board can cause transmission delays that lead to timing and synchronization problems.

capacitive That portion of the load offered by an electrical circuit that is caused by the CAPACITANCE (and not the RESISTANCE or the INDUCTANCE) of the circuit's components. It is used, for example, to describe the coupling between two neighbouring conductors.

capacitor One of the fundamental components used to build electrical circuits; its function is to store electrical charge. Most capacitors consist of a pair of closely-spaced metal plates separated by a DIELECTRIC material; opposite charges on these plates attract and retain charge within the device, but a DIRECT CURRENT cannot pass through it. However, an ALTERNATING CURRENT can pass through because it repeatedly charges and discharges the plates, and its ease of passage varies with the frequency, an effect that forms the basis of many devices (such as FILTERS and tuned circuits) used in radio and sound engineering. The same effect makes capacitors useful for smoothing fluctuations in power supplies (they act like a temporary battery). DYNAMIC RANDOM ACCESS MEMORY chips consist of millions of microscopic capacitors, and the charges stored in each of them represents one data BIT. See also CAPACITANCE.

CAPI 1 (Common API) An APPLICATION PROGRAMMING INTERFACE (API) for network ASSET MANAGEMENT software, created by the US Desk Management Task Force consortium.
2 (Common API) A digital telephony software interface developed by a consortium of German vendors to simplify writing software that accesses ISDN cards.
3 (Calendar API) An API for calendar-based software created by Microsoft as part of its Schedule+ application.

capital One of the large letter forms (often referred to as UPPER CASE) provided in most type FONTS (for example A, B, C in this font) which are used to start sentences and proper names, for emphasis, and in headings. See also SMALL CAPS, DROP CAP, CAPITALIZE.

capitalize To turn a letter from LOWER CASE to UPPER CASE. A computer program can accomplish this by subtracting 32 from the letter's ASCII code.

CAPS LOCK key A special key, situated just above the left SHIFT key on most computer keyboards which while depressed causes all letters typed to appear in UPPER CASE. The key stays down until pressed a second time – hence the name 'lock' – and typically has an indicator light close to it that alerts the user when it is engaged.

card A small PRINTED CIRCUIT BOARD fitted with an EDGE CONNECTOR or similar coupling so that it can be inserted into an EXPANSION SLOT in a computer or other device. See for example MEMORY CARD, FLASH CARD, SOUND CARD, GRAPHICS CARD, SMARTCARD.

CardBus The 32-bit version of the PC CARD expansion BUS for portable computers.

cardinal 1 In the MODULA-2 programming language, the name for UNSIGNED INTEGER data types.

2 A well-known US brand of modem made by Cardinal Technologies Inc.

cardinality In mathematics, the number of elements in a set.

caret 1 The symbol used when editing documents by hand to indicate a place where something is to be inserted: from the Latin *carere*, to lack (literally: something is missing).
2 The character ^ with ASCII code 94, whose main use is in programming and technical manuals as a prefix indicating a CONTROL CHARACTER: for example ^C is shorthand for CTRL+C.
3 In graphical word processors, sometimes used to mean the I-BEAM CURSOR, which indicates the current text insertion point.

carpal tunnel syndrome Inflammation of the sheath that surrounds a tendon in the wrist, caused by repetitive movements such as typing: see more under TENDINITIS.

carriage return The ASCII CONTROL CODE 13, which is interpreted by most computer text editors and printers as an instruction to return to the left margin. The name comes from the lever employed by the operator of a manual typewriter to return the paper carriage to the right-hand end of its track, so that typing can begin again at the left margin, and which simultaneously advances the paper upwards by one line. Under many computer operating systems, however – including MS-DOS and WINDOWS – a second code, the LINE FEED character (ASCII 10) is required to advance to the next line, so the end of each line of text is marked by a pair of characters, carriage return and line feed (0D 0A in hexadecimal), which are collectively referred to as a NEWLINE sequence. See also TEXT FILE, TEXT EDITOR, TELETYPE.

carrier 1 In telecommunications, a company that offers telephone services to the public; also called a *common carrier*.
2 A continuous signal of fixed frequency (which defines the CHANNEL of the communication) onto which data to be transmitted is imposed by modulation (see under MODULATE); also called a *carrier wave*. The two most common modulation schemes are AMPLITUDE MODULATION and FREQUENCY MODULATION.
3 Within a semiconductor, an ELECTRON or a

positive hole that can transport charge through the material.

Carrier Sense Multiple Access/Collision Avoidance See CSMA/CA.

Carrier Sense Multiple Access / Collision Detect See CSMA/CD.

Cartesian coordinates The system employed in mathematics to define the location of a point in space by specifying distances measured along perpendicular lines called AXES, first devised by the French philosopher-mathematician René Descartes. In the three-dimensional space we inhabit, the three axes are called x, y and z, and any point can be described by supplying three numbers that represent its distance from the origin (i.e. the point where these three axes meet) along each line, called the point's x, y and z coordinates. In pure mathematics, spaces with any number of dimensions can be so described, even though the human mind cannot visualize more than three perpendicular axes. See also 3D GRAPHICS, POLAR COORDINATES, DIGITIZE.

cartridge A casing that encloses some subsystem in such a way that it can be inserted into a larger system as a single unit. Examples might be a tape cartridge that contains twin reels of magnetic tape; a memory cartridge containing an array of RAM or ROM chips; the toner cartridge that contains the powdered pigment used in a LASER PRINTER; the ink cartridge employed to refill an INKJET PRINTER.

CAS Abbreviation of COLUMN ADDRESS STROBE.

cascade 1 In a GRAPHICAL USER INTERFACE that employs windows, the action of arranging all the open windows so that they overlap diagonally like a descending staircase from the top left corner of the screen.
2 A sequences of events such as program errors, in which each triggers the next.
3 A series of interconnected network devices such as HUBS which work together to give the effect of a REPEATER.

cascading menu See under SUBMENU.

cascading style sheets (CSS) An extension to the HTML page markup language that enables 'style sheets' (collections of attributes such as colour, font and size) to be attached to parts of a hypertext document in a reusable way. Styles may be included in the HTML file that describes a particular WEB PAGE, or they may be placed into a separate CSS file that can be shared by many different pages. CSS styles may be inherited in a hierarchical fashion: for example a page designer might copy a page from a template that contains CSS-defined styles, but then override some of those styles by adding a new CSS file of its own – hence the 'cascading' part of the name. See also XML, XSL, MHTML, DYNAMIC HTML.

CASE Abbreviation of COMPUTER AIDED SOFTWARE ENGINEERING.

case 1 A protective outer covering for some hardware device.
2 One of the two alphabets contained within any type FONT, that is, the LOWER CASE or the UPPER CASE (capital) letters.
3 In programming, one of the clauses of a CASE STATEMENT, which will be executed only if its associated condition is true.
4 In a CASE BASED REASONING system, one of the examples that may be consulted when making future decisions.
See also USE CASE.

Case Based Reasoning (CBR) An ARTIFICIAL INTELLIGENCE methodology used to build computerized consultation systems that refine their expertise through experience. Unlike earlier EXPERT SYSTEMS that worked from logical rules (see under RULE-BASED SYSTEM), CBR systems store successful solutions of some real-world problem, called 'cases'. When presented with a new problem, the CBR system uses an algorithm (often based on an INFERENCE ENGINE) that measures which previous cases it most resembles, then offers a suitably modified combination of their solutions. If the new problem is successfully solved, its solution is entered into the case base to improve future performance.

CASE Data Interchange Format A standard for exchanging model information between different CASE TOOLS.

case-sensitive A software system, particularly a programming language or an operating system that distinguishes between the UPPER CASE and LOWER CASE letters when interpreting commands, so that SAVE, Save, sAve and so on would each be interpreted as a different command.

Case sensitivity is often annoying to users as it places a premium on precise typing, but it also provides a much larger range of permissible identifiers. A classic instance of its implications may be experienced when attempting to construct a web site under UNIX (where filenames are case-sensitive) using files that have been created under WINDOWS (where filenames are not).

case statement Also called a MULTI-WAY BRANCH, or in c-like languages a SWITCH STATEMENT; a control structure that enables a program to branch many different ways according to the value of a test expression, rather than just the two ways offered by an IF...THEN...ELSE statement. For example:

```
CASE Size OF
1: PRINT("Small");
2: PRINT("Medium");
3: PRINT("Large");
DEFAULT PRINT("Huge")
ENDCASE;
```

would print the appropriate message for size values of 1, 2 or 3 and 'Huge' for any other value. Each of the values 1, 2 and 3 is called a case SELECTOR: in many languages including C these must be integers (or characters) while some other languages, notably VISUAL BASIC, permit strings as selectors.

CASE tool A class of software tool employed to assist in COMPUTER AIDED SOFTWARE ENGINEERING (CASE). A typical CASE tool consists of one or more visual editors that allow the programmer to draw various kinds of diagram – entity/relationship, data structure, data flow, and more, depending upon the particular METHODOLOGY that the tool supports – which describe the desired properties of the program being developed. For a database for example, one of these diagrams will be a schema that portrays the RECORD structure employed.

The CASE tool can automatically turn these diagrams into, either completed SOURCE CODE in some programming language, or a set of templates that the programmer can fill in to complete the coding. The most sophisticated CASE tools support so-called ROUND-TRIP ENGINEERING, which means that they can take the source code of a program and convert it back to diagrams, permitting it to be modified visually.

cashpoint See under AUTOMATED TELLER MACHINE.

Casio A Japanese manufacturer of programmable POCKET CALCULATORS and POCKET COMPUTERS.

cassette A plastic casing containing one or two reels of MAGNETIC TAPE with spindles that allow them to be rotated, and an aperture into which a recording HEAD can be inserted to read or write information on the tape. The Compact Cassette format invented by Philips became the most popular medium for recording and distributing music before the rise of the COMPACT DISC. Other tape technologies that use cassettes include VHS analogue video and some DIGITAL AUDIO TAPE formats. See also CARTRIDGE.

CAST (Computer Aided Software Testing) The use of a computer to test new programs, for example by automatically generating sets of test data. In many cases, CAST methods can compress hundreds of hours of manual testing into a few minutes by supplying the data faster than any human operator could, though this does not apply to REAL TIME programs. CAST may involve the SIMULATION of various real-world input streams (for example thousands of other users on a network) and the application of a TEST HARNESS to drive the parts of a program suite separately from one another.

CAST employs both static tools that analyse the SOURCE CODE of a program, and dynamic tools that check the RUN TIME behaviour of the executable code. Static checks detect errors such as undeclared or uninitialized variables, unreachable code sections and misused pointers. Some graphical representation of the CONTROL FLOW through the program is often generated, along with a list of constructs that are likely to cause problems. Dynamic testing works by actually COMPILING the program, referring to the source code to flag each problem it encounters. See also TESTING, TEST SUITE, BOUNDS CHECKING, DEBUGGING, COMPLIANT, ALPHA TESTING, BETA TESTING, METRIC, USABILITY.

cast 1 In programming, a shorthand for TYPE CAST, that is, to change the type of a data item.
2 In the DIRECTOR multimedia authoring tool, the name given to the assemblage of still

pictures, graphics and film clips that go to make up a particular presentation.

cat An abbreviation of *catenate*, a Unix command that sends the contents of multiple files to a named output device without any separating characters.

Cat 3 See CATEGORY 3.

Cat 5 See CATEGORY 5.

catalogue (*US* catalog) **1** A list or database of contents. Apple Computer Inc. at one time used the term to mean a disk DIRECTORY, and it has since been used in a similar sense applied to certain optical media such as CD-ROMs.
2 A list of the goods for sale via an E-COMMERCE web site. Management of such sites is often performed by a dedicated software system called a CATALOGUE SERVER.

catalogue server (*US* catalog server) A type of WEB SERVER specifically designed for E-COMMERCE which enables customers to electronically browse from a catalogue of goods and services, to place selected goods into a virtual 'shopping basket' and to pay for them by a secure credit-card transaction, all while remaining online.

Category 3 An ANSI standard type of UNSHIELDED TWISTED-PAIR cable used in telephone and computer networks, also called 'voice grade'. It transmits data at up to 16 MHz and is used to carry 10BASET and 100BASET4 traffic. See also CATEGORY 5.

Category 5 An ANSI standard type of UNSHIELDED TWISTED-PAIR cable used in telephone and computer networks, also called 'data grade'. It transmits data at up to 100 MHz and is used to carry 100BASETX and 100BASET4 traffic. See also CATEGORY 3.

catenate Similar to CONCATENATE, that is to join together end-to-end, as of two strings or two files.

cathode The negatively charged electrode that acts as a source of ELECTRONS within a current-consuming device such an electrolytic cell, a gas-discharge or CATHODE RAY TUBE, a TRANSISTOR or THERMIONIC VALVE. In a current-producing BATTERY, it is the electrode via which the external current returns to the battery and hence is connected to the *positive* terminal. See also ANODE.

cathode ray tube The electronic device used as a visual display unit in television sets and, until quite recently, the majority of computers. It consists of a bottle-shaped tube of strong glass, sealed and evacuated to a high vacuum, with a flat face coated on the inside with a mixture of fluorescent pigments called the PHOSPHOR. At the opposite end is an ELECTRON GUN, the beam from which can be steered by electromagnets so as to scan down the face of the tube in a RASTER pattern: modulating the strength of the electron beam produces the picture. The name is a historic relic from the 1900s when electrons, because they are emitted by a negative electrode, were called cathode rays.

CBASIC A compiled dialect of the BASIC language once widely used for business programming.

CBM Abbreviation of COMMODORE BUSINESS MACHINES.

CBR 1 Abbreviation of CONSTANT BIT RATE.
2 Abbreviation of CASE BASED REASONING.

CBT Abbreviation of COMPUTER-BASED TRAINING.

cc Originally an abbreviation for Carbon Copy, but now used in EMAIL software to send simultaneous copies of a message to a list of alternative recipients.

cc:Mail An electronic mail program published by Lotus Corporation (now owned by IBM) that is still widely used among larger businesses; cc:Mail runs on all the most important computing platforms including Windows, Unix, the Macintosh and DEC VAX.

CCD Abbreviation of CHARGE-COUPLED DEVICE.

CCITT Abbreviation of COMMITÉE CONSULTATIF INTERNATIONAL DE TÉLÉGRAPHIC ET TÉLÉPHONIQUE.

CCSD Abbreviation of CELLULAR CIRCUIT SWITCHED DATA.

CD (Compact Disc) A 4.72-inch OPTICAL disk storage format developed jointly by Sony and Philips in 1976, originally intended as a DIGITAL distribution medium for music but since extended to store still and moving video images, computer data and programs. Compact discs are made by pressing a pattern of tiny pits into a clear polycarbonate plastic disc and then coating it with a reflective aluminium coating by vacuum deposition; a solid-state LASER is employed to read the pattern of pits by reflection. The same fabrication process is used to make both audio CDs and data CD-ROMs, but there are differences in the DRIVE mechanism used to read them. The data format for audio CDs is defined in the 1982 RED BOOK published jointly by Sony and Philips.

CDC Abbreviation of CONTROL DATA CORPORATION.

CDE (Common Desktop Environment) A standardized GRAPHICAL USER INTERFACE for UNIX systems, designed by the COSE consortium to replace the multiplicity of proprietary systems. See also KDE, MOTIF, GNOME.

cdev The abbreviation normally used to describe a Control Panel Device on the Apple Macintosh, a type of software extension which is installed into the SYSTEM FOLDER to control some new hardware device or low-level machine function. See also INIT, DEVICE DRIVER.

CD-I (Compact Disc Interactive) A standard for interactive MULTIMEDIA disks based on an extension of the CD-ROM format, introduced by Philips in 1990. CD-I was intended as a vehicle for interactive movies, learning materials and games that did not require using a computer – the stand-alone CD-I player also acted as a TV SET-TOP BOX. However, lack of software support for this non-mainstream device caused its commercial failure.

CDIF Abbreviation of CASE DATA INTERCHANGE FORMAT.

CDMA (Code Division Multiple Access) Also called *spread-spectrum* and *code division multiplexing*, one of the competing transmission technologies for digital MOBILE PHONES. The transmitter mixes the packets constituting a message into the digital signal stream in an order determined by a PSEUDO-RANDOM NUMBER sequence that is also known to the intended receiver, which uses it to extract those parts of the signal intended for itself. Hence each different random sequence corresponds to a separate communication channel. CDMA is most used in the USA. See also TDMA and GSM.

CDO Abbreviation of COLLABORATION DATA OBJECTS.

CD-quality Audio data sampled at 44 KHz and 16-bit SAMPLE size, which subjectively sounds as good as a CD.

CD-R (Compact Disc Recordable) A WRITE-ONCE version of the CD-ROM disc, which can be used to distribute and back up computer data or to copy music CDS. Though it follows the same data format and can be read in standard CR-ROM drives, CD-R employs quite a different physical storage process, based on an organic dye film that is selectively bleached by a laser beam, which explains the blue or green colour of the recording surface.

Recording a CD-R, often called *burning* it, requires a special DRIVE called a CD Writer, which can also read conventional CD-ROMs (recent models may also write CD-RW discs). Writing to a CD-R disc is a delicate REAL TIME operation and even a short interruption to the process, say by another program using too much processor time, can cause the resulting disk to be unreadable (sometimes called 'burning a coaster' in an allusion to the only use for such disks).

Data written to a CD-R can be deleted (i.e. made unreadable), but not removed or altered. Most CD-Rs are now MULTISESSION so, if not full, more data can be recorded later but, in contrast to the CD-RW, the existing data cannot be overwritten.

CD-ROM (Compact Disc Read-Only Memory) A NON-VOLATILE OPTICAL DISK STORAGE medium based on the same physical disk format as the audio Compact Disc (CD), developed by Philips and Sony. Like music CDs, CD-ROMs cannot be written by a computer, only pressed from an original master, but their large capacity of around 640 megabytes has made them the most important medium for distributing software, which is now much too large for FLOPPY DISKS to be practical.

CD-ROMs employ a data format that is different from music CDs and require a different DRIVE to read them (which can also play music CDs). All PCs now come fitted with CD-ROM drives, the reading speed of which is rated as a multiple of that of the music CD – currently 24x drives are the standard, with faster to come. See also CD-R, CD-RW, DVD, WHITE BOOK.

CD-ROM XA Extended Architecture, a modification to the original CD-ROM data format that allows drives to read multi-session disks such as Kodak's PHOTO CD, and supports the interleaving of up to 16 parallel audio and video tracks so that they can be played back in synchronization.

CD-RW (Compact Disc Read-Write) An OPTICAL DISC storage format, employing the same sized medium (4.72 inches) and data format as CD-ROM, but which can be written to, erased and rewritten many times. Physically, CD-RW employs entirely different technology from the CD-ROM or the write-once CD-R: data is stored in a shiny layer of metal alloy whose reflectivity can be selectively and reversibly altered by heating with a LASER of a higher power than that used to read it. CD-RW disks can therefore be written only in a special CD-RW drive, but can be read by most modern (though not by older) CD-ROM drives.

cdwrite A Unix utility for writing to CD-R disks.

CeBIT The world's largest computer and communications trade fair, held annually in March in Hanover, Germany.

Ceefax A VIDEOTEXT system introduced by the BBC in 1974 in which textual news bulletins, sports results and program information are transmitted along with the broadcast signal for BBC 1 and BBC 2, and can be read on teletext-enabled TV sets. The Ceefax service will be replaced by a new Digital Text Service when the BBC switches over to all-digital transmissions.

ceiling 1 The highest value that some system parameter is permitted to take: in contrast to FLOOR, which is the lowest value.

2 Used in some programming languages to name a function that rounds up, i.e. returns the smallest integer that is larger than some real number. For example ceiling(1.4) = 2, and ceiling behaves correctly for negative arguments so that ceiling(-1.4) = -1 and not -2. See also FLOOR.

Celeron The name Intel has given to low-cost derivatives of its PENTIUM II family of MICROPROCESSORS that have 128 kilobytes of on-chip CACHE.

cell 1 A location in a SPREADSHEET grid in which a piece of data or a formula is displayed.

2 A small unit of data forming part of a three (or more) dimensional grid, as employed in FINITE ELEMENT ANALYSIS or SIMULATION software.

3 The standard packet of data in an ASYNCHRONOUS TRANSFER MODE network, having a fixed-length of 53 bytes.

4 An area of silicon on a chip layout that implements a specific function; for example the element on a RAM chip that stores a single bit.

5 A battery, as in ALKALINE CELL.

6 In a MOBILE PHONE system, the area served by a single transmitter.

Cello One of the first widely available WEB BROWSERS to run under Microsoft Windows, written at Cornell University Law School.

cell phone See under MOBILE PHONE.

cell reference The address of a particular data item in a SPREADSHEET. There are two widely used syntaxes for cell references: one employs letters for the column and numbers for the row, so that for example B23 means the 23rd cell in column B of the sheet; the other employs R to denote the row and C to denote column, so the same cell would be referenced as R23C2. Microsoft's Excel spreadsheet software permits the use of either syntax. Most spreadsheets provide a scheme for both absolute and relative cell references (see more under RELATIVE REFERENCE) to simplify replicating a formula across a range of cells.

cell relay See ASYNCHRONOUS TRANSFER MODE.

cellular automaton A mathematical construct consisting of a regular grid of cells, each of which can exist in one of several states. The states of all the cells are updated simultaneously to create a new 'generation' by uniformly applying a rule that in some way relates the state of each cell to that of its immediate neighbours. The most widely known example of a cellular automaton is John Conway's LIFE game. It has been demonstrated that with suitable rules cellular automata can be constructed that are equivalent to a TURING MACHINE, and hence can perform any computation.

Cellular Circuit Switched Data (CCSD) A data transfer service available over older analogue

MOBILE PHONE systems by using a dial-up modem built into or connected to a mobile phone: its maximum data rate is 9.6 kilobits per second. See also HSCSD, GPRS, GSM.

cellular phone See under MOBILE PHONE.

central processing unit See under CPU.

Centronics port Once the most common variety of 8-bit PARALLEL PORT on small computers for connecting to a PRINTER, deriving its name from the printer manufacturer who first introduced it. The Centronics port employs a 25- or 50-pin D CONNECTOR plug and socket and was fitted to most personal computers from the early 1980s through to the late 1990s. Later parallel port standards for the ENHANCED PARALLEL PORT and EXTENDED CAPABILITIES PORT offer improved performance while retaining the same connector and are backwards compatible with Centronics peripherals, though all three are now being rapidly displaced by the USB port and FIREWIRE.

CEPT (Comité européen des postes et telecommunications) A data compression scheme used in European telecommunications networks. It is named after the committee that defined it.

Cerf, Vinton (b. 1943) The inventor, along with Bob Kahn, of the TCP/IP protocols that enabled the construction of the modern INTERNET: now a vice-president of MCI, the largest Internet carrier.

CERN (Conseil européen pour recherche nucléaire) A multinational particle physics laboratory in Geneva where in 1991 Tim BERNERS-LEE invented the WORLD WIDE WEB protocols.

CERT Abbreviation of COMPUTER EMERGENCY RESPONSE TEAM.

certificate See under DIGITAL CERTIFICATE.

certificate authority A firm or institution that is a trusted source of DIGITAL CERTIFICATES. A well-known example is VeriSign Inc.

CGA (Color Graphics Adapter) IBM's first GRAPHICS ADAPTER introduced as an option for the original IBM PC, which was capable of displaying 320 x 200 pixels in 4 colours. Its feeble performance (and that of its successor the EGA) allowed the MACINTOSH to become the machine of choice for professional designers and graphical applications for over a decade. See also VGA, XGA.

CGI (Common Gateway Interface) A standard interface that enables external programs to be executed from inside a WEB SERVER, and hence allows essentially unlimited functions to be embedded into WEB PAGES, far beyond those provided by HTML. CGI defines the way that arguments to such an external program can be passed as part of the HTTP request for the page in question. Typically, an external program called via CGI returns its results as HTML text, which is passed back to the requesting BROWSER and thus appears as part of the current page. For example such a program might access a database manager to look up records that match a query passed via CGI, then format the returned records as HTML pages.

Any program that can accept COMMAND LINE arguments may be called via CGI, but very often special-purpose CGI SCRIPTS are written in interpreted languages such as PERL, PYTHON or VBSCRIPT.

cgi-bin A special directory on a WEB SERVER where CGI scripts, which provide server-side services such as hit counting or database queries, are traditionally stored. This directory name is often visible in search engine queries such as http://www.altavista.com/cgi-bin/query?q=Simpsons. The trend among more recent server software is to identify CGI scripts by their filename extension, allowing them to be stored in any directory, alongside the HTML pages that call them.

CGM Abbreviation of COMPUTER GRAPHICS METAFILE.

chain A program instruction that transfers control from the currently executing program directly to another named program, with no possibility of return to the first since its execution state is discarded. Chain was used in many early programming languages, including FORTRAN and BASIC, to break up large programs into separate, memory-sized modules, but it has now been largely superceded by more sophisticated mechanisms such as the DYNAMIC-LINKED LIBRARY. See also OVERLAY.

challenge-response Any type of AUTHENTICATION system that requires a new user to reply to challenges presented by the computer system, maybe by speaking to a voice identification system, or by typing text or number codes.

change management A set of methods and rules for regulating the evolution of the specification, design and implementation of any system, whether hardware, software or business and personnel practices. Change management might be considered as a broadening and generalization of VERSION CONTROL, that is the orderly labelling and documenting of the changes to be made, then arbitrating their concurrent implementation by multiple agents to avoid conflicts. See also CONFIGURATION MANAGEMENT.

channel 1 In general, any conduit through which signals are conveyed for the purpose of communication.

2 On the WORLD WIDE WEB, a type of distribution in which a user of a WEB SITE subscribes to a channel, and thereafter receives automatic updates of its content without asking (see also PUSH, WEBCAST).

3 In certain models of concurrent computing (for example COMMUNICATING SEQUENTIAL PROCESSES), a named data structure that is the communicating equivalent of a program variable, but transmits values from one process to another rather than storing them.

4 In semiconductor engineering, the undoped (see DOPED) region of silicon separating the SOURCE from the DRAIN of a MOS TRANSISTOR, through which current flows when the transistor is turned on.

channel bonding The combining of two ISDN 64 kilobits per second bearer channels to act as a single 128 kilobits per second data channel, for example to provide a fast link to an Internet service. The server end of the connection as well as the call initiator must support channel bonding.

channel hopping 1 A synonym for *frequency hopping*, a modulation technique used for both security and efficiency in wireless communication networks. See more under CDMA, FHSS.

2 The practice of rapidly jumping between conversations on different channels on an Internet CHAT system such as IRC.

3 Hence used metaphorically of, say, a person who changes jobs frequently, or a retailer who changes wholesalers frequently.

channel-splitting The ability of DIGITAL SUBSCRIBER LINE communication technologies to carry analogue voice data and digital data on the same line.

character 1 A single letter, numeral, punctuation mark or symbol used in a system of writing or printing.

2 In computing, any letter, numeral, etc that can be displayed on an output device and is represented by a unique binary code. Until recently these codes have typically been single byte ASCII codes, but now there are several multi-byte codes such as UNICODE and UNIVERSAL CHARACTER SET that can encode characters from more than just the Roman alphabet. See more under CHARACTER SET.

character-based A computer or TERMINAL that can display only text and not graphical images. Most business computers and their operating systems were CHARACTER-based prior to the 1990s, as graphical display ability required too much processing power and was confined to expensive engineering WORKSTATIONS.

The VDUS of character-based systems could not address individual screen PIXELS, but only character positions; a typical screen contained 80×25 characters, and the character shapes were generated in hardware, so it was not possible to alter the text FONT. By contrast modern GRAPHICAL USER INTERFACES such as Windows draw each character as a picture, pixel-by-pixel.

Operating systems such as UNIX and MS-DOS were character-based, employing a COMMAND LINE user interface and treating input and output as simple streams of ASCII codes.

character generator An INTEGRATED CIRCUIT that generates the character forms on the screen of older CHARACTER-BASED terminals or monitors. Unlike modern graphics-based software FONT systems, a character generator can display only in a single font and with a very limited number of text attributes, often just reversed and underlined. Its characters are all formed on the same, very low resolution PIXEL grid (often 8×12 or 10×18) and are therefore of fixed pitch (see FIXED-PITCH FONT) so the resulting displays have the same number of characters on every line: for example a standard MS-DOS display contains 25 lines of 80 characters each.

character orientation The direction of the characters used in a particular SCRIPT in relation to its LINE ORIENTATION. The orientation is said to be *with-stream* if characters face the same way as the line orientation, and *cross-stream* otherwise. Horizontal line orientations (whether left-to-right as in Roman, or right-to-left as in Arabic) are typically with-stream, while vertical line orientations (e.g. Chinese and some Japanese) are cross-stream.

character set A numeric encoding scheme that enables computers to handle textual data: each CHARACTER in an alphabet is represented by a number, so that words can be stored and processed as strings of numbers. A character set typically encodes all the letters, digits and punctuation symbols of an alphabet, as well as certain special characters such as Space, Tab and underscore, some symbols used in mathematics and business such as currency symbols, and various invisible CONTROL CHARACTERS whose purpose is to trigger some software action (for example perform a CARRIAGE RETURN or ring a bell) rather than to be printed or seen.

The most commonly used character set on today's computers remains ASCII, which employs 7 bits to encode each character of the Roman alphabet: for example A is number 65 in the ASCII code, while Space is 32. It is important to distinguish between a character set and a FONT – the character set determines only which number represents each character, while a font governs exactly how that character will appear on a VDU screen or printer. A is always ASCII code 65, no matter whether it is displayed in Times Roman or Univers.

For historical reasons, ASCII evolved around the English language and the Roman alphabet, which poses severe problems for languages such as Arabic or Japanese that use more characters, or are based on a different principle. Because ASCII is only a 7-bit code it can cope with only 128 characters, which is not sufficient to encode many written languages, and these have had to invent 16-bit or even 32-bit encodings. For example the Japanese have developed their own KATAKANA and KANJI character sets, which enable up to 7000 different ideograms to be built up by entering combinations of phonetic part-characters.

There is some movement toward adopting UNICODE, a 16-bit character set that can encode more than 64,000 different characters and should permit all the world's different language communities to use the same character set, printers and software versions. However, moving to a new character set is a slow business because it requires all software to be rewritten, not merely word processing software. Converting old ASCII documents to Unicode is easy, but Unicode documents cannot be read by old software. See also UTF-8, EBCDIC, ANSI.

character string See under STRING.

charge-coupled device (CCD) A class of SEMICONDUCTOR chips that convert light into electrical charge, used as the active elements in video cameras, camcorders and digital cameras. A CCD chip consists of an array of tiny photocells, the charge induced in each of which depends on the light intensity falling on it, while the number of cells determines the overall image RESOLUTION. See also MEGAPIXEL.

chart An alternative name for a GRAPH, that is, a visual representation of a set of data values. See for example BAR GRAPH and PIE CHART.

chat A conversation between two or more people conducted via networked computer systems – chat takes place in real time, by typing messages and seeing immediate responses. Chatting is supported by online systems such as AOL and over the Internet via IRC. See also CHAT ROOM.

chat room A private virtual space in which a group of people can converse electronically by typing text messages to each other in real time. To avoid hundreds of people all trying to 'speak' at once, online CHAT systems are divided up into many separate rooms, each containing a small group with some shared interest. See also INTERNET RELAY CHAT, ICQ,

BULLETIN BOARD, CONFERENCING SYSTEM, NEWS-GROUP.

chdir The command used in both UNIX and MS-DOS to change the current DIRECTORY.

check box A visual component used in GRAPHICAL USER INTERFACES such as Windows and MacOS, which enables the user to set some program option by clicking in the box using the MOUSE. When the option is set, a cross appears in the box, which can be cleared by clicking a second time.

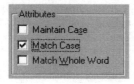

check digit A special digit inserted into a BAR CODE to verify that the code has been scanned correctly.

checksum A quantity calculated from a set of data to test whether it has been altered. For example, a crude checksum for this dictionary definition might be computed by adding up the ASCII codes of all the characters it contains. Substituting any single character would then change the value of that sum (though reordering them would go undetected). Checksums are sometimes applied as a simple security check to executable files, to determine if they have become corrupted. See also CYCLIC REDUNDANCY CHECK, ERROR DETECTION AND CORRECTION.

chiclet keyboard A nickname for the low-cost rubber membrane keyboards used on some personal computers, calculators and remote control units, whose soft keys look like pieces of chewing gum, hence the name.

child process A PROCESS started by another process (called the PARENT PROCESS) in a MULTITASKING operating system such as UNIX. Any process may create many child processes (see SPAWN, FORK), but can itself have only a single parent. The first process, called INIT in Unix, which is started by the operating system at BOOT-UP, has no parent and never terminates, all other running processes automatically becoming its children. Child processes typically inherit their parent's resources and attributes, such as PERMISSIONS and open files. See also ORPHAN PROCESS.

child record In a HIERARCHICAL DATABASE, a RECORD that belongs to a parent record one level higher in the tree.

chip A popular shorthand for a silicon chip or INTEGRATED CIRCUIT.

chip set Two or more INTEGRATED CIRCUITS (chips) that are designed to be used together: for example the chips that are used on the motherboards of IBM-compatible PCs to implement the system BUS and timing logic.

chi-square A statistical distribution, and a test derived from it that is employed to discover how well a set of theoretical predictions fit the observed data.

chmod The command used in UNIX to change the ACCESS PERMISSIONS for a file or directory.

Chomsky Hierarchy An ordering of the properties of language GRAMMARS, and the class of machine needed to parse them, derived from the linguistic discoveries of Noam CHOMSKY. The hierarchy consists of four levels in order of increasing generality: regular languages can be parsed by a FINITE STATE MACHINE; context-free languages by a STACK machine; context-sensitive languages require a linear bounded automaton; and recursively enumerable languages require a TURING MACHINE.

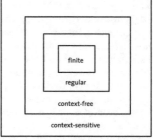

Chomsky, Noam (b. 1928) A US linguist whose findings about the structure of human language grammars have been of paramount importance in the theory of computing and programming languages: see more under CHOMSKY HIERARCHY. He is also a well-known political radical, vociferous in his support for the rights of developing nations.

chord keyboard A type of KEYBOARD that requires a combination of more than one key to be pressed to generate each single character, thus permitting a smaller number of keys overall. Some such designs (e.g. the UK-designed Agenda) had only five keys, one for each finger, requiring chords of two or three keys to generate all the required characters – a primary purpose of such designs is to enable single-handed typing. No chord keyboard has so far been widely adopted; perhaps the most successful is the machine used by court stenographers.

Chorus A modular OPERATING SYSTEM highly optimized for use in telecommunication systems, originally developed in France at the INRIA research institute and employed in many public telephone switches in Europe. Chorus features a small MICROKERNEL with a built-in communications engine, on top of which layers can be added to emulate other operating systems such as UNIX. It was purchased in 1997 by SUN, since when its profile has been very low.

chromaticity That quality of light which captures its hue and saturation characteristics, that is, the objective scientific property corresponding to the everyday concept of 'colour'.

Chromaticity can be visualized as a plane within a COLOUR SPACE of three dimensions, and there are several different systems for describing such spaces: the international standard is the CIE chromaticity diagram. Since working with a three-dimensional space is inconvenient, a 2D transformation called the CIE x, y model is used in which the achromatic component (black, white and greys) is kept separate from the chromatic component. All the fully saturated colours of the spectrum are arranged around the edges of the colour plane, and the hue of light of a particular colour is defined as the wavelength of its central frequency.

A colour's position in this 2D space can be described by giving its x and y coordinates, where x is the redness value divided by the total reflectance, and y is the greenness divided by the total reflectance. The colour

GAMUT that can be reproduced by any actual colour display device, such as a computer monitor or printer, can be depicted as a bounded area within the total CIE plane. See also COLOUR, COLOUR MODEL, RGB, CMYK, HUE, SATURATION, INTENSITY, COLOUR CORRECTION, COLOUR RETOUCHING.

chrominance A video signal that represents only the colour information contained in a picture – a second separate signal called the LUMINANCE is then used to represent the lightness and darkness information. In the COMPOSITE VIDEO system used for domestic video, chrominance and luminance information are combined into a single signal, while the semi-professional S-VIDEO system transmits them on two different wires. Some video compression schemes such as JPEG depend on separating chrominance and luminance values.

CHRP Abbreviation of COMMON HARDWARE REFERENCE PLATFORM.

Church, Alonzo (1903–95) An American logician who in 1936 proved the theorem that bears his name, showing that no mechanical process can determine in advance whether a given statement is provable from a given theory. This result is now recognized as equivalent to Alan TURING's discovery of the same year, and a combined CHURCH/TURING HYPOTHESIS has become the backbone of modern computer science. Church also invented the LAMBDA CALCULUS, which opened up the possibility of functional programming languages such as LISP and its successors.

Church/Turing hypothesis The proposal that any problem that can be computed at all can be computed by a suitably programmed TURING MACHINE given sufficient time and memory-space. In other words, all digital computers are equivalent as regards the classes of problem that they can solve (though not in how fast they can solve them), which is the informing principle of computer science, PROGRAMMING LANGUAGE design and the study of ALGORITHMS.

The result derives from the 1936 discoveries of Alan TURING and Alonzo CHURCH; it is still labelled a hypothesis rather than a theorem simply because the notion of effective computability on which it depends remains unformalized.

CICS (Customer Information Control System) IBM's TRANSACTION MONITOR suite, developed for its range of MAINFRAME computers.

CIDR Abbreviation of CLASSLESS INTERNETWORK DOMAIN ROUTING.

CIE (Commission internationale de l'éclairage) The body responsible for defining international standards for colours and lighting. See also CHROMATICITY.

CIF Abbreviation of COMMON INTERCHANGE FORMAT.

Cinepak One of the first popular video compression CODECS, now largely displaced by MPEG.

cipher, cypher A scheme for encoding messages to prevent them being read by unauthorized persons. The simplest ciphers work by substituting one letter for another as prescribed by a list of substitutions called a KEY, possession of which enables the message to be decoded and read. For example the key could be a table of random number pairs, or an agreed passage from a published book (where consecutive letters of the encyphered message are replaced by those in the equivalent position in the passage). There are endless possibilities for such ciphers, the study of which falls within the discipline of CRYPTOGRAPHY.

Machines may be devised to generate fresh substitutions for every message, but substitution ciphers still remain vulnerable to the rapid processing power of modern computers, which can try out billions of permutations and exploit unchangeable facts such as the known frequencies of occurrence of the letters (and letter pairs, triples, etc) in texts written in different languages – in English for example, the most common letter will be E. The WWII German Enigma machine was the most famous such machine, and the cracking of its codes played a crucial role in the history of computing (see BLETCHLEY PARK, COLOSSUS). Modern cryptographers depend instead on encrypting the binary representation of a text, using mathematical algorithms that exploit the difficulty of factoring huge num-

bers: see more under RSA ENCRYPTION, PUBLIC-KEY ENCRYPTION.

circuit 1 A set of electronic components connected to one another by conductors such as wires, in such a way as to create one or more paths through which a continuous electric current can flow. The name indicates that such paths must ultimately be closed (i.e. circular) so that the current can reenter its source and maintain a flow: otherwise an *open circuit* is said to exist (whether by intention due to a SWITCH or by accident due to a broken wire), and no current can flow. A *short circuit* occurs when two wires accidentally touch, so the current returns prematurely without visiting all parts of the circuit.

2 In telecommunications, a continuous path between a sender and a receiver of messages: see more under CIRCUIT-SWITCHED, CONNECTION-ORIENTED, VIRTUAL CIRCUIT.

circuit board A flat piece of insulating material onto which electronic components are mounted and connected to form a circuit. Nowadays the term is generally synonymous with PRINTED CIRCUIT BOARD.

circuit-switched A class of communication NETWORK, the most familiar example of which is the public telephone system, in which electronic SWITCHES are used to establish a temporary but exclusively owned circuit between each sender and receiver. By contrast, in a SHARED-MEDIUM NETWORK all users must contend for access to the same piece of wire. Switched networks are faster than shared-medium ones as they eliminate the complexity of arbitrating access to a shared transport, and provide each user with the full bandwidth of the medium. However, they are more costly because of the extra switching hardware required. See also CONNECTION-ORIENTED, CONNECTIONLESS.

CIS Abbreviation of COMPUSERVE INFORMATION SYSTEM.

CISC (Complex Instruction Set Computer) A term applied to all the older computer ARCHITECTURES to distinguish them from the new RISC designs introduced in the 1990s. A CISC INSTRUCTION SET contains instructions that perform several steps in one, and therefore take many CYCLES to execute – such as the Intel 8086's ADC instruction, which takes more than 20 cycles to add the contents of a REGISTER to a memory location. The concept grew through the early days of computing from a desire to make life easier for MACHINE CODE programmers, but now that most programming is done in HIGH-LEVEL languages it is less necessary and hinders hardware efficiency. RISC designs employ a larger number of simple, one cycle operations that are automatically generated by a COMPILER.

Cisco Systems Inc. A US manufacturer of network ROUTERS whose products constitute a large part of the backbone of the INTERNET.

Citrix The US software firm that developed WINFRAME and the INTELLIGENT CONSOLE ARCHITECTURE protocol that turn Microsoft's WINDOWS into a MULTIUSER operating system.

CIX **1** Abbreviation of COMMERCIAL INTERNET EXCHANGE.
2 Abbreviation of COMPULINK INFORMATION EXCHANGE.

clamshell The hinged case design typically employed for LAPTOP and NOTEBOOK computers, which is thought to resemble the eponymous bivalve.

clash A conflict between two consumers of the same resource or two bearers of the same identifier. For example a NAME CLASH occurs when a name given to an object within a program is already being used by another object within the same NAMESPACE, while a hash clash (see under HASH COLLISION) occurs when two objects produce the same value when a hash function is applied to them.

class The fundamental organizing structure of any OBJECT-ORIENTED PROGRAMMING LANGUAGE, a template or prototype that describes the properties and behaviour of all the objects, called INSTANCES, that will be created from it. A class defines a set of named variables called INSTANCE VARIABLES, of which each instance will possess a set to hold its state information, and a set of procedures called METHODS that any instance can call to implement its behaviour. The whole set of methods constitutes the INTERFACE of the class. A class definition might look something like this:

```
CLASS ComplexNumber
x: Real
y: Real
```

```
PROCEDURE ComplexAdd(a, b);
PROCEDURE ComplexMult(a, b);
PROCEDURE ComplexDiv(a, b);
ENDCLASS
```

x and y are the instance variables, and the three procedures are its private methods, which may be executed only by instances of this class (or of any DERIVED CLASS) and are invisible to all other objects. See also CLASS HIERARCHY.

class hierarchy A set of classes related to one another by INHERITANCE, defined in an OBJECT-ORIENTED PROGRAMMING LANGUAGE. A class hierarchy begins with a BASE CLASS from which descend DERIVED CLASSES that represent specializations of its properties: that is to say, they may possess additional INSTANCE VARIABLES or methods that specify properties unique to themselves. Such subclasses in turn may have descendants whose instances inherit all the instance variables and methods of the base class and other ancestors.

Class hierarchies are similar in both concept and function to the classification systems used in the biological sciences to distinguish species. A class hierarchy created to write programs about transport systems might look something like:

```
        CLASS Vehicle
         /        \
CLASS Motor    CLASS Humanpowered
   /    \          /      \
CLASS Car CLASS Bus CLASS Bike CLASS Scooter
```

Here the base class is Vehicle, and MotorCar and Bicycle are derived classes. Motor and Humanpowered are also derived classes but they are ABSTRACT CLASSES, invented to assist the specialization but not intended to have instances of their own (just as in nature there are no living instances of 'mollusc', only of particular mollusc species). See also CLASS.

class ID, class identifier (CLSID) A unique identifier employed to distinguish different object classes in object models such as Microsoft's COM or CORBA. When a client program wishes to create a new INSTANCE of a class it must pass the CLASS IDENTIFIER of the desired class to the CLASS LIBRARY that contains it. See also MONIKER.

classification problem A type of mathematical problem that involves sorting a population of objects into different classes on the basis of some similarity or shared attribute. See also DECISION PROBLEM, SATISFIABILITY PROBLEM, SEARCH PROBLEM.

Classless Internetwork Domain Routing (CIDR) An Internet ROUTING technology that does away with the older IP ADDRESS classes A, B and C and makes more usable addresses available: it is defined in RFC 1467.

class library A set of compiled CLASS definitions for some particular application domain. Programmers can link such a library into their own programs using an OBJECT-ORIENTED PROGRAMMING SYSTEM along with any inherited classes required to accomplish the job at hand, without having to redo all of the work invested in the library. MICROSOFT FOUNDATION CLASSES for Windows is a representative example.

clause A section of program code contained within a control structure which may be executed or not. For example in a construction such as:

```
IF Test THEN CodeA ELSE CodeB ENDIF
```

the segments CodeA and CodeB are different clauses. In LOGIC PROGRAMMING languages such as PROLOG, the entire program consists of a sequence of clauses. See also HORN CLAUSE.

clean room 1 A dust-free room with a filtered air supply that is used for the fabrication of the semiconductor WAFERS on which INTEGRATED CIRCUITS are built. Modern VLSI processes employ FEATURE SIZES that are an order of magnitude smaller than human hair or dust particles. So even a particle of smoke is large enough to ruin several devices during the photographic LITHOGRAPHY process that is used to copy chip layouts. Clean rooms are therefore graded by the size of smallest particle that can pass their filters, and their occupants must wear 'space suits' with a positive-pressure air supply to contain moisture and skin particles. See also FAB, MASK, PROCESS TECHNOLOGY.

2 The term is now used metaphorically (alluding to the above meaning) to describe a software or hardware development team that has been deliberately isolated from contact with a competitor's product, to avoid any suspicion of copying code and hence any breach-of-copyright suits. It is used as in 'their Windows emulator was developed using a clean room approach'.

ClearType A new FONT RENDERING technology developed by Microsoft to improve the readability of type displayed on the small LIQUID CRYSTAL DISPLAY (LCD) screens used in portable and hand-held devices, intended to promote acceptance of the EBOOK document format. ClearType is a form of ANTIALIASING that takes account of the physical reality of colour LCD displays, which is that their 'pixels' are not really dots but triplets of red, green and blue vertical stripes. A ClearType converter program performs SUBPIXEL sampling on the character forms produced by some conventional font system such as TRUETYPE, applying a series of red, green and blue filters that are slightly horizontally displaced from one other. A modest smoothing effect will also be seen on desktop cathode-ray tube monitors, but far less than is produced on an LCD. See also PIXEL, FONT RENDERING, ADOBE TYPE MANAGER, OPENTYPE.

CLI Abbreviation of COMMAND LINE INTERFACE.

click 1 The popular term for pressing the button on a computer's MOUSE to select an object on the screen such as an icon or menu option. The term is used both as a noun ('it takes two clicks to reach Exit') or a verb ('click on the first option'). A click is the most significant sort of EVENT in a modern GRAPHICAL USER INTERFACE, and especially within a WEB BROWSER where it may almost entirely replace keyboard activity. See also BUTTON-PRESS, DOUBLE-CLICK, RIGHT-CLICK, CLICK-THROUGH, CLICK-AND-DRAG.

2 A short sharp sound effect produced by some programs to indicate to the user that an attempted operation (for example selecting some screen object) has succeeded. Clicks are particularly used on hand-held computers with PEN INTERFACES to provide a positive feedback.

click-and-drag A type of interaction employed in GRAPHICAL USER INTERFACES where the user moves the MOUSE POINTER over a desired screen object, presses and holds down a MOUSE BUTTON, and the object then follows the pointer, allowing it to be moved to a different screen location.

click-through The act of clicking the mouse over a LINK embedded in a WEB PAGE and hence being taken to a different page. For advertisers and E-COMMERCE companies, who pay to have their links or BANNER ADVERTS inserted into other sites' pages, a click-through event is far more important than a mere viewing of the page that the link is embedded in, as it means a potential customer has actually been taken to their site. Therefore the number of click-throughs is the preferred measure of usage for commercial sites, rather than the overall number of PAGE IMPRESSIONS.

client 1 A computer connected to a network that obtains some resource or service (such as file storage, printing or EMAIL) from a SERVER located elsewhere on the network.

2 A program or process that calls upon services provided by another program or process called a SERVER PROCESS. The term is used to describe the user software required to access many Internet services such as EMAIL and newsgroups: see under EMAIL CLIENT, NEWS CLIENT, FTP CLIENT. See also CLIENT/SERVER, CLIENT-SIDE, SERVER-SIDE.

client/server A principle commonly used to structure computer programs and hardware systems, where the work effort is divided between CLIENTS that request services, and SERVERS that provide those services. In a purely software implementation of the client/server paradigm, client and server may form parts of the same program (for instance user interface and calculating engine), or be different programs running on the same computer, or run on different computers across a network. In both hardware and software client/server systems, the two parties must have some agreed format or PROTOCOL for exchanging messages (i.e. requests and responses to requests).

The advantages of adopting a client/server structure are severalfold:

i) It can simplify distributing a computing task over several computers, as client and server can run on different machines.
ii) There is a separation of concerns, which may simplify writing the software. For example a server might be concerned solely with

numerical computation while its client performs only graphical display of the results.
iii) It becomes easy to support multiple, heterogeneous computing environments. The client may run on one kind of CPU and OPERATING SYSTEM and the server on another, so long as they can exchange messages.
iv) It may be advantageous for maintenance purposes to keep a few servers under central control, with many clients controlled by individual users.
v) Hardware clients may require less computing resources (e.g. CPU power, memory and disk storage) and hence be cheaper, if much of their task is performed on a powerful remote server.

An example of a software-only client/server system is Microsoft's OLE, where one component of Microsoft Office such as Word may act as a client for another such as Excel to embed a spreadsheet into a business report. The Internet is an example of a hardware client/server system that supports many different kinds of client, server and protocol. See also PEER-TO-PEER.

client-side The user's (that is, the CLIENT machine's) end of a CLIENT/SERVER connection, as opposed to the SERVER. In the most common example of such a connection, a WORLD WIDE WEB connection, client-side refers to an action, such as the execution of a SCRIPT, that occurs within the user's BROWSER rather than on the WEB SITE itself. See also SERVER-SIDE.

clip See under CLIPPING.

clip-art Drawn or photographic images, typically sold on a CD-ROM or from a WEB SITE, for which blanket permission is granted to use, modify and publish them in documents without paying any copyright fee directly to their original author.

clipboard An area of memory reserved for transferring data between one running application and another under MULTITASKING operating systems such as Windows and MacOS. A region of an image or text is selected using the MOUSE and then copied to the clipboard, from where it may be PASTED into the second application's window at the cursor position (see also CUT-AND-PASTE). The Windows clipboard can also temporarily store OLE objects of various classes, such as spreadsheets or vector drawings, and paste them into another application, converting into different formats if required. See also CLIPBOOK.

clipbook, ClipBook An enhancement of the Windows CLIPBOARD mechanism for transferring data from one application to another, introduced with WINDOWS FOR WORKGROUPS and adopted in WINDOWS NT. A clipbook contains multiple pages so that it can hold more than one data item at once, allowing it to be used for cumulative operations, such as clipping out several non-contiguous paragraphs from a document to move to another document, in a single pass.

Unlike the contents of the clipboard which disappear at power-down, a clipbook can be stored permanently for use in future sessions, and it can be shared with other users over a network, so providing a simple mechanism for publishing data.

Clipper **1** An INTEGRATED CIRCUIT for data ENCRYPTION developed by the National Security Agency, whose use was strongly promoted by the US government in the 1990s. It met with determined resistance from users because it has a built-in TRAP DOOR to allow government agencies to decrypt all communications.

2 A now defunct RISC processor designed by Fairchild, most notable for being the first to employ CLOCK-DOUBLING and the HARVARD ARCHITECTURE later adopted by Intel for the PENTIUM.

clipping **1** A section of text removed from a larger document, as in 'press clipping'. See also CUT-AND-PASTE.

2 The act of reducing the size of a digital image to fit into a defined box: see also VIEWPORT.

3 In audio engineering, to drive an output device such as a loudspeaker or earphone too hard – beyond its range of faithful reproduction – which results in truncation of the peaks of the sound WAVEFORMS so that they approximate a SQUARE WAVE. The effect is a harsh distorted sound, which may cause permanent damage to the device: in the music industry it is sometimes deliberately sought as a desirable 'fuzz' effect in guitar amplifiers.

clock In computer engineering, a SEMICONDUCTOR device that emits a sequence of regular electrical pulses, used to regulate and synchronize the operation of other devices. See more under CLOCK SIGNAL, SYSTEM CLOCK.

clock cycle The basic unit of timing within a computer system, consisting of one of the stream of regular pulses generated by the SYSTEM CLOCK. Most of a computer's components, in particular its processor, bus and memory systems, operate in strict step with the clock, so the number of clock cycles their various actions occupy is of crucial importance to a computer designer.

clock-doubling A technology introduced by Intel in the early 1990s to upgrade personal computers by plugging into their CPU socket a module that contains a MICROPROCESSOR running at twice the original speed, but with a normal-speed external BUS. For example a 25 MHz 486 system could have a clock-doubled 50 MHz chip added.

clock signal The train of pulses generated by a computer's SYSTEM CLOCK chip, the transitions of which are used as timing signals by various components of the computer, including its processor and memory.

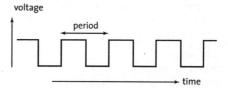

clock speed Most often used to refer to the CLOCK frequency at which a PC's CPU is running, which is typically 800 MHz to 1 GHz in the latest generation of machines. In fact different sections within the PC run at different speeds, so the external memory and system BUS are more likely to be clocked at 100 MHz while input/output channels run at yet another frequency.

The comparative clock speeds of PC systems are often quoted as indicators of their performance, in much the same way as the 0–60 mph time is quoted for cars. However, this ignores the profound effect that other architectural details, particularly CACHE size and configuration, may have on real processing throughput. It is not unknown for one CPU to outperform another running at twice the clock speed, if the task in question will fit wholly into the former's but not the latter's cache. See also CLOCK CYCLE, CLOCK-DOUBLING, CLOCK SIGNAL, SYSTEM CLOCK.

clone A computer manufactured to the same functional specification as some more famous brand so that it can run all the latter's software. The term was first coined to describe the low-cost copies of the IBM PC made in the early 1980s, whose success drove the huge growth of the personal computer market. The Apple MACINTOSH has also been cloned, but with far less success.

The term has a slightly derogatory undertone and throughout this dictionary 'IBM-compatible PC' is used instead: all today's leading PC manufacturers including COMPAQ, DELL and GATEWAY could be described as clone manufacturers, but many have grown to be technical innovators in their own right.

CLOS Abbreviation of COMMON LISP OBJECT SYSTEM.

close box A visual component used in most GRAPHICAL USER INTERFACES, which consists of a small BUTTON, usually displayed in one of the upper corners of a screen WINDOW, which causes that window to close when clicked with the MOUSE. See also SCREEN FURNITURE, MAXIMIZE, MINIMIZE, CONTROL.

close-coupled Any system whose parts have a direct, high-BANDWIDTH connection between them. For example a MULTIPROCESSOR computer with its processors on the same BUS might be so described, whereas one that has remote network connections between processors would not.

closed-loop Any system that seeks to maintain itself in equilibrium by using a FEEDBACK loop.

close tag A symbol used to mark the end of a tagged construct in HTML, XML and similar MARKUP LANGUAGES. For example </P> is the close tag for a <P>paragraph tag. See also TAG, OPEN TAG.

closure A construct supported in some FUNCTIONAL PROGRAMMING LANGUAGES whereby a function can be invoked on some of its arguments, and evaluation completed later when the remaining arguments are supplied. See also CURRIED FUNCTION.

CLP Abbreviation of CONSTRAINT LOGIC PROGRAMMING.

CLR Abbreviation of COMMON LANGUAGE RUNTIME.

CLSID Abbreviation of CLASS IDENTIFIER.

CLU An early OBJECT-ORIENTED PROGRAMMING LANGUAGE developed at MIT in 1975 whose pioneering use of ABSTRACT DATA TYPES influenced many later language designs.

cluster 1 A group of computers connected together using a very fast NETWORK, with an operating system that enables them to be treated as a single MULTIPROCESSOR computer or to provide FAULT-TOLERANT backup for one another. Running tasks may be automatically switched from one member of the cluster to another in the event of its failure: see FAILOVER.

2 A unit of space allocation used by the MS-DOS disk filing system when storing data on magnetic disk media such as floppy and hard disk drives. A cluster is of variable size, consisting of between 1 and 16 physical SECTORS. See also FAT16, FAT32, NTFS, DYNAMIC STORAGE.

3 An accumulation of data elements around a certain position in a table, caused by them having equal HASH indices.

clustered SMP A type of MULTIPROCESSOR computer created by assembling a CLUSTER of separate computers and linking them via a very fast switched INTERCONNECT network that gives each processor access to its neighbour's address spaces. Such a cluster can appear to software as a conventional SMP multiprocessor (though one with a dual-speed memory in which far accesses are slower than local accesses: see NUMA). Clustered SMP was pioneered by SEQUENT and TANDEM for building fast, fault-tolerant servers.

CMOS (Complementary Metal-Oxide Semiconductor) The most popular fabrication process for modern INTEGRATED CIRCUITS, which employs LOGIC GATES made out of complementary pairs of FIELD-EFFECT TRANSISTORS called the P-CHANNEL and N-CHANNEL respectively. The p-channel transistor is made within a well of n-type silicon, while the n-channel is made directly in the doped silicon SUBSTRATE. These two transistors are arranged so that a current flows only momentarily while the gate is switching, and none flows in its on or off states, which enormously reduces power consumption as compared with older BIPOLAR processes. It is this benign property that permits the phenomenal improvement in chip performance over recent decades that is referred to as MOORE'S LAW. See also FIELD-EFFECT TRANSISTOR, MOS, MOSFET.

CMYK The COLOUR MODEL employed by printers, which uses cyan, magenta, yellow and black inks for its four primary colours (hence the name). The CMYK primaries differ from those in the RGB model because ink on paper absorbs rather than emits light – cyan, magenta and yellow are the colours that remain when a pigment *removes* red, green or blue from the white light reflected from the paper.

In theory only cyan, magenta and yellow are necessary, as black is the mixture of all three. But in practice this yields a dark brown, so printers employ a separate black ink, which also gives a crisper result when printing text. The GAMUT of the CMYK colour space differs considerably from that of RGB, making some colours very difficult to match between print and screen.

Since computer displays are emissive, the more common GRAPHICS FILE FORMATS store RGB information for each PIXEL, but all professional DESKTOP PUBLISHING programs that create output for litho printing will offer the option to save in CMYK, for example as a TIFF or ENCAPSULATED POSTSCRIPT file.

CNC Abbreviation of COMPUTER NUMERICAL CONTROL.

coarse-grained A metaphorical term used to describe systems or processes that deal with relatively large scale data objects such as whole files or records, rather than with individual bits and bytes: see more under GRANULARITY.

coaxial cable, coax A type of cable that consists of a central insulated conductor, surrounded by an earthed layer of knitted wire mesh that shields the signal from electrical interference. Coaxial cable is used for TV aerial leads and some computer networks.

cobalt alloy A class of magnetic materials made from combinations of cobalt with other magnetic metals – a widely-used example being cobalt-nickel – which are used to coat the PLATTERS of high-performance hard disks by virtue of their high coercivity and low noise characteristics. See also FERRIC OXIDE, BARIUM FERRITE, FERROMAGNETISM.

cobalt-nickel See under COBALT ALLOY.

COBOL (COmmon Business Oriented Language) The first HIGH-LEVEL PROGRAMMING LANGUAGE designed for business, rather than scientific, applications, created by the CODASYL committee in 1960: the development effort that lead up to COBOL was led by Admiral Grace HOPPER for the US Navy. COBOL remained the language of choice on MAINFRAME computers in banking, finance and large corporations up until the late 1980s when SQL and so-called FOURTH GENERATION LANGUAGES began to supercede it, but there are still millions, if not trillions, of lines of COBOL code running throughout the world.

COBOL is a COMPILED language, though interpreted versions have existed, and its programs typically perform very simple arithmetic calculations on large amounts of data stored as records contained in files. It is a verbose language, with a syntax that tries to resemble conversational English. Programs are divided into four compulsory sections, the Identification division (which identifies the program and programmer), the Environment division (which specifies the required hardware and storage configuration), the Data division (which defines data structures) and the Procedure division (which contains the executable code). As a sample of COBOL style, consider this excerpt from a Procedure division:

```
OPEN INPUT EMPLOYEE-FILE,
OUTPUT FILE-1, FILE-2.
SELECTION SECTION.
PARAGRAPH-1. READ EMPLOYEE-FILE
AT END. GO TO FINISH-HERE.
IF FIELD-A EQUALS FIELD-B PERFORM
COMP ELSE MOVE FIELD-A TO FIELD-B.
```

COBOL has many deficiencies, not least its primitive control structures, dominated by the use of GO TO which makes a program's overall logic very hard to unravel. COBOL's crude handling of dates lay behind many of the YEAR 2000 BUG problems. There have been attempts to modernize the language, including major revisions in 1968, 1974, 1985 and now ANSI OBJECT-ORIENTED COBOL.

COCOMO (Constructive Cost Model) A set of methods for evaluating the cost of a software project, based on the number of lines of SOURCE CODE it contains. COCOMO first estimates the number of logical lines in a project: that is, excluding comments but counting multiline control structures such as 'if-then-else' as single lines. It then applies a number of multiplicative factors, called 'drivers' to this figure: the various Scale Drivers are attempts to measure contextual factors such as precedentedness/novelty, flexibility, architectural risk, team cohesion and process maturity; Cost Drivers estimate the effort involved in each part of the project, the effect of different levels of safety requirement and so on. These are all fed into a set of empirically established algebraic formulae to give a total cost. See also SOFTWARE METRICS, METRIC.

CODASYL (Conference On Data Systems Languages) The international task force responsible for defining the COBOL language in 1959, along with the first database standards.

Codd, Edgar F. The US inventor of the RELATIONAL DATABASE model. A former researcher at IBM, Codd developed a mathematical theory of data relations derived from the PREDICATE CALCULUS, and published a list of Twelve Rules for Relational Databases that must be followed for the relational model to deliver its promised benefits. Codd later turned his attention to ONLINE TRANSACTION PROCESSING for which he issued a similar set of 12 rules.

Codd's Normal Forms A set of transformations that must be applied to raw data in order to achieve a RELATIONAL DATABASE design that is efficient in terms of access speed, storage space and data integrity.

A RELATION is said to be in normal form if it satisfies certain constraints defined in CODD's original theory, which mostly have to do with removing duplicate items and flattening out many-to-one and one-to-many relationships. Codd described three normal forms called First Normal Form (1NF), Second Normal Form (2NF) and Third Normal Form (3NF), each achieved by further transformation of the previous one, but it is now accepted that there are five steps to full normalization.

code 1 A system of letters or symbols together with rules for their combination, by means of which information can be represented or communicated for reasons of secrecy (see CIPHER), brevity (see for example HUFFMAN CODING), identification (see BAR CODE), or in order to be executed by a computer.

2 Hence, the informal term used by programmers to refer to their product, namely executable computer programs (used as in 'that's really neat code') whether in the original, human readable form called SOURCE CODE, or after compilation into OBJECT CODE. The term is also used as a verb meaning to write programs, as in 'it took three weeks to code it'.

3 Sometimes used in MAINFRAME computing circles in the plural form 'codes' referring to large computer application programs.

code base 1 All of the SOURCE CODE that goes to make up a software product, including different versions, external libraries, test routines, and so on.

2 Less commonly, all the copies of all versions of a program that have been sold, used as in 'we have to remain compatible with our existing code base'.

codec 1 A contraction of *compress/decompress*, a type of software DRIVER or PROTOCOL used to create and playback compressed video and audio files: for example MPEG files require the installation of an appropriate codec before they can be viewed. (Under WINDOWS the codecs installed on a computer can be inspected in the Advanced pane of the Control Panel/Multimedia applet.)

2 A contraction of *coder/decoder*, an INTEGRATED CIRCUIT that converts between analogue and digital signals and vice versa within a communications system such as a wireless network. See also MODEM.

Code Division Multiple Access See CDMA.

code division multiplexing See under CDMA.

code generator 1 One of the final stages of a programming language COMPILER, which converts an internal representation of the program being compiled into a stream of machine code instructions for a specific processor, and then outputs them as an OBJECT

CODE file. See also LEXICAL ANALYSER, PARSER, CODE OPTIMIZER.

2 Sometimes used to refer to an automatic PROGRAM GENERATOR: see also FOURTH GENERATION LANGUAGE.

code maintenance The process of keeping a program running and fit for its purpose, which may include finding and fixing BUGS, adding or modifying features requested by users, and upgrading to new versions of the underlying operating system or libraries. A good rule of thumb is that code maintenance will eventually cost as much as all the earlier stages of development combined.

code morphing See under CRUSOE.

code optimizer A stage present in advanced programming language COMPILERS that examines the INSTRUCTION stream emitted by the CODE GENERATOR and reorders certain instruction groups to make them execute as efficiently as possible on a particular model of processor. It might, for example, place some arithmetic instructions after a slow memory access to consume the idle cycles. Most C and C++ compilers that generate Intel x86 code will now have an optimizer for various versions of Pentium.

code page, codepage A system for organizing foreign language CHARACTER SETS originally developed by IBM in the 1970s and later formalized in the international standard ISO 8859. Applications and operating systems were written to support a particular code page (or pages) which indicated what character sets they could use: for example American English is code page 437, while Latin-2 is code page 852. Software designed to run in multiple languages had to support multiple code pages, and the extra programming effort involved was a prime motivator for the development of the comprehensive UNICODE character set. See also EXTENDED ASCII, ANSI CHARACTER SET, WGL4.

code point A 16-bit number that represents a character in the UNICODE character set.

co-design The practice of designing an INTEGRATED CIRCUIT and the software to run on it in tandem with one another.

co-development A strategy for TECHNOLOGY TRANSFER that proceeds by involving the future users of a system in its development at an early stage.

codomain Also called the RANGE, the set of all the values that a mathematical FUNCTION may return for all possible values of its ARGUMENTS.

coercion An action performed by some programming language COMPILERS or INTERPRETERS, of implicitly converting one data type to another. For example where a programmer has written an expression such as $x+2.63$ but x has been declared of an integer type, the compiler might quietly coerce the value of x to FLOATING-POINT rather than complaining about the mismatch. See also CAST.

cognitive Having to do with the acquistion of knowledge.

cold boot To restart (that is REBOOT) a computer from its completely powered-off state when all its memory contents have been lost, as compared with a WARM BOOT in which the RESET BUTTON is pressed without turning the power off, so that some memory contents may be retained. Certain rare error conditions may for this reason not be cleared by a warm boot, and require a full cold boot to correct. See also BOOTSTRAP, BOOT-UP, BOOTSTRAP LOADER.

cold cathode lamp A type of fluorescent lamp widely employed for BACKLIGHTING the displays of portable computers because of its relatively low power consumption and ability to operate without getting hot. A cold cathode lamp contains metal filament electrodes at each end of a tubular glass envelope filled with a low-pressure gas, typically mercury vapour or an argon/neon mixture, through which an electric arc is struck from one end to the other: electrons and short-wave radiation liberated from the resulting plasma strike a PHOSPHOR coating on the tube walls to generate the light. While conventional domestic/industrial fluorescent tubes draw a permanent current to keep their cathode hot for instant starting, a cold cathode lamp employs instead a short high-voltage surge to start itself, hence the name. As a result cold cathode lamps require a relatively high-voltage TRANSFORMER. Historically speaking the neon tube was the first example of a cold cathode lamp.

ColdFusion A WEB AUTHORING system published by the US company Allaire.

Collaboration Data Objects (CDO) An OBJECT LIBRARY created by Microsoft to simplify building GROUP CALENDAR and WORKFLOW applications on top of its EXCHANGE and OUTLOOK applications.

collate 1 To assemble the pages of a printed or photocopied document into their correct order, and/or to group sets of such pages to form individual documents. Many WORD PROCESSORS offer the option to collate automatically when printing multiple copies of a multi-page document.
2 Hence also to arrange any stream of data into some orderly format, for example into ASCII character order. With complex CHARACTER sets such as those employed by the UNICODE and OPENTYPE systems, it becomes necessary to define many different sorting orders to take account of different sets of special characters, and such an order is then known as a *collation*: see more under COLLATION ORDER.

collation See under COLLATION ORDER.

collation order An intrinsic ordering of a set of data items, most particularly an ALPHABET or CHARACTER SET. The well-known 'alphabetic order' of English, a, b, c, d... z, is a simple example of a collation order but it ceases to be simple once numerals, punctuation characters, other languages and computer systems with many alternative character sets have to be considered. Ambiguities arise over the position and ordering of accented and other special characters, and different collation orders may become desirable for different applications. For example, in this dictionary it was decided that a word like 10BaseT should sort under T, because most people will be thinking 'TenBaseT' as they look it up.
Collation order becomes crucial for searching and pattern matching software, which has to decide whether two strings are equal, or which precedes which. The UNICODE system employs a complex algorithm supplemented by tables of 'collation elements' to make such comparisons unambiguous: a complete character ordering for a particular language is called a *collation*.

collection A general data type that acts as a container for multiple items, supporting just the operations of adding and removing items. Languages that support collections include SMALLTALK and DELPHI. See also BAG, LIST.

collector The part of a BIPOLAR TRANSISTOR to which current flows from the EMITTER when the transistor is turned on.

collision The result of two processes trying to simultaneously access the same resource: see for example HASH COLLISION.

collision-avoidance In any communications system that employs a SHARED MEDIUM, the mechanism that ensures that two workstations do not try to send messages simultaneously and corrupt each other's messages, the classic example being ETHERNET'S CSMA/CD algorithm.

collision-detection In 3D GRAPHICS and animation, the task of determining when two objects are trying to occupy the same space, i.e. have collided. For complex scenes collision -detection can become an onerous computational task.

Color Graphics Adapter See CGA.

colorimeter A device for measuring the quality of a colour by comparing it with standard colours or colour combinations.

Colossus An electronic calculating machine built at BLETCHLEY PARK during World War II for decoding German military signal traffic, and which alongside the US ENIAC machine can claim to be the world's first digital electronic computer.
Ten Colossus machines were built, designed specifically to reduce the time required to try out all the permutations needed to crack messages encoded with the German's Lorenz cipher from weeks to hours, which would enable tactical decisions to be made based on their contents. The machines were conceived by the Cambridge mathematician Max Newman and perfected by a talented UK Post Office engineer Tommy Flowers. Alan TURING was involved in their programming.
Colossus employed photocells to read 5-bit BAUDOT CODED teleprinter characters from a punched paper tape at 5,000 characters per second, and computed BOOLEAN functions of

these characters against other characters that represented a possible setting of the wheels within the original encoding machine. It exploited parallel processing by calculating five bit streams simultaneously, allowing it to perform up to 500 such Boolean operations within the 200 millisecond interval before the next character, a performance that is hard to achieve even with a modern PC. The Mark 2 Colossus employed thyratrons, gas-filled triode valves (*US*: vacuum tube) as one-bit storage elements, and contained valve-based AND and OR logic gates and 5-bit SHIFT REGISTERS. It was programmed (as was ENIAC) by setting up a pattern of switches and telephone jack-plugs by hand, and was not a STORED-PROGRAM COMPUTER in the modern sense, as it was designed for a limited range of calculations.

Unlike the ENIAC, the Colossus was kept secret by the UK government until 1970 and all the existing machines were destroyed, seriously delaying the acknowledgement of its rightful place in computing history. See also ENIGMA MACHINE, UNIVAC 1.

colour A property attributed to things as a result of the human visual system's experience of the light radiation that they emit or reflect in the visible part of the spectrum between 380 and 780 nanometres. The colour perceived depends upon the wavelength, or mixture of wavelengths, and the intensity of the light impinging on the observer's eye. A mixture of all visible wavelengths in the correct proportion is perceived as white, while an excess of some wavelengths (e.g. red) results in unsaturated colours or 'tints' such as pink.

Colour perception may vary significantly between different individuals (most extremely in colour blindness) which makes the accurate reproduction of colours in printing, photography and computer displays a complex task. Each of these technologies seeks, more or less successfully, to synthesize the full colour GAMUT from a small set of pure colored pigments or lights, according to some COLOUR MODEL. See more under COLOUR SPACE, RGB, HSI, CMYK, CIE, GAMMA CORRECTION.

colour correction The alteration of the colours in a digitized image to take account of distortions introduced at the photography or scanning stage, or by the inks used in printing, or by the phosphors used in a computer's colour display. Many devices used in professional publishing and PREPRESS work contain circuitry that performs automatic colour correction, using a stored device profile gained by calibration against a standard colour chart. Most graphics programs contain features that permit manual colour correction, including GAMMA CORRECTION and the ability to alter hue, saturation and brightness separately: see under COLOUR RETOUCHING. See also COLOUR MODEL, COLOUR SPACE, CHROMATICITY.

colour depth The number of BITS needed to specify the colour of each PIXEL in a computer graphics display. For example a colour depth of 8 bits can produce 256 distinct colours.

colour, HSI See HSI.

colour image The distribution of the component frequencies in the light emitted by, or reflected from, a coloured object. The colour balance of a particular image may alter noticeably when displayed on different computer monitors and between screen and printed copy, producing for example a red or blue cast if the median point of the distribution is shifted. The process of COLOUR CORRECTION attempts to achieve a standardized representation of an image. See also COLOUR MODEL.

Colour Look-Up Table (CLUT) A small area of memory built into those computer graphics systems (such as VGA and SVGA adapters) that store index values into a larger COLOUR SPACE rather than direct RGB values. The CLUT stores a table of 256 index values together with an RGB value (chosen from 16 million) that each corresponds to in the current PALETTE. Images in the computer's video memory are stored as arrays of these 8-bit index values, and the graphics adapter consults the CLUT to translate each index value back into RGB before sending it to the display circuitry.

CLUTs are seldom found in systems with greater than 8-bit colour depth, because the size of the CLUT required soon becomes sufficiently large that it is more economical to simply store RGB values directly.

colour model A systematic method for analysing colours into components. The RGB colour model analyses colours into the same three primary components – red, green and blue – that the retina of the human eye does, and is commonly used to specify the colour of

PIXELS on computer displays. A different class of model analyses colours into hue, saturation and intensity components, which correspond more closely to the way people think about colour, and hence are easier for colour matching and programming purposes (variants are named HSI, HSB, HSL or HSV).

Physicists tend to work with the colour spaces defined since 1931 by the CIE, especially the L*A*B* and L*U*V* systems.

colour palette A panel containing samples of different colours displayed by a computer graphics program so that the user can select a new current colour for drawing or painting by pointing to one with the MOUSE POINTER or CURSOR. See also PALETTE.

colour retouching Originally a manual process of altering the colours in a photographic image by applying transparent inks with a brush or spray to correct blemishes and add emphases. The term is now applied to the electronic altering of the colours in a scanned image, using all the FILTERS, MASKS and correction tools available in a modern BITMAP editing graphics application such as Adobe PHOTOSHOP. For this reason such programs are occasionally referred to as retouching programs.

colour space The set of colours defined by a particular COLOUR MODEL.

column One of the vertical subdivisions within a two-dimensional grid of data such as a SPREADSHEET or a database TABLE.

column address One of the two ADDRESS components that is required to locate a particular word of data within a RAM chip, the other being the ROW ADDRESS. The column address is normally placed on the memory BUS of the computer after the row address, to select which column within the selected row is to be written or read. See also COLUMN ADDRESS STROBE, ROW ADDRESS STROBE, REFRESH.

Column Address Strobe (CAS) The electrical signal used to tell a RAM chip that a new column address is ready to be selected. See also ROW ADDRESS STROBE.

column heading A name displayed at the top of a column of data, for example a directory listing or a spreadsheet. In many Windows programs clicking on the column heading triggers an action, typically to sort the data using that column as the sort KEY.

COM Abbreviation of COMPONENT OBJECT MODEL.

comb-binding A type of binding used for short-run printed documents, based on a coiled plastic tube with comb-like teeth that engage a row of holes punched into the paper. Unlike a loose-leaf binder, it is not suitable for documents whose sheets need to removed, inserted or changed.

combinator A type of function consisting of a single ARGUMENT with no free VARIABLES employed in COMBINATORY LOGIC. Any combinator can be constructed from the two primitive combinators called S, the distributor, and K the cancellator, defined thus:

$$S f g x = f x (g x)$$
$$K x y = x$$

where x and y are variables. See also LAMBDA CALCULUS.

combinatory logic A system of mathematical logic developed by Schoenfinkel and Haskell B CURRY, which reduces the notation of mathematics to the application of a sequence of functions of a single argument called COMBINATORS: it is equivalent to the LAMBDA CALCULUS and forms the basis of most FUNCTIONAL PROGRAMMING LANGUAGES.

combo box A visual component used in GRAPHICAL USER INTERFACES that consists of a TEXT BOX combined with a LIST BOX, giving the user the option of either typing in a completely new word or choosing one from the predefined list. A typical application for a combo box is to allow the user to select a file to open.

Comdex The biggest US computer show, held twice a year in Las Vegas and Atlanta.

comma-delimited See COMMA-SEPARATED.

command A name which, when entered as input to some program, causes it to perform a particular action. Commands may be typed on a KEYBOARD, or selected from MENUS by pointing with a MOUSE.

command button An on-screen BUTTON that causes some program action to occur when pressed.

command completion A feature of some software products whereby a user only needs to type the first few letters of a COMMAND and the program then pops up a MENU of possibilities to complete the command.

command-driven A style of interaction with a computer program in which the user types short sequences of commands to control the workings of the program: the area of screen in which to type the commands is marked by a special symbol called the COMMAND PROMPT. Examples include the MS-DOS operating system and the various non-graphical Unix SHELLS. Historically the command-driven style displaced BATCH PROCESSING in which the commands to control the software had to be presented all at once in a file, and it has itself been largely displaced by the graphical or EVENT-DRIVEN style of interaction in which the user points to various visual control objects using a mouse.

command interpreter A software routine that accepts COMMANDs typed by the computer's user and performs the requested action. The outer level of any non-graphical operating system such as MS-DOS, and many non-graphical applications, contains a command interpreter that presents the user with a COMMAND PROMPT at which to enter the commands. The more sophisticated command interpreters are capable of parsing a COMMAND LINE that may contain a command together with various ARGUMENTS on which to operate and SWITCHES that modify its action.

command line 1 In a non-graphical computer program, the area where the user types in commands to be executed. See more under COMMAND LINE INTERFACE.

2 A sequence of words and symbols, comprising a command and its ARGUMENTS, typed at the COMMAND PROMPT by the user of such an interface. Programs intended for command line operation are frequently controlled by typing extra arguments and 'switches' after the program's name when it is invoked, and this whole sequence is called a command line. An example is:

```
xcopy fileA.txt oldfileA.txt /m /s /v
```

command line interface (CLI) A type of user interface employed by older, non-graphical computer operating systems, consisting of a COMMAND PROMPT symbol next to which the user must type in a command word and then press the Enter key, whereupon the computer executes that command. Both UNIX and MS-DOS employ command line interfaces.

Command line user interfaces are extremely intimidating for new users, because they do not typically list all the commands available (which have to be memorized) and any misspelling of a command will prevent it from being executed, often producing a cryptic error message. A MENU (as used in GRAPHICAL USER INTERFACES) overcomes both problems by showing what commands are available and removing the need to type them. Some menu-driven programs provide an alternative CLI for experienced users.

command prompt A symbol displayed by a computer system that employs a COMMAND LINE INTERFACE to announce that it is ready to receive the next command from the user. The actual symbol used differs between different OPERATING SYSTEMS, SHELLS and applications: for example, MS-DOS uses the prompt C:\> while the standard UNIX shell uses $.

command set The collection of all the COMMANDS that a particular software system can recognize.

comma-separated A standard TEXT FILE format often used to transport data between different DATABASE or SPREADSHEET programs, in which each RECORD occupies a new line and the FIELDS within each record are separated by commas. See more under CSV; see also TAB-SEPARATED.

comma-separated values See CSV.

comment A passage of text placed in the SOURCE CODE of a program to explain its workings to a human reader, which does not generate any OBJECT CODE. Different languages use different syntactic devices to warn the COMPILER not to try and compile such comments:

```
C and Java /* This is a comment */
Visual Basic ' This is a comment
Basic REM This is a comment
Pascal (* This is a comment *)
Delphi {This is a comment}
```

comment out To temporarily remove a section of code from a program under development, by marking it as a COMMENT so that the compiler will ignore it.

commerce server A WEB SERVER specifically designed for E-COMMERCE which therefore supports secure monetary transactions via SECURE SOCKETS LAYER or some equivalent security PROTOCOL. See also CATALOGUE SERVER.

Commercial Internet Exchange (CIX) A non-profit umbrella trade association of ISPS, set up to coordinate the provision of Internet services to business and the general public. The original purpose of CIX was to gain unrestricted commercial access to the worldwide network in the days when the US government was still trying to restrict access to educational and research users. It has evolved an equally important role in persuading extra-US ISPs to connect to each other, avoiding the waste of BANDWIDTH involved in, say, EMAIL from France to Switzerland having to go via a US backbone. European CIX offices are located in Helsinki, Paris, Amsterdam, Geneva (CERN), London, and Stockholm.

Comité Consultatif International de Télégraphic et Téléphonique (CCITT) The international consultative committee whose initials appear on many telephony standards. Now defunct, replaced by the standardization division of INTERNATIONAL TELECOMMUNICATIONS UNION.

Comité Européen des Postes et Telecommunications See CEPT.

Commodore Business Machines (CBM) One of the earliest US personal computer manufacturers, whose PET machine was launched in the same month in 1977 as the APPLE II. Like the Apple, the PET was a complete system with keyboard, screen, a cassette recorder for mass storage, and a built-in BASIC interpreter – however it had only 4 KB of memory.

In 1985 Commodore launched the innovative AMIGA, a machine whose powerful multimedia features remained unsurpassed for many years, and which achieved a significant niche usage in video production studios. From the mid-1990s Commodore entered a long period of financial decline, which was not cured by switching to production of IBM-compatible PCs; the company finally expired in 1999.

Common API See CAPI.

common carrier Telecommunications industry jargon for a company that offers telephone services to the public. A phone company.

common-channel Any telecommunications system, such as ISDN, in which the voice signals and control signals are carried in different channels down the same wire. See also IN-BAND, OUT-OF-BAND.

Common Desktop Environment See CDE.

Common Gateway Interface See CGI.

Common Hardware Reference Platform (CHRP) A open specification for personal computers based on the POWERPC microprocessor, agreed in 1994 by various manufacturers including Apple and IBM. The name was later changed to the POWERPC REFERENCE PLATFORM, though very few compliant machines were ever built under either name.

Common Interchange Format (CIF) One of the two standard image sizes supported by the H.261 specification for VIDEOCONFERENCING systems, which requires a resolution of 352×288 pixels. The other supported size is Quarter CIF (QCIF) at a resolution of 176×144. See also CODEC.

common language runtime (CLR) Microsoft's new RUN-TIME SYSTEM for its programming languages VISUAL BASIC, VISUAL C++, C# and the various SCRIPTING LANGUAGES supported by the Windows Scripting Host (including PERL and JAVASCRIPT). The older language compilers have been modified to generate a form of pseudo-code known as INTERMEDIATE LANGUAGE (IL) as an alternative to native code, while C# emits IL only. IL programs running under the CLR are known as MANAGED CODE and they gain the benefit of automatic GARBAGE COLLECTION.

The CLR enables WEB SERVICES written in any of the supported languages to communicate with one another across networks or the Internet using the SOAP protocol, and to access all the same OBJECT LIBRARIES using a minimum of code. See also BYTECODE, PSEUDO-CODE, SEMI-COMPILED.

Common Lisp A dialect of the LISP programming language defined in 1981 by a consortium of computer vendors, universities and US government laboratories. Common Lisp is a large and complex language that supplements Lisp's fundamental LIST construct with user-defined data structures, arrays and several numeric types. By default it employs LEXICAL SCOPE, though DYNAMIC SCOPE is an option. The set of OBJECT-ORIENTED extensions, COMMON LISP OBJECT SYSTEM, is now incorporated into the language.

Common Lisp Object System (CLOS) An OBJECT-ORIENTED extension of the LISP language that features multiple inheritance and generic functions.

Common Object Model The earlier name for Microsoft's object model, now called the COMPONENT OBJECT MODEL.

Common Object Request Broker Architecture See CORBA.

Common User Access (CUA) The standard USER INTERFACE created by IBM for all the components of its SYSTEMS APPLICATION ARCHITECTURE.

comms The usual abbreviation for COMMUNICATIONS, in the sense of connecting different computers together.

Communicating Sequential Processes (CSP) A notation for describing CONCURRENT computation invented by Anthony HOARE in 1978. CSP describes a concurrent system as a group of purely SEQUENTIAL processes running simultaneously and sending SYNCHRONOUS messages to each other through named CHANNELS. The precepts of CSP have been implemented in CONCURRENT PROGRAMMING LANGUAGES such as OCCAM, PARLOG and some parallelized dialects of C.

communication channel Any conduit through which signals are conveyed for the purpose of transmitting information.

communication port An electronic interface through which a computer may be connected to other computers, to telecommunication equipment, or to other peripherals including printers or a mouse. For personal computers, the term normally refers to a SERIAL PORT or increasingly to a UNIVERSAL SERIAL BUS port. Under the MS-DOS and Windows operating systems, the communications ports are addressable under the names COM1, COM2, COM3, etc. See also COM PORT, FIREWIRE, FDDI, FIBRE CHANNEL.

communications A shorthand term that covers all methods of connecting computers together, from SERIAL links, through LANS, to MODEM links and WANS. Also used as a job description, for example a communications manager.

Communications of the ACM (CACM) A highly regarded journal of computer science and engineering published by the ACM.

communicator A term coined to describe a new class of hand-held devices that combine wireless telephone and personal organizer functions.

community server A type of web server that is specifically designed to support and manage a VIRTUAL COMMUNITY, its functions including registration of new member accounts and the creation and management of multiple CHAT ROOMS. The more advanced examples may offer graphical abilities such as VIRTUAL REALITY meeting spaces and AVATARS to represent members.

commutative A property of any operation on two arguments A and B, which requires that A op B = B op A for every possible A and B. For example in everyday arithmetic addition and multiplication are commutative (2+3=3+2=5), but subtraction and division are not (2/3 does not equal 3/2).

Compact Disc See CD.

Compact Disc Interactive See CD-I.

compact-disc-quality audio See under CD-QUALITY.

Compact Disc Read-Only Memory See CD-ROM.

Compact Disc Read-Write See CD-RW.

Compact Disc Recordable See CD-R.

Compact Flash A standard for removable FLASH MEMORY storage cards promulgated by a consortium of manufacturers called the Compact Flash Association (CFA) which includes Kodak, Hewlett Packard, Motorola and Polaroid. Compact Flash cards employ a 50-pin interface and measure 43 × 36 × 3.3 mm, roughly one quarter the volume of a PC CARD. They are available in capacities from 8 to 512 MB and are the most widely used storage medium for digital cameras and hand-held computers. See also SD CARD, MEMORY STICK, PC CARD.

compaction The process of rearranging a collection of data items to make best use of the available storage space, and to consolidate all the free space into a contiguous block: see also FRAGMENTATION. Examples of such items might be RECORDS in a DATABASE file, scattered memory blocks in a HEAP or used blocks on a HARD DISK.

Compaq The world's largest personal computer manufacturer, based in Texas. Compaq started its business in 1982 by making the first portable CLONE of the IBM PC, and in the 1990s took over the businesses of DIGITAL EQUIPMENT CORPORATION and TANDEM.

compare A class of primitive instruction implemented by all types of processor, which involves testing two numbers for equality and then setting one or more bits in a FLAG REGISTER to indicate the result. Varieties of this instruction compare values located in different combinations of registers, memory and immediate (i.e. included in the instruction). Conditional structures such as IF...THEN and REPEAT...UNTIL in high-level languages ultimately compile into a compare instruction followed by a JUMP ON CONDITION.

Compas A fast and compact PASCAL compiler written in Denmark by Anders Hejlsberg and others, later sold to BORLAND to become TURBO PASCAL and ultimately DELPHI.

compatibility The ability of two mechanisms, whether hardware or software, to cooperate with one another. Compatibility is not an absolute property, and may admit various degrees. For example one computer might be described as compatible with another if it can run programs written for the other, while a

hardware EXPANSION BOARD is compatible with a particular computer if it can be plugged into the computer's EXPANSION BUS and work as intended. However, it is perfectly possible for two computers to run each other's programs but not accept each other's expansion board, or even vice versa.

Compatibility has become a matter of the utmost commercial importance since the arrival of a mass market for personal computers: the question of whether or not a program is compatible with the majority of existing computers may mean the difference between hundreds and millions of copies sold. This imposes an enormous constraint on the designers of computer OPERATING SYSTEMS, who must negotiate an extremely difficult compromise between adding innovatory features and maintaining compatibility with every piece of software that ran under earlier versions. They are not always successful.

compilation The action of a COMPILER in turning the SOURCE CODE of a program, written in some PROGRAMMING LANGUAGE into EXECUTABLE code. Conceptually, compilation is a three (or more) stage process, whose principal stages are called lexical analysis, parsing and code generation. In a SINGLE-PASS COMPILER these stages are automatically performed one after the other to produce a single output file, whereas a MULTI-PASS COMPILER produces an intermediate file from each stage that must be further processed in a separate step.

The LEXICAL ANALYSER section of the compiler scans the source program and breaks it down into word-like groups of symbols called LEXEMES or tokens, which represent separate KEYWORDS, IDENTIFIERS, literal strings and numbers and punctuation characters. These are then fed to the PARSER, which determines what program structure each group of tokens represents and builds an internal data structure that describes the sequence of actions the program is meant to perform. Finally the CODE GENERATOR traverses this structure and creates the appropriate MACHINE CODE (or p-code, or bytecode, etc) to perform each described action.

In an OPTIMIZING COMPILER there is a further stage in which the output code is rearranged and reordered to exploit features particular to the target processor's INSTRUCTION SET for greater efficiency.

compile To convert the SOURCE CODE of a program into MACHINE CODE that can be executed on a particular computer, by using a COMPILER. See also LINK, COMPILE/LINK.

compiled Any programming language, scripting language or page description language, in which a program is translated in a single operation into a different, executable form. Contrast this with INTERPRETED.

compile/link To COMPILE and LINK a program into an executable file: the combination of terms reflecting the fact that these operations are combined in practice, either via a BATCH FILE or SCRIPT, or as a menu option in an INTEGRATED DEVELOPMENT ENVIRONMENT. Since a program cannot be executed or debugged (see DEBUGGING) before linking in any required libraries and other modules, the term is more pedantically correct than 'compile' on its own. See also COMPILER, LINKER, LIBRARY.

compile-once, run-anywhere A slogan coined by the JAVA community to emphasize the PLATFORM-INDEPENDENT quality of the language.

compile on demand A facility introduced into VISUAL BASIC from version 4.0 onward which compiles parts of a project only when they are required to be loaded.

compiler A program that converts the SOURCE CODE of a new program written in a HIGH-LEVEL PROGRAMMING LANGUAGE into EXECUTABLE code (which may be MACHINE CODE for a particular type of PROCESSOR or some form of INTERMEDIATE CODE. A compiler that produces machine code directly is called a NATIVE CODE compiler. Unlike an INTERPRETER, which executes each language construct immediately after converting it, a compiler converts a whole source code file at one time into a file of compiled code, which may then need to be fed into a LINKER to add any libraries that are called by the program. Most compilers are highly specific in two ways: they compile only one particular language (maybe only one version of one language) and they produce machine code for a single type of processor. Hence one may speak of a c++ compiler for the PENTIUM family of processors.

A compiler is the software developer's principal tool, the 'hammer and chisel' of programming, and consequently much research is devoted to the science of language compilation and the improvement of compiler technology. For the language designer there is a strong sense in which the compiler *is* the language – which exists otherwise only as an abstract specification – since only what can be compiled can be executed. See also COMPILATION, LINKER, LIBRARY, INTEGRATED DEVELOPMENT ENVIRONMENT.

compiler compiler A COMPILER that generates a compiler for a programming language, given a description of the language's syntax in some formal notation, typically BNF.

compiler directive A programming language statement that is merely an instruction to the COMPILER to change its mode of operation, and which therefore does not lead to the generation of any OBJECT CODE. Examples from c include the #if and #ifdef directives which state that the enclosed section of code is only to be compiled if a certain condition is met.

compiler error An error that occurs during the COMPILATION of a program, which may indicate that the program fails to comply with the definition of the language it is written in, or that it exhibits certains kinds of logical error. The most commonly encountered compiler error is the SYNTAX ERROR, caused by misspelling or other misplacement of language statements. Precisely which kinds of logical error can be caught as compiler errors constitutes an important issue for language designers. The ideal is that as many kinds of error as possible should be caught by the compiler (and hence corrected by the programmer), rather than inconveniencing the user as a RUN-TIME ERROR.

compiler/linker A program that combines the action of a COMPILER and a LINKER into one operation.

compiler optimization Any technique employed within a programming language COMPILER to make the final compiled code run faster or more efficiently.

compiler option An alternative mode of COMPILATION or resource allocation that the programmer can specify when compiling a program. Options offered by most compilers include alternative language versions, turning on or off certain language features, what MEMORY MODEL to employ, the amount of memory to devote to the program's STACK and HEAP, whether to include extra code for array BOUNDS CHECKING, and many more.

compiler switch The code or command used to select a particular COMPILER OPTION. Originally switches were short codes appended to the COMMAND LINE used to invoke the COMPILER, as for example: cc testprog -tsi which compiles the source file testprog.c with options specified by the switches t, s, and i. In modern INTEGRATED DEVELOPMENT ENVIRONMENTS, a switch is more typically a CHECK BOX contained in a TABBED DIALOGUE.

compile time One side of an important distinction made by programmers, between the time when a program is being compiled and the time when it is being run (see also RUN TIME). Options and alternatives that are selected at compile time are frozen into the program's code forever, whereas run-time options are left open for the END-USER to choose. Similarly, compile-time errors should be found and corrected by the programmer, but run-time errors may cause the program to crash with loss of data and severely inconvenience the user. The term is used in many derived expressions such as compile-time optimization, COMPILE-TIME ANALYSIS, and COMPILE-TIME EVALUATION.

compile-time analysis A feature offered by some programming language COMPILERS, in which information about the program is collected during its compilation, such as the pattern of function calls between modules, the use (or not) of declared variables and other matters that are of help to the programmer in DEBUGGING the program.

compile-time evaluation The evaluation of an EXPRESSION at COMPILE TIME, so that its result, rather than the expression itself, is compiled into the program. Compile-time evaluation can be used only for values that will remain constant for the life of the program, but it may make a program both more readable and easier to modify or write:

```
radius := 3.4;
area := pi * radius * radius;
```
rather than:
```
area := 36.317;
```

complement In mathematics or programming, the inverse (in whatever sense) of some quantity. For example, the complement of a positive number is its negative (see ONES COMPLEMENT, TWOS COMPLEMENT), while in SET theory the complement of a set means all those values that are *not* in the set, in the particular universe of discourse. As a verb, to form the complement of some entity.

Complementary Metal-Oxide Semiconductor See CMOS.

complex 1 Intricate or involved; composed of many interrelated parts.
 2 In mathematics, having a real and an imaginary part: see more under COMPLEX NUMBER.
 See also COMPLEXITY, COMPLEXITY ANALYSIS, COMPLEXITY CLASS.

complex instruction set computer See CISC.

complexity A measure of the difficulty of performing a computation in terms of the time (TIME COMPLEXITY), the number of steps or arithmetic operations (COMPUTATIONAL COMPLEXITY), or the amount of memory space (space complexity) that is required. The study of the complexity of ALGORITHMS – how their solution scales with the size of their input data – forms a central part of computer science: see more under ALGORITHMIC COMPLEXITY.

complexity analysis The analysis of an ALGORITHM to discover how the time or memory space it requires to solve a particular class of problem will vary with the size of the problem. This may be a matter of great commercial importance, since algorithms that SCALE badly (for example EXPONENTIAL-TIME ALGORITHMS) can become completely unusable even for apparently modest increases in problem size, and could therefore jeopardize a project.

Complexity analysis is performed by mathematical reasoning about a particular implementation of the algorithm, noting features such as what depth of nesting of repetitive LOOPS it requires. See also ALGORITHMIC COMPLEXITY, TIME COMPLEXITY, COMPUTATIONAL COMPLEXITY, NP-HARD.

complexity class A set of algorithms or computable functions that all have the same degree of ALGORITHMIC COMPLEXITY.

complex number In mathematics, a kind of NUMBER that possesses both a real and an imaginary (that is, a multiple of i, the square-root of minus one) part. An example is 3+4i, in which 3 is the real part and 4i is the imaginary part. To add two complex numbers, their real and imaginary parts are added separately, as in:

(3+4i) + (5+2i) = 8+6i

Complex numbers were invented for purely mathematical reasons, to give meaning to the roots of negative quantities, for example when solving QUADRATIC equations, but they have proved to have enormous application in physics in the description of FIELDS and in applied electronics where they are indispensible to calculations involving alternating currents. See also BUTTERFLY, FAST FOURIER TRANSFORM.

compliant Conforming to the indicated STANDARD, used as in 'POSIX compliant'.

component 1 In general, some part which goes into the making of a whole system (hardware or software).
2 The term has a special use in the field of OBJECT-ORIENTED software, where it refers to a pre-written MODULE that can be incorporated into a new project with little or no programming effort. VISUAL BASIC'S OCX controls, and JAVABEANS are examples of such components. See also COMPONENT ARCHITECTURE.

component architecture A style of programme construction, based on OBJECT-ORIENTED PROGRAMMING techniques, in which programs are constructed from prefabricated MODULES called COMPONENTS which may be fitted together by writing only a minimal amount of program code.

Typically components are assembled inside an INTEGRATED DEVELOPMENT ENVIRONMENT, within which prefabricated components advertise what METHODS and PROPERTIES they possess so that the programmer can decide which is appropriate for a particular task. A component may be a large program, such as a whole WEB BROWSER, TEXT EDITOR or SPREAD-SHEET grid, rather than an individual CLASS. Examples of component architectures include JAVABEANS, Microsoft's ACTIVEX and OLE DB, and CORBA.

Component Object Model (COM) Microsoft's OBJECT MODEL which underlies ACTIVEX, OLE and almost all current Windows software. For example the constituent applications of Office 2000 are all built from COM objects and expose COM interfaces, allowing them to be integrated with, or driven by, other applications.

COM is a mechanism that enables one piece of software to call services supplied by another in a uniform way, regardless of their relative locations. Calls within the same PROCESS, between different processes, to the operating system or to another remote computer across a network are all made in a similar way. All COM services are packaged as OBJECTS which have one or more INTERFACES that reveal what services or METHODS they are making available. CLIENT programs can access the services only by calling these methods, and may not directly access the data within an object. For example a dictionary packaged as a COM object might offer an interface that includes a method called GetDefinition that returns a word definition as its result. Most COM objects have more than one interface, always including one called IUnknown that gives access to all the others .

Every COM object is an instance of a CLASS, and a client program may request that a new instance be created and set running by looking up the appropriate class in a COM library (which must be present on any system that supports COM). COM supports POLYMORPHISM – that is, objects of different classes may present the same interface while implementing its methods differently – but it supports only INHERITANCE of interfaces, not of their implementations. COM is designed to support COMPONENT software deployment, where new features may be added to an application long after it was written, and without having to recompile it – implementation inheritance could compromise this goal by creating unwanted dependencies.

COM objects may be distributed in the form of DLL files, or as ActiveX APPLETS that can plug into an existing application or be embedded in a document or web page.

component software Used to describe any software system that makes use of interchangeable COMPONENTS. See also COMPONENT ARCHITECTURE.

component video An analogue video technology that records and transmits images using three separate signals, one each for the red, green and blue image components. As a result, the hardware, cabling and connectors are more expensive than those used in the COMPOSITE VIDEO and S-VIDEO systems, which employ fewer signals. Component video is used for professional camera systems such as Betacam. See also RGB.

com port Shorthand for COMMUNICATION PORT.

composite video The system used to transmit video signals between domestic televisions and video recorders, in which the CHROMINANCE and LUMINANCE information are combined into a single signal on the same cable. Professional systems such as S-VIDEO and COMPONENT VIDEO use multiple signals, which offers better picture quality but significantly increases the cost of cables and connectors.

compound document A digital document composed from separate sections created by different programs, an example being a report that has embedded graphs or voice annotations in addition to the text. There is no single universal standard for compound documents, several attempts to create one (for example OPENDOC) having failed.

Perhaps the most widely used type of compound document now is the HTML-based WEB PAGE, which may contain almost any kind of multimedia content (sound, pictures, animation, video) as well as JAVA code or ACTIVE SERVER PAGES code that performs active processing. Another widely used compound document format is Microsoft's OLE or DOCFILE format, created when content produced using two or more of the MICROSOFT OFFICE applications (for example a letter, a spreadsheet, a graph and a voice message) are embedded into the same file. See also IN-PLACE EDITING, OBJECT-ORIENTED.

compound file A file that employs Microsoft's STRUCTURED STORAGE to hold the output from several different applications at once.

compressed video Video data that has been reduced in volume using a COMPRESSION algorithm, to minimize its storage space and reduce transmission time. Compressed video

is widely used in broadcast, satellite and cable television, for computer games and on web sites.

The software or hardware system used to compress a video stream is called a CODEC, the most widely used ones including CINEPAK, INDEO and MPEG.

compression The processing of a set of data in order to reduce its size. Compression may be performed both to reduce the amount of storage space occupied (say, to fit the data onto a single CD) and to reduce the time it takes to transmit (say, over a slow telephone line). Compressed data must be decompressed by reversing the process before it can be read or modified.

There are many known compression/decompression ALGORITHMS, and the search for better ones has become commercially important since most new communications technologies (such as digital television) can only work with effective data compression. See for example RUN-LENGTH ENCODING, LEMPEL–ZIV COMPRESSION, HUFFMAN CODING, JPEG, MPEG.

All compression algorithms work by uncovering and eliminating redundancy in the data, and there is an important distinction between those that preserve all the information in the data (*lossless* methods) and those that sacrifice some information for greater compression (*lossy* methods). Lossy algorithms such as JPEG and MPEG are suitable only for final delivery of data to end users, as the information losses accumulate each time the material is recompressed and decompressed.

Compulink Information Exchange (CIX) A long-established UK online CONFERENCING SYSTEM and now also a popular ISP (www.cix.co.uk).

CompuServe Information System (CIS) One of the earliest online systems, founded in 1979, which provides information services, conferencing and EMAIL, as well as Usenet and Internet access. Taken over in 1998 by AOL.

computable A number is computable if it can be generated by some mechanical process or ALGORITHM; it is known that there are uncountably many REAL NUMBERS that cannot be so generated. A FUNCTION is computable if an algorithm can be found that calculates its output for every valid input, and again there are many functions for which this cannot be done. See also TURING MACHINE.

computation Any process that works on data to transform input into output. The concept is not confined to data expressed in DIGITAL, nor even electronic form: biological, chemical, optical, hydraulic or, for that matter, clockwork, mechanisms can all perform computation. Computation theory is a branch of computer science that uses abstract models such as the Universal TURING MACHINE to capture what is essential to the process.

computational complexity The rate at which the number of processing steps required by a particular ALGORITHM grows with the size of the input data. Like the closely related TIME COMPLEXITY, it is usually expressed in an order-of-magnitude notation, where, say, $O(N^2)$ means the steps required increase as the square of the problem size N: see also EXPONENTIAL-TIME ALGORITHM, POLYNOMIAL-TIME ALGORITHM, NP-HARD.

compute To transform INPUT data into OUTPUT data by applying a programmed sequence of calculations.

compute-bound The condition of any program whose execution time is determined solely by the speed of the PROCESSOR on which it is running rather than by the speed at which it can read or write from external data storage (that is, it is not DISK-BOUND).

compute-intensive A task that consumes a lot of a computer's PROCESSOR time, as opposed to a lot of memory space, disk or communications bandwidth. For example 3D graphics operations are very compute-intensive, whereas many database operations are instead DISK-BOUND.

computer A machine that performs COMPUTATIONS. In everyday usage the term suggests a programmable computer, which means one that can be made to perform many different computations by running different PROGRAMS. However, a chip that can only add pairs of numbers remains a computer of a simple kind.

There is an important distinction between ANALOGUE COMPUTERS, which operate on continuously variable values (such as the magnitude of a voltage, or the intensity of a light beam), and DIGITAL COMPUTERS which work only with a limited set of discrete values. The vast majority of the computers used in the world today are electronic, digital computers, which is to say they operate on electricity (rather than light, or air pressure, or mechanical motion) and they represent values by employing two different voltage levels that can be interpreted as standing for the binary numbers 0 and 1. Such computers can perform any arithmetical or logical operation by using electronic switches to combine these binary digits in various precisely defined ways. All the other forms of data that we expect computers to handle nowadays – for instance words, sums of money, pictures or sounds – must be DIGITIZED before they can be manipulated, by devising a code that can represent them as sequences of such binary numbers or BITS.

The electronic circuits that enable modern digital computers to manipulate bits are constructed on slices of silicon using Very Large Scale Integration (VLSI) techniques to put millions of circuits onto a single chip. The principle components of a computer are: a CENTRAL PROCESSING UNIT (CPU) which actually performs the computations; a working memory in which values can be stored before and after processing; and some kind of non-volatile MASS STORAGE device that can retain stored values even after the electrical supply is turned off.

In a typical PERSONAL COMPUTER, the CPU is a single MICROPROCESSOR chip, the working memory is a collection of Random Access Memory (RAM) chips, and the mass storage device is a magnetic hard disk drive. In addition to these, any computer requires some sort of input device, such as a keyboard, and an output device such as a visual display screen or a printer in order to communicate with its human user.

All these chips, disks and the wires that connect them together are called the HARDWARE of the computer, whereas the programs that the computer executes and the data they work on are called the SOFTWARE, a term intended to convey its abstract nature.

All modern digital computers are stored-program computers, which means that they store their program – i.e. the list of instructions that tells them what task to perform – in the same memory as the data that they are to process. Historically, earlier programmable machines such as the Jacquard Loom used programs (punched cards) that were quite different in form from their data (silk threads). The stored program architecture, devised by John von Neumann in 1945, allowed the computer itself to be employed as a tool in the creation of its own software, and it was this insight that empowered the phenomenal growth of the modern computer industry.

Computer Aided Design (CAD) The use of a graphical computer workstation to design new industrial products. CAD has revolutionized the field of industrial design by largely replacing the expensive, slow and inflexible process of building solid models from wood, clay or plaster, with 3D computer models that can be stress-tested, costed and taken through to final engineering drawings all within the same computer system. The resulting ease of alteration enables designers to experiment interactively with their subject, and it is no exaggeration to say that the smoothly curving forms of most modern products, from kettles and steam irons to cars and aeroplanes are the visible result of using CAD systems.

CAD, along with games software has been the driving force behind the many advances made in 3D GRAPHICS in recent decades, such techniques as SMOOTH SHADING and CUBIC SPLINES being originally invented by CAD software developers.

Computer Aided Design and Drafting (CADD) A term used by many vendors of CAD software that is heavily oriented toward document and drawing output rather than toward direct machine control.

Computer Aided Engineering (CAE) The use of computers to assist in the design and testing of machines and buildings, for example by performing stress and materials analyses, or by SIMULATION of their key operations.

Computer Aided Instruction (CAI) The use of computers to automate teaching and training courses. Such courses consist of a series of interactive lessons, usually including software tests of comprehension, and typically the student will be permitted to move on to the next lesson segment only when a satisfactory score has been achieved. The software automatically keeps a tally of test scores, and computes an overall grade at the end of the course. See also AUTHORING SYSTEM.

Computer Aided Learning (CAL) See under COMPUTER AIDED INSTRUCTION.

Computer Aided Manufacturing (CAM) The use of computers to assist in a manufacturing process, from designing the models, moulds and jigs to controlling the machine tools or whole production lines. The tendency is toward ever greater integration of the whole production chain, so that even the ordering of raw materials and components may be incorporated into an overall workflow. The term is most often encountered as the combined name CAD/CAM, because the early design stages involve the use of a 3D COMPUTER AIDED DESIGN tool whose results are passed directly into the tool or mould-making software.

Computer Aided Software Engineering (CASE) The use of computers to assist in the process of writing computer SOFTWARE. CASE typically involves organizing the work of specification, design and coding of a software project into the stages defined by some CASE METHODOLOGY, and then employing a special software suite called a CASE TOOL that automates some of these stages and assists the programmers in performing others.

computer animation The use of computers to assist in the creation of moving images. A computer may be used to store and create individual pictures or FRAMES, to assemble these frames into the desired sequence and to automatically INTERPOLATE sequences of frames between chosen start and end images to produce the illusion of smooth motion (see IN-BETWEENING).

Computer Assisted Learning (CAL) See under COMPUTER AIDED INSTRUCTION.

Computer Associates (CA) One of the largest US software vendors, whose products include the INGRES relational database.

Computer-Based Training (CBT) The use of interactive course materials running on a computer to impart new skills or to improve existing ones. For teaching computing skills, the material often consists of guided use of an actual APPLICATION PROGRAM. In other fields it may well consist mostly of live-action video sequences depicting an example of the activity in question, followed by interactive tests of comprehension.

computer crime Forms of crime committed against, or made possible by, computers. The former includes the writing of VIRUS, WORM or TROJAN HORSE programs, and HACKING into a remote system to gain illicit access to information. The latter includes forging credit cards and extortion or sabotage by programmers who implant secret code routines, for example to divert funds into a fake bank account. See also SOFTWARE PIRACY.

Computer Emergency Response Team (CERT) A group formed by DARPA in 1988 to respond quickly to Internet security emergencies such as VIRUSES and WORMS. CERT issues documents called Advisories, which alert Internet users to the presence of a new threat.

computerese The professional argot of the computer industry, composed in equal part of acronyms, neologisms and sci-fi metaphors. Its vestigial English component is remarkable chiefly for the way in which verbs and nouns regularly exchange roles.

Computer Graphics Metafile (CGM) A GRAPHICS FILE FORMAT for storing scalable VECTOR images, adopted as a standard by the ISO. Pictures in CGM format can be embedded into HTML, XML and SGML documents for use on web sites.

computerize To automate some activity using computers.

computer language A specialized language invented to simplify the task of programming computers. Computer languages are usually very restricted subsets of some human language such as English, containing a limited vocabulary of words, each of which describes a command that causes the computer to perform some particular action. See more under PROGRAMMING LANGUAGE.

computer literacy An educationalist's term meaning familiarity with the use of computers.

Computer Numerical Control (CNC) A type of automated machine tool that contains a MICROPROCESSOR or microcontroller which enables it to perform, for example, cutting, drilling, milling, turning, grinding or routing operations by following a pattern supplied as a digital data file. Many COMPUTER AIDED DESIGN programs can output directly into a CNC code file to control such a machine.

computerphobia Fear of computers.

computer program See under PROGRAM.

computer science An academic discipline that studies, among other topics, the mathematics of COMPUTATION, the properties of ALGORITHMS and the design of PROGRAMMING LANGUAGES. It should be distinguished from Computer Studies, which is a vocational course in the practical use of computers, and may include some computer science.

Computer science is a relatively new science, founded in the years after WWII in the UK and USA. Its founding fathers include Alan TURING, whose paper on computable numbers could be said to be the founding document, and John von Neuman. However, in the earliest days there was no clear demarcation between computer science and computer engineering, and so hundreds of practical electronic engineers and COMPILER writers deserve an equal place in this Pantheon. Among the most important discoveries of computer science are those that concern the time and space complexity of algorithms, which allow the limits of computation to be understood, and the adaption of Chomsky's linguistic discoveries to describe the power of different classes of computing machine. See also COMPUTATIONAL COMPLEXITY, CHOMSKY HIERARCHY, TURING MACHINE.

computer vision The use of computers to recognize specific features within an overall video image, for examples human faces, concealed weapons, or the orientation of products on a conveyor belt. It is a field that is intensively researched, particularly for security and military applications. See more under IMAGE RECOGNITION.

compute server A PARALLEL PROCESSING supercomputer that is operated as a network SERVER, so that many CLIENT workstations can share it by running computationally intensive programs on it.

concatenate Literally to join together into a chain, which in computing terms means joining two data structures such as FILES, ARRAYS or STRINGS end-to-end into a single structure.

concentrator A device that combines (i.e. MULTIPLEXES) the signals from a number of input lines onto a single output line. For example a concentrator might be used to connect up to six 9,600 bits per second serial terminals to a single 56 kilobits per second modem line.

concrete class In OBJECT-ORIENTED PROGRAMMING, a class whose METHODS are fully implemented and of which INSTANCES may be created for manipulation in a program. This is in contrast to an ABSTRACT CLASS, which is merely a shared template, defined only to allow concrete subclasses to inherit from it.

concrete syntax The actual SYNTAX of a PROGRAMMING LANGUAGE as encountered in the SOURCE CODE of a program by a PARSER, which includes all the punctuation and DELIMITERS – in contrast to some abstract syntax into which it may be converted during the process of COMPILATION. See also INTERMEDIATE LANGUAGE, PSEUDO-CODE.

concurrent Occurring at the same time. When used of a computer program or system, able to support more than one PROCESS running at the same time. On a computer, concurrency may either be *simulated*, by TIME SHARING between several processes running on a single processor, or *real*, where each concurrent process runs on a different processor. See also MULTITASKING, SCHEDULING, CONCURRENT PROGRAMMING LANGUAGE, MULTIPROCESSOR, PARALLEL COMPUTER.

concurrent programming language A PROGRAMMING LANGUAGE that contains explicit constructs for expressing CONCURRENCY, examples including ADA, LINDA, JAVA and OCCAM.

conditional The property of being executed or not depending upon the result of some test. Hence also used as a noun, meaning a programming construct that has this property.

conditional branch See under BRANCH.

conditional loop A type of program LOOP construct that keeps repeating until a test becomes true. The syntax for conditional loops varies widely between different languages, but divides into two principal varieties: those where the test is performed at the beginning of the loop, as in WHILE y!=0 DO x, and those where the test is performed at the end, as in REPEAT x UNTIL y=0. Their effects are different (for example x might be executed one more time in the second case) and so many languages provide both types, while some languages such as VISUAL BASIC employ a single flexible construct (DO...LOOP) into which an UNTIL or WHILE test can be placed at either beginning or end.

conductance The ability of a conductor to transmit an electric current, measured as the ratio of the current that flows to the potential difference that causes it. It is the reciprocal of RESISTANCE. The unit of conductance is the siemen.

conductor 1 Any substance that supports the easy passage of an electric current, examples being all metals and many aqueous salt solutions. In strict physical terms, all substances are conductors to some extent, but those that conduct very poorly are instead called INSULATORS, while SEMICONDUCTORS exhibit a conducting ability that can be altered by their environment. A substance's ability to conduct is called its conductivity.
2 A wire, cable, track on a circuit board or silicon chip, or other physical pathway made from such a conducting material.

conduit A type of DEVICE DRIVER installed onto a HOST computer by the PALM range of HANDHELD computers to enable data from Palm applications to HOTSYNC with their equivalent programs running on the host. For example, addresses from the Palm address book might sync with an address database kept in Microsoft Outlook on a PC.

Any Palm application that employs a new data file format must be supplied with a specially written conduit, which gets installed at the same time as the application. The list of currently installed conduits can be inspected in the HotSync applet's Custom menu, where they may also be turned on or off, and their synching direction controlled.

conference An online forum in which many participants may conduct discussions by reading and posting messages, supervised by a MODERATOR who vets the entries for relevance and civility. See also CONFERENCING SYSTEM.

Conference On Data Systems Languages See CODASYL.

conferencing system A type of online service that permits groups of users to conduct public or private discussion forums called CONFERENCES. Conferencing systems such as COMPUSERVE INFORMATION SYSTEM pre-dated widespread public access to the INTERNET, and were isolated DIAL-UP systems. Nowadays NEWSGROUPS serve much the same function, and stand-alone conferencing systems are on the decline. It is also possible, by deploying suitable scripts, to simulate conferencing on a WEB SITE.

CONFIG.SYS A file that is automatically read at start up by the MS-DOS operating system used to load the DEVICE DRIVERS required by the various peripherals connected to the computer, and to set the correct configuration parameters for them. CONFIG.SYS is also the place in which various EXTENDED MEMORY and EXPANDED MEMORY options are configured. Under Windows, particularly versions later than 95, its role has been taken over by other files, most notably the REGISTRY. See also AUTOEXEC.BAT.

configuration The process of setting various parameters of a computer and its software to values appropriate for its required use – also used as a noun to mean a particular set of such parameter values. The configuration of even a single-user desktop computer is becoming a matter of great significance as disk capacities increase and software grows larger and more complex, while for networks it has become the most pressing problem facing SYSTEM ADMINISTRATORS.

A particular configuration includes: all the hardware parameters such as memory size, number, size and names of the disk drives; the DIRECTORY structures and file locations on these disks; the version numbers of all the application programs, and any customizations that have been applied to them; and the versions of any libraries such as DLLs that they require.

All this information must be recorded so that the same configuration can be recreated, say after a disk failure or adding a new drive, or moving the data over to a newer machine. Mistakes in setting up the configuration are the most frequent cause of applications failing to work correctly.

A new software market has arisen in network CONFIGURATION MANAGEMENT tools that automate the central collection and maintainance of configuration information, and the distribution of application versions to users.

configuration management The activity of deploying and maintaining a range of software and hardware products among a number of networked computer users. There is now a class of software tool designed to assist with configuration management, for example automatically distributing software upgrades and licences, keeping track of inventory, and checking software versions – all of which can be performed remotely from a central administrator's workstation. See also VERSION CONTROL, REPOSITORY.

configure See CONFIGURATION.

conflict A problem caused when two computer programs or peripherals try to use the same resource at the same time. The resources that most commonly cause conflicts are SERIAL ports and IRQ lines.

conformance test To determine whether a piece of hardware or software behaves in the way laid down in some STANDARD, by running a special suite of test programs that exercise in turn each feature required by the standard. See also TEST SUITE.

congestion A problem that arises when the load on any communication channel exceeds its capacity, so that not all the traffic can be delivered. Tactics for coping with congestion include rerouting excess traffic via another path, prioritizing traffic and dropping packets from the lowest priority messages, and requiring reservation of BANDWIDTH (see for example RESOURCE RESERVATION PROTOCOL). The Internet's TCP/IP protocol tackles congestion in the first instance by dropping packets and sending back a message to the originator of those packets telling it to restart and slow down its transmissions. ASYNCHRONOUS TRANSFER MODE networks employ a so-called LEAKY-BUCKET ALGORITHM to drop packets according to the QUALITY OF SERVICE promised to each particular message stream: for some content types, such as low-fidelity voice, the loss of a small percentage of packets may be quite acceptable. See also LATENCY.

conjunction 1 In the PROPOSITIONAL CALCULUS, the operator that combines two propositions into a single proposition, equivalent to the English word 'and'. The operation is usually symbolized as A∩B. Also, the combined proposition resulting from this operation.

2 The BOOLEAN AND operator which is only true if both its arguments are true.

3 In the algebra of SETS, the set containing all those elements that are both in set A and in set B.

Connectable Objects A technology that enables two-way communication between COM (COMPONENT OBJECT MODEL) objects and their CLIENTS. Objects make services available by allowing clients to call methods in their published INTERFACES, but this is a one-way process. Connectable Objects provides a mechanism for server objects to send requests or event notifications back to a client. To become connectable, an object must support one or more outgoing interfaces (any interface for which the object can be a client) plus the *ConnectionPointContainer* interface which enables its own clients to discover what these outgoing interfaces are. Connectable Objects were originally developed to assist the working of ACTIVEX controls.

connected graph A GRAPH in which there is some path that joins any node to any other.

connection The act or state of linking two systems together so that they may exchange information. Under a CONNECTION-ORIENTED communication PROTOCOL such as the public telephone system or the Internet's TCP protocol, each connection is a discrete event, a state that must be established before communication can begin.

connectionless A communications PROTOCOL under which no preliminary negotiation with the receiving station is required before a message is sent; this means that each data PACKET transmitted must contain all the routing information necessary to find the recipient. Under a connectionless protocol there is no acknowledgement of receipt, and so message delivery is said to be on a 'best effort' basis. The Internet Protocol IP is a connectionless protocol.

Connection Machine A brand of MASSIVELY PARALLEL computer, made by the US company Thinking Machines, that had some commercial success in the early 1990s when it was for a while the world's fastest computer, used for computer animation, in defence research and for weather forecasting. The original CM-1 Connection Machine employed a SIMD architecture with up to 64,000 one-bit processing elements that could be harnessed to accelerate MATRIX ARITHMETIC operations. The later CM-5 model replaced these with a large network of SPARC microprocessors, but the company was bought by ORACLE in 1999 for its expertise in DATA MINING and has ceased to produce hardware.

connection-oriented A type of communication PROTOCOL under which each connection must be negotiated in advance to agree the parameters for transmission, and the connection so established belongs to the sender and receiver for the duration of transmission. Examples of connection-oriented services include the public telephone system, all ASYNCHRONOUS TRANSFER MODE networks, and the Internet's TCP transport layer protocol (but *not* its underlying network layer IP). Also called an END-TO-END protocol.

connectivity 1 In strict mathematical usage, a quantity that measures what proportion of the nodes of a GRAPH or network are connected to one another.

2 Used in a looser sense in the computing industry to mean the ability to connect to another computer, network or peripheral. For example the collection of PORTS on the back panel of a PC might be collectively referred to in promotional literature as its connectivity.

connector That which makes a connection: a generic term applied to anything from an electrical plug or socket, to a piece of software that enables two other programs to cooperate.

consistency 1 In mathematics, a property of a formal system which means that it does not produce contradictory statements.

2 Agreement or compatibility between the different parts of a complex system. For example in RELATIONAL DATABASES and RULE-BASED SYSTEMS, it implies that none of the stored relationships contradict one another. See also ACID.

console **1** The operator's station of a MAIN-FRAME computer from which the machine is controlled, as opposed to the TERMINALS of ordinary users.

2 In UNIX, MS-DOS and many other OPERATING SYSTEMS, a text-based system device that represents the KEYBOARD and VDU. For instance the command `copy myfile con` will display the contents of that file on the screen, while `copy con myfile` will add any keystrokes typed after it to that file, until an end-of-file character is typed.

3 A dedicated computer for playing games: see more under GAMES CONSOLE.

constant A value that does not change. Many programming languages distinguish syntactically between constants and VARIABLES, allowing the COMPILER to produce more efficient code by compiling the value rather than the address of constants.

Constant Bit Rate (CBR) The most demanding type of traffic in an ASYNCHRONOUS TRANSFER MODE network, whose bit rate must not be allowed to alter at all. This level of service might be used to carry hi-fidelity audio or video streams.

constraint A restrictive condition. In mathematics, a constraint can be expressed in the form of an inequality such as $4 < x < 8$: that is, the value of x must lie between 4 and 8. A computerized CONSTRAINT SOLVER can solve systems of simultaneous constraints and sometimes provides pragmatic solutions to classes of real-world problem (e.g. scheduling and routing) that are not easily solved by means of ALGORITHMS. See for example CONSTRAINT LOGIC PROGRAMMING.

Constraint Logic Programming (CLP) An offshoot of LOGIC PROGRAMMING in which the logical inference engine is augmented by a CONSTRAINT SOLVER that can vastly reduce the search space and render faster solutions to certain classses of problem, particularly scheduling, routing, partitioning and similar. For example a set of constraints such as $x < 100, y > 40$ would avoid consideration of any values that do not satisfy them when seeking solutions to a logical goal such as: shortestDistance(x,y). There are numerous experimental and commercial CLP languages, such as CHIP and Eclipse, and constraint solvers have been created for several domains including integer, real, finite, linear rational and Boolean arithmetics and string matching.

constraint satisfaction A method of computing by solving sets of inequality relations: see more under CONSTRAINT SOLVER.

constraint solver A computer program that solves sets of inequalities (i.e. constraints), such as $x > 4$ and $x * y < 8$ to yield a simpler constraint (in this example $y < 2$) while rejecting any constraints that are inconsistent. An incremental constraint solver is one that allows a new constraint to be added to the set without forcing all the others to be solved again. In general, different solvers are required for different types of data, e.g. integers, real numbers, strings. See also CONSTRAINT LOGIC PROGRAMMING.

Constructive Cost Model See COCOMO.

constructor **1** In OBJECT-ORIENTED PROGRAMMING, a special method that instantiates a new object by giving it a name and initializing its values. In C++, constructors have the same name as the class they instantiate. See also DESTRUCTOR.

2 In FUNCTIONAL PROGRAMMING LANGUAGES, an operator used to build data structures. For example in LISP the two constructors NIL and CONS are used to create lists.

consultancy An individual or company that provides computing advice to others for a fee. The term also refers to the act of following such advice.

consumables The collective term for all those materials that a computer system requires to be periodically replenished, such as printer paper, ink or toner, floppy disks, tape cartridges and CD-R disks. See also TOTAL COST OF OWNERSHIP.

consumer electronics The huge market sector that covers, for example, television, home video, games consoles and music reproduction equipment. Although consumer electronic devices are increasingly driven by microprocessors, both vendors and users have very different expectations from those of the computer industry concerning the cost of goods and ease of use.

container In OBJECT-ORIENTED PROGRAMMING, any object whose sole purpose is to contain other objects and possibly to provide services to those objects. A CONTAINER CLASS is a class that define objects of this kind, common examples of which might include frames, windows or forms.

container class See CONTAINER.

content A jargon term used in the computer and entertainment industries to collectively describe the words, pictures, music, speech or film that is placed on a WEB SITE or delivered over a TV channel – that is, the stuff that has to be purchased from non-suit-wearing 'creative' types.

content-addressable See under ASSOCIATIVE MEMORY.

contention Competition between two or more processes for control of a single shared resource, for example BUS CONTENTION. Unresolved contention results in reduced performance, THRASHING or even DEADLOCK, both of which can be avoided by applying some orderly ARBITRATION procedure.

content management A task, and an associated category of software, that consists of maintaining the MULTIMEDIA content of a WEB SITE, for example uploading new versions of topical documents, removing outdated ones, keeping track of versions, and updating all the necessary LINKS on the site. Some software systems for content management work from a centralized REPOSITORY, similar to those used in group software development, into which all the content is first checked and which maintains control over versions. Others take a distributed approach, enabling the authors of the content to upload it to the web site and set the necessary ACCESS PERMISSIONS themselves, using their own WEB BROWSER as the management interface. Microsoft's Commerce Server and Netscape's Enterprise Server provide examples of the latter approach.

content provider A person or company who provides text, pictures, sound, video or other components for a WEB SITE, as opposed to the INTERNET SERVICE PROVIDER who only offers access to that content.

context The environment in which a software PROCESS runs; that is, the current value of all program variables. See more under CONTEXT SWITCH.

context-free grammar A class of GRAMMARS in which the syntax for constructing a symbol does not depend upon what other symbols occur before or after it in a sentence. Creating a PARSER for a context-free grammar is simpler than for a CONTEXT-SENSITIVE one, because it need only ever inspect the current symbol. In general only artificial grammars are context-free, and natural (i.e. human) languages typically exhibit some degree of context dependence. See also CHOMSKY HIERARCHY, PRODUCTION RULE.

context-independent Any property that remains the same regardless of its surrounding context. For example the spelling of English words is largely context-independent (if capitalization is ignored), while their meaning is not. See also CONTEXT-FREE GRAMMAR.

context menu A pop-up menu whose contents may differ, depending on where it is invoked from. Under Microsoft Windows and some other operating systems a context menu is summoned by clicking the right mouse button.

context-sensitive Any property that changes in different contexts. In the software world this term is often applied to a program that offers MENUS of operations whose contents vary according to what the user is currently doing.

The term also has a technical meaning in linguistics, describing that class of languages whose syntactic rules depend on sentence content: see more under CHOMSKY HIERARCHY.

context switch The procedure by which a MULTITASKING operating system stops one PROCESS from running and starts another one. Each process runs in its own software environment or context, but the extent of that context varies between different operating systems. At its simplest, each process has its own PROGRAM COUNTER and STACK, but more sophisticated systems may protect processes from interfering with one another by giving them each a separate ADDRESS SPACE. Hence a context switch might be as simple as just refreshing two REGISTERS (program counter and stack pointer) or as complex as completely resetting the MEMORY MANAGEMENT UNIT tables. See also TASK SCHEDULING.

contextual analysis A set of techniques employed in, for example HANDWRITING RECOGNITION, OPTICAL CHARACTER RECOGNITION and VOICE RECOGNITION systems, which attempt to guess from the rules of the language concerned the likelihood of certain letters or words occurring near to each other. For example, if a recognizer is unsure whether a certain character is a Q, it might check if the next character is a U (in English, but not in Arabic).

contiguous Physically adjacent or neighbouring (literally, touching). In a computing context it is usually used to describe adjacent areas of memory or disk space without any gaps in their ADDRESS range.

continuous availability An alternative term for HIGH-AVAILABILITY, applied to computer systems that have FAULT-TOLERANT features that reduce the amount of time that they are out of service (see DOWNTIME). See also FAILOVER, CLUSTER, RAID.

continuous simulation See under SIMULATION.

continuous-speech recognition Any system of computerized SPEECH RECOGNITION that can cope with a naturally paced speaking voice in which successive words often run together into a single sound. Such systems must try to distinguish between the identical sound of, say, 'my nose' and 'mine owes'.

continuous stationery A type of paper for computer printers that has the form of a continuous folded strip (see also FAN FOLD). Such paper may be blank, but is more often preprinted with a business form such as a company's invoice or blank cheques. See also TRACTOR-FEED, PIN FEED.

continuous tone Properly describes an image in which there is an effectively infinite and continuous gradation of shades of colour, as for example in an original oil painting, watercolour, pastel, or in film-based photographic prints and transparencies.

Digital imaging techniques can depict only finite numbers of colours, (for example 256 or 16 million, depending on how many bits are used to encode each PIXEL) and so must reduce continuous tone originals to a pattern of discrete dots called a HALFTONE, by sampling their colours in a grid pattern, for example via the CCD array of a scanner or digital camera.

Some LASER PRINTERS can vary the size of dots they print, which creates many more possible shades, a process described by their manufacturers as multilevel or *contone* printing. It is not, however, truly a continuous tone as the image is still made up of regularly spaced dots. See also DITHER.

contone See under CONTINUOUS TONE.

contract programming Writing computer programs on a freelance basis.

contrast The ratio between the luminous intensity of the darkest and lightest areas in a visual image, which governs how well the human eye can discriminate different objects. The natural world often exhibits contrast ratios of more than 10,000 to 1, for example when bright sunlight is viewed from inside a dark building. Photographic film can capture contrasts of 1000:1, but photographs or type printed on paper and viewed in daylight offer only a few hundreds to one.

The best computer displays now offer contrast in the range from 100:1 to 350:1 (all television sets and computer VDUS provide a separate control to adjust the contrast). For most types of LIQUID CRYSTAL DISPLAY, the contrast diminishes greatly when they are viewed obliquely.

control 1 An abstraction that describes the stream of instructions being executed by a computer processor. See more under CONTROL FLOW, CONTROL STRUCTURE.

2 In VISUAL PROGRAMMING systems, a visual input or output mechanism such as a MENU or LIST BOX that is displayed on the screen for the user to interact with when adjusting the workings of a program. In OBJECT-ORIENTED systems such as Microsoft's ACTIVEX, a control is synonymous with a prefabricated COMPONENT, and may be a complete program in its own right, such as a small TEXT EDITOR or SPREADSHEET. For other examples of commonly used controls see TEXT BOX, COMBO BOX, CHECK BOX, RADIO BUTTON, TOOLBAR.

control character One of the ASCII codes between 0 and 31 which do not correspond to printable characters, but are interpreted by many computer programs as commands to perform some action. Most computer keyboards can generate the appropriate code when a letter key is depressed simultaneously with the CTRL KEY, hence the name, but there is no agreement on what any particular program will do as a result, and many Windows programs ignore the majority of control key sequences.

The control characters are given the name of their corresponding keyboard character (whose ASCII code is 64 or greater) prefixed by CTRL or Control, so control character 01 is Control A while A itself is code 65. A shorthand for depicting control characters is to prefix the corresponding printable character with the caret (^) symbol, so Control A may be written as ^A. (See table under CONTROL CODE.) In this dictionary the ^A notation will be used when a code value is being referred to, say in a program, and the notation <CTRL+A> when actual user keypresses are meant.

Although the original ASCII standard prescribed meanings for all the control characters in telecommunication signalling, there is no universal agreement on their interpretation by modern computer software, and many programs use control key sequences in their own ways. However, a few conventions are widely adhered to, especially by printers and at operating-system level, for example:

^H	is BACKSPACE
^I	is TAB
^J	is LINE FEED
^M	is CARRIAGE RETURN
^P	turns on a printer
^Z	marks the end of a file

control code The range of ASCII character codes between 0 and 31 which do not represent printable characters and were formerly used to control devices such as printers or teletypes (see more under CONTROL CHARACTER). These codes have mnemonic names that were given to them in the early days of telecommunications:

0	^@	NUL
1	^A	SOH Start of Heading
2	^B	STX Start of Text
3	^C	ETX End of Text
4	^D	EOT End of Transmission
5	^E	ENQ Enquire
6	^F	ACK Acknowledge
7	^G	BEL Bell
8	^H	BS Backspace
9	^I	HT Horizontal Tab
10	^J	LF Line Feed
11	^K	VT Vertical Tab
12	^L	FF Form Feed
13	^M	CR Carriage Return
14	^N	SO Shift Out
15	^O	SI Shift In
16	^P	DLE Data Link Escape
17	^Q	DC1 Device Control 1/XON
18	^R	DC2 Device Control 2
19	^S	DC3 Device Control 3/XOFF
20	^T	DC4 Device Control 4
21	^U	NAK Not Acknowledged
22	^V	SYN Synchronous Idle
23	^W	ETB End of Transmission Block
24	^X	CAN Cancel
25	^Y	EM End of Medium
26	^Z	SUB Substitute
27	^[	ESC Escape
28	^\	FS File Separator
29	^]	GS Group Separator
30	^^	RS Record Separator
31	^_	US Unit Separator

Control Data Corporation (CDC) One of the earliest US manufacturers of SUPERCOMPUTERS, now defunct.

control flow An abstract way of describing the succession of INSTRUCTIONS being executed by a PROCESSOR. Programmers visualize control as a concrete entity that flows through the program code, rather like the 'bouncing ball' used to highlight song lyrics for a sing-along. This flow of control may be altered by CONTROL STRUCTURES, so that for example after an IF..THEN..ELSE construct, control flow will be diverted down one of two different paths. During a subroutine or procedure call, one routine is said to 'pass control' to another, which 'returns control' to the caller after it terminates. To think about the flow of control is to grasp the logic of a program and see whether it does what it is intended to do.

Control key See CTRL KEY.

controller An INTEGRATED CIRCUIT specifically designed to handle the commands that control a particular peripheral device such as a DISK DRIVE or a KEYBOARD. Such a controller chip works in conjunction with a software DEVICE DRIVER.

control menu In Microsoft WINDOWS and many other graphical operating systems, a pull-down MENU that is accessed by clicking on a corner of a window border which contains commands to close, move, minimize or resize that window. See also SCREEN FURNITURE.

Control Panel 1 On older computers, a flat panel containing control knobs, switches and indicator lights (also called a FRONT-PANEL) from which the machine's operations were controlled.

2 In Microsoft WINDOWS, a special window containing various small programs or APPLETS that enable the parameters of many system devices such as modems, networks, display, keyboard, printer, clock, etc to be altered. It may be accessed from the START MENU.

Control Program for Microcomputers See CP/M.

control structure A programming language construct that determines the sequence of execution of instructions, that is, which steers the CONTROL FLOW within a program. Each language employs different names for its control structures, which is often the principal difference between languages. However, all of them are simply abstractions from – and ultimately COMPILE into – a handful of primitive processor instructions, namely the conditional and unconditional JUMP and the JUMP TO SUBROUTINE. The two main categories of control structure are *statement-level* control structures, which order the execution of individual program statements, and *unit-level* control structures which order the execution of whole SUBPROGRAM units.

Statement-level control structures may for convenience be further divided between BRANCH statements (such as GOTO, IF...THEN...ELSE, CASE or SWITCH) and ITERATION statements (such as LOOP, FOR...NEXT, REPEAT...UNTIL, DO...WHILE) though this difference is purely cosmetic. Unit-level control structures include not only explicit subroutine call statements like GOSUB and CALL, but also EXCEPTION and INTERRUPT handling statements such as ON ERROR or TRY...EXCEPT. See also STRUCTURED PROGRAMMING, STRUCTURED EXCEPTION HANDLING.

control unit The section within the CPU of a computer that regulates the fetching and execution of instructions. The control unit fetches one or more new instructions from

memory (or an INSTRUCTION CACHE), DECODES them and dispatches them to the appropriate FUNCTION UNITS to be executed. The control unit is also responsible for setting the LATCHES in various data paths that ensure that the instructions are performed on the correct operand values stored in the REGISTERS. (See also ARITHMETIC AND LOGIC UNIT, REGISTER FILE.)

In a CISC processor the control unit is a small processor in its own right that executes MICROCODE programs stored in a region of ROM that prescribe the correct sequence of latches and data transfers for each type of macroinstruction. A RISC processor does away with microcode and most of the complexity in the control unit, which is left with little more to do than decode the instructions and turn on the appropriate function units.

conventional memory The 640 kilobytes (KB) of memory which is all that can be directly addressed by an Intel processor running in REAL MODE. Some memory managers can raise this limit beyond 640 KB; see under EXPANDED MEMORY, EXTENDED MEMORY.

convergence 1 A property of a CATHODE RAY TUBE display, by which the electron beam is focused so that it becomes thinner as it approaches the screen and produces a small, sharp dot. The more expensive monitors provide a control to adjust this property.

2 The property of a mathematical series whose terms become successively smaller so that an infinite number of terms still have a finite sum.

3 A jargon term that suggests that two currently distinct technologies (for example television and computers, or telephones and computers, or TV and the Web) are about to merge into a single product.

cookie A small file containing date and other information that is stored onto the hard disk of all visitors to a particular WEB SITE, its purpose being to identify them whenever they visit that site again. Cookies are made necessary because the STATELESS nature of the HTTP protocol makes it impossible otherwise to know whether a visitor has been before, but their use is fiercely opposed by some net libertarians who see them as an insidious invasion of privacy. Most WEB BROWSERS now include a configuration option that refuses to accept cookies.

cooperative multitasking A MULTITASKING scheme under which each concurrently running program must at intervals voluntarily relinquish control of the CPU to the next program. Such programs must be specially written to suspend themselves in some non-critical section and so, conversely, programs that are not so written cannot be multitasked. This contrasts with PRE-EMPTIVE MULTITASKING in which the OPERATING SYSTEM itself periodically suspends each task, so that any program may be multitasked. Apple's MACOS is a cooperative multitasking system, whereas UNIX and WINDOWS are preemptive.

coordinate In mathematics, one of a set of numbers that defines the location of some point in space in relation to a system of axes (see under AXIS). See also CARTESIAN COORDINATES, POLAR COORDINATES.

Copland The internal codename for an operating system developed by Apple in the late 1990s to replace MACOS. Copland was intended to add multiprocessor support and enhanced memory protection among other improvements, but was cancelled after running very late because of technical problems. It is now superceded by MacOS X.

coprocessor A secondary PROCESSOR designed to perform some highly specific type of computational task, for example FLOATING-POINT ARITHMETIC or GRAPHICS. A coprocessor is installed to reduce the burden on a computer's CPU and thus free it for more general duties such as transferring data and handling multiple tasks. A coprocessor may be designed to work just with a particular type of CPU, in which case its instructions can be included in the main program and are passed on to the coprocessor by the CPU as it encounters them. In other cases, the coprocessor may require its own separate program and program memory, and communicates with the CPU by interrupts or message passing via a shared memory region. See, for example, MATHS-COPROCESSOR, DIGITAL SIGNAL PROCESSOR, GRAPHICS PROCESSOR. See also MULTIPROCESSOR, MULTICOMPUTER.

copy-and-paste An editing operation supported in all GRAPHICAL USER INTERFACES which involves copying a region of a document or a picture into a temporary storage area or CLIPBOARD, and then inserting the clipboard contents into another document or location. See also CUT-AND-PASTE.

copyfitting To make a given quantity of text fit into the available space during the layout of a document, particularly of a magazine or newspaper. The principal parameters that can be varied to make copy fit are the FONT SIZE, the character spacing, and the space between lines (i.e. the LEADING) of the text in a procedure called FEATHERING.

copyleft The legal licence under which free software from the FREE SOFTWARE FOUNDATION is released; a play on the word 'copyright'. Copyleft gives a user the right to modify, copy and distribute the code, but only on condition that they extend these same rights to the recipient. Copyleft does not preclude accepting payment for code, but does seek to prevent a user from making the code (or any code derived from it) their exclusive property.

copy protection Any scheme that prevents a data distribution medium such as a CD-ROM or FLOPPY DISK from being copied. Such schemes are frequently used to protect computer games against PIRACY, and less frequently to protect application programs.

Copy protection is controversial because it is highly desirable to keep a copy of the master disk of important software in case it becomes corrupted. This requirement is met in part by KEY DISK protection schemes that need the original disk to be in a drive for the software to run, or that use a hardware DONGLE, both of which permit copies to be made, but not given away.

copyright The exclusive right to produce copies of and otherwise control some original literary, musical or artistic work, or computer program, granted under law to its author(s) during their lifetime and for a specified number of years (currently 70) after death. Copyright in a work may be sold to another party. The fact that a work is subject to copyright is indicated by the © symbol. See also COPYLEFT, PIRACY.

CORAL A SYSTEM PROGRAMMING language developed by Woodward and Wetherall in

1970 that became a standard in the British armed forces until replaced by ADA in the 1980s. CORAL derived many of its concepts from the earlier programming languages Jovial and ALGOL 60.

CORBA (Common Object Request Broker Architecture) A standard defining OBJECT REQUEST BROKERS (ORBs), which act as go-betweens that enable objects created by different OBJECT-ORIENTED PROGRAMMING SYSTEMS (perhaps running on different processor types and operating systems) to cooperate with each other.

CORBA defines a neutral INTERFACE DEFINITION LANGUAGE, IDL as a lingua franca with which to compile the INTERFACES of objects, quite independently of what programming language the objects are implemented in. These IDL interfaces are stored in an Interface Repository within the ORB and, whenever the ORB receives a request from some object to execute an operation on another object, the ORB looks up the requisite IDL interface to see which operation is wanted. The syntax of CORBA IDL was made a subset of that of C++, to exploit the widespread familiarity of the latter.

CORBA also defines various object services that the ORB itself can provide to objects, including life cycle and TRANSACTION management, and PROTOCOLS for communicating with ORBs across networks. The General Inter-ORB Protocol is a simple generic definition of the message formats required for ORBs to converse, while the INTERNET INTER-ORB PROTOCOL is a specific implementation of this protocol that runs over TCP/IP across the Internet.

CORBA tends to be used mostly in the world of large computer systems, telecommunications and UNIX, while the PC world tends to employ Microsoft's COM which is tied to the Windows operating system.

core An old-fashioned term for a computer's MAIN MEMORY, dating from the pre-silicon days of FERRITE-CORE MEMORY.

core dump 1 A facility in some older operating systems, including UNIX, which automatically prints out the contents of memory following a system CRASH.
2 Used sarcastically of someone who shares more of their knowledge than is required.

Corel A Canadian software firm that became famous through its popular Windows drawing package CORELDRAW, but has since expanded by acquiring WordPerfect and has established a strong presence in the commercial LINUX software market.

CorelDRAW A popular Windows drawing program published by the Canadian software firm COREL. It was the first such program to offer professional quality graphics manipulation on a PC. A particular strength is its ability to create fancy text effects.

Core Wars A non-graphical computer game that involves writing small 'robot' programs that are pitted against one another, the objective being to completely occupy the computer memory that forms the 'arena' and exclude the opponent's program.

coroutine A construct used to implement or simulate CONCURRENT execution in a few programming languages, the best known of which is SIMULA. A coroutine is a type of subprogram that may at any point hand over control to another named coroutine. However, unlike a conventional SUBROUTINE or PROCEDURE, a coroutine does not automatically return to its caller and does not destroy its local data; thus when called again it resumes where it left off. Two or more coroutines may therefore repeatedly call each other and so be executed together in interleaved fashion. For example in a program to simulate a game of poker, each player might be represented by a coroutine which, after making a bet, calls the next player's coroutine; when play eventually returns to the first player's coroutine it resumes with the same cards, money and stake.

corporate A computer marketing term that refers to the market sector consisting of large corporations. The term is sometimes also employed as a noun to mean a corporation (short for 'corporate client' or customer). See also SME, SOHO.

corruption The inadvertent alteration of a data item in such a way as to damage or destroy the information it contained. See also NOISE.

COSE (Common Open Software Environment) An initiative by a consortium of UNIX vendors, including Hewlett-Packard, Sun, IBM, Novell,

Univel and SCO to encourage a common user interface and software interoperability. Its most important product is the CDE.

cost-of-ownership The total cost of running a computer, including the capital cost of purchase, the cost of all CONSUMABLES, and the labour cost for configuring, maintaining and troubleshooting both hardware and software. For a personal computer this labour element is usually the owner's own time and so is seldom adequately accounted for.

countable Capable of being counted, a property possessed by all discrete objects in the real world, but not by certain mathematical entities such as the REAL NUMBERS. Mathematically, a SET is countable if it can be put into a one-to-one correspondence with the NATURAL NUMBERS. For example the set of even numbers is countable because of the correspondence $2{\rightarrow}1$, $4{\rightarrow}2$, $6{\rightarrow}3$, $8{\rightarrow}4$ etc.

counted loop A kind of program LOOP that is repeated for a specified number of times. In most programming languages, the syntax for a counted loop is of the form FOR x = 0 TO 9 DO <y>, where x, the LOOP INDEX, is automatically incremented by one at each iteration. Most languages allow the index to be stepped by a value other than one, as in FOR x = 0 TO 9 BY 3 DO <y>, which causes x to take the successive values 0, 3, 6 and 9.

Languages vary widely in their rules for the use of counted loops, especially over such issues as whether it is permissible to leave such a loop before it has finished (say, by jumping out of it with a Goto or Break statement) and whether it is permissible to assign new values to the loop index from within the loop.

counter A hardware or software device that stores a value that may be incremented or decremented to keep a tally. A hardware counter is a type of REGISTER, while a software counter is a program VARIABLE. See for example PROGRAM COUNTER, REFERENCE COUNTING.

counting loop See COUNTED LOOP.

courseware Teaching software for use in COMPUTER AIDED INSTRUCTION courses.

CP/M (Control Program for Microcomputers) An 8-bit OPERATING SYSTEM (OS) for Intel 8080 and Zilog z80 compatible processors which

briefly became the OS of choice for business software on early personal computers, but was swept away upon the launch of the IBM PC and MS-DOS.

CP/M was created by Gary Kildall in 1974 and made available for the newly released ALTAIR 8800 (the first ready-made personal computer), providing users with a simple text editing, programming and debugging environment. It employed the newly invented FLOPPY DISK for mass storage, hard disks not being supported until 1979. A strength of CP/M was that its kernel was kept separate from the file system, which made it easy to port to an impressive 3000 different hardware platforms. Among its weaknesses were that program size could not exceed 64 kilobytes and it lacked any provision for hierarchically nested file folders, so that its file management ability was rudimentary. A multi-user version called MP/M was released in 1980 by Digital Research Inc.

CPRM (Content Protection for Recordable Media) A system of copyright protection that has been implemented for DVD disks and for some other removable digital media, which prevents the copying of information from those media. It works by placing a unique digital signature within each individual drive mechanism (and therefore cannot be easily retro-fitted to earlier hardware), so that programs, music or video recordings can be made to work only in the drive for which they were licenced. Applying CPRM also requires appropriate modifications to reading and viewing software and the operating system, to ensure that file copying, moving and deleting operations all check this unique identifier before proceeding. Proposals to implement CPRM within the mechanism of all future HARD DISK drives, in an attempt to combat software PIRACY, have caused great controversy in the industry as they could interfere with the performing of adequate BACKUPS.

CPU (Central Processing Unit) The most important component of a computer, responsible for executing programs, performing calculations and moving data between memory and long-term storage media. In modern computers the CPU is always a single-chip MICROPROCESSOR (examples of which include the Intel Pentium and PowerPC), though in older minicomputers and mainframe computers it was constructed from many simpler chips. For users, the significance of the CPU is twofold: it determines which software products can be run on the computer, and also how fast that software will run. Different brands of CPU will not in general run software written for a competitor's CPU.

Almost everything that happens inside a computer does so under the control of the CPU. Both the data to be processed and the program that describes how it should be processed are held temporarily in different areas of solid state Random Access Memory (RAM) for the duration of each computing session, and the CPU is connected to this memory by a very fast electrical pathway called the PROCESSOR BUS. At its simplest, the CPU fetches a single program instruction from memory, which in turn tells it to fetch one or more numbers from a data area of the RAM and perform some COMPUTATION on them (e.g. add them together). When this operation is completed, the CPU fetches the next instruction from memory, which may for example tell it to put the results of the addition back into RAM, and so on until the whole program has been executed. This process of reading and executing instructions takes place to a strict tempo, with pulses from a clock chip acting like a metronome. In current generation computers, this clock ticks hundreds of millions of times per second, so that its frequency needs to be measured in Megahertz (millions of cycles per second). Hence the advertisements for CPU speeds such as '850 MHz Pentium'.

The current instruction to be executed and the data it operates on are stored inside the CPU for the duration of each operation, in small internal memories called REGISTERS. Every CPU can perform a modest repertoire of basic operations (typically between 32 and 256 different ones) which are designed into its hardware and are not alterable: these constitute the CPU's INSTRUCTION SET. Typical instructions might perform arithmetic (e.g. add, multiply, divide) or logic (e.g. AND, OR, NOT) operations on pairs of numbers stored in the registers; read numbers from memory into the various registers; write numbers from registers out into memory; or move data from one memory location to another. Each of these basic operations is identified by a unique number called an OP CODE, and a whole program consists of a sequence of these opcodes stored in memory, referred to as MACHINE CODE. CPU designs from different manufacturers will typically employ different numbers of registers, different instructions and instruction codings, so that machine code written for one computer will not run on another (see BINARY COMPATIBILITY).

Everything a computer can do, from word processing to creating 3D animated pictures happens because the CPU executes a long sequence of these very primitive operations, and so non-numeric data such as letters of the alphabet or colours must first be encoded into numbers before the CPU can operate on them. All the computer's peripheral devices – e.g. the keyboard, mouse, display monitor, printer and the disk drives used for long-term storage of programs and data – are ultimately controlled by the CPU executing certain repetitive machine code sequences that comprise the computer's OPERATING SYSTEM.

CPU manufacturers' research aims to create ever faster CPUs, because ultimately speed buys everything else. To display, say, a more life-like animation, the program must execute more primitive instructions every second. One way to make a chip faster is to improve the fabrication process so that the clock can be run faster, but CPU designers also apply great ingenuity to make their CPUs do more work within each clock tick. Such tricks include executing more than one instruction at once (see under PARALLELISM, SUPERSCALAR), overlapping the execution of successive instructions (see under PIPELINE), and fetching data and instructions from memory before they are needed in order to store them in a closer, faster memory called a CACHE.

CPU time The number of CPU CLOCK CYCLES devoted to running a particular program.

cracker A person who attempts to gain unauthorized access to other people's computer systems. Coined in an attempt to deflect the pejorative connotations from HACKER, which originally merely meant someone very expert in computer programming or communications.

crash An error condition in a computer program that is so severe that the program cannot continue executing. Recovery from a crash may be possible under a MULTITASKING operating system that protects one program from another: the crashed program simply terminates but leaves others running. Under an operating system that does not provide such protection – for example MS-DOS and earlier versions of Windows and MacOS – recovery often requires the computer to be REBOOTED. A program that crashes so badly that the keyboard no longer responds to commands is said to have HUNG the computer. See also FATAL ERROR, ERROR HANDLING, GENERAL PROTECTION FAULT, BLUE SCREEN OF DEATH, PROTECTION VIOLATION.

Cray Research Inc. A US computer firm founded by Seymour Cray, whose most famous product the Cray 1 was for several decades the world's leading SUPERCOMPUTER, employed by meteorological offices and defence departments in many countries. In 1997 the firm merged with SILICON GRAPHICS INC. and its technologies, particularly in the realm of fast processor INTERCONNECTS have been incorporated into SGI's own supercomputers.

CRC Abbreviation of CYCLIC REDUNDANCY CHECK.

Creative Labs A Singapore-based hardware company best known for its popular SOUNDBLASTER range of SOUND CARD for PCs, but which also makes other multimedia products including GRAPHICS ACCELERATORS, DVD and MP3 players.

creeping featuritis A condition affecting software manufacturers who keep adding new features to products that are already too complicated.

crippleware An unattractive coinage meaning software given away on a trial basis (see SHAREWARE), but with some of its key functions disabled to encourage purchase of the full product.

crisp logic A name occasionally given to traditional LOGIC to differentiate it from FUZZY LOGIC: in crisp logic the fundamental operations AND, OR and NOT always return either True or False (i.e. 1 or 0).

crisp set A normal SET, as defined by a traditional symbolic LOGIC, which has strict membership criteria so that an object must either be completely included or completely excluded: in contrast with a FUZZY SET.

critical path analysis A mathematical method for scheduling complex projects. It identifies precisely those subtasks that must be completed before the successive stages can proceed, and whose durations therefore determine the total job time: this chain of tasks is called the critical path, and its total time is the shortest time the whole job can possibly take. Only improvements that speed up tasks on the critical path will have an effect on the overall job time, so such an analysis ensures the most efficient application of effort. The method was invented in the defence industries in the late 1950s and refined during NASA's moon-landing programme. See also PERT, GANTT CHART, SCHEDULING.

critical section A section of program code, for example a real time DEVICE DRIVER, which is not RE-ENTRANT and must therefore be executed to completion by one process at a time, without any interruption from other processes. Critical sections require some synchronization mechanism, such as a MUTEX or SEMAPHORE, to prevent two processes executing them at once.

CRM (Customer Relations Management) A branch of business computing that revolves around maintaining databases of customer information and integrating these with sales, marketing and distribution systems.

crossbar-switch An electronic device that can connect any of its multiple inputs to any of its outputs under the control of electrical signals. The name derives from its mechanical predecessor, which was once used in telephone exchanges, and literally involved a set of metal bars that joined multiple contacts. Cross-bar switches are employed in very high-speed networks where a fixed connection topology would be impractical or inefficient – for example inside a PARALLEL COMPUTER to create a temporary direct connection between a particular processor and a particular memory bank.

cross-compile To COMPILE a program for one computer using a special COMPILER that runs on a different type of computer. For example one might cross-compile a program for the PALM PILOT using a compiler running on an Apple MACINTOSH.

cross development The process of writing programs for one computer on a different kind of computer. See also CROSS-COMPILE.

cross-licensing A business arrangement under which a company allows another to incorporate or sell its product. Widely used in the software business.

cross-linked A form of damage sometimes encountered in a computer FILE, caused by the OPERATING SYSTEM erroneously allocating the same disk SECTOR to two different files. Cross-linking creates unpredictable results if an attempt is made to edit either file, and often produces spurious directory listings, for example with circularly nested subdirectories.

cross-platform Software that is able to run on more than one type of PROCESSOR or OPERATING SYSTEM. Typically applied to development systems that can generate several different BINARY executable files from the same SOURCE CODE.

cross-reference 1 A link embedded in a document that points to another location or document. This dictionary contains many cross-references indicated by printing in SMALL CAPS. The HYPERTEXT links used by document markup languages such as HTML, XML and SGML are a form of automated cross-reference. **2** The information gleaned from programming tools that locate and list every usage of the IDENTIFIERS in a program.

cross-sectional bandwidth A measure of the speed at which a MASSIVELY PARALLEL computer or network of computers can process data. It is obtained by conceptually splitting the system into two parts, each containing half the processors, and then determining the data flow per second across the boundary between them. See also INTERCONNECT, SWITCHED INTERCONNECT.

crosstalk The unwanted straying of an electrical signal from the conductor that bears it into a neighbouring conductor.

CRT Abbreviation of CATHODE RAY TUBE.

Crusoe An innovative microprocessor made by Transmeta Corporation intended for use in portable computers, which features very low power consumption (~1 watt) and can run software written for Intel's 80x86 ARCHITECTURE, that is to say, all PC software. Crusoe is not REGISTER-COMPATIBLE with Intel CPUs but instead employs a processor core that is built on VLIW principles (with 128-bit instructions) and translates x86 instructions into its own code using software – a process that Transmeta calls *code morphing*.

cryptography, cryptanalysis The science of making and breaking codes and CIPHERS. Modern cryptography has become a branch of mathematics, much concerned with number theory and information theory. See more under ENCRYPTION, PUBLIC-KEY ENCRYPTION.

C shell A replacement command SHELL and SCRIPTING LANGUAGE for the UNIX operating system, written by William Joy for BSD Unix. The C shell enhances the original BOURNE SHELL by adding a history feature that re-issues previously typed commands, and by using a more C-like syntax in its SCRIPTING LANGUAGE.

CSMA/CA (Carrier Sense Multiple Access/Collision Avoidance) A PROTOCOL similar in principle to Ethernet's CSMA/CD, used in WIRELESS networks. Both protocols work by forcing the transmitter to wait for a random interval before retrying in the event of a COLLISION. However in CSMA/CA this is achieved by adding an extra acknowledge protocol at MEDIA ACCESS CONTROL level, which causes a retransmission if reception of a FRAME is not acknowledged.

CSMA/CD (Carrier Sense Multiple Access/Collision Detect) The low-level network ARBITRATION protocol employed by ETHERNET networks that prevents the corruption of messages due to two nodes transmitting at the same time over the shared cable. If any node tries to transmit but detects collision with another transmission, it waits for a random interval before trying again, which assures fair turns while minimizing wasted BANDWIDTH. See also SHARED MEDIUM.

CSP Abbreviation of COMMUNICATING SEQUENTIAL PROCESSES.

CSS Abbreviation of CASCADING STYLE SHEETS.

CSV (Comma-Separated Values) A COMMA-SEPARATED TEXT FILE format commonly used to export and import data between different database and spreadsheet programs. Within a CSV file, each successive RECORD occupies a new line (i.e. is separated by a NEWLINE sequence) while the individual FIELDS within each record are separated by commas. Since text data in a field may itself contain commas, the whole field is normally surrounded by double quotes, as in:

```
"Clark","Jim","088-6461","34 River
St, London W7"

"Bloggs","Joe","097-278876","55
Plod Lane, Swindon"
```

CTRL key A modifier key fitted to almost all computer keyboards, which when pressed in conjunction with a letter key causes the equivalent ASCII CONTROL CODE to be emitted instead of the printable character. For example, <CTRL+C> sends the code 3 instead of 67. In the days of COMMAND-DRIVEN user interfaces, many programs were controlled entirely by issuing multiple CTRL key combinations such as <CTRL+K+C> and <CTRL+K+V>, of which there may be dozens per program. A few such combinations survive in Windows as the KEYBOARD SHORTCUTS <CTRL+C> to copy, <CTRL+X> to cut and <CTRL+V> to paste a section of selected text.

CTS Abbreviation of Clear To Send. See under FLOW CONTROL.

CU Online shorthand for See You.

CUA Abbreviation of COMMON USER ACCESS.

cubic spline A geometric construct used in many computer graphics programs to create complex curves and surfaces from assemblages of many shorter curve segments, each represented by a cubic polynomial expression of the form:

$$y = ax^3 + bx^2 + cx + d$$

Cubic expressions are chosen because they exhibit a property not shown by lower-order (for example QUADRATIC) expressions, namely, that they will always fit together perfectly

smoothly if they are joined at their points of inflection; that is, points of zero curvature. See also SPLINE, B-SPLINE, BEZIER CURVE, BEZIER SURFACE, BICUBIC SURFACE PATCH.

CUL Online shorthand for See You Later.

Curie Point A critical temperature above which a magnetic material loses its magnetism. The effect is exploited in the manufacture of MAGNETO-OPTICAL DISKS.

curly brackets See BRACES.

current directory The disk directory in which a computer's OPERATING SYSTEM will look for any files that are not specified by a full PATHNAME. In MS-DOS the command prompt can be made to reflect the name of the current directory as well as the current drive, and under both MS-DOS and Unix the CHDIR command (abbreviated to cd) can be used to change which directory is the current one.

current loop A SERIAL communications hardware standard that preceded the now ubiquitous RS-232. Current loop equipment used voltages as high as 100 volts and so should never be connected to a modern RS-232 port.

current selection An object on a computer screen – say a passage of text or part of an image – that has been picked out by the user with a MOUSE and is HIGHLIGHTED in some way to show that it has been so chosen. Many program operations, such as deletion, are performed on the current selection rather than on the whole document.

curried function In some FUNCTIONAL PROGRAMMING LANGUAGES, a type of FUNCTION that may be applied to only some of its arguments, whereupon its return value is another function that takes the rest of the arguments. For example a curried application of the function Add(x, y) such as Add(3) returns a function that adds 3 to its own argument. Named after its inventor Haskell B CURRY.

Curry, Haskell B (1900–82) A logician and inventor of COMBINATORY LOGIC, after whom the HASKELL programming language is named.

curses A UNIX programming LIBRARY for controlling the CURSOR movement on a variety of different types of TERMINAL screen.

cursor 1 A distinctive mark in a text displayed on a computer screen that indicates the place at which the next character typed will be inserted. On old CHARACTER-BASED terminals the cursor was a blinking, colour-reversed or underlined character, but in modern GRAPHICAL USER INTERFACES it is more usually a vertical line positioned between rather than over the characters (see I-BEAM CURSOR). The cursor moves along automatically after each character is typed, but may also be moved deliberately using the keyboard CURSOR KEYS or by pointing to the new location with a MOUSE.

2 In the SQL DATABASE QUERY LANGUAGE, a named variable that points to one row in a TABLE, and can be altered to select successive data records.

cursor-addressable terminal Any type of computer display device that has a CURSOR which can be moved to any point on the screen, marking the point at which typed input will appear and where output characters will be presented. All modern computer displays are cursor-addressable in this sense, whether they be CHARACTER-BASED or employ a GRAPHICAL USER INTERFACE.

The name survives from the earliest days of computing when terminals connected to a remote host computer could output only a succession of lines, rather like a printer (see GLASS TELETYPE), which scrolled irreversibly off the top of the screen. The only way of positioning the output on such screens was via the CONTROL CODES (such as CARRIAGE RETURN and LINE FEED) that were included in the ASCII character set – this did however have the advantage of being wholly independent of the terminal hardware used.

With the invention of cursor-addressable terminals, each brand created its own internal codes to position the cursor on the screen, introducing a whole new level of configuration complexity that persists today, particularly during online communication with a remote computer running a different operating system. See for example VT100, ANSI TERMINAL, CURSES, TERMCAP. See also FULL-SCREEN EDITOR, WINDOW.

cursor addressing The ability of a software system to directly control the position of the CURSOR on a computer's display.

cursor keys, cursor arrows Four keys on a computer's keyboard, marked with the up, down, left and right arrow symbols (hence the alternative name *arrow keys*) which move the screen CURSOR one place in the indicated direction. When pressed, the cursor keys emit certain CONTROL CHARACTERS that are received by the currently running software and interpreted as commands to move the cursor. Under modern graphical operating systems the cursor keys are universally recognized, but some very old software may not recognize some (or all) of the cursor keys, having been written before the introduction of the CURSOR-ADDRESSABLE TERMINAL. Other older programs may interpret cursor control characters in a different way: see more under TERMINAL EMULATION.

Most computers now have several other keys that move the cursor in addition to the arrow keys: the PGUP and PGDN keys move a whole screen up or down; and the HOME and END keys move to the start and end of a line. Some programs may interpret these keys in slightly different ways, while many programs support various combinations of these keys with the MODIFIER KEYS SHIFT, CTRL and ALT to provide related functions: for example SHIFT PGUP to go to the start of a document. See also FUNCTION KEY, TAB.

curve fitting To find the mathematical curve that best describes a set of empirically measured data points, the purpose being to then predict or INTERPOLATE further points that were not measured. Most modern SPREADSHEET programs incorporate a curve-fitting feature.

CU-SeeMe A shareware communications program that enables live video and audio to be sent over the Internet. It was written at Carnegie-Mellon University, hence the CU part of its name.

custom chip An INTEGRATED CIRCUIT designed especially for a customer, to perform a particular task. Sometimes called full-custom chips to distinguish them from semi-prefabricated solutions produced using GATE ARRAYS or FPGAS. Custom chips typically run faster than either of the latter techniques, but incur huge initial costs that make them viable only for large production runs.

Customer Information Control System See CICS.

customize To tailor the properties and behaviour of a computer program to its user's liking. Typical customizations include choosing the type FONTS, window colours and size, together with such non-cosmetic features as the default directories in which to save and look for files, keyboard SHORTCUTS, and much more. Such customization details are stored either in CONFIGURATION files or, in the case of Windows programs, in the REGISTRY, so that they are automatically restored whenever the program is started. Modern software has become so complex that customization data represents a very large investment of user's time, which may be potentially lost if a program has to be reinstalled from scratch. See also PREFERENCES, SKIN, CONFIGURATION MANAGEMENT, THIN CLIENT.

custom software Software written especially for a particular application rather than mass produced: see also BESPOKE, SHRINK-WRAP, OFF-THE-SHELF.

cut-and-paste To move a selected passage of text, part of an image or other object to a new location by copying it to a temporary storage area or CLIPBOARD (deleting the original in the same operation), then inserting the clipboard contents at a new location. Cut-and-paste is a fundamental operation provided in all GRAPHICAL USER INTERFACES, along with the similar COPY-AND-PASTE operation which does not delete the original.

cybercafe A café that provides personal computers connected to the INTERNET for hire (typically by the half-hour) to its customers.

Cybercash One of the first secure electronic payment systems, set up in 1995 to process credit-card transactions over the INTERNET. CyberCash employs its own commerce application PROTOCOL, described in RFC 1898, which encrypts and digitally signs credit-card transaction data, enabling customers to be notified of approval or denial of credit and complete a transaction within seconds

Cyberglove A US manufacturer of input devices for VIRTUAL REALITY systems, consisting of gloves that transmit the relative positions of the users' hands and fingers. See also DATA GLOVE, HEAD-MOUNTED DISPLAY.

cybernetics A rather fuzzily defined discipline founded in the 1950s by John VON NEUMANN and others to study the properties of automata and self-regulating systems, and which is now largely subsumed into COMPUTER SCIENCE.

cyberspace A term first coined by the novelist William Gibson (in *Neuromancer*, 1982) to refer to the totality of the world's networked computers, which form a huge virtual space inside which people can communicate and locate stored information.

cybersquatting The purchase of an Internet DOMAIN NAME that ought naturally to belong to some other person or company in the hope of later selling it to that person. The practice has been outlawed in the USA, so that companies can for example reclaim from cybersquatters domain names that constitute long-used trademarks. See also ICANN.

Cybiko A portable, battery-operated GAMES CONSOLE that employs short-range wireless links to play with other users, and can download free games from the Internet. It also incorporates some personal organizer functions such as an address book and appointments calendar.

cycle 1 In hardware engineering, a CLOCK CYCLE – that is, the time interval between two successive EDGES in an electrical signal – used to synchronize the occurrence of events.
2 Hence the informal use to mean CPU clock cycles, as a measure of computing power: as in 'program X can really eat cycles'.
3 In the electrical generating industry, the interval between two peaks in the voltage of an ALTERNATING CURRENT supply.
4 Used in US computer slang as in 'cycle the power': i.e. to turn a computer's power switch off and on again to REBOOT it.

cyclic redundancy check (CRC) An error-detection mechanism in which a special number is appended to a block of data in order to detect any changes introduced during storage (or transmission). The CRC is recalculated on retrieval (or reception) and compared to the value originally transmitted, which can reveal certain types of error. For example, a single corrupted bit in the data results in a one-bit change in the calculated CRC, but multiple corrupt bits may cancel each other out.

A CRC is derived using a more complex algorithm than the simple CHECKSUM, involving MODULO ARITHMETIC (hence the 'cyclic' name) and treating each input word as a set of coefficients for a polynomial. See also ERROR DETECTION AND CORRECTION.

cylinder The set of all the TRACKS on a HARD DISK drive with multiple PLATTERS that may be read at the same time. All the tracks are the same distance from the central spindle, so they can be imagined as tracing a cylinder in space. The HEADS on all the platters move together in a parallel motion – a sequence of data stored within the same cylinder can be read at optimum speed without requiring any movement.

CYO Online shorthand for See You Online.

cypher See CIPHER.

cyphertext An encrypted (see ENCRYPTION) version of a document, as opposed to its readable or PLAINTEXT version.

Cyrix Formerly a US manufacturer of Intel-compatible MICROPROCESSORS, now owned by VIA.

D

DAA Abbreviation of DISTRIBUTED APPLICATION ARCHITECTURE.

DAC Abbreviation of DIGITAL TO ANALOGUE CONVERTER.

daemon The term used in the UNIX operating system for a small program that remains in memory, running silently as a BACKGROUND TASK and waiting for some condition to occur to trigger it into action. A typical Unix system has several daemons permanently installed, handling such services as PRINT SPOOLING, FILE TRANSFER and REMOTE EXECUTION. See also TERMINATE AND STAY RESIDENT.

daisy-chain To connect several PERIPHERALS to a computer in a sequence, with each one linked to the previous one, so that only one connector on the computer itself is occupied. Not all connection technologies support daisy-chaining, those that do including USB, SCSI and FIREWIRE.

daisy-wheel printer A now obsolete type of IMPACT PRINTER that employed mechanical type FONTS in the form of small metal disks made of many spokes, each of which ends in a typewriter-like character block. Daisy-wheel printers produced crisper, darker text than DOT-MATRIX PRINTERS and were favoured by businesses before the invention of the LASER PRINTER. However, they were slow, horribly noisy, and changing fonts meant manually swapping wheels.

dangling pointer A POINTER whose referenced object has been deallocated, which leaves it pointing to an incorrect location. This is one of the most damaging of program BUGS, as following such a pointer will almost invariably cause the program to CRASH and may affect other programs too.

DAO Abbreviation of DATA ACCESS OBJECTS.

DARPA (Defense Advanced Research Projects Agency) Formerly called ARPA, the US military research agency that commissioned and funded the original development of the INTERNET and Berkeley Unix (see BSD), and has sponsored many advances in SUPERCOMPUTER technology. See also ARPANET.

Dartmouth BASIC The original version of the BASIC language, developed in 1964 at Dartmouth College, New Hampshire, by John Kemeny and Thomas Kurtz as an aid to teaching programming.

DAT (Digital Audio Tape) A magnetic tape recording system originally invented by Sony and Philips as a medium for distributing CD-quality digitized music on special tape cassettes, but now widely used for computer data backup duties.

DAT recorders employ rotary READ/WRITE heads (similar to those used in video recorders) to write diagonal stripes of data on one side of the tape only, permitting the tape to be moved more slowly than in traditional analogue tape recorders while still writing data very densely. Reduced stress on the tape prolongs cartridge life, at the cost of faster wear on the moving heads. The DDS DAT format used for computer backup enables a DAT drive to locate individual files at very high speed by writing digital markers onto the tape, and a 120-metre cartridge can hold up to 50 gigabytes of data.

data Information entered into a computer to be transformed in some way determined by the computer's PROGRAM. Strictly speaking, data is a plural form but it is widely treated as singular, and its proper singular *datum* (Latin for 'that which is given') is seldom used in computing circles.

There is an important distinction between data and a program that operates on that data but, since both are represented simply as sequences of BINARY NUMBERS, and both are stored in the same MEMORY, such a distinction cannot be made by the computer itself. For example, depending on its context, the number 65 might represent someone's age, a sum of money, the letter A, or a program instruction. The computer must be told what is a program to execute and what is data to be operated on; the human user does this by issuing appropriate commands. The computer's operating system makes it easier to remember which is program and which is data by defining different FILE TYPES. Programs are stored as a special type of file that is automatically executed when its name is invoked, whereas data files do nothing on their own and must be passed to a program that will open them or edit them.

data abstraction A data type used to represent some aspect of a real-world problem within a program. See also ABSTRACTION.

Data Access Objects (DAO) An OBJECT LIBRARY provided in early versions of MICROSOFT ACCESS and VISUAL BASIC for accessing data from a range of sources. It is now largely superceded by the ACTIVEX DATABASE OBJECTS library.

data acquisition The automatic collection of data by some electronic measuring device connected to a computer.

data alignment The placing of data items in a computer's memory so that they begin at a particular kind of ADDRESS (for example an even address, or an address that is divisible by four). Alignment is a fundamental issue, bound up with the way a particular PROCESSOR physically accesses the memory. A processor that is capable of addressing single bytes could start reading a four-byte data object at its second byte were it not correctly aligned, and thus read an incorrect value. Aligning data may involve adding meaningless extra bytes to act as padding.

data analysis The study of the form as well as the content of the data to be presented to a computer to decide what RECORD structure is appropriate to store the data in a DATABASE (see SCHEMA), what relationships exist between different data items, which items are likely to be needed as KEY FIELDS for searching, and to determine how much STORAGE is needed to hold the data. Data analysis is the most important phase of any computer project, because proceeding prematurely to the programming phase with an inadequate or incorrect structure for the data almost guarantees that the project will fail to meet its goals. It is extremely difficult and expensive to correct a poorly chosen data format after a database has been populated with huge amounts of data.

Every software design METHODOLOGY has its own scheme for performing data analysis, and there are numerous more or less formal methods that may be applied, some based on statistics, some on logic, some interactive, some supplemented by graphical charting tools (see for example STRUCTURED ANALYSIS, ONLINE ANALYTICAL PROCESSING, PIVOT TABLE, TIME SERIES). The widespread adoption of the RELATIONAL DATABASE model forced a greater emphasis on correct data analysis, as the data must be extensively transformed before it can be placed into tables (see more under CODD'S NORMAL FORMS). The introduction of OBJECT-ORIENTED techniques has further moved the emphasis away from program coding and toward deeper data analysis, since objects are nothing more than parcels of structured data whose structure determines their behaviour, leading to a whole new set of methods for OBJECT-ORIENTED ANALYSIS and OBJECT-ORIENTED DESIGN. See also SOFTWARE ENGINEERING, CASE, UNIFIED MODELLING LANGUAGE.

database A collection of DATA stored in a computer in some organized fashion, so that desired items can be quickly retrieved according to various criteria.

Almost all databases are organized as a set of identically structured RECORDS, templates that bind together several pieces of information about a single entity (for example payroll details for an employee). Each record consists of a number of FIELDS that hold the actual data items of various types, e.g. numbers, text, dates or pictures. To retrieve a particular record from the database, its user must specify the value to be found in a particular field (or fields), which is called making a QUERY to or 'against' the database. For example, the query might be: retrieve all records where the name field contains 'smith'. Retrieval can be made faster by building a sorted INDEX (similar to the index of a book) of all the values in one or more fields called the KEY fields.

There is an important distinction between a database that keeps all its records in the same disk FILE (a so-called FLAT-FILE DATABASE), and a RELATIONAL DATABASE that segregates different types of record into separate files or TABLES. When a query is issued in a relational database, these tables are recombined in ad hoc configurations to answer that particular query. See also DATABASE QUERY LANGUAGE, SQL, QUERY BY EXAMPLE, QUERY OPTIMIZATION.

database engine The core software that performs the main work of a DATABASE, creating, storing and retrieving RECORDS from disk files and maintaining the INDEXES. Professional databases separate this core engine from the user interface or FRONT-END through which users enter data and queries and view the results. In a CLIENT/SERVER database, the core engine runs on a remote server, while the user interface runs on the user's local terminal or PC. See for example SQL SERVER, ORACLE.

database index See under INDEX.

database management system (DBMS) A software system used to create, maintain and query a computer DATABASE. The simpler DBMSes are single programs that run on a personal computer and keep all data in a single FILE (see FLAT-FILE DATABASE), while at the other extreme a large distributed DBMS consists of whole suites of different programs and utilities, sometimes running on several different makes of computer and operating system. The operations supported by a typical DBMS include adding, updating and removing RECORDS from the database, creating and deleting INDEXES, searching the database and retrieving selected groups of records, and outputting such selections as formatted REPORTS.

The modern tendency in DBMS design is to separate the DATABASE ENGINE from its FRONT-END or user interface, and to provide the latter with VISUAL PROGRAMMING tools such as VISUAL BASIC or POWERBUILDER. This facilitates easy customization of the interface to specific applications without disturbing the database structure, and also integration with other software tools such as WORD PROCESSORS and SPREADSHEETS to simplify the generation of REPORTS. See also RELATIONAL DATABASE, HIERARCHICAL DATABASE, FREE-FORM DATABASE.

database manager See under DATABASE MANAGEMENT SYSTEM.

database publishing An offshoot of DESKTOP PUBLISHING in which the textual content of the documents produced is mostly extracted as records from one or more computer DATABASES and merged into the PAGE LAYOUTS, rather than being created in a word processor. Database publishing is used particularly for creating reference works, such as a telephone directory or this dictionary.

database query language A specialized PROGRAMMING LANGUAGE designed for issuing queries to a DATABASE. The most widely used such language by far is Structured Query Language or SQL.

database server A network SERVER whose main function is to support a shared DATABASE.

Datablade The proprietary name used by INFORMIX for the COMPONENT SOFTWARE model used to extend its DATABASE product.

data-bound control In a VISUAL PROGRAMMING system such as VISUAL BASIC, a prefabricated software component that can be associated with a particular DATABASE file and will then automatically populate its own FIELDS with data records drawn from that database, without any explicit program code needing to be written – such controls have revolutionized the writing of database FRONT-END software. Typically an SQL query string is entered into one of the control's properties to determine which records are retrieved, and any changes made to data displayed in the control are written back to the database to update the original record. Data-bound controls generally take the form of a

SPREADSHEET-like grid, whose successive rows become populated with records from the database; more rarely they may be in the form of a text editor or a graphics viewer.

data bus 1 In general, any set of parallel conductors (see more under BUS) that is used to transport computer data.

2 The computer bus used to carry data items to and from memory, as opposed to the separate bus normally employed to carry the memory address being accessed (see under ADDRESS BUS).

3 A bus within a computer's CPU that carries only data items rather than program INSTRUCTIONS. Some processors use a single bus for both, but others separate them because their traffic patterns are so different: instructions tend to be small and fetched regularly, while data traffic tends to be heavy but sporadic. See more under HARVARD ARCHITECTURE.

data cache A PROCESSOR CACHE that is used to cache only data and not program INSTRUCTIONS. See also INSTRUCTION CACHE, HARVARD ARCHITECTURE, UNIFIED CACHE.

datacasting Sending WEB PAGES or other digital multimedia data over a broadcast television system. See more under WEBCAST.

data cleansing A pre-processing stage applied to a set of data that is to be entered into a computer system, for example to remove duplicated, badly-formed or out-of-date entries. See also DEDUPE, PURGE, LIST MANAGEMENT.

Data Communication Equipment (DCE) In SERIAL communication systems, a device that provides a communication network connecting data sources and destinations, which are called DATA TERMINAL EQUIPMENT (DTE). The MODEM is the most common kind of DCE. DCE and DTE are typically connected by an RS-232 serial line, and before any data can be transmitted the DTR (Data Terminal Ready) signal must become active to tell the DCE that a DTE is ready to transmit and receive data. The distinction between these two categories of device is made because their connectors must be wired appropriately so that the transmitting pin of one connects to the receiving pin of the other and vice versa. The RS-232 standard requires that DCE should use a female connector, transmitting on pin two and receiving on pin three. However, according to this rule most modern modems are actually DTE rather than DCE.

data compression See under COMPRESSION.

data cube A view into a DATABASE or SPREADSHEET model that is arranged along three (or even more) different dimensions, for example by date, region and product. Such a view might be presented on a computer screen as a sequence of two-dimensional slices, or by using 3D GRAPHICS to create a rotatable solid representing the data set. Data cubes are extensively employed in ONLINE ANALYTICAL PROCESSING and DATA MINING when seeking trends and correlations in large masses of data. The term is also sometimes abused to mean a HYPERCUBE.

data definition A description of the data structures, for example the file and record formats, to be used to represent data within a computer program. The term is particularly associated with the COBOL programming language which provides a separate section within each program for the data definitions. See also DATA ANALYSIS, DATA MODEL, DATA DICTIONARY.

Data Definition Language A subset of the SQL query language that contains just those commands that are used to allocate and initialize a new database and to maintain its REFERENTIAL INTEGRITY.

data dictionary A type of file used in mainframe DATABASE software that stores the DATA DEFINITIONS separately from the files that hold actual data.

data-driven 1 A style of computer interaction in which the user mostly manipulates data files directly, rather than first explicitly executing a program and then giving it a data file. At its simplest, this might be achieved by using FILE ASSOCIATIONS to open each file with the appropriate application, but in more advanced OBJECT-ORIENTED systems it implies the IN-PLACE EDITING of different sorts of content within the same window using different applications that are started automatically as required.

2 Any computation process that is synchronized by the data becoming available, rather

than to a strict clock signal. For example in some programming languages such as PARLOG or OCCAM, a communicating process will automatically wait until an input value is supplied. See also DATAFLOW, ASYNCHRONOUS.

Data Encryption Standard (DES) A PRIVATE-KEY ENCRYPTION algorithm developed for the US federal government in the mid-1970s, which depends on the difficulty of discovering a large prime number KEY by factorization. DES has been so widely deployed (for example it is used to encrypt passwords in the UNIX operating system) that is has been implemented in special chips to speed up encryption and decryption, and the US government forbids export of advanced DES implementations to certain countries on defence grounds. DES is identical to the ANSI standard DEA(Data Encryption Algorithm) defined in X3.92-1981.

The standard version of DES employs 56-bit keys but recent increases in computer power have made these insecure, so that Triple DES, which involves making three passes using 112-bit or 168-bit keys is now preferred. See also PUBLIC-KEY ENCRYPTION, RSA ENCRYPTION.

data entry The process of entering new data into a computer, either manually typed in by a human operator or for example using an optical SCANNER, an OCR device, a BAR CODE READER or a mechanical PUNCHED CARD reader. See also VALIDATION.

data exchange The transfer of data from one computer to another.

data file A file that contains data, as opposed to one that contains executable program code. For example, a document or a picture stored on disk is a data file.

dataflow A model of CONCURRENT computation in which the execution of programs is controlled by the availability of their data rather than explicitly by the programmer. Dataflow programs consist of networks of connected concurrent processes that wait for each other to deliver a result. The dataflow model has been used to build experimental computer hardware (especially at Manchester University) and also programming languages such as LUCID.

dataflow analysis An activity that forms part of most program design methodologies in which the movement of data items between the various program modules is studied, typically with the help of data flow diagrams. See also DATA ANALYSIS, SYSTEMS ANALYSIS, FLOW CHART.

data fork Under Apple's MACOS, the part of a file that contains the actual data, as opposed to the RESOURCE FORK, which contains assorted ancillary information such as ICONS and BITMAPS.

data format The particular arrangement of data items required by a piece of computing or communications hardware or software for its correct operation. See also FILE FORMAT.

data fusion The combining or merging of two or more data sets into a single set. The term is applied particularly to the merging of large databases as used in DATA MINING and ONLINE TRANSACTION PROCESSING.

Data General A US computer manufacturer which in the 1970s was the chief competitor to DIGITAL EQUIPMENT CORPORATION in the MINI-COMPUTER market.

data glove An input device worn on the hand which tracks the positions of the fingers in three dimensions and transmits them to a computer, typically to control a VIRTUAL REALITY system. The virtual reality scene may contain a 3D representation of a hand which follows the movements of the real hand, and may be used to grasp and manipulate virtual objects and controls. Data gloves range in sophistication from those that merely detect whether the hand is open or closed, to ones that track every finger joint, wrist and elbow position.

datagram A discrete package of data that contains sufficient addressing information to be routed from a sending computer to a destination computer across a network, without needing to refer to any prior connection between those computers. The Internet's TCP/IP protocol uses the term datagram for the basic units of information that it transmits.

The datagram is a higher-level concept than the PACKET or the FRAME employed by DATA LINK LAYER protocols such as ASYNCHRONOUS

TRANSFER MODE or FRAME RELAY, and an Internet datagram may in fact be composed of a collection of such lower-level packets, depending on what sort of link it is currently traversing.

data integrity The completeness and internal consistency of a set of data. See more under REFERENTIAL INTEGRITY.

data link Informally, any connection over which data can be sent. More specifically, the DATA LINK LAYER is the second layer of the OSI REFERENCE MODEL for networks.

Data Link Escape (DLE) The mnemonic name for the CONTROL CHARACTER with ASCII code 16.

data link layer The second layer of the OSI REFERENCE MODEL for networks, consisting of those protocols that split the data stream into PACKETS, reassemble packets, and resend packets that are lost or corrupted in transmission.

data logging The automatic collection of data from some electronic instrument, for example an electricity meter or a rainfall gauge. Logging may be performed continuously via a radio or telephone link to a computer, or in batch mode where tape or other memory devices are periodically retrieved from the instrument.

data member See MEMBER VARIABLE.

data migration Moving data from one computer or software system to another, which may involve converting it into a different FORMAT.

data mining The use of computer software to examine large volumes of data – for example the sales records of a retail business – in order to extract trends and relationships that may be of use in planning the business. For example a supermarket chain might use data mining to discover correlations between certain product categories and customer DEMOGRAPHICS to help in planning special offers.

Data mining may be enormously demanding computationally, involving the comparison of every combination of millions of data points along multiple axes (see DATA CUBE), and it often requires the use of a SUPERCOMPUTER and massive disk ARRAYS. Techniques derived from ARTIFICIAL INTELLIGENCE research are often employed to extract rules from the data using methods such as INDUCTION.

data model An important stage in the design of a computer DATABASE, which specifies the DATA STRUCTURES to be used and the operations that will validate and manipulate them. Most DATABASE MANAGEMENT SYSTEMS make it expensive to change the structure of a database once the data has been entered, so constructing an effective and consistent data model is an essential preliminary.

A data model specifies what types of RECORD will be held in the database, what FIELDS each will contain, and the types of relationship between the entities these records describe (say, a one-to-one relationship between customers and accounts, but a one-to-many relationship between each customer and products). See also SCHEMA.

data packet A network PACKET that contains user data, as opposed to one that contains only control information.

data preparation **1** Readying data for processing by a computer, which typically involves both DATA ANALYSIS and DATA CLEANSING. Much of the task of data preparation consists of putting the data into the correct FORMAT for processing by a particular program.

2 Sometimes used to refer to the simple keying in of data.

data processing (DP) The use of computers to manipulate data. This term was once used to describe the whole field of commercial computing, whose practitioners therefore came to be referred to as 'DP professionals'. 'IT' is now the more fashionable term for this field, since it encompasses more branches of computing, including for example graphics and audio and telecommunications. See also TMT.

data protection Measures taken to prevent the misuse of data stored within a computer. Data protection measures may include: PASSWORD protection and other AUTHENTICATION schemes to regulate access to the SERVER on which the database is stored, ENCRYPTION of sensitive parts of the data, and regular DATA CLEANSING to make sure that out-of-date information is not treated as current (for example in a credit control or criminal record system).

Data Protection Act A 1998 act of the UK Parliament (in compliance with a 1995 EU directive) that regulates how personal details may be stored in a computer system. Its main provisions are that:

i) Personal data must not be kept without the subject's informed consent.
ii) Personal information may be used only to perform specific contracts with the subject, or for legally necessary pursuits such as tax collection and social security.
iii) The database owner must identify themself to the subject and demonstrate if asked that such personal data is being used lawfully.
iv) The subject has the right to object to use of personal data for direct marketing (i.e. junk mail) and other purposes.
v) Such personal data may be transmitted outside the EU only if the destination country itself provides 'adequate' levels of data protection.

data pump Any process or system that supplies a steady stream of data to another process or system. The term is used, for example, to describe a type of INTEGRATED CIRCUIT employed in building MODEMS whose job is to convert the data stream being transmitted from ANALOGUE to DIGITAL form and vice versa. It is also used to describe a class of software tool that is used to periodically refresh the data in a REPLICATED database to reflect any changes that have been made to the master copy.

data rate The rate at which a DATA TRANSFER between two data storage devices proceeds, typically measured in kilobytes per second or megabytes per second for PARALLEL data streams and kilobits per second or megabits per second for SERIAL data streams. See also BAUD RATE, BANDWIDTH.

data retrieval Locating and extracting data stored in a computer system.

data scrubbing See DATA CLEANSING.

data segment In a computer processor that employs a SEGMENTED MEMORY MODEL, such as the Intel 80x86 family, a segment that is used to store data rather than executable program code. In the Intel architecture a special

processor register, the DS register, is reserved for storing a pointer to the current data segment. See more under 80x86 ARCHITECTURE.

data set Any group of related data items that is to be subjected to some processing operation. Once used by IBM as the term for a FILE, but now obsolete in that usage.

data source Any file, program or device that provides a stream of data for use by another program. Under a CROSS-PLATFORM database interface such as ODBC, the data source is some named file, either local or remote, from which records will be read. See also UNIFORM DATA ACCESS, ACTIVEX DATABASE OBJECTS, OLE DB.

data storage The placing of information into some special place from which it can be retrieved as required. See also STORAGE, DISK STORAGE, MASS STORAGE.

data stream Any continuous procession of data items, for example BITS, BYTES or database RECORDS.

data striping The technique of writing a sequence of data items across a number of different HARD DISKS, to improve either performance or reliability or both. The name implies that successive data items are represented by tracks or stripes on different disk platters. Striping may be employed because a computer's PROCESSOR can generate data faster than any single disk can accept it; each disk in a STRIPE SET has time to position its heads while data is being written to the preceding one.

Striping may also be used as part of a REDUNDANCY scheme to increase reliability since, by duplicating some of the data between disks in the set, the full data can be reconstructed should any single disk fail. See more under BYTE STRIPING and RAID.

data structure A collection of simple data items (e.g. numbers, characters, strings) combined together in a specified way so that they can be manipulated as a single entity. Data structures are employed both to indicate a real-world relationship between the separate items (for example clients' names and their addresses) and to keep them close to one another in memory so the computer can access them efficiently. The ARRAY and the RECORD are the most commonly used data structures, but other examples include the LINKED LIST, the TREE and the HEAP. Data structures may be recursively embedded within one another, as in an array of arrays or a tree of records.

The correct choice of data structure for a program is as important as the correct choice of ALGORITHM to process it, these choices being intimately related since particular algorithms may demand, or work better with, particular data structures. See also ABSTRACT DATA TYPE, OBJECT.

Data Terminal Equipment (DTE) In SERIAL communication systems, a device that can act as a source or destination for data and which controls the communication line. Computers, terminals (both smart and dumb), multiplexers and protocol converters are all DTE devices and are typically connected via a serial line to some DATA COMMUNICATION EQUIPMENT (DCE) such as a MODEM. DTE and DCE are typically connected by an RS-232 serial line, and before sending data the DTE must set the DTR (Data Terminal Ready) signal to tell the DCE that it is ready to transmit and receive. The distinction between these two categories of device is made because their connectors must be wired appropriately so that the transmitting pin of one connects to the receiving pin of the other and vice versa. The RS-232 standard requires that DTE should use a male connector, transmitting on pin three and receiving on pin two. However, by this rule most modern modems are actually DTE rather than DCE.

Data Terminal Ready See under DATA COMMUNICATION EQUIPMENT, DATA TERMINAL EQUIPMENT.

data transfer The movement of data from one storage location to another, either within the same computer, between computers, or between a computer and the outside world. The rate at which such a transfer happens, the DATA RATE, is typically measured in kilobytes per second or megabytes per second.

data type An attribute of any entity in a computer program representing a value (e.g. a VARIABLE, a CONSTANT, a FUNCTION or an EXPRESSION) which specifies what kind and range of values it may take. For example a variable declared to be of data type INTEGER may represent only whole numbers, while a variable of type BOOLEAN may take only the values True or False. Data type is the most fundamental abstraction in programming, since it attributes meaning to what are physically merely strings of BITS of different lengths.

data visualization Representing a set of data using computer GRAPHICS as an aid to interpretation. Techniques range from the simple BAR GRAPH used to visualize a range in a business SPREADSHEET to three-dimensional plots of atomic energy levels produced on a SUPERCOMPUTER. An important part of visualization is the use of FALSE COLOUR to heighten contrasts and to pick out areas of importance. Interactivity is increasingly employed, for example using VIRTUAL REALITY techniques to enable users to rotate and explore 3D models of their data.

data warehouse An intermediary DATABASE used to hold items of immediate interest in the management of a business, extracted from one or more larger databases. For example a large retail chain might build a data warehouse to contain management summaries of monthly sales drawn from the huge MAINFRAME databases that hold the raw daily figures.

A data warehouse typically has live and automated communication links into its raw data sources, so that the data is always up-to-date, and it formats the data in ways most convenient to its users, for example as SPREADSHEETS or documentary reports. The implementation of data warehouses therefore tends to draw on the most leading-edge communications technologies and software AUTOMATION techniques.

See also THREE-TIER ARCHITECTURE, BUSINESS LOGIC.

date arithmetic Performing calculations upon dates, such as finding the number of days between two dates, or the date of Easter.

date stamp To append the current date and/or time of day to a document, file or other data object. Date stamping is a convenient way of distinguishing otherwise similar items, and provides a simple means of establishing the order in which events (say DATABASE updates) occurred. See also REAL TIME CLOCK, DATE ARITHMETIC.

Date Window A rule invented by Microsoft when fixing the YEAR 2000 BUG, to resolve ambiguities over two-digit years, where 20 might refer to 1920 or to 2020 (or indeed to 1820). The Date Window rule interprets two-digit years of 30 and above as lying in the 20th century (1930 onwards), but two-digit years below 30 as lying in the 21st century so 15 means 2015.

daughterboard A small PRINTED CIRCUIT BOARD that plugs directly into a socket on a larger board, and carries chips that add some extra function. Daughterboards are sometimes used to hold a PC's CPU or memory, when they plug directly into the MOTHERBOARD (hence the name). They are also used to add extra features to other expansion cards, such as GRAPHICS CARDS or SOUND CARDS.

daybook 1 In manual book-keeping, a ledger in which the day's transactions were recorded. Hence a MODULE of that name in many computer accounting software suites.

2 In US parlance, a diary of the day's events, sometimes offered as one of the functions in PERSONAL INFORMATION MANAGER programs.

DB2 IBM's RELATIONAL DATABASE software.

dBase II The first effective DATABASE MANAGEMENT SYSTEM for personal computers, written by Wayne Ratliff at the Jet Propulsion Lab for the CP/M operating system, and published in 1980 by Ashton-Tate. dBase went on to become the most popular database under MS-DOS on IBM-compatible PCs, reaching version dBase VI before being eclipsed by Microsoft's ACCESS. Its DBF FILE FORMAT is still widely used by (and imported by) other software products.

DBF (DataBase File) The FILE FORMAT used by Ashton-Tate's DBASE II database manager and its successors, and still supported as an import format by many software products. DBF is a binary file format, which stores the FIELD names used in each database at the start of the file.

DBMS Abbreviation of DATABASE MANAGEMENT SYSTEM.

DC Abbreviation of DIRECT CURRENT.

DCA Abbreviation of DOCUMENT CONTENT ARCHITECTURE.

DCC Abbreviation of DIRECT CLIENT TO CLIENT PROTOCOL.

DCE 1 Abbreviation of DATA COMMUNICATION EQUIPMENT.

2 Abbreviation of DISTRIBUTED COMPUTING ENVIRONMENT.

DCI Abbreviation of DISPLAY CONTROL INTERFACE.

DCOM The DISTRIBUTED version of Microsoft's COMPONENT OBJECT MODEL, under which an object stored on one computer can activate an object on a different computer by calling its METHODS across a network connection. DCOM employs the same invocation mechanism as COM itself (in which a PROXY within the CLIENT process calls a STUB within the SERVER process), but interposes a REMOTE PROCEDURE CALL protocol between proxy and stub, thus permitting the same code to be used to communicate between both local and remote objects (the property described as LOCATION TRANSPARENT).

D connector A type of electrical connector widely used in small computers for both serial and parallel ports and monitor cables, whose shape in cross-section is flat with two parallel rows of pins (or holes) and sloping, trapezoidal ends to prevent insertion upside down. The three most commonly used sizes have 9, 25 or 50 pins. See also SERIAL PORT, CENTRONICS PORT, SCSI, EDGE CONNECTOR.

DCS Abbreviation of DIGITAL CELLULAR SYSTEM.

DCT Abbreviation of DISCRETE COSINE TRANSFORM.

DD 1 Abbreviation of DISK DRIVE.

2 Abbreviation of double density, as in DOUBLE-DENSITY DISKETTE.

DDE Abbreviation of DYNAMIC DATA EXCHANGE.

DDS 1 (Digital Data Storage) The data storage format used by DAT data recorders designed jointly by Sony and Hewlett Packard.

2 (Digital data service) A now-obsolete type of digital LEASED LINE that supported data rates between 2,400 and 56,000 bits per second.

deadlock, deadly embrace A condition that may affect any CONCURRENT program, where two (or more) processes are waiting for the other to do something (e.g. to release some resource) and neither can proceed – think of two people standing in the same doorway both saying 'after you!' A deadlock is in effect a CRASH of the processes concerned, and requires intervention either from a human operator, or from some supervisory program such as a TIMEOUT or WATCHDOG, to close them down.

deadly embrace See under DEADLOCK.

dead tree edition The print-on-paper version of a document that is also available in electronic form.

debugger A software tool that enables a programmer to examine the workings of a program in great detail in order to locate any errors (BUGS). The minimum requirements for any debugger are the ability to 'SINGLE STEP' (to execute the program one instruction at a time) and to examine the contents of particular memory locations. Most debuggers provide the additional abilities to set BREAKPOINTS that stop the program at a particular instruction or when a certain event occurs.

There is an important distinction between a debugger that works only on the compiled or assembled MACHINE CODE of a program, and a so-called SYMBOLIC DEBUGGER that works on the SOURCE CODE of the program, displaying its execution by moving a cursor through the program text. Most modern INTEGRATED DEVELOPMENT ENVIRONMENTS have some degree of symbolic debugging ability built in, so that programmers can single step and set breakpoints from within the same editor that was used to write the code.

debugging The process of using a DEBUGGER to find and fix the errors in a computer program. The natural human tendency is to imagine debugging as a minor task confined to the end of any project, whereas all practical experience indicates that it may take up as much (even more) time than actually writing the code. See also BUG, SYMBOLIC DEBUGGER, BUG FIX, BUG LIST.

DEC Abbreviation of DIGITAL EQUIPMENT CORPORATION.

DEC Alpha More fully named the Alpha AXP, one of the first commercial RISC microprocessors, developed by DIGITAL EQUIPMENT CORPORATION to power the company's successors to its VAX range of minicomputers and first released in 1992. Several early versions of the Alpha held the title of world's fastest microprocessor, running at 166 MHz when competitors were running at less than half that speed, and for several years Alpha AXPs remained several times faster than Intel's best offerings, up to clock speeds of 275 MHz. However, Intel has since caught up with its later Pentium models. The Alpha was the first fully 64-bit processor architecture, and pioneered several new design techniques such as SUPERPIPELINING and SUPERSCALAR execution to enable it to run at higher clock speeds.

The Alpha was mostly used in Unix-based servers and workstations until the mid-1990s when Microsoft ported its WINDOWS NT operating system to run on the Alpha, leading several manufacturers to produce Alpha-based PC-compatible workstations – though such machines could not directly run Intel binary code, EMULATION software (see under FX!32) permitted them to run Intel programs at an acceptable speed thanks to the Alpha's high performance. However, Microsoft withdrew support for Alpha with WINDOWS 2000, putting the chip's future commercial viability in doubt.

decidability One of the core concepts of computability theory. A SET is said to be decidable if some program (typically, an abstract TURING MACHINE) exists that can determine whether a given number is in the set, and this program will always terminate with the answer yes or no after a finite number of steps. There exist sets that are not so decidable, as in the famous HALTING PROBLEM.

decimal notation The number representation used in everyday life: a positional notation expressed in powers of 10, so that for example 529 stands for $5\times10^2 + 2\times10^1 + 9\times10^0$. The BASE 10 was adopted because humans have 10 fingers and counting on them was the original form of 'digital' computation. However, for programming modern digital computers, notations based on integral powers of 2 (such as HEXADECIMAL NOTATION based on 16) are more convenient.

decision problem Any problem that has a yes/no answer, examples of which might include 'is X a fish' or 'is 453 a prime number'. The term is used by computer scientists to distinguish such problems from SEARCH PROBLEMS, which involve examining many potential answers (for example 'what is X's telephone number'). A decision problem requires only the application of some test to its input values, but this does not mean that such problems are always easily solved. Many decision problems are known to be NP-HARD, including some surprisingly simple jigsaw-like rearrangement puzzles.

decision tree A data structure used in many types of ARTIFICIAL INTELLIGENCE software and now in DATA MINING, which codifies a particular line of human reasoning as a tree built from questions, with branches to represent each possible answer. Such a tree may be constructed manually by interrogating a human expert, or extracted automatically from a database of examples by using some form of INDUCTION algorithm. See also RULE-BASED SYSTEM, EXPERT SYSTEM, CASE BASED REASONING.

declaration A statement within a computer program that introduces some new named data object or procedure that is to be manipulated by the program. See more under DECLARE.

declarative language Any PROGRAMMING LANGUAGE that describes relationships between data items, rather than specifying the exact sequence of steps the computer should take to process them. Logic programming languages such as PROLOG and functional languages such as HASKELL are declarative, while SQL has many declarative features. Proponents of declarative languages claim that they correspond more closely to human thinking, and hence enable programs to be written more quickly and with fewer errors. However, they are typically less efficient to execute on a computer than are conventional or PROCEDURAL LANGUAGES.

declarative semantics A way of describing the meaning of a computer program as a collection of relationships between data items rather than as a sequence of computational steps. See also DECLARATIVE LANGUAGE, OPERATIONAL SEMANTICS, DENOTATIONAL SEMANTICS, AXIOMATIC SEMANTICS.

declare To specify the type and other properties of some object such as a VARIABLE, DATA STRUCTURE or PROCEDURE in the SOURCE CODE of a program. Many, perhaps most, programming languages insist that all variables be declared before they may be used, though some versions of BASIC and FORTRAN can detect the use of a new variable and make default assumptions about its type. Compulsory declaration is helpful to programmers as it prevents them from accidentally creating a second object with the same name, which may cause hard-to-detect program errors.

decode 1 To restore to readability a document that has been encoded using a CIPHER, by reversing the encoding procedure using a KEY.
2 In a computer PROCESSOR, the stage of program execution immediately following INSTRUCTION FETCH, where the freshly read instruction word is translated by the CONTROL UNIT into a sequence of MICROINSTRUCTIONS that set-up the processor's gates, buses and registers to perform the required operation. In RISC and VLIW designs the decode stage becomes trivial, with each bit in the instruction word directly driving one of the processor's functional units.

decoder 1 In general, any device that DECODES encoded information. See CODEC.
2 Hence in satellite or cable TV systems, the SET-TOP BOX that decodes encrypted programmes for customers who have paid the fee.
3 In computer hardware engineering, a circuit that translates BIT PATTERNS into an action of some sort. For example: a processor's CONTROL UNIT decodes INSTRUCTION words and performs the specified operation; an ADDRESS decoder translates bits sent on the address lines into the signals to retrieve data from a RAM chip.

decompiler A program that can take the binary OBJECT CODE of a COMPILED program and reconstruct its SOURCE CODE in some programming language. Decompilation is far easier for SEMI-COMPILED programs, for which the names of program variables may still be present in the compiled code. For a fully compiled program, the decompiler has to invent new names for all the variables and subroutines. See also REVERSE ENGINEER, OBFUSCATE.

decompress To expand a DATA FILE that has been compressed. See more under COMPRESSION.

decouple To remove a direct dependency between two systems. For example: a CACHE decouples the timing constraints of the processor from those of its external memory system; an operating system decouples application programs from the low-level details of the hardware's operations.

decrement To decrease the value of some quantity. The amount of the decrement is often implied to be one, as when decreasing a COUNTER or when moving a POINTER to point to the previous address in a sequence. See also INCREMENT.

decrypt To retrieve the original or PLAINTEXT version of a message that has been ENCRYPTED.

DECT (Digital Enhanced Cordless Telecommunications) A wireless digital communication technology formerly used mainly in domestic cordless telephones but now being promoted for a wider range of applications. A DECT system consists of one or more fixed base stations and one or more mobile units such as telephone handsets. It employs a TIME DIVISION MULTIPLEXING cellular scheme with 10 separate carrier frequencies in the 1880–1900 MHz band, enabling up to 12 simultaneous channels of voice data to be supported by each DECT transceiver. Each such channel can carry 32 kilobits per second full-duplex, using ADCPM encoding, and several such channels can be combined into one to provide a variety of different bandwidth options.

While a typical range for indoor DECT equipment is 30–50 metres it can be extended as far as 5 kilometres with line-of-sight antennae, and it can support very large numbers of users in the same space (up to a staggering 100,000 per square kilometre). DECT is now finding favour for wireless PBX (PRIVATE BRANCH EXCHANGE) installations in large offices and factories with several thousand users. See also MOBILE PHONE, BLUETOOTH, WI-FI.

DECUS Abbreviation of Digital Equipment Computer Users Society.

dedupe, deduplicate The operation of removing duplicate entries from a DATABASE of names and addresses. Duplicate RECORDS are those that refer to the same person, even if they are not literally identical. Records that are absolutely identical are easy to find by simply SORTING the data, when they will appear next to one another.

However, the problem lies with those records that are not literally identical – for example entries for 'John Doe', 'Mr John Doe' and 'Doe, John' could sort in completely different positions. Deduplicating these cases can be helped by better organization of the data, such as storing the salutation (Mr), first name (John) and surname (Doe) in separate fields, but even that will not catch a case such as Dick Pountain versus Richard Pountain.

Deduping programs employ a variety of powerful TEXT SEARCH matching criteria to find such cases, and then present a list of those found to the human operator, who must ultimately decide whether they refer to the same person or not. See also DATA CLEANSING, LIST MANAGEMENT.

default The value that a system PARAMETER takes on before any changes the user may make to it, and which is typically restored whenever the system is started up. See also CONFIGURATION, FACTORY DEFAULT.

defect analysis A procedure used in QUALITY CONTROL that seeks to classify defects into categories and to identify their possible causes.

defect density 1 In semiconductor fabrication, the number of defects per square centimetre that are present on an average WAFER. The definition of what constitutes a defect is not absolute, but becomes tighter as the FEATURE SIZE is reduced: the same wafer might display only 5 defects per square centimeter when used for fabricating medium-scale integrated devices, but have a density of 50 defects per square centimeter at the scale of VLSI components.

2 In software development, the ratio between the number of known BUGS a program contains and its length: for example, 0.03 defects

per line. This gives a rough measure of overall program quality. See also SOFTWARE METRICS, TESTING.

Defense Advanced Research Project Agency
See DARPA.

defrag Shorthand for DEFRAGMENT.

defragger See under FRAGMENTATION.

defragment To reorganize the contents of a HARD DISK drive so that all its free areas form a contiguous block, the purpose being to speed up its operation. See more under FRAGMENTATION.

degauss To demagnetize a computer's display MONITOR and thereby restore its picture quality. Over time, the monitor's steel chassis becomes permanently magnetized by fields generated in the coils of the CATHODE RAY TUBE, and this may distort the electron beam and defocus the picture. The Degauss button on a professional monitor triggers a large pulse of high-frequency current that removes this unwanted magnetism.

delaminate A mode of failure in which the separate layers of some structure (for example a PRINTED CIRCUIT BOARD) come unstuck.

delay **1** v. To retard the occurrence of some event by a period of time.
2 n. The period by which such an event is retarded.
In computing, delay is frequently a matter that must be known with great precision, especially when REAL TIME constraints have to be met. Examples include the delay in a hard disk drive mechanism as the heads move from track-to-track, the delay in sending a packet over a network, or the delay caused by memory accesses within a microprocessor.

delayed-write A type of disk CACHE in which data written by the processor is not written immediately back to the disk, but held back until the WRITE can be most efficiently performed, for example when the drives write HEADS have moved into the correct position.

delay-sensitive traffic See under RESOURCE RESERVATION PROTOCOL.

delay slot See under BRANCH DELAY SLOT.

delegation A schema employed in some OBJECT-ORIENTED PROGRAMMING LANGUAGES (for example JAVA) to supplement or replace INHERITANCE, wherein an instance of one class acts as a proxy toward an object of another class, allowing the latter to access the former's METHODS.
For example, in the Java delegation EVENT model, one object (e.g. a button) can be registered as an event source, and another object containing code as a 'listener' whose methods get invoked whenever the source generates an event.

delimiter A symbol employed to distinguish the consecutive parts of some data structure (e.g. a RECORD) from one another. In the following example a comma is used as a delimiter:

```
Pountain, 456, green, unperforated
```

A delimiter is also sometimes called a SEPARATOR, but it is not the same as a TERMINATOR which is used only to mark the end of such a structure.

deliverable Jargon term meaning a completed software product, i.e. as delivered to a customer.

Dell Computer Corporation A highly successful US PC manufacturer that only sells direct to customers by mail order, not through shops.

Delphi **1** A VISUAL PROGRAMMING system launched by BORLAND INTERNATIONAL INC. in 1994 which combines a fast compiler for an OBJECT-ORIENTED dialect of PASCAL with a library of visual components within an INTEGRATED DEVELOPMENT ENVIRONMENT. Delphi comes supplied with its own proprietary VISUAL COMPONENT LIBRARY of controls (with full source code), but it can also incorporate controls written to Microsoft's ACTIVEX object model.
Delphi differs from VISUAL BASIC in two important respects: it compiles into standalone executable files that need no RUN-TIME LIBRARY, and its visual programming metaphor is two-directional, meaning that the textual description of any visual object can be retrieved by dragging it into an editing window. Delphi evolved out of Borland's famous TURBO PASCAL compiler.

2 One of the pioneering US online CONFER-ENCING SYSTEMS, set up in Cambridge, Massachusetts in 1983. Now an INTERNET SERVICE PROVIDER that offers web-based shared-interest 'forums' at www.delphi.com.

delta A small change between two successive sets of data, derived from the mathematical usage of the term to name small differences. Many forms of DATA COMPRESSION are based on saving only the deltas, or changes, in a data set. For example the MPEG system saves only the changes between consecutive frames of a movie, while many VERSION CONTROL systems save only the changes between successive versions of a document or programming project.

delta encoding A method of reducing storage space by saving only changes. See more under DELTA.

demand driven Any system in which activity is initiated only in response to requests, rather than to some pre-set schedule. See, for example, DEMAND-PAGED.

demand-paged Any type of VIRTUAL MEMORY scheme in which a new page is automatically loaded from disk into main memory whenever a reference is made to an address that it contains. See also MEMORY MANAGEMENT UNIT, PAGE IN, PAGE FAULT.

demo A demonstration of the operation of some hardware or software product.

demodulate To extract message information from a CARRIER wave onto which it has been superimposed in order to transmit it as a signal over some communications channel. See also MODULATE, MODEM.

demo effect An allusion to the well-known phenomenon whereby a new product that works perfectly in the lab breaks down only when it is demonstrated to outsiders. A curiously selective extension to MURPHY'S LAW.

demographic **1** Pertaining to the scientific study of human populations, especially their size and geographical distribution.
2 Hence a euphemism used in the marketing world, to describe all kinds of stored information about people, such as their age, class, ethnic origin, income and postcode.

demon See DAEMON.

demo version A version of a software product provided free of charge to allow users to examine its features. It is typically restricted in some way to prevent serious use, for example by having its ability to save data disabled, or by ceasing to work altogether after a 30-day time limit. See also CRIPPLEWARE.

demultiplex To separate out two or more signals that have been combined and transmitted down the same communications channel. See also MULTIPLEX.

demux A common abbreviation for DEMULTIPLEX. See also MUX.

denial of service attack A strategy used by HACKERS to close down a web site by writing SCRIPTS that bombard the site with fake page requests from multiple locations. The excess traffic generated may be sufficient to cause the WEB SERVER to run out of memory or disk space, and so crash. See also MAIL BOMB, TROJAN HORSE.

denotational semantics A way of ascribing a meaning to computer programs by describing them as mathematical functions that operate on other programs. See also AXIOMATIC SEMANTICS, OPERATIONAL SEMANTICS.

departmental A marketing category that describes servers and networks whose size lies somewhere between the WORKGROUP (tens of users) and the ENTERPRISE (thousands of users) levels. See also MIDRANGE SYSTEM.

depletion layer The region surrounding an np junction within a SEMICONDUCTOR, which becomes depleted of positive charge carriers when a voltage is applied, and is responsible for the CAPACITANCE of the junction.

deployment A late stage in the software development process in which the product is installed onto the computers it will be used on. Deployment is rarely as simple as merely copying the program's executable files onto the target computer, because the correct execution environment has to be established, which may involve such factors as the amount of memory present, the correct version of the OPERATING SYSTEM, establishing the identity of certain peripherals such as GRAPHICS CARDS, and the presence of any required external software LIBRARIES in a location that is visible to the program (see PATH).

For DISTRIBUTED software systems, deployment may be a major exercise as not only does the correct environment have to be established on each machine in the network but all the links between them have to be correctly configured too. See also CONFIGURATION MANAGEMENT.

depth cueing In 3D GRAPHICS, the use of ALPHA BLENDING to make distant objects progressively more blue and less saturated according to their distance from the viewer, which heightens the realism of a scene. See also FOGGING.

depth-first search A class of ALGORITHM for searching in a TREE-STRUCTURED graph, which works by extending the current search path as far as possible until a LEAF NODE of the tree is reached, then BACKTRACKING to the previous fork and trying the next alternative path, until all NODES have been visited. A depth-first search can be used to determine whether the graph contains a CYCLE, that is a circular path, by recording whether or not each node has already been visited. Depth-first search is a very old method, being the preferred way of solving mazes as long ago as the 16th century. It is generally the first method of choice unless the nature of the data suggests that the alternative BREADTH-FIRST SEARCH would be more efficient.

depth of field 1 In an optical system, the range of distances from the lens surface within which the image can be brought to a sharp focus. Depth of field increases in direct proportion as the aperture of the lens decreases.

2 A trick employed in rendering computer 3D GRAPHICS to mimic the depth of field variations of a real camera lens.

dereference To access the item pointed to by a POINTER, i.e. to follow the pointer.

derived class The name given to a SUBCLASS in C++ and some other OBJECT-ORIENTED languages.

derived type 1 In the C language, a new DATA TYPE that consists of an ARRAY, STRUCTURE, or UNION of, a POINTER to, or a FUNCTION returning, one or more simpler data types.

2 In ADA and some other programming languages, a data type that is based on an existing type and inherits all its properties but is distinct from it so that objects of the two types may not be mixed. For example a type Year might be derived from the type Integer.

DES Abbreviation of DATA ENCRYPTION STANDARD.

descender A vertical stroke in a typographical CHARACTER that projects below the line on which the characters rest, for example the stalks of the letters p, q and y in lower-case Roman fonts. See also ASCENDER.

descriptor An INTEGER, STRING or other data item attached to some software entity (for example a file, a VIRTUAL MEMORY page, a DIRECT MEMORY ACCESS transfer buffer) by the operating system to distinguish it from other similar instances. See also HANDLE, ID, CAPABILITY.

design One of the main phases of any software development, which comes after the SPECIFICATION but before the writing of any CODE. The design stage includes tasks such as breaking down the problem into manageable sub-problems, choosing suitable DATA STRUCTURES and ALGORITHMS. Program design is an intensively studied subject, and there are many competing design methodologies that claim to simplify or formalize the task.

design methodology See METHODOLOGY.

design pattern A concept used in OBJECT-ORIENTED DESIGN to refer to any program structure or scenario that is encountered sufficiently often to be worth abstracting into a CLASS, so that it can be easily modified and reused. An example of a commonly encountered pattern could be an interaction where a user picks some item from a screen list and that item is then retrieved from a disk file.

desktop 1 The screen display of a computer operating system that employs a GRAPHICAL USER INTERFACE, showing a collection of ICONS and other visual objects that the user can click on with a mouse to initiate different operations: programs thus executed appear within their own WINDOW on the desktop. The name suggests the metaphorical character of such interfaces, which loosely mimic a real desk, each window resembling a piece of paper on that desk.

2 Used as an adjective to describe computer equipment and software that is designed to operate on a (real) desktop, as distinct from portable equipment (for example LAPTOP or PALMTOP computers) and large mainframe installations that occupy a whole room.

3 A related meaning distinguishes between the horizontal or desktop style of a PC case and the vertical, floor-standing TOWER-STYLE CASE.

desktop presentation An alternative name for PRESENTATION GRAPHICS, coined by analogy with DESKTOP PUBLISHING.

desktop printer A printer that is connected directly to a personal computer, for the use of its single owner, in contrast to a printer that is shared by many users over a network.

desktop publishing (DTP) The design of publication-quality documents on a desktop computer. Desktop publishing applications (such as QUARK XPRESS or Adobe's INDESIGN) differ from WORD PROCESSORS in offering more precise placement of pictures and arrangement of text on the page, and more controllable typographic parameters such as LEADING and KERNING. Typically, raw text will be created in a conventional word processor and then imported into a DTP program for page layout. Finished layouts may then be printed on a laser printer or exported in POSTSCRIPT format for processing by professional typesetting equipment.

desktop video Editing video on a personal computer. Video data from an ANALOGUE camcorder must be digitized and stored on the PC's hard disk in some compressed format (see under VIDEO COMPRESSION) before it can be edited – however, DIGITAL camcorders, which are increasingly popular, can download straight into the computer. The latest PCs have sufficient CPU power to digitize and decompress MPEG video in software, but earlier machines require hardware assistance from an add-on VIDEO CAPTURE card.

despeckle An operation provided in many IMAGE PROCESSING and COLOUR RETOUCHING programs which removes spots – that is, very small areas of contrasting colour – left as unwanted artefacts after cut-outs, certain types of filtering operation such as POSTERIZATION, or a FLOOD FILL to a complicated boundary. See also SPECKLE.

Desqview A utility for MS-DOS, published by Quarterdeck, which enabled rapid CONTEXT SWITCHING between several programs without having to load and reload them – it was popular in the late 1980s, prior to the emergence of effective MULTITASKING in WINDOWS 3.0. See also TERMINATE AND STAY RESIDENT, CONTEXT SWITCH.

destination address **1** The memory or register address to which data is to be moved by some processor instruction. See also ADDRESSING MODE.

2 The first 6 bytes of a standard ETHERNET FRAME, which contains the ADDRESS of the WORKSTATION to which the frame is being sent.

destructor In OBJECT-ORIENTED PROGRAMMING, a special METHOD possessed by every object which is called to dismantle the object and reclaim the memory it occupied when it is no longer required. See also CONSTRUCTOR.

deterministic automaton A class of AUTOMATON that always arrives at the same finishing state whenever it is given the same starting state, initial inputs and sequence of program steps. See also NONDETERMINISTIC, CHOMSKY HIERARCHY.

Deutsche Industrie Normen See DIN.

developer A PROGRAMMER, one who develops programs.

development A contraction of 'software development', i.e. computer programming, used as a prefix in terms such as 'development system' and 'development tool' that describe products intended for programmers rather than for END-USERS.

development system **1** A suite of software used for writing computer programs, including at least a COMPILER and LINKER, a PROGRAM EDITOR and a DEBUGGER, but often containing many other software tools as well. Sometimes these components are all combined to form an INTEGRATED DEVELOPMENT ENVIRONMENT (as for example with VISUAL BASIC).

2 A computer or workstation, with software as in **1** installed on it, that is reserved for writing programs rather than for other duties.

device **1** In general, any piece of computer HARDWARE, from a single chip to a laser printer.

2 More specifically, a piece of hardware whose presence is known to a computer's OPERATING SYSTEM and for which a DEVICE DRIVER is installed to enable it to be accessed. So far as the operating system is concerned, a device is something that can act as a source or destination for data, and some devices are therefore given special names that may be used to identify them in DATA TRANSFER commands. The most familiar examples are the names of disk drives under MS-DOS and Windows, such as C: and D: (the terminating colon indicates that this is the name of a device). Similarly, the printer may be addressed as the device LPT: and the display as device CON:. Unix employs a different system for naming devices, so that, for example, a terminal might be addressed as /dev/tyy5.

device driver A small program that provides the interface between a computer and some piece of PERIPHERAL hardware such as a display adapter, disk drive or printer, translating generic requests from the computer's OPERATING SYSTEM (e.g. 'display a block of bytes') into the precise commands required by the device. Drivers require intimate knowledge of the device's internal hardware ARCHITECTURE, down to the level of PORT and REGISTER addresses and any INTERRUPTS it uses – they are therefore usually written by the device's manufacturer and supplied with it on a floppy disk or CD, to be installed by the user.

Whenever a peripheral is replaced, say a new GRAPHICS CARD is substituted for old, its device driver must also be replaced during the installation process. Manufacturers periodically issue revised device drivers for existing equipment that fix reported bugs or support extra features, and these are typically announced on and downloaded from the manufacturer's web site. See also PLUG-AND-PLAY.

device independent Capable of working with many different types of hardware. For example, the POSTSCRIPT language is device independent because a page described in it can be printed on many kinds of printer. Most of the advances in software design in recent years have involved a moving toward device independence, most notably in World Wide Web technologies such as HTML, XML, SVG and UDDI. See also OPEN SYSTEMS.

Device independence is in general more highly prized among software vendors, since it increases their potential market, than it is among hardware vendors who may have a vested interest in tying customers to their own brands.

device independent bitmap (DIB) A 24-bit GRAPHICS FILE FORMAT invented by Microsoft and used first in OS/2 and later in WINDOWS, which usually employs the filename extension .DIB. Unlike ordinary Windows BMP files, DIB files do not store their PIXEL data as BIT PLANES for any particular DISPLAY ADAPTER, but store it in an arbitrary order that is indicated in the file's header. They may therefore be displayed on any computer running Windows regardless of what graphics hardware is installed, hence the name. DIB files may be set up to apply RUN-LENGTH ENCODING to reduce their size. The format is now little used, having been largely supplanted by the JPEG, GIF and TIFF formats for most professional purposes.

Dewey decimal system A hierarchical numeric classification system used throughout most of the world's libraries to organize books by category.

D flip-flop See FLIP-FLOP.

DHCP Abbreviation of DYNAMIC HOST CONFIGURATION PROTOCOL.

Dhrystone A popular BENCHMARK that measures the INTEGER arithmetic performance of a PROCESSOR or COMPILER. (The original benchmark for FLOATING-POINT performance was called WHETSTONE, after its inventor's name, so Dhrystone is a play on words.)

DHTML Abbreviation of DYNAMIC HTML.

diacritic, diacritical, diacritical mark A series of strokes written above or below an alphabetic character or other symbol to modify its phonetic value (e.g. its length or nasality), to indicate a stress, or for any other reason. Examples of diacritics include the various accents employed in European languages (as in soigneé, soupçon, niño) and the hiatus in English (as in coïncidence).

Displaying diacritics used to present a major problem for computers since the plain

ASCII character set does not include them all (but see EXTENDED ASCII) and they occupy the same position on a line as the character they modify, thus requiring the cursor or print-head to backspace to add them. These difficulties are now largely overcome with the introduction of the UNICODE character set which includes all common character/diacritic combinations, though problems still remain over keyboard layout, and the way such characters are accessed from within popular application programs often remains awkward. See also INTERNATIONALIZATION.

diagnostic A piece of software that tests the functioning of some electronic system such as a computer or network, and reports the nature of any faults it discovers. See for example POWER-ON SELF TEST, NORTON UTILITIES, SNMP, SYSTEMS MANAGEMENT SERVER.

dialect A variant of a PROGRAMMING LANGUAGE in which some of the KEYWORDS may have different meanings.

dialler A software utility that can initiate calls on a tone-dialled telephone line by using a MODEM, and hence allows numbers held in an address database to be automatically dialled.

dialogue, dialogue box (*US* dialog) A visual USER INTERFACE component used to present information to users of a software system and elicit their response. A dialogue is a small pop-up WINDOW containing a text message, possibly an ICON indicating the type of message (e.g. error, query), and one or more BUTTONS (e.g. 'OK' and 'Cancel') that the user must press to continue. Some dialogues enforce user attention by freezing all other screen objects while they are visible (see MODAL DIALOGUE).

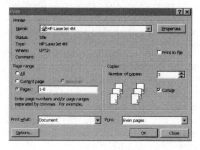

dial-up Any communications link made via a public telephone line in which the user (or a

modem) has to dial a telephone number to establish the connection – hence 'dial-up internet access', or a 'dial-up BBS'.

DIB 1 Abbreviation of DEVICE INDEPENDENT BITMAP.
   2 Abbreviation of DUAL INDEPENDENT BUS.

dice The plural of DIE.

dictionary 1 A book, such as this one, which lists words and their meanings.
   2 A data structure employed in several programming languages including POSTSCRIPT and SMALLTALK which consists of a list of pairs of keys and their values, a kind of ASSOCIATIVE ARRAY. In FORTH the dictionary consists of a list of subprograms called words, together with the code for the actions that they initiate when called. See also DATA DICTIONARY.

die The technical term for a small rectangular piece of silicon, cut from a WAFER and bearing an INTEGRATED CIRCUIT layout, that is informally called a silicon CHIP. Its plural is dice.

dielectric A material that does not conduct electric current (more precisely, it has a very large electrical RESISTANCE), but transmits electrostatic fields easily. The dielectric constant is a measure of the magnitude of this effect for a particular substance. Dielectric materials are used for separating the plates of CAPACITORS and the coils of transformers. Thin dielectric films are deposited onto glass in the manufacture of LCD displays, and flexible dielectric films are employed in some types of GRAPHICS TABLET that work by altering capacitance. The dielectric constant is closely related to refractive index, and transparent dielectric materials frequently have optical properties useful in the fields of optical communications and computing.

differential backup A variety of BACKUP regime for computer data that copies only the files that have changed since the last full backup and leaves their archive flags set. After a mishap the last full backup must be restored, but then only the most recent differential backup need be applied. Compare with INCREMENTAL BACKUP.

diffusion layer Sometimes abbreviated to 'diffusion', a region on the surface of a SILICON chip that has been DOPED to alter its conducting properties.

digerati The rich, famous, great and good of the computer industry, aka the usual suspects.

digicam Shorthand for a DIGITAL CAMCORDER.

DigiCash A Dutch firm that created one of the first electronic payment schemes. Users open an account with one of the participating banks, which issues 'ecash' that can be transmitted via EMAIL or spent on participating WEB SITES. See also MICROPAYMENT, MICROBILLING, MILLICENT.

digital Any communication or computing technology whose data may have only a finite number of discrete values. By contrast, analogue technologies work with values that vary continuously, and may take an infinity of different values. In this sense an abacus or the Roman alphabet are digital technologies, while a ruler is an analogue device. The term is normally reserved for electronic technologies that work on BINARY data composed of the two values 0 and 1. Computing and networking are digital technologies, while older public telephone and television systems were analogue.

Digital electronics made modern computing possible, and is replacing analogue electronics in most other fields because of its intrinsic resistance to error and noise. In an analogue sound system, for example, the fidelity of reproduction depends on the circuits' ability to accurately reproduce a continuously varying voltage, and every tiny deviation is heard as distortion. In a digital sound system the circuits need only be able to distinguish 0 volts (representing a 0) from 5 volts (representing a 1); if interference caused the voltage to wander, even by as much as 2 volts, this would not prevent discriminating between a 0 and a 1.

digital audio Sound stored in some electronic medium by SAMPLING it to represent it as a stream of BITS. Typically digital audio is stored on CD, MAGNETIC TAPE or computer HARD DISK. The fidelity with which such digitized data can reproduce the original sound depends on the number of samples taken per second, and the number of bits per sample (for a commercial music CD these are 44.1 KHz at 16 bits per sample). There are several different formats for encoding and storing digital audio. See also DAT, WAV, MP3, SAMPLING RATE.

digital audio tape See DAT.

digital camera A class of image recording device that employs a traditional camera lens to focus images onto a light sensitive chip (see more under CHARGE-COUPLED DEVICE) instead of photographic film, and stores the resulting images as digital data that can be loaded into a computer for processing and printing. Most current digital cameras employ some kinds of removable memory card to store images (see COMPACT FLASH, SD CARD) and a fast serial interface such as FIREWIRE to transfer them.

Digital Cellular System (DCS) A cellular wireless telephone standard derived from GSM, designed for urban applications and so employing a smaller cell size to offer higher densities of subscribers. It also operates in a higher (1800 Hz) frequency band.

digital certificate A small file of encrypted information issued by some recognized certifying authority, which can be used as a proof of the user's identity during online transactions. The certificate is used as a private key to generate a DIGITAL SIGNATURE from a message that authenticates its origin when decrypted by the receiver. Certification agencies that issue such certificates include the commercial organizations Verisign, Thawte Personal and GTE CyberTrust, plus many public authorities. Most WEB BROWSERS can now automatically store and present such certificates to sites that require them.

digital computer A COMPUTER whose operations are performed on a range of discrete values (usually finite sequences of 0s and 1s), in contrast with an ANALOGUE COMPUTER, which manipulates continuously varying physical quantities such as voltages. See also DIGITAL, BINARY NUMBER.

Digital Dashboard A software technology introduced by Microsoft that enables a number of different external information sources – say a weather forecast, a stock price ticker and a movie guide – to be easily combined together onto a single web page and published over an intranet.

digital data Quantities encoded using a range of discrete values (typically finite sequences of 0s and 1s), in contrast to ANALOGUE data, which represents quantities using continuously varying physical properties, such as voltages or magnetic fields. See also DIGITAL, DIGITAL COMPUTER.

Digital Data Storage See under DDS.

Digital Enhanced Cordless Telecommunications See DECT.

Digital Equipment Corporation (DEC) The most successful of the second-generation of computer manufacturers, whose 1967 PDP-1 was the first true MINICOMPUTER. Its PDP (Program Data Processor) and later VAX series created the market for computers in small companies and university departments. Interactive software and TIME-SHARING operating systems (including UNIX) were pioneered on DEC minicomputers, which also comprised many of the hosts on the early INTERNET. However DEC failed to adapt quickly enough to the rise of the microprocessor and the PC, and lost much of its earlier dominance, eventually merging with COMPAQ in 1998.

digital image A picture represented or stored as a sequence of BINARY NUMBERS. See also DIGITIZE, SAMPLE, BITMAP.

Digital Light Processor (DLP) An innovative chip made by TEXAS INSTRUMENTS which is the first practical application of NANOTECHNOLOGY. It contains an array of thousands of tiny, hinged aluminium mirrors, each sited over a capacitor that when charged bends the mirror and thus deflects the light reflected from it – hence each mirror becomes a PIXEL that can be turned on or off. Because it works by reflected rather than transmitted light, the DLP can employ more powerful light sources than an LCD-based system, and so it is used in powerful PC projection systems.

Digital Linear Tape (DLT) A digital magnetic tape storage format originally invented by DEC but later commercialized by Quantum. DLT does not employ rotating helical scan heads (unlike DAT) but instead writes data as longitudinal tracks (hence the name) many of which can be written in parallel. DLT applies data COMPRESSION algorithms, implemented in both software and FIRMWARE, and hardware-assisted string searching to increase both retrieval speed and capacity: DLT cartridge capacities range from 20 to 500 gigabytes and transfer speeds up to 40 megabytes per second. DLT drives are mostly used in larger computer installations and for building archival JUKEBOX systems.

Digital Nervous System Microsoft's marketing term for a group of web-based networking technologies built into WINDOWS 2000.

Digital Network Architecture (DNA) A proprietary network ARCHITECTURE developed by DEC as the basis of its DECNet product range. DNA employs a layered protocol model (see LAYER), but differs from the OPEN SYSTEMS INTERCONNECTION model in having 8 layers.

Digital Signal Processor (DSP) A type of MICROPROCESSOR specially designed for processing continuous streams of data (such as those encountered in sound and video editing) in REAL TIME, rather than fixed blocks of data stored in a memory. DSP chips provide the processing power in most modems and computer sound cards, laser printers, electronic musical instruments (e.g. to generate special effects), mobile telephones, and much radio, television and radar equipment.

DSP architectures are optimized for rapid reading of input data, and for fast execution of certain arithmetic operations that are heavily used within signal processing ALGORITHMS, such as MULTIPLY-ACCUMULATE and MULTIPLY-ADD.

digital signature A small parcel of data appended to an electronic message to authenticate the identity of its sender.

Digital signatures operate using a PUBLIC-KEY ENCRYPTION method. The sender's mail software uses a HASH FUNCTION to generate around 32 bits of signature data from the message content, and then encrypts this using a private key. The receiver's software applies the same hash function to the message, and also decodes the attached signature using the public key. Only if these are the same is the message authentic. See also AUTHENTICATION, ENCRYPTION.

Digital Subscriber Line (xDSL) A whole class of digital telecommunication technologies that can offer BROADBAND data rates, up to 50 megabits per second (Mbps), over the existing copper wires of the analogue public telephone system. By employing advanced modulation schemes, xDSL technologies support Internet or other data access simultaneously with voice telephone calls. In the meta-acronym xDSL, the x stands for the first letter of any of the individual acronyms used for these technologies: ADSL, HDSL, SDSL and VDSL.

The xDSL technologies vary in the relative speeds of their incoming and outgoing signals, and in the distance from the exchange over which they can operate, each making a different trade-off in its exploitation of the available BANDWIDTH. All are, in telecom jargon, 'last mile' technologies, designed only to carry signals over the last mile into the home or office, rather than between cities or countries.

The best-known variant ADSL (Asymmetric Digital Subscriber Line) supports a downstream data rate into the subscriber's home of 1.5 Mbps, sufficient for an MPEG compressed video signal, at up to 18,000 feet from the exchange. However the upstream rate back to the exchange is only 16–640 kilobits per second, hence the name, 'Asymmetric'. ADSL is currently being deployed commercially in several areas of the USA and in the UK.

HDSL (High-data-rate Digital Subscriber Line) employs more advanced modulation techniques to deliver 2 Mbps in both directions over two wires, at up to 12,000 feet, while SDSL (Single-line Digital Subscriber Line) delivers similar rates over a single wire.

VDSL (Very-high-data-rate Digital Subscriber Line) is asymmetric like ADSL but with a higher downstream data rate of 13 Mbps at 4500 feet and up to 50 Mbps at 1000 feet (sufficient for a high-definition television signal): its upstream rate is around 2 Mbps.

Digital to Analogue Converter (DAC) An electronic circuit that takes a DIGITAL value representing a binary number, and outputs an ANALOGUE voltage proportional to that number. DACs may be made as stand-alone chips, but they are often incorporated as part of a larger INTEGRATED CIRCUIT chip. DACs are central to the working of many types of computer output peripheral, transforming digital data that has been processed by the computer into the variable voltages required to drive physical devices such as motors, cathode ray

tubes and loudspeakers. For example in GRAPHICS CARDS a set of three DACs generates the red, green and blue colour signals to drive an ANALOGUE MONITOR, while in SOUND CARDS DACs are employed to generate the audio signal that is sent to the loudspeakers or headphones. See also ANALOGUE-TO-DIGITAL CONVERTER, RAMDAC.

Digital Versatile Disc, Digital Video Disc Abbreviation of DVD.

Digital Video Interactive (DVI) A digital video technology originally developed by RCA but bought by Intel and launched as an Intel/IBM joint venture in 1989. It ran on Intel 80x86 family CPUs and supported FULL-MOTION VIDEO at up to 30 frames per second at resolutions up to 1024 by 768 pixels and 24-bit colour. DVI required hardware assistance from a special Intel chipset to perform VIDEO COMPRESSION in real time and, with the advent of the more powerful PENTIUM family of microprocessors, it was replaced by the software-only INDEO standard which is descended from DVI.

digital watermark A scheme for applying hidden identifying marks to DIGITAL pictures, to enable copyright claims to be pursued. The watermark stores information about the author in the BITMAP data for the picture itself, encoded as small variations in the LEAST SIGNIFICANT BITS of each PIXEL that cannot be detected by the human eye but only by decoding software.

digitize To convert the ANALOGUE representation of some physical phenomenon, such as an image or a sound, into a sequence of binary numbers of fixed size, so that it may be processed by a computer. This is accomplished by SAMPLING the analogue data: measuring its amplitude at periodic intervals (in either time or space) and expressing each sample in binary form. For example a SCANNER and a digital video camera both digitize a continuous tone picture to produce a digital image file. See also ANALOGUE-TO-DIGITAL CONVERTER, SAMPLING RATE, NYQUIST FREQUENCY.

digitizer 1 In general, any device that converts an ANALOGUE quantity into a DIGITAL one.

2 Most often applied to a class of electrical devices that continuously translate the

spatial position of a pointer or pen in two dimensions into a stream of digital signals, used to manufacture GRAPHICS TABLETS, TOUCH SCREENS and pocket computers that employ a PEN INTERFACE. Many different technologies are used to construct digitizers, based for example on detecting pressure, electrical capacitance or inductance, interrupting light, infrared or ultrasonic beams, or detecting a weak radio signal transmitted from the pen.

digraph 1 A combination of two consecutive CHARACTERS such as 'ea' or 'cs'. Some types of text search operation require the examination of digraphs rather than single characters.
  2 A shorthand term for a DIRECTED GRAPH.

Dijkstra, Edsger (b. 1930) A Dutch computer scientist who, along with Anthony HOARE and O-J Dahl, invented the discipline of STRUCTURED PROGRAMMING in the early 1970s. He has also contributed several major innovations to the design of concurrent systems, including the concept of GUARDED constructs.

dimension 1 *n*. In maths and physics, one of the coordinates required to specify the location of a point in space, hence the related terms 2-dimensional (2D) and 3-dimensional (3D).
  2 *v*. In programming, to DECLARE the number of dimensions and size of an ARRAY. In BASIC this is performed using the DIM statement.

DIMM (Dual In-line Memory Module) A small PRINTED CIRCUIT BOARD with RAM chips mounted on both sides and a single edge connector, via which it can be plugged into a computer MOTHERBOARD. A DIMM differs from a SIMM in that the chips on either side have separate pins on the edge connector, permitting a wider 128-bit datapath for faster access to the memory; hence they tend to be used in more expensive systems like servers.

DIN (Deutsche Industrie Normen) The committee that issues German engineering standards.

Dining Philosophers Problem (DPP) A programming problem invented by Edsgar DIJKSTRA to illustrate CONCURRENT resource allocation and DEADLOCK. A group of very polite philosophers dine at a round table, with a fork placed between each pair of plates of food. Each philosopher may choose the left-hand or right-hand fork at whim, but only one philosopher may use any fork at one time. The task is to devise an ALGORITHM that allows the philosophers to eat.

diode An electronic device that conducts electricity in only one direction. TRANSISTORS and valves (vacuum tubes) may act as diodes.

DIP Abbreviation of DUAL INLINE PACKAGE.

DIP switch A small block of sliding switches that is fitted to many computer PRINTED CIRCUIT BOARDS to enable the user to change between alternative circuit configurations. The name DIP refers to DUAL INLINE PACKAGE, a style of chip package with two parallel rows of pins, which these switches emulate in form so that they can be fitted and soldered using the same machinery. See also JUMPER, JUMPERLESS, PLUG-AND-PLAY.

Direct3D A set of software LIBRARIES produced by Microsoft to improve the 3D GRAPHICS performance of Windows applications, particularly games. Launched in 1996, Direct3D is an operating system-level API (APPLICATION PROGRAMMING INTERFACE) that intervenes between the application and the hardware, enabling a graphics programmer to call high-level 3D graphics routines without needing to know the details of the system's 3D hardware. A program can query Direct3D to discover whether a 3D GRAPHICS ACCELERATOR is present and find out which 3D functions it supports – Direct3D's HARDWARE ABSTRACTION LAYER (HAL) then translates the program's API calls into the parameters that these functions require. Direct3D also contains a hardware emulation layer (HEL) of software routines that execute any functions that are not supported by the available hardware. See also OPENGL, MMX, DISPLAY LIST.

direct addressing See under ADDRESSING MODE.

Direct Client to Client Protocol (DCC) A PROTOCOL used on the INTERNET RELAY CHAT system which enables two users to chat privately and exchange data files directly, rather than going via the IRC server. DCC prevents a user's conversation being monitored by an IRC server operator, and economizes on available bandwidth since such conversations are no longer BROADCAST to all users.

direct current (DC) An electrical current that always flows in the same direction. Compare ALTERNATING CURRENT.

direct-dial Any type of ONLINE SERVICE that must be accessed by using a MODEM to dial its own telephone number, as opposed to INTERNET-based services which users access indirectly via telephone connection through an INTERNET SERVICE PROVIDER.

directed acyclic graph A DIRECTED GRAPH that contains no circular paths, so that if there is a route from node A to node B, there is no way back to A.

directed graph A GRAPH whose edges may be traversed only in one fixed direction.

direct mapped cache A simple CACHE design in which the CACHE LINE that stores a data block from a particular address is determined by certain bits in the address, so the same block always maps to the same line. This is easy to implement, but performs badly if a program alternately accesses two addresses that map to the same line (common enough in a program LOOP). Such cache CONTENTION, in which one block continually evicts the other, will cause a crippling string of CACHE MISSES. The more sophisticated ASSOCIATIVE CACHE was invented to avoid this and related problems.

Direct Memory Access (DMA) A scheme whereby PERIPHERAL devices are permitted to access the MEMORY of a computer directly, without having to pass requests via the CPU: such accesses are managed by a separate *DMA controller chip*. DMA is widely used to increase the DATA TRANSFER rate of disk drives, graphics and sound subsystems and printer ports, enabling them to transfer data even while the CPU is busy with other tasks. The IBM-compatible PC architecture includes a DMA controller with five channels. See also BUS MASTER.

Director The most widely used multimedia authoring program, published by Macro-Media, which supports the production of animated presentations for deployment on a CD-ROM or onto a WEB SITE by using its SHOCKWAVE and FLASH PLUG-IN.

directory 1 In most computer FILE SYSTEMS, a special type of file that contains references to other files, hence providing an organizing mechanism to group together files stored on some MASS STORAGE device such as a disk or tape. Modern graphical operating systems often refer to directories as FOLDERS, using a metaphor based on traditional office filing.
2 A type of DATABASE accessible via a computer network that dispenses information concerning individual network users and network resources such as computers and printers. See more under DIRECTORY SERVICE, LDAP, X.500.

directory service A network service consisting of a shared DATABASE that contains the NETWORK ADDRESS and other details for human users and various network resources such as printers, servers and archives. Examples of directory services on the INTERNET include WHOIS and WHITE PAGES, while large private networks often implement shared directory services accessed using protocols such as X.500 or LDAP. The information stored in a directory service is typically organized in a hierarchical fashion, either geographically (e.g. world, country, city, office) or by corporate structure (e.g. division, department, office, employee).

direct sequence modulation See under DSM.

Direct Sequence Spread Spectrum See DSSS.

DirectX A programming INTERFACE developed by Microsoft to support portability of computer games between different computers running WINDOWS (from 95 onwards). DirectX allows games programmers to bypass the Windows GRAPHICAL DEVICE INTERFACE for faster screen drawing, and to exploit the features of GRAPHICS ACCELERATORS and advanced SOUND CARDS in a device-independent fashion. Prior to the introduction of DirectX, most PC games had to be run under MS-DOS, even on Windows machines. See also OPENGL.

dirty Used to describe data, for example a document, that has been altered but not yet saved to disk. Saving the data renders it 'clean' again. May also be used to descibe the contents of a disk's WRITE-BACK CACHE or WRITE-BEHIND cache before they have been written to disk.

disassembler A program that can take the executable MACHINE CODE of another program and turn it back into ASSEMBLER MNEMONICS, that is into SOURCE CODE.

disaster recovery A professional service for computer-dependent businesses that involves instituting a rigorous BACKUP regime with copies of all data stored off the premises, and providing duplicate computing equipment at an alternative or mobile site. In the event of an emergency such as a fire, flood or robbery a client company can immediately resume normal operations from this temporary base.

disc See DISK.

Discrete Cosine Transform (DCT) A mathematical technique that expresses a WAVEFORM as the weighted sum of a set of cosines. It is the basis of several methods of VIDEO COMPRESSION and encoding including MPEG. See also DIGITAL SIGNAL PROCESSOR.

discrete event simulation See under SIMULATION.

discrete logic Simple electronic circuits such as LOGIC GATES and LATCHES that are contained in their own individual packages. Discrete logic chips were an intermediate stage in the rapid evolution of electronics that followed the invention of the TRANSISTOR: first single transistors were placed onto a chip and used to build circuits, then whole logic gates (i.e. discrete logic), and finally the modern INTEGRATED CIRCUIT combined many logic gates onto a single chip (see more under VLSI). However discrete logic components are not entirely obsolete: a scattering of such chips is incorporated into most computer designs (see GLUE LOGIC) to perform functions that could not be economically built into a VLSI chip or were added as an afterthought to correct problems. Discrete logic is also used in teaching and for constructing prototypes of new circuits that will later be turned into a more integrated chip. See also TTL, SYSTEM CHIP SET.

discrete speech recognition, discrete word recognition Any method of computerized SPEECH RECOGNITION that requires the speaker to emphasize the breaks between words. Most older recognition systems are of the discrete kind, as it requires less processing power. See more under CONTINUOUS-SPEECH RECOGNITION.

discriminant **1** In statistics and NEURAL NETWORK design, a class of FUNCTION used to classify a population of objects into different groups on the basis of several measurable parameters.
2 An integer value used to distinguish different varieties of a discriminated UNION structure in some programming languages such as C and C++ (see also VARIANT RECORD).
3 In mathematics, an algebraic expression derived from the coefficients of a POLYNOMIAL equation whose value determines whether the ROOTS of the equation are real or imaginary, equal or unequal. For example the discriminant of the quadratic equation $ax^2 + bx + c = 0$ is $b^2 - 4ac$.

disinfect A purely metaphorical term meaning to remove a VIRUS from a computer system.

disjunction **1** In logic the operator, usually symbolized as $A \cup B$, that combines two propositions A and B into a single sentence that asserts one or the other of them is true, equivalent to the English 'or'. An exclusive disjunction asserts that A or B is true, but not both. Also, the combined proposition that results from the application of this operator.
2 In BOOLEAN ALGEBRA, the OR operator that is true if either of its arguments is true.

disk Any circular rotating medium used to store data. See more under FLOPPY DISK, HARD DISK, CD-ROM, CD-R, CD-RW, DVD, ZIP DRIVE.

disk access An act of reading data from or writing data to a DISK DRIVE, as performed by a computer program. The user will normally see an indicator light flicker, to show that a disk access is taking place, and may in some cases notice a pause in the program's interaction until the access has completed.

disk-bound A computing task whose maximum speed is restricted to the rate at which it can read and write data to and from disk, as opposed to one that is PROCESSOR-BOUND, where computation speed sets the limit. Examples of disk-bound operations include sorting or searching very large files that cannot be fitted into MAIN MEMORY, and so require continuous reading of data items from disk and writing back the results. The most important measures that can be taken to accelerate a disk-bound task are to switch to a faster DISK DRIVE technology, to read more data at a time and to employ a DISK CACHE. See also VIRTUAL MEMORY.

disk cache A portion of computer MEMORY set aside by the OPERATING SYSTEM to store the contents of those SECTORS of a HARD DISK that were most recently read or written, to speed up disk operations. The cache contents are periodically written back to the disk to keep it up to date (see WRITE-BEHIND), usually while the system is otherwise idle. Cacheing introduces the risk that the computer may suffer a crash or power failure before the cache has been written back, which would cause data to be lost. See also WRITE-BACK CACHE, WRITE-THROUGH CACHE, FLUSH.

disk changer A mechanical device, sometimes called a JUKEBOX, which can automatically select one CD-ROM from a rack and mount it for reading; used to implement large archives of read-only data.

disk controller An INTEGRATED CIRCUIT or circuit board, fitted either within a DISK DRIVE or on a computer's MOTHERBOARD, which implements the set of commands required to locate and move the heads, read and write data to the disk. The computer's OPERATING SYSTEM and BIOS issue commands directly to the controller to BOOT the computer and to access files stored on the disks. See also IDE, EIDE, SCSI.

disk drive Any computer MASS STORAGE device that depends on reading and writing data from a rotating disk for its operation. There are many different disk drive technologies in current use: see for example FLOPPY DISK, HARD DISK, CD-ROM, CD-R, CD-RW, MAG-NETO-OPTICAL DISK, DVD, ZIP DRIVE, FLOPTICAL DISK, and SYQUEST drive.

diskette A FLOPPY DISK.

disk farm A collection of DISK DRIVES, typically connected either to a network of computers or to a MAINFRAME computer.

disk-full error An error raised by a computer's operating system when there is insufficient free space on a DISK for a requested save operation to proceed. The better operating systems will offer the user the opportunity to delete some files to free up space, rather than simply aborting the operation at this point. For example, under WINDOWS the user may be able to empty the RECYCLE BIN to free up more space.

diskless workstation A network WORKSTATION that has no DISK DRIVES and must download all the software it runs from a SERVER over its NETWORK connection. Diskless workstations may save money by not providing unnecessary hardware, and they also prevent employees from installing unauthorized software and thereby compromising security. However, their main rationale is to overcome the increasing difficulty of managing the software configuration in PC networks – all system and application software need be installed only once, under the control of a central network administrator. With the advent of TERMINAL SERVER systems such as those from Citrix (see WINFRAME) and Microsoft, which have small portable client software, diskless workstations do not need to run the same operating system as the server and might even be HAND-HELD computers. See also NETWORK COMPUTER, SMART TERMINAL.

disk mirroring The use of two HARD DISKS whose contents are kept identical by writing to both simultaneously, to provide a redundant BACKUP in case either disk fails. Mirroring offers protection against hardware failure only; any software failure that causes the written data to become corrupted is most likely to corrupt the contents of both disks equally. Some operating systems such as WINDOWS NT and UNIX have built-in support for mirroring, and it is one of the several forms of security through redundancy offered by RAID systems.

disk operating system See DOS.

disk partitioning To divide a single HARD DISK into two or more LOGICAL drives that appear to the user as separate disks with their own drive letters: each such logical drive is referred to as a partition.

On MS-DOS and most WINDOWS computers, partitioning is performed by the low-level system utility FDISK prior to formatting the disk. Windows NT and 2000 permit partitions to be altered in the Disk Administrator tool, and third-party tools such as PARTITION MAGIC may be used to alter partitions without destroying any data already stored on them. See also VOLUME, BASIC STORAGE, DYNAMIC STORAGE.

disk sector See under SECTOR.

disk shadowing A less-used name for DISK MIRRORING.

disk storage The collective term for the various types of rotating storage medium used to store computer data permanently after the power is switched off. Most computers now contain both a fixed and a removable DISK DRIVE, typically a HARD DISK together with one or more FLOPPY DISK, CD-ROM or ZIP DRIVE. See also MASS STORAGE, MAGNETIC DISK, OPTICAL DRIVE, MAGNETO-OPTICAL DISK, BERNOULLI DRIVE.

disk striping See under BYTE STRIPING.

disk-to-disk copy An operation that copies data from one DISK to another without having to load it into memory.

dismount To remove some storage device such as a removable DISK from a FILE SYSTEM. Also used metaphorically in some non-physically removable disk systems when making a device unavailable during, for example, maintenance.

dispatch 1 To send an INSTRUCTION to one of the functional units within a computer PROCESSOR to be executed (see also ISSUE).
2 To send a request to a SERVER that can process that request.
3 To identify an incoming command or event and then execute a section of code corresponding to that command, for example a METHOD in an OBJECT-ORIENTED program.
4 To allocate a waiting TASK to a processor or THREAD in a MULTITASKING operating system.
5 To launch a message or a PACKET onto a NETWORK.

dispatcher A software component that matches up incoming requests with processes that can service them: for example TASKS and THREADS in an OPERATING SYSTEM, errors or interrupts and their HANDLERS, or page requests within a WEB SERVER.

dispinterface A special simplified INTERFACE exposed by software applications that conform to Microsoft's COM object model, to make it easier to automate them from SCRIPTING LANGUAGES such as VISUAL BASIC. A dispinterface typically has fewer and simpler methods than the internal VTABLE interface that it ultimately calls.

display The part of a computer system on which the user views its output and software controls. See more under VDU, MONITOR, LCD, CATHODE RAY TUBE.

display adapter Another name for a GRAPHICS CARD.

display buffer A dedicated region of computer memory used to store the data that represents the image currently showing on the computer's display screen. See also FRAME BUFFER, VIDEO RAM, GRAPHICS CARD, DOUBLE BUFFERING, UNIFIED MEMORY.

Display Control Interface (DCI) An interface standard developed by Microsoft and Intel for GRAPHICS CARDS to provide hardware acceleration of full-motion video. Originally intended for Windows 95, it has been effectively superceded by Microsoft's own DIRECTX technology.

display driver A piece of software (see DEVICE DRIVER) that enables a particular OPERATING SYSTEM to direct its screen output through a particular brand of GRAPHICS CARD. Any new operating system for PCs – which support a huge diversity of graphics hardware – must have display drivers for every popular brand of graphics card if it is to succeed. For users, too, the choice of display driver can be crucial since incorrect installation can leave a blank display, making recovery rather fraught – hence Microsoft WINDOWS provides a universal VGA display driver called VGA.DRV that will produce a basic display with any card.

display list A DATA STRUCTURE used to represent a graphical image as a compact list of commands rather than as raw PIXEL data – when executed such a list generates the required scene by applying the sequence of drawing operations. The commands are primitive graphics operations, such as 'draw a line' or 'fill a polygon', and the COMPRESSION achieved may be very large because a fill command that is only a few bytes in size may produce an image that would otherwise take thousands of bytes to store as a BITMAP.

Display lists are employed by many VECTOR GRAPHICS programs, CAD applications such as AUTOCAD, and in 3D GRAPHICS systems such as Microsoft's DIRECT3D API (APPLICATION PROGRAMMING INTERFACE). They are particularly suited for use with a hardware GRAPHICS ACCELERATOR, when the list can contain hardware instructions to drive the graphics processor directly. See also FRAME BUFFER, RENDER.

Display PostScript A version of the POSTSCRIPT page description language designed to drive a screen display, thus guaranteeing that screen contents and printed output will appear identical as they are both rendered from the same code. Intended for widespread use, it required more processing power than was available from PCs in the mid-1980s and so was adopted only by the short-lived NEXT machine and in some SUN workstations.

distortion An undesired change in the shape of an electrical waveform or signal. See also ATTENUATION, SIGNAL DEGRADATION, NOISE.

distributed Any computing or storage system that is spread across several different physical locations connected by a network, used as in DISTRIBUTED DATABASE, DISTRIBUTED ENTERPRISE or DISTRIBUTED OBJECT SYSTEM.

distributed application architecture 1 A set of software technologies, including communication services, object location services, object managers and request brokers, which when combined enable different parts of an application to be run on different computers in a network, possibly under different GRAPHICAL USER INTERFACES, operating systems and over mixed network technologies. Examples of such distributed application architectures include Sun's JAVA RMI architecture, CORBA, and Microsoft's DISTRIBUTED COMPONENT OBJECT MODEL.

2 A specific distributed application architecture called DAA was developed by Data General, Sun and Hewlett Packard in the early 1990s in compliance with the OBJECT MANAGEMENT GROUP's Object Management Architecture.

Distributed Component Object Model See DCOM.

Distributed Computing Environment (DCE) An architecture for DISTRIBUTED computer systems developed under the auspices of the OPEN SOFTWARE FOUNDATION, which consists of a set of standard APPLICATION PROGRAMMING INTERFACES, conventions for naming under distributed file systems, and a REMOTE PROCEDURE CALL mechanism that enables different parts of an application to work transparently on different types of computer over a network.

distributed-data A description applicable to any system in which the data is stored on more than one computer rather than on a single central SERVER. See also DISTRIBUTED DATABASE, REPLICATION.

distributed database A DATABASE whose contents reside on more than one computer. The Internet's DNS system is the best known example, spanning the whole world and stored on thousands of separate machines.

Most distributed databases share one characteristic – while the actual data resides on different machines connected by a communications network, the user sees only a single, VIRTUAL database and does not need to know where any particular data item is physically stored. Management software is therefore free to move data around to balance the storage and BANDWIDTH requirements of the system, for example causing data to migrate to those machines from which it is most requested, or to those that have most spare disk space.

Some distributed databases maintain a single central INDEX that all the users consult, while others allow different users to work with subsets of the whole database on their local machines (see for example LOTUS NOTES), in which case the network is used to spread information about changes made on one machine to all the others: see more under REPLICATION and SYNCHRONIZATION. The WORLD WIDE WEB could be considered as a distributed database that may be queried through the various SEARCH ENGINES, which act as a distributed, continually updated (but incomplete) index.

distributed enterprise A jargon term referring to large corporations whose operations and computing facilities are geographically spread out, and which rely on their communications networks to integrate them all. See also UDDI, WEB SERVICE, E-COMMERCE.

distributed-memory computer A type of PARALLEL COMPUTER (also called a MULTICOMPUTER) in which each PROCESSOR has its own memory, so that there are many separate ADDRESS SPACES in which programs can be run. Such programs must employ MESSAGE PASSING via a communications network to synchronize with one another, since no processor can directly access the memory of another, in contrast with the alternative SHARED-MEMORY MULTIPROCESSOR. This complicates the programming of distributed-memory machines since communication code is required in addition to processing code. See also PARALLEL PROGRAMMING, PARALLEL VIRTUAL MACHINE, PARMACS, INTERCONNECT, SWITCHED INTERCONNECT.

Distributed Network Architecture Microsoft's overall name for the collection of technologies it offers for building multi-tier web-based applications, including COM+, Visual Studio and SQL Server.

distributed object system A software system that is constructed using an OBJECT-ORIENTED architecture and whose data objects may reside on different computers joined by a NETWORK.

distributed processing The execution of different parts of a computation on different computer PROCESSORS, possibly in several geographical locations connected by a network. See also PARALLEL PROCESSING.

distributed system A software system whose constituent parts run on different computers connected by a NETWORK.

dither To simulate more tones and shades than a particular display system actually supports, by mixing dots of the available colours in various ratios. The result is seldom satisfactory as the dots are often visible, and may produce unsightly MOIRÉ PATTERNS. However, dithering is rarely chosen deliberately, but more often is applied automatically by software that is attempting to emulate a graphics mode that it doesn't support directly.

Ditto drive A range of TAPE DRIVES of various capacities made by Iomega, which all employ the QUARTER-INCH CARTRIDGE format.

divide-and-conquer algorithm A type of ALGORITHM that solves a problem by splitting it into two or more simpler problems and solving those instead. The QUICKSORT algorithm is the classic example of the technique.

divide-by-zero error An ERROR CONDITION raised whenever a computer's PROCESSOR is asked to perform a division with a divisor of 0. To a mathematician the result of such division is undefined, but to a computer it is a number so large that it overflows the destination register. Many processors treat divide-by-zero as a hardware error, with its own dedicated INTERRUPT that can be trapped by the operating system and passed back to the application that caused the error. See also TRAP, SOFTWARE INTERRUPT.

divider 1 A dedicated circuit used within the ARITHMETIC AND LOGIC UNIT of many PROCESSORS to perform division operations.
2 A circuit used to divide the CLOCK SIGNAL of a system to allow some part (for instance an external BUS or CACHE) to run at a fraction of the CPU clock speed.
3 A horizontal or vertical line used to separate, for example, groups of items on a MENU, or columns in a table.

DLL (dynamic-linked library) In programming, a type of LIBRARY file that becomes LINKED to a program that uses it only temporarily when the program is loaded into memory or executed, rather than being permanently built-in when the program is COMPILED. The same DLL may therefore be shared by many different programs, rather than each program having to contain its own copy; this saves on memory usage and potentially simplifies the updating of programs.

Microsoft WINDOWS was the first operating system to make heavy use of DLLs, with large parts of the operating system itself (e.g. KERNEL32.DLL) and of Microsoft Office applications existing in DLL format. The use of DLLs should simplify the distribution of updates to programs, but in practice they are a double-edged weapon, as installing new programs can cause chaos by overwriting DLLs needed by others with incompatible versions.

Programs that call DLLs are compiled and permanently linked to a library of STUBS which at RUN TIME are replaced with the real addresses of the shared library routines.

DLL hell The most frequent reason for software failure under Microsoft's WINDOWS operating system, which arises when a newly installed program copies its own version of a shared DLL over the existing one and so causes existing programs to stop working or to work erratically. Such problems are hellish to untangle, thanks to the undisciplined way in which Windows stores DLLs. Windows 2000 has introduced features designed to ameliorate this situation, if only slightly: see under WINDOWS FILE PROTECTION, SYSTEM FILE CHECKER.

DLP Abbreviation of DIGITAL LIGHT PROCESSOR.

DMA Abbreviation of DIRECT MEMORY ACCESS.

DMA controller See under DIRECT MEMORY ACCESS.

DML (Database Management Language, Data Manipulation Language) A programming language built into some database management systems to enable the automation of maintenance tasks such as the creation and deletion of TABLES and RECORDS, and also used for writing STORED PROCEDURES.

DNA 1 Abbreviation of Distributed Network Architecture.

2 Abbreviation of DIGITAL NETWORK ARCHITECTURE.

DNA computing A novel and experimental method of chemical computation in which data items are encoded as sequences of nucleotides and can be retrieved by exploiting the intrinsic ability (upon which all living creatures depend) of DNA strands to find and bind to their complementary form. For certain classes of text search it promises excellent performance, as PATTERN MATCHING among millions of alternatives can occur in parallel, but it has yet to be refined sufficiently for commercial application.

DNS (Domain Name System, Domain Name Service) 1 The name translation service used on the Internet to translate a human-readable HOSTNAME into the numeric IP ADDRESS required to send requests to that host. For example when a BROWSER requests a WEB PAGE, such as www.yahoo.com, that request goes first to a local DNS SERVER, which may then contact other DNS servers, until the hostname can be resolved to its corresponding IP ADDRESS, say 204.71.177.71, needed to access the site.

DNS is a DISTRIBUTED system, spread across many servers throughout the world, and replicas of the same lookup data may be found on many different servers, continually updated to keep all the information correct. DNS names work in a hierarchical fashion, not unlike ordinary postal addresses: for example 'Penguin Ltd, 27 Wrights Lane, London, UK', when read from right to left, specifies country, then city, street and building.

DNS servers are connected together in a tree-like manner, with a large central root server listing all the DNS servers for each top-level DOMAIN such as .com. Requests may have to pass up this tree from local level to root and back down to local in order to resolve a particular name to an address.

DNS is defined in the Internet Architecture Board documents STD 13, RFC 1034 and RFC 1035.

2 Abbreviation of DIGITAL NERVOUS SYSTEM.

DNS server An Internet SERVER that functions as part of the global Domain Name System (see DNS).

DOC Digital Oscillator Chip, a 32-voice sound generator chip made by Ensoniq and used in early SOUND CARDS and multimedia computers such as the Apple IIGS.

doc The name commonly given to the proprietary FILE FORMAT in which MICROSOFT WORD stores its documents, referring to the .doc FILENAME EXTENSION it employs.

docfile An obsolete name for a COMPOUND FILE that uses Microsoft's STRUCTURED STORAGE.

dock To plug a PORTABLE computer into its DOCKING STATION.

docking station A desktop unit into which a LAPTOP or NOTEBOOK computer can be plugged to provide features that were omitted from the machine itself to reduce its size, for example a floppy, hard, or CD-ROM DISK DRIVE, plus a full-sized keyboard or monitor.

docking toolbar A style of software TOOLBAR that can be used either as a free FLOATING TOOLBAR or else attached to one edge of the surrounding screen or window (that is 'docked') simply by dragging it with the MOUSE to the desired location. Docking toolbars were introduced by MICROSOFT in WORD 97 and INTERNET EXPLORER 4.

document **1** *n*. Human-readable information, whether composed of text, pictures, tables, numbers or some mixture of them all, that has been written or printed on paper or stored in an electronic, magnetic or optical medium such as a computer FILE or a microfiche.
2 *v*. To describe the workings of a computer program in some human language such as English, as opposed to in a PROGRAMMING LANGUAGE. See also COMMENT, MANUAL.

documentation The instruction manuals, whether on paper or in electronic form, for some computer hardware or software system.

document-centric A style of computer USER INTERFACE in which the only visible objects are the user's documents, i.e. DATA FILES, which when selected automatically invoke the correct program with which to open themselves for editing. This is the reverse of the traditional style, where the user first chooses a program, then executes it and loads a data file from within it.
Apple's MACOS is document-centric to a degree, and Microsoft WINDOWS can be made more so by setting up a suitable FILE ASSOCIATION for every data file type.

document clustering A technique employed in some DOCUMENT MANAGEMENT SYSTEMS which automatically groups together documents that contain related ideas in order to permit more relevant information to be retrieved when they are searched. See also RELEVANCE, SEARCH ENGINE, SEMANTIC NETWORK.

Document Content Architecture A portable document format introduced by IBM in the early 1990s as part of its SYSTEMS APPLICATION ARCHITECTURE project.

document format The precise layout of the data items that compose a document, including such details as the special values used to mark the end of lines and paragraphs, changes of FONT or STYLE, MARGINS and TAB STOPS.

document management system A computerized system for storing large volumes of documentary material, such as used by large corporations and government departments to keep their archives. If the documents are already in electronic form, they may be put into a TEXT RETRIEVAL SYSTEM that enables indexed searches, or they may be transcribed into some standard notation such as SGML for uniformity of formatting.
Documents not already in electronic form may be scanned and turned into editable, searchable computer text by using OPTICAL CHARACTER RECOGNITION (OCR), or else stored as BITMAP images if they are handwritten or otherwise unsuitable for OCR. In the latter case the document management system normally provides some means of annotating each image to help in retrieving them.

Document Object Model (DOM) A specification issued by the WORLD WIDE WEB CONSORTIUM as part of the standard for DYNAMIC HTML, which describes an OBJECT-ORIENTED page layout model that enables HTML and XML elements to appear as objects and collections that expose properties and methods. DOM operates through SCRIPTING LANGUAGES such as JAVASCRIPT or VBSCRIPT to dynamically manipulate the style, content and positioning of text on an HTML web page, for example to create an animated image on the page.

Document Style Semantics and Specification Language (DSSSL) A language for defining the format of text objects for use in SGML documents. It offers great descriptive power, but employs an unfamiliar LISP-like syntax, and is likely to be displaced by the much simpler XSL and CSS used with XML documents.

Document Type Definition (DTD) An auxiliary document that defines the GRAMMAR of the TAGS used in a main document that has been laid out using the SGML or XML MARKUP LANGUAGES. A valid DTD must be supplied to any parsing program to enable it to correctly interpret and display the document. See also XSL, CASCADING STYLE SHEETS.

DoD (US Department of Defense) The US federal government agency in charge of military procurement.

DOD-STD-2167A The US Department of Defense's standard for the development and documentation of MISSION-CRITICAL software systems.

DOM Abbreviation of DOCUMENT OBJECT MODEL.

domain 1 A subdivision of a computer NETWORK, containing machines that have some part of their NETWORK ADDRESS in common.

2 More specifically, on the INTERNET a domain is a group of IP ADDRESSES all belonging to the same organization. For example if penguin.com is a domain belonging to Penguin Books, then individuals' computers within that domain might have names such as fred.penguin.com and barney.penguin.com. Domain names form a tree-like hierarchy, the last component (.com in this example) representing one of a handful of top-level domains that contain millions of computers. See also FULLY QUALIFIED DOMAIN NAME and DNS.

3 Under Microsoft's WINDOWS NT network operating system, a subdivision of a network that shares the same user account and security information, stored on a single SERVER designated as the PRIMARY DOMAIN CONTROLLER.

4 In SYSTEMS ANALYSIS, the environment or market in which a piece of software is designed to work.

5 In mathematics, the range of argument values within which a function has a defined value.

6 In solid state physics, a microscopic region within a magnetic substance in which all the magnetic dipoles are aligned in the same direction.

domain address An older term for an Internet DOMAIN NAME, dating from the period when the DNS was replacing the older BANG PATH addressing scheme.

domain architecture A concept employed in SYSTEMS ANALYSIS to describe a generic structure to which all software systems in a particular DOMAIN must adhere in order to satisfy the requirements specified in the DOMAIN MODEL.

domain controller In a network of computers running the WINDOWS NT or 2000 operating systems, a specially distinguished computer that holds a copy of the adminstrative information for a particular DOMAIN including the PASSWORDS, USER ACCOUNTS and DIRECTORY SERVICES. See more under PRIMARY DOMAIN CONTROLLER, BACKUP DOMAIN CONTROLLER.

domain model In SYSTEMS ANALYSIS, a description of the data structures, information flows, functions, controls and constraints that are required for software systems that are to be implemented in a particular problem DOMAIN, for example manufacturing or stock control. An important purpose of the domain model is to identify those features that all such software systems will have in common, and those in which they will differ.

domain name The name of a particular SERVER or group of servers on the INTERNET, formed according to the hierarchical naming scheme for Internet resources. For example in an EMAIL address such as info@penguin.co.uk, everything following the @ constitutes the domain name, which in this case has three levels: 'penguin' is identified as a subdomain within the 'co' subdomain of the 'uk' TOP-LEVEL DOMAIN. See also DNS, FULLY QUALIFIED DOMAIN NAME, DOT COM.

Domain Name System See DNS.

dongle A hardware device that prevents illegal copies of software from being used (see more under COPY PROTECTION), consisting of a ROM chip holding a unique registration code that plugs into the computer, typically via its PARALLEL PORT. The protected program reads this port periodically and will not function if the dongle code is not found: hence the software may be copied for the owner's own security but copies given to others will not work. The name dongle is just a whimsy, equivalent to 'thingamejig' or 'whatsit'.

Doom A brutal, sadistic and extremely entertaining computer game published by id Software, which introduced a new level of realism in 3D GRAPHICS. Doom was also notable for its construction, which separated the drawing engine from the environment, enabling players to create their own new scenarios: this has lead to a huge Internet following. The successor to Doom is the equally successful QUAKE.

dopant A chemical element that is introduced as a deliberate impurity into a SEMICONDUCTOR substance such as SILICON, in order to modify its electrical properties. An *n-type* dopant creates an excess of free electrons, while a *p-type* dopant creates a deficiency of electrons, which means an excess of positive charge carriers or 'holes'. Arsenic is an n-type dopant for silicon, while boron is a p-type dopant. See also DOPING.

doped A SEMICONDUCTOR such as SILICON that has been deliberately contaminated with small quantities of another element, called the DOPANT, to change its electrical properties.

doping The process whereby the electrical properties of a pure semiconductor such as SILICON, germanium or GALLIUM ARSENIDE are modified by the introduction of tiny quantities of another element such as arsenic, boron or phosphorus, called the DOPANT. Doping is performed by exposing the semiconductor WAFER to the vaporized dopant at high temperature, or more recently by bombarding the wafer with a beam of dopant ions from a particle accelerator.

DOS (Disk Operating System) A computer OPERATING SYSTEM that supports the storage of data in files on floppy or hard magnetic DISKS. In the early days of computing (and later of personal computing) this was the primary function of any operating system, so many of them had names ending in DOS, such as MS-DOS and AmigaDOS. The word DOS is sometimes used to refer specifically to MS-DOS, or as a generic reference to any operating system. Nowadays an operating system must deal with many different kinds of storage media and with networks too, and so this latter use is disappearing.

A typical disk operating system includes a FILE SYSTEM that supports the organization of data into files and directories, and it provides a number of system calls that enable application programs to create, delete, rename, open and close files, and to read and write blocks of data from them.

DOS box A mechanism provided under 32-BIT versions of Microsoft Windows to enable older 16-BIT MS-DOS and Windows programs to be run. In essence the DOS box assigns a separate VIRTUAL MACHINE to each such program. See also VDM.

dot 1 One of the spots of ink from which a printed image is composed, equivalent to a PIXEL in a screen image.

2 The pronunciation used for the full stop that separates the elements of an EMAIL address or web URL, as in DOT COM.

3 The separator CHARACTER used to divide certain IDENTIFIERS such as IP addresses or the names of objects in certain programming languages, into their constituent parts. See more under DOT NOTATION.

4 See under QUANTUM DOT.

dot com The popular term for an INTERNET-based business, derived from the way that the URL of a company registered in the TOP-LEVEL DOMAIN .com is pronounced – for example www.yahoo.com is usually spoken as 'yahoo-dot-com'.

dot command The syntax employed when issuing COMMANDS interactively at the command prompt in the original DBASE II database – each command began with a full-stop, for example . SEEK

dot-matrix printer A type of IMPACT PRINTER that dominated the early days of personal computing. It formed each character by pressing an inked ribbon against the paper using a vertical row of metal pins under program control: early models used only 9 pins, but later models had 24 for improved resolution. Though more flexible than the DAISY-WHEEL PRINTER, thanks to multiple fonts and a basic graphics ability, the dot-matrix was noisy and lacked the print quality needed for business – it was quickly swept away after the invention of the LASER PRINTER and the cheap INKJET PRINTER.

dot notation Any notation in which IDENTIFIERS are constructed by joining together shorter numbers or words using dots as separators. Such notations are for example used to represent hierarchical Internet names (e.g. penguin.co.uk), numeric IP ADDRESSES (e.g. 127.101.44.53) and to name objects in many object-oriented programming languages, as in tvwControl.Nodes.Add(ParentNode.Key). See also SLASH-DELIMITED, DELIMITER.

dot pitch A measure of the RESOLUTION of a computer's MONITOR, namely the distance between two adjacent PHOSPHOR dots of the same colour (red, blue or green) on its screen. Typical pitch values range from 0.3 mm or more for the cheapest monitors to 0.2 mm and below for professional models.

dot-separated number Any identifying number formed by joining several shorter numbers with dot characters, used for example to represent an IP ADDRESS such as 127.101.44.59. Also called DOT NOTATION.

dotted quad The four-part numeric notation used for writing an IP ADDRESS, as in 127.0.0.1. See also DOT NOTATION, DOT-SEPARATED NUMBER.

double buffering A trick used in computer ANIMATION to improve the smoothness of displays by providing twin FRAME BUFFERS whose contents can be displayed alternately, the next image being built in the non-visible buffer while the other one is visible. This reduces the minimum time between successive frames to the time required to switch buffers, rather than the time required to RENDER a whole frame, so avoiding a lengthy dark space between frames.

double-byte character, double-byte code, double-byte font A character belonging to any CHARACTER SET that requires 16 rather than 8 bits to encode, used for example in Japan, China and Korea to encode KANJI pictograms, and now standardized in the UNICODE system. See also ASCII, UNICODE, UNIVERSAL CHARACTER SET.

double-click The act of depressing a BUTTON on a MOUSE twice in rapid succession, which is interpreted by the software as a different EVENT from a single click, and hence allows alternative control functions to be performed.

Double clicks originated with the Apple MACINTOSH, which has only a single mouse button and hence needs the extra information, but they are also employed in Windows with its two-button mouse.

double-density diskette, DD diskette Two IBM PC FLOPPY DISK formats that contained twice as much data as the formats they replaced. An original 5.25-inch PC floppy contained 180 kilobytes (KB), so double-density (abbreviated to DD) disks contained 360 KB.

With the later 3.5-inch floppy, 360 KB became single-density and 720 KB became DD. Today's floppy drives all take HIGH-DENSITY DISKETTES (called HD) which hold 1.44 megabytes.

double precision Any numeric DATA TYPE that is twice the length of the default type for a particular system: so in a 16-BIT system, a double-precision integer would be 32 bits. A specially common usage of the term is to refer to IEEE FLOATING POINT numbers, where single precision is 32 bits so that double precision is 64 bits. See also PRECISION.

double quote The character ", with ASCII code 34. Professional typesetters employ separate characters for opening and closing double quotes (ANSI/Unicode 147 and 148) neither of which is this character. See also SINGLE QUOTE.

double-sided A description that applies to any DISK STORAGE medium on which data may be stored on both sides, including FLOPPY DISKS and some DVD disks.

doubleword A 32-BIT quantity. See also BYTE, WORD, QUADWORD.

doubly-linked list A LINKED LIST in which each NODE contains not one but two POINTERS, one to the next and one to the previous node. Hence such a list can be traversed equally fast in either direction (and from either end), which makes certain types of list update operation far more efficient.

down arrow One of the four CURSOR KEYS on a typical computer KEYBOARD, which makes the text CURSOR move down by one line.

downlink In SATELLITE communications, VIDEO-ON-DEMAND and interactive digital television systems, the channel that carries programme and message data to the receiver or customer, as opposed to the UPLINK which carries the customer's commands back to the sender. See also DOWNLOAD.

download To copy a FILE over a communications link from a remote SERVER into the memory or hard disk of one's local computer. Most commony used on the Internet.

downsize Originally a term meaning to transfer MAINFRAME and MINICOMPUTER software systems onto a network of PCs, but now borrowed by economists as a euphemism for reducing the labour force of a company.

downtime A period during which a computer or network is unavailable owing to system failure or maintenance.

downwardly-compatible Capable of running on earlier or less powerful versions of a computer system. See also UPWARDLY-COMPATIBLE.

doze An alternative term for the SLEEP mode provided by most portable computers to save on battery life. See more under SUSPEND.

DP Abbreviation of DATA PROCESSING.

DPA Abbreviation of DATA PROTECTION ACT.

dpi (dots per inch) A measure of RESOLUTION for printers.

DPMS (Display Monitor Power Management System) A widely adopted standard for POWER SAVING circuitry in computer monitors, developed by the VIDEO ELECTRONICS STANDARDS ASSOCIATION.

draft Short for DRAFT-QUALITY PRINTING.

draft-mode A mode supported by many types of computer printer and some graphics programs which offers fast but low-quality output for checking purposes or display.

draft-quality printing On DOT-MATRIX and INK-JET printers, a mode that offers faster output at a lower RESOLUTION, suitable for printing trial versions of documents.

drag To move the image of a displayed object across a computer's VDU screen by placing the MOUSE POINTER over it, then holding down a mouse button and moving the mouse. Along with pointing and clicking, dragging is one of the fundamental actions of any GRAPHICAL USER INTERFACE, used when copying and moving files, sections of document or pictures. See also DRAG-AND-DROP, CUT-AND-PASTE.

drag-and-drop A style of interaction used in computer programs that have a GRAPHICAL USER INTERFACE, which allows the user to DRAG the representation of a data file from one location to another using the MOUSE, and then release it (i.e. 'drop' it) to effect some action. For example, the file may be copied or moved into a different FOLDER, or dropped onto some program that will open it for editing.

drain One of the terminals of a FIELD-EFFECT TRANSISTOR.

DRAM Abbreviation of DYNAMIC RANDOM ACCESS MEMORY.

drawing program A name commonly applied to vector-based design programs such as Adobe Illustrator which are principally used for drawing lines rather than for applying colours (which is the province of bitmap-based PAINTING PROGRAMS). See also VECTOR GRAPHICS, GRAPHICS, CORELDRAW.

Dr Dobb's Full name, *Dr Dobb's Journal of Computer Calisthenics and Orthodontia (Running Light Without Overbyte)*, one of the earliest popular computer magazines, launched in 1976. *Dr Dobb's* is a highly technical magazine that specializes in ASSEMBLY LANGUAGE, C and C++ programming, algorithms and experimental programming languages, and hardware interfacing. It is favoured by HACKERS in the older, benign sense of that term.

Dreamweaver A popular web site authoring tool produced by MACROMEDIA.

drill down To traverse some nested software hierarchy displayed on a computer screen to deeper and deeper levels. For example, to descend through a TREE of SUBDIRECTORIES on a hard disk to home in on an individual file, to traverse a sequence of nested MENUS, to select successive tabs in a set of nested TABBED DIALOGUES, or to locate a field within a hierarchical database RECORD.

drive The mechanical transport mechanism of any computer storage device that employs a moving recording medium, for example a HARD DISK, FLOPPY DISK, CD-ROM or TAPE drive.

drive-array A collection of DISK DRIVES joined together to appear as one drive. See more under RAID.

drive bay A mounting point for a DISK DRIVE within a computer's casing, typically consisting of a pair of metal rails to support the drive. A rectangular aperture often enables the drive's front panel to be visible from outside the case.

drive letter Under the CP/M, MS-DOS and WINDOWS operating systems, a unique IDENTIFIER assigned to each DRIVE connected to the system, consisting of a single letter of the alphabet followed by a colon. The drive letter is used as the first part of a PATHNAME to identify any file stored on that drive, as for example c:\docs\myfile.txt. Traditionally A: and B: are reserved for FLOPPY DISKS and C: is the first HARD DISK.

driver An abbreviation for DEVICE DRIVER.

drop cap, dropped capital A typographical device mostly seen in book and magazine layouts, in which the first capital letter of the first word of a piece or chapter is greatly enlarged, usually to three or more lines in depth, and is set into a suitably-shaped INDENT in the rest of the text. (A drop cap serves the function of the illuminated capitals in medieval manuscripts, from which it no doubt derives.) All modern DESKTOP PUBLISHING programs offer the ability to create drop caps automatically and to define them in a STYLE SHEET.

drop-down menu A style of MENU that appears when the user clicks on its title using the mouse and then remains visible until a choice is made. Widely used in Microsoft Windows applications and other graphical user interfaces. See also PULL-DOWN MENU, POP-UP MENU.

dropout A temporary loss of signal or power. In an audio transmission it refers to a temporary dip in the sound level, while in a magnetic recording medium such as a tape it means a small faulty area resulting in a possible loss of data.

drum scanner A type of SCANNER used by printers and PREPRESS professionals to digitize colour transparencies.

Dr Watson A postmortem DIAGNOSTIC utility provided in Microsoft WINDOWS from the 3.1 version onwards, which, following a system crash provoked by an application, can be used to extract more information about the cause than is given in the displayed ERROR MESSAGE. Whenever an UNRECOVERABLE APPLICATION ERROR or GENERAL PROTECTION FAULT occurs, running the Dr Watson application creates a file that records the software environment (e.g. memory and register contents) and user actions that lead up to the error, and this LOG FILE may be emailed back to the software's developers to help them to try and reproduce the error. See also POSTMORTEM DEBUGGER, DEBUGGER, ERROR TRAPPING.

DSL Abbreviation of DIGITAL SUBSCRIBER LINE.

DSLAM (Digital Subscriber Line Access Multiplexer) The combined SWITCH and ROUTER units that are installed at local telephone exchanges to support DIGITAL SUBSCRIBER LINE services such as ADSL.

DSM Abbreviation of DIRECT SEQUENCE MODULATION.

DSP Abbreviation of DIGITAL SIGNAL PROCESSOR.

DSSS (Direct Sequence Spread Spectrum) A wireless communication technology widely used in wireless LANS which employs radio waves to transmit messages by broadcasting each data bit on several (typically 11) frequencies at once. A different set of frequencies is used for each successive bit, chosen according to a numeric key that must be known to receive the message. See also FHSS, WIRELESS COMMUNICATIONS, BLUETOOTH.

DSSSL Abbreviation of DOCUMENT STYLE SEMANTICS AND SPECIFICATION LANGUAGE.

DTD Abbreviation of DOCUMENT TYPE DEFINITION.

DTE See DATA TERMINAL EQUIPMENT.

DTMF Abbreviation of DUAL TONE MULTI FREQUENCY.

DTP Abbreviation of DESKTOP PUBLISHING.

DTR See under DATA COMMUNICATION EQUIPMENT, DATA TERMINAL EQUIPMENT.

dual-boot The installation of two different OPERATING SYSTEMS on a computer's HARD

DISK, so that it may BOOT-UP into either one of them. Dual-booting is most commonly encountered between two different versions of WINDOWS, or between Windows and some version of UNIX. The choice of which operating system will be booted can be made by the user from a boot menu that is presented when the computer's power is turned on. When dual-booting between Windows and Unix, special attention may need to be paid to the organization of the PARTITIONS on the hard disk to ensure that the MASTER BOOT RECORD is correctly configured.

dual-bus A class of computer architecture that contains two BUSES.

Dual Independent Bus A BUS architecture introduced by Intel for its PENTIUM Pro and II microprocessor, in which two separate buses are used for the LEVEL 2 CACHE and the MAIN MEMORY, and the processor may access both simultaneously, yielding a threefold increase in total throughput. See also FRONTSIDE BUS, BACKSIDE BUS, SOCKET 8.

Dual In-line Memory Module See DIMM.

Dual Inline Package (DIP) A type of integrated circuit PACK-AGE that is rectangular with a row of connection pins down each long side, bent like the legs of an insect so that it can be inserted into a socket on a PRINTED CIRCUIT BOARD.

dual-ported A Random Access Memory (RAM) that incorporates two independent address and data BUSES, so that two different devices can simultaneously read or write to the chip. Dual porting is used to improve performance by reducing CONTENTION, particularly in GRAPHICS systems (see VIDEO RAM), enabling the computer's CPU to write fresh data into the graphics memory at the same time that the GRAPHICS PROCESSOR is reading it and displaying it on the screen.

dual scan display See PASSIVE MATRIX DISPLAY.

Dual Tone Multi Frequency The tone-based signalling PROTOCOL used for dialling on the public telephone system.

dumb A jargon term that can be applied to any electronic device that does not contain a reprogrammable microprocessor and there-fore has a fixed function; for example, a DUMB TERMINAL. Its opposite is SMART.

dumb terminal Any computer TERMINAL that has no processor of it own, and is therefore capable only of displaying data sent to it from a remote computer and sending back keystrokes typed on its keyboard.

dump A term used indiscriminately by programmers to indicate transferring data wholesale to another place, often in some low-level format: as in HEX DUMP, CORE DUMP, BRAIN DUMP, SCREEN DUMP.

duplex 1 In telecommunications, a channel that can carry signals in both directions. A FULL-DUPLEX channel can transmit in both directions simultaneously (e.g. a public telephone), while a HALF-DUPLEX channel can transmit only in one direction at a time, while a SIMPLEX channel can transmit only in one direction.
2 Of a printer, the ability to print on both sides of the paper in one pass.

dusty deck Ironic programmer's term for ancient mainframe programs that, conceptually if not in reality, ought to be contained on a deck of PUNCHED CARDS.

duty-cycle The proportion of time during which some periodically switched device is in the 'on' state.

DVD (Digital Versatile Disc) Originally called Digital Video Disc, a read-only OPTICAL DISK STORAGE medium with the same diameter (12 cm) but a larger data capacity than CD-ROM, mostly used to distribute feature-length films in digital MPEG 2 format.

DVD disks currently hold 4.7 gigabytes (GB) per side, capable of storing two hours of FULL-MOTION VIDEO, and double-sided versions are available that hold 9.4 GB, but require removal and manual turning over to read the other side.

DVD achieves its greater capacity by using smaller, closer-spaced data pits and a shorter wavelength LASER than CD-ROM, and it can transfer data around 9 times faster. Future versions will be double layered, where the read-back laser focuses at different depths to read from one of two parallel reflective layers. Single-sided, double-layer disks will hold 8.5 GB, and double sided 17 GB.

There has been a great confusion over DVD standards and nomenclature. Current read-only DVD drives are also called *DVD-ROM* (and now also read CD-ROMs), but differing regional formats have been adopted in an attempt to prevent US DVD films being viewed outside the USA. There are four incompatible recordable DVD formats. The write-once version for computer data is called *DVD-R*, uses dye technology like that in CD-R and holds 4.7 GB per side. There are three rival rewriteable formats called DVD-RAM (2.6 GB, supported by Toshiba and the DVD Forum); DVD-RW (4.7 GB, supported by Pioneer); and DVD+RW (3 GB, supported by Sony, Philips, HP and Ricoh).

DVD-R See under DVD.

DVD-RAM See under DVD.

DVD Read Only See under DVD.

DVD Recordable See under DVD.

DVD-ROM See under DVD.

DVD+RW See under DVD.

DVD-RW See under DVD.

DVI Abbreviation of DIGITAL VIDEO INTERACTIVE.

Dvorak keyboard An improved KEYBOARD layout proposed as an alternative to QWERTY, which enables faster typing by placing the most frequently used letters adjacent to the home keys. Its three alphabet rows are:

', . p y f g c r l / +
a o e u i d h t n s -
; q j k x b m w v z

Many PC keyboards can be reconfigured to the Dvorak layout by running a utility program and then swapping the key-caps around.

DXF (Drawing Exchange Format) An export file format first introduced by the AUTOCAD technical drawing program which is now widely used as an interchange format to move drawings from one drawing system to another.

dyadic operator Any mathematical OPERATOR, such as + (addition) or * (multiplication) that takes two ARGUMENTS. Sometimes called a 'binary operator', but in computing contexts this risks confusion with the digital meaning of BINARY.

dye-sublimation printer A type of non-impact colour PRINTER that uses heated electrodes to evaporate a solid wax-like ink onto the paper. Dye-sublimation is an expensive technology that produces extremely high quality output using a special high-gloss coated paper comparable with a photographic print. It is being rapidly displaced by the colour LASER PRINTER and improvements in INKJET PRINTER quality.

dye-transfer printer An obsolescent class of colour printer that works by transferring coloured dyes from a thin plastic film onto the paper, using either heat or mechanical impact. See also DYE-SUBLIMATION PRINTER.

dynamic Used of any computing resource that is created or allocated when needed, rather than having a more permanent existence. Its opposite is STATIC. See for example DYNAMIC ALLOCATION, DLL, DYNAMIC ROUTING.

dynamic address An ADDRESS acquired by an intelligent network device such as a BRIDGE, ROUTER or SWITCH from the DATA PACKETS it has processed, as opposed to an address that has been manually entered into the device's address table by a network administrator.

dynamic allocation The allocation of extra memory to a program while it is running. Dynamic allocation is employed to build data structures whose size cannot be predicted in advance and which may grow and shrink during execution, such as LISTS and TREES. To avoid running out of memory, dynamically allocated blocks of memory should be released when they are no longer needed. See also MALLOC, GARBAGE COLLECTION, MEMORY LEAK.

dynamic binding An alternative name for LATE BINDING. See also BINDING.

Dynamic Data Exchange (DDE) A PROTOCOL once used by Microsoft to provide communication between different application programs on a CLIENT/SERVER basis. Whenever a DDE server application modifies a shared document, one or more client applications will be informed via a DDE message that contains the modified portions of data. DDE is now obsolete, replaced by COM AUTOMATION, but support for it may still be encountered in many older programs that can act as a DDE client, server or both.

Dynamic DNS (DDNS) **1** A type of INTERNET service that enables net users to create web sites or other resources that can be accessed via a normal FULLY QUALIFIED DOMAIN NAME, despite having been allocated a dynamic IP ADDRESS that changes every time they go online (say by an INTERNET SERVICE PROVIDER that has more customers than IP addresses, or by a local area network that employs DYNAMIC HOST CONFIGURATION PROTOCOL). A DDNS service provides an alias for the resource, whose DNS entry is automatically updated whenever it is put online; some DDNS services charge for this service, while others are free.
2 A facility in Microsoft's WINDOWS 2000 that integrates the functions of the proprietary WINDOWS INTERNET NAMING SERVICE with the public DNS system. When a Windows 2000 server goes online, it publishes its DNS name and IP ADDRESS automatically to its local DNS server.

Dynamic Host Configuration Protocol (DHCP) A PROTOCOL developed by Microsoft that dynamically allocates IP ADDRESSES to IBM-compatible PCs connected to a Windows NT local area network using TCP/IP. System administrators can assign a range of IP addresses to the DHCP server and configure each client PC to request an address from it at log on time.

Dynamic HTML (DHTML) An extension of HTML created by Microsoft that offers greater control over the layout of WEB PAGES and enables them to interact with the user within the client BROWSER rather than via the SERVER. Under DHTML, HTML TAGS become active objects which export methods (see DOCUMENT OBJECT MODEL), and code may be embedded directly into web pages, while the appearance of a page is kept separate from its actions through the use of CASCADING STYLE SHEETS. DHTML tags can raise EVENTS similar to those used in VISUAL BASIC to capture user interactions such as clicking on a button or moving the mouse pointer. It also supports the binding of database files to web pages to allow data to be read and written from within them. DHTML is supported in INTERNET EXPLORER versions after 4.0 and in NETSCAPE COMMUNICATOR (though they differ over some details of the implementation). The WORLD WIDE WEB CONSORTIUM is currently developing a standard for DHTML. See also VBSCRIPT, JAVASCRIPT, ACTIVE SERVER PAGES, PHP.

dynamic link A LINK between two software modules that is forged only at RUN TIME, when one of the modules needs to call the other. See also DLL, LATE BINDING.

dynamic-linked library See DLL.

Dynamic Random Access Memory (DRAM) A type of RAM chip that can retain its contents only for a very brief period (measured in milliseconds) and must therefore be continually refreshed by reading its contents at short intervals. Despite the fact that DRAM requires extra REFRESH circuitry to be designed into the computer's PROCESSOR BUS, it has until recently been the most widely used type of memory because it is so much cheaper to manufacture than non-volatile STATIC RAM.
The CELLS that store the bits in a DRAM chip are simple single-transistor CAPACITORS (whose charge leaks away, hence the refresh requirement) and more of them can be packed onto a single chip than the multi-transistor cells used in STATIC RAM, reducing the cost per megabyte. DRAM is only now falling out of favour – on the grounds of speed rather than cost, because it cannot be read fast enough to keep up with the latest generations of microprocessor.

dynamic routing Any ROUTING algorithm that automatically adjusts to compensate for changes in the NETWORK topology or TRAFFIC flow. Also called *adaptive routing*.

dynamic scope A scoping scheme (see under SCOPE) most often encountered in INTERPRETED programming languages such as LISP and BASIC, under which a particular IDENTIFIER can be referred to not only within the block in which it was DECLARED, but also from inside any function or procedure that is CALLED within that block (even though they were declared elsewhere). Dynamic scoping offers great flexibility, but is also the source of very hard-to-trace errors, compared to the alternative LEXICAL SCOPING scheme employed by most compiled languages. See also PROCEDURE DECLARATION, FUNCTION DECLARATION, FORWARD DECLARATION.

Dynamic Storage The new disk STORAGE TYPE provided in Microsoft's WINDOWS 2000 operating system. A disk initialized for Dynamic Storage is called a dynamic disk and may contain multiple VOLUMES with separate drive letters, which replace the notion of PARTITIONS used in the older BASIC STORAGE system. A volume may be allocated from the free space on a single physical disk, or from up to 32 separate disks to form a SPANNED VOLUME. Other types of volume include the STRIPED VOLUME, the MIRRORED VOLUME and the RAID 5 volume. Disks and partitions formatted under older versions of Windows are called basic volumes and can share the same FILE SYSTEM (but not the same physical disk) with dynamic volumes. Dynamic Storage permits the rearrangement of volumes on a disk without requiring a REBOOT.

dynamic storage See under DYNAMIC ALLOCATION.

E

eager evaluation In a FUNCTIONAL PROGRAM-MING LANGUAGE, the evaluation of the whole of an expression. Compare with LAZY EVALUA-TION, in which only as much as needed in the current context is evaluated.

early-adopter One who enjoys wrestling with new technologies, a neophile. See also BLEED-ING EDGE.

early binding In OBJECT-ORIENTED PROGRAM-MING, the establishing of which object a METHOD call refers to when the program is being COMPILED, as opposed to doing it when the program is run – which is called late, dynamic or run-time binding. Early-bound method calls can be compiled as conventional procedure calls, which makes early binding more efficient than LATE BINDING, but restricts the ability of a program to exploit POLYMOR-PHISM. See also BINDING.

Easter egg A secret feature hidden within a piece of software by its programmers as a joke or testament to their prowess, which either appears spontaneously under certain rare cir-cumstances or can be activated by someone who knows a certain key sequence. Among the many products known to contain such Easter eggs are MICROSOFT WORD (a pinball game) and Excel 97 (a crude flight simulator), while on early PALM PILOTS a palm tree appeared on certain dates and a small car drove across the screen.

EBCDIC Abbreviation of EXTENDED BINARY CODED DECIMAL INTERCHANGE CODE.

eBook (electronic book) A format for docu-ments that are intended to be distributed in electronic form (for example downloaded from the WORLD WIDE WEB) and read on the screen of a PC, portable computer or dedicated eBook device. The format was developed by a large consortium of manufacturers, software vendors and content providers including Adobe, IBM, Microsoft, Simon & Schuster and the Library of Congress. The specification, which is available free of charge to all publish-ers, is based around HTML, XML and CASCADING STYLE SHEETS. eBook provides for illustrations by requiring that all conforming eBook read-ers must be able to view at least JPEG and PNG pictures. Other embedded content (for exam-ple Quicktime animations) may be supported, but always with a 'fallback' still picture in JPEG or PNG for viewers that cannot handle it. See also PDF, POSTSCRIPT, CLEARTYPE, PAGE DESCRIP-TION LANGUAGE.

ECC Shorthand for ERROR CORRECTION.

echo **1** To display the results of an operating system command on the local TERMINAL screen. In the early days of computing when DUMB TERMINALS prevailed, commands exe-cuted on the remote HOST computer did not by default display their results on the local screen (which would require transmitting them back down the serial communication line), so 'echoing' them there was an option that had to be explicitly configured.
2 Hence, the name of an MS-DOS and UNIX command that merely prints its arguments on the display.

echo cancellation The use of digital SIGNAL PROCESSING techniques to remove echoes from an audio stream such as a telephone transmission or microphone input; this fea-ture is often built into speakerphone and videophone equipment.

Eckert, J Presper (b. 1919) The co-inventor in 1946, along with John Mauchly, of ENIAC, which is often credited with being the first fully electronic digital computer. He later joined Mauchly in the ECKERT-MAUCHLY COMPUTER CORPORATION and sold the first commercial computer to the US Government.

Eckert-Mauchly Computer Corporation The first commercial computer company, founded in the USA by ECKERT and MAUCHLY, the inventors of ENIAC. Its product was called UNIVAC 1, the first general-purpose data processing computer, the first example of which was delivered to the US Census Bureau on 14 June 1951. The company was later merged into the Sperry Corporation.

ECL Abbreviation of EMITTER-COUPLED LOGIC.

ECMA Abbreviation of EUROPEAN COMPUTER MANUFACTURERS ASSOCIATION.

e-commerce (electronic commerce) The use of the INTERNET for advertising, buying and selling goods and services.

ECP Abbreviation of EXTENDED CAPABILITIES PORT.

ECRC (European Computer-Industry Research Centre GmbH) An industrial research centre located in Munich and jointly founded by Bull, ICL and Siemens. The centre pursues fundamental research in computer science.

edge A TRANSITION in a digital electrical signal in which its voltage goes from high to low or vice versa. See also EDGE-TRIGGERED.

A practical problem for electronic engineers is to maintain the edges in a signal as close as possible to the vertical ideal, in the face of circuit IMPEDANCE, ringing and other phenomena that would smear them out into gradual ramps. See LATCH, TERMINATE.

edge connector A type of coupling commonly used to plug EXPANSION BOARDS into a computer's BUS. It consists of a rectangular protrusion of the PRINTED CIRCUIT BOARD that carries a set of gold-plated TRACKS arranged like the teeth of a comb. This protrusion is plugged into an elongated box or EXPANSION SLOT which contains matching springy metal strips that both mechanically grip and make electrical contact with these tracks.

edge-detection A digital FILTER algorithm provided by most computer PAINTING PROGRAMS that can locate the edges of objects within a BITMAPPED image by identifying the steepest transitions between neighbouring colours. Having found such edges, further filters may be applied to exaggerate their sharpness (see EDGE ENHANCE), to soften or blur them, or to remove all flat areas of colour, leaving an outline drawing or the impression of an embossed or engraved image. See also IMAGE ENHANCEMENT, IMAGE PROCESSING.

edge enhance To find and exaggerate the sharpest transitions between adjacent colours in a BITMAPPED image, which mostly correspond to the edges of its depicted objects, and thus make the picture appear sharper. This function is widely used to sharpen blurred images in astronomy and forensic science, and once required the use of a supercomputer; now it is offered by most PC PAINTING PROGRAMS. See more under IMAGE ENHANCEMENT.

edge-lit A type of LIQUID CRYSTAL DISPLAY that is illuminated by strip lights arranged around its periphery rather than by a flat panel that covers its whole area. COLD CATHODE fluorescent tubes are typically used for this purpose. See also BACKLIGHT, ELECTROLUMINESCENCE.

edge-triggered A type of electronic LOGIC in which every TRANSITION of the signal voltage from high to low or vice versa is regarded as a separate event that can be used to initiate some operation. This is in contrast to LEVEL-TRIGGERED logic in which entering either the high or low state is itself regarded as an event. For the same CLOCK SPEED an edge-triggered device therefore sees twice as many events and works twice as fast.

Edinburgh Prolog A dialect of the PROLOG language, invented at Edinburgh University by Robert Kowalski in 1975, whose syntax eventually prevailed over that of the original MARSEILLE PROLOG. It is essentially the language described in the standard textbook by Clocksin and Mellish. Edinburgh syntax employs the :- symbol to stand for 'is implied by', and the comma to stand for 'and', as in:

```
is_a_duck(X) :- walks_like_duck(X),
quacks(X), swims(X).
```

edit box A component of all GRAPHICAL USER INTERFACES that consists of an outlined screen area into which the user can type text, and which offers the basic editing functions such as backspacing, deleting and inserting characters, and usually CUT-AND-PASTE facilities. See also COMBO BOX, LIST BOX.

edit-compile-run-debug cycle The fundamental cycle of program development, in which the programmer writes some code using a TEXT EDITOR, COMPILES and LINKS it, runs it and discovers a mistake, then returns to the editor to correct the mistake. Modern programming tools devote much effort and ingenuity to speeding up this cycle by minimizing the changes of attention required of the programmer. See more under INTEGRATED DEVELOPMENT ENVIRONMENT.

editor The generic term for computer programs that allow a human operator to create or alter the contents of DATA FILES of a particular type. For instance a TEXT EDITOR is used to write and alter text documents, while a BITMAP EDITOR manipulates images, and a WAVEFORM EDITOR is used to manipulate sound files.

EDO RAM (Extended Data Out RAM) A type of RAM chip that provides faster access by permitting the overlapping of data reads from successive columns of cells. It does this by keeping a column's data output active even after the next column has been selected, hence the name. Special circuitry is required to exploit this ability, and is provided in Intel's PENTIUM family of MICROPROCESSORS.

EDRAM Shorthand for ENHANCED DRAM.

EEPROM Shorthand for ELECTRICALLY ERASABLE PROM.

EFF Abbreviation of ELECTRONIC FRONTIER FOUNDATION.

e-form (electronic form) A form presented as part of a WEB PAGE which visitors to the site can fill in from within their WEB BROWSER (also called a WEB FORM). E-forms are already much used on E-COMMERCE sites for taking customers' orders and credit card details, and they promise to remove the need for paper forms for many bureaucratic purposes, such

as tax returns and censuses, once all the requisite information has been put online.

An e-form works in conjunction with a server-side SCRIPT (frequently a CGI script written in PERL) that collects the visitor's inputs and stores them in a database file on the server. HTML supplies a number of tags – including FORM, INPUT, SELECT and OPTION – for drawing appropriate input boxes and buttons on the page.

EFTPoS (Electronic Funds Transfer at Point Of Sale) The widespread system that enables retailers to authorize payments made by credit card by using a card reader connected to a telephone line.

EGA (Enhanced Graphics Adapter) IBM's second GRAPHICS ADAPTER for the PC family, introduced with the PC AT in 1984, which offered a RESOLUTION of 640 × 350 PIXELS in 16 colours. EGA is now entirely obsolete and its successor the VGA has become the minimum resolution standard. It was notable as the first IBM graphics standard to be REVERSE ENGINEERED and so spawned today's vast industry in add-on GRAPHICS CARDS. See also CGA, XGA.

egosurfing Scanning the WORLD WIDE WEB looking for mentions of one's own name.

EIDE An improved version of the popular IDE disk drive interface standard that offers faster data transfer thanks to 32-BIT transactions and the option of employing DIRECT MEMORY ACCESS. EIDE was invented by drive manufacturer Western Digital in the mid-1990s and is now an ANSI standard called Fast ATA-2 (see AT ATTACHMENT). Almost all the hard drives fitted in low cost PCs are EIDE devices. See also SCSI, ESDI.

Eiffel A pure OBJECT-ORIENTED PROGRAMMING LANGUAGE, developed in 1985 by Bertrand Meyer, which features strong TYPE CHECKING, MULTIPLE INHERITANCE, PERSISTENT objects and a powerful EXCEPTION HANDLING mechanism based on ASSERTIONS, PRECONDITIONS and POSTCONDITIONS. Eiffel compilers, which are generally available for Unix systems, generate C source code as an INTERMEDIATE LANGUAGE.

eight-plus-three A shorthand which alludes to the severe file-naming limitations imposed by the MS-DOS operating system. Files can have at most an 8-letter filename coupled to a 3-letter filename extension, as in myfilnam.txt.

Eight Queens Problem A test problem much used in teaching and ARTIFICIAL INTELLIGENCE programming research, which involves writing a program to place eight chess queens onto a chessboard so that no queen threatens any other.

8080 An early 8-bit microprocessor made by INTEL in 1974, which formed the basis of the first commercial personal computer, the ALTAIR 8800.

8086 An 16-bit microprocessor made by Intel in 1980 which, although never so widely used as its 8-bit offspring the 8088 (adopted for the IBM PC), introduced most of the elements that define the 8086 architecture with which all PC software must remain compatible even today. Unlike the 8088, the 8086 possessed a full 16-bit external DATA BUS. See also 8088, I386, I486, PENTIUM.

8088 The 8-bit microprocessor employed in the original IBM PC. The 8088, which ran at 4.77 megahertz (MHz), was a reduced-cost version of the 16-bit Intel 8086: it retained the latter's 16-bit register set but shrank its DATA BUS width down to 8 bits to permit the use of existing (and therefore cheap) 8-bit peripheral chips and the easy porting of 8-bit CP/M software. It would be hard to imagine a less attractive CPU design upon which to found a trillion dollar industry.

8514/A A high-resolution GRAPHICS ADAPTER capable of displaying 1024 × 768 pixels in 256 colours, introduced by IBM as an option for its PS/2 models in 1987. The 8514/A was the first IBM adapter to employ a dedicated graphics processor chip, making it a true GRAPHICS ACCELERATOR rather than a passive display device.

CLONE manufacturers who emulated the 8514/A dubbed its display format the XVGA standard, and this later became the basis of IBM's own XGA standard.

Eighty-Twenty Rule (80:20 Rule) A rule of thumb for complex software engineering projects that the last 20% of the code takes 80% of the time.

80x86 architecture A generic shorthand used to refer to all the members of INTEL CORPORATION's family of compatible microprocessors: the 8086, 80186, 80286, 80386 and 80486. Following the 80486, Intel abandoned these series numbers, substituting the name PENTIUM, but the term should strictly cover these chips too since the same code will run on them.

The term is typically used in descriptions of software products that will run on any one of these processors, or by programmers to refer to those features of the processor architecture that all the chips have in common. Those features consist basically of: a core set of four 16-bit general REGISTERS called AX, BX, CX and DX which can also be accessed as eight 8-bit registers; four 16-bit index registers SI, DI, BP and SP the STACK POINTER; the PROGRAM COUNTER; and four SEGMENT REGISTERS CS (Code Segment), SS (Stack Segment), DS (Data Segment) and ES (Extra Segment). See also REGISTER-COMPATIBLE.

EISA Abbreviation of EXTENDED INDUSTRY-STANDARD ARCHITECTURE.

eject A command, implemented either by a dedicated mechanical button, by software or both, which causes the storage medium to be expelled from a floppy disk, cartridge, CD-ROM or tape drive so that it can be changed. A similar button or software command is used in many PC Card slots and notebook computer DOCKING STATIONS.

elastomer A contraction of 'elastic polymer', the name given to many types of synthetic rubber, some of which are used to make low-cost computer and calculator keyboards.

Electrically Erasable PROM (EEPROM) A type of ROM whose contents can be erased and rewritten *in situ* by sending a pulse of higher voltage through some of its pins. EEPROM was once widely used to store semi-permanent configuration information in various electronic devices, but it is now being replaced by FLASH MEMORY for this purpose, which is much easier for end-users to update.

electric circuit See CIRCUIT.

electrode An electrical CONDUCTOR through which electric current can enter or leave some device such as a battery, a welding arc, an electrolytic cell or a valve (*US* vacuum tube).

Hence in SEMICONDUCTOR manufacture it has become the collective term used for the constituent parts of a TRANSISTOR.

electroluminescence The emission of light by some materials in the presence of an electrical field, but without depending on the generation of heat as in an incandescent lamp. The LIGHT-EMITTING DIODE is the oldest electroluminescent device. It operates by passing an electric current through an np junction made from a SEMICONDUCTOR such as GALLIUM ARSENIDE when visible light in a narrow waveband is emitted as electrons, and holes recombine at the junction. More recently electroluminescence has been discovered in silicon that has been etched into a fine, foam-like structure, which emits a much broader spectrum.

A different kind of electroluminescence is observed in unsaturated organic polymers such as polyacetylenes, polyaniline and polypyrrole, doped with oxidizing agents such as iodine or reducing agents. Sandwiches made from thin films of these materials separated by transparent organic insulators emit green, blue or white light when a low voltage is applied.

These polymers are used to make flat-panel computer displays by placing the phosphor between two wire grids to create self-luminous pixels at each intersection: though very thin, such displays are also expensive and of low intensity. When coated onto plastic panels, such organic phosphors are also used in commercial display signs, and in place of fluorescent tubes as backlights behind a conventional LIQUID CRYSTAL DISPLAY in mobile phones, wrist-watches and pocket computers, where their low power consumption is a great asset.

electroluminescent display See under ELECTROLUMINESCENCE.

electromagnetic radiation A form of energy that can propagate through empty space at the speed of light (3×10^8 metres per second), consisting of oscillating electrical and magnetic fields oriented at right angles to one another and to the direction of travel. Visible and ultraviolet light, X-rays, infra-red and radio waves are all forms of electromagnetic radiation of different wavelengths.

electromotive force (EMF) The energy required to move a unit charge of electricity around a circuit; that is, the energy required to overcome the POTENTIAL DIFFERENCE between two points in the circuit. The unit of electromotive force is the VOLT.

electron One of the fundamental subatomic particles from which all matter is composed, and whose motion is responsible for the phenomenon of electric current – hence the name electronics for the applied science of electrical devices. Every atom consists of a nucleus surrounded by a cloud of electrons, and in atoms of electrical conducting materials such as metals, these electrons may be detached and made to flow through the metal under the influence of an electrical FIELD. The electron bears a negative charge (of 1.6022×10^{-19} coulombs) and is therefore attracted toward more positively charged regions. It has a mass when at rest of 9.1096×10^{-31} kilograms. Electrons can also travel freely through a vacuum, for example in the electron beam of a CATHODE RAY TUBE.

electron gun The device inside a CATHODE RAY TUBE that generates the beam of ELECTRONS that is scanned to form the picture. It contains a filament coated in a rare earth salt that liberates electrons when heated, and a ring-shaped high-voltage electrode to accelerate them to a high speed. Most colour tubes contain three separate guns (for the red, green and blue signals) but Sony's Trinitron tubes generate three beams from a single gun with three cathodes.

electronic book See EBOOK.

electronic commerce See E-COMMERCE.

electronic form See E-FORM.

Electronic Frontier Foundation (EFF) A non-profit, public interest organization set up in 1990 by Mitch Kapor and others to address the social and legal issues arising from the increasing use of computers in communications and information distribution. The EFF lobbies on civil liberties issues, matters concerning freedom of expression, privacy, and access to online resources and information.

Electronic Funds Transfer at Point Of Sale See EFTPOS.

electronic magazine See E-ZINE.

electronic mail See EMAIL.

electronic mail address See EMAIL ADDRESS.

Electronic Numerical Integrator and Computer See ENIAC.

electronic performance support system (EPSS) An extension of the concept of COMPUTER-BASED TRAINING in which the training software integrates with the software product being taught so that it can continue to offer assistance during real use.

Electronic Point of Sale See EPOS.

electro-optical A class of device that combines electronic circuits with optical components such as solid-state LASERS or LEDS, an example being a chip that turns digital electrical signals into light pulses for transmission down an OPTICAL FIBRE.

electrostatic Any phenomenon or device that depends upon an electrical field created by an accumulation of stationary ELECTRONS – that is, where a voltage gradient exists but no current is flowing. An example of electrostatic principles at work is the laser printer or photocopier, in which toner particles are attracted to the revolving drum on which the image is formed by an electrostatic potential of several thousand volts.

elegance An ideal espoused by many mathematicians (and rather fewer computer programmers) which means the expression of a proof, concept or design simply, without fuss or superfluous elaboration.

element The general name for a single item that is part of some larger repetitive structure, for example one value in an ARRAY or list, or one PROCESSOR in a massively PARALLEL COMPUTER.

elevator seek An optimizing technique employed to speed up the ACCESS TIME of HARD DISK drives, which involves queuing up successive access requests and sorting them into the order of the physical location of the TRACKS on the disk surface, so that the HEAD is moved in only one direction rather than skipping back and forth. The name derives from a similar strategy employed by the elevators (lifts) serving different floors of a building. See also BUFFERED SEEK.

Eliza A pioneering ARTIFICIAL INTELLIGENCE program written by Joseph Weizenbaum, which pretended in a very simplistic way to be a psychotherapist. Whenever the patient states some fact, Eliza simply turns it around into a question, as in 'I hate my father!': 'Why do you hate your father?' Surprisingly, Eliza proved immensely popular, with people confiding to it things they would not say to a real therapist.

em A printer's unit of width, used to specify spaces and rules, traditionally equal to the width of a lower case letter m in the current FONT. See also POINT, POINT SIZE, EM-DASH.

Emacs A highly capable TEXT EDITOR for computers running the UNIX operating system, written by Richard Stallman, founder of the Free Software Foundation. Emacs paved the way for the modern word processor by presenting text as a scrolling, full screen display through which the user can move the cursor to the desired edit point – previous editors had relied on typed commands rather than on cursor interaction to perform editing (see LINE EDITOR). It was also perhaps the first successful example of FREEWARE, after Unix itself. Emacs enables users to add new functions – and to modify its own functions – by writing scripts in a built-in dialect of LISP. The program has now been ported to almost every operating system. See also VI.

email, e-mail, electronic mail Textual messages exchanged between individual computer users and conveyed across a communications NETWORK (for instance a company-wide local area network or the world wide INTERNET). Each user of an email system has their own MAILBOX to receive incoming messages, which has a unique EMAIL ADDRESS that correspondents must quote when sending a message.

Email messages have traditionally been composed of plain ASCII text, though there is now a growing tendency for them to be formatted in HTML to allow different type fonts, sizes, weights and colours to be seen when read within suitably-equipped MAIL READER software. Binary data files containing for example pictures, spreadsheets or executable programs may be sent alongside such email messages as BINARY ATTACHMENTS, using an encoding scheme such as UUENCODE or MIME. See also MAIL READER, MAIL SERVER, POP3, SMTP, IMAP.

email address A unique identifier that allows EMAIL messages to be directed to a specific recipient's MAILBOX. On the INTERNET a typical email address looks like fred@sales.widgets.co.uk, where fred is the name of the user and everything following the @ symbol is the DOMAIN or HOST name of the computer on which his mailbox is stored. Some proprietary email systems use different address formats, though most of these are now becoming obsolete.

If both sender and recipient have mailboxes on the same computer, it is usually sufficient to quote only the first part of the address, i.e. fred, to deliver a message. Large corporations and universities commonly employ an alias directory that maps individual names such as fred to a full email address, to simplify redirecting mail if someone leaves or changes department.

email attachment A document or other data file that is sent alongside a textual EMAIL message. An attachment can be in any binary file format and must be specially encoded for transmission over an email link using, for example, MIME or UUENCODE. The recipient's mail reader software must be capable of accepting and opening such attachments.

email client See MAIL READER.

email virus Now the most common form of computer VIRUS, a malicious program sent as an ATTACHMENT to an email, which may cause damage to a user's computer data when opened. Email viruses are usually MACROS written in the SCRIPTING LANGUAGE of some very popular application such as Microsoft Word, which are included within a document using the normal mechanism but are designed to AUTO-EXECUTE when that document is opened and cause some damage or nuisance such as erasing the contents of a hard disk, or sending a copy of themselves to everyone in the user's address book (see for example MELISSA VIRUS). Protective measures against email viruses include turning off macro execution, and banning whole swathes of file types from being accepted as

attachments. See also WORM, TROJAN HORSE, VIRUS SCAN, FIREWALL.

embedded Of computer hardware or software, permanently built into the fabric of some non-computing device such as a car, telephone or washing machine. See also EMBEDDED SYSTEM.

embedded controller A type of small MICROPROCESSOR that is built into a piece of electrical equipment such as a washing machine or CD player to automate its functions. See more under EMBEDDED SYSTEM, MICROCONTROLLER.

embedded font See FONT EMBEDDING.

embedded system A computer system built into some larger mechanical device, such as a car or a washing machine, in order to control its operations. Embedded systems run the same program continuously with very small amounts of storage to minimize the cost. Hence, designing and programming them is a specialized discipline significantly different from programming desktop computers.

EMC Directive The European Union's Electromagnetic-Compatibility directive of 1996 that regulates the amount of electromagnetic radiation that may be emitted by electrical equipment sold in the European Economic Area. Equivalent to the US FCC regulations.

em-dash A long horizontal dash CHARACTER one EM in width (much wider than an ordinary hyphen); once commonly used as punctuation in place of commas or a colon— as in this example. Now used more often to indicate the omission of a word or part of a word.

EMF **1** Abbreviation of ENHANCED METAFILE FORMAT.
2 Abbreviation of ELECTROMOTIVE FORCE.

emitter The electrode in a BIPOLAR TRANSISTOR which emits the electrons or holes that carry the current.

emitter-coupled logic (ECL) A type of fast digital logic circuit built using BIPOLAR TRANSISTORS, which was employed in the construction of MAINFRAME computers in the 1970s. ECL devices dissipate large amounts of heat, hence the water-cooling required by those machines – the switch to CMOS integrated circuits permitted today's miniature, energy-efficient computers.

EMM Abbreviation of EXPANDED MEMORY MANAGER.

EMM386 (expanded memory manager 386) A piece of software issued with all versions of the MS-DOS operating system from version 5.0 onward to enable it to access more than the 640 kilobytes of memory to which the original IBM PC was restricted. EMM386 works only on Intel processors later than the 80386, hence the name. The program is loaded in the CONFIG.SYS file at system start up, and was still required by all versions of WINDOWS prior to NT and 2000. See more under EXTENDED MEMORY and EXPANDED MEMORY.

emoticon A jargon name for the SMILEY and other symbols used to convey the writers mood in text-only EMAIL and NEWSGROUP messages. The use of emoticons is sufficiently well established that the latest text-to-speech synthesizers can speak them.

emphasis A collective term for various visual methods of drawing attention to certain words within a text, including the use of bold, italic and underlined FONTS, colour, and animated effects such as blinking.

EMS Abbreviation of EXPANDED MEMORY SPECIFICATION.

emulation The process by which one system or device mimics the operation of another, most typically by a computer running suitable software. An emulation that must reproduce the behaviour of the original system in all respects including speed is called a REAL TIME emulation, but in many applications emulation slower than the original is acceptable. Emulation software is often used to run software written for one processor or operating system on another. See also SIMULATION.

emulator Hardware or software that imitates the behaviour of another device sufficiently well that it may be used in its place under real operating conditions. An emulator that is used only for purposes of appearance, analysis, experimentation or training is more usually called a SIMULATOR. To illustrate this distinction, consider that an emulator for the Pentium chip might be used to run actual Pentium programs, but a Boeing 747 flight simulator will not take you to actual Barbados. See also EMULATION, SIMULATION.

en A printer's unit of width, used to specify spaces and rules, traditionally equal to the width of a lower case letter n in the current FONT. See also POINT, POINT SIZE, EN-DASH.

Encapsulated PostScript (EPS) A file format used to import into different DTP applications document layouts represented in the POST-SCRIPT page description language. Pages represented in EPS remain scalable and can be adjusted to the desired size within the target application without loss of quality.

EPS files contain PostScript code for the text, BITMAP images and any VECTOR drawings, together with PRAGMAS (comments) describing details such as the page's bounding box and page number. Photographs and fonts may also be embedded in the file as tables of bitmap data.

EPS files usually also contain a low-resolution preview of the whole layout which the target application can display to help the user identify the required image and position it accurately, without waiting for a full rendering.

encapsulation **1** In OBJECT-ORIENTED PROGRAMMING, the concealment of data items contained within an object so that they may be accessed only by calling that object's own methods, and remain invisible to all other program code.
2 In hardware engineering, the sealing of chips and other devices within a plastic coating to prevent the ingress of air and moisture.

Encarta Microsoft's CD-ROM encyclopedia.

encode To convert data into a different form. The purpose of encoding data may be to prevent it being read by unauthorized eyes (see ENCRYPTION), to prepare it for transmission or storage in a different medium (see for example ASCII code), or to represent it in the minimum of space (see for example HUFFMAN CODING). See also DECODE.

encryption The encoding of data so that it may be read only by authorized persons. Data is transformed in a way that can be reversed only by someone who possesses an extra piece of information called the KEY, which is a secret shared only by authorized parties.

Encryption is one of the principal means of guaranteeing the security of financial transactions performed over networks such as the INTERNET.

The search for new encryption techniques and algorithms forms an important and fast growing field known as CRYPTOGRAPHY. The currently most widely used methods of encryption are variants of PUBLIC-KEY ENCRYPTION which depend for their effectiveness upon the difficulty of factorizing large numbers. See also RSA ENCRYPTION.

en-dash A horizontal dash character one EN in width that is used as punctuation – like this.

endianism In any computer system that can ADDRESS memory a single byte at a time, an ambiguity arises over how quantities larger than one byte should be stored. As an example imagine storing the 16-bit quantity FE09h at the address 1000h. The two possible ways to do this are:

```
        1000: FE    1001:09
or      1000:09     1001:FE
```

Neither is more efficient nor more obvious than the other, so the decision between them is an arbitrary design choice. However, once this choice is built into the PROCESSOR hardware it is irrevocable, and a processor that chose the first way would read data stored in the second way as completely scrambled. Hence this arbitrary choice creates an incompatibility between processor families as deep as that caused by different INSTRUCTION SETS; not only can they not run each other's programs, but they cannot even read each other's data. The industry, with characteristic irony, chose to name this dilemma after the warring Big Endian and Little Endian boiled-egg eaters described in Swift's *Gulliver's Travels*. See also BIG-ENDIAN, LITTLE-ENDIAN.

END key A key on most modern computer keyboards that moves the screen cursor to the end of the current line or to the last field on a form. See also HOME KEY, CURSOR KEYS.

endnote Notes commenting on points made in a document, which are listed at the end of each chapter or of the whole document, unlike FOOTNOTES, which are placed at the bottom of the page on which they are referred to. Attention is drawn to the existence of each endnote by a reference mark (typically a SUPERSCRIPT number) placed in the body of the text.

End Of File See EOF.

End Of Line (EOL) See LINE-END CHARACTER.

end station The WORKSTATIONS at both ends – that is, the caller and the called – of a network communication.

end-to-end See under CONNECTION-ORIENTED.

end-user The person who uses a computer application program to perform actual work, as distinct from those persons involved in the designing, writing and maintenance of the application. See also DEVELOPER, OEM.

energy-saving The preferred marketing term for those automatic power-management features, found in most modern PCs and monitors, that turn themselves off after some prescribed interval of non-use.

Engelbart, Douglas (b. 1925) A pioneer of computer user interface design who invented the MOUSE and foresaw the GRAPHICAL USER INTERFACE at Stanford Research Institute in 1963. He also developed one of the first HYPERTEXT document retrieval systems, called Augment.

Enhanced DRAM (EDRAM) A type of RAM that has a region of CACHE built into in each chip to speed access. The main storage portion of each chip is conventional DRAM, but the smaller cache part is fast STATIC RAM, which enables frequently accessed items to be retrieved more quickly.

Enhanced Graphics Adapter See EGA.

Enhanced Integrated Drive Electronics See EIDE.

Enhanced Metafile Format (EMF) An improved version of the WINDOWS METAFILE FORMAT that employs a superior compression method to achieve much smaller file sizes.

Enhanced Parallel Port (EPP) An extension of the PARALLEL PORT into an EXPANSION BUS, defined in the IEEE 1284 standard, which enables the connection of up to 64 peripherals such as disk drives, scanners and printers at the same time, with a maximum data rate of 1.5 megabytes per second in both directions.

EPP employs a 25-pin connector compatible with the standard CENTRONICS PORT printer port. See also EXTENDED CAPABILITIES PORT.

Enhanced Small Disk Interface See ESDI.

ENIAC (Electronic Numerical Integrator and Calculator) The first general-purpose digital computer, built during World War II by John MAUCHLY and J Presper ECKERT and unveiled in 1946 at the University of Pennsylvania. ENIAC was created to calculate the tables of ballistic trajectories used by artillery gunners, a very similar purpose to that for which Charles BABBAGE's Difference Engine was invented a century earlier.

ENIAC employed 19,000 vacuum tubes and 1,500 mechanical RELAYS as its logic elements, consumed 200 kilowatts of power (which necessitated forced-air cooling) and weighed over 30 tonnes. It anticipated all the basic hardware circuits employed in modern computers, including the digital AND and OR LOGIC GATES and the FLIP-FLOP as a storage element. It could add, subtract, multiply, divide, extract square roots and compare numbers for equality, and could store up to 20 10-digit decimal numbers in its vacuum tube memory. It was not software programmable, the type of computation it performed being determined by manual alteration of hardware switches and cable connections. However, it was while working on ENIAC in 1947 that John VON NEUMANN thought of several enhancements which lead to the STORED-PROGRAM COMPUTER concept that remains the model for almost all modern computers.

Controversy persists over whether ENIAC or the British COLOSSUS machines built at BLETCHLEY PARK for code-breaking deserve the title of first electronic computer, and this is complicated by the fact that Colossus remained a state secret until the 1970s. On balance, both machines deserve to share this honour.

Enigma machine An electro-mechanical CIPHER generator employed by the German armed forces during World War II, the secret cracking of whose code is seen by some historians as the turning point of the war, since it helped to break the U-boat blockade of the Atlantic. The Enigma was originally a commercial device, invented and exhibited in 1923 and openly used by many banks in several countries. However, a secret military version had greatly enhanced capabilities.

Enigma was a box fitted with a typewriter keyboard, which created substitution ciphers by displaying a different letter whenever a key was pressed. However, unlike simple table-based ciphers, Enigma's substitution scheme changed at every keypress, thanks to a set of brass rotors that rotated to create a new electrical circuit path and light up a different letter. The machine's operators could change the order and starting positions of these rotors, and the settings of plugs in a plugboard, at the start of each working day to create a wholly new family of ciphers. Later in the war, more rotors were added, and the operators could choose them from a larger set.

The complexity of the Enigma cipher was such that manual decoding proved impossible, but cryptanalysts in Warsaw and Britain's BLETCHLEY PARK discovered a tiny weakness, derivable if a message was repeated, which could be exploited given the aid of a powerful mechanical calculator that did not then exist. The effort to build such a calculator, lead by the Cambridge mathematician Alan TURING, was one of the seminal moments in the history of the development of the electronic computer. See more under BOMBE, COLOSSUS, CRYPTOGRAPHY. See also ENIAC, VON NEUMANN.

Enter key The key used to terminate lines of text and commands on a computer keyboard. See more under RETURN KEY.

enterprise A term used to distinguish the kinds of computers and software purchased for use within large corporations from those intended for small and one-person businesses. Describing a product as 'enterprise level' implies that it can operate across a network to support multiple users and shared databases. See also DEPARTMENTAL, MIDRANGE SYSTEM, SOHO.

Enterprise Memory Architecture A technology developed by Microsoft and Intel that enables applications that are 'large memory aware' to CACHE their data in high memory addresses on servers fitted with more than 4 gigabytes of RAM.

enterprise server A powerful SERVER that can cope with the load imposed by a whole corporation, with perhaps hundreds or thousands of users.

entity-relationship model A DATA ANALYSIS methodology invented by P Chen in 1976, which works by separating the items to be represented in a DATABASE into two logical groupings: *entities* such as 'customer' and 'product', and *relations* such as 'orders' and 'pays for'. The resulting entity-relationship diagram captures most significant aspects of the transactions that may be expected to take place, and can be used as a basis for designing and coding the actual software system. The entities tend to become FIELDS in the database, while the relations will become the software routines that operate on those fields. See also METHODOLOGY, UNIFIED MODELLING LANGUAGE, CASE, BOOCH METHOD, YOURDON METHOD, OBJECT-ORIENTED ANALYSIS.

entry-level The marketing term for a low-cost system.

entry-point The ADDRESS of the INSTRUCTION at which execution of a program, or a routine within a program, must begin. A LIBRARY has multiple entry-points, one for each routine it contains.

enumerated type, enumeration type A DATA TYPE whose declaration consists of an exhaustive list of all the values it may represent. Despite the name, these values need not be numbers, although the compiler converts them to integers. For example, an enumerated type called WeekEndDay might have the values [Saturday, Sunday]. Enumerated types are supported in C++, PASCAL and ADA among other languages.

environment 1 The set of facilities provided to the user by a particular computer program: see for example INTEGRATED DEVELOPMENT ENVIRONMENT.
2 In the MS-DOS and UNIX operating systems, a set of variables maintained within the SHELL that may be read by any application program, containing for example the location of important libraries, the names of shared directories, and other global information. For example the MS-DOS PATH forms part of the environment. See also ENVIRONMENT VARIABLE.
3 In programming, the set of VARIABLE BINDINGS with which an EXPRESSION is to be evaluated.

environment mapping An extension of the technique of TEXTURE MAPPING to create more realistic 3D images, in which the textures to be applied are calculated dynamically from the surrounding objects in a scene, rather than stored as static BITMAPS. This allows a highly realistic depiction of shiny objects that carry reflections of their surrounding environment.

environment variable A mechanism used in many operating systems including MS-DOS and UNIX to store global information that is required by many different programs, such as the current date and time, or the location of important libraries, configuration files and shared system directories. Environment variables are stored within the operating system's SHELL, and may be accessed by any application program or script that needs them.

For example the MS-DOS PATH is stored in an environment variable that may be accessed from the command prompt or from a BATCH FILE under the name %PATH%. The MS-DOS SET command enables users to define their own new environment variables, so:

```
C:\> set dick=good chap
C:\> echo %dick%
good chap
```

EOF (End Of File) A special CHARACTER that is appended to the end of a file to inform software that there is no more data to come. The character employed differs under different operating systems: MS-DOS uses ^Z (ASCII code 26) while Unix often uses ^D (ASCII code 04). See also CONTROL CHARACTER.

EOL (End Of Line) See LINE-END CHARACTER.

EPIC (Explicitly Parallel Instruction Computing) The architecture of Intel's 64-bit ITANIUM processor, based on VLIW principles. The PROCESSOR executes groups of three instructions at a time, and allows a COMPILER or an ASSEMBLY LANGUAGE programmer to explicitly indicate which ones can be executed together. A hugely extended REGISTER set with 128 general registers, 128 FLOATING-POINT registers and 128 application registers ensures that most code can execute with all its variables in registers and no contention. See also PARALLEL PROCESSING.

EPOC 32 A 32-bit MULTITASKING operating system for hand-held computers and mobile telephones, originally developed by PSION and then spun off into the separate company SYM-BIAN in collaboration with NOKIA and ERICS-SON. EPOC was originally written for the ARM and STRONGARM processor families but has now been ported to Intel and Motorola chips. EPOC employs a strongly OBJECT-ORIENTED architecture, structured as a collection of application servers in which the user interface is rigorously separated from data-processing code. It is optimized for REAL TIME telephony applications such as GSM decoding, featuring a small real-time KERNEL that offers very rapid INTERRUPT HANDLING. See also REAL TIME EXEC-UTIVE, WINDOWS CE.

EPoS (Electronic Point of Sale) A class of computer system designed for use in shops and other retail premises in which the cash registers are computer TERMINALS connected by a NETWORK to an accounting system that logs all the cash transactions, a price database to look up the cost of items, and a stock control system that reduces the stock level record as items are sold and permits automatic re-ordering.

EPP Abbreviation of ENHANCED PARALLEL PORT.

EPROM (Erasable Programmable Read Only Memory) A type of ROM chip that can be erased and reprogrammed. The process of programming an EPROM is often called BURN-ING, and the box into which it is plugged to program it an EPROM burner.

To erase its contents, the most popular and cheapest kind of EPROM has to be removed from its socket in the computer and placed under an ultraviolet light. Such UV-erasable EPROMs have a round glass window on top of the chip package through which radiation passes and discharges the memory cells on the silicon chip. EPROM is relatively cheap and was once widely used for prototyping and to hold FIRMWARE that was subject to frequent revision. It is now being displaced by ELECTRI-CALLY ERASABLE PROM, which can be erased *in situ* by raising the voltage on one or more pins, and more recently by FLASH MEMORY.

EPS Abbreviation of ENCAPSULATED POST-SCRIPT.

epsilon (∈) The fifth letter of the Greek alphabet, used in mathematics as the symbol to represent an extremely small quantity, tending toward zero. It is often encountered in calcula-tions of error and precision, to represent a small discrepancy.

EPSS Abbreviation of ELECTRONIC PERFORM-ANCE SUPPORT SYSTEM.

equation A mathematical statement that asserts that two EXPRESSIONS have the same value, for example: $x^2+7 = 7x-5$

An equation such as this one, which contains a VARIABLE x, is said to be 'solved' when a value is found for x that makes the statement true (in this case $x=3$ or $x=4$). These values are called the 'roots' of the equation.

equation-solver A computer program that can find solutions to a set of EQUATIONS. See also SOLVER.

equipment check A software INTERRUPT provided in the BIOS of an IBM-COMPATIBLE PC, which an application program can call to determine what hardware facilities are available: for example whether or not a MATHS-COPROCESSOR is present. The data returned by equipment check is collected during the POWER-ON SELF TEST routine.

erasable A description applied to any data storage medium that is capable of having its contents erased, which does not necessarily imply that the contents may be rewritten after such erasure – for example a CD-R disk is erasable but not rewriteable. See also WRITE-ONCE, READ-ONLY, READ-MOSTLY.

Erasable Programmable Read Only Memory Abbreviation of EPROM.

ergonomic keyboard A KEYBOARD designed with ERGONOMIC principles rather than merely speed of typing in mind. This means maintaining the hands, wrists and lower arms in positions that are as close as possible to their natural ones, so most such keyboards split the keys between twin, angled keypads – one for each hand – and tilt the keyboard away from the user. Microsoft's NATURAL KEYBOARD is the most widely available such device.

ergonomics The study of the work environment and its effects on the human body. Its findings impinge on the computer industry particularly in the areas of seating, lighting, KEYBOARD and VDU design. See ERGONOMIC KEYBOARD.

Ericsson A Swedish company that is one of the world's leading makers of MOBILE PHONES and other telecommunications equipment.

Erlang 1 Agner Erlang, a Danish mathematician (1878–1929) who developed a theory of random processes in statistical equilibrium that is widely employed in the simulation and design of telecommunication systems.

2 A concurrent FUNCTIONAL PROGRAMMING LANGUAGE designed for creating large telecommunication programs, for example to drive automatic telephone exchanges, developed at ERICSSON's research laboratories and named in honour of the above.

ERM Abbreviation of ENTITY-RELATIONSHIP MODEL.

ERP (Enterprise Resource Planning) A branch of business computing that integrates purchasing, planning, production, distribution and accounting software systems. Among the chief vendors of ERP software suites are SAP and BAAN.

error 1 A measure of the discrepancy between the intended value of some quantity and an estimate or approximation to it, whether computed or measured. See also PRECISION, ACCURACY.

2 An abnormality in the operation of, or a premature termination of, a computer program due to some condition arising that the program's authors had not foreseen, or to some mistake in the program's logic. See also ERROR MESSAGE, ERROR HANDLING, EXCEPTION, BUG, DEBUGGER, BUG REPORT, PROGRAM CORRECTNESS, FORMAL METHODS.

error checking The process of detecting whether errors have been introduced into information that has been transmitted over a communications channel or stored in a device. Error checking is performed by using techniques such as a PARITY test or a CYCLIC REDUNDANCY CHECK. See more under ERROR CORRECTION, ERROR DETECTION AND CORRECTION.

error condition Any state that deviates from the intended behaviour of a piece of software or hardware.

error correcting memory A type of RAM that adds ERROR DETECTION AND CORRECTION circuitry to automatically detect and correct a single BIT ERROR in any of the chips. Such errors are often induced, for example, by stray alpha particles emitted from minute amounts of radioactive elements in the chips' packaging.

If fitted at all, error correction schemes for personal computers work by adding a single extra parity BIT to every BYTE (which is why RAM is built from banks of nine rather than eight chips). The memory circuitry calculates the PARITY, odd or even, of the bits in each bank, so any single bit error will be detected and a PARITY ERROR signalled. MAINFRAME and MINICOMPUTER error correction schemes typically add multiple parity bits that allow the exact location of the changed bit to be identified, so that it can be corrected. See more under ERROR DETECTION AND CORRECTION.

error correction (EC) See ERROR DETECTION AND CORRECTION.

error detection and correction The application of methods derived from INFORMATION THEORY to the detection and correcting of errors in DIGITAL data streams. Error correction is of the utmost importance in most areas of computing and communications technology. For example: Internet's TCP protocol provides error detection, CD-ROMS devote around 14% of their total data capacity to redundant error correction information (and music CDS only a little less), and modem speeds above 28 kilobits per second would be impossible over public telephone lines without error correcting PROTOCOLS such as V.90.

All error detection methods involve adding redundant (i.e. non-data) bits to each data word, and up to a point the more redundancy added the more errors can be detected and corrected. For example adding a single redundant bit and calculating the PARITY of a message allows the fact that a single bit has changed to be detected, but not to be located for correction. Using more redundant bits allows multiple bit errors to be both detected and corrected. For example a REED-MULLER CODE employed by NASA to send image data from interplanetary probes sends 32 bits for each 5-bit PIXEL value, and can detect and correct corruption of up to 7 of those bits. The related REED-SOLOMON CODE provides the redundant bits on CD-ROM and hard disk drives.

error diffusion A widely-used dithering technique (see under DITHER) for digitized pictures, which averages adjacent pixel values to avoid conspicuous dot patterns.

error handling The provision of code in a computer program that enables it to recover from errors. See more under EXCEPTION HANDLING.

error message A message displayed by a program to inform its user that it has malfunctioned or cannot interpret the user's input. The ideal error message would state exactly what caused the problem and how to cure it, but this is seldom possible in practice because in a modern computer there are many layers of software between the user and the hardware, and no application program can be written to anticipate all the possible errors that might occur in the levels beneath it. Hence error messages vary widely in their helpfulness, depending on how deep the source of the error is. Errors from an APPLICATION PROGRAM itself may be relatively informative and couched in terms of objects meaningful to the user, such as 'The printer is not ready. Make sure it is turned on and online', whereas errors that originate in the lowest layers of the operating system are intended to provide diagnostic information to programmers and are phrased in terms of abstract entities, such as 'Protection violation in module GDI.EXE at address $3D99:9E00'. Error messages consisting simply of numbers, such as 'I/O Error 34' originate in the programming language system used to write an application, and are evidence of very poor program design.

error propagation The spreading of an error condition when it causes errors in other connected regions, for example software modules or network nodes.

error trapping The ability of a program to catch an ERROR CONDITION while retaining control, so that corrective actions may be taken.

escape (ESC) **1** The character with ASCII code 27, formerly used as a signal to terminate the operation of programs and operating system operations. It may be sent from most computer keyboards by pressing the *escape key*. Modern GRAPHICAL USER INTERFACES seldom use escape to terminate a whole program, but often use it to dismiss a dialogue box or terminate other types of temporary user interaction.

2 ESC is also employed as the prefix character for ESCAPE SEQUENCES which are interpreted by some operating systems and printers as commands, for example to change a text font or screen background colour.

escape key See under ESCAPE.

escape sequence A numeric code used to control peripheral devices such as printers or VDU screens. Non-graphical operating systems such as UNIX and MS-DOS send escape sequences, say, to switch the printer into bold type or to change the screen's background colour. Escape sequences may be embedded into documents to achieve formatted printing (see also WYSIWYG). The name derives from the fact that such sequences by convention begin with the ESC or escape character (ASCII 27). For example, the sequence ESC [2J clears the screen on an ANSI terminal.

ESDI (Enhanced Small Disk Interface) A HARD DISK controller standard developed between 1983 and 1990 by a consortium of US drive manufacturers. Derived from the ST506 interface but faster than both that and SCSI, ESDI supported hard, floppy, optical and tape DRIVES in the same controller. However, unlike the system-level, hardware-independent SCSI, ESDI was a device-level interface built into the drive mechanism. Controllers had therefore be certified to work with every sort of drive, and DEVICE DRIVERS written for every controller/drive combination. For this reason ESDI remained confined to high-performance applications (including servers from Compaq and Dell, and IBM's PS/2), and lost the battle for the mainstream PC market to IDE and later EIDE.

ESPRIT (European Strategic Programme for Research in Information Technology) An EU-sponsored initiative that ran from 1984 to 1998 to encourage collaboration between university and industrial research.

etaoinshrdlu The letters that appeared on the first row of keys of an old Linotype hot-metal TYPESETTER, which were arranged in descending order of their abundance in typical English text (and hence provide a useful mnemonic for these frequencies).

etching The process of removing surface layers, using corrosive chemicals or beams of particles, employed in the manufacture of INTEGRATED CIRCUITS and PRINTED CIRCUIT BOARDS.

e-text A paper document, for example a novel or play, that has been transferred into some electronic format (often HTML or SGML) so that it can be disseminated and read online. See also EBOOK.

Ethernet The most popular LAN medium, invented by Xerox at PARC and co-developed with Digital Equipment and Intel. Ethernet has become the industry standard for smaller networks, and is the subject of IEEE standard 802.3. The invention of single-chip Ethernet controllers has made Ethernet cards very cheap, and many modern PCs have it built-in on the MOTHERBOARD.

Ethernet is a SHARED MEDIUM network technology, where all the workstations are connected to the same cable and must contend with one another to send signals over it. The algorithm used to resolve collisions – that is, when two workstations try to speak at the same time – is called CSMA/CD, and works by forcing both workstations to back off for random (and hence probably different) intervals before trying again.

The maximum data rate of the original Ethernet technology is 10 megabits per second (Mbps), but a second generation FAST ETHERNET carries 100 Mbps, and the latest version called GIGABIT ETHERNET works at 1000 Mbps. SWITCHED ETHERNET involves adding switches so that each workstation can have its own dedicated 10 Mbps connection rather than sharing the medium, which can improve network throughput – it has the advantage over rival switched technologies such as ASYNCHRONOUS TRANSFER MODE that it employs the same low-level protocols, cheap cabling and NETWORK INTERFACE CARDS as ordinary Ethernet.

Ethernet station Any addressable device or NODE connected to an Ethernet network that is capable of transmitting, receiving and/or repeating data PACKETS. It may be a WORKSTATION or some peripheral such as a HUB or a PRINTER.

Euclid A programming language derived from PASCAL, designed for the creation of verifiable software systems. It dispenses with difficult-to-verify features such as global assignment and nested procedures.

Eudora A popular MAIL READER program published by Qualcomm Inc., which is available for Windows PCs and the Apple MACINTOSH and supports MIME attachments.

EULA (End-User Licence Agreement) The term used by Microsoft and other software vendors for the licence specifying the conditions under which their software products may be used. See more under SOFTWARE LICENCE.

EUnet A network with infrastructure spread throughout Europe that forms the largest European component of the INTERNET BACKBONE.

Eurocard A family of standard sized PRINTED CIRCUIT BOARDS ranging from Normal Eurocard at 100 × 160 mm, through Extended double at 233.4 × 220 mm to Hyper extended double Eurocard at 233.4 × 280 mm. Eurocards are mostly used in industrial VME bus and STEbus computers rather than in PCs.

European Computer Manufacturers Association (ECMA) A trade association that issues computing technology standards.

European Strategic Programme for Research in Information Technology See ESPRIT.

eval A function provided in many INTERPRETED programming languages – for example, some BASIC dialects, PERL and LISP – which evaluates an EXPRESSION supplied as a text string and returns the result.

evaluate To compute the current value of a function or expression, given the current values of any variables it contains.

evangelize To preach the virtues of a particular computer, PROCESSOR, OPERATING SYSTEM or PROGRAMMING LANGUAGE. Supposedly metaphorical, but often approaches the literal.

Evans and Sutherland A firm founded in 1969 that was the pioneer of 3D GRAPHICS in both hardware and software, and still manufactures some of the most advanced professional flight simulators.

even-byte boundary A memory address that is an even number. See also DATA ALIGNMENT.

even parity See PARITY BIT.

event **1** Any time-dependent occurrence that is of significance to a program or task, for example the updating of a file, a hardware INTERRUPT, or the completion of an ASYNCHRONOUS output operation.

2 More specifically in programs that employ a GRAPHICAL USER INTERFACE, any significant action performed by the user (such as moving the mouse pointer over a window or clicking a mouse button) that can be interpreted by the program as a command. See also EVENT-DRIVEN.

event-driven A type of computer program that is always ready to respond to one of many possible user inputs, in contrast to one that responds only to a predefined sequence of COMMANDS and inputs. The term typically applies to programs with a GRAPHICAL USER INTERFACE in which the user may arbitrarily select any one of several controls displayed on the screen by pointing with a mouse or touch screen. Each such selection is treated as a separate EVENT by the program code, hence the name.

event handler A section of program CODE designed to respond to the occurrence of a particular EVENT.

event log A file that is automatically generated by many computer OPERATING SYSTEMS and SERVERS which provides a permanent record of the system's status, including any abnormal occurrences during the starting, running and closing of programs.

event loop The heart of any GRAPHICAL USER INTERFACE, a section of program code that loops continually, watching for the occurrence of user EVENTS such as mouse movements or button clicks, and activates the appropriate EVENT HANDLER to perform a response whenever it detects one. Control always returns to the event loop after any response is completed. See also EVENT-DRIVEN.

event partitioning A software design method used for REAL TIME applications, in which the problem is conceived as a collection of concurrent and sequential EVENTS.

event queue A collection of EVENTS arranged in time order to await processing. The event queue is a crucial DATA STRUCTURE in many kinds of MULTITASKING software environment, used to prevent any events being ignored because the task that should process them is busy doing something else. See also EVENT HANDLER, EVENT-DRIVEN, EVENT PARTITIONING, SCHEDULING.

event source Any entity or subsystem that generates EVENTS to which a program needs to respond – for example a human user, a peripheral device, or the operating system.

exabyte 2^{60} BYTES of information (that is 1,152,921,504,606,846,976) or 1024 PETABYTES.

Excel The SPREADSHEET component of the MICROSOFT OFFICE software suite.

exception An EVENT that changes the normal FLOW OF CONTROL in a program. Exceptions may be raised by both hardware and software subsystems, and they may represent ERROR conditions (for example attempting to divide a number by zero) or unpredictable but legal events such as a user pressing the RESET button, or a memory manager chip reporting a PAGE FAULT. The process of dealing with exceptions in such a way that the program can continue running afterwards is called EXCEPTION HANDLING.

exception handler See EXCEPTION HANDLING.

exception handling That aspect of a computer program that copes with unusual events and errors, collectively called EXCEPTIONS, and hence allows the program to continue running. Many early programming languages lacked any provision for exception handling, merely stopping the program with the display of a RUN-TIME ERROR message. Modern programming languages, such as C++, VISUAL BASIC and DELPHI, provide special control structures that execute a certain section of code, called an *exception handler*, whenever a particular exception occurs. Such handlers try to correct the condition that caused the exception, and repair any damaged data.

Exchange The EMAIL component of MICROSOFT BACKOFFICE, sold in both CLIENT and SERVER versions.

Excite A popular Internet SEARCH ENGINE.

exclamation mark (*US* exclamation point) The ! character, ASCII code 33, used in text to terminate sentences that are to be emphasized or dramatized. (Use in moderation!) In journalists' and programmers' slang it is often called 'shriek', 'pling' or 'bang'.

exclusive OR See under XOR.

EXE The FILENAME EXTENSION reserved for executable files under the MS-DOS and WINDOWS operating systems. Any file whose name ends in .EXE can be executed by typing the first part of its name, so to run EDIT.EXE one types EDIT.

Internally, a .EXE file differs from the earlier and simpler .COM type of executable file in that the code it contains must be RELOCATABLE (that is, must be capable of running from any address), and may be divided into many separate sections that can be loaded on demand in a manner invisible to the program's user.

exec **1** A UNIX system call that executes another program from within the one that makes the call. See also CHAIN.

2 On IBM mainframe computers, a type of BATCH FILE or SHELL SCRIPT.

executable Capable of being executed by a computer's PROCESSOR, that is, a valid processor INSTRUCTION or sequence of such instructions. The term is often used as a noun to mean a file that contains such a sequence of valid instructions, and therefore constitutes a PROGRAM. Used as in 'the second disk contains all the executables'.

executable content Material placed on a WEB PAGE that contains EXECUTABLE code, which is downloaded into the BROWSER of anyone who views that page and is executed there. JAVA, JAVASCRIPT and ACTIVEX are examples of technologies used to implement executable content, which typically takes the form either of animated graphics, or some kind of interactive control such as a calculator or search facility. Executable content can pose severe security problems, because it offers an entry point for maliciously intended code such as a VIRUS or TROJAN HORSE that performs destructive actions when executed on the local computer. A possible solution is the SANDBOX.

execution The performance by a COMPUTER of the operations specified in a list of INSTRUCTIONS called a PROGRAM (or SCRIPT), as a result of which input data is turned into output data.

execution profiler A software tool that enables a programmer to see which parts of a program are being executed most often. The output from a PROFILER provides the basis on which improvements to the program can be most productively made. A small time saving in the most often executed routine is worth far more than a huge saving in one that is rarely executed. Profiling is often employed to determine whether a chosen ALGORITHM is effective, or should be replaced by a better one.

executive An alternative name for an OPERATING SYSTEM, mostly applied to the small REAL TIME systems used for EMBEDDED control applications.

exit condition A test that determines when to terminate the repetition of a program LOOP.

expanded memory See EXPANDED MEMORY SPECIFICATION.

expanded memory manager The special software required by IBM-COMPATIBLE personal computers using the MS-DOS operating system and INTEL processors, to enable them to address more than 640 kilobytes of memory. The most commonly used expanded memory manager is EMM386, which is supplied by Microsoft with MS-DOS and loaded from the CONFIG.SYS file – there are, however, enhanced products from other manufacturers such as Quarterdeck's QEMM. The expanded memory manager is no longer required under later versions of Windows, which perform their own memory management. See more under EXPANDED MEMORY SPECIFICATION and see also EXTENDED MEMORY.

Expanded Memory Specification (EMS) A complex scheme developed jointly by Lotus, Intel and Microsoft in the late 1980s to enable IBM-compatible PCs to access more than the 640 kilobytes (KB) of memory available in REAL MODE. EMS is a paged memory scheme in which the extra memory is accessed by swapping ranges of addresses at least 64 KB in length into and out of a so-called PAGE FRAME stored in the high memory region from 640 KB to 1 megabyte. Access to this memory is enabled by a software add-in called an EXPANDED MEMORY MANAGER. Early PCs also required a hardware ADAPTER CARD to access EMS memory, but Intel processors from the

80386 onward perform the necessary address mapping for themselves. See also EXTENDED MEMORY.

expansion board An alternative name for an EXPANSION CARD.

expansion bus A computer BUS that contains several sockets, each of which can accept an EXPANSION CARD and connect it to the rest of the computer's systems. In modern designs the expansion bus is not normally the same bus that the CPU uses to access MAIN MEMORY, as the contention this would cause could slow the whole system down. Expansion cards may also be allowed to use DIRECT MEMORY ACCESS to avoid involving the CPU in most of their memory operations.

Examples of expansion buses include the ISA BUS and PCI BUS in the PC world, the VME-BUS for UNIX systems and the NUBUS for the Apple MACINTOSH.

expansion card A small PRINTED CIRCUIT BOARD that is plugged into the EXPANSION BUS of a computer to add extra hardware features: also called variously an *expansion board*, *adapter card* or *add-in card*. The most widely used categories of expansion cards include GRAPHICS CARDS, SOUND CARDS and NETWORK INTERFACE CARDS.

expansion slot A socket on a computer's MOTHERBOARD or BACKPLANE that accepts EXPANSION CARDS, and connects them to the computer's EXPANSION BUS.

expert system A computer program that contains, in encoded form, the expertise of a human expert from some domain (e.g. engineering, medicine) and which may be consulted to help solve problems in that domain. The human expertise is typically codified as a set of rules that are applied to any new query in order to deduce an answer. Expert systems formed one of the earliest subjects for ARTIFICIAL INTELLIGENCE research, but enthusiasm for them has waned somewhat owing to the difficulty of obtaining such rules and ensuring their consistency and completeness.

explicit parallelism A style of PARALLEL PROGRAMMING in which the programmer must indicate which parts of the program are to run concurrently.

exploded pie A type of PIE CHART in which some or all of the segments are withdrawn slightly from the disk and surrounded by white space, for emphasis.

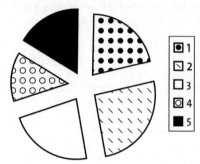

exploit In Internet HACKER slang, a loophole in the security measures of a MAIL READER, WEB BROWSER or other communications program that leaves it open to invasion by an EMAIL VIRUS. See also TROJAN HORSE, WORM.

Explorer Microsoft's visual SHELL, its file browsing and management utility in versions of WINDOWS from 95 onwards. The classic Explorer view presents a window that contains two horizontally adjacent panes, the left-hand one showing a TREE VIEW of all the disks in the system and the FOLDERS they contain, while the right-hand one shows the contents of the folder currently selected in the left pane. There are several other options for the level of detail displayed, and how it is set out. In versions of Windows from 98 onwards the left-hand pane of Explorer can also display the contents of many types of file when their name is clicked on with the mouse.

exponent The power to which a number is to be raised. Exponents are written as a second number, normally as a SUPERSCRIPT, which states how many times the first number is to be multiplied by itself: for example 10^2 means 10×10, or 100. Exponents are used to express very large or very small quantities in SCIENTIFIC NOTATION, and to represent FLOATING-POINT numbers for a computer.

exponential A class of mathematical function that raises some number to the power of its ARGUMENT, for example $y = 2^x$. The value of an exponential functions increases with the size of its argument more quickly than any merely POLYNOMIAL function. Exponential growth is encountered in nature in the growth of unconstrained animal populations (a so-called 'population explosion') and in chain-reactions such as the combustion of an explosive substance.

exponential smoothing A class of statistical techniques for modelling TIME SERIES, especially effective on data that shows seasonal variation and trends superimposed over a background of randomness. See also BOX-JENKINS.

exponential-time algorithm Any ALGORITHM whose time of execution increases exponentially with the size of the problem. For example, the time might be proportional to 2^N where N is the number of items to be processed. Such algorithms are rarely usable because the processing time they require may exceed the age of the known universe, even for quite modest-sized problems. Many algorithms for exact solutions to optimization and routing problems fall into this category, and in such cases an APPROXIMATION ALGORITHM has to be found to achieve a practical program. See also ALGORITHMIC COMPLEXITY.

export To save the working data from a DATABASE or other APPLICATION PROGRAM in a file format other than its own, to enable the data to be processed by some other program.

expose In OBJECT-ORIENTED PROGRAMMING, to make some or all of the methods of a particular class visible to, and hence callable by, other classes.

expression Some conjunction of CONSTANTS, VARIABLES and LITERAL values, combined together by arithmetical and logical OPERATORS or FUNCTION calls, that has a value at a particular time during the execution of a program. Examples of expressions are:

```
2 + 3 / 9
(a + b)*sqrt(c - 20)
price - cost_of_goods + overhead
```

Extended Architecture 1 See CD-ROM XA.
2 A standard for distributed TRANSACTION PROCESSING create by the X/OPEN group.

extended ASCII Any version of the ASCII CHARACTER SET that employs 8 bits instead of 7 to encode each CHARACTER, allowing for 256 characters in all. ISO Latin 1, the most commonly seen extension to ASCII, devotes the 128 extra characters to the accents and LIGATURES used in European languages, plus some extra mathematical and currency symbols. Many African and Asian countries have developed extended ASCII codings for their own language characters.

Extended Binary Coded Decimal Interchange Code (EBCDIC) A CHARACTER SET proprietary to IBM and still used in some of its MAINFRAME computers as recently as the 1990s. EBCDIC is different from, and incompatible with, the ASCII character set used by all other computers. EBCDIC was adapted from the character codes used in IBM's pre-electronic PUNCHED CARD machines, which made it less than ideal for modern computers. Among its many inconveniences were the use of non-contiguous codes for the alphabetic characters, and the absence of several punctuation characters such as the square brackets [] used by much modern software.

There have been six or more incompatible versions of EBCDIC, the latest of which do include all the ASCII characters, but also contain characters that are not supported in ASCII:

	0	1	2	3	4	5	6	7	8	9	A	B	C	D	E	F
0	control codes															
1	control codes															
2	control codes															
3	control codes															
4	â	ä	à	á	ã	å	ç	ñ	¢	.	<	(	+	|		
5	&	é	ê	ë	í	î	ï	ì	ß	!	$	*	)	;	^	
6	-	/	Â	Ä	À	Á	Ã	Å	Ç	Ñ	¦	,	%	_	>	?
7	ø	É	Ê	Ë	È	Í	Î	Ï	Ì	`	:	#	@	'	=	"
8	Ø	a	b	c	d	e	f	g	h	i	«	»	ð	ý	þ	±
9	°	j	k	l	m	n	o	p	q	r	ª	º	æ	¸	Æ	¤
A	µ	~	s	t	u	v	w	x	y	z	¡	¿	Ð	[	Þ	®
B	¬	£	¥	·	©	§	¶	¼	½	¾	Ÿ	¨	´	]	´	×
C	{	A	B	C	D	E	F	G	H	I	-	ô	ö	ò	ó	õ
D	}	J	K	L	M	N	O	P	Q	R	¹	û	ü	ù	ú	ÿ
E	\	÷	S	T	U	V	W	X	Y	Z	²	Ô	Ö	Ò	Ó	Õ
F	0	1	2	3	4	5	6	7	8	9	³	Û	Ü	Ù	Ú	

See also EXTENDED ASCII, ANSI CHARACTER SET, UNICODE.

Extended Capabilities Port (ECP) A variety of PARALLEL PORT defined in the IEEE 1284 standard for connecting computers to printers, which is capable of bi-directional data transmission at up to 4 megabytes per second in both directions. See also CENTRONICS PORT, ENHANCED PARALLEL PORT.

Extended Data Out RAM See EDO RAM.

Extended Graphics Array See under XGA.

Extended Industry-Standard Architecture An EXPANSION BUS for IBM-compatible personal computers, launched in 1988 by a consortium of vendors including COMPAQ, DEC and HEWLETT-PACKARD, as a counter to IBM's misguided attempt to impose its proprietary MICRO CHANNEL ARCHITECTURE on the industry. Like MCA, EISA is a 32-bit bus that supports multi-processing, and though less elegant than MCA in such respects as self-configuration, it could accept all the older ISA bus cards and so was briefly successful.

extended memory All the memory beyond the first megabyte of the ADDRESS SPACE of an IBM-COMPATIBLE PC fitted with an Intel 80286 or later CPU. In REAL MODE, extended memory cannot be directly addressed by the processor, and therefore cannot be used to hold executable code, only data, which may be accessed through schemes such as EMS (EXPANDED MEMORY SPECIFICATION) and XMS (EXTENDED MEMORY SPECIFICATION). In PROTECTED MODE the CPU can address extended memory directly to run programs larger than 1 megabyte under the supervision of a protected-mode operating system such as Microsoft Windows and an EXTENDED MEMORY MANAGER such as HIMEM. See also EXPANDED MEMORY, HIGH MEMORY, UPPER MEMORY BLOCK.

extended memory manager (XMM) A software DRIVER that enables an IBM-compatible PC to address memory above the 1 megabyte limit. The official Microsoft extended memory manager is called *HIMEM.SYS* and is distributed with both MS-DOS and WINDOWS. See more under EXTENDED MEMORY SPECIFICATION.

Extended Memory Specification (XMS) A scheme developed by Lotus, Intel and Microsoft which enables an IBM-compatible PC to address memory above the 1 megabyte limit. See EXTENDED MEMORY.

extended precision Any data type which is larger, and hence can express a wider range of values, than the default type for a particular system. For example the IEEE FLOATING POINT standard specifies 32-bit and 64-bit default types, with extended precision types of 80 and 128 bits.

extensible Any system that can be enlarged by addition rather than by complete replacement. Most modern computer hardware is extensible by adding more RAM and larger HARD DISKS. Software systems are said to be extensible if they can be expanded by adding new MODULES without requiring the whole program to be recompiled. Examples of such extensible systems include programs written using Microsoft's ACTIVEX or Sun's JAVABEANS technologies.

Extensible Link Language See XLL.

Extensible Markup Language See XML.

Extensible Style Language See XSL.

extent A unit of space allocation on a magnetic storage disk under some disk operating systems (including MS-DOS and MACOS) which consists of a sequence of physical data blocks or sectors joined together into a list. In MacOS an extent has two components, a pointer to the first block in the sequence, and the number of blocks in the sequence. In MS-DOS an extent is a subdivision of a CLUSTER. See also TRACK, SECTOR, FORMAT.

external, external reference An IDENTIFIER that is declared in some program module other than the current one. Resolving such references is one of the jobs of a LINKER.

extract To remove a file from a compressed ARCHIVE such as a ZIP FILE.

extranet An extension of an organization's INTRANET to permit selected outside users (such as a travelling salesforce, home workers, suppliers or customers) to access it via the INTERNET.

extrapolate To estimate further values belonging to some data set based on the known values; to estimate the value of some variable quantity beyond the range over which it has been actually measured. Extrapolation is often performed graphically, by extending the length of a line or curve representing the data. See also INTERPOLATE.

extrusion **1** In 3D GRAPHICS, the process of moving a 2-dimensional figure perpendicularly to its own plane so as to create a long solid 'tube' with that figure as its cross-section. For example, extruding a triangle produces a prism.

2 A solid produced in the above manner.

e-zine (electronic magazine) A magazine whose content is available only via the INTERNET and not as ink-on-paper.

F

fab SEMICONDUCTOR industry slang for a FABRI-CATION plant where INTEGRATED CIRCUIT chips are made. Also called a *wafer fab*.

fabless Used to describe companies that design INTEGRATED CIRCUIT chips, but do not have their own FABRICATION plants.

fab SEMICONDUCTOR industry slang for a FABRI-CATION plant where INTEGRATED CIRCUIT chips are made. Also called a *wafer fab*.

fabless Used to describe companies that design INTEGRATED CIRCUIT chips, but do not have their own FABRICATION plants.

fabric In a communication network, a broad term that describes the combination of the physical conductors (i.e. the wires) and the low-level PROTOCOLS that define the signals used to represent the DATA being transmitted. For example ETHERNET, ATM or Fibre Channel might be referred to generically as network fabrics without specifying more detail.

fabrication The whole process of manufacturing an INTEGRATED CIRCUIT, from slicing purified silicon into WAFERS, through the many stages of doping, ETCHING and deposition of metal layers, to the final cutting up of the wafer into individual chips. See also FAB, FABLESS, PROCESS TECHNOLOGY, FEATURE SIZE, VLSI, PACKAGE.

face recognition A specialized area of IMAGE RECOGNITION that seeks to identify human beings from a video image containing their face, using key dimensional ratios in a manner similar to that of FINGERPRINT RECOGNITION. See also BIOMETRICS.

face-time A face-to-face encounter with someone with whom one normally communicates electronically.

facsimile, facsimile transmission See FAX.

factor **1** *n*. In mathematics, one of several EXPRESSIONS that are combined by multiplication. The act of separating a number or expression into some combination of such factors (e.g. $6 = 2 \times 3$) is to factorize it.
2 *v*. In programming, to partition a program into separate subprograms by identifying within it sections that perform discrete operations. Each such section is said to have been 'factored out'.

factory default The configuration parameters for some piece of programmable equipment (e.g. a MODEM) that were originally set by the manufacturer, and hence are guaranteed to work in a basic manner. The option to 'restore factory defaults' is often employed as a means of recovery from unsuccessful modifications.

fail-over A process whereby one computer, typically a network SERVER, automatically hands over control to a duplicate back-up machine after encountering a hardware or software failure. Fail-over is a feature built into many FAULT-TOLERANT computing systems. See also CLUSTER, REDUNDANCY, HIGH-AVAILABILITY.

fail-safe A principle of system design that requires that the total failure of a system should leave it in a safe state rather than a dangerous one. For example a fail-safe car engine control system should stop the engine if it fails, rather than causing it to run at full throttle.

failure analysis A phase of testing in many engineering disciplines which seeks to discover, and to predict, the cause of failures.

Fairchild One of the earliest semiconductor manufacturers which in 1961 sold the first commercial INTEGRATED CIRCUIT. Its employees included Gordon Moore and Robert Noyce, who left in 1968 to found INTEL CORPORATION. See also TEXAS INSTRUMENTS.

fall over Used of a computer system that has CRASHED, as in 'the main server just fell over'.

fall through A term used of any program CONTROL STRUCTURE that does not entirely specify the path that control must take, so that in some cases execution will simply continue at the next instruction. It is most often used in connection with the C language's SWITCH STATEMENT. For example given the switch:

```
switch(x)
{
case 1:
case 2:
case 3: DoIt; break;
case 4: DoSomethingElse;
}
```

then DoIt will be executed whenever x is 1, 2 or 3 since the 1 and 2 cases fall through. Falling through is also a rich source of errors since, if a break is accidentally omitted, unwanted actions are invoked.

false colour A DATA VISUALIZATION technique used to render complex computer-generated pictures more readily understandable by applying strongly contrasting colours that need not reflect the real-world colours. For example the topography in an aerial photograph might be heightened by changing colour at each 100 metre contour step. The most familiar examples of false colour are those employed in thermal and satellite imaging.

family filter A facility provided by most online services and web PORTALS which seeks to prevent children from viewing unsuitable materials. Methods employed to regulate which sites may be accessed, include lists of proscribed addresses and pattern-matching on certain key words (e.g. sex, porn) occurring in an address.

fan-cooled Any piece of equipment that employs electric fans to circulate air and remove excess heat, in contrast to using a circulating liquid, radiation or unassisted air convection. All IBM-compatible PCs are now fan-cooled, and many now contain more than one fan, with separate fans for the power supply and the CPU chip. See also AIR-COOLED, OVER-CLOCKING.

fan fold A kind of paper used by older TRACTOR-FEED printers, which consists of a continuous strip, perforated between sheets and folded like a concertina, usually with rows of holes down each edge to engage with the printer's sprocket teeth. See also CONTINUOUS STATIONERY.

fan-out **1** The number of connections that leave a particular NODE on a network.
2 In an integrated circuit design, the number of logic gates whose inputs are connected to the output of some given gate. The maximum permissible fan-out is limited by the delays introduced by sharing the available charge among several gates.

FAQ (Frequently Asked Questions) A list of commonly asked questions and their answers, posted in a NEWSGROUP or on a WEB SITE to preempt these questions and so avoid much boring and repetitive discussion. It is considered good manners to read the FAQs before attempting to participate in any discussion. See also NETIQUETTE, FLAME.

farad (F) The SI unit of CAPACITANCE, defined as that of a capacitor between whose plates a charge of 1 coulomb creates a potential of 1 volt.

far call In a computer that employs a SEGMENTED ADDRESS SPACE, any procedure CALL whose target address does not lie within the current segment, and which therefore incurs the additional overhead of having to change the SEGMENT REGISTER.

farm A collection of SERVERS, PROCESSORS or other devices.

far pointer On a computer whose PROCESSOR employs a SEGMENTED MEMORY MODEL (for example the Intel x86 family), an ADDRESS that refers to a location that is not in the current segment. A far pointer consists of a segment address and an OFFSET concatenated, for example 3E45:0089h, and so is longer than an intra-segment pointer. On a 16-bit machine it might be 32 bits long.

FAST Abbreviation of FEDERATION AGAINST SOFTWARE THEFT.

Fast Ethernet The common name for 100 megabits per second (Mbps) ETHERNET, as distinct from the original 10 Mbps version.

Fast Fourier Transform (FFT) An ALGORITHM that efficiently computes the mathematical FOURIER TRANSFORM which is much used in SIGNAL PROCESSING applications, for example to analyse sounds into different frequency bands. The crucial repeated calculation involved in the FFT is the multiplication of two COMPLEX NUMBERS – called the BUTTERFLY operation because the cross-multiplication of their two halves, when drawn diagrammatically, suggests that insect's wings. Various hardware solutions have been devised to accelerate the butterfly operation, including the inclusion of special processor instructions such as MULTIPLY-ACCUMULATE and MULTIPLY-ADD.

Fast Infra Red The 4 megabits per second INFRARED link fitted to many modern NOTEBOOK computers.

Fast Page Mode RAM (FPM RAM) A type of RAM that provides faster access to successive data items if they are contained on the same RAM PAGE. FPM has been largely superceded by EDO RAM.

Fast SCSI See under SCSI.

Fast Wide SCSI See under SCSI.

FAT Abbreviation of FILE ALLOCATION TABLE.

FAT16 See under FILE ALLOCATION TABLE.

FAT32 See under FILE ALLOCATION TABLE.

fatal error A RUN-TIME ERROR condition from which recovery is either impossible or inadvisable, so that the offending process must be terminated. The choice of name is unfortunate, as it may suggest to inexperienced PC users that their life is in danger.

fat binary A file that contains two or more versions of a program's BINARY CODE to run on different CPUs. Fat binaries require an operating system that can choose the right version to execute at run time, MACOS being one example

(uses Motorola 68000 and PowerPC code) and NEXTSTEP being another (uses Intel, SPARC and 68000 code).

fatbits The magnification of the individual PIXELS in an image to allow pixel-by-pixel editing: see also ZOOM. The name was first coined in the MacPaint program that came with the original Apple MACINTOSH.

fat client The opposite of a THIN CLIENT, that is a normal, lavishly-equipped PC.

fat pipe A slang term for a high-BANDWIDTH Internet connection.

fault An abnormal or specially distinguished condition encountered during the execution of a computer program. See also EXCEPTION.

fault-tolerant Capable of some degree of automatic recovery from an ERROR CONDITION or physical failure. A widely adopted strategy for achieving fault-tolerance is redundancy: two systems (for example PROCESSORS or HARD DISKS) are run in parallel and, should a fault occur in one, the other automatically takes over its function. See for example RAID.

fault tree A data structure used in many fault tracing systems that consists of a sequence of yes/no questions; answering each of these leads the user to further questions, and eventually to one of a number of possible diagnoses. For example:

```
Is the red light on?
no: Is the device plugged into a
power socket?
...
yes: Is the device making any
sound?
...
```

See also DECISION TREE, EXPERT SYSTEM, RULE-BASED SYSTEM.

fax The universally employed abbreviation for *facsimile transmission*, a system for sending images over public telephone lines which predates the personal computer. Despite being slower and less flexible than EMAIL, fax remains the favoured information channel for many businesses thanks to its extremely simple user interface: a single button press sends, while receiving requires no user intervention at all.

At a functional level, a fax machine consists of a combination of a small SCANNER, a dedicated MODEM and a simple printer. Source documents are scanned to produce a BIT-MAPPED image which is then compressed and transmitted using a slow but reliable PROTO-COL. Most computer modems can now also send and receive documents in fax format using this protocol: see FAX MODEM.

fax-back A type of unmanned information service that enables customers to request information over the telephone by selecting from pre-recorded, voice or tone activated telephone menus; the requested documents are then automatically faxed to them. Briefly popular in the early 1990s, the technology has been made almost redundant by the advent of web sites.

fax modem A MODEM that can transfer fac-simile (fax) images between computers and fax machines. Special fax software is required on the computer to turn documents and scanned picture files into the standard fax data format for transmission. Fax modems work to the Group 3 digital fax standard, according the the the CCITT's T.30 specification.

fax server A dedicated computer connected to a local area network (LAN) and to the public telephone system, which enables network users to send faxes via one or more shared FAX MODEMS. Typically a fax server will also perform management functions such as logging all the faxes sent and keeping a central shared directory of fax numbers. It may also convert documents from a specific computer fomat, such as a spreadsheet, into a faxable form.

FC-AL See under FIBRE CHANNEL ARBITRATED LOOP.

FCC (Federal Communications Commission) The US governmental body that regulates all US broadcasting and telephony and enforces controls on RADIO FREQUENCY EMISSIONS.

FCS error packet See under FRAME CHECK SEQUENCE.

FDDI Abbreviation of FIBRE DISTRIBUTED DATA INTERFACE.

FDISK A utility supplied with the MS-DOS operating system to FORMAT and PARTITION HARD DISK drives. Capable of doing great damage in unfamiliar hands.

FDMA Abbreviation of Frequency Division Multiple Access; see under FREQUENCY DIVISION MULTIPLEXING.

FEA Abbreviation of FINITE ELEMENT ANALYSIS.

Fear, Uncertainty and Doubt See FUD.

feathering 1 In typography, the introduction of extra space between the lines of a document (that is an alteration to the LEADING) to make it fill a given space.
2 In printing, a defect in which the ink runs and causes blurring of individual CHARACTERS.
3 In computer graphics, a function provided in many BITMAP EDITORS that softens or blurs the edge of a selected region of an image to a chosen degree, often used to disguise the join when pasting into another image.

feature connector A 26-pin socket fitted to all VGA-compatible GRAPHICS CARDS to deliver PIXEL data from external devices such as VIDEO CAPTURE boards.

feature recognition, feature extraction Processing the binary data that represents an image to discover geometric components (for example lines, circles and edges) within that image. The most widely encountered example is the recognition of alphabetic characters within a BITMAPPED document image, as performed by OPTICAL CHARACTER RECOGNITION programs. See more under IMAGE PROCESSING, NEURAL NETWORK, PATTERN RECOGNITION.

feature size The average size of an active element such as a transistor in an INTEGRATED CIRCUIT chip layout. Today's feature sizes are on the order of 0.1 MICRONS or one ten-thousandth of a millimetre, and they shrink with each generation of fabrication technology (see MOORE'S LAW). See also SUBMICRON PROCESS, FABRICATION, PROCESS TECHNOLOGY.

featuritis A less severe form of CREEPING FEATURITIS.

Federation Against Software Theft (FAST) A computer industry organization founded in the UK to enforce the copyright laws on software and to detect and prosecute software PIRACY.

feedback 1 Diverting part of the output of a system back into its input. In *positive feedback* this results in amplification of the output in a vicious spiral, the 'howl round' effect heard when a microphone is placed too close to a loudspeaker. In *negative feedback* the output is subtracted from, rather than added to, the input. This provides a control mechanism of great versatility, widely used to stabilize the output of electrical devices from electronic amplifiers and disk head ACTUATORS to household ovens and central heating systems.

2 The term is also now universally used in a metaphorical sense, meaning to offer an opinion, favourable or not, on any topic.

feed-forward 1 A class of NEURAL NETWORK in which the outputs from each layer of processing units are connected to the inputs of the *next* layer, but not to the previous layer: hence it is the opposite of FEEDBACK.

2 A technique employed in some deeply PIPE-LINED processor ARCHITECTURES, whereby results computed in an early pipeline stage may travel ahead, bypassing the next few stages, to an instruction at a later stage that needs to know them: also called REGISTER BYPASS.

female Any type of electrical plug or socket that contains holes to accept the pins of a matching MALE connector.

femtosecond 10^{-15} seconds, or one millionth of a NANOSECOND: the time-scale of some processes in particle physics.

fence-post error A common error made when programming, so-called because it results from counting things instead of the gaps between them. For example given an ARRAY of numbers, how many LOOP iterations are needed to process items m to n? The immediately obvious answer n-m is wrong, the correct answer being n-m+1. See also OFF-BY-ONE ERROR.

Fermat prime A PRIME NUMBER that has the form:

$$2^{2^n}+1$$

for example 17 (n=2).

Ferranti A UK electronics firm based in Manchester that was among the world's first commercial computer manufacturers – at the end of World War II it took on key staff from BLETCHLEY PARK including Alan TURING.

ferric oxide A magnetic oxide of iron, thin coatings of which form the recording medium in TAPE, FLOPPY DISK and some HARD DISK drives.

ferrite A class of ceramic materials made by mixing oxides of iron, cobalt and zinc, whose strongly magnetic properties are exploited, for example, as cores for miniature tuning coils and TRANSFORMERS, and in recording HEADS for tape and disk drives. Before the invention of semiconductor memory chips, tiny rings of ferrite threaded onto a mesh of copper wires were used as memory in early computers, called FERRITE-CORE MEMORY.

ferrite-core memory The principle form of electronic MEMORY used in computers prior to the invention of semiconductor memory chips. It consisted of thousands of tiny rings called cores, made from a magnetic FERRITE material and each threaded onto three fine copper wires: the whole formed a two-dimensional mesh much like a knitted textile. By passing current down the two appropriate vertical and horizontal wires, a particular core could be addressed and its direction of magnetization either read or altered using the third wire, so it behaved as a RANDOM ACCESS memory. The size of its components restricted the amount of core memory that could fit into a computer to thousands rather than millions of bytes.

ferromagnetism One of the three fundamental modes of behaviour that may be displayed by any substance in the presence of a magnetic field (the other modes being paramagnetism and diamagnetism). In a ferromagnetic material, the magnetization induced by an external field increases with the field's strength, and may in a few materials such as iron (hence the name) become permanent. Ferromagnetism is the result of the spins of the electrons throughout small regions called DOMAINS all becoming aligned in the same direction. It is formally defined as having a relative magnetic permeability much greater than one. Ferromagnetic materials are much rarer in nature than the other two types, and are sought out for the manufacture of magnets and data storage media such as recording TAPE and computer DISKS. See also CURIE POINT, FERRITE.

FET Abbreviation of FIELD-EFFECT TRANSISTOR.

fetch-ahead See under PREFETCH.

fetch–execute cycle The basic sequence of actions that lies at the heart of all computers: the next instruction in a program is fetched from the computer's memory into a processor register where it is executed; that is, the operation that it specifies is carried out. See also INSTRUCTION FETCH, CONTROL UNIT, INSTRUCTION DECODING, CISC, RISC.

FFT Abbreviation of FAST FOURIER TRANSFORM.

FH Abbreviation of FREQUENCY-HOPPING.

FHSS (Frequency Hopping Spread Spectrum) A wireless communication technology originally developed for military purposes but now used in many wireless LANS. In contrast to the competing DSSS technique, it employs radio waves of a single frequency to transmit messages, but continually changes this frequency to avoid interception. See also WIRELESS COMMUNICATIONS, BLUETOOTH.

Fibonacci series A mathematical SERIES constructed by continually adding together the previous pair of terms, thus:

1 1 2 3 5 8 13 21 34....

This sequence is frequently observed in nature, in examples that range from the numbers of seeds in successive rows of a sunflower head to the diameters of the coils of a snail's shell. The ratio between successive terms of the series CONVERGES toward the value 1.61803..., the so-called Golden Section or Golden Mean employed as the ideal proportion by painters, sculptors and architects for many centuries.

fibre See OPTICAL FIBRE.

Fibre Channel Arbitrated Loop, Fibre Channel (FC-AL) A fast SERIAL BUS that seeks to replace SCSI for very high performance applications such as large servers. FC-AL is faster than SCSI, capable of speeds from 100 to 800 megabits per second, and many FC-AL devices are DUAL-PORTED for twice the throughput and increased FAULT-TOLERANCE. FC-AL devices are also self-configuring and permit HOT SWAPPING. Despite its name, FC-AL can use ordinary COAXIAL CABLE for runs up to 30 metres, but OPTICAL FIBRE extends this to 10 kilometres, with a maximum of 126 devices per port.

Most FC-AL adapters also support SCSI-3 and HIPPI (HIGH PERFORMANCE PARALLEL INTERFACE) and so can use software designed for

SCSI devices. However FC-AL is too expensive for desktop PCs, for which FIREWIRE is a more likely future standard.

Fibre Distributed Data Interface (FDDI) A fast network technology based on optical fibre cabling which is widely used for building BROADBAND local area network (LAN) backbones to carry multimedia traffic such as videoconferencing and studio-quality audio. FDDI supports very long cable runs of up to 2 kilometres and transmits data at 100 megabits per second. It employs the TOKEN RING arbitration method for CONFLICT resolution, but has twin rings so that tokens can be passed in both directions. FDDI is the subject of ANSI standard X3T9.5. See also GIGABIT ETHERNET, FIBRE CHANNEL, FIREWIRE.

fibre-optic An adjectival form derived from fibre optics (see OPTICAL FIBRE), applied to many devices, technologies, interfaces and other entities that employ optical fibre somewhere in their operation.

fibre optics See under OPTICAL FIBRE.

FidoNet A pioneering electronic BULLETIN BOARD and email network hosted on personal computers which was popular in the mid-1980s and pre-dates the rise of the WORLD WIDE WEB as a means of communication between computer hobbyists. See also USENET, HOTLINE, PEER-TO-PEER, NAPSTER, CONFERENCING SYSTEM.

field 1 In computing, one of several predefined areas for storing data items within some larger data structure such as a database RECORD or a data entry form.
2 The brutal world inhabited by actual computer users, as opposed to the cushioned environment of the manufacturer's workshop: as in 'but how will it perform out in the field'. Hence also FIELD-PROGRAMMABLE.
3 In a television set or other INTERLACED DISPLAY device, one of two or more sets of SCAN LINES that go to make up each full screen picture.
4 A region of space that is under the influence of some physical force such as gravity, electrical potential or magnetism. See for example FIELD-EFFECT TRANSISTOR.
5 In mathematical logic, the set of all the arguments and values of a FUNCTION: the union of its DOMAIN and its CODOMAIN.

6 In set theory, a set whose members form a COMMUTATIVE group under addition and, with the exception of the zero element, under multiplication.

field-effect transistor (FET) A TRANSISTOR formed by creating two adjacent DOPED regions on the surface of a SEMICONDUCTOR, called the SOURCE and the DRAIN, the gap between which is bridged by an isolated conducting layer called the gate. A voltage applied to the gate alters the conductivity of the gap by creating a DEPLETION LAYER, and hence can start or stop current flowing from source to drain. FETs waste far less power than BIPOLAR TRANSISTORS, since almost no current flows when they are switched off. MOSFETs, that is FETs implemented in metal-oxide-semiconductor (MOS) fabrication technology, are the basis of all modern VLSI chips.

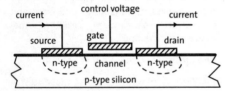

field-programmable Said of a hardware device whose mode of operation may be fundamentally changed by its end user: for example a FIELD-PROGRAMMABLE GATE ARRAY.

field-programmable gate array (FPGA) A type of SEMICONDUCTOR chip whose function is not fixed at the manufacturing stage, but can be redefined by an engineer 'in the field' (hence the name) by loading new software into it that defines the connections between all its LOGIC GATES. FPGAs are useful when testing prototypes of new devices, allowing modifications to be quickly applied, but are generally replaced by dedicated chips in the final product. The inventor and largest producer of FPGAs is XILINX INC.

field rendering A facility supported by many computer 3D GRAPHICS rendering systems, which enables output in an INTERLACED half-frame field format as required for playback on video recorders and television.

field upgrade The replacement of components of a system carried out in its operating environment rather than at the maker's factory.

FIFO (First In–First Out) **1** The acronym commonly used to describe a QUEUE data structure, through which data items proceed in that order.

2 In electronic engineering, a type of circuit that implements a queueing function in hardware, as used in serial communication chips such as a UART. See also BUFFER, STACK.

Fifth-generation Project A project sponsored by the Japanese government in the 1980s to develop a 'fifth generation' of computers that could think like human beings. It pursued the development of MASSIVELY PARALLEL architectures and LOGIC PROGRAMMING languages, but with disappointing results that led to its eventual abandonment.

56k modem A shorthand term for a MODEM capable of transferring data at 56 kilobits per second (Kbps). There were two rival 56k modem standards between 1997 and 1999; these were k56flex and US Robotic's rival X2, but there is now a single ITU-approved 56 Kbps standard called v.90, to which all such modems should conform. See also V STANDARDS.

file The most important data structure used for storing data on MASS STORAGE devices such as hard disks and tapes. Whenever an application program is employed to create a new document, spreadsheet, picture, musical work or whatever, the result will typically be saved onto a hard disk as a file, which can be opened (i.e. reloaded into MAIN MEMORY) at some future time to edit the work.

A file consists of a finite sequence of BYTES to which the user or application must give a FILENAME by which it can be distinguished from other files. A part of the computer's operating system called the FILE SYSTEM is responsible for allocating the appropriate number of physical disk SECTORS to store a particular file, and for recording its name and other attributes (such as time and date of creation, size, and ACCESS PERMISSIONS) in a DIRECTORY or FOLDER. Directories may be employed to group together files of a similar nature, or belonging to a similar job, so that they can be more easily found (rather like putting paper files into the same drawer of a filing cabinet). Under most operating systems you may not have more than one file of the same name in the same directory.

On the disk or in memory a file physically consists of an undifferentiated sequence of bytes, but particular application programs may interpret certain byte values as dividers to split the file contents up into more complex structures – such a scheme is called a FILE FOR-MAT belonging to that application. Different applications employ different formats, and so often cannot process files created by other applications. There is no single universal file format that can be read by every application, but the nearest to this ideal is the TEXT FILE which contains only human-readable ALPHA-NUMERIC characters, divided up into lines or paragraphs by CARRIAGE RETURNS. All other file formats, which may contain non-alphanu-meric characters are collectively described as BINARY FILES.

File Allocation Table (FAT) A data structure employed in the FILE SYSTEMS of Microsoft's MS-DOS and Windows operating systems to locate individual files stored on hard and floppy disks. When a disk is FORMATTED it is divided up into many physical SECTORS of equal size grouped together into CLUSTERS. Whenever a new file is created, the file system allocates a number of these clusters to hold that file's data – the FAT is a table that contains the name of each file and the addresses of the clusters that it occupies. When a file is deleted, only its FAT entry, rather than the data itself, is erased, which is why UNDELETE utilities can usually recover the file.

The FAT is stored on the first track of each disk and is read into memory whenever the disk is in use, to be updated and written back whenever the computer is switched off (or one removable disk is swapped for another). Should the FAT become corrupted during this process, then all the files on that disk may be lost.

MS-DOS and versions of Windows prior to WINDOWS 98 used 16-bit pointers in their FAT (hence called *FAT16*) which restricted the size of the largest disk PARTITION they could address to 2 Gigabytes. Windows 98 intro-duced the *FAT32* system, with 32-bit pointers so it can support partitions larger than 2 Giga-bytes, which also makes more economical use of disk space by storing the data in more, but smaller, clusters. However FAT16 and FAT32 are incompatible, and may not be deployed on the same hard disk partition.

file association The linking of a file to some APPLICATION PROGRAM that can open it, so that clicking on the file's name automatically launches that application. Some operating systems such as Apple's MACOS perform such associations via links stored within the file, while others including Microsoft Windows associate particular FILENAME EXTENSIONS with each application – for example the extension .doc in MyDocument.doc would normally associate that file with the MICRO-SOFT WORD program. See also DATA-DRIVEN.

file compression A class of techniques for shrinking the size of a data file to reduce its storage requirement, by processing the data it contains using some suitably reversible algo-rithm. Compression methods tend to be more effective for a particular kind of data, so that text files will typically be compressed using a different algorithm from graphics or sound files. For example RUN-LENGTH ENCODING is very effective for compressing flat-shaded computer graphics, which contain many long runs of identical PIXEL values, but is quite poor for compressing tonally rich photographic material where adjacent pixels are different. Dictionary-based algorithms such as LEMPEL–ZIV COMPRESSION are very effective for com-pressing text, but perform poorly on binary data such as pictures or sound.

Compression may be applied automatically by an operating system or application, or applied manually using a utility program such as PKZIP, TAR, LHA or STUFFIT. See also JPEG, MPEG.

file conversion The act of converting a file from one FILE FORMAT to another so that it may be processed by a different application: for example a MICROSOFT WORD document might be converted into WORDPERFECT format. Many applications now have built-in file con-version facilities for the most frequently used formats in their particular domain, and some can accept new format converters as PLUG-INS. Alternatively, there are dedicated file conver-sion utilities that convert between many pop-ular formats, or else a conversion program can be written for a particular job using a SCRIPT-ING LANGUAGE such as VISUAL BASIC or PERL.

file format A convention for structuring the contents of a computer FILE containing BINARY data. All such files ultimately consist of a continuous string of 0 and 1 bits, but by choosing to interpret certain bit patterns as markers, files may be viewed as containing structured data. A particular file format is useful only in relation to a piece of software that can create or read the format and, if such a file is opened with the wrong software, its contents will appear meaningless.

For example, in TEXT FILE format the data is treated as a stream of 8-bit values representing ASCII characters, and the two special characters 10 (line feed) and 13 (carriage return) are considered to be separators between successive lines of text; any text editor program will then display such a file on a computer screen as wrapped lines of text. A file containing a picture must be interpreted as a sequence of rows and columns of PIXELS, but there are so many different ways this can be done that a plethora of different graphics formats has been invented, each one associated with a particular software product that is required to view the picture. Commonly encountered graphical formats include JPEG, GIF, BMP/DIB, PIC and TIFF.

file locking The process of granting one user exclusive access to a shared file, to prevent other users from making simultaneous updates and overwriting each other's changes: the exclusive user must relinquish the lock when finished to allow others access. Some form of locking is an essential feature of any MULTIUSER computer system, but locking at the level of whole files is nowadays regarded as drastic and harmful to efficiency. Instead, some system of RECORD LOCKING is preferred, which enables many users to access the same file simultaneously, though not the same record within it. See also LOCK, LOCK MANAGER, GRANULARITY.

FileMaker A best-selling DATABASE application for the Apple MACINTOSH, later ported successfully to IBM-COMPATIBLE PCS.

filename The identifier by which a computer file may be distinguished from others. Most computer operating systems set some limits on what characters may be used and on the length of permissible file names, and all forbid the existence of two files with the same name within the same DIRECTORY or FOLDER. For example MS-DOS filenames are restricted

to a main name of up to eight characters plus an optional FILENAME EXTENSION of up to three characters (as in myfile.txt) while Windows and Apple Macintosh files may have names containing spaces such as *My Accounts for December 1999*. Some operating systems use a filename extension to identify the type of a file and automatically assign a program to open it, so that, say, .xls files are associated with Microsoft Excel.

filename extension A short name (typically three letters) appended to the main FILENAME following a dot. It is used by many operating systems including MS-DOS, UNIX and VMS to indicate the type of file, and sometimes to associate it with the application that created it. There are a few widely accepted conventions, such as .txt (e.g. readme.txt) indicating a TEXT FILE, .ps a POSTSCRIPT file and .c a C language source file.

file operation Any of the basic operations that may be performed on a computer file, including create, delete, open, close, read, write, append and seek operations.

file recovery Salvaging data files that have been deleted in error, or which have become unreadable owing to corruption of their format or hardware failure of their STORAGE MEDIUM. The techiques used for file recovery are as varied as the causes of loss, ranging from a simple UNDELETE utility, through manual inspection of the BINARY data with a disk SECTOR EDITOR, to the use of specialized electronic equipment that can read faint magnetic signals from a damaged disk surface.

file server A network SERVER that holds a central store of data files, so that they can be accessed by many different network users. Keeping all files on a server avoids having multiple copies of the files spread around on individual computers, minimizes the total disk space required to store them, and simplifies the process of making BACKUPS or distributing updates. File serving is the most popular role for network servers, and the major network operating systems Unix, Windows NT and Novell Netware all support such file sharing.

Modern file servers are usually specially designed machines with large power supplies, multiple bays to allow the installation of many hard disks, and enhanced cooling facilities. They may be MULTIPROCESSOR machines, and are typically fitted with more memory (hundreds of megabytes) than are single-user PCs.

file sharing A fundamental service provided by most computer networks, under which many users may gain access to the same files, which are stored in a designated shared directory on the SERVER.

file system 1 The part of an OPERATING SYSTEM that enables access to data stored in files on some non-volatile medium, such as a HARD DISK, CD-ROM or flash RAM card. In simple operating systems such as MS-DOS the file system constitutes a large and permanent part of the operating system, but for more powerful operating systems the file system may be an installable subsystem that can be replaced by another.

The job of a file system is to maintain a connection between the hardware addresses used by, say, a hard disk drive mechanism to locate its blocks of stored data, and the human-readable file and directory names that you see on your screen. All but the very simplest of file systems enable files to be collected together into named directories or FOLDERS, which can be nested within one another so that large numbers of files can be organized in an intelligible manner – operating system utilities allow the user to view and manipulate such hierarchical directory structures via a TREE VIEW or diagram. Ideally a file system should present files stored on different media such as floppy disks, hard disks, CD-ROM, tape cartridge, flash card (or even on remote computers connected by a network) in exactly the same way, disguising the fact that completely different underlying mechanisms are involved in accessing each type.

The file system and its associated disk formats are what govern whether a disk written on one computer can be read by another, so changing the file system is a matter with serious implications for compatibility, and is undertaken only at major operating system revisions.

Microsoft's operating systems have undergone four major changes of file system since the first 8-bit FILE ALLOCATION TABLE system that was used in MS-DOS 1 to hold the links between named files and physical disk blocks.

MS-DOS version 6 introduced FAT16 which allowed bigger disk drives and more numerous unique file names; FAT32 was introduced in 1998 as a modification to Windows 95, to support single hard disk partitions larger than 1 Gbyte. WINDOWS NT has its own file system (NTFS), which has sophisticated fault tolerance, data recovery, and file compression features lacking in the FAT systems. Apple's MACINTOSH employs HFS (Hierarchical File System) and most UNIX systems use NFS, the NETWORK FILE SYSTEM. None of these file systems are compatible with one another, though Apple's HFS can write disks that are readable under MS-DOS, and there are utilities that can achieve the same for Unix.

2 On computers running the Unix operating system, file system is also used to describe the collection of files and directories stored on a particular drive. Such a file system can be added to or removed from the total file hierarchy by using the mount and dismount commands.

file transfer The act of moving a file from one computer to another, either by means of some kind of communication link (e.g. a LAN or the INTERNET) or by using a removable storage medium such as a floppy disk.

File Transfer Protocol See FTP.

file type The kind of data that a FILE can store: examples include text, bitmaps, database records, sounds and executable program code. Most OPERATING SYSTEMS provide some way of distinguishing the type of a file, often by using a distinctive extension to the file name, as in MyDocument.txt or MyPicture.bmp.

fill 1 To store the same value into every location of some area of a computer's memory: see also BLOCK MOVE.

2 In computer graphics, to apply a particular colour or pattern throughout an area within an image. See for example FLOOD FILL, GRADIENT FILL.

filter 1 In general a program that inputs a set of data items, performs some operation on each item, and outputs the modified results. Often the operation involves removing certain items, hence the name.

2 In an EMAIL program, a facility that enables the user to automatically reject messages, for example those emanating from a

list of prohibited addresses or whose text contains certain undesirable key words.

3 In a WEB BROWSER, a similar facility that prevents access to a list of prohibited sites, or to any site whose URL contains a prohibited word, or some other criterion based on content. See also FAMILY FILTER.

4 Under most computer operating systems, a mechanism that enables a DIRECTORY listing to show only those files that meet some specified criterion. See more under WILDCARD.

fine-grained A metaphorical term used to describe data structures or processes that deal in details at the BIT and BYTE level. See more under GRANULARITY.

finger A Unix and Internet utility program that displays information about a user when given their EMAIL ADDRESS. Used as in finger fred@penguin.com, it typically provides the user's full name, last login time, idle time, and terminal line and location for multi-user systems.

fingerprint recognition The use of IMAGE PROCESSING software on a computer to look for a matching fingerprint amongst millions of others held in a database.

finite difference algorithm A class of algorithms often used in mechanical and electrical simulation that work by treating change as a sequence of tiny discrete steps, rather than by applying some continuous algebraic function. For example, the ballistic trajectory of a moving particle might be simulated by determining its position at every millisecond interval.

finite element analysis (FEA) A technique for modelling the behaviour of complex systems by dissecting them into many tiny cells, small enough for their properties to be treated as uniform. It is then possible to solve the differential equations that describe the position and motion of the boundaries between these cells and obtain an approximation to the motion of the whole system.

Finite element analysis is used, for example, to simulate the detonation of nuclear devices, to model atmospheric movements for weather forecasting, and to simulate collisions during car design. There are so many equations to solve that massive computing resources are required, and the more effective implementation of FEA methods has been a principal motive driving the evolution of SUPERCOMPUTERS.

finite state machine, finite state automaton A class of computing machine that exists always in one of a finite set of possible states, and input signals drive it from one state to another. A transition function prescribes which state it will enter next for every possible state/input combination, and what its output will then be. Certain so-called *terminal states* cause the machine to stop. The finite state machine is a computing device, but one of less power and generality than the TURING MACHINE. See also CHOMSKY HIERARCHY.

firewall A special type of GATEWAY server that monitors all traffic passing between a LAN within a company or institution and the outside world, to prevent security breaches. The firewall allows users within the company to communicate with each other using relatively relaxed security precautions, and to send email out across the Internet, but it prevents malicious persons from outside accessing or damaging the company's private data. A firewall is often implemented by a modest PC running Linux or Unix firewall software, which has no other duties except possibly VIRUS SCANNING of email attachments. See also NAT, TUNNEL.

FireWire The popular name for the High Speed Serial Bus (now IEEE 1394), a SERIAL peripheral interface introduced in 1995 for Apple Macintosh and IBM-compatible PCs. FireWire can transfer data at 100, 200 or 400 megabits per second and is designed to support PLUG-AND-PLAY automatic configuration and HOT SWAPPING of peripherals. This has led to its increasing adoption for connecting digital cameras and camcorders to PCs. Cable length is restricted to 4.5 metres but up to 16 cables can be connected in a DAISY-CHAIN to span up to 72 metres. FireWire employs a 6-wire cable that is thinner than a SCSI cable and can supply up to 60 watts of power to a peripheral, so eliminating the need for a separate power cord. See also USB.

firmware Software stored in a ROM chip that forms a permanent part of a piece of electronic equipment. Examples include the BIOS of a PC, the head-positioning software embedded within a HARD DISK drive or the error-correcting and compression software within a MODEM. The name is meant to suggest something midway between hardware and software. There is an increasing tendency to place firmware into FLASH MEMORY rather than ROM so that it can be updated by the end user whenever improved versions become available, by running an installation program from a floppy disk or CD: see FLASH-UPDATABLE.

First In–First Out See FIFO.

first silicon The SEMICONDUCTOR industry term for the first examples of a new chip design to emerge from the fabrication process.

fixed disk An older name for a non-removable HARD DISK drive.

fixed length field A FIELD within a database RECORD whose length must be declared when the record type is defined and may not be changed once the database has been populated with data. In many database management systems, numeric, date and most other field types must be of fixed length; only text or MEMO FIELDS are allowed to be of variable length.

fixed-length record The basic component of some older database storage schemes in which the same amount of disk space is allocated in advance for all records. Such a scheme is very efficient for storing numeric data but not for textual data, where any text that does not exactly fill the pre-allocated space must either be truncated if too long or PADDED with spaces or NULL characters if too short, resulting in wasted space compared to the alternative of a VARIABLE-LENGTH RECORD structure.

fixed media Any form of MASS STORAGE device that is not removable from the computer, most commonly referring to a HARD DISK drive.

fixed-pitch font A text FONT, such as Courier, in which every character has the same width – like this. Such fonts were all that could be displayed in the days of CHARACTER-BASED terminal screens, but modern graphical screens and printers permit the display of PROPORTIONAL FONTS as employed in professional typesetting (see for example TRUETYPE, ADOBE TYPE MANAGER, POSTSCRIPT). Fixed-pitch fonts are now rarely used to display or print long documents because the resulting appearance is tiring to read, but there are still some applications – particularly programming tools – that employ them because they guarantee that characters will line up vertically in columns. See also LEADING, FEATHERING.

fixed-point A number representation scheme, in which a fixed number of bits are designated as representing the fractional part of a number – in effect, a constant scaling factor is applied to turn all fractions into integers. Contrast to FLOATING-POINT representations.

For example representing sums of money as numbers of pence (so that 3178 means £31.78) is a kind of fixed-point notation that assumes a decimal point between the second and third digits, which is equivalent to scaling by 100. Most computer fixed-point formats are, however, binary, and scale by powers of two. Fixed-point was once extensively used in DIGITAL SIGNAL PROCESSORS and GRAPHICS chips for the sake of speed, since it manipulates fractional quantities using only integer arithmetic, but the speed of modern floating-point processors has made this application redundant. The disadvantage of fixed-point schemes is they can represent only a limited range of values without causing an OVERFLOW.

flag A single bit whose value is read as a signal for some condition within a program or piece of hardware (for example that data has been changed), or used as a switch to determine which of two actions should be performed (for example save/don't save). See also FLAG BIT, FLAG REGISTER.

flag bit A BIT used by a program to indicate one of two different conditions according to whether it is set to 0 or 1. See also FLAG and FLAG REGISTER.

flag register A processor REGISTER, each bit of whose content represents a FLAG for some program condition. For example a particular flag bit might be set or unset to indicate the result (e.g equal/not equal, greater than/not greater than) of a comparison test on the numbers held in two other registers.

flame An abusive or overly-emotional email message or posting to an Internet discussion group. Sometimes more sophisticated users will explicitly bracket the more inflammatory parts of a message with FLAME ON and FLAME OFF.

flame off Used in online discussions to indicate a return to rational discussion.

flame on Used in online discussions to signal the start of an intemperate outburst.

flame war A protracted exchange of increasingly insulting messages in an online discussion group, often triggered by some relatively trivial comment.

Flash A popular graphics tool for producing streaming animation sequences in web pages, acquired by MacroMedia as an add-on for its DIRECTOR authoring program. Flash animations can be viewed in any web browser that has Director's SHOCKWAVE plug-in installed.

Flash animation files, with the filename extension .SWF, contain VECTOR GRAPHICS information in an extremely economical format that keeps file sizes to a minimum and reduces the required download time. This is achieved by storing only flat colour information rather than bitmaps, and by not storing any lines or areas that are not visible; for example, a solid coloured area that is crossed by a line of different colour will be stored as three non-overlapping objects. Flash files also include script code for animating interactive elements such as ROLL-OVER buttons. See also LIVEMOTION, SVG, ANIMATED GIF.

flash card A plug-in memory card containing FLASH MEMORY chips, used to store either user data or software. Flash cards are employed by several brands of hand-held computer, and in digital cameras to store pictures. Unlike RAM-based storage cards, they do not require an internal battery to retain their contents. See also COMPACT FLASH, MEMORY STICK.

Flash EPROM An alternative name for a FLASH MEMORY chip. See also ROM, PROM, EPROM, ELECTRICALLY ERASABLE PROM.

flash memory A type of RAM that, like a ROM, retains its contents when the power supply is removed, but whose contents can be easily erased by applying a short pulse of higher voltage. This is called *flash erasure*, hence the name. Flash memory is currently both too expensive and too slow to serve as MAIN MEMORY, but is used as removable storage cards for digital cameras and pocket computers.

Flash is also fast replacing ROM as a storage medium for semi-permanent information – for example the BIOS code on PC motherboards or the FIRMWARE in modem and network cards – which may therefore be periodically updated by the end-user merely by running a piece of software. Such hardware is then said to be *flash-updatable*.

flash-updatable See under FLASH MEMORY.

flat address space A memory architecture within which any location can be selected by supplying a single integer value chosen from a contiguous range. Compare with a SEGMENTED ADDRESS SPACE. See also ADDRESS, ADDRESS SPACE.

flatbed scanner An optical SCANNER in which the source document is laid on a flat sheet of glass similar to that in a photocopier, as opposed to being fed into a slot, wrapped around a rotating drum or traversed with a hand-held device. See also DRUM SCANNER, HAND-HELD SCANNER.

flat-file database A computer database in which all the data is stored within the same single file or table, as compared with a RELATIONAL DATABASE in which the data is split into several separate tables each containing a different but related type of item.

flat memory model A memory architecture in which the processor can address any memory location using just one kind of ADDRESS, as opposed to a SEGMENTED MEMORY MODEL in which the processor must specify a segment and then an address within that segment. Motorola's 680x0 family, PowerPC and most other RISC processor employ flat memory models, but the commercially dominant Intel x86 family employs a segmented model.

flat-panel display Any display technology such as an LCD or a PLASMA SCREEN which is much thinner than it is wide and is hence suitable for building into portable equipment such as notebook or pocket computers, or for hanging on a wall. The term is used mostly to differentiate it from the CATHODE RAY TUBE used in conventional monitors, which is usually as deep as it is wide and occupies a great deal of desk space.

flat-screen display Most often used as a synonym for a FLAT-PANEL DISPLAY, but also occasionally used to describe certain brands of conventional CATHODE RAY TUBE monitor in which the tube is made with a flat rather than convex front face.

flavour (*US* flavor) **1** An enhancement to a software system. See also VANILLA.

2 The name for a CLASS in some early versions of object-oriented LISP.

FLC A FILENAME EXTENSION used by animations created in Autodesk Animator.

Flesch-Kincaid Index A formula based on word and sentence lengths that computes the difficulty of reading a document in terms of US school grades, so a score of 7.0 would mean that readers in the 7th grade or higher could understand the document. MICROSOFT WORD can calculate the Flesch-Kincaid score of documents.

FLI A FILENAME EXTENSION used by animations created in Autodesk Animator.

flicker A rapid visible fluctuation in the brightness of a VISUAL DISPLAY UNIT which may cause annoyance and eye-strain to the user. Flicker can be avoided by increasing the REFRESH RATE of the device beyond 60 Hz, which is done for most modern computer displays.

flip-book A simple technique for creating animations by making a semi-transparent copy of an existing frame and superimposing it over the original so that the artist can modify it appropriately. It is named by analogy with the paper toy whose pages are flicked to animate a drawing.

flip-flop A digital logic circuit that can store a single BIT of information, and is therefore used as the basis for the construction of MEMORY chips, LATCHES and the REGISTERS within processors. A flip-flop can exist in two states, with either a high or low voltage at its output, and flips from one state to the other at each pulse of a CLOCK SIGNAL. Two different implementations of flip-flop are commonly used, called the *D flip-flop* and the *J-K flip-flop*.

float The keyword used in C and related computer languages to describe the FLOATING-POINT data type.

floating-point A number format widely used to represent non-integral values in computer hardware and software.

A floating-point representation of a number consists of a MANTISSA, M, an EXPONENT, E, and an implied number BASE, B, the number's value then being

$M \times B^E$ for example 2.5×10^6 The base is normally 10 for human calculation, but is 2 for BINARY computer representations. Many different formats for representing the mantissa and exponent are possible, but the most widely used on computers are those laid down in the IEEE FLOATING POINT standard 754, which is employed by many hardware floating-point processors.

The term is also used adjectivally to distinguish those hardware and software devices that perform FLOATING-POINT ARITHMETIC from those that perform INTEGER (i.e. whole number) arithmetic: see for example FLOATING-POINT ACCELERATOR, FLOATING-POINT UNIT. Many modern microprocessors have special hardware for floating-point calculations, which are heavily used in GRAPHICS, so floating-point representation is rapidly making older FIXED-POINT representations obsolete.

floating-point accelerator Additional hardware provided to speed the processing of FLOATING-POINT arithmetic operations such as trigonometric and logarithmic functions. Many modern microprocessors – such as the Intel Pentium family – have such a FLOATING-POINT UNIT built into the chip, and so the term is generally reserved for older computers where the accelerator was a separate chip or even a whole circuit board. See also MMX.

floating-point arithmetic Arithmetic operations performed on FLOATING-POINT numbers, which in a modern computer are typically performed by different hardware units than those performed on INTEGERS.

floating-point-intensive Any computing task that requires many FLOATING-POINT calculations, a prime example being 3D GRAPHICS.

Floating-Point Operations Per Second See FLOPS.

floating-point underflow See under UNDERFLOW ERROR.

floating-point unit (FPU) An auxiliary computer processor that is devoted to speeding up the performance of FLOATING-POINT ARITHMETIC operations. Such operations are used extensively when computing financial and scientific problems, and for 3D GRAPHICS, and so most modern microprocessors such as the Intel Pentium and PowerPC have an FPU built into the chip. Formerly FPUs were sold as separate chips that fitted into a socket next to the main CPU.

floating toolbar A style of TOOLBAR that is a self-contained window full of icons or buttons which the user can position anywhere on the screen. See also DOCKING TOOLBAR.

flood fill A type of tool used in computer drawing and painting programs to fill a whole area with colour in a single operation. Flood fill algorithms work by colouring outwards from a central point – like spreading water (hence the name) – and stopping only where a boundary of a different colour is encountered. The more sophisticated flood-fill tools allow the user to choose a tolerance range for this boundary colour, so the fill can penetrate more deeply into variably-bounded areas, and also to define GRADIENT FILLS in which the colour changes progressively in a variety of ways across the filled area.

floor **1** The lowest value that some system parameter is permitted to take (in contrast to CEILING, which is the highest value).
2 Used in some programming languages to name a function that rounds down, i.e. returns the largest integer that is smaller than some real number. For example floor(1.4) = 1, and floor(−1.4) = −2 and not −1. See also CEILING.

floppy disk A cheap removable storage medium widely used in personal computers which consists of a disk of flexible plastic coated with a magnetic oxide layer, like thick recording tape. The earliest such disks (of 8 inches and later 5.25 inches in diameter) were contained within a very flexible outer plastic envelope with a slot to admit the read/write HEAD, which is how the name arose. Modern 3.5 inch floppy disks are housed in a rigid plastic case with a sliding metal shutter for head access so the name is no longer appropriate, but it persists as a convenience to distinguish them from HARD DISKS.

Floppy disks retrieve data far more slowly than hard disks because they rotate at lower speed (300 rpm as against 10,000+ rpm) and their head mechanism is cruder, so tracks must be written further apart and capacity is much smaller. The original IBM PC used 360 Kb 5.25 inch floppy disks, while modern 3.5 inch disks hold 1.44 Mb. Floppy disks became the main medium for software distribution during the formative years of personal computing, and historical traces of this remain in IBM-COMPATIBLE PCS, which still reserve the drive letters A: and B: for two floppy drives.

Floppy disks are in the process of being displaced by higher capacity removable disk technologies such as Iomega's ZIP DRIVE and various optical technologies such as CD-ROM, CD-R and CD-RW.

FLOPS FLOATING-POINT operations per second, a measure of a computer's processing speed that is particularly indicative of its performance when running graphical and scientific software.

floptical disk A hybrid removable storage technology which enhances the older FLOPPY DISK drive by using optics to guide the HEAD mechanism, permitting tracks to be written and read faster and placed closer together, so more data to be packed onto a disk. Stripes printed onto the disk surface are tracked by a laser servo mechanism in the head. In the early 1990s Insite made a 20 megabyte (MB) floptical drive that could also read MS-DOS and Macintosh floppies, while more recently Compaq and Matsushita have tried a 100 MB floptical drive.

flow chart A visual notation used to depict processes and information flows when planning computer systems or designing programs. The principal components of a flow chart are boxes that depict particular statements or sections within a program, joined by lines that indicate the FLOW OF CONTROL. Whenever a CONDITIONAL statement (for example an IF–THEN–ELSE) occurs, a lozenge-shaped symbol with one input and two or more outputs is employed to split the path and depict all the possible outcomes. There are several different sets of standard flow chart symbols developed by computer manufacturers and standards bodies such as ISO, as well as many sets created specifically to support particular design METHODOLOGIES such as UNIFIED MODELLING LANGUAGE.

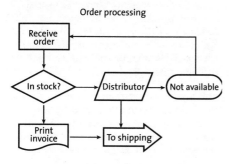

Order processing

flow control The various PROTOCOLS used in SERIAL communications to prevent the sender from sending more data until the receiver is ready to accept it, and thus avoid OVERRUN errors. The receiver typically has a fixed size BUFFER for received characters and, when this fills beyond a critical point, a signal is sent to the sender to stop transmitting until sufficient data has been read from the buffer to make more space. Under *software flow control* the signal is a special character added to the message stream – see for example XON/XOFF. With *hardware flow control* separate pins in the interface are reserved for these signals – in RS-232 they are called Request to Send (RTS) and Clear To Send (CTS). See also HANDSHAKE.

flow of control See under CONTROL FLOW.

flush To empty the contents of some temporary memory BUFFER, whose contents are usually saved onto another medium. For example the contents of a DISK CACHE are flushed back to the disk, while the contents of a processor cache are flushed back into MAIN MEMORY.

flyback In any visual display based on the CATHODE RAY TUBE, that phase of the scanning of the screen when the dot returns to begin another scan. There is a horizontal flyback at the end of each SCAN LINE to the start of the next line, and a vertical flyback from the bottom right hand corner to the top left hand corner to start a new FIELD (i.e. screen). A computer can use the time taken for the dot to return, called the *flyback interval*, to modify the contents of its graphics buffer without causing visible interference.

flyback interval See under FLYBACK.

fly-by-wire Aircraft control system, in which there is no mechanical or hydraulic linkage from the pilot's control stick to the plane's ailerons, rudder and elevator. Instead, digital signals generated by the stick are relayed over wires (or OPTICAL FIBRES) to control motors that adjust these surfaces. The latest generations of jet fighter would be unflyable without fly-by-wire – human reactions are not fast enough to maintain the attitude of the inherently unstable craft – so computers are interposed between stick and control surfaces. Most commercial airliner designs are also moving over to fly-by-wire.

FM Abbreviation of FREQUENCY MODULATION.

FMV Abbreviation of FULL-MOTION VIDEO.

focus **1** Under any window-based user interface, the window that appears in front of all the others and receives any user input such as mouse clicks or typed text is said to 'have the focus'. Similarly, within the window an individual control may have the focus. The focus can be given to another window by moving the MOUSE POINTER into it and clicking.
2 In an optical system, to adjust the configuration of a series of lenses in order to bring the rays of light passing through them to a point and create an image.

fogging In 3D GRAPHICS, the use of alpha blending (see ALPHA CHANNEL) to create the effect of a haze over a scene. See also DEPTH CUEING.

folder A named entity that holds a collection of related files in graphical operating systems such as WINDOWS and Apple's MACOS. A folder is the visual equivalent of the SUBDIRECTORY employed in older non-visual operating systems such as MS-DOS and UNIX. The name is metaphorical, playing on the reassuring familiarity of the cardboard folders used to hold papers in an old-fashioned filing cabinet.

font A complete set of typographical characters of a single TYPEFACE and size, an example being Times Roman 12 point. The term originated in the printing industry as 'fount', where it meant one whole set of lead type blocks purchased from the foundry. In computing too a font is the basic unit in which type is purchased, but modern computer type representations such as TRUETYPE and POST-SCRIPT mean that many different sizes may be derived from a single font file (see OUTLINE FONT). Hence the term font is often used in a looser sense by computer users to mean a typeface, regardless of size.

The BITMAPPED FONT which consists of a simple bitmapped picture of each character, and hence cannot be scaled effectively to different sizes, is still employed by some older software and in low-level operating system functions (for example a DOS box under WINDOWS), but these are seldom used any longer in document creation.

A minimal font file will contain two whole alphabets – the lower case and upper case letters – plus many punctuation and other symbols (see under CHARACTER SET). An outline font system such as TrueType can transform a single font into different styles (e.g. bold and italic) with some loss of letter quality but, for professional use, bold and italic versions of the typeface are usually supplied as separate font files. Hence there is some ambiguity as to whether setting a word in, say, bold, really represents a 'change of font'.

Modern computer operating systems are approaching a typographical sophistication that until recently was the preserve of professional typesetters. A troubling by-product of this progress is that one must consider what fonts the recipient will have available before transmitting highly formatted documents. FONT EMBEDDING schemes supported by some operating systems offer a partial solution to this problem.

font box A user interface component that enables a program's user to visually select a new FONT from a DROP-DOWN MENU.

Albertus Medium
ALGERIAN
Antique Olive
Arial
Arial Black

font caching Storing the data that describes a type FONT in memory so that it does not need to be reloaded from disk every time it is used. In most IBM-compatible PCs font caching is performed by the GRAPHICS CARD as part of its GUI ACCELERATION capabilities. See also CACHE.

font embedding The process of merging the data contained in a computer FONT file into a document in which the font has been used, so that the recipient of the document does not need to have that particular font installed on his/her computer to view it correctly. MICROSOFT WORD is among the document editors that offer this facility.

font family A group of related FONTS that share the same name (e.g. Times Roman) and have similar character forms, differing only in size and style – that is bold, italic and so forth. See also FONT OUTLINE, FONT SUBSTITUTION.

font manager A software component that is responsible for the appearance of the characters displayed on a computer's screen. This may include selecting the appropriate FONT, size and style, RENDERING the individual characters, and applying any special effects such as ANTIALIASING. Examples of font managers include ADOBE TYPE MANAGER and Microsoft's TRUETYPE engine (which is integrated into the operating system).

font metrics The widths and weights of each individual character in a PROPORTIONAL FONT, which are stored in a separate file or a table within the font file. In a font-rendering system such as POSTSCRIPT or TRUETYPE which supports FONT SUBSTITUTION (replacing a missing font with a similar and compatible one), only the font metrics rather than the whole font need be embedded in a document that is to be transferred to another computer system. Similarly, when printing on a device such as a laser printer that contains its own fonts, sending the font metrics enables the same visual layout (margins, etc) to be maintained.

font outline A file containing the data needed to reproduce the characters of an OUTLINE FONT. A font outline contains geometric descriptions of the shape of each character, which can be used to RENDER that character at various sizes. It may also contain HINTING information that slightly modifies the character shape at certain sizes, for example by thickening or thinning particular strokes, to improve its appearance. A single font outline may be used to generate all the styles (bold, italic, etc) of a particular style by geometric transformation, but for the highest quality reproduction a separate outline is provided for each style. See also FONT, TRUETYPE, POST-SCRIPT, ADOBE TYPE MANAGER.

font rendering The process of turning a FONT OUTLINE description into a BITMAP of a particular size ready to display or print. See also HINTING.

font scaling Altering a single FONT OUTLINE to produce characters of different sizes.

font size The size of the characters in a particular FONT, expressed in printer's points (see more under POINT SIZE).

font substitution A feature supported by several FONT RENDERING systems, including ADOBE TYPE MANAGER, POSTSCRIPT and TRUETYPE, which enables a document to be printed on a different computer from the one it was created on, and any font that is not installed to be replaced by a similar and compatible font that is available. This permits only the FONT METRICS rather than the whole font to be embedded into such portable documents, which greatly reduce their size.

font weight The thickness of the strokes that form the characters in a particular FONT. Most computer fonts are supplied in two weights called regular (or medium, or normal) and bold. Many professional fonts offer a third weight called light which is thinner than regular, and some offer a wide range of weights.

foo bar zot Nonsense syllables once popular with programmers as variable names when writing quick test programs.

footer A line of text, often containing the page and chapter number, that is printed or displayed at the foot of every page of a document. Most WORD PROCESSORS offer automatic insertion of a footer and a HEADER on each page, with automatic incrementing of the page numbers.

foot-lambert A now obsolete unit of LUMINANCE, equal to one lumen per square foot.

footnote A note commenting on a point made in a document, printed at the bottom of the page, to which attention is drawn by some reference mark (typically a SUPERSCRIPT number) placed in the body of the text. Most modern WORD PROCESSORS can assist with the management of footnotes and the similar ENDNOTES, for example automatically renumbering them if they are moved or deleted, and automatically gathering them together should footnotes need to turned into endnotes or vice versa. Footnotes may remain hidden when not required and appear only when the mark is clicked on.

footprint Used metaphorically to mean the space occupied by a particular object, for instance the area of desktop space taken up by a computer, or the amount of memory occupied by a particular data structure.

force feedback A technique used in advanced VIRTUAL REALITY systems that employ DATA GLOVES, to lend an illusion of solidity to objects: in addition to monitoring the user's finger positions, a force feedback glove contains motors or hydraulic joints that can resist the user's hand movements, conveying the impression that a solid object is being grasped. Simple force or vibration feedback is also offered by some JOYSTICKS.

fork **1** In the UNIX operating system, a system call used by one process (called the PARENT PROCESS) to make a copy of itself (the CHILD PROCESS). The child process receives a different PROCESS IDENTIFIER from its parent, but is otherwise identical.
2 In the Apple MACINTOSH file system (see MACOS), one of the two subdivisions within every file. The DATA FORK contains the data proper, which would be the sole contents of the file under other operating systems, while the RESOURCE FORK contains a number of arbitrary attribute/value pairs that include segments of program code, BITMAP data representing ICONS, and various other parameters. This divided structure poses problems when transferring files from the Macintosh to other systems such as MS-DOS or Windows, and it is common to transfer only the data fork, or to convert the whole file into another format before transfer.

form **1** A structured document that contains blank fields that must be filled in with information being sought from the user. Forms may be presented on a computer screen as well as on paper, as for example when creating a DATABASE QUERY or via a web page (see under WEB FORM).
2 In a VISUAL PROGRAMMING LANGUAGE such as VISUAL BASIC, the name given to the blank

window into which prefabricated components are placed to create a new program.

formal logic See under SYMBOLIC LOGIC.

formal methods Mathematically derived techniques for specifying, implementing and verifying software and hardware systems. Formal methods depend upon the existence of specially designed languages which have the property of REFERENTIAL TRANSPARENCY, so that programs can be mathematically proved correct, and submitted to mathematical transformations that preserve their correctness. The difficulty of designing such languages to cope with problems of real-world complexity means that formal methods have so far found little application.

formal parameter A variable name used as a place-holder for the value of a PARAMETER that will be passed to a subprogram.

format 1 Most generally, a style, plan or arrangement, for example of a television programme or a magazine.
2 Of computer data, the exact manner in which data items are arranged within a file, which determines what software can and cannot read that file. See also FILE FORMAT.
3 Of a magnetic storage medium, such as a HARD DISK, FLOPPY DISK or TAPE, the exact arrangement of data items on the recording surface, as determined by the hardware specification of the particular recording device. Hence also, the act of preparing the recording surface to receive data, an operation that destroys any data already present. See also HARD SECTORED, SOFT SECTORED, LOW-LEVEL FORMAT.
4 Of a document stored on a computer, the aggregate of all the type FONTS and STYLES, MARGINS, INDENTS, line, paragraph and section breaks; in short all its cosmetic attributes as opposed to its textual content. See also REFORMAT.

format string, format expression A string of characters that acts as a template to describe how numbers, dates or times are to be output by a computer program. For example in VISUAL BASIC the format string ####.## would cause the value 5 to be output as 5.00, each # character indicating a digit before or after the decimal point.

form designer A kind of software tool used by programmers to create the USER INTERFACE portion of a program without having to write any code, by drawing boxes to represent the various fields and/or by dragging prefabricated components into a window from a visual TOOLBOX. The best-known example of such a facility is that in VISUAL BASIC.

form factor A standard shape and size for some item of computing equipment such as a HARD DISK or an EXPANSION BOARD.

form feed (FF) The ASCII CONTROL CHARACTER with code 12, used to instruct a printer to advance the paper by a whole sheet.

form letter A mechanically reproduced letter, created by inserting personal details such as name and address into a pre-written template.

forms A shorthand for FORMS PROCESSING.

forms-based Descriptive of any computer system whose principal source of input data is provided by forms filled in by users. These may be paper forms that have to be read using OPTICAL CHARACTER RECOGNITION, but more often are on-screen forms distributed via a network or web site. Much of modern business software is forms-based in a loose sense – consider for example sending an EMAIL that requires filling in the 'address', 'copies to' and 'message' fields of an on-screen form. See also FORMS PROCESSING.

forms-driven Any computer application whose operation depends upon the user entering data into on-screen FORMS. Most business software is of this kind, in particular those applications that are based on DATABASE maintenance such as sales ledgers, accounting or stock control. See also FORMS-BASED, FORMS PROCESSING, FORMS GENERATOR.

forms generator A software module supplied with some of the larger DATABASE MANAGEMENT SYSTEMS which uses information from a DATA DICTIONARY to automatically create data entry forms.

forms processing A specialized area of DATABASE management in which bulk data entry is performed by extracting information contained in forms filled in by customers. These may be paper forms (say for a census, opinion poll, or in a billing application for a utility supplier) or on-screen forms from a WEB SITE. In the former case, forms processing applications often employ OPTICAL CHARACTER RECOGNITION to read the paper forms.

formula A mathematical expression typed into a SPREADSHEET CELL in place of a number, whose value is automatically calculated and entered into the cell. A typical formula calculates a value that depends on the contents of other cells in the sheet, for example to add up the contents of a row or column. See also RELATIVE REFERENCE, RECALCULATE.

Forth An extensible programming language created by Charles MOORE in 1971 to control telescopes at the Kitts Peak observatory. Forth is SEMI-COMPILED and generates extremely compact programs, suitable for embedding in devices such as cameras and robots. Unlike ASSEMBLY LANGUAGE, Forth is INTERACTIVE and encourages program development by experimentation and prototyping. Forth stores temporary results on a STACK rather than in named variables, and employs REVERSE POLISH NOTATION for arithmetic, both of which can make programs hard to read.

FORTRAN (FOrmula TRANslator) One of the first HIGH-LEVEL PROGRAMMING LANGUAGES, developed in 1954 by BACKUS, Herrick and Ziller for scientific computing applications. It is still widely used in fields such as space exploration and particle physics. FORTRAN is a COMPILED language that supports both integer and FLOATING-POINT data types. The original dialect had a line-oriented syntax governed by the format of punched-cards, and had only a few primitive control structures such as IF, GOTO and a counted DO loop. However successive versions such as FORTRAN IV, FORTRAN 77 and FORTRAN 90 have enhanced its features to include modern BLOCK STRUCTURED control, modularity and user-defined data types.

fortune cookie A joke, maxim or item of trivia randomly selected for display from a large file of such items, for example when a computer system is rebooted, when a certain program is executed, or when some operation is completed.

forum An alternative name for an online CONFERENCE; i.e., a service that supports discussions in which participants exchange messages that may be read and replied to by all.

forward chaining One of the two major styles of reasoning used in ARTIFICIAL INTELLIGENCE programs, which proceeds from a collection of known facts to infer new solutions or predictions. It is a data-driven technique which may produce a new solution every time a new fact arrives. The alternative style, called BACKWARD CHAINING, proceeds by deduction from a set of rules until only facts that can be proven remain.

forward declaration In COMPILED programming languages such as C and PASCAL that employ LEXICAL SCOPING, a partial declaration of a procedure or function that consists merely of the heading describing its name, parameters and return types, which is made at the start of a source file to enable calls to that procedure to be compiled before the body of its definition is defined further on in the program. See also PROCEDURE HEADING, PROCEDURE DECLARATION, FUNCTION DECLARATION, BINDING, EARLY BINDING.

four-colour separation The action of decomposing a coloured image into four separate cyan, magenta, yellow and black components, for printing using a four-pigment CMYK process.

4GL Abbreviation of FOURTH GENERATION LANGUAGE.

Fourier transform A mathematical function that takes an arbitrarily complex waveform and dissects it into the sum of a collection of regular sine waves. Fourier transforms are much used in sound and image processing (see under DIGITAL SIGNAL PROCESSOR) and in COMPRESSION algorithms to isolate different signal components so that they can treated individually. A highly efficient ALGORITHM for calculating them has been devised, called the FAST FOURIER TRANSFORM.

Fourth Generation Language (4GL) A special-purpose PROGRAMMING LANGUAGE used for rapid creation of business software systems, which typically is closely coupled to a DATABASE MANAGEMENT SYSTEM. Programming with a 4GL normally involves visually drawing layouts for the various forms (e.g. orders and invoices) used to hold business information, and for the relationships between them, from which the 4GL then automatically generates most of the code (possibly outputting it in a conventional language such as BASIC or C).

The name was coined in the 1980s to distinguish such products from so-called THIRD GENERATION LANGUAGES such as COBOL and C, (the second generation language was ASSEMBLY LANGUAGE and the first was raw MACHINE CODE itself).

Early 4GLs were mostly text-based, but nowadays they tend to be more graphical, making it difficult to draw any sharp distinction between them and general-purpose VISUAL PROGRAMMING environments such as VISUAL BASIC, DELPHI and POWERBUILDER which are tending to supercede them.

FoxPro   An interactive relational DATABASE MANAGEMENT SYSTEM, developed by Fox Software in 1990, which was originally created to be compatible with dBase IV but later added an OBJECT-ORIENTED DATABASE language. It was bought by Microsoft in 1992 and turned into VISUAL FOXPRO by adding interactive form creation similar to that in VISUAL BASIC.

FPGA   Abbreviation of FIELD-PROGRAMMABLE GATE ARRAY.

FPL   Abbreviation of FUNCTIONAL PROGRAMMING LANGUAGE.

FPM RAM, FPM DRAM   Abbreviation of FAST PAGE MODE RAM.

FPU Abbreviation of FLOATING-POINT UNIT.

FQDN   Abbreviation of FULLY QUALIFIED DOMAIN NAME.

fractal, fractal figure   A geometric figure whose parts are like small copies of the whole figure: hence a fractal figure appears roughly the same no matter what the scale at which it is examined – they are 'self similar'. Such figures are considered to exhibit fractional dimensionality (say 2.56 dimensions rather than 2 or 3). The name was coined by Benoit MANDELBROT in 1975 from the Latin 'to break'. The appearance of the natural world exhibits many examples of fractal form, from the structures of plants and animals to clouds, flames and water turbulence (the standard analogy is that of a coastline). An important application of fractals is in computer graphics, where they are generated to simulate natural-looking landscapes and textures.

Fractal figures can be plotted by the ITERATIVE evaluation of simple mathematical functions, which is practical only with the aid of computers: Mandlebrot discovered the set that bears his name (see under MANDELBROT SET) by plotting millions of iterations of the simple squaring of a COMPLEX NUMBER.

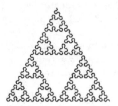

fractal compression   A powerful technique for reducing the storage size of graphical images, discovered by the UK mathematician Michael Barnsley and now marketed by the US software firm ITERATED SYSTEMS. The method works by identifying all those components of an image that have a FRACTAL structure, then storing just a set of suitable mathematical functions and their arguments (called an *Iterated Function System*) that when repeatedly evaluated will regenerate those shapes. See also COMPRESSION.

fragmentation   A problem affecting any storage system, such as a disk-based FILE SYSTEM or a memory HEAP, that allocates and deallocates space in arbitrary order – eventually all its free space will exist as small, randomly distributed, non-contiguous pieces. Fragmentation may render it impossible to satisfy a request for a large contiguous block, even though the total space free would appear to be sufficient. The cure is to move all the used areas into one contiguous block (since this changes their addresses, it is only possible if they are referenced indirectly). For a memory heap this procedure is called compacting the heap, while for disks the cure is performed by running a utility called a defragmenter or DEFRAGGER.

frame 1 In web design, a scheme invented by NETSCAPE to permit several independent pieces of content to be displayed in the same HTML page, for example a fixed menu bar sitting down the side of a variable content pane. Frames are defined using the <FRAME> and <FRAMESET> tags which are now incorporated into the HTML version 4 standard. A frameset divides the page into several areas, each of which can display a frame representing a different URL.

2 In networking and telecommunications, a packet of information at the DATA LINK LAYER, which contains the header and trailer information required by the physical transmission medium. Many NETWORK LAYER packets may be bundled together into a single frame for transmission. See also FRAME RELAY.

3 In film and animation, one single picture from a sequence that makes up a moving image.

4 In video engineering, one complete scan or refresh of the display screen. On an INTERLACED DISPLAY each frame will consist of two or more separate FIELDS each consisting of a subset of the total displayable SCAN LINES. See also FRAME RATE, INTERLACED DISPLAY.

5 In computer graphics, the PIXEL data representing one complete scan of the display screen, as stored in a FRAME BUFFER.

6 A data structure used to store information about the objects represented in a KNOWLEDGE-BASED software system.

frame buffer A region of memory that is set aside to store the PIXEL information representing the current contents of a computer's screen display. For high-performance GRAPHICS systems, a dedicated high-bandwidth BUS is often provided to connect the computer's CPU (or a dedicated GRAPHICS PROCESSOR) to the frame buffer, to enable the display to be updated as fast as possible. See also BUFFER, DOUBLE BUFFERING, RENDER, ACCELERATED GRAPHICS PORT.

frame check sequence An integrity test automatically performed on every packet sent over an ETHERNET network (based on a CYCLIC REDUNDANCY CHECK value appended to every packet) to detect transmission errors.

frame grabber A hardware device that captures single frames from an analogue video sequence or TV programme and stores them in a computer's memory, where they may be used in digital VIDEO EDITING.

FrameMaker A professional cross-platform DESKTOP PUBLISHING application for Unix, also available for Macintosh and PC systems.

frame rate For any form of animated visual display, the number of times per second the picture is renewed. For example, for cinema film the frame rate is 24 frames per second (Fps), which is around the minimum required to give an impression of smooth motion. Most broadcast television systems employ INTERLACED DISPLAYS so that the frame rate is the rate at which all the FIELDS making up a single picture are displayed: for example European television uses a frame rate of 25 Fps with two fields, that is 50 Fps or 50 Hz, while US television displays 30 Fps (i.e. 60 Hz field rate). Most computer MONITORS now support variable frame or REFRESH RATES, ranging up to 90 Hz for the most expensive, FLICKER-free models.

Frame Relay A type of fast, CONNECTION-ORIENTED packet network technology used mainly by telecommunication companies to build wide-area networks (WANs). Frame Relay differs from ASYNCHRONOUS TRANSFER MODE (which is sometimes called Cell Relay to distinguish the two) by employing variable length packets and an IP-based addressing scheme. Frame Relay is typically used over T1 (1.5 megabits per second) and T3 (45 megabits per second) leased lines, but a faster variant capable of 155 megabits per second has been defined, as has a standard for carrying voice data. See also X.25, VOICE-OVER-IP, PACKET SWITCHING, T1 LINE, T3 LINE.

frameset See under FRAME.

framework See APPLICATION FRAMEWORK.

framing error A type of error encountered during a SERIAL communications session when badly formatted data is received. Serial data streams employ certain combinations of bits to mark the start of a new data item (see under START BIT, STOP BIT) and if one of these is lost or corrupted a framing error will result. Framing errors are normally detected in hardware by the UART chip used to implement the SERIAL PORT.

FreeBSD A FREEWARE version of BERKELEY UNIX.

free-form database, free-text database A type of DATABASE that is used mainly to store text rather than numeric data, whose individual RECORDS need not consist of a rigidly ordered set of FIELDS, but may simply be documents in any format. Such a database differs from a mere collection of documents by INDEXING some or all of the words in the documents it contains, and offering search facilities that are typically much more powerful than those offered by the computer's operating system (for example supporting WILDCARDS, BOOLEAN search expressions, PROXIMITY SEARCHES or SOUNDEX searches). Examples of free-form databases include askSam, Lotus Agenda, Idealist and Folio Views. See also TEXT RETRIEVAL SYSTEM.

free list A data structure often employed in the management of scarce or shared program resources such as MEMORY blocks, HANDLES and DESCRIPTORS, in which all those resources that are not currently in use are joined together into a LINKED LIST – a resource is removed from this list whenever it is allocated, and returned to it when it is no longer in use. An empty free list signifies that all resources are in use and avoids costly searching.

Free Software Foundation (FSF) An organization set up in 1984 by a group of UNIX programmers lead by Richard STALLMAN to promote the spread of free software – that is, software that is free from licencing fees and whose source code is available to the user. The main work of the FSF is the development and maintenance of the GNU programming tools and operating system.

free-text database See FREE-FORM DATABASE.

freeware Software that is distributed for use absolutely without payment, in contrast to SHAREWARE which is distributed for free trial, but with a request that payment be made if the product is adopted for regular use. Freeware may still, however, be subject to COPYRIGHT restrictions that limit its modification and/or resale. See also OPEN SOURCE, GNU, FREE SOFTWARE FOUNDATION.

freeze-frame The ability to make a television programme or video playback stop at a particular FRAME. Freezing a frame requires all the picture information describing that frame to be temporarily stored in an internal FRAME BUFFER so that it can be redisplayed 50 or 60 times per second. Television sets or video recorders with a freeze-frame capability contain several megabytes of RAM for this purpose.

frequency The number of times that some periodic event repeats itself within a specified time interval. The unit of frequency is the HERTZ, which equals one cycle per second. Frequency is related to wavelength by the equation:

$$\text{frequency} \times \text{wavelength} = \text{velocity}$$

See also BANDWIDTH, FOURIER TRANSFORM.

Frequency Division Multiple Access (FDMA) See FREQUENCY DIVISION MULTIPLEXING.

frequency division multiplexing (FDM) The sending of two or more signals through the same shared physical link – such as a wire, optical fibre or light beam – by MODULATING the separate signals onto different frequency bands and adding the resulting waveforms linearly, before or during transmission. The combined signals can be amplified, shifted in frequency and ROUTED as if a single signal, which allows for efficient transmission. The receiving equipment separates the multiplexed signals by applying frequency passing or rejecting filters, and demodulates the resulting signals individually according to the modulation scheme used for that particular band. Different frequency bands may be joined to form groups.

Analogue broadcast radio, television, and cable services all employ FDM, as did the long distance telephone system in pre-digital days. The more recent TIME DIVISION MULTIPLEXING schemes are, however, more suitable for DIGITAL data. See also MULTIPLEX, DEMULTIPLEX.

frequency domain That domain of measurement that involves FREQUENCIES and BANDWIDTHS, as opposed to the spatial domain, which involves distances and lengths.

frequency-hopping See under FHSS.

frequency modulation (FM) Any signalling scheme in which the FREQUENCY rather than the amplitude of the CARRIER wave is varied to encode the information to be sent. Frequency modulation is more resistant to noise corruption than the alternative AMPLITUDE MODULATION scheme, and so it is used for high-quality radio and television sound broadcasting, for most computer networks, and in internal computer systems such as hard disks. See also MODULATE.

frequency shift keying (FSK) The tone-based protocol by which one MODEM interrogates another when first negotiating a connection. The characteristic FSK tones can often be heard as a protracted period of warbling and whistling when a connection is being established.

Frequently Asked Questions See FAQ.

friction feed printer A type of computer printer that prints onto a continuous roll of paper, which is propelled through the printer by a rubber-covered platen exactly like that of an old manual typewriter. Friction feed used to be a feature of the very cheapest of DOT-MATRIX PRINTERS, and is now found only in the small printers used inside point-of-sale terminals and data logging equipment.

friend function A C++ function declared to be a friend of a particular CLASS can access the data within INSTANCES of that class, even though it does not itself belong to the class.

Frogger One of the pioneering arcade GAMES in which a frog has to hop across a busy 6-lane motorway.

front-end A computer system or program that offers users an interface to some larger system such as a remote MAINFRAME database or SUPERCOMPUTER, or even to some other piece of software running on the same machine. Typically a front-end is designed to appear simpler and easier to use than the BACK-END machine or program, in which case it is often referred to as a 'friendly front-end'.

front-end processor A small computer connected to some larger computer such as a MAINFRAME or SUPERCOMPUTER, whose job is to interact with users and send data to the larger machine for processing. The classic example of a front-end processor is a UNIX workstation that runs programming tools and VISUALIZATION software, connected to a remote supercomputer that actually executes the programs that are written and processes the large data sets. See also FRONT-END, SMART TERMINAL, CLIENT/SERVER, THREE-TIER ARCHITECTURE.

front-panel A board containing rows of switches and lights fitted to all early computers, which functioned as both primitive display and input device. The patterns of lights revealed the binary values currently in the machine's registers, and the switches could be set to enter binary quantities into the registers. In the very earliest pioneering days

before ROM chips were invented, computer operators had to enter the BOOTSTRAP LOADER code in this fashion every time the machine was started.

frontside bus The name given to the conventional PROCESSOR BUS that leads to main memory in any microprocessor (such as the Pentium II) which also has a separate BACKSIDE BUS to access its LEVEL 2 CACHE. See also SOCKET 8, SLOT 1, SLOT 2.

FSF Abbreviation of FREE SOFTWARE FOUNDATION.

FSK Abbreviation of FREQUENCY SHIFT KEYING.

FTP (File Transfer Protocol) A client/server PROTOCOL used to transfer files from one computer to another over a TCP/IP network. FTP was originally developed as a utility for the UNIX operating system, hence its abbreviation is often written in lower case, ftp, following the normal Unix convention. FTP is the principal protocol used to download files from the Internet, especially from web sites and archive sites, and so a limited FTP client capability is built into most WEB BROWSERS. The URL of a file that is to be transferred via FTP starts by naming the protocol, server and directory path
so:ftp://info.cert.org/pub/cert_adv
isories/c567.txt
The protocol is defined in the Internet standard STD 9.

FTP archive Also called an archive site, an Internet server that holds a large quantity of documents, free programs, source code files, emails or newsgroup messages, which is thrown open to public access via ANONYMOUS FTP or some other distribution mechanism such as GOPHER or the WORLD WIDE WEB.

FTP by mail See under FTPMAIL.

FTP client A program that enables files to be transferred between two computers over a TCP/IP network using the FTP protocol. An FTP CLIENT is needed to download files from web sites and archive sites on the Internet, and may be integrated into a WEB BROWSER.

FTPmail A specially modified MAIL SERVER that permits users who have only email access to the Internet to nevertheless obtain files from FTP ARCHIVES by sending the requisite FTP commands in an email message. The requested files are returned as attachments to a replying email in MIME or UUENCODED form. Widespread access to the WORLD WIDE WEB has rendered it more or less obsolete.

FTP server A computer connected to the Internet that allows users to upload and download files using the FTP protocol. The term is also used for the FILE TRANSFER software that is used to run such a server. A typical application for an FTP server is to support an FTP ARCHIVE of free Unix software.

fubar (Fouled Up Beyond All Repair) Broken. US forces slang from World War II that has passed into programmers' argot.

FUD (Fear, Uncertainty and Doubt) A marketing tactic reputedly employed by certain large computer companies, which works by starting rumours that a certain rival technology is about to become obsolete to scare the rival's customers into delaying their purchasing decision.

full colour An alternative term for 32-bit, that is, TRUE COLOUR.

full-duplex Any communications channel that can carry messages in both directions at the same time, for example a public telephone line. Some computer network technologies are capable of being operated in either a full-duplex or a HALF-DUPLEX mode. See also SIMPLEX.

full-motion video Video sequences that are displayed on a computer screen at the broadcast-quality rate of 30 (or more) frames per second, rather than the greatly reduced frame rates that were until recently all that could be managed on a personal computer.

full record locking See under RECORD LOCKING.

full-screen Occupying the whole of a computer's monitor screen, rather than being contained within its own WINDOW. The term is a shorthand that describes an old-fashioned style of software (for example, MS-DOS software) that was CHARACTER-BASED and took over the whole computer screen, as compared with modern programs with graphics-based interfaces that can run in separate windows and multitask with other programs. See also TERMINAL WINDOW, GLASS TELETYPE.

full-screen editor The now-dominant style of TEXT EDITOR in which the user is presented with a scrolling text that fills either the whole screen or a window within it, through which they can move a CURSOR (using the cursor keys or a MOUSE) to reach the point at which an alteration must be made. The name is a survival from the days when LINE EDITORS prevailed, which permitted the user to edit only one line at a time. See also WORD PROCESSOR, EMACS, VI.

full stroke seek time Also called the MAXIMUM SEEK TIME, the time taken for a DISK DRIVE to move its head from the first track to the last track on a disk – that is, for a full stroke of the head-positioning mechanism. See also SEEK TIME, AVERAGE SEEK TIME, TRACK-TO-TRACK SEEK TIME.

full-text retrieval, full-text search, full-text indexing Any data retrieval technique that permits searching for any word in the documentary content of a DATABASE, rather than just for a few KEY fields. Web SEARCH ENGINES are examples of distributed full-text retrieval systems. See more under TEXT RETRIEVAL SYSTEM, FREE-FORM DATABASE.

fully associative cache See under ASSOCIATIVE CACHE.

fully qualified domain name (FQDN) The full identifying name of a networked computer, constructed from the name of its local HOST and the name of the DOMAIN to which it is attached; an example might be bigserver. penguin.com

function 1 Informally, any feature of a program, used as in 'Word provides a powerful search function'.

2 In mathematics, a formula or expression that can be evaluated to yield a single result. More formally, a many-to-one relation between two sets that associates each element (called an argument) in the first set with exactly one element (called the value) in the second set. A function f with argument x is written as $f(x)$, and the value of $f(x)$ for the case $x = 2$ is written $f(2)$.

3 A name given to subprograms in many programming languages, including C, C++, Lisp, Pascal, Visual Basic and APL. Some languages including Pascal and Visual Basic make a distinction between functions, which return a

result, and procedures, which do not; while Lisp and so-called functional programming languages only permit functions that return results. C and C++ functions may return a result or not. Functions must be declared before they can be used: see under FUNCTION DECLARATION.

functionality An ugly coinage meaning the capabilities of a system: to 'add new functionality' merely means 'to add new abilities'.

functional programming language, functional language Also called *applicative languages*, a class of PROGRAMMING LANGUAGES in which the only type of computation permitted is the application of FUNCTIONS to their arguments and the returning of results. Functional languages offer the advantage of REFERENTIAL TRANSPARENCY but, since their performance is generally inferior to that of conventional PROCEDURAL LANGUAGES, they have rarely been adopted for commercial programming. LISP was the first functional programming language, though it was only partially functional. Purer examples include ML, MIRANDA and HASKELL.

function body Those lines of source code that actually define the action performed by a program FUNCTION or PROCEDURE, in contrast to its heading, which defines its name and PARAMETER types.

function call An alternative name for a PROCEDURE CALL, preferred by C programmers since all subroutines are called functions in that language.

function declaration A programming language statement that tells the compiler or interpreter that a new FUNCTION of a particular name is to be defined, the names and types of its arguments, its RETURN TYPE, and how its return value is to be calculated. An example is:

```
function Square(x: integer): integer;
begin
return x*x
end Square;
```

See also FUNCTION HEADING, PROCEDURE DECLARATION, FORWARD DECLARATION.

function definition A statement describing the way a function calculates its value. See also FUNCTION DECLARATION.

function heading The first line of the declaration of a FUNCTION in a programming language, which states the name of the new function, the names and types of its arguments, and its RETURN TYPE. See more under PROCEDURE HEADING, FUNCTION DECLARATION.

function key A key on a computer KEYBOARD that, when pressed, does not produce a fixed ALPHANUMERIC character, but some action determined by the software currently running. Frequently function keys cause a MENU or DIALOGUE BOX to be displayed, as a substitute for pointing with the MOUSE. IBM-COMPATIBLE PCS have a set of 12 such function keys running along the top of the keyboard.

function unit One of the subunits within a computer PROCESSOR that performs a single function, such as an ADDER, MULTIPLIER, BUFFER or BRANCH PREDICTION unit.

fuzzy inference In software systems based on FUZZY LOGIC, the process of using degrees of partial truth to select which PRODUCTION RULE to execute.

fuzzy logic An extension of BOOLEAN LOGIC to handle partial truths (that is fractional TRUTH VALUES lying between True and False) invented by Dr Lotfi Zadeh at Berkeley University in the 1960s for modelling the ambiguities inherent in NATURAL LANGUAGE descriptions.

Fuzzy logic replaces the Boolean truth values with degrees of truth that resemble probabilities (except that they need not always sum to one). Rather than asserting that X has property Y, fuzzy logic instead assigns a degree of truth to that assertion, that is, a degree of confidence with which one believes it to be true. Fuzzy truth values can be combined arithmetically, one possible set of rules being:

```
Truth(not X) = 1.0 - Truth(X)
Truth(X and Y) = Lesser_of
(Truth(X), Truth(Y))
Truth(X or Y) =
Greater_of(Truth(X), Truth(Y))
```

If truth values are confined to 0 and 1, these reduce to their Boolean counterparts.

Fuzzy logic has attained some importance in the fields of ROBOTICS and machine control, where it is more suited to describing the logic of imprecise operations in the real world than traditional logic is.

fuzzy search Any text search algorithm that can cope with some degree of partial mismatch between target word and text. The term is often used in promotional literature to loosely describe methods ranging from PROXIMITY SEARCHES, SOUNDEX searches and FUZZY LOGIC proper even to simple WILDCARD searches.

fuzzy set A mathematical set that has been constructed using relationships derived from FUZZY LOGIC. Such sets allow partial degrees of membership, so for example John Doe might be 0.45 Young and 0.36 Rich. See also SET, SET THEORY.

FWIW Online shorthand for For What It's Worth.

FX!32 A software EMULATOR developed by DIGITAL EQUIPMENT CORPORATION to enable Windows executable programs compiled for Intel processors to run on its ALPHA processors. FX!32 works by combining translation and interpretation: it translates some Intel instructions into NATIVE Alpha instructions – saving the result in a separate DLL file – but intercepts all SYSTEM CALLS and redirects them into a library of Windows routines written in native Alpha code. By this technique it can typically achieve over 40% of the speed of a native program.

FYI Online shorthand for For Your Information.

G

GaAs Chemical formula for GALLIUM ARSE-NIDE.

gain The multiple by which a signal is increased by some amplifying device.

GAL Online abbreviation for Get A Life!

gallium arsenide (GaAs) A semiconducting compound of gallium and arsenic with chemical formula GaAs, which supports INTE-GRATED CIRCUITS that run much faster than those made of SILICON. GaAs chips are, however, more difficult and expensive to fabricate than silicon ones, which limits them to premium applications such as network and satellite communications chips that must operate at multi-gigahertz frequencies.

game A computer program designed to entertain the computer's user. Computer games can be divided into several main categories:

a) Computerised versions of traditional card and board games such as chess, bridge, backgammon, poker or Patience (Solitaire) in which the computer plays the part of one or more players against the human user. Computers are now sufficiently powerful to beat the best human players at some of these games.
b) Arcade games emulate the operation of amusement arcade slot machines. These games usually involve driving fast vehicles or shooting fast-moving targets, and require great hand-to-eye coordination. They may also require special input hardware such JOY-STICKS, pistol grips or steering wheels to be plugged into a PC.
c) SIMULATIONS of real-life sports such as football, tennis, pool or snooker, car racing or flying an aircraft. These games employ the latest

3D GRAPHICS and audio techniques to make the simulation as life-like as possible.
d) Adventure games that involve the player pursuing a quest through a fantastic virtual world created within the computer: monsters are encountered and fought, and problems solved by finding and correctly employing magic objects.
e) Simulation games that require the player to build and manage a virtual world, complete with virtual inhabitants. Such worlds range from humble railway systems, through cities, up to whole planets or galaxies, and from the warlike to the ecologically sound.
f) Multiuser role-playing games in which a number of human players share the same virtual world over Internet connections, each player being represented in the game space by a more or less realistic graphical figure called an AVATAR. Players interact verbally by exchanging text-based messages.
g) Abstract games that have no equivalent in the real world, and depend solely on computer graphics for their attraction (Tetris and its imitators are prime examples).

Games employ increasingly sophisticated graphics and animation techniques and have become a major driver of technical advance in PC design. The above categories are continually merging and blurring so that in the longer term they seem destined to converge around multi-player role-playing games in cinematically (sur)realistic virtual playgrounds.

Game Boy A battery-operated pocket games console made by NINTENDO.

game port Also called a game control port, a 15-pin connector used to connect a JOYSTICK to an IBM-COMPATIBLE PC.

games console A computer-based electronic device dedicated to the playing of GAMES and exemplified by the Sony PLAYSTATION, NINTENDO Ultra and SEGA Dreamcast. Consoles lack keyboards; instead they have special input devices such as JOYSTICKS, guns or steering wheels, and they typically output to a domestic television set. New games are loaded either via solid-state cartridges or on CD-ROM disks. Internally, modern consoles contain extremely advanced hardware, including 64-bit and even 128-bit RISC microprocessors and GRAPHICS ACCELERATOR chips.

games machine A personal computer with a specification suited for playing GAMES, which essentially means lots of memory and the fastest GRAPHICS ACCELERATOR available.

gamma correction An adjustment applied to a digital image displayed on a computer monitor to compensate for the fact that the light intensity produced by a CATHODE RAY TUBE is not linearly proportional to its input voltage, but rather to the input voltage raised to the power of a constant called gamma whose value varies between one tube and another (typical values of gamma are around 2.5). For accurate colour matching, therefore, the gamma curve of the particular monitor needs to be established and the correction applied to image data. Many SCANNERS, GRAPHICS CARDS and monitors have gamma correction circuitry built in, and most graphics programs such as PHOTOSHOP permit the correction to be performed in software.

gamma curve See under GAMMA CORRECTION.

gamut The entire range of colours that can be depicted by a display or printer, or that can be represented by a particular COLOUR MODEL.

Gantt chart A specialized type of BAR GRAPH used for scheduling complex projects. It consists of a set of overlapping horizontal bars that represent the sequence of actions involved in various concurrent tasks, with time plotted along the horizontal axis. Most computer scheduling software can display its results in the form of a Gantt chart. See also SCHEDULER, CRITICAL PATH ANALYSIS, PERT.

garbage collection The process of automatically reclaiming areas of memory that are no longer in use by a program, so that they may be used again. A few programming languages such as JAVA, OBERON, LISP and SMALLTALK employ garbage collection, but more traditional languages such as C, C++ and FORTRAN require the programmer to write code to explicitly deallocate any dynamically allocated memory, and omitting this is the cause of a common class of bug called a MEMORY LEAK.

Garbage collection is a time-consuming task since the program must determine which objects are still referred to by others, and this involves scanning the whole memory space. A garbage collector may run continuously as a BACKGROUND TASK, or be invoked periodically when free memory falls below a preset level.

garbage in, garbage out (GIGO) A homily from the early days of data processing, reminding that computers merely manipulate the data they are given, and if fed with faulty information will produce useless answers.

gas plasma display See under PLASMA SCREEN.

gate **1** One of the three constituent parts of a FIELD-EFFECT TRANSISTOR: an electrical conductor so positioned that any voltage applied to it either increases or decreases the current flowing between two other conductors called the SOURCE and the DRAIN. Hence the transistor acts as a switch, controlled by the voltage at its gate.

2 An abbreviation of LOGIC GATE, one of the primitive circuit elements from which INTEGRATED CIRCUITS are built.

gate array A silicon chip that contains a large number of LOGIC GATES that can be connected together to create any desired circuit. Gate arrays may be used to produce small quantities of an INTEGRATED CIRCUIT that would be too expensive to fabricate as a full CUSTOM CHIP, though they involve a considerable sacrifice of component density. In a FIELD-PROGRAMMABLE gate array, the gates are connected together electrically using software, and may therefore be changed later, whereas in other types the connections are made permanent by breaking fusible links.

gate-level The level of detail in the design or simulation of an INTEGRATED CIRCUIT that encompasses individual LOGIC GATES.

Gates, Bill (William Henry) (b. 1955) President and co-founder with Paul ALLEN of MICROSOFT CORPORATION. Gates started the company after dropping out of Harvard, co-writing with Allen the MICROSOFT BASIC interpreter that was supplied with many of the earliest personal computers, including the IBM PC. His personal contribution to Microsoft's current world-leading position is undeniable, and it made him for a while the richest man in the world.

gateway 1 A computer that connects two different networks and can translate between the different data formats or PROTOCOLS they may employ. Also called a PROTOCOL CONVERTER.
2 An obsolete name for what is now called a ROUTER.

Gateway 2000 A US manufacturer of low-cost personal computers.

Gaussian blur An operation provided in many IMAGE PROCESSING and COLOUR RETOUCHING programs that blends together the PIXELS in a selected region in a manner that follows a Gaussian or bell-shaped distribution; that is, dense in the centre of the region and becoming sparser toward the edges.

Gaussian distribution In statistics, a continuous distribution of the values of a random variable whose mean, median and mode are all equal, also called the NORMAL DISTRIBUTION. The graph of such a distribution displays the well-known BELL CURVE shape. The distribution is named after the great German mathematician Carl Friedrich Gauss, who first described it.

The Gaussian distribution is frequently encountered in nature, for example in the heights of randomly chosen human beings or the weights of apples, and also in science and technology when measuring quantities with a degree of error. In fact it is seen in any phenomenon that clusters around a typical value rather than permitting any value. See also POISSON DISTRIBUTION.

gaze-controlled A class of advanced experimental USER INTERFACE in which the direction of the user's gaze can be determined – either by analysing a video image of the subject's eyes or by reflecting infrared beams from the surface of the eyeball – and used as input to a software system, say to steer a CURSOR or control a motor. While such interfaces have been implemented for game playing and controlling software, the most advanced versions are produced by the military for aiming weapons systems.

GB Symbol for a GIGABYTE.

Gbit Abbreviation of GIGABIT.

Gbps Abbreviation of GIGABITS PER SECOND.

gcc See under GNU C.

GDI (Graphical Device Interface) The section of Microsoft's WINDOWS operating system that contains all the primitive commands for creating a screen display by drawing lines, rectangles, fonts, arcs, bitmaps, windows and their borders. Windows application programs are supposed to perform all output to the screen by making GDI calls rather than by directly accessing video memory (but see also DIRECTX). The GDI is packaged as a separate DLL called GDI.DLL.

geek A person who is deemed to have an excessive interest in computers, to the detriment of their social life. See also NERD.

gender An attribute of an electrical connector which may either be MALE (with pins) or FEMALE (with sockets).

gender changer An adapter that converts an electrical connector (for example for a printer or serial cable) from MALE to FEMALE or vice versa.

General Magic The US creator of Magic Cap, a graphical operating system for hand-held communicating devices.

General Packet Radio Service (GPRS) The latest generation of mobile phone technology, which employs PACKET SWITCHING to enable mobile phones and pocket communication terminals to connect directly to remote networks via the Internet, at much higher rates than at present. Unlike the older CELLULAR CIRCUIT SWITCHED DATA services, GPRS is an 'always on' service that does not require the use of a modem, and it will transmit data up to 20 times faster.

GPRS works by overlaying a packet-switched data service on top of a CIRCUIT-

SWITCHED digital GSM telephone connection, which means that channel BANDWIDTH is consumed only when users are actually sending or receiving data: rather than dedicating a whole channel to one user for a fixed period, the available bandwidth is shared between several users in the same cell. GPRS can theoretically transfer data at a maximum speed of 172.2 kilobits per second, but the speed attainable in practice may be less, depending on the number of current users, the application being used and how much data is being transferred. GPRS does not work with existing GSM phones and requires a dedicated GPRS handset, and a telephone service provider who has installed GPRS hardware and software. See also CIRCUIT-SWITCHED, PACKET SWITCHING, HSCSD.

General Protection Fault (GPF) A hardware ERROR CONDITION generated by the MEMORY MANAGEMENT UNIT of Intel microprocessors whenever a program tries to write data outside of its assigned memory SEGMENT, usually because a bug has caused it to run out of control. This error underlies the well-known message *'This program has performed an illegal operation and will be shut down'* which appears when an application crashes under Microsoft's Windows operating systems from 95 onwards. See also PROTECTED MEMORY, ERROR MESSAGE, ERROR TRAPPING.

General Public License See GNU GENERAL PUBLIC LICENSE.

General-Purpose Interface Bus (GPIB) See under HPIB.

generic programming A kind of program design applicable to OBJECT-ORIENTED PROGRAMMING LANGUAGES and FUNCTIONAL PROGRAMMING LANGUAGES, in which parameterized TEMPLATES are created that can be later instantiated into real classes and algorithms. The intention is to create a body of more general, and hence more reusable, program components. For example, a generic class template called `Array(t)`, where t is any data type, might be instantiated as `Array(bitmap)`, a real class that describes an array of bitmaps, from which in turn individual instances can be created.

genetic algorithm A type of ALGORITHM that improves itself according to the principles of evolution, by creating many different possible solutions, choosing the best ones and 'breeding' them – that is combining them in random way – to produce an improved solution. Genetic algorithms have been shown to achieve excellent results in problem areas such as routing and optimization.

genlock An electronic circuit that enables a computer's display signal to synchronize with an external video signal from a camera or recorder to allow the two signals to be mixed or the computer display to be seen on camera with flicker or interference bars.

GeoCities A pioneering American ISP which hosts personal web sites for millions of people, who call themselves HOMESTEADERS. Now owned by YAHOO!

Geoforce A maker of high-performance 3D ACCELERATOR graphics cards.

geometric transformation A mathematical function that modifies the shape, size or orientation of a geometric figure when applied to that figure's coordinates. See also CARTESIAN COORDINATES, POLAR COORDINATES, AFFINE TRANSFORM, MATRIX ARITHMETIC.

geometry 1 The branch of mathematics that studies the properties of points, lines, curves and surfaces. Also, any subdiscipline within this study, such as analytical geometry, solid geometry or non-Euclidean geometry
2 A shorthand meaning the shape, configuration or arrangement of some objects in space. See also TOPOLOGY.
3 In computer graphics, that part of the information describing a scene which relates to the shape, size and position of the objects in the scene rather than to the surface appearance of these objects. See more under 3D GRAPHICS, GEOMETRY ENGINE, 3D ACCELERATOR.

geometry engine The portion of a GRAPHICS ACCELERATOR that processes the coordinates describing the shape and position of figures which are then 'coloured in' by a RENDERING engine. The geometry engine performs FLOATING-POINT operations on sets of real numbers representing points in 2D or 3D space, and much of its work consists of MATRIX multiplication applying AFFINE TRANSFORMS to an object in order to move, scale or rotate it to fit the current viewpoint. See more under 3D GRAPHICS.

geostationary Any SATELLITE that remains above the same spot on the Earth's surface.

geosynchronous satellite (GEO satellite) A type of artificial Earth SATELLITE that orbits at precisely 22,238 miles above the Earth's equator, so that its period of orbit is 24 hours and it stays above exactly the same point on the Earth's surface. (This orbit is called a Clarke orbit after the sci-fi author Arthur C Clarke, who first posited its possibility in 1945.) Most communication satellites are GEOs. Also called GEOSTATIONARY.

gesture-based interface A class of advanced experimental user interface which enables a computer program to be controlled by the user gesturing with hands, arms or whole body movements. These movements are recorded by a video camera and interpreted by the system software to select one of a repertoire of commands. See also HEAD-MOUNTED DISPLAY, GAZE-CONTROLLED.

gesture recognition 1 An advanced computer input technique that involves tracking the position of a user's head, limbs and body, and interpreting their gestures as commands. Such tracking can be performed using IMAGE PROCESSING algorithms on a live video feed, by the wearing of special garments such as the DATA GLOVE, and in future possibly using phased-array radar (see PHASED-ARRAY ANTENNA) or infra red techniques.
2 In a more restricted sense, a technique used by many PEN INPUT computers that interprets certain strokes and flourishes of the pen (e.g. crossing-out or underlining a passage) as commands.

GFLOPS See GIGAFLOPS.

Ghostscript   A software interpreter for Adobe's POSTSCRIPT page description language that enables PostScript files to be printed from a personal computer that is not attached to a PostScript printer. Published by Aladdin Enterprises, Ghostscript is distributed free of charge under a type of OPEN SOURCE licence.

Ghostview An add-on viewer for GHOSTSCRIPT that can be used to read and print POSTSCRIPT files under MS-DOS, OS/2 and WINDOWS.

GHz Symbol for GIGAHERTZ.

giant magnetoresistive head   See under MAGNETO-RESISTIVE HEAD.

GIF (Graphics Interchange Format) A popular compressed GRAPHICS FILE FORMAT developed originally for use on the CompuServe online service but now used extensively on the World Wide Web. GIF compresses 256-colour bitmapped images by first creating an 8-bit PALETTE and reducing each PIXEL value to an index value, then applying LZW COMPRESSION to the resulting data set. For pictures with lower colour depths, GIF can reduce the palette size accordingly, down to two colours. GIF files may contain more than one image, which has led to their extensive use on the web for the short animated sequences called ANIMATED GIFS. Because the LZW algorithm has been patented by Unisys, software that employs the GIF format can no longer be sold without a royalty, and to overcome this the public-domain alternative PNG format was created. See also JPEG, IMAGE COMPRESSION.

gigabaud A DATA RATE of one thousand million bits per second. See also BAUD RATE.

gigabit Literally 1,073,741,824 BITS (that is 2^{30} bits). However, the term is most often encountered as a shorthand for GIGABIT ETHERNET.

Gigabit Ethernet The latest version of ETHERNET networking technology which supports a data rate of 1024 megabits per second.

gigabits per second (Gbps) A measure of data throughput that is used for FIBRE-OPTIC communication networks, and will very soon be required for computer systems too. See also GIGABIT, GIGABAUD, GIGABIT ETHERNET.

gigabyte (GB) 1,073,741,824 BYTES, that is 2^{30} bytes, or 1024 MEGABYTES. Now the standard measure for HARD DISK capacities.

gigaflops 1,000,000,000 (10^9) Floating-Point Operations Per Second (FLOPS), a measure of computation speed. Only a decade ago this was the speed of the world's fastest supercomputer; now Intel's latest Pentium III is capable of 2 gigaflops.

gigahertz (GHz) 1,000,000,000 cycles per second, a unit of FREQUENCY.

GIGO Abbreviation of GARBAGE IN, GARBAGE OUT.

GKS (Graphical Kernel System) An ANSI and ISO standard 2D graphics software interface, consisting of a set of high-level drawing functions that are implemented via a RUN-TIME LIBRARY. GKS-3D extends the standard with 3D GRAPHICS commands and supports HIDDEN SURFACE REMOVAL.

GL Abbreviation of GRAPHICS LANGUAGE.

glass-ferrite A recording head technology used in some TAPE DRIVES

glass teletype, glass tty An ironic and informal name for the kind of simple text-based user interface found on a remote MAINFRAME or MINICOMPUTER with a serial TERMINAL – or in a non-graphical PC operating system such as MS-DOS or Unix – in which all typed user input and system output scrolls off the top of the screen, just like the paper in an old TELE-TYPE printer.

glibc See under GNU C.

GlidePoint A proprietary brand name for a TOUCHPAD input device widely used on LAPTOP and NOTEBOOK computers in place of a MOUSE. The patent holder and licensor is the US company Cirque Corporation of Salt Lake City.

Glint A range of high-performance 3D ACCEL-ERATOR chips made by 3D Labs.

glitch A transient and minor fault.

global 1 Accessible from all parts of a program, a term applied to the individual components of a program such as its VARIABLES and PROCEDURES. See also LOCAL, LOCAL VARIABLE, SCOPE.
2 Often used by programmers as a noun, as shorthand for GLOBAL VARIABLE.

Global Positioning System See GPS.

Global System for Mobile communications See GSM.

Global Unique Identifier See GUID.

global variable A VARIABLE that is visible throughout a whole program and whose value may be modified by any PROCEDURE in the program. Compare with LOCAL VARIABLE.

glueless interface An interface between INTE-GRATED CIRCUITS that does not require any GLUE LOGIC.

glue logic A collection of DISCRETE LOGIC components such as gates, inverters and latches that are often required to correct minor mismatches of polarity, timing or word size when connecting larger INTEGRATED CIRCUITS together to form a system – for example to interface a microprocessor to a personal computer's motherboard. See also SYSTEM CHIP SET.

glyph The graphical image that represents an alphabetic CHARACTER on a computer screen or printer. Hence a glyph is the *appearance* of an actual instance of the character, as distinct from its alphabetic name (say 'a') or its ASCII code (say 65). A FONT is therefore a complete set of glyphs of a particular size and TYPEFACE.
   In most fonts each character is represented by a single glyph, but some specialized fonts may have more than one glyph for a single character, while markup notations such as SGML employ multi-character codings that correspond to a single glyph – for example, é to represent the accented character é.

glyph scaling The varying of letter widths, in addition to the inter-word and letter spacing, to achieve the most pleasing appearance for a line of JUSTIFIED text. See also GLYPH, MICRO-JUSTIFICATION, INDESIGN.

GNOME (GNU Network Object Model Environment) A part of the GNU project which is developing a graphical user interface for Unix based entirely on free software components. The GNOME desktop consists of a collection of utility programs and larger applications, such as editors and browsers, which share a common look and feel. See also CDE, KDE, MOTIF.

GNU (Gnu's Not Unix!) A cooperative programming project initiated by the pioneering MIT programmer Richard STALLMAN, which aims to create a free version of the UNIX operating system and its software development tools under the auspices of Stallman's FREE SOFTWARE FOUNDATION. Any program created as part of a GNU project must be distributed under the GNU GENERAL PUBLIC LICENSE or GPL.

The GNU project began in 1983 and to date has produced the popular EMACS text editor, the GNU C compiler and many other widely used software tools. There is not as yet a full GNU Unix, because work is still in progress on the GNU Hurd KERNEL. Many advocates of the GNU philosophy therefore build their systems around the free LINUX kernel, which though created independently of the GNU project was developed under the terms of the GPL. See also OPEN SOURCE.

GNU C Strictly those versions of the C and C++ languages that can be compiled by the free software COMPILER created as part of the GNU project. However the term is used more narrowly to refer to the compiler itself (the program *GCC*) or more broadly to include the GNU C RUN-TIME LIBRARY *GLIBC* which supports a superset of ANSI C and a large subset of the POSIX.2 interface.

GNU General Public License The licence under which free software developed as part of the GNU project is released for use. It grants the legal right to use the product, to give copies to other people (either free or for payment), to possess and modify the source code of the product and to distribute under this same licence any further software developed using the product. This principle has been dubbed COPYLEFT, a pun on the conventional notion of copyright.

GNU/Linux The preferred name for the LINUX operating system, since strictly speaking only the kernel is Linux, the rest being derived from GNU Unix.

GNU Network Object Model Environment See GNOME.

Gnu's Not Unix! See GNU.

goal-seeking A feature offered in many SPREADSHEET applications, including Microsoft EXCEL, in which the user specifies the desired answer to some formula calculation and the program works backward to find the input value that would produce that result. For example, the goal might be a particular level of profit, and the formula might involve the price and sales of a product. Goal-seeking

in the general case is difficult, because some mathematical functions have no inverse, and because there may be multiple inputs that would produce the same output. Excel's Goal Seek feature requires that just one input be singled out to be varied. To attempt multi-input goal seeking, ITERATIVE methods may be employed to alter each input by a small amount and check whether the output moves in the desired direction, but such methods do not always converge to an answer. See also SOLVER, CONVERGENCE, CONSTRAINT, CONSTRAINT SATISFACTION.

Gödel, Kurt (1906–78) A Swiss mathematician who revolutionized 20th-century mathematics (and thought) with his famous theorem that any formal system strong enough to contain arithmetic cannot be both complete and consistent. The implication of Gödel's result destroyed at a stroke long-standing dreams that the pursuit of mathematical truth might be automated. At the same time, it impelled Alan TURING and Alonzo CHURCH into studies that would lead to a more modest dream, the DIGITAL COMPUTER.

Gopher A client/server PROTOCOL used to publish documents over the Internet, which users can access by searching through a series of text-based hierarchical menus. Gopher does not support graphical browsing, and so the introduction of the WORLD WIDE WEB is gradually rendering it redundant. Most web browsers do not support Gopher, so a separate Gopher client program is required.

goto An unconditional branch command provided in most programming languages for transferring control directly to a different place in the program, which is specified either by giving its line number or a textual LABEL. Directly equivalent to a machine code JUMP instruction, goto can be used to simulate more complex control structures including call and return from a SUBROUTINE, thus:

```
10 goto 50
20 ...
...
50 do subroutine
60 goto 20
```

However, excessive reliance on goto can lead to programs whose logic is almost impossible for a human reader to follow (see SPAGHETTI

CODE), and its elimination was one of the chief objectives of the STRUCTURED PROGRAMMING movement. See also SUBPROGRAM, PROCEDURE, PROCEDURE CALL, CONDITIONAL BRANCH.

Gouraud shading An algorithm employed in 3D GRAPHICS to fool the eye into seeing as a smoothly curving surface an object that is actually constructed from a mesh of polygons. Gouraud's algorithm requires the colour at each vertex of a polygon to be supplied as data, from which it INTERPOLATES the colour of every PIXEL inside the polygon: this is a relatively fast procedure, and may be made faster still if implemented in a hardware GRAPHICS ACCELERATOR chip. See also PHONG SHADING, RAY TRACING, RADIOSITY, TEXTURE MAPPING.

GPF Acronym for GENERAL PROTECTION FAULT.

GPIB Abbreviation of General-Purpose Interface Bus. See under HPIB.

GPL 1 Abbreviation of GENERAL PUBLIC LICENSE. **2** Abbreviation of GNU GENERAL PUBLIC LICENSE.

GPRS Abbreviation of GENERAL PACKET RADIO SERVICE.

GPS (Global Positioning System) A system originally created by the US military under which a GPS receiver can determine its latitude and longitude on, and altitude above, the Earth's surface to a precision of about 10 metres by calculating the difference in arrival time of radio signals from several SATELLITES. The GPS system consists of 24 satellites equipped with radio transmitters and atomic clocks; three or more of these satellites may be visible to any GPS receiver at one time depending on its geographic location. Portable GPS receivers are now fitted in cars and sold as consumer items for hikers and sailors, but special GPS signals reserved for military use offer a higher precision (better than 3 metres) for guiding miltary vehicles and missiles.

grab To capture into a computer some set of data, for example a video frame.

graceful degradation A highly desirable mode of system behaviour in which overloading manifests itself as a *gradual*, *visible* and *controllable* reduction of performance rather than as a sudden catastrophic failure.

gradient In computer graphics, a smooth and gradual variation in a colour. See also GRADIENT FILL.

gradient fill A variety of the FLOOD FILL algorithm in computer graphics that causes an area within an image to be filled not with a single colour but with a tint that varies smoothly between two specified colours. Programs that offer a gradient fill feature may also offer a choice of different geometries for the colour gradient, including linear, radial, rectangular and circular or 'sunburst' effects. More sophisticated versions also offer control over the steepness and profile of the gradient.

Graffiti A system of simplified handwritten characters employed to enter data into a computer with a PEN INTERFACE. Graffiti was the first commercially viable HANDWRITING RECOGNITION system, thanks to the success of the PALM computer family, though it was originally developed at XEROX CORPORATION (a matter which provoked a lawsuit). Graffiti characters must be entered one at a time, not as continuous handwriting, and are written in a prescribed direction.

grammar The rules that govern the way words may be combined in a language (whether natural or an artificial PROGRAMMING LANGUAGE), and hence allow well-formed sentences to be distinguished from badly formed ones. The grammar of most human languages is complex and fluid and admits of many exceptions, but programming languages have simple regular grammars that can be compactly described in a formal notation such as BACKUS-NAUR FORM. See also SYNTAX.

grammar checker A feature provided in some modern WORD PROCESSORS which checks certain aspects of the grammar of the document currently being edited, including capitalization of words, hyphenation, subject/verb agreement (for example for plurals), misuse of the apostrophe, and double negatives. Some grammar checkers such as the one in MICROSOFT WORD can also be instructed to point out problems of prose style, such as long sentences, clichés, or excessive reliance on the passive voice.

granularity A metaphorical term, meaning the relative size of the items processed or examined by a computer hardware or software system. For example a program that processes a file one BYTE at a time is exhibiting a finer granularity than one that processes whole RECORDS at once. See also FINE-GRAINED, COARSE-GRAINED.

graph 1 A drawing that depicts the relationship between two or more sets of numbers by plotting them as dots, lines or areas relative to a set of reference lines called AXES. Also called a CHART: see PIE CHART, BAR GRAPH, STACKED BAR CHART, SCATTER PLOT.

2 In mathematics, a geometric figure consisting of a set of lines called arcs or edges joining a set of points called vertices (see under VERTEX) or nodes. If the arcs have an indicated direction, the figure is called a DIRECTED GRAPH. The study of such figures, called GRAPH THEORY, finds application in many different areas of computer science.

grapheme A letter or combination of letters in a particular written human language that serves to distinguish one word from another, typically representing a PHONEME in the spoken language. For example, the 'f' in fish, the 'ph' in phone, and the 'gh' in tough are three different graphemes that correspond to the same phoneme. Computerised SPEECH RECOGNITION and SPEECH SYNTHESIS systems may be based around either graphemes or phonemes, and may convert one to the other.

Graphical Device Interface See GDI.

Graphical Kernel System See GKS.

graphical user interface (GUI) An INTERACTIVE outer layer presented by a computer software product (for example an operating system) to make it easier to use by operating through pictures as well as words. Graphical user interfaces employ visual metaphors, in which objects drawn on the computer's screen mimic in some way the behaviour of real objects, and manipulating the screen object controls part of the program.

The most popular GUI metaphor requires the user to point at pictures on the screen with an arrow pointer steered by a MOUSE or similar input device. Clicking the MOUSE BUTTONS while pointing to a screen object selects or activates that object, and may enable it to be moved across the screen by dragging as if it were a real object.

Take, for example, the action of scrolling a block of text that is too long to fit onto the screen. A non-graphical user interface might offer a 'scroll' command, invoked by pressing a certain combination of keys, say CTRL+S. Under a GUI, by contrast, a picture of an object called a SCROLLBAR appears on the screen, with a movable button that causes the text to scroll up and down according to its position. Similarly, moving a block of text in a WORD PROCESSOR that employs a GUI involves merely selecting it by dragging the mouse pointer across it until the text becomes HIGHLIGHTED, then dragging the highlighted area to its intended destination.

There is now an accepted 'vocabulary' of such screen objects which behave in more or less similar ways across different applications, and even across different operating systems. These include: WINDOWS, ICONS, pulldown and pop-up MENUS, BUTTONS and button bars, check boxes, dialogues and tabbed property sheets. Variants of these GUI objects are used to control programs under Microsoft Windows, Apple's MacOS, and on Unix systems that have a windowing system such as Motif or KDE installed.

GUIs have many advantages and some disadvantages. They make programs much easier to learn and use, by exploiting natural hand-to-eye coordination instead of numerous obscure command sequences. They reduce the need for fluent typing skills, and make the operation of software more comprehensible, and hence less mysterious and anxiety-prone. For visually-oriented tasks such as word processing, illustration and graphic design they have proved revolutionary.

On the deficit side, GUIs require far more computing resources than older systems. It is usual for the operating system itself to draw most of the screen objects (via SYSTEM CALLS) to relieve application programs from the overhead of creating them from scratch each time, which means that GUI-based operating systems require typically 100 to 1000 times more working memory and processing power than those with old text-based interfaces.

GUIs can also present great difficulties for people with visual disabilities, and their interactive nature makes it difficult to automate repetitive tasks by batch processing. Neither do GUIs *automatically* promote good user interface design. Hiding 100 poorly-chosen commands behind the tabs of a property sheet is no better than hiding them among an old-fashioned menu hierarchy – the point is to reduce them to 5 more sensible ones.

Historically, the invention of the GUI must be credited to Xerox PARC where the first GUI-based workstations – the XEROX STAR and XEROX DORADO – were designed in the early 1970s. These proved too expensive and too radical for commercial exploitation, but it was following a visit to PARC by Steve Jobs in the early 1980s that Apple released the LISA, the first commercial GUI computer, and later the more successful MACINTOSH. It was only following the 1990 release of Windows version 3.0 that GUIs became ubiquitous on IBM-compatible PCs.

graphics Pictures on a computer display, or the process of creating pictures on a computer display. The term came into use when there was still a distinction between computers that could display only text and those that could also display pictures. This distinction is lost now that almost all computers employ a GRAPHICAL USER INTERFACE.

Since a computer can ultimately deal only with binary numbers, pictures have to be DIG-ITIZED (reduced to lists of numbers) in order to be stored, processed or displayed. The most common graphical display devices are the CATHODE RAY TUBE inside a monitor, and the PRINTER, both of which present pictures as two-dimensional arrays of dots. The most natural representation for a picture inside the computer is therefore just a list of the colours for each dot in the output; this is called a BIT-MAPPED representation. Bitmapping implies that each dot in the picture corresponds to one or more bits in the computer's video memory.

An alternative representation is to treat a picture as if it were composed of simple geometric shapes and record the relative positions of these shapes; this is called a vector representation (see more under VECTOR GRAPHICS). A typical vector representation might build up a picture from straight lines, storing only the coordinates of the endpoints of each line.

Vector and bitmapped representations have complementary strengths and weaknesses. Most modern output devices work by drawing dots, which makes it more efficient to display bitmapped images. There are a few, mostly obsolete, display technologies, such as the GRAPH PLOTTER or the VECTOR DISPLAY tube, that can draw lines directly, but it is more typical for a vector image to be first converted into bitmap (the process called RENDERING) before displaying it on a dot-oriented device. Rendering involves extra work for the computer, which is performed either by software or by special hardware called a GRAPHICS ACCELERATOR.

Vector representations are easily edited by moving, resizing or deleting individual shapes, whereas in a bitmap all that can be changed is the colour of the individual pixels. Vector images can easily be rotated and scaled to different sizes with no loss of quality, the computer simply multiplying the endpoint coordinates by a suitable factor. A bitmap, on the other hand, can be magnified only by duplicating each pixel, which gives an unsightly jagged effect.

Vector representations are most suitable for pictures that are actually drawn on the computer (such as engineering drawings, document layouts or line illustrations), and for images that must be reproduced at various sizes (such as fonts). On the other hand, bitmaps are more suitable for manipulating photographs of real world scenes and objects that contain many continuously varying colours and ill-defined shapes – both scanners and digital cameras produce bit-mapped images as their output. See also BITMAP EDITOR, GRAPHICS ADAPTER, GRAPHICS TABLET, 2D GRAPHICS, 3D GRAPHICS.

graphics accelerator A chip or expansion card added to a computer to speed up the display of graphic images. Such accelerators are nowadays classified into 2D accelerators and 3D ACCELERATORS. A 2D accelerator, sometimes called a GUI ACCELERATOR, is much the simpler device, its main function being to speed up the BIT BLOCK TRANSFER operations used in windowed user interfaces, and the colour interpolation (see INTERPOLATE) operations used in shading figures. In addition to these

2D operations, a 3D accelerator must be able to perform fast trigonometric transformations and apply SMOOTH SHADING algorithms. Popular graphics accelerators include those made by Matrox, nVidia, 3DLabs, S3 and 3Dfx. See also GRAPHICS, 2D GRAPHICS, 3D GRAPHICS, GRAPHICS PROCESSOR, GEOMETRY ENGINE.

graphics adapter An EXPANSION CARD that enables a personal computer to create a graphical display. The term harks back to the original 1981 IBM PC which could display only text, and required such an optional extra card to 'adapt' it to display graphics.

The succession of graphics adapter standards that IBM produced throughout the 1980s (CGA, EGA, VGA) both defined and confined the graphics capability of personal computers until the arrival of IBM-compatibles and the graphical Windows operating system, which spawned a whole industry manufacturing graphics adapters with higher capabilities.

Nowadays most graphics adapters are also powerful GRAPHICS ACCELERATORS capable of displaying 24-bit colour at resolutions of 1280 × 1024 pixels or better. Providing software support for the plethora of different makes of adapter has become an onerous task for software manufacturers.

graphics card See under GRAPHICS ADAPTER and GRAPHICS ACCELERATOR.

graphics file format Any computer FILE FORMAT designed for storing pictures rather than text or other data. There are many different graphics file formats, often developed to work with specific display hardware, though some are designed to be hardware-independent, and allow pictures to be viewed on different types of computer. There is, however, no graphical equivalent of the text file – no format sufficiently universal that any operating system can view it unassisted. Each different graphics file format requires the presence of a suitable application program to open it.

There are two main categories of graphics file format: VECTOR GRAPHICS formats which contain geometrical descriptions from which a picture can be reconstructed, and BITMAPPED graphics formats, which contain the actual PIXEL values representing the picture. See more under GRAPHICS.

Widely used vector file formats include .DXF (AutoCAD exchange format), .HGL (Hewlett Packard Graphics Language), and .CDR (CorelDRAW), while the most popular bitmap formats include .JPG, .GIF, .TIF and .BMP files.

Graphics Interchange Format See GIF.

Graphics Language (GL) Originally a GRAPHICS package produced by SILICON GRAPHICS INC. for its own machines, but now incorporated into the cross-platform OPENGL standard.

graphics processor An auxiliary computer PROCESSOR optimized to perform those operations most heavily used in generating graphic displays, including certain FLOATING-POINT ARITHMETIC operations and BIT BLOCK TRANSFERS freeing up the main CPU for other tasks. See also GRAPHICS ACCELERATOR.

graphics tablet A computer input device consisting of a flat board over which a pen is moved to produce corresponding movements of a CURSOR on the display screen. This provides finer control than a MOUSE can offer. Tablets are used by architects and engineers for creating plans and drawings, as well as by graphics artists and animators. Sophisticated tablets are sensitive to both pressure and speed, so that pressing harder with the pen or moving it faster can be interpreted by painting programs to create thicker or thinner lines, or other effects.

graphics workstation A single-user computer with powerful GRAPHICS abilities used, for example, in engineering, drawing, architecture and COMPUTER AIDED DESIGN applications. Such machines are typically connected to a network and store their data on a central server. Graphics workstations manufactured by firms such as SUN, APOLLO and HEWLETT-PACKARD dominated the field of computer graphics throughout the 1970s and 80s, pioneering many of the attributes of today's personal computers, including INTERACTIVE software and GRAPHICAL USER INTERFACES. However, modern PCs now have sufficiently powerful graphics to threaten this once lucrative market.

graph plotter A computer output device that draws lines rather than dots, by moving a pen in two dimensions across a flat bed holding the paper. Typically, it will have a rack of several different coloured pens available. The name derives from the days when plotters were mostly used by mathematicians to plot graphs, but nowadays they are mostly used by architects and engineers to create hard copy from plans and drawings created using VECTOR drawing software.

graph reduction An evaluation strategy for FUNCTIONAL PROGRAMMING LANGUAGES in which an expression is represented as a DIRECTED GRAPH, more specifically an inverted tree in which every node is a FUNCTION CALL and its subtrees are the ARGUMENTS to that call: evaluation then proceeds from leaves to root of this tree.

graph theory A branch of mathematics that studies the connectedness of networks, which it represents as collections of lines called arcs that meet one another at junctions called nodes. Many of the results discovered by graph theory have direct practical application in computer science, particularly in the design of communication networks and in processor and compiler design. For example, many searching and resource allocation problems can be solved by algorithms that visit and manipulate the nodes of a graph. Pure graph theory is itself a subject of great interest to computer scientists, as so many of the problems for which no POLYNOMIAL-TIME ALGORITHM is known arise in this domain. See also GRAPH, DIRECTED GRAPH, GRAPH REDUCTION, DEPTH-FIRST SEARCH, SPANNING TREE, DECISION PROBLEM, NP-HARD.

greek 1 Nonsense text used by compositors and graphic designers when creating trial page layouts, which has roughly the same appearance as normal English text (e.g. the proper ratio of ASCENDERS, DESCENDERS and CAPITALS). The text traditionally used for this purpose is not actually Greek but a garbled passage of Cicero's Latin beginning 'Lorem ipsum dolor sit amet'.
2 In computerized DESKTOP PUBLISHING the term can refer both to the use of dummy text, or to the use of meaningless squiggles or shading to represent text (particularly in greatly reduced preview images). Hence the term is also used as a verb, meaning to render text as squiggles or shading, as in 'at sizes below 5 point the preview display will be greeked'.

Green Book A standards document released in 1986 by Sony and Philips to define the data format for the CD-I multimedia system. See also RED BOOK, YELLOW BOOK, ORANGE BOOK, WHITE BOOK.

green machine Jargon term for a computer that employs power-saving features, recyclable materials, and so forth.

green monitor A computer monitor fitted with circuitry that switches it into a low-power standby mode after an interval of non-use.

green-screen A short-hand term for those old-fashioned computer systems that can display only text and not graphics; it alludes to the green-on-black displays employed by many of the TERMINALS used with mainframe computers. See also FULL-SCREEN, CHARACTER-BASED, GLASS TELETYPE, TERMINAL EMULATION.

grep A UNIX utility program that searches through a group of files to find all lines that match a given REGULAR EXPRESSION. Its name was derived from a command sequence used within an older LINE EDITOR used for this purpose, namely *g*lobally search for a *r*egular *e*xpression and then *p*rint the result. Versions of grep are now available for most operating systems. See also TEXT SEARCH, SEARCH ENGINE.

greyed-out (*US* grayed-out) A visual technique that indicates that an option on a software menu is not currently active, by changing its colour from black to grey.

grey level One of the degrees of darkness that taken together form a GREY SCALE.

grey scale 1 In computer GRAPHICS, an image that is composed from a finite number of discrete shades of grey, or a display device that presents such images. Grey scale pictures work in an analogous way to colour pictures, the number of BITS representing each PIXEL determining how many GREY LEVELS can be portrayed. So with 8 bits per pixel, 256 shades of grey are possible. A grey scale display that stores only one bit per pixel (i.e. black or white) is called MONOCHROME.

2 A table of evenly darkening shades of grey used as a reference in photography and for calibrating printers and displays.

group **1** In a VECTOR GRAPHICS program, to select several objects within an image and make them behave as a single object (so that for instance they can be FILLED or DRAGGED from one location to another as a single unit). **2** A construct used to simplify account management in multi-user databases and operating systems, consisting of named collections of users who all share similar security status and access permissions.

group calendar A computerized appointments calendar that is shared by a group of colleagues who can use it to organize meetings. Typically a group calendar is a networked application, with date information stored on a central SERVER that is capable of examining all the users' individual appointment schedules and automatically locating those periods when all are free at once. There is now a flourishing business in WEB-based group calendars that can be consulted from anywhere in the world over the Internet using a LAPTOP computer and a WEB BROWSER, enabling travelling employees to be continuously updated with new schedule information.

group scheduler A shared calendar program that can be used by a group of co-workers to arrange meetings and plan projects.

Group Separator See GS.

groupware A category of software designed to enable groups of people to collaborate on the same project, a popular example being LOTUS NOTES. At the centre of all groupware products is a LAN and a set of shared DATABASES, editing software that renders visible any revisions made to documents; VERSION CONTROL for revised documents, exchange of memos by EMAIL and sometimes a BULLETIN BOARD for broadcast messages, and shared diaries, calendars and address books. More advanced features may include an electronic WHITEBOARD facility to permit remote viewing of software demonstrations, and a database REPLICATION ability which makes it feasible for remote users to participate using slow modem connections. A VIDEOCONFERENCE facility is likely to become a ubiquitous feature of groupware as network bandwidths improve.

GS (Group Separator) The CONTROL CHARACTER with ASCII code of 29.

GSM (Global System for Mobile Communications) An international communications network that joins together various mobile phone networks and which now covers large areas of the world throughout Europe and Asia (though it has less presence in the USA and Japan). GSM is a digital telephone system that employs TDMA encoding in the 890–960 MHz radio frequency bands.

In addition to voice calls, GSM mobile phones can send and receive SHORT MESSAGE SERVICE text and access the Internet via the WAP protocol, permitting data transfers at a modest 9600 bits per second. However next-generation data services, HSCSD and GENERAL PACKET RADIO SERVICE, promise much faster data connections over GSM phones.

guard A mechanism supported in a few programming languages which consists of a BOOLEAN expression prefixed to some other program construct, which will consequently be executed only whenever the guard is true.

GUI Acronym of GRAPHICAL USER INTERFACE.

GUI acceleration Also called 2D acceleration, an extra function built into most 3D ACCELERATOR graphics cards specifically to speed up those common 2D graphics operations that are heavily used by GRAPHICAL USER INTERFACES such as Windows – for example the drawing of window borders and menus – which might otherwise actually become slowed down by being treated as 3D objects. GUI acceleration essentially consists of hardware assistance for the BITBLT operation that is used to move bitmapped images quickly onto the screen. See also VIDEO ACCELERATION.

GUID (Global Unique Identifier) A unique name given to a software object to distinguish it from all others; used by distributed programming systems such as DISTRIBUTED COMPUTING ENVIRONMENT, CORBA and Microsoft's COMPONENT OBJECT MODEL. GUIDs need to be unique in both space and time and so are typically formed by concatenating a time-stamp (which distinguishes them from others on the same computer) with the network name of the machine on which they were created.

gun See ELECTRON GUN.

guru A person with great expertise in some esoteric branch of computing, such as writing UNIX SHELL SCRIPT.

gutter The vertical white space that separates blocks of text in columns or facing pages of a printed document such as a book or magazine. See also MARGIN.

GW-BASIC A version of the MICROSOFT BASIC interpreter that was shipped with many early IBM-COMPATIBLE PCS.

gzip A free FILE COMPRESSION utility for UNIX and several other operating systems, produced as part of the GNU project to get around the fact that the official Unix compress utility is patented and therefore not free software. Like the PKZIP in the PC world, it employs a copyright-free version of the LZ COMPRESSION algorithm.

H.261 A VIDEO COMPRESSION standard promulgated in 1992 by the ITU for transmitting video images over ISDN lines.

hack 1 *n*. A quick fix for a programming problem, or a clever programming trick.
2 *v*. To gain illicit access to a computer system or network. See also HACKER.
3 *v*. To create program code, particularly of a 'quick-and-dirty' quality.

hack attack An attempt by HACKERS to gain unauthorized access to a computer system or network. The main types of attack are the DENIAL OF SERVICE ATTACK which seeks to close a system down by overloading it, and SPOOFING Internet addresses to take control of someone else's server to use as a relay point for distributing stolen software or mounting SPAMMING attacks on further victims.

Hackers may guess PASSWORDS by writing a program or SCRIPT that tries out millions of permutations, or set traps to capture passwords from legitimate users by impersonating an operating system service.

hacker Originally, a dedicated and skilful computer programmer – many of the pioneers of modern programming at MIT and Stanford so described themselves. However, its current usage, particularly in the popular press, has been shifted to describe persons who gain unauthorized access to computer systems and networks. The connection between the old and new usages is that much skill and dedication used to be required to break into computers, though modern tools have made this less true (see for example SCRIPT KIDDY). Many programmers still consider the term not to be derogatory, and would like to reclaim it by employing the alternative term CRACKER for those who perform illegal acts.

hacker humour A defence mechanism against the boredom and anxiety induced by too-close contact with computers.

hacking Gaining unauthorized access to a computer or network. See also HACKER.

HAL Abbreviation of HARDWARE ABSTRACTION LAYER.

half-duplex Any communications channel that can transmit in both directions but only in one direction at a time, a familiar example being 'walkie-talkie' radio systems where the user must press a button to reply to a message. SHARED-MEDIUM NETWORKS such as many versions of ETHERNET are often operated in a half-duplex mode to avoid excessive CONTENTION. See also FULL-DUPLEX, SIMPLEX.

half-height A generation of HARD DISK, FLOPPY DISK, TAPE and CD-ROM drives (in both 5.25 inch and 3.5 inch FORM FACTORS) introduced in the late 1990s that are only half as thick as their predecessors.

halftone The process by which CONTINUOUS TONE photographs are reproduced in print (for example in newspapers and magazines) by reducing them to a grid of tiny dots. (The resulting image is also commonly known as a halftone.) Each individual dot is printed using a single coloured ink of fixed intensity, and the intensity of colour the reader perceives is controlled by varying the size and density of the dots to reveal more or less of the underlying white paper.

The superficial similarity between this use of dots in printing and the PIXELS that constitute computer images is misleading, since pixels actually vary in colour and intensity rather than size. When computer-generated pictures are prepared for printing, each pixel gets broken up into a sub-grid of halftone dots that simulate its tonal value spatially. The pixel and halftone grids may interfere with each other and cause the problem called SCREEN CLASH.

halting problem An important problem in COMPUTATION theory. Every program written for a TURING MACHINE must when executed either eventually halt or continue running forever, and the halting problem asks whether it is possible to create another program that can predict, *a priori*, whether a particular Turing Machine program will ever halt. A consequence of the CHURCH/TURING HYPOTHESIS is that no such program can exist, and that the only way to find out whether a program will ever halt is to start it and wait. This turns out be another way of stating GÖDEL's theorem, and contains a profound insight into the nature of mathematical and logical truth.

Hamming code An important class of techniques (named after their inventor, R W Hamming, one of the pioneers of INFORMATION THEORY) for performing ERROR DETECTION AND CORRECTION on communication channels by adding REDUNDANT bits to each word transmitted. By adding sufficient bits, multiple bit errors can be detected and corrected: in some codes used by interplanetary probes, redundant bits outnumber the message bits by five to one. See also HAMMING DISTANCE.

Hamming distance The number of BITS that differ between two HAMMING CODED numbers.

hand-coded Written in ASSEMBLY LANGUAGE rather than being COMPILED from a HIGH-LEVEL programming language, the implication being that such code is therefore more efficient.

hand-held A category of computer smaller than a NOTEBOOK or LAPTOP which may be carried about in a pocket or briefcase. Examples include the PALM and PSION ranges, and various models that run Microsoft WINDOWS CE.

hand-held scanner See under SCANNER.

hand-holding Measures, such as HELP SCREENS and verbose messages provided to assist novice users of a particular software or hardware product.

handle A type of POINTER often used to refer to instances of dynamically-allocated resources such as memory blocks or windows. A handle is doubly indirect (it is a pointer into a table of pointers to resources), which allows the addresses of the actual resources to be altered (for example by compacting a fragmented HEAP) without invalidating the handle.

handler A software routine designed to be invoked whenever a particular kind of event occurs, the most frequently encountered examples being an ERROR handler, an INTERRUPT handler or an EVENT HANDLER.

A handler is often invoked indirectly via a table of handler addresses called a vector (see for example INTERRUPT VECTOR) which enables the handler code to be changed without having to recompile the whole system.

handshake An exchange of signals between two pieces of communicating equipment that announces that each is ready to talk to the other, and on what terms. A familiar example is the sequence of audible chirruping sounds exchanged between two MODEMS before they open a connection, in which they seek to discover what speed, compression and error-correction method each other supports. Simpler handshakes include the signals used for FLOW CONTROL under serial protocols such as RS-232. See also XON/XOFF.

hands-on The experience gained by actually using a software or hardware product, rather than reading about it.

handwriting recognition A technology that enables data to be input into a computer by writing with an electronic pen, onto either the screen or some other designated area. By removing the need for a KEYBOARD, handwriting recognition permits much smaller device sizes, vital in the POCKET COMPUTER and mobile telephone markets.

Some handwriting recognition technologies, such as the GRAFFITI system used in PALM computers, require the user to write in a special simplified script using discrete characters, while others such as that employed in Apple's NEWTON recognise cursive (i.e. 'joined-up') writing. The latter approach requires far more processing power and needs to be trained to a particular individual's handwriting.

In hardware terms, a further distinction exists between those systems that use an active pen containing electronic components, and passive systems such as the Palm whose pen is merely a stick (so a finger or toothpick will work).

Technically two fundamentally different approaches to recognition are in use, one involving constantly monitoring the direction and acceleration of the pen, while the other treats the writing as a BITMAP and uses NEURAL NETWORK technology to discriminate the intended character.

hang Any computer failure that causes it to stop responding to the keyboard or mouse, and hence requires a RESET to regain control. The usual cause is a program that has become stuck in an endless loop that consumes so much of the available processing time that there is none left in which to service the input devices. Under a genuinely MULTITASKING operating system, or within a MULTITHREADED application, it should be possible to switch away from the hung program and regain control without requiring a reboot, but some kinds of hardware error can still prevent this. See also CRASH, BUG, GENERAL PROTECTION FAULT, BLUE SCREEN OF DEATH.

hard-coded Said of information that is written into the body of a program where it cannot be altered by the user. For example a poorly designed financial program might have the rate of some tax hard-coded into it, and so would become obsolete if the rate was changed.

hard copy A copy of some data printed on paper, as opposed to an electronic copy on, say, a floppy disk or CD.

hard disk, hard disk drive, hard drive A type of storage device that is now the most popular form of MASS STORAGE for all computers, from personal computers to workstations and mainframes. The hard disk is a magnetic storage device which stores each individual data BIT as a tiny magnetized dot on the surface of a rapidly rotating metal disk or PLATTER that is coated with a film of magnetizable material. A movable recording HEAD containing coils that can both magnetize (to write a dot) or detect magnetism (to read a dot) can be slid rapidly back and forth along a radius of the rotating platter, without ever making contact with its surface, to read and write billions of dots in concentric rings called TRACKS.

The name 'hard disk' was coined to contrast with the lower capacity FLOPPY DISK which is made of a flexible oxide-coated plastic rather than rigid metal. Modern hard disk drives have data capacities of tens of gigabytes, which they achieve by mounting 5 to 10 platters on the same spindle (like a pile of plates) with heads on both sides, and by making the heads tiny (in both area and thickness) to write smaller dots. The speed at which a hard disk can locate a single byte among all this data continues to improve, achieved by faster rotation of the platters: 10,000 rpm is now common, which is comparable with the speed of a jet engine.

The hard disk drive is certainly the most sophisticated mechanical device ever to be put into mass production. The read/write heads are far thinner than a piece of tinfoil and hover only micrometres above the surface of the furiously spinning platter – if they touch it while it is rotating they will be destroyed instantly, an event that is called a 'head crash' and renders the drive useless. Compared with this head gap a human hair, a grain of dust or even a particle of smoke look like huge boulders, so the whole mechanism has to be confined in a sealed case with a filtered recycled air supply. Yet you can purchase this device in a high-street shop for the price of a small transistor radio and it will probably operate without error or maintenance for five years or more.

The most important physical characteristics of any hard disk drive are: its capacity after formatting (see FORMAT), the type of computer INTERFACE it employs (e.g. IDE, EIDE or SCSI), its average SEEK TIME, LATENCY and total ACCESS TIME. The usable capacity of a hard disk is always less than the manufacturer's claimed nominal capacity because, before use, the drive must be formatted for a particular operating system, which means some of its platter area will be devoted to system purposes (such as error correction and head positioning information) and will not be available for user data. The most important manufacturers of hard disk drives include IBM, Fujitsu, Quantum, Seagate, Hitachi, Maxtor and Western Digital.

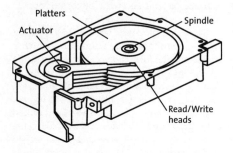

Platters
Actuator
Spindle
Read/Write heads

hard reset See under RESET.

hard return A CARRIAGE RETURN character, embedded into a stream of text by the user pressing the RETURN KEY, which always forces a new line at that point. Most modern text editors and word processors employ automatic WORD-WRAP, which removes the need to insert hard returns and allows for more flexible formatting of the text. The presence of hard returns is often to blame for the ragged appearance of some emails or documents downloaded from the Internet.

hard sectored An early and obsolete type of FLOPPY DISK on which the divisions between SECTORS were marked by holes punched in the medium.

hardware Physical equipment, that is machines made of metal, plastic, silicon and so on, as opposed to the abstract SOFTWARE that may animate and control such machines. What distinguishes digital electronic devices from earlier generations of machinery is their ability to alter their mode of operation by loading different software. Computers, keyboards, monitors, printers, scanners are all hardware devices, but their operation relies on software to a greater or lesser extent.

At the engineering level, this hardware/software distinction reduces to whether or not to create a new CHIP to perform a particular computational task (a hardware solution) or to write a PROGRAM that performs the same task on a general-purpose computer chip (a software solution). It is a strong consequence of Alan TURING's theorem, which founded COMPUTER SCIENCE, that such a choice is always available: any computation that can be performed in hardware may be emulated in software (given sufficient time and memory).

Hardware Abstraction Layer (HAL) A layer of low-level code within Microsoft's Windows NT operating system that contains all the processor-specific ASSEMBLY LANGUAGE routines, all the higher layers being written in C. Its purpose is to ease the task of creating versions of the operating system for new types of processor: in theory only the HAL needs to be totally rewritten for the new processor, while the higher layers merely need to be re-compiled.

hardware-accelerated An operation for which a dedicated CHIP has been provided to make it run faster; examples include many GRAPHICS and AUDIO operations.

hardware compatibility list A list of all the hardware devices (such as sound and graphics cards, disk drives) that are known to work under various versions of Microsoft's Windows NT and 2000 operating systems.

hardware dependent Any feature of a computer program that will work only on a particular kind of hardware, for example because it presupposes the presence of a particular make of chip or a particular memory configuration. The aim of most computer operating systems is to confine hardware dependency as far as possible to special DEVICE DRIVER programs and then to present to application programs a set of APPLICATION PROGRAMMING INTERFACES that hide the precise details of the hardware. This can simplify both program portability and hardware UPGRADES. See also HARDWARE ABSTRACTION LAYER.

Hardware Description Language (HDL) A class of MARKUP LANGUAGES used to define INTEGRATED CIRCUIT layouts in automated circuit design systems – examples include VERILOG and VHDL.

hardware interrupt An interrupt that is triggered by some hardware event, such as a keypress or a mouse movement, rather than by the execution of a program instruction. See also SOFTWARE INTERRUPT.

hardware platform A jargon term which, depending on the context, may mean a particular brand of computer, computer architecture or CPU type. Most computer software is written to run on only one specific hardware platform (though see CROSS-PLATFORM). See also PLATFORM-INDE-PENDENT, PLATFORM-NEUTRAL.

hard-wired 1 Originally, a function that is permanently built into the structure of a hardware system, as opposed to one that can be reconfigured by changing software. For example the dialling mechanism of a telephone handset is typically hard-wired.

2 The term is now frequently used in a metaphorical sense in all-software systems: a 'hard-wired' feature of an application program is one that cannot be customized by the user, but can be changed only by the original programmer recompiling the program.

Harvard Architecture A type of processor architecture in which the DATA CACHE and INSTRUCTION CACHE and their respective BUSES are kept separate; this offers superior performance, because the patterns of memory access for data and instructions are quite different and may interfere with one another when a UNIFIED CACHE is used. The disadvantage is that self-modifying programs may no longer work because they require access to instruction code as if it were data. Nevertheless a Harvard Architecture is used in most modern microprocessors, including all of Intel's PENTIUM family and in many later versions of the POWERPC.

The name arises from a debate in the earliest days of computing, when the Princeton team of John von NEUMANN advocated unified data and instruction storage, whereas the 1950 Harvard Mark III employed a separate magnetic drum to store its program.

hash 1 v. See under HASHING.

2 n. The # character, ASCII code 35, which has a bewildering variety of names and uses: in music it is the sharp sign; in the USA it is often called 'pound' and replaces the £ sign on US layout keyboards; telephone companies call it 'square' on telephone keypads. In both everyday life and programming it is used as a prefix to mean 'number' (e.g. #23, number 23).

hash clash, hash collision See HASHING.

hash function A function that transforms a KEY value, which might be numeric or textual, into a number that is then used as an index into a HASH TABLE to locate the associated data record. A good hash function should distribute keys as evenly as possible over the table, while minimizing the number of keys that 'hash' to the same table slot. See also HASHING.

hashing A class of algorithm that helps to provide very rapid access to data items that can be distinguished by some KEY value, for example a person's name, or a filename. This key value is passed through a HASH FUNCTION which creates from it a number that is used as an index into a HASH TABLE containing pointers to the actual data items.

A simple hash function might be the alphabetic order of the first letter of a person's name, so that, say, Pountain would hash to the 16th slot in the table. However, this would be a very poor hash function since every name beginning with P would hash to the same slot, an occurence known as a *hash clash* or *hash collision*. Whenever such a collision occurs, the new item that caused it must be stored either in the next free adjacent table slot, or on a LINKED LIST pointed to by the table slot. If too many such collisions occur, the algorithm degenerates into a case of LINEAR SEARCH. Designing a good hashing algorithm involves choosing a hash function that distributes the items widely and evenly, without requiring too large a hash table.

hash table An array holding pointers to a set of data items, arranged in order of some KEY value that has been put through a HASH FUNC-TION. See also HASHING.

Haskell A pure, LAZY, FUNCTIONAL PROGRAM-MING LANGUAGE created in 1990 which features POLYMORPHIC types, HIGHER-ORDER FUNCTIONS and user-defined ALGEBRAIC DATA TYPES.

HAVi Abbreviation of HOME AUDIO-VIDEO INTEROPERABILITY.

Hayes A pioneering US manufacturer of MODEMS and the inventor of the AT command set that has become the universal way for computers to communicate with modems. See more under HAYES-COMPATIBLE.

Hayes-compatible Any MODEM that is controlled by commands from the *AT command* set invented by HAYES, which consist of the letters AT (short for ATtention) followed by a string of letter and number combinations. Some basic AT commands are common to all such modems, but others are added by a particular manufacturer to drive a new feature. Some of the basic commands are:

ATDxxxxxxx: Dial the telephone number xxxxxxx.

ATLn: Set modem speaker volume, where n ranges from 0 for low to 3 for high.

ATF: Select connection mode, where F0 means AUTO-DETECT and F1 upwards select the various V STANDARDS.

ATZ: Restore modem to its FACTORY DEFAULT settings.

ATSn: Access the contents of internal register number n. Modems may contain many such registers in which they store everything from their running parameters to passwords and telephone numbers.

Strings of AT commands are employed as modem INITIALIZATION strings by email and other communications programs, and setting wrong commands there is a common source of communication problems.

HBI Abbreviation of HORIZONTAL BLANKING INTERVAL.

HCI Abbreviation of HUMAN-COMPUTER INTERFACE.

HCL Abbreviation of HARDWARE COMPATIBILITY LIST.

HD See under HIGH-DENSITY DISKETTE.

HDD Abbreviation of HARD DISK DRIVE.

HDL Abbreviation of HARDWARE DESCRIPTION LANGUAGE.

HDLC Abbreviation of HIGH-LEVEL DATA LINK CONTROL.

HDSL See under DIGITAL SUBSCRIBER LINE.

HDTV Abbreviation of HIGH DEFINITION TELEVISION.

head 1 The part of a magnetic or optical DISK DRIVE or tape drive that records and reads data by changing the surface state of the recording medium. In a disk drive the heads move across the rotating disk surface to find data. See more under HEAD POSITIONING, HEAD ALIGNMENT, TRACK.

2 The first element in a LINKED LIST.

head alignment The orientation of the recording HEAD of some STORAGE device (for example a tape recorder, floppy, hard disk or CD drive) relative to the data tracks written on the recording medium. Misalignment may result in an increased error rate, or at worst a complete failure to read the data.

head crash A catastrophic failure of a HARD DISK drive which renders all the data on it unreadable, caused by the fragile recording HEAD touching the rotating disk surface.

header 1 In word processing, a line of information – often containing page number, chapter number, document title or author name – that is printed or displayed at the top of each page of a document. Most WORD PROCESSORS offer automatic insertion of a header and possibly a corresponding FOOTER.

2 A section prefixed to a larger package of data to convey important information about its contents. Many of the data structures used in computing, from FILES, to network PACKETS, to EMAIL messages employ a header that reveals their size, format, location, route and so on.

header file A type of file used by many programming languages, most notably C and C++, which contains definitions and declarations of commonly needed functions and constants that may be included in many different programs.

head-mounted display A computer display device worn over the eyes like a visor, typically with a separate display for each eye to give a stereoscopic view. Such displays are employed in VIRTUAL REALITY systems to create the impression that the viewer is immersed in the depicted scene (see IMMERSIVE), or in a transparent form for military 'head up' aiming and navigation systems.

head positioning The act of placing the read or write HEAD of a rotating storage device such as a FLOPPY or HARD DISK drive above the TRACK that contains the desired data. See also SEEK, SEEK TIME, BUFFERED SEEK, ELEVATOR SEEK.

headroom The amount of spare capacity available in a communication CHANNEL or a STORAGE device.

head-select time The time taken to determine which of the HEADS of a HARD DISK drive with multiple PLATTERS is the one required to access a particular SECTOR. See also SEEK TIME, HEAD-SETTLE TIME.

headset Any electronic equipment worn on the head, such as acoustic earphones, an earphone/microphone combination, or a HEAD-MOUNTED DISPLAY for viewing computer data or a VIRTUAL REALITY environment.

head-settle time The time required for the HEAD of a storage device such as a FLOPPY or HARD DISK drive to orient itself precisely to the required TRACK. The momentum of the mechanical heads causes them to slightly overshoot the target and the time for any oscillation to cease (typically a few milliseconds) must be added to the SEEK TIME when measuring performance.

head-to-disk distance The gap between the read/write HEAD of a HARD DISK and its rotating PLATTER, which is typically measured in fractions of a MICRON.

head-tracking The use of magnetic, optical or other types of sensor to determine in what direction a human user is looking, to enable the picture to be synchronized with head movements in various types of HEAD-MOUNTED DISPLAY. See also GAZE-CONTROLLED.

heap 1 An ordered BINARY TREE data structure employed in the HEAP SORT algorithm.
2 More commonly, an area of memory from which an operating system or program can dynamically allocate blocks, of arbitrary size and in arbitrary order, to act as temporary storage areas. The name is intended to suggest this lack of order, in contrast to an orderly STACK or QUEUE. When no longer needed, such memory blocks are returned to the heap, and this eventually results in the heap suffering FRAGMENTATION.

heap sort An efficient sorting ALGORITHM that works by inserting the data items to be sorted into a BINARY TREE data structure, in such a way that the largest value is stored at the tree's ROOT and the value stored at any parent NODE is greater than either of its children: the items may then be removed via the root in sorted order.

heat sink A block of metal that is pressed firmly against an INTEGRATED CIRCUIT package to conduct away the heat it generates. Heat sinks are routinely fitted to microprocessors of the Intel PENTIUM class and similar. Heat sinks often have deep fins cut into them so that heat from the chip is rapidly dispersed by the airstream from a cooling fan.

Hebbian learning One of the earliest methods for training NEURAL NETWORKS, invented by Donald Hebb in 1949. The simple rule involves increasing or decreasing the weight of only the active inputs, to activate or deactivate their corresponding outputs.

helical-scan A technique used in various types of TAPE DRIVE in which the recording heads travel in a small circle as the tape is pulled past them, thus writing diagonally inclined instead of linear TRACKS onto the tape and packing in more data for a given length of tape. The technique was pioneered for analogue video tape recorders such as VHS but is employed in some computer digital data tape drives, including DAT drives.

hello world! A programmer's tradition in which the first program to write when encountering a new language is one that writes 'hello world!' on the VDU screen.

help Explanatory and reference information provided with a computer program which is accessed from within the program by pressing Help buttons provided at various points in the USER INTERFACE. At its simplest, a help facility merely consists of a database of short instructional paragraphs with an index and table of contents, but most modern software provides CONTEXT-SENSITIVE help that detects what operation the user is currently engaged in and automatically presents the correct help text. Help pages also typically contain HYPERLINKS that lead the user directly to related topics.

helpbot Derived from help+robot, a semi-autonomous software AGENT that assists the users of a WEB SITE or CHAT ROOM. The meaning of this once-fashionable term has become so diluted that it is often used to describe conventional HELP systems.

helpdesk A service provided by most computer hardware and software manufacturers that enables users of the firm's products to make technical enquiries by telephone or email. The term is now also applied to a class of software product used to automate such enquiry systems, for example using VOICE ACTIVATED telephone menus to enable users to request technical documents that are then returned by FAX-BACK. Many of the functions of the helpdesk have now moved to companies' web sites; these include lists of frequent queries and their answers (see FAQ), discussion and self-help forums, download areas for PATCHES, BUG FIXES and DEVICE DRIVERS, and email access to technical assistance staff.

help screen A page of instructional information that can be displayed by pressing a key or on-screen button when a difficulty is encountered. On IBM-compatible PCs the F1 FUNCTION KEY is traditionally used to summon help screens. See also HELP, HELPBOT.

Herbrand Universe In the PROPOSITIONAL CALCULUS, the collection of CLAUSES produced by substituting every possible combination of variable values into the AXIOMS of a problem.

hertz (Hz) A unit of FREQUENCY equal to one cycle or occurrence per second.

heterogeneous network A computer NETWORK that is running more than one NETWORK LAYER PROTOCOL, for example IP alongside Novell's IPX or Microsoft's NETBEUI.

heterostructure A device made from layers of different semiconducting materials: such structures are the objects of much research into new kinds of light-emitting diode (LED) and SOLID-STATE laser.

heuristic A rule of thumb or approximation that narrows the range of possible solutions in some only-partially-understood problem domain, as compared to an ALGORITHM which is a precise sequence of steps that leads to a definite solution. An example of a heuristic from everyday life might be that if there are black clouds in the sky, it may rain – a heuristic is not guaranteed to provide an accurate, nor even a workable solution.

Heuristic methods are very often associated with some form of learning procedure, so that the rule can be progressively improved to produce better and better solutions. This is particularly true in the field of NEURAL NETWORKS where heuristic methods are the norm. See also STOCHASTIC, CASE BASED REASONING.

Hewlett-Packard One of the largest US manufacturers of computers and printers, which started out by making scientific instruments in the proverbial garage.

Hewlett Packard Graphics Language See HPGL.

hexachrome A colour printing system that provides a better colour reproduction quality than the traditional CMYK process, by employing six-ink colours instead of four. The two extra colours are an orange and a lime green, which typically lack adequate saturation when simulated in the four-colour process, and their addition enhances the impact of the red and green portions of an image. Hexachrome is as yet relatively little used, since both the machinery and the setup costs are more expensive than for four-colour printing, which results in a higher price to the customer.

hexadecimal notation A numeric notation widely used in computer programming, which employs the BASE 16 instead of the base 10 used in ordinary DECIMAL NOTATION. Hexadecimal notation therefore requires symbols to be invented for a further six digits, and the letters A (standing for decimal 10), B (11), C (12), D (13), E (14) and F (15) are used for this purpose. For example the decimal number 45 ($4\times10 + 5\times1$) is 2D ($2\times16 + 13\times1$) in hexadecimal.

Computer programmers use hexadecimal because of its close practical relationship with BINARY NOTATION, stemming from the fact that 16, unlike 10, is an integral power of two (2^4). Binary quantities – which ASSEMBLY LANGUAGE programmers must deal with continually, for example, as BIT MASKS or graphical PIXEL data – convert very easily into hexadecimal. Each group of four BITS in the binary quantity translates directly to a single digit of the hexadecimal version, so the binary number 101100010101 (2837 in decimal) is B15 in hexadecimal because 1011=B, 0001=1, 0101=5.

Because a number such as 23 could represent either a valid decimal or hexadecimal number, several conventions have been devised to distinguish hexadecimal numbers in computer documentation and program text. This dictionary writes 23 hexadecimal as 23h, Unix documents and the C language use the convention 0x23 and Microsoft VISUAL BASIC uses &23H.

hex dump A listing of a program or data file in HEXADECIMAL NOTATION, the lowest level at which the contents of a computer's memory are typically viewed by a programmer. 'Staring at hex dumps' is regarded as the last resort in trying to locate a BUG. See also CORE DUMP.

HFC Abbreviation of HYBRID FIBRE-COAXIAL.

hidden layer A layer within a NEURAL NET-WORK that is connected to the outside world only via other layers. See more under MULTI-LAYER PERCEPTRON.

hidden line removal One of the early stages in the construction of a realistic 3D image on a computer. Once a WIRE-FRAME model of the desired object has been created, all those lines that should not be visible from the current viewpoint (i.e. those that define surfaces that are facing away from the viewer) can be erased, leaving only the front-facing surfaces to be RENDERED. The operation may be delayed until after the faces have been rendered, when it is called *hidden surface removal*.

Hidden-line removal is a time-consuming operation which involves sorting the data-base of vertices that describe the model in order of distance from the current viewpoint. It can slow down the display of complex objects to a point where interactive manipulation such as rotating the object in real time becomes sluggish. For this reason some draft-ing and design programs allow hidden line removal to be switched off during such manipulations and reapplied once the object is in the desired postion. See also HIDDEN SUR-FACE ALGORITHM, Z-BUFFER.

Hidden Markov Model (HMM) A technique used in SPEECH RECOGNITION software to iden-tify words. An HMM is a table of states, con-structed by analysing a number of spoken samples of a word, which distils information about the variability of various segments of the word. The HMM describes the probability that any state will follow another state, and a candidate word presented to the recognizer follows a path through this table that meas-ures how well it matches.

hidden surface algorithm A class of 3D GRAPHICS RENDERING algorithm that never draws any surface that could not be visible from the current VIEWPOINT because it faces away from the viewer (as opposed to algo-rithms that draw such surfaces and later draw over them). Many such algorithms rely on the use of a Z-BUFFER. See also HIDDEN LINE REMOVAL.

hidden surface removal See under HIDDEN LINE REMOVAL.

hierarchical Any system consisting of a sequence of ordered groupings, examples of which can be found in social affairs, botanical classification, and extensively in computing. For example, FILES are hierarchically organ-ized into FOLDERS and SUBFOLDERS in all the major computer operating systems. The advantage of hierarchical classification sys-tems – which may be visualized as TREE struc-tures – is that when properly designed they can minimize the number of items that need to be examined to locate a particular element.

hierarchical database A kind of DATABASE MANAGEMENT SYSTEM that links records into a family tree, where parent records own child records, so that any record type has only a sin-gle owner. For example, an order is owned by a single customer. Widely used in the 1950s on early MAINFRAME computers, but now almost entirely replaced by the RELATIONAL DBMS, because their restrictive structure was often incapable of modelling complex real world relationships.

hierarchical file system Any FILE SYSTEM which permits files to be nested within other files, to assist in managing large numbers of them. A file that is a container for other files is called a DIRECTORY, and the whole hierarchy resembles a notional TREE in which the branches and twigs are directories, while the leaves are the data files. All modern operating systems including Windows, Unix, MacOS and MS-DOS employ such hierarchical file sys-tems.

hierarchical storage management (HSM) An advanced storage scheme employed by some MAINFRAME and MINICOMPUTER operating sys-tems, in which data is automatically moved closer or further away from the CPU according to how often it is being accessed. Data required for daily use is kept on HARD DISKS but after a period of disuse it may be removed to a slower but more capacious CD-R disk, and ultimately onto TAPE for archival storage. The HSM software makes this a transparent proc-ess, so that old data is requested in exactly the same way as yesterday's data, though it will take longer to access.

high-availability Those computer and com-munication systems used in critical applica-tions, that employ FAULT-TOLERANT techniques to reduce their DOWNTIME to a minimum.

High Definition Television (HDTV) A name that covers several different technology standards for the next generation of broadcast television sets. These standards have in common a greatly increased resolution (close to that of cinema film) and a widened 'cinemascope' style of picture format (for example an aspect ratio of 16:9 in place of the current 4:3).

high-density diskette (HD) The current IBM-compatible format 3.5-inch FLOPPY DISK, labelled HD, that holds 1.44 megabytes of data.

high-end Computer industry jargon for 'most expensive' or 'of highest performance'.

higher-order function In FUNCTIONAL PROGRAMMING LANGUAGES, a function that can accept one or more FUNCTIONS as arguments and can return another function as its result.

high-level At a level of abstraction far removed from the manipulation of individual bits. The term is most often applied to PROGRAMMING LANGUAGES, but may also be encountered as a prefix to INTERFACE, SOLUTION and other terms. See also HIGH-LEVEL PROGRAMMING LANGUAGE.

High-level Data Link Control (HDLC) A general-purpose control PROTOCOL defined by the ISO for use in both POINT-TO-POINT and MULTIPOINT communication links, which forms the DATA LINK LAYER for many telephony standards such as X.25, ISDN and FRAME RELAY, and is also used extensively in computer networks.

high-level programming language A PROGRAMMING LANGUAGE that provides the programmer with abstractions that are closer to real-world operations than to the bit-level operations of ASSEMBLY LANGUAGE – for example the ability to manipulate complex named data structures. PROLOG, LISP, 4GL database , VISUAL BASIC and PASCAL are (in decreasing order) all high-level languages, while C is a lower-level language because it supports explicit POINTERS and BIT FIELDS. See also SEMANTIC GAP.

highlight To indicate on a computer screen that a region of text or other material has been successfully selected by the user. Highlighting might involve reversing the foreground and background colours of the highlighted text, or making it brighten or blink: this varies between different programs and operating systems.

high memory Regions of memory at the upper end of the ADDRESS SPACE of a particular computer, which are frequently reserved by the operating system for storage of special data. In an IBM-compatible PC running MS-DOS, the term carries the extra meaning of memory beyond the 640 kilobyte limit on conventional memory. See also UPPER MEMORY BLOCK, EXTENDED MEMORY, EXPANDED MEMORY.

high memory area (HMA) In an IBM-compatible PC running in REAL MODE with an 8026 processor or later, the first 64 kilobytes of EXTENDED MEMORY (less 16 bytes) starting from the 1 megabyte threshold. Due to a quirk in the Intel memory architecture this area can be addressed by the processor and used to store executable code such as device drivers and other DOS components, if a high memory manager such as HIMEM.SYS is installed. See also EXPANDED MEMORY SPECIFICATION.

high order bit See MOST SIGNIFICANT BIT.

high-pass filter An electronic FILTER that allows through only frequencies above some threshold value. See also LOW-PASS FILTER.

High Performance File System The file system employed by IBM's OS/2 operating system.

High Performance Fortran A dialect of FORTRAN 90 that has extensions for data PARALLELISM, specially created by a consortium of industrial and academic users in 1993 for programming SUPERCOMPUTERS.

High Performance Parallel Interface (HIPPI) A high-speed network technology developed at the Los Alamos National Laboratory for connecting SUPERCOMPUTERS to peripherals such as ROUTERS, FRAME BUFFERS and disk arrays, and to other computers.

HIPPI is a SWITCHED network technology that uses a CONNECTION-ORIENTED protocol, and is capable of speeds of 800 megabits per second one-way or 1.6 gigabits per second FULL-DUPLEX over distances up to 10 kilometres. It is now an ANSI standard, X3T9/88-127. See also ASYNCHRONOUS TRANSFER MODE, SYNCHRONOUS OPTICAL NETWORK, FIBRE CHANNEL.

high-resolution As applied to an image, printer or monitor, the term used to describe whatever is the current upper range of RESOLUTION. At present this means any picture or display with a resolution of 1024 × 728 PIXELS or more, or any printed image of 600 dots per inch or better. A very relative and historical term, given the rapid progress of computer graphics systems. (Twenty years ago, 320 × 240 was considered high-resolution.) See also RESOLUTION, DOT PITCH.

High Speed Digital Subscriber Line See under XDSL.

High Speed Serial Bus See under FIREWIRE.

hill climbing A class of OPTIMIZATION algorithms that move closer to a solution by incrementally changing several problem parameters. If the parameters are depicted as a three (or more) dimensional plot, the problem terrain resembles a rugged landscape in which the summits of hills (or the bottoms of valleys) represent various solutions. Such algorithms are prone to become stuck if they discover a local maximum or minimum (e.g. a small hill on the lower slopes of the best solution) and may need to be jolted out of it by applying a larger random perturbation.

The operation of Darwinian natural selection can be viewed as a hill-climbing algorithm in a multi-parameter terrain where the hills represent different ecological niches and height represents survival 'fitness'. See also SIMULATED ANNEALING, GENETIC ALGORITHM.

HIMEM The DEVICE DRIVER supplied with Microsoft's MS-DOS and WINDOWS operating systems that enables programs to access EXTENDED MEMORY, and also allows portions of MS-DOS 5+ to be relocated to the HIGH MEMORY AREA.

hinting **1** A mechanism for improving the appearance of text printed in an OUTLINE FONT at small POINT SIZES. It consists of instructions to alter certain features of a particular character (say, the crossbar of an A) to avoid unsightly overhangs or stray pixels. Both ADOBE TYPE MANAGER and TRUETYPE fonts have built-in hinting schemes.

2 A mechanism supported by some processors (such as the latest Pentiums) to reduce cycles wasted through PIPELINE BREAKS or CACHE MISSES. Hints are special bits provided within an OP CODE, which the programmer may set to tell the processor, for example, that this data item will be used only once.

HIPPI Abbreviation of HIGH PERFORMANCE PARALLEL INTERFACE.

hires Abbreviation of HIGH-RESOLUTION.

histogram A type of BAR GRAPH that uses lines or rectangles of proportional lengths to represent the distribution of a range of discrete values of a variable.

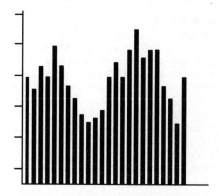

history list A facility provided in many program USER INTERFACES that allows the user to view a list of the most recently issued commands and reuse any of them.

hit rate The number of people requesting a particular WEB PAGE during a certain period, usually per day.

HLS See HSB.

HMA Abbreviation of High Memory Area, see under HIGH MEMORY.

HMM Abbreviation of HIDDEN MARKOV MODEL.

Hoare, Anthony (b. 1934) Oxford professor of computing, co-founder of STRUCTURED PROGRAMMING, inventor of the QUICKSORT algorithm and COMMUNICATING SEQUENTIAL PROCESSES.

hobbyist One who uses computers for pleasure rather than business. Among the computer sales fraternity, this is a derogatory term.

hole A missing electron within the crystal lattice of a semiconducting substance, which behaves as though it were a positively-charged particle, migrating through the lattice toward the negative electrode and effectively carrying a single positive charge with it.

Holes are created by the presence of certain electron-hungry DOPANT atoms which steal electrons from the neighbouring SEMI-CONDUCTOR atoms. See also MOS, CMOS, TRANSISTOR.

Hollerith, Herman (1860–1917) Inventor of the PUNCHED CARD for data storage, used in the 1880 US census. In 1924 Hollerith's Tabulating Machine Company was acquired by a younger firm called International Business Machines (IBM).

hologram A type of photographic record produced by exposing film – without any intervening lens – to two light sources simultaneously, a coherent light beam from a laser, and this same beam reflected from the object of interest. Interference patterns are formed within the film, which when illuminated by the original coherent light source reproduce a three-dimensional image of the object.

Despite much research into the hologram as a store for computer data, none has so far reached commercial production. See also HOLOGRAPHIC MEMORY.

holographic memory The use of a HOLOGRAM, typically formed within a transparent matrix impregnated with a light-sensitive dyestuff, to store digital data. Holographic storage potentially enables very large amounts of data to be stored within the same volume of material, as separate pages each of which is stored and retrieved by a tiny alteration in the angle of the illuminating light beam. No such device has yet found commercial use. See also BIO-COMPUTING.

Home Audio-Video interoperability (HAVi) A specification for communication protocols, software components and APIs (APPLICATION PROGRAMMING INTERFACES) to enable digital household electronic appliances such as TVs and video recorders to be connected together. It was developed by a consortium including Philips, Sun, Sony and Grundig. HAVi employs Sun's JINI distributed processing technology to transmit uninterrupted real-time data streams, and to provide remote control of appliances via the Internet.

home banking Schemes in which a bank provides its customers with software to run on their home computers and makes available some of its banking facilities (such as checking balances or making transfers between accounts) via a WEB SITE or other ONLINE SERVICE.

Home Highway British Telecom's brand name for its domestic ISDN service.

HOME key A key on most modern computer keyboards that moves the screen CURSOR to the start of the current line. See also END KEY, CURSOR KEYS.

home office A computer marketing term that defines a business sector occupied by single users working from home, whose equipment requirements include a personal computer, a small LASER PRINTER, a MODEM, a SCANNER and an office software suite. This sector is also referred to as the SOHO (Small Office/Home Office) sector. See also SME, MIDRANGE SYSTEM, CORPORATE.

home page 1 The root page of a WEB SITE, to which visitors are first directed, and from where the other pages can be reached. The URL given out for any web site is that of its home page, which is normally contained in a file called index.html.

2 A web page created by a private individual that contains personal details and content.

homesteader A person who has a web site hosted by GEOCITIES.

homogeneous network A computer network that runs the same NETWORK LAYER PROTOCOL throughout.

hook 1 A point of access deliberately created within a computer program to allow other programs (possibly ones that have yet to be written) to interact with it. Used as in 'it contains hooks for attaching a spell-checker'.

2 To capture an INTERRUPT and employ it for a different purpose. For example a program might replace the address of a computer's keyboard interrupt routine (see under INTERRUPT VECTOR) with its own address, then inspect each keystroke that the user types, before passing it on to the original keyboard routine for normal processing. The program is then said to have 'hooked the keyboard vector'.

hop A direct link between two HOST computers in a large routed NETWORK such as the INTERNET. The 'distance' a message has travelled can thus be specified as the number of hops it passed through. Some network protocols may set an upper limit to the hop count that any message is allowed to incur, as a mechanism for detecting and avoiding routing loops (see SPANNING TREE).

Hopper, Grace (1906–92) An Admiral in the US Navy who was also a pioneer of computer programming. She co-invented the COBOL language in the 1950s and is credited with introducing the term BUG to mean a program error.

horizontal application An application program that is of broad use in many different fields of endeavour, the best examples being the WORD PROCESSOR and SPREADSHEET. Compare this with a VERTICAL APPLICATION written for use in a particular activity or trade.

horizontal blanking interval The period during which the dot on a CATHODE RAY TUBE is turned off to allow it to return to the left after tracing each SCAN LINE. See more under BLANKING INTERVAL.

horizontal scan rate The number of SCAN LINES that a computer monitor can display in one second, normally expressed as a frequency between 20 and 100 kilohertz. See also HORIZONTAL BLANKING INTERVAL, VERTICAL REFRESH RATE, INTERLACED DISPLAY.

Horn clause A restricted form of logical proposition used in LOGIC PROGRAMMING languages such as PROLOG.

host 1 Most generally, a computer that runs a certain piece of software, as in 'we are using it as a host for Unix'. Also as a verb as in 'we are using it to host Unix'.

2 A computer connected to a network, particularly to the INTERNET, which has its own network address, forwards various types of network traffic to other hosts, and may also act as a SERVER for remote data services. The opposite of CLIENT. See also NODE, HOSTNAME.

3 A remote mainframe or minicomputer to which users connect using a DUMB TERMINAL.

4 A piece of software that acts as a platform into which another (typically smaller) piece of software is loaded and executed. For example an operating system hosts application programs; a web page might host a Java applet.

host adapter The name given to a SCSI interface card.

hostname The unique name given to each computer in a network to identify it when sending ELECTRONIC MAIL or other types of electronic communication to its users. On the INTERNET, hostnames are text-based, for example penguin.co.uk, and constructed from a local part (penguin) plus a wider DOMAIN ADDRESS (co.uk). Such hostnames are translated into numeric IP ADDRESSES which are used to route the messages: see under DOMAIN NAME SYSTEM.

host-to-host connection A connection between two adjacent SERVERS that form part of a large routed network such as the INTERNET. See also ROUTING, HOP.

HotBot A popular Internet SEARCH ENGINE created by the US magazine WIRED.

hot cathode A wire coil, coated with rare earth metal salts, which emits electrons when heated to red heat, and is used as a source in the THERMIONIC VALVE and the CATHODE RAY TUBE. See also COLD CATHODE LAMP.

HotJava A WEB BROWSER published by SUN which was one of the first applications written entirely in its JAVA language.

hot key Another name for a KEYBOARD SHORTCUT that can be used instead of clicking the MOUSE on screen.

Hotline A communications software product that supports both online CHAT and file transfer, and which employs a distributed, PEER-TO-PEER architecture so that anyone can host a Hotline server on their personal computer. The result is a fast-growing network entirely separate from the WORLD WIDE WEB. See also NAPSTER.

hot link A connection created between two files such that changes made to one file are automatically replicated in the other. For example an extract from a SPREADSHEET embedded as a table in a report might be hot linked to the original sheet so that whenever the original is altered, the figures in the report are automatically brought up to date.

Hot links are also used in some DESKTOP PUBLISHING programs to display an illustration within a page layout while leaving it in fact stored in its original separate graphics file; if the picture is edited in a drawing program, the view of it on the page also changes. Before printing, the picture must eventually be merged into the page. See also OBJECT LINKING AND EMBEDDING.

hot spot An area within a screen display that responds to MOUSE CLICKS.

hot swapping The ability offered by some computer systems to replace hardware units (such as a failed HARD DISK drive or EXPANSION CARD) while the system is running, without stopping the processor or REBOOTING the system. Hot swap ability is required, for example, in applications such as public telephone exchange switches and large web servers which cannot be conveniently taken off-line for such routine repairs. See also FAULT-TOLERANT, FAIL-OVER, HIGH-AVAILABILITY.

HotSync A term proprietary to PALM Computing Inc. that describes the action of equalizing file contents between a Palm organizer and a PC, and also the software that performs this action.

hourglass A special icon that replaces the MOUSE POINTER in the Windows and Apple Macintosh operating systems to indicate that a program is busy processing and cannot accept any keyboard or mouse input from the user.

housekeeping Routine periodic data management tasks performed by a computer's operator, such as removing unwanted files and reorganizing folders. The term is also applied by programmers to various 'clean up' activities performed by a program itself, such as reclaiming no-longer-used memory blocks or compacting a HEAP.

HPA (High Performance Array) A superior variant of PASSIVE MATRIX DISPLAY screen technology which offers picture quality close to that of an ACTIVE MATRIX DISPLAY. It is fitted to many budget-priced NOTEBOOK computers.

HPFS Abbreviation of HIGH PERFORMANCE FILE SYSTEM.

HPGL (Hewlett-Packard Graphics Language) A set of commands for printing VECTOR GRAPHICS on Hewlett Packard's plotters and laser printers that has become an industry-standard, supported or emulated by many other manufacturers. HPGL consists of short command sequences that draw geometric figures including circles, arcs, polygons and wedges. It has to a degree been rendered obsolete by the increasingly widespread use of POSTSCRIPT, except in drafting and architectural drawing applications where it is used by AUTOCAD.

HPIB (Hewlett-Packard Interface Bus) An 8-bit parallel BUS originally devised for connecting Hewlett-Packard's own electronic measuring instruments to computers. Now standardized as IEEE-488 (also called GPIB) and widely used by laboratory equipment of all makes. Up to 15 HP-IB devices can share a single bus at data rates of around 1 megabit per second.

HP-UX, HP/UX Hewlett Packard's dialect of UNIX, as supplied with all the company's WORKSTATIONS.

href A shorthand description for the HTML tag used to introduce HYPERTEXT links into web pages, used as in:`<A HREF="../member-ship.html" TARGET="_top">`

HSB Abbreviation of Hue, Saturation, Brightness, a commonly used COLOUR MODEL. Also called HLS, HSV, HSC. See under HUE, SATURATION, LIGHTNESS, BRIGHTNESS.

HSCSD (High-Speed Circuit-Switched Data) A CIRCUIT-SWITCHED data transmission system for GSM mobile telephone users that enables data to be sent and received at up to 38.4 kilobits per second – four times faster than an ordinary GSM connection. It requires only software modifications to an existing GSM network infrastructure and handsets, and is available as an extra-price service from several GSM operators.

HSI Abbreviation of Hue, Saturation, Intensity, see under HUE, SATURATION, LIGHTNESS, BRIGHTNESS.

HSL Abbreviation of HUE, SATURATION, LUMINANCE.

HSM Abbreviation of HIERARCHICAL STORAGE MANAGEMENT.

HSV Abbreviation of Hue, Saturation, Value, see under HUE, SATURATION, LIGHTNESS, BRIGHTNESS.

HTML (Hypertext Markup Language) The PAGE DESCRIPTION LANGUAGE used to describe documents that are to be published over the

WORLD WIDE WEB (WWW). The HTML description of a document page defines the placement of text and images on the page, and also the HYPERTEXT links that lead visitors from this page to other pages on the web. When you go to a page on the web, what is actually received by your computer is the HTML-coded text describing that page. The main function of a WEB BROWSER is to interpret these HTML descriptions and render them into text and graphics on a computer screen. Most of the content on the web is stored in HTML format files, with filenames such as penguin.htm or penguin.html.

HTML is an OPEN STANDARD that does not depend on the facilities of any particular brand of editing software, or on the display abilities of any particular computer. This, and the creation of low-cost or free browsers, are what encouraged the phenomenal expansion of the web seen today. HTML is one of the crucial components of the web, and the standardization of its functions is overseen by the WORLD WIDE WEB CONSORTIUM.

HTML is a subset of the richer and more complex document description language Standard Generalized Markup Language (SGML). Like SGML, it works by embedding TAGS into the text of a document which define different document elements and their styles. Tags consist of code words called directives enclosed in angle brackets, for example <BODY>, and they are mostly deployed in matched pairs to surround the text they apply to, as in <B>Penguin Dictionary</B> which specifies bold text thus, **Penguin Dictionary**. In this way HTML separates the content of a document from its format. Browsers are free to ignore any tags whose meaning they don't understand, without serious loss of document content.

The most commonly used tags provide document structure. For example: <P> for a paragraph and <H1>, <H2>...<H6> which define six levels of heading. HTML cannot assume that any particular font (such as Times Roman or Univers) is available at the receiving end, and although it does permit preferences to be expressed, the typeface and size used to display headings <H1> through <H6> is determined by each individual browser.

Hypertext links are defined using the tag <A> for Anchor, which defines their departure and destination points. Links conventionally appear as underlined text on the browser screen, which when clicked with the mouse cause a jump to their destination. For example, the tag <A HREF="info.html"> Information</A> displays a link called 'Information' which jumps to a new page called info.html on the same web site.

The HREF (for Hypertext Reference) parameter of the <A> tag can also be the address or URL of a document held elsewhere on the web. For example the line

<A HREF="http://www.penguin.com/
dictionary.html">Dictionary</A>

creates a link called Dictionary that jumps to a page on the www.penguin.com site.

HTML offers only simple page formatting facilities that are not as powerful as those in DESKTOP PUBLISHING programs. For example, it is difficult to position graphical elements precisely on an HTML page, or to run text around them in complex layouts. Successive versions of HTML (4.0 is current) have added extra features, and extensions such as XML and DYNAMIC HTML add more still, but each advance must wait for a new generation of browsers to process their new abilities, and some new features may threaten the ideal of portability.

HTTP (Hypertext Transfer Protocol) The protocol used to request and transport WORLD WIDE WEB pages across the INTERNET. HTTP is a high-level CLIENT/SERVER protocol running on top of the Internet TCP/IP protocols, which requires the presence of an HTTP client program (a WEB BROWSER) at one end and an HTTP server program (a WEB SERVER) at the other end of a connection.

HTTP is TRANSACTION-oriented, treating each web page as a new transaction in which a request for the page with a particular URL is sent to the server, and an HTML representation of that page together with associated files holding pictures, sounds or other multimedia content are sent back to the browser. It is also a STATELESS protocol, that after each page breaks the connection to the server and retains no memory of it. A fresh TCP connection is remade to retrieve each page. These characteristics were deliberately chosen to make HTTP sufficiently responsive to follow hypertext jumps, while conserving the Internet's available BANDWIDTH. A protocol that allowed every web browser to remain connected to a server for hours would quickly saturate the network.

There are two types of HTTP messages, requests and responses. *Requests* contain commands such as GET, PUT and DELETE that ask the server to retrieve, store or remove the information at a particular URL. *Responses* report back the success or failure of such actions. HTTP itself performs no error correction or routing, relying on the underlying TCP/IP protocols for these functions.

HTTP can work either via direct end-to-end TCP connection between client and server, or indirectly via intermediary systems, such as a PROXY, a GATEWAY, a FIREWALL or a TUNNELLING PROTOCOL.

httpd (Hypertext transfer protocol daemon) A small and simple WEB SERVER program for computers that run UNIX.

HTTPS A variant of the HTTP protocol used on the WORLD WIDE WEB to handle secure transactions. A web site that supports HTTPS may be addressed using a URL that starts with https:// in place of the normal http://. HTTPS actually consists of normal HTTP running on top of the SECURE SOCKETS LAYER protocol.

hub A hardware device for joining together the various components of a local area network (LAN) and passing data packets from one to the other. It consists of a box into which the cables from many different network devices (such as workstations, printers, other hubs) can be plugged. The resulting layout resembles a wheel with spokes, hence the name.

At its simplest a hub merely connects the devices plugged into all its ports into a single network, and acts like a junction box for network cabling. The modern tendency, however, is to put some intelligence into the hub by adding a microprocessor, memory and firmware, so that it can actively route packets from one network to another. A *managed hub* is capable of partitioning the various connected devices into different sub-networks, and of collecting diagnostic information such as the network traffic passing through each port or the incidence of malformed packets. This information may be read through a serial port mounted on the hub, or over the network

itself using a network management protocol such as SNMP.

A *switching hub* can divert traffic from any of its ports to any other under software control, which reduces contention for the available bandwidth, and brings many of the benefits of a SWITCHED network. Switching hubs are often used to connect older 10 megabits per second Ethernet devices and newer 100 megabits per second devices into the same network. See also ROUTER, BRIDGE, GATEWAY.

hub-and-spoke A network TOPOLOGY in which a central server has many clients connected to it, each by a separate cable run.

Hue, Saturation, Intensity See under HUE, SATURATION, LIGHTNESS, BRIGHTNESS.

Hue, Saturation, Lightness, Brightness The COLOUR MODEL that best describes the way human subjects experience colour. *Hue* corresponds to the experience of pure colour (red as against blue) and *saturation* to the strength of that colour (red as against pink). Lightness and brightness both describe the experience of darkness versus brightness. *Lightness* is an inherent property of the viewed surface (the percentage of the incident light it reflects), while *brightness* is a measure of the total light received from the surface, and so varies with the intensity of external illumination.

Luminous television and computer displays (such as the CATHODE RAY TUBE) make it difficult to separate lightness from brightness, and so programmers and engineers tend to employ three other component models in which the third component represents various measures of lightness and is given different names in different disciplines: video engineers tend to use *Hue, Saturation, Value*, while programmers use *Hue, Saturation, Intensity* or HUE, SATURATION, LUMINANCE. See also GAMMA CORRECTION.

Hue, Saturation, Luminance (HSL) A computer COLOUR MODEL that is offered as an alternative to RGB and CMYK in the COLOUR PALETTES of most computer graphics programs as it makes selecting ranges of harmonizing tints much easier. A basic colour (hue) is chosen and then a range of tones created by adding white (saturation) and a range of shades by adding black (luminance). See more under HUE, SATURATION, LIGHTNESS, BRIGHTNESS.

Hue, Saturation, Value See under HUE, SATURATION, LIGHTNESS, BRIGHTNESS.

Huffman coding A data compression algorithm described by D A Huffman, one of the founders of INFORMATION THEORY, in 1952. It assigns codes of different lengths proportional to the information content of the symbols to be encoded – so the most frequently used symbols receive the shortest binary representations. For example a Huffman encoding of the alphabet for English text should assign the shortest code to letter 'e', the next to 'a' and so on.

Human-Computer Interface (HCI) A formal term used in computer science to describe a USER INTERFACE.

human-readable form Data encoded in ASCII text form, which is more intelligible to humans than a pure BINARY FORMAT which is merely a string of numbers.

100baseFX A standard for 100 megabits per second FAST ETHERNET cabling which employs OPTICAL FIBRE (see XBASEY).

100baseT4 A less-used standard for 100 megabits per second FAST ETHERNET cabling which employs four pairs of the cheaper voice-grade CATEGORY 3 UTP cable (see XBASEY).

100baseTX The most popular 100 megabits per second FAST ETHERNET cabling system, which employs CATEGORY 5 UTP cables (see XBASEY).

100baseVG A less-used standard for 100 megabits per second FAST ETHERNET cabling which employs voice-grade CATEGORY 3 UTP cable (see XBASEY).

hung A program is hung when it is stuck in an endless LOOP and cannot respond to an exit command. Some software crashes may prevent the computer from receiving any keyboard commands at all, in which case the user must switch off the power or press the reset button to REBOOT it.

Hungarian naming convention A convention for constructing unique names for variables, procedures, classes and methods, invented by Charles Simonyi and used by Microsoft when specifying APPLICATION PROGRAMMING INTERFACES. The convention is to prefix and append short qualifiers to a base name to indicate data type and other properties. For example in cpMacPrev, the cp says that this variable is of character pointer type. 'Hungarian' is a self-mocking reference to the inventor's nationality and to the very un-English-like names it generates.

Hybrid Fibre-Coaxial A networking scheme adopted by many CABLE TV companies which employs OPTICAL FIBRE cabling from the studio to a few neighbourhood junctions, and COAXIAL CABLE from there to individual homes or streets.

HyperCard A MULTIMEDIA authoring program distributed with the original Apple MACINTOSH and widely used for CD-ROM-based publications.

hypercube A mathematical construct for describing cubes with more than three dimensions. For example a 4-hypercube has 16 corners and in our world can be visualized only as a 3D PROJECTION that looks like two ordinary cubes one inside the other with all their corresponding corners joined.

The hypercube has significance in computing when used as a NETWORK TOPOLOGY, offering an optimal trade-off between the total number of LINKS and the number of HOPS between any two nodes.

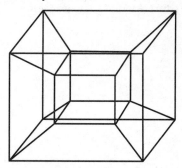

hyperdocument A document, such as a WEB PAGE, that contains HYPERLINKS.

hyperlink A cross-reference embedded in a HYPERTEXT document which may be followed into another document, or to another place in the same document. The best-known examples are the links embedded into pages published on the WORLD WIDE WEB which, when viewed in a suitable WEB BROWSER, can be clicked on with a mouse to automatically jump to the document to which they refer.

hypermedia A collective term for all the publishing technologies, including graphics, video and sound, that are associated with the WORLD WIDE WEB.

HyperSparc A 64-bit version of Sun's SPARC microprocessor built by Cypress Systems from 1992 onwards.

hypertext A document containing LINKS that cause a jump to a different place in the document, or into another document altogether. Hypertext documents are not effective when printed on paper, but must be read in a BROWSER running on a computer for the links to be active. The hypertext concept was first explored by Ted NELSON in the early 1960s in his XANADU project, but came to fruition only at the end of the 1980s with the invention of HTML and the WORLD WIDE WEB.

Hypertext is a powerful medium for any work of reference. For example if you were reading this dictionary in electronic form, clicking your mouse on a cross-reference would carry you straight to its definition. Despite many atrocious experiments, hypertext has yet to be successfully applied to fiction or narrative.

Hypertext Markup Language See HTML.

Hypertext Transfer Protocol See HTTP.

hyphen A punctuation mark (-) used to join two words that are to be used in combination (e.g. 'self-esteem') or to break a word between lines. In computer text the character with ASCII code 45, called hyphen or minus is typically used, but the extended ASCII character 173 may be used instead to represent a non-breaking hyphen.

hyphenation The process by which a text-processing program decides where to split those words that will not fit at the end of the line. Hyphenation is employed only in the more sophisticated WORD PROCESSORS and DESKTOP PUBLISHING programs. Simpler text editors merely WORD-WRAP the whole word onto the next line. Hyphenation is particularly important when a passage of text is to be fully JUSTIFIED to some fixed line length, but it may be applied to unjustified or partially justified text to split long words that project so far that they are visually displeasing. Hyphenation systems may work by employing a set of rules to define where a hyphen is permitted, or from a disk-based dictionary containing acceptable hyphenations for thousands of commonly used words, or by a combination of both these methods. See also NONBREAKING HYPHEN, NONBREAKING SPACE, HARD RETURN.

i18n A bizarre abbreviation for the word INTER-NATIONALIZATION, the 18 signifying the number of characters between the i and the n: a symptom of advanced acronymania, like its fellow abbreviation L10N meaning localization.

i386 The short name for Intel's family of 32-BIT microprocessors, which began with the iAPX 80386 microprocessor, introduced in 1985. The 80386 was Intel's first full 32-bit processor, with both 32-bit address and data bus, full hardware support for multitasking through its PROTECTED MODE, and a demand-paged virtual memory system (VMS). The introduction of the i386 made possible the huge success of Microsoft's WINDOWS 3.0 operating system, which exploited these new hardware features to overcome the previous limitations of MS-DOS and earlier Windows versions, particularly with regard to the amount of memory that could be addressed. With multi-megabyte programs possible, Windows could finally challenge the Motorola 68000-based Apple MACINTOSH and UNIX workstations in memory-hungry applications such as desktop publishing. See also 80x86 ARCHITECTURE.

i486 The short name for Intel's family of 32-BIT microprocessors which began with the iAPX 80486 microprocessor, launched in 1989 as a follow-up to its highly successful I386. The 80486 added to the 80386's features an ON-CHIP CACHE and FLOATING-POINT UNIT, together with a PIPELINED execution path which enable it to achieve more than twice the previous chip's performance at equivalent clock rates.

IAB Abbreviation of INTERNET ARCHITECTURE BOARD.

IANA (Internet Assigned Numbers Authority) The body that until 1999 handed out and recorded the various ASSIGNED NUMBERS used by Internet software, including INTERNET PROTOCOL parameters such as PORT, PROTOCOL and ENTERPRISE numbers. IANA was funded by the United States government, which was deemed to be inappropriate, given the increasingly international nature of the Internet, and it was replaced by ICANN in 1999.

IAP (Internet Access Provider) Any company or institution that provides access to the INTERNET. An IAP is typically either a commercial company or an academic institution. Commercial IAPs lease fast lines from some larger company that is directly connected to the Internet BACKBONE, and resell portions of the leased bandwidth to the public. IAPs are now frequently also INTERNET SERVICE PROVIDERS.

I-beam cursor In graphical window-based TEXT EDITORS and WORD PROCESSORS, a thin vertical line (often flashing) that marks the point at which new text will be inserted. An I-beam cursor sits *between* two characters, unlike cursors in older CHARACTER-BASED editors, which are positioned over the current character. On a PC, pressing the DEL key removes the character to the right of the I-beam and pressing BACKSPACE removes the character to its left.

IBM (International Business Machines) The world's oldest and largest computer hardware firm, and also a leading software vendor. IBM still dominates the MAINFRAME computer market, and created the modern personal computer market with its 1981 IBM PC. The company went through difficult times in the late 1980s having lost its monopoly of the PC standard and failed to establish its alternative PS/2 and MICRO CHANNEL ARCHITECTURE, but it has now returned to prosperity with the best-selling ThinkPad range of NOTEBOOK computers and Netfinity network servers. IBM's purchase of LOTUS DEVELOPMENT CORPORATION has given it a powerful presence in the GROUP-WARE and web software markets.

IBM-compatible PC Any personal computer, from whatever manufacturer, that can execute programs for the MS-DOS or WINDOWS operating systems and accept expansion cards for one of the popular PC buses. Such a machine needs to contain at least the following components: a microprocessor that can execute code written for processors compatible with the INTEL 80x86 ARCHITECTURE, a motherboard based on a SYSTEM CHIP SET that is compatible with PC peripherals, a PCI or ISA expansion bus, and some version of MS-DOS or Windows.

The definition of what constitutes an IBM-compatible PC is a little vague since the original IBM PC has not been in use for two decades, and IBM's own current machines employ a variety of different components that make them neither more nor less 'PC compatible' than those from other manufacturers. Some machines (such as DEC Alpha-based workstations or notebooks based on the Transmeta CRUSOE processor) use microprocessors that are not register-compatible with Intel's but employ some form of EMULATION. It might in theory be possible to define degrees of PC compatibility by comparing the number of programs and peripherals that do *not* work on each particular machine, but manufacturers are hardly likely to undertake such an arduous and profitless task.

IBM PC The first PERSONAL COMPUTER made by IBM in 1981, which was responsible for making PCs respectable to businesses and thus sparked off a vast expansion of the market. The IBM PC itself was not a technically innovative machine. With only 64 kilobytes of memory and a FLOPPY DISK drive for storage, it was underspecified even for its time (it was rapidly followed by the IBM PC XT which contained a HARD DISK and was more suitable for business use). However, the IBM PC's architecture (based on the INTEL 8088 microprocessor, the MS-DOS operating system and the ISA BUS)

attracted many other firms to copy it, leading to a vast market for CLONE PCs and forcing down the price of computing to current levels. This process also secured dominance of the software industry for MICROSOFT CORPORATION, but did little for IBM's own revenues.

IBM PCjr A cut-down version of the IBM PC launched in 1983 and aimed at home users. Unlike the original PC, it offered colour graphics (see MCGA) but it was widely criticized for its horrible rubber CHICLET KEYBOARD and sold poorly.

IBM PC XT IBM's second personal computer model, launched in 1983, which added a 10 megabyte hard disk to the specification of the original IBM PC and thus made it suitable for use as a business computer.

IBM Type 1 cable See under SHIELDED TWISTED-PAIR.

IC Abbreviation of INTEGRATED CIRCUIT.

ICA Abbreviation of INTELLIGENT CONSOLE ARCHITECTURE.

ICANN (Internet Corporation for Assigned Names and Numbers) The non-profit body which, since 1999, has been given responsibility for the duties of IP ADDRESS allocation, protocol parameter assignment, domain name system management, and root server system management that formerly were performed under US Government contract by IANA, INTERNIC and other institutions.

ICE Abbreviation of IN-CIRCUIT EMULATOR.

ICL (International Computers Ltd) Once the UK's only MAINFRAME computer manufacturer, ICL was created in 1968 by merging English Electric and International Computers and Tabulators. It was purchased by Fujitsu in 1990 and its name was finally dropped in June 2001.

Icon A programming language designed for manipulating textual data, designed by RE Griswold as a successor to SNOBOL.

icon A small picture displayed on a computer screen to represent a particular program, data file or directory. When pointed at and clicked with a MOUSE or other input device, the icon acts like a control button to activate the associated object. The name was coined to suggest an element in a pictorial language.

Icons were first employed at Xerox PARC in the 1970s, but the concept found widespread use only with the launch of the Apple MACIN-TOSH in 1984. It is now employed by all computers that have a GRAPHICAL USER INTERFACE.

Add New Hardware

Add/Remove Programs

Joystick

Keyboard

iconify, iconize See MINIMIZE.

ICQ An online CHAT system that is specifically designed to enable people to find each other quickly all over the world; the name is a pun on 'I seek you'. Now owned by AOL.

ID An abbreviation for IDENTIFIER, frequently found in the names of the labels used to distinguish different instances of software entities, as for example process ID and USER ID.

IDE **1** See INTEGRATED DEVELOPMENT ENVIRON-MENT.

2 (Integrated Drive Electronics) A HARD DISK drive interface employed by most personal computers during the 1990s, which was based on the original IBM PC's 16-bit ISA BUS. IDE defines the power and data signal lines running between the computer's MOTHERBOARD (which must contain an IDE disk controller chip) and disk drives which may be added as peripheral devices connected via a ribbon cable. Each IDE controller can support only two such devices – one master and one slave. IDE was developed by COMPAQ in the mid 1980s in collaboration with Western Digital and other drive manufacturers, and ratified by ANSI in 1990 as a standard under the name AT ATTACHMENT. See also EIDE, ESDI, SCSI.

Identichip A small INTEGRATED CIRCUIT that may be implanted under the skin of farm livestock or pets (such as dogs) to transmit a unique identification code when passed close to a reader device. Such chips are PASSIVE and require no power source.

identifier (ID) A character string created to uniquely identify some entity used in a pro-gram, such as a VARIABLE, CONSTANT, PROCE-DURE, CLASS or METHOD.

Most programming languages restrict the characters that may be employed in identifiers. Almost all prohibit spaces, because the COMPILER uses spaces to distinguish one identifier from the next, and most permit only ALPHANUMERIC characters and the underscore, as in My_New_Identifier2. The region of a program within which an identifier must be unique is called its SCOPE, and the collection of all possible, legal, unique identifiers is called a NAMESPACE.

ideograph, ideogram A compound symbol that directly represents a concept rather than a word sound, as used in the writing systems of China, Japan, Korea and neighbouring countries. See also KANJI, KATAKANA, UNICODE.

IDL Abbreviation of INTERFACE DEFINITION LANGUAGE.

idle The condition of a computer's operating system when it is not executing a user program. Idling does not mean the processor is doing nothing at all, as it always has to do some work to watch for user input, and there may be BACKGROUND TASKS scheduled to run during idle time to perform housekeeping duties such as reindexing files or DEFRAG-MENTING a disk. See also BUSY WAIT, IDLE TIME.

idle time Those periods during which a computer program is not actively processing data. In a WORD PROCESSOR for example, most of the time between each user KEY PRESS is idle time; even for the fastest typist this means millions of CPU cycles. A well-designed program will use this idle time to perform useful work – say to SPELLCHECK the last-typed word.

IE Abbreviation of INTERNET EXPLORER.

IEEE (Institute of Electrical and Electronics Engineers) An influential professional society based in the USA which promotes STANDARDS and publishes technical papers covering aerospace engineering, computers and communications, biomedical technology, electric power and consumer electronics. Founded in 1884, the IEEE now has more than 400,000 members in 150 countries. Many of the connectors and cables employed in computer networking and communications are standardized by the IEEE. For example, GPIB is IEEE 488 and FIREWIRE is IEEE 1394.

IEEE 488 See GPIB.

IEEE 754 The IEEE FLOATING POINT standard.

IEEE 802.11b See WI-FI.

IEEE 802 The classification group for those IEEE standards that cover local area networking (see LAN). For example, ETHERNET is IEEE 802.3, while IEEE 802.11 covers wireless networks such as WI-FI.

IEEE 1284 An IEEE standard defining various enhanced PARALLEL PORT operation modes all of which support bidirectional operation, with a BACK CHANNEL that allows a device to send messages back to the computer. Nibble mode and byte mode provide for a slow back channel that transmits 4 or 8 bits at a time; ECP (see under EXTENDED CAPABILITIES PORT) offers 4 megabytes per second in both directions; and EPP (see under ENHANCED PARALLEL PORT) treats the parallel port as an extension of the system bus, to which multiple peripherals such as CD-ROM drives, scanners and hard disks can be connected at up to 1.5 megabytes per second in both directions. See also FIREWIRE, UNIVERSAL SERIAL BUS.

IEEE 1394 See FIREWIRE.

IEEE floating point A set of binary FLOATING-POINT number formats for use in computers, defined in the IEEE standard 754-1985, and now widely implemented in processor hardware. Each format consists of three fields: a sign bit, an EXPONENT and a significand. The sign bit is 0 if the number is positive and 1 if it is negative. The exponent field specifies the power of 2 by which the significand must be multiplied to get the actual floating-point value being represented. The significand field contains either the MANTISSA of the number, or just its fractional part with the top bit omitted since IEEE numbers are 'normalized' by adjusting the exponent so that the high bit of the significand is always 1.

The lengths of the fields differ between the two main IEEE formats. A SINGLE PRECISION number occupies 32 bits: 1 for sign, 8 for exponent and 23 for significand. A DOUBLE PRECISION number occupies 64 bits: 1 for sign, 11 for exponent and 53 for significand. The EXTENDED PRECISION single and double formats are a minimum of 50 or 80 bits, but manufacturers are free to make them longer. The standard also defines the effect of arithmetic operations including addition, subtraction, multiplication, division and square root on these numbers, and bit patterns to represent certain special values, such as an exponent of all ones meaning NOT A NUMBER or infinity, and exponents of all zeroes meaning zero or an infinitesimally small value.

IESG Abbreviation of INTERNET ENGINEERING STEERING GROUP.

IETG Abbreviation of INTERNET ENGINEERING TASK FORCE.

ifdef A construct used to create different versions of a program in the C and C++ languages that compiles a section of code only if some other named function is defined.

IFF Abbreviation of INTERCHANGE FILE FORMAT.

IFS Abbreviation of Iterated Function System. See under FRACTAL COMPRESSION.

IF–THEN–ELSE The simplest and most important control construct in most high-level programming languages. It causes execution to choose one of two branches, depending on whether a test condition is true or false. For example, in:

```
IF x>0 THEN a=x ELSE a=0
```

if the test condition 'x is greater than zero' is true, the code 'a=x' will be executed. Otherwise 'a=0' will be executed.

See also CONDITIONAL, CONDITIONAL BRANCH, BRANCH.

IID Abbreviation of INTERFACE IDENTIFIER.

IIOP Abbreviation of INTERNET INTER-ORB PROTOCOL.

IL Abbreviation of INTERMEDIATE LANGUAGE.

i.link The name given by Sony to its version of the fast SERIAL IEEE 1394 interface, because the most-used name FIREWIRE is copyrighted by APPLE COMPUTER INC.

ILLIAC The first SUPERCOMPUTER, built at the University of Illinois in the early 1950s.

iMac APPLE's current range of POWERPC-based MACINTOSH models, distinguished by their striking translucent plastic cases and elegant industrial design.

image **1** A picture or other visual representation.

2 In programming, the complete set of bits in a computer's memory that represents the currently running program, more properly called a BINARY IMAGE of the program.

image analysis The use of computers to identify meaningful content within a still or moving video image (see also IMAGE RECOGNITION), which requires great processing power and sophisticated algorithms.

Image analysis is important for military applications (e.g. to identify missiles or tanks in a satellite photo), but also has more mundane uses. For example, the MPEG video compression algorithm needs to identify the moving portions of a picture in order to compress the background.

image capture The creation of a digital picture in a computer's memory, using for example a digital camera, a SCANNER or a FRAME GRABBER.

image compression The use of COMPRESSION algorithms to reduce the size of the binary data representing a picture. Image compression techniques have become central to the operation of many modern communication systems. For example DIGITAL television depends on MPEG compression to fit the data into the available BANDWIDTH. On the INTERNET pictures are compressed into GIF, JPEG or PNG files to enable them to be DOWNLOADED in an acceptable time.

image enhancement The use of computers to extract more detail from an image, as used for example on surveillance images or images transmitted from space probes. Once the image is DIGITIZED and stored in memory, digital FILTERS can be applied to increase the contrast, improve colour balance and remove distracting artefacts. EDGE-DETECTION filters are particularly effective for emphasizing any faint structures present in the picture.

image processing Using computer software to manipulate and enhance images. A large repertoire of well understood image-processing algorithms operate at the level of the individual PIXEL by comparing its value with that of its immediate neighbours; many of these operations, such as sharpen, soften, blur, edge detect, COLOUR CORRECTIONS and geometric distortions and transformations are nowadays built into popular BITMAP editing programs such as PHOTOSHOP. Image processing is widely employed in PREPRESS work for publishing and printing, in science and space exploration to enhance weak images, and in military intelligence, security and forensic applications.

Another branch of image processing deals with the content of pictures, attempting to isolate the different objects depicted; it is perhaps more useful to distinguish this by the name IMAGE RECOGNITION.

image recognition The use of computer software to identify individual objects within a DIGITIZED image. Even at its simplest (say, attempting to recognize and count identical spanners on a moving conveyor belt), recognition demands sophisticated algorithms and fast processing. For example spanners on a conveyor belt may be lying in any orientation, so a recognition program must first employ EDGE-DETECTION filters to find a dark area in the frame that is a candidate, then incrementally rotate this area to see how well it can be made to match a standard spanner template stored in memory. With objects at different distances, of different sizes, or oriented in three dimensions, the difficulties of recognition escalate dramatically and involve scaling and rotating to seek a fit (FUZZY LOGIC may be employed to find the best partial fit). For the most challenging objects, such as human faces, trainable NEURAL NETWORKS offer the best solution.

image sensor A type of INTEGRATED CIRCUIT that contains an array of devices that are sensitive to light, and which can be used to capture a pixel-by-pixel image of a scene projected onto its surface. Such chips are at the heart of digital cameras, webcams and camcorders. Most such image sensors employ the CHARGE-COUPLED DEVICE as their sensing elements, but some recent designs use light-sensitive CMOS cells.

imagesetter See under TYPESETTER.

IMAP (Internet Message Access Protocol) An EMAIL protocol that allows users to read their messages on the remote SERVER, rather than by first downloading them to a local machine, as happens with protocols such as POP3. IMAP supports operations for creating, deleting and renaming mailboxes on the remote server, for searching and selectively reading parts of messages. However, it does not specify a means of sending messages, which must be handled by a separate mail transfer protocol such as SMTP. The current version, IMAP 4, is defined in RFC 1730.

IME Online shorthand for In My Experience.

IMHO Online shorthand for In My Humble Opinion.

immediate addressing See under ADDRESS-ING MODE.

immersive A term applied to VIRTUAL REALITY systems in which the observer wears a head-mounted display that gives the illusion that they are actually inside a three-dimensional scene.

impact printer Any type of printer that forms images by moving a mechanical part to make contact with the paper, which includes the old TELETYPE, the DAISY-WHEEL PRINTER and the DOT-MATRIX PRINTER.

impedance An overall measure of the opposition a CONDUCTOR presents to the passage of an ALTERNATING CURRENT, combining the effects of RESISTANCE (R), CAPACITANCE (C) and INDUCTANCE (L) into a single quantity, calculated by the formula:

$$Z = \sqrt{(R^2 + (\omega L - 1/\omega C)^2)}$$

where ω is 2π times the frequency of the current in HERTZ. Digital circuits can be considered as carrying alternating current in this sense, so their impedance is more important than their resistance alone. See also TRANSMISSION LINE, WAVEGUIDE.

imperative language See under PROCEDURAL LANGUAGE.

implement To put into practice and create a working example of some hardware or software system described in a specification document.

implementation A particular applied instance of some technology, standard or language specification. For example ISDN is a communications standard but BT's Home Highway is an implementation of that standard.

The term carries special significance in programming language design, because many (if not most) language specifications are incom-plete, leaving certain details up to the imple-mentor. Such details are said to be IMPLEMENTATION-DEFINED or IMPLEMENTATION-SPECIFIC.

implementation-defined Used of features in a PROGRAMMING LANGUAGE that are not laid down in its standard, but are to be decided by each implementer.

implementation-specific Used of some feature of a PROGRAMMING LANGUAGE that is present only in a particular implementation.

implicit parallelism A style of PARALLEL PROGRAMMING in which the system allocates processes to different processors without direction from the programmer.

import To introduce into a computer program data that was created by a different program. This operation has considerable commercial significance because, when a software system is replaced, unless the data can be imported from the old system it will need to be re-entered by human operators at great expense.

There is no such thing as a general importa-tion facility – each importing program has to specify precisely which FILE FORMATS it can import, and automatically performs any nec-essary conversion to make the data fit into its own file format. However, certain file formats have achieved something approaching uni-versal importability through widespread use. For example, most text editing programs can import TEXT FILES, and databases can normally be transferred as text files containing COMMA-DELIMITED or TAB-DELIMITED records, or in the DBASE II .DBF format, for example.

in-band A term that originated in telecommu-nications engineering, but which is now widely used in computing and means any kind of control signal that is embedded within the data it controls. For example, printer codes embedded in a document could be so described, as could HTML tags.

The term is used in expressions such as in-band management, which refers to a network device such as a ROUTER that can be reconfig-ured over the network itself by using TELNET. See also OUT-OF-BAND.

in-band management See under IN-BAND.

in-betweening A term used in ANIMATION to describe the process of drawing all the intermediate FRAMES that lie between two key positions in a motion sequence, to create the impression of smooth motion. Originally performed manually by teams of assistant animators, in-betweening is now performed automatically by powerful computer animation programs such as SOFTIMAGE and MAYA. See also INVERSE KINEMATICS, KEY FRAME.

Inbox A software component of most EMAIL and other communications programs, typically represented by an icon installed on the user's DESKTOP, which gives the user access to any incoming messages. See also UNIFIED MESSAGING.

in-circuit emulator (ICE) A hardware device that plugs into the PROCESSOR socket of a circuit board under development and imitates the action of the central processor while enabling the system's designer to set both hardware and software BREAKPOINTS, inspect its register contents and examine the timing windows for critical EVENTS such as bus transfers – in effect it is a DEBUGGER for hardware circuits. ICEs are widely used in the design of EMBEDDED systems.

include file, include In programming, a file of SOURCE CODE that is to be used in several different programs. The include file is simply mentioned by name, normally at the beginning of any program that will use it, and the COMPILER treats it as if its whole text were present at that point.

increment To increase the value of some quantity, often by one, as when increasing a COUNTER (see under BUMP) or when moving a POINTER to point to the next address in a sequence. See also AUTO-INCREMENT, PRE-INCREMENT, POST-INCREMENT, DECREMENT.

incremental backup A particular class of BACKUP regime for computer data in which only those files whose contents have changed since the last full or incremental backup are copied into the backup set, and these files then have their ARCHIVE FLAG reset to false. An incremental backup therefore copies the minimum number of files strictly necessary, and is the fastest option. After a mishap the last full backup must be restored and then all subsequent incremental backups must be applied, in strict date order. Compare with DIFFERENTIAL BACKUP.

incremental compiler A programming language COMPILER that compiles each new PROCEDURE as the programmer writes it, rather than forcing recompilation of the whole program after every alteration.

indent In typography, the displacement of the start of one or more lines of text toward the right MARGIN, often used to distinguish a quoted passage or the start of a new paragraph. In some PROGRAMMING LANGUAGES indentation is employed as a syntactic element to mark the boundaries between structures.

Indeo A video compression CODEC developed by INTEL CORPORATION, designed to exploit the MMX extensions of PENTIUM processors.

InDesign ADOBE'S successor to its groundbreaking PAGEMAKER desktop publishing program. InDesign provides greatly enhanced controls over typographical quality, including GLYPH SCALING, OPTICAL MARGIN ADJUSTMENT and multiple line composition, all features designed to produce justified text in the way that is most pleasing to the human eye rather than being merely mathematically correct. See also QUARK XPRESS.

index 1 A separate file that contains the locations of all the RECORDS in a database file. Just as the index of a book helps to locate words in the book, an index enables data to be retrieved more quickly than by searching the whole database file from the beginning; any record that is listed in the index can be retrieved directly. Indexing also permits very fast SORTING of the database, since only the index information need be sorted, with no need to move the much larger data records themselves. See also INVERTED INDEX.

2 A number used to select one element of a sequential data structure such as an ARRAY or LINKED LIST. For example the expression Weekdays[7] refers to the 7th element of an array called Weekdays and thus the index is 7.

indexed addressing See under ADDRESSING MODE.

Indexed Sequential Access Method (ISAM) A type of FLAT-FILE DATABASE technology that permits records either to be retrieved directly via an INDEX, or else sequentially, in ascending or descending order of the value of a particular FIELD. ISAM databases have now been largely displaced by the RELATIONAL DATABASE, but the term is still used to describe products such as BTRIEVE.

index field Another name for a KEY FIELD in a database, that is one whose contents are used in building an INDEX.

indirect addressing A class of ADDRESSING MODES supported by most processors in which an INSTRUCTION contains not the address of its OPERAND, but the address of another location that contains the address of the operand, called the 'effective address'. In REGISTER INDIRECT addressing it is a REGISTER that contains the effective address. Indirect addresses are indicated in many ASSEMBLY LANGUAGES by writing the operand in parentheses, for example: MOV B, (A) writes the contents of register B to the location pointed to by the address in register A.

Indirect addressing instructions may also include a PRE-INCREMENT or POST-INCREMENT (or DECREMENT) feature that allows the operand address to be automatically increased or decreased after each access; this simplifies 'walking' through the items in an ARRAY.

indirection The identification of some resource by supplying the location of a pointer to its location, rather than the location itself. Consider an everyday example: you might tell a friend that 'Jim lives at number 12' (direct addressing), but an alternative is to say 'Jeff at number 5 knows where Jim lives' (indirect addressing).

Indirection is widely employed in all aspects of software design because of its ability to isolate unwanted dependencies. In the example, were Jim to move to another street your first advice would immediately become false, but the second would remain true if Jim told Jeff where he had moved to.

In programming, POINTERS are the principal mechanism used for indirection, and programs frequently contain a pointer to a pointer, or a pointer to a pointer to a pointer etc, adding two or more levels of indirection.

inductance That property of an electric conductor by which any change in the current flowing causes an ELECTROMOTIVE FORCE to be generated, either in the same conductor (self-inductance) or in some neighbouring conductor (mutual inductance). The unit of induct-

ance is the Henry. See also RESISTANCE, CAPACITANCE, IMPEDANCE, TRANSFORMER.

induction, inductive inference A process of reasoning in which a general conclusion is drawn from a set of premises derived by experience or experiment: the conclusion may go beyond the information contained in the premises and need not follow necessarily from them. Inductive arguments may therefore be highly probable, but still lead to a false conclusion.

In computing, inductive algorithms work by processing a database of facts to identify any general rules that they imply: such an algorithm seeks correlations or common factors among the properties of the objects involved to derive probabilistic rules such as:

```
if (income > 10000) and (occupation
= professional) then owns_car >
0.88
```

Such rules may be made more palatable for users by converting them into a DECISION TREE which asks a sequence of questions based on the probabilities to enable predictions to be made. INFERENCE ENGINES based on such techniques are used in the growing fields of DATA MINING and in some types of CASE BASED REASONING system.

industry-standard A product that is so widely used as to become an effective, or *de facto*, standard.

Industry Standard Architecture See ISA.

infect To pass on a computer VIRUS from one machine to another.

inference engine The part of a RULE-BASED SYSTEM that compares all the conditional parts of the rules (of the form IF condition THEN action) with a KNOWLEDGE BASE of currently known facts about the world. Of all those rules that match some fact, one is chosen to be executed, and the action it takes may change the facts in the knowledge base. See also EXPERT SYSTEM, INDUCTION.

Inferno A small, modular real time operating system developed by LUCENT TECHNOLOGIES for communication via hand-held devices such as mobile telephones. Inferno treats all the online resources available to it (even displays, printers and disks) as FILES organized into distributed FILE SYSTEMS that can be grouped into reconfigurable NAMESPACES, regardless of where they are located.

infinite loop A program LOOP that can never terminate because its EXIT CONDITION can never become true. The ultimate cause of most HUNG programs.

infinite set Any set such as 'all the integers' that contains an infinite number of elements. Some FUNCTIONAL PROGRAMMING LANGUAGES that support LAZY EVALUATION can manipulate such sets, by generating only those elements of the set required for a particular calculation.

infinity An uncountably large number. Mathematicians, since the work of Cantor, have a more precise definition of uncountability and in effect can distinguish many different 'infinities'. The size of memory and WORD LENGTH of any computer restricts it to representing finite numbers (though execution time may be theoretically infinite), and so several programming languages use infinity to denote the largest value that can be represented in a particular variable or register.

infix notation The familiar arithmetic notation in which each operator is placed between its operands, as in 2+3. The alternatives to infix notation are PREFIX NOTATION and POST-FIX NOTATION, examples of both of which are encountered in various computer programming languages.

infobahn A once fashionable but now, thankfully, obsolete jargon term for a future BROAD-BAND Internet.

information The raw material of the computing industry. See more under INFORMATION THEORY.

information hiding An important principle employed when computer programs are written by teams, in which each programmer is given only as much information as needed to use some piece of code and no more. The intention is to prevent them making assumptions that might be invalidated by future revisions. The normal way to hide information is by partitioning the code into separate INTER-FACE and IMPLEMENTATION sections: MODULAR programming and OBJECT-ORIENTED PRO-GRAMMING techniques are both forms of information hiding.

Information Superhighway An obsolete jargon term for a future BROADBAND-capable INTERNET. The term was invented by journalists and politicians during the early 1990s and now sounds as dated and embarrassing as 'The War to End all Wars'.

Information Technology (IT) The blanket term that describes all the products and activities of the computing and telecommunications industries.

information theory Originally a branch of applied mathematics dealing with the transmission of information over imperfect communication channels, information theory is now finding unexpected new applications in fields as diverse as genetics and particle physics. The founder of information theory was Claude SHANNON, whose discoveries at BELL LABORATORIES after World War II, along with the work of R W Hamming (see HAMMING CODE), lie behind all modern ERROR DETECTION AND CORRECTION techniques. Shannon sought to make telephone and telegraph lines (and the relatively new radio communications systems) more reliable, and chose a scientific rather than an empirical approach. His key insight was that information can be treated as a mathematical quantity like any other and measured in binary digits (or BITS), each of which is the answer to a single yes/no question. The amount of information in a message is its degree of uniqueness, that which distinguishes it from all other possible messages of the same size, and can be established by asking a sufficient number of such questions. Shannon formulated an elegant equation relating information to entropy or disorder, which can be expressed most simply as:$I = \log_2 N$

where I is the number of bits of information a message carries and N is the number of possible different messages. For example, using only the letters of the English alphabet it is possible to invent 11,881,376 different five-letter words such as 'fsnix' (ignoring whether or not they mean anything†), so the information content of a five-letter message is $\log_2(11,881,376)$ or roughly 24 bits. Any method that seeks to encode a five-letter word in less than 24 bits must necessarily throw away some information (as for example in LOSSY data compression methods) and the discarded information can not be recovered – Shannon's equation in effect restates the Second Law of Thermodynamics. Information theoretic arguments can be applied similarly to any field, say genetics (DNA sequences as messages) or physics (particle spins as messages).

(† The parenthetical comment about meaning hints at a great unresolved philosophical paradox raised by information theory, namely that this definition of information cannot include any notion of SEMANTICS – the meaning of a message to human beings – and indeed becomes rather unstable if such considerations are introduced. It would seem intuitively that a list of travel directions in, say, Italian conveys more information to an Italian speaker than to a non-Italian speaker, but its bit content remains the same to both.)

Informix One of the principal vendors of RELATIONAL DATABASE MANAGEMENT software for Unix systems.

info-tainment Originally meaning information presented in an entertaining form, the word is now frequently used in a derogatory way of information that has been 'dumbed down' so far as to become a joke.

infrared 1 The region of the electromagnetic spectrum with longer wavelengths than red light and shorter wavelengths than radio waves: that is, radiation of wavelengths from 0.8 micrometres to 1 millimetre.

2 Hence used as a shorthand for any communication system that employs radiation of these wavelengths as its carrier medium, as used in TV remote controls, portable computers and wireless networks.

Infrared Device Association (IrDA) The standard for INFRARED communication links between portable computers.

infrastructure The basic support services needed to keep a computer or network of computers running, such as the power supply, documentation, service engineers, spare parts and telephone system.

Ingres One of the principal vendors of RELATIONAL DATABASE MANAGEMENT software for Unix systems.

inheritance In OBJECT-ORIENTED PROGRAMMING, the mechanism by which a new CLASS of object is created by taking an existing class as a template and writing only the desired new features. Inheritance can achieve great economies of programming time, but it also brings the risk that some future modification to the template class may cause all its descendants to malfunction.

in-house Work performed by an organization's own staff rather than put out to contract.

init 1 Under the Unix operating system, the name of the first PROCESS that is started when the system starts, and is the PARENT PROCESS of all other processes.

2 Under the Apple Macintosh MACOS operating system, a MEMORY-RESIDENT system extension or utility that is loaded when the machine is started up.

3 In many OBJECT-ORIENTED PROGRAMMING LANGUAGES, including C++ and JAVA, the name of the METHOD used to INITIALIZE newly-created objects.

initialization The process of putting sensible default values into the system parameters or VARIABLES when starting a piece of hardware or software. Initialization is made necessary because computers employ VOLATILE memory which does not retain its contents from previous sessions, and also because a program variable might be allocated at an ADDRESS that contains a value put there by a previous program.

initialization string A string of commands that a communications program sends to a MODEM prior to making a connection in order to set up the desired communications parameters (e.g. speed, compression method) for a particular link. Nowadays such initialization strings invariably consist of HAYES-COMPATIBLE AT commands, a typical example being AT&FX4&C1&D2E1$0D

Initial Program Loader (IPL) See under BOOTSTRAP LOADER.

inkjet printer A popular type of printer that works by propelling tiny droplets of ink at the paper without making any mechanical contact with it. The term encompasses both the BUBBLE-JET PRINTER and printers that use the PIEZOELECTRIC EFFECT to propel the droplets. Inkjet printers offer print quality comparable to that from a LASER PRINTER but they are slower (owing to the time required for the liquid ink to dry) and require frequent replacement of expensive ink cartridges, so they are uncompetitive for long print runs.

inline A COMPILER DIRECTIVE supported by some programming languages (e.g. C and TURBO PASCAL) which indicates that the following function or procedure is to be compiled as INLINE CODE.

inline code In a compiled program, the replacement of a FUNCTION or PROCEDURE CALL with the actual code of the FUNCTION BODY. Inlining is an optimization provided in some programming languages to speed up execution by saving the time consumed in a call-and-return, at the cost of increasing the size of the compiled code.

Inmos A UK semiconductor manufacturer that designed the TRANSPUTER. The company later merged with SGS-Thomson.

i-node The data structure employed to identify individual files in a UNIX file system. It is essentially a POINTER to the list of disk blocks allocated to hold that file's data.

in-place editing A facility provided by OBJECT-ORIENTED computer programs, whereby an object of one class embedded in a CONTAINER object of another class can invoke its own editor within the editor of its container. In-place editing is supported, for example, in MICROSOFT WORD documents – clicking on a picture or a spreadsheet embedded in a document will cause Word's menus to be replaced by those of a picture editor or Excel, allowing the embedded item to be modified without having to leave Word.

in-process Running within the same PROCESS. In OBJECT-ORIENTED and CLIENT/SERVER structured applications, a CLIENT and SERVER running within the same process can call each other by using an ordinary PROCEDURE CALL (as they would to call a library routine). However, when they are in different processes – perhaps on different host computers – they must instead use INTERPROCESS calls or REMOTE PROCEDURE CALLS. See also OUT-OF-PROCESS, PROXY, STUB, MARSHAL.

input **1** *n*. One of the values that must be supplied for a computer program, process or procedure to be executed, used as in 'this procedure requires a date, a name and an amount as its inputs'.

2 *n*. An electrical connector through which signals can be transmitted into some hardware device, for example an amplifier, a computer or a printer.

3 *v*. The act of entering data into a computer so that it can be processed. There are many different ways to input data. See more under INPUT DEVICE, I/O.

input device Any type of hardware employed to enter DATA or COMMANDS into a computer. The most common input device is the KEYBOARD, which was inherited from the manual typewriter. The next most common input device is the MOUSE, which is used only to input cursor positions and to select commands. For drawing and painting applications a GRAPHICS TABLET is often employed that allows pen strokes to be entered directly, while games typically employ a JOYSTICK to move the cursor.

Pictures or photographs may be entered using a SCANNER, and preprinted text documents using OPTICAL CHARACTER RECOGNITION on scanned images.

VOICE-ACTIVATED interfaces are becoming increasingly popular, using a microphone to dictate text or commands into the computer. For hand-held computers PEN INPUT with HANDWRITING RECOGNITION is commonly employed to reduce the overall size of the equipment by eliminating the keyboard. Computers used in hazardous or dirty factory environments, or exposed in public places such as bank cashpoints and street information kiosks, frequently use a TOUCH SCREEN for input to avoid the fragility of keyboards.

Future input devices may include GESTURE RECOGNITION and HEAD-TRACKING devices that detect where the user is looking, or induction devices for direct detection of electrical impulses from muscles and even the brain.

input-process-output The simplest possible model of computing, corresponding to the old notion of BATCH PROCESSING where a file of data is processed and then printed out. Modern interactive systems seldom follow such a simple model, typically running multiple concurrent processes and being always ready to receive inputs from a variety of sources.

INRIA Abbreviation of INSTITUT NATIONAL DE RECHERCHE EN INFORMATIQUE ET AUTOMATIQUE.

insanely great A term of approbation, coined by Steve JOBS to describe the Apple MACINTOSH, that has passed into the industry argot.

insert 1 The action of adding a new element to an existing structure (e.g. a word to a document, a record to a database) by making space between existing elements. An inserting editor is one in which any new text that is typed does not OVERWRITE the existing text, but pushes it out of the way to the right. See also APPEND.

2 A key on the computer KEYBOARD, usually labelled 'Ins', that TOGGLES the input behaviour of text editing software between inserting and overwriting modes.

insertion point The point at which any text typed at the keyboard will be inserted into an on-screen document. In a system with a GRAPHICAL USER INTERFACE, this is typically marked by a flashing I-BEAM CURSOR between characters. On an older CHARACTER-BASED terminal it is marked by a flashing block cursor or underline positioned at the character which the new input will displace to the right.

insertion sort A very simple sorting algorithm (essentially the one people use to sort a hand of cards) in which items are put into their correct place in an initially empty list by comparing against the already sorted items until one that is larger is encountered, then inserting just before it. The insertion sort is very inefficient for more than the smallest quantities of data. See also QUICKSORT, HEAP SORT.

inspector In an OBJECT-ORIENTED software system, a utility that enables the user to examine the contents and properties of an object. Each class of objects typically has its own inspector which may, for example, be summoned by clicking on an object's ICON in a visual user interface.

install To introduce new hardware or software into a computer system. This is seldom as simple as plugging in the hardware or copying the software: hardware may need a particular DEVICE DRIVER to be added, while software may need various LIBRARY files to be stored in the correct directory. It may also be necessary to register the new addition so that the operating system knows it is there. For these reasons most vendors now supply a special installa-

tion program with their products that performs all these necessary steps automatically. See also UNINSTALLER, REINSTALL.

installed user base The number of users of a particular software or hardware system.

instance An object whose structure has been copied from an abstract template such as a CLASS or an ABSTRACT DATA TYPE: that is, a variable of that class or type. An instance is a real data structure that can hold information, whereas the template is only a pattern, of which only one copy exists. See also INSTANTIATE, INSTANCE VARIABLE, OBJECT-ORIENTED.

instance variable In OBJECT-ORIENTED PROGRAMMING, the named compartments within an object, which is an INSTANCE of a particular CLASS, into which the object's private data is stored. Consider a class definition such as:

```
CLASS xyCoordinate
x: Integer
y: Integer
ENDCLASS
```

This defines two instance variables named x and y, and every newly created instance of a xyCoordinate object will receive its own copy of both of them, and hence be capable of storing two integers.

In a pure object-oriented language the instance variables are invisible from outside the object and may be accessed only by its own METHODS. However, in hybrid languages such as C++, they may be accessed by other procedures by referring to them by name:

```
ANewXyCoordinate.x
```

where ANewXyCoordinate is an instance of the class xyCoordinate. See also DOT NOTATION.

instantiate To create an INSTANCE of some abstract template such as a CLASS or an ABSTRACT DATA TYPE.

Institute of Electrical and Electronics Engineers See IEEE.

Institut National de Recherche en Informatique et Automatique (INRIA) The premier French research institution for computer science.

instruction The basic unit from which all computer programs are constructed, consisting of a binary number code that causes the computer's PROCESSOR to perform a particular operation. Each different make of processor supports different operations, and encodes them by different instruction numbers (see INSTRUCTION SET), so a program written for one make will not run on another.

For example instruction number 64 (40h or 1000000 binary) causes an Intel 8086 processor to increment by 1 the contents of a REGISTER called AX. Such numbers are very hard for humans to remember, so programmers prefer to write a name such as INC AX (see under ASSEMBLER MNEMONIC), which is translated back into the number 64 by a program called an ASSEMBLER before it can be executed.

Modern processors typically employ a 32- or 64-bit wide instruction BUS, and since they do not have enough different instructions to use up so many bits, they pack data and addresses needed by the operation (or more than one instruction) into the same instruction WORD.

instruction cache A PROCESSOR CACHE that is used only to cache program INSTRUCTIONS and not data. See also DATA CACHE, HARVARD ARCHITECTURE, UNIFIED CACHE.

instruction decoding The step in the execution of a computer program that occurs immediately after a new INSTRUCTION has been fetched from memory into the processor's instruction register.

Decoding identifies the class of operation to perform and the operands to perform it on, prior to execution.

instruction fetch That part of the operation cycle of a computer's processor during which it reads the next instruction to be executed from memory. See also FETCH–EXECUTE CYCLE, INSTRUCTION PREFETCH.

instruction mnemonic Also called an *assembler mnemonic*. A short name or acronym used in place of the binary number of a MACHINE CODE instruction when writing ASSEMBLY LANGUAGE programs for a particular type of computer processor. An ASSEMBLER program translates the list of mnemonics back into numbers. Such mnemonics are typically chosen so that they offer some suggestion of their function, as in LD for Load, ST for Store, CMP for Compare, MOV for Move and so on.

instruction prefetch A scheme to minimize the time a processor must wait for the next instruction to be fetched from memory, whereby several following instructions are also fetched in anticipation that they will soon be needed. If the processor employs a PIPELINE, these following instructions can even be decoded (see INSTRUCTION DECODING) while the first is still executing. However, in the event of BRANCH being taken, all the instructions in the pipeline or prefetch queue must be discarded, and new ones fetched from the branch target address: see PIPELINE BREAK.

instruction scheduling A late phase in the COMPILATION of a program in which the COMPILER adjusts the order of the INSTRUCTIONS it has generated so as to maximize the number of FUNCTION UNITS that can be kept working simultaneously on a PIPELINED or SUPERSCALAR processor. For example it may move an instruction to fill a BRANCH DELAY SLOT; it may alternate FLOATING-POINT with INTEGER arithmetic instructions to keep both units busy; or it may separate instructions that write to memory to avoid overfilling the WRITE BUFFER.

instruction set The complete repertoire of operations that a computer's PROCESSOR can perform, and the numeric codes used to invoke those operations.

There is no single standard instruction set, every make of processor having its own: moreover there is no general agreement about what instructions need to be in an instruction set. The choice of instructions is up to the processor's designers and is as much an art as science, involving much compromise between elegance, efficiency and available silicon space (see for example CISC versus RISC). See also OP CODE, MACHINE CODE, ASSEMBLY LANGUAGE, ORTHOGONAL INSTRUCTION SET.

insulator A substance that does not conduct electricity (or more precisely, conducts electricity very poorly).

integer In mathematics, one of the positive or negative whole numbers ... −4, −3, −2, −1, 0, 1, 2, 3, 4 ... A computer has to represent integers as binary BIT strings of a fixed and finite length, so that programmers speak of a 16-bit integer (which can represent integers only up to 65,535) or a 32-bit integer (which can represent integers only up to 4,294,967,295). Many programming languages support more than one length of integer, and are given such names as int, unsigned int, LONG INTEGER, long or longint to distinguish them. See also WORD, QUADWORD, CARDINAL.

integer multiply A processor instruction that multiplies two INTEGER quantities, such as 3 times 4. Within a computer's processor, integer multiply is a different operation from a FLOATING-POINT multiply and is performed by an entirely separate FUNCTION UNIT.

integrate 1 To build a large computer system using separate parts purchased from different vendors: for example a SERVER from one manufacturer, a printer from another, and WORKSTATIONS from a third. The job of connecting these parts, configuring them correctly and installing the software to make them work together is known as SYSTEM INTEGRATION, and sustains a whole branch of the computer consultancy business.

2 To put together various parts of a computer program written by a team of different programmers so that they work as a whole. Integration is normally performed relatively late in the development cycle after each part has been tested as far as possible on its own. Various SOFTWARE ENGINEERING methodologies prescribe disciplined, stepwise techniques for integrating the components of large projects.

integrated circuit An entire electrical circuit created on a single thin slice of SEMICONDUCTOR material, popularly known as a chip. The MICROPROCESSORS, MEMORY chips and GRAPHICS ACCELERATORS found in personal computers are all examples of integrated circuits.

An integrated circuit is constructed by creating many microscopic electronic components together on the surface of the substrate by a kind of printing process called LITHOGRAPHY, similar in principle (though not in scale!) to those used to print books and magazines. The most common material that integrated circuits are made of is SILICON, but for special purposes other substrates such as GALLIUM ARSENIDE or SILICON ON SAPPHIRE may be used.

Images of the desired circuit layouts, called MASKS (which look something like city street maps), are optically reduced in size and projected onto a silicon surface covered in a light-sensitive varnish called *photoresist*.

Unexposed areas of resist are then washed away with a solvent, and the bared areas treated by various chemical processes. Different electronic components are created by selectively DOPING the substrate with different elements, then oxidizing the surface to create insulating films, and etching away unwanted parts. Repeating these operations several times, using different masks and different chemical processes, forms a multi-layer sandwich with transistors at the intersections of the 'streets'. Layers of aluminium or copper are deposited by evaporation, and etched away using yet more masks, to form the wires or TRACKS that connect these millions of transistors together. The most highly integrated circuits in use today may contain a whole computer (including its memory) or a MODEM on a single chip. See also VLSI.

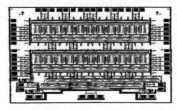

Integrated Development Environment (IDE) A program that combines a COMPILER or INTERPRETER for some programming language with a TEXT EDITOR and various other programming tools such as smart LINKERS and MAKE utilities, form designers, project and object browsers and symbolic debuggers, so enabling the programmer to write, compile and debug a program without leaving the same single user interface. Examples of widely used IDEs include those provided by VISUAL BASIC, VISUAL C++ and DELPHI. See also RAPID APPLICATION DEVELOPMENT, EDIT-COMPILE-RUN-DEBUG CYCLE, CASE TOOL.

Integrated Drive Electronics See under IDE.

Integrated Services Digital Network See ISDN.

Intel 8oxx processors See 8086, 8088, 80x86 ARCHITECTURE.

Intel 8088 See 8088.

Intel Corporation US company that is the world's largest manufacturer of MICROPROCESSORS. Founded in 1968 by Gordon Moore and

Robert Noyce to manufacture the then new semiconductor memory chips, in 1971 it introduced the world's first processor on a single chip, the Intel 4004 (which was used in a Japanese desktop calculator). The company now manufactures the Pentium family of 32 and 64-bit processors which power most of the world's personal computers, as well as many other types of chip used in communications and video.

intellectual property (IP) Copyrights and patents; that is, the ownership of ideas rather than material objects.

intelligent A term often used to describe electronic devices that contain a microprocessor and so may be programmed to perform more than one function, or even to learn autonomously: see for example INTELLIGENT TERMINAL. Its common synonym is SMART (as in SMART TERMINAL) and its opposite is DUMB.

Intelligent Console Architecture (ICA) A protocol devised by the US firm CITRIX that permits Microsoft WINDOWS programs to be run on a remote server while their user interface is displayed on any non-Intel, non-Windows computers for which an ICA CLIENT exists. These include most UNIX and Apple MACINTOSH machines and many SMART TERMINALS, NETWORK COMPUTERS and some hand-held computing devices.

Like the X WINDOW SYSTEM, ICA works by reducing user interface displays to a stream of compact commands rather than sending a bitmap of the whole screen, and so can operate over relatively low-bandwith links including 10 megabit per second ETHERNET or even a MODEM connection. See also WINFRAME, TERMINAL SERVER.

intelligent terminal A computer TERMINAL that contains its own microprocessor and can therefore execute programs locally as well as on the HOST computer to which it is connected. Intelligent terminals have effectively been replaced by personal computers running suitable TERMINAL EMULATION software for most purposes. Intelligent terminals are colloquially referred to as SMART TERMINALS, the opposite of which is a DUMB TERMINAL. See also THIN CLIENT, NETWORK COMPUTER.

IntelliMouse A brand of MOUSE manufactured by Microsoft which, in addition to the customary mouse buttons, features a thumbwheel that scrolls the current document when turned and also acts as a third button. See also WHEEL MOUSE.

IntelliPoint The DEVICE DRIVER software employed by Microsoft's INTELLIMOUSE.

IntelliSense The proprietary name of a set of features in the MICROSOFT OFFICE software suite that attempts to guess what the user is currently doing and offer unprompted assistance. Such features include automatic correction of certain common spelling errors, and automatic capitalization of the initial words of sentences.

Intel processor Any microprocessor manufactured by INTEL CORPORATION, for example one of the PENTIUM family.

inter- A prefix that means 'between'. Compare this with intra-, which means 'within'.

interactive Capable of being controlled or modified by the user.

1 When used of computer software it means that the program undertakes a dialogue with the user, requesting data and replying with answers or further requests. This is in contrast to older forms of BATCH PROCESSING where the user must enter a command and source of data and the computer then works with no further communication until the results are returned.

2 When applied to television or other entertainment systems, the term implies that the user can make changes to the course of programmes (by selecting options using a remote control) rather than observing them passively.

interactive video Video recordings in which the user can intervene to alter the sequence in which the pictures are displayed. Interactive video is shown on a computer monitor with graphical overlays that enable the user to enter commands and make MENU selections. For example an interactive video training course might ask the user questions and analyse the answers to determine what video sequence to show next. Another popular application is for information kiosks, where a TOUCH SCREEN may be substituted for the computer KEYBOARD. See also WEB TV.

Interchange File Format (IFF) A multimedia METAFILE invented by Electronic Arts in 1985 as an OPEN STANDARD, intended to be portable across different computing platforms. IFF files may contain a number of 'chunks' so that different kinds of data can be embedded. There are different types of chunk for audio, graphics and animation data.

interconnect The conductors that join together a group of electronic devices, for example the TRACKS that connect the various functional units on an INTEGRATED CIRCUIT chip, or the BUS that connects the processors inside a MULTIPROCESSOR computer. See also AUTO-ROUTING, SWITCHED INTERCONNECT, HYPERCUBE.

interface A common boundary where two different domains join: hence that term has several specialized meanings in computing.

1 An electrical connection between two devices, as in SERIAL interface or SCSI interface.

2 Short for USER INTERFACE, that part of a computer program that manages interactions with the user.

3 In OBJECT-ORIENTED PROGRAMMING, a set of METHODS that a class of objects makes visible for communicating with other objects. An interface contains only the names and PARAMETER lists of the methods, not their implementations, so objects of different classes may display the same interface while providing a different implementation. For example many classes may have a method named Print, but the precise details of how to print objects of each class will be different. Separating interface from implementation in this way enables programmers to write economical POLYMORPHIC code that can handle many different classes of object.

Interface Definition Language (IDL) The language used to define the INTERFACES through which CORBA and Microsoft's COMPONENT OBJECT MODEL and DCOM objects call each other's methods. IDL is used only to define the interface, not to implement the methods themselves, and various IDL compilers have been developed that compile IDL descriptions into target languages such as PASCAL, ADA or C++. Microsoft IDL is almost identical to CORBA IDL: both derive from the IDL developed for the OSF DISTRIBUTED COMPUTING ENVIRONMENT, and both employ a syntax that is a subset of C++.

Interface Identifier A unique 16-byte name given to every new INTERFACE created in a system that employs Microsoft's COMPONENT OBJECT MODEL. IIDs are not meant to be read by humans but only by the software that needs to call that interface: interfaces all have alternative human-readable names such as ILookUpWord. IIDs are a type of GUID. See also INTERFACE DEFINITION LANGUAGE.

interlaced display A RASTER DISPLAY in which each FRAME is drawn in two stages, first all the odd lines, then the even lines. The advantage of interlacing is that it halves the BANDWIDTH required to transmit each image while maintaining the FRAME RATE (important for smooth depiction of motion) and the VERTICAL RESOLUTION (important to preserve detail). For this reason interlacing was adopted for broadcast analogue television standards. The disadvantages of interlacing are that it introduces undesirable visual artefacts such as TWITTER and FLICKER of thin horizontal lines, and that it makes digital manipulation of TV video more difficult, because computer displays are not interlaced.

interleave To intersperse or alternate two or more sets of objects like the pages of a book. Interleaving is a strategy frequently employed in computer design to reduce the LATENCY of access to some resource, such as the SECTORS of a hard disk (see under SECTOR INTERLEAVE), different BANKS of memory or data PACKETS on a network. The effect is always to make ready a second resource during the otherwise dead time required to access the first. For example many GRAPHICS PROCESSORS alternately load data into odd and even memory banks, performing the data I/O while one bank is in its PRECHARGE phase.

Interlisp One of the two main families of LISP dialects (the other being MACLisp) developed from 1967 onwards at Bolt, Beranek and Newman. Xerox PARC later went on to create a version called Interlisp-D which featured perhaps the first true INTEGRATED DEVELOPMENT ENVIRONMENT.

intermediate code Program instructions emitted by a programming language COMPILER that are not in the NATIVE CODE of the target processor but in some INTERMEDIATE LANGUAGE. See also PSEUDO-CODE, P-CODE.

Intermediate Language (IL) The particular INTERMEDIATE LANGUAGE generated by those Microsoft programming languages (including VISUAL BASIC, VISUAL C++ and C#) that share the new COMMON LANGUAGE RUNTIME. IL is a form of stack-oriented BYTECODE.

intermediate language Any programming language, other than native MACHINE CODE, which is generated by the COMPILATION of a SOURCE program written in a different language. For example programs written in the EIFFEL language are compiled into C source code (the intermediate language) which must then be further compiled using an ordinary C COMPILER.

The reason for using an intermediate language is that it can shorten and simplify the task of writing a new language compiler. The compiler writers need write only a parser for the new syntax, and can leave code generation to the intermediate language's compiler (which is typically a mature and efficient one). See also BYTECODE, PSEUDO-CODE.

International Business Machines See IBM.

International Computers Ltd See ICL.

internationalization The modification of a software product for use by speakers of a different (human) language. Internationalization involves more than merely translating menus, dialogues and documentation into the new language: other important differences might include a different CHARACTER SET, keyboard layout (e.g. the French use of AZERTY), different numeric notations (e.g. the European use of point rather than comma to separate thousands, as in 123.323.456) and more subtle cultural differences. Some modern operating systems and development tools try to assist internationalization by isolating all such affected data items into replaceable modules.

International Organization for Standardization See ISO.

International Telecommunications Union See ITU.

Internet A network of computer networks that now spans the whole world, connecting all the major public, private and university networks. The Internet permits email to be sent to and from anywhere in the world that has access to it via an INTERNET SERVICE PROVIDER.

The Internet was first created in 1966 by ARPA, the US government's defence research agency, to provide a highly decentralized, resilient communications network that could not be destroyed by a nuclear attack on any single 'nerve centre'. At first it connected only government defence laboratories, but under the Reagan administration it was expanded to include the major universities and give them access to the expensive supercomputers deployed at these laboratories. As it grew, the Internet was gradually opened up to more and more institutions, and eventually to the public.

The Internet is built around a three-level hierarchy of carriers, organized in tree-like fashion so that long-distance messages travel via a few high-speed, high-capacity networks that form its trunk. These so-called INTERNET BACKBONE networks are mainly the original military networks such as ARPAnet, NSFnet and MILNET, along with high-speed lines belonging to the major telephone companies. The branches and twigs are called 'mid-level' networks and 'stub' networks respectively. Hence the Internet works over many different kinds of hardware and with many different low-level protocols, the unifying factor being the Internet Protocol IP and its INTERNET ADDRESS scheme, together with the DOMAIN NAME SYSTEM.

Many thousands of people have contributed to the building of the Internet, which is run and maintained by non-governmental bodies such as the INTERNET ENGINEERING TASK FORCE, the INTERNET ENGINEERING STEERING GROUP, the INTERNET ARCHITECTURE BOARD, the INTERNET ASSIGNED NUMBERS AUTHORITY and the INTERNET SOCIETY and INTERNIC. Some of the most important software utilities and protocols used on the Internet, including SENDMAIL, the APACHE web server and the WORLD WIDE WEB protocols, have been developed by volunteers for no payment. There is therefore no single inventor of the Internet, though pivotal figures include Bob Taylor who negotiated funds for the initial ARPA project, JCR Licklider who worked out the topology, Vint

Cerf who invented the ROUTERS and TCP/IP protocols, and Larry Roberts the father of ARPAnet.

internet A network of networks. A group of networks connected together by BRIDGES or ROUTERS so that data may be passed from one network into another, which allows users of all of these networks to communicate and share data with one another. *The* INTERNET (note the capital I) is a world-wide internet. See also INTRANET.

Internet Access Provider See IAP.

Internet address See IP ADDRESS.

Internet Architecture Board (IAB) The technical body that keeps the Internet open by overseeing all development work on the INTERNET PROTOCOLS, issuing its findings in a series of standards documents called STDS. The IAB has two working groups, the INTERNET ENGINEERING TASK FORCE and the INTERNET RESEARCH TASK FORCE, which perform software development work on new protocols.

Internet Assigned Numbers Authority See IANA.

Internet backbone The high-speed, high-capacity networks that carry Internet traffic around the world. The backbone networks include the military networks that formed the original core of the Internet (ARPANET, NSFnet and MILNET) together with commercial optic fibre networks owned by the large carriers AT&T, Sprint, MCI, Netcom, UUNet, IBM and GTE. The backbone networks meet at points called NETWORK ACCESS POINTS. Only the largest Internet Service Providers (ISPS) are connected directly to the backbone; the smaller ISPs connect indirectly via a connection to a larger ISP.

Internet Corporation for Assigned Names and Numbers See ICANN.

Internet Engineering Steering Group The governing body of the INTERNET ENGINEERING TASK FORCE, composed of the task force's area directors and chair.

Internet Engineering Task Force (IETF) An international group of network software vendors, designers, operators and researchers that manages the development of the Internet PROTOCOLS and resolves any disputes over ARCHITECTURE and IMPLEMENTATION. The IETF produces proposals which are sent to the INTERNET ARCHITECTURE BOARD for final approval.

Internet Explorer Microsoft's WEB BROWSER software, currently available in version 5.5.

Internet Information Server Microsoft's main WEB SERVER product.

Internet Inter-ORB Protocol (IIOP) A communication protocol developed to enable CORBA 2.0 objects to exchange messages with one another over the Internet and access web pages, and to permit CORBA objects to be manipulated within a WEB BROWSER. NETSCAPE COMMUNICATOR contains the only browser that currently supports IIOP.

Internet Network Information Center See INTERNIC.

Internet Printing Protocol (IPP) A protocol that enables print jobs to be submitted to a remote printer over an INTERNET or INTRANET connection. An IPP-enabled BROWSER can search for printers on the Internet and interrogate them concerning properties such as the paper size they use and their current busy status.

Internet Protocol See under IP.

Internet Protocol Control Protocol (IPCP) The PROTOCOL within the TCP/IP protocol suite that controls all the routing functions: an IPCP PROTOCOL STACK runs inside each ROUTER in the network. Defined in RFC1332.

Internet Public Library A project sponsored by the University of Michigan to provide a 24-hour online library on the Internet.

Internet Relay Chat See IRC.

Internet Research Steering Group The governing body of the INTERNET RESEARCH TASK FORCE.

Internet Research Task Force The body chartered by the INTERNET ARCHITECTURE BOARD (IAB) to coordinate research work on future Internet technologies, such as MULTICASTING and VIDEOCONFERENCING.

Internet Server Application Programming Interface (ISAPI) A programming interface into Microsoft's INTERNET INFORMATION SERVER (IIS) which permits SCRIPTS embedded within web pages to make calls into external DLLS to perform data processing tasks. Such scripts may be written in VBSCRIPT, JAVASCRIPT or PERL. ISAPI is more efficient than the standard CGI gateway because it is specifically designed for IIS and can exploit knowledge of IIS's internal structure.

Internet Service Provider See ISP.

Internet Society (ISOC) A non-profit professional society set up to support the development of the INTERNET. It promotes interest in the Internet among the scientific and academic communities, industry and the general public by holding discussion forums, running an annual conference, INET, and publishing a quarterly newsletter, *Internet Society News*.

Internet telephony See under VOICE-OVER-IP.

internetwork 1 *n.* A network of networks, also called an INTERNET.
2 *a.* Existing on, or acting upon several networks.
3 *v.* To connect different networks together, using ROUTERS or GATEWAYS.

inter-network Taking place between two or more different networks. See more under INTERNET.

Internetwork Packet Exchange (IPX) A widely used network-layer PROTOCOL made popular by its use in the NOVELL NETWARE network operating system. Originally developed by XEROX CORPORATION, the IPX protocol can also be used in ROUTERS to interconnect different LANS.

Internet Worm A VIRUS-like program that travels across the Internet from server to server, replicating itself within each server. The most famous example appeared in 1988 and clogged large parts of the Internet for several days. Ironically its perpetrator, who was jailed for the episode, was the son of a high-ranking US intelligence official.

InterNIC (Internet Network Information Center) A cooperative body set up in 1992 to administer the registration of Internet DOMAIN NAMES, and to provide directory and information services to Internet users. InterNIC is a collaboration between the US Government (via the NATIONAL SCIENCE FOUNDATION),

AT&T and the private firm NETWORK SOLUTIONS Inc. InterNIC's domain registration functions have now been taken over by the non-profit organization ICANN.

interoperability The ability of software and hardware on machines from different vendors to communicate with one another.

interpolate 1 In mathematics, to introduce additional data points between two measured points by calculation rather than measurement.
2 When used of a SCANNER or DIGITAL CAMERA in computer graphics, to give the illusion of a higher RESOLUTION picture by generating more PIXELS than were actually imaged, by using an algorithm that estimates the colour for each extra pixel according to those surrounding it.

interpreted A programming language whose programs are executed by an INTERPRETER in their SOURCE CODE form, rather than being compiled into an executable form. Examples of purely interpreted languages include older dialects of BASIC and LISP. Some benefits of an interpreted language are the ease of changing and experimenting with a program (without incurring a lengthy compilation) and the ability to run the code on any brand of computer for which the interpreter is available. However, writing in a purely interpreted language requires that the program's source code be distributed to end-users, which is unacceptable to commercial software vendors, who regard the source code as their private property. Interpreted programs also typically run more slowly than their compiled equivalents because the effort of translation is incurred every time the program is run.

Some interpreted languages mitigate both of the above problems by first compiling programs into an INTERMEDIATE LANGUAGE that is not native MACHINE CODE (and hence not restricted to a single type of processor), and then running this code on an interpreter. Such languages are called SEMI-COMPILED and the intermediate form is often called *pseudo-code*. Languages that employ this technique include VISUAL BASIC, JAVA, SMALLTALK, FORTH and many dialects of LISP and PROLOG. Such pseudo-code programs may run almost as fast as fully compiled programs if, as with Visual

Basic, most of the hard work is actually performed by machine-coded LIBRARY routines. Furthermore the pseudo-code is not human readable, and hence distributing it does not constitute giving away the source code.

interpreter A program that executes the SOURCE CODE of another program by translating its statements one at a time into MACHINE CODE instructions and executing them immediately. Contrast with a compiler, which translates the whole source program in advance to produce a separate file of executable machine code, which is then executed directly. See also SEMI-COMPILED, INTERPRETED, PSEUDO-CODE.

interprocess Taking place between two different PROCESSES: see for example INTERPROCESS COMMUNICATION.

interprocess communication (IPC) The exchange of data between one PROCESS and another that is running concurrently, either on the same computer or remotely across a network. Processes that occupy a common MEMORY SPACE can communicate simply by sharing a number of memory locations and taking turns to update them. However, only the simplest of operating systems permit this since it conflicts with the requirement to protect processes from interfering with one another (see PROTECTED MEMORY). Hence under MULTITASKING operating systems, each process typically occupies its own private memory space and interprocess communication must be carried out by MESSAGE PASSING between them.

The use of message passing brings an extra advantage. It erases any essential difference between processes running on the same computer and those running on a remote computer, which encourages software to be written in a LOCATION TRANSPARENT fashion. Various PROTOCOLS have been devised to manage such exchanges, including the Unix SOCKET protocol, Novell's SPX and Windows DDE. See also IN-PROCESS, OUT-OF-PROCESS, DCOM, CORBA

interrogate When used of a piece of software or hardware, to ask of another what its properties are: for example what speed it can run at or what PROTOCOLS it supports. See also AUTO-DETECT, HANDSHAKE, PLUG-AND-PLAY.

interrupt An event that causes a computer processor to temporarily stop executing its current program and execute another instead, finally returning control to the original program. The purpose of an interrupt is to ensure that high-priority tasks are carried out promptly and not delayed by slower, less important tasks. For example a REAL TIME device such as a HARD DISK drive might interrupt the execution of a word processing program to deliver a block of data – the user would notice nothing except perhaps a momentary hesitation in cursor movement.

Interrupts may be raised in hardware by sending a signal down a dedicated wire, or in software by executing an INT instruction. In either case the processor pushes its current REGISTER contents onto the STACK to preserve them, and starts to execute a new program known as an INTERRUPT HANDLER, on completion of which the processor restores its registers from the stack and continues as before. One interrupt may interrupt another, and so on, to many levels.

interrupt controller A type of integrated circuit whose purpose is to manage the raising and servicing of hardware INTERRUPTS from PERIPHERAL devices within a computer. The controller acts like a switchboard, receiving signals from various interrupting devices and placing their identifying INTERRUPT VECTOR onto the DATA BUS: the CPU uses this value as an index into a table of addresses of INTERRUPT HANDLER routines. An interrupt controller can also be programmed to allow certain types of interrupts to be ignored temporarily (a MASKABLE INTERRUPT). An interrupt controller designed for MULTIPROCESSOR systems can also be programmed to balance the system load by fairly distributing interrupts among the processors.

interrupt-driven A style of computer architecture in which all the peripheral devices compete for the CPU's attention by raising INTERRUPTS, which are dealt with according to the priority assigned to each device. The alternative is a POLLING architecture where the operating system asks each device in turn whether it needs attention.

When a higher-priority device interrupts one of a lower priority, the latter's servicing is temporarily suspended, to be resumed when the higher-priority one has finished. So long as sufficient processing power is available, all devices will be served (albeit at different speeds) and an impression of concurrency is maintained. The IBM-COMPATIBLE PC architecture is to a large extent interrupt-driven. See also IRQ, INTERRUPT CONTROLLER, MASKABLE INTERRUPT, REAL TIME EXECUTIVE.

interrupt handler A section of program code that is executed only in the event of the computer's processor receiving a certain INTERRUPT signal.

interrupt request See under IRQ.

interrupt vector The address of the INTERRUPT HANDLER code that will be executed when a computer's processor receives a certain INTERRUPT signal. Interrupt vectors are stored in a table and, when it receives interrupt number *N*, the processor immediately jumps to the *N*th slot in this table, and then to the address found in the table to begin executing the handler routine. The advantage of using such an indirect scheme is that the interrupt handling behaviour of the system can be changed by simply writing the address of a new routine into the table, without having to RECOMPILE the whole operating system. See also HOOK.

intersection An operation performed on two SETS that returns just those elements that are members of both. See also UNION.

intra- A prefix that means 'within'. Compare this with *inter-*, which means 'between'.

intractable Those classes of problem for which the only known algorithms require execution time that increases too quickly with the problem size (for example exponentially) for any but the smallest examples ever to be solved. See more under NP-HARD, EXPONENTIAL-TIME ALGORITHM, POLYNOMIAL-TIME ALGORITHM, TRAVELLING SALESMAN PROBLEM.

intranet A private network that to its users appears similar to the public Internet because it is implemented using the same TCP/IP protocols, web servers and web browser software, but which is accessible only within one organization.

introspection A mechanism built into Sun's JAVABEANS component standard that allows VISUAL PROGRAMMING tools to discover the public INTERFACE of a Bean automatically and connect it into a new program without the user having to write any code.

invalid 1 Badly formed, not conforming to some accepted rule of construction: for example 14/223/98 is an invalid date.
2 In electronic engineering, a digital signal whose voltage has not yet settled into a definite 0 or 1 state.

inventory management The task of keeping track of what hardware and software is installed on a company's computer network. This may include recording the location and abilities of all the workstations, servers, printers and other resources, all the software that is installed on them, and possibly also the licensing information for that software (see LICENSE MANAGER). Inventory management is one of several management functions that are now becoming automated as a function of NETWORK MANAGEMENT software suites. See also CONFIGURATION MANAGEMENT, DIRECTORY SERVICE, ACTIVE DIRECTORY, LDAP.

inverse 1 Having an opposite or contrary effect.
2 In mathematics, the inverse of a FUNCTION is a second function that reverses its effect – for example, the inverse of the square function is the square root function, because $\sqrt{x^2} = x$.
Only one-to-one functions have inverses, and it is in most cases difficult to discover them, a fact that is exploited in certain CRYPTOGRAPHY techniques: see TRAP DOOR FUNCTION.

inverse kinematics A technique used in computer 3D GRAPHICS for animating jointed limbs. It permits the animator to interactively move an extremity such as a hand or foot to a desired location and have the software calculate the appropriate angles for each of the joints automatically, within the constraints of their fixed length and rigidity. In effect, inverse kinematics allows the animator to manipulate the screen image as if it were a real object. The most sophisticated animation programs can even take account of gravity, friction and elasticity in their inverse kinematic calculations.

inverted file A powerful indexing technique used in TEXT RETRIEVAL SYSTEMS, in which each document is decomposed into all its constituent words and an INDEX constructed by listing all these words alongside the positions of all their occurrences. An inverted file thus contains a sequence of locations in word order, rather than a sequence of words in location order, hence its name. An inverted file index offers fast and comprehensive searching abilities, but has the disadvantage that the size of the index may approach or even exceed that of the original document.

inverted index The most commonly used technique for creating an INDEX for a DATABASE file, under which one or more of the FIELDS that make up each RECORD in the database is designated a KEY field to be indexed. The resulting INDEX file contains pairs consisting of the contents of a key field together with the location of the corresponding record in the database. For example if the 47th record in a database were:

```
47, Penguin, London, publisher
```

then an index on the Name field would contain an entry

```
Penguin, 47
```

The index is kept in sorted order of key values, so that a record may be located via its key rather than vice versa, hence the name 'inverted'. A database may be indexed on several fields (e.g. Name and Town) but typically the key values are required to be unique (i.e. there can be only one record with Name= Penguin).

inverter A digital LOGIC GATE that reverses the value of its input, outputting a 0 whenever it receives a 1 and vice versa. It is equivalent to the Boolean function NOT and its TRUTH TABLE is:

A	NOT A
True	False
False	True

invoke To cause a software routine to be executed.

I/O (Input/Output) Any communication between a computer and the outside world inhabited by the user.

1 Applied to a whole computer, the term covers all those devices (KEYBOARD, MOUSE, VDU, DISK DRIVE, SERIAL PORT and so on) that may be used to put data in or take data out.

2 Applied to a lone microprocessor it refers to any subsystem such as a PORT or BUS that

moves data on and off the chip as opposed to processing it within the chip.

3 Applied to an operating system, application program or programming language, it refers to those commands responsible for creating and manipulating files or communication channels. See also BIOS, I/O redirection.

Iomega A US manufacturer of removable disk storage devices, best known for its ZIP DRIVE and JAZ DRIVE. See also BERNOULLI DRIVE.

ion implantation The process of infusing a DOPANT substance, for example arsenic, into a SEMICONDUCTOR such as SILICON by bombarding its surface with a beam of high-speed ions from a particle accelerator.

I/O redirection A facility provided by most computer operating systems to greater or lesser degree, which enables data to be rerouted from one of its defined input or output devices to another by issuing a suitable command. For example text typed at the keyboard might be redirected from screen into a disk file, or the contents of a file redirected to the screen. UNIX provides the most powerful example in its STANDARD INPUT/OUTPUT concept, which permits the output of any program to be piped into any other (or to a disk, screen, printer or communication port).

IP **1** Abbreviation of INTELLECTUAL PROPERTY.

2 Abbreviation of Internet Protocol. The NETWORK LAYER component of the TCP/IP protocol suite that controls all traffic carried via the INTERNET. IP is a CONNECTIONLESS, packet routing protocol which determines the routes that packets will take to get to their destination. The sender, the receiver and each ROUTER that the packets pass through during the journey between them, are each assigned a unique IP ADDRESS, which is a 32-bit number (normally written in a dot-separated format such as 198.83.41.77). These addresses are stored in routing tables that provide the 'roadmap' for the network.

IP is also responsible for fragmentation, the splitting of large message packets into smaller units as and when required by the underlying network hardware (for example by ASYNCHRONOUS TRANSFER MODE) and their subsequent reassembly to reconstitute the original packets. IP does not perform any error detection or correction; this is performed at the higher TRANSMISSION CONTROL PROTOCOL level.

Today's Internet is built around version 4 of IP which employs 32-bit addresses. IPv6 will employ 128-bit addresses (and hence will be capable of providing many more addresses) and is already in use on some private networks. It would however take several years to convert the whole Internet to IPv6. IP is defined in the document STD 5 (RFC 791).

IP address Also called an *Internet address*, a unique number (currently 32 bits in size) that is assigned to every HOST computer connected to the INTERNET to distinguish it from all the others.

IP addresses are normally represented as four groups of decimal digits in DOT NOTATION, for example 123.134.2.7, in which each of the four groups is interpreted by ROUTERS on the network to direct traffic to the host it represents. The different ways in which parts of an address can be interpreted are defined in Internet standard STD 5 (RFC 791).

Demand for unique IP addresses currently outstrips supply, forcing various reuse strategies such as dynamic address allocation. Version 6 of the Internet Protocol (see under IP) should eventually rectify this by increasing the length of addresses to 128 bits. See also DNS, DYNAMIC DNS

IPC Abbreviation of INTERPROCESS COMMUNICATION.

IPCP Abbreviation of INTERNET PROTOCOL CONTROL PROTOCOL.

IPL 1 Abbreviation of Initial Program Loader, see under BOOTSTRAP LOADER.
2 Abbreviation of INTERNET PUBLIC LIBRARY.

IP Multicast A variant of the IP protocol that can send a single data stream to multiple recipients, where normal IP would require a separate connection for each recipient and hence generate much traffic. IP Multicast is at present available only via experimental networks such as MBONE, but once it is supported by most ROUTERS on the Internet it will enable world-wide VIDEOCONFERENCING and television- style entertainment sites. IP Multicast is defined in RFC 1112.

IPP Abbreviation of INTERNET PRINTING PROTOCOL.

IPv6 The latest version of the Internet Protocol (IP), which when fully introduced will increase the number of available network addresses by employing 128 rather than 32-bits to encode them.

IPX Abbreviation of INTERNETWORK PACKET EXCHANGE.

IRC (Internet Relay Chat) A communication system that runs over the Internet, allowing participants to chat in real time. IRC users can create virtual CHAT ROOMS in which a number of people may have private discussions. IRC works via networks of dedicated servers that have the ability to locate chat rooms and to route callers automatically to the correct server. IRC also requires special client software, rather than a WEB BROWSER or MAIL READER. There are several different IRC networks, examples being Effnet and Undernet.

IrDA Abbreviation of INFRARED DEVICE ASSOCIATION.

iris recognition A BIOMETRIC AUTHENTICATION technique that uses a computer imaging system to scan the iris of each subject's eye, the patterns in which are as unique as fingerprints (see also FINGERPRINT RECOGNITION, RETINA SCAN).

IRIX The variety of UNIX created by SILICON GRAPHICS to run on its Iris (and other) workstations. It is essentially a MULTIPROCESSOR and MULTITHREADED variant of Unix SYSTEM V releases 4.1 and 4.2.

iron oxide See under FERRIC OXIDE.

IRQ (Interrupt Request) An input line or pin present on many computer processors, which when active causes the processor to stop executing the current program and execute an INTERRUPT HANDLER instead.

The original IBM PC architecture provided eight hardware IRQ lines into its Intel processor (numbered IRQ0 to IRQ7), and this was increased to 16 in later models. Any peripheral device, such as a GRAPHICS CARD, that needs to interrupt the CPU must be assigned a unique IRQ to itself. As several of them are already assigned to system devices such as SERIAL PORTS and PARALLEL PORTS, this is a common cause of conflict when new devices are added.

irrational number Those REAL NUMBERS that cannot be expressed as the ratio of two integers, and therefore would require an infinite number of decimal places to specify completely, pi and the square root of two being common examples. Sometimes referred to in older texts as a *surd*.

IRSG Abbreviation of INTERNET RESEARCH STEERING GROUP.

IRTF Abbreviation of INTERNET RESEARCH TASK FORCE.

ISA, ISA bus (Industry Standard Architecture) The 8-bit (and later 16-bit) EXPANSION BUS introduced in the original IBM PC in 1981. One or two ISA EXPANSION SLOTS are still fitted to most IBM-compatible PCs, to enable older expansion cards to be used in them, but all new cards employ the newer 32-bit PCI BUS instead. Because of its narrow data path and low clock speed, the ISA bus is too slow to keep up with modern processors, and ISA cards cannot be detected by WINDOWS' PLUG-AND-PLAY system for automatic configuration.

ISAM Abbreviation of INDEXED SEQUENTIAL ACCESS METHOD.

ISAPI Abbreviation of INTERNET SERVER APPLICATION PROGRAMMING INTERFACE.

ISAPI filter A small user-written software routine that processes requests for web pages made to Microsoft's INTERNET INFORMATION SERVER, for example to exclude attempts to hack the site, or to redirect certain types of request to a different server. See also INTERNET SERVER APPLICATION PROGRAMMING INTERFACE.

ISDN (Integrated Services Digital Network) A public digital data network that was intended eventually to replace our present analogue telephone system. ISDN uses the existing telephone wiring and switches to carry voice, digital data and video down a single copper wire or optic fibre, at a typical maximum speed per channel of 64 kilobits per second (Kbps). ISDN users do not need a modem to perform file transfers or to access the INTERNET as the network carries digital rather than analogue data,

but a TERMINAL ADAPTER is required to join a PC to the ISDN line.

A simple ISDN connection, on ordinary phone wires, employs the BASIC RATE INTERFACE (BRI) which consists of three separate channels: two 'bearer' or B channels capable of 64 Kbps and a single 9.6 Kbps 'delta' channel used by control signals. For data calls it is possible to combine the two B channels into a single 128 Kbps link, a process called 'channel bonding'. For business use there are several faster ISDN lines available: for example the PRIMARY RATE INTERFACE (PRI) consists of 23 (US and Japan) or 30 (Europe and Australia) B channels and a single delta channel.

ISDN is now widespread in Japan, Singapore, continental Europe and Australia, with the USA and UK lagging further behind. When the ISDN standards were published in the late 1980s it was envisaged that the whole telephone network would be converted by now, but the slow deployment means that ISDN is at risk of being superceded by ADSL and CABLE MODEMS before it ever becomes established.

ISO An international, non-governmental organization, founded in 1947 and based in Geneva, Switzerland, which is responsible for creating and promulgating many of the world's most important technical STANDARDS. The ISO is a federation of national standards bodies from some 130 countries (one body from each country) and is financed by member countries' subscriptions and by revenues from the sale of standards publications. Note that strictly speaking the short-form name ISO is not an acronym (which would be IOS in English, OIN in French, etc) but a pun on the Greek prefix iso- meaning 'the same'.

The ISO is responsible for numerous scientific and industrial standards, including many in the computing industry. The best-known are the SI units system, metric screw threads, photographic film speeds, credit card formats, paper sizes and the universal symbols that identify car controls. In the computing world the ISO has issued standards for hardware connectors, CHARACTER SETS, network PROTOCOLS and programming languages. The government standards body ANSI is the member of ISO for the USA. See also IEEE.

ISO 10646 The international standard defining the 32-bit UNIVERSAL CHARACTER SET.

ISO 8859 An international standard defining a group of 8-bit EXTENDED ASCII character sets that incorporate all the accents, DIACRITICS and LIGATURES used by most languages that employ the Roman alphabet. The standard includes six character sets: LATIN 1 Western; Latin 2 Central European; Latin 3 Esperanto; Latin 4 Baltic; Latin 5 Turkish; and Latin 6 Extended Baltic. See also UNICODE, CODE PAGE.

ISO 9660 The international standard that describes the structure of the logical file system to be used on CD-ROM discs: their physical data format is described in the Sony/Philips YELLOW BOOK.

ISOC See INTERNET SOCIETY.

isochronous Any data transmission scheme in which successive packets are separated only by a whole number of bit-length intervals, unlike ASYNCHRONOUS transmission in which the intervals may be of random length (or SYNCHRONOUS transmission where the intervals are constant). In effect an isochronous service transmits asynchronous data over a synchronous link, which is necessary for satisfactory transmission of time-dependent data such as video and voice. ASYNCHRONOUS TRANSFER MODE can provide isochronous service, but the Internet's IP protocol at present cannot.

isometric A method of projecting a drawing into three dimensions in which the three chosen AXES are equally inclined to the viewer and all the lines are drawn to the same scale rather than in perspective. Isometric projection is offered as an option in many 3D drawing and drafting programs, because it preserves measurements. It is employed in some types of computer action game as it requires less computing power than an IMMERSIVE 3D view.

isomorphic Having the same form. In mathematics an isomorphism is said to exist between two structures when for every component of one there is a corresponding component in the other, and vice versa. See also FUNCTION, MAP.

isotropic Having the same physical properties in all directions. Its opposite is ANISOTROPIC.

ISP (Internet Service Provider) A company that provides INTERNET services, such as hosting WEB SITES, and usually also sells access to the Internet (i.e. is also an IAP). Most ISPs are resellers who lease connections to the Internet backbone from one of the large telecommunications companies and share this leased BANDWIDTH among their paying customers. Larger ISPs offer a choice of DIAL-UP access via a modem for home users and permanent connections for businesses, and they typically charge on a flat-rate basis (i.e. regardless of usage) rather than by call time as telephone service operators do.

issue Of a MICROPROCESSOR, to place a new instruction into the PIPELINE ready to be executed. A multiple-issue processor architecture is one in which more than one such instruction may be issued per CLOCK CYCLE.

Itanium Formerly codenamed Merced, Intel's first full 64-bit MICROPROCESSOR, due for release in 2001. Itanium departs significantly from the established 80x86 ARCHITECTURE and so has to employ hardware emulation to run older PC software. Its new processor core architecture, called EPIC, is based on VLIW principles, contains 4 integer and 2 FLOATING-POINT execution units and three levels of on-chip CACHE. Itanium employs a FLAT ADDRESS SPACE and can address up to 16 Gigabytes of memory.

iterate 1 To repeatedly execute the same program statements, that is to enter a program LOOP. The term is frequently used by programmers in the phrase to 'iterate over' some data set, such as a file or array, which means to perform the same operations on each item in that set.
2 The term is also widely used in a metaphorical sense when speaking of the progress of a project, to imply the repetitive nature of evaluating results, making corrections and re-presenting the results, as in 'we got it right at the third iteration'. See also ITERATOR, CONDITIONAL LOOP.

Iterated Function System See under FRACTAL COMPRESSION.

Iterated Systems The software firm founded by Michael Barnsley to commercially exploit the discovery of his FRACTAL COMPRESSION technique.

iteration   A single pass through some repeated section of a program. See also ITERATE, ITERATIVE, ITERATOR.

iterative   Used of an algorithm, program or control structure that explicitly repeats the execution of groups of instructions, in contrast to a RECURSIVE equivalent.

iterator   A type of abstract CONTROL STRUCTURE provided in certain advanced programming languages (such as CLU and SATHER) that extracts individual elements from some collection, for example records from a file or objects from an array, without requiring the explicit writing of a loop with a numeric index variable. For example an iterator called employees() might be defined to return one employee record from a file each time it is called:

```
foreach employee in employees
("widgetco") do
. . . .
```

It returns some special value when the end of the file is reached. See also ITERATE, LOOP, LAZY EVALUATION.

ITU   (International Telecommunications Union)   The international body responsible for issuing the technical standards for global communication systems, in particular the X STANDARDS for computer networks and the V STANDARDS for modems.

Iverson, Ken   The inventor of the APL programming language.

IYSWIM   Online shorthand for If You See What I Mean.

J   A mathematically-oriented programming language derived from APL, which employs ordinary ASCII-based command names in place of the former's unorthodox CHARACTER SET. J INTERPRETERS are available for MS-DOS, Unix, Windows and MacOS.

Jackson method   One of the first structured program design METHODOLOGIES, invented in 1975 by Michael Jackson.

Jacquard loom   A silk weaving loom invented in France in 1797 by JM Jacquard which was the world's first truly programmable machine. Complex weave patterns prepared by a human artist were recorded as holes punched into a sheet of paper (in much the same way as a Pianola roll or a musical box) and these sheets were joined together into a continuous belt, which was fed through a reading mechanism in the loom. Pins in the reader controlled the raising and lowering of the threads to produce the required pattern, though the loom itself was still manually operated by treadles. The modern, fully automatic version of the Jacquard loom is still used to make reproduction carpets and fine silk textiles for expensive neckties. See also BABBAGE, HOLLERITH, PUNCHED CARD.

jaggies   See ALIASING.

JANET (Joint Academic Network)   A private wide-area network (WAN) linking all the universities and research institutes in the UK. JANET is an internetwork connecting many subnetworks, based on an ASYNCHRONOUS TRANSFER MODE packet-switched backbone. A BROADBAND subnetwork of JANET, called SUPERJANET employs ATM over FIBRE-OPTIC cabling to achieve 140 megabit per second bandwidth and is capable of supporting vide-oconferencing and transporting the huge data sets used in physics and medical imaging.

Java   An OBJECT-ORIENTED PROGRAMMING LANGUAGE invented by SUN MICROSYSTEMS and intended for programming DISTRIBUTED applications to be deployed across the INTERNET. Java is a semi-compiled language that compiles down to a platform-independent BYTECODE which can be run on any kind of processor, provided that there is a JAVA VIRTUAL MACHINE available for that processor. Files of Java bytecode can therefore be sent from one computer to another across the Internet without worrying about the make of computer at either end. This is summed up in Sun's slogan, 'Write Once, Run Anywhere.' Java was first applied in small so-called APPLETS embedded into web pages, which download themselves into a user's BROWSER and execute there (often to provide animated graphic effects). More recently Java is being used for full-scale applications that run on client, server or both, and communicate using a range of protocols.

The syntax of Java resembles a simplified C++, but unlike the latter it is a pure object-oriented language. It supports concurrency via synchronized THREADS, and permits INTERFACES to be separated from their implementation. The language has its own component architecture called JAVABEANS. The definition of Java is currently proprietary to Sun, an attempt to have it standardized by ISO having failed. There are, however, many COMPILERS available from other vendors, including Borland and Microsoft.

JavaBeans   The name given to the COMPONENT ARCHITECTURE employed by the JAVA language. Individual prefabricated Java components are called beans, and they may be assembled to form an application program within a suitably-equipped Java compiler. JavaBeans possess the ability (dubbed INTROSPECTION) to reveal their inner workings to the development environment, which assists in connecting them together. They can communicate with one another by sending EVENTS, and they can be made PERSISTENT so that any customization of their properties is automatically saved for future use.

Java Card An APPLICATION PROGRAMMING INTERFACE for software to run on SMARTCARDS, based on the JAVA language.

Java Database Connectivity (JDBC) A standard interface for accessing SQL databases from JAVA programs, which has formed part of the the JAVA DEVELOPMENT KIT since version 1.1.

Java Development Kit (JDK) The official JAVA compiler, complete with CLASS LIBRARIES and APPLICATION PROGRAMMING INTERFACES, published free of charge by SUN MICROSYSTEMS. The JDK is available for many operating systems including most varieties of Unix, Microsoft Windows and Apple MacOS.

Java Native Interface A programming interface that allows Java BYTECODE programs running in a JAVA VIRTUAL MACHINE to call NATIVE CODE routines, such as operating systems services or native applications and libraries.

JavaScript An interpreted SCRIPTING LANGUAGE devised by NETSCAPE for creating interactive elements to be embedded into web pages, a typical application being to capture the words typed by a user into a WEB FORM and store them into a database record on the server. Despite its name, it is only very loosely related to the far more powerful JAVA language. JavaScript is now very widely used, particularly on Windows-based SERVERS, as it is supported by all the popular browsers. See also VBSCRIPT, PERL, PHP.

Java SDK See under JAVA SERVLET DEVELOPMENT KIT.

Java Server Pages (JSP) A SERVER-SIDE scripting system that automatically generates and executes a SERVLET from a section of Java code embedded into an ordinary HTML web page. JSP can simplify the maintenance of server-side applications, as servlets are generated on-the-fly and therefore do not need to be RECOMPILED every time a change is made. See also ACTIVE SERVER PAGES.

Java Servlet Development Kit The official SUN MICROSYSTEMS development kit for creating SERVER-SIDE JAVA applications.

Java Virtual Machine (JVM) A key component of Sun's JAVA programming system, the interpreter that must be installed on each client computer to execute the BYTECODE files produced by compiling Java source programs. The JVM was originally designed as a plug-in for web browsers, for executing Java APPLETS downloaded with a web page. It is designed to prevent malicious or badly-written applets from directly accessing the local hardware (see more under SANDBOX) and takes complete responsibility for memory allocation to a running applet. As the Java language has expanded to encompass stand-alone applications, other forms of JVM have become available, for example built into the operating system of portable computers or held in ROM in peripheral devices. Most recent JVMs incorporate a performance optimization that translates the bytecode for a CLASS into native MACHINE CODE the first time it is run (see more under JUST-IN-TIME).

Jaz drive A removable HARD DISK drive made by IOMEGA, which takes removable 1 or 2 gigabyte cartridges.

JCL Abbreviation of JOB CONTROL LANGUAGE.

JDBC Abbreviation of JAVA DATABASE CONNECTIVITY.

JDK Abbreviation of JAVA DEVELOPMENT KIT.

Jeeves The original codename for JavaSoft's Java Web Server, (published as freeware) which is written entirely in JAVA and supports the running of server-side SERVLETS.

jewel-case The clear plastic boxes with hinged lids in which audio CDS and CD-ROMS are stored.

Jini A mechanism, based around the JAVA language, for dynamically locating services such as printers, webcams or scanners on a network. Jini supports both software and hardware services, and eliminates manual configuration by dynamically registering services and automatically installing their drivers over the network. Since Java code may be run on different platforms, a Java object implementing a device driver, a PROXY or even a whole user interface can be stored within the device that it applies to and automatically retrieved and executed on any remote computer that connects to it via the Jini lookup service.

JIT Abbreviation of JUST-IN-TIME.

jitter Random variation in the timings of a signal such as a clock pulse. In a packet-switched network, it refers to the random variation in the LATENCY of successive packets.

J-K flip-flop See under FLIP-FLOP.

JNI Abbreviation of JAVA NATIVE INTERFACE.

job control language (JCL) A type of primitive SCRIPTING LANGUAGE used to control BATCH PROCESSING jobs on IBM MAINFRAME computers.

Jobs, Steve (b. 1955) Co-founder, along with Steve WOZNIAK, of APPLE COMPUTER INC. Following management disputes, Jobs left Apple in 1985 and launched the innovative but commercially unsuccessful NEXT computer. He rejoined a troubled Apple in 1997 and returned the company to profit by commissioning the stylish and innovative IMAC range.

Jog Dial A one-finger input device for mobile telephones and hand-held computers invented by Sony. It consists of a cylindrical roller which, when turned, causes a cursor to move up or down a screen menu and, when pressed in, acts as the Enter command. See also TRACK-BALL, TRACKPOINT, ARROW KEYS.

join An operation performed on two TABLES in a RELATIONAL DATABASE that share a common field: the result is a new table that combines the contents of all the rows that have the same value in that field. The join operation is the crux of the relational model, allowing data items to be stored separately and uniquely but also to be combined as and when required. An SQL statement such as

```
SELECT customer.name, cus-
tomer.phone, invoice.date,
invoice.total FROM customer,
invoice WHERE customer.customer_id
= invoice.customer_id
```

extracts data from the two tables customer and invoice via the customer_id field which they have in common.

Joint Academic Network See JANET.

Joint Photographic Experts Group See JPEG.

Josephson junction An electronic circuit that once showed promise for creating high-speed computer LOGIC GATES. It consists of a pair of superconducting metal electrodes separated by a thin insulating film. When cooled to near absolute zero in liquid helium, the current through the junction becomes extremely sensitive to the strength of the surrounding electrical or magnetic field. Fabrication problems prevented commercial application of Josephson devices in computing, but similar technology is employed to make the SQUID (superconducting quantum interference device) used in some brain scanners. See also SUPERCONDUCTOR, TRANSISTOR, CMOS, ECL.

journal A special file into which some software systems write every transaction that takes place so that, in the event of a system CRASH, the status of all recent changes is preserved. A journal saves time when recovering from a crash by eliminating the need to check the whole system for consistency; as the journal's contents can be used to identify any transactions that had not completed. Some MAINFRAME operating systems incorporate a journal within their FILE SYSTEM that permits the reversal of disk activity such as copying or deleting files.

journalling The recording of all the transactions and changes made within some software system, to assist with recovery from errors: see more under JOURNAL.

joystick An INPUT DEVICE that consists of a hand-held stick, pivoted at one end, which transmits its angle in two dimensions to a personal computer or GAMES CONSOLE. Joysticks are used mainly for controlling games and so typically contain a trigger and several push-buttons for firing weapons. Most IBM-compatible PCs have a 15-pin joystick port, called the game port, on their motherboard, and for those that do not, many SOUND CARDS are fitted with one.

JPEG, JPG 1 Joint Photographic Experts Group, the committee that designed the IMAGE COM-

PRESSION algorithm that forms the basis of the most popular GRAPHICS FILE FORMAT for displaying photographs on the WORLD WIDE WEB.

2 The abbreviation of JPEG File Interchange Format, the graphics file format mentioned in 1, whose identifying FILENAME EXTENSION is JPG. JPEG employs a very efficient, but LOSSY, compression scheme to achieve compression ratios as high as 25:1 for CONTINUOUS TONE images with a little loss of fine detail. The degree of compression is adjustable to trade off size against image quality.

JPEG compression is a five-stage process that begins by converting the image into the L*A*B* COLOUR SPACE which handles colour and luminance separately. The chrominance channels are resampled at lower resolution (the human eye responds less to changes in colour than brightness) reducing the data by 50% with almost no perceivable loss of quality. The image is then divided into 8×8 pixel blocks to which a DISCRETE COSINE TRANSFORM is applied, and then each block is quantized according to the user's chosen quality setting, on a scale of 1 to 100. The resulting set of coefficients is finally losslessly compressed using HUFFMAN CODING.

The forthcoming JPEG 2000 standard (ISO15444) will employ new WAVELET compression algorithms to produce higher compression ratios while sacrificing less image quality. It is expected to find wide use in future digital cameras.

JSDK Abbreviation of JAVA SERVLET DEVELOPMENT KIT.

JSP Abbreviation of JAVA SERVER PAGES.

JSR Abbreviation of JUMP TO SUBROUTINE.

Jughead A local index to the contents of a GOPHER document archive. Named after a character in a US cartoon strip. See also ARCHIE, VERONICA.

jukebox A term applied to very large data storage devices that contain many separate storage volumes (for example CD-ROMS or TAPE cartridges) and which employ a mechanical transport mechanism to locate and mount a requested volume. The name alludes to the old-style Rockola music jukebox with its rotating record rack.

jump See under BRANCH.

jumper A crude type of switch employed to select alternative circuit configurations on a computer PRINTED CIRCUIT BOARD. It consists of a set of metal pins with removable links that can join different pairs; the links must be altered manually, which often requires tweezers and considerable dexterity. See also DIP SWITCH, JUMPERLESS, PLUG-AND-PLAY.

jumperless A type of computer PRINTED CIRCUIT BOARD that allows alternative circuit configurations to be made without needing JUMPERS to be moved from one pin to another. The term normally implies that the configuration is performed in software, possibly stored on the board in FLASH MEMORY. See also PLUG-AND-PLAY.

jump on condition A class of processor instruction that either transfers control to another location or not, according to a value held in a FLAG register: see also CONDITIONAL BRANCH.

jump to subroutine (JSR) A class of processor instruction that causes program execution to transfer to a SUBROUTINE, with the PROGRAM COUNTER contents stored on a STACK. A matching RTN or RETURN FROM SUBROUTINE instruction at the end of the subroutine restores the program counter contents, and causes execution to resume from the instruction following the original jump. The instruction is not always called JSR: for example on Intel microprocessors its mnemonic is CALL.

junk mail Unsolicited postal or electronic mail.

junkmailer A software product that takes a list of EMAIL ADDRESSES and automatically sends a message to all of them, the main use of which is for sending unsolicited or 'junk' mail.

justify In typography, to cause one or both of the margins of a column of text to be aligned vertically in the interest of readability or visual design. Most newspaper, magazine and book text in European languages is either justified to the left margin (also called 'ranged left' or 'ragged right') or to both left and right margins (fully justified). Right justification is encountered less often, and is used mostly in fancy graphical layouts, picture captions, and by Arabic and Asian languages. Full justification is performed by altering the spacings between words, or between words and letters, or adjusting space and letter widths (see under GLYPH SCALING) until the text fits the line. Excess words are moved to the next line (see WORD-WRAP) or broken with a hyphen where necessary (see HYPHENATION). All WORD PROCESSORS and DESKTOP PUBLISHING programs, but not simple TEXT EDITORS, can perform justification automatically. See also MICROJUSTIFICATION, OPTICAL MARGIN ADJUSTMENT.

just-in-time 1 Any operation that is performed no sooner than it needs to be. For example a just-in-time reordering system in manufacturing employs computers to order new parts just before they are required, to keep stock levels to a minimum.

2 (JIT) A type of COMPILER technology used especially for the JAVA language. Whenever the JAVA VIRTUAL MACHINE loads a new program's classes, a JIT compiler will translate their BYTE-CODE into NATIVE MACHINE CODE on the spot and then CACHE this machine code in memory so that the translation need not be repeated if the program is run again.

3 MICROSOFT TRANSACTION SERVER employs just-in-time INSTANTIATION, in which an object is left in memory for a short while after it has been used, in case another access to it is required immediately.

4 Whenever a RUN-TIME ERROR occurs in a debug version of a program, a just-in-time DEBUGGER presents a dialogue box, which offers the choice of terminating the program immediately, or entering the debugger with its source window showing the offending code line.

JVM Abbreviation of JAVA VIRTUAL MACHINE.

K

K6 The model number of AMD's second Pentium-compatible MICROPROCESSOR introduced in 1997 and still employed in many low-cost PCs.

kanji A Japanese CHARACTER SET, based on Chinese character forms, that is widely used in written and printed texts, and on computer displays.

katakana A Japanese CHARACTER SET, based on Chinese character forms, that is mainly used for the syllabic transcription of foreign words and phrases.

Kay, Alan (b. 1940) A visionary computer scientist who lead the Software Concepts Group at Xerox PARC in the 1970s, which developed the SMALLTALK language and pioneered both OBJECT-ORIENTED PROGRAMMING and the GRAPHICAL USER INTERFACE. Kay also devised the concept of a mobile, communicating computer he called the Dynabook, which is only now coming to fruition with the Internet-connected hand-held computer and mobile telephone.

Kbaud See KILOBAUD.

KB (Kb) Abbreviation of KILOBYTE

Kbps Abbreviation of KILOBITS per second.

KBS Abbreviation of KNOWLEDGE-BASED SYSTEM.

KDE (Kool Desktop Environment) A GRAPHICAL USER INTERFACE for GNU/Linux systems that is distributed as freeware but is based on the Qt widget set by Troll Tech which requires a licence. KDE is network-aware and can view any file tree, local or remote, in Internet URL format. It also has the ability to render HTML pages and can function as a web browser. See also CDE, GNOME, MOTIF.

Kerberos A system developed at MIT for AUTHENTICATION of network users based on the issuing of virtual tickets. A potential user of a remote network service must first log on to a dedicated Kerberos server: if the presented password is accepted, a 'ticket' will be issued into the user's browser which (until its expiry) may in turn be presented to gain admittance to the desired server. The name alludes to Cerberus the three-headed dog of Greek mythology who guarded the entrance to Hades.

Kermit A FILE TRANSFER protocol developed at Columbia University that works over both FULL-DUPLEX and HALF-DUPLEX, 7- or 8-bit serial connections, and offers recovery from transmission errors through selective retransmission. It has been somewhat eclipsed by ZMODEM and the Internet's FTP.

kernal A simple misspelling of the word KERNEL, which became institutionalized via the documentation of COMMODORE BUSINESS MACHINES computers which referred to 'kernal calls'.

kernel That part of a computer OPERATING SYSTEM which handles the most fundamental 'low-level' activities, including the allocation of memory, scheduling of THREADS and TASKS, timing functions, and sometimes the interface to crucial hardware devices such as DISK DRIVES, COMMUNICATION PORTS and NETWORKS. In many operating systems the kernel runs in a protected ADDRESS SPACE, separate from that in which user programs run, and user programs must access all resources via the operating systems APPLICATION PROGRAMMING INTERFACE routines, which in turn call the kernel.

kernel call A PROCEDURE CALL made directly to an operating system's KERNEL, usually to obtain faster performance by bypassing the routines supplied in some APPLICATION PROGRAMMING INTERFACE. Kernel calls are most often used by programs (such as telecommunications programs) that have real- time constraints, or games that employ animated 3D graphics (see for example DIRECTX). See also SYSTEM CALL, SOFTWARE INTERRUPT.

Kernel calls may be dangerous to the system in several ways: a crash in the application program that issues them may crash the whole operating system; if they bypass the operating system's resource allocation mechanisms they may deprive other important programs of, say, memory or processor time; and they strongly couple the program that uses them to a particular version of the operating system, so that it may not work after a system update. Operating systems designed for real time tasks, such as CHORUS and EPOC 32, provide a managed way for crucial programs to have direct kernel access, for example by installing a server or driver in KERNEL SPACE rather than user space.

kernel space The PROTECTED ADDRESS SPACE in which an operating system's KERNEL (and sometimes its DEVICE DRIVERS) run. User programs are normally forbidden to access kernel space except via a small set of approved KERNEL CALLS.

kernel thread A mechanism employed in many recent OPERATING SYSTEMS whereby multiple THREADS are supported in the KERNEL as well as within user programs. INTERRUPT HANDLING is greatly simplified, since DEVICE DRIVERS may be run on prioritised kernel threads, allowing time-critical user tasks (for example video or voice capture) to be briefly granted higher priority than, say, kernel disk operations.

kerning In typography, the alteration of the spacing between particular letter pairs to create a more pleasing visual impression. For example the letters VA look best when they are close enough for their bounding boxes to overlap. In lead type this required overhangs created by hand filing of the blocks, but in an electronic system kerning is performed automatically by software that refers to a stored table of pair spacings.

The term is often misused to mean the distance between all the successive letters in a text, which is properly called TRACKING. See also FEATHERING, LEADING.

key 1 A finger-operated switch employed to enter characters and commands into a computer. A typical computer KEYBOARD contains around 106 such keys, some of which perform control functions or user-assigned functions.
2 In CRYPTOGRAPHY, a piece of secret additional information that must be known in order to DECODE an encrypted message. See also PUBLIC-KEY ENCRYPTION.
3 A value that identifies one particular RECORD in a DATABASE. A key may simply be the value of a single FIELD from the record, or it might be computed as some combination of the values in several fields (possibly by applying a HASH FUNCTION). A set of keys for all the records in the database is called an INDEX.

keyboard An input device used to enter numbers, text and commands into a computer. A typical keyboard consists of one hundred or more lightly-sprung switches called KEYS fitted into a shallow tray. Most computer keyboards employ a layout that is descended indirectly from that of the manual typewriter, via the electromechanical telegraph/teletype machine, featuring a block of 52 alphanumeric characters that in English-speaking territories is arranged in QWERTY order. This block is surrounded by further keys that have application only in computing, including additional SHIFT keys called the CTRL KEY and the ALT KEY, an ESCAPE KEY, 10 or 12 FUNCTION KEYS, and often a separate NUMERIC KEYPAD arranged to mimic a desk calculator which may be used when entering long sequences of numbers.

The keyboard of IBM-compatible PCs is an intelligent device that contains its own microprocessor; this allows it to be reconfigured by software, for example to a different national layout or to an alternative layout such as the DVORAK KEYBOARD. However, the letters depicted on each key have to be physically changed by swapping their caps.

Keyboard layout has become controversial owing to the occupational disease REPETITIVE-STRAIN INJURY, which may be causally linked to typing for too long with the wrong posture. Modern ERGONOMIC KEYBOARDS position the hands, wrists and arms more naturally by splitting the alphanumeric portion into separate, angled left-hand and right-hand keypads and by tilting the keyboard away from the user.

keyboard buffer A small memory area – typically holding a few hundred characters – that temporarily stores the KEYSTROKES typed by a computer user, and from which they are removed as the computer's CPU processes them. The buffer permits the user to type faster than a particular program can accept input, and so is alternatively called a *typeahead buffer*. It is nevertheless possible for a very slow or crashed program to cause the keyboard buffer to overflow. This is signalled on many machines by a beep whenever a key is pressed.

keyboard mapping The process of changing the codes assigned to each key on a computer's KEYBOARD, and also used as a noun to mean a stored set of such keycode assignments.

keyboard shortcut See SHORTCUT.

key code A unique numeric CODE generated by each key that is pressed on a computer KEYBOARD. Key codes are not the same as ASCII codes, and are typically converted, where appropriate, into ASCII values by low-level operating system routines. Raw key codes are often intercepted by software, to detect key combinations such as <CTR+ALT+F1> that correspond to no ASCII character, and this also permits the effective layout of the keyboard to be altered by software.

key disk A removable storage medium such as a FLOPPY DISK or CD-ROM that must be present in the drive in order for the software it contains to run, even if the software has been copied onto a hard disk. Key disks are used as a method of COPYRIGHT enforcement, since any copies given away cannot be run without the original disk. Various techniques are employed to create key disks, including secret identification codes hidden in the BOOT SECTOR or other areas of the disk invisible to the user, or deliberate damage to certain sectors of the disk. See also COPY PROTECTION, DONGLE, SOFTWARE PIRACY, SOFTWARE LICENCE.

key escrow In a data security system employing PUBLIC-KEY ENCRYPTION, the entrusting of copies of the private keys to a third party so that documents can be DECRYPTED in the event of, say, their authors forgetting a password, dying or leaving the company.

key field A FIELD in a database RECORD whose values are used in the building of an INDEX.

key frame In a VIDEO COMPRESSION system such as MPEG, one of the video frames that is stored in full, whereas all the frames in between key frames are stored only as their difference (or DELTA) from the previous key frame. The essential key frames are those that contain a major change in the content (say a cut to a different scene) rather than just small movements within a scene that is mostly unchanged. The MPEG compression software automatically identifies which frames are to become key frames.

key holder In a data security system that employs PUBLIC-KEY ENCRYPTION, one of the people entrusted with the public and private keys.

keypad A small set of keys arranged for a particular task, which may form part of a larger KEYBOARD or constitute a separate device. Keypads are typically used for rapid entry of numeric data (see NUMERIC KEYPAD), for programming devices that do not required a full QWERTY keyboard, and on communications devices such as telephones and TV remote controls.

key press The action of depressing and releasing a KEY on a computer KEYBOARD. The ease of use of different USER INTERFACES is sometimes measured by comparing how many keypresses are required to execute particular operations. The keypress is also one of the fundamental events in any EVENT-DRIVEN software as produced by VISUAL BASIC or DELPHI, where it may be further decomposed into separate Key Down and Key Up events for finer control.

key recovery The ability to extract the private key and hence DECRYPT messages protected by a PUBLIC-KEY ENCRYPTION system. Some governments, including that of the USA, would like all encryption products to include a key recovery loophole for use by law enforcement agencies.

keystroke See KEY PRESS.

keyword **1** One of a fixed set of words employed in the SYNTAX of a PROGRAMMING LANGUAGE (also called a RESERVED WORD). Each language is distinguished by its own set of keywords, but some are used in many languages, including `if`, `then`, `else`, `goto` and `while`. Most languages forbid the use of a keyword as a name for a user-defined object such as a variable.

2 A word picked out as representative of the meaning of a technical document or web page, and then listed separately to assist in performing searches.

KHz (kHz) See KILOHERTZ.

Kilburn, Tom (1921–2001) A British computer scientist who designed and built one of the world's first electronic computers at Manchester University in 1948, and wrote what was probably the first true SOFTWARE, a program that was stored in a CATHODE RAY TUBE memory. Kilburn later designed the Manchester Mark 1 on which Alan TURING worked, and founded the UK's first computer science department where he remained professor until his death in 2001. See also ENIAC.

killer app An APPLICATION PROGRAM that proves so popular that it becomes a reason for buying the platform on which it runs; for example LOTUS 1-2-3 became a killer app for the IBM PC.

kill file A mechanism supported by many Usenet NEWS READER programs to allow selective reading. The kill file (sometimes called a *bozo filter*) contains a list of boring or troublesome participants in a NEWSGROUP whose postings the user does not wish to read. A kill file may reject postings solely on the name of the author, or by pattern-matching on the subject description (e.g. 'block any mention of Star Trek+regalia').

kilobaud A data rate of one thousand bits per second. See more under BAUD RATE.

kilobit 1024 BITS of data. Often abbreviated to kb, while KB is reserved for KILOBYTE.

kilobyte (KB) A unit of computer memory equal to 1024 BYTES. Confusion often arises because the prefix kilo normally means 1000 (as in kilometre) but for computing purposes 1024 was chosen because it is an integral

power of 2 (2^{10}) and thus is a round number in both BINARY NOTATION (10000000000) and HEXADECIMAL NOTATION (400h).

kilohertz (kHz) One thousand cycles per second, a unit of FREQUENCY.

kiosk A special-purpose computer designed for public access in a street or other public space, for example providing information services such as street maps or tourist guides. Kiosks intended for outdoor use are typically weather-proofed and employ a TOUCH SCREEN or MEMBRANE KEYBOARD for user input. Increasingly they employ a web browser software interface to retrieve the information from a central web server. See also AUTOMATED TELLER MACHINE.

KISS Principle Programmers' shorthand for Keep It Simple, Stupid.

Klamath The internal code-name for Intel's PENTIUM II processor series.

kludge Programmer's argot for a hasty and inelegant solution to a problem, also called a HACK.

knapsack problem Given a knapsack of unknown weight and a pile of assorted weights, choose a subset of the weights that adds up exactly to the weight of the bag. Knapsack problems, and many others with a similar structure, belong to the class of NP-HARD problems – only EXPONENTIAL-TIME ALGORITHMS are so far known to solve them. As a result, variants of the problem have been employed in PUBLIC-KEY ENCRYPTION systems. Some knapsack problems can be solved in reasonable time using CONSTRAINT LOGIC PROGRAMMING techniques.

knowledge base **1** A large database of technical hints, advice, release notes, BUG REPORTS and BUG FIXES, posted on a web site by a software manufacturer for access by users of its product, as part of its technical support operation.

2 A collection of facts about the chosen problem domain, used in conjunction with a set of inference rules in a KNOWLEDGE-BASED SYSTEM.

knowledge-based system A software system that attempts to accumulate and exploit knowledge rather than raw data. This requires a degree of understanding of the SEMANTICS of the data being handled – for example the relationship between a vendor and a customer – and this is achieved by marking up the data with some formal knowledge representation language, the result being called a knowledge base. Knowledge-based systems are employed as advanced diagnostic aids in as such diverse fields as medicine and aero-engineering.

Knowledge-based systems can be further classified into RULE-BASED SYSTEMS (also called EXPERT SYSTEMS), which codify knowledge by extracting rules that can be applied to solve new problems, and CASE BASED REASONING systems, which solve problems by comparison with an accumulated body of previous solutions. See also ARTIFICIAL INTELLIGENCE, DATA MINING.

knowledge elicitation The process of collecting the knowledge required for the practice of some human skill for use in a KNOWLEDGE-BASED SYSTEM. Typically the process involves interviewing one or more human experts using an appropriately compiled questionnaire, or analysing examples of diagnoses made by such experts. See also CASE BASED REASONING, EXPERT SYSTEM.

knowledge representation The format in which knowledge (that is, facts and rules) is stored within a KNOWLEDGE BASE. Various data structures have been tried in this role, including SEMANTIC NETS, FRAMES, BLACKBOARDS and DECISION TREES. See also KNOWLEDGE-BASED SYSTEM, ARTIFICIAL INTELLIGENCE.

Knuth, Donald (b. 1938) One of the most influential of computer scientists, and author of the monumental reference work *The Art of Computer Programming* (which is still in progress). Knuth was also the inventor of the TEX typesetting and formatting system.

Kohonen, T. A Finnish computer scientist who has been a pioneer of NEURAL NETWORK research.

Korn shell A replacement command shell for the UNIX operating system which uses the same syntax as the BOURNE SHELL but improves on it by adding a LINE EDITOR for commands and the ability to create command ALIASES.

Kylix Borland International's version of its DELPHI programming language for the LINUX operating system.

L

L1 cache See LEVEL 1 CACHE.

L2 cache See LEVEL 2 CACHE.

L2F (Layer 2 Forwarding) A protocol for creating VIRTUAL PRIVATE NETWORKS over the Internet developed by CISCO (see more under TUNNELLING PROTOCOL). Unlike the rival POINT-TO-POINT TUNNELLING PROTOCOL from Microsoft, L2F requires support in both the access server and all intervening routers, so the chosen ISP (Internet Service Provider) must offer an L2F facility. However it does provide for secure AUTHENTICATION at both tunnel endpoints, which PPTP does not.

l10n A bizarre abbreviation for LOCALIZATION, the 10 signifying the number of characters between the l and the n. See also I18N.

L*a*b* Also called CIELAB or Uniform Colour Space, a standard COLOUR SPACE defined by the CIE in 1976 to specify colours to be reproduced in subtractive media such as dyes or ink on paper. The colour of any sample can be defined relative to a standard white source by stating three coordinates in this colour space: L* (lightness, the cube root of luminance), a* (red–greenness) and b* (yellow–blueness). See also L*U*V*, CHROMATICITY, COLOUR MODEL, RGB, HSV.

label In ASSEMBLY LANGUAGE programming, a symbolic name give to a particular memory location so that jumps can be made to this name rather than to the numeric address. The advantage is that, if such a label is subsequently moved, the jump instruction does not need to be altered as it would with an absolute address. Also a symbolic name given to a location within a program written in a high-level programming language such as C, Basic or Pascal, which can be used as the destination for a GOTO statement. Most languages use a similar syntax for labels, which is to suffix the label name with a colon, for example:

```
if x > 0 then goto here
. . .
here: inc(x)
```

See also INDIRECTION.

lambda calculus A branch of mathematical logic developed by Alonzo CHURCH in the late 1930s that deals with the application of FUNCTIONS to their arguments. Like Russell and Whitehead before him, Church sought to found mathematics on a simpler basis, in his case by confining it to quantities that could be constructed by an 'effective procedure'. The pure lambda calculus therefore admits no constants (neither numbers, nor mathematical functions such as plus) and consists solely of lambda abstractions, functions, variables and applications of functions to one another. The natural numbers were to be constructed by the function that applies its first argument to its second argument n times. In the light of GODEL's result, Church abandoned the project, but the lambda calculus survives (with the addition of constants) as the basis for many of the FUNCTIONAL PROGRAMMING LANGUAGES (such as LISP) used on computers.

lambda expression A term in the LAMBDA CALCULUS which represents a mathematical FUNCTION. A lambda expression such as: $\lambda x\,y.x+y$ represents a function of two formal arguments, x and y, which when applied to actual arguments returns the term $x+y$ with x and y replaced by their actual values. See also COMBINATORY LOGIC.

LAN (Local Area Network) A system for connecting many computers together so that they can exchange and share data, where all the computers are located within the same or closely adjacent buildings. This is in contrast to a wide-area network (WAN), in which the computers are located in different cities or countries, so long distance communications technologies are needed to connect them. LANs are normally used to connect PCs together within a single office or firm, and the network cabling can be purchased from and installed by PC vendors. By far the most popular network technology for LANs is ETHERNET (which is now capable of data rates from 10 to 1000 megabits per second), followed by TOKEN RING. The most widespread LAN protocols are TCP/IP and Novell's IPX.

land-line A conventional telephone line, as opposed to a SATELLITE or other WIRELESS COMMUNICATION link.

LAN emulation (LANE) The use of a software layer to emulate local area network (LAN) protocols on top of some other carrier protocol. LANE is most often encountered to allow ETHERNET or TOKEN RING networks to be connected to a high-speed switched ASYNCHRONOUS TRANSFER MODE (ATM) network backbone, or to carry Internet TCP/IP traffic over ATM. LANE software is run inside the ATM switches to emulate the other network's protocols.

language See PROGRAMMING LANGUAGE and NATURAL LANGUAGE.

language-neutral Not tied to a particular programming language; able to be manipulated by programs written in different languages.

LAN Manager Microsoft's first attempt at a NETWORK OPERATING SYSTEM, released in 1988 as an application running under the OS/2 operating system. LAN Manager enabled basic file and printer sharing and employed the HIGH PERFORMANCE FILE SYSTEM which could also read and write MS-DOS files. Microsoft produced an OEM version called LAN Manager/X for Unix systems, IBM released its own LAN Server version and 3Com produced a portable version called 3+Open. However, LAN Manager failed to displace NOVELL NETWARE as the dominant PC networking OS, and in 1992

version 2.2 was incorporated into Windows NT as an integral part of the operating system.

Laplink A series of popular communications utilities published by the US firm Traveling Software Inc. and originally used to connect LAPTOP computers to DESKTOP PCs, hence the name. More recent versions of Laplink provide extensive file transfer, synchronization and remote control facilities between any two computers, via a variety of channels that includes serial, parallel and USB ports, and network and modem connections.

laptop The largest of the size categories applied to portable computers, so-called because they may be conveniently used balanced on the knees, but not in the hand while standing (compare with PALMTOP). The category has recently further subdivided to embrace NOTEBOOK computers (which by convention are smaller in area than an A4 magazine) and SUBNOTEBOOK computers (which are still too large to use in one hand).

Laptop computers typically consist of a CLAMSHELL style case, which opens to reveal a keyboard, with an LCD display inside the lid, and hard disk, floppy disk and CD-ROM drives. They are powered by internal rechargeable batteries that give a few hours of operation away from an electricity outlet.

large memory aware Software that is capable of exploiting Intel's PHYSICAL ADDRESS EXTENSIONS to address more than 4 gigabytes of memory when running on a Pentium Pro or later processor.

laser An acronym for Light Amplification by Stimulated Emission of Radiation, a class of optical devices that generate coherent, monochromatic light (that is, light of a very pure colour whose waves are all in step). All lasers require a source of light as input and amplify it by repeatedly passing it through a crystal or volume of gas. SOLID-STATE lasers, also called laser diodes, incorporate a LIGHT-EMITTING DIODE, which emits light when an electric current is applied; these devices are used in LASER PRINTERS, OPTICAL FIBRE networks and CD players.

laser disc A term now generally used to mean the almost obsolete 12 inch optical disc format introduced in the the early 1990s for storing video information. Makers of laser disc players included Pioneer, RCA and Sony. Strictly speaking the name could equally be applied to any form of CD, DVD or MINIDISC, all of which rely on LASERS to read the stored information.

laser printer A type of printer that employs a dry powder toner instead of liquid ink, and prints with fine resolution in black and white or colour. Similar in principle to the xerographic photocopier (Xerox machine), except that a laser beam writes the dots that compose the image directly onto the rotating light-sensitive drum.

Last In, First Out An ordering principle used both by programmers, in the form of the STACK data structure, and by many firms as a redundancy policy.

last mile See under LOCAL LOOP.

latch A digital circuit that temporarily stores one or more BITS, allowing them to be reliably read by other devices. A latch consists of a data input, a CLOCK input and an output. When the clock signal goes active, all data bits present at its input are 'latched' and transferred to the output when the clock goes inactive – the output retains its value until the clock goes active again. Latches are the universal glue of digital electronics, employed wherever signals are conducted from one device or chip to another (for example at both ends of a parallel BUS) to give the connected devices a stable set of bits to read rather than rising and falling signal voltages.

late binding In OBJECT-ORIENTED PROGRAMMING, the deferral until RUN TIME of the decision as to which object a particular METHOD call refers to. This permits the writing of POLYMORPHIC programs that can work on many different types of object, at the cost of some loss of efficiency, since extra work must be done at run time to identify the actual object of the call. For example given a call such as X.PrintFormatted, the decision as to which object X refers to would be left until the program is run, and so X might be any object of a class that possesses a PrintFormatted method. The opposite of late binding is EARLY BINDING or compile-time binding. See also BINDING.

latency **1** In communications, the delay between the start of transmission and the start of reception of a message sent across any communications link. For PACKET SWITCHING networks, latency is the time taken by a single packet to cross from sender to receiver. For network devices that BUFFER packets, latency is the delay between receiving a packet and forwarding it.
2 For a disk drive, latency is the delay from the time a HEAD arrives at the correct track till the required data rotates under the head. Faster spindle rotation reduces the latency.

LaTeX An enhanced and simplified version of the TEX document creation system.

Latin 1 An 8-bit EXTENDED ASCII character set, adopted as part of the ISO 8859 standard which adds the accented characters used in French, German and Spanish.

launch To load and execute an APPLICATION PROGRAM.

Launcher The part of the Apple Macintosh operating system MACOS which lists all the executable programs on the computer and allows them to be run by clicking with the mouse.

Lawrence Livermore National Laboratory A US government research establishment based in Fremont, California which pursues world-class work in many fields, including SUPERCOMPUTERS, thermonuclear fusion and the human genome. See also LOS ALAMOS NATIONAL LABORATORY, SANDIA NATIONAL LABORATORY.

layer **1** A section of software that collaborates with other software, information flowing between them in such a way that one can be conceived as being 'wrapped around' the other. Operating systems, for example, consist of many such software layers.
2 One of the levels in a hierarchy of abstractions used to describe a complex system such as a communications network. See for example OSI REFERENCE MODEL. A layer in this sense should exhibit most of the following properties:
• Functions that are obviously similar belong in the same layer.

• The functions in a layer may be divided into subsets, which may be bypassed if not required.

• Each layer provides well-defined services to the layer above, and receives services from the layer below.

   • Changes made to one layer should not affect the layers above and below it.

   • Interfaces between layers should be simple and standardized.

   • The number of layers should be reduced to the minimum consistent with the above.

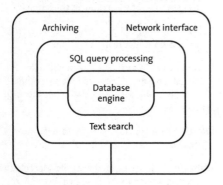

lazy A programming language that supports LAZY EVALUATION. See also STRICT.

lazy evaluation In a FUNCTIONAL PROGRAM-MING LANGUAGE, the evaluation of just so much of an expression as is required by the current context, as compared to EAGER EVALU-ATION, which always evaluates the whole expression. Lazy evaluation enables a program to manipulate ostensibly infinite objects, such as the set of all INTEGERS, because only those parts of the set actually used are ever evaluated.

LCD Abbreviation of LIQUID CRYSTAL DISPLAY.

LCP Abbreviation of LINK CONTROL PROTOCOL.

LDAP Abbreviation of LIGHTWEIGHT DIRECTORY ACCESS PROTOCOL.

lead 1 Any wire or cable used to supply electric current to a device, but particularly applied to those used for connecting audio and video equipment, and for connecting to mains power outlets.

2 In the semiconductor industry, the fine gold wires that connect the contact PADS

around the edges of an INTEGRATED CIRCUIT chip to the PINS that protrude from its PACK-AGE and make external connection with a PRINTED CIRCUIT BOARD.

leading Extra spacing introduced between the lines of a typeset document. The term derives from the days when lead strips were inserted between rows of lead type to achieve the effect.

leading spaces Spaces inserted before the first non-space character in a word. In computer processing, leading spaces may cause unwanted results, for example in a search routine that works by inspecting only the first character of each word – therefore many programs automatically strip off leading spaces and discard them when text is being input. See also TRAILING SPACES.

leading zero A zero character at the start of the representation of a number which is not strictly necessary, and does not affect its value. When displaying decimal fractions less than one, it is customary to start with a leading zero for clarity (so 0.456 rather than .456). Leading zeroes may even be added to whole numbers (for example 09) to adjust their length for tabulation (so 09 lines up with 12) or when sorting STRING representations of numbers to prevent 9 from sorting higher than 89. See also TRAILING ZERO, FORMAT STRING.

leadless chip carrier A type of integrated circuit PACKAGE that consists of a square plastic or ceramic tile with metal contact pads rather than pins. The package is fitted into a socket that consists of a matching square depression with sprung contacts. See also PIN GRID ARRAY, QUAD FLAT PACK.

leaf node In any TREE-STRUCTURED hierarchy, one of the terminal points of a branch from which there are no further descendants. See also TWIG, ROOT, TREE.

leak See under MEMORY LEAK.

leaky-bucket algorithm A class of algorithm used for FLOW CONTROL in several types of network (particularly ASYNCHRONOUS TRANSFER MODE) to combat CONGESTION. A router or switch that employs such an algorithm will queue up packets from messages that are using more than their allocated bandwidth, but the queue is of limited depth, and any packets that fall off the end are discarded. The analogy is with a bucket with a hole in its bottom, where water can leak out only at a constant rate (the allocated rate) regardless of how fast it comes in; if water comes in too fast, the bucket may overflow. See also QUALITY OF SERVICE, RESOURCE RESERVATION PROTOCOL.

learning curve A term imported from cognitive psychology that originally meant a graph of expertise against time plotted for some learning process. Such a curve starts shallow reflecting initial unfamiliarity, becomes steeper as learning progresses faster, then levels off once the task is fully learnt.

Hence a 'steep learning curve' actually means that a lot of learning is taking place very quickly, which is abused in computer jargon to mean that something is difficult to learn.

leased line A private communication line permanently connecting two sites, for which the telecom company charges a fixed monthly rental rather than the normal per-minute usage charge. Leased lines are used to implement private wide-area networks (WANs) between branches of a large company. They are also rented by ISPs who then divide and sub-let their BANDWIDTH to numerous DIAL-UP customers for Internet access.

least-recently-used algorithm (LRU algorthim) An ALGORITHM often used in space or memory management problems (including human dwellings). To make more room when space runs out, discard the item that has remained unused for longest.

least significant bit The rightmost bit in the binary representation of a number. In the byte 10101100 the least significant bit is 0. So called because its value contributes least to the value of the whole.

LED (light-emitting diode) A SOLID-STATE electronic device that emits light when an electric current passes through it, via an efficient quantum process that (unlike a conventional light-bulb) generates little heat. LEDs made from different combinations of SEMICONDUCTOR materials can be made to emit light at various frequencies in the visible and infra-red ranges. Cheap red LEDs are used as power indicator lights on all kinds of electrical equipment, while infra-red LEDs are used in remote-control handsets.

LED printer An alternative to the LASER PRINTER in which, rather than a scanning laser head writing dots onto the photosensitive drum, a row of fixed light-emitting diodes (LEDs) is employed for the purpose. LED printers were sold by Alps, Kyocera, Panasonic and Okidata in the early 1990s, but they are now rare as laser printers have become cheaper, faster and more reliable.

legacy code A collection of APPLICATION PROGRAMS inherited from some now-replaced computing system, perhaps written in obsolete languages, for obsolete hardware, or by authors who no longer work for the company. See also LEGACY DATABASE, WRAPPER.

legacy database A computer database inherited from an older computer system, often one hosted on a MAINFRAME or MINICOMPUTER system, that contains too much valuable data to be discarded and so must be converted to run on a newer system. See also IMPORT.

Lempel–Ziv compression (LZ compression) A method that lies behind many of the most widely used COMPRESSION algorithms for textual data, discovered by Jacob Ziv and Abraham Lempel in 1977–78.

LZ compression works by adding any repeated patterns it encounters in the data to an ever-growing dictionary, and then replacing any future occurrence of that pattern by its dictionary position. For typical human languages this method may compress text to as little as 25–30% of its size, though it is less efficient on graphical material.

Lempel–Ziv Welch compression See LZW COMPRESSION.

letter-quality printing (LQ) A printing mode supported by many types of PRINTER, that is of higher quality than the faster but less visually pleasing DRAFT-MODE.

Level 1 cache (L1 cache) A processor CACHE that is fabricated on the same chip as the processor itself. Modern microprocessors typically have 64 kilobytes or more of on-chip cache memory, and for high performance systems this communicates not directly with main memory but the much larger off-chip LEVEL 2 CACHE.

Level 2 cache (L2 cache) A processor CACHE which is not integrated onto the same chip as the processor itself, but stores data that is accessed by an on-chip LEVEL 1 CACHE. For maximum performance, modern microprocessors often incorporate a dedicated ultra-wide memory BUS to access the Level 2 cache. See also STORAGE HIERARCHY, CACHE COHERENCY.

level-sensitive See under TRANSITION.

level-triggered A type of electronic LOGIC in which either the high or the low signal voltage is designated as the 'on' state (see ACTIVE-HIGH) and entering this state constitutes an EVENT that can be used to initiate some operation. Compare this with EDGE-TRIGGERED logic in which the TRANSITION from high to low or vice versa is regarded as the event.

lex To analyse a text into LEXEMES, which are fundamental units of meaning such as words and phrases. See also LEXICAL ANALYSIS.

lexeme 1 In linguistics, the smallest meaningful unit of any language, whose meaning is lost if it is broken down any further. A lexeme might be a word, or a prefix or suffix. See also PHONEME.
  2 In a computer programming language, the smallest permissible statements of the language, namely all its individual KEYWORDS and punctuation symbols, plus any user-defined IDENTIFIERS, LITERAL strings and numbers. See also LEXICAL ANALYSIS, GRAMMAR.

lexical analyser The section of a language COMPILER that breaks down the source program into meaningful words or LEXEMES.

lexical analysis One of the earliest phases in the COMPILATION of a computer program, in which the SOURCE text of the program is split up into separate words called TOKENS or LEXEMES, which are then classified into RESERVED WORDS of the language, literal constants, and programmer-created IDENTIFIERS. Lexical analysis is simplified by the severe restrictions that most programming languages place on the formation of names (for example the almost universal rule that they may not contain spaces). The LEXICAL ANALYSER and the PARSER are the parts of a compiler that implement the SYNTAX of the language.

lexical scope The SCOPE rule employed by most compiled BLOCK STRUCTURED programming languages, under which the scope of every IDENTIFIER is governed solely by its location within the program's text, extending from the place where it is first declared to the end of its innermost surrounding block. See also DYNAMIC SCOPE, FORWARD DECLARATION, PROCEDURE DECLARATION, FUNCTION DECLARATION.

lexicon A vocabulary: the set of all words that have meaning in some language system, such as a PROGRAMMING LANGUAGE.

LHA A FILE COMPRESSION utility for MS-DOS computers, called LHARC in its earlier manifestations.

LHARC See under LHA.

lhz The FILENAME EXTENSION of ARCHIVE files compressed using the LHA utility.

library A collection of commonly used routines that may be called from within newly written programs to save having to write the routines again. Libraries of specialized functions for, say, graphics, mathematics or communications, are crucial to the modern program development process. If programmers had to reinvent everything from scratch, there would be very little software in the world.

Library routines kept in source code form may be incorporated into a new program using an INCLUDE statement that makes a compiler treat library code as if it were part of the new source file. When, as is more usual, libraries are kept in machine code form, it is the job of a LINKER program, following compilation, to discover which routines in the new program are EXTERNAL (i.e. not defined within the new source file), to find their code in the library and to correctly incorporate it into the new program's machine code.

license manager A type of management software used on computer NETWORKS that allocates to network users the licences purchased for an application that allow the software to run on their workstations. For example a company with many network users might purchase a licence for program X for only 50 users, and once 50 people are using the software the license manager will prevent anyone else from using it.

LIF Abbreviation of LOW-INSERTION FORCE.

life-cycle The succession of phases required to accomplish any engineering project, whether hardware or software, which can be summed up as SPECIFICATION, DESIGN, IMPLEMENTATION, TESTING, DEPLOYMENT and MAINTENANCE. See also WATERFALL MODEL, SPIRAL MODEL.

Life, Game of An early computer game devised by the British mathematician John Conway in 1970, which is an animated graphical representation of a simple two-dimensional CELLULAR AUTOMATON. On a rectangular grid of cells, three simple rules determine whether any given cell will live or die: a dead cell with precisely three living neighbours comes to life; a live cell with less than two, or more than three, living neighbours dies; no other cells change. From these rules extraordinarily complex behaviours emerge, resembling living processes (hence the name) such as the growth of bacteria or animals – populations fluctuate wildly, stable configurations emerge, and forms appear that can move across the grid.

LIFO Abbreviation of LAST IN, FIRST OUT.

ligature In typography, a pair of characters that are fused into a single character, such as æ.

light-emitting diode See LED.

light pen A POINTING DEVICE consisting of a light-sensitive pen, connected by a wire to a computer, that may be pointed at the monitor screen to direct movement of the CURSOR. It has been largely replaced by the MOUSE, the TOUCH SCREEN or the GRAPHICS TABLET.

Lightweight Directory Access Protocol (LDAP) A protocol for accessing on-line DIRECTORY SERVICES defined by the INTERNET ENGINEERING TASK FORCE to simplify the implementation of x.500 directories, whose original DAP protocol was too complex for use within web browsers running on PCs. LDAP defines a simple mechanism for updating and searching directories over a TCP/IP connection, and is now supported by many software products, including Microsoft's WINDOWS 2000.

LDAP directory entries are arranged into a hierarchy along geographical and organizational boundaries, with country at the top of the tree, then national organizations, branches, individual people and finally resources such as computers, printers and documents. Each entry may contain name, address, email addresses, pictures and, in the case of resources, hardware details.

lightweight process Also called a THREAD in many systems, a PROCESS that has its own STACK but shares its ADDRESS SPACE and GLOBAL data with other processes.

Limbo The programming language provided in Lucent's INFERNO operating system, which supports concurrency via threads and communication channels, and provides high-level data structures such as lists and TUPLES that are useful in communications-oriented programming tasks.

limited-vocabulary recognition A branch of VOICE RECOGNITION that confines itself to a restricted vocabulary of commands for a particular application domain. Such a restriction permits fast and reliable REAL TIME recognition, using a stored dictionary of sounds, with modest processing requirements that make it suitable for mobile telephones or for production line equipment such as post-office sorting systems.

Linda A CONCURRENT PROGRAMMING LANGUAGE, invented in 1982 by David Gelernter at New York University, Stonybrook, that runs only on SHARED-MEMORY MULTIPROCESSORS. Linda is a conceptually simple language consisting of just six statements, and hence it is normally implemented as an extension to some other language such as C, C++ or ADA. It works by maintaining a pool of data items called a TUPLE space, from which any processor may fish out an item, do some processing on it and then put it back.

linear 1 Literally, having the form of a straight line.
2 In mathematics, an expression or function containing no powers greater than the first, so called because the GRAPH of such a function is a straight line.
3 In electronics, a circuit whose output is strictly proportional to its input, so that a graphical plot of output against input is a straight line.

linear address space Computer memory that is organized into a single contiguous sequence of addresses, rather than a SEG-MENTED ADDRESS SPACE.

linear predictive coding (LPC) A SIGNAL PROCESSING algorithm employed to compress voice data with little loss of information. It works by outputting a list of coefficients for a linear equation that predicts the FREQUENCY spectrum of each short interval of speech (for example one hundredth of a second) based on the coefficients from previous samples. The result is a stream of FLOATING-POINT values. See also AUDIO COMPRESSION, ADAPTIVE PULSE CODE MODULATION, ATRAC.

linear programming A mathematical technique for solving OPTIMIZATION problems involving many variables. Linear programming is a well-studied area because the class of problems it can solve include many of the most difficult and industrially-important ones, such as scheduling tasks in a complex manufacturing process or determining the flow of fluids through pipe networks.

A linear program is a set of variables related by equations called CONSTRAINTS, together with an 'objective function' that relates just those variables whose values are to be optimized within the given constraints – in an industrial example 'throughput' might be maximized, or 'cost' and 'wastage' minimized. The constraining equations must all be linear (hence the name): that is, no variable must be raised to a power greater than 1. With just two variables, each constraint can be represented as a straight line that divides the plane in two so that the desired solution must lie on one side or the other. After plotting the various constraints, the intersection of all their lines outlines a convex region called a SIMPLEX, which forms the basis of an algorithm to find the optimum solution.

The *simplex method* considers the objective function as another line, of known slope but unknown position. Sliding this line about while maintaining its slope will eventually cause it to touch one corner of the simplex, which is the desired optimum solution. For more than two variables the same principles apply, but depicted by planes and solids in a multi-dimensional space, hard for humans to visualize but possible for a computer to calculate.

linear search The simplest possible search ALGORITHM, which involves traversing the data sequentially, comparing each in turn with the sought value. Its running time is directly proportional to the number of items to be searched. See also BINARY SEARCH.

line editor A simple type of TEXT EDITOR that was prevalent in the early days of computing before the widespread availability of CURSOR-ADDRESSABLE TERMINALS, and which may still be encountered today in some COMMAND LINE based online systems. Examples include the Unix editor VI and the MS-DOS editor EDLIN. To alter a piece of text, the user types in commands that identify in which line the alteration is to be made, followed by the change to be made. For example a typo such as 'tehre' for 'there' in line 203 might be corrected with a command such as:

```
s203 teh/the
```

where the s is an abbreviation for the command 'substitute'. The text can be read by typing a command such as 1100-200 to list lines 100 through 200 to the screen.

With dozens of commands to learn, line editors are deeply counter-intuitive and pose formidable learning problems, but they are surprisingly rapid to use once learned. They are also amenable to non-interactive, automated use (for example from a BATCH FILE) in which the user supplies the name of one or more text files to edit and a command file containing the operations to perform. For instance vi is still often used by Unix programmers from a command script to perform bulk file operations, though few people would choose to write a novel with it. See also WORD PROCESSOR, EMACS.

line-end character Also called END OF LINE or NEWLINE, a character defined as signifying to computer software the end of a line of text. There is no universally agreed standard for line-end characters, but the CARRIAGE RETURN (ASCII code 13) or LINE FEED (ASCII code 10) characters, or a sequence of the two, are widely used in TEXT FILES under most operating systems. The proprietary file formats employed by many word processors sometimes use line-end characters other than these, so such documents appear completely jumbled if viewed in a plain ASCII text editor.

line feed, linefeed (LF) ASCII character 10, originally used as a control code to make a printer advance its paper by one line. A separate code, ASCII 13 or CARRIAGE RETURN was used to return the print head to the left margin, and so two codes, a carriage return followed by a line feed, were needed to start a new line. This usage still survives in the TEXT FILE formats of much MS-DOS and Windows software.

line noise Spurious information introduced into a communications line, for example by interference from stray electrical and magnetic fields, or by random thermal effects. The term is often used in particular to describe spurious characters received via a serial MODEM link caused by such NOISE. See also SIGNAL-TO-NOISE RATIO.

line orientation The direction in which text flows within a line written in a particular human language script. For example English is normally written with a left-to-right orientation, Arabic with right-to-left, while Japanese employs either top-to-bottom or left-to-right. See also CHARACTER ORIENTATION, OPEN-TYPE, UNICODE.

line printer A type of printer used for low-quality, high-speed output that prints a whole line of characters in a single operation, rather than by moving a scanning head as in a LASER PRINTER or INKJET PRINTER. Line printers are typically employed in MAINFRAME installations for listing the contents of large databases.

line wrap See under WORD-WRAP.

Lingo The OBJECT-ORIENTED SCRIPTING LANGUAGE that is built into Macromedia's DIRECTOR multimedia authoring program.

linguistics The scientific study of language. The results of linguistic studies have relevance to many aspects of computing, including VOICE RECOGNITION, ARTIFICIAL INTELLIGENCE and particularly in the construction of new PROGRAMMING LANGUAGES.

link **1** In communications, any connection between a sender and a receiver over which data flows.
2 On the Internet, an address embedded in a WEB PAGE which, when activated by a mouse click, causes the BROWSER to jump to a different page.
3 In programming, the act of joining together a number of compiled code modules, libraries and other components to form a single executable file.

Link Control Protocol (LCP) A protocol that forms part of the PPP protocol suite for accessing the INTERNET over a SERIAL link. The job of LCP is the initial establishment, configuring and testing of such a link, after which it hands over to one of the NETWORK CONTROL PROTOCOLS.

linked list A sequence of data items each of which points to the next in the list. A list is built from NODES, each of which contains one data item and a POINTER to the next node. The linked list is an important data structure in computer programming, which offers several notable virtues: a new item can be inserted at any point without having to move all the others along as in an ARRAY; it can grow to any size (which need not be specified at compile time); and its items may be of various data types. The disadvantages are that the pointers constitute a significant memory overhead, and accessing any element after the first involves traversing the whole list to that point, which is slower than directly accessing an array element. The linked list is the fundamental data structure manipulated by programming languages of the LISP and PROLOG families.

linker A program that takes a collection of OBJECT CODE modules (perhaps produced using several different COMPILERS and ASSEMBLERS) and combines them, together with any required libraries, into a single executable file. In a modern INTEGRATED DEVELOPMENT ENVIRONMENT the activity of the linker may not be visible as a separate stage, but may be concealed behind a menu option called 'make' or 'build'. In traditional command-line programming environments, the linker is normally invoked after the compiler via a script or batch file.

The modern tendency toward writing programs as a large number of small modules makes great demands on linkers, which have to resolve not only references to LIBRARY routines, but also references between program modules. They achieve this by using the

SYMBOL TABLES that compilers and assemblers produce: these are separate files that list all the routines defined within each module. A *smart* linker is one that links in the code for just those library routines that are actually called by a program (rather than incorporating the whole library), which reduces the size of the final executable file.

link level A less formal synonym for DATA LINK LAYER.

link-support layer One of the components of Novell's ODI network driver standard.

Linotype A principal manufacturer of hot-metal, phototypesetting and now imagesetting equipment, notably its Linotron range. See more under TYPESETTER.

LINPACK Originally a library of linear algebra routines written in FORTRAN by Jack Dongarra. Now best known as a BENCHMARK suite derived from those same routines which is widely respected as a test of the FLOATING-POINT performance of scientific processors.

lint A programmers' utility supplied with the Unix operating system that checks a C program for errors prior to compilation. It not only finds syntax errors and mismatches between source files, but also warns over matters such as variables that are declared but not used. The name is a joking allusion to picking bits of lint off a sweater.

Linux A UNIX-compatible operating system KERNEL originally written by the Norwegian programmer Linus TORVALDS (hence the name, from 'Linus Unix'), that has become the basis of a huge free software project to which thousands of programmers contribute via the Internet. Linux supports almost all the most advanced features of Unix, including MULTI-TASKING with multiprocessor support, VIRTUAL MEMORY, shared libraries, demand loading of DEVICE DRIVERS, and TCP/IP networking.

Linux, along with its source code, may be downloaded free of charge from the Internet under the terms of the GNU public licence. There are also many commercial distributions that are typically bundled together with large collections of GNU and other utilities and applications and sold on a CD-ROM for a modest fee. The most widely used distributions include Red Hat, Caldera, Debian, and Mandrake. The latest version of the Linux kernel is

2.2, which is available for Intel, Sun SPARC and ULTRASPARC, DEC ALPHA, Motorola 68K family and POWERPC-based computers.

liquid crystal display (LCD) A type of VDU that is flat and consumes little power compared to the CATHODE RAY TUBE, and is hence widely used in portable and battery operated equipment, including all mobile telephones, laptops and pocket computers.

The operation of an LCD display depends on passing polarized light through a thin film of a viscous liquid that has semi-crystalline properties. Applying a small voltage to this material changes the orientation of its long molecules, which in turn twists the plane of polarization of the transmitted light. When viewed through a polaroid filter, this results in dark or light areas (see also SUPERTWIST). By adding suitable colour filters an RGB display, functionally similar to a cathode ray tube, can be constructed.

LCD displays that employ a separate TRAN-SISTOR switch behind each individual pixel (so-called ACTIVE MATRIX DISPLAYS) are more expensive, but have better colour saturation and contrast, than PASSIVE MATRIX DISPLAYS, in which transistors are deployed only around the edges, and pixels are created by the intersection of the thin-film wires that join them.

Lisa Apple's first attempt to build a personal computer with a GRAPHICAL USER INTERFACE, launched in 1983 and loosely based on ideas pioneered by the XEROX STAR. Lisa was too expensive to be a commercial success, and lacked any significant software base, but it tested the concepts that lead to the successful MACINTOSH two years later.

Lisp (LISt Processing language) The first programming language to be designed specifically for symbolic, rather than numeric, computation, invented in 1957 by John MCCA-RTHY at MIT. Variants and descendants of Lisp provided the backbone of ARTIFICIAL INTELLI-GENCE research for many years, but the language has never become important in commercial programming because to achieve adequate performance it demanded more memory and processing power than was available until the late 1990s. Though Lisp was originally an INTERPRETED language, most modern dialects are COMPILED, while retaining an interactive programming environment.

Lisp is a conceptually simple and elegant language, in which all programs are expressions that return values, and RECURSION is preferred to ITERATION. It is based around three fundamental operations that may be performed on LISTS of data items: extracting the 'head' or first item from a list; returning the 'tail' (i.e. the rest of the list); and constructing a new list. Lisp employs a bracketed PREFIX SYNTAX where, say, (myfunc a b) means 'apply myfunc to the arguments a and b'. Since such FUNCTION CALLS are themselves just lists, Lisp programs can manipulate other Lisp programs as data, which is the root of its popularity for artificial intelligence applications.

list 1 On the INTERNET, shorthand for MAILING LIST.

2 In programming, shorthand for the LINKED LIST data structure.

list box A visual component employed in most GRAPHICAL USER INTERFACES, which is presented whenever the user is required to choose between one of a limited set of parameters, for example choosing which font to apply in a word processor. A list box consists of a vertical list of items that can be scrolled up and down using a SCROLLBAR; items in the list are selected by clicking on them, usually with a MOUSE. See also COMBO BOX, TEXT BOX, EDIT BOX.

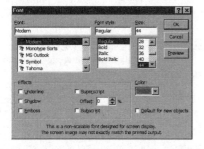

list management The process of collecting and selling lists of names, usually for the purposes of direct marketing. Computer systems for list management employ special software for sorting and deduplicating the lists of names, a difficult task since (unless told otherwise) to a computer Mr. John Doe, John Doe and Doe, John are all different entries. See also DEDUPE, DATA CLEANSING.

list processing Computation using the LINKED LIST as the primary data structure. Lists can be made to stand in for any of the major data structures – ARRAYS, RECORDS, TREES, STACKS and QUEUES – and they offer great economy of expression using just a handful of manipulation operators. Languages such as LISP and PROLOG support list operations as a built-in feature, but lists can be implemented in almost any language as library routines or COLLECTION classes.

Listserv A popular LIST SERVER program.

list server A type of Internet server that broadcasts email messages to all the members of a MAILING LIST. Every message and every reply is sent to all members, providing a NEWSGROUP-like discussion forum while requiring only an email account rather than full Internet access. Listserv and Majordomo are the most widely used list servers.

literal A constant value that is stated explicitly in the text of a program and which cannot change when the program is run, in contrast to a named variable or other symbolic reference whose underlying value may change. A literal may be of any data type, so 28, "Penguin" and [dog,cat,pig] might be examples of a literal number, string and list.

lithium ion battery A type of rechargeable battery widely employed in notebook and laptop computers for its favourable properties, which include holding 50% more charge by volume and 80% more by weight than the NICKEL METAL HYDRIDE CELL while also having a lower self-discharge rate and being free from the MEMORY EFFECT. Its disadvantage is that the lithium metal it contains is highly reactive and inflammable, and so requires great care in disposal.

lithography 1 Any method of printing that works by creating images on a flat (rather than raised or engraved) surface, by causing different areas to attract or repel the ink.

2 In the SEMICONDUCTOR industry, the process used to create INTEGRATED CIRCUITS by coating a silicon wafer with a light-sensitive varnish and then exposing it to light through a MASK that depicts the desired circuit layout.

little-endian Said of any computer memory addressing scheme in which multi-byte data words are stored so that their least significant byte is stored at the lowest address: that is, data is stored 'small end' first. Intel microprocessors, DEC's PDP-11 and VAX families of minicomputers are little-endian. See also BIG-ENDIAN, ENDIANISM.

livelock A condition in which each of two or more concurrent processes changes its state in response to the other, so they become stuck in an endless loop where none has stopped but none can perform useful work. The situation differs from DEADLOCK in that the processes are running rather than waiting, and so are consuming processor time. If deadlock resembles two people stuck in the same narrow doorway, then livelock resembles people chasing each other around a revolving door.

LiveMotion An animated graphics authoring program created by Adobe Systems as an attempt to counter MacroMedia's highly successful FLASH product. LiveMotion supports more bitmapped features than Flash does, and allows shading, gradient and glow effects, at the cost of larger file sizes. It can output files in various formats including Flash's SWF format, SVG and HTML.

live video A stream of video information produced by a camera, rather than from a recording.

LLC (Logical Link Control) The higher of the two sublayers into which the DATA LINK LAYER of the OSI REFERENCE MODEL for networks has been split by the IEEE 802.2 standard. The LLC sublayer controls the flow of DATA PACKETS and handles ERROR CHECKING and retransmission of corrupted packets, while the lower MEDIA ACCESS CONTROL (MAC) sublayer is responsible for network access and sharing of the medium, for example by TOKEN passing or COLLISION-DETECTION.

LLNL Abbreviation of LAWRENCE LIVERMORE NATIONAL LABORATORY.

LMA See LARGE MEMORY AWARE.

load **1** *n.* The percentage of a computer's processing capacity that is being used by its current tasks. See also LOAD BALANCING.
2 *v.* To copy binary information from some external storage device such as a DISK DRIVE into a computer's MAIN MEMORY. See also LOAD/STORE ARCHITECTURE.

load balancing The task of fairly sharing the workload between several processors connected by a network, or within a PARALLEL or SYMMETRIC MULTIPROCESSOR computer.

loader A small program whose function is to LOAD another program or set of DATA.

load/store architecture A processor architecture, most often implemented in RISC designs, in which all memory data must be brought into a REGISTER before it is operated on, and must be written back to memory afterwards: that is, no instruction is allowed to operate directly on the data at a memory location.

local Effective, meaningful or available only within a particular computer, program or process. The opposite of GLOBAL.

Local Area Network See LAN.

local bus A BUS that connects a computer's processor to its main memory and which, for maximum speed, is constructed directly on the computer's motherboard. A local bus may contain EXPANSION SLOTS for adding EXPANSION CARDS.

Most current personal computers employ proprietary designs for their local buses, the most widely used being the PCI BUS employed both by IBM-COMPATIBLE PCs and some models of the Apple MACINTOSH – the VESA LOCAL BUS may still be found in some older PCs. Portable computers typically employ a proprietary local bus that has no expansion slots, instead using PC CARD slots for expansion.

locale **1** A geographical region that shares a particular set of date, time, language and character code conventions, defined for purposes of INTERNATIONALIZING software products, for example in WINDOWS or the UNICODE system.
2 In some programming languages, a type of module or private NAMESPACE.

localhost A dummy DOMAIN NAME given to an Internet server, which refers to the server itself: it resolves to the reserved IP address 127.0.0.1 and is often used by LOOPBACK diagnostic utilities that test whether the server is operating correctly. Localhost is often quoted in HTML pages and other web SCRIPTS to identify resources located on the client machine on which the script is running.

localization Adapting a hardware or software product for sale in a foreign market. This typically involves translating all the software prompts and messages, HELP SCREENS and documentation into the local language, adapting the keyboard and display to take account of that language's CHARACTER SET and orientation (see for example UNICODE, KANJI, KATAKANA), and the appropriate currency and date formats. Modern operating systems such as WINDOWS increasingly include support for this level of localization through a set of LOCALES, which can simply be selected from a list.

It may also be necessary to modify hardware for the local power supply characteristics and prevailing climate – by providing measures against, say, excessive humidity or against sand ingress.

local loop The telecommunications industry term for those sections of the public telephone system that join individual subscribers' homes to their local exchange. Also referred to as the *last mile* because that is roughly the average length of the cables involved. The word loop refers to the completion of an electrical circuit to the exchange whenever the telephone is in use. See also ADSL, DIGITAL SUBSCRIBER LINE.

local loopback address The special IP ADDRESS 127.0.0.1, reserved by the Internet Protocol (IP) for any HOST to send messages to itself.

local memory Memory that is directly connected to a particular computer processor, in contrast to memory attached to a different processor (in a multi-processor system), installed in a peripheral device or in a remote computer connected by a network.

local procedure call (LPC) A PROCEDURE CALL made to a routine that is stored in the same ADDRESS SPACE as the calling routine, in contrast to a REMOTE PROCEDURE CALL.

local variable A VARIABLE defined, used and visible only within the body of a procedure or function, and which retains its value only for the duration of each CALL to that procedure. Within different procedures, different local variables may be declared with the same name, which eases the task of finding unique names, and avoids a whole class of errors in which a GLOBAL VARIABLE is inadvertently altered by the wrong procedure. See also SCOPE.

location transparent Any resource or process that behaves in the same way regardless of where it is located – for example, whether it is stored on the local machine or on a different network node.

lock A software object, possession of which grants exclusive access to some resource such as a FILE, a PROCESSOR or a BUS in the face of competition from other potential users of that resource. Locking is absolutely essential in any CONCURRENT system to prevent the problems of inconsistency that arise if one agent overwrites the changes just made by another before they can be made permanent. The absence of locking code is the principal difference between the single-user and multi-user versions of many software applications. See also FILE LOCKING, FILE SHARING, LOCK MANAGER, MUTEX, CAPABILITY, CONTENTION.

locked up The condition where a software CRASH has frozen a computer's keyboard preventing further input. See HANG.

lock manager A component employed in multiuser DATABASE MANAGEMENT SYSTEMS and in the operating system of MULTIUSER or MULTITASKING computers, which is responsible for the locking and unlocking of memory, disks, files and other resources to permit safe shared access to them by different processes (see more under FILE LOCKING). In MULTIPROCESSOR computers, the lock manager regulates the access of the different processors to all the system's resources. In MASSIVELY PARALLEL computer architectures, the design and performance of the lock manager can become a crucial issue, since so much time is spent executing it. A lock manager may be a single centralized service, but in networked systems it is frequently distributed over many machines.

log **1** A file in which the output of some monitoring process is stored. For example a telephony program might store the number of each phonecall made in a log, while a WEB SERVER often logs each page request it receives. See also JOURNAL.

2 In mathematics, an abbreviation for LOGARITHM or LOGARITHMIC.

logarithm The logarithm of a number is the power to which a fixed number, called the base of the logarithm, must be raised to obtain the given number. So for example, since $10^{3.5} =$

3162 then the logarithm of 3162 to the base 10 (written $\log_{10}3162$) is 3.5. Tables of base 10 logarithms used to be employed to simplify multiplication and division, because to multiply two numbers one can add their logarithms. The calculation of log tables was one of the important spurs to the invention of the mechanical computer (for example BABBAGE's difference engine).

logarithmic Any type of proportionality that involves the LOGARITHM of some quantity, that is, one that can be described by a curve of the form $y = \log(x)$. A logarithmic curve has the property of starting off steeply but levelling off at high values of x; that is, it is the exact inverse of EXPONENTIAL. Logarithmic scales can be useful as compact representations for large ranges: for example historical time can be 'telescoped' by plotting along a logarithmic axis on which the last 10 years occupies the same amount of space as the previous 100 years, the 1000 years before that, and so on.

log file A file of data written automatically by some monitoring software application, for example to record disk transactions, or error events. See also DATA LOGGING.

logic 1 Those branches of philosophy that investigate human reasoning in the abstract: that is, the way that conclusions may be properly drawn from premises without considering their meaning or content.

2 In mathematics, a formal system that proceeds from a set of AXIOMS by applying rules of inference to derive new results or theorems. See also FORMAL LOGIC, CALCULUS, PROPOSITIONAL CALCULUS, PREDICATE CALCULUS.

3 In computer engineering, a shorthand term that describes any kind of LOGIC GATE or LOGIC CHIP used to implement some computing function in hardware.

4 In computer programming, a type of calculation that applies the rules of BOOLEAN ALGEBRA to variables that may only take one of the truth values, true or false.

logical 1 Concerning, or used in, the practice of LOGIC. Following from a valid argument in logic.

2 Conceptual or virtual, as opposed to PHYSICAL or actual. This sense is much used in computing. For example, a LOGICAL ADDRESS is an address in a VIRTUAL MEMORY system, that need not correspond to any actual memory

chip; a logical DISK DRIVE may be merely one of several partitions on a single physical drive.

logical address In a system that employs VIRTUAL MEMORY, any address that does not correspond to a real memory location and which must therefore be converted to a PHYSICAL ADDRESS by the MEMORY MANAGER before its contents can be accessed.

Logical Link Control See LLC.

logical shift A type of processor instruction that moves all the bits making up a binary WORD one or more places to the left or right. Bits that move off the end of the word are discarded, and zeroes are introduced to fill the vacated positions. Unlike the otherwise similar ARITHMETIC SHIFT operations, logical shifts do not preserve the word's sign – they treat the word as a string of bits rather than as a number, and are therefore useful for manipulating BIT MASKS (especially in BITMAPPED GRAPHICS) rather than for calculation. See also ROTATE.

logical-to-physical translation The process of transforming a VIRTUAL address (or other parameter) used internally by a computer into an actual quantity that will be recognized by an external device. This takes place, for example, within the MEMORY MANAGEMENT UNIT of a computer with VIRTUAL MEMORY, or within an IDE hard disk CONTROLLER; in both cases a notional LOGICAL ADDRESS employed within the software is finally converted to a real memory location or disk sector address.

logic analyser An instrument (often based around an oscilloscope) that may be used to study the shape and timing of the signals in an electronic circuit by inserting PROBES to make contact with the conductors of interest.

logic board An alternative name for a MOTHERBOARD.

logic bomb A section of secret program code, hidden within a BESPOKE computer application by a hostile programmer, which will disable that application on a certain date, or when a certain condition is fulfilled (for example if that programmer's name is removed from the payroll). Logic bombs have been employed for the purposes of revenge or blackmail, and are now declared to be illegal, constituting a form of criminal damage. See also VIRUS, TROJAN HORSE.

logic chip 1 A generic term for all the integrated circuits that implement BOOLEAN LOGIC function in hardware. It is most often applied to the many varieties of TTL chip.

2 More loosely, any VLSI chip that implements various key peripheral functions (such as DRAM REFRESH and BUS control) for a particular microprocessor such as the Intel PENTIUM. Such chips are employed by PC manufacturers to reduce the overall chip-count and hence the cost of a system. See more under SYSTEM CHIP SET.

logic gate The fundamental component of a digital computer. A type of electronic circuit that accepts one or more binary-valued inputs, and outputs some BOOLEAN function of their values. Physically the input and output values of a logic gate are two distinct voltages, and the gate itself is a configuration of TRANSISTORS that switches these voltages in an appropriate fashion. In the design of computer circuits, these voltages are interpreted as logical truth values, so 0 volts might stand for False and +5 volts for True.

The principal types of logic gate are the AND gate, the OR gate and the NOT gate or INVERTER. The behaviour of any logic gate can be described by constructing its TRUTH TABLE, which lists the outputs for every possible combination of inputs. For example the truth table for an AND gate is:

A	B	A&B
F	F	F
F	T	F
T	F	F
T	T	T

where T represents True and F represents False.

The gate will only ever output True if both input A *and* input B are True, hence the name. In practice semiconductor engineers seldom employ all three of the AND, OR and NOT gate circuits as such, because all these functions can be synthesized as combinations of a single circuit type – typically a NAND (ie. NOT AND) or NOR (NOT OR) gate – and such an approach greatly simplifies the process of automated circuit layout.

logic probe An electronic instrument used in testing and fault diagnosis whose fine probes can be brought into contact with the pins and junctions of a circuit to measure voltages and examine wave-forms. Semiconductor manufacturers employ logic probes so fine that they can test the INTEGRATED CIRCUITS on a finished WAFER by applying voltages to the various devices and measuring their response. Coarser probes connected to an oscilloscope are employed to test PRINTED CIRCUIT BOARDS while they are running.

logic programming A model of computation based on SYMBOLIC LOGIC (to be more precise first-order PREDICATE CALCULUS) in which a program consists of a collection of facts about, and relationships between, various objects. Computation then proceeds by asking questions, which are answered by logical inference from these facts. This procedure differs sharply from orthodox PROCEDURAL LANGUAGE programming via step-by-step ALGORITHMS, in particular because logic programs (in theory at least) are not concerned with the order in which the facts are arranged, and can tolerate ambiguity since questions may receive multiple answers. Logic programming is particularly expressive when applied to conceptual data, as in an EXPERT SYSTEM or a language PARSER.

The best-known logic programming language is PROLOG which is based on a restricted form of predicate calculus called clausal form in which each clause is an implied CONJUNCTION, and there is an implied DISJUNCTION between separate clauses, so that the two clauses:

```
animal(X), male(X)

animal(X), female(X)
```

can be interpreted as 'X is an animal AND X is male, OR, X is an animal AND X is female'. See also HORN CLAUSE, CONSTRAINT LOGIC PROGRAMMING.

login, log in Another term for LOG ON.

log/linear A type of GRAPH in which one AXIS is LOGARITHMIC and the other is LINEAR. Such a graph is often used to accommodate very large value ranges along the log axis within the available space: a classic use is to depict archaeological or cosmological time periods along a logarithmic horizontal axis.

log/log A type of GRAPH in which both AXES are LOGARITHMIC, used to compress very wide ranges of values into a viewable space.

Logo A programming language devised by the educational psychologist Seymour Papert for teaching programming and general deductive skills to small children. Logo is a LIST PROCESSING language, based on a greatly simplified dialect of LISP, which employs TURTLE GRAPHICS for its screen output. It was originally used with a small wheeled robot called a hardware turtle as its output device, and drew pictures on large sheets of paper placed on the floor. Here is a sample Logo procedure to draw a 10 × 10 square:

```
TO SQUARE
REPEAT 4 [FORWARD 10 RIGHT 90]
END
```

Though briefly popular in schools in the early 1980s, Logo failed to become more widely adopted.

log off, logoff To terminate a computing session by typing a command that closes all running programs and deprives the user of access until they LOG ON again.

log on, logon To start a new session on a computer system by presenting one's USER NAME and PASSWORD, which must match those stored in the user's ACCOUNT, previously set up by the SYSTEM ADMINISTRATOR.

logout Another term for LOG OFF.

log to disk To record the occurrence of some error or other type of event in a LOG file.

long integer A whole number represented as a 4-byte (32-bit) quantity. The largest value expressible as a long integer is 4,294,967,295 (FFFFFFFFh).

look-ahead 1 When reading a stream of data items (for example PARSING a stream of text within a programming language COMPILER) the action of inspecting the next few items to establish the context of the current one.
2 In the programming of computer GAMES, especially chess, the investigation of possible moves beyond the current one, and their consequences: see for example ALPHA/BETA PRUNING, MINIMAX ALGORITHM.

look-and-feel Those properties of a computer program that relate to its screen appearance and the specific ways in which it interacts with the user. Such properties may now be protected by copyright law. See also USER INTERFACE, GRAPHICAL USER INTERFACE, INTERACTIVE.

loop A group of program statements that is executed repeatedly, together with the CONTROL STRUCTURE that is used to specify such a repetition. The term is also now widely used in a metaphorical sense, to mean the repetitive everyday activities of a business, as in 'I'll keep you in the loop'.

There are two main kinds of program loop, the COUNTED LOOP which repeats itself a specified number of times, and the CONDITIONAL LOOP, which repeats itself until a test becomes true. In most programming languages the counted loop is introduced by the keyword FOR, but the syntax of conditional loops varies widely from one language to the next, variants including DO...LOOP, LOOP...ENDLOOP, WHILE...ENDWHILE, REPEAT...UNTIL and many more. See also ITERATE, ITERATOR, LOCAL LOOP.

loopback A kind of test applied to NETWORK and other communication links that involves the sender sending a test message to itself.

loop index When programming a COUNTED LOOP construct, the variable that keeps count of the current ITERATION. So in

```
FOR x = 1 TO 10 DO squares[x] := x*x;
```

x is the loop index.

loop invariant An expression placed within a program LOOP whose value does not vary from one ITERATION to the next.

loop optimization A relatively easy compiler optimization that involves identifying LOOP INVARIANT statements and moving them out of the body of the LOOP. For example the code fragment:

```
FOR i = 1 to 4 DO
y := w + 9
z := i + y
```

could be optimized to:

```
y := w + 9
FOR i = 1 to 4 DO
z := i + y
```

loop unrolling A program optimization, which may be performed either manually or by a compiler, which reduces the number of iterations performed by some program LOOP by creating multiple copies of the loop body. For example:

```
FOR i = 1 TO 100 DO
A[i] = A[i] + 9
```

might be optimized to:

```
FOR i = 1 TO 100 BY 2 DO
A[i] = A[i] + 9
A[i+1] = A[i+1] + 9
```

Even on a single processor, unrolling saves a little time by reducing the number of branches taken, but it is most effective on PARALLEL or SUPERSCALAR processors where the multiple copies may be scheduled to execute concurrently.

Lorenz attractor In the mathematical theory of chaotic systems, a region within a space that appears to draw the paths of chaotically moving particles toward itself.

Lorenz cipher A CIPHER invented by the German firm Lorenz for the German Army High Command during World War II, which worked on the 5-bit digital BAUDOT CODE used by teleprinter machines, rather than on the normal alphabet used by the Navy's ENIGMA MACHINE. The cipher encrypted a message by adding to each letter another letter chosen from a random sequence, using bitwise modulo-2 addition (see under MODULO ARITHMETIC) which has the effect of performing a logical EXCLUSIVE OR: if the recipient added exactly the same letter sequence to the ciphertext, the original was restored. Given a truly random sequence, this cipher would be unbreakable, but it requires the same long sequence to be securely distributed to both sender and receiver – difficult to achieve in wartime. Lorenz instead made a machine containing ten numbered wheels that generated PSEUDO-RANDOM sequences, and at each end operators with identical machines set their wheels in a new order for each new message.

The code was cracked by the cryptanalysts at the UK's BLETCHLEY PARK interception station after a tired German operator broke regulations by transmitting the same message twice with minor differences, but *without* first resetting the wheels. This gave a tiny clue to the machine's structure, but to exploit it required the assistance of the world's first electronic computers, ten COLOSSUS machines, working for several hours to decode each message. See also ENCRYPTION, CRYPTOGRAPHY, TURING, ALAN, ENIAC.

Los Alamos National Laboratory A US government research establishment based in New Mexico, originally built to house the US nuclear weapons programme but which now also pursues world-class work in SUPERCOMPUTERS and other areas of computing. See also LAWRENCE LIVERMORE NATIONAL LABORATORY, SANDIA NATIONAL LABORATORY.

lossless Any COMPRESSION algorithm that preserves all the information in the data, so that it is fully recovered when it is decompressed. See LZW COMPRESSION.

lossy Any method of DATA COMPRESSION that results in loss of information: see for example JPEG. Its converse is LOSSLESS.

Lotus 1-2-3 The first commercially successful SPREADSHEET program for IBM-compatible PCs, launched in 1982. Mirroring the earlier success of VISICALC on the Apple II, it was demand for 1-2-3 among businessmen that contributed in a major way to the success of the IBM PC standard.

Lotus Development Corporation The US software firm whose principle products are the LOTUS 1-2-3 spreadsheet and the LOTUS NOTES groupware product. It is now a division of IBM.

Lotus Notes The first and most popular GROUPWARE program, produced by LOTUS DEVELOPMENT CORPORATION and now owned by IBM. Notes enables multiple users on a network to exchange mail and memos, share calendars, diaries and address books, and to work on the same documents. Notes' REPLICATION feature allows sections of the shared data to be taken away and worked on remotely on a portable computer, then automatically reconciled with any changes made by the other participants.

Lovelace, Ada (1815–52) Daughter of the poet Lord Byron, and accomplished mathematician and collaborator of Charles BABBAGE, Lovelace is credited with being the first computer programmer because of the programs she wrote for Babbage's unfinished Analytical Engine. The Ada programming language was named in her honour.

lower case The alphabet of small letter forms included in most type FONTS, as opposed to the capitals (that is the UPPER CASE) letters. The name dates from the days of lead type when these letters were kept in the bottom part of the wooden type box or 'case'.

low-insertion force (LIF) A type of socket used for mounting microprocessors that have very large numbers of PINS onto a PRINTED CIRCUIT BOARD. Instead of gripping the pins by simple friction, which would make insertion and removal almost impossibly awkward, a LIF socket provides a lever that opens and closes a sliding shutter to grip or release the pins.

low-level format To FORMAT a hard disk by using an operating system command that erases its contents byte-by-byte and rebuilds all the formatting information. This is in contrast to formatting the disk with a higher-level utility that merely resets the DIRECTORY or FILE ALLOCATION TABLE pointers and leaves the previous content present but inaccessible (except to a disk SECTOR EDITOR). A low-level format is normally required only when a new disk is first installed, in the aftermath of a truly catastrophic software failure, or to ensure absolute destruction of data for privacy purposes.

low-level programming language A programming language that permits direct manipulation of memory addresses, processor registers and bit-level operations, in contrast to a HIGH-LEVEL PROGRAMMING LANGUAGE, which hides such details behind abstractions. Low-level languages are needed for writing OPERATING SYSTEMS and DEVICE DRIVERS which must control the 'bare' hardware without assistance. For example the c language was invented specifically for writing the Unix operating system.

low-pass filter An electronic FILTER that allows through only frequencies below some threshold value. See also HIGH-PASS FILTER

LP Abbreviation of LINEAR PROGRAMMING.

LPC 1 Abbreviation of LINEAR PREDICTIVE CODING. **2** Abbreviation of LOCAL PROCEDURE CALL.

LQ Abbreviation of LETTER-QUALITY PRINTING.

LRU Abbreviation of LEAST-RECENTLY-USED ALGORITHM.

ls The UNIX command for listing the contents of a disk DIRECTORY.

LSB Abbreviation of LEAST SIGNIFICANT BIT.

Lucent Technologies The telecommunications company created as a spin-off of AT&T's microelectronics division, and which inherited the famous BELL LABORATORIES from its parent. The company is at the forefront of electronic and optical communications research.

Lucid An experimental DATAFLOW programming language that performs all computation on streams of simple data types by applying filters.

luggable The semi-humorous name given to the earliest portable computers, such as the Osborne and first Compaqs, which were contained in sewing-machine-sized cases and weighed more than 10 kilograms.

luminance 1 The brightness of a point on a surface that is radiating or reflecting light, measured in a direction orthogonal to the surface.
2 That component of a video signal or colour-encoding scheme that conveys information about light intensity. In the S-VIDEO and COMPONENT VIDEO systems, luminance is transmitted on a separate channel from CHROMINANCE.

lurker Someone who reads the messages in an online discussion group but does not contribute or reply to any.

L*u*v* Also called CIELUV or Uniform Colour Space, a standard COLOUR SPACE defined by the CIE in 1976 to specify colours to be reproduced in additive media such as lights, or phosphors on a computer monitor screen. The colour of any sample can be defined relative to a standard white source by stating three coordinates in this colour space: L* (lightness, the cube root of luminance), u* (red–greenness) and v* (yellow–blueness). See also L*A*B*, CHROMATICITY, COLOUR MODEL, RGB, HSV.

Lycos One of the earliest SEARCH ENGINES for the World Wide Web, created at Carnegie-

Mellon University in 1994, which permits the content of web pages to be searched for KEY-WORDS. Now converted into a fully-fledged PORTAL.

Lynx One of the earliest WEB BROWSERS, written at the University of Kansas, which can display only text. Lynx is available for almost every known operating system and is still used where speed and low memory usage are more important than graphics ability.

LZ compression See LEMPEL–ZIV COMPRESSION.

LZH compression Lempel-Ziv-Haruyasu compression, a variant of LEMPEL–ZIV COMPRESSION

used by the utility LHA which adds an extra level of compression by HUFFMAN CODING its output.

LZW compression (Lempel–Ziv Welch compression, LZW) A compression algorithm derived from the LEMPEL–ZIV COMPRESSION method by Terry Welch in 1984. It is employed in many popular file compression and archiving programs including PKZIP, and has been implemented in hardware in disk and tape controllers. Originally distributed free, this algorithm is now copyrighted by UNISYS CORPORATION, a situation that has led to other variants being used for free software.

M

M The new name for the MUMPS system.

MAC 1 Shorthand for MULTIPLY-ACCUMULATE.
2 Abbreviation of MEDIA ACCESS CONTROL.

Mac The nickname for the Apple MACINTOSH personal computer.

Mach A multiprocessor operating system kernel developed at Carnegie Mellon University and employed as the core of several UNIX-compatible operating systems including NEXTSTEP.

Mach bands Visible steps in the intensity of colour on a computer display that is intended to be smoothly graded, most noticeable in shadows on slightly curved surfaces. Mach bands are a kind of spatial ALIASING caused by sampling the colours at too small a sample size (i.e. with too small a COLOUR DEPTH). Named after the Austrian physicist/philosopher Ernst Mach. Mach bands are clearly seen when typical photographic scenes are shown on an 8-bit display, but are much less visible on 24-bit or 32-bit (so-called TRUE COLOUR) displays. More powerful shading algorithms can delay their appearance in computer-generated images, so for instance PHONG SHADING is less prone to banding than the simpler GOURAUD SHADING. See also POSTERIZE, QUANTIZATION, SAMPLING.

machine 1 A computer. The term is used particularly to distinguish between the hardware and the software running on it: for example 'close to the machine' means a very low-level routine.
2 Used adjectivally to mean either specific to a particular computer (as in MACHINE CODE) or performed by a computer (as in MACHINE TRANSLATION).

machine code, machine language A computer program stored in the form of a stream of binary numbers representing INSTRUCTIONS that may be executed directly by the computer's PROCESSOR. (This is in contrast to a program stored in the form of text written in some PROGRAMMING LANGUAGE, which must be translated before it can be executed.) Most commercial programs are purchased in machine code form: for IBM compatible PCs such program files have names ending in the extension .EXE. See also SOURCE CODE.

machine-readable Capable of being read by a computer. The term may refer to data that are already in digital electronic form (for example held on a disk, tape, bar code or magnetic stripe) or to printed documents that are written in a typeface that can be read by an OPTICAL CHARACTER RECOGNITION system (for example a specially-designed cheque, questionnaire or census form).

machine room A room specially designed to house one or more computers, frequently equipped with air-conditioning and a stabilized power supply.

machine translation The translation of documents or speech from one human language to another by a computer. This is extremely difficult, because human languages have far more complex structures than computer programming languages, with words changing their meanings according to context, so a word-by-word translation is useless.

Machine translation programs have to PARSE sentences into their grammatical components, and be capable of recognizing multiple word forms (such as plurals or verb tenses) created by adding prefixes and suffixes to a single word stem contained in the dictionary.

Some translation systems work via a language-independent intermediate representation which is then converted to the target language. Other approaches include looking for the closest match to a text in a huge database of previously translated documents, and statistical methods that extract the probabilities of various word sequences by analysing such a database.

The best translation programs now achieve an accuracy of around 95%, but that still means that on a typical page of text every line might contain a translation error that requires manual correction.

Macintosh A range of personal computers, first launched by APPLE in 1984 and still produced (now under the name of iMac). The Macintosh was the first commercially successful personal computer to feature a GRAPH-ICAL USER INTERFACE that made it easier for novices to operate, succeeding where its predecessor the expensive LISA had failed. The first Macintosh contained a 32-bit MOTOROLA 68000 microprocessor with 128 kilobytes of memory, and came with a MOUSE and drawing software as standard features.

Though the Macintosh has never attracted enough software development to displace the IBM-COMPATIBLE PC in the business market, it carved a niche for itself among graphic designers and other creative artists which it still retains. The name Macintosh derives from a variety of red eating apple popular in the USA.

MacOS The OPERATING SYSTEM employed by Apple's MACINTOSH computers. MacOS was the first widely-available personal computer operating system to provide a GRAPHICAL USER INTERFACE. It employs the visual metaphor of a desktop on which folders contain files, icons represent files and programs, and a waste bin ('trash can') is used to dispose of unwanted data. Many of these cosmetic aspects of MacOS have been incorporated in Microsoft's WINDOWS operating system.

Versions of MacOS up to 9 were single-user and provided only the simplest form of COOP-ERATIVE MULTITASKING. They lacked hardware memory protection to prevent tasks from interfering with one another and did not offer support for multiple processors. However, MacOS X represents a break with the past, being derived from the Unix-based NEXTSTEP operating system. It is truly multitasking and protected, and runs older MacOS programs via software EMULATION.

macro 1 A set of stored commands that can be replayed at will to automate some frequently performed computing task. A macro is often produced by recording the keystrokes that a human operator uses to perform the task (see under macro recorder). Some macro systems also include a macro language in which macros can be edited or written from scratch without recording. See also script, scripting language.

2 A programmer-defined abbreviation inserted into the source code of a computer program, which immediately prior to compilation is expanded by a macro preprocessor into valid source statements in the appropriate language. The best known example is the C language's macro preprocessor. For example, a C macro definition such as:

```
#define RED 0x3400

#define BLUE 0x9800
```

allows the programmer to use the mnemonic colour names RED and BLUE wherever these colours need to be specified, but what is actually compiled is the value 3400 or 9800 hexadecimal.

Macros offer a convenient shorthand; by avoiding a function call in favour of a macro expansion that happens at compile time, they allow a program to be made more readable at no cost in runtime performance. They may be used to modify the SYNTAX of the programming language, or even to implement a different language within the existing one. Macros are commonly used to create early prototypes of new languages. See also COMPILER.

macrocell See STANDARD CELL.

macro-expansion The action of a language PREPROCESSOR as it expands MACROS before the resulting code is compiled: a feature of many C compilers.

macroinstruction A term applied by designers of CISC microprocessors to an ordinary MACHINE CODE instruction, to distinguish it from the MICROINSTRUCTIONS from which it is composed. See more under MICROCODE.

macro language A type of simple programming language used to automate the operation of some pre-existing application program, or to harness together several different applications, rather than create stand-alone programs. For example the applications in Microsoft's Office suite all contain an embedded macro language called VISUAL BASIC FOR APPLICATIONS. See also MACRO RECORDER.

MacroMedia US publisher of one of the most popular multimedia authoring programs DIRECTOR, and its widely used web animation add-on SHOCKWAVE.

macro preprocessor A feature provided in certain language compilers (for example, most C compilers) which expands programmer-defined abbreviations called MACROS into sequences of SOURCE CODE statements immediately before the program is compiled. See more under MACRO.

macro recorder A program that captures all the keystrokes and mouse movements used to perform a computer software procedure, and stores them so that they can be replayed on future occasions to automate that procedure. Some macro recorders allow such stored keystroke sequences to be inspected and edited by the user, and may include a full MACRO LANGUAGE, which permits macros to be written from scratch rather than recorded.

macro virus A type of computer VIRUS which, instead of being written in machine code, is written in the MACRO LANGUAGE of an application such as Microsoft Word, and hence can infect only documents produced with that application. The virus is triggered on opening the document and, such is the power of modern macro languages, that it is able to do much damage including erasing files or whole disks. Such viruses can be spread via the Internet in documents attached to email messages. The MELISSA VIRUS which infected thousands of computers in 1999 was a macro virus.

MADD Shorthand for MULTIPLY-ADD.

magnetic core See FERRITE-CORE MEMORY.

magnetic disk Any data storage device, such as the FLOPPY DISK or HARD DISK, whose mode of operation depends upon a rotating metal or plastic disk coated with a FERROMAGNETIC material such as iron oxide. A recording head is moved radially across the disk in order to read and write concentric TRACKS on its surface.

magnetic tape A data storage medium that consists of a long narrow plastic band coated with a FERROMAGNETIC material such as iron oxide, and which is moved past a read and write head while winding it on and off a reel or spool (which may be enclosed within a protective CASSETTE or CARTRIDGE).

magneto-optical disk (MO) A rotating data storage device that combines both optical and magnetic elements to achieve high capacity and rewriteability. MO disks are coated with an alloy of terbium, iron and cobalt whose surface reflectivity alters when it is magnetized. A powerful infra-red LASER is used to heat a spot on this coating beyond its CURIE POINT; this allows its direction of magnetization to be altered by a magnetic recording head, and a bit to be written. The disk is read like a CD, using reflected light from a weaker laser.

Unlike purely optical read/write media, MO disks may be erased and rewritten millions of times, and they offer longer archival permanence than purely magnetic media. Capacities from 640 Mb to 2.6 Gb are available.

magneto-resistive head (MR) A technology invented by IBM for making hard disk heads. It reads the magnetized data dots not by inducing current in a coil – as in older technologies – but by altering the resistance of certain alloys in the presence of a magnetic field. The heads consist of sandwiches of very thin layers of alternating magnetic and non-magnetic metals, such as manganese/iron, cobalt, copper and nickel/iron. Their extreme sensitivity allows the size of data dot to be reduced, increasing the areal density of data to more than a gigabit per square inch. Further refinements of the technology called the GIANT MAGNETORESISTIVE HEAD (GMR) and SPIN VALVE HEAD increase the areal density further to 10–20 gigabits per square inch, making possible the current generation of low cost, miniature 20+ gigabyte drives.

mail Short for EMAIL, as in 'You have mail'.

mail bomb The sending of an email message that has a huge BINARY ATTACHMENT – which may tie up the receiver's computer for hours in the downloading – either as as an act of aggression or as punishment for some perceived misdemeanour such as SPAMMING. See also NETIQUETTE, LOGIC BOMB, VIRUS, WORM, DENIAL OF SERVICE ATTACK.

mailbox A location on a network SERVER used to store messages intended for a particular user. The address of the mailbox constitutes that user's EMAIL ADDRESS. Mail messages may be read and stored on the server itself (for example using the IMAP protocol), or downloaded to the user's machine for reading (as under the POP3 protocol). Many email systems permit each user to maintain several different mailboxes and to employ FILTERS to direct mail of a certain kind or from certain sources into different ones.

mail client See under EMAIL CLIENT.

mail delivery agent (MDA) Also called a *mail user agent*. The term used under UNIX for a program that enables users to read and write EMAIL messages – an MDA provides the software interface between the user and the *mail transport agent* (MTA) which actually delivers the messages over a network. The MDA collects incoming messages from the user's mailbox where the MTA deposits them, though on a single-user machine the MDA may instead use POP3 to collect mail. Widely used MDAs include ELM, Pine, smail and rmail. See also IMAP, SMTP.

Mail Exchange record (MX record) A type of record used in the Internet's DOMAIN NAME SYSTEM to indicate which host computer will handle all electronic mail sent to a particular DOMAIN.

mail filter A function provided by many EMAIL client programs which enables the user to specify actions that will be performed only on certain received messages, triggered by, for example, the address contained in the From: field of the message's header, or the presence of certain key words in the message body. Filters can be used to file messages of the same type in the same place, or to block all messages from an unwanted source (see SPAMMING).

mail gateway A computer that connects two or more, perhaps incompatible, EMAIL systems and translates messages between their various formats.

mail header A header automatically attached to every message that is sent by an EMAIL system, which specifies who the message is from and the time and data of sending. INTERNET email headers may contain far more information than this, listing the name of every server that the message passed through on its route to the destination, along with details of any BINARY ATTACHMENTS to the message, and their encoding methods.

mail hub Another name for a MAIL SERVER.

mailing list A list of subscribers' EMAIL ADDRESSES for use by a LIST SERVER, which broadcasts all members' messages to all others. In scientific and academic circles, mailing lists are frequently used to disseminate research findings.

mail merge A procedure for automatically addressing large numbers of identically formatted letters to a list of recipients contained in a computer file or database. The name, address (and perhaps other details) of each recipient are automatically substituted for special placeholders created for that purpose in the template document, and the combined result is printed. Most modern WORD PROCESSORS offer a built-in mail merge facility. See also LIST MANAGEMENT, DEDUPE, SPAMMING.

mail reader Software used to read and compose EMAIL messages, popular examples of which include Eudora, Microsoft Outlook and Netscape Messenger. A mail reader usually provides several extra facilities, such as storing and retrieving old mail in a local database, and maintaining an address book of email contacts.

mail server A network SERVER whose main function is to send, receive and store EMAIL messages. Mail servers may be employed in a LAN to provide a shared mail service to all its users and avoid each user having their own access route to the outside world (e.g. via a modem and telephone line) – such a mail server typically supports a FIREWALL to prevent unauthorized outside access to the LAN. On the Internet, mail servers relay email messages from one to another using the SMTP protocol, and support user accounts and mailboxes from which mail may be retrieved using the POP3 or IMAP protocols.

mail transfer protocol A network protocol that controls the sending and receiving of EMAIL messages. See for example POP3, IMAP, SMTP.

mail transport agent (MTA) Also known as a *message transfer agent*. A program that transports EMAIL messages between one UNIX computer and another. See more under MAIL DELIVERY AGENT.

mail user agent (MUA) See under MAIL DELIVERY AGENT.

mainframe, mainframe computer The class of large computer first manufacturered in the 1950s, and which only the biggest corporations could afford. Mainframe computers featured central processors consisting of many separate circuit boards (each containing many DISCRETE LOGIC chips) and MAGNETIC CORE memory, all of which generated so much heat that the computer was housed in a special air-conditioned room and may even have required water-cooling. The name originally referred only to the wardrobe-sized cabinets in which these components were housed but after the invention of the MINICOMPUTER in the early 1970s, it came to be applied to the computer as a whole. Perhaps the most famous mainframe models are IBM's 390 and Digital Equipment's DEC 20.

Mainframes are still manufactured by companies such as IBM and Fujitsu, but they now employ the INTEGRATED CIRCUITS and miniature disk drives developed since the personal computer revolution of the 1990s. They are mostly used for massive administrative jobs such as processing census data or electricity bills. The astounding progress in microprocessor design has meant that, on paper at least, a desktop PC now seems capable of as many raw MIPS (millions of intstructions per second) of processing power as older mainframes were, while a network of PCs can match a mainframe's I/O bandwidth and storage capacity. However PC operating systems are only now beginning to approach the reliability, maintainability and security

features of mainframe operating systems such as MVS, OS/390 and VMS.

main loop The outermost LOOP of any interactive computer program, which continually accepts commands from the user until instructed to quit.

main memory The memory area within a computer into which the current program and the data it is working on are loaded, as opposed to any specialized memories such as a processor or disk CACHE, or other regions of memory contained within peripheral devices such as printers or video adapters. The ADDRESS by which a data item is located, or at which a progam instruction is executed, is an address within this main memory. See also ADDRESS SPACE, SEGMENTED MEMORY MODEL, SHARED MEMORY.

maintainability The comparative ease of modifying and re-configuring a program. Increasing maintainability is one the chief goals for programming language designers.

maintenance The business of keeping a computer system working once it has been installed and configured. Hardware maintenance is much like that for any other machine – replenishing CONSUMABLES and replacing defective parts. However, software maintenance is an entirely new discipline, and involves installing each new full VERSION of the product as it is released, removing outdated and unwanted files, adding PATCHES to fix specific bugs and, in the case of a BESPOKE application, compiling BUG REPORTS and WISH LISTS for its programmers. However most of the day-to-day work of software maintenance lies in sorting out unwanted interactions between one program and another or with new hardware, and repairing damage done to one program by the installation of another. See also COST-OF-OWNERSHIP, DLL HELL, VERSION CONTROL.

Majordomo A popular free LIST SERVER program.

major release A new version of a software product that contains significant new features. It has become a general convention to signify each major release by incrementing the leading digit of the version number – for example, v2.2.8 becomes v3.0. See also VER-SIONING, VERSION CONTROL.

Make **1** A software tool that automates the procedures required to compile a program. The interdependencies between different source modules are stored in a MAKEFILE which enables Make to recompile only those modules that have been changed. Make was originally provided as part of UNIX but there are now equivalent utilities for most programming environments and operating systems.
  2 Used as a noun as in '...next time I do a Make'; in other words, '...next time I compile the program'.

makefile A text file containing information about what source modules constitute a particular program, which is supplied as a parameter to the MAKE utility to automate the compilation process. A typical makefile contains lines of the form:

```
vesa.obj: vesa.c vesa.h
```

(which says that to create the file vesa.obj you must compile the two files vesa.c and vesa.h), and

```
c:\tc\tcc -mt -Ic:\tc\include -
Lc:\tc\lib -c vesa
```

(which invokes the COMPILER with the necessary command line switches).

male Any electrical plug or socket that contains protruding pins. Freudian symbolism at its most obvious. See also FEMALE.

malloc The c language function that allocates memory for storing data, from within a program at run-time. Malloc takes size in bytes as a parameter, and returns a pointer to a memory block of that size on the system HEAP. Memory allocated using malloc must be explicitly released (using the 'free' function) when it is finished with, to make it available for reuse by future malloc calls.

malware Malign software that combines the attributes of a VIRUS with those of a WORM: that is, a virus that can use networks to propagate itself. Like viruses, malware programs arrive in a downloaded file or an email attachment, but once activated they connect to the network and, for example, send copies of themselves to everyone in the victim's address book (see MELISSA VIRUS). The term

was coined for an article in the *Dr. Dobbs'* journal and has passed into wider usage.

MAN (Metropolitan Area Network) A high-speed public network which is confined to a particular city and permits individual companies' LANS to communicate with one another. Once touted as an important growth area, but the Internet seems destined to displace the few such systems that currently exist.

man The UNIX help utility which searches for topics in an online MANUAL (hence the name) and presents the appropriate pages of information.

managed code Program code in Microsoft's INTERMEDIATE LANGUAGE that is running under the COMMON LANGUAGE RUNTIME environment, which gives it the benefit of automatic GARBAGE COLLECTION and the ability to retrieve runtime type information from libraries of prefabricated components called ASSEMBLIES.

managed hub See under HUB.

Mandelbrot, Benoit (b.1924) A French mathematician who, while working as an IBM fellow at Yorktown Heights New York, applied modern computer graphics to the visualization of figures from FRACTAL geometry and greatly popularized the subject. The MANDELBROT SET that he discovered is still the best-known fractal image.

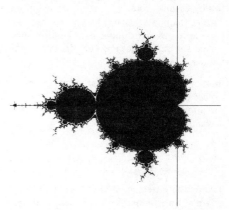

Mandelbrot set A mathematical set discovered by Benoit MANDELBROT. Its beetle-like graphical representation has become the best known example of a FRACTAL figure. The set is generated by repeatedly squaring a COMPLEX NUMBER and plotting the resulting values on the complex plane.

man-machine interface (MMI) A field within COMPUTER SCIENCE that studies the principles of USER INTERFACES.

man page A page of information returned by the UNIX MAN utility.

mantissa The fractional part of a logarithm or of a number that has been expressed in SCIENTIFIC NOTATION or a FLOATING-POINT representation.

manual 1 Originally, a book containing instructions for the use of, or describing the specification of, some device such as a computer or computer program. The term is now also applied to such information presented in electronic form, say on a CD-ROM or a web site. Under UNIX the entire reference manual is available as an online resource: see MAN.

2 The term applied to any part of a task that must be performed by a human being rather than by the computer or a peripheral, used as in 'the sheets must then be manually collated'.

many-to-many relation A relationship in which each participant may be related to many others, as for example a nephew may have many aunts and an aunt many nephews. See also MANY-TO-ONE RELATION.

many-to-one relation A relationship in which many participants may be related to a single one, as for example many children may have the same mother. See also MANY-TO-MANY RELATION.

map 1 In mathematics or computer science, to place the elements of a SET into a one-to-one relationship with members of another set. For example the relation:

```
A -> London
B -> Manchester
C -> Sheffield
```

maps the letters A, B and C onto the city names. A mathematical expression that performs such a mapping is called a FUNCTION.

2 In the everyday use of the word (to mean a diagram that depicts an area of land on a reduced scale), the two sets involved are points on the actual ground (measured by a surveyor) and the corresponding points on the piece of paper.

MAPI (Messaging Application Programming Interface) A Microsoft programming interface that enables EMAIL messages to be sent directly from within non-mail application programs such as word processors and spreadsheets.

margin The strips of white space left around the edges of a page of text. In a word processor the margin width is one of the basic parameters that makes up a paragraph or document STYLE, and variations such as automatic indentation of first lines are often supported. See also JUSTIFY.

marker A special value inserted among other data values to indicate their beginning, end or a boundary between different DATA SETS.

Markov Chain A mathematical construct invented by the Russian AA Markov in 1913 to describe the sequences of letters encountered in Russian words. A Markov Chain can model any sequence of events where each event in the chain determines the probability of the next event. For example, in English the letter 'q' has a high probability of being followed by 'u' and a low probability of being followed by 'x'.

markup language A formal notation for describing the appearance and function of text documents and their components. Markup languages (the best known examples of which are HTML, SGML and XML) usually work by embedding textual directives called TAGS into the text; these are then interpreted and acted upon by the software used to display or print the document. This means that the document as a whole remains a plain text file, with all the advantages that this brings in terms of inter-platform portability and ease of transmission via EMAIL systems. The following extract is example of an HTML tagged document:

```
<H2><A NAME = "POISON TREE">A Poi-
son Tree (<A HREF = "note-
sexp.html#POISON
TREE">Notes</A>)</A></H2>

I was angry with my friend:<BR>

I told my wrath, my wrath did
end.<BR>
```

This differs from the proprietary document formats employed by word processors, in which the formatting information is stored as binary data. It is harder to draw the distinction between a markup language and a RICH TEXT format such as RTF or a PAGE DESCRIPTION LANGUAGE such as POSTSCRIPT, but in general, HTML and XML have a simpler construction, and are sometimes written 'by hand', but RTF and PostScript are more complex and are almost always generated mechanically as the output of some word processor or desktop publishing program.

marquee A visual device used to mark out an area on a computer screen. It usually consists of a rectangle of alternating light and dark dashes that march around its periphery like a line of ants: the dashes may be black and white, or a reversal of the underlying screen colours. Marquees are used in most graphics editors to select the area of an image to which some operation is to be applied. The name is an allusion to the strips of moving lights displayed over the entrances to US cinemas, theatres and night-clubs.

Marseille Prolog The first version of the PROLOG language, written at the University of Marseille in 1973 by Alain Colmerauer and Phillipe Roussel.

marshal To assemble a group of data items prior to sending them in a message over some communication channel. Hence, for example, in Microsoft's COM object model, to package the parameters for a remote method call so that they can be sent to the server object using a REMOTE PROCEDURE CALL is to marshal them.

Martin, James A US computer consultant and author, influential in the emergence of SOFTWARE ENGINEERING as a serious discipline.

MASCOT Acronym for MODULAR APPROACH TO SOFTWARE CONSTRUCTION OPERATION AND TEST.

mask **1** A pattern of bits used to change the value of selected bits in some register or memory location by performing a logical AND or OR operation. See also BIT MASK.
2 In the manufacture of INTEGRATED CIRCUITS, an optical transparency bearing the design for a single layer of a circuit layout, employed in the LITHOGRAPHY process. For ease of handling, the mask is many times larger than the actual chip, and is reduced as it is projected onto the wafer surface.
3 In a graphics application, a feature that permits part of an image to be protected from alterations made to the rest of the image.

maskable interrupt A type of hardware INTERRUPT that may be enabled and disabled under software control, by setting a special bit in the processor's FLAG REGISTER. Maskable interrupts are typically disabled during the execution of an interrupt service routine, to avoid further nested interrupts with the possibility of stack overflow. See also NON-MASKABLE INTERRUPT.

Massachusetts Institute of Technology See MIT.

massively parallel A class of computer that employs hundreds or even thousands of processors to execute different parts of the same program at the same time. Most modern SUPERCOMPUTERS employ a massively parallel architecture, which is well suited to the kinds of repetitive calculations encountered in science and engineering. See more under PARALLEL PROCESSING and PARALLEL COMPUTER. See also VECTOR PROCESSOR, ARRAY PROCESSOR.

mass storage The generic term used to refer to any type of storage device on which data can be permanently stored once a computer has been switched off. The most commonly used mass storage devices are magnetic media such as HARD DISKS and TAPE DRIVES, various types of OPTICAL DISC, and SOLID-STATE storage devices such as FLASH MEMORY cards.

master boot record (MBR) Under Microsoft operating systems, a small data area on TRACK 0 of the boot disk of a computer system which points to the location of a PARTITION on that disk whose BOOT SECTOR in turn contains the location of the operating system. This indirect arrangement allows different operating systems to be booted from the same disk.

master disk The disk(s) containing a software product that was actually purchased from the vendor, in distinction to any copies made from it for security purposes.

master/slave A relationship between two pieces of hardware or software in which one completely controls the other's operations. Examples abound in computing, and include disk controllers, network devices and processors in a parallel computer.

MathCAD A program for performing SYMBOLIC MATHEMATICS and VISUALIZING the results. See also MATHEMATICA.

Mathematica A powerful mathematics program developed by Wolfram Research Inc. that permits the manipulation of SYMBOLIC MATHEMATICS expressions and sophisticated visualization of the results. Originally written for the Apple Macintosh, Mathematica is now also available for Unix and Windows machines. See also MATHCAD.

maths coprocessor Also called a FLOATING-POINT ACCELERATOR. A special-purpose computer processor (see COPROCESSOR) whose sole function is to perform FLOATING-POINT ARITHMETIC calculations.

Maths coprocessors were once manufactured as separate chips which could be installed as an option, widely used examples include Intel's 80387 and the Weitek 4167. However, this created extra complexity for software writers, since many programs needed to determine whether or not such a coprocessor was present and execute equivalent software arithmetic routines (called floating-point emulation) if it were not. This problem has largely faded since most of the recent generations of microprocessor (for example the Pentium and PowerPC families) include an on-chip FLOATING-POINT UNIT.

MatLab A mathematics program for performing complex scientific numeric calculation and VISUALIZATION, optimized for MATRIX ARITHMETIC and SIGNAL PROCESSING operations.

matrix **1** In mathematics, a rectangular table of quantities arranged in rows and columns, which may be manipulated by applying the rules of MATRIX ARITHMETIC. An example of a matrix is:

2 4
3 6
5 1

The *order* of a matrix is its number of rows and columns, so the above example is of order 3×2. Matrices are extensively used in statistics, and in computer graphics where they are used to describe geometrical transformations such as rotations or deformations. The most efficient manipulation of matrices is a major problem for both hardware and software designers. See also AFFINE TRANSFORM.

2 Used by cybertheorists and sci-fi writers to describe the totality of all the world's interconnected communication networks.

matrix arithmetic The combination of two matrices (see MATRIX) using a set of operations that work on all the elements of each matrix. Two matrices of the same order may be added by adding their corresponding elements to form a new matrix. Multiplication of matrices involves summing the cross products of each row with each column, and is permitted only if the number of columns of the first matrix is the same as the number of rows of the second.

Most of the computations employed in SIGNAL PROCESSING and in 3D GRAPHICS involve matrix arithmetic, for example when computing the geometry of scenes or calculating the light intensity reflected from each point when a coloured surface is RENDERED. For this reason much effort has been devoted to devising special hardware to speed up matrix arithmetic: see for example MMX, VECTOR PROCESSOR, ARRAY PROCESSOR.

Mauchly, John (1907–80) Co-inventor in 1946, with J Presper ECKERT, of ENIAC, the first general-purpose digital computer.

maximize **1** To increase as far as possible the value of a variable that describes an attribute of a system: for example profit, efficiency, satisfaction.

2 In a program that employs a GRAPHICAL USER INTERFACE, to click on an ICON that represents some hidden program or open data file and so cause it to expand into a window again. See more under MINIMIZE.

maximum seek time See FULL STROKE SEEK TIME.

Maya Formerly called Alias Wavefront, the leading 3D animation program for SILICON GRAPHICS workstations, which now runs under Windows NT as well as Unix. It supports many advanced features such as RAY TRACING, volumetric lighting, INVERSE KINEMATICS, and PARTICLE SYSTEMS.

MB Abbreviation of MEGABYTE. Sometimes incorrectly written as Mb.

MBASIC A disk-based version of MICROSOFT BASIC that was supplied with many CP/M and MS-DOS systems.

MBasic See under MICROSOFT BASIC.

MBE Abbreviation of MOLECULAR BEAM EPITAXY.

MBONE A technology that permits real time video and audio to be broadcast over the Internet. MBONE is short for *multicast backbone* (see MULTICAST and BACKBONE), and it depends upon a modification of the normal IP routing protocol called IP MULTICAST. MBONE-enabled routers form a small subnetwork within the Internet – currently there are some 4000 sites from which MBONE is available. To attach to the MBONE requires an operating system (such as Sun's SOLARIS) with multicast capability and a very fast Internet connection capable of carrying about 1 megabit per second.

Mbps Abbreviation of MEGABITS PER SECOND.

MBR Abbreviation of MASTER BOOT RECORD.

MC68000 Abbreviation of MOTOROLA 68000.

MCA Abbreviation of MICRO CHANNEL ARCHITECTURE.

McCarthy, John (b. 1927) A pioneer of ARTIFICIAL INTELLIGENCE and inventor at MIT in 1957 of LISP, one of the first truly high-level programming languages.

MCGA (Multi Colour Graphics Array) One of the early IBM GRAPHICS ADAPTERS, capable of displaying 320 × 200 pixels in 256 colours, which was built into the unsuccessful 1983 PCjr model. MCGA format is now very rarely used.

MCI (Media Control Interface) The programming interface in Microsoft WINDOWS via which MULTIMEDIA devices are controlled by sending device-independent commands such as Open, Close, and Play. MCI supports the loading and control of third-party MPEG CODECS for video playback.

MCSE Abbreviation of MICROSOFT CERTIFIED SYSTEM ENGINEER.

MDA 1 See MAIL DELIVERY AGENT.
2 See MONOCHROME DISPLAY ADAPTER.

ME Abbreviation of MOTION ESTIMATION.

Mead, Carver (b. 1934) Professor of Computer Science, Electrical Engineering and Applied Physics at CALTECH, one of the leading pioneers of VLSI design, and co-author of a definitive textbook.

mean time between failures See MTBF.

mechanical mouse A computer MOUSE that employs moving parts (typically a large metal ball-bearing that rotates two small metal rollers set at right angles). By contrast an *optical mouse* employs light beams and photocells to read a grid pattern printed on the MOUSE MAT.

Media Access Control (MAC) The lower of two sublayers into which the DATA LINK LAYER of the OSI REFERENCE MODEL for networks has been split by the IEEE 802.2 standard. The MAC sublayer controls network access and sharing of the medium (for example, whether by TOKEN passing or by COLLISION-DETECTION), while the upper LOGICAL LINK CONTROL sublayer handles flow control and error checking.

Media Control Interface See MCI.

medium 1 The physical material used to store data: for example a magnetic disk or tape, an optical disc, a RAM card.
2 The material used to carry signals: for example radio or infra-red waves, optical fibre or copper wire.
3 The combination of the physical and data-link layers of a network PROTOCOL (i.e. the cabling and electrical signal types), which carries individual data bits.

meg A colloquial abbreviation for MEGABYTE.

mega In most scientific usage a prefix meaning one million (1,000,000), from the Greek from 'huge'. However in computer usage the term has come to mean 1024 × 1024 or 1,048,576 for conformity with the KILOBYTE of 1024 BYTES. See for example MEGABYTE.

megabit 1,048,576 bits, commonly abbreviated to Mb or Mbit. The unit used when specifying the data capacity of a digital communication link or computer network.

megabits per second (Mbps) The most commonly used measure for the throughput of computer system buses and communication networks. See also BIT, MEGABIT.

megabyte 1,048,576 BYTES (that is, 2^{20}) or 1024 KILOBYTES, commonly abbreviated to MB or more informally to *meg*. The megabyte is still, but only just, the unit most used to specify a computer's RAM capacity, though for hard disks it has already given way to the GIGABYTE. This entire dictionary contains around one megabyte of text.

megaflops One million FLOPS (Floating-Point Operations Per Second), a measure of computation speed.

megahertz (MHz) One million cycles per second, a unit of FREQUENCY.

megapixel A unit of RESOLUTION, used particularly when specifying digital cameras, which consists of 1,048,576 PIXELS.

Melissa virus A Microsoft Word MACRO VIRUS let loose on the Internet in April 1999, Melissa arrived as an EMAIL attachment which, if opened, sent copies of itself to the first 50 people in the victim's email address book. As it did no harm to the victim's computer, Melissa is strictly speaking a WORM rather than a virus.

member function The name given to a METHOD belonging to a CLASS in C++. See also MEMBER VARIABLE.

member variable Also called a DATA MEMBER, the name given to an INSTANCE VARIABLE of a CLASS in the C++ language. See also MEMBER FUNCTION.

membrane keyboard A type of computer keyboard that presents a smooth and flat surface covered with a flexible and impermeable plastic sheet on which the key labels are printed: switches mounted under the sheet operate when a key area is pressed. Membrane keyboards are used for outdoor applications such as AUTOMATED TELLER MACHINES and KIOSKS, and in harsh environments such as factory floors or boats, to keep out water and other contaminants that would damage the switches of a conventional keyboard. Even when a full QWERTY layout is employed, typing on a membrane keyboard is slow and tiring because of its stiff action and lack of tactile feedback.

membrane switch A type of electrical switch covered with a sheet of sealed flexible plastic that enables it to be operated safely in wet or dirty environments. Such switches are used to make sealed MEMBRANE KEYBOARDS.

memo field The name given to a special field type used to store long passages of continuous text, supported by many DATABASE MANAGEMENT SYSTEMS including DBASE II and MICROSOFT ACCESS.

memory In general any type of device that can store information. In practice the term tends to be reserved for semiconductor-based devices such as the RANDOM ACCESS MEMORY chip used for temporary working storage in a computer, rather than for more permanent storage devices such as the various forms of MAGNETIC DISK and TAPE, which are properly referred to as MASS STORAGE. See also VOLATILE STORAGE, DYNAMIC RANDOM ACCESS MEMORY, FLASH MEMORY, ROM.

memory address See under ADDRESS.

memory allocation The most crucial activity of any computer OPERATING SYSTEM: the assignment of each program to be executed to a different range of memory addresses, ensuring that programs do not overwrite each other's space.

memory bank 1 One of several different sets of RAM chips that make up a BANK SWITCHED computer memory system. See also INTERLEAVE.
2 A term commonly employed in non-technical parlance (e.g. popular newspapers) to mean a computer DATABASE. It is meant as a metaphor that compares stored data to money in a bank vault, but since money itself is merely data nowadays it may be literally true.

memory board See MEMORY CARD.

memory card A small PRINTED CIRCUIT BOARD containing RAM chips, inserted into a computer to increase its memory size. See also EXPANSION CARD.

memory contention A situation where two processors are trying to access the same memory area in a SHARED-MEMORY MULTI-PROCESSOR system.

memory effect A defect of certain rechargeable battery technologies (most notably the NICKEL-CADMIUM and NICKEL METAL HYDRIDE CELLS) where, if the battery is repeatedly recharged when only partly discharged, it 'remembers' this amount of charge and will refuse to recharge fully, and so gradually diminishes in capacity. The effect can be avoided by never recharging the battery before it is completely discharged.

memory expansion The addition of extra RANDOM ACCESS MEMORY to a computer, typically by plugging SIMM or DIMM packages into slots provided on the MOTHERBOARD.

memory leak A common type of BUG in which a program dynamically allocates some memory (see DYNAMIC ALLOCATION) but fails to release it after use – so the program consumes more and more memory the longer it is run. If the leak is small, it may take weeks to consume enough memory to crash the program, and this is often a cause of hard-to-trace errors in SERVER applications which are seldom rebooted.

Memory Management Unit (MMU) A special-purpose processor used to implement VIRTUAL MEMORY in a computer by translating VIRTUAL ADDRESSES into actual memory locations. In a MULTITASKING system, an MMU may also map concurrent processes into different address spaces, thus preventing them from overwriting each other's data. A third function is to overcome memory FRAGMENTATION by mapping scattered chunks of physical memory to a single contiguous virtual address range.

Modern microprocessors of the Intel PENTIUM or POWERPC class have a built-in MMU interposed between the CPU proper and the memory bus. In earlier computers, it was contained on a separate chip, board or cabinet.

memory manager The component of a computer's OPERATING SYSTEM that controls the way in which memory is allocated to run new programs. Most modern operating systems are MULTITASKING, so many programs may be running at once, and programs are RELOCATABLE so they may load and execute at any address. It is the job of the memory manager to find a suitably-sized region of memory that is not being used by any other program, and to reclaim it once the new program has been terminated (some of the memory so allocated might be VIRTUAL MEMORY). See also FRAGMENTATION, COMPACTION, ADDRESS TRANSLATION.

A memory manager may work purely as a software process, or it may work in conjunction with a hardware MEMORY MANAGEMENT UNIT. See for example EMS, EMM386, HIMEM.

memory-mapped A memory-mapped PERIPHERAL device is one that communicates with its host computer by reading and writing to a range of memory locations reserved for this purpose, rather than by using a COMMUNICATION PORT.

memory model A concept employed by language compilers that generate code for processors (such as the Intel 80x86 family) that employ a SEGMENTED MEMORY MODEL. Different memory models allocate different amounts of memory to program and data, and determine whether NEAR POINTERS or FAR POINTERS will be compiled for function calls and data references. For example a *small* memory model allocates just one segment to be shared by both program and data, while a *huge* memory model permits compilation of data structures that are bigger than a single segment. See also FLAT MEMORY MODEL.

memory-resident A type of program that remains in a computer's memory even after it has ceased to execute, so that it may be reactivated without having to reload it from disk. Many extensions of the operating system (such as DEVICE DRIVERS) operate in this way. Under the UNIX operating system such programs are referred to as DAEMONS, while under MS-DOS so-called TERMINATE AND STAY RESIDENT utility programs were once deployed as a substitute for a true MULTITASKING ability.

memory space A region of computer memory occupied by a particular program and its data.

Memory Stick A portable, solid-state medium for the temporary storage and transfer of digital data, invented by Sony to handle data for pocket and hand-held devices such as digital cameras and portable MP3 music systems. Memory Sticks are small narrow cartridges ($21.5 \times 50 \times 2.8$ mm) containing FLASH MEMORY chips, with capacities currently up to 64 megabytes (but regularly rising as flash technology advances). To reduce the size of the connector required, they employ a SERIAL interface to communicate with the host device.

memory test A utility program that runs through the whole of a computer's memory, writing and reading each location in turn to detect any malfunctioning chips. On IBM-compatible PCs a memory test is automatically performed at BOOT-UP time, and can be cancelled by pressing the ESC key. See under POWER-ON SELF TEST.

memory-to-memory interconnect A technique used in the construction of CLUSTERED SMP servers, in which several separate computers have their memory systems joined together to form a single shared ADDRESS SPACE that can be accessed by all the processors. Typically a very high speed bus is used for this purpose (see SWITCHED INTERCONNECT), but some systems employ a relatively slow SERIAL interconnect, making memory accesses between cluster members slower than those within the same machine. See more under NUMA.

menu A component of many software USER INTERFACES, which consists of a list of commands or 'menu options' from which the user may select by moving a highlighted bar. A menu both reminds the user what commands are available and removes the need for the user to type them (possibly incorrectly).

Menus were employed even in the days of text-only displays, when the up and down cursor keys were used to move the selector bar and the Return key pressed to make a selection. In modern GRAPHICAL USER INTERFACES menus may appear when a mouse button is pressed over their name (the PULL-DOWN MENU or DROP-DOWN MENU), or appear at the current mouse pointer position when a button is clicked (a POP-UP MENU).

menu bar A strip running along the top of an application's window that displays the names of that application's main MENUS. Moving the mouse pointer over, or clicking a name causes the corresponding DROP-DOWN MENU to unfold. For programs that follow Microsoft's WINDOWS design guidelines, the menu bar very often starts with three menus called File, Edit and View.

menu-driven Any software system that is controlled by choosing among commands presented as a MENU.

merge To combine two sets of data to make a single larger set.

merge sort A very efficient sorting ALGORITHM that works by dividing the items to be sorted into two parts, sorting each part recursively, and then merging the parts. Merge sort has the advantage over QUICKSORT of being STABLE, but it is somewhat slower and requires memory space equal to twice the total data size – which may prove restrictive for huge data sets.

Mersenne prime A PRIME NUMBER that has the form 2^n-1, for example 31 (2^5-1).

mesh The grid of polygons that makes up a WIRE-FRAME representation of a 3D object.

MESI protocol The protocol employed to maintain CACHE COHERENCY in most SHARED-MEMORY MULTIPROCESSOR computers. The name is an acronym for Modified, Exclusive, Shared, Invalid: the four states with which any particular CACHE LINE can be labelled (using two extra bits in the cache TAG). The meanings of the terms are, briefly:

Modified: some processor has altered this line; if another processor requests an address cached here, send this altered data instead and mark it Shared.

Exclusive: no other processor is currently caching this line; any processor may write to it and mark it as Modified.

Shared: a processor may not write to this line, but must instead broadcast to all other caches holding it, telling them to mark it Invalid.

Invalid: this line must be re-read from main memory and then marked Exclusive.

Under MESI, each processor mostly reads and writes to its own or another processor's cache, and changed data is written back to main memory only when a cache is FLUSHED.

A MESI cache controller uses BUS SNOOPING to discover what locations each processor is reading and writing to.

message A communication between a sender and a receiver. See also MESSAGE PASSING.

message packet See under PACKET.

message passing Used to describe a class of MULTIPROCESSOR computer architectures in which each processor has its own separate address space, so that the different processors cannot communicate by sharing memory. Instead, they must send messages to one another over some type of inter-processor communication network. See also MULTICOMPUTER, PARALLEL VIRTUAL MACHINE.

Message Passing Interface See MPI.

message queue A type of communications MIDDLEWARE that manages message traffic between distributed applications running on a network of computers. It stores messages in the event of a lost connection, and resends them once connection is restored (see STORE-AND-FORWARD). Examples include IBM's MQSERIES and Microsoft's MESSAGE QUEUE SERVER.

Message Queue Server (MQS) A software component, first introduced by Microsoft as part of WINDOWS NT 4.0 Enterprise Edition, which provides an ASYNCHRONOUS application-to-application messaging service. Data may be transmitted between sender and receiver applications in any format that is understood by both, and the asynchronous nature of the service means that messages will be automatically retransmitted or rerouted following any application or network failure. MQS is intended to be used in conjunction with MICROSOFT TRANSACTION SERVER to implement reliable, mainframe-style transaction processing systems.

message routing 1 The process of determining the route that a message will take when traversing a network with multiple nodes. See ROUTER, ROUTING, ROUTE.

2 A class of large communications MIDDLEWARE suite that provides reliable distribution of messages across WANs. Such as suite typically offers such features as MULTICASTING of company-wide memos, and PUBLISH-AND-SUBSCRIBE services that send the latest versions of selected documents to the appropriate individuals. See also MESSAGE QUEUE, MIDDLEWARE, LOTUS NOTES.

message transfer agent Another name for a MAIL TRANSPORT AGENT.

Messaging Application Programming Interface See MAPI.

metadata Literally data about data: for example the name of a database field, rather than the value that field contains. The Document Type Definitions (DTD) and style sheets that describe how to interpret an XML document transmitted via the Internet are a powerful form of metadata, and the importance of metadata continually increases with the rise in the use of such transportable notations. There is also an increasing tendency to use the term in a looser sense to refer to the entire contents of a REPOSITORY which may contain all of a company's online resources. In this case, the boundary between what is data and what is metadata becomes unclear. See also SCHEMA, DATA DICTIONARY, DATA WAREHOUSE, DIRECTORY SERVICE, UDDI.

metadirectory A network DIRECTORY SERVICE which provides access to, and management for, several other disparate directories. See also LDAP, ACTIVE DIRECTORY.

metafile Literally a file that contains information about files, though the term has come to be used to describe various hybrid VECTOR GRAPHICS/BITMAPPED GRAPHICS file formats that contain both a geometric description of an image and raw binary data. Examples include the WINDOWS METAFILE FORMAT, COMPUTER GRAPHICS METAFILE, 3D METAFILE and ENCAPSULATED POSTSCRIPT.

metalanguage 1 In logic, a language used to examine the truth of statements in another language.

2 In computing, a programming language used to manipulate logical proofs: languages such as LISP and PROLOG are often employed as such metalanguages. The term is also applied

to languages such as XML and SGML that can be used to define other, more task-specific languages.

metal oxide semiconductor See MOS.

metal oxide semiconductor field effect transistor See MOSFET.

metal-oxide varistor (MOV) See under VARISTOR.

metaphor A scenario drawn from the real world which is imitated on a computer screen to make some operation feel more familiar to the user. The classic example is the DESKTOP metaphor employed by the graphical user interface of most modern operating systems. Since computers typically handle only representations of the world rather than real objects, the choice of suitable metaphors plays an important part in software design.

metasyntactic variable A name chosen by a programmer for the purposes of illustration, intended to represent an abstract example of the entity being explained (for example, a variable, a file, a database or a procedure) or a random member of a collection of such entities. Programmers tend toward whimsy in their choice of these names: *foo*, *bar* and *zot* are timelessly popular, while names drawn from *The Flintstones*, *Star Trek*, *Lord of the Rings* or Lewis Carroll's *Jabberwocky* may reveal rather too much about the cultural achievements of their user.

meta tag An HTML TAG that may contain arbitrary name/value pairs that will not be interpreted by a web browser. A meta tag provides a space in which to store keywords for SEARCH ENGINES to index, to store commands intended for non-browser utilities (e.g. for access control), or simply to describe the contents or ownership of a site. For example:

```
<meta name=company value="Penguin">
```

method The name given by an OBJECT-ORIENTED PROGRAMMING LANGUAGE to a procedure or function that is associated with a CLASS of objects. Methods may be executed only by creating an instance of the class and calling the method through it, typically by suffixing the method name to the object name, as in MyDocument.print. This is a reversal of traditional programming practice, where procedures perform actions on data. Instead, objects perform actions on themselves, and their methods are the actions they know how to perform.

The term method is applied both to the name of such a procedure, as it appears in a class's INTERFACE, and to its implementation, i.e. the actual code that performs its action.

method call In OBJECT-ORIENTED PROGRAMMING the equivalent of a PROCEDURE CALL, in which an object invokes the program code contained in one of its own, or another object's METHODS.

methodology A formalized and documented sequence of steps and guidelines for performing one or more stages of the software development process (such as DATA ANALYSIS or design). Many methodologies start out from a graphical notation that uses diagrams to describe the system under development at the appropriate levels of abstraction – computerized tools may be used to help draw these diagrams and translate them into program templates. A methodology usually prescribes a step-by-step approach to carrying out the necessary tasks, and a set of criteria for judging the acceptability of the results. Well-known methodologies include the YOURDON METHOD, the BOOCH METHOD, and the UNIFIED METHOD.

me too An allusion to the slavish copying of competitor's product features, used as in 'that's just a "me too" feature'.

metric Also called a *software metric*, a procedure for quantitatively evaluating a software project by measuring various aspects such as its overall size and complexity, the understandability of its source code, and its amenability to testing. Most metric procedures work by examining the structure of – and linkage between – the larger modules that make up a project, rather than working at the level of individual lines of code.

The two most widely used metrics are *Halstead's software science counts* (which calculates the executable code volume by counting the operators and operands used) and *McCabe's cyclomatic complexity measure* (which measures the number of nodes and edges in a diagram of the program's CONTROL FLOW). With both methods, the most complex (and therefore hardest to test) parts of a program will yield the highest metric value, and a project supervisor may decide to split up and rewrite such modules until their metrics fall below some prescribed limit.

Benchmark suites used for assessing execution performance, and methods such as COCOMO for estimating the cost of a project may also be describes as metrics. See also ALPHA TESTING, BETA TESTING, DEBUGGING, USABILITY.

MFC Abbreviation of MICROSOFT FOUNDATION CLASSES.

MFLOPS Shorthand for MEGAFLOPS.

MHTML (MIME email encapsulation of HTML documents) An Internet standard developed by the INTERNET ENGINEERING TASK FORCE that permits images, forms and multiple fonts to be embedded within an email message as a single file (using the MIME encoding scheme). It permits existing web pages to be sent as email messages without modification, but viewing the embedded content of such messages requires an HTML-enabled email program such as recent versions of Eudora and Microsoft Outlook Express. The same message may also contain a plain ASCII version for reading in older mail programs. Microsoft employs MHTML under its own proprietary name of Web Archive. See also WEB FORM, XML, DYNAMIC HTML, ENCAPSULATED POSTSCRIPT.

MHz Abbreviation of MEGAHERTZ.

MIB (Management Information Base) A database used to store status information collected by an SNMP network management system.

mickey The unit of MOUSE movement employed by Microsoft that consists of 1/65535 of the height and width of the display screen. The name pays tribute to Walt Disney's popular hero.

microarchitecture The internal structure of a microprocessor, so named to distinguish it from the architecture of the whole computer inside which it operates. The term microarchitecture covers the physical layout of the REGISTERS, CACHES, BUFFERS and BUS, and also the processor's INSTRUCTION SET and SCHEDULING logic. See also MICROCODE, RISC, CISC.

microbilling Charging an extremely small sum of money for viewing the contents of web pages. For example, a microbilling system might charge 0.1p for each page viewed on a site. Such small sums must be accumulated in a credit account until the cost of collecting them becomes significantly less than the sum to be collected. Also called *micropayment*.

microcash The tiny sums of money that are exchanged in MICROBILLING systems.

Micro Channel Architecture (MCA) IBM's proprietary 32-bit EXPANSION BUS launched in its PS/2 range of personal computers in 1987. In its support for multiple processors and self-configuration to avoid hardware conflicts, MCA is superior to the ISA BUS that it replaced, but it is not backward-compatible and could not use the millions of existing ISA-bus expansion cards. As a result MCA was never adopted by CLONE manufacturers, and by 1993, Intel's PCI BUS had effectively killed it.

microchip A vernacular term for INTEGRATED CIRCUITS or VLSI chips, used in the popular Press but rarely in the industry.

microcode A sequence of stored steps that together implement a single instruction in a COMPLEX INSTRUCTION SET COMPUTER. Microcode can be considered as a very specialized form of software, which is stored in an area of ROM within the processor's CONTROL UNIT and is not replaceable. Microcode instructions are not concerned with the manipulation of user data, but only with the coordination of the operation of the sub-units within the processor itself; such as connecting a particular buffer to a bus or moving a word of data from one register to another.

microcommerce The activity of selling information viewed on a web site at low prices but high volumes, using a MICROBILLING system.

microcomputer An obsolete name, originally applied to what are now called PERSONAL COMPUTERS that employ a MICROPROCESSOR as their central processing unit (CPU). It was coined to suggest their status as successors to the MINICOMPUTER. The term was also used to refer to the microprocessor itself.

microcontroller A type of integrated circuit designed to act as a processor for EMBEDDED SYSTEMS (e.g. for controlling machinery or toys) which is typically smaller, simpler, cheaper and uses less power than a general purpose MICROPROCESSOR. Most microcontrollers contain a small amount of on-chip RAM and ROM in which all the required software is stored and run, removing the need for any external memory. Many microcontrollers (such as the PIC range) remain 8-bit devices, which offers sufficient computing power for their restricted applications.

microelectromechanics The official name for NANOTECHNOLOGY, an engineering discipline that exploits the new fabrication techiques developed by the semiconductor industry to build tiny machines, motors and sensors.

microelectronics The study and creation of miniature electronic circuits such as the MICROPROCESSOR.

microinstruction One of the instructions that makes up the MICROCODE of a COMPLEX INSTRUCTION SET COMPUTER.

microjustification Altering the spacing between the characters of a text by fractions of a normal space, which enables even letter spacing to be achieved in a JUSTIFIED document. This feature is supported by all professional DESKTOP PUBLISHING and TYPESETTING programs.

microkernel An operating system KERNEL that performs only the most basic of functions (typically only memory allocation and task scheduling) and hence is very small in size. Operating systems designed around a microkernel provide all their higher-level services as separate modules that operate outside the microkernel, allowing them to be configured more easily for a variety of roles, from handheld devices with minimal memory up to desktop computers. Examples of operating systems that employ microkernels include CHORUS, NEXTSTEP, Apple's MacOS and Symbian's EPOC 32.

micron One millionth of a metre. The term is officially obsolete, having been replaced by an identical SI unit called the micrometre (10^{-6} m), but it is still used informally within the semiconductor industry to describe the FEATURE SIZE of integrated circuits.

microparallelism The ability of a microprocessor to perform several internal operations at once. See also SUPERSCALAR, SUPERPIPELINE.

micropayment See under MICROBILLING.

microprocessor A computer integrated onto a single piece of silicon or CHIP, often referred to informally as a *microchip*, or the *silicon chip*. The microprocessor was the invention that sparked the revolution in computing and communications which began in the late 1970s. The first commercial microprocessor was the Intel 4004 launched in 1971, which was designed to be used in a Japanese desk calculator.

Microprocessors lie at the heart of all modern computers, not only personal computers, and are also EMBEDDED as controllers in many industrial and domestic appliances, from cars to washing machines. A single microprocessor chip, together with some memory chips, forms the basis for a simple computer (and for some embedded applications may even have the memory integrated onto the same chip). The electronic components of a modern microprocessor chip are very densely packed, cramming some 100 million transistors onto a silicon die around 15 mm square, and this density rises with every generation (in accordance with MOORE'S LAW).

The main components of a typical microprocessor chip are: INTEGER and FLOATING-POINT arithmetic units which actually perform the calculations; a bank of REGISTERS that hold both the numbers currently being worked on, and the results; an INSTRUCTION FETCH unit which gets the next instructions to be executed from external memory; one or more CACHES to speed up access to data and instructions that are anticipated to be needed soon; and a CONTROL UNIT which choreographs the operations of all these other units. Together, these core units act as the central processing unit (CPU) of a computer. Mainstream microprocessors, such as those of the Intel PENTIUM or the POWERPC families, often integrate several additional functional units such as a MEMORY MANAGEMENT UNIT, INTERRUPT CONTROLLER and BUS control unit onto the chip. There is also a tendency toward adding special units and instructions to assist specific tasks such as graphics or sound processing.

microprogrammable A type of computer processor in which the user can replace the MICROCODE after manufacture and customize the instructions that the processor can execute. Microprogrammability is not a feature of commercial microprocessors, and is found only in a very few specialist chips such as SIGNAL PROCESSORS, MICROCONTROLLERS, MPEG decoders and similar devices.

microsecond (μs) One millionth of a second.

microsequencer 1 A simple type of MICROCONTROLLER chip used in CNC machine tools, which is barely a fully-fledged computer but can merely open and close a set of switches by reading a list of instructions.
2 The part of the CONTROL UNIT of a COMPLEX INSTRUCTION SET COMPUTER that orders the execution of the MICROINSTRUCTIONS.

Microsoft Access (Access) The RELATIONAL DATABASE MANAGEMENT SYSTEM supplied as part of the MICROSOFT OFFICE software suite. Access employs a graphical user interface that enables a user to design the layout of data TABLES, FORMS and REPORTS in an interactive, visual way. Access can automatically generate several predefined form layouts, and provides an interactive WIZARD that elicits the user's preferences in step-by-step fashion. It also provides built-in VISUAL PROGRAMMING tools that enable forms to be designed on screen by dragging and dropping prefabricated controls onto a blank form template.

Access integrates strongly with VISUAL BASIC, exposing most of its functions as objects accessible to other programs, and it contains the VISUAL BASIC FOR APPLICATIONS subset as its MACRO LANGUAGE. Powerful applications can be constructed with little extra programming by combining Access with the other Office applications such as WORD and EXCEL using the COM-based AUTOMATION mechanism. Access is suitable for creating single user databases of small to medium size, but for distributed CLIENT/SERVER systems SQL SERVER is to be preferred.

Microsoft BackOffice A suite of server software for WINDOWS NT that includes SQL SERVER, INTERNET INFORMATION SERVER and EXCHANGE server. It is intended to support the creation of complete networked CLIENT/SERVER systems.

Microsoft Basic An interpreter for a dialect of the BASIC programming language, originally written by Bill GATES and Paul ALLEN as Microsoft's first product. An early version of Microsoft Basic for the APPLE II supported graphics, while a version called BASICA was built into the ROM of the original IBM PC. A disk-based version called GWBASIC (reputedly for Gee Whizz) introduced a full-screen PROGRAM EDITOR and DEBUGGER and was bundled with most MS-DOS computers. Later versions included MBASIC (which incorporated a COMPILER) and QBASIC. VISUAL BASIC is a different language entirely, with little in common with other Microsoft Basics.

Microsoft Certified System Engineer (MCSE) A qualification issued by Microsoft-approved training courses in the company's operating systems and servers.

Microsoft Corporation (Microsoft) The world's largest publisher of personal computer software and OPERATING SYSTEMS, founded in 1975 by Bill GATES and Paul ALLEN, two Harvard computing students. Gates and Allen wrote an interpreter for the BASIC language that was small enough to run on the new breed of tiny computers based on microprocessor chips, and they sold it to all the earliest vendors including APPLE and COMMODORE BUSINESS MACHINES.

The IBM PC was launched in 1981 with Microsoft's PC-DOS operating system (rather than the then industry-standard CP/M) and this became the foundation of the company's fortune. When IBM-compatible CLONE PCs appeared in the 1980s, Microsoft sold a copy of the generic version of MS-DOS with every one of the millions of machines.

Following the 1984 launch of Apple's MACINTOSH, Microsoft added a graphical layer over MS-DOS called WINDOWS, and this is now the world's most widely used operating system in its own right (the underlying MS-DOS having been finally abandoned by WINDOWS 2000). Microsoft also publishes the best-selling suite of application software for Windows,

MICROSOFT OFFICE. The company is now numbered among the richest in the world by revenue, and its founders are among the world's richest men.

In May 2000 the US Justice Department ruled that Microsoft had established a monopoly, and that it should be split into two parts, one for operating systems and one for applications. This ruling was partially overturned on appeal in June 2001 but hearings continue and various US states have added antitrust actions.

Microsoft Excel (Excel) The SPREADSHEET component of the MICROSOFT OFFICE software suite. Excel provides many sophisticated mathematical and statistical functions, easy-to-use interactive graphing and charting facilities, and powerful analytical tools such as PIVOT TABLES and a constraint SOLVER.

Excel integrates strongly with VISUAL BASIC, exposing most of its functions as objects accessible to other programs, and it contains the VISUAL BASIC FOR APPLICATIONS subset as its MACRO LANGUAGE. Powerful applications can be constructed with little programming effort by combining Excel with the other Microsoft Office applications, for example using Excel to display records retrieved from a MICROSOFT ACCESS database.

Microsoft Foundation Classes A C++ CLASS LIBRARY that encapsulates all the basic components used in Microsoft's Windows operating systems, and may be used to speed the writing of ACTIVEX controls and other COM (COMPONENT OBJECT MODEL) objects in VISUAL C++.

Microsoft Network See MSN.

Microsoft Office (Office) Microsoft's best-selling suite of application software currently available for the company's own WINDOWS operating systems and for the APPLE MACINTOSH. There are various versions, intended for single users, multiple networked users and software developers, which contain some or all of the following programs: the MICROSOFT WORD word processor; MICROSOFT EXCEL spreadsheet; INTERNET EXPLORER web browser; POWERPOINT presentation program; OUTLOOK mail and personal organizer program; MICROSOFT ACCESS database manager; Publisher desktop publishing; Front Page web authoring program; Project time manager; and several other utility programs.

The popularity of Office stems from the fact that several of its components are the best in their market, and all of them share a similar user interface. They can also be easily automated and integrated to create complex business systems by using the built-in MACRO LANGUAGE called VISUAL BASIC FOR APPLICATIONS. For example, functions of Access, Word and Excel might be combined to produce accounting or document management systems.

Office is a prime example of an OBJECT-ORIENTED software system, as many of its components share their core modules and make many of their internal operations available to other programs via a METHOD interface.

Microsoft Point-to-Point Encryption An encryption protocol that may be used with the POINT-TO-POINT TUNNELLING PROTOCOL to provide a secure connection.

Microsoft Transaction Server (MTS) A software component, first released for WINDOWS NT 4.0 but now incorporated into Windows 2000, which serves as a TRANSACTION MONITOR for COM-based (see COMMON OBJECT MODEL) Windows programs. MTS provides full transactional semantics to programs that run under it, including automatic ROLLBACK in the event of failure to complete, queuing of requests, load balancing on multiple processors, and automatic THREAD management via a pool of threads that are recycled after use.

Microsoft Windows See WINDOWS.

Microsoft Word (Word) The WORD PROCESSOR component of the MICROSOFT OFFICE application suite. Word for Windows offers features that were previously confined to DESKTOP PUBLISHING programs. These include WYSIWYG display of proportionally-spaced FONTS, and multi-column layouts with headlines, illustrations and tables embedded in the text. Word has the ability to automatically create tables, and can output documents as HTML for use on web sites. Using the built-in VISUAL BASIC FOR APPLICATIONS Word can be integrated with databases and other applications to create customized DOCUMENT MANAGEMENT SYSTEMS.

microsystem A complete electronic data processing system implemented on a single chip. Designed to perform specialized tasks such as gas analysis, GPS direction finding, or radio transmission and reception, microsystems are increasingly (for reasons of size, power-consumption and cost) used to build hand-held devices. They typically combine various solid-state SENSORS with a microprocessor and software stored in ROM.

middle-tier application A program that runs on the middle tier of a CLIENT/SERVER networked application that employs a THREE-TIER ARCHITECTURE. Middle-tier software mediates between users requesting or entering data (the first tier) and the BACK-END database (the third tier), converting data into suitable formats and performing those shared and business-specific tasks that are often collectively referred to as BUSINESS LOGIC.

middleware An extra layer of software interposed between a user's application program and a network to manage transactions that may involve several different SERVERS and SERVER-SIDE applications. Middleware is often employed to provide fault tolerant features (see MESSAGE QUEUE), to translate between applications that use different data formats, or to REPLICATE a remote database onto a local machine.

MIDI (Musical Instrument Digital Interface) A standard interface for controlling electronic musical instruments. MIDI provides both a hardware specification for synthesizers, music keyboards and other electronic instruments, and a software protocol that lets them exchange note and sound-effect information with a SEQUENCER program running on a computer. The connection is made via a high-speed SERIAL link that employs separate connections for *MIDI in, MIDI out,* and *MIDI through* to allow devices to be DAISY-CHAINED.

The fundamental units of MIDI information are the *note on* and *note off* EVENTS, which include both a note's number (pitch) and its key velocity (loudness). Hence MIDI completely specifies a particular musical performance, unlike conventional musical notation, which represents the composer's ideal intention. The MIDI description of a piece can be captured merely by playing it on a keyboard into a sequencer. The MIDI file format simply contains a dump of the data stream sent over the MIDI PORT.

There are many other MIDI message types that describe events such as pitch bend (i.e. glissando), PATCH changes (i.e. different instrument sounds) and control events specific to a particular synthesizer, say to load a new patch from disk.

midrange system The computer marketing term for systems that are larger than a PERSONAL COMPUTER but smaller than a MAINFRAME, and which thereby inhabit roughly that market sector once occupied by MINICOMPUTERS. See also DEPARTMENTAL, ENTERPRISE, SOHO.

Millicent A sophisticated MICROBILLING system developed by DIGITAL EQUIPMENT CORPORATION. It works by exchanging a virtual currency called scrip, which is ultimately redeemed by a credit-card company or bank for real cash.

Milnet The unclassified part of the US military network which, along with the ARPANET, was a forerunner of today's Internet.

MIMD (multiple-instruction multiple-data) A generic description that can be applied to any MULTIPROCESSOR computer architecture in which each processor is able to execute a different program, as distinct from a SIMD architecture in which each processor executes the same program on a different data item (see also VECTOR PROCESSOR). With a MIMD architecture, the deployment of the program code onto the different processors and the interconnection TOPOLOGY of the processors become visible to the programmer, and complicate the writing of programs. See more under PARALLEL PROGRAMMING, TOPOLOGY, HYPERCUBE. See also MULTICOMPUTER, MESSAGE PASSING.

MIME (Multipurpose Internet Mail Extensions) A protocol and file format used to send multimedia documents (which may include images, video clips, sounds, facsimile images and executable files) in email messages across the Internet. MIME encodes BINARY FILES, such as images, into a stream of ASCII characters using the BASE64 encoding scheme, so that they can pass through text-only Internet mail GATEWAYS. MIME supports the splitting of large documents into several smaller sections to overcome any size restrictions on particular network connections, and a MIME-enabled mail reader will normally reassemble such sections automatically without user intervention. MIME is defined in RFC 1341.

The MIME protocol identifies many different kinds of file content, called MIME TYPES, by adding a unique identifier to the encoded file. The recognized types include many graphics, sound, and compressed archive formats, such as text/plain, text/html, or video/mpeg.

MIME type A unique identifier allocated to each type of file that can be transmitted across the Internet as MIME-encoded email or via HTTP, to enable the recipient to associate it with a program that can open it. Examples of MIME types include application/pdf (an Adobe Acrobat document) and image/jpeg (a JPEG-encoded graphic). New MIME types may be registered with the Internet authorities as explained in RFC 2048.

minicomputer A term coined to distinguish a new generation of computers introduced from the 1960s onward by companies such as DIGITAL EQUIPMENT CORPORATION (DEC) and DATA GENERAL. These computers were smaller and cost much less than the IBM MAINFRAMES that then dominated the very restricted market. Minicomputers such as those in DEC's PDP series were cheap enough to be used by small businesses or to be dedicated to process control, and in some universities they were used as personal computers to write early interactive software.

A mainframe CPU occupied a whole cabinet, but a typical minicomputer CPU consisted of a single board. This size decrease continued through to the 1980s when the minicomputer itself was displaced by the personal computer (for a while called the *microcomputer*) which had its CPU on a single chip.

MiniDisc (MD) An OPTICAL DISC storage format introduced by Sony in 1992, which at present is mainly used for music and consumer electronics rather than for computer storage. The format was intended to replace the compact tape CASSETTE for home recording, rather than to replace the CD as a distribution medium.

A MiniDisc is 64 mm in diameter and, like a floppy disk, permanently enclosed in a plastic cassette. Two types are available: one read-

only, and one eraseable and rewriteable using MAGNETO-OPTICAL technology. Both types hold 74 or 80 minutes of digital music (the same as the much larger CD) by employing ATRAC compression. When used for data storage they can hold 140 megabytes of data. Unlike the music CD, a writeable MiniDisc's table of contents is editable by the user, so that the play order and title of the tracks can be altered. MiniDiscs are used mostly in personal record players, significantly smaller than a Walkman, and as yet there have been few applications to portable computers. See also MEMORY STICK, CD-RW.

minimax algorithm An algorithm used in computer games, to choose the best next move in a two-player game such as chess. It chooses that move which minimizes the maximum (hence the name) combined value of the opponent's possible next moves.

minimize To cause a screen window within a program that employs a graphical user interface to collapse down into a single ICON on the desktop, TASKBAR or some other temporary parking area. Clicking on the icon causes the window to reopen to its previous state with all its contents intact. Programs that are minimized remain in memory and continue to run (perhaps executing some lengthy processing job as a BACKGROUND TASK), so minimizing is usually a purely visual matter performed to avoid screen clutter. See also MAXIMIZE, MULTITASKING.

minimum seek time See TRACK-TO-TRACK SEEK TIME.

Ministry of International Trade and Industry (MITI) The Japanese government department whose promotion and sponsorship helped create the country's strong electronics industry.

MIP mapping A refinement of the TEXTURE MAPPING technique for creating realistic 3D images. Three or more differently-sized copies of the same texture are stored, and the version appropriate for each different magnification of a scene is used in order to avoid degrading the texture by stretching it too far. See also BUMP MAPPING, ENVIRONMENT MAPPING.

MIPS (Millions of Instructions Per Second) A widely used measure of processing speed.

Miranda A strongly typed (see under TYPE CHECKING), LAZY, purely FUNCTIONAL PROGRAMMING LANGUAGE developed at the University of Kent in 1980.

mirror To duplicate the contents of one hard disk on a second disk to provide a safe backup in the event of one disk failing. Some operating systems (such as WINDOWS NT) offer an automatic mirroring facility which routes all the data written to both disks simultaneously. See also RAID, FAULT-TOLERANT, JOURNALLING, BACKUP, RELIABILITY, AVAILABILITY.

mirrored volume Under Microsoft's DYNAMIC STORAGE system, a type of VOLUME that consists of space on two disks, each holding exactly the same data to provide fault-tolerance through duplication. See also DISK MIRRORING and RAID.

misprediction In a processor that employs BRANCH PREDICTION, a wrong 'guess' (that is, predicting branch taken when not taken, or vice versa) that results in a PIPELINE BREAK. If the processor also employs SPECULATIVE EXECUTION, then many clock cycles may be wasted while the correct instruction stream is fetched; this is called the 'misprediction penalty'.

mission-critical Any hardware or software system whose continuous operation is essential to the workings of a business. For most modern businesses the telephone and fax equipment, and possibly a computer database or network server might be so described. The term originated at NASA and the space program in the 1960s, hence the name.

MIT (Massachusetts Institute of Technology) One of the premier American technical colleges, located in Cambridge Massachusetts, and the origin of many important innovations in computing, including the first graphical computer displays and the first interactive OPERATING SYSTEM.

MITI Abbreviation of MINISTRY OF INTERNATIONAL TRADE AND INDUSTRY.

MITS Altair See ALTAIR 8800.

M-JPEG See MOTION JPEG.

ML A STRICT, purely FUNCTIONAL PROGRAMMING LANGUAGE invented at Edinburgh University in 1978.

MMI (Man-Machine Interface) An alternative term for USER INTERFACE, favoured in academic circles.

MMU Abbreviation of MEMORY MANAGEMENT UNIT.

MMX (MultiMedia Extensions or Matrix Math Extensions) A set of additions to the INSTRUCTION SET of Intel's PENTIUM family of microprocessors, designed to speed up their performance when running multimedia and graphics software such as games, while retaining compatibility with older software.

MMX consists of 57 new instructions that apply simple arithmetic and logic operations to a set of eight 64-bit REGISTERS, which are shared with the Pentium's FLOATING-POINT UNIT (an MMX operation cannot be therefore be executed concurrently with a floating point operation). These registers hold PACKED integer values – eight bytes, four 16-bit, two 32-bit or a single 64-bit value – which typically represent PIXELS, thus enabling as many as 8 pixels to be processed in a single cycle in the manner of a VECTOR PROCESSOR. Common graphics and sound processing algorithms such as the DISCRETE COSINE TRANSFORM, FOURIER TRANSFORM or WAVELET compression can exploit such concurrency to run several times faster. However, in order to benefit from this acceleration, programs must be rewritten and recompiled with an MMX-aware compiler.

mnemonic An abbreviation chosen to assist in remembering some longer phrase. Examples abound in computing including LIFO (Last In, First Out), FIFO (First In, First Out) and in particular the ASSEMBLER MNEMONICS used by programmers to remember machine code instructions.

mobile phone Also known as a *cellular phone*, *cell phone*, or *mobile*. A wireless, battery-operated mobile telephone handset that communicates via a nationwide network of closely-spaced transmitters. The area served by each such transmitter is called a 'cell'. Each mobile phone contains computerized circuitry that switches frequencies from one transmitter to its neighbour as the user travels around between cells.

The first mobile phone systems employed analogue signals but increasingly such systems are moving to digital technology, which provides both better speech quality and security, and enables the use of SHORT MESSAGE SERVICE or TEXTING in addition to voice calls. Most mobile phones are capable of storing a limited number of telephone numbers in an internal memory, which can be searched and dialled automatically using a built-in LCD display and browser buttons. There is an increasing trend to employ larger LCD displays so that the phone can be used to connect to the INTERNET and read EMAILS, and even to integrate all the functions of a hand-held computer such as an address database, appointment calendar and note-taking facilities. See also SMARTPHONE, WAP, GSM, CDMA, GPRS.

mod The MODULUS operator which returns the remainder following a division; for example 5 mod 3 is 2.

modal dialogue A type of DIALOGUE that renders all other screen windows inaccessible so long as it is visible, and allows no other action to be performed until its OK BUTTON has been pressed. Under the latest versions of Windows with more sophisticated MULTITASKING, only windows belonging to the same application may be affected. Contrast this behaviour with that of a MODELESS dialogue.

mode One of several possible manners of operation of a piece of hardware or software. For example Intel processors can execute code in REAL MODE or PROTECTED MODE. Most WORD PROCESSORS have two different modes: newly typed words either overwrite existing words, or push them to the right.

Since actions that are desirable in one mode may be inappropriate in another, some software designers see modes as a source of error and propose MODELESS systems as the ideal. See also MODAL DIALOGUE.

mode bit A single bit, often stored in a hardware register, whose value alters the mode of operation of some program or device. For example, inside a microprocessor, a mode bit might cause a switch between 31-bit and 32-bit addressing. See also FLAG.

model A set of data stored in a computer to represent the attributes of some real world system, for example a set of data concerning a business that are stored in a SPREADSHEET, or the 3D GRAPHICS coordinates describing an object that are stored in an engineering or architectural CAD program. See also MODEL-VIEW-CONTROLLER PARADIGM.

modeless A style of USER INTERFACE in which there are no different MODES of operation, so every action that is permitted can be initiated from the same screen display by selecting the appropriate CONTROL. See also MODELESS DIALOGUE.

modeless dialogue A type of DIALOGUE that does not render other screen windows inaccessible while it is visible; so the user may move away and perform some other activity (such as locate a file or check free disk space) before completing the details requested in the dialogue and pressing its OK BUTTON. See also MODAL DIALOGUE.

model-view-controller paradigm (MVC) A style of software architecture for graphics systems in which the USER INTERFACE (the *view*) is kept rigorously separate from the data (the *model*) and the functions that work on it (the *controller*). The scheme promotes the creation of many different kinds of view onto a single data MODEL, and allows the functionality to be changed without disrupting the model. The concept was first explored in the SMALLTALK language at Xerox PARC in the 1970s, and has influenced to greater or lesser extents all modern GUIs including WINDOWS.

modem Short for modulator/demodulator, an electronic device that converts DIGITAL computer data into ANALOGUE audio signals, and vice versa, thus allowing computers to communicate with one another over the public telephone system. The earliest modems, called ACOUSTIC COUPLERS, turned computer data into actual sounds that were played into the mouthpiece of the telephone handset. Modern modems send an audio-frequency electrical signal directly into the telephone line, bypassing the handset altogether.

There is a limit to the speed at which signals can be sent over traditional copper telephone wires, but modern modems employ a range of clever modulation, error correction and data compression schemes to push this limit up to 56 kilobits per second. Such a modem contains its own microprocessor, memory and software and is capable of several functions. It may be able to send and receive faxes and store voice messages like an answering machine, in addition to handling computer data. Modems are capable of dialling and answering the phone automatically, and AUTO-SENSING the speed of another modem at the other end of the line. Conformance to standards issued by the ITU now ensures that modems of any make, from anywhere in the world can talk to one another. See more under V STANDARDS.

Digital telephone networks such as ISDN can carry computer data directly, without conversion into an audio signal, and so no modem is required to communicate over these networks. A TERMINAL ADAPTER, which converts the computer data into the proper format and handles dialling, replaces the modem. See also CABLE MODEM, FAX MODEM, NULL MODEM, SOFTWARE MODEM.

moderator The person who is responsible for maintaining order and civility in an online FORUM such as a NEWSGROUP or CONFERENCE.

modifier key Any key on a computer keyboard that can be pressed simultaneously with another key to alter its function: this includes the universally present SHIFT KEY, the almost ubiquitous CTRL KEY and ALT KEY, and various other keys specific to certain manufacturers such as the Apple key on MACINTOSH keyboards, the Windows key on PCs and the Fn key found on many reduced-size LAPTOP keyboards.

Modula-2 A programming language designed by Niklaus WIRTH in 1978 as the successor to PASCAL. Modula-2 introduced the concept of a MODULE, with a well-defined and separately compiled INTERFACE, which encapsulates a group of procedures and data structures and hides their implementation from the rest of the program. This assists in the development of large programs by teams of programmers. Modula-2 also supported a limited form of concurrency using COROUTINES.

modular Constructed from several separate, and by implication replaceable, MODULES. See also MODULARITY.

Modular Approach to Software Construction Operation and Test (MASCOT) A design METHODOLOGY for REAL TIME EMBEDDED SYSTEMS software developed at the Royal Signals and Research Establishment at Malvern in the UK.

modularity The most powerful concept available for managing the complexity of large systems (whether hardware or software, living or dead), which involves dividing them into smaller units called MODULES. For example in the evolution of living things, the cell (a *biological module*) was the first structure to emerge and was the basis of all higher life forms.

Modularity is not a matter of size, as simply chopping a complex system into arbitrary smaller pieces does not necessarily simplify it. The crucial point is that the modules must be independent so that they can be constructed separately, and more simply than the whole. For instance it is much easier to make a brick than a house, and many different kinds of house can be made from standard bricks; but this would cease to be true if the bricks depended upon one another like the pieces of a jigsaw puzzle.

modulate To alter some property of a communication SIGNAL in a systematic way so that it conveys information. In AMPLITUDE MODULATION the property so altered is the magnitude of an electromagnetic CARRIER wave, while in FREQUENCY MODULATION it is the wave's frequency that is altered: both schemes are widely used in radio frequency communication. Modern telephone systems such as XDSL rely on extremely complex and sophisticated modulation schemes based on the relative PHASE of waves.

module A self-contained unit (either hardware or software) that may be joined to other such units to form a larger system. The exploitation of MODULARITY is a fundamental principle of all modern engineering disciplines, from cars and aircraft to washing machines and computers.

A hardware module, such as a memory or processor module, contains several components mounted on a single circuit board, with a standard connector so that it can be plugged into a matching socket on other equipment. A software module (such as a DLL) is a file containing one or more subprograms whose implementations are hidden, but whose names and parameters are made visible so that they can be called from a main program (see also INTERFACE). Hence changes may be made to the implementation of a module without affecting programs that use it.

modulo arithmetic Arithmetic on a finite and cyclically repeating range of INTEGERS. For example in arithmetic modulo 3, only the numbers 0, 1 and 2 are represented, so 1 + 2 = 0 and 2 + 2 = 1. Any natural number can be converted to modulo n by dividing it by n and taking the remainder, so that 7 modulo 3 is 1.

The finite WORD LENGTH imposed by computer hardware means that all arithmetic performed by a computer is in fact modulo arithmetic. For example, a computer that has only 8-bit REGISTERS can perform only arithmetic modulo 256 (2^8) in a single operation, and the result of adding 6 to a register containing 254 would be 4.

See also ONES COMPLEMENT, TWOS COMPLEMENT, WRAP-AROUND.

modulus 1 An INTEGER that divides exactly into the difference between two other integers: so 2 is a modulus of 11 and 3. See also MOD, MODULO ARITHMETIC.

2 In the RSA ENCRYPTION method, the product of the two large primes used in calculating the private and public keys.

3 The absolute value of a COMPLEX NUMBER. The modulus of the number a+bi is defined as $\sqrt{(a^2+b^2)}$.

Moiré pattern A pattern of concentric fringes or stripes that appears when two identical or very similar rectangular grids are superimposed slightly out of alignment. It is caused by the interference of two-dimensional spatial waveforms. Unwanted Moiré effects often arise when a picture that is already composed of dots is digitized for a second time or when DITHERING is applied to its colours.

The term originally referred to a variety of silk cloth that uses such patterns for decorative effect.

molecular beam epitaxy (MBE) A semiconductor FABRICATION process that creates composite materials by depositing layers of different materials a single molecule thick on top of one another, by firing a beam of particles at the target in a vacuum chamber.

MBE is used to make specialized chips with complex 'sandwich' structures of different elements that have light-emitting properties that are useful in OPTOELECTRONIC applications. However, at present MBE is too slow and too expensive to make high-volume chips.

monadic operator An arithmetic or logical OPERATOR that takes only a single argument. An example is the negation operator, as in -3 or NOT P.

moniker A COM (COMMON OBJECT MODEL) object whose sole purpose is to create and initialize another COM object, hiding from its client the details of how this is done.

Monikers contain PERSISTENT data that is preserved from one session to the next: for example, a file moniker contains the name of its associated file. Monikers are used to store the information about linked documents under OLE, for example when a graphic is embedded into a text document.

monitor 1 An alternative name for a VDU.

2 A type of software utility that runs continuously as a BACKGROUND TASK to collect data on the working of a part of its computer system, such as hard disk usage or the volume of network traffic.

3 A data structure employed in CONCURRENT programming to regulate access to a resource that must be shared by several processes. A monitor is implemented as an ABSTRACT DATA TYPE that encapsulates input and output QUEUES, and the competing processes must explicitly relinquish control to one another by calling its `delay` and `continue` routines. See also SEMAPHORE, MUTEX.

monochrome An image or display that employs only a single colour against a contrasting background.

Monochrome Display Adapter (MDA) The DISPLAY ADAPTER supplied with the original IBM PC in 1981, which generated a text-only display of 80×25 characters. The character forms on the MDA display were far superior to those on the alternative graphical CGA adapter as they were created on a 9×14 rather than 4×8 matrix.

monospace font A FIXED-PITCH FONT that uses the same width for all CHARACTERS.

monotonic Varying always in the same direction, whether increasing or decreasing, whether smoothly or in discrete steps.

Monte Carlo algorithm A class of algorithms that employ statistical techniques based on the generation of RANDOM NUMBERS (hence the name, which alludes to gambling). An example might be a radiotherapy simulation that calculates the patient's total received dose by generating millions of random rays and tracing their individual paths through a software model of the body.

MOO See under MULTI-USER DUNGEON.

Moore, Charles H (b. 1938) The inventor of the FORTH programming language, which he originally developed to control telescopes at Kitt's Peak observatory.

Moore's Law The observation that the number of TRANSISTORS that can be fabricated on a single INTEGRATED CIRCUIT chip doubles roughly every 18 months, first pointed out by Gordon Moore, one of the founders of INTEL. This 'law' has held true for 25 years and shows little sign of failing.

Moore's Law is largely a consequence of the benign electrical properties of the CMOS transistor which both becomes faster and consumes less power as it is made smaller. The economic consequence of Moore's Law is the astonishing increase both in absolute computing power and in 'MIPS-per-dollar' which underpinned the personal computer revolution of the 1980s and 1990s.

morphing A technique that has become a mainstay of the movie special effects industry: one photographic image is made to smoothly transform itself into another via an animated sequence of intermediate images. Morphing software automatically computes a trajectory for each of a set of corresponding key points chosen by the user in the starting and finishing images, and then displaces all the rest of the PIXELS by suitable fractions of this movement to generate each intermediate frame.

MOS (Metal-Oxide-Semiconductor) A technology for fabricating INTEGRATED CIRCUITS in which the TRANSISTORS are formed as sandwiches of conducting POLYSILICON and DOPED bulk SILICON separated by a thin insulating layer of silicon oxide.

There are two major variants of the MOS process called NMOS and PMOS depending on whether n-type or p-type (see under SEMICONDUCTOR) DOPING is employed for the conducting channel. These processes are used to make the FIELD-EFFECT TRANSISTORS or MOSFETS used in audio amplifiers and other electronic goods.

A further modification of the process called Complementary MOS (see under CMOS) uses pairs of n- and p-type transistors, configured so that no current flows except during their brief switching period. The low power consumption of the resulting circuits made them the basis of the modern microprocessor, and hence the computer industry.

Mosaic The first popular graphical browser for the WORLD WIDE WEB, developed at the NCSA in 1993. Written by Marc ANDREESEN (later a founder of Netscape) and Eric Bina, Mosaic was distributed as freeware for Unix, Macintosh and Windows computers.

Both the current leading browsers, NETSCAPE NAVIGATOR and Microsoft INTERNET EXPLORER have inherited many design features from Mosaic.

MOSFET (Metal Oxide Semiconductor Field-Effect Transistor) The fundamental building block of modern VLSI chips such as microprocessors and memory chips. A microscopically small FIELD-EFFECT TRANSISTOR formed on the surface of a prepared silicon wafer by exposing it to a succession of chemical treatments through a sequence of masks.

Each transistor consists of a GATE formed from POLYSILICON, separated by a thin layer of silicon oxide insulation from the underlying DIFFUSION LAYER in which the SOURCE and DRAIN are formed by DOPING the silicon surface.

Thin tracks formed in a final metal layer (of aluminium or copper) join all these transistors together to form a complex electronic circuit.

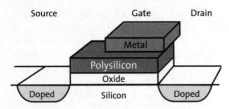

most significant bit (MSB) The leftmost bit in the binary representation of a number. For example, the MSB of a byte such as 10101100 is 1. So called because its value contributes most to the value of the whole.

motherboard The main PRINTED CIRCUIT BOARD within a personal computer, containing all the principal electronic components. These typically include one or more MICRO-PROCESSORS, a SYSTEM CHIP SET, some MEMORY chips, a DISK CONTROLLER, several COMMUNICA-TION PORTS, and often several EXPANSION SLOTS into which EXPANSION BOARDS carrying additional functions (such as a GRAPHICS ADAPTER or a SOUND CARD) may be plugged. The architecture of IBM-COMPATIBLE PCS has now become sufficiently modular that it is quite feasible for an enthusiastic end user to purchase a bare motherboard and other components and construct their own PC without the need for any soldering – or to UPGRADE an old PC by replacing the motherboard with a new one.

Motif A GRAPHICAL USER INTERFACE for UNIX computers running the X WINDOW SYSTEM, developed by the OPEN SOFTWARE FOUNDA-TION.

motion blur A special effect offered by most 2D GRAPHICS editing programs that simulates the appearance of a photograph of a fast-moving object by softening the image only in the direction of motion.

motion detection The ability to automatically identify areas within a video image that represent moving objects. This feature is built into some of the more recent IMAGE SENSOR chips as a hardware function. See also MOTION ESTIMATION.

motion estimation The process of distinguishing those parts of a moving video picture that depict moving objects from those that depict a static or almost-static background. It is performed as a step in the process of compressing the video stream using the MPEG method.

Motion estimation works by repeatedly comparing a rectangle of PIXELS from one frame of the video with a reference frame, sliding the rectangle both horizontally and vertically to find the position that creates the best match by summing the differences between those pixels that overlap (if an exact match exists there will be no difference between source and reference pixels, so this sum will be zero). To perform in REAL TIME, this operation requires a very powerful CPU, or the use of a dedicated DIGITAL SIGNAL PROCESSOR chip.

Motion JPEG (M-JPEG) A simplified version of the JPEG IMAGE COMPRESSION scheme for use on moving pictures. It applies compression to whole sequences of frames rather than to each frame separately. It is *not* the same as MPEG compression and employs different algorithms. See also COMPRESSED VIDEO, COMPRES-SION.

motion path In a 3D GRAPHICS drawing system, a line drawn by the user to define the path to be taken by some object moving through the picture space.

Motorola 68000 A MICROPROCESSOR created by the MOTOROLA CORPORATION in 1980. It became the second most important processor in the personal computer arena, thanks to its incorporation into the original Apple MACIN-TOSH and into early models of SUN WORKSTA-TION. The 68000 was a 32-BIT processor internally (though it used only a 16-bit external address bus) and, unlike its rival, the Intel 8088 used in the IBM PC, it employed a FLAT ADDRESS SPACE with no segmentation. This made it much easier to write programs for, and accounts for Apple's early lead in memory-hungry graphical applications.

The 68000 was succeeded by a whole family of full 32-bit microprocessors (68010, 68020, 68030, and 68040) which are collectively referred to as the 68k family. Apple ceased to use them beyond the 68040, moving over to the POWERPC family, but descendants are still used in the PALM range of hand-held organizers.

Motorola Corporation A major US manfacturer of WIRELESS COMMUNICATION systems, semiconductors and other electronic systems and services, which started in the 1930s making car radios, hence the name. Its many product lines include cellphones, pagers, automotive, defence and space electronics, computers, satellite communications systems, and two-way radio systems for police and emergency services. The company is known in the computer industry as the second most important maker of MICROPROCESSORS after INTEL, creating the MOTOROLA 68000 family of chips used in the original Apple MACINTOSH (and still used in the PALM range of pocket computers). It collaborated with IBM to make the POWERPC chip family used in modern Macintoshes.

mount To insert a removable storage device into a FILE SYSTEM so that its contents become visible.

mouse A computer INPUT DEVICE consisting of a small box or puck held in the hand; moving this in a horizontal plane causes a small pointer symbol on the computer screen to make matching movements. The upper surface of the mouse contains one or more buttons that the user may press or 'click' to select the screen object being pointed to. The invention of the mouse is credited to Doug ENGELBART in 1963, though a commercial version did not go on sale until 1982.

Most mice are still mechanical, driven by a ball-bearing that rolls over a special rubber MOUSE MAT to generate a signal that is transmitted to the computer over a connecting wire. Some mice, however, are optical, using a laser to read a grid pattern printed on the mouse mat, and some newer designs are cordless, eschewing the connecting wire in favour of a wireless infra-red link.

mouse ball A large ball-bearing deployed inside a mechanical MOUSE that translates the linear motion of the mouse into a rotary motion of two internal sensor wheels that generate streams of x and y coordinates. See also OPTICAL MOUSE.

mouse button A switch positioned along the front edge of a computer MOUSE beneath the user's fingers, which sends a signal to the computer when pressed. A mouse may have one, two or three buttons and the way that their button presses are interpreted depends on the make of the computer to which it is attached and the software currently running. With a two-button mouse the buttons may be referred to as the primary and secondary mouse buttons, or right and left mouse buttons. Single button mice such as those for the Apple Macintosh simulate secondary mouse button functions by pressing an additional keyboard key. See also BUTTON-PRESS, CLICK, DOUBLE-CLICK, RIGHT-CLICK.

mouse click The act of moving a MOUSE POINTER over some object on a computer screen and then pressing one of the MOUSE BUTTONS.

mouse elbow A variety of repetitive-strain injury (RSI) allegedly caused by using a computer MOUSE.

mouse mat A rectangular rubberized pad placed on a desk top to provide a suitable surface for rolling a computer MOUSE. Like tee shirts, mouse mats have become vehicles for marketing messages and wacky slogans.

mouse pointer A small cursor symbol, normally an arrow, which can be moved around the VDU screen by moving the MOUSE. It is used to point to and activate icons, buttons, menus and other interactive screen objects.

mouse wheel A thumb-wheel control fitted to a computer MOUSE input device, used to scroll a document up and down the computer screen. See also WHEEL MOUSE, INTELLIMOUSE.

MOV Abbreviation of metal-oxide varistor, see under VARISTOR.

Moving Pictures Experts Group See MPEG.

Mozilla The project set up by NETSCAPE in 1998 to coordinate the release and development of its Communicator web browser as an OPEN SOURCE product. The name is a pun on 'Mosaic Killer' and 'Godzilla', and was coined in 1994 as the codename for Netscape NAVIGATOR, the new rival to NCSA's MOSAIC.

MP3 (MPEG-1 Layer 3) The part of the MPEG 1 standard for compressed video that carries the soundtrack information, and which is now the preferred file format for downloading music from the Internet, because of its small file sizes and efficient compression algorithm, rather than for its audio quality.

The format is sufficiently popular for several manufacturers to produce tiny portable MP3 music players that contain only RAM chips and have no moving parts. Music can be downloaded from the Internet to a PC and thence into the player. As a result MP3 files have become a vehicle for massive international copyright violation. See also NAPSTER.

MPC Abbreviation of MULTIMEDIA PC.

MPEG 1 (Moving Pictures Experts Group) The committee that designed the most widely employed VIDEO COMPRESSION algorithm, which is used to deliver feature movies on DVD and via BROADBAND communications links.

2 The various video FILE FORMATS defined by this committee:
• *MPEG-1* is optimized for compressing video for storage on CD-ROM. It first removes redundant spatial information from each individual frame of the video using a DISCRETE COSINE TRANSFORM followed by HUFFMAN CODING, then removes redundancy in the temporal dimension by retaining only those portions of the image that change between frames. The audio soundtrack is also compressed using MPEG-1 LAYER 3 (see MP3) compression.
• *MPEG-2* is a variant optimized for compressing broadcast video signals.
• *MPEG-3* was originally intended for HDTV applications at resolutions up to 1920 x 1080, at 30 Hz and bit rates of 20–40 megabits per second, but was merged into MPEG-2, and no longer exists.
• *MPEG-4* is a future version still in preparation. It will support complex interactive multimedia applications – such as mobile VIDEOCONFERENCING, multimedia electronic mail, electronic newspapers and games – at bit rates up to 64 megabits per second.

MPEG-1 Layer 3 See MP3.

MPI (Message Passing Interface) A widely-used LIBRARY of software routines that enable programs running on different NODES of a PARALLEL COMPUTER that employs a DISTRIBUTED MEMORY architecture to communicate with one another to perform collaborative parallel processing. MPI routines can be called from FORTRAN and C programs, and the programs so created are portable because a version of the MPI routines has been written for every distributed memory architecture in current use.

MPOA (Multi-Protocol over ATM) A routing protocol for ASYNCHRONOUS TRANSFER MODE (ATM) networks defined by the ATM Forum. See also LAN EMULATION.

MPP Abbreviation of MASSIVELY PARALLEL.

MPPE Abbreviation of MICROSOFT POINT-TO-POINT ENCRYPTION.

MQS Abbreviation of MESSAGE QUEUE SERVER.

MQSeries IBM's MESSAGE QUEUE software product, as used on most of its MAINFRAME computer systems.

MSB Abbreviation of MOST SIGNIFICANT BIT.

MS-DOS The OPERATING SYSTEM produced by MICROSOFT for the original IBM PC (see PC-DOS) and its compatibles, the huge success of which provided the basis of Microsoft's currently dominant market position. MS-DOS was a simple text-based, single-user, single-tasking operating system which supported little more than a disk file system and program loading. It was developed in 1980 from a hasty copy of the CP/M operating system called QDOS.

MS-DOS had many limitations, the most serious being its inability to address more than 1 megabyte of memory (only 640 kilobytes of which was available to application programs). This limit, initially imposed by the architecture of the INTEL 8088 microprocessor, stunted the development of PC software (and Intel's chips) for many years owing to the commercial imperative to remain BACKWARD COMPATIBLE.

Subsequent MS-DOS versions added UNIX-style HIERARCHICAL file directories and various tricks to work around the memory limit (see under EXTENDED MEMORY and EXPANDED MEMORY). MS-DOS employed a cryptic COMMAND LINE user interface resembling a far less powerful version of Unix.

Microsoft's WINDOWS began life as a GRAPHICAL USER INTERFACE layer running on top of MS-DOS, but gradually consumed its host to become an operating system in its own right. Windows version 3.0 finally overcame the memory limit and added multitasking, while versions of Windows from Windows 2000 onward have no underlying MS-DOS presence at all. The last stand-alone version of MS-DOS was 6.22.

MSN (Microsoft Network) Originally created as an ONLINE SERVICE by Microsoft as a commercial rival to the INTERNET, but now merely one of several Internet PORTALS.

MTA Abbreviation of MAIL TRANSPORT AGENT.

MTBF (mean time between failures) A common measure of reliability of mechanical and electronic systems, normally expressed in hours, and calculated by dividing the total number of failures observed during a test period by the operating hours observed. For hard disks, for example, MTBF is on the order of 20,000 to 30,000 hours, roughly the time for which the system can be used before faults should be expected.

MTS Abbreviation of MICROSOFT TRANSACTION SERVER.

MUD Abbreviation of MULTI-USER DUNGEON.

multicast A NETWORK technology that enables a single stream of data from a provider to be read by multiple recipients, generating far less traffic than if each recipient used a separate connection. Multicast involves manipulating network addresses at a low level, and must be supported within the network's ROUTERS. Receivers of a multicast have to identify themselves to the network as members of a multicast group.

Multicast differs from BROADCAST in that a multicast-enabled router will forward multicast traffic into a network segment only if it contains active receivers. Once the last receiver in a particular segment leaves the multicast group, the router will cease forwarding data to that segment, reducing the burden on the overall network.

multicast addressing A special address format available on ETHERNET networks that causes any packets that use it to be received by every NODE on the network (or by all nodes of a particular type). The scheme works by setting a particular bit in the packet header.

multichip module A hardware MODULE in which several unpackaged chips are glued onto a single base and wired together, so that the whole assembly can be plugged into a single socket.

Multi Colour Graphics Array See MCGA.

multicomputer A computer that contains multiple processors that each have their own private MEMORY SPACE, rather than all sharing the same memory as in a MULTIPROCESSOR. To cooperate on the same computing task, these processors typically employ MESSAGE PASSING to exchange data and synchronize with one another. See also MPI.

Multics An ambitious but over-complex early TIME SHARING operating system for MAINFRAME computers, developed at MIT and BELL LABORATORIES and released in 1969. It was his experience of working on Multics that persuaded Ken THOMPSON to create UNIX, and to give it a rhyming name.

multilayer perceptron A class of NEURAL NETWORK in which some or all of the outputs of each layer are connected to one or more of the inputs of another layer. The first layer is called the input layer and the last one the output layer, and between these there may be several HIDDEN LAYERS with no direct outside connection.

multimedia The combination of sound, still and moving pictures and computer software to produce interactive presentations, for example for entertainment or training applications. The term is less used than it was a decade ago because so much modern software now employs all these elements (especially on web sites), but it is still meaningful among software developers because special authoring software is required to combine the different components. Popular multimedia authoring tools include MACROMEDIA Director and MatchWare's Mediator.

Multi Media Extensions See under MMX.

Multimedia PC (MPC) A specification devised in 1990 by a consortium of manufacturers called the Multimedia PC Marketing Council to encourage adoption of a standard MULTIMEDIA computing platform. In 1993 this was upgraded to MPC Level 2, and both specifications remain in effect today.

MPC Level 1 certification requires at least a 16 megahertz (MHz) I386-class processor with 2 megabytes (MB) of memory, a 30 MB HARD DISK drive, and a CD-ROM drive capable of transferring 150 kilobytes per second (kbps) sustained. The minimum display resolution is 640 × 480 in 16 colours, and both MIDI and JOYSTICK ports must be fitted. The 8-bit digital sound system must be capable of SAMPLING at up to 44.1 kilohertz (while using no more than 15% of the CPU's BANDWIDTH) and contain a 6-note multi-voice, multitimbral SYNTHESIZER with MIDI playback.

MPC Level 2 raises these minimum requirements to a 25 MHz I486-class processor with 4 MB of RAM, a 160 MB hard drive, a CD-ROM XA-compatible drive capable of 300 kbps sustained, display resolution of 640 × 480 in 65,536 colours and 16-bit stereo digital sound with 8-note synthesizer.

multi-pass compiler See under COMPILATION.

multi-platform Capable of running on more than one type of PROCESSOR and/or OPERATING SYSTEM.

multiple inheritance In OBJECT-ORIENTED PROGRAMMING, the ability to derive a new CLASS that inherits its properties from more than one parent class: for example a class called Car might inherit from both MotorVehicle and PersonalTransport. There is heated debate amongst language designers about the desirability of multiple inheritance, which to some extent subverts the purpose of inheritance, namely to control complexity. For example, C++ supports multiple inheritance while SMALLTALK and JAVA do not.

multiple-instruction multiple-data See MIMD.

Multiple Master Font A FONT system introduced by Adobe in 1992 that enables many TYPEFACES with differing character weights and sizes to be created from a single, scalable font design. Based on Type 1 POSTSCRIPT fonts (see under ADOBE TYPE 1 FONT), Multiple Master fonts allow, for example, the regular, medium, condensed, expanded, bold, and semibold variants of a single face to be economically generated from the same master, and they form the basis of FONT SUBSTITUTION schemes which match some existing font by altering the parameters of a master to fit.

multiplex To combine two or more signals so that they can be transmitted down the same communications channel (such as a telephone line). There are several different ways of combining the signals, the most important being TIME DIVISION MULTIPLEXING, FREQUENCY DIVISION MULTIPLEXING and CODE DIVISION MULTIPLEXING. Under all of them the total BANDWIDTH of the channel remains the same, but multiplexing can ensure its full utilization, and may reduce the LATENCY for individual messages. See also DEMULTIPLEX.

multiplier 1 A sub-unit within a computer's central processor that multiplies pairs of numbers as a single operation.

2 In mathematics and statistics, the number by which another number, the multiplicand, is to be multiplied.

multiply-accumulate A specialized instruction, often built into microprocessors intended for SIGNAL PROCESSING applications, that multiplies two numbers and then adds the result to a running total in a single step. The operation takes three operands, and can be depicted as A×B+C→C. Multiply-accumulate is heavily used in the most important algorithms for 3D graphics, video and sound processing. See also MULTIPLY-ADD.

multiply-add A specialized instruction that is built into many DIGITAL SIGNAL PROCESSORS and modern microprocessors such as the PENTIUM and POWERPC to improve their graphics performance. Multiply-add combines its three operands thus: A×B+C→D, and stores its result as a separate value (in contrast to the otherwise similar MULTIPLY-ACCUMULATE). This operation is heavily employed in the matrix multiplications that form the basis of 3D GEOMETRY processing.

multipoint Any communication system that permits multiple listeners to receive a transmission at the same time: used particularly with reference to VIDEOCONFERENCING networks. Its opposite is POINT-TO-POINT.

multiprocessor A computer that contains several processors capable of running at the same time. Multiprocessors may be categorized into two main groups: SYMMETRIC MULTIPROCESSORS, in which all the processors are of a similar type and function, and ASYMMETRIC MULTIPROCESSORS, in which each processor is of a different type and devoted to a special job.

Almost all personal computers nowadays could be classified as asymmetric multiprocessors since they invariably employ a separate graphics processor to accelerate screen display, and many also contain extra processors in network cards, disk controllers, modems and printer interfaces.

multi-protocol over ATM See MPOA.

Multipurpose Internet Mail Extensions See MIME.

multiquery optimization A class of algorithms used in real time distributed information systems (such as package-tracking systems) to optimize the simultaneous, incremental evaluation of multiple queries such as 'monitor the total weight, for all cities in Europe, of all large, high-priority packages'. The difficulty of the problem lies in efficiently combining dynamic web-based information (such as where a particular package is now) with static information stored in a conventional RELATIONAL DATABASE (the list of cities).

multiscan monitor A computer monitor that can synchronize to more than one HORIZONTAL SCAN RATE and frame REFRESH RATE and so is capable of displaying images at different resolutions and from different display cards. Most monitors now have this capability, supporting dozens of different resolution/refresh rate combinations.

multisession A feature of writeable CD-R disks and of CD-ROM mastering software, by which further data may be added to an already-written disk, until it becomes full. In the case of multisession CD-ROMs, each new session has to contain a new file system for the whole disk, which consumes some valuable storage space.

multisync monitor Often used as a generic term, though strictly speaking it is NEC's proprietary name for its own brand of MULTISCAN MONITOR.

multitasking The ability of a computer OPERATING SYSTEM to execute more than one program at the same time. Multitasking is a fundamental property that must be built into the operating system at the deepest level, because every subsystem must be designed to take into account the possibility that it may be shared. For example a disk FILE SYSTEM must be able to cope with two programs trying to read the disk at once.

Under a PRE-EMPTIVE MULTITASKING system (also called a TIME SHARING system) the computer's processor executes each program in turn (see TIME SLICE) under control of the operating system's task scheduler (see TASK SCHEDULING). In a COOPERATIVE MULTITASKING system, each program must be specially written so as to cede the processor to other programs at convenient points in its execution. WINDOWS and UNIX are pre-emptive systems, while Apple's MACOS is a cooperative system.

multithreading The ability of an OPERATING SYSTEM to support the simultaneous execution of several lightweight processes called THREADS, which either share time on a single CPU with other executing threads, or run on separate CPUs in a MULTIPROCESSOR system. Multithreading is valuable when executing interactive programs, as it enables a program to accept unhindered user input on a separate thread while other processes such as printing or calculation are occurring. It also enables, for example, a communications program to spawn separate threads that wait for the completion of remote data transfers without forcing the whole program to wait.

Threads differ from TASKS in that they share more of their program execution context, having their own STACK POINTER and PROGRAM COUNTER but otherwise sharing the same address space and global data: hence they can be switched faster than tasks, as there is less state information to save, but they are also less protected from each other than tasks. In order to access shared data, threads must be synchronized using some mechanism like a SEMAPHORE or MUTEX that ensures that only one thread at a time may modify a shared data object, and others are forced to wait their turn. Operating systems that support multithreading include Windows NT/2000 and Unix. See also MULTITASKING.

multiuser Any computer or software product that can be operated by more than one user, by maintaining separate accounts with different user names, passwords and data storage spaces. A multiuser system may also be CONCURRENT, permitting many users to share it simultaneously, or not, in which case one user at a time logs into their own account in succession, as for example with Microsoft OUTLOOK. Many multiuser OPERATING SYSTEMS, such as UNIX, support such concurrent use (see more under MULTITASKING) while others, such as Windows 95, do not.

All the older MAINFRAME and MINICOMPUTER operating systems were multiuser systems because the hardware was then too expensive to devote to a single user. Personal computer operating systems tend to be single-user, or non-concurrent multiuser, though Microsoft Windows NT and 2000 can be used concurrently by multiple users through their TERMINAL SERVER facility.

Multi-User Dungeon (MUD) A class of multiuser interactive adventure games, first developed by students at the University of Essex in 1979. MUDs are text-based and resemble a series of CHAT ROOMS comprising different virtual locations, in which many players can move around and interact, via the Internet or dial-up telephone connections. MUDs include traps, puzzles and opportunities for 'combat', as well as a simple economy based on finding and exchanging treasure. An object-oriented MUD, which enables more sophisticated character representations, is called a MOO. The most popular MUD sites include Ultima Online, Meridian 59 and The Realm, and a list of MUD sites is available at www.mudconnect.com.

multivalued 1 A data object that can contain multiple values at once, for example some kinds of database FIELD or SEMAPHORE.

2 A class of logic (most notably FUZZY LOGIC) that deals in other values than just true or false.

multivariate analysis In statistics, any analytical procedure that involves the use of several distinct (though not always independent) random variables. For example, multivariate regression uses the past values of several variables (say age, gender and income) to predict the future value of another variable (say sales).

multi-way branch A special type of BRANCH instruction that involves more than two possible outcomes, as employed in a few advanced VLIW processor architectures to reduce the number of BRANCH DELAYS that must be incurred.

MUMPS (Massachusetts General Hospital Utility Multi-Programming System) A combined DATABASE MANAGEMENT SYSTEM and programming language originally developed to track hospital medical records but later more widely used by, for example banks, stock exchanges and travel agencies as a multiuser database for textual data. The system has now been renamed as M.

When MUMPS was written for the PDP-11 in the late 1960s it acted as its own complete operating system but modern implementations run under a normal host operating system such as WINDOWS or UNIX.

mung (mash until no good) To mistreat or break something, usually applied by programmers to abstract entities such as files or pointers.

μP An abbreviation for MICROPROCESSOR.

Murphy's Law Anything that can go wrong, will go wrong.

μs See MICROSECOND.

Musical Instrument Digital Interface See MIDI.

mutex, mutual exclusion A software technique used to regulate access to some shared resource (such as a disk file or a memory block) by the multiple THREADS of a multi-threaded program. A thread that succeeds in acquiring the mutex locks it, and any other threads trying to access it will remain blocked until it is unlocked again. The name is an abbreviation for *mutual exclusion*. See also SEMAPHORE, MONITOR.

mutual recursion Two or more procedures are said to be mutually RECURSIVE if they call one another. Mutual recursion is often employed as a programming technique when traversing hierarchically-nested data structures.

mux A common abbreviation for MULTIPLEX. See also DEMUX.

MVC Abbreviation of MODEL-VIEW-CONTROLLER PARADIGM.

MVS (Multiple Virtual Storage) One of the earlier MULTITASKING operating systems written for IBM 390 series MAINFRAMES in the late 1960s. The name alludes to its technique of running different programs in different virtual address spaces.

MX record Short for MAIL EXCHANGE RECORD.

N

nag screen A DIALOGUE or other display raised by a SHAREWARE program to remind the user that it has not been paid for. Nag screens are typically displayed when the program first starts up, sometimes when it exits, and occasionally at random intervals during its use. Entering the registration key delivered when the program is paid for removes the nag screen permanently. See also NAGWARE.

nagware A SHAREWARE program that, each time it is started up (and maybe at other times also, see NAG SCREEN), reminds the user that it has not been paid for. Once the program has been paid for, the user is given a registration key that puts a stop to the 'nagging'.

naive user A user with very little experience of a computer system, to whom certain sections of the DOCUMENTATION ought to be addressed.

NAK Abbreviation of NOT ACKNOWLEDGE.

name clash A condition that arises when the name given to an object within a program is already being used by another object within the same NAMESPACE. How this condition is dealt with depends on the programming language in question. In some languages the new name will prevent the older named object from being visible, while in other languages an error will be signalled. See also MODULE, INTERFACE, UNIQUE IDENTIFIER.

named pipe A UNIX PIPE that has been given a FILENAME by using the *mknod* command. Named pipes enable wholly unrelated processes to communicate with one another, whereas ordinary un-named pipes can connect only child or sibling processes created from the same parent using FORK.

named range A facility provided by many SPREADSHEET programs that permits a rectangular region of cells to be given a meaningful name, and any future references to those cells to be made by using that name.

name resolution The conversion of a human-readable name into a computer-readable numeric ADDRESS, as for example by the Internet's DNS system.

name service Software that converts human-readable names into computer-readable ADDRESSES. See also NAME RESOLUTION, DNS.

namespace A set of names that are all required to be unique. For example each FOLDER on a computer's hard disk constitutes a separate namespace, since it is not permissible to put two files with the same name in the same folder. See also SCOPE, MODULE, ENCAPSULATION.

NaN (Not a Number) A special value returned by IEEE FLOATING POINT library routines to indicate that the result of a calculation is not a valid number: perhaps an INFINITY or the value of an uninitialized variable. NaN is represented by setting all the EXPONENT bits to 1.

NAND (Not AND) A BOOLEAN operator that negates the AND operation, being false only when both its operands are true:

A	B	A and B
F	F	T
T	F	T
F	T	T
T	T	F

(where T stands for True and F for False). Any other Boolean operation can be synthesized from some combination of NANDs, and so

NAND GATES are often used to simplify the design of INTEGRATED CIRCUIT layouts.

nanometre (nm) One thousand-millionth of a metre (10^{-9}m), a unit used for measuring the wavelength of light and, increasingly, for the feature size of INTEGRATED CIRCUITS.

nanosecond (ns) One thousand-millionth of a second (10^{-9}sec), the timescale of typical operations in a modern INTEGRATED CIRCUIT.

nanotechnology The use of fabrication techniques invented in the semiconductor industry, such as ETCHING and vacuum deposition, to make microscopic mechanical and electrical devices such as motors and gears on a single slice of silicon. Enthusiasts for nanotechnology predict a time when tiny dredging devices can be injected into the human bloodstream to treat medical conditions such as atherosclerosis. The existing state of the art remains far short of this ideal, however, and the only commercially available nanotechnology device is Texas Instruments' DIGITAL LIGHT PROCESSOR chip.

NAP Abbreviation of NETWORK ACCESS POINT.

NAPLPS Abbreviation NORTH AMERICAN PRESENTATION-LEVEL-PROTOCOL SYNTAX.

Napster A dedicated server program that allowed many users to share music files across the INTERNET in MP3 format by direct PEER-TO-PEER transfer. Napster was forced to cease operating in 2001 following copyright suits brought by the music industry.

narrowband Wireless communications systems that employ a large number of channels each covering a very small range of frequencies, as used for two-way radio systems by the military, emergency services and air transport operators. Its converse is WIDEBAND not BROADBAND, which refers to high data rate telephone lines.

n-ary operation An operation that takes n ARGUMENTS.

NAT (Network Address Translation) An Internet standard that enables a local area network (LAN) to use one set of IP ADDRESSES for internal traffic and a second set of addresses for external traffic. A NAT converter, which may be dedicated hardware or software running on a PC, is located where the LAN meets the Internet and makes all the necessary IP address translations. NAT fulfills two main purposes. It adds to security, acting as a type of FIREWALL by hiding internal IP addresses from the external world, and it enables a company to employ a large number of internal IP addresses without worrying whether any of them will conflict with IP addresses used by other companies and organizations. NAT is frequently employed in large organizations to combine multiple ISDN connections into a single Internet connection. See also VIRTUAL PRIVATE NETWORK, TUNNELLING PROTOCOL, ROUTER.

National Cash Register See NCR CORPORATION.

National Center for Supercomputing Applications (NCSA) A US government research institution best known as the place where the MOSAIC graphical browser was created, and hence as one of the birthplaces, along with CERN, of the modern WORLD WIDE WEB.

National Research and Education Network (NREN) A proposed network linking all US universities and research laboratories at gigabit speeds, similar to the UK's SUPERJANET.

National Science Foundation (NSF) A US government agency responsible for funding scientific research and infrastructure projects such as NSFNET.

National Science Foundation Network A high-speed communication network, funded by the NATIONAL SCIENCE FOUNDATION, which spans the USA and forms a major part of the backbone of the Internet. NSFNET is a network-of-networks whose 16 top-level nodes are connected by 45 megabits per second lines – from these depend mid-level networks, and from those campus and local networks. NSFNET also has connections to Canada and Mexico, and outside the continental USA to Europe and the Pacific Rim.

National Security Agency (NSA) The US government agency responsible for electronic surveillance, interception of communications, decoding and CRYPTOGRAPHY.

National Semiconductor (NatSemi) One of the oldest and largest semiconductor manufacturers which makes a wide range of chips from Ethernet controllers to Flash memory. Though it had little success in the general purpose microprocessor market with its own designs in the 1990s, the 1998 acquisition of CYRIX has now placed it firmly in the Intel-compatible market.

National Television Standards Committee See NTSC.

native Intimately coupled to a particular hardware system, in contrast to CROSS-PLATFORM.

native code A program written in MACHINE CODE for a particular type of processor, in contrast to hardware-independent intermediate codes such as P-CODE, or interpreted source code.

native format The data format that is normally used by a piece of software or hardware, rather than other PORTABLE formats that it can also deal with. For example, the DOC file is the native format for documents in MICROSOFT WORD, though Word can open many other file types such as text files and WordPerfect files.

NatSemi Abbreviation of NATIONAL SEMI-CONDUCTOR.

Natural Keyboard Microsoft's proprietary name for its ERGONOMIC KEYBOARD with separate keypads for the left and right hands.

natural language The 700 or more languages spoken by human beings, rather than 'artificial' computer languages. The term is often used adjectivally, as in NATURAL LANGUAGE PROCESSING or NATURAL LANGUAGE INTERFACE.

natural language interface A computer user interface that employs NATURAL LANGUAGE PROCESSING software to interpret commands from the user expressed in everyday language, such as 'show me all restaurants in South West London'.

Such interfaces are used on some web sites and database products, but the most advanced examples are found in text-based adventure games. Even the best of such interfaces have a limited understanding of subtle sentence order and are capable only of picking out a known verb ('show') and a few significant nouns ('restaurant', 'London').

natural language processing The use of a computer to process human speech or writing in ways that involve understanding the meaning of the words, in contrast to processing a specially restricted PROGRAMMING LANGUAGE or merely manipulating words as character strings. Hence a word processor does not perform natural language processing, but an English-to-French translation program does.

True natural language processing is a branch of ARTIFICIAL INTELLIGENCE research. It is very difficult, and progress in the field has been relatively slow because the redundancy and ambiguity of human language assumes huge amounts of remembered context information on the part of the listener/reader that is not easily transferrable to a computer.

However the term is used in a rather loose sense to describe database engines that can parse queries presented as whole sentences. See also MACHINE TRANSLATION.

natural number One of the positive whole numbers 1, 2, 3, 4, etc.

navigate To find one's way around a software system and locate the desired function or information. The term is particularly applied to multi-page web sites. See also NAVIGATION BAR.

navigation bar A strip, arranged along one or more edges of a WEB PAGE, that contains LINKS or BUTTONS that lead to other pages.

Navigator The first graphical WEB BROWSER to find mass market use, created by NETSCAPE in 1994. Its ability to run on Unix, Windows and Macintosh systems provided the kick-start needed to turn the WORLD WIDE WEB into a mass medium.

NCD Abbreviation of NETWORK COMPUTING DEVICES.

n-channel See CMOS.

NCP Abbreviation of NETWORK CONTROL PROTOCOL.

NCR Corporation (National Cash Register) A company, founded in 1884 to make mechanical cash registers, which began manufacturing

MAINFRAME computers in the 1950s and still manufactures high-performance SERVERS.

NCS Abbreviation of NETWORK COMPUTING SYSTEM.

NCSA Abbreviation of NATIONAL CENTER FOR SUPERCOMPUTING APPLICATIONS.

NDIS (Network Driver Interface Specification) A protocol-independent standard for network driver software, created by a consortium led by MICROSOFT and 3COM. It permits multiple protocols to be run on the same network interface card so that different network hardware can be connected together. See also ODI.

NDS Abbreviation of NETWARE DIRECTORY SERVICE.

near call In a computer that employs a SEGMENTED ADDRESS SPACE, a procedure call whose target address lies within the current segment.

near-field recording A recording technology used in certain MAGNETO-OPTICAL DISK drives that employs a solid immersion lens (a region of different refractive index implanted within a larger lens) to focus the laser beam into a very small spot, which enables higher bit densities to be written.

Near Letter Quality (NLQ) An old-fashioned term for certain printing technologies, such as the 24-pin DOT-MATRIX PRINTER, which produced output nearly as sharp as that of an electric typewriter. The term survives in some makes of printer as a command that selects a mode of higher quality than DRAFT-MODE.

near pointer In a computer that employs a SEGMENTED ADDRESS SPACE, a pointer whose value is an address lying within the current segment.

neat hack A clever or elegant piece of programming.

NEC (Nippon Electric Company) One of Japan's largest companies and a leading manufacturer of personal computers. It has a stronger presence in the home market than it has abroad.

negation In arithmetic, the operation of making a number negative; in logic, the operation of inverting the truth value of a proposition.

Nelson, Ted (b. 1937) One of the pioneers of HYPERTEXT research whose still-unrealized XANADU project begun in the mid-1960s anticipated many of the features of the WORLD WIDE WEB. His 1974 book *Computer Lib* prefigured many of the attitudes of the personal computer revolution and today's Internet culture.

nerd Derogatory term for a person who is fascinated by computers to the detriment of their social life.

nested folders Folders (that is, disk DIRECTORIES) that contain other folders as well as files.

nesting The containment of one data structure within another, as for example with a set of NESTED FOLDERS, or a RECORD that contains a further record as one of its fields. See also HIERARCHICAL, DRILL DOWN.

.NET Microsoft's new strategic architecture for DISTRIBUTED computing that combines a range of existing technologies, including the SOAP protocol, XML, the BIZTALK application framework, and the new scripting language C#. All of Microsoft's programming languages will henceforth share a COMMON LANGUAGE RUNTIME, allowing them to exchange data with each other over the Internet using SOAP messages.

'net, net Shorthand for INTERNET.

NetBEUI (NETBIOS Extended User Interface) The principal TRANSPORT LAYER network protocol employed by Microsoft's networking operating systems from LAN Manager to Windows 2000, and also by IBM's LAN Server.

NetBIOS An APPLICATION PROGRAMMING INTERFACE originally developed for exchanging data across a network between applications running under Microsoft's MS-DOS operating system, but now also supported by most other network operating systems.

netcam See WEBCAM.

net.cops See NET.POLICE.

net.god A person of great eminence in the USENET online culture, usually qualified by long service or having moderated important NEWSGROUPS.

netiquette A code of politeness recognized by participants in the USENET and MAILING LISTS, to prevent discussions becoming bogged down in acrimony or irrelevancy. These rules include: read the FAQ list before asking a question; don't post messages to groups where they are not relevant; carry on personal discussions by EMAIL, not in the group; quote only short and relevant excerpts when replying to a posting; use a spell checker. The penalty for breaching netiquette is often to be FLAMED.

netlist A data structure used to store circuit layouts in electronic circuit design software.

Netnews The Unix server software that enables the USENET to operate. Sometimes used as a synonym for the Usenet itself and its contents.

net.police Also called net.cops. USENET users who feel an obligation to discipline others by flaming (see FLAME) what they consider to be offensive postings. Not a term of endearment.

Netscape Communications Corporation The publisher of NETSCAPE NAVIGATOR, which was for a while the leading WEB BROWSER software. The company's founders, who included Marc ANDREESEN, were the authors of MOSAIC, the first graphical web browser and former employees of the NCSA. The company is now merged with AOL and is a leading supplier of business web server software as well as browsers.

Netscape Communicator A suite of communications programs published by Netscape that includes the Navigator web browser, mail and newsgroup clients, voice conferencing, groupware and calendar applications.

Netscape Navigator One of the two leading WEB BROWSER programs (the other being Microsoft's INTERNET EXPLORER). Developed from the earlier free browser MOSAIC, Navigator was the first browser to achieve commercial success. Unlike Internet Explorer, Navigator is available on several computing platforms besides Intel/Windows and the Apple MACINTOSH, including UNIX and Vax VMS. On the PC platform Navigator has now been absorbed into Netscape's Communicator suite of programs.

Netware See under NOVELL NETWARE.

Netware Directory Service (NDS) The DIRECTORY SERVICE provided in the NOVELL NETWARE network operating system from version 4 onwards. NDS offers a hierarchical organization of a network in which all the available network resources such as workstations, servers and printers are displayed like a directory tree. See also ACTIVE DIRECTORY, LDAP.

Netware Loadable Module (NLM) The format in which programs are supplied for installing onto servers running the NOVELL NETWARE network operating system.

network **1** Most generally, any collection of entities connected together by some form of conduit (for example roads, rivers, air or shipping routes, veins, wires, lines) to form a coherent group.
2 In computing, a collection of computers connected together via cables or wireless links so that they can exchange data with one another.
3 In telecommunications, a system of permanent cables and switching stations distributed throughout a territory, to which subscribers are permitted to make a temporary connection in order to communicate with others.
4 In broadcast media, a group of radio or television stations that all transmit the same programmes at the same time.
5 In mathematics, a finite, non-zero set of arcs, no two of which intersect except possibly at their end points, which are called vertices. In some disciplines the term is reserved for a directed, weighted GRAPH.

Network Access Point (NAP) Also called a *peering exchange*, point or centre. A major junction on the Internet where two or more BACKBONE networks are connected together through ROUTERS to transfer data from one sector to another. There were originally four such main exchanges, located in New Jersey, Washington, Chicago and San Francisco, but now smaller private exchanges are proliferating around the world, including all of the European capitals.

network address 1 A unique identifier used to distinguish different destinations within a communications NETWORK. On a small LAN, addresses may simply be unique numbers assigned to each server and workstation. On a WAN, network addresses have a more complex format that encodes information about sub-networks and routing. For example the IP ADDRESS used to identify a site on the INTERNET starts with one or more bytes that identify a particular network, followed by further bytes that identify a particular host connected to that network.

2 The term is also occasionally used to mean an EMAIL ADDRESS.

Network Address Translation See under NAT.

network-aware A software product that can access data stored on a LAN as well as on the local machine.

network-centric A computing application that depends on the presence of a NETWORK, whether local area or wide area.

network computer A type of computer, also called a *thin client*, that contains its own screen, keyboard, processor and memory, but no local mass storage. All its software is kept on a remote APPLICATION SERVER. In some schemes the software is downloaded to execute in local memory, while in others it executes on the server via a remote user interface system such as the X WINDOW SYSTEM or Citrix ICA. The attraction of network computers is not only that, being diskless, they cost less, but more importantly that all their software installation and maintenance is under the central control of a network administrator. This prevents users from becoming entangled in configuration problems, from inadvertantly introducing viruses, and from wasting company time on games.

Network Computing Devices (NCD) A manufacturer of NETWORK COMPUTERS.

Network Computing System A REMOTE PROCEDURE CALL system developed by the workstation manufacturer APOLLO, and later adopted by DEC, Hewlett Packard and the OSF.

Network Control Protocol (NCP) One of a family of protocols that contribute to the working of the PPP protocol for accessing the Internet through a SERIAL link. PPP handles packets from different network layer protocols (such as IP, Novell IPX and APPLETALK) by encapsulating them using the appropriate version of the Network Control Protocol.

Network Driver Interface Specification See under NDIS.

Network File System (NFS) A distributed FILE SYSTEM protocol developed by SUN MICROSYSTEMS which has become a standard (defined in RFC 1094) for all Unix systems. NFS allows a networked computer to access files on a remote computer exactly as if they were on one of its own local disk drives.

network interface card (NIC) An EXPANSION CARD fitted into a computer to enable it to be connected to a network. An NIC translates data from the computer's memory into the electrical signals required by a particular network, and similarly receives into memory data PACKETS transmitted over the network. Nowadays most NICs contain their own microprocessor which handles the lower level network protocols, so that network activity has little impact on the computer's own CPU loading.

network layer The third and most important LAYER of the OSI REFERENCE MODEL, which includes the protocols for routing packets between computers and for interconnecting different networks. For example, the Internet protocol IP is a network layer protocol.

network management The task of running and maintaining a computer NETWORK, which includes creating new USER ACCOUNTS, allocating SERVER storage space to them, deploying and updating software, and backing up user and system data. Management is easier if it can be performed remotely from a central administrator's station, and many dedicated software tools are now available to support this, for example those based on the SNMP protocol.

Network News Transfer Protocol The protocol employed to distribute USENET newsgroup information over the Internet.

network operating system (NOS) A computer operating system that has the ability to communicate with other computers across a network built into it. Examples include Microsoft WINDOWS NT, UNIX and NOVELL NETWARE. A NOS is by definition a MULTIUSER operating system, since many users may share the same disks, files and programs, and it must also support MULTITASKING to permit network transfers to proceed at the same time as other processing. Other constraints include a need to support a locking mechanism for shared resources (see under LOCK MANAGER).

network protocol Strictly, any communications PROTOCOL that can be used across a computer network, but the term is generally used to refer to NETWORK LAYER and TRANS-PORT LAYER protocols such as TCP/IP, IPX and NETBEUI.

network segment A region within a computer network (for example, one based on ETHER-NET technology) in which all message PACKETS transmitted by any node are inspected by all the others. Typically a segment will consist of a single continuous cable (see under SHARED MEDIUM), so the network protocol employed must be able to determine whether any message was successfully transmitted without interference from other nodes (see COLLISION-AVOIDANCE). Messages intended for a node on a different segment must be delivered to it via a ROUTER.

Network Solutions The private US company that was originally given charge of allocating DOMAIN NAMES on the Internet, a responsibility that has since 1999 been taken over by ICANN.

Neumann, John von See VON NEUMANN, JOHN.

neural network A class of computing devices unlike the conventional STORED-PROGRAM COMPUTER, that instead operates on principles analogous to those of the human nervous system. A neural network is constructed from numerous very simple processing units connected together by communication links. Each processor has an activation threshold above which it will fire a communication, and all the links entering it have variable 'strengths' – a measure of their ability to activate the processor.

Neural networks excel at classifying complex patterns into sets and picking out one pattern among millions. They are increasingly finding use in graphical applications (such as recognizing printed characters or human

faces) and for identifying trends in long data sequences (such as stock market prices) that a human observer might miss.

A neural network is not programmed like a conventional computer, but rather is *trained* by being presented with numerous solved examples from the problem domain (say, many different samples of the characters A, B, C...). This selectively strengthens and weakens various links, so that once trained the network can solve new problems – when presented with a new character form it returns the letter that it fits best. Unlike a conventional computer, a neural network will still yield a result when presented with 'fuzzy' data such as badly written characters.

Most neural networks are currently implemented by software running on a conventional computer, but there is much research devoted to the design of dedicated neuron chips, using both DIGITAL and ANALOGUE technologies.

A weakness of neural networks is that they have no 'program' or 'memory' that can be inspected, so it is difficult to verify independently the correctness of their conclusions.

neuron One of the processing elements in a NEURAL NETWORK.

newbie A slightly derogatory term for a novice user of the Internet, particularly in a NEWS-GROUP.

newline The character or sequence of characters used by a computer's operating system to mark the end of each line of text within a TEXT FILE. Unfortunately different operating systems (and even different application programs) may use different sequences for this purpose, which is a source of great inconvenience when transporting data between systems, and particularly in telecommunications.

The term newline comes from the UNIX world, which uses the LINE FEED character (ASCII code 10) for this purpose. MS-DOS and Windows use a pair of characters, CARRIAGE RETURN (ASCII code 13) followed by line feed, while yet other systems use carriage return alone.

news client See under NEWSREADER: also USENET, NEWSGROUP.

newsgroup An online discussion forum on the USENET, consisting of a scrolling list of messages contributed by the group's subscribers. Special NEWSREADER software is required to participate in such groups, and enables a subscriber to browse just the message HEADERS before deciding which ones to read in full. Newsgroups are wholly text-based, but BINARY FILES may be uploaded and downloaded from a group.

Newsgroups may be unmoderated – that is, open for anyone to contribute – or may have a MODERATOR who must approve all submissions before posting them to the group. News groups are organised hierarchically into subject areas, with names such as comp.lang.c (computers, languages, the C language) and rec.outdoors.fishing. Newsgroups on offbeat, outrageous and unsavoury subjects are collected under the heading alt for alternative, as in alt.barney.dinosaur.die.die.die.

newsrc The configuration file for the Unix NEWSREADER program, which contains a list of all newsgroups subscribed to and which articles have been read.

newsreader, news reader Also called a *news client*, a program that enables the reading and writing of messages to a USENET newsgroup. All newsreaders offer the ability to download just the HEADERS of the postings to a group, so that the user can decide whether to read the whole message or not. Most offer additional management functions, including the ability to filter newsgroup contributions by author or subject, and to display and read multiple discussion THREADS separately from one another. Some WEB BROWSERS have a limited built-in newsreader capability.

Newton An innovative hand-held computer introduced by Apple in 1993, which featured a pen instead of a keyboard for input, and easy-to-use operating software based on advanced programming techniques: the term personal digital assistant or PDA was coined to describe it. Contemporary processor and battery technology did not allow the Newton to be made small enough, nor the handwriting recognition accurate enough for the device to be a commercial success. Some of the Newton design team left to create the PALM Pilot, which fulfilled both goals using less ambitious software.

NeXT The company set up by Steve JOBS after he left Apple in 1985 to produce a powerful multimedia personal computer of the same name. The NeXT featured extremely high quality sound and graphics and an advanced UNIX-based operating system called NEXTSTEP, but was too expensive (and perhaps too novel) to succeed commercially. The NEXTSTEP OS survived the demise of the company; ironically it is now owned by Apple and forms the basis of MACOS version X.

NextStep An innovative OBJECT-ORIENTED operating system originally produced for Steve JOBS' NEXT computer but later ported to IBM-compatible PCs as OPENSTEP. NextStep is now owned by Apple and forms the basis of MACOS version X.

NextStep employs many low-level features of BSD Unix, including its virtual memory and file system, and is built on top of the multi-threaded MACH kernel. It features a sophisticated GRAPHICAL USER INTERFACE built up from OBJECT LIBRARIES that are supplied with the system, along with powerful programming tools for building new applications rapidly by reusing these prefabricated components. NextStep's Interface Builder, Application Kit and Objective C programming language prefigured many of the ideas now found in products such as VISUAL BASIC and DELPHI. Much of the early work on the World Wide Web, including the first browsers, was carried out using NextStep at CERN in the early 1990s.

NFS Abbreviation of NETWORK FILE SYSTEM.

nibble Four bits, or half a BYTE (hence the name). More rarely spelled *nybble* by analogy with byte.

nibble-mode DRAM A type of DYNAMIC RANDOM ACCESS MEMORY (no longer made) that retrieved data 4 bits at a time.

NIC Abbreviation of NETWORK INTERFACE CARD.

NiCAD Abbreviation of NICKEL-CADMIUM CELL.

nickel-cadmium cell (NiCad) One of the most widely used rechargeable battery technologies, employed in all kinds of portable devices from cameras and cordless power-tools to pocket computers. The cells employ a nickel anode and a cadmium cathode with an alkaline gel electrolyte. NiCad cells suffer badly from the MEMORY EFFECT if recharged before fully discharged, and so have been largely replaced for laptop and notebook computer applications by the NICKEL METAL HYDRIDE CELL (which suffers less) or by the even better LITHIUM ION BATTERY.

nickel metal hydride cell (NiMH) A type of rechargeable battery often used to power portable computers, but now rapidly being displaced by the superior LITHIUM ION BATTERY. Nickel metal hydride cells suffer from the MEMORY EFFECT, though not as badly as NICKEL-CADMIUM CELLS.

Nil 1 The byte or word with binary value 0, also called NULL. Note that Nil is not the same as the zero character '0' (which has the ASCII code 48): it is ASCII control character NUL, code 0.

2 In programming, a special value chosen to represent the end of a linked LIST, or some forbidden value such as a badly-formed date. The value 0 may be used, or any other value that is not as valid as data in that context.

3 In LIST-PROCESSING languages descended from LISP, the empty list. All lists are created by adding nodes to Nil.

niladic A FUNCTION that takes no ARGUMENTS. See also MONADIC OPERATOR, DYADIC OPERATOR.

Ninety-Ninety Rule A cynical parody of the EIGHTY-TWENTY RULE, stating that the first 90% of the code accounts for the first 90% of the development time while the remaining 10% of the code accounts for the other 90%.

Nintendo A Japanese manufacturer of a highly successful range of GAMES CONSOLES.

Nippon Electric Company See NEC.

NLM Abbreviation of NETWARE LOADABLE MODULE.

NLQ Abbreviation of NEAR LETTER QUALITY.

nm Abbreviaton of NANOMETRE.

NMH Abbreviation of NICKEL METAL HYDRIDE CELL.

NMI Abbreviation of NON-MASKABLE INTERRUPT.

NNTP Abbreviation of NETWORK NEWS TRANSFER PROTOCOL.

node 1 Any addressable device connected to a network, i.e. at which some network link terminates. Workstations, servers, hubs, routers and switches are all kinds of node.

2 In GRAPH THEORY, an intersection of arcs (a vertex) in a graph.

3 In programming, a data structure that combines a data value and one or more POINTERS to other nodes. Used in the building of dynamic data structures such as LINKED LISTS and TREES.

noise Unwanted information. In telecommunications and information theory the term means any spurious frequencies introduced into a signal during its transmission, due to stray electromagnetic and thermal effects in the conductors. The SIGNAL-TO-NOISE RATIO is the crucial measure of the quality of any connection. Many communication systems employ active noise reduction software running on DIGITAL SIGNAL PROCESSORS to filter out the unwanted parts of the signal.

Nokia A Finnish company that is the world's leading maker of MOBILE PHONES.

non-algorithmic See under HEURISTIC.

nonblocking Any kind of process, whether in hardware or software, that does not hold up other processes if it fails to complete. For example, a nonblocking communication process will wait for a reply without preventing other processes using the same line; a nonblocking cache does not hold up the CPU when a CACHE MISS occurs; a nonblocking network hub allows packets destined for one server to jump queues for a different server.

nonbreaking hyphen A special hyphen character that is not permitted to appear at the end of a line, so that the word it hyphenates must always be displayed as a whole by wrapping onto the next line. This feature is offered in most word processing and DESKTOP PUBLISHING programs. See also HYPHENATION, NONBREAKING SPACE.

nonbreaking space A special space character that is not permitted to occur on its own at the end of a line, so that the two words it separates are forced to appear on the same line. It is used to maintain the formatting of tables in many

DESKTOP PUBLISHING and WEB AUTHORING applications. See also NONBREAKING HYPHEN.

nonbuffered Any form of communication that lacks a temporary storage capacity, so that a message may be lost if the receiver is not ready or cannot keep up. See also BUFFER.

noncacheable memory See under CACHEABLE.

nondestructive Any modification to a data structure that preserves all the information it originally contained. For example changing the contents of a spreadsheet cell is destructive, because the previous contents are lost; but some graphics programs permit nondestructive additions as overlayed layers that preserve the underlying picture information.

nondeterministic 1 Any computation whose final output is not completely determined by its inputs and starting state – it may produce multiple results, for example, or a different result each time it is executed.

2 In ALGORITHMIC COMPLEXITY theory the term has a more precise meaning, describing a hypothetical kind of 'magic' algorithm that, when faced with two choices, always takes the better of the two according to some criterion. The significance of such nondeterministic algorithms is that, were they to exist, certain classes of problem that require unreasonable amounts of time to solve when all the possible paths have to be explored, could instead be solved in reasonable, that is, polynomial time (see POLYNOMIAL-TIME ALGORITHM). This class of algorithms, which includes many important decision and search algorithms is therefore called NONDETERMINISTIC POLYNOMIAL TIME or NP. See more under NP-COMPLETE, NP-HARD.

nondeterministic polynomial time (NP) In ALGORITHMIC COMPLEXITY theory, a set of DECISION PROBLEMS that can be solved by a NONDETERMINISTIC TURING MACHINE using a number of steps that is a polynomial function of the size of the input. NP is a superset of P, the set of problems solvable by a deterministic Turing Machine in POLYNOMIAL TIME. Whether or not every problem in NP can actually be solved in polynomial time remains to be proven. See also NP-HARD, NP-COMPLETE.

non-linear Literally, not describable by a straight line graph. A function or device whose outputs do not vary in simple proportion to its inputs is said to exhibit non-linear behaviour. Non-linearity makes equations more difficult to solve and makes effects more difficult to predict. Non-linear relationships are observed in many of those natural phenomena such as fluid flow, turbulence and gravitational attraction that are the most difficult to analyse mathematically, and such systems often exhibit chaotic or unpredictable behaviour. Many electronic components and circuits such as transistors and valves display non-linear behaviour outside of their normal range of working parameters. See also FEEDBACK.

non-maskable interrupt (NMI) An INTERRUPT of the highest priority that is always serviced immediately and cannot be interrupted by any other. Many types of processor, including all of Intel's 8086 family, provide a dedicated NMI PIN for raising this interrupt. An NMI is most often employed by REAL TIME peripheral devices (such as a disk drive, where it ensures that a data transfer is started while the drive's heads are in the right position); by power management and suspend/resume systems to shut down the processor; by some critical ERROR HANDLING routines; and by DEBUGGING tools to interrupt a hung program to examine its current state.

nonprocedural language A programming language that does not require the programmer to specify explicitly the order in which events must happen.The term is applied to LOGIC PROGRAMMING languages, FUNCTIONAL PROGRAMMING LANGUAGES and to some DATABASE QUERY LANGUAGES such as SQL.

Non Uniform Memory Architecture See NUMA.

non-volatile Any type of storage medium that is capable of retaining its contents after its power supply is removed – for example a ROM chip or a hard disk. Compare this with a computer's DRAM memory, which loses it contents when the power is switched off. See also VOLATILE STORAGE, CMOS.

non-volatile RAM (NVRAM) Any form of RAM that retains its contents when system power is removed. These range from FLASH MEMORY to ordinary CMOS static RAM provided with a battery for backup power (see BATTERY-BACKED), as used to store PC BIOS settings.

no-op, NOP No Operation, that is, a null instruction code that does nothing. All computer processors supply such an instruction in their instruction set. It may be used, for example, as 'padding' when a following instruction or data structure needs to be aligned on a certain address, or when the processor needs to be made idle for a set number of cycles. See for example BRANCH DELAY SLOT.

normal distribution An alternative name for the GAUSSIAN DISTRIBUTION.

normal form See under CODD'S NORMAL FORMS.

North American Presentation-Level-Protocol Syntax (NAPLPS) An enhanced TELETEXT standard developed in the USA in the 1980s for sending text and graphics over a telephone line. It was rendered obsolete by the growth of the World Wide Web.

Norton Utilities A set of utility programs, launched by Peter Norton for the MS-DOS operating system in 1982, for diagnosing and correcting faults and altering system parameters. The original utilities performed various useful operations that DOS did not provide, such as UNDELETING files and directories, changing volume labels and editing disk sectors; they also included an enhanced visual directory browser. The utilities were later moved over to Windows and given many more features, and they have spawned a whole range of related, Norton-branded products for VIRUS protection, disk image copying and CONFIGURATION MANAGEMENT.

NOS Abbreviation of NETWORK OPERATING SYSTEM.

Not Acknowledge (NAK) The CONTROL CHARACTER with ASCII code 21, formerly used to signal a reception error.

Not a Number See under NAN.

notation A collection of symbols that may be used to stand for the elements of some other system, such as numbers, musical notes or voiced sounds. See, for example, BINARY NOTATION, DOT NOTATION, ALPHABET.

notebook Short for notebook computer. A size category for portable computers smaller than a LAPTOP, and generally defined as having a footprint size similar to or smaller than that of an A4 magazine or notepad, hence the name. See also SUBNOTEBOOK.

Notepad The simple TEXT EDITOR supplied with Microsoft Windows for inspecting and editing system files.

notepad A very basic text editor with minimal functions, that is used to write notes and view text files. A notepad is often provided as one component of some larger software suite, an example being the Windows NOTEPAD.

Novell Data Systems The Utah-based software company that developed the NETWARE network operating system.

Novell Netware A NETWORK OPERATING SYSTEM produced by NOVELL DATA SYSTEMS that is widely used for implementing small to medium-sized personal computer LANS.

NP See NONDETERMINISTIC POLYNOMIAL TIME.

NP-complete (NPC) A computational problem that is NP-HARD and also a member of the class NP.

NP-hard Any computational problem for which, if a way were found to solve it in POLYNOMIAL TIME, then all the problems in class NP could also be solved in polynomial time. NP-hard problems that are also in NP are called *NP-complete*, though not all are. In simple terms NP-hard problems are those for which no POLYNOMIAL-TIME ALGORITHM is known, and which therefore cannot be effectively computed for any but the smallest of examples, such as the TRAVELLING SALESMAN PROBLEM and the KNAPSACK PROBLEM. See also ALGORITHMIC COMPLEXITY.

NREN Abbreviation of NATIONAL RESEARCH AND EDUCATION NETWORK.

NRN Online shorthand for No Response Necessary.

nroff A text formatting language and interpreter for UNIX systems that accepts document files prepared with the typesetting program TROFF and outputs them to a terminal or printer.

ns Abbreviation of NANOSECOND.

NSF Abbreviation of NATIONAL SCIENCE FOUNDATION.

NSFNET Abbreviation of NATIONAL SCIENCE FOUNDATION NETWORK.

NT File System (NTFS) The new file system introduced with Microsoft's WINDOWS NT operating system to replace the older FAT file system inherited from MS-DOS. NTFS offers several major enhancements over FAT including: the ability to address hard disks larger than 2 gigabytes, more secure file-level ACCESS PERMISSIONS across a network, the ability to automatically compress directories, and its fault-tolerant support for data STRIPING across multiple disk sets.

NTFS Short for NT FILE SYSTEM.

NT LAN Manager (NTLM) The security protocol employed by the Microsoft WINDOWS NT operating system (prior to WINDOWS 2000). NTLM provides secure user AUTHENTICATION by encrypting passwords on their way to the SERVER.

NTLM Abbreviation of NT LAN MANAGER.

NTSC **1** (National Television Standards Committee) The body that defines the video standard for US analogue television, and hence by association the video standard itself, which is 525 lines by 30 frames per second, interlaced.
2 (Never Twice the Same Colour) A play on the name of the US television standard that comments on its relatively poor colour quality.

n-type See under SEMICONDUCTOR.

NuBus An expansion bus introduced by Apple for MACINTOSH models from the Mac II onward. More recent POWERPC-based models have adopted the PCI BUS, as used in IBM-compatible PCs, in its place.

null A byte of value 0, used to terminate strings and lists in many programming languages including C and C++. See also NULL-TERMINATED, NIL.

null modem A cable (or plug adapter) that allows two computers to communicate directly, rather than via MODEMS, by connecting their SERIAL PORTS together. The specification of the RS-232 serial connector requires both computers to send on pin 3 and receive on pin 2, so a null modem is simply a cable with a cross-over that connects pin 3 of one computer to pin 2 of the other, and vice versa.

null pointer A pointer to memory location 0, sometimes used to mark the end of a list, or returned by certain operating systems to signify the failure of some request (e.g. to allocate memory). To DEREFERENCE such a null pointer can cause a system CRASH. See also DANGLING POINTER.

null-terminated Any data structure, most usually a character STRING or a LIST, whose end is marked by a byte of value 0.

NUMA (Non Uniform Memory Architecture) A memory architecture used by TANDEM, SEQUENT and other companies to build CLUSTERED SMP servers, in which each processor has its own local memory, but also has access to the local memory of its neighbours via a fast switched network. Software therefore sees a single ADDRESS SPACE, but one where near memory accesses are faster than far ones, hence the name.

number An abstraction of the concept of quantity on which arithmetic is based. Historically numbers arose from the activity of counting, which gave rise to the NATURAL NUMBERS that we represent in Arabic numerals as 1, 2, 3, 4... The concept of absence was later formalized as the zero or 0 symbol. Mathematicians further extended the notion of number to encompass negative numbers -3, -2, -1..., fractions such as 3/4, and imaginary numbers, which were invented to extend the notion of a square root to negative numbers. Mathematics now employs a hierarchy of number classes: every number is a COMPLEX NUMBER; a complex number is composed of an imaginary and a real part; a REAL NUMBER is either rational or irrational; a rational number is either an INTEGER or a fraction; an irrational number is either transcendental or algebraic. See also CARDINAL, ORDINAL.

number crunching Programmer's slang for mathematical calculation, rather than, say, text-oriented processing.

numeric Pertaining to numbers rather than text or other types of data.

numeric keypad An array of keys – typically 15 or 16, including all the numerals and arithmetic operators – placed to the right of the ordinary alphanumeric keys on many computer keyboards. The keys are arranged in a square that mimics the keys of a desk calculator. Its purpose is to speed the entry of numbers and calculations in accounting and mathematical applications.

NUMLOCK key A special key on the keyboards of IBM-COMPATIBLE PCS which, when pressed, switches the 15 numeric KEYPAD keys to cursor navigation functions. On laptops and other portable computers with small keyboards, the NUMLOCK key switches 15 of the alpha-numeric keys to simulate a missing numeric keypad.

NVRAM Abbreviation of NON-VOLATILE RAM.

n-well A small region of n-type SEMICON-DUCTOR within a larger area of p-type semiconductor.

nybble An alternative spelling of nibble (i.e. 4 bits) that emphasizes its analogy with BYTE.

Nyquist frequency The frequency at which an ANALOGUE signal can be SAMPLED to extract all the information it contains in DIGITAL form. The Nyquist frequency is twice the BAND-WIDTH occupied by the analogue signal, so a 4 kilohertz (kHz) voice signal must be sampled at 8 kHz for adequate digital reproduction. Sampling at less than the Nyquist frequency introduces errors known as ALIASING effects, and any harmonic components of the signal above the Nyquist frequency should be fil-tered out to avoid these effects. The Nyquist Sampling Theorem, of which this is a conse-quence, is one of the core theorems of INFOR-MATION THEORY. See also SAMPLING RATE.

O

Oberon A strongly typed programming language (see under TYPE CHECKING) developed by Niklaus WIRTH as the successor to MODULA-2. Oberon and its successor Oberon 2 support a form of OBJECT-ORIENTED PROGRAMMING via *type extensions* and *type-bound* procedures.

obfuscation The process of scrambling or encrypting the BYTECODE of a JAVA program to prevent its modification and to protect the author's copyright. Java bytecode is not human-readable, but it can easily be turned back into SOURCE CODE by a DECOMPILER, and obfuscation defeats this process by altering the order of instructions, and by introducing illegal character combinations into variable names so that they will not compile.

object 1 In object-oriented programming, the data structure used to store and manipulate data. See more under OBJECT-ORIENTED, OBJECT-ORIENTED PROGRAMMING.
    2 More generally and informally, any data element that is manipulated by a program, such as a variable, an array, a record, or a file.

object cache A software technique that makes DISTRIBUTED OBJECT SYSTEMS run more efficiently by holding the objects to be manipulated in local memory, rather than repeatedly reading and writing them from the network.

object code The list of MACHINE CODE instructions produced by passing the SOURCE CODE of a computer program through a COMPILER or an ASSEMBLER. Typically it must be linked to other object code files that form parts of a larger project, or to one or more run time LIBRARY files, before it can be run. See also LINKER, DYNAMIC-LINKED LIBRARY.

object database management system, object database (ODBMS) A type of DATABASE MANAGEMENT SYSTEM that stores data in OBJECTS rather than in records or tables. An ODBMS can more easily contain complex and hierarchically-structured data sets (such as the collection of parts that make up a jet engine, or a 3-D image for an animated film) than a RELATIONAL DATABASE can. On the debit side, the ODBMS lacks the rigorous mathematical underpinning of the relational database model, may introduce duplication of data, and cannot be queried so efficiently as a relational system can. As the use of object-oriented languages such as JAVA and C++ becomes more widespread, the ODBMS becomes an attractive way to make program objects PERSISTENT by storing them on disk.

object inspector A software tool supplied by an OBJECT-ORIENTED PROGRAMMING SYSTEM to examine the properties and methods of objects.

Objective-C An OBJECT-ORIENTED dialect of the C language created for use in the NEXTSTEP operating system, which is in some respects similar to, but not compatible with C++. The powerful user interface building abilities of NextStep are implemented as Objective-C libraries.

object library A LIBRARY that provides a set of predefined OBJECTS that programmers can incorporate into their own programs by calling them from an OBJECT-ORIENTED PROGRAMMING LANGUAGE or SCRIPTING LANGUAGE. Much of Microsoft's development software is now distributed in the form of ACTIVEX object libraries for use with their various server and Office products (examples include DATA

ACCESS OBJECTS and COLLABORATION DATA OBJECTS) which can be deployed by writing minimal programs in VISUAL BASIC or VBSCRIPT.

Object Linking and Embedding See OLE.

Object Management Architecture See OMA.

Object Management Group A consortium set up to create standards for object-oriented programming. Its main project has been to publish the Common Object Request Broker Architecture, CORBA.

object model In OBJECT-ORIENTED PROGRAM-MING, the precise physical format in which data is stored within objects, and the mechanism used to call methods, that a particular programming system employs. In the early days, each object-oriented language used a different object model, which made it impossible for programs written in one system to use objects created with another. Standards such as CORBA, COM and JAVABEANS attempt to remedy this situation and facilitate cooperation between object-oriented programs written using different systems.

Object Modelling Technique An OBJECT-ORI-ENTED DESIGN method developed by James Rumbaugh, that provides a graphical symbolism for drawing CLASS and INSTANCE diagrams.

object-oriented Any computer program built by combining many self-contained software structures called OBJECTS, instead of writing a single long list of instructions. Objects have both properties and behaviour, which makes them powerful tools for modelling events and processes in the real world. Each object possesses its own private data describing its properties (e.g. 'size', 'colour') and also a collection of private subprograms, called METHODS (e.g. 'print', 'display', 'move') for manipulating that data. The set of methods that an object understands is called its INTERFACE, and is the only means by which one object is allowed to interact with others.

Any kind of software can be designed in an object-oriented way, but the technique is particularly effective for programs that closely mimic the real world, such as SIMULATIONS, 3D design and animation, planning and control software and GRAPHICAL USER INTERFACES. By following strict disciplines, object-oriented programs may, in theory, be written in almost any programming language, but it is very much easier to write them in an OBJECT-ORI-ENTED PROGRAMMING LANGUAGE such as C++ that offers explicit support for the technique.

Properly designed object-oriented programs gain several advantages, owing to the self-contained nature of objects:

a) Such programs can be extended or upgraded by adding new objects or replacing old ones, without the whole program needing to be re-compiled (see COMPONENT SOFTWARE).

b) Altering such programs is less likely to cause unexpected side-effects (i.e. BUGS) because the scope of a change is confined within a single object. A programmer may completely change the internal workings of some object (say to improve its efficiency) but, so long as its interface remains unchanged, the rest of the program should not be aware that anything has altered.

c) Designing object-oriented programs can be a more intuitive process than with traditional programming techniques. Several OBJECT-ORI-ENTED DESIGN methodologies have been devised to help ascertain which items are important in the real world problem domain (say banks, customers, accounts, and cheques) and then to create equivalent software objects. At risk of oversimplifying, the properties of these objects correspond to the *nouns*, and their methods correspond to the *verbs* used in an English (or French, etc) description of the process being modelled – as in 'customer X withdraws amount Y from her account'.

d) The fact that objects can have behaviours greatly simplifies many programming tasks. Consider for example a sophisticated WORD PROCESSOR that allows images or charts to be placed within a document. Internally, text, images and charts are represented by different kinds of object, but if each of these understands a method called 'print', then when printing out the document, the main program can simply ask each type of object to print itself without becoming concerned with the details of how this is to be accomplished. This property of objects is called POLYMORPHISM.

e) Important objects within an object-oriented program may expose their interfaces to external inspection, enabling an end-user to customize the workings of the program – or to integrate it with another program to perform some special task – using a simple SCRIPTING

LANGUAGE and without needing to possess the full SOURCE CODE of the program.

Object-orientation is widely employed in today's commercial software, Microsoft's Office 2000 suite provides a good example: all its constituent applications (Word, Excel, Outlook and PowerPoint) expose their internal object interfaces, allowing them to be 'glued together' to create customized applications using VISUAL BASIC FOR APPLICATIONS as the scripting language.

object-oriented analysis The first phase of an OBJECT-ORIENTED DESIGN process: to identify what relevant objects are present in the real world system being modelled. Methodologies such as Shlaer-Mellor and Coad-Yourdon provide support for both analysis and design through graphic symbolism.

Object-oriented COBOL A set of extensions to the COBOL programming language defined in ANSI technical report X3J4.1 and finalized in 1997. They add classes, inheritance, encapsulation and polymorphism to the language (see more under OBJECT-ORIENTED).

object-oriented database See OBJECT DATABASE MANAGEMENT SYSTEM.

object-oriented design A way of designing software systems that involves modelling real world processes as systems of cooperating objects. Object-oriented design methods typically proceed by drawing diagrams to identify which objects are relevant to the problem solution and their persistent properties (the *object structure model*). They then describe the way these react to external events and to each other (the *object behaviour model*). Such diagrams are eventually translated into CLASS and INTERFACE definitions in an object-oriented programming language to assist in writing the software. At least 50 different

object-oriented design methods have been developed, mostly named after their authors (Booch, Shlaer-Mellor, Coad-Yourdon, for example). Most of these have now been subsumed into the UNIFIED MODELLING LANGUAGE, which provides a set of standard symbols for object modelling.

object-oriented programming The writing of programs using an OBJECT-ORIENTED PROGRAMMING LANGUAGE and/or OBJECT-ORIENTED design methods.

object-oriented programming language (OOPL) A programming language specifically designed to support the writing of OBJECT-ORIENTED programs. Such languages typically support three features not found in traditional programming languages: CLASSES, ENCAPSULATION and INHERITANCE, though the actual constructs that embody these features may have different names in different languages. The first such OOPL to be invented was SIMULA, and the most widely used OOPL today is C++, which is a derivative of the C language with added object-oriented features. Other important OOPLs include JAVA, OBJECT PASCAL, EIFFEL, and the historically important SMALLTALK.

A class is a template that describes the structure and behaviour of any number of similar objects, which are bundles of related data values. A class definition is in two parts, a data part and a code part. The data part describes a collection of named slots called INSTANCE VARIABLES, copies of which will be contained in every INSTANCE (i.e. object) of that class. At run time these will be filled with different values representing the properties of each individual object. Imagine a class as being like a cheque book; then creating a new instance means tearing out one cheque and filling it in.

The code part defines a collection of named subroutines called METHODS which have access to the instance variables and may manipulate their contents. ENCAPSULATION refers to the fact that, in a purely object-oriented language, the only way to access the data stored in each object is by executing one of these methods, as the data is otherwise entirely hidden from other objects in the program. When a program that uses several classes is run, it creates named INSTANCES of these classes, and it is these objects and the data that they contain that are manipulated by the program, not the classes themselves (just as you give the grocer a cheque, not your chequebook). Execution proceeds by objects calling each others' methods, and data may be transferred between objects via the PARAMETERS passed in such calls.

INHERITANCE permits new classes to be derived from previously defined classes, and is a powerful conceptual tool for organizing related classes in a hierarchical fashion. Suppose that a class called 'aircraft' has been defined, with instance variables 'wingspan' and 'number_of_engines'. A new SUBCLASS called 'airliner' that inherits from 'aircraft' would automatically have these instance variables (and all the methods too) without having to redefine them, but may add to them some more specific variable such as 'number_of_passengers' that does not apply to all aircraft. Inheritance proceeds by specializing, from the general to the particular.

In a pure object-oriented programming language, all data must be contained in objects, and programs consist solely of method calls, whereas a hybrid language permits object references and method calls to be mixed with conventional program code that may access the data inside objects directly, and may employ other data structures besides objects. JAVA and SMALLTALK are pure OOPLs whereas C++, OBJECT PASCAL and VISUAL BASIC are hybrids.

object-oriented programming system

(OOPS) An OBJECT-ORIENTED PROGRAMMING LANGUAGE, together with a large LIBRARY of pre-defined object classes, that provides most of the constructs commonly required by programmers. These are typically accessed within an integrated programming environment that enables easy browsing of the class library. Examples include Microsoft's VISUAL C++ or IBM's Visual Age.

Object Pascal

An extended version of the PASCAL language that adds CLASS and OBJECT declarations to support OBJECT-ORIENTED PROGRAMMING. Apple and Microsoft both produced Object Pascal versions in the 1980s, but now the only commercial example is to be found in Borland's DELPHI system.

object-relational database management system

(ORDBMS) A hybrid type of database that can handle both textual data (kept in RELATIONAL tables and queried via SQL) and complex objects such as multimedia documents with graphics or video clips. Such databases generally work either by using SQL queries to retrieve individual components and then wrapping these up into objects, or via mapping tools that generate a layer of code that transparently translates between a relational record schema and an object model (and vice versa).

Object Request Broker (ORB) A software layer that translates between the different method call and data formats to enable objects created under different OBJECT-ORIENTED PROGRAMMING SYSTEMS, perhaps running on different processors and operating systems, to collaborate with one another. The CORBA standard defines the services that an ORB should provide and defines protocols to allow ORBs to communicate with one another across networks. In a heterogeneous DISTRIBUTED OBJECT SYSTEM an ORB is required to run on every SERVER and every CLIENT.

Object System Adapter (OSA) A type of software tool employed to install objects created by a foreign object system such as COM into a CORBA-compliant system. Each OSA acts as a preprocessor to the INTERFACE DEFINITION LANGUAGE compiler, translating calls from the foreign object system to those of the host system.

object technology Software systems that employ OBJECT-ORIENTED techniques.

occam A low-level, explicitly PARALLEL PROGRAMMING language developed by David May in 1982 to be used like an assembly language for programming parallel computers built from arrays of TRANSPUTERS. An occam program consists of multiple processes that communicate with one another over named, self-synchronizing channels. Occam was named after the 14th century Oxford philosopher William of Occam (of OCCAM'S RAZOR) because it is conceptually very simple.

Occam's Razor A principle of economy of thought which holds that, among competing explanations, always choose the one that requires the fewest assumptions. This principle, which still guides scientists today, was named after the 14th century English nominalist philosopher William of Occam, who expounded it in the Latin: *'Entia non sunt multiplicanda praeter necessitatem'* or literally 'entities should not be multiplied further than needed'.

OCR (Optical Character Recognition) A class of software that enables computers to read printed texts and convert them into computer data, recognizing the individual characters and converting them to a stream of equivalent ASCII or UNICODE values.

The OCR process for printed documents typically starts with a scanner producing a bitmap image of the page, which is then fed through software that identifies the character forms within the bitmap. This is a difficult task, given that letters may be encountered in different fonts, sizes and orientations, and may be badly reproduced. Nevertheless highly effective OCR software is now available for personal computers, examples including Omnilage and Fine Reader. OCR for handwritten text is even more difficult, and typically only possible if special input forms are used that force the characters to be written within aligned boxes.

octal notation A number representation that employs the base 8 rather than BASE 10 and is used mostly by programmers of DEC minicomputers, most other systems preferring HEXADECIMAL NOTATION. As an example, 23 decimal becomes 27 in octal ($2 \times 8^1 + 7 \times 8^0$). See also DECIMAL NOTATION, BINARY NOTATION.

octet Another name for a BYTE or 8 bits, more frequently used in the telecommunications and networking industries than in computing.

OCX (OLE Custom Control) The filename used by Microsoft's ACTIVEX system for reusable software components.

ODBC (Open Database Connectivity) An APPLICATION PROGRAMMING INTERFACE published by Microsoft which, by loading the appropriate ODBC driver at run time, enables the same program code to have access to data from many different brands of database. This driver performs all the conversions necessary between the record format of the source database and the destination database. ODBC also provides access to server-specific database extensions, and enables programmers to write code that can automatically determine exactly what extensions are available. ODBC has become a widely adopted standard, with drivers available for all the major Windows RELATIONAL DATABASE products and many UNIX products including Oracle. See also JDBC, CORBA.

ODBMS Abbreviation of OBJECT DATABASE MANAGEMENT SYSTEM.

odd parity See PARITY BIT.

ODI, ODLI (Open Datalink Interface) A protocol-independent standard for network driver software created by Novell and Apple, which permits multiple protocols to be run on the same NETWORK INTERFACE CARD (allowing, for example, a Macintosh with APPLETALK to be connected to a NETWARE network). See also NDIS.

OEM (Original Equipment Manufacturer) A maker of computer-related products. The term is used by software companies to label versions of their products that are for sale to computer manufacturers, but not for direct sale to the END-USER, i.e. the public. Used as in 'The OEM version of Windows 95'.

off-by-one error Perhaps the most common source of programming errors, the result of counting some collection from 1 when it should be counted from 0, or vice versa, so that the result is in error by one place. See also FENCE-POST ERROR.

office automation A marketing term that embraces various computer technologies such as WORD PROCESSING, DATABASE MANAGEMENT SYSTEMS and DOCUMENT MANAGEMENT SYSTEMS that can be used to automate business activities.

office suite A marketing category that describes a set of BUNDLED software products containing, at a minimum, a WORD PROCESSOR, a SPREADSHEET, a PRESENTATION GRAPHICS package, EMAIL and FAX software, and usually also a simple DATABASE MANAGEMENT SYSTEM. Examples of office suites include MICROSOFT OFFICE, Lotus Smartsuite and Corel's WordPerfect suite.

off-line Not connected to a remote HOST computer. See also OFF-LINE READER.

off-line reader A type of communications program that enables its users to download information from a remote HOST computer, then to disconnect and read the information at leisure on their local machines. Off-line readers are most often used with DIAL-UP services to save telephone costs. See also BLINK.

offset 1 The distance, measured in bits, bytes or words, from the start of some data structure to a required location within it. An offset is therefore a form of relative ADDRESS.
 2 In computers that employ a SEGMENTED MEMORY MODEL, that portion of each address that selects a particular word within a memory SEGMENT rather than selecting a particular segment. See also SEGMENT ADDRESS.

off-the-shelf Of software or hardware, general purpose rather than BESPOKE; in other words, not created specially for the particular application.

ohm The unit of electrical RESISTANCE. One ohm is the resistance of a conductor across which a potential difference of one VOLT occurs when a current of one AMPERE flows through it.

OK button A visual component employed in most software DIALOGUE boxes, which the user must press to confirm or accept the offered action and dismiss the dialogue. To refuse the action, the user presses the neighbouring CANCEL BUTTON instead.

OLAP (Online Analytical Processing) The use of computers to extract useful trends and correlations from large databases of raw data. OLAP may involve consolidating and summarizing huge databases containing millions of items (such as all the sales figures from all branches of a supermarket chain) and making this data viewable along multidimensional axes, while allowing the variables of interest to be changed at will in an interactive fashion.
 Hence OLAP systems require great processing power, large memory and disk arrays and sophisticated VISUALIZATION software. Nevertheless OLAP can now be performed with the more powerful desktop PCs and servers; tools such as the PIVOT TABLE in Microsoft Excel, and numerous add-on products, are aimed at such applications.

OLE (Object Linking and Embedding) Originally the name for Microsoft's system of OBJECT-ORIENTED component software (now called ACTIVEX). OLE now refers specifically to those parts of ActiveX technology that are involved in embedding visual objects, such as images and charts, into COMPOUND DOCUMENTS. For example, embedding an Excel spreadsheet in a Word report using drag-and-drop is an OLE operation.
 A *linked* object is stored in a separate file, but any changes made to it are reflected in the file it is linked to (a so-called HOT LINK). An *embedded* object is a copy of the original, stored in the same file as the document in which it is embedded. Changes to the original are not reflected in an embedded copy.
 OLE achieves its effects by making use of several underlying ActiveX technologies including STRUCTURED STORAGE, UNIFORM DATA TRANSFER and MONIKERS.

OLE custom control See OCX.

OLE DB The COM-based component architecture that underlies Microsoft's ACTIVEX DATABASE OBJECTS database access APPLICATION PROGRAMMING INTERFACE. OLE DB provides access to many different kinds of structured and unstructured data source by using existing ODBC drivers.

OLI See under ODI.

Olivetti A large Italian manufacturer of computers and printers.

OLTP (Online Transaction Processing) The use of computer and communications equipment to handle business transactions, such as bank deposits and withdrawals, or purchases of goods. See also TRANSACTION, E-COMMERCE.

OMA (Object Management Architecture) The overall name given by the OBJECT MANAGEMENT GROUP to a collection of technologies for implementing distributed object systems, whose main component is the CORBA object model. Other components include CORBA services and CORBA facilities, which provide class and instance management, print services and email.

OMG Abbreviation of OBJECT MANAGEMENT GROUP.

OMT Abbreviation of OBJECT MODELLING TECHNIQUE.

on-board Fitted to a computer's MOTHER-BOARD, and hence not requiring to be added via an EXPANSION CARD. A common example is 'on-board VGA graphics controller'.

on-chip Fabricated on the same piece of silicon, rather than being made as a separate chip: for example, an 'on-chip FLOATING-POINT UNIT'.

one-liner A very short program that achieves an effect out of proportion to its size. Certain programming languages such as APL, PERL and FORTH are notorious sources of amazing one-liners.

one-pass A software tool, for example a compiler, that performs its job by traversing its input data only once.

ones complement A scheme for representing negative numbers in BINARY NOTATION by inverting all the bits of the corresponding positive binary value (i.e. replacing 0 by 1, and 1 by 0). For example, in the case of an 8-bit WORD LENGTH, then –3 would become 11111100 – the inverse of 3 (binary 00000011). The disadvantage of the ones complement scheme is that it yields two different representations for zero, for example 00000000 and 11111111; this problem is remedied by the more commonly used TWOS COMPLEMENT scheme.

One Time Programmable Read Only Memory (OTPROM) A type of memory similar in function to EPROM, but which has no provision for erasing its contents, and so can be written to only once.

one-way function A mathematical FUNCTION whose input (i.e. ARGUMENT) cannot easily be deduced from its result. Such functions are often employed as HASH functions for passwords in security systems.

online 1 Connected and available for use, as in 'the printer is now online'.
2 Accessible via some communication link or network, as in 'an online information service'.

on line See ONLINE.

on-line See ONLINE.

online analytical processing See OLAP.

Online Media A British manufacturer of the SET-TOP BOXES used in one of the first VIDEO-ON-DEMAND trials using an ASYNCHRONOUS TRANSFER MODE network.

Online Public Access Catalogue (OPAC) The online version of the British Library's catalogue, which permits readers to order books via a web site (though not yet to view their contents).

online service A type of electronic business, once typified by COMPUSERVE and AOL, in which paying subscribers log-in directly to the company's server via a DIAL-UP telephone connection to read a range of content (e.g. financial, weather, entertainment and traffic news), to participate in online conferences, and to send and read EMAIL. Such systems were popular in the early 1990s, but the rise of the WORLD WIDE WEB has rendered them obsolete, since the same functions are now fulfilled by free web sites that are accessible by anyone with Internet access and a browser. Compuserve and AOL remain in business, but now as INTERNET SERVICE PROVIDERS and PORTALS. See also CONFERENCING SYSTEM, BULLETIN BOARD SYSTEM.

online shorthand The use of recognized acronyms that stand for cliches and interjections when corresponding by EMAIL, NEWSGROUP or other online systems, in order to save typing. Examples include OTOH for 'on the other hand' and IYSWIM for 'if you see what I mean'. There are many other examples throughout this dictionary.

online transaction processing See OLTP.

on-the-fly Performed dynamically, as and when required. For example an on-the-fly encryption scheme is one that encodes each word immediately before it is transmitted, rather than encoding whole documents before sending them. See also JUST-IN-TIME.

OO Abbreviation of OBJECT-ORIENTED.

OOA Abbreviation of OBJECT-ORIENTED ANALYSIS.

OOD Abbreviation of OBJECT-ORIENTED DESIGN.

OODB Abbreviation of OBJECT-ORIENTED DATABASE.

OOP Abbreviation of OBJECT-ORIENTED PROGRAMMING.

OOPL Abbreviation of OBJECT-ORIENTED PROGRAMMING LANGUAGE.

OOPS Abbreviation of OBJECT-ORIENTED PROGRAMMING SYSTEM.

OOPSLA (Conference on Object-Oriented Programming Systems, Languages and Applications) The principal forum at which developments in OBJECT-ORIENTED PROGRAMMING are aired. It is held annually in the USA.

OPAC Abbreviation of ONLINE PUBLIC ACCESS CATALOGUE.

op-amp A type of electronic amplifier that is used as the processing element in ANALOGUE COMPUTERS and in many electronic instrumentation systems.

op code Short for operation code, the informal term used by programmers for an INSTRUCTION MNEMONIC. See also ASSEMBLY LANGUAGE, ASSEMBLER.

open architecture Any computer hardware or software ARCHITECTURE for which all the SPECIFICATIONS and PROTOCOLS are published so that, without seeking a licence or paying royalties, any vendor can create new components and add-ons that will work with it. Examples include the IBM-COMPATIBLE PC architecture and the Internet's TCP/IP protocol. See also OPEN SYSTEMS, OPEN SOURCE, OPEN SOFTWARE FOUNDATION, OPEN GROUP, THE, PROPRIETARY FORMAT.

OpenCard An interface standard promoted by IBM, Netscape and Oracle that allows different SMARTCARDS to operate with each other.

open-collector A type of logic chip whose output is directly connected to the COLLECTOR of an output transistor, so that with an external load the output voltage goes low when the device is on (i.e. it is active-low, see under ACTIVE-HIGH). Hence also used to mean the active-low signal associated with such a device. Open-collector outputs are found in, for example, many INTERRUPT CONTROLLERS and hard disk interfaces, because active-low signals are easier to share between multiple devices by connecting them to a shared load.

Open Database Connectivity See under ODBC.

Open Data-Link Interface See under ODI.

Open Desktop A GRAPHICAL USER INTERFACE developed by the SANTA CRUZ OPERATION for SCO UNIX, based on the MOTIF component libraries.

OpenDoc A COMPOUND DOCUMENT architecture developed in the late 1990s by a consortium that included Apple, IBM, Novell, Oracle, Taligent, WordPerfect and Xerox. It used the CORBA object model to embed features created by different application programs working under different graphical desktop platforms into a single working document. It failed to attract sufficient developers in the face of competition from WINDOWS and ACTIVEX.

OpenGL (Open Graphics Library) A powerful hardware-independent 3D GRAPHICS programming environment originally developed by SILICON GRAPHICS INC. for its own Iris range of workstations but since ported to many other platforms including the X WINDOW SYSTEM and Microsoft WINDOWS NT. The OpenGL APPLICATION PROGRAMMING INTERFACE presents programmers with an abstract graphics environment, so that any OpenGL program can run on any hardware at any resolution without explicit reference to hardware details: OpenGL confines all hardware optimization measures to the level of the DEVICE DRIVER. OpenGL supports advanced RENDERING operations such as SMOOTH SHADING and TEXTURE MAPPING. See also DIRECT3D, QUICKDRAW.

Open Group, The An umbrella organization formed in 1996 to promote open software standards. Its members includes groups such as the X CONSORTIUM, X/OPEN, and the OPEN SOFTWARE FOUNDATION. Its international headquarters is in Cambridge, Massachusetts.

Open Software Foundation (OSF) A consortium of nine large computer manufacturers (Apollo, DEC, Hewlett-Packard, IBM, Bull, Nixdorf, Philips, Siemens and Hitachi) set up in the 1980s to develop a unified and non-proprietary dialect of the UNIX operating system. The resulting OSF Unix was first released in 1990.

open source A movement or business model for developing software products. It is based on the premise that purchasers of any computer program should receive its SOURCE CODE, together with permission to modify and further distribute the program under the same conditions. The movement evolved from a schism within the OPEN SOFTWARE FOUNDATION and its GNU project, stimulated by the LINUX phenomenon: its founding statement is Eric Raymond's essay 'The Cathedral and the Bazaar'. See also OPEN ARCHITECTURE.

open standard A STANDARD that is independent of any single institution or manufacturer, and to which users may propose amendments.

OpenStep A version of the NEXTSTEP operating system that runs on IBM-compatible PCs.

open systems A movement among computer and software vendors, dating from the 1970s, to create operating systems that were not the sole property of a single corporation. The term became something of a coded synonym for 'open UNIX systems', since that was the operating system of choice. The OPEN SOFTWARE FOUNDATION, a consortium of nine computer companies, including IBM and DEC, was set up organize the effort and in 1990 released an OPEN STANDARD version of Unix.

Open Systems Interconnect The original name for the OPEN SYSTEMS INTERCONNECTION initiative.

Open Systems Interconnection A subcommittee of the International Organization for Standardization (ISO) created in 1978 to develop a framework of standards for computer-to-computer communication. The result of its work is the OSI REFERENCE MODEL, which is an abstract description of the communication process partitioned into seven separate layers, and provides a terminology that is used in defining concrete communication standards.

open tag A symbol used to mark the start of a tagged construct in HTML, XML and similar MARKUP LANGUAGES. For example <P> is the open tag for a new paragraph. See also TAG, CLOSE TAG.

OpenType A FONT system developed jointly by Adobe and Microsoft which combines the best aspects of TRUETYPE and ADOBE TYPE 1 FONT systems. OpenType supports all the UNICODE international character sets and, as with POSTSCRIPT, OpenType fonts are independent of any particular operating system. However, they differ from PostScript Type 1 fonts in being each contained in a single file.

The OpenType font rendering system employs a highly sophisticated new GLYPH model that can accommodate all the subtleties of those Arabic and Indic scripts that may require letters to be reordered according to the context in which they occur – it performs extra pre- and post-processing passes to achieve the correct letter forms. See also INDESIGN, DESKTOP PUBLISHING, FONT.

operand 1 In mathematics, a value to be operated on by an OPERATOR. In the expression 3 + 4, 3 and 4 are the operands and + is the operator.

2 In ASSEMBLY LANGUAGE programming, an entity to be operated on by a machine instruction which is indicated as part of the instruction. An operand may be a LITERAL number or string, a REGISTER name or a memory ADDRESS. For example in the instruction MOV AL, 8 both AL (the name of a register) and 8 (a literal number) are operands.

operating system (OS) The software that enables the user of a computer to run all their other software. The operating system is a program that is loaded automatically, typically from a hard disk, when the computer is first turned on, in a process called bootstrapping or booting (see under BOOTSTRAP). The operating system performs several levels of function: it interacts with the user by receiving and acting on their commands; it is responsible for managing all the hardware in the computer, including main memory, disk storage and the peripherals connected to it; and it is responsible for loading other APPLICATION PROGRAMS to perform specific jobs (e.g. a word processor, a spreadsheet) as and when the user requests them.

The operating system affects program COMPATIBILITY between different makes of computer. Two computers may contain the same CPU (e.g. an Intel PENTIUM) but if they are running different operating systems (e.g. UNIX and WINDOWS) then in general they cannot run the same software.

When no application program is running, the operating system provides the user's basic interface with the computer. In older operating systems such as MS-DOS and UNIX this interface consists of a prompt at which the user must type commands, while modern operating systems such as Microsoft WINDOWS and Apple's MACOS offer instead a graphical DESKTOP from which the user issues commands and runs programs by clicking ICONS with a MOUSE (see under GRAPHICAL USER INTERFACE). The operating system normally provides UTILITY programs that allow the user to locate and execute application programs, to list all the files stored on disk drives, and to manage these files by copying, deleting or moving them

Beneath the surface presented by this user interface, the operating system manages the computer's hardware. It allocates an area of memory in which to run a new program, loads the binary code for the program from disk storage into that memory, and then sets the new program running.

A computer that contains only a single CPU (the great majority) can execute instructions from only one program at a time. However, operating system designers have devised many ingenious strategies whereby the CPU executes a few instructions from each of several programs in turn, and does this so quickly that all the programs appear to be running simultaneously. This capability is called MULTITASKING and is an essential feature for modern interactive operating systems, since the user interface must remain receptive to user commands even while one or more applications are running.

Given this ability to multitask, some operating systems can support several users running different programs at the same time, employing separate terminals to display their user interfaces; these are MULTIUSER operating systems. In a further refinement, the most advanced operating systems are capable of running different parts of the same program simultaneously, a feature called MULTITHREADING (each separate program part is a single THREAD). Multithreading improves the interactivity of application programs, allowing, say, a word processing program to perform multiple computations (such as indexing and formatting) as a BACKGROUND TASK, unnoticed by the user who is at the same time typing in a document.

For those computers that contain more than one CPU (see MULTIPROCESSOR and PARALLEL PROCESSING), the operating system must also be able to allocate different programs, or even different threads within a single program, to different CPUs for truly simultaneous execution.

As well as managing the hardware and processing user commands, the operating system provides services to application programs (for example, the ability to read characters typed on the keyboard, to display text on a VDU screen and to store data on disk), so that these fundamental actions do not need to be reinvented by every new application. To use one of these services, the application program executes a SYSTEM CALL, and a collection of these system calls is called an APPLICATION PROGRAMMING INTERFACE (API) of the operating system.

Modern operating systems tend to be modular in design, consisting of many subsystems that can be replaced independently of one another. Typically these will include a KERNEL, responsible for memory allocation, task scheduling and possibly INTERPROCESS COMMUNICATION; a file system that controls some form of non-volatile storage; and a network subsystem that gives access to files stored on other computers. No designer could possibly anticipate the variety of different peripheral devices (visual displays, printers, drawing pads, scanners, etc) that a computer may be required to control in the future, so the operating system controls each such peripheral through a small add-on program called a DEVICE DRIVER (typically supplied by the manufacturer of the peripheral). Nowadays users can install device drivers like any other program, without making any changes to the operating system code itself.

Operating systems vary hugely in size depending upon their intended field of application. At one end of the scale an enterprise-level server operating system such as Unix or Windows 2000 may consumer more than 64 megabytes of main memory and occupy hundreds of megabytes of disk storage, whereas an EMBEDDED operating system for a portable device such as a mobile telephone may occupy less than a megabyte, and be responsible for continuously running only a single program.

General purpose operating systems such as Windows and Unix are immensely complex software systems, and creating a new one is a project comparable in scale to designing a new airliner or a large building. It typically takes 5 years to introduce a new operating system from first conception, and 10 years before it is fully established and stable.

operational semantics A way of describing the meaning of a computer program using a set of rules that specify the sequence of states that a computer will pass through in executing the program. A single state consists of the collective contents of several components such as the processor REGISTERS, the STACK, and the HEAP, and each rule may impose PRE-CONDITIONS and POSTCONDITIONS on the values of these contents. The TURING MACHINE offers one possible notation for describing operational semantics. See also DENOTATIONAL SEMANTICS, AXIOMATIC SEMANTICS.

operator 1 In mathematics, any symbol used to stand for an operation or process, for example + is the addition operator.

2 In programming, a symbol that may be used like a FUNCTION, typically using INFIX NOTATION if it has two ARGUMENTS and PREFIX NOTATION if it has one argument. For example the arithmetic addition operator is infix, as in 3+4, while the Boolean NOT operator is prefix, as in NOT P. See also OPERATOR OVERLOADING.

operator overloading A feature of some programming languages in which the same OPER-ATOR may be used on different data types with different, but analogous, results. For example most languages permit the same operator + to add either INTEGER or FLOATING-POINT numbers, and many further allow it to be used to CONCATENATE strings, so that 'rag' + 'mop' produces 'ragmop'. A few languages, including C++, allow the programmer to create new operator overloadings.

optical Operated by light waves, rather than electrons.

Optical Character Recognition See OCR.

optical disc (*US* optical disk) The generic name for any kind of flat rotating storage medium that employs light to read or write the data. The most widely used examples are the various Compact Disc formats (CD, CD-ROM, CD-R, CD-RW and DVD) but there are a number of less-used formats including several MAGNETO-OPTICAL DISK formats, the Sony MINIDISC and the almost obsolete 12 inch Philips LASER DISC.

The term embraces a wide variety of different technical mechanisms, but almost all of them involve reflecting the beam from a solid state LASER off the disc surface and measuring the intensity of the reflected beam. The differences lie in the way that the surface's reflectivity is modulated to create the data bits. In a CD this is achieved by physical pits, in a CD-R by bleaching a light-sensitive dye, in a CD-RW by melting a soft alloy, and in magneto-optical disks by exploiting the effect of magnetic fields on the surface of a special alloy.

optical drive A disk drive for reading or writing one or more types of OPTICAL DISC. See more under DVD, COMPACT DISC, CD-R, CD-RW, MAGNETO-OPTICAL DISK.

optical fibre (*US* optical fiber) A hair-thin glass or plastic fibre down which signals can be sent, encoded as ultra-rapid flashes of light. Total internal reflection (i.e. light bouncing off the inner surface of the glass at a shallow angle) prevents the light signals escaping from the fibre.

Optical fibre can carry more signals, and faster, than copper wire can; hundreds of millions of telephone calls can travel down a single fibre at the same time. As well as providing higher capacity and speed, optical fibre is far less prone to interference from external magnetic and electrical fields than copper wire is, and costs less to manufacture.

On the other hand, optical fibre is very much more difficult and expensive to join than wire, as it cannot be clamped, soldered or welded. Instead the cut ends of the fibre (which is thinner than a human hair) must be very precisely mated together, or the signal will not cross the join. Another drawback is that all existing communication and computing devices remain electronic rather than optical, so data must be translated from electrical into optical form (using solid-state LEDS or lasers) for transmission down the fibre, and back into electrical form again every time it has to be switched, filtered or otherwise processed. Despite many years of research, all-optical computing systems are not yet commercially viable.

Public telephone companies and large data networks were the first to use optical fibre, for implementing long-distance BACKBONES with throughputs measured in the order of gigabits per second. Optical fibre is finding increasing use in fast LANS, INTERCONNECTS in multiprocessor computers, and to connect high capacity storage devices.

optical margin adjustment Minute alterations to the margins of successive lines of a passage of JUSTIFIED text, to make them appear straight to the human eye rather than merely geometrically aligned. Such adjustments are necessary because of the varying visual weights of different characters: for example a full stop occurring at the end of a line is pushed slightly over the margin to avoid the appearance of a slight indent. See also MICROJUSTIFICATION, GLYPH SCALING, INDESIGN, DESKTOP PUBLISHING.

optical mouse A computer MOUSE that employs light sensors rather than rotation sensors to track its current position. The advantage is said to be that its smooth operation is less easily disrupted by dust and fluff in the moving parts. Some optical mouse designs have to be used on a special MOUSE MAT that is printed with a grid-pattern, while others instead employ a MOUSE BALL that has a grid of dots printed on its surface.

optimistic record locking See under RECORD LOCKING.

optimization A vast class of problems that involve finding a set of values for multiple variables within a system that maximize or minimize the value of a particular chosen variable. Many, if not most, of the commercially important problems in industry and finance can be considered optimization problems – controlling the yield of a chemical process or the output of a factory, the contents of a stock portfolio or the tax policy of a whole nation – hence their solution by computer is a subject of great economic interest. Many problems within computing itself (e.g. register allocation by compilers and network routing) fall into this class.

The number of related variables makes many optimization problems (e.g. the KNAPSACK PROBLEM and TRAVELLING SALESMAN PROBLEM) INTRACTABLE but in many cases good APPROXIMATION ALGORITHMS can be found that yield almost-optimum results. Some can be tackled by LINEAR PROGRAMMING and the SIMPLEX METHOD, while CONSTRAINT LOGIC PROGRAMMING is effective for others.

optimizing compiler See under COMPILATION.

optoelectronic Operating with both electricity and light, an example being the LED (light-emitting diode).

optomechanical Any device that has moving parts and manipulates or is activated by light, for example an OPTICAL MOUSE or Texas Instrument's DIGITAL LIGHT PROCESSOR chip.

OR A BOOLEAN operator that is true if either or both of its operands are true. See also XOR, AND.

Oracle A large US software publisher best known for its UNIX-based database software.

Orange Book 1 A standard issued by the US Federal Government's National Computer Security Council defining four levels of security for computer products that are to be accepted as trusted systems. Its official title is *Trusted Computer System Evaluation Criteria, DOD standard 5200.28-STD, December 1985.*

In decreasing order of stringency, the four security levels are called A, B, C and D. D is a wholly non-secure system; C1 requires users to log on, but groups may share a password; C2 requires individual passwords and auditing of access; B and A require Department of Defense security clearance of users. The highest level, A1, requires the whole system to be described by a mathematical model that can be proven correct.

2 A standards document created in 1993 by Sony and Philips that defines the physical data format for MAGNETO-OPTICAL DISKS and write-once CD-R discs. See also RED BOOK, YELLOW BOOK, GREEN BOOK, WHITE BOOK.

ORB Abbreviation of OBJECT REQUEST BROKER.

ORDBMS Abbreviation of OBJECT-RELATIONAL DATABASE MANAGEMENT SYSTEM.

order In mathematics, the size of a MATRIX or determinant expressed as the product of the numbers of its rows and columns.

order processing That part of an accounting software suite which deals with customers' orders, forming a bridge between the sales ledger, stock control and shipping modules.

ordinal Denoting a particular position in some numbered sequence. See also ORDINAL TYPE.

ordinality See under ORDINAL TYPE.

ordinal type A subdivision of the DATA TYPES supported in certain programming languages (including PASCAL and MODULA-2) that represent values that have certain ordering properties. All the simple data types except REAL NUMBERS are ordinal types, and have the property of forming an ordered set, where each possible value has a position or ordinality that is a whole number. For integers the ordinality is simply the number itself, while for user-defined ordinal types, such as *(red, blue, green, yellow)*, each value is has an ordinality starting with 0 for *red*, 1 for *blue* etc. Values of an ordinal type can be manipulated using standard functions *Pred* and *Succ* (to find their preceding and succeeding values) and *Ord* (to determine their ordinality). So *Pred(green)* would be *blue*, and *Ord(blue)+Ord(green)* would be 1+2 (=3).

O'Reilly and Associates A major publisher of technical books and manuals for the UNIX operating system.

organic phosphor See under ELECTROLUMINESCENCE.

organization chart A diagram of the management structure of a company or some other institution that shows the responsibilities of each department, the relationships of each department to other departments, and the hierarchies of command. Many computer applications for drawing FLOWCHARTS offer an organization chart as one of their supported formats, since both kinds of chart are composed of boxes joined by lines. See also CHART, PERT, GANTT CHART.

original equipment manufacturer See OEM.

orphan process A UNIX process whose parent process has terminated, which automatically becomes a child of the first process INIT. See also SPAWN.

orthogonal 1 In geometry, forming a right angle.
2 In logic, mathematics and computer science, two concepts or quantities that are mutually independent – that is, able to be plotted along axes at right angles to one another. See for example ORTHOGONAL INSTRUCTION SET.

orthogonal instruction set A processor INSTRUCTION SET in which all the different instruction types have the same format and may seek their OPERANDS from any of the REGISTERS, so that choice of instruction and register become independent (hence the name: see ORTHOGONAL). This is in contrast to, for example, those older Intel and Zilog instruction sets where different groups of instructions had to use particular sets of registers.

orthographic Having to do with spelling.

OS Abbreviation of OPERATING SYSTEM.

OS/2 A single-user, 32-BIT, MULTITASKING OPERATING SYSTEM for IBM-COMPATIBLE PCS created by IBM in partnership with Microsoft for its new PS/2 range in 1988. OS/2 could also execute both MS-DOS and Windows programs. The partners later fell out, and Microsoft turned what should have become OS/2 version 3 into WINDOWS NT, while IBM released its own v3 in 1994 as OS/2 Warp. OS/2 v4 Merlin turned it into a full network operating system. IBM will support OS/2 until 2001, but now ships Windows with most of its PCs.

OS-9 A REAL TIME OPERATING SYSTEM for personal computers developed by the US company Microware. It has been used in multimedia players conforming to Philips CD-I specification.

OS/400 The OPERATING SYSTEM developed by IBM for its AS/400 series of minicomputers.

OSA Abbreviation of OBJECT SYSTEM ADAPTER.

OSCAR (Orbiting Satellite Carrying Amateur Radio) A group of Earth-orbiting communication satellites that have been fitted with TRANSPONDERS for relaying amateur radio frequencies. OSCAR satellites are used to carry repeaters and mailboxes for the world-wide PACKET RADIO network.

oscillator An electronic circuit that generates an alternating current, often used to generate sound or radio waves.

Oscilloscope An electrical instrument for visualizing electronic waveforms. It typically has a display screen and two or more pairs of terminals to which varying voltage sources may be connected, with a built-in 'time-base' function to display graphs of voltage against time at various pre-selectable speeds.

OSF Abbreviation of OPEN SOFTWARE FOUNDATION.

OSI Abbreviation of OPEN SYSTEMS INTERCONNECTION.

OSI Reference Model (Open Systems Interconnection Reference Model) Also called the ISO/OSI Reference Model. An abstract model of communication between computerized systems. It was developed from 1978 onward by a subcommittee of the ISO in conjunction with other international standards bodies, principally the CCITT and ECMA. The model is defined in ISO standard 7498.

The OSI model provides a terminology for distinguishing seven different LAYERS of PROTOCOL that may be needed to permit electronic devices such as telephones and computers to communicate with one another. Each layer performs a specified set of functions, cooperates with the layers above and below it via standardized interfaces, and communicates with its equivalent layer on remote devices. The boundaries between layers may sometimes correspond with real boundaries within equipment (e.g. between different computers or circuit boards) and sometimes with different layers of software, but sometimes they are purely conceptual and may be blurred in a particular real network. The layers are as follows:

Physical layer (the lowest layer) The hardware (cables, sockets, plugs) and its electrical characteristics, signalling patterns and modulation schemes.

Data link layer Flow control, PACKET creation and sequencing, correction of bit-level errors.

Network layer ROUTING of traffic between nodes and networks, gateways and segmentation, control information.

Transport layer Addressing, QUALITY OF SERVICE management, resending lost messages, security and VPN implementation.

Session layer The opening and terminating of sessions, management of the dialogue between applications, recovery from loss of connection.

Presentation layer Converting between different computer's data formats, appearance of data on screen.

Application layer The interaction between application programs and with the end user. Services such as file transfer and printing.

There are many separate ISO standards for protocols and interfaces at all these levels but, regardless of whether or not particular commercial products conform to one of these standards, the terminology of the layered model is frequently used to describe its function and relationship to other products.

OSI seven layer model See under OSI REFERENCE MODEL.

OTOH Online shorthand for On The Other Hand.

OTPROM Abbreviation of ONE TIME PROGRAMMABLE READ ONLY MEMORY.

Outbox The name given to the receptacle for outgoing messages in various EMAIL programs, including Microsoft's OUTLOOK and Oulook Express.

outline font A computer FONT that permits many different sizes of type to be generated from the same font file without loss of quality. An outline font file contains a geometrical description of each character, in contrast to a BITMAPPED FONT, which contains an image of each character (which becomes jagged if enlarged or reduced). Even though they demand considerably more processing power to RENDER them onto the screen or printer, outline fonts are preferred for modern graphical operating systems, as they permit the size of text to be easily altered. A true outline font describes each character as a collection of line and curve segments. A less common variant is the vector or STROKE FONT, which contains such a description of only the spine of each character and the relative weight to be used to trace that spine.

The most widely used outline font rendering systems are the TRUETYPE system used in Microsoft Windows, and the ADOBE TYPE MANAGER and POSTSCRIPT systems used on Unix and Macintosh machines. Examples of popular outline fonts include Times New Roman and Arial on IBM-compatible PCs. Outline font systems frequently employ HINTING to improve the rendition of characters at the smaller font sizes. See also FONT SCALING, ADOBE TYPE 1 FONT, VECTOR GRAPHICS.

outliner A type of specialized TEXT EDITOR that permits the construction of documents as lists of hierarchically-nested headings that can be expanded and collapsed to reveal and hide their contents. Its purpose is to assist in writing a sketch (i.e. outline) of a complex document by allowing the author to jot down topics and then progressively add further layers of detail. An example is the outline view in MICROSOFT WORD.

Outlook The personal organizer and communications component of the MICROSOFT OFFICE software suite, and now perhaps the world's most widely used EMAIL program. Outlook integrates an email client with an address database, diary, To Do list and calendar facilities, and can also send faxes. There are several versions, including Outlook 97, Outlook Express, Outlook 98 and Outlook 2000, and much confusion surrounds their compatibility or otherwise.

out-of-band A term that originated in telecommunications engineering, but is now used in computing. It refers to any system of control signals that are sent via a channel separate from that which carries the data itself. For example, ISDN lines contain a separate delta channel to carry control signals.

The term is used in expressions such as out-of-band management (applied to network devices such as ROUTERS that have separate serial ports for configuration) or, say, to an UNINTERRUPTIBLE POWER SUPPLY that calls an administrator's pager in the event of a power failure.

out-of-band management See under OUT-OF-BAND.

out-of-house Performed by outside contractors rather than a company's own staff.

out-of-memory error A type of error condition raised when a program requests more memory and none is available. Rather than simply aborting the program, a friendly operating system will invite the user to close down some other program to free up more memory.

out-of-order execution An optimization mechanism employed in the MICROARCHITECTURE of high-performance microprocessors, in which instructions are not necessarily executed in the order in which they appear in the program. If an instruction is waiting for the result of a previous, slower, instruction, the processor may proceed immediately to execute the next instruction rather than risk stalling the PIPELINE, and this latter instruction may therefore finish executing before its predecessor, reversing the order in which they appear in the program. To avoid this trick

changing the intended result of the program, such completed instructions are queued up in a special hardware unit called the REORDER BUFFER from where they can be RETIRED (that is, made to write their results back to their destination register) in original program order. The latest processors from Intel, Cyrix, AMD and PowerPC all support such reordering.

out-of-process Not running within the same PROCESS. See more under IN-PROCESS.

out-of-tolerance A system parameter that has strayed out of the range of allowable values.

output The act of transferring data out of a computer system after processing. The principal channels via which output occurs are text and graphic images on a VDU screen or PRINTER; sounds created by a loudspeaker; as FILES stored on some removable STORAGE MEDIUM; or by transmission over a NETWORK connection or SERIAL PORT. See also INPUT, INPUT DEVICE, I/O.

outsource Jargon term meaning to buy in a service, particularly a computing service, from an outside contractor.

over-clocking The practice of running the CPU of a computer or a GRAPHICS PROCESSOR at a higher CLOCK SPEED than its manufacturer recommends. The batch process used to fabricate microprocessors means that even nominally the same model will display a significant spread of performance characteristics. The manufacturers test the chips and sort them into broad categories with average, usually rather conservative, speed ratings. Therefore any given sample may be capable of running much faster than its recommended speed before exhibiting errors (for example due to overheating), at the cost of overall reliability. Over-clocking has become a hobby, similar to hot-rod car tuning, and its adherents may go to extreme lengths such as adding liquid (even cryogenic) cooling systems to extract the last cycle of performance.

OverDrive A trademark of INTEL CORPORATION applying to a special upgrade socket fitted to PC MOTHERBOARDS so that the user can fit a faster CPU after purchase.

overflow A class of computer error condition caused by some quantity exceeding the space allocated for its storage. Most often encountered due to a FLOATING-POINT ARITHMETIC operation whose result exceeds the size of its destination REGISTER. Other examples include STACK OVERFLOW, which is a common cause of program crashes, and KEYBOARD BUFFER overflow (when a keyboard beeps and refuses to accept more characters). Well-written software should trap and cope with overflows of any kind. See ERROR TRAPPING.

overflow bit A FLAG BIT provided in many processor architectures which is set to 1 to indicate that a calculated result is too large to fit in its destination REGISTER.

overhead 1 Any expenditure of a computing resource that does not contribute to the immediate task being performed. For example storing data in COMPRESSED form on a disk saves space but imposes a time overhead, since the data has to be uncompressed every time it is used. Compiling a program with extra DEBUGGING information imposes a space overhead. Calculating the overheads created by various operations forms an important part of choosing an appropriate solution to a particular problem, and ignoring them may defeat even the most apparently efficient ALGORITHM.
2 A slide for an overhead projector.

overlay 1 In graphics, to superimpose one image over another.
2 In programming, a section of MACHINE CODE that is loaded into memory so as to overwrite part of an existing program and change its operation. Overlaying was the first, most primitive, technique for running a program

larger than the computer's memory, and depended on programs loading at a known and fixed ADDRESS. Modern operating systems use more sophisticated schemes such as VIRTUAL MEMORY and the DYNAMIC-LINKED LIBRARY.

overload See under OPERATOR OVERLOADING.

override In OBJECT-ORIENTED PROGRAMMING, to replace a METHOD of a CLASS that is being inherited from with a new method of the same name but different behaviour.

overrun A type of error encountered on SERIAL communication lines when data is sent faster than it can be received, and some characters are lost. The cure is to be found in FLOW CONTROL measures.

overstrike To print a horizontal dash through an already printed character to signify its deletion. Most computer word processors and printers avoid having to move backward to overprint characters by supporting overstrike as an separate FONT style similar to bold or italic. Overstrike is used mainly for legal documents, in which the deletions must remain visible. Also called STRIKEOUT or STRIKE-THROUGH.

overwrite 1 To replace data stored in some medium with new data. For example, to replace the contents of a file with new contents.
2 In the context of WORD PROCESSING, overwrite is a mode of data entry where each character typed replaces the one at the CURSOR, in contrast to INSERT mode where the character under the cursor is pushed to the right by a newly typed character.

P3P Abbreviation of PLATFORM OF PRIVACY PREFERENCES PROJECT.

PABX (Private Automatic Branch eXchange) A telephone system that handles all the internal and outgoing calls for a building or a company without the manual intervention of an operator. Modern versions are also capable of automatically routing incoming calls to the appropriate extensions. See also PBX, TELEPHONY.

package 1 An informal name for an APPLICATION PROGRAM, used as in 'a popular word processing package'.
  2 In several programming languages (including ADA and versions of LISP), the syntactic term used for a software MODULE.
  3 In semiconductor manufacturing, the outer casing in which an INTEGRATED CIRCUIT is embedded for distribution purposes. The package serves not only to protect the chip, but also carries the pins that enable the chip to be connected to other components. For chips of low-heat output, packages are made of plastic, and for chips that generate much heat they are ceramic. See also SINGLE INLINE PIN PACKAGE, DUAL INLINE PACKAGE, QUAD FLAT PACK, PIN GRID ARRAY.

packed A data structure from which all superfluous characters or bits have been removed to save space. For example a STRING format that represents each character by a byte could be further packed to 7/8ths of its size by representing characters in only 7 bits, assuming only ASCII characters are present. See also PACKED PIXEL, BINARY CODED DECIMAL.

packed decimal See BINARY CODED DECIMAL.

packed pixel Any BITMAPPED GRAPHICS format in which the bits representing the red, green and blue components for each PIXEL are stored contiguously, in contrast to BIT PLANE formats where all the red bits are stored together, then all the green bits, then all the blue.

packet A generic term for the basic unit of data transmitted across a network, that is, a collection of data bits that travels as a single unit. A packet typically consists of a HEADER section containing control information (such as the destination address) followed by the data itself. Packets may be constructed at various different layers of network PROTOCOL, higher-level packets sometimes being assembled from smaller ones at a lower layer. More specific names such as FRAME or CELL may be used to describe the packets under some protocols.

Packet Assembler/Disassembler (PAD) A hardware or software device that splits up a stream of data into PACKETS for transmission over a network (particularly an X.25 network) and recombines them at the receiving end.

packet driver The part of a NETWORK OPERATING SYSTEM that divides data into PACKETS before routing them out onto the network. The driver also processes all incoming data from the network, reassembling the packets into a continuous data stream that can be read by APPLICATION SOFTWARE as if it came from a file. Different network protocols can therefore be supported by changing only the packet driver, rather than the applications themselves.

packet header A data sequence attached to the start of each PACKET of data conveyed over a communications network, which conveys details such as the size and format of the following data, its destination, and desired routing. See also ROUTER, ROUTING, IP ADDRESS.

packet radio (PR) A free, world-wide wireless network that allows computers to communicate using the radio frequencies set aside for amateur use. PR provides facilities similar to those on the INTERNET, such as EMAIL, FILE TRANSFERS, CHAT and BULLETIN BOARDS.

PR messages are in the main transmitted via satellites that carry amateur traffic (see under OSCAR). They may pass through sections of the Internet *en route* but, to preserve their amateur status, PR resources are not allowed permanent connection to the Internet. PR users must possess an amateur radio operator's licence and have a globally unique call sign.

packet switching An important communication technique in which messages are decomposed into many small portions called PACKETS, which are then individually transmitted to the destination following a route determined by a ROUTING algorithm. Routing algorithms may take account of transient conditions such as CONGESTION or failure of a particular link to choose an alternative route, so not all the packets belonging to the same message will necessarily follow the same route. Software on the destination computer knows how to reassemble the packets into their correct sequence.

Packet switching allows packets from many different messages to be interleaved, helping to smooth out BURSTY traffic patterns and make best use of the available network BANDWIDTH. It also minimizes network LATENCY, since the start of any particular message can only ever be delayed by a few packets, not by whole prior messages. Forms of packet switching are employed in networks of all levels, from world-wide data networks to local area networks such as ETHERNET, and even at the level of the BUS inside individual computers.

Packet-switched communication is also known as CONNECTIONLESS communication because it does not reserve a particular connection for each message. This contrasts with the public telephone system, which employs the alternative, CIRCUIT-SWITCHED or CONNECTION-ORIENTED technology. See also VIRTUAL CIRCUIT, X.25.

packet writing A scheme for writing data to CD-R and CD-RW disks in short segments, smaller than the BUFFER in the writing software, rather than as a continuous stream. This prevents the buffer underrun errors that used to frequently result in spoiled disks. It is packet writing that enables the UDF file system to support the DRAG-AND-DROP of files onto CD media as if they were ordinary disk drives. Windows 2000 now contains packet writing ability at the operating system level.

PAD Abbreviation of PACKET ASSEMBLER/DISASSEMBLER.

pad To add extra bits or characters to a data structure to make it exactly fit the allotted space. For example, in a database that uses FIXED-LENGTH RECORDS, text might be padded by appending spaces to fill a field.

padded string A character STRING that has been extended by adding spaces to its end so that it becomes a predefined length. Padded strings were generated by the output routines of certain programming languages (for example C's PRINTF function), and by older types of database that employed FIXED-LENGTH RECORDS, in order to produce aligned print or displays on devices such as TELETYPES that did not support cursor addressing.

PAE Abbreviation of PHYSICAL ADDRESS EXTENSIONS.

page 1 *n.* A subdivision of the text within a document, which will fill one side of one sheet of paper when the document is printed. See also REPAGINATE.

2 *n.* A unit of memory allocated by a VIRTUAL MEMORY system. See also DEMAND-PAGED.

3 *n.* A subdivision of the data within a RANDOM ACCESS MEMORY chip. See for example FAST PAGE MODE RAM.

4 *v.* To send a message via an electronic PAGER system.

page description language (PDL) A formalism for describing the layout of text and images on a printed page, the most widely used example being Adobe's POSTSCRIPT language. A PDL description is in effect a program for creating the page, which is executed by an INTERPRETER running on a particular printer. Most PDLs aim for hardware independence so that publishing applications can output without needing to know what hardware the page will finally be printed on. See also MARKUP LANGUAGE.

PAGE DOWN key A key on most modern computer keyboards that moves the screen CURSOR down by a whole screen's height (or to the end of the current document if shorter). See also PAGE UP KEY, CURSOR KEYS.

page fault See under VIRTUAL MEMORY.

page frame A 64 kilobyte (KB) region in upper memory on a PC running MS-DOS that is reserved for use by an EXPANDED MEMORY MANAGER, which can swap-in pages of data occupying memory addresses beyond the 640 KB upper memory limit.

page impression A unit for measuring the usage of a WEB SITE, consisting of one request for (i.e. viewing of) a particular page. See also CLICK-THROUGH.

page in To fetch a new page of memory from disk in a VIRTUAL MEMORY system.

page layout The set of properties such as font size, margin width, number of columns and position of pictures that defines a particular page of a document. Also the activity of choosing these properties.

PageMaker The first true DESKTOP PUBLISHING program, created by Aldus for the Apple MACINTOSH in 1985 but later purchased by ADOBE SYSTEMS. PageMaker revolutionized graphic design by for the first time providing interactive DRAG-AND-DROP editing of page layouts. The program was almost entirely responsible for establishing the Macintosh among professional publishing users (though it has since been ported to Windows PCs too). See also QUARK XPRESS, INDESIGN.

page mode See under FAST PAGE MODE RAM.

page out To write out to disk a page of memory in a VIRTUAL MEMORY system to make room for other pages.

pager 1 A pocketable wireless communication device that can receive, but not send, short messages. On receiving a call, the first pagers merely emitted a beep to alert the user and displayed the caller's number. Modern pagers can display text messages several lines long. Some PALMTOP computers can now receive information bulletins over wireless pager networks.

2 A software utility that displays the contents of a TEXT FILE one page at a time, as for example with the More command under UNIX and MS-DOS.

page scraping A technique that extracts just those parts of a web page that do not change over time. Invented to bypass certain measures (such as placing a real-time clock on the page) taken to thwart automatic page readers.

page table A table that stores the locations of the disk sectors that hold the pages of data associated with VIRTUAL ADDRESSES. Such a table is stored in the main memory of any computer that employs a VIRTUAL MEMORY system. See also ADDRESS TRANSLATION, TRANSLATION LOOK-ASIDE BUFFER.

PAGE UP key A key on most modern computer keyboards which moves the screen CURSOR up by a whole screen's height (or to the start of the current document if shorter). See also PAGE DOWN KEY, CURSOR KEYS.

paging file On a computer system that employs VIRTUAL MEMORY, a file used to hold memory pages that need to be temporarily written out to disk because physical memory is full. See also SWAP FILE.

painting program, paint program An alternative name for a BITMAP EDITOR such as PHOTOSHOP. The name is used to emphasize that such programs are largely concerned with applying colour, rather than with drawing lines (which is the province of a vector graphics editor or DRAWING PROGRAM). See also BITMAP, GRAPHICS.

PAL 1 Abbreviation of PROGRAMMABLE ARRAY LOGIC.

2 (Phase Alternating Line) One of the world's three major broadcast analogue television standards, developed in the UK and first deployed in 1967. It is used in countries including the UK, much of Europe, China and Australia. A PAL display consists of 625 lines refreshed at 50 frames per second. See also NTSC, SECAM, HDTV.

palette 1 A set of colours used to render an image in a computer graphics system, enabling a system with limited COLOUR DEPTH to display more colours than would be possible if the bits representing each PIXEL were treated directly as RGB values. For example a system with 8 bits per pixel can display only 256 distinct colours, but by using a palette these may be individually chosen from some larger COLOUR SPACE. The graphics hardware contains a small memory chip called a COLOUR LOOK-UP TABLE which stores 256 16-bit (or larger) RGB values and interprets each 8-bit pixel value as an index into this table. The palette for each individual image is stored along with its pixel data, using a GRAPHICS FILE FORMAT such as GIF or Microsoft's BMP/DIB, and is loaded into the lookup table whenever the picture is loaded into memory.

A great disadvantage of palettes is that, when images that use different palettes share the same screen, all but one will show in the wrong colours if the overall number of colours is too great. The technique becomes pointless at colour depths of 16 bits and over, as the stored palette becomes too large, and the advent of 24- and 32-bit GRAPHICS ADAPTERS has made palettes largely redundant, except on the World Wide Web where the compact size of GIF files offers a worthwhile reduction in download time.

2 A table of colour samples displayed by a computer program to allow its user to select the current colour for text, background or drawing.

Palm A range of pocket computers manufactured by Palm Computing Inc. (a division of 3COM CORPORATION). They are notable for using the GRAFFITI handwriting recognition system instead of a keyboard, for their small size (they fit into a shirt pocket), and for their ability to HOTSYNC with a desktop computer by pressing a single button – this equalizes between the two machines any alterations that have been made to addresses, appointments or notes. The machines were originally named Palm Pilots, but this was dropped because of a trademark dispute.

Palm Pilot See under PALM.

palm rest A broad, sometimes padded, area at the front edge of a computer keyboard on which the operator may rest the balls of the hands to relieve pressure on the wrists and forearms while typing. See also REPETITIVE-STRAIN INJURY.

palmtop A marketing term used to describe the smallest class of HAND-HELD computers.

Palo Alto Research Center See PARC.

PAM 1 Abbreviation of PLUGGABLE AUTHENTICATION MODULE.
2 Abbreviation of PULSE AMPLITUDE MODULATION.

pan To move a displayed image in the plane of the screen. The term originates in the movie industry where it means to swivel the camera in the horizontal plane, and is probably a contraction of panorama. However, some software products also apply it to vertical movement. See also ZOOM.

Panasonic A Japanese electronics manufacturer that has pioneered OPTICAL and MAGNETO-OPTICAL disk drives.

pane A rectangular subdivision within the screen window displayed by a computer program.

Pantone A set of standard colours devised for the printing industry. Each is specified by a single number, which enables designers to select colours from a Pantone swatch book and send a detached swatch or its number to the printer. Most professional DESKTOP PUBLISHING programs allow colours to be specified by Pantone number in addition to CMYK, RGB, HSV or other schemes, and can generate spot-colour separations that specify Pantone colors. The PHOSPHORS used in computer VDUS and standard CMYK printing inks can however only approximate many of the colours in the Pantone range (see more under COLOUR SPACE).

paperless office The notion that computers would remove the need for paper documents in the office (in much the same way that cars have removed the need for legs).

paper-parking A facility provided on some types of DOT-MATRIX PRINTER that enabled single sheets or envelopes to be printed without having to unthread the FAN FOLD paper first.

paper size The computer industry employs an eclectic selection of paper sizes for PRINTERS, drawn from the traditional stationery, printing and publishing industries on both sides of the Atlantic. For example, most popular WORD PROCESSORS include the following sizes in their Print Setup DIALOGUE:

European A4 210×297 mm
European B5 176×250 mm
US Letter 8.5×11 inches
US Legal 8.5×14 inches

paradigm 1 A pattern or model. In computing, frequently misused as a more pretentious substitute for metaphor or architecture, as in the 'client/server paradigm' or the 'desktop paradigm'.
2 In science, a very broad conception or set of assumptions, as in 'the Newtonian paradigm', 'the Quantum Mechanical paradigm'.
3 In linguistics, the set of all the inflected forms of a word.

paragraph style A formatting mechanism used in some WORD PROCESSORS and DESKTOP PUBLISHING systems, under which various unique combinations of font, margin setting, line spacing and other typographical variables may be saved as named styles that can then be applied to new documents, but at the level of whole paragraphs only.

parallel 1 Electronic components, such as resistors or capacitors, that are connected side-by-side (rather than in SERIES).
2 In digital communication, the carrying of multiple bits via multiple wires rather than sending them one after another (i.e. in SERIAL fashion) down a single wire. See, for example, PARALLEL PORT.
3 Capable of performing more than one computation at the same time. See for example PARALLEL COMPUTER, PARALLEL PROCESSING.

Parallel C An extended version of the c programming language with added constructs for programming PARALLEL COMPUTERS. There have been several such extensions, including a commercial one from the company 3L.

parallel computer A computer with multiple processors that can all be run simultaneously

on parts of the same problem to reduce the solution time. The term is nowadays mostly reserved for those MASSIVELY PARALLEL computers with hundreds or thousands of processors that are used in science and engineering to tackle enormous computational problems.

There are two fundamental divisions in parallel computer architecture. The first is between those architectures in which each processor has it own memory space and communicates with others by MESSAGE PASSING, and those architectures in which all the processors communicate through a shared memory (SHARED-MEMORY MULTIPROCESSORS). The increasing number of high-end PCs and servers that contain more than one processor fall into this latter category.

The other fundamental division is between those computer architectures in which each processor executes the same program on a different data item (SINGLE-INSTRUCTION MULTIPLE-DATA or SIMD) and those in which each processor executes a different program (MIMD or multiple-instruction multiple-data). Within these subdivisions, the processors can be connected together in many different ways (their TOPOLOGY) which profoundly affect the efficiency of communication between them. See more under SCALABILITY, CROSS-SECTIONAL BANDWIDTH, SWITCHED INTERCONNECT, HYPERCUBE. See also PARALLEL PROGRAMMING.

Parallel Fortran An extended version of FORTRAN created at Houston University for programming PARALLEL COMPUTERS.

parallel interface Another name for a PARALLEL PORT.

parallelism The degree to which a particular computer program permits its activities to be performed simultaneously, i.e. in PARALLEL.

parallelize To modify a program designed to run on a single PROCESSOR so that it may be run on multiple processors.

Parallel Macros See PARMACS.

parallel port Any kind of computer communication PORT that transfers data several bits at a time rather than one bit after another (see SERIAL, SERIAL PORT). If not further qualified, the term normally refers to a PC's printer port, but it is equally applicable to other communication technologies such as SCSI, IDE and HPIB.

parallel processing Employing more than one processor to speed up the course of a computation. Parallel processing introduces important problems that are not encountered with single-process computation, such as what should happen when two processors wish to update a shared resource. Special techniques of PARALLEL PROGRAMMING have been developed to cope with such problems. Another important issue is how best to decompose a given computational problem into separate processes so as to extract the maximum PARALLELISM and hence achieve the greatest increase in speed. See more under PARALLEL COMPUTER.

parallel programming The creation of programs to be executed by more than one processor at the same time. Parallel programming is more difficult than ordinary SEQUENTIAL programming because of the added problem of synchronization (see SYNCHRONIZE). A sequential program has only a single FLOW OF CONTROL and runs until it stops, whereas a parallel program spawns many CONCURRENT processes and the order in which they complete affects the overall result. A second problem is that parallel programs may become dependent on the connection TOPOLOGY of the multiple processors they run on, which makes them difficult to port to a different parallel architecture.

To synchronize parallel processes using a conventional programming language, a programmer typically employs SEMAPHORE or MONITOR data structures, but much research has been devoted to creating special programming languages that simplify the task. Some of these languages (including OCCAM and PARALLEL C) support EXPLICIT PARALLELISM using novel control structures, while others (such as LINDA and Parlog) employ an IMPLICIT PARALLELISM which is concealed from the programmer.

parallel-to-serial converter An electronic circuit that turns a parallel data stream (for example a stream of bytes or WORDS) into a sequence of bits, by placing each in turn into a SHIFT REGISTER. Such a circuit forms the transmitter part of a UART chip. See also PARALLEL, SERIAL, SERIAL-TO-PARALLEL CONVERTER.

Parallel Virtual Machine (PVM) A distributed processing software system developed at several US universities that enables a network of individual engineering workstations or PCs (which need not be all of the same make) to be used as a single PARALLEL COMPUTER. PVM is available as a C and C++ library for Unix and Windows systems. See also MESSAGE PASSING INTERFACE, PARMACS, MIDDLEWARE.

param, parm Abbreviation of PARAMETER.

parameter 1 Informally, any property of a computer system that can be varied by a user; for example the disk buffer size might be a system parameter.

2 In mathematics, an auxiliary variable in terms of which the other variables in some functional relationship can be expressed. For example the relation $x^2+y^2=1$ can be rewritten as $x = \sin(t)$ and $y = \cos(t)$ where t is a parameter. This meaning is also used in describing certain types of COMPUTER AIDED DESIGN software (*see* PARAMETRIC).

3 In programming, a value passed into a function or procedure by its caller. It is also called an ARGUMENT. Consider a simple function defined in an imaginary programming language:

```
def sum(x, y): num
x+y
```

x and y are called the FORMAL PARAMETERS of the function, and they act as place holders for the actual values that will be passed to the function when it is used. In a call to the function – say sum(2,3) which returns the result 5 – the 2 and 3 are called the ACTUAL PARAMETERS. Parameterized procedures and functions enable the same piece of code (in this trivial example x+y) to be used in many different circumstances, which can both significantly reduce the size of programs and make the program easier to handle by giving names to its subtasks.

The precise mechanism used to pass parameters, called a PARAMETER PASSING CONVENTION, is of great importance in the design of programming languages.

parameter passing convention The mechanism employed by a programming language to pass the PARAMETERS or ARGUMENTS into a PROCEDURE CALL or FUNCTION CALL. Different conventions are distinguished by the way in which they evaluate the parameters, and whether this is done by the caller or the called. For example a procedure declared as MyProc(x) might be called with a variable, say N, as its actual parameter and the question arises whether the value of N will be changed by the call.

Under a *call-by-value* convention, only a copy of N's value is passed to MyProc(N), which returns leaving N itself unchanged. Under a *call-by-reference* convention, the address of N is passed to MyProc(N) so that value of N itself may be changed by actions performed within the procedure. Most popular programming languages support both of these conventions. c and c++ are call-by-value by default, but support call-by-reference by passing a POINTER to N as the parameter. PASCAL employs call-by-value by default, but call-by-reference if the parameter is preceded by the keyword VAR. VISUAL BASIC on the other hand uses call-by-reference by default, but call-by-value if the parameter is surrounded by parentheses or preceded by the keyword ByVal.

There are several other less frequently used conventions employed in some INTERPRETED languages including SCRIPTING LANGUAGES and experimental FUNCTIONAL LANGUAGES. *Call-by-result* changes the value of a variable parameter, as call-by-reference does, but only *after* the call has returned – all intermediate calculations being performed on a local copy. Under *call-by-name*, arguments that are expressions (e.g. MyProc(N+M)) are passed unevaluated as a pointer to code that will evaluate the argument. *Call-by-need* only evaluates as much of the argument as is required for the current calculation step, which enables notionally infinite arguments – such as a list of all the integers – to be represented. It is used in functional languages such as Hope and Miranda.

parameter RAM A small CMOS memory chip, fitted to all IBM-COMPATIBLE PCS, whose contents are preserved by a battery when the computer's power is switched off. The parameter RAM stores fundamental information about the PC's configuration required by the system's BIOS in order to BOOT-UP the operating system, including the number and type of HARD DISKS fitted, the identity of the BOOT DRIVE, and instructions to turn on or off certain processor features such as an external

CACHE. It is sometimes referred to simply as the 'CMOS settings'.

parametric Any hardware device or software program whose behaviour can be specialized by changing a set of PARAMETERS. For example a parametric drawing program enables a whole family of drawings (such as a set of spanners) to be derived from a single master drawing by merely altering the size parameters appropriately.

PARC (Palo Alto Research Center) An immensely influential computer science research institution set up by the XEROX CORPORATION in the early 1970s. During a remarkable few years around 1981, PARC researchers invented most of the elements of the modern personal computer, including the GRAPHICAL USER INTERFACE with ICONS, MOUSE and pull-down MENUS, and ETHERNET networking. Xerox funded PARC sufficiently generously that researchers were able to test these concepts not only by designing a series of experimental machines (called Alto, Mesa, Dorado and Dolphin), but also to put them into limited production for internal use only.

Unfortunately these ideas were years ahead of the market, of volume production technology, and of comprehension by Xerox's own management – only one machine, the XEROX STAR, was launched commercially, and at a price that guaranteed failure. It was left to APPLE COMPUTER INC. to capitalize on these ideas in the MACINTOSH, for which it poached many ex-PARC scientists.

PARC researchers also pioneered the OBJECT-ORIENTED PROGRAMMING techniques that were needed to tame the complexity of graphical interfaces, first expressed in the SMALLTALK language. See also Alan KAY, INTERLISP, UNICODE, RESOURCE RESERVATION PROTOCOL.

paren Abbreviation of PARENTHESES.

parent–child relationship A hierarchical relationship between a data object and one or more dependent objects, such that any change made to the parent object is automatically propagated to all the 'children'. The objects in question might be database records, or graphical objects in a 3D graphics system.

parentheses (*sing.* parenthesis) The punctuation symbols (and), ASCII characters 40 and 41. Sometimes informally called BRACKETS. Parentheses may be used to enclose a phrase (like this one) to show that it represents a digression from the main narrative. In mathematics, parentheses are used to group together elements within an expression and modify the order of their evaluation, as in (2+3)×5 versus 2+(3×5).

Parentheses play an important part of the syntax of computer programming languages, where they are used not only in the mathematical way but often to enclose the PARAMETERS of a function or procedure, as in: SetFillStyle(SOLIDFILL, 50);

parent process Under a MULTITASKING operating system such as Unix, a PROCESS that has created one or more other processes called CHILD PROCESSES. All processes except INIT (the very first one launched at system startup) must have been created by a parent process. See also SPAWN, FORK.

parity Oddness or evenness (i.e. divisibility by two). A property of numbers that is employed in many types of ERROR DETECTION AND CORRECTION scheme, on the principle that the unwanted addition or removal of a single item from any collection will change the parity of the total number of items. Such simple parity checks cannot, however, detect the addition or removal of two items, which leaves the parity the same. See also PARITY BIT, PARITY ERROR, CHECKSUM, CYCLIC REDUNDANCY CHECK.

parity bit An extra bit appended to a data word for the purpose of error detection. The number of 1s in each data word is counted by the software, and an extra 1 or 0 bit appended so as to make this total (called the PARITY of the word) always, say, odd. If a single bit should inadvertently be changed during storage or transmission, such an error can now be detected because it will change the parity of the received word (in our example, from odd to even). The scheme works similarly using an even parity that changes to odd, but neither variation will detect two corrupted bits (or any even number) as they have no net effect on the parity. See more under ERROR CORRECTING MEMORY, ERROR CORRECTION, ERROR DETECTION AND CORRECTION, PARITY ERROR, CYCLIC REDUNDANCY CHECK.

Under SERIAL communications protocols such as RS-232, a parity bit may be appended to each character for the same purpose of error detection. Whether or not such a parity bit is used is one of the crucial communication parameters that must be set correctly for a particular remote service to enable connection to be made. See also START BIT, STOP BIT.

parity error An error in the digital representation of some stored or transmitted quantity, as detected by the addition of an extra PARITY BIT. For example in a computer fitted with ERROR CORRECTING MEMORY, a parity error signals that a bit stored somewhere in the memory has had its value changed by some unwanted process (for example a cosmic ray passing through the chip). Similarly a parity error in a data stream received through a SERIAL PORT would indicate that a bit had become corrupted in transmission.

Parlog A dialect of PROLOG, developed at Imperial College, London, in 1983, which supports PARALLEL evaluation of queries.

PARMACS (PARallel MACroS) A portable library of MESSAGE PASSING functions that enables the same PARALLEL program code to be executed on a PARALLEL COMPUTER or on a network of WORKSTATIONS.

parse To analyse a text into meaningful units, according to the rules of a language SYNTAX.

parser A computer program that analyses a text into meaningful units, according to the rules of some language SYNTAX. An important application of parsing is in computing itself, as the first action of the COMPILER used to create new programs. The parser first breaks down the SOURCE CODE into a stream of TOKENS representing actions, which are then translated into EXECUTABLE machine instructions by later stages of the compiler. (See more under RECURSIVE DESCENT.)

A parser for a NATURAL LANGUAGE such as English breaks down sentences into parts of speech – nouns, verbs, adjectives and so on – and identifies clause structures. Such parsers are hard to implement because of language ambiguity and the lack of a complete, formalized syntax. Nevertheless language translation programs, advanced database QUERY engines and adventure games contain greatly simplified parsers.

parser generator A program that accepts a description of a programming language grammar written in a formal notation (typically BACKUS-NAUR FORM) and outputs the source code for a PARSER for that language. The best known example is perhaps the UNIX system's YACC.

Partial Response Maximum Likelihood (PRML) A technique used in HARD DISK drives to more accurately translate the weak ANALOGUE signal produced by the reading head into a DIGITAL signal. Rather than setting an absolute peak threshold to distinguish 0 from 1, PRML correctly interprets even small changes in the signal by weighting them against their context of surrounding values. Correctly decoding weaker signals permits higher recording densities.

particle system A trick used in 3D GRAPHICS to simulate the appearance of a collection of a large number of small objects, such as clouds of sparks, debris or snow, or even swarms of insects. When hundreds or thousands of such particles are required it becomes far too expensive to give each one of them an entry in the GEOMETRY database as a fully fledged 3D object. So instead an algorithm is employed to generate the objects at rendering time with varying sizes, orientations and trajectories whose constraints are defined by user-specified parameters.

Such algorithms are typically implemented as a SCRIPT within the graphics software, which may offer the ability to simulate complex behaviours such as following a swarm leader, explosive dispersal, or a fountain under the influence of gravity. See also PROCEDURAL TEXTURE, RENDERMAN.

partition 1 A portion of a hard disk drive that is presented to the operating system as a separate LOGICAL disk drive. Also used as a verb for the act of splitting a disk into such partitions.
2 In mathematics, to divide a set into subsets such that each element lies in only one subset.
3 Hence in computing, a portion of a data set that has been so divided, which may be

processed using a DIVIDE-AND-CONQUER ALGORITHM or allocated to a different processor in a MULTIPROCESSOR or PARALLEL computer.

Partition Magic A disk utility program, published by the US company PowerQuest, which can alter the size of a PARTITION on a hard disk without destroying any data that is stored on it. See also FDISK.

Pascal A programming language designed by Niklaus WIRTH in 1970, and named after the French mathematician Blaise PASCAL. It is a strongly typed (see under TYPE CHECKING), BLOCK STRUCTURED language that supports user defined data types called RECORDS. Pascal has been displaced by C and C++ for commercial programming purposes, but is still used in the teaching of programming and as the language of Borland's DELPHI visual programming environment. Its clear syntax has been an influence on many subsequent languages, including VISUAL BASIC.

passive Incapable of initiating an action. In hardware terms, a device may be described as passive because it lacks a processor or power supply of its own, and can therefore only respond to a dialogue initiated by some other device. For example: a passive radio transponder contains no battery, but can reply to signals from another, active, transmitter using solely the power from the received signal. A passive BACKPLANE merely contains slots to accept expansion cards and a bus to connect them, but no processor.

passive matrix display The cheapest type of LIQUID CRYSTAL DISPLAY for portable computers. It has its TRANSISTOR switches arranged around its periphery, connected by twin grids of thin-film wires so that a PIXEL is lighted at the intersection of two addressed wires. This structure makes it cheaper and easier to manufacture than the superior ACTIVE MATRIX DISPLAY (which places a transistor behind every pixel), but results in relatively poor contrast. As a result, a second set of switches and address lines is usually added to produce the so-called DUAL SCAN DISPLAY.

pass-through To process a data stream while allowing the original stream to continue onward so that other processors may also have access to it. The ease with which digital data can be copied means that the continuing stream is not diminished in any way. A common example from the hardware field is a type of plug used to connect, say, a scanner to a computer's PARALLEL PORT, which bears an identical vacant socket so that the printer can still be plugged in. See also DAISY-CHAIN.

password A secret word or phrase used as proof of authorization to gain admission to a computer or network. A password is typically a string of numbers and letters of some minimum length (e.g. 6 letters). The ideal password is one that is easy for the user to remember but hard for others to guess: as with so many ideals, this proves elusive.

Most operating systems implement a password protection system that requests a USER NAME and password during the LOG ON procedure, and some permit extra passwords to be applied to individual files or directories.

paste To insert data that has been temporarily stored in a CLIPBOARD into a document at the current cursor position. Pasting concludes the two-stage procedure that is used to copy (COPY-AND-PASTE) or move (CUT-AND-PASTE) a section of a document. Some programs offer a choice of different modes when pasting data; for example a choice of font in a word processor, or a choice of location in a graphics program.

patch A piece of program code that is added to an existing program file to correct a BUG or to add a new feature. Applying a patch does not require access to the program's SOURCE CODE or full recompilation. Software vendors typically supply a patch as an executable file that, when run, automatically edits the executable file of the target application. See also BUG FIX, SERVICE PACK, OVERLAY.

path 1 Under any operating system that employs a HIERARCHICAL FILE SYSTEM, the full route that must be taken through its nested DIRECTORY structure to arrive at a particular file. For example under MS-DOS or WINDOWS the full *pathname* required to identify a file called mydoc.txt might be c:\documents\ letters\mydoc.txt, which begins by naming a DRIVE C: which contains a FOLDER documents that contains a folder letters that contains the file. See also ENVIRONMENT VARIABLE.

2 In VECTOR-based drawing programs such as Adobe Illustrator, the name given to the strokes that define the shape of any on-screen object. The path is composed of one or more line segments with their start and end NODES joined. Many such programs allow any arbitrarily curved line drawn by the user to be used as a path along which text or brush-strokes can be forced to flow. See also VECTOR GRAPHICS, OUTLINE FONT.

3 In computer ANIMATION, an arbitrarily curved line drawn on the screen that a moving object can be made to follow as its trajectory.

4 In a GRAPH or NETWORK, a sequence of contiguous arcs that can be traversed to get from one NODE to another. Less formally, any route that joins two or more nodes.

pathname See under PATH.

pathological case A particular example of a problem that is very badly behaved and not typical of the problem. For example some highly efficient SORT algorithms may become very slow in the special pathological case when the data is already in sorted order. See also WORST CASE.

pattern See under PATTERN MATCHING, PATTERN RECOGNITION, BIT PATTERN, DESIGN PATTERN.

pattern matching The process of comparing two data objects – for example character strings or bitmapped images – to identify similarities in their structure. Pattern matching is one of the most fundamental computer operations, employed, for example, to locate files in a disk directory, to SEARCH AND REPLACE text in a word processor, to retrieve records from a DATABASE, or by ANTI-VIRUS SOFTWARE to identify virus code.

Pattern matching algorithms for character strings all depend upon some notation (such as WILDCARDS or REGULAR EXPRESSIONS) for describing patterns. For example the wildcard ? in the pattern D?CK can stand for any single letter, so the pattern would match DECK, DICK, DOCK or DUCK.

Some specialized programming languages, including PERL, AWK, ICON and SNOBOL, are designed with pattern matching as their main purpose. Many DECLARATIVE LANGUAGES employ pattern matching to identify the type of the

ACTUAL PARAMETERS supplied in a FUNCTION CALL and bind them to the correct FUNCTION BODY.

Pattern matching between images is an altogether more difficult task, involving APPROXIMATION ALGORITHMS that measure the difference between shapes. See more under PATTERN RECOGNITION.

pattern recognition An area within ARTIFICIAL INTELLIGENCE research that aims to extract structure from raw digital data, for example trying to locate individual objects within a picture or video, to identify a particular human face, or to find regularities in a sequence of seemingly random stock prices. Some pattern recognition systems employ statistical methods to find regularities in the data set, while others work from a set of examples of previously recognized structures. The latter approach is used by NEURAL NETWORKS, which are among the most favoured tools for pattern recognition: the examples are presented to train the network.

pause 1 A key fitted to all IBM-COMPATIBLE PC keyboards that was originally intended to temporarily suspend execution of the current program. While it does have this effect in most older, text-based MS-DOS programs, few Windows programs respond to it.
2 One of the standard set of keys for operating tape recorders and CD players, which causes playing to be temporarily suspended until pressed again. It is frequently emulated in software player interfaces, bearing the ‖ symbol.
3 In some programming languages that support COOPERATIVE MULTITASKING, a command that causes the currently executing task to suspend itself and allow other tasks to run until they execute a pause statement of their own, in ROUND ROBIN fashion.

payload data In any PACKET-SWITCHED communications system, the portion of each packet which contains the actual data being transmitted, as opposed to headers that contain routing and other system information.

PBX (Private Branch Exchange) A local telephone exchange, owned by a company or organization, which routes calls between the outside telephone lines and all the internal extensions. See also PABX.

PC 1 Abbreviation of PERSONAL COMPUTER.
2 Abbreviation of PROGRAM COUNTER.

pcAnywhere A REMOTE CONTROL program for IBM-compatible PCs published by Symantec. It allows one PC to be used as a workstation to run programs on another remote PC connected by a direct serial or parallel cable, by a network, or via a MODEM connection.

PCB Abbreviation of PRINTED CIRCUIT BOARD.

PC Card The standard for miniature EXPANSION CARDS to be used in notebook and laptop computers, developed by the Personal Computer Memory Card International Association (PCMCIA) and formerly called PCMCIA cards. The cards are credit-card-sized plastic boxes with a 68-pin electrical interface and are most often used to add computer memory, MODEMS and NETWORK INTERFACE CARDS. Most notebook computers are fitted with two PC Card slots, which may hold two separate Type 1 or 2 PC cards or one double-thickness Type 3 PC card. The slots can also act as input/output ports for attaching external devices (such as digital cameras) via a cable.

PCD Abbreviation of PHOTO CD.

PC-DOS Often simply called DOS, the official name given by IBM to its proprietary version of Microsoft's MS-DOS operating system, as shipped with the original IBM PC and its successors. PC-DOS differed little from generic MS-DOS internally, though some of its commands such as FORMAT and MODE made calls to the PC's ROM-based IBM BASIC whereas MS-DOS instead supplied the disk-based MS-Basic or GW BASIC.

p-channel See under CMOS.

PCI bus (Peripheral Component Interconnect bus) A 32-bit EXPANSION BUS introduced by Intel in 1993 which has almost completely displaced the original ISA BUS in IBM-compatible PCs, and has also been adopted by Apple for MACINTOSH models later than 1995.

Strictly speaking, PCI is not a SYSTEM BUS but a BRIDGE (sometimes called a 'mezzanine bus') which isolates the local PROCESSOR BUS from the peripherals, allowing the CPU to run much faster than the 33 megahertz of PCI itself. PCI's great advantage over ISA, apart from faster throughput, is that it supports automatic PLUG-AND-PLAY configuration of expansion cards.

PCL Abbreviation of PRINTER CONTROL LANGUAGE.

PCM Abbreviation of PULSE CODE MODULATION.

PCMCIA (Personal Computer Memory Card International Association) The computer industry body responsible for developing the PC CARD standards.

p-code Short for PSEUDO-CODE.

PC/SC (PC Smart Card) An interface standard that provides interchangeability between different SMARTCARDS. Promoted by the Smart-Card Forum, which includes Microsoft and several computer manufacturers.

PC Write A fast and elegant word processor for MS-DOS computers created by Bob Wallace, a Microsoft compiler writer. It became one of the very first successful SHAREWARE products, but Wallace declined to port it to Microsoft Windows and so development ceased in the late 1980s.

PCX The native GRAPHICS FILE FORMAT of ZSoft's PC Paintbrush painting program, which became a widely used import format for PC applications, until the Windows bitmap (BMP) format displaced it.

PDA (Personal Digital Assistant) A term coined by John Scully of Apple to describe its NEWTON pocket computer, intended to convey the idea of more than just a combined calculator, diary and address book, and imply that it would make intelligent connections between data. Since the Newton's demise, the term is still sometimes applied to personal organizers such as those from PALM Computing.

PDC Abbreviation of PRIMARY DOMAIN CONTROLLER.

PDF (Portable Document Format) An electronic document format invented by ADOBE. It enables documents containing both text and graphic images to be viewed and printed in a uniform manner on different computer systems, independently of the resolution of the display device. PDF files must be viewed in Adobe's ACROBAT reader program, which is widely available free of charge. PDF format is often chosen on the Internet for downloadable documents whose design cannot be accurately reproduced in HTML.

PDF files encode their contents using a simplified variant of Adobe's POSTSCRIPT page description language. They may contain embedded fonts that can be substituted if any font originally used to create the document is missing on the target machine. Such embedded fonts may lose details of some ornate characters, but maintain the metrics of the original so that layout and line breaks are preserved. If the original fonts are embedded in the PDF file then text remains editable to a limited degree.

PDH Abbreviation of PLESIOCHRONOUS DIGITAL HIERARCHY.

PDL Abbreviation of PAGE DESCRIPTION LANGUAGE.

PDP-11 The most popular of the family of MINICOMPUTERS produced by DEC in the 1970s. In some ways the PDP-11 was the forerunner of the personal computer because of its popularity with university departments, where users were granted relatively free access. A lot of the earliest interactive software, including UNIX, the C programming language and much of the INTERNET software, were first developed for the PDP-11.

PDS Abbreviation of PROCESSOR DIRECT SLOT.

peak The highest value attained by some system parameter, rather than its average value. Used as in 'peak throughput' or 'peak memory-usage'.

peak-to-peak A measurement of the momentary amplitude of a waveform (such as an alternating current or audio signal) that is taken between the highest positive and the lowest negative peak in the chosen time interval, rather than from the zero axis.

peek A command provided in most versions of the BASIC programming language which returns the contents of a specified memory location. When used in conjunction with the related POKE command, it permits a very limited degree of MACHINE CODE level programming to be performed from within a Basic program.

peephole optimization A class of COMPILER OPTIMIZATION that examines only short sequences of adjacent MACHINE CODE instructions at a time (hence the name), seeking to replace them with a more efficient single instruction or shorter sequence. For example a pair of instructions such as:

```
ADD Reg, 1
ADD Reg, 2
```

can clearly be performed more efficiently by the single instruction ADD Reg, 3.

peering exchange See under NETWORK ACCESS POINT.

peer-to-peer A network architecture in which any pair of connected computers may communicate directly with one another, each acting as either SERVER or WORKSTATION as required. This contrasts with a CLIENT/SERVER architecture in which these roles are separate and fixed (i.e. a server is always and only a server).

The term has also been applied more recently to Internet-based services such as the music-sharing NAPSTER network, in which all the participants can act as either client or server.

pen input Entering data into a computer by using a stylus to write either onto a touch-sensitive screen or onto a separate tablet, rather than by typing on a keyboard. Pen input was first used for entering drawings in Computer Aided Design applications. With the addition of HANDWRITING RECOGNITION software, it has become a popular mode of data access for pocket computers which are too small to incorporate a usable keyboard.

pen interface A computer USER INTERFACE that requires data to be written with a stylus rather than typed on a keyboard. See under PEN INPUT.

Pentium The name given by Intel to the generation of 32-BIT general purpose MICROPROCESSORS it launched in 1993 to replace the Intel 80486. The next number in that sequence should have been 80586 but, following a US court ruling that numbers cannot be trademarked, Intel chose instead to adopt a name, which can.

The Pentium also marked a turning point in Intel's design strategy, as it employed many of the techniques used in rival RISC-based designs to increase its execution speed, including SUPERSCALAR execution via two integer and one floating-point PIPELINES. However, it retains the older 8086 register structure (see under 80x86 ARCHITECTURE) for compatibility. Any 80x86 program should run unchanged on a Pentium, but many will run faster if recompiled using a Pentium-specific compiler to exploit the multiple pipelines.

The Pentium family now extends to Pentium II, Pentium Pro, Pentium III, Pentium 4 and the Celeron, some chips running at clock speeds in excess of 1 gigahertz (GHz). Processors from Pentium III onward feature the STREAMING SIMD EXTENSIONS for enhanced FLOATING-POINT performance.

perceptron A simple type of NEURAL NETWORK first studied in the 1960s, which consists of three layers of NEURONS; an input layer, a middle layer and an output layer. It has been shown that a perceptron can never solve certain kinds of classification problem (the so-called XOR problem), and so the model has been superceded by networks that employ BACK-PROPAGATION to enhance their learning ability.

performance Of a computer or communications system, generally the rate at which the system can move and/or process data. Additional factors such as RELIABILITY, LATENCY or USABILITY may also be included in estimating performance in some cases. See also BENCHMARK.

performance tuning Enhancing the performance of a system by adjusting various parameters, such as CACHE or BUFFER sizes, to eliminate bottlenecks. See also LOAD BALANCING, STARVATION, TWEAKING.

peripheral, peripheral device Any part of a computer that lies outside its CPU and MAIN MEMORY. The KEYBOARD, MOUSE, DISPLAY, DISK DRIVES, TAPE DRIVE, PRINTER, MODEM, SCANNER, and many more, are all types of peripheral device.

Peripherals must be connected to the CPU, either via an EXPANSION BUS or via a PORT such as a SERIAL PORT, SCSI port, PARALLEL PORT or USB port. In most cases a peripheral also requires a special piece of software called a DEVICE DRIVER to make it visible to the computer's operating system.

The term has a commercial significance, in that peripheral devices may frequently be purchased from manufacturers other than the manufacturer of the computer itself.

Peripheral Component Interconnect See PCI BUS.

Perl (Practical Extraction and Report Language) An INTERPRETED SCRIPTING LANGUAGE originally developed under UNIX by Larry Wall and distributed free via the USENET, but now available for most operating systems. Perl is a powerful and concise language designed to manipulate text data by PATTERN MATCHING using REGULAR EXPRESSIONS and ASSOCIATIVE ARRAYS. It is widely used to write SERVER-SIDE CGI scripts for web servers.

Perl script A program written in the PERL scripting language, which typically runs on a web server, and may be invoked from a web page via the CGI interface.

permission A level of access privilege granted to a computer's user by the operating system either for individual FILES or for whole DIRECTORIES. For example *read permission* allows the user only to read a file's contents, *write permission* allows the contents to be altered, *execute permission* allows a program to be run. Many operating systems, such as UNIX and WINDOWS NT, enable each file to have different permissions for different users and groups of users.

persistent Maintaining an existence over time. The term is applied, for example, to network connections or other system configurations such as DRIVE LETTER substitutions that remain intact between separate computing sessions. In programming the term describes various kinds of data structure that retain their existence from one invocation of the program to the next – unlike ordinary variables whose contents are lost when the program terminates.

For example, the JAVA language supports persistent objects, which must be stored on a permanent medium, such as a hard disk.

Unlike the traditional disk file, however, the programmer does not need to write explicit code to open, read, write or close them.

personal computer (PC) A computer designed to be operated by and for one person. This is in contrast to MAINFRAME or MINICOMPUTERS, which have to be shared between many users. The first personal computers were built in the late 1970s, as a direct consequence of the invention of the MICROPROCESSOR, which for the first time made it economically possible to provide electronic computing power to a single person.

A typical personal computer consists of four essential units: a *system unit* containing the microprocessor CPU, a power supply, some MEMORY and one or more DISK DRIVES for permanent program and data storage; a MONITOR to display information generated by the computer's software; a KEYBOARD on which the user can enter data; and a MOUSE or other pointing device to select data and operations from a GRAPHICAL USER INTERFACE displayed on the monitor. Different designs may combine several of these functional units. So for example some Apple MACINTOSH models combine system unit and monitor into one box, while LAPTOP computers cram them all into a single hinged unit.

Various other PERIPHERAL devices add to the utility of a personal computer, the most ubiquitous being a printer to produce hard copy, a MODEM for communicating via the telephone system and Internet, and increasingly a SCANNER for inputting pictorial material. For game playing, alternative input devices such as JOYSTICKS and steering wheels are available, as well as HEAD-MOUNTED DISPLAYS for 3D games.

Early personal computers were adopted by technically proficient enthusiasts, but they found favour among businesses following the invention of the SPREADSHEET in the early 1980s. Once effective methods of networking personal computers together were invented, PC networks began to displace minicomputers – and even occasionally mainframes – in the running of large corporations. The late 1990s saw a huge increase in home ownership of personal computers for entertainment and educational use, and for accessing the Internet. Ironically, the enormous demands that modern 3D computer games make on the hardware have ensured that home PCs frequently have equivalent or even superior specifications to those used in business.

Historically, the first personal computers were kits of parts that enthusiasts had to assemble themselves, the first commercially successful one being the MITS Altair 8800 of 1975. The first ready-built personal computers were the Apple II and the Commodore PET 2001 of 1978. Both these machines originally came with 4 kilobytes (KB) of memory and used ordinary cassette tapes for mass storage, though floppy disk drives that held 160 KB had become affordable by 1979. By 1983, 5 MB hard disk drives could be had for a mere $3000.

IBM's introduction of its own Intel-powered PC in 1981 made personal computers respectable among business users and, by allowing (or at least by failing to prevent) other companies to copy its hardware architecture IBM triggered the growth of a huge PC industry. The majority of today's so-called IBM-COMPATIBLE PCS still employ the Intel family of CPUS and a BUS architecture that derives from that original IBM PC, though some of the constraints on memory and disk sizes and bus BANDWIDTH have been removed over the decades by evolutionary improvements to the hardware and the OPERATING SYSTEM.

In 1985 Apple replaced the Apple II with the innovative MACINTOSH which pioneered commercial application of the easy-to-use graphical user interface. Microsoft later introduced this concept to IBM-compatible PCs through its Windows operating system. The IBM-compatible and the Macintosh remain the only important (though incompatible) standards in personal computing.

Personal Computer Memory Card International Association See PCMCIA.

Personal Digital Assistant See PDA.

personal identification number See PIN.

personal information manager See PIM.

personality A complete set of characteristics of a hardware or software system that can be substituted by an alternative set. For example some operating systems employ 'personality modules' that allow them to emulate other systems, while a hardware device such as a printer might have plug-in 'personality modules' that adapt it to fit different makes of computer.

personal organizer A pocket computer used to carry personal addresses and phone numbers, calendar dates, reminders and notes. The term is sometimes also used of software on a desktop computer that fulfils the same functions. See also PDA, PIM.

perspective 1 In many computer action games, such as DOOM and QUAKE, one of several viewpoints that the player may adopt by pressing a key. A first-person perspective shows the world through the eyes of the protagonist, while a second-person perspective is through the eyes of a spectator some distance to the side of the action. There may be also a third perspective that surveys the whole scene from above.
2 A feature of some graphics programs that automatically transforms a selected figure into vanishing-point perspective.

perspective-correct Any 3D GRAPHICS effect, such as TEXTURE MAPPING or BUMP MAPPING, to which geometric transformations are applied so that it continually changes to match the perspective of the viewer. See RENDER, MIP MAPPING.

PERT (Program Evaluation and Review Technique) A mathematical method used for planning, controlling and checking the time taken to finish important parts of a complex project such as making a new aircraft, ship, bridge or computer program. The PERT equation estimates the size and duration of the whole project, and establishes a standard deviation to assess the risks of overshooting by combining estimates for the individual parts. In a computing context, this means calculating the Equivalent Delivered Source Instructions and their deviation from analysts' estimates of the smallest possible size, the most likely size, and the greatest possible size of each component of the program. See also CRITICAL PATH ANALYSIS, GANTT CHART.

Pet One of the earliest personal computers. See more under COMMODORE BUSINESS MACHINES, its manufacturer.

petabyte 2^{50} BYTES, that is, 1024 TERABYTES.

petaflops 1,000,000,000,000,000 (10^{15}) FLOPS (Floating-Point Operations Per Second), the next significant milestone for supercomputer designers, which has yet to be achieved.

Petri net A type of DIRECTED GRAPH, invented by Carl Adam Petri, which can be used to model the behaviour of concurrent computation and communication systems. Each node in a Petri net represents either a place (usually shown as a circle) or a transition (shown by a rectangle). The net is then loaded by placing TOKENS on the places. Whenever all the places connected to a particular transition (its 'input' places) have received a token, that transition 'fires' by removing a token from each input place and adding one to each output place (i.e. those places pointed to by the transition). Petri nets are sometimes used to model network PROTOCOLS.

PGA Abbreviation of PIN-GRID ARRAY.

PgDn key See PAGE DOWN KEY.

PGP Shorthand for PRETTY GOOD PRIVACY.

PgUp key See PAGE UP KEY.

phase The relative position within its cycle that has been reached at a particular instant by some cyclically varying quantity, such as a wave. Phase is therefore usually expressed as an angle between 0° and 360°. See for example PHASE SHIFT KEYING, QUADRATURE AMPLITUDE MODULATION, THREE-PHASE POWER SUPPLY.

phased-array antenna A type of radar transmitter that, instead of physically rotating its antenna to scan an area, rotates the beam electronically by cyclically varying the PHASE of the signals supplied to a grid of separate, fixed antennae. Miniaturized phased arrays have been tried as input devices in some experimental VIRTUAL REALITY systems to locate all solid objects in the vicinity.

phase encoded A recording method used in some large MAGNETIC TAPE systems.

phase-locked loop (PLL) An electronic circuit that locks onto an external CLOCK SIGNAL and outputs some multiple of its frequency (for example, multiplying a 50 MHz clock signal to 200 MHz). PLLs are used as internal timers inside all modern microprocessors to allow the use of slower peripheral chips and to avoid the difficulties of propagating such high-frequency clock signals around a motherboard.

phase shift keying (PSK) A class of encoding techniques that depend on changes in the PHASE of a CARRIER wave to transmit information. Shifting the carrier's phase by 90° increments (relative either to a reference phase, or to the phase of the previous cycle) creates four possible states, and so can encode two bits per carrier cycle; 45° increments create 8 states, and hence encode three bits, and so on. PSK increases the apparent BANDWIDTH available, and variants are employed in high-speed MODEMS and DIGITAL SUBSCRIBER LINE technologies.

PHIGS Abbreviation of PROGRAMMERS HIERARCHICAL INTERACTIVE GRAPHICS SYSTEM.

Philips A large electronics company based in Holland, which in association with SONY has been responsible for developing many of the major recording formats of the last 50 years, including the Compact Cassette and various CD standards.

phoneme The smallest unit of sound used in human speech; part of the set of speech sounds that distinguish one word from another in any particular language.

Phong shading An algorithm employed in 3D GRAPHICS to fool the eye into seeing an object as a smoothly curving surface when it is actually constructed from a mesh of polygons. It differs from GOURAUD SHADING in calculating the light reflected normal to the surface for every pixel in the interior of each polygon, rather than interpolating from the EDGE values, which makes it too slow for REAL TIME displays, but yields a smoother result with more accurate reflections and highlights.

phosphor Fluorescent chemical compounds, used to coat the inside of the screen of a CATHODE RAY TUBE, which glow when struck by the tube's beam of electrons. For a colour tube, groups of three dots or stripes, each of a different phosphor, are deposited, glowing red, green or blue according to which the beam strikes. In addition to colour, an important property of a particular phosphor compound is its persistence, that is, the length of time it keeps glowing once the beam has left it: persistence must be sufficient to avoid FLICKER between frames, but not so long as to smear moving images.

Photo CD (PCD) A system developed by Kodak for transferring photographs taken on conventional photographic film onto a CD-ROM as high-definition digital image files (up to 2048 × 3072 pixels at a COLOUR DEPTH of 24 bits). The GRAPHICS FILE FORMAT employed for Photo CD permits variously sized images to be extracted from the same file without loss of quality.

photocell An opto-electronic component, usually made of silicon, which generates an electrical voltage proportional to the amount of light falling upon it. Photocells are used to measure and detect light and to generate electrical power. See also CHARGE-COUPLED DEVICE.

photonics In communications and computing, the use of circuits based on light rather than electrons. Optical signal transmission is already a well-established technology using OPTICAL FIBRE, but the other required functions such as switches and storage devices for light signals remain at an experimental stage.

Photonic switching technologies exist, for example based on dichroic materials whose refractive index can be altered by an external stimulus, but few are amenable to the kind of high volume fabrication techniques on which the semiconductor industry was founded. In the meantime, hybrid OPTOELECTRONIC designs enable optical transmission to be combined with electronic processing circuits to produce usable devices.

photo-realistic A computer graphics display that approximates to a photograph of a real scene, as used for example in movie special effects.

Photoshop The most widely used digital PAINTING PROGRAM, published by ADOBE. Photoshop was originally designed for photographic editing and retouching (hence its name), but it is now used as a general-purpose creative tool for everything from illustration to web site design. Its success is due in part to the large number of FILTERS and other PLUG-IN utilities sold by third-party vendors to enhance its abilities.

phototypesetter An obsolete kind of TYPESETTER that stored its FONTS on film and reproduced the characters optically.

PHP A UNIX-based SCRIPTING LANGUAGE for creating dynamic web pages which is available in both commercial and FREEWARE versions. According to conflicting sources, the name either stands for Personal Home Page or is a RECURSIVE ACRONYM for PHP: Hypertext Processor. See also PERL, ACTIVE SERVER PAGES.

physical When used as the opposite of LOGICAL, this refers to a real, material piece of equipment rather than some software abstraction erected to disguise it. For example a single physical disk drive may be configured to appear to an operating system as two or more logical drives. Similarly, when describing multi-layered communication structures the physical level refers to the level of wires carrying electrical currents rather than to software protocols.

physical address In a system that employs VIRTUAL MEMORY, an address that corresponds to an actual location in the computer's MAIN MEMORY, rather than to a VIRTUAL ADDRESS that lies beyond the physical memory range. A MEMORY MANAGEMENT UNIT is responsible for converting virtual into physical addresses. See also LOGICAL-TO-PHYSICAL TRANSLATION, PAGE TABLE, TRANSLATION LOOK-ASIDE BUFFER.

Physical Address Extensions (PAE) A mechanism introduced by Intel with the PENTIUM Pro and later processors, to enable them to address more than 4 gigabytes of PHYSICAL MEMORY by increasing the page size of the VIRTUAL MEMORY system from 4 kilobytes to 2 megabytes. To use additional PAE memory, software requires operating system support via the ADVANCED WINDOWING EXTENSIONS. Processors from the Pentium II Xeon onward can also employ true 36-bit physical addresses, which can be exploited directly by software running under WINDOWS NT Enterprise Server Edition, WINDOWS 2000 or UNIX.

physical memory In a computer that supports VIRTUAL MEMORY, the actual RAM into which the larger ADDRESS SPACE is mapped by swapping in data from disk as required. See also PHYSICAL ADDRESS, LOGICAL ADDRESS, ADDRESS TRANSLATION.

piano-roll A view provided in most MIDI SEQUENCER programs in which a playing tune is portrayed as a moving strip with small rectangles representing the notes, like the holes in an old Pianola roll.

PIC **1** A FILENAME EXTENSION used by several different GRAPHICS FILE FORMATS including the ones used by LOTUS 1-2-3 and the SOFTIMAGE 3D animation program.
2 An abbreviation for PROGRAMMABLE INTERRUPT CONTROLLER.
3 The name of a range of 8-bit MICROCONTROLLERS made by Microchip Technology.

Pick An operating system, marketed by its inventor Dick Pick for most of the available brands of MINICOMPUTER, which was popular in the 1970s for commercial data processing. Pick featured a built-in database manager with a powerful dialect of BASIC integrated into it, enabling business systems to be constructed without purchasing any extra software. Though ported to the IBM PC, Pick failed to make the transition to personal computers.

picosecond 10^{-12} (US one trillionth) of a second, a timescale used to measure events in subatomic physics.

PICT A GRAPHICS FILE FORMAT used on the Apple MACINTOSH.

PID Abbreviation of PROCESS IDENTIFIER.

pie chart A type of GRAPH that takes the form of a disk divided into sectors, like slices of a pie, whose areas are proportional to the values being plotted. Pie charts are effective for

illustrating individual shares of a total resource.

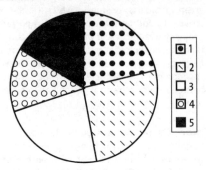

piezoelectric effect A phenomenon that creates a high ELECTROSTATIC voltage between opposite faces of crystals of certain materials (such as quartz) when they are mechanically stressed. Conversely, a small physical contraction of the crystal occurs when a high voltage is applied. This phenomenon is exploited to make the quartz OSCILLATORS that beat time in battery-powered wrist watches and computers, and in some INK-JET PRINTERS to propel the ink droplets out of the nozzles.

PIF (Program Information File) A type of configuration file created by Microsoft Windows to assist in the running of older MS-DOS programs in a separate DOS window. Each such program has its own PIF file, containing details such as the size of its screen, the screen font to use, the amount of memory to allocate to the program, and its mode of termination.

PIM (personal information manager) A category of software that aims to replace the function of a pocket or desk diary by storing the data used by a person in everyday life (both home and business), such as addresses and telephone numbers, appointments and calendar dates, a TO DO LIST for reminders, and a note-taking facility. Some PIM products attempt to duplicate the appearance of a paper diary for the sake of familiarity, for example by using alphabetic index TABS in the address book section.

A PIM typically offers some degree of integration between its different functions, so that, for example, an item on the To Do list that falls due might automatically appear in that day's calendar. Moreover, with the rise in importance of EMAIL and the Internet there has been a tendency for PIM programs to become absorbed into larger communications software suites – the most popular example being Microsoft's Outlook – and to support group and remote functions (see GROUP CALENDAR, CALENDAR SERVICE). Hence it is common to refer to the 'PIM functions' of a larger program, meaning essentially its Contacts, Diary and To Do functions.

pin 1 One of the metal conductors used to convey electrical signals into and out of an INTEGRATED CIRCUIT package. The name was coined in the early days of the semiconductor industry when circuits came in packages with two parallel rows of sharp metal 'legs' that plugged into holes in a socket. It is still used, even though most chips now have flat metal pads instead.

2 (personal identification number, personal information number) A unique numeric identifier that the bearer of a credit card, bank card or other electronic identification system must memorize and enter on request to AUTHENTICATE their identity. See also PASSWORD, USER NAME, AUTOMATED TELLER MACHINE, KERBEROS.

pin-compatible A product sufficiently similar to an equivalent product that it is able to plug into the same socket, and work.

pincushioning A form of distortion seen on CATHODE RAY TUBE monitors, in which the edges of the picture are slightly concave rather than straight. The opposite distortion (i.e. convex edges) is called BARREL DISTORTION.

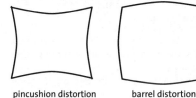

pincushion distortion   barrel distortion

pin feed An alternative name for a TRACTOR-FEED printer.

ping (Packet Internet Groper, Packet Internet Gopher) A widely-used utility program for TCP/IP networks that sends a dummy message to check whether a remote computer is currently online and working correctly. It is the network manager's first recourse as a diagnostic tool. Ping was originally written for UNIX, but versions are now available for all operating systems and even for other network protocols. The term is also used as a verb, meaning to employ ping to check whether a network connection is working, as in 'I pinged the server but it's down'.

The ping command is issued with the IP address of the equipment to be tested as its argument, and it reports the time taken to receive the acknowledgement (if any) of its dummy message. Various ping implementations offer extra options that alter the number of times to ping, how often, how long to wait, and how much data to send.

pin grid array, pin-grid array (PGA) A type of INTEGRATED CIRCUIT package consisting of a roughly square slab of plastic or (more usually) ceramic, the lower face of which bears a densely-packed grid of metal pins resembling the bristles of a brush. The pin grid array (and the related BALL GRID ARRAY) offer the most pins for a given area of any packaging technology, and as a result are used for most modern microprocessors, including the earlier Intel PENTIUMS, which require hundreds of pins. Pin grid array chips are normally deployed in a ZERO INSERTION FORCE socket, since they would be too difficult to insert into conventional sockets. See also PACKAGE, QUAD FLAT PACK, SURFACE MOUNT.

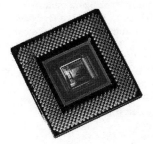

pin-out The numbers of, and functions assigned to, the PINS on an INTEGRATED CIRCUIT PACKAGE or a cable CONNECTOR.

pipe 1 A mechanism for streaming the output from one program into another program (or file), invented in UNIX but now copied in many other operating systems. At the command shell level, a pipe is represented by the | symbol, so for example the command sequence:

```
type myfile.txt | sort
```

pipes the output of type into the sort program, resulting in a sorted list of the contents of myfile.txt being displayed. Pipes are implemented behind the scenes via temporary and anonymous buffers or files created by the operating system. See also NAMED PIPE, SOCKET.

2 Increasingly used as a slang term for a telecommunications line, used as in 'we really need to install a fatter pipe'.

pipeline A principle employed to improve the efficiency of many kinds of processing task, such as the arithmetic units in most modern microprocessors. It involves dividing the task into several discrete stages and overlapping these in time by passing them through a sequence of independently operating units.

Pipelining is the same principle employed in a factory production line where many workers simultaneously fit different parts to a moving line of cars. The pipeline does not reduce the overall time to complete one item (each car might still take an hour to pass through the line) but more items can be completed in a given time: with 10 workstations a finished car emerges every 6 minutes.

Pipelining exploits the PARALLELISM inherent in a task by bringing multiple processing units to bear on it, but is effective only if the line is kept full and all the units busy. If one stage halts, the pipeline downstream will empty and cause a delay while it refills before flow can be restored (in the car analogy, that could take up to an hour). Computer engineers call this situation a *pipeline break* or *pipeline stall* and much ingenuity is applied to avoiding it.

pipeline break See under PIPELINE.

pipeline burst cache A type of processor CACHE in which reading or writing from a new location takes several clock cycles, but consecutive locations can then be accessed in a single cycle each, thanks to the use of PIPELINED STATIC RAM chips. Pipeline burst caches are

typically used as LEVEL 2 CACHE with a processor that has an ON-CHIP cache.

pipeline stall See under PIPELINE.

PIPEX One of the first and largest UK ISPs.

piracy Using or selling computer software without paying for it. A somewhat overdramatic term for breach of copyright.

pivot To change the axes along which a set of data involving multiple variables is viewed. The term is much employed in ONLINE ANALYTICAL PROCESSING and in working with spreadsheets. See also PIVOT TABLE.

pivot point A systematic way to interpret ambiguous two-digit years, employed in solving the YEAR 2000 problem in software. Some arbitrary year is chosen as the pivot point and all two-digit years below it are assumed to be in the 21st century while those above it are put in the 20th. For example Microsoft chose a pivot point of 30; so a date 65 is assumed to mean 1965, but the date 24 is assumed to refer to 2024. The scheme yields wrong results for dates too far removed from the present: for example a birth date in 1921 that had been written as 21 will be wrongly interpreted as 2021.

pivot table An advanced analysis feature provided by MICROSOFT EXCEL which permits the data from several SPREADSHEETS or DATABASE tables to be combined and quickly crosstabulated along different dimensions. Given, for example, sales data for several products, sales people and regions, a pivot table permits the switch from a view by region and product to a view by salesperson and total sales using a single mouse click.

pixel One of the dots, or picture elements from which the image on a computer screen is composed.

Computer displays are categorized by how many pixels form a whole screen image (say 1024×768 pixels) and by how many BITS of information describe the colour of a single pixel, which is called the COLOUR DEPTH. For example, a display with 8-bit colour depth permits each pixel to take on one of 256 (2^8) different colours.

The physical attributes of a pixel vary between different display technologies. On a

CATHODE RAY TUBE, each pixel is formed from three spots of PHOSPHOR that illuminate when struck by electron beams. An LCD display works on transmitted light, each pixel being a square region containing transparent red, green and blue stripes.

pixellation The coarse, blocky appearance produced when a BITMAPPED picture is enlarged too far, because there is not enough information present for the increased resolution. The effect is sometimes introduced deliberately to disguise people's faces, for example in television programmes. See also JAGGIES, ALIASING, ANTIALIASING.

pixel-mapped A less commonly used alternative term for BITMAPPED, which has the advantage that it remains correct no matter how many bits are actually employed to store each pixel.

pizza box A nickname given to any equipment packaged in a low, flat case, such as many ROUTERS, HUBS and even some PRINTERS.

PKunzip See under PKZIP.

PKWare The US software publisher of the widely used PKZIP FILE COMPRESSION utilities.

PKZip A widely used FILE COMPRESSION utility for MS-DOS files manufactured by the US software publisher PKWare. The corresponding decompression program is called *PKUnzip*.

PLA Abbreviation of PROGRAMMABLE LOGIC ARRAY.

placeholder A data item that has no intrinsic meaning, but is inserted into a document to indicate where a real value will later be stored. For example:name = "<yournamehere>"

plain ASCII A document format that contains nothing but the printable ASCII characters – no invisible formatting information concerning typefaces, font sizes, or styles such as bold or italic.

Plain Old Telephone Service See POTS.

plaintext The decoded or unencrypted version of a document. See ENCRYPTION.

plain-vanilla See VANILLA.

Plan 9 An innovative NETWORK OPERATING SYSTEM developed at BELL LABORATORIES by a team of researchers who had previously worked on UNIX. Plan 9 is a distributed and highly scalable operating system based around a collection of SERVERS that divide up the functions. For example multiprocessor CPU servers provide computing power, while file servers provide data storage. Users access these servers from SMART TERMINALS with graphical displays that run a Unix-like windowing user interface. Everything in the system is treated as a file, each server appearing as a tree of files. Every user possesses a NAMESPACE into which they can connect all the resources they need, regardless of where in the network these are actually located. Plan 9 is very much better than the low-budget, cult sci-fi film from which it takes its name.

planar 1 All in the same plane, flat.
2 IBM's proprietary term for what everyone else calls a MOTHERBOARD.

plasma screen Also called a *gas plasma display*, a type of digital display in which each illuminated PIXEL is formed by a tiny cell containing gas that emits light when a high voltage is discharged through it – like a miniature neon tube. Plasma screens can display in full colour and, unlike LCDs, can be manufactured in large sizes of several metres square. However, their high cost limits application to demonstrations and public display rather than day-to-day computer use.

platform A particular combination of computer hardware and operating system for which software may be developed: for example the WINTEL platform, or the MACINTOSH platform.

platform-independent Capable of working on any processor and under any operating system. For example web pages described in pure HTML are platform-independent.

platform-neutral Any feature of a programming language or other software system that does not depend upon, nor need to be aware of, what processor or operating system it is currently running on.

Platform of Privacy Preferences Project (P3P) A project of the WORLD WIDE WEB CONSORTIUM to give Internet users some choice over the collection, use and disclosure of their personal data when browsing on the web. P3P publishes vocabularies of privacy norms against which web sites can be rated for 'privacy-friendliness', so that browser software can be set to different levels of privacy protection.

platter One of the several thin metal disks, coated with a magnetic material and mounted on a common spindle, that make up a HARD DISK drive.

PlayStation A hugely successful GAMES CONSOLE produced by Sony that employs a domestic TV set as its monitor and runs games supplied on CD-ROM.

PLC Abbreviation of PROGRAMMABLE LOGIC CONTROLLER.

Plesiochronous Digital Hierarchy (PDH) A transmission technology used in European digital voice telephony systems that is currently being replaced by the faster SYNCHRONOUS DIGITAL HIERARCHY. The term plesiochronous means 'almost synchronized', a reference to the fact that it employs fixed-length time slots but does not require them all to be filled with data.

PL/1 An ambitious high-level programming language created by IBM in 1964 in an attempt to improve on COBOL, FORTRAN and ALGOL while maintaining their best features. As a result, the language became very large and complex, and has never found much currency beyond the world of IBM MAINFRAME programming. One of its most notable constructs was ON <condition> <action>, a mechanism for responding to infrequent program occurrences that prefigured modern EVENT-DRIVEN programming practices, but which caused great difficulties in tracing a program's flow of control.

PLL See PHASE-LOCKED LOOP.

plot To draw a GRAPH from a set of data. Also a graph so drawn.

plotter A type of computer output device that draws pictures by moving a pen in two dimensions across a sheet of paper. Some plotters can draw in several colours by selecting new pens from a rack, but they are more suitable for line drawings than for extensive solid-shaded areas, and therefore find most use in architecture, engineering and cartography.

plug-and-play The ability of a computer's operating system to detect what hardware PERIPHERALS are connected during start-up, and to automatically configure them. Without plug-and-play, each peripheral must be separately configured and made known to the operating system by manually setting JUMPERS or DIP SWITCHES and then editing the contents of one or more CONFIGURATION files (see for example AUTOEXEC.BAT under MS-DOS). Plug-and-play is supported in versions of Microsoft Windows 95, 98 and 2000. See also JINI, AUTO-DETECT.

plug-compatible A degree of hardware similarity between two computers such that PERIPHERALS and EXPANSION CARDS from one can be plugged into the other. Also said of two components that will plug into each other's sockets and work correctly. Plug-compatibility was first achieved in certain MAINFRAME and MINICOMPUTERS of the 1970s, but became a whole industry with the emergence of the IBM PC and its thousands of clones.

Pluggable Authentication Module (PAM) A standardized system for authenticating the identity of users as they log on to a computer running the UNIX operating system. System entry components – for example the log on procedure of a GUI desktop such as the CDE – that are PAM compliant permit different user authentication schemes to be added at will. PAM supports stacking of such plug-in schemes so that a SMARTCARD system, RSA ENCRYPTION and KERBEROS might be used on the same system.

plug-in 1 A small program that adds an extra function to some larger application. Plug-ins are extensively used with WEB BROWSERS, to enable them to display or play special kinds of multimedia content such as STREAMING VIDEO or audio. They are also used by graphics programs such as PHOTOSHOP, to which they add extra visual effects and filters.

2 The term is less often used for a hardware

module that adds a new function to a hardware device such as a hand-held computer.

PMMU Abbreviation of Paged Memory Management Unit. See VIRTUAL MEMORY, DEMAND-PAGED, MEMORY MANAGEMENT UNIT.

PNG (Portable Network Graphics) A compressed GRAPHICS FILE FORMAT that is becoming increasingly popular on the Internet. It was originally created and placed in the public domain by the WORLD WIDE WEB CONSORTIUM to get around copyright restrictions placed on the earlier GIF format. Like GIF, PNG is a BIT-MAPPED format, and can store pixel data either as 8-bit palette indexes or in 16-bit RGB form. It employs Phil Katz's lossless Deflate compression algorithm, in place of GIF's LZW algorithm, and applies predictive filtering to achieve superior compression of vertical and diagonal lines. PNG files are divided internally into a number of separate 'chunks', some of which may be used to hold GAMMA CORRECTION, ALPHA CHANNEL, chromaticity and other arbitrary types of information such as text labels.

PnP Abbreviation of PLUG-AND-PLAY.

pocket calculator A battery-operated portable computing device that is pre-programmed to perform the most common arithmetic functions such as addition, subtraction, multiplication and division. Programmable pocket calculators enable the user to add new functions by storing sequences of their built-in operations. A calculator is distinguished from a hand-held computer by having a numeric rather than an alphabetic keyboard and display, though the most advanced programmable calculators blur this distinction.

pocket computer A category of computer even smaller than a hand-held computer, and which can be carried about the person, in a shirt or jacket pocket. To qualify as a pocket computer, such a machine must be able to load and run new software, unlike a fixed-function POCKET CALCULATOR. Examples include the PALM range, various models based on Microsoft's POCKET PC specification, and several models from PSION and Casio.

Pocket PC A hardware and system software specification for POCKET COMPUTERS, based around Microsoft's WINDOWS CE operating system, and optimized for the very small screens and PEN INPUT used in pocket machines. Pocket PC contains trimmed-down versions of Microsoft's Office programs Word and Excel, along with communications software such as a web browser and email reader. Computers built to the Pocket PC specification included Hewlett Packard's Jornada models and the Compaq iPaq.

point 1 In geometry, a location in space that can be defined by a unique set of numeric COORDINATES. See also CARTESIAN COORDINATES, POLAR COORDINATES.
2 A printer's measurement unit equal to 1/72 of an inch or 0.35mm, used to specify the size of characters and the spaces between them when typesetting documents. See also TYPESETTER, FONT, FONT SIZE.

point-and-click A style of software interface that invites the user to choose, say, a menu option or a file-name from the screen by positioning a MOUSE POINTER over it and clicking a mouse button, rather than by typing it at the keyboard. Point-and-click is therefore the key principle behind most GRAPHICAL USER INTERFACES.

pointer 1 A visual device used as an indicator on a computer display screen – for example, a MOUSE POINTER.
2 In programming, the address of some object in memory, used by a program to locate the object. The act of following a pointer back to the object it refers to is called DEREFERENCING the pointer. When manipulating a large data structure it is more efficient to pass pointers than to pass the object itself (just as it is easier to give a friend the address of your house than the house itself).

System programming languages such as C, designed for writing device drivers and operating systems, make extensive use of pointers, and provide pointer arithmetic operations that enable the programmer to rapidly traverse large data structures by incrementing a pointer to their starting address.

Pointers are also a rich source of program BUGS, because like jump instructions they may transfer control to a remote part of the program, and if the destination is wrong for whatever reason (see NULL POINTER, DANGLING POINTER) then the program is likely to crash. Languages such as PASCAL, VISUAL BASIC and OBJECT-ORIENTED languages discourage the explicit manipulation of pointers by the programmer.

pointing device Any device that enables a computer user to point to the image of objects on a visual display. By far the most common such device is the MOUSE, followed by the TOUCHPAD, TRACKBALL and TRACKPOINT devices fitted to portable computers. Professional graphics systems typically employ pen-based TABLETS for pointing as well as data input, while street kiosks and public information systems employ TOUCH SCREENS. Advanced pointing devices include the DATA GLOVES used in VIRTUAL REALITY systems, and military head-up displays that can determine what the user is looking at.

point of presence (PoP) A site containing a number of MODEMS connected to LEASED LINES and ROUTERS, maintained by an Internet Service Provider (ISP) as an access point to the Internet. For DIAL-UP Internet users, a PoP manifests itself simply as a public telephone number, and a large ISP will have many PoPs spread around its market area so that users can connect using a local phone call.

point-of-sale terminal (POS terminal) A type of combined cash register and network workstation that is used in shops and other retail premises to perform cash transactions. A POS terminal is typically connected to a server that logs all the transactions for accounting purposes, permits prices to be looked up in a database, and in the more sophisticated systems may also be integrated with the stock control and re-ordering systems.

point size The average height of the characters in a particular FONT, measured in printer's POINTS (1/72 of an inch) from the top of the highest ASCENDER in the alphabet (typically the h) to the bottom of the lowest DESCENDER (typically the p). 10 or 12 point is a typical size for books and newspapers. In pre-electronic days, the point size referred to the size of the body, i.e. the rectangular metal slug on which each letter was cast. See also X-HEIGHT, EM, EN.

point-to-point Any communication that takes place between a single sender and a single receiver, as for example a telephone call. See also BROADCAST, MULTICAST.

Point-to-Point Protocol See PPP.

Point-to-Point Tunnelling Protocol See PPTP.

Poisson distribution A statistical distribution that describes the behaviour of events that occur randomly and independently of one another, such as bolts of lightning or radioactive decays. See also GAUSSIAN DISTRIBUTION.

poke 1 A command in the BASIC programming language that writes a value to a given absolute memory ADDRESS and can therefore be used to modify programs in memory. See also PEEK.
2 Hence to cheat at a computer game by discovering the storage locations of key game statistics and poking new values into them. The locations themselves are sometimes called pokes.

Pokémon A children's game invented in Japan which involves collecting a large number of monsters and staging fights between them on linked GAME BOY consoles.

polar coordinates A COORDINATE system that locates each point in the plane by stating the radius r of a circle about the origin that passes through the point, and the angle θ that this radius makes with a single fixed AXIS. Some mathematical expressions are more naturally and simply expressed in polar coordinates than in the two-axis CARTESIAN COORDINATE system. For example the equation of a circle about the origin becomes simply $r=k$ (a constant) instead of $x^2+y^2=k^2$. See also COMPLEX NUMBER.

polling The process of periodically inspecting a DATA SOURCE, such as an I/O port or a network adapter, to see whether any new data is available. Polling suffers the disadvantage that it consumes processor time even when no data is present, unlike the alternative strategy of using an INTERRUPT to signal whenever new data arrives. See also BUSY WAIT, INTERRUPT-DRIVEN.

polygon In mathematics, a closed-plane geometrical figure with three or more sides. In computer GRAPHICS, a polygon (typically with three or four sides) is the primitive unit from which more complex images are constructed, so that the number of polygons that can be RENDERED (i.e. coloured) per second becomes an important measure of a graphics system's performance.

polygon-fill A function provided in many programming languages and graphics systems that, given the coordinates of its corners as parameters, draws a filled POLYGON.

polygon mesh Also called a WIRE-FRAME representation. A grid of lines that dissects a three-dimensional surface into small polygonal cells, allowing the surface to be described by a list of numbers (the coordinates of the corners of each POLYGON). Such a mesh is the principal means of representing objects in computer 3D GRAPHICS systems.

polygons per second The preferred measure of RENDERING performance for 3D GRAPHICS systems. For the latest graphics cards, this is now into the tens or hundreds of millions. See also POLYGON, 3D GRAPHICS, SHADE.

polymorphic Capable of working on more than one type of object, applied to program components such as PROCEDURES, FUNCTIONS or OPERATORS. For example, in many programming languages the + operator can be used to add several different data types, including integers, real numbers and strings. In OBJECT-ORIENTED PROGRAMMING the term describes variables that can hold objects of different CLASSES, or methods that can take objects of different classes as parameters. In FUNCTIONAL PROGRAMMING LANGUAGES, the term describes functions or type constructors that can work on values of any type (for example to count the items in a 'list of anything'). See also POLYMORPHISM.

polymorphism One of the three key concepts of OBJECT-ORIENTED PROGRAMMING (the others being ENCAPSULATION and INHERITANCE). The ability for the same variable to hold objects of different types that are not known until RUN TIME. Polymorphism permits programmers to write generic code that may be inherited by future classes, without needing to know in advance every type of object they will operate on (an approach that conventional TYPE CHECKING systems render almost impossible).

polynomial A mathematical expression consisting of the sum of terms each formed by multiplying a constant (called a coefficient) by one or more variables raised to a positive or zero integral power: an example is x^3+2xy^2+5y.

When used in connection with the COMPLEXITY of computer algorithms, the signifi-cance of a polynomial expression is that it involves only powers that are constant (however large) and not variable, and therefore grows in less explosive fashion than an EXPONENTIAL expression. See POLYNOMIAL-TIME ALGORITHM.

polynomial-time algorithm Any ALGORITHM whose time of execution increases as a constant power of the size of the problem – for example the polynomial time might be proportional to N^2 (a polynomial function) where N is the number of items to be processed. Such algorithms are eagerly sought by computer scientists because they require only reasonable amounts of processing time. See also ALGORITHMIC COMPLEXITY.

polysilicon Already short for 'polycrystalline silicon', but shortened further to 'poly' by semiconductor engineers. A form of SILICON that can be deposited as a thin layer during the fabrication of INTEGRATED CIRCUITS (typically by thermal decomposition of a volatile silicon compound). This differs from the chip itself, which is a slice from a single crystal of bulk silicon. Poly conducts electricity well enough to be used to form the gates of the TRANSISTORS. Wherever a poly track crosses a DOPED diffusion track, a transistor is formed.

Pong The first electronic ARCADE GAME, published by ATARI, which consisted of a simulated table tennis game for two players.

pool A collection of resources from which items may be removed for use and returned later, such as a pool of memory, or modems, or window HANDLES. See also FREE LIST, DYNAMIC ALLOCATION, ALLOCATION.

POP Abbreviation of POST OFFICE PROTOCOL.

PoP Abbreviation of POINT OF PRESENCE.

pop The action of removing a data object from a STACK, its opposite being to PUSH an object onto the stack.

POP3 (Post Office Protocol 3) The most widely used version of the POST OFFICE PROTOCOL which enables mobile and home computer users to dial in to a remote MAIL SERVER and read their mail. POP3 downloads mail to the local machine and optionally removes it from the server, so that it cannot be read from elsewhere, unlike IMAP which reads mail in place on the server. POP3 is defined in RFC 1081.

POP-11 A programming language designed in 1975 by Robin Popplestone for ARTIFICIAL INTELLIGENCE and teaching applications. POP-11 combined a PASCAL-like syntax with interactive, dynamically-typed list-processing features like those of LISP.

pop-up menu A style of MENU that appears at the particular place on the display screen where the MOUSE POINTER is currently located, triggered for example by pressing the right mouse button. See also PULL-DOWN MENU.

port **1** One of several types of CONNECTOR provided on the outer casing of a personal computer for the attachment of PERIPHERAL devices. More formally called I/O ports (because they support input and output of data from the computer), the most widely encountered types are the KEYBOARD and MOUSE port, SERIAL PORT, PARALLEL PORT, USB and SCSI ports.
2 A dedicated REGISTER or memory address forming part of a channel used to read and write data words to and from an INTEGRATED CIRCUIT of some kind (for example a timer chip or a disk controller). Such a channel might typically contain three ports, for reading and writing data, status and control words.
3 In networking, a LOGICAL communication channel whose traffic is MULTIPLEXED with others over a single network interface. The TCP/IP protocol, for example, assigns fixed, unique port numbers to many well-known APPLICATION LAYER services such as TELNET (port 23) and FTP (port 21), which may be used to distinguish their traffic from others. A new TCP application must specify what port number it wishes to work on, chosen from outside the range 0 to 255 allocated to these well-known applications. Port numbers may optionally be quoted following a colon in a URL thus:

```
http://www.penguin.com:8080/
images/map.gif
```

4 To convert a piece of software to run on a different processor and/or operating system. Coined by computer programmers to provide a verbal form of PORTABLE, it is often also used as a noun, as in 'I'm waiting for the new port of Linux', meaning a particular instance of such conversion.

portable **1** In the physical sense, capable of being carried from one place to another.
2 When said of software, capable of being easily translated from one PLATFORM to another. See also CROSS-PLATFORM.

Portable Document Format See PDF.

Portable Network Graphics See PNG.

Portable Operating System Interface See POSIX.

portal A WEB SITE that offers free entry to a multitude of other sites by presenting screens full of LINKS to them. Popular examples include YAHOO!, LYCOS and MSN. Many web users make such a portal the default HOME PAGE in their browser for convenience, and so access all other sites via its links, which enables the portal's owner to garner substantial revenues by displaying BANNER ADVERTS to them on the way, paid for by other site owners. See also SEARCH ENGINE.

PoS Abbreviation of POINT-OF-SALE TERMINAL.

positional notation Any system of representation in which the value of each symbol within a message is altered according to its place in the message. For example, the DECIMAL NOTATION for numbers we use in everyday life is a positional notation. It employs only ten distinct digits, and multiplies each digit in a number such as 839 by a power of ten proportional to its place in the number ($8\times10^2 + 3\times10^1 + 9\times10^0$). The Roman numeral system, on the other hand, is not a positional notation, since V always represents 5 and I represents 1 wherever they occur in a number, such as VII or IV.

position sensing Locating the position of an object in space and turning this information into an electrical signal. For example, the head-mounted devices in VIRTUAL REALITY systems that determine the direction of the user's gaze are performing position sensing, as are tape or disk drives that can determine the current position of the recording medium using some form of index mark.

POSIX (Portable Operating System Interface) A set of standards devised by the IEEE to provide application portability between different variants of the UNIX operating system: any POSIX-COMPLIANT program should run on any POSIX-compliant Unix system. In practice POSIX provides such compatibility only for non-graphical applications with character-based interfaces. The latest version is POSIX.2, whose three main components are the Unix-compatible operating system interface defined in IEEE 1003.1, command SHELLS and utilities such as AWK, GREP and LEX defined in IEEE 1003.2, and REAL TIME extensions defined in IEEE 1003.4.

POST Abbreviation of POWER-ON SELF TEST.

postcondition An ASSERTION about the values of a program's variables placed at the exit from a block of program statements: if this assertion is not true at runtime then an error condition is raised. An example might be that $x < 1000$ on leaving a certain routine. Postconditions, and the related PRECONDITIONS; thus enable a limited amount of checking of a program's SEMANTICS, and they are a built-in feature of certain safety-conscious programming languages including EIFFEL and OBERON. See also AXIOMATIC SEMANTICS, SYNTAX, SYNTAX CHECKING, TYPE CHECKING.

Postel, John (1943–98) One of the inventors of ARPANET, pioneer of the Internet and founder of IANA, the body originally responsible for administering the Internet and allocating ADDRESSES.

posterize To reduce the tonal range of a digital image such as a photograph so far that previously smoothly-shaded areas are transformed into a few broad bands of solid colour, and so resemble a silk-screen printed poster. This effect, which is provided in most BITMAP EDITING programs such as Photoshop, can usually be varied by the user and becomes most striking when the tones are reduced to just three or four. See also SOLARIZE, MACH BANDS, IMAGE PROCESSING.

postfix notation Also called *reverse polish notation*, an arithmetic notation in which an OPERATOR follows its OPERANDS, as in 2 3 +. It is mostly encountered in systems that pass operands via an open STACK, such as the programming languages FORTH and POP-11, and certain models of Hewlett-Packard scientific CALCULATOR. Numbers are entered, and then an operation is issued that implicitly works on whatever numbers it finds on the stack.

post-increment A class of processor instruction that performs an operation and then INCREMENTS an address pointer, in contrast to a PRE-INCREMENT instruction, which increments the address and then performs the operation.

postmaster The person responsible for running an EMAIL system at a site connected to the Internet: any queries about the mail service must be addressed to the postmaster, for example, postmaster@widget.net. Any email that fails to be delivered to its addressee for whatever reason is BOUNCED back to its sender with an explanatory message from the postmaster, though this function is typically automated by scripts rather than handled personally. See also WEBMASTER, SYSTEM OPERATOR, SYSTEM ADMINISTRATOR.

postmortem debugger A programmer's utility that helps to discover the cause of a program's failure only after it has terminated in an error. A postmortem debugging system causes the contents of memory and processor registers to be dumped into a disk file that the debugger can examine to locate the cause. It may also preserve the screen contents that were displayed at the time of the crash, which may otherwise be difficult to catch. Postmortem debuggers are often used in conjunction with a programming language that supports the use of ASSERTIONS, so that a controlled termination can be triggered whenever a certain wrong condition occurs and the postmortem debugger applied to the results. Another kind of postmortem utility is Microsoft's DR

WATSON, as supplied with Windows, which creates an error LOG that can be returned to the software's developer. See also ERROR TRAPPING, ERROR CONDITION.

Post Office Protocol (POP) The most widely used EMAIL protocol, which enables a computer user to connect temporarily to a remote MAIL SERVER and download mail from a MAILBOX for reading on a local machine. There have been three (not entirely compatible) versions of the protocol, of which the latest POP3 is by far the most used. POP does not provide any means to send mail or to reply to mail, which must be done using a different protocol, normally SMTP.

A POP server typically has a permanent connection to the Internet, and the client computer periodically connects to collect the mail that has accumulated, often via a modem and dial-up telephone link. POP generally deletes mail from the remote server once it has been downloaded, which is inconvenient for travelling users who may log on from different sites and as a result find their mail spread over several computers. The alternative IMAP protocol allows mail to be read, managed and stored on the remote server, which is more convenient (assuming sufficient connection BANDWIDTH is available).

Post Office Protocol 3 See POP3.

postprocess To use a separate software tool to modify data that has been output from another program, most often a COMPILER or a TEXT EDITOR. For example the rendering of a POSTSCRIPT file output by a DESKTOP PUBLISHING program is one kind of postprocessing.

PostScript A widely used PAGE DESCRIPTION LANGUAGE developed by ADOBE in the early 1980s to drive the new generation of LASER PRINTERS. PostScript allows pages of highly formatted text and graphics to be described in a device independent fashion so that the hard copy produced will appear more or less the same when printed on any compatible printer. Professional publishing jobs, including books, magazines and academic papers, are commonly created as PostScript files output from DESKTOP PUBLISHING software, and fed to a high-quality printer or printed out by a TYPESETTER onto film for making litho plates.

The PostScript description of a page consists of a sequence of textual drawing commands, which a PostScript printer interprets to recreate the appearance of the page. To speed up this operation such printers usually contain their own dedicated processor and many megabytes of working memory. PostScript supports its own system of scalable OUTLINE FONTS which are downloaded into the printer along with the page description (see more under ADOBE TYPE 1 FONT and ADOBE TYPE 3 FONT). BITMAPPED images such as magazine photographs are embedded in the textual PostScript code as tables of BINARY data. See also PDF, DISPLAY POSTSCRIPT, ENCAPSULATED POSTSCRIPT.

Post, Telephone and Telegraph administration See PTT.

potential difference The difference in electric potential between two points, measured by the work that must be done to move a unit electric charge from one to the other. It is measured in VOLTS.

POTS (Plain Old Telephone System) An acronym coined to concisely distinguish the traditional analogue telephone system from newer digital systems such as ISDN.

PowerBuilder A VISUAL PROGRAMMING environment published by Powersoft for MS-DOS, Microsoft Windows, Apple MacOS and Unix systems. Powerbuilder is designed for building the user interfaces of CLIENT/SERVER applications that employ ORACLE, SYBASE or a variety of other RELATIONAL DATABASES as their BACK-END.

power-on self test (POST) An automatic test of the memory chips and certain key system functions that is performed whenever an IBM-COMPATIBLE PC is started up. The code to perform these tests is stored in ROM along with the computer's BIOS code. If the POST detects a fault serious enough to prevent the computer completing its BOOT-UP, it signals this to the user either via a coded sequences of BEEPS from the PC's sound generator or by lighting up a coded sequence of LEDs on the motherboard, since no screen display may be available. If desired, the POST can be cut short by pressing the ESCAPE KEY during the boot sequence. See also BLUE SCREEN OF DEATH, PARITY ERROR.

PowerPC A family of microprocessors jointly launched by IBM, APPLE and MOTOROLA in 1994 in an attempt to counter INTEL's dominance of the industry, and to serve as a replacement for the near-obsolete MOTOROLA 68000 family in the MACINTOSH line.

PowerPC employs a RISC architecture with 32 INTEGER and 32 FLOATING-POINT registers, on-chip CACHE and deep execution PIPELINE. PowerPC failed to break Intel's hold on the industry but is still used by Apple, the latest version being the 64-bit, 500 MHz PowerPC 7400 used in the Macintosh G4 models.

PowerPC Reference Platform (PPCP or PReP, formerly CHRP) An OPEN SYSTEMS standard devised by IBM in 1995 to promote compatibility between POWERPC-based computers built by different companies. However Apple's IMAC range failed to support PPCP and it has faded from sight, with little enthusiasm even within IBM.

PowerPoint The PRESENTATION GRAPHICS component of the MICROSOFT OFFICE suite. PowerPoint enables presentations to be created simply by dragging and dropping text and images created in other applications (such as Word and Photoshop) onto a sequence of blank pages. PowerPoint provides an extensive library of prefabricated background patterns, FONT styles and TRANSITION effects such as fades and dissolves that can be introduced between pages. The finished presentation can be viewed as a SLIDE-SHOW which changes to the next page whenever the space bar or mouse button are pressed, and is typically deployed on a laptop computer connected to a projector.

power saving Various measures taken to reduce the electrical power consumed by a computer and its peripherals, such as automatic entry into a STANDBY MODE and the selective 'spinning down' of hard disk drives if no activity is detected for some predefined interval. The latter case requires power saving support to be incorporated into the operating system itself. Power saving at processor and disk level is most often used in portable computers, to extend the useable period before the batteries need recharging, but power saving MONITORS are now the rule even for desktop systems (see DPMS, ACPI).

powerset The SET of all possible subsets of a given set.

power-up The moment of turning on a computer's power supply, which, if it is working correctly, will be immediately followed by the BOOTSTRAP sequence. See also POWER-ON SELF TEST.

power user One who exploits the full capabilities of a personal computer to perform exacting tasks.

PPCP, PReP Abbreviation of POWERPC REFERENCE PLATFORM.

PPP (Point-to-Point Protocol) The standard Internet protocol for transmitting TCP/IP packets or datagrams over a SERIAL link, such as a modem link. PPP has some advantages over the alternative SLIP, in that it can dynamically configure its IP ADDRESS once connection is made, and it can work over both ASYNCHRONOUS links, such as a dial-up telephone link, and SYNCHRONOUS serial lines. See also WINSOCK.

PPTP (Point-to-Point Tunnelling Protocol) A TUNNELLING PROTOCOL used to connect clients and servers running Microsoft's Windows operating systems to form a VIRTUAL PRIVATE NETWORK. PPTP was developed by Microsoft and 3Com, and works by embedding its data (which may be encrypted using a separate service) within standard TCP/IP packets. A PPTP transmission may be client-initiated and requires no special support from the ISP or from the intervening ROUTERS, unlike its rival L2F. However, it does require Windows to be running at both client and server ends of the connection.

PQFP (Plastic Quad Flat Pack) See under QUAD FLAT PACK.

pragma A special type of COMPILER DIRECTIVE that supplies optimization hints to the compiler, in languages including C and ADA.

precharge A period in the operation cycle of a DYNAMIC RANDOM ACCESS MEMORY chip during which the contents are not accessible because the ROW and/or COLUMN select circuits are being reset.

precision In mathematics, the number of decimal places to which a REAL NUMBER is specified. In programming, the term is used with a related meaning to describe the storage size of FLOATING-POINT numbers (as in SINGLE PRECISION, DOUBLE PRECISION and EXTENDED PRECISION) and informally to mean the RANGE of an integer data type. Precision should be distinguished from ACCURACY, which means the degree to which a measurement approximates the object measured.

precompiler A program that processes a source file and outputs SOURCE CODE in some other programming language, which must then be further COMPILED into an executable file. Common examples would be the precompilation of an SQL database query, or a COM IDL specification, into C++ source code which is then compiled with a regular C++ compiler.

precondition An ASSERTION about the values of a program's variables placed at the entry to a block of program statements: if this assertion is not true at runtime then an error condition is raised. An example might be that $x > 0$ on entry to a certain routine. Preconditions, and the related POSTCONDITIONS, thus enable a limited amount of checking of a program's SEMANTICS, and they are are a built-in feature of certain safety-conscious programming languages including EIFFEL and OBERON. See also AXIOMATIC SEMANTICS, SYNTAX, SYNTAX CHECKING, TYPE CHECKING.

predicate **1** In logic, a property that some entity can be definitely either affirmed or denied to possess. For example, the sentence 'all dogs are brown' attempts to connect the predicate *is a dog* with the predicate *is brown*. See also PREDICATE CALCULUS.
2 In logic programming languages such as PROLOG, the name given to a relationship between objects. For example in the clause `likes(John, haggis);` the predicate, which takes two arguments, is `likes`.

predicate calculus A system of SYMBOLIC LOGIC that looks beyond the truth or falsehood of whole propositions (as in the PROPOSITIONAL CALCULUS) to the relationships and properties of individual names within a proposition.

pre-emptive multitasking A technique for MULTITASKING on a single processor, which permits the operating system to interrupt the currently running task at any time to let another task run. This is in contrast to a COOPERATIVE MULTITASKING system where each task must explicitly relinquish the CPU to give the next task a turn. Pre-emptive multitasking greatly simplifies programming, as each task may be written as if it had the CPU to itself. Each task in a pre-emptive system is assigned a PRIORITY level, which the operating system's SCHEDULER considers when deciding when to interrupt it. To adjust the amount of CPU time the task gets this priority may be altered – manually by the computer's user and/or dynamically by the operating system. Most modern operating systems such as UNIX, WINDOWS NT and OS/2 support pre-emptive multitasking.

Preferences A MENU topic found in many software applications that offers access to a collection of program parameters that can be altered by the user. See also CONFIGURE.

prefetch Also called *fetch-ahead*. The fetching by a computer's PROCESSOR of one or more INSTRUCTIONS that follow the next one to be executed, with the aim of saving memory access time if these are also to be executed. However, if the next instruction is a BRANCH which is taken, these prefetched instructions will not be required, and must be discarded. See also SPECULATIVE EXECUTION, BRANCH PREDICTION, PIPELINE, PIPELINE BREAK.

prefix notation An arithmetic notation in which the OPERATORS precede their OPERANDS, as in + 2 3. See also PREFIX SYNTAX.

prefix syntax The syntactic style used by most programming languages, which requires OPERATORS to be written before their ARGUMENTS (which are often enclosed in parentheses). The FUNCTION and PROCEDURE CALL syntax used in most languages is prefix, as in `DrawLine(10,10,20,20)`. A few languages even employ prefix syntax for their arithmetic operators, for example +(2,3) but most support the use of the more familiar INFIX NOTATION (that is, 2+3) in expressions. See also POSTFIX NOTATION, OPERATOR OVERLOADING.

pre-increment A class of processor instruction which first INCREMENTS an address pointer before performing an operation, in contrast to a POST-INCREMENT instruction which performs the operation and then increments the address.

preload 1 To load a program or data into computer memory before it is actually required, in order to save time later. This technique is often applied in multimedia software; images or sound clips are preloaded while the user is otherwise engaged, thus avoiding a distracting pause when they are eventually required. See also CACHE.
2 To install an OPERATING SYSTEM and/or APPLICATION SOFTWARE onto a computer prior to its sale to a customer.

prepend To insert a new data item at the beginning of an existing DATA STRUCTURE, rather than APPENDING it at the end.

prepress Shorthand for all those processes required to prepare a document or publication for printing by a commercial printer. Prepress activities include making film from the CAMERA-READY artwork, COLOUR RETOUCHING and separating photographs and transparencies, performing knock-outs and undercolour removal for graphics and spot colours, assembling film into pages, page imposition and plate making.

preprocessor A software tool that is run before a COMPILER to modify the SOURCE CODE that is to be compiled. A typical reason for running a preprocessor is to expand MACROS in the source code, as is done by the C language's cpp program. Other reasons for preprocessing are to check for correct SYNTAX, as with Unix's LINT utility, or to translate one programming language into another, for example FORTRAN 90 into FORTRAN 77.

presentation graphics A category of application software used to create slide shows to illustrate lectures, seminars and business presentations. Presentation graphics packages such as Microsoft's POWERPOINT enable images and text produced in other programs to be assembled into sequences of slides, then displayed using a laptop computer connected to a projector – clicking the mouse button to step from one slide to the next.

presentation layer Layer six of the OSI REFERENCE MODEL of network PROTOCOLS, which deals with conversion between different data formats.

Pretty Good Privacy (PGP) A widely used FREEWARE encryption program created in defiance of the US government's attempts to restrict civilian access to high-security encoding algorithms such as RSA ENCRYPTION.

pretty print To output data, especially program SOURCE CODE, in a human-readable form whose structure is revealed by appropriate addition of carriage returns, tabs, spaces and upper and lower case lettering. Pretty printers are often available as POSTPROCESSING utilities for a particular programming language.

price/performance ratio A simple measure of the value-for-money offered by a piece of equipment. Somewhat counter-intuitively, smaller values indicate a better deal. As a comparative index it is only as good as the measure of performance employed. See under BENCHMARK.

primary cache In a processor that employs two or more levels of CACHE, the cache that is closest to the PROCESSOR CORE and from which data and instructions are passed directly into the processor's REGISTERS. This is most often an ON-CHIP cache, fabricated on the same silicon DIE as the rest of the processor core.

primary domain controller (PDC) In a network running the WINDOWS NT operating system, a single server that is designated as containing the master copy of all the user account information and passwords. Other servers within the same DOMAIN may be designated as BACKUP DOMAIN CONTROLLERS, and the PDC will then periodically replicate its account information onto them, which enables the burden of validating user LOG ONS to be spread more evenly across the network.

primary key The KEY on which selection and sorting of a DATABASE will be performed first. For example a data set might be sorted on a primary key of Age and a secondary key of

Name, to give a list of age groups, alphabetical by name within each group.

Primary Rate Interface (PRI) A grade of ISDN line supplied to larger businesses that can support up to 23 separate connections (23 B channels and one D channel).

Prime Computer A US manufacturer of MINI-COMPUTERS.

prime number A number that is exactly divisible only by itself and 1. The first ten primes are 1, 2, 3, 5, 7, 11, 13, 17, 19 and 23. Primes are of great intrinsic interest to pure mathematicians, but their study has recently gained commercial importance because of the role they now play in PUBLIC-KEY ENCRYPTION. To discover whether a number is prime, attempt to divide it in turn by all the primes smaller than its own square root (so to test whether 83 is prime, divide by 2, 3, 5 and 7). The largest known primes are now so huge that SUPER-COMPUTERS are required to find them and prove their primality. See also FERMAT PRIME, MERSENNE PRIME, SIEVE OF ERATOSTHENES.

primitive One of the built-in statements of a programming language, rather than a user-defined procedure.

printed circuit board (PCB) A flat insulating board on which a complete electronic device may be assembled from INTEGRATED CIRCUIT packages connected by a pattern of thin copper conductors. The PCB was one of the key enabling technologies for the revolution in miniature electronics. A photo-etching process is used to transfer circuit designs onto copper-covered, resin-impregnated boards, after which automated machinery drills arrays of holes, inserts the chips and solders them in place.

printer In the computing world, a PERIPHERAL device for transferring computer representations of text and images onto paper. Most current printing technologies build an image on the paper from many tiny dots of pigment, analogous to the PIXELS used to depict BIT-MAPPED images on a display screen. They differ only in the way these dots are made, for example by depositing drops of liquid ink (see INKJET PRINTER), with toner powder (see LASER PRINTER), by pressing metal pins onto an inked ribbon (see DOT-MATRIX PRINTER), or by evaporating a solid dye (see DYE-SUBLIMATION PRINTER). The exceptions are the GRAPH PLOTTER, which draws lines rather than dots, and the now obsolete DAISY-WHEEL PRINTER, which printed whole characters at a time using typewriter-like metal type blocks.

Printers are typically connected to a computer via either a SERIAL PORT or a PARALLEL PORT. Most computer operating systems recognize a generic printer device to which simple text may be sent without inquiring what type of printer is present. However, to print graphics, use printer FONTS, or for colour printing, then special printer driver software must be installed to inform the operating system about these capabilities. Many printers understand some special control language (see PRINTER CONTROL LANGUAGE, POSTSCRIPT) or ESCAPE SEQUENCES that may be sent by an application program to turn on such features.

Printer Control Language (PCL) A page description language used by HEWLETT-PACKARD Laserjet printers which is a superset of HPGL.

printer driver A DEVICE DRIVER that enables a computer system to print on a particular make of printer.

printer-plotter A now rarely-used device that combines the functions of PRINTER and GRAPH PLOTTER.

printer port An output PORT through which a computer may be connected to a printer. In the personal computer field the term most often refers to a parallel port.

printf The formatted output function supplied in the C programming language's standard library. The SYNTAX of printf is so familiar to so many programmers that it has been widely emulated by other languages and applications. In a call such as printf('%4d', mysalary) the first argument is a FORMAT STRING, which in this example specifies that mysalary is to be printed as a 4-digit decimal number.

print preview A facility offered by most modern application programs that enables the user to see on screen what a printed document will look like before actually committing it to paper. Many print preview facilities, such as that in MICROSOFT WORD, also allow certain formatting changes such as margin adjustments to be made interactively on the preview, rather than re-editing the document.

print queue A list of files waiting to be printed which is maintained by an OPERATING SYSTEM or PRINT SERVER, enabling users to add new files to the queue and proceed with other tasks rather than waiting for the printer to become free.

Print Screen key (PrtSc) A special key on the keyboard of IBM PC-compatible computers that once caused the current contents of the screen to be sent to the printer. Under Windows, pressing <PrtSc> alone copies the whole screen to the CLIPBOARD, while <ALT+PrtSc> captures just the contents of the top screen window, providing a convenient way to capture screen displays into a drawing or PAINTING PROGRAM.

print server A computer that connects one or more printers to a network and therefore enables all the network's users to share access to the printers. A print server may be a fully specified PC with its own hard disks, used to store spool files (see under PRINT SPOOLING), it may simply be an EXPANSION CARD or modem-sized external box with printer and network sockets but no screen or keyboard, or even just a piece of software, in which case printer output files are built and stored on the remote workstation before sending to the server. Increasingly, print servers are being built into the printer itself. See also PRINT QUEUE, PRINT SHARING, INTERNET PRINTING PROTOCOL, POSTSCRIPT, WINDOWS PRINTING SYSTEM.

print sharing A network service that allows many users to send their documents to the same central printer for printing. Documents are automatically placed into a PRINT QUEUE to await their turn to be printed. Apart from FILE SHARING, print sharing is the most frequent use for a LAN. The printer to be shared may be connected to a computer that acts as the PRINT SERVER, but there is an increasing trend toward each printer having its own NETWORK INTERFACE CARD and ADDRESS, and becoming a stand-alone NODE on the network.

print spooling The writing of data that is to be printed into a temporary disk file, which is then added to a PRINT QUEUE for later printing. The advantage of print spooling is that it immediately frees up the application program (such as a word processor) that requested the printing, so it is ready for other tasks. See also SPOOL, SPOOLER, SPOOL FILE.

priority A measure of importance, attached to a procedure or data item such as a network PACKET or a processor TASK, that determines how soon it will be served in any competition for access to a shared resource such as a PROCESSOR or a ROUTER. In the simpler priority schemes, all priorities are fixed in advance. More sophisticated schemes may alter the priorities of different items dynamically to ensure fair treatment. See more under PRIORITY SCHEDULING, PRE-EMPTIVE MULTITASKING, REAL TIME EXECUTIVE.

priority scheduling A scheduling algorithm employed by many MULTITASKING operating systems in which tasks are assigned PRIORITY levels and run in order of priority, so that the most important tasks get the most processor time. A SCHEDULER may assign priorities statically when each task is created, but many schedulers dynamically modify a task's priority while it is running. Often a task's priority is progressively reduced the longer it runs (called 'task aging') to ensure that even the least important tasks get some CPU time eventually.

private A KEYWORD used in many programming languages to denote that some entity should be visible only within the MODULE or CLASS in which it is declared. For example C++ permits both data members and member functions to be declared private to a class; VISUAL BASIC allows functions and procedures to be private to a module; in Java classes, methods and instance variables may be private. See also PUBLIC, PROTECTED.

Private Automatic Branch Exchange See PABX.

Private Branch Exchange See PBX.

private-key encryption Any ENCRYPTION scheme that depends on both parties to the communication possessing the same secret key, as compared to PUBLIC-KEY ENCRYPTION methods.

privileges An alternative name for ACCESS PERMISSIONS.

PRML Abbreviation of PARTIAL RESPONSE MAXIMUM LIKELIHOOD.

probabilistic Any system, process or algorithm whose behaviour cannot be predicted with absolute certainty, but only with some degree of probability. PSEUDO-RANDOM NUMBERS are often employed in programs to simulate such probabilistic behaviour. See also STOCHASTIC, NONDETERMINISTIC, HEURISTIC.

probability An estimate of the degree of confidence one may place upon the occurrence or not of some event, measured on a scale that runs from zero (impossible) to one (certain). Probability may be estimated theoretically as the ratio of the favourable outcomes to the total number of equally likely possibilities, or observed empirically as the ratio of favourable outcomes to total events in a sample.

probability theory The branch of mathematics that deals with the calculation and manipulation of PROBABILITIES.

proc Short for PROCEDURE.

procedural language Any computer programming language that sets out a precise sequence of computational steps needed to manipulate each data item; sometimes called an *imperative language* because programs consist essentially of a list of orders to be obeyed. This is in contrast to DECLARATIVE LANGUAGES, in which programs consist of lists of descriptions of the relationships between data items. All the most commonly used languages such as C, C++, VISUAL BASIC and FORTRAN are procedural. See also ASSIGNMENT, PROCEDURE, ALGORITHM.

procedural texture In computer 3D GRAPHICS, a texture created on a surface by executing a mathematical algorithm rather than by supplying a 2D picture of the desired effect. FRACTAL algorithms are frequently employed for this purpose to generate realistic rock, snow or water effects. Procedural textures are a feature of RENDERMAN and other such rendering systems. See also TEXTURE MAPPING, PARTICLE SYSTEM, BITMAP TEXTURE.

procedure The name used to describe a SUBPROGRAM in many programming languages, for example PASCAL and its descendants, and VISUAL BASIC. Pascal and Visual Basic both distinguish between FUNCTIONS, which return a result, and procedures, which do not, and employ a different RESERVED WORD to define each.

procedure call The invocation of a named, parameterized SUBPROGRAM by stating its name with actual values supplied in place of any FORMAL PARAMETERS. For example given that a procedure called DrawPixel(x, y: Integer) has been defined, then a call to the procedure could look like:

```
DrawPixel(100, 200);
Halt;
```

Following a procedure call, execution always returns to the routine from which the call was made, at the following statement (Halt in the above example).

procedure declaration In compiled programming languages such as C, PASCAL and BASIC, a statement that tells the COMPILER that a new PROCEDURE of a particular name is to be defined, the names and types of its PARAMETERS, and the actions it will perform. See also PROCEDURE HEADING, FUNCTION DECLARATION, FORWARD DECLARATION.

procedure heading In most compiled programming languages, the first line of the declaration of a new PROCEDURE, which states the name of the procedure and the names and types of its PARAMETERS. In some languages, the heading alone may be placed at the beginning of a program to permit calls to the procedure to be compiled before the full declaration of its actions is encountered further down the program (see FORWARD DECLARATION). Here is an example of a procedure heading in Pascal:

```
PROCEDURE GetTextCoords(Angle,
Radius: Real; X, Y: Integer);
```

In languages that support the separate compilation of MODULES, the headings of all the procedures defined in a particular module may be collected into a separately-compiled module that is called the INTERFACE to the module. See also PROCEDURE DECLARATION, FUNCTION HEADING, INTERFACE DEFINITION LANGUAGE.

process A computer PROGRAM that is being executed. A process consists of a copy of the program's INSTRUCTION codes stored in memory, together with various other temporarily owned resources, such as a PROCESS IDENTIFIER, some private data space (and possibly some data shared with other processes) and perhaps one or more open disk FILES. Under many OPERATING SYSTEMS, more than one process can execute at the same time (see MULTITASKING), and more than one process may be executing a single copy of the instruction codes at the same time (see RE-ENTRANT).

process control The use of computers to control industrial equipment.

process identifier The unique identifying number allocated by a MULTITASKING operating system to each new process that it starts, by which the process can be distinguished from others for the purpose of placing it in a QUEUE, or terminating it.

processor Shorthand for information processor or data processor. A device that inputs information, performs some transformation on it according to a set of instructions called a PROGRAM, and then outputs the results. A computer is constructed from a processor connected to a memory system for storing information, and devices for the input and output of information (see I/O).

A processor may be general purpose, capable of performing any kind of transformation that can be specified in a program (which must therefore be supplied), or it may be designed to perform only one particular task. An example of the former kind is the MICRO-PROCESSOR used in personal computers, while an example of the latter might be a digital filter chip installed in a CD player to modify its sound characteristics. Between these two extremes lie processors that are programmable but designed to be particularly efficient at certain types of task, an example being a GRAPHICS PROCESSOR. See also CPU, PROCESSOR CORE, PROCESSOR BUS.

processor-bound Any computing task whose maximum speed is limited by the speed of the PROCESSOR available, rather than by the amount of memory space or the speed of DISK STORAGE. Examples of processor-bound tasks include those that require many INTEGER or FLOATING-POINT calculations such as rendering 3D GRAPHICS. The only ways to speed up a processor-bound task are to use a faster processor, a more efficient CACHE, or to find a better ALGORITHM. The opposite of processor-bound is DISK-BOUND.

processor bus The high-speed BUS that connects a computer's CPU to its memory system,

in contrast to a separate I/O bus that connects to the disk drives and to expansion slots. The processor bus is typically the fastest and widest bus in any system, and is connected directly to any LEVEL 2 CACHE memory. See also PCI BUS, AGP, BUS SNOOPING, CACHE.

processor core Those crucial components of a MICROPROCESSOR that actually execute instructions and alter data values, principally the ARITHMETIC AND LOGIC UNIT, the CONTROL UNIT, the REGISTER FILE, the ADDRESS GENERATION circuitry and the BUS interfaces.

It is this core that determines the software compatibility of a processor. Some microprocessor cores are small enough to be combined on the same chip with different special purpose peripheral circuits such as graphics or communications processors, to create a whole family of code-compatible designs. See more under STANDARD CELL, ASIC.

Processor Direct Slot An EXPANSION BUS employed in the Apple MACINTOSH range of computers.

processor farm A collection of computer processors connected together via a network so as to act as a single PARALLEL COMPUTER.

process scheduling A most important function performed by the KERNEL of any MULTITASKING operating system, which consists of deciding which of many competing PROCESSES should be allowed to run at any given time. Processes corresponding to currently running programs are kept in a queue, from which each in turn is allowed to run for a brief period determined by the process SCHEDULER. The scheduler must ensure that all processes get a fair allocation of processor time and that none is prevented from running at all. See also PRIORITY, PRIORITY SCHEDULING.

process technology The blanket name given to the materials, designs, techniques and machines for making a particular family of INTEGRATED CIRCUITS. It encompasses everything from the SEMICONDUCTOR SUBSTRATE employed, the DOPANTS employed to create devices, the layouts of the TRANSISTOR and LOGIC GATE circuits, the FEATURE SIZE and type of LITHOGRAPHY used, and the materials and techniques used to etch and deposit the various circuit layers and interconnects. For examples of different process technologies see CMOS, ECL, BIPOLAR, BICMOS.

Prodigy An early US ONLINE SERVICE and later ISP that began life as a VIDEOTEXT system.

production rule 1 A class of statement used to define the grammar of a language, by specifying the permissible order of constituents and sub-constituents in sentences of that language. The left-hand side of each rule is a SYMBOL that names a particular syntactic object – for example a 'noun-phrase' in a natural language grammar – while its right-hand side is composed from symbols defined elsewhere (for example 'noun' and 'verb') that define the structure of such an object. Production rules form a hierarchy that descends from a single top-level rule defining the structure of a whole sentence, and ends with a collection of TERMINAL SYMBOLS that correspond to single LEXEMES of the language (that is, atomic entities that have no further internal syntactic structure). For a computer language, the terminal symbols are the PRIMITIVE statements and operators of the language like IF, THEN, + and =. Non-terminal symbols are the left-hand sides of intermediate rules. See also BACKUS-NAUR FORM.

2 One of the rules in a RULE-BASED SYSTEM that is executed whenever the condition it contains is fulfilled by the current data.

productivity software A blanket term that covers several different categories of single-user application software (including the WORD PROCESSOR and SPREADSHEET, address book and EMAIL) all of which are intended to improve the productivity of individual users rather than of whole companies. See also OFFICE SUITE, ENTERPRISE.

profiler See EXECUTION PROFILER.

program A list of instructions to be executed by a computer, also referred to as CODE or SOFTWARE. Programs are what make computers useful; a typical computer has no pre-ordained function, but can be made to perform an almost unlimited number of different functions by running different programs.

To computer users the term program normally means a file, supplied on FLOPPY DISK or CD-ROM, that can be executed by issuing an appropriate command to the OPERATING SYS-TEM; word processors, spreadsheets, database managers and games are all examples of such programs. To a computer programmer however, the term program may refer equally to the SOURCE CODE – written in a human-readable programming language – and to the final BINARY version which is delivered to users. Source code is turned into binary code by running it through a third program called a COMPILER. Most programs are delivered in a binary format for two reasons. Firstly, binary programs are more efficient because the machine code instructions are directly executable by the computer's CPU. Secondly, the user cannot modify programs supplied in binary form, which goes some way toward protecting the copyright of the program's author (a practice that is challenged by advocates of FREEWARE and OPEN SOURCE).

The fundamental behaviour of any program is to start, perform some computations and then stop. But to do anything useful, a program normally needs to obtain INPUT data from outside itself, which it transforms into OUTPUT data in a manner that defines the purpose of the program. Early computers required the user to append the name of a file containing input data to the command used to execute a program, and the program would process this data, placing the results in another file, and then stop. This style of working is called BATCH PROCESSING, and is still employed by utility programs under operating systems such as MS-DOS and UNIX.

Most programs nowadays, however, are designed to be INTERACTIVE, which means that they ask the user to specify which input data to process (e.g. which document to open in a word processor) by choosing it from a visually displayed list. Moreover, the program does not stop after processing it, but continues to interact with the user until dismissed by an 'exit' command. Such programs are structured so that they spend much of their timing executing the same repeated LOOP of instructions, awaiting new commands from the user.

Programs large enough to do useful work are very complex entities, and so may behave in ways that were unintended by their authors, when they are said to exhibit a BUG or error. Some kinds of error can be detected by the program's own logic and reported to the user as an ERROR MESSAGE. Other kinds may cause the program to execute a repeated loop of instructions that ignores user commands: the program is then said to have HUNG or CRASHED.

program code The sequence of executable instructions that constitutes a computer PRO-GRAM. See also SOURCE CODE, OBJECT CODE, BINARY CODE, COMPILED, INTERPRETED.

program correctness The ability of a program to meet its specification – that is, to do what it was intended to do. There has been much research into program SEMANTICS to permit proofs of correctness, and into FORMAL METHODS for creating unambiguous specifications and automatically turning them into programs. FUNCTIONAL PROGRAMMING and LOGIC PROGRAMMING were both invented with such ideas in mind, as was the Z language. However, so far no such system has achieved widespread commercial use.

program counter A dedicated register employed by every processor, which acts like a bookmark by always containing the address of the next program instruction to be executed. Every time a new instruction is fetched, the processor automatically increments the program counter. The program counter is not normally modified directly by programs: instead special JUMP and CALL instructions are employed to change its contents.

program editor A TEXT EDITOR specially designed to assist programmers in writing program SOURCE CODE. Such editors typically feature multiple editing windows, powerful SEARCH-AND-REPLACE facilities based on REGU-LAR EXPRESSIONS, a system of TEMPLATES or command completion to speed up the entry of commonly used words and phrases; an ability to automate repetitive tasks by writing MACROS, and perhaps SYNTAX CHECKING and/or SYNTAX COLOURING for one or more PROGRAMMING LANGUAGES.

Widely used stand-alone program editors include EMACS and BRIEF, though increasingly programmers are working in the built-in editor of some INTEGRATED DEVELOPMENT ENVI-RONMENT. Programmers become so highly accustomed to the keyboard commands of a particular editor with which they work day-in, day-out, that most program editors now emulate the keyboard command sets of all the most popular editors.

Program Evaluation and Review Technique See PERT.

program generator A type of software tool used by programmers that automatically translates some kind of visual representation of a program into SOURCE CODE in a programming language. See also VISUAL PROGRAM-MING, FORM DESIGNER.

Program Information File See PIF.

programmable Any device that is capable of having its behaviour altered by its user through entering a sequence of instructions.

Programmable Array Logic (PAL) See under PROGRAMMABLE LOGIC ARRAY.

programmable logic array (PLA) A type of INTEGRATED CIRCUIT whose function is not fixed in advance but may be configured by a system designer using software. PLAs offer a cheap and convenient way to prototype new designs, and to make production parts when the quantity required is too small to justify designing and fabricating an ASIC. See also GATE ARRAY, FIELD-PROGRAMMABLE GATE ARRAY.

programmable logic controller (PLC) A class of simple computing device used largely to automate industrial plant and machinery. It is less powerful than a general purpose microprocessor, and simply opens and closes a set of switches in a programmed sequence. See also MICROSEQUENCER, MICROCONTROLLER, COM-PUTER NUMERICAL CONTROL.

Programmable Read Only Memory (PROM) A type of memory chip whose contents can be altered once, by programming it in a device called a PROM burner or programmer: fusible links within the chip are permanently opened or closed by passing a high current through them to create the desired data patterns.

The term is also nowadays used in a broader and looser sense to cover to all types of write-once, or 'write-occasionally' memory chips, including UV-erasable EPROMS and even 'flash PROM'. See also ROM, EEPROM, OTPROM.

programmer A person who writes computer programs.

Programmers Hierarchical Interactive Graphics System (PHIGS) A computer GRAPHICS standard developed jointly by the

ISO and ANSI that permits complex objects to be defined as a hierarchy of constituent parts. For example when drawing a car, a wheel need be drawn only once, and then included four times. PHIGS has been implemented mostly on large UNIX systems, and has been largely displaced by OPENGL.

programming environment A particular set of software tools, for example a TEXT EDITOR, COMPILER and DEBUGGER, used to write computer programs. See also INTEGRATED DEVELOPMENT ENVIRONMENT.

programming fluid Coffee.

programming language An invented language used to write computer programs, and designed to be more readable by humans than binary MACHINE CODE instructions are. The purpose of any programming language is to ease the task of writing error-free programs. There is no single universal programming language, but hundreds of different ones tailored to different kinds of computer application, and new ones are being developed all the time. The most widely used languages today are C, C++, BASIC, COBOL and FORTRAN.

Programming languages are described as being high-level or low-level, according to how closely they resemble the machine instructions of the computer on which they run on (machine code itself being the lowest possible level). The highest possible level would be a real human language such as English, but no computers can yet understand such languages, and all our existing programming languages rate very low on this scale.

Programs written in any programming language must be translated into the machine code for a particular computer (which is all that computers can actually execute) and this translation is performed by another computer program, called a COMPILER or an INTERPRETER. The original high-level program is called the SOURCE CODE of the program. Each instruction written in a high-level language (i.e. each source code instruction) will typically translate into many simple machine code instructions.

COMPILED languages such as C, C++, PASCAL and FORTRAN convert the whole high-level program at once into a file of binary machine code, which can then be executed without requiring access to the source code. This is the form in which all commercial software for typical Windows PCs and Macintoshes is sold.

INTERPRETED languages such as BASIC, PERL and LISP translate instructions of a high-level program one at a time into machine code, and execute it immediately. Such interpreted programs run more slowly than compiled programs owing to the time taken in translation before executing every instruction, and they also require that you possess the source code of the program; for both reasons, interpreted languages are not favoured for commercial software production. Languages such as VISUAL BASIC, JAVA and FORTH take a middle road, first compiling source programs into an intermediate PSEUDO-CODE which can be more efficiently interpreted.

All programming languages provide a small set of RESERVED WORDS that describe the actions they can perform, together with a set of rules or SYNTAX that prescribes how these words may be combined. A programmer writing in the language invents new words to describe data items and actions relevant to the problem being solved, within the confines of this syntax. The programmer must also learn the SEMANTICS of the language, that is, precisely what action each word performs: the syntax and semantics of a programming language must be set down in a reference document. At the minimum, a language consists of this document together with a compiler or interpreter that implements it, though it may include other optional software tools such as source code editors, debuggers and libraries of pre-written code for commonly needed operations.

Programming languages employ different reserved words and syntaxes that make them look very different, but beneath this surface they control the execution of programs in broadly similar ways. Most languages will offer some way to branch conditionally (if A is true, do B, else do C) and to loop (keep doing A until B becomes true), plus some way of turning frequently-executed sections of code into named sub-programs that can be used like new reserved words.

In addition to these fundamental control techniques, programming languages may contain special actions to solve particular kinds of problem. OBJECT-ORIENTED PROGRAM-MING LANGUAGES handle complex structured data, CONCURRENT PROGRAMMING LANGUAGES create programs to run on many CPUs at once, and DECLARATIVE LANGUAGES and LOGIC PROGRAMMING languages solve problems concerned with knowledge and reasoning rather than arithmetic.

See also SCRIPTING LANGUAGE, MACRO LANGUAGE, PAGE DESCRIPTION LANGUAGE.

program variable See under VARIABLE.

progress bar A visual software component that shows the user of a program how much time some activity such as saving a file to disk or downloading a file from a network is likely to take. It typically consists of a horizontal BAR GRAPH that moves in real time in exact proportion to the amount of the action that has been completed. Sometimes it may be accompanied by various textual displays giving, for example, the percentage completion, the number of bytes transferred so far and remaining, the current transfer rate and the amount of time remaining at that rate.

1023 of 3451 bytes transferred

projection 1 In geometry, a view of an N-dimensional object using only $N-1$ dimensions. For example a photograph is a 2D projection of a 3D object.

2 In programming, an ALGORITHM for optimizing searches in an N-dimensional data set by examining each dimension separately to constrain the search area.

3 A construct introduced in the OBERON programming language that allows only selected fields of a RECORD structure to be made visible.

project management The process of keeping track of all the different phases of some complex activity over time. Project management software enables such activities to be broken down into many separate subtasks, and then displays the way that these tasks overlap in time, often using some standard model such as GANTT CHARTS, CRITICAL PATH ANALYSIS or, in the case of software projects, a PERT diagram.

Prolog The most widely known LOGIC PROGRAMMING language, invented at the University of Aix-Marseilles in 1973 by Alain

Colmerauer and Philippe Roussel. Though Prolog has never been widely accepted as a commercial programming language, it is used in ARTIFICIAL INTELLIGENCE research, most particularly for NATURAL LANGUAGE processing applications. A Prolog program works by storing a database of known facts about the problem domain, expressed in the form of predicates of the form male(Tarzan), female(Jane), and deduction rules expressed as conjunctions of the form apelike(X): hairy(X), longarms(X), shortlegs(X). The program then deduces the answers to user queries by applying the rules to the facts. Unlike conventional programming languages, Prolog can provide multiple solutions to the same query, thanks to its ability to BACKTRACK and find any further answers. See also EDINBURGH PROLOG, PREDICATE CALCULUS, RESOLUTION, UNIFICATION.

PROM See PROGRAMMABLE READ ONLY MEMORY.

proof 1 In logic and mathematics, a sequence of statements or deductive steps that establish the truth of a proposition from a set of given AXIOMS. See also THEOREM PROVER.

2 A preliminary copy of a printed document, made ('pulled', in printer's jargon) to establish that the PAGE LAYOUTS are correct before committing to printing a larger quantity. In DESKTOP PUBLISHING the proofs are often printed on a LASER PRINTER before sending final layouts to a litho printer. Also used as a verb meaning to make such a proof, or as a shorthand for proofread, meaning to examine such a proof for errors.

proofing The process of making a trial or PROOF copy of a document or picture before it is committed to a printer to produce a large number of copies.

propagate To spread or distribute some change, event, condition or state throughout a system. See for example ERROR PROPAGATION, BACK-PROPAGATION.

property The name given to user-configurable system parameters in operating systems with GRAPHICAL USER INTERFACES such as WINDOWS and MACOS. Rather than having to type strings of configuration commands to change, say, the FONT used by a word processor, the user can visually inspect and alter pages of properties (displayed in the form of a TABBED DIALOGUE when more than one page is involved) by pointing and clicking with the mouse.

property sheet   A type of on-screen DIALOGUE that displays the current values of the internal PARAMETERS of some software object, and allows the user to modify them. Examples can be seen by selecting Properties from the RIGHT-CLICK MENU of many Windows objects such as icons. See also PROPERTY, TABBED DIALOGUE, INSPECTOR.

proportional font   A FONT in which each CHARACTER may be of a different width, in contrast to a FIXED-PITCH FONT in which all characters occupy the same width. Proportional fonts are essential for achieving professional print quality, and most of the fonts employed in such systems such as TRUETYPE and POSTSCRIPT are proportional. The widths of the individual characters are called the FONT METRICS, and are typically stored in a table within the font file.

proposition   In LOGIC, a sentence affirming or denying some state of affairs, which is capable of being true or false. See more under PROPOSITIONAL CALCULUS.

propositional calculus   A system of SYMBOLIC LOGIC that deals solely with relations between whole propositions, and ignores their internal structure. Contrast with PREDICATE CALCULUS.

proprietary format   A data FILE FORMAT that has been created by a software vendor especially for a particular program, and which is not routinely employed by other programs. See also IMPORT, INDUSTRY-STANDARD.

protected   Not allowed to be changed without the appropriate PERMISSION.

protected memory   A memory space having the property that no PROCESS running within it may access any address outside its bounds. The intention is to prevent processes accidentally overwriting each other's code or data, so that a CRASH in one process need not bring down the whole system. Protection is ultimately enforced by a hardware MEMORY MANAGER, which is built into most modern

microprocessors, but requires additional support from the operating system.

protected mode   A mode of operation supported by all Intel's 80x86 family of microprocessors from the 80286 onward, and still used by today's PENTIUM models.

As in REAL MODE, all addresses are computed by adding an OFFSET to the value held in a SEGMENT REGISTER, but in protected mode the segment register contains not the ABSOLUTE ADDRESS of a segment but an index into a table of segment descriptors. These descriptors may contain memory protection information, such as limits on the permitted offsets, enabling the processor to prevent certain memory accesses. Operating systems such as Microsoft WINDOWS exploit this mechanism to prevent different processes from overwriting each other's memory space, hence the name. Attempts by faulty software to violate this protection are responsible for the all-too familiar GENERAL PROTECTION FAULT error message. See also 80x86 ARCHITECTURE.

protection violation   An attempt by a computer's processor to write or read an address that lies outside the bounds of the PROTECTED MEMORY area assigned to the currently executing program. A protection violation is normally a FATAL ERROR, which results in the PROCESS that caused it being terminated, because otherwise memory spaces belonging to other programs (including the operating system itself) might be overwritten and corrupted. However, a competent operating system should be able to prevent other running processes from being affected by the error. See also PROTECTED MODE, MEMORY MANAGEMENT UNIT, GENERAL PROTECTION FAULT, UNRECOVERABLE APPLICATION ERROR.

protocol   A set of formal rules governing the way that two communicating devices (such as computer systems or telephones) can exchange data with one another. There are hundreds of different protocols in current use, at every level of communication from local area computer networks to the world-wide telephone system and the Internet. A sample of commercially important protocols might include TCP/IP, HTTP, IPX, CDMA and TDMA.

In the absence of any protocol, senders would just dispatch messages in any arbitrary format down a channel and then forget about them, as when you post a letter. The simplest possible protocol requires the receiver to return a short standard message acknowledging receipt of the first message. Real life protocols are typically much more complex, involving rules for resending messages that were not received, and for detecting whether the message has been corrupted during transmission.

A *low-level protocol* defines the physical and electrical characteristics of the communication, such as the medium (e.g. wire, radio, infrared, optic fibre), how many channels it employs, and how different sequences of, say, light or voltage pulses are to be interpreted as signals. *High-level protocols* define the data formats to be employed to encode messages and control information, the syntax of messages and of the dialogues between the communicating devices, and any facilities for flow control, error detection and correction.

The ISO has defined an abstract model of communication called the OSI REFERENCE MODEL, which supplies the terminology for describing seven different levels of protocol, starting at the Physical layer and ending at the Application layer.

protocol analyser (*US* protocol analyzer) An electronic instrument that can capture the signals passing over a network for the purpose of diagnosing network faults. A protocol analyser measures overall data rates, detects bit-level errors and decodes the various different layers of the network protocol used to encode the data PACKETS. Some protocol analysers are dedicated portable devices, while others are implemented as software running on a portable computer.

protocol converter A hardware device or software layer that converts data between two different network protocols. Such a device is now more often referred to as a GATEWAY.

protocol layer One of the various levels of encoding and control employed in any communication between two systems. All networks employ a number of different layers of protocol, starting at the level of the kinds of electrical signal employed by the raw hardware at each end of the connection, and rising up to the application level, where users must specify account names and passwords. The

protocols in each layer use the protocols below, and provide service to the layers above, the advantage of such an organization being that a change to a protocol in one layer need not affect the others. See also OSI REFERENCE MODEL.

As a possibly helpful analogy, compare the ordinary activity of writing. Here the lowest level 'protocol' is the alphabet, which controls what letters you may use (chosen from, say, A to Z). The next layer is the layer of words, dictated by the vocabulary of the language, which will differ between, say, English, French or Italian, even though using the same basic alphabet. Higher layers govern sentence structure (i.e. grammar), punctuation, prose style and so on.

protocol stack A set of communication protocols organized into separate layers which are used together to control some communication channel. The best known examples are the five-layered protocol stack that constitutes the TCP/IP suite used on the INTERNET, and the seven-layered protocol stack prescribed in the full OSI REFERENCE MODEL.

While the very lowest levels of a protocol stack may be supported directly by the network hardware, its higher layers are typically implemented in software running on both the machines that are party to a communication. Each network PACKET to be transferred must

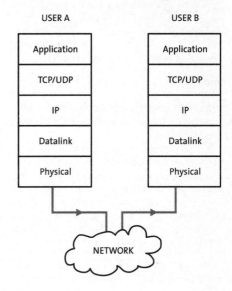

first pass down through the layers of the stack on the sending machine, and on arrival at the destination machine it passes up the stack, being interpreted at successively higher levels. For example the five levels of the TCP/IP stack are (from the bottom) bits, frames, datagrams, segments and messages.

prototype 1 A preliminary version of a software product, created to enable its design to be tested and improved. Also used as a verb, to create such a first version. See also RAPID PROTOTYPING.

2 In C++ and ANSI C, a function declaration that explicitly shows the function's ARGUMENT types and RETURN TYPE, as in:

```
Boolean DemoProc( int Arg1, float
Arg2 );
```

prototyping The process of making a PROTOTYPE of a software system.

provably difficult A problem for whose solution it can be proven that only EXPONENTIAL-TIME ALGORITHMS exist.

provably unsolvable A problem for whose solution it can be proven that no ALGORITHMS exist at all; an example is the HALTING PROBLEM for TURING MACHINES.

proximity search A type of search facility employed in TEXT RETRIEVAL SYSTEMS and FREE-FORM DATABASES that locates the target words only when they occur within a specified number of words of one another, for example: find fox within 10 grapes. See also RELEVANCE, SYNONYM RING, SEARCH ENGINE.

proxy 1 Any software entity that substitutes itself for, or stands in for, some other entity. The term is widely applied to INTERNET technologies – see PROXY SERVER, proxy FIREWALL and PROXY GATEWAY.

2 In a DISTRIBUTED OBJECT SYSTEM, an object located on the CLIENT that stands in for a similar object located on a remote SERVER. The proxy accepts any METHOD call intended for the remote object and transmits it via a communications link to a small code STUB on the remote server that invokes the appropriate methods in the actual object.

proxy gateway A computer running software that passes on any requests for WEB PAGES it receives to other WEB SERVERS, and returns the results to the user. The main reasons for employing a proxy gateway are: to act as a CACHE that provides quicker and cheaper access to frequently viewed web pages, to act as a FIREWALL that prevents HACKERS gaining access to a company's INTRANET, and to prevent internal users from accessing external sites that are forbidden for economic, moral or security reasons.

Web browsers may be configured so that users are unaware of the proxy gateway's intervention, and may employ a different proxy (or no proxy at all) for accessing different URLS, or for FTP, GOPHER, WAIS or NEWSGROUPS. See also PROXY SERVER.

proxy server A term applied both to the software used to implement a PROXY GATEWAY on a WEB SERVER, and to a server running such software. Proxy server software is sometimes also deployed as a local CACHE on a CLIENT computer, enabling it to download a whole web site and access it from its local hard disk to save time and money.

ps The abbreviation for PICOSECOND.

PS/2 IBM's second generation of personal computers, introduced in 1987 to replace the older XT and AT models. The PS/2 introduced the VGA graphics standard and a technically superior, but overly expensive, new EXPANSION BUS called the MICRO CHANNEL ARCHITECTURE, which failed to be accepted by the marketplace. The PS/2 was also the platform on which the new OS/2 operating system was introduced. The only part of the PS/2 architecture that has survived into today's PCs is its small-diameter MOUSE connector socket.

pseudo-code, pseudocode 1 A type of 'fake' programming language employed merely to illustrate ALGORITHMS and programming techniques, and not intended to be executed on a computer. Most of the program examples in this dictionary employ a PASCAL-like pseudo-code.

2 (p-code) An alternative name for the INTERMEDIATE LANGUAGE or BYTECODE generated by semi-compiled programming languages such as JAVA or VISUAL BASIC. The name was originally coined in connection with the UCSD PASCAL language. See more under INTERPRETED.

pseudoprime A very large number that statistical methods suggest is probably a PRIME NUMBER but whose primality has not been proven.

pseudo-random number A number generated by a computer as part of a sequence created by an algorithm that attempts to generate each permitted value with equal frequency, and to avoid any correlation between successive values. Such numbers are only pseudo-random because re-running the same algorithm with the same initial values will generate the same sequence. Generating truly random numbers is far more difficult, and requires the exploitation of some random natural phenomenon such as radioactive decay or thermal noise. See also RANDOM NUMBER GENERATOR, SEED.

Psion A pioneering UK manufacturer of hand-held computers, and developer of the EPOC 32 operating system employed in MOBILE PHONES. The company started in business producing software for Sinclair personal computers, but its 1985 Organiser was the first commercially successful pocketable electronic storage device and transformed the company's fortunes. The later Series 3, 5 and Revo models were also commercially successful. However in July 2001, faced with overwhelming competition from Palm and Microsoft, Psion announced it was abandoning further developments in hand-held computers. See also PSION ORGANISER, SYMBIAN.

PSTN Abbreviation of PUBLIC SWITCHED TELEPHONE NETWORK.

ptr Abbreviation of POINTER.

PTT (Post, Telephone and Telegraph administration) The generic name for pre-privatization national telephone companies. See also TELCO.

p-type See under SEMICONDUCTOR.

public A KEYWORD used in several programming languages, including C++, VISUAL BASIC, JAVA and DELPHI, to indicate that a CLASS, VARIABLE or METHOD is to be made visible to all other program objects. See also PRIVATE.

publication-quality Of a quality suitable for professional publication. The term is applied to digital photographs, diagrams and FONTS that have been reproduced to some minimum RESOLUTION (roughly 300 dots per inch or better).

public domain (PD) The total renunciation of COPYRIGHT protection. A work placed in the public domain is free for anyone to copy and use in any way they wish. The term is often inaccurately applied to FREEWARE, SHAREWARE and OPEN SOURCE software, all of which are subject to some form of copyright, however lenient, but are distributed without requiring any advance payment. In some countries (including the UK) public domain may have no legal force, as the author will be deemed to have automatic copyright. See also COPYLEFT, CRIPPLEWARE, NAGWARE.

public-facing A jargon term for those parts of a WEB SITE or other Internet resource that are open to access by anyone, in contrast to those parts that are accessible only to internal staff.

public-key encryption A method of enciphering messages in which all the communicating parties receive a pair of KEYS: a public key and their private key. The public key may be freely published to all interested parties, while the private key must be kept secret. Any new message is encrypted using the intended recipient's public key, but can be decrypted only by using the private key. Hence there is never a need for sender and receiver to exchange their secret keys via a secure channel as with older ciphers: communication involves only the public keys, and no private key is ever transmitted.

Public-key encryption was invented in 1976 by Diffe and Hellman, and is now widely used for computer AUTHENTICATION and in DIGITAL SIGNATURES, the RSA ENCRYPTION method being the most widely used variant.

Public-key encryption works because the keys are both FACTORS of some large prime number, but unreasonable amounts of computing time are required to calculate one from the other. 128-bit keys are considered secure given today's computing power, but the US government regards encryption as a defence technology and restricts the export of encryption software that uses keys longer than 56 bits.

public switched telephone network (PSTN) The ordinary public telephone system used throughout the world, which works by sending ANALOGUE voice signals over copper wire conductors and employs switches installed at centres called telephone exchanges to create a temporary end-to-end circuit between each caller and recipient. See also POTS, ISDN, BROADBAND.

publish To make data available so that it may be read by another person or computer program. See also PUBLISH-AND-SUBSCRIBE.

publish-and-subscribe A communication paradigm in which one party (e.g. person or computer program) releases new data and then notifies a list of interested recipients called subscribers that it is available. This is in contrast to a BROADCAST system, which sends the data to everyone without notification, or a CLIENT/SERVER system in which each subscriber must explicitly request the data. See also PUSH, PULL, MIDDLEWARE.

pull A jargon term used to describe any type of network transaction (such as an FTP file transfer, viewing a WEB PAGE or reading a NEWSGROUP) in which the CLIENT must specifically request some resource from a remote SERVER. Contrast with PUSH technologies, in which the server takes the initiative by feeding information automatically down some pre-defined channel.

pull-down list A visual user interface component that consists of a list of items (for example file names or fonts) of which all but the first are initially hidden. The list unfolds downwards when the user clicks with the MOUSE on a BUTTON attached to the list, which is typically marked with a down-arrow symbol. See also LIST BOX, COMBO BOX.

pull-down menu A style of MENU that appears only when its name is clicked with the MOUSE but remains visible only so long as the mouse button is kept depressed, disappearing if a choice is made. Used widely in Apple Macintosh software and certain other graphical user interfaces. See also DROP-DOWN MENU, POP-UP MENU.

Pulse Amplitude Modulation A modulation scheme that is widely used in digital telephone systems. The amplitude of an ANALOGUE voice signal is sampled at regular intervals and these values are converted to a stream of pulses of equal length but varying heights that convey the information. See also PULSE CODE MODULATION, NYQUIST FREQUENCY.

Pulse Code Modulation (PCM) A modulation scheme widely used in music reproduction and digital public telephone networks that samples the amplitude of an ANALOGUE signal at regular intervals and then encodes a binary representation of the obtained value as different patterns of consecutive pulses. This is in contrast with PULSE AMPLITUDE MODULATION in which the heights of successive pulses encode the information. See also ADPCM, CODEC, NYQUIST FREQUENCY.

pulse width The duration of the higher voltage portions of a SQUARE WAVE signal (that is, the tops of the waves), which may be varied in length to carry information (see MODULATE). For example many LASER PRINTERS vary the pulse width of the laser beam used for writing in order to alter the dot size for ANTIALIASING and DITHERING purposes. Pulse width encoding is also used frequently to vary the speed of electric motors used in control systems.

punched card One of the earliest forms of data storage, which encodes data items as different patterns of holes punched through a sheet of thin cardboard. Punched card systems may be purely mechanical (using metal pins to read the holes, as in the JACQUARD LOOM or HOLLERITH'S census machine) or may use a light beam and photodiode to read them, as in early MAINFRAME computers.

Pure Java A certification initiative launched by SUN MICROSYSTEMS to promote the development of JAVA applications that eschew operating-system dependent features, and hence are portable to different platforms.

purge To remove a data object from a computer memory or other storage system. The term is often used in connection with a DATABASE, which may be purged of duplicated or deleted records, or of a VIRTUAL MEMORY system to mean the replacement of an old page by a new one. See also FLUSH, BUFFER, COMPACTION.

push A jargon term used to describe a type of network transaction in which the SERVER feeds information down a pre-defined channel without waiting for it to be requested. Examples include the US PointCast news service, or the way that AOL distributes upgrade PATCHES for its communication software. Contrast with typical Internet transactions such as viewing a web page or making an FTP file transfer, where the CLIENT must specifically request the resource from the server.

PVM Abbreviation of PARALLEL VIRTUAL MACHINE.

Px64 A standard for real-time VIDEOCONFER-ENCING, more usually referred to by the name of the video compression CODEC it employs, H.261.

Python An interpreted, OBJECT-ORIENTED, SCRIP-TING LANGUAGE invented by Guido van Rossum in 1991, which is mainly used to write SERVER-SIDE scripts for use on the World Wide Web. Python is distributed as FREEWARE for all major computing platforms including Unix, MS-DOS, Windows, Macintosh, BeOS and Amiga, and is supported by an online community of its users.

Q

QA Abbreviation of QUALITY ASSURANCE.

QAM Abbreviation of QUADRATURE AMPLITUDE MODULATION.

QBasic See under MICROSOFT BASIC.

QBE Abbreviation of QUERY BY EXAMPLE.

QC Abbreviation of QUALITY CONTROL.

QCIF See under COMMON INTERCHANGE FORMAT.

QDOS **1** (Quick and Dirty DOS) A hastily assembled, CP/M influenced, 16-bit operating system for the IBM PC which Microsoft bought from its author in 1980 and turned into MS-DOS 1.0.
2 The operating system used by the Sinclair QL.

QEMM An EXPANDED MEMORY MANAGER produced by the US software company Quarterdeck as an alternative to Microsoft's EMM386. It offered automatic optimization of HIGH MEMORY usage, plus data COMPRESSION and VIRTUAL MEMORY techniques to make programs load faster. Later versions of WINDOWS have rendered such programs redundant. See also DESQVIEW.

QFP Short for QUAD FLAT PACK.

QIC (quarter-inch cartridge) A once-popular format of MAGNETIC TAPE cartridge used as a backup medium for smaller computer systems. QIC cartridges are of roughly similar size to an audio cassette but have a thick steel backing plate for greater rigidity. They may have capacities up to 10 gigabytes. Travan and Ditto are popular brands of tape drive that use QIC format cartridges.

QNX A REAL TIME DISTRIBUTED operating system for Intel processors developed in Canada, that employs a MICROKERNEL small enough to be run from ROM in EMBEDDED SYSTEMS. Network communications are built into the QNX kernel, with support for TCP/IP, NFS and the X WINDOW SYSTEM. QNX is MULTIUSER and MULTITASKING with a UNIX-like, POSIX-compatible shell, and it can run WINDOWS software as a guest process.

QoS Abbreviation of QUALITY OF SERVICE.

quad **1** A prefix meaning four, as in QUAD-WORD or QUAD FLAT PACK.
2 The term used for a board containing four PENTIUM Pro PROCESSORS used as the building block in Sequent's NUMA range of multiprocessor servers.

quad flat pack (QFP) A type of integrated circuit PACKAGE that takes the form of a square tile with connecting pins around all its four edges. It offers a cheaper package than the PIN GRID ARRAY, but provides a lower pin density and is suitable only for chips with 100 to 200 pins. QFPs are made in both plastic (called *PQFP*) and in ceramic. Ultra-thin versions of this package type (called thin quad flat packs or *TQFP*), in which the L-shaped pins are soldered directly to a circuit board, are used for SURFACE MOUNT applications.

quadratic A POLYNOMIAL expression of the second degree, that is, containing no powers higher than 2, such as x^2+3x+4.

quadratic prime A PRIME NUMBER that leaves the remainder 3 when divided by 4, such as 31, 43, 59 or 67.

quadrature amplitude modulation (QAM) An advanced modulation scheme employed in most modern modems and in DIGITAL SUB-SCRIBER LINE technologies, which exploits phase as well as amplitude information to encode four bits at each signal transition.

quadword A 64-bit quantity; that is, four 16-bit WORDS.

Quake A gory and entertaining computer game published by id Software as its successor to DOOM, and which is frequently played by teams interacting over the Internet.

qualifier Any word or phrase prefixed or appended to some other term to modify (particularly to narrow) its meaning. In a programming language, qualifiers are often one or more names of MODULES, CLASSES or OBJECTS prefixed to the name of a method or variable using DOT NOTATION, to indicate ultimate ownership – for example TextControl-lers.NewReader.Init. Almost all modern languages including C++, VISUAL BASIC, JAVA and DELPHI support this form of syntax.

quality assurance (QA) A systematic programme of work practices and tests designed to give confidence that a product will meet a customer's specification. Quality assurance in the software industry may involve the use of special programming METHODOLOGIES, program code checking tools, organized peer-review practices such as code WALK-THROUGHS, and extensive programs of both alpha and beta TESTING.

quality control (QC) An activity that involves uncovering and fixing the BUGS in a software or hardware product (including processing user BUG REPORTS) and then using the knowledge gained to improve future product design and production techniques. Most large manufacturing organizations maintain a separate department to pursue quality control, and the certificates issued by such a department are frequently to be found in the box or attached as a sticker to electronic equipment of many kinds. See also QUALITY ASSURANCE.

Quality of Service (QoS) The level of performance offered by a particular network as measured by combining several parameters, which include the total data throughput, the LATENCY, and the priority of a particular data stream vis-à-vis other traffic. Some network protocols such as ASYNCHRONOUS TRANSFER MODE allow the quality of service required to be specified and enforced for individual PACK-ETS or data streams, while extensions to the Internet's TCP/IP protocol permit a certain quality of service to be reserved in advance (see under RESOURCE RESERVATION PROTOCOL).

quantization 1 The collating of data values into a series of discrete value ranges as part of the process of ANALOGUE-TO-DIGITAL CONVER-SION. *Uniform quantization* places each sample individually into the storage 'bin' appropriate to its value. For example, with 8-bit samples there will be 256 such bins. In *vector quantization* an entire set of samples is stored at a time: this is used in VIDEO COM-PRESSION algorithms including JPEG and MPEG because, although it needs more computing power at the compression stage, it allows for faster decompression via a simple table lookup.
2 A feature of many MIDI SEQUENCERS that adjusts the length of notes played in via an instrument to the nearest whole note value.

quantization noise A type of undesirable artefact that may appear when analogue data (especially sound or pictures) are digitized. It manifests itself as a spurious noise or visible banding in areas that should be smooth. It is caused by the samples clumping around a series of discrete values instead of being evenly distributed. See also SAMPLING, ALIAS-ING, MACH BANDS, NYQUIST FREQUENCY.

quantum computing The use of QUANTUM EFFECTS to perform computation. The quantum property exploited is that of 'superposition'. Suppose a subatomic particle can exist in two spin states, up and down: these can be taken to stand for 0 and 1, a digital BIT. However, quantum mechanics predicts that such a particle can also be put into a *superposed* state that is both up and down at the same time, and has no equivalent in classical physics. In computing terms, this represents a bit that is both 0 and 1 at once. Adding the contents of two quantum REGISTERS each containing four such superposed bits should simultaneously compute all the possible sums of pairs of the numbers between 0 and 15 inclusive. It is thought that such quantum computers could therefore be EXPONENTIALLY faster than classical computers at certain operations (such as factorizing large numbers) that have significance in communications and CRYPTOGRAPHY.

However, much work remains before workable quantum computers can be produced. Superposed states collapse if one particle comes in contact with others, which poses formidable (possibly insurmountable) obstacles to their construction.

quantum dot An electronic device that uses quantum effects to store one BIT with an extremely fast switching time.

quantum effect Physical phenomena encountered as INTEGRATED CIRCUITS are made ever smaller. The conductors contain so few electrons that they cease to behave predictably according to Ohm's Law, and begin to exhibit quantum mechanical behaviour, where current, voltage and resistance are no longer proportionally related.

Quark XPress A powerful DESKTOP PUBLISHING program popular in the professional publishing industry.

quarter-inch cartridge See QIC.

quarter-inch tape drive A class of TAPE DRIVE that takes QIC (quarter-inch cartridge) tapes.

quartile In statistics, one of the divisions of a data set that has been split into four non-overlapping ranges delimited by 25, 50, 75 and 100% of some significant property. Hence a phrase such as 'in the third quartile by income', which means receiving between 50% and 75% of the average income of some group.

query A request made to a computer DATABASE to retrieve a particular set of data RECORDS. Queries may be written in a programming language such as SQL, or performed interactively via a QUERY BY EXAMPLE interface. In the former case, a query may be stored so that it can be used again in future. Queries frequently exploit PATTERN MATCHING techniques such as WILDCARDS and BOOLEAN operators (AND, OR and NOT) to retrieve a whole group of related records at the same time. See also QUERYDEF, QUERY OPTIMIZATION, INDEX, KEY.

query by example (QBE) A style of user interface provided as an alternative in many computer DATABASE MANAGEMENT SYSTEMS. It enables users to retrieve records simply by entering the values they wish to find into one or more fields of a blank record, rather than by typing a logical expression or an SQL query: those fields left blank may contain any value in the result set. For example typing 'Jones' into the Last_Name field might retrieve all records for customers named Jones. Query by example does not offer the degree of precision and flexibility of full SQL queries, but it is intuitively obvious and well-suited to fast, interactive applications such as an address book.

querydef An object that represents an SQL QUERY in Microsoft's DATA ACCESS OBJECTS database object model.

query optimization The automatic restructuring of an SQL database query in order to increase the efficiency of the search process. This might be done by making better use of any INDEXES that exist, or for example, by PREFETCHING and precomputing partial results and CACHING them in memory.

queue A data structure with the property that the first element that can be removed is the first one that was put in. Hence a queue enables a number of items to wait for the occurrence of an event, or access to a rationed resource, while maintaining the strict order in which they arrived. See also FIFO, STACK.

quick-and-dirty A solution to a problem that is thrown together quickly, and without concern for elegance.

QuickDraw The library of graphics routines employed by Apple's MACINTOSH operating system, contained in the system ROM. QuickDraw was ahead of its time in being independent of screen resolution and supporting display across multiple monitors.

Quicksort A very efficient sorting ALGORITHM that works by swapping pairs of items to partition them into those larger than and those smaller than some chosen item. The same process is applied to each of these two sets, until eventually many sets of only two items each will be arrived at, and these sets can be put into order by a simple comparison operation. Quicksort is not only fast but space efficient, as it sorts the data in place, without having to duplicate it.

QuickTime The part of the Apple MACINTOSH operating system that performs full motion video and animation. QuickTime drivers are now available for other computers and it has become a popular format for distributing animated sequences. Since 1995 QuickTime has been extended with QuickTime 3D for 3D GRAPHICS. See also 3D METAFILE, AVI, DVI, OPENGL, DIRECT3D.

QWERTY The standard keyboard layout for typewriters and computers in English-speaking countries, so called after the characters that appear in its top right letter row. The arrangement was devised in the early days of the manual typewriter to separate frequently-typed letter pairs and so avoid their typebars tangling during rapid typing. Now this is no longer a consideration it is clear that QWERTY significantly restricts typing speed, but reformed layouts such as the DVORAK KEYBOARD have been unable to overcome the inertia of billions of typing courses. Some countries use slightly modified versions of QWERTY, such as the AZERTY layout favoured in France.

R

race condition A problem encountered in the design of electronic circuits, where the output of some LOGIC GATE has an unwanted dependence on which of two or more input signals is received first.

rack mounting A highly space-efficient method for housing multiple items of electrical equipment by installing them as a vertical stack held within a standard 19-inch wide rack. Components for rack mounting normally have heights that are integer multiples of the U unit (1.75 inches) so a 2U case is 3.5 inches high. The equipment must be specially designed for rack mounting, in a case of the proper width with mounting lugs on its front panel. In computing and telecommunications, the items most often rack mounted are SERVERS, ROUTERS, SWITCHES, HUBS and MODEMS.

RAD (rapid application development) A school of computer program design that emphasizes a cycle of building, testing and improving a series of test programs, rather than first attempting to produce a complete and correct specification on paper. RAD is made feasible by the invention of interactive program development tools and COMPONENT ARCHITECTURES such as VISUAL BASIC, POWERBUILDER, DELPHI and JAVABEANS, which enable programmers to build and rebuild a prototype system in hours, or at most days. The term RAD has been applied to a broad spectrum of practices, ranging from simple trial-and-error through to elaborate methodologies based on diagrammatic specifications supported by CASE TOOLS, reusable TEMPLATES or DESIGN PATTERNS.

rad hard Short for RADIATION HARDENED.

radiation Energy emitted in the form of electromagnetic waves. In a computer, the main sources of radiation are the light emitted by its display screen, followed by radio frequency emissions from the circuit boards and magnetic fields from the VDU's cathode ray tube.

radiation hardened (rad hard) A grade of electronic component whose operation cannot be disrupted by pulses of ionizing radiation (such as cosmic radiation, or gamma radiation from a nuclear explosion), unlike normal commercial CMOS chips which may be destroyed by such radiation. Rad hard chips are made specially for the armed forces and for space exploration. Since they achieve radiation resistance by employing GALLIUM ARSENIDE or SILICON ON SAPPHIRE fabrication processes in place of ordinary bulk silicon, they are far more expensive than civilian equivalents.

radio button A visual user interface component that acts as a switch, turned on or off by clicking with a MOUSE. When a group of radio buttons is present, only one may be on at a time, and clicking any other will turn it on and the former off. This resembles the behaviour of the station buttons on a car radio, hence the name.

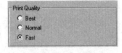

radio frequency emissions, radio frequency interference The radio frequency energy radiated by computer circuit boards and by the computer's MONITOR. In the USA, the FCC enforces a strict regulatory testing regime to limit such emissions, to prevent them from interfering with wireless communications. For example a 600 megahertz microprocessor radiates in bands used for portable WIRELESS COMMUNICATIONS in aircraft and by the emergency services. To comply with FCC regulations, most PCs have a case made either of metal or metal-coated plastic. See also EMC DIRECTIVE.

radiosity A technique for RENDERING photorealistic scenes in 3D GRAPHICS that gives a more natural appearance than the alternative RAY TRACING method by treating every object in a scene as a source of radiation that illuminates every other object, using equations borrowed from heat transfer engineering. The algorithm requires substantially more computing power than ray tracing, and can handle only diffuse illumination because it includes no concept of direction, so images tend to have a matte appearance. The ideal is to apply ray tracing as well to add SPECULAR HIGHLIGHTS, which requires more calculation still. Radiosity is supported only in the most advanced graphics software such as SOFTIMAGE and MAYA.

radix In mathematics, the formal name for the number BASE of a POSITIONAL NOTATION such as BINARY NOTATION (radix 2) or DECIMAL NOTATION (radix 10) – that is, the integer by powers of which the successive digits of a number must be multiplied.

radix sort A class of highly efficient SORT algorithms that work by viewing the sort KEYS as BINARY NUMBERS and then sorting by individual groups of BITS within these keys.

RAID (Redundant Arrays of Independent (or Inexpensive) Disks) A technique for building very large disk storage systems by combining large numbers of small HARD DISK drives of the sort used in personal computers.

The RAID concept was conceived at the University of California at Berkeley by Katz, Ousterhout and Patterson in 1989, and has now become the standard way to provide storage in the hundreds and thousands of gigabytes range for large SERVER FARMS.

RAID works by dividing the data to be written to the disk array between the constituent disks in different ways, depending on whether the aim is maximum speed or maximum security. MIRRORING writes the same data to two disks to provide a backup should one fail. STRIPING writes each data item across several disks, together with ERROR CORRECTION information so that the data can be reconstructed should any of the drives fail. Striping may be performed at different levels, writing each successive bit, or byte, or sector to a different drive, which can reduce retrieval times since all the drives' HEADS can seek in parallel. These techniques are combined in various ways to produce five levels of RAID specification:

RAID 0: Data striped across all drives without redundancy, so the array appears as one large disk.

RAID 1: Data mirrored onto pairs of drives.

RAID 2: Data striped in bits with multiple error-correcting disks for redundancy.

RAID 3: Data striped in bytes with one drive reserved for parity information.

RAID 4: Data striped in sectors with one drive reserved for parity information.

RAID 5: Data striped in sectors with parity information rotated among all drives.

Security and fault-tolerance is best achieved at RAID level 5 and so many SCSI disk controllers, and operating systems such as WINDOWS NT and 2000 and UNIX, now support the construction of RAID 5 arrays.

RAM (Random Access Memory) A readable and writeable electronic data storage medium that permits equally rapid access to any stored data item. Its somewhat misleading name (arbitrary access memory would perhaps be more accurate) is a historic remnant, originally chosen to distinguish RAM from various SEQUENTIAL ACCESS media (such as magnetic tape or magnetic disk) whose mechanical moving parts make it much slowers to access non-sequential data.

Modern RAM is a type of INTEGRATED CIRCUIT, manufactured by fabrication techniques similar to those used to build microprocessors and other chips. Individual RAM chips have standard capacities that increase every few years with each new technology generation – currently these range from 64 megabits to 256 megabits per chip. For convenience of installation, several RAM chips are mounted together onto small printed circuit boards called Single or Double Inline Memory Modules (SIMMS or DIMMS) so they will fit into a single memory socket inside the computer.

Most random access memory is volatile (it loses all its contents when electrical power is switched off), and so programs and data must be stored for the long term on some non-volatile medium (typically a HARD DISK) and loaded into RAM only temporarily, when required for use. RAM is hundreds of times faster to access than a magnetic disk and, while modern operating systems allow computers to run programs that are larger than the amount of RAM fitted (see VIRTUAL MEMORY), performance will always be faster if the whole program and data can fit into RAM. For this reason typical PCs come fitted with 64 megabytes or more of RAM.

RAM provides the main memory of all modern computers; it is the place from where programs are executed and where data is loaded while it is being processed. The presence of some RAM is quite fundamental to the whole design philosophy of microprocessors, which are capable of generating the address signals required to retrieve data from external RAM (i.e. that is not on the CPU chip).

Physically, a RAM chip consists of millions of CELLS, each composed of one or more TRANSISTORS, and each capable of storing a single bit. These cells are organized as a two dimensional grid, and individual cells can be addressed – to read or to change the value of their bit – by supplying a row and a column address, rather like a microscopic spreadsheet.

There are two main types of RAM, DYNAMIC RANDOM ACCESS MEMORY (DRAM) and STATIC RAM (SRAM). Dynamic RAM is so called because it can store bits only very briefly, so the CPU or memory controller must constantly read and then rewrite the information stored in each RAM chip, a process called *refreshing* (see under REFRESH). Static RAM does not require refreshing, and retains its contents so long as electrical power is applied, but it employs several more transistors to build each cell, so fewer cells can be fitted on a chip, and hence it costs more per megabyte.

There are many varieties of dynamic and static RAM technology, differing in the way they handle ADDRESSES, the size of data words that they read and write, whether they oper-

ate synchronously or asynchronously, and the pattern of usage for which they work most efficiently. Examples include FAST PAGE MODE RAM, EDO RAM and Burst EDO RAM, DRDRAM, SLDRAM, ESDRAM , JEDEC, PC100 and DDR SDRAM. In recent years CPU speeds have been improving more quickly than RAM speeds, so the speed of RAM access has become a bottleneck and a critical factor in the price/performance trade-off – in general, faster RAM is more expensive RAM.

Rambus DRAM Also Direct Rambus DRAM or DRDRAM. A very fast DRAM technology invented by the Californian firm Rambus, which can attain 500 megahertz (MHz) throughput and hence keep pace with the latest generation of MICROPROCESSORS. It achieves this by employing three separate 8-bit buses (one each for ROW ADDRESS, COLUMN ADDRESS and data), a 250 MHz clock signal with both edges used, and a 4-stage pipeline for row accesses.

RAMDAC Abbreviation of RANDOM ACCESS MEMORY DIGITAL-TO-ANALOGUE CONVERTER.

RAM disk See under SOLID-STATE STORAGE DEVICE.

R&D Short for RESEARCH AND DEVELOPMENT.

random access A mode of accessing a storage medium in which single items may be selected and retrieved independently of the others, as for example in a RAM chip or a HARD DISK drive. See also SEQUENTIAL ACCESS.

random-access machine A class of abstract computing device that is equivalent in computational power to a TURING MACHINE, but whose structure more closely resembles that of real digital computers. Its memory contains a collection of words with ADDRESSES that enable them to be accessed directly, and it has a set of REGISTERS into which a word can be moved to perform arithmetic operations. See also FINITE STATE MACHINE, CHOMSKY HIERARCHY.

random access memory See RAM.

Random Access Memory Digital-to-Analogue Converter (RAMDAC) A type of INTEGRATED CIRCUIT employed in computer graphics systems. It contains three DIGITAL TO ANALOGUE CONVERTERS (DACs), one each for red, green and blue, together with a small quantity of STATIC RAM, and its purpose is to generate the signals to drive an analogue MONITOR. Its RAM component stores a colour lookup table or PALETTE that relates colour numbers stored in the computer's video memory to a particular set of red, green and blue components.

random number A number generated by a computer for the purpose of simulating some random process or distribution (e.g. the next card drawn from a pack in a card game). In fact even the best computer algorithms generate only PSEUDO-RANDOM NUMBERS because, given the same starting value or SEED, they will always produce the same sequence of numbers. To create genuinely random numbers it is necessary to use a hardware device that exploits some random physical process such as electronic noise or radioactive decay.

random number generator A software routine that generates a sequence of PSEUDO-RANDOM NUMBERS for use by a larger program, for example in a game or a simulation to represent shuffled cards or random events. Given the same starting values, a random number generator always produces the same sequence of numbers, but this behaviour is useful during DEBUGGING of a program since it allows the same conditions to be recreated at will. A pseudo-random SEED value is supplied to generate different sequences when the program is in actual use.

A simple and commonly used algorithm for generating random number sequences is to multiply the first number by an integer constant, add one, then divide by a second constant and take the remainder as the next number. Expressed as a formula:

```
randnum := (randnum * k₁ + 1) MOD k₂
```

This method produces a random integer between 0 and k_2-1. Such sequences always eventually repeat themselves, but the length before this happens can be increased by a good choice of values for k_1 and k_2 (try, for example, 421 and 10). The constants also affect the distribution of the random numbers, some values producing very poor sequences whose last digits cycle through a very few values. Much research has been devoted to the study of random number generators, because of their importance in statistical simulations:

a poorly performing generator may produce severely skewed and misleading results.

random-read A data access operation that can read a record from any arbitrary position within a file. See also RANDOM-WRITE, SEQUENTIAL ACCESS.

random-write A data access operation that can write a record into any arbitrary position within a file. See also RANDOM-READ, SEQUENTIAL ACCESS.

range 1 In communications and networking, the distance over which some medium (e.g. a wireless transmitter or a cable run) is effective.

2 A region of data within a SPREADSHEET, specified by the addresses of its top left and bottom right CELLS, to which an operation can be applied. Ranges may also be named and addressed by name.

3 In mathematics, another name for the domain of a function.

4 In some PROGRAMMING LANGUAGES, a numeric expression with prescribed limits on its value. For example in PASCAL the expression 0...8 stands for any integer between zero and eight.

rapid application development See RAD.

rapid prototyping The creation of a quick working program that demonstrates some desired feature of a larger software system. A whole series of such PROTOTYPES may be created, tested and rewritten as the specification of the desired system evolves. If a modern interactive VISUAL PROGRAMMING system is employed, such prototypes may often be further refined to form the basis of the actual production code. See more under RAPID APPLICATION DEVELOPMENT.

RAS 1 Abbreviation of ROW ADDRESS STROBE.
2 Abbreviation of REMOTE ACCESS SERVICE.

raster The area of a CATHODE RAY TUBE display that is scanned by the moving electron beam to draw a series of lines that make up one picture FRAME. For television and computer displays, the raster is scanned from top to bottom in left-to-right horizontal lines, then scanning returns to the top left corner during the FLYBACK INTERVAL ready to draw the next frame. See also SCAN LINE.

raster display Any visual display device in which the image is drawn as a sequentially scanned set of stripes called the RASTER. For example, the CATHODE RAY TUBE, as employed in television sets and computer monitors. See also SCAN LINE.

raster font See BITMAPPED FONT.

raster graphics An obsolete term for a BIT-MAPPED computer image that is composed from horizontal rows of PIXELS. Compare with VECTOR GRAPHICS.

raster image processor (RIP) A MICROPROCESSOR or GRAPHICS ACCELERATOR employed in LASER PRINTERS to speed up the rendering of a document page described in POSTSCRIPT (or some other PAGE DESCRIPTION LANGUAGE) into bands of printable pixels. A RIP is an essential component of professional imagesetting equipment.

rasterizer A hardware device or software process that converts a geometric description of, for example, a font or a 3D object into PIXELS that can be displayed on a display screen or printed. See also RASTER IMAGE PROCESSOR, RENDER, GEOMETRY ENGINE.

raster scan See under RASTER DISPLAY.

rate-pacing The function within an ASYNCHRONOUS TRANSFER MODE network switch that controls the number of cells being transferred per second.

rate-sensitive traffic See under RESOURCE RESERVATION PROTOCOL.

RATFOR (RATional FORtran) A programming language based on FORTRAN with additional CONTROL STRUCTURES, implemented as a PREPROCESSOR that outputs ordinary FORTRAN. RATFOR has rarely been used for real-world programming; it is known chiefly as the language used for the examples in Kernighan and Plauger's famous 1976 programming textbook *Software Tools*.

Raw Iron The name given by ORACLE to version 8i of its RELATIONAL DATABASE MANAGEMENT SYSTEM which runs on top of a small MICROKERNEL operating system rather than on a general-purpose operating system such as WINDOWS or UNIX. Raw Iron performs its own memory allocation, network interfacing and file storage, the intention being to enable it to run on cheap hardware, and to eliminate the cost of an operating system licence.

ray tracing An advanced technique for RENDERING scenes in 3D GRAPHICS. It works by starting from the observer's eye and tracing backwards the path of each notional light ray as it reflects off the various objects in the scene, until it reaches a source (e.g. a light bulb) or disappears to infinity. Ray tracing produces highly realistic results, but is very demanding of processor time and is not suitable for real time animation.

RBOC Abbreviation of REGIONAL BELL OPERATING COMPANY.

RDBMS Abbreviation of RELATIONAL DATABASE MANAGEMENT SYSTEM.

RDO (Remote Data Access) A CLASS LIBRARY published by Microsoft to simplify programming CLIENT/SERVER database applications from later versions of VISUAL BASIC (see also DATA ACCESS OBJECTS). Now largely superceded by ACTIVEX DATABASE OBJECTS.

RDRAM Abbreviation of RAMBUS DRAM.

RDS Abbreviation of REMOTE DATA SERVICE.

read To retrieve data from a storage device. For example, a computer's processor might read data from its RAM or from an external MAGNETIC DISK. The term is also used as a noun, short for read operation, as in '25 reads per second'. See also WRITE.

read-after-write A common method of VERIFICATION, used for example by many TAPE BACKUP systems, in which each data item is read immediately after it is written to check that it was correctly recorded.

reader The hardware device that reads some form of portable data storage medium such as a SMARTCARD or a BAR CODE.

read-mostly A description applied to applications (and to data storage media used in those applications), where the stored data is mostly referred to, and only infrequently updated. Examples might include price or address lists that are updated only monthly or annually. It implies that efficiency of reading is paramount and that a slower writing process may be tolerated, so that flash memory or CD-R and CD-RW discs might be preferred, on cost or power consumption grounds, to RAM or a HARD DISK.

read-only A description applied to any data storage medium whose contents can be read but not written by their current user, examples being a ROM chip, a CD-ROM or a file for which write permission has been disabled. In some instances the data content must be introduced either by using a special writing method that is not available to the end-user (for example burning a ROM: see under BURN) or by copying from a master, as with CD-ROM. See also READ-MOSTLY.

read-only memory See ROM.

read/write Any data storage medium that can be written to as well as read back. Examples include RAM chips, MAGNETIC DISKS and MAGNETIC TAPES and CD-RW disks. Contrast with READ-ONLY media such as ROM or CD-ROM.

read/write head The component within a magnetic or optical disk or tape drive that both reads and writes data tracks on the recording surface. Often abbreviated to head.

RealAudio A proprietary compressed data format developed by REALNETWORKS for sending STREAMING audio over the Internet with the aid of a PLUG-IN added to a web browser.

real estate A jargon term for the area of a silicon die that is available to build components on. Used as in 'we shrank the write buffer to free up some real estate'.

real mode An operation mode supported by all Intel's 80x86 family of microprocessors in which memory addresses are formed by adding an offset to the current contents of the SEGMENT REGISTER to yield a 20-bit absolute address within that segment. The MS-DOS operating system runs in real mode, hence its 1 megabyte memory limitation, since that is all that can be addressed using 20 bits. Windows and Unix running on Intel processors use the alternative PROTECTED MODE, which overcomes this limitation. See also 80x86 ARCHITECTURE, SEGMENTED MEMORY MODEL, EXTENDED MEMORY, EXPANDED MEMORY.

RealNetworks The US software company, formerly called Progressive Networks, which invented the widely used REALAUDIO, REALVIDEO and REALPIX protocols and data formats for sending STREAMING multimedia data over the Internet. The company also markets a range of client player software including RealPlayer, RealJukeBox and RealSlideshow.

real number A fractional number used to measure continuously variable quantities (such as length, mass or temperature). Compare this with the natural numbers or INTEGERS that are used to count discrete objects. Mathematics defines real numbers as the rational numbers (i.e. fractions such as 2.367), together with the irrational numbers (such as pi and the square root of 2) that have infinitely long fractional representations. The real numbers have the disturbing property of infinite divisibility, for between any two real numbers there is an infinite number of further real numbers.

Computers can represent real numbers only approximately as FLOATING-POINT numbers, so the REAL data type provided in a few languages such as PASCAL and OBERON corresponds to the FLOAT type in other languages such as C, ADA and JAVA.

RealPix A data format created by REALNETWORKS for sending a sequence of still images as a STREAMING slideshow over the Internet.

Real Programmer A mythical creature of conservative instincts who refuses to use any modern programming aids. Subject of an extensive online literature.

Real Soon Now Sarcastic dig at manufacturers who repeatedly claim that a product is nearly ready. Coined by Byte columnist Jerry Pournelle but now part of the language.

real time Time constraints imposed by the world of physical objects, rather than the virtual world of computer software.

In a computer SIMULATION of a real world process, time is under the computer's control – the process may be slowed down, speeded up, paused or reversed at will. However, once the computer is connected to a real mechanical system (perhaps via a STEPPER MOTOR or TRANSDUCER), this freedom disappears, and the process must meet critical deadlines imposed by physical events. For example, commands to move the head of a HARD DISK drive to a particular track must be completed within a tiny interval determined by the rapid rotation of the disk PLATTER.

Real time software is the most difficult kind to program, because delaying or interrupting it at all may cause the desired operations to fail. Complex desktop computer operating systems are typically unable to respond fast enough for real time operation, and so a stripped-down REAL TIME EXECUTIVE specially designed for the purpose is often employed instead.

real time clock A special chip fitted into a computer to maintain the current date and time of day, for use by the computer's software (for example, to date-stamp files). A real time clock requires either a small battery (and perhaps some NON-VOLATILE memory) to enable it to continue keeping time while the computer is switched off, or increasingly, an Internet connection over which to resynchronize itself to a remote standard clock. The limitations of some old or low-cost real time clock chips were responsible for some instances of the YEAR 2000 BUG.

real time executive A class of compact and efficient OPERATING SYSTEM for use in EMBEDDED SYSTEMS, whose prime requirement is to respond to external events quickly and predictably. Real time executives are designed to perform a few critical functions reliably, not for extensive user interaction or to support many different peripherals as large operating systems such as UNIX and WINDOWS are. A typical application might involve running just a single program stored in ROM for ever, monitoring its progress and restarting it if it should fail.

RealVideo A proprietary compressed data format developed by REALNETWORKS for sending STREAMING video over the Internet with the aid of a PLUG-IN added to a web browser.

real world Net slang for the everyday, physical world we live in, in contrast to the abstract CYBERSPACE of the Internet.

rear panel The back wall of a computer's case, which traditionally carries all the COMMUNI-

CATION PORTS, EXPANSION SLOTS and the power connectors.

reboot To cause a computer to reload its operating system and reinitialize all its systems (see also BOOTSTRAP).

A reboot is typically performed to escape from a software CRASH that has rendered the computer inoperable, or to confirm an alteration made to some fundamental system parameter that takes effect only at start up time. Rebooting is a drastic option that destroys any data not yet saved onto a permanent medium (e.g. a disk file).

POCKET COMPUTERS and mobile telephones (which lack disk storage), and publicly accessible or MISSION-CRITICAL network SERVERS, are increasingly expected to operate for months at a time without rebooting, which will favour operating system designs that can be reconfigured without forcing a reboot.

recalculate In a SPREADSHEET program, to cause the values in all its CELLS to be recomputed to take account of newly entered data.

receiver 1 The incoming portion of any communication hardware system such as a network, a telephone or a radio link. Compare this to a TRANSMITTER.

2 In a communications software system, the program or agent that accepts incoming messages. Compare this with a SENDER.

recognition The use of a computer to identify various sorts of pattern found in the real world. See more under SPEECH RECOGNITION, IMAGE RECOGNITION, PATTERN RECOGNITION, FACE RECOGNITION, IRIS RECOGNITION, FINGERPRINT RECOGNITION.

recompile To COMPILE a program again from its SOURCE CODE, for example to correct bugs, to incorporate improvements, or to run on a different processor type.

reconfigure To alter the characteristics of a hardware or software device. See more under CONFIGURATION.

reconnect To remake a network connection that has been broken.

record A data structure consisting of a collection of FIELDS, possibly each containing data of a different type, which is employed as the basic unit of information to be stored in a DATABASE. For example a simple personnel database might contain records with the structure:

```
name: STRING
address1: STRING
address2: STRING
age: INTEGER
birthdate: DATE
```

and an INSTANCE of such a record in the database with its fields filled in might look like:

```
Fred Nurk
2 Acacia Avenue
London NW12
45
12/12/1955
```

All the languages used in commercial programming (e.g. COBOL, C, VISUAL BASIC, DELPHI) provide some kind of record structure as a user-definable data type.

record locking A mechanism employed in multi-user databases to avoid conflicts when different users are trying to update the same RECORD. While one user is editing a particular record, all other users are prevented from accessing that record and will be shown a message to that effect.

There are two commonly used modes of record locking. *Full record locking* prevents all other users from accessing a record for as long as that record is locked for modification. *Optimistic record locking* allows two users to modify the same record simultaneously, locking the record only when one user writes it back to the database, and giving the other user a warning message with an option to override the lock. See also FILE LOCKING, FILE SHARING, LOCK MANAGER.

recovery 1 The actions taken by a program or its user to regain control after an ERROR CONDITION has arisen. Recovery may involve closing down the errant process, restoring damaged data structures to a known state and, as a last resort, restarting the program completely.

2 The retrieval of data that has been lost because of a program or hardware CRASH. For example using special tools to read the data from a hard disk that has suffered a HEAD CRASH. See also DISASTER RECOVERY.

recurrence relation An equation that defines the value of one element of a mathematical SERIES in terms of its predecessors and/or successors. For example the well-known FIBONACCI SERIES could be defined by the recurrence relation:

$$fib(0) = 1$$
$$fib(1) = 1$$
$$fib(n) = fib(n-1) + fib(n-2)$$

Recurrence relations often lead to highly memory-efficient algorithms.

recursion In a program or subprogram, the act of calling itself. Recursion may be employed in many (though not all) circumstances instead of ITERATION to repeatedly execute the same section of code. However, a program that calls itself unconditionally will remain stuck in an INFINITE LOOP, so it must contain a test to determine when the recursive calls should cease.

Recursion is the natural and elegant way to implement certain ALGORITHMS, the classic example being the factorial function:

```
define factorial(n) -> num
factorial(0) = 1
factorial(n) = n * factorial(n-1)
```

Here the first case of factorial(0) ensures that the recursion will terminate (for positive values of n).

Recursion is possible only in those programming languages (most modern ones) that store their function ARGUMENTS on a STACK, as otherwise each recursive call would obliterate the previous argument value. The stack thus grows at each recursive call, so that stack OVERFLOW becomes a limiting factor for recursive solutions. Recursion is the preferred programming style in functional and logic languages such as LISP and PROLOG. See also MUTUAL RECURSION, TAIL RECURSION, RECURSIVE FUNCTION.

recursion (see recursion) An old joke beloved of computer lexicographers, but one that will not be repeated here.

recursive Employing RECURSION.

recursive acronym An ACRONYM that includes itself in its own expansion, the best-known example being GNU (Gnu's Not Unix). An expression of rarified hacker humour that verges on the sad.

recursive descent A powerful algorithm frequently employed to PARSE texts that are constructed according to a rigorous GRAMMAR, for example program code to be processed by a COMPILER. The algorithm mirrors the PRODUCTION RULES of the grammar itself by treating the text as being composed of components, which in turn are composed of subcomponents and so on, and employs mutually recursive functions (see MUTUAL RECURSION) to recognize these components.

recursive function In mathematics, a FUNCTION that uses itself in its own definition. For example the factorial function $n! = 1 \times 2 \times 3 \times 4 ... \times n$ could be defined recursively as

$$\text{factorial}(n) = n \times \text{factorial}(n-1)$$

Alonzo CHURCH and Alan TURING showed that any function that can be computed by a machine must be expressible as a recursive function.

recursive type A STRUCTURED DATA TYPE whose definition contains an instance of itself. For example a LINKED LIST of items might be defined as being either empty, or an item followed by a list of items:

type list(item) = NIL or item :: list(item)

Only a few FUNCTIONAL PROGRAMMING LANGUAGES support recursive data types directly, but they may be defined indirectly in any language that supports POINTERS, as in this PASCAL definition of a list:

```
TYPE ListNodePtr = ^ListNode;
ListNode = RECORD
Data: Integer;
NextNode: ListNodePtr
END;
```

recycle bin An ICON on the desktop of Microsoft Windows that effectively deletes any file that is dropped onto it, but preserves the 'deleted' files so that they can be UNDELETED later if required. To free the disk space that deleted files consume, the user must periodically empty the recycle bin. See also WASTEBASKET.

Red Book The document published in 1982 by Sony and Philips that defines the standard data format for audio CDs. See also YELLOW BOOK, GREEN BOOK, ORANGE BOOK, WHITE BOOK.

Red Hat A commercial vendor of a version of the LINUX operating system.

redirection The act of changing a reference to some location or resource so that it points to a different destination. Everyday examples include redirecting post to another address or redirecting phone calls to another telephone number, but in computing the process is ubiquitous: operating systems routinely redirect data from keyboard to file to screen; routers redirect network PACKETS; and PROXY SERVERS redirect web page requests to a different web site, to mention only a few.

red-lining 1 Placing a red line through the black text to mark those parts of a document that have been deleted or altered. This feature, which is supported by MICROSOFT WORD, enables multiple collaborators to quickly see what each has done.
2 Slang for running a system to the limit of its capabilities, by analogy with the red danger line on an car's rev counter.

reduced instruction set computer See RISC.

redundancy 1 The duplication of the hardware or software components of a system to improve its reliability, the principle being that if one component fails, another can take over its function. See also RAID, CLUSTER, FAILOVER, FAULT-TOLERANT.

Software redundancy is employed in highly safety-critical applications such as aircraft control systems, by using two or three different programs, possibly running on different processors, to perform the same calculation and flagging an error (or accepting the majority result) if there is any discrepancy between them. Ideally these programs are written in different languages and by different programmers to reduce the likelihood of all containing the same systematic error. See also SAFETY-CRITICAL SYSTEM.
2 The provision of extra information in a data stream to permit ERROR CORRECTION techniques to be applied. See for example CYCLIC REDUNDANCY CHECK, HAMMING CODE, and also INFORMATION THEORY.

redundant arrays of independent disks, redundant arrays of inexpensive disks See RAID.

Reed-Muller code See under ERROR DETECTION AND CORRECTION.

Reed-Solomon code See under ERROR DETECTION AND CORRECTION.

reengineering See under BUSINESS PROCESS RE-ENGINEERING.

re-entrant, reentrant A section of program code is said to be re-entrant if it may safely be executed simultaneously by more than one PROCESS or THREAD. Re-entrant code is a requirement for all PARALLEL and CONCURRENT systems. Obstacles to re-entrancy include sharing of GLOBAL data structures, where the ordering of updates may become problematic, and access to REAL TIME hardware devices. For example, a routine that writes sectors of a hard disk must not be re-entrant, because interruption by another process after the HEADS have been positioned would write data in the wrong place.

reference 1 In any HIGH-LEVEL PROGRAMMING LANGUAGE, an invocation of the name of a program VARIABLE to stand for its current value, so the expression A+B contains two references, one each to A and B. The code that a COMPILER generates from such an expression contains the ADDRESS of A and B rather than their value (that is, a POINTER to their value). See also DEREFERENCE, CALL-BY-REFERENCE, REFERENCE COUNTING.
2 In C++, an instance of a REFERENCE TYPE that is an alias for (i.e. contains the address of) another OBJECT.
3 In a SPREADSHEET, an address used in a formula to indicate a particular cell: for example A1 in the syntax of MICROSOFT EXCEL.

reference counting A GARBAGE COLLECTION algorithm that maintains, for every object in a program, a count of how many other objects are currently pointing to it. If this count reaches zero, that object's memory space can safely be reclaimed, and any objects that it points to will then have their own reference counts decremented by one. The algorithm has difficulty with objects that point to each other in circular fashion, as their counts will never fall below 1.

reference type In C++, a type of variable that contains the ADDRESS of another variable, used mainly to pass PARAMETERS whose values are to be modified. For example

```
void demo(int& x)
```

declares demo's formal parameter x to be a reference to an integer. When called, as say demo(y), the address of y rather than its value is passed into demo, and any assignment to x will change y's value. Ultimately references are POINTERS, differing only in the syntax used to manipulate them, so the above declaration is identical in effect to

```
void demo(int *x)
```

referential integrity A set of desirable properties concerned with consistency and completeness that should be possessed by the data contained in a RELATIONAL DATABASE. For example if Homer has been entered as the spouse of Marge, then Marge should also be recorded as the spouse of Homer, and if one end of this relationship should ever be deleted, then the other end must also be removed. The SQL DATA DEFINITION LANGUAGE contains constructs such as TRIGGERS that help in dealing with such issues of integrity.

referential transparency A program or expression is referentially transparent if any SUBEXPRESSION can be replaced by its value without changing the value of the whole: that is, when there are no hidden side effects that can change the value. Mathematical reasoning, transformations and proofs of correctness can be applied only to expressions with this property, but programs written in conventional PROCEDURAL programming languages are not transparent as assignment to global variables causes hidden side effects. The design goal of FUNCTIONAL LANGUAGES is the achievement of such transparency.

reformat To erase the contents of some rewriteable data storage medium such as a FLOPPY DISK, HARD DISK or tape CARTRIDGE. Quick methods of reformatting a disk simply reset its DIRECTORY pointers, leaving all the data present but inaccessible, to be gradually overwritten by new data. To actually obliterate the data, a much slower LOW-LEVEL FORMAT must be performed, which rewrites the formatting markers that separate every SECTOR.

refresh To update or regenerate the contents of some hardware or software device. The term is used, for example, to describe the redrawing of successive picture frames on a CATHODE RAY TUBE or LCD display (see REFRESH RATE, VERTICAL REFRESH RATE, HORIZONTAL SCAN RATE), and the periodic reading and rewriting of the contents of a DRAM chip to prevent them from being lost. The term is also employed to mean downloading once more a web page whose contents have changed. See also REFRESH RATE.

refresh rate The number of FRAMES per second that can be displayed on a computer's MONITOR screen. To avoid visible FLICKER the refresh rate needs to be above 60 Hz (i.e. frames per second) and on high quality monitors it may exceed 100 Hz.

Regional Bell Operating Company (RBOC) The collective name for the seven US regional telecommunications companies (Bell Atlantic, Nynex, Bell South, Southwestern Bell, Pacific Bell, Ameritech and US West) that were formed as a result of the government-enforced break up of AT&T in 1984. Several have since been absorbed in takeovers; Southwestern Bell and Bell Pacific are now known as SBC, and Nynex merged with Bell Atlantic. See also BABY BELL.

register A storage area, capable of holding a single number, that forms part of some INTEGRATED CIRCUIT such as a MICROPROCESSOR. Since a register is built on the same piece of silicon, the chip's circuits can access its contents more quickly than they can off-chip RAM. The CPU of every computer contains a relatively small cluster of registers (typically in the region of 8 to 64) called its REGISTER FILE, in which it temporarily holds just those data items that are currently being worked on. Because registers are so much more efficient than external memory, they are a precious resource whose pattern of utilization crucially affects the overall performance of any program. Enormous ingenuity is applied both in hardware architecture and COMPILER design to maximize their availability (see REGISTER VARIABLE, REGISTER ALLOCATION, REGISTER ASSIGNMENT, REGISTER RENAMING, REGISTER BYPASS, REGISTER WINDOWING). Other kinds of chip, such as communications chips or sound chips, also often contain registers, which they use to store their working parameters.

register addressing See under ADDRESSING MODE.

register allocation The task of deciding which program VARIABLES should be stored in processor REGISTERS for maximum speed and which should be left in external memory, performed during the compilation of a program

by the COMPILER software. There are typically far fewer registers than variables, and the relative importance of some variables may change during the execution of a program, so this is a complex resource allocation problem that requires advanced mathematical techniques to optimize.

register assignment The final phase of REGISTER ALLOCATION, where particular program variables are matched up with particular REGISTERS.

register bypass A shortcut employed in some RISC processor designs, whereby an instruction that is stalled waiting for the result of a calculation that is occurring later (i.e. further back) in the PIPELINE is allowed to read that result directly, before it has been written back into the REGISTER FILE. This allows the pipeline to be advanced one cycle sooner than otherwise. See also SPECULATIVE EXECUTION.

register-compatible The highest level of compatibility between two different hardware devices that contain INTEGRATED CIRCUITS (for example MICROPROCESSORS or UARTS). It implies that they contain the same number of hardware REGISTERS at the same addresses and therefore, to other software, appear identical. For example many GRAPHICS CARDS and NETWORK INTERFACE CARDS for IBM-compatible PCs are register-compatible even though they use chips from different manufacturers and have different internal architectures. A microprocessor such as the AMD Athlon is register-compatible with Intel's Pentium, which is necessary for it to run the same programs. See also BINARY COMPATIBILITY.

register file That part of the CPU of a computer that contains the REGISTERS in which the values currently being worked on are temporarily stored. The number of registers in the register file has been increasing with each successive generation of microprocessors, 64–128 now being typical. The tendency is to make registers general-purpose so that they can be used interchangeably by programs. However, integer and floating-point values are still stored in separate register files. See also REGISTER ALLOCATION, REGISTER RENAMING, FLOATING-POINT UNIT.

register indirect A processor ADDRESSING MODE under which an instruction contains not the data itself, but rather the name of the REGISTER that holds the address of the data. In ASSEMBLY LANGUAGE, this is conventionally signified by placing the register name in parentheses, so that MOV B, (A) might mean 'load register B with the word whose address is contained in register A'. See also DIRECT ADDRESSING, INDIRECT ADDRESSING, INDEXED ADDRESSING.

register-level Concerning the arrangement of the REGISTERS of a computer.

register renaming A technique employed in many modern microprocessor designs, including the Intel PENTIUM family and many RISCS, to assist in SPECULATIVE EXECUTION of instructions. The chip includes more physical REGISTERS than are nominally contained in the processor's REGISTER FILE, allowing the results of several speculatively executed instructions to be kept in 'spare' registers. Once the outcome is known, the names of these registers are swapped to make them 'real' registers, thus avoiding having to move data from register to register.

register variable In C or C++ programming, a VARIABLE that is declared with the prefix 'register', which forces the compiler to keep its contents in a processor REGISTER for greater access speed.

register windowing A processor architecture feature introduced by Sun's SPARC family of microprocessors, in which only a portion of the physical REGISTER FILE is made visible to programs at any one time, via a moveable 'window' of register addresses. By moving this window, a different set of registers can be brought into play without any data having to be physically moved. See also REGISTER RENAMING.

registry A large data structure employed by all versions of Microsoft's WINDOWS operating system from 95 onwards to store a variety of crucial configuration parameters such as the locations of program files and libraries, file type associations, network passwords and more. The registry is contained in the two files USER.DAT and SYSTEM.DAT, the corruption of either of which can cause Windows to fail to BOOT.

regression testing One of the phases of testing a software product in which a new MODULE is integrated into a larger program, and its added functions tested. The program's previous functions are then re-tested to ensure that the new code has not altered their behaviour. See also TESTING, ALPHA TESTING, BETA TESTING, TEST SUITE.

regular expression A notation for describing patterns in a text, used in the SEARCH-AND-REPLACE functions of the more powerful TEXT EDITORS and SCRIPTING LANGUAGES.

A regular expression is a string of symbols constructed using three principal operations: *concatenation* (where spo matches the first three letters of spot); *alternation* (where sp[io] matches the first three letters of spot or of spit; and *closure* which matches multiple occurences, so a* matches a or aa or aaa and so on. For example the regular expression [ch]o*p would match cop, coop, hop and hoop but not hip, while the expression ="[A-Za-z0-9"]* will find quoted strings preceded by an equal sign, such as ="CREF" or ="Name". The UNIX operating system and the AWK and PERL languages make heavy use of regular expressions, while MS-DOS and many popular word processors support a simpler and weaker subset called WILDCARDS.

Regular expressions were first studied by the mathematician Stephen Kleene in the 1950s as the class of expressions that may be parsed using a FINITE STATE MACHINE.

reinstall To install a computer software product afresh, typically in an attempt to correct some malfunction that may have arisen due to the loss or corruption of one or more of its files. See also INSTALL, UNINSTALLER, DLL HELL.

rekey To retype the contents of a written or printed document into a computer. See also OPTICAL CHARACTER RECOGNITION.

relation 1 In mathematical SET theory, an association between an ordered pair of objects, an example being *is greater than*. Also, a set of such associations between ordered pairs. A relation R is said to be *symmetric* if a R b implies b R a and *transitive* if a R b and b R c implies a R c.

2 In DATABASE engineering, one of the TABLES of data employed in a RELATIONAL DATABASE. This is closely related to meaning 1, as the theory of relational databases was developed on a mathematical basis by Edgar F CODD. The purpose of organizing such data into Codd's

NORMAL FORM is that it permits the mathematical rules of relations to be applied.

relational Designed according to the precepts of the RELATIONAL CALCULUS. See for example RELATIONAL DATABASE.

relational calculus A methodology derived from the PREDICATE CALCULUS by Edgar F CODD, which enables relations between data items to be rigorously defined and which forms the basis of the theory of the RELATIONAL DATABASE. See also RELATION, NORMAL FORM.

relational database A database that is designed using a technique for storing data with minimum redundancy and maximum flexibility of access, based on the relational data model introduced by Edgar F CODD in the early 1970s. Most of the larger business DATABASE MANAGEMENT SYSTEMS, including ORACLE, MICROSOFT ACCESS and SQL SERVER, INGRES and SYBASE, are relational databases.

The most important principle of the relational database is that data is stored in a number of separate TABLES, each of which contains a single RELATION. A table is organized by rows and columns, each row or RECORD containing the same columns or fields. For example a Customers table might contain records that relate Customers to their Addresses, like this:

Customer	Address
A. Jones	2 Acacia Avenue
B. Smith	10 Laburnum Grove

while a second table called Sales relates Customers to products they have purchased:

Customer	Product
A. Jones	spanner
A. Jones	screwdriver
B. Smith	spanner

and a third table, Prices, relates products to their prices:

Product	Price
spanner	34.50
screwdriver	23.50

A conventional FLAT-FILE DATABASE would have stored all this data in a single file, but the relational model requires one relation (Customer/Address, Customer/Product, Product/Price) per table, to maximize the flexibility with which the data can be queried. The SQL query language contains commands such as JOIN and SELECT that pull data items out of different tables and combine them into one result. For example to create an invoice for A. Jones you could perform a join between the Customers and the Sales table, using their shared Customer field, to discover all the products that Jones has purchased, then a join between the Sales and Prices tables on their shared Product field to find the prices. The important point is that such joins are created only temporarily, at runtime during the execution of a query. Data is brought together only when needed for a particular report, and so the structure of the database contains no assumptions about what sort of reports might be required in future.

Another powerful feature of the relational model is that each data item (e.g. customer's address and product price) appears only in a single place in the tables and so needs to be updated only in one place when it changes. Codd defined a preparation process called Normalization, which must be performed on data in order to build an efficient relational database. Normalization involves removing duplication of various different kinds from the data as a sequence of steps called First, Second and Third Normal Forms. This insistence on uniqueness is a strength of the relational model for typical business data structures, but it can also be its biggest weakness when trying to describe complex hierarchical structures (such as the assemblage of parts that goes into making an airliner), and for such tasks the OBJECT DATABASE is now thought by many to be more suitable.

relational database management system, relational DBMS (RDBMS) A software system used to create, maintain and query a RELATIONAL DATABASE. It typically supports the addition, updating and deletion of RECORDS from the database, the creation and deletion of INDEXES, the retrieval of selected groups of records by constructing SQL queries, and the outputting of such selections as a formatted REPORT. Many RDBMSs also contain utilities for QUERY OPTIMIZATION and some type of SCRIPTING LANGUAGE for creating STORED PROCEDURES. All the larger database software in current use, from MICROSOFT ACCESS and SQL SERVER, ORACLE, INFORMIX, SYBASE to IBM's DB2, can be classed as an RDBMS. See also DATABASE MANAGEMENT SYSTEM, RELATIONAL CALCULUS, TRIGGER, QUERY.

relative address **1** A partial memory address that must be added to some BASE ADDRESS to calculate the actual address. See also OFFSET.

2 An alternative name for a RELATIVE REFERENCE in a SPREADSHEET formula.

relative pathname A file PATHNAME that specifies a DIRECTORY other than the current working directory without explicitly stating the location of the latter. So a relative pathname such as src\newprog.pas could equally refer to the file c:\turbo\src\newprog.pas or to the file d:\delphi\src\newprog.pas depending on whether the CURRENT DIRECTORY happens to be c:\turbo or d:\delphi. By using the .. convention for a parent directory, relative pathnames may be made to refer to directories at the same or higher level in the tree than the current directory. Relative pathnames are very useful in BATCH FILES that are to be used in many different contexts.

relative reference In a SPREADSHEET, a cell reference within a formula having the property that, if the formula is copied to another cell, the reference changes to point to the cell in the equivalent relative position. For instance, using the syntax of MICROSOFT EXCEL, suppose cell A1 contains the formula B1+C1. If the formula is copied into cell A2 then the formula automatically changes to B2+C2 (though not if it is *moved* to A2, which is a source of many errors). In Excel all references are relative by default, and to indicate an absolute reference (which always points to the same cell) a $ symbol must be added, as in B1+C1.

relay An electromechanical device that uses an electrical current flowing in one circuit to switch the current in another circuit. Relays were the basic component in older telephone exchanges, but have now mostly been displaced by SOLID-STATE electronics.

release **1** A version of a software product that is on sale to the public. Also the act of putting such a version on sale. See also VERSION, VERSIONING, VERSION CONTROL, ALPHA RELEASE, BETA RELEASE.

2 A legal document that grants permission to use some product, or frees a person of some responsibility.

3 A press release, announcing some event or product.

release candidate A version of a software product under development, typically one that is undergoing late BETA TESTING, that is considered fit to be released for sale.

relevance A measure of how closely some object, such as a file, web page or database record, matches a user's query. Relevance algorithms range from simply looking for the presence of the words contained in the query, counting such occurrences, looking for derivatives (e.g. plural forms) of the query words, through to consulting a thesaurus or dictionary of synonyms, perhaps even in multiple languages. Most SEARCH ENGINES return their results sorted in decreasing order of relevance, and some, such as WAIS, display the numeric relevance score of each found item.

reliability The ability to perform a specified task in a dependable and predictable manner. In many engineering disciplines there is an important trade-off between reliability and AVAILABILITY, in which less reliable components may have to be employed to keep a system permanently ready for use. For example a racing car is required to be 100% reliable when it runs, but needs to run only at infrequent intervals, whereas a public telephone system must be constantly available, but its users may tolerate relatively frequent short faults.

relocatable A computer program that can be loaded into memory and executed at any starting ADDRESS. For a program to be relocatable its MACHINE CODE must use only instructions (for example branches and moves) whose destinations are relative to the start address, and not to absolute addresses. Most modern operating systems require all programs to be written in a relocatable manner. See also EXE.

REM Short for 'remark'. A keyword used in many dialects of the BASIC language (and in MS-DOS BATCH FILES), placed at the start of a line to indicate that the following text is a comment and is not to be executed. Hence the verb 'to REM out' meaning to temporarily remove a line from a program.

remailer An Internet MAIL SERVER that receives emails and forwards them to their destination under a different name to provide anonymity to their sender.

remark See REM.

remote 1 Situated on another computer at the far end of a network or other communication link. The opposite of LOCAL.
2 Shorthand for a REMOTE CONTROL handset.

Remote Access Service (RAS) A service provided in the WINDOWS NT operating system that allows users of a LAN to log in to it via a modem and telephone line from a remote location. RAS does not require such remote users to run Windows NT on their own computers, as there are RAS clients for other versions of Windows.

remote component In a DISTRIBUTED application that is built using a COMPONENT ARCHITECTURE, a software component that resides elsewhere on the network than the local computer, and must either be downloaded or executed remotely when it is called into use. See also DISTRIBUTED APPLICATION ARCHITECTURE, DISTRIBUTED OBJECT SYSTEM, CORBA, DCOM.

remote control 1 A class of software that allows a user to run a distant computer via a communications link. The remote computer's display appears on the local machine's screen, and the user may type input as if they were sitting in front of the remote machine.
2 An electronic device used to control an appliance such as a television, hi-fi or video recorder, usually sending the user's commands via an INFRARED link.

Remote Data Service A Microsoft software technology, formerly known as the Advanced Data Connector (ADC), that enables processes running on remote computers to gain access to data from an OLE DB data source. See also UNIFORM DATA ACCESS.

remote execution To cause a program to be run on a distant computer connected to the local computer via a network or other communication link. See REMOTE CONTROL.
There is a sense in which a user sitting at a DUMB TERMINAL connected to a MAINFRAME computer is performing remote execution, but the term is more usually applied to networked CLIENT/SERVER systems in which users have a choice of whether to run a program locally or on a remote server. Systems such as the X WINDOW SYSTEM, Citrix WINFRAME and Microsoft TERMINAL SERVER exist to support this type of remote execution.

remote login The act of operating, via a network link, a remote computer as if one were sitting at its keyboard. The most commonly used protocols for remote login are TELNET and RLOGIN.

remote management The management of network SERVERS, ROUTERS, printers and other infrastructural devices from an administrator's WORKSTATION elsewhere on the network. Management tasks that may be performed remotely include setting up new user accounts, deleting unwanted data, backing up and defragmenting disks, receiving notifications of paper jams, and setting up address filters and other parameters for a router. The term is mostly reserved for server management tasks, rather than the business of installing software on users' workstations, which is instead labelled as software distribution, or asset or inventory management. See more under NETWORK MANAGEMENT, SNMP, SYSTEMS MANAGEMENT SERVER, CONFIGURATION MANAGEMENT, ASSET MANAGEMENT, INVENTORY MANAGEMENT.

remote method invocation A function provided by the JAVA programming language that enables a Java program running on one computer to execute a method of a Java object running on a different computer, via a network connection. See also REMOTE PROCEDURE CALL.

remote procedure call (RPC) A type of network protocol that permits a program running on one computer to cause code to be executed on a remote computer, and to pass PARAMETERS to it as if it were a local program, without the programmer needing to explicitly write the details of the communication. RPC was invented by SUN MICROSYSTEMS, INC. as part of the NETWORK FILE SYSTEM, and an enhanced version was adopted for the OSF's DISTRIBUTED COMPUTING ENVIRONMENT. RPC is used to implement many kinds of CLIENT/SERVER system, including those based on the Internet, and most modern network operating systems support some version of it.

remote server A network SERVER that is located in a different building, city or country and which may be accessed by means of the INTERNET or other WAN.

removable disk Any disk storage system such as the FLOPPY DISK, ZIP DRIVE or SYQUEST drive in which the storage medium may be removed from the drive and replaced with another.

render To create an image suitable for outputting on a VDU or printer from a geometrical description of that image. Rendering therefore consists of processing a set of numbers that describe locations in some abstract space into a set of PIXEL coordinates and colour values for a real device. The term is employed in computer GRAPHICS and also in typography, where it means to produce a printable BIT-MAPPED character image from an OUTLINE FONT description.

In 3D GRAPHICS, rendering is the last and most time-consuming of the chain of operations required to produce a two-dimensional coloured picture from the internal model of the objects. Scenes from photo-realistic movies such as *Jurassic Park* and *Toy Story* might take hours or even days to render.

render farm A collection of computers, sometimes connected together to form a single parallel computer, used to render the frames of a movie that employs 3D animation sequences.

RenderMan A 3D graphics rendering system developed by Pixar corporation that is widely used to create photo-realistic special effects for movies and computer games. It provides a MARKUP LANGUAGE in which animators can write scripts that perform complex shading operations (see under PROCEDURAL TEXTURE). It also supports ANTIALIASING, RAY TRACING, TEXTURE MAPPING, DEPTH OF FIELD cueing, MOTION BLUR and 3D TRANSPARENCY MAPPING in 24-bit colour. RenderMan is available as a plug-in or extension for the main 3D modelling and animation programs including AUTOCAD.

rendezvous An interaction between two concurrent tasks in which they both pause to establish a point of synchronization, exchange information and then continue with their individual activities. The concept is supported in certain CONCURRENT PROGRAMMING LANGUAGES, most notably in ADA where it is implemented by a specialized form of procedure call defined using the entry and accept constructs.

A named entry defined within one task gives access to some resource, and may be called by another task that wants that resource. However an entry is executed only when the called task is ready, which it signals by executing a corresponding accept statement. In the meantime, the calling task is kept suspended. Accept marks the point of rendezvous at which the calling task is permitted access to the resource.

reorder buffer See under OUT-OF-ORDER EXECUTION.

repaginate To re-divide a document into separate pages following an editing operation such as inserting or deleting text that may have moved the page boundaries. Many modern word processors repaginate continuously and automatically as a BACKGROUND TASK.

repeater In telecommunications and computer networks, a device placed between two stretches of cable to amplify the signal and compensate for any ATTENUATION caused by the length of its journey. Many repeaters are required for a transatlantic telephone cable, while computer LANS may require one in cable run as short as 100 metres, and for this reason most LAN HUBS fulfill the function of a repeater.

repetitive-strain injury See RSI.

replication The copying of all or part of a server-based database onto a remote client computer, the intention being to reduce network traffic by allowing the client to read and alter the data from its local hard disk. Any changes made are later written back to the master database. A typical application for replication would be for a travelling salesperson who needed to consult a company's prices and orders database (from a portable computer) and would otherwise have to do so via a slow and expensive dial-up telephone connection.

The most sophisticated replication schemes treat distributing copies of the database as a TRANSACTION under a full TWO-PHASE COMMIT, to permit recovery from communication failures.

report A printed summary of the results obtained by querying a DATABASE or other software system.

report generator A software module supplied with most database management systems, accounting suites and other kinds of business software, whose purpose is to assist with the formatting of printed output. Nowadays such report generators usually incorporate a degree of VISUAL PROGRAMMING ability that enables a user to design output formats by dragging the required database fields into position on a blank form.

Report Program Generator See RPG.

repository A database used to store all the components of a complex collaborative project. A repository is typically used in conjunction with a VERSION CONTROL system to manage the making of revisions, and to assist this process the repository maintains records of everything checked out and replaced. The contents of a repository may include source code files, compiled library routines and objects for reuse, documents, pictures and videos, workflow statistics and personnel records.

representation A data structure that acts like (or stands in for) some real world entity or quality. For example, a collection of digital bits might stand for the colours in a picture, or for the air pressure changes that constitute a sound wave. The choice of an appropriate representation for the data is the most important part of designing any computer program. See also MODEL, SIMULATION, DATA ANALYSIS, OBJECT-ORIENTED.

re-purpose An ugly coinage, which describes the process of converting text and graphics created with a desktop publishing application for print-on-paper publication so that they can be used on a web site. Re-purposing is typically accomplished by exporting the document from its authoring program in HTML format, and creating a style sheet that applies appropriate fonts and formatting.

request A signal that invites some form of reply from its recipient.

Request For Comments See RFC.

research and development (R&D) The activity of discovering and refining new products.

reserved word In a programming language, any word that has a special meaning within the language and therefore must not be employed by the programmer as an IDENTIFIER: it is *reserved* for use by the computer. For example in BASIC, IF and WHILE are both reserved words.

reset An operation that causes a computer processor to cease executing the current program, clear all its register contents to zero, and begin executing the program again from its first instruction. This is sometimes called a HARD RESET, in contrast to the SOFT RESET provided by some processors which restarts the program without clearing the register contents.

Reset is performed by sending an electrical signal on a processor pin reserved for that purpose, typically activated whenever the computer's power switch is turned on. Many manufacturers also provide a RESET BUTTON, separate from the power switch, which the user can press to escape if a program fault causes the computer to HANG. See also REBOOT.

reset button A switch, usually fitted on the front panel of a computer, which when pressed causes a HARD RESET of the CPU, typically causing the computer to reload its operating system from disk (see under REBOOT). See also HANG, CRASH, THREE-FINGER SALUTE.

resistance A measure of the opposition of an electrical conductor to the flow of electric current. The unit of resistance is the OHM; if a current of one ampere flows when a potential of one volt is applied, the resistance is one ohm.

resistor An electronic component used to add a known RESISTANCE to a circuit. Resistors may be made from carbon, wire or metal film depending on the current they are required to carry. Some are painted with colour coded stripes that indicate their value in OHMS.

resize To alter the size of a screen window or other graphical object by dragging on some kind of visual HANDLE using the MOUSE POINTER.

resolution 1 In an optical instrument (e.g. a telescope) or a computer input or output device, the power to distinguish between different points. For example the resolution of a computer MONITOR is the maximum number of distinct PIXELS it can display, measured in horizontal and vertical rows, say 1024×768.

The resolution of a printer is the fineness of the ink dots that it can reproduce, usually measured in DPI (dots per inch).

2 In logic, a mechanical technique for proving statements by elimination, employed in the PROLOG computer language.

3 In networking, the translation of a human-readable computer name (for example a URL or FULLY QUALIFIED DOMAIN NAME) into a numeric network address that computer hardware can use. See, for example, more under DNS.

resource 1 In general, any facility required to support the course of a computation, most notably processor time, memory and disk storage space, but also often extended to include operating system services, device drivers and utility programs.

2 Under many operating systems, the name given to data (particularly FONTS and ICONS) that are stored within an executable program rather than as separate files.

Under the Windows operating system in particular, a type of data structure used to store DESCRIPTORS for graphical and other objects stored in memory. Running out of resources was a common cause of system CRASHES under 16-bit versions of Windows.

resource compiler A special kind of compiler provided in several GRAPHICAL USER INTERFACES (GUI), notably Microsoft WINDOWS and Apple's MACOS, which does not compile executable program code but rather data items (namely scripts that define GUI components such as MENUS, DIALOGUES, ICONS, help files and message texts), which may then be included in executable files. See also RESOURCE, RESOURCE FORK.

resource fork A separate partition within each data file on the Apple MACINTOSH that contains a collection of program CODE segments, ICONS, BITMAPS and various parameter values, in contrast to a DATA FORK, which contains the file's actual data.

resource-hungry A computer program that makes heavy demands on memory space, disk space or processor time.

Resource Interchange File Format See RIFF.

Resource Reservation Protocol (RSVP) A network-control protocol that will one day enable Internet applications to request a special QUALITY OF SERVICE (QoS) for their data transmissions. It was invented at the University of Southern California and Xerox PARC, and is currently being standardized by the INTERNET ENGINEERING TASK FORCE. RSVP is not a ROUTING protocol but works in conjunction with routing protocols, installing its own dynamic access lists along the routes that routing protocols calculate – it occupies the TRANSPORT LAYER of the OSI REFERENCE MODEL. However, it is not yet implemented over large parts of the Internet.

Under RSVP, each application's data flow is regarded as a sequence of messages having the same source, destination(s) and QoS requirement. The latter is communicated by a flow specification, a data structure used by Internet hosts to request special service from the network. RSVP supports three traffic types – best-effort, rate-sensitive and delay-sensitive – but the precise type of flow-control used to support these traffic types may depend on the implementation of a particular network's transfer protocol (e.g. whether ASYNCHRONOUS TRANSFER MODE (ATM) or FRAME RELAY).

Best-effort traffic is traditional IP traffic, as used for FILE TRANSFER and EMAIL transmission. *Rate-sensitive traffic* is willing to accept a variable arrival time for a guaranteed data rate; if an application requests 100 kilobits per second (kbps) of BANDWIDTH but actually sends 200 kbps for extended periods, the router may choose to delay its delivery (applications, such as videoconferencing, that were originally designed for ISDN or ATM may need this type of traffic). *Delay-sensitive traffic* requires timely delivery, but will accept a variable rate. MPEG 2 video is of this type, where only the sporadic KEY FRAMES require a guaranteed arrival time and the in-between frames can tolerate a variable rate. See also CONGESTION, TUNNELLING PROTOCOL, IP MULTICAST.

resource sharing The sharing of data files and peripherals such as printers and modems between different users of a network.

response time The delay before a response to some REQUEST or COMMAND is received.

restart 1 To cause a program, process or transaction to be executed again from the beginning. If that program is the computer's

OPERATING SYSTEM, the act is more often called a REBOOT.

2 A stage in the process of resetting a computer's processor in which the processor visits an address called the *restart vector* that contains the first program instruction that it is to execute. For example, in a Pentium Pro system the reset procedure sets the CS register to OFFFF:OFOooh and the EIP register to OFFFOh, forcing the first code fetch to be from the restart vector at OFFFF:FFFOh. See also RESET.

restart vector See under RESTART.

restore 1 To replace lost or damaged data with a copy retrieved from a BACKUP set.

2 To cause a screen window to return to its previous size after it has been MINIMIZED or MAXIMIZED.

restore window button A visual user interface component used in operating systems such as WINDOWS and MACOS. It returns to its original size a screen window that has been MINIMIZED or MAXIMIZED. It is typically a small square button in one of the upper corners of the window border. See also CLOSE BOX, CONTROL MENU.

result code See under RETURN CODE.

resume In general, to continue some process from where it left off after an interruption. For example, many portable computers have a SUSPEND mode that freezes all running programs in their current state. Pressing Resume restarts them all where they left off.

Some programming languages and operating systems employ a pair of commands called suspend and resume to implement CO-OPERATIVE MULTITASKING. A task calls suspend and then 'goes to sleep' until some other task calls resume to awaken it. For example THREADS in JAVA support such a mechanism.

retardation film A layer introduced into an LCD display to improve its contrast.

retina scan A BIOMETRIC identification method that recognizes unique patterns of capillaries in the retina of the human eye. Retina scan is more accurate than the more commonly used IRIS RECOGNITION, and cannot be deceived by wearing contact lenses. However it requires placing the eye a centimetre from the camera and holding the head still, which is too intrusive for any but the most draconian of security regimes.

retire See under OUT-OF-ORDER EXECUTION.

retransmit To send a message again because of an error in its previous transmission. See ERROR DETECTION AND CORRECTION.

retrieve To extract an item of data from some storage device or data structure.

retrofit Originally, to fit an improved part from a later version to an older version of some machine such as an aircraft. Now applied by analogy to software systems.

retry To re-attempt some failed act of communication or data access.

return 1 To supply a found or calculated value (called the *return value*) to an entity that has requested it. For example a database query returns records located from the database to the user, or the value of a FUNCTION is returned to the program that called it.

2 A common abbreviation for CARRIAGE RETURN.

return channel In a CLIENT/SERVER system, the communication channel that returns a user's responses from the client to the server. The term is typically used of those services (such as web access via satellite or cable television) in which the return channel is of a different kind to the down channel, for example by public telephone and modem. See also BACK CHANNEL.

return code Also called a *result code*, a numeric code returned by certain program functions or subroutines (particularly DEVICE DRIVERS, communications functions and file I/O functions) to indicate the success or failure of the operation.

return-delimited A standard TEXT FILE format often used to transport data between different database or spreadsheet programs in which each RECORD occupies a separate line – that is, the records are separated by CARRIAGE RETURNS. The individual fields within each record might, for example, be COMMA-DELIMITED or TAB-DELIMITED, both of which formats are typically return-delimited between records.

return from subroutine (RET or RTN) A class of MACHINE CODE instruction employed to terminate execution of a SUBROUTINE and restore execution to its previous course. See more under JUMP TO SUBROUTINE.

RETURN key A large key situated on the right-hand edge of a computer keyboard which is used both to end lines of typed text (like the CARRIAGE RETURN on a typewriter, hence the name) and also to signal that a current command is complete and should now be executed. Hence on older keyboards it may be labelled Return or Enter (see ENTER KEY), but nowadays it is typically marked with the internationally recognized, language-independent symbol ↵.

return type The data type of the value to be returned by a FUNCTION, which in STRONGLY TYPED programming languages must be declared when the function is declared. See also FUNCTION DECLARATION.

return value See under RETURN.

reusability A property of a section of program CODE that permits it to be reused within a different program. Reusability is highly desirable, to reduce program creation time by building libraries of frequently used routines. However, it is difficult to achieve in practice, partly owing to differences between languages, hardware and operating systems, but more so because to be reusable, a section of code must be free of dependencies on the rest of the program it inhabits. The goal of much programming language research, for example in OBJECT-ORIENTED PROGRAMMING, is to promote reusability.

reverse engineer 1 To examine a COMPILED computer program and attempt to reconstruct its SOURCE CODE so that its operations can be imitated or modified. One reason for doing this is for purposes of PIRACY, but reverse engineering may have legitimate purposes, including the maintenance or updating of LEGACY CODE whose source has been lost, or the construction of an interface between new code and some commercial program whose source code is not available. See also DECOMPILER, DISASSEMBLER, OBFUSCATION, ROUND-TRIP ENGINEERING, CASE TOOL.

2 To examine an INTEGRATED CIRCUIT, using for example X-rays and electron microscopes, to discover how it works. Using such knowledge to duplicate the chip exactly would be a clear violation of any patent and/or copyright, but the practice is nevertheless widespread in the semiconductor industry for intelligence-gathering purposes. For example it might be used to determine how a rival is implementing some new feature, which may then be provided in a different way. See also CLEAN ROOM.

Reverse Polish Notation See POSTFIX NOTATION.

revert To restore the contents of the current working file to what they were before the last Save command. This facility is offered on the File menu of many text processing and graphics programs. See also UNDO.

rewritable Any type of storage medium that is capable of having data written, deleted and rewritten to it. For example, hard and floppy disks are rewritable.

REXX (Restructured EXtended eXecutor) A powerful SCRIPTING LANGUAGE created by IBM for its VM and MVS mainframe operating systems, but now available on almost all computing platforms.

RFC (Request For Comments) A series of documents in which the technologies used to build the INTERNET are defined and discussed, starting from RFC 1 in 1969 and now running beyond RFC 2580. The development of the Internet has been a unique example of a distributed, democratically controlled project: a technical expert puts forward an RFC proposing some change or innovation, and the whole community discusses, criticizes, and possibly participates in its implementation. Not all RFCs become standards, but all Internet standards are expressed in RFCs (which also have an alternative STD number). Crucial RFCs include 791, which defines the IP protocol, 793, which defines Transmission Control Protocol (TCP) and 822, which defines the Internet EMAIL format. RFCs may be read at http://ds.internic.net/rfc/ though they are also held at many other MIRROR sites.

RFI See RADIO FREQUENCY INTERFERENCE.

RGB A shorthand used to describe binary data or electrical signals that are encoded according to the RGB COLOUR MODEL (red, green, blue). Hence:

1 (software) A file of RGB data contains triplets of numbers, representing the intensities of red, green and blue light at one point in an image.

2 (hardware) An RGB signal requires three wires, one each for the red, blue and green components.

RGB colour model Short for Red, Green, Blue. A COLOUR MODEL in which these are the three primary colours, and other colours can be created by mixing them in different proportions. The human eye operates according to an RGB model, having separate cone receptors in the retina for red, green and blue light. RGB is also the colour model employed by all computer VDUS, based on the use of red, green and blue PHOSPHORS in a CATHODE RAY TUBE, or red, green and blue filters over an LCD screen.

RGB is not, however, the appropriate colour model for describing printed or painted materials, whose appearance depends on absorption from reflected light rather than emission. For reflected light the primary colours are cyan, yellow and magenta, as used in printing inks. See also CMYK, HSV.

Rhapsody The name once given to the latest version of Apple's MACOS operating system, now called MacOS X.

rich text Any text file format that offers more formatting options than PLAIN ASCII. In addition to the character and line-break information, it may specify type styles such as bold and italic, different FONTS and character sizes, and higher-level document structures such as tables, mathematical formulae, tables of contents and hyperlinks. Strictly-speaking, MARKUP LANGUAGES such as HTML and SGML can be described as rich text formats (since they are not binary formats and contain only ASCII characters), but the term is often taken to refer to Microsoft's RTF format.

Rich Text Format See RTF.

RIFF (Resource Interchange File Format) A class of file storage format employed by Microsoft and various other vendors to store audio and image information. Like TIFF, RIFF is a 'chunk' based scheme in which many different pieces of data may be stored within the same file, with a HEADER that explains how to find and interpret them. An example is the WAV audio file format which contains PCM audio data along with a RIFF header.

right-click The action of clicking the right-hand button of a two-button MOUSE.

right-click menu A context-dependent menu that appears in Microsoft WINDOWS applications whenever the right-hand MOUSE BUTTON is clicked. See also CONTEXT MENU.

ring 1 In the Intel 80x86 family of microprocessors from the 80386 onwards, one of the four internal protection levels called rings 0 to 3. All application software and ordinary DEVICE DRIVERS run at ring 3 protection, whereas ring 0 is reserved for the most privileged code (such as the operating system KERNEL), and offers direct access to I/O ports and disk drives.

2 Any NETWORK TOPOLOGY that takes the form of a closed circle. See, for example, TOKEN RING.

3 An undesirable condition in which a signal reflects back from the termination of a communication line to interfere with subsequent signals – named by analogy to the long fading of a bell note.

RIP 1 In computer graphics and printing, an abbreviation of RASTER IMAGE PROCESSOR.

2 In networking, an abbreviation of ROUTING INFORMATION PROTOCOL

rip 1 To render a document page for printing using a RASTER IMAGE PROCESSOR (RIP).

2 To copy the contents of a commercial music CD onto a CD-R using a CD writer.

RISC (reduced instruction set computer) A class of PROCESSOR ARCHITECTURE, developed out of research at Berkeley in 1980, in which instructions that perform complex calculations are eschewed in favour of simple instructions that execute in a single CLOCK CYCLE. Complex tasks must be performed by a succession of such simple instructions (see also INSTRUCTION SET). Thus streamlined, the hardware can run at faster clock rates, at the cost of larger, more complex software (dealt with by writing more intelligent COMPILERS).

RISC processors such as Motorola's POWER-PC and the DEC ALPHA were once thought to threaten Intel's market lead, but Intel cleverly incorporated many of the better features of RISC into its PENTIUM architecture, and maintained supremacy.

The basic principles that constitute the RISC design philosophy are:

• All instructions to execute in one clock cycle.
• No MICROCODE – instruction bits act directly to control processor subunits.
• Provide lots of REGISTERS for working data. All data must be loaded into a register for processing, then stored back into memory (the so-called LOAD/STORE ARCHITECTURE) with no register-to-memory operations.

Processors that do not follow these principles, such as older Intel designs, are called CISC (Complex Instruction Set Computers).

RISC OS The operating system employed by ACORN'S ARCHIMEDES and subsequent ARM-based personal computers. It was a multitasking, graphical operating system that in some respects (for example memory management and graphics performance) was superior to either WINDOWS or MACOS.

RISC PC A range of personal computers, produced by ACORN from 1994 until 1998, that contained both Intel and ARM processors and could run both the Windows and RISC OS operating systems.

Ritchie, Dennis (b. 1941) The co-inventor with Ken THOMPSON of the UNIX operating system, and inventor of the C programming language, both at BELL LABORATORIES in the early 1960s. Ritchie is also the co-author with Brian Kernighan of the first and definitive text book on matters of C syntax *The C Programming Language*, sometimes referred to by C programmers simply as the *White Book*.

Rivest, Shamir, Adleman encryption See RSA ENCRYPTION.

RLE Abbreviation of RUN-LENGTH ENCODING.

rlogin (remote login) A Unix software utility that enables computer users to LOG ON to remote computers over a network. See also TELNET.

RMI Abbreviation of REMOTE METHOD INVOCATION.

road-warrior A mock-heroic term for frequent travellers (such as business executives and salesmen) who 'arm' themselves with the latest computer and mobile telephone technology.

robot 1 A mechanical device that performs physical tasks under control of a computer program. Derived from the Slav word for a worker, the term was coined in 1920 by Czech playright Karel Capek to describe a humanoid machine. Modern robots – which are widely used to assemble, for example, cars and computers – tend to imitate only the human arm and hand rather than the whole body. The discipline that designs and programs robots is called ROBOTICS.
2 Another name for the class of SPIDER or crawler programs that can be sent out onto the Internet to collect information. This usage is often abbreviated to 'bot.

robotics The branch of engineering that designs and programs ROBOTS.

robust Able to operate in the face of adverse conditions. Of a software product in particular, it implies an ability to recover from most ERROR CONDITIONS and from badly-formed input data.

Rockwell A US SEMICONDUCTOR manufacturer that specializes in making MODEM CHIP SETS.

ROFL Online shorthand for Rolls On Floor Laughing. Used in online discussion groups to indicate amusement.

role-playing game See under GAME.

rollback, roll back, roll-back The ability to undo a network TRANSACTION that has failed so that none of the data involved is left in a damaged state. See also ATOMIC, ACID, TRANSACTION COMMIT.

roll-forward The opposite of ROLLBACK, that is, to restore the values of some TRANSACTION that has been undone.

roll out, rollout Computer industry jargon for the deployment of a new product to its users.

roll-over A type of on-screen button, much used on WEB SITES, that changes its colour, shape or other features whenever the MOUSE POINTER passes over it. The name comes from the illuminated buttons set into the deck of a mechanical pinball machine.

ROM (read-only memory) A type of memory chip whose contents, once written, cannot be erased, and is therefore used to store permanent information that must persist even when the computer is switched off. For example ROM is used to store the program needed to BOOTSTRAP a computer's operating system from disk.

The earliest types of ROM worked using fusible metal links that could be selectively broken by passing current, and the process of storing information into a ROM is still called 'blowing a ROM' even though most modern ROMs are electrically erasable devices. See also PROM, EPROM, FLASH MEMORY.

root 1 The first NODE in any TREE-STRUCTURED hierarchy, from which all the other nodes are descendants.

2 A shorthand for ROOT DIRECTORY.

3 Under UNIX and many other operating systems, a privileged USER ACCOUNT that is granted the power to override all access PERMISSIONS. An administrator who logs on as 'root' may access all the system's resources for maintenance purposes. Also called the SUPER-USER account.

4 The principal form of a word, from which other forms or inflections may be derived by adding suffixes and prefixes. For example from the root 'go', forms such as 'goes', 'gone' and 'going' are derived.

root directory The first DIRECTORY in a HIER-ARCHICAL FILE SYSTEM, of which all other directories are SUBDIRECTORIES. On a typical PC for example, C : \ is the root directory of the boot drive.

root node The single first NODE from which a TREE structure is constructed.

rotate 1 To turn around an axis, to revolve.

2 To exchange a group of items (for example daily BACKUP tapes) in a circular fashion so that the last eventually becomes first again.

3 A class of BITWISE arithmetic operations that shift bits to the left or right along a REGIS-TER but preserve any that get shifted out and reintroduce them at the other end, like the rotation of a continuous chain. Compare this with SHIFT operations, which lose the bits that fall off the end.

round To remove the fractional part of a number, leaving an INTEGER remainder. If this is the next integer larger than the original number it is said to be 'rounded up' while if smaller it is 'rounded down'. In mathematics the convention is that numbers whose fractional part is .5 or greater round up, while .49999... or smaller rounds down. See also FLOOR, CEILING, TRUNCATE.

round robin The simplest possible scheduling algorithm, under which each participant is given an equal turn in strict rotation. Round robin schedulers are usually encountered in systems that employ a COOPERATIVE MULTI-TASKING scheme.

round-trip engineering The ability of an automated software design tool or CASE TOOL to extract a design SCHEMA from a program's SOURCE CODE, as well as to produce program code from a schema. This ability enables new products to be developed by REVERSE ENGI-NEERING existing programs and adding new sections to them, all within the same development environment.

route 1 *n*. The sequence of network NODES that a message traverses to reach its final destination.

2 *v*. To steer messages through a communication network toward their intended destination. In a packet-switched network, routing is performed by reading address information stored in the header of each PACKET. This happens within a series of intermediate computers along the route called ROUTERS, each of which passes on the packet to the next, like a relay baton. See also ROUTING TABLE, ROUTING INFORMATION PROTOCOL, PACKET SWITCHING.

router A hardware device that connects two or more NETWORKS or NETWORK SEGMENTS to form a single internetwork, by forwarding data PACKETS from one network into another. A router is a small dedicated computer with its own memory, microprocessor and multiple network connectors. The router examines the HEADER of each packet addressed to itself, and calculates which outgoing connection offers the best route toward that packet's destination, by consulting ROUTING TABLES stored in its memory that describe the layouts of the networks. A router, unlike a GATEWAY, normally requires the same network PROTOCOL to be used on all the networks it connects.

Routers may be used to break up a large LAN (local area network) into several more manageable segments, to join a LAN to the Internet or other WAN (wide-area network), and to make DIAL-UP connections via the public telephone networks. Some routers are capable of performing extra processing duties, such as encrypting packet headers for a VIRTUAL PRIVATE NETWORK, or other security and access-control tasks. See also HUB, BRIDGE.

routine A self-contained section of program code with a well-defined action: a SUBROUTINE.

routing The process by which network traffic is guided from one SWITCH or ROUTER to the next until it reaches its final destination. In a complex network such as the public telephone system there will be many alternative paths between any two points, making routing a demanding discipline. Routing algorithms employ various criteria to optimize routes, seek perhaps the minimum number of steps, or to avoid the most loaded links.

Routing Information Protocol 1 (RIP) An Internet routing protocol that operates by seeking the shortest route to a destination, as defined in Internet standard STD 34. See also ROUTING, ROUTER.

2 A routing protocol, wholly unrelated to **1**, that is used by NOVELL NETWARE.

routing table A list stored in the memory of a network ROUTER, containing the addresses of the other routers to which it is connected. The router inspects certain bits in the HEADER of each message PACKET it receives, uses these as an index into the routing table, then forwards the packet to the address so retrieved. See also ROUTING.

row One of the horizontal sections into which a TABLE or SPREADSHEET is divided. See also COLUMN.

row address An address placed on the memory BUS of a computer to select which row of the RAM is to be read from. Once this address has been accepted, the COLUMN ADDRESS can be set and data read or written. See also ROW ADDRESS STROBE, COLUMN ADDRESS STROBE.

Row Address Strobe The electrical signal used to tell a RAM chip that a new ROW ADDRESS is ready to be selected. See also COLUMN ADDRESS STROBE.

row-and-column format Any grid-like arrangement of data such as a SPREADSHEET or a database TABLE.

row heading In a SPREADSHEET, the title given to a row, which appears in its leftmost cell.

RPC See REMOTE PROCEDURE CALL.

RPG (Report Program Generator) One of the earliest automatic PROGRAM GENERATORS, released by IBM in 1965 for its 360 series of minicomputers to simplify the production of sophisticated reports. RPG/400 is still used on many AS/400 machines.

RPN See REVERSE POLISH NOTATION.

RS-232 The most commonly employed standard for ASYNCHRONOUS SERIAL communications. Almost every personal computer has at least one RS-232 port which is typically labelled as a SERIAL PORT or COMMUNICATION PORT, and can be used to connect modems, mice, printers and other peripheral devices.

RS-232 is an Electronics Industry Association 'Recommended Standard' (hence the RS) which defines only the gender and pin usage of the connectors but not their shape (which is most commonly either a 9 or a 25 pin socket). The electrical signals are the subject of a separate standard called RS-423. The RS-232 standard originally classified all equipment as being either DATA COMMUNICATION EQUIPMENT (DCE), which historically meant a modem, or Data Terminal Equipment (DTE), which meant the computer or terminal, but this distinction is frequently ignored nowadays.

RS/6000 IBM's RISC processor and the range of Unix WORKSTATIONS built around it.

RSA encryption (Rivest, Shamir, Adleman encryption) A widely used algorithm for PUBLIC-KEY ENCRYPTION, named after its authors.

RSI (repetitive-strain injury) A class of muscular and nervous injuries caused by repeatedly performing some operation that enforces the same set of limb movements. Long periods of typing at a keyboard may cause such injury unless care is taken to achieve a suitable position and posture. See also TENDINITIS, TENO-SYNOVITIS and CARPAL TUNNEL SYNDROME.

RSVP Abbreviation of RESOURCE RESERVATION PROTOCOL.

RTF (Rich Text Format) A text format developed by Microsoft to permit interchange of documents between its Word WORD PROCESSOR and other document-processing software, while preserving layout features such as fonts and headlines, bold and italic (but not embedded pictures or other Office documents). Unlike Word's native .DOC file, which is a BINARY file format, RTF files are TEXT FILES that contain all their formatting information in the form of embedded TAGS, as in:

```
\f21\froman\fcharset186\fprq2
Times New Roman Baltic;
\par This is some \lquote Rich Text
\rquote
```

RTFM (read the f***ing manual) An exhortation often directed at online users who ask too many obvious questions.

RTN See RETURN FROM SUBROUTINE.

RTOS See REAL TIME EXECUTIVE

RTS Abbreviation of Request To Send. See under FLOW CONTROL.

rubber-banding A visual device employed in many GRAPHICS and COMPUTER AIDED DESIGN programs in which lines or boxes drawn on the screen behave as if made of elastic, allowing the user to stretch them to the desired size and position. A rubber-band box is typically used to select an area of an image for copying See also MARQUEE.

rule A proposition of the form 'if this condition holds, then do that action' that is employed as means of encoding human expertise in a type of EXPERT SYSTEM program known as a rule-based system. See also BACKWARD CHAINING, INDUCTION.

rule-based system, rule-driven system The preferred name for the most popular type of EXPERT SYSTEM, which encodes human skills collected from some particular domain as a database of hierarchical PRODUCTION RULES of the form:

```
IF <has wings> THEN <try bird, bat,
insect>.
```

The technical challenges that rule-based systems face are firstly to extract the knowledge from a human expert in useable form, and secondly to ensure that the database of rules is self-consistent, which is an inherently difficult task. For this reason, in recent years rule-based systems have to some extent given way to more empirical approaches such as CASE BASED REASONING.

rule-driven See under RULE-BASED SYSTEM.

ruler, ruler bar A line or bar bearing unit marks that is displayed along the edge of a graphics or word processing program's screen to enable the user to accurately estimate the size of parts of the document or image. In a WORD PROCESSOR the ruler may also be the place where TAB STOPS are set and MARGINS altered.

runes Sarcastic description of highly cryptic command sequences, particularly those created by Unix GURUS.

run-length encoding (RLE) A simple DATA COMPRESSION algorithm that looks for repeated elements and replaces them with a single element followed by a count. Hence a character string such as aaaaaabbbcccc could be compressed to a6b3c4. RLE is effective only on data with long repeated runs, because turning, say, aabbcc into a2b2c2 achieves no compression. It is therefore very effective on flat-shaded computer graphics that contain long sequences of identical PIXEL values, but very poor on continuous tone photographs, where each pixel tends to differ from its neighbour.

run time, runtime, run-time Any occasion when a program is being operated by a user, in contrast to those occasions when it is being COMPILED from its SOURCE CODE by a programmer. The significance of the distinction is that aspects of the program that might be alterable at COMPILE TIME are frozen at run time, and some classes of error that might be intercepted by a DEBUGGER at compile time may cause the program to crash with loss of data if encountered at run time.

run-time environment The context that a computer program encounters when it is executed by a user. Factors that form part of this context include the particular VERSION of the OPERATING SYSTEM and its various subsystems, the amount of free memory and disk space available and the presence of other running programs. A program's developers must try to anticipate all such factors, and failure to do so gives rise to a whole class of BUGS.

run-time error Any error that occurs during the use of a program, rather than while it is being written. The ideal of programming would be to catch all errors at COMPILE TIME and eliminate them, but in practice this is not possible and the best that can be done is to TRAP run-time errors in such a way that they do not CRASH the whole computer or lead to data loss.

run-time library In an INTERPRETED programming language, a collection of MACHINE CODE routines that must be supplied along with all programs written. The language INTERPRETER (which may be contained in the LIBRARY file) calls these routines to execute each source instruction in the program. An example is the VBRUN.DLL file required by VISUAL BASIC programs.

run-time system A piece of auxiliary software that must be present in order to run a program. Programs that are written in INTERPRETED languages such as VISUAL BASIC or JAVA require a run-time system that contains the INTERPRETER.

S

SAA (Systems Application Architecture) A family of standard interfaces devised by IBM for its range of MAINFRAME and MINICOMPUTERS, which are intended to enable the same applications to be run on various processor types running the VM, MVS, OS/2 or AS/400 operating systems. The standard has attracted little adherence in the personal computing world.

safety-critical system Any mechanical or electronic system upon whose correct functioning human lives depend. Examples include steering mechanisms for vehicles from cars to aeroplanes, medical equipment, escape equipment such as fire escapes and ship's lifeboats.

Over the centuries, engineers have developed certain principles for such systems, including the concept of FAIL-SAFE design and the duplication of key components to provide backup. A continuing inability to produce guaranteed-correct software complicates the design of safe computerized systems, but these older principles still apply. Safety-critical hardware and software systems employ fail-safe operation modes and REDUNDANCY – multiple copies of crucial chips and programs.

Samba A suite of free UNIX software that enables files and printers to be shared with computers running other operating systems such as WINDOWS. Samba is a CLIENT/SERVER system that employs the Server Message Block (SMB) protocol.

sample To measure the magnitude of some ANALOGUE quantity at a particular instant, and then to create a DIGITAL representation of the value so obtained. For example, the voltage output by an analogue microphone might be sampled thousands of times per second to make a digital sound recording, or a digital scanner used to sample the reflectivity of a picture over a grid of points. Also used as a noun to describe one such measured value. See also SAMPLING RATE.

sampling 1 The process of turning an ANALOGUE signal into a DIGITAL signal by taking SAMPLES at fixed time intervals.
2 In electronic music production, the process of taking a short sequence from an existing audio recording and incorporating it into a new recording.

sampling rate The number of measurements made per second when converting an ANALOGUE signal into a DIGITAL one. For example, the ordinary music CD contains sounds sampled at 44 thousand 16-bit samples per second. The sampling rate should be sufficiently high to capture all the required level of detail from the analogue signal, which as a rule means twice as frequent as the highest frequency in the signal being sampled: this is called the NYQUIST FREQUENCY. See also SAMPLE, CD-QUALITY.

SAN 1 Abbreviation of STORAGE AREA NETWORK.
2 Abbreviation of SYSTEM AREA NETWORK.

sandbox A concept introduced by the JAVA programming language to guard against malicious damage inflicted by programs shared over the Internet. Any Java APPLET downloaded from a remote computer is forced to run within a highly constrained software environment called the sandbox (by analogy with a safe play area for children) which for example prevents it from writing to a local disk drive and so nullifies any attempted VIRUS or TROJAN HORSE attack.

Sandia National Laboratory A US Government research establishment based in Albuquerque, New Mexico, that pursues world-class work in SUPERCOMPUTERS and other areas of computing. See also LAWRENCE LIVERMORE NATIONAL LABORATORY, LOS ALAMOS NATIONAL LABORATORY.

sanity check A rough interim check performed during the development of a program (or mathematical calculation) to see that the results are reasonable and no gross error has been made.

sans serif, sans A typeface, such as Univers or Arial, that does not employ SERIFS.

Santa Cruz Operation US vendor of the SCO UNIX operating system for INTEL processors.

SAP (Service Advertisement Protocol) A protocol used by NOVELL NETWARE networks to resolve the textual names of network services, such as printers and fileservers, into real network addresses. Each service sends out periodic SAP requests that register its type and name, and clients can access services by sending an SAP request for services of a given type, or by searching the BINDERY for registered services.

SAP AG A German software firm that develops large business automation suites for MAINFRAME and MINICOMPUTERS. Its R/3 suite is widely used in factory and business resource planning and automation.

SAPI **1** (Speech Application Programming Interface) Microsoft's standard APPLICATION PROGRAMMING INTERFACE for writing SPEECH SYNTHESIS and SPEECH RECOGNITION software to run under Windows versions from 95 onward.
   2 Abbreviation of SCHEDULING APPLICATION PROGRAMMING INTERFACE.

SASI (Shugart Associates System Interface) A fast hard disk interface developed by NCR and Shugart Associates in 1981. The ANSI X3T9 standards committee adopted SASI as a working document for what became the SCSI interface.

SATAN (Security Administrator Tool for Analysing Networks) A software tool that can simulate various types of HACK ATTACK on a network. It may be used to test and improve the system's security measures. See also FIREWALL.

satellite, satellite communications The sending of radio, television, voice telephone and data signals around the world by relaying them through TRANSPONDERS contained within Earth-orbiting artificial satellites. Satellite communication can potentially reach the most remote parts of the Earth's surface without costly terrestrial cable laying, though it incurs the enormous capital cost of building and launching satellites.

Current satellite television and telephone systems operate at radio frequencies beyond 10,000 gigahertz, allowing them to carry many BROADCAST channels and potentially to offer superior BANDWIDTH for Internet connections (trial systems offer up to 40 megabits per second). However such speeds are possible only in one direction, from SERVER to user, owing to practical limitations on domestic aerials. Signals in the reverse direction currently have to be carried by terrestrial telephone link. This limitation can be overcome by hybrid systems that use MOBILE PHONE networks to concentrate signals onto long-distance satellite links, as in the GSM phone system and its successors based on PACKET RADIO. The highly successful GPS (Global Positioning System) works via satellite communication.

Sather An advanced experimental OBJECT-ORIENTED PROGRAMMING LANGUAGE developed at Berkeley that supports STRONG TYPE CHECKING and separate INHERITANCE of types and their implementations.

satisfiability problem A class of LOGIC problems that require values to be found for the variables in a BOOLEAN expression that make the whole expression true. Such problems are known to be computationally INTRACTABLE, and have been proved to be NP-COMPLETE.

saturate To send as much data down a communication channel, or to a computer processor, as it can handle.

saturation That aspect of a perceived colour that represents its content of pure chromatic colour. See also COLOUR MODEL, HUE, SATURATION, LIGHTNESS, BRIGHTNESS.

save The act of copying wanted data from a computer's volatile internal RAM onto some more permanent storage medium such as a magnetic or optical disk. This prevents the loss of the data when the computer's power is switched off (hence the name) and allows the data to be retrieved for future reading or editing when it is turned on again. Saving data in named FILES is a principal purpose of a computer's OPERATING SYSTEM, though the user typically performs the save action from within each separate application program using a menu option or command called Save. It is good practice to save very frequently to avoid losing valuable data because of a software CRASH or power failure. Some applications allow saving to be performed automatically at prescribed intervals.

Save As... A menu option presented by almost all application programs that permits the current DATA FILE to be saved to disk as a new file under a different name. See also SAVE, REVERT.

SB AWE32 A WAVETABLE version of the popular SOUNDBLASTER sound card.

SBus The EXPANSION BUS used in SUN workstations for adding peripherals such as printers.

scalability The ability of a system to be extended in size while maintaining proportional performance – for example, a MULTIPROCESSOR computer is said to be scalable if doubling the number of processors roughly doubles its processing speed. Scalability always has limits beyond which diminishing returns are encountered. Good scalability is a matter of utmost concern to NETWORK, SERVER and PARALLEL COMPUTER designers, since in its absence, adding new users or processors will not be cost effective and may even degrade existing performance. The term has become somewhat devalued in current marketing jargon, being used as if merely synonymous with expandability.

Scalable Processor ARChitecture (SPARC) A RISC processor architecture devised in 1985 by SUN MICROSYSTEMS, INC. and licenced to various semiconductor manufacturers to make a family of microprocessors that are still used in its own WORKSTATION products. The innovative feature of SPARC was its concept of REGISTER WINDOWING, whereby a large number (128 or more) of physical registers is provided, but only 32 are visible at any time – moving the location of this 'window' (rather than the actual register contents) permits very fast CONTEXT SWITCHING and the sharing of registers between processes. Later enhancements to the architecture went by the names Super-SPARC and HyperSPARC.

scalar 1 In mathematics, a quantity that has only a magnitude, in contrast to a VECTOR quantity which has both a magnitude and a direction. For example, temperature is a scalar quantity whereas velocity is a vector quantity.
2 In computer programming, a simple number as opposed to a compound data structure or collection such as an ARRAY or a RECORD.

scale 1 To change the size of a graphic object. Scaling is one of the most fundamental graphical operations. See also AFFINE TRANSFORM.
2 To multiply or divide a set of data items by the same constant factor in order to make them fit within a desired range of values.
3 To increase the size of a hardware system. See more under SCALABILITY.

scan code The unique numeric code sent to a computer by its keyboard whenever a key is pressed. See more under KEY CODE.

ScanDisk A utility program supplied with recent versions of Microsoft's Windows operating system that checks floppy disks and hard disks for corrupted DIRECTORY structures, bad SECTORS, cross-linked files and other kinds of error.

scan line One of the horizontal lines that form the picture on a RASTER DISPLAY like that of a television set or computer monitor. See also RASTER SCAN, FLYBACK.

scanner 1 A computer input device that digitizes an optical image and turns it into a stream of binary data, using a light sensor to SAMPLE the intensity of reflected or transmitted light along narrow strips of the original.

Scanners are categorized according to the traversal method they employ. A FLATBED SCANNER resembles a photocopier, moving its light source and scanning head under a glass sheet bearing the original; a HAND-HELD SCANNER is propelled manually across the original image; the DRUM SCANNER used in professional studios attaches transparent originals to a rotating drum.

Key parameters of a scanner's performance are its optical resolution (the smallest dot it can distinguish) and the size of digital samples it creates. Typical values for a medium range device are 1200 × 2400 dots per inch with 36-bit samples. See also TWAIN, OCR.

2 An alternative name for the LEXICAL ANALYSER employed in language processing and COMPILER technology to decompose a text into its smallest meaningful units.

scanning frequency　The frequency with which the lines that compose the image on a VDU are redrawn. See also SCAN LINE, HORIZONTAL SCAN RATE, VERTICAL REFRESH RATE.

scanning spot　The illuminated point at which the electron beam in a CATHODE RAY TUBE hits the screen. By moving and modulating the intensity of this spot the picture is traced on the screen's PHOSPHOR coating. See also RASTER SCAN.

scatter-gather　A strategy employed by high-performance HARD DISK controllers, in which many separate READ or WRITE requests are collected together and sorted into SECTOR order to optimize the access time.

scatter plot, scatter graph, scatter chart　A style of GRAPH often used by statisticians in which the data values are represented by isolated individual points with no joining lines. The overall trend of the data in a scatterplot is sometimes rendered more obvious by adding a TREND LINE. See also BAR GRAPH, PIE CHART.

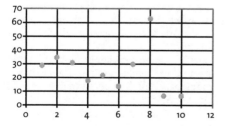

scheduler 1 An application program that simulates an automated diary in which its user can record appointments and meetings. Such software may have sophisticated abilities to rearrange meetings to avoid clashes, and some products can use a LAN or INTRANET to consult the schedulers of other potential participants to find mutually acceptable times (see GROUP SCHEDULER).

2 A piece of system software that controls the time order in which a group of related activities takes place, often by placing them in and removing them from a QUEUE. An important example is the TASK or PROCESS scheduler in the kernel of any MULTITASKING operating system, which determines the order in which a group of processes sharing the same CPU are allotted processing time. Another example is the PACKET scheduler in a network ROUTER which sorts packets into order of priority before forwarding them.

3 The hardware subsystem within a computer's CPU that determines the order in which INSTRUCTIONS are executed.

scheduling　**1** The process of planning a project and allotting the time for each of its various sub-tasks.

2 Within a computer's central processor, operating system or language compiler, the process of deciding in what time order a sequence of instructions or processes should be executed. See also SCHEDULER, PRIORITY SCHEDULING, TASK SCHEDULING.

Scheduling Application Programming Interface (SAPI) An APPLICATION PROGRAMMING INTERFACE defined by Microsoft for its Schedule+ work scheduling application.

schema 1 A description of the relationships between the various data items stored in a DATABASE, typically expressed in a diagram that shows the number and data type of the FIELDS that compose each kind of RECORD.

2 A template describing the structure of documents of a particular type created in the XML language, and the meanings to be ascribed to the formatting TAGS they may contain. See also DOCUMENT TYPE DEFINITION, XSL.

Scheme　A dialect of the LISP programming language designed by Steele and Sussman in 1975 for elementary teaching purposes.

science fiction A literary form beloved of people in the computer industry. Many of the names of products, programming languages and concepts are derived from sci-fi comics, dramas such as *Star Trek*, and the novels of William Gibson. Examples include 'warp', 'zap', 'vape' and CYBERSPACE.

scientific notation A concise notation used in science and engineering for expressing very large numbers, by representing them as a real number between 1 and 10 multiplied by an integral power of 10. For example the number 123,700,000,000 would be written as 1.237×10^{11}.

SCO Abbreviation of SANTA CRUZ OPERATION.

scope The region of a program's SOURCE CODE within which a particular IDENTIFIER is visible, and hence within which it must be unique. The simplest imaginable scheme would be for all identifiers to be visible throughout the whole program, but for programs with multiple authors this would make selection of unique names intolerably difficult. Hence BLOCK STRUCTURED languages support LOCAL identifiers whose scope is confined to the subprogram in which they are declared, and GLOBAL identifiers whose scope is the whole program:

```
VAR temp
...
procedure A
VAR temp
...
procedure B
VAR temp
....
```

These three declarations of temp all represent different variables, and within procedures A or B a REFERENCE to temp refers to the local one, which is said to 'mask' the global version. The concept of a MODULE, so important in modern programming languages, is largely concerned with controlling the scope of identifiers. See also DYNAMIC SCOPE, LEXICAL SCOPE.

SCO Unix A version of the UNIX operating system for INTEL processors, developed by the SANTA CRUZ OPERATION, and formerly called XENIX.

scramble To render a message unintelligible by deliberately mixing up its component parts. Such a message must be unscrambled by the receiving equipment in order to be read. See also ENCRYPTION.

scratchpad A temporary storage area in which a program can write intermediate results, deleted data items, etc. In INTERACTIVE systems it may actually be an area of screen or memory where the human user can store such items.

screen capture, screen dump To store the temporary contents of a computer's screen as a GRAPHICS file that can be retrieved later and edited. It is often done in order to capture ERROR MESSAGES following a crash, or for documentation purposes. See also PRINT SCREEN KEY.

screen clash An unsightly visual artefact produced when two overlayed dot grids interfere to produce Moiré patterns. This may happen, for example, when an image captured from a computer screen is screened as a HALFTONE for printing, or between two of the colours in an image separated into CMYK components. Screen clash can be minimized by rotating one of the grids to an optimum angle with respect to the others, and all professional DESKTOP PUBLISHING programs will perform such *screen angling* automatically when colour separations are generated.

screen font A FONT that is designed specifically to be used on a computer's display, rather than on its printer. Examples include those BITMAPPED FONTS (e.g. MS Sans Serif, Small Fonts) once used by default for Windows dialogues and menus for faster display. See also WYSIWYG.

screen furniture The various permanently-visible devices and areas of interaction that are displayed on the screen of any program that employs a GRAPHICAL USER INTERFACE, and via which a user can control the program, particularly its appearance. Some screen furniture is presented by the operating system itself and remains the same for every program. Such areas include the WINDOW BORDERs that are used for moving and resizing each window, the SCROLLBARS used to move a text up and down within a window, and the close and MINIMIZE boxes that remove or hide a window from the screen. Each program may then present its own MENU BARS, TOOLBARS and similar devices that give control over its own internal operations. See also WINDOW MANAGER, CONTROL, ICON, TASKBAR, MOUSE CLICK.

screening The reduction of an image to a regular grid of coloured dots to enable its reproduction by various printing processes. See more under HALFTONE.

screen saver A software utility that blanks a computer's screen, or displays an amusing animated image, after a certain period with no user input: pressing any key restores the original display. The rationale for screen savers (and the origin of their name) was that a static image, say of the Windows DESKTOP, left on the screen for a protracted period could become permanently 'burnt' into the PHOSPHOR of the monitor tube. This is unlikely to happen in normal PC use, but the choice of screen saver has now become a vehicle for personal expression, much as desktop WALLPAPER has.

screen scraping A crude technique for converting data into some new format by capturing the contents of an older application's screen displays and reading the contents of any data fields in them. Screen scraping has mostly been used to access data from old MAINFRAME applications where there is no possibility of running the software on a PC.

script **1** A writing system for creating a visual representation of a human language, consisting of a set of CHARACTERS with rules on how to combine them. The most widely used scripts include Roman, Chinese and Arabic.
2 A file containing stored commands that can be executed by invoking its name. Scripts are often used to automate the operation of another program (such as an OPERATING SYSTEM, WORD PROCESSOR or SPREADSHEET) by executing a sequence of commonly-used operations. Scripts are usually INTERPRETED rather than COMPILED, but otherwise the distinction between a script and a program is often somewhat blurred. Interpreted programs written in PERL tend to be called scripts, while those written in JAVA are called programs. See also MACRO, SCRIPTING LANGUAGE, SHELL SCRIPT.

scripting language A type of INTERPRETED programming language used to automate the operation of an existing application program or operating system. Scripting languages are usually distinguishable from general-purpose programming languages in that they provide relatively few, but very HIGH-LEVEL, commands specialized for a particular task, such as text manipulation or graphics. This distinction is not clear cut, however, and SCRIPTING LANGUAGES such as PERL, PYTHON, TCL, AWK and VBSCRIPT are quite broadly applicable.

script kiddy A derogatory term for a novice HACKER who merely downloads from newsgroup scripts written by others, and uses them to attempt illicit access to remote computer systems, but is deemed to be incapable of writing them.

scroll To move a screen display, up, down or to either side in very small increments, giving the illusion that it is a real document behind the screen that is moving. On a graphical display if the increments are small enough, the process is called SMOOTH SCROLLING, whereas on older text-only displays it may proceed one text line at a time.

scrollable Capable of being scrolled. A screen window capable of holding a text or image that is longer and/or wider than its visible area. See also SCROLL, SCROLLBAR.

scrollbar A visual component employed in GRAPHICAL USER INTERFACES to scroll a text or graphic that is larger than the window it is displayed in, by dragging a small box (called the THUMB) along its track using the MOUSE POINTER. Often a horizontal scrollbar is provided in addition to a vertical one, for example, when viewing a very wide SPREADSHEET.

Scroll Lock key A MODIFIER KEY on the keyboard of all IBM-compatible PCs which, when engaged, forces the display to SCROLL when the CURSOR KEYS are pressed. The cursor, however, remains in the same relative position within the document – it would have been better named 'cursor lock'. Few modern programs define any action for the Scroll Lock key – those that do include SPREADSHEETS such as EXCEL where it confines the selection cursor to its current cell while the sheet scrolls.

SCSI (Small Computer System Interface) A standard interface for connecting intelligent peripherals such as hard, floppy and CD-ROM disk drives, printers and scanners to a computer, independently of what type of CPU or operating system the computer employs.

The original SCSI 1 standard (ANSI X3.131-1986, ISO/IEC 9316) specified an 8-bit parallel BUS capable of connecting up to seven such devices to each controller or HOST ADAPTER, and could operate in either ASYNCHRONOUS or SYNCHRONOUS modes, delivering up to 5 megabytes (MB) per second in the latter mode. A succession of later SCSI standards have increased performance by making the bus wider, faster or both, which has lead to some convoluted names:

SCSI-1: 8-bit, 5 MB per second
Fast SCSI: 8-bit, 10 MB per second
Fast Wide SCSI: 16-bit, 20 MB per second
Ultra SCSI: 8-bit, 20 MB per second
Wide Ultra SCSI: 16-bit, 40 MB per second
Ultra2 SCSI: 8-bit, 40 MB per second
Wide Ultra3 SCSI: 16-bit, 80 MB per second
Ultra3 SCSI: 16-bit, 160 MB per second

SCSI remains the most popular disk interface for network SERVERS, though it is being displaced by FIBRE CHANNEL ARBITRATED LOOP in the very largest systems. See also IDE, EIDE.

scuzzy A popular nickname for the SCSI disk interface.

SD 1 Abbreviation of SINGLE-DENSITY DISKETTE. **2** Abbreviation of STRUCTURED DESIGN.

SD Card (Secure Digital Card) A tiny solid-state MEMORY CARD format for digital cameras and hand-held computers, created by a consortium of more than 200 consumer electronics manufacturers including Sanyo, Canon, Casio, Pioneer and Palm (but not Sony). SD media, which are around the size of a postage stamp, are made from non-volatile FLASH MEMORY and are available in capacities from 32 to 256 megabytes. They can be read and written at 10 megabytes per second, and an SD SLOT implements a full I/O bus, so active devices such as network adapters can use it. A built-in ENCRYPTION scheme prevents the copying of copyrighted materials distributed in SD format. See also COMPACT FLASH, MEMORY STICK, PC CARD, CARDBUS, SMARTCARD.

SDDI 1 (Shielded twisted-pair FDDI) A version of the FIBRE DISTRIBUTED DATA INTERFACE that works over copper cable rather than over OPTICAL FIBRE. **2** (Sony Digital Data Interface) A SERIAL communications interface fitted to Sony's Betacam professional video cameras.

SDH Abbreviation of SYNCHRONOUS DIGITAL HIERARCHY.

SDK Abbreviation of SOFTWARE DEVELOPERS KIT.

SDL Abbreviation of SPECIFICATION AND DESIGN LANGUAGE.

SDLC (Synchronous Data Link Control) A SYNCHRONOUS serial communication protocol invented by IBM for MAINFRAME applications. It may be used in FULL-DUPLEX or HALF-DUPLEX, switched or non-switched forms.

SDRAM (synchronous DRAM) A type of RAM that achieves high access speeds by using a separate clock signal in addition to the usual RAS and CAS control signals. SDRAM chips can deliver data in BURST-MODE at 150 megahertz.

SDSL See under DIGITAL SUBSCRIBER LINE.

Seagate One of the largest (and earliest) manufacturers of low-cost HARD DISKS for personal computers.

seamless integration The combined use of two distinct programs in such a way that they behave as if one.

search-and-replace To automatically locate some or all occurrences of a word or phrase in a document and replace them by another word or phrase. All WORD PROCESSORS and all but the very simplest of TEXT EDITORS support such an operation, usually with the ability to use WILDCARDS or REGULAR EXPRESSIONS that will find many variant spellings in a single operation. Modern word processors, such as MICROSOFT WORD, which support sophisticated typography and formatting, will also allow search-and-replace on particular FONTS and paragraph STYLES.

search engine One of several services provided on the WORLD WIDE WEB that enable users to locate web pages via their content, by entering search strings such as 'poodle clipping' or 'booksellers'. Search engines are multiuser applications that can serve many hundreds of users simultaneously, and typically run on very large, very fast servers. The most famous search engines include YAHOO!, ALTA VISTA, LYCOS, HOTBOT and EXCITE.

All search engines work by constructing a huge INDEX that takes in millions of web sites, but they differ in how this is collected. Some (such as Alta Vista) send out automatic software agents called SPIDERS that prowl the net for new sites, while others (such as Yahoo!) employ human compilers to construct hierarchical directories of sites categorized by content.

search problem Any problem that involves examining a large list of data items, looking for those that match some criterion, an example being 'what is X's telephone number?' Computer scientists distinguish search problems from DECISION PROBLEMS that have a simple yes/no answer. Much effort has been expended to discover the most efficient search algorithms, since so much of commercial computing involves finding items in databases. See also INDEX, LINEAR SEARCH, BINARY SEARCH.

seasonality The tendency of a data set to vary in a predictable way throughout the year. For example holiday and heating oil sales exhibit strong seasonality.

SECAM (Système Électronique pour Couleur avec Mémoire) One of the world's three major broadcast analog television standards, developed in France and first deployed in 1967. It is used in countries including France, Russia, Greece and much of Africa. A SECAM display consists of 625 lines refreshed at 50 frames per second. See also NTSC, PAL, HDTV.

secondary cache An alternative name for LEVEL 2 CACHE.

secondary key In a database query, any KEY value apart from the principal one used to identify the information to be retrieved. In a query such as SELECT name, phonenumber FROM customer for example, phonenumber is a secondary key. See also SORT, INDEX, INDEX FIELD.

second source An alternative manufacturer of some electronic part, especially an INTEGRATED CIRCUIT, that serves as a guarantee of continued supply should the first close down or discontinue the part. Also used as a verb meaning to locate such a supplier, as in 'We're second-sourcing the disk controller from Taiwan'.

section A unit used to divide up long documents in MICROSOFT WORD and other WORD PROCESSORS.

sector A subdivision of the physical storage space on a rotating storage medium (such as a HARD DISK or FLOPPY DISK) employed when formatting the disk. Each recording surface is divided into concentric TRACKS, and each track is divided into a number of sectors (see also PLATTER). For example a standard PC 1.44 megabyte floppy disk is formatted into 80 tracks, each containing 18 sectors. See also CLUSTER, EXTENT, LOW-LEVEL FORMAT.

sector editor A software utility that can inspect and alter the data stored on a hard disk or floppy disk directly, a byte at a time, completely bypassing the computer's FILE SYSTEM. Such a tool can be used by the *very* knowledgeable to recover lost files or repair damaged ones, but in less experienced hands it is more likely to wreak havoc.

sector interleave A technique employed in the design of HARD DISK drives to speed the retrieval of information. It involves staggering the arrangement of the concentric SECTORS into which the data is organized with respect to their neighbours. For example, sectors 0–8 might actually be laid down in the order 0,3,6,1,4,7,2,5,8 (the so-called *sector mapping*). This avoids the drive's read/write HEAD having to wait for a full revolution of the PLATTER to locate the beginning of the next sector, which would be the case if they were radially aligned.

sector map The order in which the SECTORS on a HARD DISK are arranged. See more under SECTOR INTERLEAVE.

sector size The number of bytes stored in each SECTOR of a magnetic disk storage medium such as a HARD DISK or FLOPPY DISK. The typical range is from 512 to 2048 bytes.

Secure HyperText Transmission Protocol
See S-HTTP.

Secure Sockets Layer (SSL) A secure communications protocol designed by NETSCAPE that enables encrypted connections to be made over the Internet. SSL occupies a software layer below the APPLICATION LAYER protocols (such as HTTP, FTP and SMTP), but above the TCP/IP TRANSPORT LAYERS. See also HTTPS, SECURE HYPERTEXT TRANSMISSION PROTOCOL, OSI REFERENCE MODEL.

security A blanket term used to describe all aspects of regulating access to, and ensuring the preservation of, computer data. Routine security measures fall into three broad and intertwined areas: ensuring that persons requesting access to the data are who they say they are (see AUTHENTICATION), ensuring that whoever they say they are is allowed to access the data (see PERMISSION), and ensuring that no third party can eavesdrop on the eventual transaction (see ENCRYPTION).

Another branch of security is concerned with preventing malicious attempts to damage data or bring down a computer system (see for example FIREWALL, VIRUS, EXPLOIT, TROJAN HORSE, HACK ATTACK). Finally, it is arguable that data BACKUP and DISASTER RECOVERY should fall under the heading of security, since accidental loss is the ever-present and most dangerous enemy of all. See also PASSWORD, HTTPS, KERBEROS, SECURE SOCKETS LAYER, DIGITAL SIGNATURE.

seed An initial number supplied to a computer's RANDOM NUMBER GENERATOR to begin a new number sequence. A commonly-used trick for creating pseudo-random seeds is to supply the current time from the computer's REAL TIME CLOCK, in 1/100ths of a second. See also PSEUDO-RANDOM NUMBER.

seek 1 In hardware, the process of moving the HEAD of a DISK DRIVE to locate a particular data TRACK. See more under SEEK TIME, AVERAGE SEEK TIME, TRACK-TO-TRACK SEEK TIME, FULL STROKE SEEK TIME.

2 In software, an operating system call that gives access to a particular record within a RANDOM ACCESS file system. A Seek call typically takes a numeric expression as its parameter and moves the file pointer to that position in the file. A Get or Put call may then be issued to read or write the record stored at that location. See also RANDOM-READ, RANDOM-WRITE.

seek time The time taken by a DISK DRIVE to move its HEAD from one TRACK to another, which is a key determinant of its overall data retrieval speed. Total seek time is affected by the mass of the head assembly, the number of tracks to be traversed, and the time it takes for the head to align itself over the new track stably enough for reading or writing to begin (the so-called HEAD-SETTLE TIME). The seek time varies between makes of drive and is an important criterion of suitability for a particular style of work.

A low seek time is important in those applications in which a large number of small files or different database records will be frequently consulted. For an application that reads sequentially from a single large file, overall transfer rate is more important. See also AVERAGE SEEK TIME, TRACK-TO-TRACK SEEK TIME, FULL STROKE SEEK TIME.

Sega A Japanese manufacturer of a highly successful range of GAMES CONSOLES.

segment 1 A group of computers on a network that are all connected by the same cable. See more under NETWORK SEGMENT.

2 A portion of the BINARY IMAGE of an executable program that is independently RELOCATABLE. Many operating systems require programs to keep their code and data in separate segments.

3 A subdivision of the total MEMORY SPACE of a computer's processor that must be accessed using a two-part address: a SEGMENT REGISTER is set to the required SEGMENT ADDRESS, and then short addresses may be issued to access locations only within that segment. Intel's 80x86 architecture is the best known example of such a scheme. See more under SEGMENTED MEMORY MODEL.

4 A set of memory pages within a VIRTUAL MEMORY system.

segment address In computers that employ a segmented address space, that portion of each ADDRESS that selects a particular segment rather than a word within that segment, and which would be specified as an OFFSET from the start of the segment. For example for an Intel processor, in an address such as 1027: 889 the 1027 portion represents the segment address. See also SEGMENTED MEMORY MODEL, SEGMENT REGISTER, FLAT ADDRESS SPACE.

segmented address space See under SEGMENTED MEMORY MODEL.

segmented memory model A PROCESSOR ARCHITECTURE in which the physical ADDRESS SPACE is subdivided into many smaller areas called SEGMENTS. The processor addresses a particular location by first loading the address of its SEGMENT into a SEGMENT REGISTER, and then issuing an address which lies within that segment.

The original purpose of segmentation was to reduce the size of the processor chip, as shorter addresses need fewer ADDRESS LINES. For example 16 megabytes of total memory might be addressed using only 16-bit addressing within each 64 kilobyte segment, while to address it using a FLAT ADDRESS SPACE would require 24-bit addresses. However, segmentation severely complicates programming owing to a forced distinction between far and near locations, and makes data structures larger than one segment very inefficient. It is at least arguable that IBM's adoption of the segmented Intel architecture stunted the development of Microsoft's operating systems.

See also NEAR POINTER, NEAR CALL, FAR POINTER, FAR CALL, MEMORY MODEL.

segment ordering The order in which the separate SEGMENTS are stored within a WINDOWS .EXE or DLL file. This order is stored in a mapping file written by the LINKER whenever a program is COMPILED.

segment register In a computer processor that employs a SEGMENTED ADDRESS SPACE, the REGISTER that holds the address of the current segment.

select 1 To identify one group of data items among many as being the current focus of interest, to which some action may be applied. In programs that employ a GRAPHICAL USER INTERFACE, selection is typically carried out interactively on the screen by pointing with a MOUSE (see POINT-AND-CLICK), and selected items become highlighted in some way to signify this status.

2 In the SQL query language, the most important KEYWORD, which has the effect of extracting all the RECORDS from a DATABASE that fit the criteria supplied as its parameters.

Select All An option that is offered on the Edit MENU of almost all Windows programs. It causes the whole of the current document or image to become the current SELECTION.

selection A set of data items, for example a group of words within a document or an area within an image, that has been identified by the program's user as the current focus of interest to which some operation should be applied. See also FOCUS, SELECT, SELECTION HANDLE, MARQUEE, RUBBER-BANDING.

selection handle A small square box that appears on part of a drawing in a GRAPHICS program to signify that the part is currently SELECTED. Clicking the MOUSE BUTTON and holding it within this box allows the part to be moved, resized or otherwise manipulated. A widely used convention enables several parts to be selected at a time, the current target displaying solid black handles while the others display empty white handles. See also VECTOR GRAPHICS.

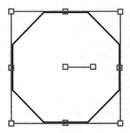

selector 1 In OBJECT-ORIENTED PROGRAMMING, an operation that returns the state of an object without altering that state.

2 In the SMALLTALK language, a message sent to an object to execute one of its METHODS.

self-calibrating Any hardware device, such as a MONITOR or SCANNER, that can automatically adjust its own operating parameters.

self-documenting code A claim made for programs written in some relatively verbose programming languages that implies that they do not need any COMMENTING. It is seldom true.

self-extracting archive A type of compressed ARCHIVE file that unpacks its own contents when its name is invoked. Several popular FILE COMPRESSION utilities, including PKZIP, can create such archives. Self-extracting archives are highly effective for distributing software products that employ multiple files, since they remove the need for inexperienced users to place files into the correct subdirectories. They are equally effective for performing UPDATES and PATCHES to existing software products, where they can be designed to automatically overwrite certain files with newer versions.

self-test A test of correct functioning that a device performs automatically on itself. See more under POWER-ON SELF TEST.

semantic gap The huge disparity between the complex objects and properties encountered when dealing with real world problems – for example people, life, love, money – and the simplistic representations of these objects that computers can deal with, which are expressed in terms of INTEGERS, FLOATING-POINT numbers and alphabetic characters. The vastness of the gap is what makes computer programming such a difficult and time-consuming task. The term is particularly used by designers of HIGH-LEVEL PROGRAMMING LANGUAGES whose daunting task is to attempt to close the gap by inventing ever more expressive representations. See, for example, OBJECT-ORIENTED PROGRAMMING, FUNCTIONAL PROGRAMMING, LOGIC PROGRAMMING.

semantic network A data structure favoured in certain areas of ARTIFICIAL INTELLIGENCE research that attempts to relate the meaning of words constituting a sentence to all the unspoken context information that is required to understand a particular usage. A semantic network consists of a DIRECTED GRAPH whose NODES contain concepts related to or inherited by one another. For example a portion of a network might contain relationships such as:

```
Jim --employs--> John --married_to
--> Jane
--is_a--> person --has_a--> name
```

The nodes of a semantic net are often implemented as FRAMES: records containing slots that hold the properties of each entity, and which may be progressively filled as more information is learned.

semantics In general, that branch of linguistics that deals with the relationship between the structure of sentences and their meaning. The difference between SYNTAX and semantics is beautifully summed up in Noam Chomsky's famous example:

a Colourless green ideas sleep furiously.
b Furiously sleep ideas green colourless.

Neither of these sentences has any meaning (semantics), but sentence a is grammatical while sentence b is not (syntax).

As applied to programming languages, semantics means ·the result of executing a program – its behaviour rather than its syntactic form. A program's syntax can be checked by the computer itself (see under SYNTAX CHECKING, SYNTAX ERROR), and any language COMPILER or INTERPRETER must verify that a program is well-formed. However, it is not in general possible to check the semantics of a program (i.e. that it does what it is supposed to do) by any shorter means than testing it with all conceivable inputs and in all contexts. Much computer science research has been devoted to devising languages with formally describable semantics. See also FORMAL METHODS, DENOTATIONAL SEMANTICS, OPERATIONAL SEMANTICS, REFERENTIAL TRANSPARENCY.

semaphore A data structure often employed to control access to some shared resource (for example a communications channel or a printer) when multiple PROCESSES are contending for it. The semaphore consists of a variable whose value is the number of units of the resource available, together with two ACCESS FUNCTIONS that allow processes either to test whether the resource is free (and claim it if it is), or to return it after use, decrementing and incrementing the value of the variable accordingly.

semi-acronym An abbreviation for a phrase that is not strictly composed of the first letters of each word. For example PING is a semi-acronym for Packet Internet Groper.

semicolon The punctuation character ; with ASCII code 59. A semicolon is used in many programming languages as a terminating or separating character to mark the end of each line of code.

semi-compiled A programming language that does not COMPILE source programs into NATIVE CODE, but into an intermediate PSEUDO-CODE which is then executed by an INTERPRETER. Examples include JAVA, VISUAL BASIC and C#.

semiconductor A class of substances, the best-known being SILICON and germanium, whose electrical conductivity lies between that of a metallic CONDUCTOR and that of an INSULATOR. Junctions formed between a semiconductor and a metal or another semiconductor exhibit many useful properties, such as conducting in one direction only (a DIODE) or having a conductance that can be varied by applying a control voltage (a TRANSISTOR). The modern electronics industry is based around these properties of semiconductor junctions, which have almost completely replaced the THERMIONIC VALVE.

The electrical properties of a semiconductor can be tailored by mixing small amounts of an impurity into it, a process called DOPING. Some DOPANTS liberate an excess of mobile electrons to produce an *n-type* semiconductor, while others remove free electrons to produce a *p-type* semiconductor. For example, phosphorus and arsenic are n-type dopants for silicon, while boron is a p-type dopant. All the electronic devices (such as transistors) from which modern INTEGRATED CIRCUITS are built consist of complex junctions between n-type and p-type regions formed on the surface of a thin semiconductor WAFER.

semicustom chip A special-purpose INTEGRATED CIRCUIT that is produced by modifying a standard template – or by combining predefined partial circuits called STANDARD CELLS – rather than being designed completely from scratch. Semicustom chips take less time to develop, and therefore have lower startup costs, than full CUSTOM CHIPS and may therefore become commercially viable for smaller production runs. However they tend to use greater amounts of silicon and may therefore not be as cheap at large production volumes. See also GATE ARRAY, PROGRAMMABLE LOGIC ARRAY.

sender The party to an act of communication that sends information. See also RECEIVER.

sendmail A MESSAGE TRANSFER AGENT originally written for BERKELEY UNIX but now used as the EMAIL agent on most Unix systems. Sendmail works via the TCP/IP and SMTP protocols and so is used to handle most of the email traffic across the Internet.

Sendmail was one of the first important examples of OPEN SOURCE software and is always distributed in SOURCE CODE form. It is also famous for the opacity of its CONFIGURATION scripts, which are impenetrable to all but the keenest of GURUS.

Send To A mechanism supported in versions of Microsoft WINDOWS from 95 onwards. It enables the user to send the currently selected files to any one of several different applications, which may be selected from the RIGHT-CLICK MENU.

sense amplifier A type of ANALOGUE amplifier circuit that is introduced into some fast RAM technologies. Its function is to save fractional amounts of access time by anticipating the settling of the DIGITAL signal levels.

sensor An electronic device that converts into an electrical signal some physical property of its environment – for example temperature, pressure, motion, light intensity, oxygen concentration or acidity. Sensors are core components of all computerized DATA LOGGING applications, industrial control systems and robots.

A vast range of different mechanical, electrical, magnetic, optical and chemical effects are exploited in the design of sensors. The only unifying theme is an accelerating tendency to integrate sensor and computer circuitry onto the same silicon chip. See more under MICROSYSTEM.

separated A stream of data items that has a well-defined SEPARATOR character to mark the end of one item and the start of the next. For textual data, the COMMA-SEPARATED and TAB-SEPARATED formats are two widely used conventions. For binary data, NULL characters are often used as separators.

separator A special value that is used to divide up a stream of data values into individual items, or to mark off individual STATEMENTS within a program text. A value chosen as a separator should not itself be a valid data item. For example in ordinary written language the space character is used to separate words, and therefore space cannot occur within a word.

In programming languages there is a subtle distinction between a separator character, used to separate consecutive statements, and a TERMINATOR character used to end statements. This manifests itself at the very end of a program where a terminator would need to be used, but a separator would not. See also COMMA-SEPARATED, TAB-SEPARATED.

Sequel An early name for Structured Query Language, intended to be a pronounceable version of the acronym SQL.

sequencer 1 Also called a MIDI sequencer, an application program that permits MIDI music files to be edited and played on a computer. A typical sequencer permits editing of multiple separate music tracks which may be assigned different synthesized instrument 'voices'. It also permits the music to be displayed in a variety of formats including conventional musical notation, a list of MIDI events, or an animated 'piano roll' display. More sophisticated sequencers also enable sampled DIGITAL AUDIO, for example WAV files, to be integrated into a piece of MIDI music.

2 See MICROSEQUENCER.

Sequent A US manufacturer of high-performance SERVERS which pioneered research into CLUSTERED SMP and NUMA architectures. Now owned by IBM.

sequential Proceeding one after another, rather than in PARALLEL.

sequential access Any method of accessing a storage medium that requires the items to be written and read in strict order, so that many items may have to be traversed in order to find the desired one. Magnetic TAPE is a typical sequential access medium, owing to its physical form – consider finding a particular tune on a music cassette. This is in contrast with a RANDOM ACCESS medium such as a hard disk.

serial 1 Arranged sequentially in time or space.

2 More specifically, a DIGITAL data stream in which the individual bits follow one another in time down some communication channel, rather than being transmitted in PARALLEL groups of 8, 16 (or however many) bits.

serial bus Any interface between a computer and its peripherals that transfers data in a BIT-SERIAL fashion, notable examples being UNIVERSAL SERIAL BUS, FIREWIRE and FIBRE CHANNEL.

serialize 1 In general, to convert a stream of PARALLEL data into a stream of BITS for transmission over a SERIAL interface.

2 In the JAVA language, to flatten out the data content of an OBJECT into a bit stream that can be transmitted over a network to another computer.

Serial Line Internet Protocol See SLIP.

serial port A type of communication channel that inputs and outputs data from a computer as a sequential stream of single BITS (in contrast to a PARALLEL PORT, which transfers a whole WORD at a time). Serial ports are cheap to implement, take up little space on a computer's MOTHERBOARD and require only a thin cable, consisting at a minimum of just three wires. For these reasons, they are almost universally fitted to small computers, for connecting the mouse and possibly a printer, scanner and modem.

Serial ports must employ a serial PROTOCOL (usually RS-232) to differentiate the continuous stream of 0 and 1 bits into separate data words, by defining a certain pattern of bits as representing the STOP BIT (i.e. an end marker). Certain parameters of the bit stream are configurable; these include whether a stop bit is sent after each 7 or 8 bits, and whether an extra bit is added as a PARITY BIT for error checking purposes. The transfer speed of a serial port is measured in bits per second, also known as its BAUD RATE. See also FRAMING ERROR, UART. In the early days of computing, serial cables were used to connect user TERMINALS to MAINFRAME computers, and as a result most of the ASCII character codes below 32 were originally interpreted as serial line CONTROL CODES.

All IBM-COMPATIBLE PCs are fitted with one or more RS-232 ports, and the newer USB and

FIREWIRE ports are faster types of serial port. Under the MS-DOS and Windows operating systems the serial ports are visible as system devices called COM1, COM2, COM3, and so on.

Serial Storage Architecture See SSA.

serial-to-parallel converter An electronic circuit that turns a SERIAL bit stream into a stream of PARALLEL data by collecting groups of successive bits into a small memory BUFFER. Such a circuit forms the receiver part of a UART chip. See also PARALLEL-TO-SERIAL CONVERTER.

series 1 In electronics, a way of connecting components such as RESISTORS or CAPACITORS end to end so that a current flows through them one after the other, in contrast to connecting them in PARALLEL, where the current splits to flow through them all at once.
2 In mathematics, a sequence of numbers that are all generated by a common formula: see, for example, the FIBONACCI SERIES. Hence also a sequence of data items representing the same scenario or process, as in TIME SERIES.

serif A small line placed at the ends of each main stroke in a type character to improve readability. Hence the word is also used to refer to any typeface, such as Times Roman or Plantim, that employs serifs. See also SANS SERIF.

server 1 In the context of hardware, a computer that is designed to provide shared services to other computers on a network (called WORKSTATIONS), rather than to be directly accessed by users. Since servers must serve many workstations simultaneously, they require an efficient MULTITASKING operating system, a powerful CPU and large amounts of memory and disk storage. They often need no screen or keyboard, since they can be remotely administered from a workstation.
The most common role for a server is as a FILE SERVER, to hold data files that can be accessed by many users. Other common roles are the PRINT SERVER, DATABASE SERVER, MAIL SERVER, APPLICATION SERVER and FAX SERVER, each of which allows many users to share access to its eponymous resource.
2 A software program that does not interact directly with users, but instead provides services that can be requested by CLIENT programs. Server programs may run on the same computer as their clients, as in OBJECT-ORIENTED software systems such as Microsoft's OLE, or they may run on different machines receiving requests over a LAN or the Internet. See CLIENT/SERVER model.

server farm A group of SERVERS connected to the same network so that many users can access the resources they contain. The purpose of building a farm may be both to increase overall capacity and to provide fault-tolerant features that automatically divert requests away from a failed machine to the ones that are still working.

server process A software PROCESS that provides services to CLIENT processes in a MULTITASKING software environment such as Unix or Windows NT. For example a WEB SERVER is typically structured so that it spawns a new server process to handle each new incoming page request. In OBJECT-ORIENTED computational models, such as CORBA and Microsoft's COMPONENT OBJECT MODEL, every application is treated as a combination of server and client processes.

server-side Taking place at the server end of a CLIENT/SERVER relationship. Often used to specify the location of execution of a PROGRAM or SCRIPT.

service 1 In general, any computation performed, or offered to be performed, by a SERVER process on behalf of a separate CLIENT process. See CLIENT/SERVER.
2 Under the UNIX and WINDOWS NT operating systems, services are BACKGROUND TASKS with a special status, which may be loaded and started at BOOT time and continue to run as if part of the operating system. An example is NT's REMOTE ACCESS SERVICE.

Service Advertisement Protocol See SAP.

service level agreement An agreement between a customer and their APPLICATION SERVICE PROVIDER that stipulates what percentage of DOWNTIME is acceptable (for example, less than 1%), and specifies financial penalties if this is exceeded.

service pack, service release A collection of software PATCHES, additional modules and documentation released by a software company to correct BUGS and add new features to a large complex software suite such as an operating system. A service pack is normally given an identifying version number. For example, Microsoft numbers its series of packs for the Office suite and Windows operating systems SR-1, SR-2 and so on.

servlet A small program written in the JAVA language that runs on a WEB SERVER. It accepts HTTP requests coming in from client BROWSERS, performs a requested action (for example retrieving some data from a database) and returns any result in HTML form, which may be integrated into a web page. The name is intended to suggest a complementarity to the client-side Java APPLET. Like applets, servlets are platform-independent, but they can be run only inside web servers that are specifically designed to support them, such as Java-Soft's Jeeves. See also JAVA SERVER PAGES, ACTIVE SERVER PAGES, CGI.

servo-motor An electric motor that accepts a set of electronic commands that stop and start it, move it to an absolute position (i.e. shaft angle), reverse its direction and control its speed. Servo-motors supply the motive force behind most kinds of remotely controlled mechanical system, from car windows to aircraft controls, and from industrial robots to toys. See also STEPPER MOTOR, ACTUATOR, ROBOT.

session **1** A period of interaction with a program or computer that has a distinct beginning and end.
2 A lasting connection between a NETWORK user and a remote SERVER that involves the exchange of many data PACKETS. Sessions are often managed by a separate layer within a particular network PROTOCOL STACK, such as TELNET or FTP in the case of TCP/IP. Protocols (such as UDP) that lack a session layer and protocols (such as HTTP) that create very short-lived sessions may create a virtual session by leaving user information in a COOKIE stored at the client end of the connection, or via some other kind of persistent session ID. See also SESSION LAYER.

session layer The fifth layer of the OSI REFERENCE MODEL for communications networks, within which services from the TRANSPORT LAYER are employed to establish and maintain a connection between processes running on different HOST computers. Session layer code is responsible for handling SECURITY measures and for creating individual SESSIONS. See also PRESENTATION LAYER, APPLICATION LAYER.

session-oriented A style of communication (and a class of PROTOCOL) that assumes that each connection will persist for a significant period, and may involve the transfer of many blocks of data in either or both directions. This is in contrast to STATELESS protocols, for example HTTP, in which each connection persists only for the downloading of a single web page. A session-oriented protocol offers the possibility of moving the whole session to a different server, in the event of overloading or failure of the original server.

set A collection of entities, called the ELEMENTS of the set, that is so described so that it is possible to tell whether or not any given entity belongs in the collection. For example {1, 2, 3} is a set with three elements, the numbers 1, 2 and 3. Sets are not ordered, so {1, 2, 3} and {3, 2, 1} are the same set, and repetition is not significant, so {1,2,3,3} is also the same set. Every set may have associated with it a property or PREDICATE that is true for exactly those entities that are elements of the set.

A set may have an infinite number of elements, as for example N, the set of NATURAL NUMBERS {0, 1, 2, ...} and Z, the set of INTEGERS {..., -2, -1, 0, 1, 2, ...}. The empty set {} contains no elements; the INTERSECTION of two sets A and B is the set containing all the elements that are both in A and B; the UNION of A and B is the set of all the elements that are in either A or B. The rules governing the manipulation of sets are collectively called SET THEORY, and form one of the fundamental bases of modern mathematics.

Some programming languages of the PASCAL family support sets as a built-in DATA TYPE, allowing the programmer to perform tests such as:

```
IF Month In [April, June, September,
November] THEN MonthDays := 30;
```

where In is the set membership operator. The other set operations are A + B for the union of sets A and B, and A * B for their intersection.

set-associative cache See under ASSOCIATIVE CACHE.

set theory See under SET.

set-top box (STB) A dedicated computer employed by SATELLITE and CABLE television companies as an interface to their network. It usually takes the form of a wide, shallow box that sits above or below the television set that is used as a display, hence the name. Set-top boxes typically contain a MODEM or network adapter, a slot that accepts SMART-CARDS for AUTHENTICATION and billing purposes, decoding circuitry to unscramble encoded pay-TV channels, and a MICROPROC-ESSOR running a simple operating system that provides a selection of MENUS and handles user commands.

setup The process of configuring a hardware device or program by setting the values of all relevant PARAMETERS. Hence also the set of relevant parameters produced by this process.

seven layer model See under OSI REFERENCE MODEL.

SFC Abbreviation of SYSTEM FILE CHECKER.

SGI Abbreviation of SILICON GRAPHICS INC.

SGML (Standard Generalized Markup Language) A non-proprietary language for marking up documents so that they can be stored and read by any computer system, while still preserving their structure. SGML is an international standard defined in ISO 8879, and is the document-storage format required by many governmental organizations, such as the US Department of Defense. SGML documents are stored as plain ASCII text, with embedded TAGS that distinguish various components and attributes of the document.

Proprietary word processor file formats merge the presentation of a document with its structure, whereas SGML keeps these aspects separate by specifying the document's logical elements (paragraphs, chapters, sections, etc) and what functions are to be performed on them. A document marked up in SGML may be sent over any communications link and printed in different styles on different systems, since attributes such as font size, typeface and emphasis (e.g., bold, italics or small caps) can be quickly and globally changed to suit new circumstances. Many proprietary word processors and DESK-TOP PUBLISHING programs can read or save in SGML format (in fact the master text of this dictionary is stored in SGML).

SGML tags have no intrinsic meaning, as SGML is actually a METALANGUAGE for creating more specific markup languages. The meanings of the tags for a particular application of SGML must be defined in a separate file called a DOCUMENT TYPE DEFINITION or DTD. For example, HTML, the markup language used to describe WEB PAGES, is a single SGML application that defines a fixed set of tags that users cannot change. Normally, SGML documents are written using a special editor that can read the DTD and check that the text complies with it. Any other computer system can read the content of such an SGML document, since it is in ASCII format. However, to reproduce its structure, the HOST computer must have available an SGML PARSER that can interpret the DTD and perform appropriate formatting actions. See also XML.

SGRAM Abbreviation of SYNCHRONOUS GRAPHICS RANDOM ACCESS MEMORY.

shade To colour the POLYGONS that make up a WIRE-FRAME representation of a 3D object in such a way as to give the appearance of a solid surface. SMOOTH SHADING algorithms such as those invented by GOURAUD and PHONG take account of the direction and colour of external light sources. They graduate the colour intensity across each polygon so that the boundaries between them cease to be visible, giving the appearance of a smoothly curving surface. See also RENDER, RAY TRACING, RADIOS-ITY, SPECULARITY.

shadow-mask tube The mechanism used in most colour CATHODE RAY TUBES, in which a perforated screen of thin metal foil (the shadow mask) is placed immediately behind the PHOSPHOR dots deposited inside the tube's face. The holes are of the precise size and orientation to allow the beam from each

ELECTRON GUN (coming from slightly different angles) to fall only on a dot of the appropriate colour. See also APERTURE GRILLE.

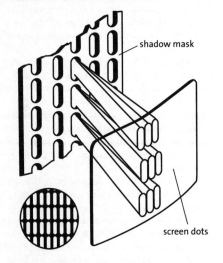

shadow mask

screen dots

shadow RAM A region of random access memory (RAM) into which the contents of a ROM are copied to permit faster access. The concept was introduced in the early days of IBM PC-compatibles to speed up access to crucial BIOS routines.

Shannon, Claude (1916–2001) A US engineer/mathematician whose work has contributed inestimably to the development of reliable electronic communications. Working at BELL LABORATORIES in the late 1940s, Shannon developed the theory of ERROR CORRECTION for noisy communication channels. In so doing, he discovered an elegant relationship between information and entropy that forms the foundation of modern INFORMATION THEORY.

share 1 The shorthand term used by network administrators and users for a *shared* DIRECTORY on a SERVER, that is one whose files are accessible to other network users.

2 A TERMINATE AND STAY RESIDENT system utility called SHARE.EXE that is supplied with the MS-DOS operating system. It must be installed to allow files to be shared by more than one program over a network.

shared medium A style of communication where many users may send messages simultaneously over the same physical CHANNEL – which might be a single wire, an OPTICAL FIBRE, or the 'air waves' (in the case of radio or infrared-based technologies). This is in contrast to communication methods in which each sender–receiver pair is assigned a separate channel, as happens with a switched public telephone system.

A shared medium requires some mechanism for separating the various messages so that they do not corrupt one another, and this is called MULTIPLEXING. See also ARBITRATION, CONNECTIONLESS, CONNECTION-ORIENTED, TIME DIVISION MULTIPLEXING, FREQUENCY DIVISION MULTIPLEXING.

shared-medium network A class of LAN in which all the WORKSTATIONS are connected to the same length of CABLE, and must compete for access to it in order to send messages. If two workstations were to transmit at the same time their signals would become mixed together and corrupted, so an ARBITRATION scheme must be adopted to ensure that only one sender 'talks' at a time. ETHERNET and TOKEN RING are the most common examples of shared-medium networks, and are largely defined by the different arbitration methods they employ. See also CSMA/CD.

shared memory A region of memory that is accessible by two or more different software processes, and which therefore enables these processes to communicate with one another by leaving messages in it. Some locking mechanism such as a SEMAPHORE or MUTEX must be provided to prevent the two processes trying to write simultaneuously to the same address. See also SHARED-MEMORY MULTIPROCESSOR, SHARED VARIABLE.

shared-memory multiprocessor (SMP) The most widespread MULTIPROCESSOR computer architecture in which all the multiple processors access the same physical memory, and hence may work on the same data items. Programs written for a single processor can be easily adapted to run on such an architecture since they still see only a single ADDRESS SPACE. Hence the SMP architecture is supported by operating systems such as WINDOWS NT and certain UNIX variants to accelerate MULTITHREADED commercial software in a transparent fashion. See also PARALLEL PRO-GRAMMING.

shared-nothing A class of MULTIPROCESSOR computer in which neither the memory nor disk storage is shared between different processing units.

shared variable A variable whose value may be changed by two or more CONCURRENT PROCESSES. Shared variables provide a simple means of communicating between processes, but they raise difficult SEMANTIC issues because their final value depends on the exact time sequence of the updates. See, for example, SEMAPHORE, MUTEX, MONITOR, LOCK, LOCK MANAGER, RECORD LOCKING. See also MESSAGE PASSING.

shareware Software distributed free of charge, usually over the Internet, under a licence that permits people to use it for a trial period and give copies to friends, but requests them to pay a registration fee if they decide to use it regularly. Several different strategies may be employed to encourage users to register a shareware product. Positive incentives include notification of periodic free updates and the supply of printed manuals and floppy or CD master disks. Negative sanctions include: irritating NAG SCREENS that can be banished only by entering the registration key; disabling some functions in the unregistered version (see CRIPPLEWARE); or most drastically, disabling the program altogether after some fixed time interval, typically 30 days.

Shareware is frowned upon by many computer professionals, and certainly varies widely in quality, but the best shareware products compare well with commercial offerings. See also FREEWARE, OPEN SOURCE.

shear A drawing tool that distorts a selected image area by pulling two opposite edges in different directions. See also SKEW.

shell The part of a computer OPERATING SYSTEM that interprets commands typed by the user. Before the widespread adoption of graphical user interfaces such as Microsoft Windows and MacOS, the shell provided the only way of interacting with the computer, and many operating systems (for example, all versions of UNIX) offer a shell as well as a graphical user interface. In addition to carrying out single commands typed by the user (for example to execute a program, copy or delete a file) most shells can execute lists of commands called SHELL SCRIPTS or BATCH FILES that permit automation of long or frequently used command sequences. Unix can be fitted with a variety of different shells, the best known being the BOURNE SHELL, C SHELL and KORN SHELL.

shell out To execute a copy of the operating system's command SHELL from inside an application program, in order to execute an operating system command or other program.

shell script An INTERPRETED program that can be executed by the command SHELL of an operating system, usually some variant of UNIX. MS-DOS BATCH FILES are a very weak form of shell script. Unix shell script languages have most of the features of a full-blown programming language, and some of the standard Unix utilities are written as shell scripts.

shell sort A more efficient variant of the simple INSERTION SORT. It compares the item to be inserted, not against adjacent items, but against widely separated ones, their spacing being reduced on successive passes through the data. For reasons that are not well understood, certain sequences of spacings (such as 40, 13, 4, 1) give the best results.

shielded twisted-pair See STP.

shift 1 On a keyboard, the action of holding down a special key that modifies the meaning of the next key pressed. Manual typewriters had only a single SHIFT KEY that produced upper case letters. Computer keyboards generally have at least two additional ones, the CTRL KEY and the ALT KEY, which generate nonprintable command sequences.

2 In programming, the action of moving all the BITS in a WORD one or more places to the left or right, as in LOGICAL SHIFT and ARITHMETIC SHIFT.

shift-click The action of holding down the SHIFT KEY while clicking a MOUSE BUTTON, which may be used to modify several commands in the WINDOWS operating system. For example, shift-clicking rather than simply clicking a filename before performing a DRAG-AND-DROP causes the file to be moved rather than copied.

SHIFT key A MODIFIER KEY present on all typewriter and computer keyboards that changes between LOWER CASE and UPPER CASE character sets. There are typically two SHIFT keys (situated to fall beneath the little fingers of each hand), and also a CAPS LOCK KEY which when engaged makes upper case the default state.

SHIFT LOCK The equivalent on manual typewriters of the computer's CAPS LOCK KEY, which worked by physically locking the SHIFT KEY in the down position.

shift register One of the fundamental electronic circuits, which converts BIT-PARALLEL to BIT-SERIAL data, or vice versa. It stores a string of BITS that may be accessed either as a whole (i.e. as parallel data), or by adding and removing bits from one end of the register and moving all the rest along (i.e. as a serial stream). Many kinds of chip, including VIDEO RAM, UARTS and the CCD chips in digital cameras, depend on shift registers for their operation.

ShockWave A plug-in program that enables web browsers to view animated sequences created with MacroMedia's DIRECTOR authoring tool. Such sequences are delivered in the FLASH file format.

shortcut **1** A combination of keystrokes that can be used in place of a MENU selection for convenience. Also called a KEYBOARD SHORT-CUT.
2 On a computer that employs a graphical user interface, an ICON representing a particular program or data file, placed onto the DESKTOP so that the user can activate it quickly without having to search for it.

Short Message Service See SMS.

shrink-wrap A popular shorthand term for the full release version of a software product, as shipped to the shops. Coined because the boxes that contain the disks and manuals are shrink-wrapped to prevent tampering.

S-HTTP, SHTTP (Secure HyperText Transmission Protocol) An extension to the World Wide Web's HTTP protocol that enables WEB BROWSERS and WEB SERVERS to encrypt and authenticate all data transfers for security. Invented by Enterprise Integration Technologies, S-HTTP is now built into servers and browsers supplied by Netscape, Microsoft and most other vendors.

Shugart, Al (b. 1930) An electronic engineer who pioneered the miniature floppy disk and hard disk drives on which all personal computers depend. He founded Shugart Technology in the 1970s, which later became SEAGATE, and was deeply involved in developing the SCSI and ESDI disk interfaces.

sidebar **1** In a document layout, a region arranged down the side of page that contains related but separate information.
2 A graphical user interface component consisting of a strip down the side of a window that contains buttons or other information.

Siemens Nixdorf International (SNI) Germany's leading computer company.

Sieve of Eratosthenes An algorithm, invented by the ancient Greek mathematician Eratosthenes, for finding all the PRIME NUMBERS up to some set limit. There is no formula that always generates a prime, so the method involves testing all the numbers up to the limit, by repeated division, to see whether they are prime, and rejecting them if not (hence the name 'sieve'). This process requires much computation, and so the Sieve has often been used as a BENCHMARK for the integer arithmetic performance of computers.

SIG See SPECIAL INTEREST GROUP.

sig Slang term for an email SIGNATURE file, derived from the filename extension it commonly employs.

SIGGRAPH See under SPECIAL INTEREST GROUP.

signal A sign, gesture, image or other mechanism used to communicate information from one place to another. In the engineering sense it refers to a unique pattern created by causing deliberate variations in some medium, such as an electrical or magnetic field, or a beam of light. The resulting WAVE is made to carry a message through the process called modulation (see under MODULATE). The same word signal is used to refer to both the means of carrying and the information carried. See also WAVEFORM, CARRIER, CHANNEL, NOISE, SIGNAL-TO-NOISE RATIO, SIGNAL PATH, SIGNAL PROCESSING, INFORMATION THEORY.

signal-compatible Two pieces of hardware that share the same electrical signalling PROTOCOL and are therefore able to communicate.

signal degradation The loss of information from a transmitted SIGNAL because of NOISE, ATTENUATION or other factors.

signal path A continuous conducting route via which electrical or optical SIGNALS are conveyed through a system.

signal processing A specialized branch of computing that deals with continuous streams of data (such as encountered in audio, video, telecommunications, radar and radio engineering) that must be processed in REAL TIME. See more under DIGITAL SIGNAL PROCESSOR.

signal processor See under DIGITAL SIGNAL PROCESSOR.

signal skew A problem that results when parallel electronic SIGNALS travelling via paths of different lengths become out of step with one another.

signal-to-noise ratio One of the most important characteristics of any communications CHANNEL, a measure of how much unwanted NOISE is added to the desired information in a message during its transmission. The lower the signal-to-noise ratio, the more difficult it becomes to accurately recover all the information contained in a message, but ERROR CORRECTION techniques can assist with this recovery. Signal-to-noise ratio is usually expressed in decibels on a LOGARITHMIC scale.

signature 1 A file containing a name and address or other information that is automatically appended to EMAIL messages (see under SIG).

2 A characteristic pattern of bytes in the code of a computer VIRUS that is used by ANTI-VIRUS SOFTWARE to recognize that virus.

3 A special encrypted data value embedded into a document to authenticate its origins when sent over a network. See under DIGITAL SIGNATURE.

4 In OBJECT-ORIENTED PROGRAMMING, a mechanism implemented in the GCC language, similar to an ABSTRACT CLASS but which separates the functions of SUBTYPE and SUBCLASS.

sign bit The MOST SIGNIFICANT BIT of a bit string that is to be interpreted as a signed binary number, which is set to 1 to indicate a negative value and zero to indicate a positive value. Using 8-bit numbers as examples, the bit string 11111111 would represent -127 and 1111111 would represent 127. See also UNSIGNED INTEGER, ONES COMPLEMENT, TWOS COMPLEMENT, BINARY NOTATION, BINARY NUMBER.

significance The position occupied by each digit of a number expressed using a POSITIONAL NOTATION. For instance in the decimal number 5728, 5 is the most significant digit and 8 is the least significant. See also MOST SIGNIFICANT BIT, LEAST SIGNIFICANT BIT.

SIGPLAN See under SPECIAL INTEREST GROUP.

silicon The 14th element in the Periodic Table and second most abundant element in the Earth's crust, a constituent of most rocks, clays and sands. It is a SEMICONDUCTOR, whose electrical properties have made it the most important material for fabricating INTEGRATED CIRCUITS. Silicon dioxide, better known as the mineral quartz and as glass, is a good insulator, a fact that enables a LITHOGRAPHY technique (similar to printing) to be employed to selectively oxidize the surface of a silicon chip and form separate TRANSISTORS and conductors. See also WAFER, BOULE, MOS, DOPANT.

silicon chip See MICROPROCESSOR.

silicon foundry A firm that fabricates INTEGRATED CIRCUIT chips designed by other companies. Named as an ironic allusion to old iron foundries.

Silicon Graphics Inc. (SGI) Manufacturer of the most powerful GRAPHICS WORKSTATIONS, including those used in the movie industry to create 3D GRAPHICS, and a pioneer of VIRTUAL REALITY hardware and software. Its best known products are the Iris and Onyx workstation ranges, Origin servers, and the Reality Engine 3D ACCELERATOR, all of which run SGI's own IRIX version of Unix. In 1998 SGI absorbed CRAY RESEARCH INC., the premier manufacturer of supercomputers. See also MAYA.

silicon on insulator A group of semiconductor fabrication technologies that employ a thin layer of SILICON deposited on an insulating SUBSTRATE (for example SILICON ON SAPPHIRE) rather than solid, SINGLE-CRYSTAL SILICON. They are more resistant to ionizing radiation than ordinary bulk silicon devices and are therefore favoured for military and space applications despite their greater expense.

silicon on sapphire An expensive fabrication technology for INTEGRATED CIRCUITS that tolerates higher operating temperatures and levels of ionizing radiation than conventional MOS circuits, and is used for military and space applications.

Silicon Valley The region of California extending south from San Francisco through Palo Alto to San Jose in which most of the US semiconductor industry and much of the computer industry is concentrated.

sim 1 See SIMULATION.
   2 See SIM CARD.

SIM card (Subscriber Identity Module) A small printed circuit card that must be inserted into a mobile phone to activate the owner's account.

SIMD (single-instruction multiple-data) A class of PARALLEL COMPUTER architectures in which the same simple instruction is executed by multiple processors on different items of data (for example all the elements of an array). This contrasts with the MIMD architectures, in which each processor executes a different program. SIMD machines, such as the CONNECTION MACHINE are best suited for repetitive matrix and array processing problems, as encountered in weather forecasting or FINITE ELEMENT ANALYSIS.

SIMM (Single In-line Memory Module) A small printed circuit board with RAM chips mounted on one or both sides and a single edge connector via which it can be plugged into a computer MOTHERBOARD. Because a SIMM stands up vertically, it permits more chips to be crammed into a given area than if the RAM chips were soldered flat onto the motherboard. The latest SIMMs hold 64 megabytes each.

Simple Mail Transfer Protocol See SMTP.

Simple Network Management Protocol See under SNMP.

simple volume A type of VOLUME under Microsoft's DYNAMIC STORAGE system that consists of free space on the same physical disk.

simplex 1 A communications channel that can transmit only in one direction. See also DUPLEX, HALF-DUPLEX.
   2 In programming, a geometric construction used in solving LINEAR PROGRAMMING problems. It consists of a polygon representing the area of possible solutions, one of whose corners is an optimum solution. See more under SIMPLEX METHOD.

simplex method, simplex algorithm An algorithm for solving OPTIMIZATION problems of many variables by using a geometric representation that can be efficiently computerized as an exercise in matrix arithmetic. It is widely used in industry to schedule production flows, and in the financial arena. See more under LINEAR PROGRAMMING

SIMULA The forerunner of all OBJECT-ORIENTED programming languages, invented by Kristen Nygaard and Ole-Johan Dahl in 1964. Simula was designed for writing discrete simulation programs and introduced the concepts of CLASS and DATA ABSTRACTION.

simulated annealing An algorithm for solving OPTIMIZATION problems that approaches an optimum via repeated steps of variable size. Initially the steps are made large for speed of solution, but they become smaller as the optimum is approached, for stability. This process resembles the annealing of a metal by raising it to a high temperature (large steps) and then allowing it to cool (small steps), hence the name.

simulation The use of a computer to imitate the behaviour of another physical system, such as a machine, a chemical reaction or a living being. Simulation always involves building a computer model of the system to be simulated – a set of software objects that represent those attributes of the physical system deemed to be important, plus a set of rules and constraints controlling their permitted values, to simulate the effect of external forces such as gravity or friction. Simulation involves executing this software model, and recording data that describes its behaviour over time.

There are two main classes of simulation: continuous and discrete. A *continuous simulation*, for example of the trajectory of a missile, calculates the values of all its variables at regular time intervals. A *discrete event simulation*, on the other hand, recalculates the values of its variables only when some significant event occurs – such as a product entering a machine, or a user pressing a button.

The main continuous simulation methods are based on either FINITE ELEMENT ANALYSIS or FINITE DIFFERENCE ALGORITHMS, while for discrete simulations, MONTE CARLO ALGORITHMS are frequently employed.

Simulations may be performed by either an interactive or a batch program. An *interactive simulation* involves building a model visually (perhaps by drawing, dragging and dropping objects) and altering their parameters during the simulation by adjusting on-screen controls. The results will typically be viewed as graphs or animations. In a *batch simulation*, the user feeds a file of starting parameters to the software and gets back a file of results.

Simulation is increasingly used in the computer games industry, where some of the flight simulation games are beginning to approach the sophistication of those used to train real pilots. Even adventure games such as DOOM and QUAKE now incorporate elements of real-time simulation such as realistic gravity, ballistics and elastic behaviours.

simulator A hardware or software system that imitates the behaviour of some other system. For example, computer software that imitates the control panel of an aeroplane. See also SIMULATION, EMULATOR, EMULATION.

simulcasting To broadcast over two different communications media at the same time. The term is most often used to describe a TV or radio programme that is simultaneously published onto the WORLD WIDE WEB. It has also been applied to simultaneous television transmissions in normal and HDTV formats, and to data transmissions via PACKET RADIO systems.

Sinclair computers A series of small and inexpensive personal computers, launched in 1979 by the UK company Sinclair Research (founded by Clive SINCLAIR). The ZX80 was the first computer in the world to sell for less than £100. Based on the 8-bit ZILOG Z80 processor it used a membrane keyboard with no moving parts, 1 kilobyte of RAM, and employed a TV set as its monitor and an audio cassette player for mass storage. Its successor, the ZX81, employed a memory expansion pack with an alarming tendency to overheat or fall off, but the next machine, the Sinclair Spectrum, featured a rubber CHICLET KEYBOARD and a colour graphics display, and was responsible for introducing a whole generation to hobby computing and programming.

Sinclair, Sir Clive A British electronics entrepreneur who in the 1970s pioneered the commercial exploitation of the TRANSISTOR and the INTEGRATED CIRCUIT (particularly SEMICUSTOM CHIPS) to create low-cost consumer devices such as hi-fis, calculators, digital watches, miniature radios and personal computers. His ZX80 was the first ever computer to retail for less than £100, though its capabilities faithfully reflected its price. The marginally superior Spectrum launched in 1981 did for the UK market what the Apple II had done in the USA, opening up personal computing as a hobby.

single-crystal silicon The material from which most INTEGRATED CIRCUITS are manufactured. A single crystal is required because the boundaries between crystals adversely affect silicon's conducting properties by scattering signals. See also BOULE, WAFER.

single-density diskette The name given to two FLOPPY DISK formats used in IBM-COMPATIBLE PCS: the original 5.25-inch floppy which contained 180 kilobytes (KB) and the later 3.5-inch floppy, which held 360 KB. Both formats were later replaced by a DOUBLE-DENSITY DISKETTE (DD) holding twice as much data, and later still by the current HIGH-DENSITY DIS-KETTE (HD) which holds 1.44 megabytes.

Single In-line Memory Module See SIMM.

Single Inline Package (SIP) A type of package for INTEGRATED CIRCUITS that contains several separate chips with a single row of connecting PINS down one edge. SIPs were once used for holding PC memory chips, but they have been replaced by the SIMM, and are now seldom found outside of ultra-miniaturized pocketable devices.

Single Inline Pin Package (SIPP) A type of integrated circuit PACKAGE that has only a single row of connection pins down one side.

single-instruction multiple-data See SIMD.

single keystroking The publishing of documents in such a way that only the original author types the words, and all subsequent editing and layout is performed on an electronic copy.

single-pass compiler See under COMPILATION.

single precision A 32-bit IEEE FLOATING POINT number, rather than a 64-bit DOUBLE PRECISION number. See also PRECISION.

single quote The character ', with ASCII code 39. Owing to the limited resolution of computer displays, this character is often mistaken for or used in place of the apostrophe character (ASCII code 44) or both of them may be used as opening and closing quotes. Professional typesetters employ different characters for opening and closing single quotes (Unicode 145 and 146), neither of which is this character. See also DOUBLE QUOTE.

single step A mode of operation supported by most development environments and DEBUGGER software. It permits programmers to execute a program one instruction at a time (for example by repeatedly pressing the spacebar), enabling them to inspect the contents of variables between steps and locate the exact point at which some error occurs. See also BREAKPOINT, WATCH, SYMBOLIC DEBUGGER, BUG.

single-threaded program A program in which there is only a single flow of control, so that it can perform only one action at a time.

For example, it may not be able to accept user input from the keyboard while it is processing (see HOURGLASS). The opposite is a multi-threaded program: see THREAD, MULTITHREADING.

single-user application A software application that may be used by only one person at a time.

sink An abstraction used to describe the consumer of a data stream emanating from some SOURCE.

SIP See SINGLE INLINE PACKAGE.

SIPP See SINGLE INLINE PIN PACKAGE.

SIRDS Abbreviation of Single Image Random Dot Stereogram. See under AUTOSTEREOGRAM.

16-bit Used to describe a hardware or software system (for example a MICROPROCESSOR or an OPERATING SYSTEM), designed to manipulate numbers that are 16 BITS in length. Microsoft's MS-DOS is a 16-bit operating system, as was WINDOWS prior to Windows NT (Windows 95 and 98 are mixed 16-bit and 32-BIT). 16-bit microprocessors are now rarely found outside EMBEDDED applications. See also 64-BIT.

16-bit application An APPLICATION PROGRAM written to be executed under a 16-BIT operating system, and which therefore may need special support to run on a 32-BIT operating system. The term is often encountered in connection with programs written for Microsoft's MS-DOS, or versions of WINDOWS prior to 95, which can be run on modern 32-bit versions of Windows only by the use of a special DOS BOX. See also THUNK.

68k A shorthand used to refer to any member of the MOTOROLA 68000 family of MICROPROCESSORS.

64-bit Used to describe any digital technology that works with a basic word length of 8 bytes or 64 bits, as in a 64-bit MICROPROCESSOR or a 64-bit OPERATING SYSTEM.

sizing handle A visual user interface component that permits a screen object to be resized by dragging on it with the mouse. The appearance of such handles varies between different operating systems and applications. They may appear as small boxes at the corners and midpoints of a MARQUEE denoting a selected area of an image, triangular buttons placed in the corners of a screen WINDOW, or double-headed arrows that replace the MOUSE POINTER as it passes above a moveable boundary line.

skew A drawing tool that slants a selected image area in any direction.

skin A mechanism used in some application programs that make heavy use of GRAPHICAL USER INTERFACES. It enables the user to load a new file (the 'skin') that instantly changes the colour scheme, the shape of important controls and various other factors that constitute the application's LOOK-AND-FEEL. Some applications even supply a TOOLKIT that allows users to create their own new skins without requiring access to the SOURCE CODE of the program – such skins are then exchanged on user web sites.

skunk works A detached research and development facility created to allow creative workers to operate free of corporate constraints on dress, time keeping (and, by implication, personal hygiene).

SLA See SERVICE LEVEL AGREEMENT.

slash-delimited A type of identifier in which the separate parts are separated by slash (/) symbols. Such identifiers are used in many operating systems to specify directory PATHS (e.g. root/usr/bin), while Internet URLS such as http://www.doh.com/index.html employ a format that combines DOT NOTATION with slash-delimited sections.

slave Any device whose operation is completely controlled by another master device: see also MASTER/SLAVE, BUS MASTER.

SLDRAM A type of RAM created by a consortium of major RAM manufacturers called SyncLink, whose design is a royalty-free, open standard. SLDRAM achieves 800 megabytes per second bandwidth by employing twin internal BUSES, while offering a lower pin count than rival RAM technologies.

sleep A dormant state used to save power on battery-operated portable computers of all kinds. In the sleep state all running programs are suspended and most major hardware systems (including the DISPLAY, DISK and COMMUNICATION PORTS) are shut down to reduce power consumption. The CPU itself may reduce its clock speed or enter some special low-power mode. The machine is typically reawakened from a sleep state either by pressing any key on the keyboard, or on the receipt of a message over a network.

slice A small portion of some resource. See for example TIME SLICE.

slider, slider control A visual component employed in many GRAPHICAL USER INTERFACES that mimics the operation of a sliding switch, and is typically used to control some continuously variable quantity such as sound volume or colour brightness.

slide-show A sequence of pages of information, possibly containing both text and images, presented on a computer screen or projector to accompany a business presentation or lecture. PRESENTATION GRAPHICS applications such as PowerPoint simplify the creation of such slide-shows, and allow the speaker to advance to the next page by simply pressing a key (such as the spacebar) or a mouse button.

SLIP (Serial Line Internet Protocol) A protocol that enables TCP/IP packets to be carried over a serial line, such as an RS-232 port, rather than over a network such as Ethernet. Hence SLIP (or the alternative PPP), is the software that enables most home users to connect to the Internet, using a modem and public telephone line to reach their ISP's server. SLIP works by appending an extra end character to each packet so that successive packets can be distinguished from one another.

SLIP requires that an IP ADDRESS be allocated before each connection is made – unlike PPP, which can dynamically obtain an IP address after connection.

slot **1** A type of socket fitted to a computer's MOTHERBOARD into which expansion cards can be plugged. See more under EXPANSION SLOT, EXPANSION CARD, EXPANSION BUS.

2 A short time interval during which some scheduled event must occur – for example a packet of information must be inserted into a network stream, or a process must be allowed to run. See also TIME SLICE.

3 The term adopted by INTEL for its proprietary processor buses (see under SLOT 1 and SLOT 2) from the PENTIUM II chip onwards.

Slot 1 A new PROCESSOR BUS developed by Intel for the Pentium II processor in 1997 to replace the SOCKET 7 and SOCKET 8 interfaces used by previous Pentium chips and by compatible chips from AMD and Cyrix. Slot 1 is in effect a DAUGHTERBOARD interface. It does not accept the processor chip's pins directly but instead the CPU and its LEVEL 2 CACHE memory chips are sealed within a plastic cartridge that plugs into the slot via a single-ROW EDGE CONNECTOR with 242 contacts. Slot 1 is electrically equivalent to Socket 8 and includes a BACKSIDE BUS running at half the processor's core clock speed. See also SLOT 2.

Slot 2 A new PROCESSOR BUS developed by Intel for the Pentium II family of processors in 1997 which is a faster, slightly larger version of the SLOT 1 interface. It can hold more LEVEL 2 CACHE memory than Slot 1, and its BACKSIDE BUS runs at full processor core speed, which makes it more suitable for high-performance applications such as multiprocessor servers.

Slot A A processor interface developed by AMD for its earlier Athlon microprocessors. Like Intel's SLOT 1 and SLOT 2, Slot A accepts cartridges carrying the CPU and CACHE MEMORY, rather than bare CPU pins. However, it is not electrically compatible with Intel's sockets, but is instead based on the EV-6 BUS specification developed by Digital Equipment for its Alpha 21264 processor. For more recent Athlon and Duron designs, AMD has reverted to a simpler processor interface called *Socket A*, which accepts bare PIN-GRID ARRAY CPU chips.

small caps Letters in any font that are in the form of the capitals from that font but are the same height as its LOWER CASE letters. They are used as an extra mode of emphasis after bold, italic and underline. In this dictionary they are used to mark out cross-references (for example: see also FONT).

Small Computer System Interface See SCSI.

Smalltalk The first OBJECT-ORIENTED PROGRAMMING LANGUAGE, developed at Xerox PARC in 1972 by a group including Alan Kay and Larry Tesler. The Smalltalk project profoundly influenced the subsequent course of computing. It introduced the concept of object-orientation, and the Xerox Star and Dorado workstations that were built to run it pioneered the BITMAPPED DISPLAY, GRAPHICAL USER INTERFACE, WINDOWS, MENUS, ICONS and the use of a MOUSE as pointing device.

Smalltalk is a purely object-oriented language that represents everything, even the numbers, as objects with their own methods. It is a semi-compiled language that compiles to a BYTECODE that is then interpreted. It has a simple syntax based on a POSTFIX NOTATION, where the name of an object is followed by a message or SELECTOR that invokes one of its methods. In the example:

```
CurrentAccount payIn: 1000 reason:
"salary mar 1999"
```

`CurrentAccount` is an object representing a bank account that receives a message (with the selector `payIn: reason:`) to add an amount to it, and to record the reason for this payment. Note that Smalltalk also introduced the style of embedding capital letters to break up long names, which has become so prevalent in computer brand-names. The definitive version of the language was released in 1980 as Smalltalk-80.

Though Smalltalk is not much used for commercial programming, it introduced all the concepts – CLASS, METHOD, INHERITANCE, ENCAPSULATION – that are now embodied in the most widely used language C++, as well as in many others such as JAVA, DELPHI and to a lesser extent VISUAL BASIC.

smart A jargon term that can be applied to any electronic device that contains a MICROPROCESSOR and which can therefore be programmed to perform more than one function: for example a SMARTCARD or a SMART TERMINAL. Its opposite is DUMB.

smartcard A credit-card-sized slip of plastic, containing an embedded memory chip (and possibly a tiny MICROPROCESSOR), that can be used to store personal information. The smartcard is inserted into a reader device that makes contact either via brass contacts on the card's surface or by induction, allowing its contents to be read or altered. The data capacity of smartcards expands yearly, with megabytes now possible.

Applications for smartcards include storing ENCRYPTION keys and billing details for mobile telephones and pay-per-view television systems; in high-security identification systems, where for example fingerprint data may be stored in the card; for storing medical records; and for online electronic payment schemes where a cash balance can be downloaded to the card and debited automatically as purchases are made. See also JAVA CARD, PC/SC and OPENCARD.

SmartDrive The DISK CACHE program supplied with Microsoft's MS-DOS operating system. SmartDrive stores recently accessed disk sectors in memory so that any subsequent accesses will be faster, and diverts any data written to disk into memory for later writing (so-called WRITE-BEHIND cacheing). The latter feature may cause data loss if the computer should crash before write-back has occurred. SmartDrive was also a REAL MODE program, which complicated its use under later versions of WINDOWS.

smartphone A mobile phone handset that incorporates the functions of a hand-held computer, including an address database, appointment calendar, note-taking facilities, fax, SHORT MESSAGE SERVICE and WEB BROWSER software. See also WAP, GSM, GPRS, MOBILE PHONE.

smart terminal A computer terminal that contains its own processor and memory, and so can perform some local processing: for example to run a GRAPHICAL USER INTERFACE such as the X WINDOW SYSTEM, Citrix WINFRAME or a WEB BROWSER. See also DUMB TERMINAL.

SMB 1 (Server Message Block) A file and printer sharing network protocol developed jointly by Microsoft and Intel, and employed in the former's NETBIOS, LAN MANAGER and WINDOWS NT network systems. SMB is also available for other operating systems, for example under Unix via the SAMBA utility suite.

2 Abbreviation of Small to Medium Business.

SMDS (Switched Multimegabit Data Service) A high-speed, SWITCHED public data network technology developed by Bellcore and now widely used by US telephone companies in the backbone of their data networks. SMDS is capable of transmission speeds from 56 kilobits per second up to 34 megabits per second and differs significantly from ASYNCHRONOUS TRANSFER MODE in using variable-length DATAGRAMS rather than fixed-length cells as its unit of transmission. See also FRAME RELAY, SYNCHRONOUS OPTICAL NETWORK, SYNCHRONOUS DIGITAL HIERARCHY.

SME (Small to Medium Enterprise) A computer marketing category that is distinguished from the CORPORATE and the home (SOHO) sectors.

smiley A symbol composed from several punctuation characters, appended to an EMAIL or other message to convey mood, particularly to indicate that the writer is joking or commenting ironically. Smileys resemble smiling faces if viewed with the head tilted to the left. Popular forms include a smile :-) a wink ;-) a broader smile :)) and a frown ">:-(

smoothing 1 The removal of SPIKES and other irregularities from a power supply.

2 The application of a mathematical transform to a set of data points to make them more closely approximate to a smooth curve or line.

3 In some graphics and type rendering programs, an alternative term for the ANTIALIASING of lines and characters. See also ALIAS, JAGGIES.

4 In VECTOR-based drawing programs, a feature that makes a curve appear less angular by reducing and optimizing the spacing of the nodes from which it is composed.

smooth scrolling The ability of a computer display that is larger than the physical screen to be moved in increments of a single pixel (rather than by some larger unit), giving the appearance of smooth movement. Most modern computers with GRAPHICAL USER INTERFACES support smooth scrolling, while older text-based terminals permit scrolling only by a whole line of text at a time.

smooth shading A group of methods employed by 3D GRAPHICS software that render objects in such a way as to disguise the fact that they are constructed from a collection of flat polygons rather than truly curved surfaces. The edges where the adjacent polygons join are made invisible by creating exactly that gradient of darkness across the surface of each polygon that it would display if it were due to shadow on an obliquely-lit curved surface. This requires calculating a shade for each point within the polygon that is an interpolation between the known colours of its corners or edges due to the incident light. Special algorithms such as GOURAUD SHADING or PHONG SHADING have been developed to do this.

SMP (symmetric multiprocessor) A computer that contains multiple processors all of the same type, and typically all sharing the same bank of memory. See more under SHARED-MEMORY MULTIPROCESSOR, see also MULTIPROCESSOR, MULTICOMPUTER.

SMS 1 (Short Message Service) A telecommunication service offered on GSM digital MOBILE PHONES, often referred to by the popular name of TEXTING, which enables alphanumeric messages of up to 160 characters (similar to those sent to a PAGER) to be displayed on the handset. Like a pager, SMS may be used not only as a person-to-person messaging system, but by commercial services that provide regular updates of stock prices, news flashes, sports results and so on. The GSM network stores up all the messages directed to a particular phone until that phone is switched on and comes within signal range. SMS works as a channel within the TDMA digital transmission system, using standard data compression techniques to reduce the amount of bandwidth consumed. See also TIME DIVISION MULTIPLEXING.

2 Abbreviation of SYSTEMS MANAGEMENT SERVER.

SMTP (Simple Mail Transfer Protocol) A protocol used to transfer EMAIL from server to server and between client and server on networks, especially the Internet. SMTP activity is normally a background task under the control of a message transport system such as SENDMAIL. SMTP delivers mail only as far as the server, so some additional protocol such as IMAP or POP3 is required to access and read the messages from there. SMTP does not guarantee delivery, issue return receipts, allow mail to be 'unsent' or handle attachments to messages. SMTP is defined in RFC 821.

smurf attack A type of DENIAL OF SERVICE ATTACK used by HACKERS to bring down an Internet server, by causing it to be bombarded with thousands of replies every second to a faked PING request.

SNA (Systems Network Architecture) A set of network protocols released by IBM in 1974 for connecting its MAINFRAME computers together. SNA is a layered system, but its seven layers are not compatible with those described in the OSI REFERENCE MODEL.

SNAFU Situation Normal, All F***ed Up. US armed forces slang for an error condition, which has passed into programmer's parlance.

snail mail Online slang for the ordinary postal services (i.e. surface or air mail), alluding to the superior speed of EMAIL.

snapshot A record of the state of a system at a particular instant. If the system is a computer's display screen, this coincides with the everyday notion of a snapshot (a quickly-taken picture), but the term can equally well be applied to abstract and non-visual information such as the contents of a program's working memory.

sneakernet No network at all. The implication is that you exchange data by walking to a colleague's machine carrying a floppy disk.

SNI Abbreviation of SIEMENS NIXDORF INTERNATIONAL.

SNMP (Simple Network Management Protocol) A high level protocol used for the remote management of network devices over the Internet, defined in STD 15 (RFC 1157). SNMP works via software agents embedded into network devices that collect information about events, traffic volumes, and device status and store them in a database. SNMP v2 is the current, enhanced version of the protocol.

SNMP can be run on top of protocols other

than TCP/IP, and may be used to configure or monitor any kind of equipment, from computers, hubs and routers to domestic appliances such as central heating and light switches.

Snobol (StriNg Oriented symBOlic Language) An interpreted programming language specifically designed for manipulating text data, invented by Farber, Griswold and Polonsky at BELL LABORATORIES in 1963. Some of its innovative operations live on today in PERL.

snooping See under BUS SNOOPING.

SOAP (Simple Object Access Protocol) A communications protocol launched by Microsoft in 2000. It enables objects created under different systems (such as DCOM and CORBA) to invoke each other's METHODS by exchanging plain text messages in an XML-based format over an ordinary HTTP connection (as used to access web sites). SOAP is intended to play a crucial role in integrating distributed applications, as part of Microsoft's future Internet strategy: see also .NET, WEB SERVICE, UDDI.

socket 1 An opening or hollow into which some other component may be fitted. For example, a processor socket or power socket.
2 A mechanism for creating virtual connections between two UNIX processes, originally developed for Berkeley Unix but now available for all versions, and for other operating systems such as WINDOWS.

Sockets effectively extend Unix's STANDARD INPUT/OUTPUT system to cover remote communication, so that the inputs and outputs of any program can be redirected onto the network. There are two kinds of socket connection, a bi-directional STREAM or a fixed-length DATAGRAM. Sockets provide the APPLICATION PROGRAMMING INTERFACE to the Internet for Unix systems, connecting email and web browsing software to the network. When it is created, each new socket receives a unique address consisting of a PORT number and the IP ADDRESS address of its host computer.

Socket 7 A 296-pin processor socket and bus interface, running at 66 MHz, which was introduced by INTEL for the original PENTIUM chip. Socket 7 was adopted by the various Pentium-compatible chip makers (such as AMD

and Cyrix) as an industry standard, and this for a while enabled PC MOTHERBOARDS to accept any manufacturer's CPU chip. Intel replaced Socket 7 with faster and more proprietary patented interfaces (SLOT 1 and SLOT 2) for its P6 class processors from the Pentium II onward, resulting in the loss of such interchangeability. See also SOCKET 8.

Socket 8 A 387-pin processor socket developed by Intel for the Pentium Pro in 1997. It enhanced the previous SOCKET 7 interface by splitting the processor bus in two: a 64-bit FRONTSIDE BUS connected to main memory, and a separate 64-bit BACKSIDE BUS for accessing the LEVEL 2 CACHE memory. Socket 8 did not accept a 'naked' processor chip, but rather a multichip module containing the CPU and L2 cache chips, mounted in a conventional PIN-GRID ARRAY package. Socket 8 was rapidly replaced by the DAUGHTERBOARD-based SLOT 1 interface, with which it is electrically identical. See also PENTIUM, PACKAGE, PIN, ZIF.

Socket A The processor socket employed by AMD's latest Athlon and Duron processors. See also SLOT A, SLOT 1, SLOT 2.

soft boot To reset a computer's operating system to its start-up status without erasing all the contents of memory. Soft booting is typically possible only under operating systems that are executed from ROM (as with pocket computers such as those from PALM and PSION).

Softimage A professional 3D animation program, now owned by Microsoft, that was used to produce the dinosaurs in the film *Jurassic Park*. Softimage supports many advanced features including volumetric lighting, INVERSE KINEMATICS and PARTICLE SYSTEMS for dust and smoke effects.

soft reset See under RESET.

soft sectored A type of FLOPPY DISK on which individual SECTORS are distinguished only by data patterns stored on its surface, rather than by physical perforations as with the older HARD SECTORED formats. All modern disks are soft sectored. See also FORMAT, TRACK.

software   A collective term for all the programs that a computer can execute and the data on which these programs operate. It is useful to distinguish several different classes of software. APPLICATION SOFTWARE performs useful tasks for the computer's user, such as word processing, accounting or drawing. SYSTEM SOFTWARE (such as an operating system or a device driver) performs tasks to control the computer, or to assist application programs perform their tasks. Development software (such as a language COMPILER or a DEBUGGER) is used by programmers to write more software.

There is a clear distinction between software and HARDWARE (if you can stub your toe on it, it's hardware), but software and hardware are nevertheless intimately connected because software requires hardware on which to exist. Software must be stored on some physical medium (such as a floppy disk, CD-ROM or tape) and it has no meaning without a hardware computer on which it can be executed. The connection runs deeper than this, for it is an almost universal truth of computer engineering that any job that can be performed by specially designed hardware could also be done by software running on a sufficiently powerful general-purpose computer.

Software is a profoundly abstract concept because, although we imagine it to consist solely of long strings of 0s and 1s, in reality these numbers are themselves abstractions from physical quantities. When a program is stored on a floppy disk, the 0s and 1s are represented by tiny areas of magnetized iron oxide, whereas on a CD-ROM they are tiny pits in a piece of plastic – and once the program is loaded into main memory they are represented by the electrical charges stored in microscopic silicon transistors. Nevertheless there is a strong sense in which we may call all these forms the *same* piece of software. This interchangeability of representation is what gives digital technologies their astonishing power; a piece of music can be recorded, transmitted across the world via a satellite link, and reproduced with no loss of quality at all, so long as all its bits are transcribed accurately into each different medium. In the end, software is any information that can be stored in digital form, on whatever medium.

Software AG   Germany's largest software house, specializing in database and networking products.

software audit   The process of inspecting all the software products installed on a company's computers, to ensure that the appropriate licence fees have been paid.

software bloat   The phenomenon in which successive versions of a software product tend to grow ever larger as more features are added. Also called CREEPING FEATURITIS.

software bus   A term once used by enthusiasts of OBJECT-ORIENTED PROGRAMMING to describe their goal – a software environment in which the same set of independent software modules can be connected to each other via well-defined interfaces to build different products. This is analogous to a hardware bus into which various expansion cards and components can be plugged.

Software Developers Kit (SDK)   A set of software tools (normally containing a programming language COMPILER or INTERPRETER, DEBUGGING tools, DEVICE DRIVERS, APPLICATION PROGRAMMING INTERFACE libraries and their documentation) that is published by the vendor of a forthcoming hardware or software product to assist third party programmers in creating applications for it. An SDK will typically be released for any novel language, operating system, hardware device (such as a GRAPHICS CARD) or a programmable application. Examples include the JAVA SDK and WINDOWS SDK.

software engineering   A profession that attempts to apply the systematic approach of other engineering disciplines to the analysis, specification, design, construction and maintenance of software products. Software engineering tends to deal with only the larger programming projects, and has devised a variety of management schemes (see METHODOLOGY) for the different phases, often supported by a flow-chart style of notation and partially automated using a CASE TOOL.

Software engineering is also used in a slightly looser sense to describe that collection of principles about good programming practice (such as MODULARITY, INFORMATION HIDING and the separation of INTERFACE from

IMPLEMENTATION) that have emerged from the reformist movements of STRUCTURED PROGRAMMING and OBJECT-ORIENTED PROGRAMMING.

software handshaking A HANDSHAKE between two pieces of communicating equipment in which the signals exchanged are generated by the programs running at either end of the link (rather than by the hardware itself: for example by a UART chip). The most commonly used software handshake protocol is called XON/XOFF, and requires the programs to exchange the ASCII CONTROL CODES 17 and 19 to start and stop transmission.

software interrupt An INTERRUPT raised deliberately by a program, by causing the processor to execute a special machine instruction (for example the Intel 80x86 family's INT, or the POWERPC's TRAP) rather than by some hardware event. Software interrupts are used to gain the processor's immediate attention to service an urgent or unusual event. The processor handles software interrupts just like hardware interrupts – by storing its current REGISTER state on the STACK and passing control to an INTERRUPT HANDLER routine. See also TRAP, EXCEPTION, EXCEPTION HANDLING.

software licence A legal document that grants the purchaser of a computer software product the right to use that product. Most such licences give the user the right to run the software on only a single computer (or a specified number of computers, depending on the price paid) and do not permit the user to pass on copies of the product to others. Software products are therefore treated as INTELLECTUAL PROPERTY and are possessed by their purchaser only in the same sense that they possess the text of a book, but not the right to reproduce it. Most such licences contain clauses that seek to limit the vendor's responsibility for incidental or consequential damage incurred because of flaws in the product.

There are several schools of thought advocating less restrictive licencing conditions. A SHAREWARE licence permits copies of software to be passed on to others for trial purposes, but still requires payment if the product is adopted for prolonged use. An OPEN SOURCE licence grants the purchaser the right to own the SOURCE CODE of the program, to modify it and to distribute it to others under the same terms. See also EULA.

software life-cycle The process of software creation considered in its entirety, which proceeds through a sequence of discrete stages: specification, design, coding, testing, deployment and integration, and maintenance.

software metrics The application of systematic techniques to measure the size, complexity and performance, and project the cost, of large software projects. See more under METRIC.

software modem A MODEM whose functions are performed by software running on the host computer's CPU rather than by dedicated hardware, the computer's SOUND CARD being used to generate the necessary audio signals. Software modems became feasible once microprocessors achieved sufficient processing speed, roughly speaking beyond 200 MHz. The advantage of a software modem is its low cost, but its disadvantage is that it consumes large amounts of CPU time, making it unsuitable for use in MULTIUSER or SERVER environments.

software piracy The unauthorized use of, or distribution of, proprietary computer programs without purchasing a SOFTWARE LICENCE for them.

software tool A program whose purpose is to assist in the creation of other programs or in the maintenance of a computer system. There is a huge variety of such tools, the most widely-used including language COMPILERS and INTERPRETERS, DEBUGGERS, PROFILERS, FORM DESIGNERS, PROGRAM GENERATORS, text manipulation tools (such as EDITORS, MACRO processors and search-and-replace utilities), and monitoring tools such as network analysers and logging utilities. See also UTILITY, APPLET.

SoftWindows A software emulator created by by Insignia Solutions that enables WINDOWS programs to be executed on UNIX systems.

SOHO (Small Office/Home Office) A term used to identify the computer market sector that includes the self-employed and small home-based businesses.

Solaris SUN MICROSYSTEMS' proprietary variant of the UNIX operating system.

solarize A special effect offered in many BIT-MAP EDITING graphics programs. It turns to negative all the colours in a digitized image (such as a photograph) that are above a certain (moveable) lightness value called the threshold. The effect is similar to that created by accidentally exposing photographic film to the light, hence the name. See also POSTERIZE, THRESHOLDING, IMAGE PROCESSING.

solder A low-melting point alloy of lead, tin and other metals used as a 'glue' to make conducting connections between metal components.

solid modelling The use of 3D GRAPHICS software on a computer to construct realistic images of real-world objects, for example in engineering or architectural design. Solid modeling involves first building a WIRE-FRAME representation of the object and then RENDERING it to create a realistic surface appearance. See also MODEL, COMPUTER AIDED DESIGN, SMOOTH SHADING.

solid-state 1 In physics and electronics, a system whose behaviour (for example the flow of ELECTRONS) takes place solely within solid matter, rather than within a gas, liquid or a vacuum.
2 Hence also those classes of device (such as INTEGRATED CIRCUITS and LEDS) that consist solely of metal and semiconductor, in contrast to devices (such as the CATHODE RAY TUBE or THERMIONIC VALVE) where electrons pass through gas-filled or evacuated spaces, or to mechanical devices with moving parts (such as DISK DRIVES).
3 In marketing, the term is applied to various miniature storage devices such as the FLASH CARD.

solid-state storage device (SSSD) Also called a *RAM disk*. A plug-in card or cartridge containing memory chips (typically STATIC RAM, ELECTRICALLY ERASABLE PROM or FLASH EPROM) that is employed in place of a magnetic disk as a mass storage device on many hand-held and pocket computers. SSSDs were once thought likely to supercede disk drives with moving parts, given their much greater robustness

and longer life. But the remarkable fall in the cost of hard disk space has rendered them commercially viable only where space is at a premium.

solution An application of computers and software to a particular problem.

solution provider A jargon term for one who buys ready-made computer hardware and packaged software and customizes them to create bespoke systems. See also VALUE-ADDED RESELLER.

Solver An add-in analysis tool for Microsoft's EXCEL spreadsheet application that attempts to find an optimal value for the formula in one cell by changing the values in a specified set of other cells. The adjustable cells must be related, either directly or indirectly, to the formula in the target cell, and CONSTRAINTS may be applied to further restrict their permissible values. A typical use for Solver would be to maximize the profit of some operation by altering adjustable factors such as advertising expenditure, cost of goods and overheads.

The Solver uses an ITERATIVE procedure that tries out different combinations of values and checks whether the goal is closer. It offers a choice of algorithms, precision and convergence conditions to achieve a solution in a reasonable amount of time. See also GOAL-SEEKING.

SOM (System Object Model) An obsolete OBJECT MODEL developed by IBM for its OS/2 operating system. It differs from Microsoft's COMPONENT OBJECT MODEL in supporting inheritance, and in being fully CORBA-compliant. SOM was the object technology underlying the OPENDOC compound document format.

SONET (Synchronous Optical Network) The US technology standard for BROADBAND FIBRE-OPTIC telecommunication networks, equivalent to the European SYNCHRONOUS DIGITAL HIERARCHY. SONET carries circuit-switched digital data at rates that are multiples of 51.84 megabits per second, the fastest currently being 48 times (2.488 gigabits per second). See also ASYNCHRONOUS TRANSFER MODE, FRAME RELAY, SMDS.

Sony A Japanese electronics company, founded in Tokyo in 1946, which is now a partner in one of one of the world's largest media conglomerates. Sony pioneered many of the most popular electronic product categories from transistor radios to video recorders, the Walkman portable personal stereo cassette player to the Gameboy games console. The firm now also has a major presence in the notebook and handheld computer markets.In collaboration with the Dutch firm PHILIPS, Sony has also defined many of the most widely used recording formats, including the various CD standards. See for example RED BOOK.

Sony Playstation A best-selling GAMES CONSOLE that plugs into a domestic television set and runs two-player games supplied on CD-ROM, using a pair of supplied JOYSTICKS for control. The PlayStation, especially version 2, incorporates some of the most advanced 3D GRAPHICS acceleration chips ever made, capable of 128-bit calculations.

sort To arrange a collection of items into order, according to some well-defined criterion (for example by alphabetical order). Sorting is one of the most fundamental operations in computing, and sorting ALGORITHMS are the most studied and best understood. Many computer applications depend for their operation on the data being in sorted order, the most obvious being the INDEX for a database file.

If the items in the collection are larger than single words or numbers, one part of each item must be chosen to sort by, and this is known as the sort KEY. For example in a database RECORD, the key would be a single FIELD (for example the Name field). If the items do not all have unique keys, then all items having the same key will be sorted into the same position. In this case a SECONDARY KEY can be chosen (for example First Name) and all the duplicated items further sorted by this key. This process may be continued for many levels of key.

Sorting efficiency is acutely sensitive to the choice of the correct algorithm for the kind of data. Choosing a better algorithm can often reduce the sorting time by many orders of magnitude. See also QUICKSORT, INSERTION SORT, BUBBLE SORT, HEAP SORT, TREE SORT, MERGE SORT and SHELL SORT.

sound See under SOUND CARD, SYNTHESIZER, DIGITAL AUDIO, CD-QUALITY, SAMPLING, MIDI, WAV, MP3, REALAUDIO.

SoundBlaster A popular and inexpensive range of SOUND CARDS manufactured by CREATIVE LABS.

sound card An expansion card used to add sound reproduction capabilities to IBM-compatible PCs. A typical low-cost sound card contains a simple MIDI SYNTHESIZER chip (capable of generating musical notes and sound effects under program control), an A-to-D converter and small audio amplifier, along with stereo sockets to input analogue audio signals from a microphone and to output to external loudspeakers or headphones. Such cards also enable music CDs to be played via the PC's CD-ROM drive, and sounds to be recorded as WAV files on the hard disk.

More expensive cards may contain interfaces to control MIDI musical instruments, direct digital audio inputs and outputs, and WAVETABLE synthesizers that generate music from recorded samples of actual instruments, stored either in ROM or downloaded into RAM on the card.

soundex A search algorithm, used in some TEXT RETRIEVAL SYSTEMS, that attempts to find words that are pronounced similarly. Soundex works by throwing away all the vowels in a word and examining just the consonants, while making certain simplifying substitutions, so that for example cool, coal and kale might all reduce to the same form kl. This rather crude scheme can be surprisingly effective when, say, searching for foreign terms whose transliterations are very variable. It might for example find Khashgai, Quashgai, Qashgi and many other varied spellings in a database of oriental textiles. See also PROXIMITY SEARCH, SYNONYM RING, SEARCH ENGINE, FUZZY SEARCH.

source 1 In programming, an abbreviation for SOURCE CODE.
2 An abstract term meaning the producer of a stream of information that is continually consumed by a corresponding SINK.

source code A textual description of a computer program, written in a programming language. Source code is not directly executable by a computer, and must first be translated into MACHINE CODE either by passing it through a COMPILER or loading it into an INTERPRETER that translates and executes it one statement at a time.

A program's source code (often shortened to *source*) is the representation of the program that is most intelligible to humans, and in general it is necessary to possess the source of a program in order to modify it, or even to understand how it works internally. Hence ownership of the source code is effective ownership of the program, while most users of off-the-shelf PC software possess only a licence to use an executable copy of the machine code. See also OBJECT CODE, OPEN SOURCE, REVERSE ENGINEER.

source control The management of the SOURCE CODE of a programming project, to ensure that the changes made by programmers working on different parts of the program are all recorded correctly and integrated into the whole, without overwriting or undoing each others' work. Source control systems typically work by storing all the source code files in a central REPOSITORY, from which each programmer must check them out, so that a log of who did what to each file can be automatically maintained. See also VERSION CONTROL.

space The ASCII character with code 32, which by convention appears on a computer screen or printer as a blank space, and is used to separate words. It may be entered into a text by pressing the SPACEBAR. The fact that space is a real character with a code, not merely an absence, creates some important differences between the manual and computerized handling of text: see for example LEADING SPACES, TRAILING SPACES.

spacebar, space-bar An elongated key, normally placed at the centre of the bottom row of typewriter and computer keyboards, that is used to type the SPACE character.

space-efficient Requiring a minimum of MEMORY to store.

spaghetti code A mocking description coined by advocates of STRUCTURED PROGRAMMING when criticizing programs written in early programming languages such as COBOL and FORTRAN. Excessive reliance on the GOTO statement as the main instrument for changing CONTROL FLOW made the course of execution in such programs extremely difficult to visualize, allegedly as hard as tracing the strands in a plate of spaghetti.

spamming The sending of an unrequested and unwanted EMAIL to multiple recipients, usually for the purpose of advertising. The practice is severely frowned upon in net circles, and may provoke retaliation (see for example MAIL BOMB). The name derives from a popular Monty Python sketch containing a song whose lyric, 'spam, spam, spam, spam...' suggests the repetitive element of the practice.

spanned volume A type of volume under Microsoft's DYNAMIC STORAGE system that consists of free space from several physical disks.

spanning tree In GRAPH THEORY, any path that connects all the vertices of a network. If the edges of the network are assigned weights, then the 'minimum spanning tree' is that with the smallest sum of edge weights, i.e. the 'shortest' path through the network. Hence in computer network engineering an algorithm employed by a ROUTER to reroute around a failed node (see under SPANNING TREE ALGORITHM). See also TREE, TRAVELLING SALESMAN PROBLEM.

spanning tree algorithm 1 In general, an algorithm for finding a path that completely traverses a particular network structure. See also SPANNING TREE, GRAPH THEORY.

2 A particular ROUTING algorithm for both local and wide area networks defined in IEEE standard 802.1d, which seeks to avoid the formation of closed loops when bridging between different networks. When the switches or routers in a network are so connected that a circular path exists (say A→B →C→A), it becomes possible for data PACKETS to travel around this loop forever if no router is smart enough to prevent it, and such loops can lead to a catastrophic increase in traffic.

The spanning tree algorithm, which is implemented in hardware within the routers, prevents this mishap by assigning different path costs to any parallel links it detects between two routers: say A→B→A and A→C→A. The algorithm automatically turns off the ports of the links with the highest path cost, thus disabling that path and avoiding a loop. If the primary link should fail, the algorithm can switch back on the port that connects the currently redundant path. See also ROUTER, SWITCHED, SWITCHING HUB, CONGESTION.

SPARC Abbreviation of SCALABLE PROCESSOR ARCHITECTURE.

SPARCstation A range of powerful GRAPHICS WORKSTATIONS manufactured by SUN MICROSYSTEMS, INC. and powered by the firm's own SCALABLE PROCESSOR ARCHITECTURE family of processors.

sparse matrix A data structure used to save memory in applications that employ tables, most especially in SPREADSHEETS. A naive approach to storing a 10 × 10 table would be to reserve space for 100 cells even if some of the cells are empty – so a spreadsheet with only two numbers, one in cell A1 and another in J10, would consume as much memory as one containing 100 numbers. A sparse matrix implementation employs DYNAMIC ALLOCATION of memory to store only those cells that are actually filled.

spawn To create and start a CHILD PROCESS in a MULTITASKING operating system. For example under UNIX the FORK system call may be employed for this purpose.

speaker dependent Any SPEECH RECOGNITION system that requires prior training to recognize each different user's voice.

speaker independent Any SPEECH RECOGNITION system that can recognize voice commands without prior training (though it may improve by adapting with continued use).

spec Shorthand for SPECIFICATION.

SPECfp A benchmark for FLOATING-POINT performance. See more under SPECMARK.

Special Interest Group (SIG) Any of several specialized technical subgroups run by the ASSOCIATION FOR COMPUTING MACHINERY. The best-known is *SIGPLAN* (Special Interest Group on Programming Languages) and *SIGGRAPH* (Special Interest Group for Computer Graphics).

specification 1 A detailed description of the tasks that some system is intended to perform. The fundamental aim of all engineering disciplines is to correctly specify a system and then ensure that the finished system meets the specification by testing.
2 (spec) A listing of the features fitted to a computer system, such as the PROCESSOR speed, amount of RAM, number and size of HARD DISKS and video system. A typical spec, as printed in a retailer's advertisement, might begin 'Pentium III 850 MHz, 256 MB RAM, 20 GB HDD, 32 MB ATI AGP graphics...'

Specification and Design Language (SDL) A graphically-based programming language created by the INTERNATIONAL TELECOMMUNICATIONS UNION (ITU-T recommendation Z100) for the purpose of specifying and describing the behaviour of complex telecommunications systems.
SDL supports two different ways to represent any program, *Graphic Representation* (called SDL/GR) and a textual form called *Phrase Representation* (SDL/PR), which provide equivalent representations of the same system SEMANTICS. Graphical tools have been produced that permit a system to be drawn as a form of FLOW CHART, which can then be automatically checked for consistency and turned into a program text. SDL defines systems as collections of communicating FINITE STATE MACHINES, and provides a special notation for describing the events that trigger state TRANSITIONS. The language is equally applicable to PROCESS CONTROL and embedded REAL-TIME systems.

SPECint A benchmark for INTEGER arithmetic performance. See more under SPECMARK.

speckle Small unwanted spots of colour left behind in a digital image as a result of slight inaccuracies in certain image processing operations, for example around the edges of an area to which a MASK has been applied. They can be removed by applying a DESPECKLE filter.

SPECmark A widely used benchmark suite for measuring both the FLOATING-POINT ARITHMETIC and INTEGER performance of a computer's processor, developed by SPEC (Standard Performance Evaluation Corporation), a non-profit body located in California. The suite contains separate benchmarks for floating-point and integer performance called *SPECfp* and *SPECint* respectively. Successive versions of these programs are labelled with their year of release, as in SPECfp95.

specular highlights Bright areas on the surface of an object rendered in 3D GRAPHICS to simulate the direct reflection of the incident light toward the viewer. Such highlights may be sharp, suggesting a hard shiny surface, or progressively more diffuse to suggest rougher surface textures. Some rendering algorithms (such as PHONG SHADING) support specularity, while less demanding ones (such as GOURAUD SHADING) do not. See also SMOOTH SHADING, TEXTURE MAPPING.

specularity The size and intensity of the SPECULAR HIGHLIGHTS on an object rendered in 3D GRAPHICS. See also SMOOTH SHADING, SHADE.

speculative execution A performance-enhancing technique employed in some of the latest microprocessor designs to avoid PIPELINE BREAKS caused by wrongly predicted conditional BRANCH instructions (see more under BRANCH PREDICTION). Instructions from both possible branch outcomes are PRE-FETCHED and executed before the condition is even evaluated, to keep the pipeline flowing. Once the condition result is known, the instructions from the branch that failed are discarded along with their results; this is usually achieved by some kind of REGISTER RENAMING scheme.

Speech Application Programming Interface See SAPI.

speech recognition, speech processing Also called *voice recognition*. The ability of a computer to identify words spoken by a human and convert them into digital text, for example to support automated dictation. There is a profound distinction between such recognition and the far more difficult task of 'understanding' human speech (see NATURAL LANGUAGE PROCESSING), which remains a far-off prospect.

DISCRETE SPEECH RECOGNITION systems require the speaker to pause after uttering each word, while CONTINUOUS-SPEECH RECOGNITION systems can cope with a normally inflected voice, but consume more computing power. Continuous recognition is nevertheless now possible on the more powerful PCs, fitted with the equivalent of a fast Pentium CPU and more than 32 megabytes of memory. Products such as IBM's ViaVoice and Dragon Dictate's Naturally Speaking recognize continuous speech, and can input the resulting text into many different PC applications such as word processors and databases.

PC-based speech recognition products typically make use of a SOUND CARD already fitted to the PC, inputting speech via its microphone socket. The recognition software must be trained to recognize each individual user's voice, by repeatedly reading prepared texts to it. Continuous speech recognition software typically employs a dictionary of more than 200,000 words stored on disk.

A different class of speech recognition applications (such as issuing commands to machinery, or voice-controlled telephony services) need to handle only very restricted vocabularies of short commands, and this may drastically reduce the memory and computing power required, and even eliminate the need for training. Such systems store acoustic templates (averaged samples from many speakers) against which to compare the input commands.

The first challenge for any speech recognition software is to match words despite the slight differences in speed, pitch, emphasis and emotion that are experienced even with the same speaker. Among the currently favoured recognition algorithms are statistical HIDDEN MARKOV MODELS and NEURAL NETWORKS. Such algorithms attempt to analyse an acoustic signal into PHONEMES by matching it against a database of acoustic samples, allotting different probabilities to different possible matches.

Such *acoustic matching* is only the first step, and further computation is devoted to resolving ambiguities (such as 'to' versus 'two') and to identify whole words and sentences. This second phase is called *linguistic matching*, and typically employs a model of the grammar of the human language being recognized. Finite state grammars consist of a network of states and transitions that specify which words follow one another in a given context (known as the active vocabulary), and they work well for the restricted vocabularies employed for voice control of machines or telephony. For unstructured dictation applications, statistical language models are more suitable. These calculate the probability that a particular word was uttered by considering the identity of its preceding word (a *bigram model*) or two words (a *trigram model*).

The separation of acoustic matching from linguistic matching has enabled good progress to be made toward multilingual speech recognition, which works with a dictionary of all the phonemes encountered in human languages.

speech synthesis The creation of sound waveforms that imitate human speech, from either phonetic or plain text descriptions (the latter being called TEXT-TO-SPEECH). By reading aloud the text from the screen and command menus, speech synthesis software may be used to assist visually and verbally disabled people to communicate with a computer. Hardware speech synthesizers are often embedded in toys, household appliances and information kiosks, and are employed to automate telephone services such as directory inquiries.

Modern PCs have sufficient computing power to perform speech synthesis in software alone, using the sound chip on a multipurpose SOUND CARD to generate the waveforms. High quality synthesizers are also available as dedicated EXPANSION CARDS, or external units that plug into a PC serial or parallel port that contain specialized sound chips and DIGITAL SIGNAL PROCESSORS. Such units offer unlimited vocabularies and a range of different, realistic human voices.

Speech synthesis is not such a difficult computing task as SPEECH RECOGNITION, but it still requires several separate processing stages. First the text is normalized, to remove punctuation and verbalize numerals and other symbols (so £2.30 becomes 'two pounds and thirty pence'). The words are then stripped of any suffixes and prefixes to obtain word roots so that a memory-resident dictionary can be employed to translate them into a stream of PHONEMES. In high quality systems a final stage parses the text for intonation and stress, to avoid the flat, robotic monotone often associated with synthesized speech. The resulting stream of phonemes is fed to a sound chip, which employs a series of filters that mimic the human vocal tract to produce the final sounds.

SpeedStep The name given by Intel to those members of its range of PENTIUM III class processors that are optimized for use in portable computers and employ intelligent power monitoring circuitry to slow down the processor clock and shut down those subunits that are not currently being used in order to preserve power.

spellchecker A software utility that tests that words typed by the user are spelled correctly, by referring to one or more built-in dictionaries. Spellcheckers are now included as standard in all WORD PROCESSORS, but are increasingly to be found in other types of program too, especially EMAIL CLIENT software, DESKTOP PUBLISHING applications and WEB AUTHORING tools.

Most spellcheckers have two (or more) modes of operation: a *check-as-you-go* mode in which each word is checked as soon as the user types a following space, and a *whole-document* mode that scans a finished document and highlights those words it thinks are wrongly spelled. Owing to the impossibility of containing every proper name, jargon term or user-defined identifier within a dictionary, spellchecker interfaces typically consult the user before actually changing any spellings. They also offer the user the opportunity to add unknown words to the dictionary for future reference. See also AUTO-CORRECT, GRAMMAR CHECKER.

Sperry One of the oldest US computer companies, now absorbed into UNISYS CORPORATION.

spider A program that automatically visits millions of web sites to analyse their contents, and create an index for use by a SEARCH ENGINE: see for example ALTA VISTA.

spike A sharp but transient change in the voltage of a power supply, typically caused by the switching of a large CAPACITIVE or INDUCTIVE load (such as the electric motor in a lift or refrigerator) elsewhere on some connected circuit. Such power spikes can seriously damage sensitive INTEGRATED CIRCUITS in a computer, and their elimination is one of the prime functions of a UPS.

spin button An alternative name for a SPINNER CONTROL.

spin down To allow the PLATTERS of a HARD DISK to stop rotating, a process that takes several seconds owing to their high rotation speed and low friction. Portable computers typically spin down their disks after some preset interval of disuse, to save power. See also SPIN UP.

spine The centreline of each segment that composes a character in a STROKE FONT.

spinner control A visual user interface component used to enter numbers into a program. It contains a small TEXT BOX where the user can either type a number, or alternatively INCREMENT or DECREMENT the number already displayed by clicking with the mouse on one of the attached up and down arrow BUTTONS. The latter mode saves typing while guaranteeing that a valid number has been entered.

spin up The action of bringing the PLATTERS of a HARD DISK drive up to their correct operational speed after power is applied. During this period, which takes several seconds, the drive is inoperative. See also SPIN DOWN.

spin valve head See under MAGNETO-RESISTIVE HEAD.

spiral model A class of models of the software development process, so called because they stress both its cyclic nature (involving repeated testing and re-implementation) and the fact that there is nevertheless overall progress toward a goal (to make the product work to the original SPECIFICATION). This is in contrast to the now discredited WATERFALL MODEL, which implied a linear progress with success achieved at the first attempt. See also LIFE-CYCLE, METHODOLOGY, CASE.

splash screen A panel displayed on a computer's screen when an application program is first started up. It typically shows the name and VERSION of the program and the name and company logo of its publisher, and is often accompanied by diverting graphics, animations or even sound effects. The more thoughtful authors provide an option to hide the splash screen once its charm has faded.

spline A long, thin and flexible strip of metal once used by draughtsmen during aircraft and ship design to mark out complex curved surfaces. The term was adopted to describe its virtual equivalent, a computer-generated curve as employed in COMPUTER AIDED DESIGN software. See also CUBIC SPLINE, B-SPLINE, BEZIER CURVE.

split box, splitter bar, split pointer See SPLITTER.

splitter **1** An electronic device used in ADSL (and other XDSL) telephone systems to separate analogue voice signals from digital signals that share the same copper wire. The splitter is a wall-mounted box installed at the customer's premises, which significantly increases the installation cost of such systems. **2** Any adapter that enables two or more cables to plug into the same socket, for example a power outlet, a telephone wall socket or a serial port. **3** A visual user interface component (also called a *split box*, *splitter bar* or *split pointer*) that may be dragged to split a screen window into two parts with a moveable boundary between them.

spoiler **1** A message posted to an online discussion forum that gives away the plot or ending of a film, TV show, game or novel. NETIQUETTE requires the author to put 'spoiler' in its header to warn those who don't wish to read it. **2** A product that is hastily (even prematurely) released or announced in order to take attention away from the launch of a rival product.

spoofing 1 To trick a device into believing that it is still connected to a remote network. Certain network protocols send out PACKETS at frequent intervals to check their connection status, but if this is via a WAN such as the Internet it can be costly of both money and BANDWIDTH. Spoofing involves causing a local ROUTER to masquerade as the remote network, fooling the device that it is still connected, even when it is not.

2 A malicious version of the above in which intruders create packets with fake IP ADDRESSES to allow them access to those remote applications that use an authentication method based only on IP. See also HACK ATTACK

spool To send the output of a program or process to a temporary disk file rather than directly to the device (such as a printer) for which it is ultimately destined.

spooler A software utility that accepts output from other programs (typically printer output) and stores it in a temporary disk file to be processed as a BACKGROUND TASK, so permitting the first program to proceed as if the operation were complete. See also SPOOL, SPOOL FILE, PRINT SPOOLING.

spool file A disk file used to hold data that is being QUEUED for later processing, typically printing. See also SPOOL, PRINT SPOOLING.

spreadsheet A program designed to manipulate numbers arranged as a table of rows and columns. A spreadsheet enables the value contained in each CELL of such a table to be related to the values in other cells by mathematical formulae, so that changing one value will automatically change all the others. This makes possible 'what-if' analyses, where the user can experimentally change some value (e.g. a price or a tax rate) and then inspect the consequences, an ability that is equally useful to businessmen, accountants, scientists and engineers.

Historically, the early spreadsheets VISICALC and LOTUS 1-2-3 were in large part responsible for making personal computers popular among the business community. With the coming of GRAPHICAL USER INTERFACES such as Microsoft WINDOWS and the Apple MACINTOSH, the ability to produce graphs instantly from a range of cells became an important enhancement to the power of spreadsheets. Microsoft's EXCEL is now by far the most widely used spreadsheet, and comes supplied with a very large built-in library of predefined mathematical functions, including financial and engineering formulae and many of the statistical operations that would previously have been performed by dedicated statistics software. Excel also introduced a new capability called the PIVOT TABLE, which enables you to interactively analyse complex tables of figures by dragging and dropping the desired axes that relate them.

Spreadsheets can display text as well as numbers in their cells, and may be used to display records extracted from a relational database.

spread-spectrum See under CDMA.

SprintNet An international PACKET SWITCHING data network run by the US operator Sprint.

sprocket feed See under TRACTOR-FEED.

spy, spy-point See under WATCH.

SQL (Structured Query Language) A standardized language for expressing queries to RELATIONAL DATABASES. SQL was developed by IBM in the 1970s for its MAINFRAME computers, but is now the subject of both ISO and ANSI standards, and is widely used on every kind of computer. SQL is typically used in CLIENT/SERVER database environments, where it can vastly reduce the network loading that is imposed by many users querying a multi-user database. Each user needs to send to the server only a short text containing an SQL query, and will receive back from the server only the few records required, rather than a copy of the whole database.

SQL consists of a set of statements for extracting data from relational database tables, and for creating and deleting whole tables and records. It is a DECLARATIVE LANGUAGE in that queries describe the data that a user wishes to retrieve, rather than precise details of *how* it is to be retrieved. The most important SQL command is SELECT which locates a set of fields or records from one or more database tables, according to some selection criteria. For example the single SQL query:

```
SELECT name, phone FROM customer
WHERE country = "UK" ORDER BY name
```

will return the name and phone fields of all the UK customers whose records are stored in the table customer, after sorting them into name order. When an INTO clause is added to a SELECT command, the results of the query are put into a new table, so SQL can be used to modify databases as well as query them. The JOIN command returns elements from two tables that have the same value in some shared field. The INSERT, DELETE and UPDATE commands permit the addition and removal of records and allow mass changes to be made to whole tables (for example, to update price lists by a fixed percentage). Another subset of SQL commands (including CREATE TABLE and CREATE INDEX), collectively called DATA DEFINITION LANGUAGE is used to define and modify the structure of database tables and to maintain their REFERENTIAL INTEGRITY.

The latest version of SQL (version 3) adds many new commands for OBJECT-ORIENTED PROGRAMMING, including user-defined data types, encapsulation and inheritance.

SQL Server Microsoft's multiuser RELATIONAL DATABASE manager for enterprise-level computing systems. SQL Server lies at the heart of Microsoft's UNIFORM DATA ACCESS software strategy for the future, intended to provide the underlying data management system for all its networked and web-based information systems, and a repository for reusable ACTIVEX components. See also RELATIONAL DATABASE MANAGEMENT SYSTEM, SQL.

square brackets See BRACKET.

square wave Any signal that periodically alternates between a high and a low state by making abrupt, essentially instantaneous, transitions rather than smooth, sinusoidal ones. All DIGITAL data signals are ideally conceived as being electrical square waves, with the high (or low) states representing the successive bits. However, in practice their transitions deviate considerably from the absolutely vertical because of IMPEDANCE effects, and this is a matter of significance to engineers trying to design stable circuits (see

LATCH). In the medium of sound, square waves have a very unpleasant rasping quality, and may cause physical damage to loudspeakers.

SQUID (superconducting quantum interference device) An extremely sensitive detector of magnetic fields used in some kinds of medical brain scanner. See SUPERCONDUCTOR.

SR Abbreviation of SERVICE RELEASE.

SRAM Abbreviation of STATIC RAM.

SSA (Serial Storage Architecture) A high-speed interface designed by IBM for connecting external disk drives, clusters of drives and RAID arrays to a host computer, using a FULL-DUPLEX SERIAL protocol. SSA breaks data into packets to permit simultaneous multiplexed transfers from more than one disk or array, at rates of 20 megabytes per second in both directions. Despite IBM seeking an ANSI standard for SSA, support for the interface remains confined to its own equipment. See also FIREWIRE, SCSI, USB.

SSADM (Structure Systems Analysis and Design Method) A software engineering methodology and toolset whose use has been required for contracts with UK Civil Service agencies.

SSE Abbreviation of STREAMING SIMD EXTENSIONS.

SSH (Secure Shell) A suite of network utility programs originally written for UNIX (but now available under Windows too) that, unlike the Unix utilities it replaces, encrypts all its network traffic, including PASSWORDS, to prevent eavesdropping and other forms of attack. The main component of the suite, SSH itself, provides a more secure replacement for both RLOGIN and TELNET for remote log in and execution, while another component called SCP replaces FTP for secure file transfers. SSH employs a version of the RSA ENCRYPTION algorithm and is distributed both in OPEN SOURCE and commercial forms.

SSL Abbreviation of SECURE SOCKETS LAYER.

ST506 One of the first small computer HARD DISK interfaces, developed by Shugart Associates in 1980 and used in the 5 megabyte (MB) hard drives fitted in many early personal computers. It was soon revised to support BUFFERED SEEKS and renamed ST412, used in the popular 10 MB drive fitted in the IBM AT. Both interfaces had a data transfer rate of 5 MB per second. See also SASI, SCSI, SHUGART.

stable 1 Said of a software product that is sufficiently free of BUGS to be capable of running for prolonged periods without crashing.
2 Said of any algorithm whose behaviour changes in a steady and predictable way with the size and quality of the supplied data, rather than suddenly revealing some catastrophic failure mode. Contrast with NONLINEAR.

stack A data structure with the property that the first element that can be removed is the last element that was put in (sometimes summarized in the acronym LIFO) and therefore resembles, say, a stack of plates in a cafeteria – hence the name. The stack is extensively used as a means of storing the current state of some computation whenever it must be temporarily interrupted to do something else. For example when a machine code program jumps to a subroutine, certain REGISTER contents are preserved on the stack to be restored on return from the subroutine. Many high-level programming languages employ a stack to store the local variables and parameters of all procedures and functions, destroying them after the procedure call returns. This permits nested and RECURSIVE procedure calls.

stack-based A style of programming language architecture that employs a STACK to allocate space for the temporary storage of LOCAL VARIABLES. Most modern languages (such as C, C++, PASCAL, JAVA and VISUAL BASIC) are stack-based in this sense. The advantage of using stack allocation is that it automatically handles the nesting of function calls, and so makes the use of RECURSION possible. Only a handful of languages (for example FORTH and POP-11) expose the stack to the programmer for explicit manipulation. See also RECURSIVE DESCENT.

stacked bar chart A variant of the BAR GRAPH in which each bar is divided up into differently coloured zones, each representing a different quantity, so that the bar's overall length is proportional to their sum. A stacked bar graph is effective, for example, for depicting the monthly sales of several different product

lines, each bar showing at a glance both the total sales and the share of each line.

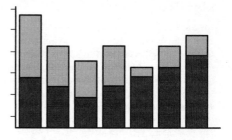

stack frame See under ACTIVATION RECORD.

stack overflow An error condition caused when a STACK exceeds the amount of memory allocated for its growth. Overflow often occurs because the procedure calls made by a program are too deeply nested, or RECURSIVE.

stack pointer A POINTER to the current top object held on a STACK. Incrementing and decrementing this pointer makes the stack work.

Stallman, Richard (b. 1953) Author of the EMACS text editor, pioneer of free software and founder of the GNU project and the FREE SOFTWARE FOUNDATION.

stand-alone A term that can be applied to any subsystem (hardware or software) that is also available integrated within another system or product. For example a TEXT EDITOR that was originally created as part of a programming environment might subsequently be sold in a 'stand-alone' version, or a personal computer that is not connected to a network might be described as a 'stand-alone PC'.

standard A documented agreement containing technical specifications or other precise criteria to be used consistently as rules, guidelines or definitions of characteristics, in order to ensure that materials, products, processes and services are fit for their purpose. (This is the ISO definition, upon which I cannot improve).
Standards are of great importance in the computer industry, as the ability to interchange hardware components and exchange data between different manufacturers' computers depends upon mutual adherence to standards. However, computing is a fast moving and highly creative industry, and there is always a tension between the desire to inno-

vate (and hence to own a new standard) and the often lengthy process of establishing true international standards.

standard cell Also called a *macrocell*, a portion of an INTEGRATED CIRCUIT layout that is sufficiently self-contained to be reused in the design of many different products. Functional units that are good candidates to be treated as standard cells include CPU cores, UARTs, and graphics and display processors.

Standard Generalized Markup Language See SGML.

standard input/output (stdio) A set of three predefined input and output channels that every PROCESS under the UNIX operating system receives when it is created. The channels are called *stdin* for input, *stdout* for output, and *stderr* for carrying error messages. All three stdio channels are initially connected to the terminal, but they may be redirected to a communications port, disk file or other storage device. They may also be connected by a PIPE into another process, which makes it easy to combine programs and scripts into a single application. The C language supports stdio through a standard header file stdio.h.

Standard Template Library (STL) A CLASS LIBRARY, containing the definitions of frequently-needed data structures and algorithms in the C++ programming language, that has been incorporated into the language standard. The library contains abstract, generic implementations of operations and structures (such as LINEAR SEARCH and BINARY SEARCH, LINKED LISTS, STACKS and HEAPS) that work with all reasonable data types, and the programmer modifies these routines to fit a specific job. Much use is made of ITERATORS to implement generic loops. See also APPLICATION FRAMEWORK, OBJECT LIBRARY, MICROSOFT FOUNDATION CLASSES.

standby mode A mode of operation, supported by many different types of computer and peripheral device, in which power consumption is reduced by shutting down some key subsystems but the system can be restored to full service more quickly than from a cold start. Standby modes are typically invoked by pressing a special button or key combination, and are signified by an indicator light. See also POWER SAVING, GREEN MACHINE.

star A network TOPOLOGY in which many client workstations are connected directly to a single central SERVER or HUB.

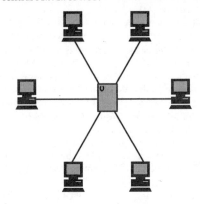

start bit In a serial communications protocol such as RS-232, a bit whose value indicates the start of transmission of each new character. For example if the line voltage is normally held low when idle, then a 1 bit (i.e. a low-to-high voltage transition) would be used to start every character. The number of start bits is one of the crucial parameters that must be set correctly for a particular remote service to enable connection to be made. See also STOP BIT, PARITY BIT.

Start Menu A central component of Microsoft's WINDOWS user interface from version 95 onwards. It consists of a hierarchical tree of MENUS accessed by pressing the Start Button that pops up whenever the mouse pointer is moved to the bottom of the screen. The Start Menu contains by default four SUBMENUS (though the user may customize it by adding more) called Programs, Documents, Settings and Find. The Programs submenu contains entries that invoke all the APPLICATION PROGRAMS that have been installed on the computer, plus various operating system utilities, and so offers an alternative to launching programs by clicking desktop ICONS. The Documents submenu allows the most recently opened data files to be instantly reopened. The Settings submenu gives access to the CONTROL PANEL and printer, network and TASKBAR bar setup options, while the Find submenu enables searching of the local hard disks, network or Internet for particular files.

start-up A newly-formed company, particular in the computer or Internet-based industries.

starvation 1 A situation in which a hardware device or software process is not receiving a flow of data sufficient to keep it working to its full capacity. For example, a processor in a MULTIPROCESSOR computer may become idle, even though there is much work to do, because the data has not been appropriately distributed. See also LOAD BALANCING.

2 A situation in which, because of an unfair allocation algorithm, one process is repeatedly denied access to some shared resource such as a processor or communications channel.

state diagram See under STATE TRANSITION DIAGRAM.

stateful The opposite of STATELESS. Said of a computer program or a communications protocol that retains some memory of its previous states or history.

stateless Having no memory of any previous state; beginning each operation anew without retrieving any stored parameters. Stateless operations have the desirable property that, if interrupted or abandoned, they may be recommenced without the need to clean up any corrupted information. On the debit side, they typically generate more communication traffic, as the same information must be sent each time they are invoked. HTTP is an example of a stateless communication protocol. See also STATEFUL.

state machine See under FINITE STATE MACHINE.

statement The basic unit of any program, consisting of a prescription for performing a single action. For example $x := y + 24$ is a statement, more precisely an ASSIGNMENT statement.

state transition diagram (STD) A DIRECTED GRAPH that represents all the states in which some system can exist as its nodes, with the transitions between states depicted as arcs joining them. Each arc is labelled with the condition that causes that transition to occur. See also FINITE STATE MACHINE, TRANSITION.

static 1 Most generally, any computing resource whose properties are fixed and persist between sessions. The opposite of DYNAMIC.

2 Used in particular in programming to describe quantities whose value was set when the program was COMPILED – or else when it was first loaded into memory – and which remain subsequently unchanged.

3 In C programming, the KEYWORD used to declare a STATIC VARIABLE.

static binding See under BINDING.

static RAM (SRAM) A type of fast RAM that retains its contents so long as a power supply is maintained, and hence does not require periodic refreshing as DRAM does. Each SRAM cell is a FLIP-FLOP switch built from up to six transistors, which makes it less dense than DRAM and so more expensive per megabyte. SRAM is mostly used for special applications such as fast LEVEL 2 CACHE, and in some battery-powered hand-held computers.

static variable In C and C++, a LOCAL VARIABLE that retains its value between successive invocations of the function that it is declared in.

statistical time division multiplexing (STDM) An efficient method for sending multiple messages down a single communication link. The simple TIME DIVISION MULTIPLEXING method allocates an equal TIME SLICE even to a channel that is not currently transmitting, and thus wastes BANDWIDTH. STDM employs a variable-length time slice, and allows all the channels to compete for any free time, using a BUFFER memory to temporarily store excess data during periods of peak traffic. Under STDM, each message must therefore carry an IDENTIFIER saying which channel it will use. To reduce the overhead this imposes, characters destined for the same channel are grouped together before transmission.

statistics The mathematical study of the quantitative properties of large populations, using methods derived from probability theory.

status The values of all the system PARAMETERS of some hardware or software system at a given moment.

status bar A narrow strip, usually situated in the lower border of a program's screen window, that is used to display status information such as the amount of memory in use, the name of the currently open file, or the state of various switches such as the CAPS LOCK KEY or an insert/overwrite TOGGLE.

STB Abbreviation of SET-TOP BOX.

STD 1 An Internet standards document. All STDs originate as RFC documents, but receive a different number once they acquire the status of accepted standards.
2 Abbreviation of STATE TRANSITION DIAGRAM.

stderr One of the Unix STANDARD INPUT/OUTPUT channels which carries ERROR MESSAGES: its default destination is the terminal screen.

stdin See under STANDARD INPUT/OUTPUT.

stdio Abbreviation of STANDARD INPUT/OUTPUT.

stdio.h The c header file that declares all the library functions for file input and output, and which must be included in most programs.

STDM Abbreviation of STATISTICAL TIME DIVISION MULTIPLEXING.

stdout See under STANDARD INPUT/OUTPUT.

step-and-repeat The process by which a silicon wafer is moved under the lens of a LITHOGRAPHY machine so that multiple, side-by-side copies of the same chip layout can be made on it (like a sheet of postage stamps).

stepper motor A type of electric motor that, in response to a digital input signal, can be made to turn its output shaft to any desired angle with high precision and keep it there. Stepper motors are used in optical SCANNERS and in various kinds of DISK DRIVE to accurately position the reading and writing heads, as well as in ROBOT arms. See also SERVOMOTOR, ACTUATOR.

stepwise refinement See TOP-DOWN DESIGN.

stereo-pair 1 A pair of microphones, arranged at right angles to one another, which may be used to make stereo recordings.
2 A pair of images which are viewed one by each eye to produce a stereoscopic or 3D effect.

stereoscopic Capable of being viewed as a 3-dimensional image.

sticky A description applied to a WEB SITE that induces visitors to view it for a long time, or to revisit it frequently.

sticky key A special mode of operation of a computer's keyboard (supported, for example, by Microsoft Windows) in which MODIFIER KEYS such as SHIFT, CTRL and ALT remain engaged once pressed, until released by a second press. This permits two-key and three-key combinations (e.g. <CTRL+ALT+DEL>) to be typed using a single finger, which is of great assistance to users with hand injuries or missing digits. See also ACCESSIBILITY OPTIONS.

STL Abbreviation of STANDARD TEMPLATE LIBRARY.

stochastic Involving randomly chosen values with a known probability distribution.

stop bit Under a SERIAL communications protocol such as RS-232, an extra 1 BIT or pair of 1 bits inserted into the data stream after every 7th or 8th bit to mark the end of each character. The number of stop bits is one of the crucial parameters that must be set correctly for a particular remote service to enable connection to be made. See also START BIT, PARITY BIT.

stopword A very commonly occurring word such as 'a', 'the', 'and' or 'but' for which it is not desirable to compile an entry when INDEXING a text. A list of such excluded words is typically supplied to the indexing software in a file.

storage 1 Most generally, any device or medium into which data, whether analogue or digital, can be entered, kept and then retrieved. See for example DISK STORAGE, VOLATILE STORAGE, NON-VOLATILE, STORAGE HIERARCHY.
2 In Microsoft's STRUCTURED STORAGE system, a partition within a file that can hold one or more STREAMS of data belonging to a particular object or application. See also DOCFILE.

storage area network (SAN) A computer system in which large mass storage devices (e.g. RAID arrays, TAPE DRIVES, CD-ROM JUKEBOXES) are connected to the central processor via a high-speed network technology such as FIBRE CHANNEL ARBITRATED LOOP, rather than being connected to the SYSTEM BUS as usual. SANs are increasingly used for online transaction processing (OLTP) systems where large capacity, reliability and performance are important. The SAN permits several CPUs to share the same storage devices, and minimizes the impact of making backups on transaction performance. A SAN may move data at up to 100 megabits per second over distances up to 10 kilometres, using special drives with built-in Fibre Channel interfaces.

storage density The number of bits than can be stored per unit area (e.g. per square centimetre or inch) of a storage medium such as a disk or silicon chip surface. In (still experimental) three-dimensional storage technologies, density is measured in bits per unit volume rather than per unit area.

Storage density is an engineers' term for comparing the capabilities of different technologies, and has little direct relevance for users as it applies only to the actual recording surfaces and takes no account of the drive mechanism and its casing.

storage device Any device, whether mechanical, electrical, magnetic, optical or some combination, that can be used to store data for later retrieval. See also MASS STORAGE.

storage hierarchy The layers of different storage media used to hold data, which become faster as the data approaches the processor. For example, a data item might be kept on a slow TAPE DRIVE for archival storage, loaded onto a HARD DISK for easier accessibility, loaded into fast RAM for processing, then into even faster CACHE MEMORY and finally into an on-chip processor REGISTER.

storage medium Any physical system that can be employed to record information and store it over time. Some storage media (e.g. photographic film) record only ANALOGUE data while others (e.g. CD) store only DIGITAL data and others again (e.g. magnetic recording tape) may store either.

storage type The storage system in use on a particular disk, under operating systems such as Windows 2000 or Unix which can support several alternative systems. The storage type is distinct from a FILE SYSTEM, and exists at the lower level of physical disk format and data layout. A computer system may contain various different storage types, but all volumes on the same physical disk must be of the same storage type. See also BASIC STORAGE and DYNAMIC STORAGE.

store 1 *n.* A shorthand term used by programmers to refer to any form of computer MEMORY. See also BACKING STORE.
2 *v.* To preserve data for later retrieval, for example in RAM or on a DISK DRIVE.

store-and-forward A style of MESSAGE PASSING mechanism under which each message must be wholly received into a particular network NODE before it is passed on to the next. Store-and-forward operation offers reliable communication because, should any link fail, messages waiting at the nodes remain intact and may be resent when the link is restored. However, it requires more BUFFER memory at each node than alternatives such as WORMHOLE ROUTING – sufficient to hold the largest anticipated message. See also ROUTING, MESSAGE QUEUE.

stored procedure A set of instructions to perform a frequently-required QUERY or other operation that is stored alongside the data in a computer database. Such stored procedures may be invoked automatically by a TRIGGER, that is, when some condition is fulfilled during a database operation (for example, for the purpose of validating a data input, or to maintain DATA INTEGRITY by removing orphaned records created by deleting a record). See also WRAPPER.

stored-program computer The modern notion of a computer in which the PROGRAM to be executed is stored in exactly the same MEMORY SPACE as the data it is to work upon. This distinguishes it from earlier computers whose functions were built immutably into the hardware, or whose programs existed in a different medium from their data (for example on punched cards). Sometimes also called the VON NEUMANN architecture, after its inventor.

storyboarding A technique that originated in the film industry, in which the bare plot of a movie is depicted as a sequence of artists' sketches, whose details may be filled in later by director, cameraman, lighting engineer, etc. The same technique is applied in computer MULTIMEDIA production, using either special storyboarding software or a standard PRESENTATION GRAPHICS package. The technique may even be applied as a planning aid for business operations, such as a sales campaign or conference.

STP (shielded twisted-pair) A type of network cable that uses a grounded shielding layer in addition to entwining its multiple conductors to protect itself from interference by external fields. It is equivalent in performance to data grade (i.e. CATEGORY 5) UNSHIELDED TWISTED-PAIR cable. IBM Type 1 is a version of STP employed for TOKEN RING networks. See also COAXIAL CABLE, TWISTED-PAIR.

stream 1 An abstraction employed to describe any continuous flow of data down a communication channel; by convention this originates in a SOURCE and is consumed in a SINK.
2 In programming, a data structure used to perform input and output, which may be attached to a file or to any other storage destination. A program may simply read and write data items to and from the stream, unaware of their ultimate destination, and with any required BUFFERING handled automatically. Streams are supported in many programming languages, including C++, SMALLTALK, JAVA and DELPHI.

streaming The ability to play sound or video files in REAL TIME as they are received from a web site, rather than having to download the whole file to a local disk before playing it. Streaming is accomplished by adding a PLUG-IN to web browsers such as NETSCAPE NAVIGATOR or INTERNET EXPLORER that DECOMPRESSES the highly compressed data stream and plays it as fast as it arrives. Hence successful reception of streaming media requires both a fast Internet connection, and a very fast CPU to perform the decompression. See also REAL-AUDIO, REALNETWORKS.

streaming media The collective term for streaming video and streaming audio technologies. See more under STREAMING.

Streaming SIMD Extensions (SSE) An extension to the Intel 80x86 architecture, introduced in microprocessors from the PENTIUM III onward, that enhances FLOATING-POINT ARITHMETIC performance by processing several items in parallel in a new set of eight dedicated 128-bit floating point REGISTERS. See also SIMD, VECTOR PROCESSOR, MMX.

streaming video See under STREAMING.

stream-oriented Said of a program or language that uses STREAMS for input/output.

stress testing Testing a hardware or software system by imposing loads as large (or larger) than any it is likely to encounter in service. See also WORST CASE.

strict In functional programming, a FUNCTION whose evaluation depends on, and may therefore not terminate before, the evaluation of its ARGUMENTS. See also EAGER EVALUATION, LAZY EVALUATION.

strikeout, strikethrough See OVERSTRIKE.

string Short for *character string*. The programmer's term for textual data that in everyday life would be called words, phrases or sentences. Programming languages rely on the separating spaces to identify individual words, and therefore require that string data be marked as such by enclosing it in single or double quotation marks – to a program, 'hello world!' is just a single string of length 12 characters.
The term is used to avoid confusion with the quite different meaning that WORD takes in computer engineering, while also tacitly acknowledging the fact that computer programs do not in general understand the sentence structure of human language.

string-search An algorithm or routine that locates a particular character STRING within a mass of textual data – as used, for example, to implement the SEARCH-AND-REPLACE function of a WORD PROCESSOR.

string variable A variable whose value is a character STRING rather than a number.

stripe See under DATA STRIPING.

striped volume A type of VOLUME under Microsoft's DYNAMIC STORAGE system whose data is interleaved – that is allocated alternately and evenly – between two or more physical disks. See also DISK STRIPING and RAID.

stripe set A particular configuration of HARD DISKS and operating system software, set up to perform DATA STRIPING.

striping See under DATA STRIPING.

strobe 1 A digital signal that is used like a clock to synchronize some repetitive activity, particularly the retrieval of data from a RAM chip. See, for example, ROW ADDRESS STROBE, COLUMN ADDRESS STROBE.

2 An abbreviation for stroboscope, a light with an adjustable flicker rate that is used by engineers to apparently 'freeze' the motion of rotating objects.

stroke One of the lines that make up each character form in an OUTLINE FONT.

stroke font A kind of computer FONT, midway between an OUTLINE FONT and a BITMAPPED FONT, that contains a description of the spine of each character in terms of lines and curves, together with the pen width to be used to trace that spine. Stroke fonts are more compact and take up less processor time to RENDER than true outline fonts, but can reproduce only a few crude TYPEFACES, such as Courier, that employ strokes of uniform width with simple round or square ends. They are now rarely encountered.

StrongARM A 32-bit MICROPROCESSOR jointly developed by DEC and ARM plc (but now owned by INTEL) that employs ARM's RISC architecture but adds improved PIPELINE technology to achieve far higher clock speeds (more than 200 MHz) than earlier ARM models. The chip is now finding widespread use in pocket computers, mobile communicators and TV SET-TOP BOXES. See more under ARM.

strongly typed See under TYPE CHECKING.

Stroustrup, Bjarne (b. 1950) The Danish inventor of the c++ programming language.

struct The keyword used to declare a STRUCTURE in c and c++.

structure **1** In general, an abstraction of the arrangement of the parts of a complex system from the actual content or details of those parts. Since much of computing is concerned with representing and abstracting from real world systems, structure is one of its most crucial concepts for conceptualizing both DATA and PROGRAMS. See for example DATA STRUCTURE, STRUCTURED DATA TYPE, DATA ANALYSIS, STRUCTURED ANALYSIS, STRUCTURED PROGRAMMING, CONTROL STRUCTURE.

2 The name given to the RECORD data structure in the c and c++ programming languages. See also STRUCT.

structured analysis A systematic method of determining the requirements for a new software system by identifying the entities, processes and relationships that are significant in the particular application DOMAIN.

structured data type A DATA TYPE that consists of a collection of simpler data types joined together in a well-defined way: examples include the ARRAY, the RECORD and the LINKED LIST. See also DATA STRUCTURE.

structured design One of the earliest systematic methods for designing programs, developed by YOURDON and others in the late 1970s and early 80s in the wake of the STRUCTURED PROGRAMMING movement. Structured Design begins by identifying all the significant entities in the particular problem domain and the relationships between them (called STRUCTURED ANALYSIS), and then refines these in progressively more and more detail until program code can be written. See also TOP-DOWN DESIGN, SOFTWARE ENGINEERING.

structured exception handling A set of features of many modern PROGRAMMING LANGUAGES that enable the programmer to specify in a single place what is to happen in the event of an error throughout whole regions of a program. A typical example is the try..except construct, which protects the whole block of code between those two KEYWORDS. If the execution of any statement within that block causes an EXCEPTION to be raised, control immediately passes to the code that follows except, which can identify and deal with its cause. Languages that support structured exception handling include c++ and DELPHI.

structured programming A programming philosophy that seeks to make program code easier to understand (and thus to reduce the number of errors introduced) by applying several techniques that give structure both to the flow of CONTROL through the program and to the data it works on. Structured programming was invented in the early 1970s in an effort to reform the poor programming practices and low productivity that the first generation of HIGH-LEVEL languages COBOL and FORTRAN had encouraged. In particular these early languages allowed the use of crude jump statements (such as GOTO) to transfer program control to some other part of the program, leading to what came to be called SPAGHETTI CODE that made it very difficult for humans to follow the logic.

The introduction of structured programming accompanied the design of a new generation of languages that supported some or all of its precepts: the founding document of the structured programming movement was a 1972 paper by Ole-Johan Dahl, Edsger DIJKSTRA and Anthony HOARE, who had been involved in designing ALGOL 60. Niklaus WIRTH designed a family of languages descended from Algol (the first being PASCAL) which encouraged the use of structured methods.

Structured programming advocates the replacement of GOTO with BLOCK STRUCTURE, which involves organizing program statements into related groups that make the flow of control obvious. For example a block structured conditional statement might look something like:

```
IF x > 100
THEN y := x - 100
    PRINT "Hopper overflow"
ELSE y := x
    PRINT "Filling..."
ENDIF
```

It can be seen at a glance that only two outcomes are possible. Either the statements between THEN and ELSE, or those between ELSE and ENDIF, must be executed, but never both. By contrast, an unstructured version makes it harder to understand what the code does, and more prone to error if additional lines are added:

```
100 IF x > 100 GOTO 300
200 y := x
250 PRINT "Filling..."
270 GOTO 400
300 y := 100 - x
350 PRINT "Hopper overflow"
400 .....
```

Another structured programming precept is to have only a few statements within any particular block so that it is easier to reason about what the block does. This is achieved by extracting a frequently-used group of statements as a named and parameterized SUBPROGRAM, creating a hierarchically-nested overall program structure.

A third principle is INFORMATION HIDING, whereby a programmer may know what a subprogram does, but is not concerned with the internal details of how it does it – this can be enforced by dividing the program into MODULES with well-defined INTERFACES.

A fourth precept is to use appropriate DATA STRUCTURES (for example Pascal RECORDS or C STRUCTURES) to group related data items together. Structured programming encourages TOP-DOWN DESIGN and STEPWISE REFINEMENT, in which emphasis is placed on choice of algorithms and data structures, the writing of code being delayed as long as possible.

Almost all modern programming languages (including C++, JAVA and VISUAL BASIC) support block and data structuring concepts, and OBJECT-ORIENTED PROGRAMMING could be viewed as an even stricter successor to the structured programming discipline.

Structured Query Language See SQL.

structured storage Microsoft's OBJECT-ORIENTED file system, which enables many COMPONENT OBJECT MODEL (COM) objects to store their persistent data in the same shared disk file. Structured Storage is used by Windows applications (such as Word) that are built from several cooperating COM objects, so that the user sees only a single output file. It is used to contain OLE compound documents that may include many objects created by different applications (e.g. text, images, spreadsheets or sound clips).

Structured storage involves dividing a single disk file internally into a tree-structured hierarchy of parts, called STORAGES and STREAMS, which behave like directories and files respectively; in effect each file is treated like a whole disk, with its own private file system. Such files are called COMPOUND FILES or DOCFILES. Each separate application or COM object that must share a single compound file gets assigned its own stream or storage in which to keep its own data. Word .DOC and Excel .XLS files are examples of compound files that employ structured storage.

stub 1 A short piece of program code that either does nothing or else prints an identifying message such as 'FileOpenStub', that is inserted into a program under development as a substitute for a function that is not yet written.

2 In a DISTRIBUTED OBJECT SYSTEM such as DCOM or CORBA, a short piece of code within a server object that receives method calls sent

by remote client objects and uses them to execute the equivalent method in the server object. See also PROXY, REMOTE PROCEDURE CALL.

StuffIt A FILE COMPRESSION utility popular with MACINTOSH users.

style A specification for the typographical appearance of a piece of text, consisting of a set of choices for FONT and size, line spacing, alignment, indentation and justification. Modern word processing and DESKTOP PUBLISHING programs allow such styles to be given names and saved for future use, when they can be picked from a menu and applied to characters, whole paragraphs, graphics and documents as required. See also STYLE SHEET, PARAGRAPH STYLE.

style analysis The use of a computer to analyse writing style, for example to determine the reading age of a text using the FLESCH-KINCAID INDEX, or to establish authorship of a manuscript. The fundamental operations of style analysis are counting and comparing frequency of word use, sentence length and size of the overall vocabulary. More sophisticated analyses count the relative occurrence rates of pairs and triplets of words.

style sheet A data structure that contains various formatting details that can be applied to a passage of text, for example the TYPEFACE and FONT SIZE, line spacing, indentation and tabulation. All modern WORD PROCESSOR applications employ style sheets to simplify the formatting of documents. Standard style sheets are created for, say, body text, several levels of headline, quotations and so on, and each can be applied to a whole paragraph or document with a single click or keystroke, replacing dozens of individual formatting decisions. Typically the user can create new named style sheets as required, or modify those supplied with the product.

The greatest advantage that style sheets offer is that they enable a setting (such as the font size) to be changed in just one place, and that change will then appear everywhere that the style has been applied. See also CASCADING STYLE SHEETS.

stylus The inkless writing instrument used to write either on the screen of a POCKET

COMPUTER that employs PEN INPUT, or onto a GRAPHICS TABLET. Styluses may be active (that is, containing electronic components, a battery or a connecting wire) or passive. In the latter case other objects such as a finger or toothpick may be used in their place. See also HANDWRITING RECOGNITION.

subclass In OBJECT-ORIENTED PROGRAMMING, a new CLASS that inherits attributes from a parent class, including both the parent's INSTANCE VARIABLES and the implementations of its METHODS. Hence also the term's use as a verb, to create such a subclass, as in 'You just need to subclass TWinControl'.

subdirectory A disk DIRECTORY or FOLDER that is contained within another directory. See more under HIERARCHICAL FILE SYSTEM.

subexpression A component of an EXPRESSION that is capable of being independently evaluated. Hence, in the expression $(x+3)/(y+4)$, $x+3$ is a subexpression but $3)/(y+$ is not.

subfolder A FOLDER that is contained within another folder. An alternative name for a SUBDIRECTORY.

sublimation-transfer printer See under DYE-SUBLIMATION PRINTER.

submenu A MENU that is accessed as an option from within another enclosing menu. Submenus typically appear slightly displaced to the right of their parent menu so that both can be read at once, producing what is often called a CASCADING MENU sequence.

submicron process A semiconductor fabrication process that employs a FEATURE SIZE of less than a MICRON (one millionth of a metre), which includes almost all current processes.

subnet A section within a network that shares the same main NETWORK ADDRESS with other sections, but is distinguished by an additional subnet number. See also SUBNET MASK, NETWORK ADDRESS, IP ADDRESS.

subnet address In a network that is divided up into SUBNETS, that part of the host portion of an IP ADDRESS that identifies a particular subnet. See also SUBNET MASK.

subnet mask A BIT MASK used to extract those bits from an IP ADDRESS that correspond to the SUBNET ADDRESS and NETWORK ADDRESS.

subnotebook A size category for portable computers that is substantially smaller than a NOTEBOOK computer (i.e. smaller than an A4 magazine), as typified by the Toshiba Libretto and the smaller Sony Viao models. See also LAPTOP, HAND-HELD, POCKET COMPUTER.

subpixel A unit smaller than a PIXEL that is employed, for example, in ANTIALIASING. If the BITMAP data is stored at a higher RESOLUTION than that displayable, then each display pixel may be represented by, say, a 4×4 or an 8×8 grid of subpixels. The path of a line is computed to the nearest subpixel to yield information that can be used to appropriately colour the actual screen pixel.

subprogram A self-contained part of a program that can be executed independently of other parts. The simplest kind of subprogram is the SUBROUTINE, which is just a range of addresses within a program to which execution can be transferred. HIGH-LEVEL PROGRAMMING LANGUAGES offer the facility to give names to subprograms, and usually also to pass PARAMETERS into them. Different languages employ different syntax for creating named subprograms, but in most languages subprograms are called either PROCEDURES or FUNCTIONS (or both).

The invention of named, parameterized subprograms is probably the most important advance ever made to the art of programming, because programs created as a collection of short subprograms, rather than as one long list of code, are easier to design, write, debug and maintain. Choosing what subprograms are needed to create a program to solve a particular problem is to FACTOR the problem, and this exercise forces the programmer to think about the structure of the problem rather than rush into a hasty implementation. Named parameterized subprograms are in effect customized extensions to a language, chosen by the programmer to solve the particular problem at hand.

All the important programming techniques, including both TOP-DOWN DESIGN and BOTTOM-UP DESIGN, depend on the availability of named subprograms.

subrange type A data type provided in several programming languages (including PASCAL and MODULA-2) that represents a finite range of values taken from some ORDINAL TYPE. For example a variable of subrange type 2...8 may have values only between 2 and 8, and will raise a COMPILER ERROR if assigned any other value.

subroutine The simplest kind of SUBPROGRAM, which is simply a section of program code with labelled entry and exit points. Program execution can be forced to jump to the entry point, and then to return to where it left off after the subroutine has been completely executed. All computer INSTRUCTION SETS support two (maybe more) instructions that force a jump to and a return from a subroutine, so that subroutines exist at MACHINE CODE level. To enable execution to return from a subroutine, the address following the JUMP TO SUBROUTINE instruction (the return address) must be stored either in a hardware REGISTER or on a software STACK.

subsample 1 To extract a sample from a larger sample.
2 To display a graphic image at a lower RESOLUTION than its stored data would permit.

subscribe To declare an interest in receiving regular updates of certain data items that are provided on a LAN or from a web site. See more under PUBLISH-AND-SUBSCRIBE, and also PUSH.

Subscriber Identity Module See SIM CARD.

subscript A text character printed below the line (for example the 2 in H_2O) – a device used extensively in writing mathematics (to distinguish between different variables) and in chemical formulae. See also SUPERSCRIPT.

subset In mathematics, a set all of whose members also belong to some larger set. As applied to computing, the term is frequently used to mean a portion of the abilities of some software product. So a simplified version of a programming language or APPLICATION PROGRAMMING INTERFACE may be described as a subset of the larger original. See also SUPERSET.

subst An MS-DOS command that creates VIRTUAL disk drives by associating a directory PATH with a DRIVE LETTER. For example the command:

```
C:> subst K:=D:\documents\letters
```

allows programs to access an imaginary drive called K: which contains all the files in the letters subdirectory. As with the older ASSIGN command (which subst was introduced to replace) many low-level disk operations will not work correctly on a substituted drive; examples include formatting a disk or using the DOS Backup utility. Subst employs the same underlying mechanisms that are used to map network drives, so any operation which may be performed on a network drive can be applied to a subst drive. See also APPEND.

substrate The material used to make the WAFER onto which INTEGRATED CIRCUITS are fabricated. The most common substrate is SILICON, but other more exotic substrates include GALLIUM ARSENIDE, gallium nitride and SILICON ON SAPPHIRE.

substring search A program routine that searches for the position of one text STRING within a longer string. For example, a substring search for 'it' within the word 'position' might return the value 4.

subsystem A portion of a larger SYSTEM with sufficient coherence (either of structure or function) that its operation may be examined separately from the whole.

subtask A subordinate TASK spawned by some controlling task to perform a part of the work that has to be done.

subtree A coherent portion of a TREE structure consisting of a single branch and all its dependents, out to leaf level.

subtype In those programming languages that support INHERITANCE, a type that inherits the INTERFACE of an existing type, so that an expression of the subtype can be used anywhere that an expression of the parent type would be valid. There is a subtle and poorly-observed distinction between a subtype and the related concept of SUBCLASS – a subclass inherits not only the interface but also the IMPLEMENTATION of its parent's methods. Many OBJECT-ORIENTED languages including SMALLTALK and C++ conflate class and type, which obscures this distinction and can be a cause of tricky semantic errors.

Sun Microsystems, Inc. US computer manufacturer specializing in graphics workstations, microprocessors and operating systems. It is the birthplace of the JAVA language.

Sun OS The original name given to the SUN version of UNIX (now called SOLARIS) supplied with the company's workstations. It was based on the Berkeley extensions (see under BSD).

superclass In OBJECT-ORIENTED PROGRAMMING, the CLASS from which a SUBCLASS inherits its attributes.

supercomputer A computer with very fast numeric processing abilities used for scientific and engineering tasks (for example atmospheric modelling for weather forecasts or FINITE ELEMENT ANALYSIS) and to render complex graphic images. The exact performance level that constitutes a supercomputer continually rises with advancing processor design. Today it is in the order of TERAFLOPS, or several thousand times the performance of contemporary PCs.

VECTOR PROCESSORS like the famous CRAY models were once employed for supercomputing, but most modern supercomputers are PARALLEL COMPUTERS that employ hundreds or thousands of processing elements.

superconductor A material that conducts electricity essentially without RESISTANCE. All currently known superconductors are complex metal alloys that display this behaviour only at very low temperatures, but the search continues for a room-temperature superconductor. Research into superconducting computer circuits such as the JOSEPHSON JUNCTION has so far led to no commercial applications.

However, superconductors provide the basis for a type of extremely sensitive magnetic field detector called the superconducting quantum interference device or SQUID, used in medical imaging.

superfloppy A generic term for removable multi-megabyte storage media such as IOMEGA's Zip disks or Imation's Superdisks, but which excludes the various writable CD formats and removable hard disks like those made by SYQUEST.

SuperJANET A BROADBAND extension to the UK universities data network JANET, consisting of a 140 megabits per second ASYNCHRONOUS TRANSFER MODE network running over OPTICAL FIBRE.

superminicomputer A marketing term coined to describe computers made in the 1970s (such as DEC's VAX series) that employed MINICOMPUTER construction techniques, but were almost as powerful as MAINFRAMES.

superpipeline A processor architecture that employs a very deep PIPELINE to improve throughput, an example being the Intel PENTIUM Pro's 12-stage pipeline. See also SUPERSCALAR.

superscalar A computer processor architecture that can launch more than one instruction for execution at each CLOCK CYCLE, so that the hardware may be fully utilized for maximum throughput. For example, a processor that has both INTEGER and FLOATING-POINT execution units would endeavour to launch one integer and one floating point instruction every cycle to keep both working. Most modern microprocessor designs are superscalar to a greater or lesser degree. For example the Intel PENTIUM II is capable of dispatching up to five instructions per cycle. See also PIPELINE.

superscript A character printed above the line, used (as with the 6 in 10^6) to represent powers of numbers, and for footnote and endnote references. See also SUBSCRIPT.

superset In mathematics, a set that includes all of the members of some smaller set called a SUBSET. As applied to computing, the term refers to a piece of software, or an interface, that contains all the features of a predecessor while adding some extra ones.

supertwist Short for 'supertwist nematic', a type of LIQUID CRYSTAL DISPLAY in which the transmitted light is rotated through more than 90°, resulting in better contrast and faster REFRESH times than older types of TWISTED-NEMATIC LCD.

superuser See under ROOT.

Super VGA (Super Video Graphics Array, SVGA) A set of PC graphics display modes that go beyond the resolution and colour depth of the VGA standard. Pioneered by independent GRAPHICS CARD manufacturers who were impatient with IBM's slow development program. The mode originally called Super VGA was 800×600 pixels in 16 colours (i.e. 4-bit) but various other modes (including 640×480 ×256, 800×600×256, 1024×768×256 and 1280× 1024×256) are also so described. See more under VESA.

supervisor mode A privileged mode of execution provided by many computer processors, in which all types of instruction may be executed, even those that are forbidden in other modes. In some cases a supervisor mode also gives access to a different ADDRESS SPACE that is used for special programs such as DEVICE DRIVERS, or to an extra set of processor REGISTERS. The operating system typically runs in supervisor mode so that it can control all parts of the hardware, while application programs run in a less privileged USER MODE.

support To provide assistance to the users of some hardware or software product, usually by accepting BUG REPORTS, issuing BUG FIXES and answering technical queries.

surd An archaic name for an IRRATIONAL NUMBER.

surface modelling The process of constructing within a computer a representation of a 3-dimensional object. Such modelling begins by building a WIRE-FRAME representation, and then SHADING it to produce smooth surfaces (see for example PHONG SHADING, GOURAUD SHADING). See also 3D GRAPHICS, CUBIC SPLINE.

surface mount A technology for constructing miniature PRINTED CIRCUIT BOARDS (as used in mobile telephones and hand-held computers) in which the INTEGRATED CIRCUITS have connection pins that are flush with their package and do not protrude through the board in older methods. Instead the chips are attached to connection pads printed on the board's surface by a thin film of solder.

surfing Also 'web surfing' or 'net surfing', a slang term for browsing on the WORLD WIDE WEB. The surfing allusion probably stems from the combination of pleasure and unpredicability.

suspend 1 To reduce the power supply to a computer in such a way that its memory contents are preserved but processing ceases, so that work may be resumed later at the point it was left off. This avoids a REBOOT, and having to relaunch all programs and open all files again. This type of suspension is typically supported on LAPTOP, NOTEBOOK and other types of portable computer. See also SUSPEND-TO-DISK, SLEEP.

2 To cause a TASK running under a MULTITASK-ING operating system to stop executing and hand over the processor to the next task in the queue.

suspend-to-disk To capture the current execution state of a computer by saving its entire memory contents and processor REGISTER state in a disk file, allowing its power supply to be reduced almost to zero. Upon pressing a RESUME key, the disk image is reloaded, so that work can continue where it was left off, with all the same applications and files open. Suspend-to-disk saves more power than a simple SUSPEND, but takes longer to perform. It requires special extensions to the computer's BIOS which are present in most modern LAPTOP and NOTEBOOK PCs.

Sutherland, Ivan (b. 1938) Inventor of computer graphics and virtual reality, co-founder of EVANS AND SUTHERLAND and Turing prize winner. At MIT in the 1950s, he wrote Sketchpad, the first interactive GRAPHICS program.

SVC Abbreviation of switched VIRTUAL CIRCUIT.

SVG (Simple Vector Graphics) A new GRAPHICS FILE FORMAT being developed by the WORLD WIDE WEB CONSORTIUM to improve the presentation of images and type on web pages. Unlike the bitmapped GIF and JPEG formats currently used for most web illustration, SVG is a VECTOR format that enables images to be

scaled and zoomed to any size without loss of quality, and also permits both fonts and bit-mapped images to be embedded within its images. SVG is based on the XML page markup language, so its files are text-based, platform-independent and may be edited with a text-editor. They may also be generated as output from DRAWING PROGRAMS, such as the latest versions of Adobe Illustrator. In this and other respects, SVG resembles a PAGE LAYOUT language such as POSTSCRIPT more than a traditional graphics format.

Among the many enhancements that SVG promises are more extensive PALETTES of up to 16 million colours, panning and zooming to any magnification without pixelation, and advanced colour handling that includes gradients and masking effects. SVG supports advanced typographic controls including kerning, text paths and ligatures, and the ability to embed hinted fonts into an image (see more under OUTLINE FONT, HINTING). SVG supports UNICODE international character sets, and all text within an SVG image remains both searchable and editable. Support for interactive and animation features via embedded SCRIPTS means that images can be made to respond to user actions with highlighting, movement and special effects. Here is a small sample of SVG code, which draws a red box:

```
</g><!-- MoscowMETRO -->
<g id="RedBox" style="dis-
play:inline;">
<path
style="fill:none;stroke:#FF0000;
stroke-width:0.5;stroke-miter-
limit:4;"
</g><!-- RedBox -->
```

See also CASCADING STYLE SHEETS, XSL.

SVGA See SUPER VGA.

S-Video A technology that records and transmits analogue video images using two separate signals, called LUMINANCE (light intensity) and CHROMINANCE (colour content), in contrast to the single signal used in COMPOSITE VIDEO and the three signals of COMPONENT VIDEO. S-Video offers better image quality than composite video, and is used in some studios, closed-circuit security systems and semi-professional Hi-8 cameras.

SVR4 See SYSTEM V.

swap To move the contents of a section of a computer's MAIN MEMORY out into a disk file (called a SWAP FILE), replacing them with other data read in from the same file. This process permits the running of programs, or the processing of data files, that are larger than the computer's memory capacity and forms the basis of VIRTUAL MEMORY systems. Slower response times and visible disk activity may indicate to the computer user that swapping is taking place. When swapping is performed in units of a fixed size, it is often called *paging*. See also DEMAND-PAGED.

swap file An area of HARD DISK used to store the state of a program and its working data that have been swapped out of memory (see SWAP) under a MULTITASKING operating system such as Windows or Unix.

swappable A section of a computer's program or data memory that the operating system is permitted to SWAP out of memory to make more space (see VIRTUAL MEMORY). Certain crucial system programs, for example the operating system KERNEL itself, may be locked so that they cannot be swapped out.

swapped in, swapped out See under SWAP.

SWF See under FLASH.

Swing A new GRAPHICAL USER INTERFACE toolkit for the JAVA language, which replaces the older AWT. Swing is a set of visual components that forms a part of the Java Foundation Classes library. Its most innovative ability is the 'pluggable look-and-feel' feature, which enables a programmer to mimic the appearance and behaviour of different user interfaces (such as Windows, UNIX, or the Macintosh) from the same application, by merely loading the correct module at start up.

switch 1 In electronics, a mechanical or electrical device for opening and closing a circuit, or for diverting current from one circuit to another.
2 In telecommunications and networking, a hardware device for making and breaking a data connection between two endpoints. In the analogue public telephone system, a sequence of switches is employed to set up a temporary connection between each caller and receiver. In CIRCUIT-SWITCHED data networks, switches are employed to create a VIR-TUAL CIRCUIT between pairs of endpoints, fulfilling a role equivalent to the ROUTER in a CONNECTIONLESS network by diverting data PACKETS toward their intended destination. See also SWITCHING HUB.
3 In software, an extra argument appended to a typed COMMAND to modify its operation. For example the MS-DOS command DIR that lists the contents of a disk directory might be followed by the 'w' switch, which makes it list in a wider format: C:> DIR /W

switched When used of a communications network, a shorthand for CIRCUIT-SWITCHED, rather than ROUTED or CONNECTIONLESS. See also CONNECTION-ORIENTED.

switched Ethernet A modification of ETHERNET networking technology (normally a shared-medium system) to incorporate SWITCHES, so that each workstation or group of workstations has a separate cable connection to the SERVER, reducing the incidence of collisions (see under CSMA/CD). Switched Ethernet offers a more predictable BANDWIDTH, which is important for time-critical multimedia applications that involve transferring video and audio data streams. See also GIGABIT ETHERNET.

switched interconnect A type of high-speed system bus used in PARALLEL COMPUTERS that employs switched circuit technology to eliminate contention between the different processors for access to the memory. A CROSS-BAR-SWITCH connects each processor to the appropriate memory bank via a dedicated (i.e. non-shared) route. The use of switched interconnects allows parallel computers to be designed whose processor-to-memory BAND-WIDTH scales almost linearly with the number of processors (see CROSS-SECTIONAL BAND-WIDTH, SCALABILITY).

Switched Multimegabit Data Service See SMDS.

switched network See under CIRCUIT-SWITCHED.

switched virtual circuit See under VIRTUAL CIRCUIT.

switching hub See under HUB.

switch statement The syntactic form taken by a CASE STATEMENT in C, C++, JAVA and related languages. An example might be:

```
switch (Operator)
{
case _AND: Result = A & B; break;
case _OR: Result = A | B; break;
case _XOR: Result = A ^ B; break;
default: return TRUE; break;
}
```

The code following `default` is executed if the value of `Operator` matches none of the other cases, while the keywords `break` or `return` cause control to pass immediately to the end of the switch BLOCK, following the final bracket. If `break` is omitted, then control passes to the code for the next case, after the colon – it is said to FALL THROUGH. Accidental omission of a `break` is a common source of errors, particularly in deeply nested switch statements.

Sybase A US vendor of RELATIONAL DATABASE MANAGEMENT SYSTEMS.

Symantec A US software house best known for its programming tools and the NORTON UTILITIES.

Symbian A joint venture company launched by PSION, ERICSSON, NOKIA and MOTOROLA to develop and promote a new operating system for wireless information devices and next generation mobile telephones. The operating system is based on Psion's real time EPOC 32 OS developed for its Series 5 hand-held computers.

symbol 1 Most generally a sign, character or figure used in mathematics, science, music, etc to represent a quantity, phenomenon or operation.
2 In programming, a character string that represents some other quantity or operation (for example a variable or procedure name) rather than a LITERAL string or number.
3 In compiler theory, and in text-oriented programming languages such as LISP, a word rather than a number. Programs that operate on words rather than numeric values are often described as *symbolic*.

symbol font A FONT that consists entirely of symbols rather than alphabetic characters.

symbolic See SYMBOL.

symbolic debugger See under DEBUGGER.

symbolic expression A mathematical expression that contains abstract identifiers that stand as placeholders for the current value of the variables they represent. Hence the value of the symbolic expression $x + y$ is the sum of the current values of x and y and can be obtained by substituting the current values for the identifiers. A symbolic expression may also contain actual values (called LITERAL values) as in $x + y + 8$. Most computer programming languages permit the evaluation of symbolic expressions, but algebraic manipulation of such expressions (e.g. to factorize them) can be performed only in SYMBOLIC MATHEMATICS programs such as MATHEMATICA.

symbolic logic Also called *formal logic*. A blanket term for various systems of deductive argument in which symbols are used to represent precisely defined categories of expression, such as the PROPOSITIONAL CALCULUS, the PREDICATE CALCULUS and BOOLEAN ALGEBRA.

symbolic mathematics Mathematical manipulations performed using named variables rather than numbers: in other words, what at school used to be called algebra rather than arithmetic. For example, reducing the expression x^2+3x-4 to its factors $(x-1)(x+4)$ is an act of symbolic mathematics. Computers, being essentially numeric calculating devices, cannot intrinsically perform symbolic maths, and to do so require some very high-level software product such as MATHEMATICA or MATHCAD which can PARSE symbolic expressions.

symbol table A data structure created by a language COMPILER to record the association between the IDENTIFIERS used in a program's source code and the memory locations or objects that they refer to. The symbol table is typically stored in a separate file from the OBJECT CODE output by the compiler. It is normally required only during program development and debugging, and does not form part of the EXECUTABLE file delivered to users.

symmetric 1 Possessing symmetry, behaving the same way in all directions.

2 When applied to a MULTIPROCESSOR computer, having all its processors dedicated to the same type of computing task.

3 In mathematics, any RELATION that holds between *x* and *y* if and only if it also holds between *y* and *x*. 'Equals' is a symmetric relation, but 'greater than' is not.

See also its opposite, ASYMMETRIC.

symmetric multiprocessor See SMP.

synapse The name given to a processing element in some NEURAL NETWORK systems. See also NEURON.

sync **1** An abbreviation for SYNCHRONIZE, or synchronization, as in 'out of sync'.

2 The action of equalizing the contents of the files held on two different computers by exchanging their contents across a communications link. See also HOTSYNC.

synchronize Literally, to cause to occur at the same time. However, in computing contexts the term may also mean to cause one PROCESS to wait for the completion of another. Synchronization is an important problem in any CONCURRENT system because the order in which different processes complete may change the system's overall behaviour. For example, an operating system that permits concurrent accesses to a hard disk drive must ensure that head positioning commands and their associated read or write commands occur in the correct order. Many programming techniques have been devised to achieve synchronization, including the QUEUE, SEMAPHORE, MONITOR and CHANNEL data structures.

synchronous Occurring at the same time as, or at the same rate as, or with some other defined time relationship to another event. It is the opposite of ASYNCHRONOUS. When applied to communications systems, the term describes any type of protocol in which messages are transmitted in step with a regular timing signal. When applied to two PROCESSES, it means that they depend upon some common timing event to synchronize them.

Synchronous Data Link Control See SDLC.

Synchronous Digital Hierarchy (SDH) A European technology standard for BROADBAND FIBRE-OPTIC telecommunications networks, equivalent to the US SONET standard.

SDH specifies the FRAME format into which payload data must be organized, and a framing rate of 8 kilohertz (resulting in data rates that are multiples of 51.84 megabits per second). Three such channels, carrying 155 megabits per second, constitute an STS-3 line and are being widely installed in telecommunication backbone routes to carry ASYNCHRONOUS TRANSFER MODE traffic.

synchronous DRAM See SDRAM.

Synchronous Graphics Random Access Memory (Synchronous Graphics RAM, SGRAM) A special variety of SDRAM that is optimized to provide the very high throughput rates (up to 640 megabytes per second) needed for graphics operations such as 3D rendering and full-motion video. Unlike ordinary DRAM, it does not need special STROBE signals, but works directly from the system clock signal, and allows whole blocks to be written at once via BURST-MODE access.

Synchronous Optical Network See under SONET.

synonym ring A set of words with similar meanings used to broaden the scope of searches in a TEXT RETRIEVAL SYSTEM or web SEARCH ENGINE: for example 'car, automobile, motorcar, vehicle'. A QUERY using a synonym ring might return documents that contain any word in the same synonym ring as any of the target words. Synonym rings are compiled by humans rather than computers, and they are typically confined to some narrow domain of knowledge, such as computing terms or legal terms.

syntactic sugar A term applied to those features of a programming language that make it easier to understand or remember (i.e. 'sweeter') for a human programmer, without adding anything to the underlying SEMANTICS of programs. For example in C the compact array notation x[2] is syntactic sugar that disguises a pointer operation *(x+2).

syntax In computer programming, a set of rules that govern precisely which arrangements of IDENTIFIERS and RESERVED WORDS written in a particular programming language constitute legal, and therefore executable, programs. The syntax of a language is the practical expression of its underlying GRAM-

MAR, and may sometimes be expressed in a formal notation such as BACKUS-NAUR FORM.

syntax checking A feature of some programming language compilers that checks the current program for SYNTAX errors without actually outputting any object code.

syntax colouring A feature of the program editors in many modern programming language systems, in which different kinds of program entity are distinguished on screen by appearing in different colours to assist programmers in more quickly grasping the program's structure. Syntax colouring is specific to a particular programming language: for example all the language's KEYWORDS may be picked out in a different colour from that of the user-defined IDENTIFIERS. See also SYNTAX.

syntax error A class of error introduced by the programmer during the development of a program, caused for example by misspelling a KEYWORD or IDENTIFIER, misplacing a punctuation symbol, wrongly ordering some construct or supplying the wrong number of parameters in a FUNCTION CALL – in other words, any mistake that causes the program not to be correctly formed according to the SYNTAX of the programming language used. Syntax errors are always trapped during the writing of the program, since the program will not COMPILE correctly (see SYNTAX CHECKING). This is in contrast to a RUN-TIME ERROR, which may survive into the distributed executable program and cause it to crash in use.

synthesizer An electronic device that generates musical note WAVEFORMS under the control of electrical signals. A synthesizer can imitate the sounds of conventional musical instruments by generating the appropriate combinations of frequencies and the correct shape or 'envelope' for each note (i.e. the way it starts, sustains and finishes). Each such imitation is called a *voice*.

Single chip synthesizers form a core component in computer SOUND CARDS, and can be used with appropriate SEQUENCER software to create music. A synthesizer that can play multiple notes at once is called *polyphonic*, while one that can play multiple voices at the same time is called *multi-timbral*. A WAVETABLE SYNTHESIS synthesizer stores the data describing each voice in RAM, and so can load new voices from disk. See also MIDI.

SyQuest A US manufacturer of removable HARD DISK drives. See REMOVABLE DISK.

sysadmin Short for SYSTEM ADMINISTRATOR.

SYSmark A widely used BENCHMARK suite for PCs running Windows, produced by the US firm Bapco. It is an applications-based suite that times the running of programs including Microsoft Word, Excel and PowerPoint, Lotus WordPro and Freelance Graphics, Borland Paradox, CorelDraw and Adobe PageMaker. See also WINSTONE.

sysop Short for SYSTEM OPERATOR.

system Any assembly of interacting components that forms a single collective entity whose behaviour transcends that of its parts.

system administrator The person responsible for running and maintaining a multi-user computer system or network. The administrator's responsibilities include creating and managing USER ACCOUNTS, installing new software, allocating disk space, supervising the BACKUP of data, and restoring service after a hardware or software failure. See also SYSTEM MANAGEMENT, REMOTE MANAGEMENT, SNMP, SMS.

System Area Network (SAN) **1** A proprietary name used by TANDEM COMPUTER INC. to describe an architecture in which a packet-switched, POINT-TO-POINT network is used inside a multiprocessor server to connect its different processors. See also PACKET SWITCHING.

2 A proprietary name used by Microsoft for a feature in Windows 2000 Datacenter Server that allows two or more servers to be joined by a FIBRE CHANNEL network and to use direct SOCKET connections to communicate.

system bandwidth The maximum rate at which data can move through a computer system. While this is affected by the clock speed of both the processor and the system bus, it is not identical with either since there may be multiple processors, multiple buses and CACHES present (particularly in a SERVER). For complex MULTIPROCESSOR computer systems, the CROSS-SECTIONAL BANDWIDTH is the most useful measure of system bandwidth.

system bus The main electrical pathway via which a computer's CPU communicates with its MEMORY to read and write data, and with various PERIPHERAL devices. Examples of standard system buses from the IBM-compatible PC world include the ISA BUS and the PCI BUS.

The system bus is a parallel interface, typically as wide or wider than the WORD SIZE of the processor (e.g. 32-bit or 64-bit), but it carries data at a rate far lower than the CPU can supply it. In most modern PCs the bus runs at 100 megahertz, while the processor may run 10 times faster. For this reason one or two levels of CACHE memory are normally introduced between the processor and the system bus to partially smooth out the speed disparity. Some computer architectures incorporate several buses, for example an ultra-wide, ultra-fast one connected to the GRAPHICS subsystem, or a slower, narrower one that carries the EXPANSION SLOTS. See also BUS, BUS CONTENTION, ARBITRATION.

system call A CALL to a subroutine in the computer's OPERATING SYSTEM that performs some fundamental operation. The operating system manages many important activities such as keyboard input and output, disk access and communication ports, and it would be both dangerous and inefficient to duplicate this code within every program that needs these services. Under a MULTITASKING operating system where several application programs might need to access the same hardware, it is doubly important that they do not access it directly, but do so via system calls. A collection of all the system calls required for a particular service is called an APPLICATION PROGRAMMING INTERFACE.

system chip set A set of two or three INTEGRATED CIRCUIT chips that contain almost all the LOGIC required to implement a PC motherboard, requiring only the addition of a microprocessor and some RAM chips. Functions typically implemented include all the BUS and memory REFRESH logic, timers, INTERRUPT CONTROLLER and DMA CONTROLLER, parallel and serial port, keyboard and floppy disk controllers. System chip sets are now a mainstay of the commodity PC motherboard business, and a handful of manufacturers such as Intel, Via, Cypress, VLSI Logic and Opti supply them for most of the world's PCs.

system clock An INTEGRATED CIRCUIT that generates a stream of regular electrical pulses that act as the timing reference for all the components in a computer. The basic clock frequency is multiplied within various circuits to drive faster components such as the microprocessor (which may run at up to 10 times faster). The clock signal must be disseminated to every part of the computer without significant lag or SIGNAL SKEW. As systems get ever faster, this presents an increasing engineering challenge.

Système Électronique pour Couleur avec Mémoire See SECAM.

system failure A breakdown of operation of some system caused by the failure of one or more of its parts.

system file Any file that is maintained for the internal purposes of a computer's OPERATING SYSTEM, as opposed to files containing the user's data. See, for example, AUTOEXEC.BAT.

System File Checker (SFC) A utility that is run whenever a Windows 2000 system is booted. It checks all the system files that are being protected by the WINDOWS FILE PROTECTION system and the catalogue files that store important version information about these protected files. It also performs maintenance jobs such as rebuilding the protected file cache. See also DLL HELL.

System folder A special FOLDER on the Apple MACINTOSH used as the location for all hardware-specific device drivers and operating system extensions.

system font The default FONT employed by an OPERATING SYSTEM for its own displays, for example COMMAND LINES or DIALOGUES. In non-graphical operating systems (such as Unix or MS-DOS) the system font is typically a BITMAPPED FONT of fixed pitch and size. Windows has a font called Fixedsys that is rarely seen except when running old MS-DOS programs in a window.

system integration 1 Most generally, the act of incorporating some new element into a working system.
2 More specifically, in software development, to add a new MODULE to a program and ensure that the new combination works as intended.

system management The process of ensuring the most efficient use of the resources available on a computer NETWORK. The tasks involved include the fair allocation of disk space, LOAD BALANCING between multiple SERVERS, fault diagnosis and correction, and software installation and maintenance. There are now computerized tools available to assist with system management, most notably the SNMP protocol and Microsoft's SYSTEMS MANAGEMENT SERVER. See also INVENTORY MANAGEMENT, ASSET MANAGEMENT, CONFIGURATION MANAGEMENT.

system memory That part of a computer's RAM that is occupied by the operating system, its tasks and data, rather than the part occupied by user programs.

System Object Model See SOM.

system-on-a-chip A complete electronic device integrated onto a single piece of silicon. Examples include MODEMS, GPS receivers, CELLULAR PHONES and many types of scientific instrument. See also MICROSYSTEM.

system operator Often abbreviated to SYSOP. The person in charge of an online BULLETIN BOARD or CONFERENCING SYSTEM, who is responsible for maintaining the software and keeping some order among its users.

system programming The writing of operating systems, device drivers and other low-level programs, rather than APPLICATION SOFTWARE for users. It requires different software tools and often different programming languages from those used in application programming.

systems analysis A type of investigation performed as the first step in any major computer project. Its purpose is to identify those entities and processes that are of significance in some real-world activity, to enable suitable computer hardware and software to be selected or written to assist in the performance of that activity. A full systems analysis should always precede the specification and design (let alone the actual writing) of any software system, to avoid overlooking or misunderstanding any vital aspects of the job that would be expensive to correct once the system is built. A crucial part of any systems analysis is that it must consult and observe the people who actually perform the activity, rather than rely on computer engineers and programmers.

Numerous formal techniques have been invented for performing systems analysis (see more under METHODOLOGY), but all of them involve identifying the most important objects, relationships and flows of data that make up the particular activity, and then representing these in some kind of graphical notation such as a FLOW CHART. See more under DATA ANALYSIS, OBJECT-ORIENTED ANALYSIS, PERT, CRITICAL PATH ANALYSIS, BUSINESS PROCESS RE-ENGINEERING.

systems analyst One who performs SYSTEMS ANALYSIS.

Systems Application Architecture See SAA.

systems integration A branch of business computer consultancy that involves combining different hardware and software products (possibly from different manufacturers) so that they can work together and exchange data. Systems integration may also involve a considerable amount of programming to overcome incompatibilities between products, for example converting data from one FORMAT to another or from one communications PROTOCOL to another. See also VALUE-ADDED RESELLER.

Systems Management Server (SMS) A network service provided in later versions of Microsoft's WINDOWS NT and 2000 to assist in distributing and installing software onto users' workstations from a central administrative server. SMS also maintains an inventory of the hardware and software installed in the network, and supports remote DIAGNOSTIC and other NETWORK MANAGEMENT functions. Later versions offer Intelligent Mirroring, which preserves details of each user's software installation and configuration on a central server so that they can be restored to the same (or a different) workstation in the event of a problem. This feature may also be employed when making large-scale changes to the network architecture. See also SYSTEM MANAGEMENT, INVENTORY MANAGEMENT, ASSET MANAGEMENT.

Systems Network Architecture See SNA.

system software Software that is used by a computer for its own housekeeping purposes and to assist with the running of user programs, rather than directly to perform tasks on behalf of the user (which is the job of APPLICATION SOFTWARE). The OPERATING SYSTEM is the most important piece of system software, followed by the DEVICE DRIVERS that control all the peripheral hardware (such as printers and disk drives) connected to the computer. See also SYSTEM PROGRAMMING, UPDATE, CONFIGURATION.

system timer 1 The quartz clock chip used to provide the CLOCK SIGNAL that regulates the working of a computer's processor.
  2 A software process provided by a computer's OPERATING SYSTEM that provides a timing mechanism to other programs, by counting pulses from the clock chip. See also REAL TIME CLOCK, DATE STAMP.

System Tray In Microsoft WINDOWS versions 95 and later, an area situated at the right-hand end of the TASKBAR in which frequently-used utilities and applications may display a small ICON that provides instant access to them. Tray entries are automatically loaded when Windows is started without requiring any intervention from the user.

System V One of the two important historical strands of development of the UNIX operating system, the other being Berkeley Unix or BSD. System V was created by AT&T and its Release 4 (often called *SVR4*) introduced major improvements in networking, graphics and a JOURNALLING file system. Modern Unix versions such as SOLARIS combine the best features from BSD and System V.

systolic processor A type of PARALLEL COMPUTER in which many processors are arranged in a PIPELINE or grid through which the data items are made to flow in a succession of waves.

T1 line One of the standard types of LEASED LINE offered by telephone service vendors, which can carry 1.5 megabits per second in both directions. A T1 line is typically shared by allocating up to 24 64 kilobits per second channels to different users, or groups of 64 kilobits per second channels to single applications (for example 8 could be combined into a 512 kilobits per second VIDEOCONFERENCING link).

T3 line One of the standard types of LEASED LINE offered by telephone service vendors, which can carry 44.7 megabits per second in both directions. A T3 line is typically shared by allocating up to 673 64 kilobits per second channels to separate users, or by bonding groups of channels (see CHANNEL BONDING) to support higher BANDWIDTH applications. A T3 line's capacity is equivalent to 28 T1 LINES.

TA Abbreviation of TERMINAL ADAPTER.

TAB The ASCII CONTROL CHARACTER with code 9. In many programs this inserts a multiple space by moving the CURSOR to the next TAB STOP.

tabbed dialogue A visual USER INTERFACE component that contains several separate overlaid pages of information distinguished by protruding name tabs along one of their edges that mimic the style of a paper address book with alphabetic index cutouts. Clicking one of these named tabs makes its associated page visible. Tabbed dialogues are heavily used in Microsoft Windows to access CONFIGURATION parameters, for example in the CONTROL PANEL's System APPLET.

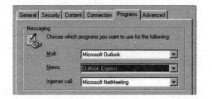

tab-delimited See under TAB-SEPARATED.

table 1 In a RELATIONAL DATABASE, the main data structure in which information is stored. It consists of a collection of RECORDS constructed from similar FIELDS, which may therefore be displayed as a two-dimensional table with different records forming its rows and different fields forming its columns. Physically, a table may well be stored in a conventional disk file.

2 In Microsoft WORD FOR WINDOWS and some other word processing programs, a way of arranging text into a two-dimensional grid of boxes, which may be performed automatically by selecting an area, then specifying the number of rows and columns.

table-of-contents 1 (ToC) A feature supported by most modern WORD PROCESSING programs that constructs a contents page for a document by gathering together copies of all its chapter and section headings. Contents page numbers are then managed automatically whenever alterations are made to the document.

2 (TOC) The directory of files stored on a CD-ROM or MINIDISC.

tablet See GRAPHICS TABLET.

tab-separated A standard text file format, often used to transport data between different database or spreadsheet programs, in which each RECORD occupies a new line and the FIELDS within each record are separated by TAB characters. See also COMMA-SEPARATED, RETURN-DELIMITED.

tab stop On a manual typewriter, a small movable metal peg that causes the carriage to stop when the TAB key is pressed, allowing text to be vertically aligned in tabular form. Hence by analogy, in a computer TEXT EDITOR or WORD PROCESSOR, one of several positions at which the CURSOR will stop when the TAB key is repeatedly pressed. The tab stops are often designed to simulate a manual typewriter, as small pointers that the user can drag along a RULER to the desired postions. See also TAB, MARGIN.

TACACS (Terminal Access Controller Access-Control System) A protocol for administering authentication, authorization and accounting data for the users on a network, as employed in all Cisco routers. The system works from a central server that contains either a dedicated TACACS database or a modified Unix PASSWORD file with TACACS protocol support, into which all authentication, authorization, and accounting data is directed when a user tries to log on. TACACS is defined in RFC 1492.

tag 1 In document MARKUP LANGUAGES such as HTML, SGML and XML, a directive inserted into the text to specify some aspect of its appearance (such as font size) or to describe its function within the document. Some special symbol combination must be chosen to distinguish the tags from the text proper: in all the above languages <angle brackets> are employed for this purpose.
2 In a processor CACHE, a group of bits used as an index into the stored CACHE LINES. Whenever the CPU requests a memory access, some bits of the requested address must be compared against all the tags in the cache to look for a hit.
3 In a few experimental computer architectures, an extra group of bits appended to each memory address to indicate the type of the data item stored at that address.
4 In general, any short sequence of bits appended to a data object to distinguish it from others within some temporary and local context such as a priority QUEUE.

Tagged Image File Format See TIFF.

tag switching A networking technology invented by CISCO to improve the efficiency of routing Internet traffic over an ATM (ASYNCHRONOUS TRANSFER MODE) backbone network. Routers that can perform tag switching add a TAG to each IP packet they pass on, to indicate what route it belongs to, and the data flows from many different routes may be MULTIPLEXED onto a single switched ATM link before demultiplexing and removing the tags for final delivery.

tail recursion The use of a RECURSIVE call (that is, a call to itself) as the last statement in a procedure or function definition, so that the procedure terminates immediately on return from each recursive call, as in the example:

```
function factorial(num: int): int;
if num = 0 then 1
else num * factorial(num-1);
```

A tail recursive call can always be replaced by an ITERATIVE loop, and some language compilers perform this substitution as an optimization to reduce stack usage. See more under RECURSION.

Tandem Computer Inc. A US computer manufacturer noted for its expertise in FAULT-TOLERANT SERVER technology, now owned by COMPAQ.

Tandy The brand name for computers and other electrical goods sold by the US Radio Shack chain stores (in the UK, the stores themselves are called Tandy).

tape A magnetic recording medium, consisting of long strips of thin polymer film coated with a ferromagnetic substance, that is moved past a recording head to write magnetized regions along its length. These regions can be detected by a separate read head to retrieve the stored information. The magnetic recording material is commonly a mixture of cobalt, iron and nickel oxides, or a finely powdered metal or alloy of those metals. Tape may be stored on a single spool that has to be threaded past the heads by hand (so called *reel-to-reel*), or in a self-contained CARTRIDGE or CASSETTE that encloses one or both reels and offers access for the heads through a small shutter or window.

Tape is widely used to store ANALOGUE audio and video information as well as DIGITAL audio, video and computer data. There are many different standard tape widths in use, the QUARTER-INCH CARTRIDGE being common in computing applications. To maximize storage capacity, advanced recorders (including domestic video recorders) employ a rotating record head to write diagonal tracks that exploit the width of the tape as well as its length.

The great disadvantage of tape for computer applications is that it is inherently a sequential access medium – to find a particular data item requires traversing all the tape up to that point – which is much slower than the random access offered by MAGNETIC DISK media.

tape archive A collection of magnetic tapes containing all the information that has passed through a computer system that is no longer needed for instant access. Typical BACKUP regimes consign data to a tape archive once the disk space it occupies is required for new data. MAINFRAME computer installations may employ automated tape archives to store large volumes of data such as census records or customer accounts, using a JUKEBOX or other mechanical mechanism to locate and load a desired tape reel.

tape backup The copying onto magnetic tape of the contents of the magnetic disks that a computer uses for its working storage, so that the data may be retrieved in case of a disk failure. In computer networks, the TAPE DRIVE is typically installed in the server and backup is performed for all users automatically. Since backing up to tape is a slow process, this is often carried out at night or at weekends when the network traffic is low.

tape drive A mechanism for storing and retrieving data from magnetic tape. It consists of motors that wind the tape, and recording and erasing HEADS over which the tape is passed. There are many different types of tape drive: some use open reels of tape and in others the tape is contained within a CASSETTE or CARTRIDGE. See also DAT.

tape library An alternative name for a TAPE ARCHIVE.

tape streamer A type of tape drive that enables very rapid BACKUP of hard disk drives by using a special streaming device driver that bypasses the computer's file system and makes a direct bit-by-bit copy of the disk's contents. Of course such a copy can be restored only by using the same driver, and cannot be read by the computer's operating system (which creates a possibly undesirable dependency on the continued existence of the tape drive manufacturer).

tape tensioning A mechanism built into most magnetic tape drives that maintains the tape at an even tension, hence avoiding read errors due to friction and inertia effects caused by stretching.

TAPI (Telephony Application Programming Interface) Microsoft's telephony programmer's interface to WINDOWS. It is used to control MODEMS, to make dial-up networking connections, and to manage VOICEMAIL messages.

tar A popular FILE COMPRESSION utility on Unix-based computer systems, and hence on the INTERNET.

Targa format See TGA

Targa graphics adaptor One of the earliest professional-quality graphics and VIDEO CAPTURE boards for IBM-compatible PCs, launched by Truevision of Indianapolis in 1985. Its widespread use in science and the TV industry has lead to its proprietary TGA file format becoming one of the de facto industry standards.

task A computer program, or section of a program, that can be run simultaneously with, and independently of, other such programs under a MULTITASKING operating system. A task typically owns all the resources associated with a full program, including its own PROGRAM COUNTER, which keeps track of what instruction to execute next, and its own STACK for saving temporary data. Many multitasking operating systems seek to prevent different tasks from accidentally overwriting each other's data by giving them separate address spaces (see more under PROTECTED MEMORY). Tasks may also be assigned different levels of PRIORITY, which determine how soon and how often they get to run.

If the computer has only a single processor, then only one task can run at any given time. However, the operating system switches between the various waiting tasks sufficiently quickly to create the illusion that they are all running simultaneously (see more under TASK SCHEDULING). If more than one processor is present, each task may be assigned to a different processor and so tasks can actually run simultaneously.

A task may exist in one of three states: running, ready to run, or blocked waiting for some event to occur (typically the completion of an I/O operation). Tasks that are ready to run are kept in a QUEUE, from which they are removed to be run in an order determined by the scheduling algorithm in use.

See also BACKGROUND TASK, PRE-EMPTIVE MULTITASKING, COOPERATIVE MULTITASKING, THREAD, MULTITHREADING, SPAWN.

Taskbar A visual user interface component used by WINDOWS (but with equivalents in several other operating systems) that displays all the currently running programs as ICONS. Clicking on an icon maximizes the corresponding program's window and gives it the FOCUS. The Windows Taskbar pops up automatically when the MOUSE POINTER is moved to whichever edge of the screen the user has currently DOCKED the taskbar on.

task scheduling The procedure whereby a MULTITASKING operating system decides which of several waiting TASKS is to be allowed to run on an available processor. The method used for making the decision should be fair, so that no task is permanently prevented from running. It must also be efficient, so that more important tasks are not impeded by less important ones. Many different scheduling algorithms have been employed by various operating systems, the best known being ROUND ROBIN scheduling (which simply runs each task in turn) and PRIORITY SCHEDULING (which gives preference to more important tasks). Other possibilities are to run the shortest tasks first, or to measure and equalize the total CPU time consumed by each task.

task switching A technique used as a substitute for true MULTITASKING, in which several programs are kept in memory simultaneously and the user switches from one to another using a single keystroke. Only the currently selected program runs, and no processing occurs in any of the others. Before the advent of WINDOWS, task switching utilities such as DESQVIEW were popular additions to MS-DOS on PCs.

TCal Abbreviation of THERMAL RECALIBRATION.

TCL (Tool Command Language) A powerful SCRIPTING LANGUAGE for the Unix operating system that is specially designed for automating the execution of otherwise interactive programs by feeding command strings to them. See also AWK, PERL, PYTHON.

TCO Abbreviation of TOTAL COST OF OWNERSHIP.

TCP (Transmission Control Protocol) The higher level of the two main communication protocols on which the INTERNET is based (see also IP). TCP was originally developed at ARPA, the US Defense research agency, but it was released to the public in 1983, whereupon it became the standard protocol for connecting Unix computer systems together.

TCP is a CONNECTION-ORIENTED, TRANSPORT LAYER protocol that includes facilities for error detection and correction and flow control to ensure reliable communication. While IP decides the precise route that blocks of data (called SEGMENTS) will take between the various computers and routers to their final destination, TCP manages the flow of these segments. It can detect when a segment has been corrupted in the lower layers of the communication, and arrange for it to be resent. TCP also resends any segment that is not acknowledged within a variable time limit, and can rearrange segments delivered out of order so that they resume their proper sequence.

Application-level Internet protocols such as TELNET, HTTP and FTP run on top of TCP, which is defined in the document STD 7 (RFC 793).

TCP/IP The protocol suite upon which the INTERNET is based. TCP/IP was invented in 1973 by Vinton CERF and Bob Kahn to enable different (and incompatible) educational and defence computer networks to be connected to the US defence network ARPANET, which was converted to TCP/IP in 1983 and became the core of the modern Internet.

TCP/IP is now frequently employed as a protocol for LANS (local area networks) too, particularly those referred to as INTRANETS, which employ web browser technology to distribute documents around a company.

TCP/IP consists of two parts, with IP (Internet Protocol) operating at the NETWORK LAYER beneath TCP (Transmission Control Protocol) which operates at the TRANSPORT LAYER.

The term TCP/IP is often loosely used to refer to the entire suite of Internet protocols, including the various APPLICATION LAYER protocols such as TELNET, FTP, UDP and RDP.

TDM Abbreviation of TIME DIVISION MULTIPLEXING.

TDMA (Time Division Multiple Access) The transmission technology used throughout Europe and most non-US countries for digital MOBILE PHONE services such as GSM. See more under TIME DIVISION MULTIPLEXING.

team development The activity of developing a software product using more than one programmer. Compared to the task of a single programmer, team development requires an extra level of discipline concerned with the synchronization of alterations made by different programmers to the same SOURCE files, the choice of IDENTIFIER names, the integration of components written by different programmers, the communication of intentions between designers and programmers, and the measurement of progress. All these factors are in addition to the personnel management problems found in any group enterprise. Various software tools and programming language features have been invented to help with these tasks. See for example VERSION CONTROL, SOURCE CONTROL and MODULARITY.

techie A derogatory term for someone who understands how computers work.

technical support The department within a computer hardware or software company that assists users with the operation of its products, providing such facilities as a telephone HELPDESK, an online KNOWLEDGE BASE and, in the case of more expensive products, even site visits from support personnel. Technical support is the department to which BUG REPORTS are usually sent.

technology transfer The process of introducing a new technology to another company, institution or country.

telco Shorthand for a telephone or telecommunications company.

telecommunication The transmission of audio or video information by means of electrical or optical signals through a cable, or via radio waves. See also WIRELESS COMMUNICATIONS.

telemarketing Selling products or services via the telephone.

telemedicine The practice of medical diagnosis and treatment at a distance, using a two-way videoconferencing link. Experimental systems have even employed IMMERSIVE VIRTUAL REALITY techniques to allow an expert surgeon to guide surgery on a remote patient. See also TELEPRESENCE.

telephony The long-distance transmission of spoken information by means of electrical signals conveyed over wires or radio waves. When used in a computing context, the term refers to the integration of computers with the public telephone system, and their use to manage phone calls.

Telephony Application Programming Interface See TAPI.

teleport To move a network user's customized desktop environment onto a remote WORKSTATION at which he or she is currently working.

telepresence Using computers and telecommunications to give a human operator the experience of being present at some remote location. Telepresence systems may in future be employed to enter hazardous environments (such as nuclear reactors), for space exploration, and to enable experts such as surgeons or engineers to deal with remote emergencies. Some telepresence techniques work with live video, via a camera and a BROADBAND network. Others employ a VIRTUAL REALITY reconstruction of the remote site. Most use IMMERSIVE head-mounted displays to convey their effect.

teleprinter A type of telegraph apparatus, also used as a very early form of computer terminal, whose mechanism evolved from the manual typewriter. A keyboard converted keystrokes into electrical impulses, which were conveyed down a SERIAL connection to a similar apparatus that converted the impulses back to motion of the printing head. See also TELETYPE

teletext A system for transmitting textual information alongside broadcast or cable TV programmes, which can be viewed on TV sets that have a teletext decoder built in. See more under VIDEOTEXT.

teletype (tty) The earliest kind of computer TERMINAL, adapted from the telegraph and manufactured by the Teletype Corporation of Skokie, Illinois. A teletype could produce only alphanumeric printed output onto continuous paper, and its text formatting commands were confined to the CARRIAGE RETURN, LINE FEED and TAB. Many features of the ASCII character set, and of scrolling COMMAND LINE operating system interfaces, are historic relics of the restricted capabilities of the teletype (see also GLASS TELETYPE).

telnet **1** The standard Internet protocol for logging into a remote computer, which runs on top of TCP/IP and is defined in RFC 854.
2 A utility program, originally provided in Unix but now available for most operating systems, that acts as a TERMINAL EMULATOR, using the telnet protocol to log on to remote computers. Often used to reconfigure remote SERVERS or ROUTERS from a portable computer.

temp file Shorthand for TEMPORARY FILE.

template **1** A master pattern from which copies may be taken to simplify the task of creating a new document or other object. Since copying and editing digital data is so easy, templates are widely employed throughout computing, from word processing to programming.
2 In word processors such as Microsoft Word, templates are complete business documents (for example, letters complete with letterhead/logo, or invoices) with space left for the user to add specific content. They may also include FIELDS which, when filled in by the user, activate a MACRO (for example to automatically compute the invoice total). When creating a new document, the user is offered a list of templates as an alternative to starting from a blank document. See also WORD PROCESSOR, STYLE SHEET, MACRO LANGUAGE.
3 In programming, templates are routines and data structures that have been defined in a generic way so that they will work on many different data types, and which programmers can adapt to the details of a specific project by making relatively few simple edits. See, for example, STANDARD TEMPLATE LIBRARY. See also CLASS LIBRARY, OBJECT LIBRARY.

temporary file A disk file written by an APPLICATION PROGRAM while it is running, to hold some of its working data, but which is auto-matically deleted when the application terminates. A typical function for such temporary files is to hold UNDO information, before the changes made to a document are committed by saving the document. If an application terminates abnormally, such temp files may be left on the disk, and are often to be seen with unreadable computer-generated names such as ~$df5446.tmp.

10base2 Also called *Thin Ethernet*. An older standard for 10 megabits per second Ethernet cabling that uses thin COAXIAL CABLE with a maximum run of 185 metres (see XBASEY).

10base5 Also called *Thick Ethernet*. The original cabling standard for 10 megabits per second Ethernet that uses thick (usually yellow) COAXIAL CABLE with a maximum run of 500 metres (see XBASEY).

10baseT The most popular 10 megabits per second Ethernet cabling system, which employs TWISTED-PAIR cabling with a maximum run of 100 metres (see XBASEY).

tendinitis A painful inflammation of tendons, usually in the wrist, which can be caused by repetitive movements such as typing. This and related ailments such as *tenosynovitis* and CARPAL TUNNEL SYNDROME are now being recognized as an occupational hazard, under the collective name of RSI.

tenosynovitis See under TENDINITIS.

terabyte 1024 GIGABYTES, or 2^{40} (approximately one thousand billion) BYTES.

teraflops A unit of processor speed equal to one million, million (i.e. 10^{12}) FLOPS (Floating-Point Operations Per Second). One teraflop is the most recent milestone speed for supercomputer designers, surpassed in 1996 by an Intel parallel computer at the Sandia National Laboratories. The next milestone is one PETAFLOPS. See also GIGAFLOPS.

termcap A utility program, developed as part of Berkeley Unix, that configures the operating system to display correctly on different types of TERMINAL. Termcap operates by processing a text-based configuration file in which are described the capabilities (hence the name) of the current terminal device. It has been largely rendered obsolete by the advent of the GRAPHICAL USER INTERFACE. See also TERMINAL EMULATION, CURSOR-ADDRESSA-BLE TERMINAL, CURSES.

terminal 1 An electronic or electromechanical device for entering data into a computer or other communication system and for displaying data received. The first computer terminal was an adapted teleprinter called the TELETYPE, later replaced by the VISUAL DISPLAY UNIT containing a CATHODE RAY TUBE display. A terminal is typically linked to a remote computer via a SERIAL line, and can display only ALPHA-NUMERIC information. If it can display images, it is normally explicitly described as a GRAPH-ICS terminal. See also DUMB TERMINAL, SMART TERMINAL, TERMINAL EMULATION.

2 In electronic engineering, the end of a communications link at which signals are either transmitted or received, or any point along the link at which the signal is made available to an external apparatus. It also refers to the apparatus used to send and receive such signals.

Terminal Access Controller Access-Control System See TACACS.

terminal adapter (TA) An interfacing device used to connect a computer to a digital telephone network such as ISDN. A terminal adaptor does not work with audio signals as a MODEM does, but merely converts the already digital signals from the computer into an appropriate format.

terminal emulation See under TERMINAL EMULATOR.

terminal emulator A piece of software that allows a personal computer to imitate the behaviour of a DUMB TERMINAL and so to connect to a MAINFRAME or MINICOMPUTER, or to some other SERIAL communication source. The terminals most widely emulated are the standard ANSI TERMINAL and various DEC terminals such as VT100, VT220 and VT52.

terminal server A hardware device (typically a computer running suitable server software, but sometimes a HUB) that allows users to log into it using a SMART TERMINAL or other THIN CLIENT and to access shared network resources or run programs remotely on the server. A good example is Microsoft's Windows Terminal Server, which permits low-powered PCs or even pocket computers to run WINDOWS NT software remotely on the server. See also WIN-FRAME, X WINDOW SYSTEM, REMOTE CONTROL.

terminal symbol In a system of PRODUCTION RULES describing the syntax of a language, one of those symbols that has no further inner structure, but forms part of the LEXICON of the language.

terminal window On a computer whose operating system employs a graphical user interface, a window within which an older style of character-based, full-screen display is simulated. Terminal windows are particularly used in Unix systems that employ, for example a Motif or KDE-based interface, to give access to a traditional Unix SHELL. See also TERMINAL, TERMINAL EMULATION.

terminate 1 To cause a software process to stop executing. See also TSR.

2 To apply a small electronic device to the end of a network cable or other signal path to prevent signals being spuriously reflected back down the line.

3 To mark the end of a data structure such as a STRING or a LINKED LIST by adding a special value. See NULL-TERMINATED.

terminate and stay resident See TSR.

terminator A small hardware device containing a RESISTOR that must be attached to any free ends of a network cable or SCSI cable to suppress reflection of the signals that may cause data to become corrupted. Terminating resistors are also placed on PRINTED CIRCUIT BOARDS at the end of BUS tracks, for the same reason.

tessellation The decomposition of a two-dimensional image into a collection of polygons in the process of creating a WIRE-FRAME representation of an object.

test-and-branch See under CONDITIONAL BRANCH.

test-and-set The generic name for a class of processor instructions that compare the values in two registers and then set a FLAG that indicates the result.

testbed An apparatus into which other devices (such as car engines) can be fitted for testing, and which supplies all the external inputs required by the device under test. The term is also used metaphorically for a specially-configured computer or program SHELL that is used to test software products. See also TEST HARNESS.

test harness A short program written to test component routines destined eventually to be built into some larger system. The harness must often provide STUBS that imitate the behaviour of any missing routines that the routine under test communicates with: for example to accept (and discard) outputs, or to supply dummy inputs.

testing The process of exercising a new hardware or software product to determine whether it meets its SPECIFICATION. Testing in the computer industry involves unprecedented difficulties because of the uniquely flexible nature of the products. For example, it is not possible to test a computer against all the software products it will be required to run, because most of them are not yet written. It is equally impossible to test a complex software product for every possible combination of user inputs, because these are effectively infinite in number. It is, however, possible to use computers themselves to assist with the testing – for example to generate huge volumes of test data or to run TEST HARNESSES that drive a program through millions or billions of input combinations. The testing process is nowadays highly organized into various different phases, including ALPHA TESTING, BETA TESTING and USABILITY studies. See also VERSIONING, RELEASE CANDIDATE.

test program A program that is written to test the workings of another program, for example by automatically delivering different inputs and contexts.

test suite A set of programs designed to test various aspects of the operation of some hardware or software system. See also TESTING, TEST PROGRAM, CONFORMANCE TEST, TEST HARNESS.

TeX A powerful and complex TYPESETTING and TEXT FORMATTING program for Unix systems created by the computer scientist Donald KNUTH and widely used in academic publishing. TeX is not an interactive program, but works by TAGS embedded in the text that describe its desired format and appearance. TeX devotees are hypersensitive about the pronunciation of its name ('tek' not 'tex') and its spelling, which should be with a subscript E as in T$_{\text{e}}$X, though a lower case e is grudgingly accepted. Widely used TeX derivatives include the simplified LATEX, and MuTeX for music publishing.

Texas Instruments (TI) The earliest major semiconductor manufacturer, founded by Jack Kilby in 1958 on the strength of his patenting of the INTEGRATED CIRCUIT. TI began by manufacturing analogue circuits for miniature devices such as hearing aids, and created the world's first pocket calculator in the 1960s. In the early 1970s TI joined Intel, Zilog and Motorola in manufacturing MICROPROCESSORS, and has produced its own branded PCs for many years. Texas Instruments remains one of the largest manufacturers of memory chips, and of special chips for embedded applications such as DIGITAL SIGNAL PROCESSORS, but has largely abandoned the general-purpose microprocessor market to Intel and the cloners of Intel CPUs. See also DIGITAL LIGHT PROCESSOR.

texel Short for texture element, a geometric shape (such as a square or triangle) used as the primitive building brick to construct a texture for use in TEXTURE MAPPING. See also PIXEL and VOXEL.

text A data type that consists of a collection of STRINGS of alphanumeric characters, separated by spaces, which represent words in a human or computer language. In a PLAIN ASCII text the only other permissible characters are the CARRIAGE RETURN and LINE FEED that indicate the beginning of a new line, and the TAB character used to format tabular matter. RICH TEXT, HTML and SGML are all forms of text that introduce special character combinations called TAGS that can be interpreted by suitable software to display different FONTS, FONT SIZES and EMPHASES such as bold, italic or underline. See also TEXT FILE.

text alignment The arrangement of lines of text on a page. The most used possibilities include making the left- or right-hand margins line up vertically (called left or right aligned or justified), centring the text so that margin spaces are the same on left and right, or fully justifying the text by making every line the same length. In many WORD PROCESSORS, these options may be applied by simply clicking one of a set of adjacent buttons. See also MARGIN, JUSTIFY, HYPHENATION, OPTICAL MARGIN ADJUSTMENT.

text box An alternative name for an EDIT BOX. A screen area into which the user can type text, and which offers basic text editing functions, as found in the user interface of most modern computer applications. See also LIST BOX, COMBO BOX, GRAPHICAL USER INTERFACE.

text compression The use of software to reduce the amount of space required to store a passage of text. See, for example, LEMPEL–ZIV COMPRESSION, PKZIP and TAR.

text editor A computer program that enables its user to perform a set of basic editing functions on the contents of a text file. These functions typically include: displaying the file's contents (with scrolling to view documents larger than the screen), backspacing to delete misstyped characters, overwriting old text with new and insertion of new text in the middle of existing text, the selection of whole passages to delete or move them, automated searching to find all occurrences of a word or phrase and replace it by another, and often automatic WORD-WRAP of lines wider than the screen. Typically simpler than a WORD PROCESSOR, a text editor is not concerned with the appearance of text and does not support multiple FONTS or complex formatting. Most computer operating systems provide a basic text editor for modifying important system files. For example, Windows supplies NOTEPAD, while Unix supplies VI and/or EMACS.

text file A file that contains nothing but printable ALPHANUMERIC characters (e.g. ASCII characters 33–126), plus SPACE, CARRIAGE RETURN, LINE FEED or TAB characters. Text files can be created and viewed using a simple TEXT EDITOR, and support only the simplest of formatting – namely line breaks and simple tabulation. Text files do not support different typefaces, font sizes or emphases such as bold and italic type. Text files are often useful as a 'lowest common denominator' when transferring textual data between different and incompatible computer systems, since every computer has a simple editor that can read them. For this reason most application programs include an option to export data in text file format.

text formatting The process of arranging text into lines, paragraphs, sections, chapters and so on, and applying different fonts, emphases, indentation, tabulation, headlines, and other features. Such formatting cannot be expressed using plain ASCII-encoded characters, but requires additional format information to be embedded in the document file. See also RICH TEXT, PAGE DESCRIPTION LANGUAGE, MARKUP LANGUAGE, REFORMAT.

texting, text messaging The use of the Short Message Service (SMS) on a MOBILE PHONE to send short text messages to another person. The limited keyboards and displays of mobile phones encourage the creation of a new kind of shorthand (e.g. CU@8 for 'see you at eight') similar to, but more extreme than, the online shorthand used in emails and newsgroups.

text retrieval system A computerized system for storing textual information. It differs from a conventional database in that individual documents are not normally divided up into separate FIELDS, but are treated as single RECORDS – such a system may often be described as a FREE-FORM DATABASE. A text retrieval system typically INDEXES every word in all the documents it contains (barring a list of common STOPWORDS such as 'the' and 'but') to permit rapid search and retrieval, so it is also sometimes called a FULL-TEXT RETRIEVAL system. Such systems are often used, for example, as a catalogues for libraries and collections.

Querying a text retrieval system consists of searching for groups of the KEYWORDS from this index, often using sophisticated combination methods such as BOOLEAN expressions, WILDCARDS or REGULAR EXPRESSIONS.

text search An operation that locates a particular word or words within a large volume of text such as a long document, a document database or a collection of web pages. The algorithms employed for text searching are quite different from those used to search numeric data, since where the latter are usually precise (two numbers are equal or they are not), in a text search partial or multiple matches are often of interest. For example when searching for 'apple', a variant such as 'apples' is usually of interest and could be found by using a WILDCARD search (see more under PATTERN MATCHING, REGULAR EXPRESSION).

Other special types of search such as PROXIM-ITY SEARCH, SOUNDEX searches and SYNONYM RINGS offer still more flexibility in retrieving related words. Powerful text search functions are built into modern WORD PROCESSORS, and may be supplemented by external utilities such as GREP. See also TEXT RETRIEVAL SYSTEM, SEARCH ENGINE, RELEVANCE.

text-to-speech (TTS) The use of a computer to read aloud documents displayed on its screen or stored in a file. Most computer sound cards contain a SYNTHESIZER chip that can be used for this purpose, in combination with suitable text-to-speech software. See more under SPEECH SYNTHESIS.

texture mapping A technique for adding realism to 3D GRAPHICS displays at relatively little computational cost by wrapping two-dimensional BITMAP images around objects to convey the impression of complex surface texture. For example, photographs of the walls of a brick-built house might be wrapped around a simple box frame, which is far more economical than creating each individual brick as a true 3D object. To create a realistic impression, texture maps must be applied early in the graphics PIPELINE so that they pass through its geometric transformation stage and are rendered in correct perspective. Modern 3D ACCELERATOR cards contain a large amount of memory for storing texture maps, and employ BILINEAR or TRILINEAR FILTERING to very rapidly warp the bitmaps into correct perspective. Further refinements of the texture mapping trick include ENVIRONMENT MAPPING, BUMP MAPPING and MIP MAPPING.

TFT (thin-film transistor) A type of TRANSISTOR employed to build ACTIVE MATRIX LCD displays, formed by depositing thin layers of silicon and metal directly onto a sheet of glass.

TGA (TarGA) A 24-bit graphics file format for bitmapped images that supports ALPHA CHAN-NELS and data compression. It was originally developed for Truevision's TARGA GRAPHICS ADAPTOR, but is now a widely used inter-change format, especially for professional video capture.

The Open Group An industry standards body formed in 1996 by a merger of the X/OPEN group and the OPEN SOFTWARE FOUNDATION. Its purpose is to promote standards for the portability of applications between different operating systems. In 1997 Microsoft handed over control of its ACTIVEX standards to a working party of The Open Group. See also OPEN SYSTEMS.

theorem prover A program that can apply logical deduction to prove the consistency of sets of propositions expressed in a suitable format, as used in some types of ARTIFICIAL INTELLIGENCE application, and in some advanced language COMPILERS. See also RULE-BASED SYSTEM, FORWARD CHAINING, BACKWARD CHAINING, CONSTRAINT SOLVER, LOGIC PRO-GRAMMING.

thermal recalibration (TCal) A process in which a HARD DISK drive periodically recali-brates itself to compensate for expansion and contraction of the moving parts caused by changes in internal temperature. The brief interruption to reading or writing while TCal takes place may have a disruptive effect on some REAL TIME applications such as music editing, and is one of the rationales for the manufacture of AV DRIVES.

thermal-transfer printer A class of computer PRINTER technologies in which heat is employed to melt or evaporate a coloured pig-ment onto the paper. The DYE-SUBLIMATION PRINTER and DYE-TRANSFER PRINTER belong to this group, but both are now threatened with obsolescence by the improvements in colour LASER PRINTERS.

thermionic valve (*US* vacuum tube) A now almost obsolete class of electronic component that formed the basis of all audio, radio and computer equipment prior to the 1960s. Valves act as switches or amplifiers, regulat-ing the electrical current they conduct by applying voltages to various configurations of ELECTRODES contained within their evacuated glass envelope. The current is carried by elec-trons emitted from a heated wire filament, hence the name thermionic.

Valves are fragile, power-consuming and have a very short service life, so the practically indestructible SOLID-STATE TRANSISTOR rapidly displaced them. However, they are still employed by some committed hi-fi enthusi-asts who enjoy the distinctive sound quality they impart.

thick client The ordinary personal computer, heavily laden with a large operating system and applications. Coined as an ironic counterpart to the term THIN CLIENT, as advocated by enthusiasts of network-centric computing.

thick Ethernet An informal name for Ethernet run over 10BASE5 coaxial cabling, which is thick and yellow.

thin-and-wide A style of NOTEBOOK computer first introduced in the late 1990s by, for example IBM, Compaq and Hewlett Packard. It features a large display screen and keyboard, but is made extremely thin to reduce the weight.

thin client A jargon term for a minimal network WORKSTATION that contains only a screen, processor, keyboard and memory, and runs all its software on a remote SERVER via a network, using some remote display protocol such as the X WINDOW SYSTEM or Citrix's ICA. The name alludes to the low specification (and hence low cost) of such a workstation compared to a general-purpose PC. Thin clients also improve security as, lacking local disk drives, they cannot be used to install any new software. See also NETWORK COMPUTER.

thin Ethernet An informal name for Ethernet run over the thinner 10BASE2 coaxial cabling.

thin-film transistor See TFT.

ThinkPad A highly successful range of NOTE-BOOK computers made by IBM.

third generation language A description applied to the first generation of HIGH-LEVEL PROGRAMMING LANGUAGES such as FORTRAN, COBOL, C and PASCAL – the first two generations being by implication raw machine code, and then assembly languages. The term was seldom used in practice until the advent of FOURTH GENERATION LANGUAGES, when it became a useful distinction.

third-party A company other than the original manufacturer of a computer or software product that provides an ADD-ON, PLUG-IN or other enhancement for that product. Used, for example, as in 'a third-party display driver'. The original manufacturer and the customer are assumed to be the other two parties.

32-bit Of a hardware or software system (for example a microprocessor or an operating system), designed to handle numbers that are 32 BITS in length. UNIX has always been a 32-bit operating system, as are Microsoft WINDOWS NT and WINDOWS 2000 (but not earlier versions). See also 16-BIT, 64-BIT.

32-bit application An application program written to be executed under a 32-bit operating system such as current versions of Windows, MacOS and older versions of Unix. The term is used only to maintain a distinction when other versions (e.g. 16-bit or 64-bit) of that operating system also exist.

Thompson, Ken (b. 1943) Co-inventor, along with Dennis RITCHIE, of the UNIX operating system, at BELL LABORATORIES in the early 1960s.

thrashing A weakness of many automated systems that may become trapped in a cycle of repeatedly switching between two equally attracting states. This behaviour can be seen by standing in front of an automatic shop or lift door but refusing to enter. Thrashing can be a problem for computer disk or memory systems, when an object only just smaller than the CACHE gets repeatedly loaded and unloaded, with devastating effects on overall throughput.

thread **1** In an online discussion forum such as a NEWSGROUP, CONFERENCING SYSTEM, BULLETIN BOARD or MAILING LIST, a sequence of messages that forms a separate strand of discussion within a larger group. The more sophisticated client programs can identify separate threads and display them using a different colour or level of indentation.
2 In a MULTITHREADING operating system, a lightweight PROCESS that shares the CPU with other executing threads. Threads differ from TASKS in sharing more of their execution context – each has its own stack pointer and program counter, but otherwise shares the same address space and global data. Operating systems that support threads include Windows NT and 2000 and Unix. See more under MULTITHREADING.

thread-aware A program written in the knowledge that it may encounter multiple THREADS of execution. See also THREAD-SAFE.

threaded code A type of PSEUDO-CODE generated as output by certain programming languages, the best-known being VISUAL BASIC and FORTH. Rather than being a sequence of actual MACHINE CODE instructions, threaded code consists of a list of the entry addresses of machine code routines that perform certain primitive actions. The threaded code is executed by an INTERPRETER that executes each primitive routine in the list in turn by simply jumping to the address.

Threaded code can be made more efficient than other types of INTERPRETED language, and may even approach the speed of a fully COMPILED language if the primitive routines are well chosen and implemented. For example, Visual Basic programs achieve acceptable speed even for heavily graphical programs because most of their processing time is actually spent executing NATIVE Windows routines. See also TOKEN-THREADED, TOKEN, INTERPRETED, STACK-BASED.

thread pool A mechanism used to support THREAD management in MICROSOFT TRANSACTION SERVER. Rather than each application programmer having to define their own execution threads, and allocate memory and other resources to them, the system automatically maintains a pool of predefined threads, which an application program can claim and use to execute a task, and which are recycled when the application releases them.

thread-safe A program written with the knowledge that it may encounter multiple THREADS of execution. It is therefore designed to acquire any shared resources it needs by using the proper request protocol, and to release them promptly when finished. See also THREAD-AWARE.

three-address architecture A class of processor architecture in which every INSTRUCTION requires the ADDRESS of three REGISTERS: two source registers and a destination register to hold the result, as in an operation such as:

```
ADD reg1, reg2, reg3
```

Some RISC designs employ this highly regular instruction format.

3Com Corporation A manufacturer of LAN and communications equipment, founded in 1979, and best known for pioneering ETHERNET chipsets. In 1997, 3Com merged with US Robotics, the leading US MODEM manufacturer, and thus acquired the PALM range of hand-held computers.

3D accelerator 1 A chip or chip-set specially designed to speed up 3D GRAPHICS operations by relieving the CPU of some of the more time-consuming processing tasks. Accelerator chips fall into two main categories: *geometry processors*, which handle the trigonometric calculations needed to determine the current viewpoint, and *rendering chips*, which assist the later stages – namely triangle setup (converting 3D POLYGON coordinates to 2D screen coordinates), TEXTURE MAPPING and rasterizing (painting the actual pixels). The leading manufacturers of 3D accelerator chips include ATI Technologies, Matrox, S3, 3Dlabs, Real 3D, Trident and Nvidia.

2 A PC EXPANSION CARD that incorporates one or more such accelerator chips (typically geometry and rendering chips), along with some memory and driver software in ROM. Well known brands include 3Dfx, Diamond and Matrox.

3Dfx Manufacturer of the popular Voodoo 3D graphics cards.

3D graphics The process of producing images on a computer display that appear to represent solid, three-dimensional objects that can be viewed from different angles. Whereas 2D GRAPHICS is concerned solely with colouring areas of PIXELS on a display screen, 3D graphics starts from an abstract representation of the depicted object in space, and the computer must rapidly calculate how this should appear from each viewpoint.

3D effects are employed for computer games, in COMPUTER AIDED DESIGN, in SIMULATORS and VIRTUAL REALITY systems, and in the film industry to create 'virtual actors' and special effects for movies from *Jurassic Park* to *Titanic*. Displaying 3D images requires far more computing power than displaying 2D images because of the recalculation required when the viewpoint is changed.

3D images start out from a WIRE-FRAME representation of each object that will appear in the scene: a mesh of triangles, squares or other polygons is drawn to conform as closely as possible to the object's surface. The three-dimensional X, Y and Z coordinates of every point (or VERTEX) where these polygons meet is stored in a database, as a description of the volume occupied by the object.

In the GEOMETRY processing phase, the computer calculates what all these wire-frame objects look like from the observer's current viewpoint (i.e. the screen), taking account of perspective. This requires a trigonometrical transformation to be applied to every single vertex – there might be tens of thousands of vertices in a complex scene – and these are FLOATING-POINT calculations which consume a lot of CPU time.

This projected view is then shaded to determine the colour of each polygon, according to its surface properties (e.g. glossy, matte, metallic) and the colour and position of all the light sources, details of which are stored in the database along with the vertices. Sophisticated shading algorithms invented by Gouraud or Phong can create smoothly varying shadow and reflection across each polygon to give the illusion of a smoothly curved surface. Finally the shaded view is RENDERED by converting all this polygon colour information into sequences of actual pixel values for display on a screen or printer.

Many ingenious tricks have been invented to increase the realism of 3D scenes while minimizing the amount of computation. Determining which surfaces hide others is accelerated by adding extra memory as a Z-BUFFER. Thousands of tiny polygons would be needed to accurately depict finely textured surfaces such as hair, grass, sand or wood grain. To avoid this, a bitmapped photographic image of real hair, grass, etc is wrapped around the wire-frame image in a process called TEXTURE MAPPING. Ideally this happens during the geometry stage so the texture is transformed into correct perspective. Another trick called BUMP MAPPING can, by modifying the shading algorithm, convey the illusion of a lumpy surface, even though the underlying geometry is actually a smooth sphere or cylinder. ENVIRONMENT MAPPING cheaply creates realistic reflections on shiny or metallic surfaces, by computing a view from that surface (rather than from the observer's position) and using it as a texture map. Atmospheric effects such as fog and haze are faked by reducing the intensity of pixels during rendering, and do not correspond to objects in the database.

The realism that can be achieved in 3D graphics is determined by processing time constraints. A film such as *Jurassic Park* can aim for maximum realism because the rendering does not have to be done in real time.

However, in an interactive, animated 3D game such as Doom or Quake each frame must be rendered in real time (30 times per second to achieve smooth motion) because the program cannot predict where the player will go next. Games have been a driving force in the development of 3D rendering tricks, and in the design of GRAPHICS ACCELERATOR hardware; cheap games consoles such as the Sony Playstation and Nintendo 64 contain state-of-the-art RISC CPUs and geometry-transform chips. See also OPENGL, DIRECT3D, RENDERMAN, SOFTIMAGE, MAYA.

3D Metafile (3DMF) The VECTOR GRAPHICS file format employed by Apple's QuickDraw 3D graphics system for the Macintosh. A 3DMF file contains not only the geometry of each object in a scene but also its lighting and texture-maps, which enables graphics applications to copy-and-paste and drag-and-drop whole 3D objects into other applications. See also QUICKDRAW.

3DMF See 3D METAFILE.

3D spreadsheet A SPREADSHEET that has, in addition to the usual rows and columns, a third dimension that is usually depicted by notionally stacking a set of conventional 2D spreadsheets on top of one another and permitting their formulae to relate CELLS on different sheets in the pile. An example of its use might be to consolidate a series of monthly spreadsheets each showing sales for a range of products. See also PIVOT TABLE, DATA CUBE, OLAP.

three-finger salute An ironic reference to the three-key combination <CTRL+ALT+DEL> used to REBOOT IBM-compatible PCs, which must be used whenever a crashed program has caused the system to HANG.

three-phase power supply An industrial power supply, as typically used to drive high-powered industrial machinery – including large computers such as MAINFRAMES and SERVER FARMS.

three-tier architecture A variant of the classic CLIENT/SERVER architecture for networked computer applications in which a third level of server is interposed between the clients and the main data store. A typical application for such an architecture might be to allow many users with PCs running web browser software to access data held on a MAINFRAME computer. The middle-tier servers run software that translates users' requests into a format (such as SQL queries) that the BACK-END system can understand, while hiding the complexities of its operating system from the users. A middle tier provides a useful isolating function, enabling a LEGACY DATABASE to be incorporated into a modern system with minimum alteration to its code, and keeping all the BUSINESS LOGIC in a separate place where it can be easily modified without affecting the back end.

three-valued logic A type of logic that admits the three values True, False and Unknown, as employed, for example in SQL. The Unknown value may be returned when an item is absent from the database, and the action that then results is determined by contingent, extralogical considerations.

thresholding An IMAGE-PROCESSING operation employed in many graphics programs that increases contrast, transforming areas of continuously varying colour into two colours. For example, all PIXELS whose value is below a chosen threshold might become black, and all those above might become white. A common application for this function is in OCR software, to remove grey tints from SCANNED pages and leave solid black type on a solid white background.

thumb 1 The square movable box contained within a SCROLLBAR, which the user drags to scroll the window contents.
2 Sometimes used as a shorthand for THUMB-NAIL.

thumbnail A greatly reduced (hence the name) copy of a digitized picture that is used when quickly previewing and selecting pictures from a large collection, to fit many pictures onto a single screen, or to reduce DOWNLOAD times for web pages.

thunk 1 A term used since the days of ALGOL-60 for a piece of code generated by a COMPILER to calculate the address of some object at run time, such as the value of an expression provided as an ACTUAL PARAMETER to a procedure.
2 More recently used to describe a programming trick that lets 16-BIT and 32-BIT Windows applications call one another under Windows 95 and later versions.

TI Abbreviation of TEXAS INSTRUMENTS.

tick-list features A marketing term meaning those features of a new product that are important enough to feature in a tick-list in an advertisement: that is, whose inclusion is considered by most users to be mandatory and beyond debate.

tier A level or layer within a multi-layered system or enterprise. The term is often used for the levels of a CLIENT/SERVER network application (see more under THREE-TIER ARCHITECTURE).

TIFF (Tagged Image File Format) A graphical file format used to store BITMAPPED images that is portable between different computer systems. As the name indicates, TIFF achieves portability by storing image components in tagged fields (e.g. for different COMPRESSION methods), from which different viewer programs can use just those they support, and ignore others. This has lead to a proliferation of different TIFF subformats, and the cruel parody 'Thousands of Incompatible File Formats'.

tilde (~) The character ~ with ASCII code 126. It is used in mathematics to signify approximation, so ~2 means 'close to two'. It has no standard meaning in computing, but is employed in many SYMBOLIC LOGIC notations to indicate negation, so ~A means NOT A.

tile 1 To cause a set of overlapping windows on a computer's display to resize and rearrange themselves side by side so that they exactly fill the available space without overlapping.
2 In geometry, a figure that when repeatedly reproduced fills a given space exactly. For example, hexagons may be used to tile a two-dimensional surface.

tilt-and-swivel The most popular type of mounting for computer MONITORS, which permits easy adjustment in two dimensions.

time base A source of timing signals, as for example used to control the FRAME RATE of a video monitor.

time bomb A piece of code inserted into a computer program, typically by a disgruntled ex-employee, that causes the program to fail on a particular date. Such practices have now been declared to constitute illegal damage. See also LOGIC BOMB.

time complexity The rate at which the time required by a particular algorithm to solve a particular problem grows with the size of that problem. Time complexity is usually expressed in an order-of-magnitude notation, where, say, $O(N^2)$ means that the time taken varies as the square of the problem size N. Hence a SORT algorithm of time complexity $O(N^2)$ would take four times as long to sort 20 numbers as to sort 10. The classification of algorithms by time complexity is one of the most important areas of computer science: see COMPLEXITY ANALYSIS, EXPONENTIAL-TIME ALGORITHM, POLYNOMIAL-TIME ALGORITHM, NP-HARD,

Time Division Multiple Access See under TDMA.

time division multiplexing (TDM) The sending of two or more different messages simultaneously down the same physical link by allowing them to take turns – separate time intervals called time SLOTS or TIME SLICES are allocated for the transmission of data from each CHANNEL. A periodic synchronizing signal is typically employed to enable the receiver to distinguish between the channels. TDM is inefficient for carrying intermittent or BURSTY traffic because a time slot will be allocated even when that channel has no data to put in it, which wastes BANDWIDTH. For such traffic patterns STATISTICAL TIME DIVISION MULTIPLEXING is a more efficient scheme. See also FREQUENCY DIVISION MULTIPLEXING, CODE DIVISION MULTIPLEXING.

timeout An error condition raised after a fixed period of waiting for some desired event to occur. Timeouts are widely employed to handle uncertain environments (such as attempting to log on to a remote computer service) where a failure might otherwise HANG the program by causing it to wait for ever. A program that raises such an error is said to have 'timed out'.

time-out To invoke the operation of a TIMEOUT mechanism.

timer A hardware device or a software process that measures the amount of time that has elapsed.

time series A set of measurements taken at regular intervals to permit the prediction of future activity based on a statistical analysis of past history. The aim of time series analysis is to uncover SEASONALITY effects and long-term trends, and to identify irregularity and randomness.

time sharing, time slicing A method of sharing a resource, such as a computer's processor, between several competing consumers of that resource by allowing them to take turns for short periods (whether fixed or variable) called TIME SLICES. The same technique may be used to share communication links (see under TIME DIVISION MULTIPLEXING).

The first computers were capable of running only a single program, and the invention of time sharing in the 1960s allowed multiple users to run programs at the same time, creating the MAINFRAME computer in its present form. Most modern operating systems implement MULTITASKING by using some form of time sharing (see more under TASK SCHEDULING).

time slice Also called a time SLOT; a short interval during which access is granted to some shared resource such as a processor or a communication link. See also TIME SHARING.

time stamp A small piece of data that encodes the current time of day, and may be attached to another data item such as a file or a network packet. Time stamping, say with a resolution of 0.01 second, is a useful strategy for distinguishing between otherwise anonymous data items. It may also be employed to endow an item (for example a PASSWORD) with a finite lifetime, beyond which it is no longer valid and must be disposed of.

Tiny BASIC Possibly the first ever FREEWARE program, a BASIC interpreter for z80 compatible processors that ran in 2 kilobytes of memory, distributed from 1976 via DR DOBB'S journal.

title bar A strip along the top of each window on a computer display in which the name of the program associated with the window and its current data file are displayed. Under most operating systems dragging on the title bar with the mouse pointer moves the window around on the screen. The title bar may also display various control buttons that enable the user to close, MAXIMIZE or MINIMIZE the window. The exact nature and disposition of these buttons varies between different operating systems and is a major contributor to their individual LOOK-AND-FEEL. See also WINDOW BORDER.

TLA (Three Letter Acronym) An ironically self-referential comment on the computer industry's love of acronyms.

TLB Abbreviation of TRANSLATION LOOK-ASIDE BUFFER.

TMT (Technology, Media and Telecommunications) A category employed by stock market analysts to encompass all hi-tech stocks.

TOC Abbreviation of TABLE-OF-CONTENTS.

To Do list One of the core applications within any suite of personal information software. It consists of a list of tasks to be accomplished, with completion dates and priorities; the list is automatically kept sorted in order of priority, and tasks may be crossed off once completed. To Do list applications are frequently integrated with an appointments calendar application, so the completion dates of tasks appear in the latter's daily diary. See also PERSONAL INFORMATION MANAGER, CALENDAR SERVICE, SCHEDULER, PROJECT MANAGEMENT.

toggle A type of switching mechanism that alternates between the on and off states with each successive key press. A familiar hardware example is the CAPS LOCK KEY on most computer keyboards.

token 1 In the TOKEN RING network system, a special data packet that is passed around from workstation to workstation. The workstation that possesses the token is able to transmit data onto the network.
2 A fundamental, grammatically indivisible unit of a programming language, i.e., a RESERVED WORD, OPERATOR or other IDENTIFIER used by the system itself. Tokens are the entities extracted by the PARSER of any language compiler or interpreter.
3 In certain interpreted programming languages that emit THREADED CODE, an INDEX into a table of routine addresses that is used in place of the actual address.

tokenize To analyse a file of SOURCE CODE into a stream of TOKENS as part of the work of a PARSER.

Token Ring One of the two main local area networking technologies, developed and

promoted by IBM from 1985. Though Token Ring is less popular than its rival, ETHERNET, it is used in many installations.

Token Ring employs an entirely different type of arbitration scheme for avoiding message conflicts from that of Ethernet. Only one workstation is allowed to transmit at a time – the one that currently possesses a circulating software key called the TOKEN. After it finishes transmitting, that workstation then passes the token to its neighbour. Token Ring also employs a FRAME format for its data packets that is different from that of Ethernet (IEEE 802.5 rather than 802.3), which makes the two systems radically incompatible. Networks of the two types can work together only via a BRIDGE or HUB.

token-threaded A variation on the THREADED CODE concept employed by some interpreted programming languages, under which the addresses of primitive routines are not used directly in the code, but instead are replaced by indexes (called TOKENS) into a table of such addresses. See also INDIRECTION.

tolerance The permitted variation in some measured attribute of an object or system. See also OUT-OF-TOLERANCE.

toner The powdered solid pigment employed in LASER PRINTERS and photocopiers.

tool A commonly used shorthand for any frequently used APPLICATION PROGRAM or UTILITY.

toolbar A component of many visual user interfaces, which consists of a horizontal strip at the top of a program's window containing a set of ICONS or BUTTONS that perform frequently required operations (as seen for example in MICROSOFT WORD). Many programs allow the user to customize such toolbars by changing the operations they contain, and to have different toolbars for different tasks. The position of toobars may be also altered (see, for example, DOCKING TOOLBAR).

toolbox 1 A term often used to describe a set of software (particularly programming) UTILITIES.
2 In visual programming languages such as VISUAL BASIC, a window or sidebar that displays all the prefabricated components that are currently installed, and from which they can be dragged and dropped onto a FORM to create a new program.

Tool Command Language See TCL.

toolkit A set of related software tools, libraries and other components that are collected together to assist in writing programs for a particular operating system or APPLICATION PROGRAMMING INTERFACE. Also called a SOFTWARE DEVELOPERS KIT or SDK.

toolset A collection of SOFTWARE TOOLS employed for a particular task, or built into a particular program.

ToolTip A helpful message that appears when the MOUSE POINTER is allowed to rest over a screen BUTTON in most recent Microsoft Windows applications. A typical ToolTip briefly describes the function of the button.

top-down design Any software design method that proceeds from an abstract, high-level description of the problem by subdividing each topic into progressively finer details (a process called stepwise refinement) until it reaches a level where coding in a programming language can begin.

For example a process 'make tea' might be refined into 'boil water; warm pot; add tea; add water'. Then 'boil water' might be further refined to 'fill kettle; plug in kettle; switch on kettle', while 'fill kettle' itself refines to 'remove lid; place under tap; turn on tap', and so on. Eventually the design arrives at a level of operations sufficiently primitive to be performed by the available machinery. Top-down design is a central concept in STRUCTURED PROGRAMMING.

top-end Marketing jargon for the most highly specified, and hence most expensive, end of a product range.

topic thread In an online CONFERENCING SYSTEM, a sequence of replies to one particular message, which together comprise a complete discussion. The conference reader software (for example a NEWS CLIENT) distinguishes such threads from one another on screen by using some graphical or textual notation, such as tree-like connecting lines or numbering.

top-level domain The last and most significant part of an Internet FULLY QUALIFIED DOMAIN NAME (i.e. the part that follows the last dot). For example in penguin.co.uk the top-level domain is .uk (for United Kingdom).

Every country has its own top-level domain, including for example .us for the USA and .de for Germany. Within such top-level domains there may be subdomains, so within .uk there is .ac for academic sites and .co for commercial ones, while within .us there are subdomains for the fifty states of the union.

The most widely used top-level domains are not, however, these national ones but the following list, all of which originated in the USA:

.com for commercial organizations (see DOT COM

.edu for educational institutions
.gov for US government
.mil for US armed services
.net for network operators
.org for any other organization

The .com domain has become heavily overpopulated, as every company throughout the world wishes to register its company or brand name as a subdomain within this easy-to-remember (or guess) domain. As a result the Internet naming authority ICANN created a further set of top-level domains in 2001:

.aero for aviation
.biz for business
.coop for cooperatives
.info for information services
.museum for museums
.name for private individuals
.pro for professionals such as lawyers, doctors, accountants

topology 1 A branch of mathematics that studies those properties of objects in space that do not involve distance, and remain unchanged under continuous deformations.
2 The arrangement of the connections between the nodes that make up a communication NETWORK or PARALLEL COMPUTER. Particular configurations (such as chains, rings and stars) are referred to as network topologies. Knowledge of the network topology is necessary for routing messages through it.

torus The three-dimensional surface formed by rotating a circle around an axis that does not intersect it. The best-known example is a doughnut. Some parallel computers connect their processors in toroidal TOPOLOGY.

Torvalds, Linus (b. 1969) The Norwegian programmer who, beginning in 1991, wrote the original LINUX operating system kernel that lies at the heart of the GNU and OPEN SOURCE free software movements.

Toshiba A Japanese electronics company best known for portable computers, CD-ROM and DVD drives.

total cost of ownership (TCO) The full cost of purchasing and running a computer system. This should include not only the initial capital outlay but also the cost of consumable items such as diskettes, printer paper and cartridges, of technical support, training and maintenance charges, and the cost of work hours lost while reconfiguring and trouble-shooting the system.

touchpad A POINTING DEVICE widely used in place of a MOUSE on laptop and notebook computers. It consists of a touch-sensitive area situated below the space bar, on which movement of the user's finger causes a corresponding movement of the on-screen pointer. Typically the pad is flanked by one or more buttons that may be pressed with the thumb to give the effect of mouse buttons. Touch-pads are sometimes called *trackpads*, or by a proprietary name such as GLIDEPOINT.

touch screen A computer display screen that doubles as an input device by enabling the user to select displayed items by touching them with a finger. Touch screens are widely used in applications such as outdoor information KIOSKS and AUTOMATED TELLER MACHINES, where a conventional keyboard would be too vulnerable to moisture and accidental damage.

Various different technologies have been used to implement touch screens, including stretching a transparent film DIGITIZER over the screen, interrupting infrared beams projected from the screen frame, ultrasound reflection, and pressure sensors fitted in the swivel base of a monitor.

tower-style case A personal computer case that is designed to stand vertically on the floor, rather than horizontally on a desktop beneath the monitor. Tower-style cases were introduced to make room for more DRIVE BAYS and EXPANSION SLOTS, and so tend to be used for the more powerful workstations and for servers. See also DESKTOP.

TPC-C (Transaction Processing Performance Council benchmark C) A widely respected benchmark suite for TRANSACTION PROCESSING computer systems, which was created by a non-profit consortium of vendors and users. TPC-C simulates a wholesale supplier managing 10 districts each serving 3000 customers who continually place new orders and request the status of existing orders.

The system records payments, processes orders and monitors stock levels. This has the effect of testing the simultaneous execution of multiple transaction types and execution modes, multiple terminal sessions, disk I/O speed, and contention over data access and update. Its rules require a response time of less than 5 seconds for 90% of new orders, payments, deliveries, and status requests, and less than 20 seconds for 90% of stock-level transactions. Breaching this invalidates the test. On completion, TPC-C produces two results: the sustained system throughput (tpmC) and a price/performance ratio.

TQFP See under QUAD FLAT PACK.

trace 1 *n*. On a PRINTED CIRCUIT BOARD or INTE-GRATED CIRCUIT chip, another name for a TRACK, i.e. a conductor.

2 *v*. In programming, to follow the detailed workings of a running program in order to locate the site of an error. Tracing typically works by displaying the program's SOURCE CODE with a special cursor that shows which instruction is currently being executed. Important tracing techniques include executing the program one instruction at a time (see under SINGLE STEP), setting BREAKPOINTS to freeze execution at critical points, and monitoring the contents of particular memory locations (see under WATCH). See also SYM-BOLIC DEBUGGER, DEBUGGING, BUG.

3 *v*. To convert part of a BITMAPPED image into a VECTOR-based outline by using a EDGE-DETECTION algorithm to determine its boundaries.

track 1 One of the concentric rings into which the recording surface of a computer storage disk is divided when the disk is formatted (see under FORMAT). Data can be written to the disk or read back from it by positioning a recording head above the appropriate track as the disk rotates (see under HEAD POSITIONING). The tracks are typically themselves further sub-divided into SECTORS.

2 A metal line deposited on the surface of an

INTEGRATED CIRCUIT chip or a PRINTED CIRCUIT BOARD that is used instead of a wire to conduct electric currents.

trackball, tracker ball A computer POINTING DEVICE that consists of a small plastic ball that may be freely rotated in its socket, causing the on-screen pointer to move in a corresponding direction. Trackballs are widely used in computer games controllers, and are also used in certain models of portable computer in place of a MOUSE or TOUCHPAD. Like the touchpad, a trackball requires the movement of only finger rather than the whole arm, which makes it suitable for use in confined spaces.

track buffering A technique used in DISK CONTROLLERS in which the last track read from the disk is stored in a small RAM so that further access to data in that track can proceed without reading from the disk again. If multiple tracks are stored, then the scheme is better described as a DISK CACHE.

tracker ball Another name for a TRACKBALL.

tracking The distance between successive letters in a run of typeset text. See also KERNING, FEATHERING, LEADING.

trackpad See under TOUCHPAD.

trackpoint A computer POINTING DEVICE for laptop and notebook computers, invented by IBM but used by certain other manufacturers including Toshiba. It consists of a small plastic button inserted in the space between the G, H and B keys on the keyboard. Exerting a light pressure on this causes the screen pointer to move in a corresponding direction, and buttons that mimic the action of mouse buttons are sited immediately below the space bar.

track-to-track seek time Also called the *minimum seek time*, the time that a disk drive takes to move its read/write head from one track to the next. See also SEEK TIME, AVERAGE SEEK TIME, FULL STROKE SEEK TIME.

tractor-feed Also called SPROCKET FEED, an obsolete paper transport mechanism for computer printers in which two toothed wheels engage with perforations down the edges of the folded but continuous paper to pull it through the printer. See also FAN FOLD.

traffic The stream of data transmitted over a communications link. Different kinds of traf-

fic may be distinguished (such as control traffic and data traffic) and may be accorded different priorities.

traffic monitoring The process of recording the variations in the loading of a network over time, performed by utility software running on a server.

trailing spaces Space characters after the last non-space character in a word. In computer processing, trailing spaces may cause unwanted results (for example by altering the margins or WORD-WRAP of a piece of text) and many text processing programs automatically discard them when a document is saved. See also LEADING SPACES.

trailing zero Zero characters appended to the end of the representation of a number with a fractional part (as in 9.456000) and which therefore do not affect its value. Some software products add trailing zeros to make all the numbers the same length for tabulation purposes. See also LEADING ZERO, FORMAT STRING.

transaction An exchange of data between two parties, which may include both humans and computer programs. Examples might be the retrieval of a record from a database, or the depositing of a sum of money into a bank account. Computer software should ideally treat transactions as ATOMIC events that must either proceed to completion or else be undone: it is unacceptable to leave them in a part-finished state if an error occurs. Each transaction should also be completed independently of other transactions.

transaction commit The crucial point in a database TRANSACTION where the software decides that the operation has succeeded, and makes permanent changes to the data. At any point prior to this step, a transaction that is deemed to have failed may be rolled back (see under ROLLBACK) and any changes to the data undone. See more under TWO-PHASE COMMIT, TRANSACTION MONITOR, TRANSACTION PROCESSING.

transaction monitor A class of system software employed by large interactive computer networks (for example a bank's cash machine system) to maintain the integrity of TRANSACTIONS. A transaction monitor can be considered as an extension of the operating system that imposes ROLLBACK semantics on all file operations so that no data is ever overwritten up until the point at which a transaction is finally committed (see TRANSACTION COMMIT). In the event of loss of communication, this permits operations to be restarted without any loss of data. A transaction monitor is often used in conjunction with MESSAGE QUEUE software to create resilient communications that automatically resend or reroute in the event of a lost connection.

Transaction monitors typically also take responsibility for security and AUTHENTICATION, and for LOAD BALANCING between the different servers on a network. Widely used transaction monitors include IBM's CICS, BEA System's TUXEDO and latterly MICROSOFT TRANSACTION SERVER.

transaction processing The branch of computing that manages large, widely distributed networks that must operate in REAL TIME and for which data integrity and reliability are paramount (examples of which include airline booking systems, bank cash machine networks, and large point-of-sale systems). Transaction processing is one of the most demanding of all computer applications, requiring very fast servers with large disk arrays and sophisticated software assistance from TRANSACTION MONITORS and MESSAGE QUEUES.

transceiver An electronic component that can both transmit and detect signals. Used, for example, in a NETWORK INTERFACE CARD to inject signals into the network cabling, and in many other kinds of communication system.

transcendental function A mathematical FUNCTION whose result cannot be exactly represented by a finite number of arithmetic operations. For example the trigonometric functions sine and cosine can be represented only as infinite (though converging) series.

transducer Any device that transforms one form of energy, such as light, heat, motion, pressure or electric charge, into a different form. Examples including a microphone (sound into electrical), an electric motor (electrical into motion) or a temperature sensor (heat into electrical).

transform In mathematics, a procedure that changes some object, such as a matrix or a waveform, into a different but related object. See for example FOURIER TRANSFORM.

transformer An electrical device that changes the voltage of an ALTERNATING CURRENT by exploiting the mutual INDUCTANCE effect between two wire coils, which are wound on a shared magnetic core. The varying current in the primary winding induces a magnetic field, which produces a voltage in the secondary winding, greater or less than the original voltage in the same ratio as the number of turns in the coils.

transient A short-lived change in the level of a signal. See also SPIKE.

transistor An electrical device made from a SEMICONDUCTOR material such as SILICON, which has three separate electrodes, arranged so that the current flowing between two of them is controlled by the voltage or current applied to the third, thus making the device capable of acting either as a SWITCH or an AMPLIFIER of signals. Transistors can be fabricated in huge numbers on the surface of a single silicon chip, using the techniques of LITHOGRAPHY, and this forms the basis of the modern electronics industry. See also BIPOLAR TRANSISTOR, FIELD-EFFECT TRANSISTOR.

transistor–transistor logic (TTL) The most commonly used semiconductor technology for building INTEGRATED CIRCUITS (ICs) that implement discrete digital LOGIC functions, such as AND gates or inverters. So-called because it connects the electrodes of its constituent transistors directly, with no intervening components. TTL was invented by TEXAS INSTRUMENTS in 1965.

TTL chips are often used in GLUE LOGIC to interface larger ICs, and in PROTOTYPING new designs. There are several series of TTL chips with different power consumption, speed and temperature ratings, identified by their code numbers. See also CMOS, BICMOS, ECL.

transition A passage from one state to another. In DIGITAL electronic communications, a transition is a change in the voltage on a conductor (from high to low or vice versa), which may be used to convey one BIT of information. There is an important distinction between *level-sensitive* signalling in which, say, the higher voltage is taken to represent a 1 and the lower voltage a 0, and EDGE-TRIGGERED or *transition-sensitive* signalling in which it is the transitions themselves that carry the information.

Various formal notations have been invented to assist in thinking about state transitions, the most important being the FINITE STATE MACHINE and the STATE TRANSITION DIAGRAM.

translate 1 To convert from one language into another; see more under MACHINE TRANSLATION. The term is also used in connection with programs written in an INTERPRETED programming language, as a synonym for 'interpret'.

2 To move an object from one location to another without rotating it or altering its size. Translation is one of the fundamental geometric operations employed in computer graphics. See more under AFFINE TRANSFORM.

translation look-aside buffer (TLB) A special register in the core of a processor that employs VIRTUAL MEMORY, which is used to store the physical address corresponding to the last virtual address translated. Whenever a fresh memory access is requested, the processor inspects the TLB first so that, if the same address has been requested, it can jump straight there and bypass the lengthy translation procedure. See also LOGICAL ADDRESS, ADDRESS TRANSLATION, LOGICAL-TO-PHYSICAL TRANSLATION, PAGE TABLE, MEMORY MANAGEMENT UNIT.

transmission control protocol See under TCP.

transmission line A type of conductor used to convey ALTERNATING CURRENTS (for example digital signals) whose frequency is sufficiently high for inductance and capacitance effects to become as important as resistance. As a result, the geometry of the conductor becomes significant; in particular, the radius of its bends will alter its conduction characteristics. The clock frequencies of modern computers are high enough for the TRACKS on their printed circuit boards to be treated as transmission lines rather than as simple resistive circuits. See also CLOCK SIGNAL, SKEW, WAVEGUIDE.

transmit To send a signal from one place to another.

transmitter A device that acts as the source for a communication signal, such as a radio wave or a network packet.

transparency mapping In computer GRAPHICS, applying to a 3D surface, a 2D image whose density indicates the desired degree of transparency or opacity of the finally rendered object. Transparency maps are typically stored in an ALPHA CHANNEL associated with the 3D image. See also ALPHA BLENDING, TEXTURE MAPPING, BUMP MAPPING, ENVIRONMENT MAPPING, PROCEDURAL TEXTURE.

transparent 1 Permitting the uninterrupted passage of light. In computer graphics, transparency (and translucency) are simulated by combining the colour of the PIXELS that form the image of an object with the colour of any underlying objects, in differing proportions according to the desired degree of transparency. See ALPHA BLENDING, ALPHA CHANNEL, FOGGING, TRANSPARENCY MAPPING.

2 Often used in a metaphorical way when describing some intermediate software layer that is not visible to a computer's user, as in 'transparent mail redirection' – that is, mail that is being redirected from a different address without the user being aware of this fact.

transponder A combined receiver and transmitter of radio or radar signals that sends an automatic reply upon receiving certain predetermined signals. Used, for example, in aircraft identification systems, and for relaying messages in satellite radio systems. See for example OSCAR.

transport The physical MEDIUM over which signals are carried in a communication network. Another term for FABRIC.

transport layer The fourth layer of the OSI REFERENCE MODEL for network protocols, which is responsible for addressing, service quality and security.

transpose 1 To interchange two objects or values.

2 In mathematics, the result of interchanging the rows and columns of a MATRIX.

3 In music, to alter the key of a piece by modifying the pitch of all its notes equally.

transputer A novel type of microprocessor invented by the UK firm Inmos in the early 1980s. It contains built-in network links and was intended to simplify the building of PARALLEL COMPUTERS by joining the links together. The name, a combination of *trans*istor and com*puter* was intended to convey this role as a replicated component. The chip failed to achieve commercial success. See also OCCAM.

trap A SOFTWARE INTERRUPT raised by some exceptional condition arising within an executing program, such as a divide-by-zero error or an access to a VIRTUAL MEMORY page that is not in memory. The operating system intercepts this interrupt and performs some corrective action (such as loading the memory page) before returning control to the user program. The term is sometimes employed as an intransitive verb ('the scheduler traps on buffer-full') meaning to cause such a trap. See also INTERRUPT-DRIVEN, EXCEPTION HANDLING.

trap door 1 Also called a BACK DOOR, a deliberate loophole left in a computer security system (e.g. in an authentication or encryption scheme) to provide instant access for those who know that it exists.
2 See TRAP DOOR FUNCTION.

trap door function A mathematical FUNCTION, also called a ONE-WAY FUNCTION, whose value is easy to compute but whose INVERSE is extremely difficult to compute, and which is for that reason useful as the basis for encryption. The widely used RSA ENCRYPTION scheme, for example, depends on the fact that, though it is easy to multiply two large PRIME NUMBERS together, it is very hard to factor the resulting large number into its prime factors. Knowledge of one of the primes thus becomes a key to the cipher. See also PUBLIC-KEY ENCRYPTION, CIPHER, CRYPTOGRAPHY.

trap-handler A HANDLER for software SOFTWARE INTERRUPTS. See also TRAP.

Trash The earlier name for what is now called the WASTEBASKET on the Apple MACINTOSH.

travelling salesman problem A much-studied problem in which a travelling salesman has clients in a number of cities and must plan the shortest possible circular trip that passes through each city. The obvious brute force solution of measuring all possible routes and then picking the shortest consumes time that explodes exponentially with the number of cities, and no POLYNOMIAL-TIME ALGORITHM has been discovered that gives an optimum solution (it is in fact known to be NP-COMPLETE). However, there are many efficient APPROXIMATION ALGORITHMS that give good, if

not best, solutions much of the time. The problem is the archetype for a whole class of similar and commercially important problems in scheduling, routing and resource allocation.

Travelling Software US publisher of the popular LAPLINK utility for connecting laptop to desktop computers.

tray See under SYSTEM TRAY.

tree A fundamental data structure that consists of a ROOT NODE that points to two or more other nodes, each of which in turn points to more nodes. The result resembles the branching of a tree, hence the name. A tree is the appropriate data structure to describe any kind of hierarchically structured data that must be decomposed into its constituent elements, such as a sentence being parsed, or a search being refined into ever more layers of detail.

tree sort A class of sorting algorithms that involve building a tree structure from the data items by comparing their KEY values, and then traversing or dismantling this tree in order to output the items in sorted order. HEAP SORT is one popular type of tree sort. See also QUICKSORT.

tree-structured Possessing the form of a tree, that is with many separate branches diverging from a single ROOT.

tree view 1 A view of the contents of some hierarchically nested data structure (such as a hard disk containing files organized into NESTED FOLDERS) that depicts the data in the form of a tree with branches. A tree view is typically collapsible, so 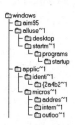 only one full branch is seen at a time. Clicking on a particular branch opens or closes the content beneath it. WINDOWS EXPLORER and the MACINTOSH Finder both employ tree views.
2 A prefabricated software component provided in many VISUAL PROGRAMMING systems (such as VISUAL BASIC and DELPHI) that simplifies the implementation of such tree-structured displays by automatically managing the creation and removal, hiding and revealing of branches.

trend The overall direction of variation of some set of data points.

trend line Also *trendline*. When plotting a graph from sets of widely scattered data points, a line drawn through all the mean values to reveal the overall tendency. See also SCATTER PLOT.

tricorder A fictional hand-held communication device invented for the *Star Trek* TV series, whose real implementation has become something of a goal for a generation of hand-held computer and mobile phone designers.

trigger A mechanism provided in many DATABASE MANAGEMENT SYSTEMS, whereby some pre-specified condition (such as a particular value appearing in a particular FIELD) can cause the execution of a built-in function or a user-written STORED PROCEDURE, which then alters the database contents. Triggers are most often employed to VALIDATE input data, and to maintain DATA INTEGRITY, for example by automatically finding and deleting any orphaned dependent records after a record has been deleted.

trilinear filtering, trilinear interpolation A SAMPLING technique used in computer graphics systems to calculate the colour values of PIXELS, for example when warping a TEXTURE MAP to fit onto a 3D surface. The values of pixels are interpolated within a 3D cubic region (along three axes, hence the name trilinear) from the values at each corner of the cube, so each new pixel is the average of eight neighbours. See also BILINEAR FILTERING, SAMPLING, BICUBIC SURFACE PATCH, TEXTURE MAPPING.

Trilogy A CONSTRAINT LOGIC PROGRAMMING language invented in Canada.

troff One of the earliest and most widely used TYPESETTING and TEXT FORMATTING tools for the Unix operating system. It has now to a large extent been displaced by TEX and by graphical DESKTOP PUBLISHING programs such as FRAMEMAKER. Troff is most often used in conjunction with the NROFF program or an equivalent that formats its output for display on a terminal.

Trojan horse A type of malicious computer program, similar to a VIRUS, that masquerades as a normal program but causes damage (such as erasing a hard disk drive) when the unsuspecting user executes it. A virus, on the other hand, typically spreads unseen, hides in inaccessible areas of the computer, and causes its damage spontaneously at predetermined times or dates. Most EMAIL VIRUSES are in fact Trojans, since they rely on the user opening them to execute. See also WORM.

TRON An unsuccessful experimental Japanese MULTIMEDIA computer architecture named after the eponymous sci-fi film.

TRS-80 The first personal computer from TANDY, launched in 1977.

true colour A computer display that supports a 24-bit or 32-bit COLOUR DEPTH and is therefore capable of adequately reproducing all the tones in typical photographic material. This is in contrast to 8-bit and 16-bit displays which employ a restricted colour PALETTE and cannot display smoothly varying colour gradients without the appearance of artefacts such as MACH BANDS.

TrueType A FONT RENDERING system originally developed by Apple for the MACINTOSH, but later adopted by Microsoft and built into the WINDOWS operating system from version 3.0 onwards. TrueType fonts are OUTLINE FONTS, which can be scaled to different sizes with little loss of quality: the system supports the inclusion of HINTING information in font files to adjust the letter forms for better reproduction at small sizes. From Windows 95 onward, TrueType fonts support ANTIALIASING of characters on screens with 16-BIT or greater colour depth. The Windows font manager contains an option to display only TrueType fonts in the font selection lists of application programs.

Windows 2000 introduced the new OPENTYPE font system, which combines the best features of TrueType and its main competitor, the ADOBE TYPE 1 FONT system. See also ADOBE TYPE MANAGER, POSTSCRIPT, WINDOWS PRINTING SYSTEM, CLEARTYPE.

truncate To shorten an object or quantity by removing one or more of its extremities. For example, to remove the fractional part of a number and leave an INTEGER remainder. See also ROUND.

truth table A table that lists the return value for every possible combination of input and output for a BOOLEAN function. See, for example, the truth tables under AND and OR.

A truth table may be used as the definition of a Boolean function.

truth value One of the two values true or false, which are the only possible results of evaluating an expression in BOOLEAN LOGIC.

TSR (terminate and stay resident) The term used under the MS-DOS operating system to describe a MEMORY-RESIDENT program that remains in memory even when not executing, and can be reactivated by pressing a particular HOT KEY combination. It then temporarily suspends the current application and superimposes its own display. To make this work, each TSR program in memory has to 'hook' the keyboard INTERRUPT VECTOR and inspect every KEYSTROKE sent to the main application, looking for its own hot key: this proved to be a rich source of clashes and instability. The technique was popular in the early 1990s, enabling, say, a spelling dictionary or a notepad to be accessed without quitting the current application, but the introduction of effective MULTITASKING with WINDOWS 3 rendered TSRs redundant (though some DEVICE DRIVERS still operate as non-interactive TSRs).

TTL Abbreviation of TRANSISTOR–TRANSISTOR LOGIC.

TTS Abbreviation of TEXT-TO-SPEECH.

tty Abbreviation of TELETYPE.

tube See THERMIONIC VALVE.

tuner An electronic device that receives radio or television signals and outputs audio and video signals to an external amplifier, loudspeaker and display.

tungsten plug A technique employed in the fabrication of INTEGRATED CIRCUITS to make the connections between an overlying aluminium INTERCONNECT layer and the electrodes of the underlying TRANSISTORS. It involves etching holes and filling them with tungsten metal before depositing the aluminium layer.

tunnel 1 *n.* A type of Internet GATEWAY computer that passes on all the data packets it receives unchanged, and without inspecting their contents. See also TUNNELLING PROTOCOL.

2 *v.* To create a connection between two computers across the Internet in such a way that they appear to each other to be directly connected, and the traffic between them is not readable by any other Internet users. See also TUNNELLING PROTOCOL, POINT-TO-POINT TUNNELLING PROTOCOL, L2F, VIRTUAL PRIVATE NETWORK.

tunnelling protocol A technique for creating VIRTUAL PRIVATE NETWORKS across the Internet, for example to link the world-wide staff of a large company by a secure and private messaging service. A tunnelling protocol works by creating a stream of private data packets, encrypting them, wrapping them within standard TCP/IP packets and then sending them like any other Internet data. The receiving HOST computer strips out the data, decrypts it and then passes it on to its addressee like normal LAN data. Tunnelling protocols may be supported in software only, as with Microsoft's PPTP, or they may require hardware assistance to be installed in the ROUTERS, as with L2F.

tuple A data structure containing two or more components that may be of different data types. Unlike a LIST, whose type is the same regardless of length, each size of tuple (the pair, the triple, the quad) is considered to be a different data type. Tuples are employed in the theory of RELATIONAL DATABASES, as an abstraction for the rows in a table, and they are directly supported by a few programming languages, including LINDA, LIMBO and many FUNCTIONAL LANGUAGES.

Turbo Pascal A small, fast compiler for the PASCAL language, originally written for CP/M but later ported to MS-DOS and then WINDOWS. Its high sales helped establish BORLAND INTERNATIONAL as a major software house. DELPHI is its modern descendant.

Turing, Alan Mathison (1912–54) The founding father of computer science. Turing's work in mathematics culminated in his 1936 paper 'On Computable Numbers' in which he invented an imaginary number-manipulating machine (now called a TURING MACHINE) that is still the archetype for most computers manufactured today. During World War Two, Turing applied his insights at BLETCHLEY PARK, helping to crack the CIPHERS employed by the German armed forces to encode their messages.

Turing Machine An imaginary computing device, invented by Alan TURING for his seminal 1936 paper 'On Computable Numbers', that is the archetype of all computers. Any function that can be computed at all can in theory be computed by a Turing Machine given sufficient time. The 'machine' was imagined to consist of an infinitely long paper tape along which a head moves reading and writing symbols according to a built-in set of rules or PROGRAM. Turing went on to postulate a universal machine whose program was supplied as symbols on a second tape, and so could compute many different functions. This insight lead to the modern computer.

See also STORED-PROGRAM COMPUTER, HALT-ING PROBLEM, CHURCH/TURING HYPOTHESIS.

turnkey system A computer system set up so that, when it is started, it will automatically execute a particular APPLICATION PROGRAM, relieving the user of any responsibility for choosing and loading programs. Turnkey systems are sometimes employed in specialized business applications (such as point-of-sale terminals or booking systems) where the computer is required to perform only a single task.

turtle graphics An output mechanism originally devised for the LOGO programming language. It consists of a small triangle on the screen called the 'turtle', which can be instructed to move forward and backward or turn through a specified angle: as it moves, the turtle draws a line behind it. For educational uses, various hardware turtles have been devised, each consisting of a small wheeled robot fitted with a pen, which runs across a sheet of paper on the floor to draw a figure.

Tuxedo A widely used TRANSACTION MONITOR published by BEA Systems.

TWAIN A standard interface that allows Microsoft WINDOWS and Apple MACINTOSH graphics programs to acquire digital images directly from an external scanner or a digital camera without having to leave the program. The acronym is said to stand for Technology Without An Interesting Name (an example of programmers' whimsy at its most emetic).

tweaking Fiddling with the parameters of a hardware or software system to improve or customize its performance.

tweening Short for IN-BETWEENING.

twig In any TREE-STRUCTURED hierarchy, a node that is at the very end of a branch, so there are no further nodes attached to it. Sometimes also called a *leaf node*. See ROOT, TREE.

twip A unit of length equal to one twentieth of a printer's POINT (that is 1/1440th of an inch) invented by Microsoft and employed in VISUAL BASIC and VISUAL C++ for specifying the size of screen displays.

twisted-nematic LCD The most widely used type of LIQUID CRYSTAL DISPLAY whose full name is the 'twisted nematic field effect LCD'. When no voltage is applied to a particular PIXEL, the rod-like liquid-crystal molecules rotate polarized light through 90 degrees and allow it to pass through a polarizing filter. When a voltage is applied, the molecules realign themselves parallel to the light direction, so that no rotation takes place, and the pixel appears dark. Extra layers that rotate light by more than 90 degrees are used in SUPERTWIST displays.

twisted-pair A type of low-cost electrical cable originally developed for telephone use, but now used for computer networks. It is so called because it protects the signals from external interference by entwining its twin conductors. See more under UNSHIELDED TWISTED-PAIR, SHIELDED TWISTED-PAIR, COAXIAL CABLE.

twitter A degradation of image quality that arises because analogue television employs an INTERLACED DISPLAY in which each frame is displayed in two separate passes, odd lines first, then even lines. Any thin horizontal line that straddles an odd number of consecutive SCAN LINES may appear to 'twitter' up and down at the frame rate, and this has a particularly noticeable and unpleasant effect on text characters. See also ANTI-TWITTER.

2D graphics In contrast to 3D GRAPHICS, any form of computer graphics that concerns itself solely with shapes or areas of PIXELS on the screen that depict a single viewpoint. In 2D graphics, such groups of pixels are themselves the main objects to be manipulated, whereas in 3D graphics they are only the end-result of a series of transformations performed on a stored model of a solid object. All the popular

VECTOR and bitmapped DRAWING PROGRAMS and their file formats are concerned with 2D graphics.

2D acceleration See under GUI ACCELERATION.

two-phase commit, 2PC A protocol employed in distributed TRANSACTION PROCESSING systems to guarantee the integrity of transactions that involve multiple participants. One participating site (designated the *controller*) confirms that all the participating sites are ready to make changes to their databases, commits the change at all sites (see TRANSACTION COMMIT), and then waits for all sites to confirm that their commit succeeded. If any sites fail to confirm, the controller ROLLS BACK the transaction at all sites in order to keep them all synchronized with the ones that failed.

twos complement A scheme for representing negative numbers in BINARY notation in which a positive number is made negative by inverting (i.e. replacing 0 by 1, and 1 by 0) each of its bits and then adding 1 (throwing away any OVERFLOW). For example, in the case of an 8-bit word length then –3 would become 11111101, the inverse of 3 (binary 00000011). The advantage of the twos complement scheme over the alternative ONES COMPLEMENT is that it yields a unique representation for zero (for example 00000000), and the bit-string 11111111 represents –1.

two-valued logic Ordinary BOOLEAN logic in which every expression must evaluate to either true or false; in contrast to a multi-valued or FUZZY LOGIC.

Tymnet One of the earliest US PACKET SWITCHED digital data networks, using the X.25 protocol. Now owned by British Telecom/MCI.

type 1 In printing, originally the cast lead blocks carrying the shape of alphabetic characters, once used by printers to compose documents. Hence, also any characters printed on paper or displayed on a computer screen. See ADOBE TYPE MANAGER, POSTSCRIPT, TRUETYPE.
2 In mathematical logic, a class of expressions (or the entities they represent) that all share a similar syntactic relationship. The use of the term in computing derives from this sense – namely, the kind of values that may be

taken on by some object in a computer program. See more under DATA TYPE, ABSTRACT DATA TYPE, TYPE CHECKING, STRONGLY TYPED, TYPE CAST, TYPELESS.

Type 1 font See under ADOBE TYPE 1 FONT.

Type 3 font See under ADOBE TYPE 3 FONT.

type-ahead buffer See under KEYBOARD BUFFER.

type cast In C and related programming languages, the operation of converting a data item from one DATA TYPE to another, often called a CAST for short. For example the statement

```
*c = (char) 65;
```

casts the integer 65 into type char, a character, and hence leaves *c pointing to a capital 'A'. See also COERCION, TYPE CHECKING, STRONGLY TYPED.

type checking The process of ensuring that all the objects manipulated by a computer program are of compatible DATA TYPES. The intention is to catch errors in program logic, for example, a program that tries to add a time to a weight is clearly flawed.

COMPILED programming languages typically employ STATIC type checking, refusing to compile any program that contains type errors. INTERPRETED languages typically leave type checking until the program is run, which is less secure. A programming language that enables all type checking to be performed statically is said to be *strongly typed*. Languages that contain constructs that cannot be so checked, or automatically convert between different types, are *weakly typed*.

typeface The basic design of a set of printed or displayed characters. The term originally referred to the actual printing surface of a wood or metal type block. A particular typeface such as Times Roman exists as a family of different sizes and styles (for example normal, bold and italic) each of which is referred to as a separate FONT. In computing literature the two terms are often used as though interchangeable.

typeless 1 A programming language that has no concept of data type, and in which variables can accept values of any type. The opposite of strongly typed (see under TYPE CHECKING).

2 Any data item that has no interpretation other than as a string of BITS, used as in 'a typeless constant'.

type library 1 In various OBJECT-ORIENTED programming systems (including CORBA and Microsoft's COMMON OBJECT MODEL), the name given to a file containing compiled object INTERFACES.

2 A collection of FONTS.

type-safe In programming, any operation that is TYPE CHECKED to ensure that mistakes arising from mixing incompatible DATA TYPES cannot occur.

typesetter A very high-quality output device (typically capable of resolutions of more than 2400 dots per inch) that is used to produce the final film from which printers' plates are made for lithographic and other commercial printing processes. Modern digital typesetting machines, known in the printing trade as IMAGESETTERS, can accept as input a POSTSCRIPT file representing the document to be printed. Well-known brands of typesetter include those made by Linotron, Hell and Agfa. See also HALFTONE, CAMERA-READY, PROOFING.

typo See TYPOGRAPHICAL ERROR

typographical error An error caused by incorrectly typing a word.

U

UAE Abbreviation of UNRECOVERABLE APPLICATION ERROR.

UART (universal asynchronous receiver/transmitter) A type of integrated circuit used to implement SERIAL communication links (such as computer RS-232 ports). It consists of a parallel-to-serial converter connected to a serial-to-parallel converter, each running off its own CLOCK SIGNAL. The parallel side of the chip is connected to a computer's SYSTEM BUS and the serial side is connected to the communication line, so the chip disassembles data bytes to produce a stream of bits and reassembles received bits into bytes. A UART typically raises a hardware INTERRUPT to tell the computer that a byte has been received, or that it is ready for a new byte to send. High-speed UARTs such as the widely used Intel 16550 contain some on-chip BUFFER memory between their two sides, to smooth out any brief gaps or overflows in the data stream.

ubiquitous computing (UC) **1** The ability to access one's personal computer data via the Internet from anywhere in the world, indoors or out, by using, for example, a hand-held computer and a mobile phone.
2 A reference to the widespread use of MICROPROCESSORS in the design of household and industrial electrical equipment such as washing machines and video recorders.

UBR **1** In data networking, an abbreviation of UNSPECIFIED BIT RATE.
2 In data sharing, an abbreviation of UDDI BUSINESS REGISTRY.

UCB Abbreviation of University of California at Berkeley.

UCS (Universal Character Set) A 32-bit CHARACTER SET, defined in 1993 as ISO Standard 10646, that aims to include all the characters of all the world's languages. Its full name is the Universal Multiple-Octet Coded Character Set, because the standard permits both 32-bit and 16-bit encodings of the UCS characters, called UCS-4 (because it employs four OCTETS, i.e. 32 bits to encode each character) and UCS-2. Development of UCS was begun in 1983, before the invention of UNICODE, but took so long to standardize that for several years the two schemes were in competition. However UCS now incorporates Unicode v1.1 as a subset.

UCS-4 is structured as multiple UCS-2 character sets called planes, the only such plane so far defined being the *Basic Multilingual Plane*, which contains Unicode, and covers all major world language characters including ASCII, all the ISO Roman sets, Greek, Cyrillic, Chinese, Japanese hiragana and katakana, Indian Devangari, and many more. In practice only 16-bit UCS-2 implementations are currently in use, and various compaction schemes (such as UTF-8) permit 8-bit characters to be used for compatibility with older software.

The full 32-bit UCS has space for up to 28,672 CONTROL CHARACTERS, which is more than enough room to include the codes employed by all the world's other computer character sets. By contrast, the Unicode subset has room for only 65 control codes, 32 of which are occupied by the ASCII codes.

UCSD Pascal A semi-compiled dialect of the PASCAL programming language invented at the University of California San Diego. It pioneered the use of a PSEUDO-CODE interpreter (as now employed in JAVA and C#) to produce cross-platform applications, and was briefly popular and influential on the Apple II computer in the early 1980s. The code generated was called p-code, and so the system was also known as the UCSD p-system. Further language compilers for FORTRAN and BASIC produced the same p-code.

UCSD p-system See under UCSD PASCAL.

UCS Transformation Format 8 (UTF-8) A method of encoding multi-byte UNICODE or UCS characters so that the characters of the ASCII set may still be represented by single bytes in the range 0–127; all non-ASCII characters encode to values greater than 128. UTF-8 is needed to enable older ASCII-based text processing tools and operating systems to work correctly with 16 or 32-bit characters that might contain byte values that would otherwise be misinterpreted as CONTROL CODES or illegal characters (for example in UNIX file names). The related *UTF-7* encoding is employed to send UCS texts via the SMTP email protocol, which permits only 7-bit characters.

UDA (uniform data access, universal data access) Microsoft's technology for accessing data from a range of sources. UDA consists of three main component technologies (ACTIVEX DATABASE OBJECTS, OLE DB and ODBC), and its intention is to enable data from many sources, and in many different formats (e.g. database records, HTML, Microsoft Office documents) to be transparently combined – potential UDA sources include RELATIONAL DATABASES, multimedia archives, web sites, mail and file servers and spreadsheets.

UDC Abbreviation of UNIVERSAL DECIMAL CLASSIFICATION.

UDDI (universal description, discovery and integration) A standard format for exchanging and sharing business information over the World Wide Web, developed by a consortium of major computing vendors including Microsoft and IBM. To use UDDI, companies place details of the WEB SERVICES they wish to advertise into a type of repository called the UBR (see UDDI BUSINESS REGISTRY), which may be queried by other companies seeking a particular service via a web PORTAL, a SEARCH ENGINE or directly from within a custom-made application. UDDI employs XML as its document format for transferring data and metadata, and sends data to and from the UBR using Microsoft's HTTP-based SOAP protocol. See also .NET.

UDDI Business Registry (UBR) A type of data REPOSITORY used to exchange and share business information and services over the World Wide Web. The UBR is stored in distributed fashion across a worldwide network of web servers, where data entered at one node is automatically REPLICATED to all the others – this scheme both spreads the network load and provides resilience when a UBR server fails.

The UBR is divided internally into three sections: the *White Pages*, which hold company details (name, address, etc.); the *Yellow Pages*, which classify companies by type of business, geographic location, etc; and the *Green Pages*, which contain the technical details of how to use each particular web service and the schemas needed to access online purchasing systems and so on. See also UDDI.

UDF (universal disk format) A file system for CD-R and CD-RW optical discs that enables them to appear in the operating system like ordinary disk drives, to and from which files can be copied by DRAG-AND-DROP like any other disk, rather than having to BURN the whole disk in a single uninterrupted session. UDF requires a special device driver to be installed on a host computer before CD-RWs can be read in this fashion.

PACKET WRITING technology, which makes the data rate less sensitive, underpins UDF. In early versions, a CD-RW could be erased only as a whole, but subsequent versions (including that built into Windows 2000) permit individual files and folders to be erased.

UDMA Abbreviation of ULTRA DMA.

UDP (User Datagram Protocol) A CONNECTIONLESS transport protocol used by some Internet applications as a layer on top of IP. It is simpler and more efficient than the normal Transmission Control Protocol (see more under TCP/IP) but far less reliable, leaving all error correction and recovery to the application itself.

For example, UDP is used by Internet VIDEO-CONFERENCING applications such as CU-SEE ME to obtain the maximum throughput. Typically, normal TCP is used to make an initial connection reliably and then the application switches to UDP for the actual data transport. See also DATAGRAM.

UDT (Uniform Data Transfer) A mechanism by which Microsoft Windows programs can exchange data with one another, which renders obsolete the older DYNAMIC DATA EXCHANGE mechanism. UDT can be used only between COMPONENT OBJECT MODEL objects that implement an interface called IDataObject. This provides a standardized means to access that object's data, whatever its source, via its GetData and SetData methods. The QueryGetData method enables clients to inquire what types of data a particular object supports.

UHF (ultra high frequency) The band within the radio spectrum from 0.3 to 3 gigahertz used by broadcast television transmissions.

UI Abbreviation of USER INTERFACE.

UID See UNIQUE IDENTIFIER.

uid See USER IDENTIFIER.

Ultra2 SCSI See under SCSI.

Ultra DMA, Ultra ATA Also called ATA-4. An enhancement to the AT ATTACHMENT hard disk interface specification, which gives nearly twice the maximum data rate of ATA-3, offering up to 33 megabits per second by using a SYNCHRONOUS transfer PROTOCOL. See also IDE, EIDE, SCSI.

ultra high frequency See UHF.

Ultra SCSI See under SCSI.

UltraSPARC A family of 64-bit MICROPROCESSORS launched by SUN MICROSYSTEMS, INC. in 1994 to power its own range of WORKSTATIONS. The UltraSPARC is a RISC design that extends Sun's SPARC architecture by adding several special graphical instructions that can move 64 pixels in a single operation, similar to (but predating) Intel's MMX graphics extensions for the Pentium. See also HYPERSPARC.

ultraviolet (UV) Energetic electromagnetic radiation of wavelengths just beyond (shorter than) the blue end of the visible spectrum, from 10^{-6} to 10^{-8} metres. It is present in sunlight and has damaging effects on living beings and organic materials. UV illumination is employed in the LITHOGRAPHY process used to make INTEGRATED CIRCUITS, where its shorter waves permit a smaller FEATURE SIZE than does visible light. It is also used for erasing some types of EPROM chip.

Ultra Wide SCSI See under SCSI.

Ultrix A version of UNIX derived from Berkeley Unix (see BSD) by DIGITAL EQUIPMENT CORPORATION to run on its VAX and DECstation ranges of hardware.

UMA See UPPER MEMORY.

UMB (upper memory block) Under the MS-DOS operating system, regions of memory up to 64 kilobytes in size within the expanded memory PAGE FRAME in HIGH MEMORY. It can be used to store device drivers and other memory-resident programs to free up the lower memory area for conventional programs. UMBs are created by an EXPANDED MEMORY MANAGER such as EMM386, and programs are loaded into them via LOADHIGH commands placed in the AUTOEXEC.BAT file. See also EXPANDED MEMORY SPECIFICATION.

UML Abbreviation of UNIFIED MODELLING LANGUAGE.

unbundle To sell separately software that was previously available only BUNDLED with a particular computer.

UNC (Uniform Naming Convention, Universal Naming Convention) Microsoft's convention for naming servers and other resources in a PC network. An example name is \\bigserver\myshare, where the first part names a server and the second part names a network shared directory on it. UNC is an extension of the notation used in the MS-DOS system of PATHNAMES, so the directory \\bigserver\myshare might also be mapped to, say, the DOS directory f:\users\dp\myshare.

undelete To restore a file that has been 'deleted' from a hard or floppy disk. Under Windows and on the Apple Macintosh, deleted files are temporarily held in a RECYCLE BIN or WASTEBASKET from which they can be undeleted merely by clicking their name (in

Windows) or dragging their icons out of the Wastebasket (on a Mac) at any time before the bin is emptied.

Under many other operating systems, deleting a file only marks the disk space it was occupying as free, and does not actually remove its data immediately. Successful undeletion is possible up until the point where some other program writes over the same space. After that point the only way to recover a deleted file's contents is by using a disk SECTOR EDITOR or equivalent utility, which may enable some part of the data to be retrieved (see under FILE RECOVERY). A command may be provided to undelete files by name, but, under some operating systems (such as MS-DOS), part of the file's name is lost when it is deleted, and so the user must inspect a list of recently deleted files to try to identify the one required.

See also DIRECTORY, FILE ALLOCATION TABLE.

underflow error A kind of computer error condition caused by some quantity becoming smaller than the smallest value that can be represented. Underflow is typically caused by a FLOATING-POINT ARITHMETIC result with a negative EXPONENT (e.g. 10^{-99}) that exceeds the size of its destination register, and hence is really a kind of OVERFLOW error in disguise.

underscan A mode of operation of a CATHODE RAY TUBE display in which the RASTER SCAN does not reach the edges of the tube face, and a black border is visible around the picture region.

underscore The character _ with ASCII code 95. The character was once used by computer printers to underline text, by backspacing and overprinting. It is now mostly used to substitute for the space character in those programming languages and applications that do not permit IDENTIFIERS to contain spaces – as for example in my_long_filename.

undo To reverse the most recent operation performed by a computer program, for example to remove the last typed character or drawn line. Undo is an important feature psychologically as it gives users the confidence to try out new operations without risk. Most programs now support at least a single level of

undo, and a few (such as Microsoft Word and Adobe Photoshop) support unlimited levels so that whole editing sessions may be progressively unwound. There is no universal command for undo but in WINDOWS programs it is performed by CTRL+Z or ALT+BACKSPACE.

undocumented call A SYSTEM CALL whose existence is not revealed in the documentation. One of the charges levelled at Microsoft is that it uses such calls in Windows to give its own programmers an advantage over other competitors.

undocumented feature A feature that the manual writer forgot to mention. The term is also a euphemism for a BUG.

unicast Any communication that takes place between a single sender and a single receiver, as for example a telephone call. See also BROADCAST, MULTICAST.

Unicode A 16-bit universal CHARACTER SET intended eventually to replace ASCII. It permits 65,536 characters to be encoded, and can hence support the alphabets of most written languages. Unicode was invented by researchers at Xerox PARC in 1987, and is now maintained by the non-profit consortium Unicode Inc. whose members include Microsoft, Sun and Adobe. In Unicode, every character is allocated a unique 16-bit number called a CODE POINT, and no characters require more than one number, so there are none of the embedded ESCAPE SEQUENCES needed to add non-standard characters to an ASCII text.

The first 8192 Unicode codes are given over to the characters of most of the world's alphabetic languages, plus some ancient scripts such as Sanskrit and Hebrew. All the printable 7-bit ASCII characters are included, as are the ASCII CONTROL CODES for compatibility (though control codes have no meaning in Unicode itself). The following 4096 codes are punctuation, mathematical and graphical symbols. 5632 codes are reserved for Unicode developers to define their own characters, and 495 'compatibility' codes assist developers who are converting to Unicode. Most of the remaining codes, some 27,000, are devoted to the Han Chinese characters, as defined by Chinese National Standard GB 13000. The remaining codes are unused, providing space to add characters to the existing languages as linguists see fit.

Since Unicode character codes are twice the length of ASCII character codes, they cannot be processed by existing ASCII editing software, which must therefore be rewritten to take advantage of Unicode. For this reason Unicode is not yet widely used, but Microsoft's support for it in Windows NT/2000 and Sun's support for it in the Java language should help it to spread more quickly. See also UCS, OPENTYPE.

unidirectional 1 Of a communication link, capable of transmitting data in only one direction, in contrast to BIDIRECTIONAL.

2 Of an impact or inkjet printer, having a print head that only prints on the forward pass across the paper, as opposed to printing on both forward and return passes.

unification The fundamental mathematical operation on which LOGIC PROGRAMMING is based. It consists of finding a set of variable bindings that will make two logical expressions equivalent to one another. See also PROLOG, PATTERN MATCHING.

unified cache A single PROCESSOR CACHE that holds both data and instructions. See also DATA CACHE, INSTRUCTION CACHE, HARVARD ARCHITECTURE.

unified memory A type of computer display architecture that employs a region within main memory for assembling and manipulating the image data to be displayed on the screen, rather than providing a separate VIDEO MEMORY. In the PC world, unified memory tends to be seen as a cheap option with downgraded performance compared to a GRAPHICS CARD with dedicated video memory. However, in the most powerful GRAPHICS WORKSTATIONS it has always been standard practice, as it both simplifies the job of programmers (see FLAT ADDRESS SPACE) and offers greater flexibility over image size. See also FRAME BUFFER, DOUBLE BUFFERING, DISPLAY BUFFER, DISPLAY LIST.

unified messaging The ability to store and manage FAX, VOICEMAIL, EMAIL amd SMS messages within the same software system and INBOX. Some PC communication products (such as Microsoft Exchange) already support the storage of these different message types in different folders. Large corporations that have various pre-existing mail systems normally need to install some type of MIDDLEWARE product to integrate the different message flows. The most advanced of these systems may go so far as converting between one message type and another using OCR, SPEECH RECOGNITION and SPEECH SYNTHESIS programs.

Unified Modelling Language, Unified Method An OBJECT-ORIENTED DESIGN method, created by Rational Inc. but now adopted by the OMG as an open standard. It combines the best elements from the Booch Method, Rumbaugh's OMT and Jakobson's OOSE methods for specifying, building and documenting software systems.

uniform data access See UDA.

uniform data transfer See UDT.

Uniform Naming Convention See UNC.

Uniform Resource Locator See URL.

Uniform Resource Name Any Internet UNIVERSAL RESOURCE IDENTIFIER that is not a URL. It represents a new category of identifier that is intended to be deployed in some enhanced future system and will be more persistent than a current web page URL, attaching to the service sought rather than simply to its current location. See also XLL, UDDI.

uninstaller A utility program supplied with many Windows applications that can remove that application from the user's computer. Uninstallers are needed because of the complexity of Windows configuration. It is no longer sufficient simply to delete an application's files: changes made to the REGISTRY must also be reversed and its DLLs may need to be removed from various directories. The application's INSTALL program typically leaves a file that records all such changes, and the uninstaller can read this file in order to undo them.

uninterruptible power supply See UPS.

union 1 In SET THEORY, an operation performed on two sets that returns all those elements that are members of one set or the other. See also INTERSECTION.

2 In the C and C++ languages, a STRUCTURE definition that contains more than one kind

of structure, whose first element is an integer used as a selector to specify which member is meant in a particular context. It is equivalent to the VARIANT RECORD in Pascal.

3 In the SQL language, an operation that forms a new table by combining rows from two database TABLES that share a common FIELD.

uniprocessor A computer that has only a single CPU (compare this with a MULTIPROCESSOR).

unique identifier (UID) A name used to distinguish, for example, a particular computer or program object from others of its kind, and which is required to be unique within a particular NAMESPACE. See also USER IDENTIFIER, CLASS IDENTIFIER, GUID.

unique key A restriction imposed by many DATABASE MANAGEMENT SYSTEMS that no two records may contain the same value in an indexed KEY field.

Unisys Corporation A large US computer corporation formed by the merger of BURROUGHS and SPERRY Univac in 1985.

unit 1 An amount of some quantifiable physical property (such as length or mass) that is adopted as a standard, so that multiples of it may employed in measuring magnitudes of that property. Examples include the metre for length and the gram for mass.

2 In computing, the name given to a separately compiled MODULE in some programming languages such as Turbo Pascal and Delphi.

UNIVAC 1 (Universal Automatic Calculator 1) To quote the United States Census Bureau 'The world's first electronic general purpose data processing computer', delivered to the bureau on June 14, 1951 by the ECKERT-MAUCHLY COMPUTER CORPORATION, which later became part of Sperry Univac (now Unisys). UNIVAC had 1000 words of storage space and was capable of performing 3000 additions per second. See also COLOSSUS, ENIAC, ATLAS, VON NEUMANN.

universal description, discovery and integration See UDDI.

universal asynchronous receiver/transmitter See UART.

Universal Character Set See UCS.

universal data access Another name for uniform data access, see UDA.

Universal Decimal Classification A hierarchical classification system for libraries that extends the DEWEY DECIMAL SYSTEM by permitting the inclusion of symbols other than the Arabic numerals in its notation. Also called the Brussels Classification, it was first published in 1905 and is used throughout Europe (and by the United Nations) especially in science and technology libraries.

universal disk format See UDF.

Universal Plug and Play (UPP, UPnP) An industry-wide initiative, lead by Microsoft and Intel, to create a new architecture for connecting peripherals to computers across different platforms, without the need for DEVICE DRIVERS. UPnP is a networking technology that is intended to be invisible to the user, and will provide for automatic discovery – a new device can dynamically join a network, obtain an IP ADDRESS, broadcast its own capabilities and discover the presence and capabilities of other devices, then quit the network without leaving behind any unwanted state (e.g. device drivers or DLLs). UPnP is based on the Internet protocols TCP/IP, UDP, HTTP and XML, with optional use of DYNAMIC HOST CONFIGURATION PROTOCOL and DNS if available. See also JINI.

Universal Resource Identifier (URI) Defined by the INTERNET ENGINEERING TASK FORCE as 'a compact string representation of a location (URL) or name (URN) for use in identifying an abstract or physical resource'. Hence URI is the generic term for any identifier used to distinguish resources on the Internet, of which the URL is currently the sort most commonly encountered. URIs are defined in RFC 1693. See also UNIFORM RESOURCE NAME.

Universal Serial Bus See USB.

Unix A general purpose multiuser, multitasking computer operating system that is most widely used on Internet servers, engineering workstations, on commercial MINICOMPUTERS and in university computer networks. Unix was created at BELL LABORATORIES in 1969 by Ken THOMPSON and Dennis RITCHIE and its adoption by universities and research institutions caused its use to spread quickly throughout the world.

Between 1972 and 1974, Unix was completely rewritten in the C programming language, making it very much easier to port to different processor types than any rival operating system. AT&T, the original owner, gave away the Unix SOURCE CODE free to many universities, which eventually lead to the emergence of several differing and barely-compatible variants such as Berkeley Unix, Version 7, Unix Systems Group Unix, Xenix, Ultrix, Linux, and GNU. Unix supports a vast range of powerful development tools, many of them also free.

Modern Unix versions support GRAPHICAL USER INTERFACES as an add-on feature, but the underlying operating system employs a COMMAND LINE user interface with many cryptically named commands, which is enormously powerful in skilled hands, as it permits the automation of complex sequences of tasks by means of SHELL SCRIPTS. However, it is quite baffling to the novice, and, despite many attempts over the years, Unix has never become widely used on personal computers – an overwhelming majority of which run Microsoft WINDOWS. Unix is technically superior to Windows in several respects. It has more robust task scheduling and memory protection mechanisms; it is easier to extend it to run on multiple processors, and it has a more extensible and less hardware-dependent FILE SYSTEM. On the other hand, because Unix runs on various brands of processor, executable programs are not in general portable between systems in the way that Windows programs are portable between PCs. Unix users instead RECOMPILE programs from the source code, which is not a job that most PC users would relish.

The tradition of free Unix software that dates from its early scientific and technical application persists today, and the OPEN SOURCE and FREEWARE movements are all based around versions of Unix.

Unix-to-Unix Copy See UUCP.

UnixWare The brand name used by NOVELL for its short-lived version of Unix SYSTEM V.

unpack **1** To uncompress a file ARCHIVE and restore the individual files it contains. See also ZIP FILE, TAR, UNZIP.

2 To expand data that has been encoded for more efficient storage into its original format. See also PACKED, PACKED DECIMAL.

unrecoverable application error (UAE) An error message announcing a fatal error that will terminate the execution of the current program under Microsoft WINDOWS version 3. In versions of Windows from 95 onwards, the UAE has been replaced by the equally terminal GENERAL PROTECTION FAULT. See also ERROR MESSAGE, ERROR CONDITION, ERROR TRAPPING.

unshielded twisted-pair (UTP) A type of cabling used for both telephones and computer LANs that is thinner and less expensive than COAXIAL CABLE. In place of the latter's woven wire shielding layer, UTP twists its pairs of conductors around one another. This has several beneficial effects: radiation from, and hence cross-talk between, the conductors is minimized; fluctuations in impedance are evened out, which reduces signal reflection at boundaries; and any external interference affects both conductors equally, making it easier to remove by subtraction in the attached circuitry.

The most commonly used varieties of UTP are called CATEGORY 3 or voice grade and CATEGORY 5 or data grade and they typically employ four such pairs of conductors within the same cable sheath. See also SHIELDED TWISTED-PAIR, THIN ETHERNET, 10BASET, XBASEY.

unsigned integer Any INTEGER DATA TYPE that does not employ a bit to indicate its sign. Hence an 8-bit unsigned integer can represent any number in the range 0 to 255 (00000000 to 11111111). See also SIGN BIT, ONES COMPLEMENT, TWOS COMPLEMENT, BINARY NOTATION.

unspecified bit rate The lowest quality of ASYNCHRONOUS TRANSFER MODE traffic, where the network offers no guarantee that the user's data will be delivered.

unZIP To restore the original files contained in a compressed ZIP FILE produced by PKZIP or a compatible COMPRESSION utility. See also ARCHIVE.

update To alter some stored quantity such as a database field, a disk file or the contents of a processor register to a new value. The term is also used as a noun meaning an individual act of such alteration, as in 'examine recent updates to the allocation table'.

upgrade To enhance a computing (or other) system by replacing various hardware or software components with newer or more powerful versions. In the software business, upgrades are frequently provided to existing users at a price lower than the full product cost.

uplink In VIDEO-ON-DEMAND, interactive digital television and SATELLITE communication systems, the channel (also called a *backchannel*) that carries the customer's commands (for example to stop or fast forward a film, or respond to a programme choice) back to the video server. Compare this with DOWNLINK, which carries the programme data to the customer. In some systems the uplink has a lower BANDWIDTH than the downlink (see for example ADSL). Some satellite TV systems employ completely different transport media for their downlink (radio waves) and their uplink (a conventional telephone line). See also ASYMMETRIC.

upload To transfer a file from a local computer onto a remote SERVER, from where other network users may be permitted to access it.

UPP Abbreviation of UNIVERSAL PLUG AND PLAY.

upper bound The largest value that some variable quantity may assume. See also ARRAY BOUNDS.

upper case The alphabet of large letter forms (also called CAPITALS) that is included in a FONT, as opposed to the small or LOWER CASE letters. The name dates from the days of lead type, when these letters were kept in the top section of the wooden type box or 'case'. See also CAPITALIZE, DROP CAP.

upper memory, upper memory area (UMA) The region of memory between 640 kilobytes and 1 megabyte in an IBM-compatible PC running its processor in REAL MODE. Normally graphics cards, BIOS ROMs, hard disk controllers and network interfaces are mapped into this region, but there are some gaps in the memory map that can be exploited by sophisticated memory managers to provide a little extra CONVENTIONAL MEMORY in upper memory blocks (UMBS). See also EXTENDED MEMORY, EXPANDED MEMORY SPECIFICATION, EMM386, HIMEM.

upper memory block See UMB.

UPS (uninterruptible power supply) An auxiliary power supply connected to computer and networking equipment to maintain their operation in the event of mains power failure. A UPS contains rechargeable batteries capable of running the equipment for several minutes, which is long enough to ride out brief cuts and 'brownouts' or to close the system down in orderly fashion in the event of a longer outage. When the UPS detects a falling mains voltage, it raises audible and online alarms to the equipment's operators, while simultaneously switching over to its own supply.

uptime The time during which a system is available to perform its specified task. The term is often used as a synonym for AVAILABILITY, and expressed as a percentage. Its opposite is DOWNTIME.

upwardly-compatible Capable of working with a later or a more powerful version of some hardware or software system. For example programs written for the Intel 386 processor are upwardly compatible with the Pentium. See also BACKWARD COMPATIBLE.

URI Abbreviation of UNIVERSAL RESOURCE IDENTIFIER.

URL (Uniform Resource Locator) Formerly called a Universal Resource Locator. The string of characters used to identify some resource on the Internet such as a server, a file, a web page or a newsgroup. Various items of Internet CLIENT software such as WEB BROWSERS, NEWSREADERS and FTP clients accept URLs and then locate and return the resource they refer to. Some people pronounce the acronym to sound like 'earl'. URLs are a kind of UNIVERSAL RESOURCE IDENTIFIER. An example of an URL is:

http://www.penguin.com/index.html

The first section (before the colon) names the PROTOCOL that must be used to access this resource, and the section following twin slashes names a host computer. Further sections following single slashes name the directory path to a particular file on the host computer.

URLs may contain only the alphanumeric characters A to z, 0 to 9, the symbols $ – _ .& and the reserved characters :/?#">< >%+ (which have special meanings). Any other character must be encoded by following a % character with the character's ASCII code as two hexadecimal digits, so that the pound sign £ for example must be inserted as %A3.

URLs may also contain strings of parameters to be fed into CGI scripts (or other executable programs embedded in web pages such as ASP objects). See, for example, this search for Marge Simpson

```
http://www.altavista.com/cgi-
bin/query?pg=q&kl=XX&q=%22Marge+Si
mpson%22&;search=Search
```

usability A property of any complex system in which humans interact with machines that measures how comprehensible and convenient the operator finds the USER INTERFACE. In the software industry, usability studies are a formal part of the development process, and are of the utmost importance since poorly designed user interfaces have a distastrous effect on productivity. Both quantitative and qualitative methods may be employed, and include measuring delays, counting the keystrokes needed to perform different tasks, or asking users how to access a particular command or what they expect to happen next in various situations.

USB (Universal Serial Bus) A relatively fast SERIAL communications architecture for attaching peripheral devices to computers, developed by Intel to avoid the configuration conflicts that plague normal PC EXPANSION SLOTS.

USB operates at 12 megabits per second and can support up to 127 devices either by DAISY-CHAINING or using a USB HUB. USB cables may be up to 5 metres long and carry the power supply for low-powered devices such as digital cameras and mice. All new PCs and Apple Macintoshes are now fitted with USB ports, and a growing number of keyboards, monitors, mice, printers and removable storage disks employ the interface. However, it cannot cope with faster devices, for which SCSI and FIREWIRE are more suitable.

use case A technique employed in some OBJECT-ORIENTED program design methodologies (most notably the Jacobsen method) that attempts to uncover all the dependencies involved in a particular business activity by describing the activity step-by-step in a format that resembles the script of a play: people, their roles and the actions they perform. A use case description is often accompanied by diagrams that show the messages flowing between participants. The strength of the method is that recording a use case for a particular event may reveal an attribute that was omitted from an object that participates in the event. See also OBJECT-ORIENTED DESIGN, YOURDON METHOD, CASE TOOL.

Usenet A worldwide client/server information network that predates the Internet. It consists of thousands of online discussion forums called NEWSGROUPS in which anyone who has NEWSREADER client software can participate.

Created in 1979 at Duke University, Usenet is a network of Unix servers running the NET-NEWS server software, used extensively by universities, government agencies, Unix programmers and private individuals alike – more than 50 megabytes of new contributions are added every day.

To read Usenet groups requires an account either on one of the Usenet servers, or (more often) with an ISP that provides a Usenet feed (i.e. that publishes daily copies of the contents of many Usenet groups). The Usenet nowadays overlaps considerably with the Internet, but there are still Usenet servers that are not connected to the Internet, and not every ISP carries all newsgroups.

user The person for whom computer systems are allegedly designed.

user account An authorization and record of a person or company's usage of some computing or communications service, for both access control and payment purposes: e.g. a public telephone or ISP account.

user base 1 The number of users of a particular hardware or software product, as in 'a user base of 10,000'.

2 The users of such a product, when considered as a collective as in 'a feature that will please the user base'.

User Datagram Protocol See under UDP.

user-defined A name (or other data object) that was selected by the user rather than being predetermined or created by a computer program.

user-friendly A much overused jargon term, applied to any software or hardware that has a well-designed USER INTERFACE. The most important elements of such friendliness are providing the user with adequate feedback about what the device is currently doing, and being patient and flexible when incorrect inputs are attempted.

user identifier, user id (uid) A unique name or number by which each user of a computer or network of computers is recognized by the system. The uid is used as the internal representation of that user, for example to mark their ownership of resources such as files or processes. The operating system typically maintains a user database that maps these uids to other information stored about the user, including real name, USER NAME, PASSWORD, EMAIL ADDRESS and home directory.

user interface The part of a computer program that is devoted to accepting instructions from the human operator and feeding back information about the program's current state and the progress of the current task. Early software user interfaces relied on short commands, either supplied as parameters when first starting the program or typed at a COMMAND PROMPT in the running program. This style of interface is still to be found in some MS-DOS and Unix programs, but is daunting for beginners, as all the commands must be learned, and then typed correctly. The introduction of MENU-DRIVEN programs removed these obstacles by making all the available commands visible and allowing them to be selected without typing. The modern GRAPHICAL USER INTERFACE goes further still by providing wholly non-verbal ways to instruct a program, such as pressing BUTTONS and selecting screen objects by pointing and clicking with a MOUSE. See also USABILITY.

user mode A mode of execution provided by most computer processors for running application programs (rather than system programs) in which certain REGISTERS are not visible and certain instruction types cannot be executed – these being reserved for the privileged SUPERVISOR MODE in which the operating system runs. See also RING, PROTECTED MODE, TRAP.

user name The unique name by which each user of a shared computer system is known. This user name, along with a PASSWORD must be supplied in order to LOG ON to the system. Most systems employ a shortened or encoded form of this user name (often a number) called a USER IDENTIFIER for the purpose of identification in internal operations.

user-programmable Any hardware device or software application that is capable of having its mode of operation altered by the end-user, rather than only by a professional programmer or engineer. For example a video recorder is user-programmable (but only by those under 20 years old).

US Robotics (USR) A subsidiary of 3COM CORPORATION that is the leading US manufacturer of MODEMS, best known for its Courier and Sportster model ranges. In 1996 USR bought PALM Computing and its name appeared on early models of the hand-held Pilot range, but it has since floated Palm as separate entity again.

UTF-8 Abbreviation of UCS TRANSFORMATION FORMAT 8.

utility A small computer program that automates some frequently required task.

utilization The proportion of some limited resource, such as memory, disk space or processor time, that is currently in use.

UTP Abbreviation of UNSHIELDED TWISTED-PAIR.

uucp (Unix-to-Unix copy) A Unix messaging protocol and utility program that enables one Unix computer to send files to another directly over a SERIAL cable, or via MODEMS and a public telephone line. Uucp may also be used over a local area network (LAN) or the Internet, but generally other protocols such as

FTP, SMTP or NNTP are preferred for this purpose. See also UUCPNET.

UUCPNET   An international computer network, parallel to, but in part pre-dating, the Internet. It consists of all the connected Unix computers that can exchange files using the UUCP protocol. UUCPNET is still employed to transfer some EMAIL and USENET messages.

uudecode   See under UUENCODE.

uuencode   A Unix program that encodes BINARY data as 7-bit ASCII characters for transmission over communications channels that cannot handle 8-bit data. Uuencode was originally created to be used in conjunction with the UUCP protocol for transferring binary files over serial links that strip the eighth bit from characters. However, it later became important as a tool for attaching binary files to email messages sent over the Internet (see BINARY ATTACHMENT), or for uploading to NEWSGROUPS and versions are now available for almost all operating systems, including Windows. Its sister program *uudecode* reverses the encoding to recreate the original binary file. Uuencode is being supplanted by MIME.

UUNET PIPEX, uunet   One of the earliest and largest ISPs.

UV   Abbreviation of ULTRAVIOLET.

V

V.90 The latest dial-up MODEM standard, capable of transmitting at 56.7 kilobits per second. See more under V STANDARDS.

vacuum tube US term for THERMIONIC VALVE.

validation The act of determining whether a data item entered into a computer program is in the format expected by the program. Validation is frequently performed by applying an input MASK that forces the user to type only in the correct format: for example when a telephone number or credit card number is expected, the input box may be divided into several parts each with the correct number of places, such as XXX-XXX-XXXX. Other programs may reject an incorrect input and request that it be re-entered before the program will proceed.

value The item of data, such as a number, a character, a text string, a date, etc. that is currently to be stored in a program VARIABLE.

value-added reseller A purveyor of computer equipment who integrates hardware and software from different vendors and sells them as complete systems.

valve Common shorthand for THERMIONIC VALVE.

vanilla The simplest version of a product (or the version with the lowest specification) – by analogy with ice-cream flavours.

vapourware (*US* vaporware) Software that is talked about, but not yet released.

VAR See VALUE-ADDED RESELLER.

variable In most HIGH-LEVEL PROGRAMMING LANGUAGES, a stored value that can be referred to by a symbolic name. A variable is an abstraction that ultimately refers to a particular memory address. The value of a variable can be altered at any time using an ASSIGNMENT statement, so that for example:

```
ThisVar := 10
```

makes 10 the current value of ThisVar, and the name can then be used in arithmetic expressions (e.g. log(ThisVar+20)) to stand for its current value. In many programming languages, variables must be DECLARED to be of a specific DATA TYPE before they can be used, as in:

```
VAR ThisVar: Integer;
```

which says that ThisVar can contain only whole numbers. In most languages a variable has four important attributes: its name, its value, its lifetime and its SCOPE. The lifetime of a variable means the interval of time during which its value is meaningful (that is, during which the name is bound to that particular memory location). GLOBAL variables live for the whole duration of a program's execution, while LOCAL variables live only during the execution of the SUBPROGRAM in which they are declared. See also PERSISTENT, STATIC.

Variable Bit Rate A type of ASYNCHRONOUS TRANSFER MODE traffic that declares upper and lower limits on the BANDWIDTH it will require, which is useful for time-critical data such as voice or video.

variable-length record A type of database record for which no fixed amount of storage space is allocated in advance, typically used to store passages of text rather than numbers. See also FIXED-LENGTH RECORD.

variable-zone recording See ZONED-BIT RECORDING.

variant 1 The default data type in VISUAL BASIC. It can be used to represent any numeric or string type, with automatic conversion between them as needed.
2 One of the alternative structures defined for a VARIANT RECORD type in programming languages of the PASCAL family.

variant record A more flexible type of RECORD provided in several programming languages (including PASCAL) that may be defined as existing in several different forms each of which is identified by a TAG. A new record instance may be created in any one of these forms by supplying the appropriate tag at the time of its creation. For example an employee record could be created in two variants for weekly or monthly paid staff, selected perhaps by a tag called pay_period.

varistor A special type of RESISTOR whose resistance rises very rapidly with applied voltage, which can be employed in surge-suppression circuits to protect computers against power SPIKES.

VAX A range of 32-BIT MINICOMPUTERS launched by DIGITAL EQUIPMENT CORPORATION in 1978 to replace the aging PDP-11. The VAX was extremely successful until the late 1980s, and pioneered many of the concepts that are now commonplace in the industry such as VIRTUAL MEMORY and CLUSTERED SMP. Its robust and capable operating system VMS influenced the design of many modern operating systems, from MS-DOS to WINDOWS NT. See also DEC ALPHA, DATA GENERAL.

VB Abbreviation of VISUAL BASIC.

VBA Abbreviation of VISUAL BASIC FOR APPLICATIONS.

VBI Abbreviation of VERTICAL BLANKING INTERVAL.

VBR Abbreviation of VARIABLE BIT RATE.

VBScript A subset of the VISUAL BASIC language that is employed as a client and server-side SCRIPTING LANGUAGE in Microsoft's ACTIVE SERVER PAGES system.

VBX (Visual Basic Extension) The original VISUAL BASIC file format for reusable software components, which has since been replaced by the more fully object-oriented OCX format. VBX files were in fact plain DLL files given a different name, and as such did not support INHERITANCE, which OCX files do.

VC Abbreviation of VERSION CONTROL.

VCL Abbreviation of VISUAL COMPONENT LIBRARY.

VDL Abbreviation of VIENNA DEFINITION LANGUAGE.

VDM (Virtual DOS Machine) A 640 kilobyte software VIRTUAL MACHINE that is created whenever a 16-bit program is run under a 32-bit version of WINDOWS or OS/2. Multiple 16-bit applications may run in separate VDMs, each one believing it has the computer to itself.

VDSL Abbreviation of very high bit-rate DIGITAL SUBSCRIBER LINE.

VDU (visual display unit) Also called a *monitor*. A device based on either a CATHODE RAY TUBE or, more recently, an LCD, that displays the output from a computer. The important statistics of a VDU from the user's point of view are: its size (measured diagonally across the screen), its RESOLUTION (that is the number of PIXELS on its screen), the number of colours it can display, its DOT PITCH, and its REFRESH RATE (which determines whether its display will appear to flicker or not). Other factors such as uniformity of focus over different parts of the screen, and distortions such as PINCUSHIONING can greatly affect the subjective experience of using a VDU. See more under DISPLAY ADAPTER, GRAPHICS ADAPTER, VGA.

vector 1 In mathematics and physics, a quantity that has both a magnitude and a direction. Examples include velocity or magnetic field, but not temperature. See also SCALAR.
2 In computer graphics, a line defined by the coordinates of its endpoints rather than as a list of PIXELS. See more under VECTOR GRAPHICS.
3 A memory location that contains the address of an executable program (for example an INTERRUPT HANDLER or a DEVICE DRIVER).

Changing the contents of this single location thus changes the routine that will be executed, without recompiling the whole program. See more under INTERRUPT VECTOR.

4 In some programming languages, the name given to a single dimensioned ARRAY. A certain class of SUPERCOMPUTER (e.g. the Cray) is optimized for processing such arrays, and is hence called a VECTOR PROCESSOR.

vector display An almost obsolete type of display device that consists of a CATHODE RAY TUBE that draws lines at any angle, rather than being scanned in a regular RASTER grid. Vector displays are typically monochromatic, drawing green or orange lines on a black background. A few are still employed in radar sets, and they were used in very early arcade game machines.

vector font A type of OUTLINE FONT, so-called because each character is specified by a set of lines (i.e. VECTORS) rather than by a BITMAP.

vector graphics A type of computer representation for images in which a picture is described as a collection of geometrical shapes (e.g. lines, circles, triangles, polygons) rather than as a set of coloured PIXELS (as in BITMAPPED graphics). A vector graphics representation is typically far more compact than a bitmap, as a line can be represented in two dimensions by just four numbers (the X and Y coordinates of its two ends) rather by every pixel it contains. A picture represented in vector format remains editable in a way that a bitmap image does not, so the length and angle of any of its geometric components may be altered later, and it may be scaled to any size without loss of clarity. However, vector representations are less effective than bitmaps for storing photorealistic images that have continuously varying colours. DRAWING PROGRAMS and COMPUTER AIDED DESIGN programs such as Adobe Illustrator and AutoCAD employ vector graphic internal representations and file formats. With the growth of the World Wide Web, vector graphics formats such as MacroMedia's FLASH have grown in importance, as their compact size reduces download times. There is a trend toward drawing programs and file formats that combine both bitmapped and vector editing

capabilities, typified by Macromedia's Fireworks, Deneba Canvas and the SVG file format. See also POSTSCRIPT.

vectorize To rearrange a computer program so that it can be most efficiently executed on a VECTOR PROCESSOR such as a Cray supercomputer. This typically involves unrolling the loops it contains so that each iteration is performed by a separate processor. See also LOOP UNROLLING, LOOP OPTIMIZATION, FORTRAN, SIMD.

Vector Markup Language See VML.

vector processor A type of MULTIPROCESSOR computer architecture (sometimes called an *array processor*) that contains a large number of identical simple CPUs that simultaneously perform the same operation on different elements of an array of numbers. Vector processors are particularly effective for accelerating MATRIX ARITHMETIC operations such as those employed in computer graphics: the famous CRAY 1 supercomputer and its descendants were vector processors. See also PIPELINE, PARALLEL COMPUTER, SIMD, SUPERCOMPUTER.

vector quantization See under QUANTIZATION.

verb A name sometimes applied to the COMMANDS provided in a particular programming language, the implication being that these are words that specify an action, and that the data items or arguments they work on are the nouns.

verification The process of establishing whether some operation (such as the writing of a file to disk or the inputting of a data item into a database) was satisfactorily completed. One technique used for verification of disk writes is the READ-AFTER-WRITE method. See also VALIDATION.

Verilog A HARDWARE DESCRIPTION LANGUAGE for the design and gate level SIMULATION of INTEGRATED CIRCUITS.

Veronica Alleged to stand for Very Easy Rodent-Oriented Net-wide Index to Computerized Archives. A distributed index to all the GOPHER document archives on the Internet. Veronica may be used via Gopher CLIENT software, allowing KEYWORD searches that return a menu of matching files from Gopher sites anywhere on the Internet. See also ARCHIE, JUGHEAD.

Versa Module Europa See VMEBUS.

version One particular historical configuration of a developing software product, identified by a version number. Software products are so complex (and may contain so many BUGS) that the problem of naming each altered version becomes equally complex – it is seldom possible to simply release version 1, followed by version 2 and so on.

A large program such as an operating system has scores of SUBSYSTEMS, each of which may be developed by a different team at a different site, so it is commercially unrealistic to wait for changes in all subsystems to catch up before releasing a new version. Hence software vendors adopt hierarchical numbering schemes (e.g. 2.15.03) that can distinguish many levels of major and minor revision and BUG FIX.

There is no universally accepted standard for such version numbering, but there are a few widely used conventions, such as that version numbers beginning with 0 denote BETA RELEASES while the full releases start from 1.0. Usually the first digit group indicates a major version while the second counts minor revisions, and the third counts bug fixes.

Managing versions (for example to ensure that everyone within a company is using the same version) forms part of the problem of DEPLOYMENT, and is increasingly being automated. A serious problem arises from the fact that OBJECT-ORIENTED component systems such as COMPONENT OBJECT MODEL (COM) and JAVABEANS have no built-in versioning support (the GUID of a COM interface doesn't change between versions), and this can lead to system configuration problems when incompatible versions are introduced. See also VERSION CONTROL, BUILD NUMBER.

version control The use of computers to assist in managing the revisions made to a collaborative project. A version control system automatically numbers and retains successive versions of every component file as revisions are made; it keeps track of which worker is working on which file (preventing several

from altering a file simultaneously); it merges revised files back into the main project without overwriting anyone else's revisions; and it permits coherent versions of the whole product to be assembled and maintained, as sets of known component file versions. These functions are frequently achieved by storing all the components in a central database called a REPOSITORY, from which they must be formally logged out before working on them, and logged back in afterwards. Version control systems are mostly employed for programming, where the files are SOURCE CODE files and the final product is a BUILD made up of many compiled and linked files. However, version control is equally applicable to complex documents written by many authors, or to film and music editing.

versioning The systematic naming and management of modifications and corrections made to a software product.

vertex A point at which two lines in a geometric figure meet.

vertical application A computer application that is designed around the working practices of a particular trade or industry, in contrast to a general-purpose tool such as a SPREADSHEET or WORD PROCESSOR (which are sometimes therefore referred to as HORIZONTAL APPLICATIONS). See also VERTICAL MARKET.

vertical blanking interval (VBI) The period during which the dot on a CATHODE RAY TUBE is turned off to allow it to return to the top left-hand corner after scanning a full image FIELD. See more under BLANKING INTERVAL.

vertical market Computer industry jargon for a particular trade or industrial sector (e.g. car manufacturing).

vertical refresh rate The number of times per second that a CATHODE RAY TUBE completes the scanning of one FIELD contributing to the screen image. Typical rates are 50 hertz (Hz) for European television sets, 60 Hz for US television sets, and 90 Hz or more for high quality, flicker-free computer monitors.

vertical resolution For any kind of VDU, the number of PIXELS in the vertical dimension of the displayed image. In the case of an analogue monitor based on a CATHODE RAY TUBE, the vertical resolution is strictly measured in SCAN LINES rather than pixels, though the two normally coincide. For example a UK analogue television set has a vertical resolution of 625 lines, while for a VGA-quality (640 × 480) computer display the vertical resolution is 480 pixels. See also INTERLACED DISPLAY, TWITTER.

vertical scan rate The same as VERTICAL REFRESH RATE.

Vertical TAB (VT) ASCII character 11, once used as a command to move teleprinter paper up by several line feeds at once.

very high bit-rate Digital Subscriber Line (VDSL) See under DIGITAL SUBSCRIBER LINE.

very high frequency See VHF.

Very Large Memory (VLM) The ability of an operating system to use 64-bit addresses to access up to 18.4 TERABYTES of memory. It is supported by several current variants of UNIX and by WINDOWS 2000. See also PHYSICAL ADDRESS EXTENSIONS.

very large scale integration See VLSI.

Very Long Instruction Word See VLIW.

VESA (Video Electronics Standards Association) An industry organization created in 1989 by a consortium of US and Japanese GRAPHICS CARD and VDU manufacturers to advance the standards of graphics hardware for IBM-compatible PCs. The first VESA standard was the 800 × 600 pixel SVGA display mode and its software interface. VESA also produced the now obsolete VESA LOCAL BUS to offer faster data connection for graphics cards, and video equipment standards including the VESA Media Channel (VMC) and VESA Display Power Management Signalling (DPMS).

VESA local bus (VL bus) An EXPANSION BUS for IBM-compatible PCs developed by VESA in 1993 to replace the slow ISA BUS and so improve the performance of GRAPHICS CARDS (which were VESA's main product). It failed in competition with Intel's PCI BUS, which remains the current standard. See also AGP, LOCAL BUS.

VGA (Video Graphics Array) IBM's first truly successful GRAPHICS ADAPTER, introduced in 1985 with the PS/2 model. Its 640 x 480 resolution in 16 colours became a universal display standard that spread beyond the confines of the PC market. The popularity of CLONE VGA cards opened the way for Microsoft's graphical Windows operating system, which previous IBM graphics standards had been inadequate to support.

VGA compatible modes are still offered as a 'lowest common denominator' standard by most display cards and monitors that are capable of much higher resolutions. See also CGA, EGA, XGA, SUPER VGA.

VHF (very high frequency) The band within the radio frequency spectrum from 30 to 300 MHz used by both broadcast and short range radio systems.

VHSIC Hardware Description Language (VHDL) A high-level design language for INTEGRATED CIRCUIT development that employs a syntax based on that of ADA. Its use is mandatory for products commissioned by the US Department of Defense, and it is the subject of IEEE standard 1076.

vi A text editor supplied with most versions of the UNIX operating system. Vi is not a FULL-SCREEN EDITOR, but is operated by typing commands that modify a particular line of text. However, once its many arcane commands are learnt, vi is extremely powerful and can be used in non-interactive batch mode to automate the processing of multiple files.

Via Technologies Inc. A Taiwanese semiconductor manufacturer that started by making CHIP SETS for PCs, but entered the microprocessor market with its purchase of CYRIX.

video acceleration A function provided in some of the more powerful GRAPHICS ACCELERATOR cards that speeds up live video replay by providing hardware assistance for any required COLOUR SPACE conversion and image SCALING operations. This frees the host CPU to maintain a steady flow of frame data. See also GUI ACCELERATION, 3D ACCELERATOR.

video adapter Another name for a GRAPHICS ADAPTER.

video capture The process of digitizing a sequence of frames from an ANALOGUE video stream (such as a video tape recorder, TV transmission, or video camera), so that they can be stored and edited on a computer. Video capture is performed by a PLUG-IN card (see FRAME GRABBER) that contains ANALOGUE-TO-DIGITAL CONVERTERS and a large amount of memory in which to store the digitized frames. Many GRAPHICS CARDS now include this function.

video compression The use of compression algorithms to reduce the volume of a stream of video data so that it can be transmitted down a channel of limited BANDWIDTH. Most modern visual communication media, from digital television to computer multimedia applications, VIDEOCONFERENCING and the WORLD WIDE WEB, are wholly dependent on video compression techiques, as the bandwidth available from a CD-ROM, a telephone line or even the broadcast airwaves is insufficient to carry uncompressed, real time video at acceptable quality. See also MPEG, MOTION JPEG, REALVIDEO, QUICKTIME, STREAMING.

videoconference A form of telecommunication that relays the image as well as the voice of the caller. Videoconferencing requires far greater communication bandwidth than does voice telephony, which is why no successful video telephone systems have so far emerged. Even using the best video compression techniques, only a small low-resolution picture updated at around a frame per second can be carried over the public copper telephone lines. BROADBAND telephony systems such as ISDN and ADSL are capable of carrying satisfactory videoconferencing streams, using video compression standards such as MPEG and H.261, but commercial success remains elusive.

A personal computer connected to the Internet can perform videoconferencing relatively cheaply, using a cheap WEBCAM with software such as Microsoft's NetMeeting or the shareware program CU-SEEME.

videodisc A disc used to store moving video pictures. This is now an ambiguous term as it could refer either to the newest digital DVD format or to the obsolete analogue Philips 12-inch laser disc format.

video editing Altering the length and sequence of the images making up a video recording. Video sequences that have been stored in DIGITAL form may be edited using a computer. Typical video editing software permits the reordering of frame sequences and the introduction of transitions such as fades, wipes and other special effects between sequences. The edited result may be either kept in the digital domain or output as an analogue video stream for recording onto video tape. See also VIDEO OUT, VIDEO CAPTURE.

Video Electronics Standards Association See VESA.

Video Graphics Array See under VGA.

video in A communication PORT provided on some computer GRAPHICS CARDS and most video tape recorders that accepts input of an analogue video signal.

video memory A region of computer memory set aside for storing image information that is to be displayed on the VDU screen. In IBM-compatible PCs, the video memory typically resides within a GRAPHICS CARD and is constructed using specially optimized VIDEO RAM chips. However, in computers that use so-called UNIFIED MEMORY, video memory is simply a designated region within main memory. See also FRAME BUFFER, DOUBLE BUFFERING, DISPLAY BUFFER, DISPLAY LIST.

video mixing The superimposition of two electronic images by combining the video signals that represent them.

video-on-demand (VoD) A method of distributing video over a broadband communications link (such as a DSL telephone line or a cable TV connection) that enables a customer to request an individual film from a large library stored on a server and start watching it almost immediately in real time, rather than having to wait while it downloads. Video-on-demand depends on MPEG encoding to achieve the necessary data rates, and this requires a link bandwidth of 1 to 2 megabits per second, which is beyond the capability of analogue public telephone lines.

While it is possible in principle to start a fresh copy of a film for each customer, this places a huge load on the video server's memory. It is more usual to run a small number of copies simultaneously (at, say, 15-minute staggered intervals) so no new customer need wait longer than this. See also STREAMING VIDEO.

video out A communication port provided on some computer GRAPHICS CARDS and most video tape recorders that outputs an analogue video signal.

video overlay The superimposition of an analogue video image onto a digital computer display, for example to display a live television broadcast or VIDEOCONFERENCE feed within a screen window. Video overlaying used to require expensive special hardware but many modern GRAPHICS CARDS can digitize the video stream 'on-the-fly' and perform overlaying entirely within the digital domain.

video port A connector provided on most notebook and laptop computers that enables external display devices such as desktop PC monitors or projectors to be attached to support larger displays. The term also applies to the COMPOSITE VIDEO connectors provided on some multimedia computers for input and output from a video camera or recorder. See also ZOOMED VIDEO.

video RAM (VRAM) A type of RAM chip specially designed for use as computer VIDEO MEMORY. VRAM chips are DUAL-PORTED, so that the graphics processing circuitry can read their contents even while the CPU is updating them. This reduces contention and increases display speed. See also DOUBLE BUFFERING, BANK SWITCHING.

videotext The sending of text and low-resolution graphical information over public telephone lines, as in the French Minitel system or the US PRODIGY system. The rise of the World Wide Web has rendered both types of system almost obsolete. See also TELETEXT.

Vienna Definition Language (VDL) A high-level METALANGUAGE invented by IBM that has been used to specify the SEMANTICS for programming languages such as PL/I. See also FORMAL METHODS.

viewer A computer program used to inspect the data files produced by some other program,

but which cannot alter them. For example, scores of viewers have been written to display the contents of the many different GRAPHICS FILE FORMATS.

viewpoint The position of the observer's eyes within a 3D picture space.

viewport In computer 3D GRAPHICS, the area of the screen in which a 3D object is currently displayed: that is, a 2-dimensional window into a 3-dimensional model. The operation of removing those parts of the image that cannot be seen through the current viewport is called CLIPPING, and a whole class of algorithms is devoted to its more efficient accomplishment. Many graphics programs permit the opening of multiple viewports that can be interactively moved, PANNED and ZOOMED by the user.

virtual A term used to describe any entity that does not really exist, but is simulated by the action of a computer. It is frequently applied to graphical simulations of real-world objects, as in VIRTUAL REALITY or VIRTUAL COMMUNITY. It may equally refer to objects within the computer itself. For example, VIRTUAL MEMORY refers to a computer's ability to swap data rapidly between memory and disk storage so that it appears to have more memory than it actually has. The term is borrowed from the field of optics (from 'virtual image') and its opposite is PHYSICAL, i.e. having material existence.

virtual address An address that lies outside the range of real physical memory addresses in a computer that employs VIRTUAL MEMORY. The processor accesses such addresses by sending them to a MEMORY MANAGEMENT UNIT that locates the page that contains that virtual address (moving it from disk into main memory if it is not already loaded) and returns a corresponding PHYSICAL ADDRESS. See also DEMAND-PAGED, ADDRESS TRANSLATION, PAGE TABLE, PAGE FAULT, TRANSLATION LOOK-ASIDE BUFFER.

virtual circuit A network connection that appears to both sender and receiver to belong exclusively to them. Whereas in reality it is simulated in software, PACKETS from many separate connections are interleaved across the same physical link and diverted to their final destinations using SWITCHES (see under PACKET SWITCHING). Virtual circuits may be employed to share a high-bandwidth connection (for example a T1 or T3 LINE) between several different users, while still giving each user the impression of a dedicated connection with separate charging accounts. ISDN and ASYNCHRONOUS TRANSFER MODE networks create virtual circuits on-the-fly, for example in public telephone systems. See also VIRTUAL PRIVATE NETWORK, TAG SWITCHING.

virtual community Any group of people that habitually communicates via the Internet to share a common interest. Such a community may communicate by ordinary exchange of EMAIL, or by a MAILING LIST, NEWSGROUP or CONFERENCING SYSTEM. The ultimate expression of the concept is to be found in those online services that enable participants to create online personalities (purely textual or represented by a graphical AVATAR) that interact socially and persist from session to session.

virtual device driver (VxD) A type of high-performance DEVICE DRIVER employed by Microsoft Windows from versions 3.0 up to 98, to assist such applications as graphics, sound and communication services. A VxD driver runs at the most privileged processor protection level (see under RING 0). This enables it to trap accesses to I/O ports made by less privileged programs and redirect them to its own routines, so that it can mimic any hardware device such as a modem or a sound card. VxDs are not supported by the new driver model introduced with WINDOWS 2000, and are the reason why some older programs fail to install under it.

Virtual DOS Machine See VDM.

virtual machine 1 A technique used by some MULTITASKING operating systems, in which each concurrent application appears to be running on its own computer. Examples include IBM's VM, Microsoft's WINDOWS NT, and earlier versions of Windows when running MS-DOS programs.
2 A mechanism supported by all the Intel 80x86 family of microprocessors from the 80386 onward that allows the processor to emulate multiple virtual 16-bit computers with their own private address spaces: this

mechanism is used by the Windows/386 Virtual Machine Manager WIN386.EXE to run 16-bit programs in a so-called DOS BOX. See also VDM, REAL MODE, PROTECTED MODE.
3 A processor emulated in software that executes the instructions of an invented MACHINE LANGUAGE or PSEUDO-CODE. The purpose of a virtual machine is usually to make programs portable between different brands of hardware. Only the virtual machine itself need be rewritten for each CPU family (either in ASSEMBLY LANGUAGE or in a portable language such as C) and, that done, any pseudo-code program can then be run on that CPU. The JAVA language uses a virtual machine in this way. A different motive for using virtual machines is to speed the design of COMPILERS for experimental programming languages, because generating a simple invented pseudo-code is easier than generating real machine code. The drawback of such virtual machines is inefficiency: the more the pseudo-code differs from the CPU's native code, the more work must be done to execute each instruction.
4 Sometimes applied to a software emulator used either to run programs written in the machine code of one CPU on a different CPU type (for example DEC's FX!32), or to run programs written for one operating system under a different one (for example SOFTWINDOWS).

virtual memory (VM) A technique that enables a computer to run programs and load data sets larger than the amount of RAM it has available. Virtual memory works by swapping chunks of code and data, called pages, between RAM and a file stored on disk. When the running program tries to access an address that lies in a page not currently in memory, an error called a PAGE FAULT occurs. This is intercepted internally by the virtual memory manager, which swaps the required page back into memory so that execution can continue. For efficiency, the virtual memory manager is normally implemented partially in hardware, as part of a MEMORY MANAGEMENT UNIT (MMU).

On a computer that supports virtual memory, programs may access any memory address within a huge virtual address space. The MMU translates each such access back to a physical memory address 'on-the-fly' before it is executed; hence virtual memory is completely transparent to software. The MMU maps the physical address space representing the actual RAM onto the much larger VIRTUAL ADDRESS space using a set of PAGE TABLES that it maintains in real memory. To improve efficiency, the most recently translated addresses are often cached in a TRANSLATION LOOK-ASIDE BUFFER (TLB) contained within the MMU. Whenever a memory access is processed the MMU looks first in the TLB, and only if the address is not there need it consult the external page tables. For more efficient addressing of very large and very small objects, some virtual memory systems employ a hierarchy of pages of differently sizes, and multi-level page tables.

Virtual Memory System See VMS.

virtual money Any type of notional currency employed by an online payment system, typically stored in a digital WALLET on the user's computer. Virtual money is not as yet legal tender, and must be converted into a real currency when bills are finally settled.

Virtual Network Computing (VNC) A remote display technology created by AT&T (and distributed as FREEWARE) that enables a user to view (via the Internet) the desktop environment running on one computer on the screen of a different computer. It may be used, for example, by a network administrator to monitor the operation of remote servers in another city. VNC is cross-platform, so a Windows machine may display the desktop of a Unix server. Moreover, VNC stores no state at all on the viewing machine, which may therefore be very small, even a hand-held computer. See also X WINDOW SYSTEM, WINFRAME, TERMINAL SERVER.

virtual private network (VPN) A wide area network (WAN) that connects private subscribers (for example employees of the same company) together using the public Internet as the transport medium, while ensuring that their traffic is not readable by the Internet at large. All the data is encrypted to prevent others from reading it, and authentication measures ensure that only messages from authorized VPN users can be received.

A VPN joining two widely separated local area networks (LANS) belonging to the same

company typically employs a TUNNELLING PROTOCOL to send PACKETS that do not interact with any Internet host except the destination gateway at the other end of the link. Encryption need only be applied to the data as it passes through each gateway to and from the Internet, and not within the local networks. See also POINT-TO-POINT TUNNELLING PROTOCOL, L2F.

virtual reality (VR) An advanced form of 3D GRAPHICS that tries to create the illusion of a real three-dimensional space. The most ambitious form of VR, called IMMERSIVE virtual reality, employs a head-mounted stereoscopic LCD display, resembling a large ski-goggle. This tracks movements of the observer's head, and continually redraws the displayed scene to compensate for the continually changing viewpoint. This gives the impression that the observer is completely surrounded by, and is moving through, a collection of real three-dimensional objects, complete with lighting, shadows and perspective. An additional refinement is to have the observer wear a DATA GLOVE whose embedded sensors track the position of the fingers, allowing them to grasp and manipulate virtual objects in the virtual world. Immersive VR systems are used in simulations (for example of complex engineering layouts), in computer games, and for TELEPRESENCE applications where a surgeon or repair engineer can examine a virtual model of some remote problem site.

In the less ambitious, non-immersive form of VR, the 3D scene remains confined behind a conventional VDU screen, but the observer can travel through it at will, navigating with a mouse, joystick or other steering device. Again the display is continually adjusted to the correct viewpoint, giving the impression that the VDU is the windscreen of a vehicle travelling through the scene. This form of VR is extensively used by architects and planners to allow people to walk through models of new developments, and in simulators for training aircraft pilots, soldiers and sailors.

It is important to distinguish between the 3D graphical effects employed in films such as *Jurassic Park*, and virtual reality proper. A film with 3D effects presents only a single viewpoint, which the audience cannot vary, and the film-makers may have had the luxury of taking hours to create the image for each single frame. A virtual reality system must draw every frame in real time, as the software cannot know in advance where the observer will wish to go – this requires extraordinarily high performance of the graphics system. Every detail of every object in the virtual world must be recorded in a database of 3D information, the size of which sets limits both to the extent of the virtual world and to the level of realism that can be depicted.

Virtual Reality Modelling Language See VRML.

virus A small computer program that is capable of copying itself from one computer to another, thus emulating a biological virus that infects new hosts. Viruses are almost always written with malicious intent, and may inflict damage on the computer they infect. The damage ranges from temporarily corrupting its screen display or slowing down its operation, through deleting certain files, up to erasing its entire hard disk. The most dangerous viruses do not act immediately after infection but often lie dormant for long periods until triggered by some event, such as reaching a particular date (Friday the 13th is popular) or running a certain program.

Writing a virus is technically demanding, so they are always written for the most popular brands of computer, where there exists a reasonable chance that they will replicate. Historically they have been mainly confined to IBM-COMPATIBLE PCs and the Apple MACINTOSH. The first virus was probably the 1987 Lehigh virus, followed by the more widely infectious Stoned, Jerusalem and Cascade viruses, all of which infected PCs running MS-DOS.

These early viruses disseminated themselves via a FLOPPY DISK, copying themselves into the BOOT SECTOR of the HARD DISK of any computer that was booted from that floppy. Their spread was exacerbated by people taking floppy disks to work to play games, and exchanging pirated software on floppies. Once software became too big for floppies, this class of virus almost died out, as they cannot infect the read-only CD-ROM. Now almost all viruses are disseminated via the INTERNET, either by the downloading of files that they have infected, or hidden in an ATTACHMENT to an EMAIL (see for example MELISSA VIRUS).

There are three main categories of virus. *Boot sector viruses* infect that hidden region of a hard or floppy disk, and are mainly spread via removable media. *File viruses* attach themselves to program or data files (which therefore increase slightly in size, a fact that is used to detect the virus) and may be spread via removable media, a LAN or the Internet. Script or *macro viruses* are written in the SCRIPTING LANGUAGE of a popular application such as Microsoft Word and can be simply included in any document without resorting to programming trickery. They are almost always spread via email attachments (see EMAIL VIRUS).

A whole industry has arisen to produce ANTI-VIRUS SOFTWARE that detects and removes viruses. However, virus writers keep one step ahead with ever more devious tricks, such as encrypting the VIRUS SIGNATURE to foil detection, or mutating into different variants. See also WORM.

virus scan The process of searching a hard disk, or a network data stream, to detect the presence of computer viruses. ANTI-VIRUS SOFTWARE software typically offers at least two modes of operation: the operator may explicitly order a scan to take place, or the software may perform continuous scanning as a BACKGROUND TASK, inspecting all file movements between computers as they occur. The latter mode can impinge on system performance, since there are thousands of VIRUS SIGNATURES that need to be searched for.

virus signature A sequence of bytes that is characteristic of a particular computer VIRUS, and which can therefore be used by ANTI-VIRUS SOFTWARE to detect its presence.

Visicalc The first SPREADSHEET program for personal computers, written in 1979 by Dan Bricklin and Bob Frankston for the APPLE II only. Visicalc was the first truly mass-market software product (see KILLER APP), and its success made the fortunes of Apple as well as its authors.

vision See under COMPUTER VISION.

Visual Basic (VB) The first widely used VISUAL PROGRAMMING LANGUAGE, launched by Microsoft in 1991. To write a program in Visual Basic, the programmer first constructs its USER

INTERFACE by dragging and dropping prefabricated control objects (such as BUTTONS, LIST BOXES and TEXT BOXES) from a palette called the Toolbox onto a blank form. Clicking on such a control opens an editor window into which the programmer may type Basic language commands that specify what is to happen when this control is activated (e.g. when a button is pressed). Visual Basic is an INCREMENTALLY COMPILED language and a program that is partially developed can be tested at each step by running it.

Visual Basic programs are partially INTERPRETED and are therefore not as fast as fully compiled C++ programs, but the speed penalty is within acceptable bounds for many classes of application. Later versions of Visual Basic added powerful database access and CLIENT/SERVER features, and the latest version 7 can generate fully distributed applications that run from a web site.

Syntactically, Visual Basic resembles a hybrid of old-fashioned BASIC and PASCAL, and supports most of the features needed for structured and OBJECT-ORIENTED programming.

Visual Basic Extension See VBX.

Visual Basic for Applications (VBA) A subset of the VISUAL BASIC programming language that is embedded into all the applications in the MICROSOFT OFFICE suite (e.g. Word, Excel and Outlook) as their SCRIPTING LANGUAGE.

Visual C++ A VISUAL PROGRAMMING environment and C++ compiler published by Microsoft.

Visual Component Library (VCL) The CLASS LIBRARY supplied with Borland's DELPHI programming language.

visual display unit See VDU.

Visual Foxpro See under FOXPRO.

Visual InterDev An Internet development tool from Microsoft that enables WEB SITES to be constructed and connected to databases using VISUAL BASIC, VBSCRIPT, JAVA and ACTIVE SERVER PAGES.

visualization The use of computer graphics to analyse numeric data and present it in flexible and comprehensible forms, particularly using 3D effects and rotation of models to reveal different aspects. The term is usually applied to those large systems that employ SUPERCOMPUTERS to create interactive animated models in domains such as meteor, particle physics and engineering. However, modern multimedia PCs are now powerful enough to perform visualization. See also SIMULATION, FALSE COLOUR.

Visual J++ A VISUAL PROGRAMMING environment published by Microsoft for the JAVA language.

visual programming language (VPL) A programming language in which the user interface parts of a program may be rapidly constructed by dragging prefabricated graphic images (buttons, icons, list boxes and so on) onto a blank form, rather than by writing textual descriptions of them. Some of these CONTROLS are supplied with the language, but others may be purchased as accessories and added to the toolbox. Visual programming is typically used to speed the creation of user interfaces for database systems, a notable exception being SDL which is used for designing complex telecommunications equipment and applications.

Widely used examples include Microsoft's VISUAL BASIC, VISUAL C++ and VISUAL J++, Borland's DELPHI and Powersoft's POWERBUILDER.

VL bus See under VESA LOCAL BUS.

VLIW (Very Long Instruction Word) A type of computer processor that is constructed as a group of separate subunits (such as integer, floating point, load, store) whose operations are synchronized with one another only by the INSTRUCTIONS themselves, which consist of long strings of primitive operations. VLIW can be viewed as an extreme extension of the RISC principle, where scheduling is devolved away from the hardware and put into the software. The disadvantage of VLIW architectures is that they demand complex and 'intelligent' language compilers, and make software compatibility across different hardware generations very difficult to achieve. There have been no commercially successful VLIW implementations so far, though Intel and Hewlett Packard have adopted certain aspects for their next generation of CPUs.

VLM Abbreviation of VERY LARGE MEMORY.

VLSI (very large scale integration) A collection of techniques for building miniaturized electronic circuits on single chips of silicon. microprocessors, memory chips and other computer components are all built using VLSI techniques, and the current generation squeezes as many as 10 million TRANSISTORS onto a single chip.

VLSI fabrication is a batch process, in which several dozen chips are formed simultaneously on the same saucer-sized slice of pure crystalline silicon called a WAFER. The factory in which VLSI manufacturing is carried out is colloquially called a wafer fab or simply a fab. Applying all the many different layers of metal and chemical processing to each wafer can take several weeks, and has to take place in conditions of great cleanliness. The tracks on an Intel PENTIUM chip, for example, are only a few millionths of an inch apart, and even a single particle of smoke or dust is big enough to ruin the chip. The fab employs a filtered air supply, and the human workers, who supervise moving wafers from one processing station to another, must wear hermetically-sealed 'bunny suits' to prevent them from contaminating the chips, rather than vice versa. At the end of the process each wafer is cut up with a diamond saw to make individual chips, or DIES.

VLSI is only the latest step in an evolutionary sequence that began with the invention of the solid-state TRANSISTOR in 1947 by Bardeen, Brattain and Shockley at Bell Labs. Once it was realized that you could make a transistor from silicon alone, by DOPING different parts of it with elements such as arsenic, phosphorus and boron, it soon followed that you could form several transistors on the same piece of silicon and combine them to make a LOGIC GATE – the INTEGRATED CIRCUIT was born. Large scale integration followed in the 1970s, with thousands of transistors on a chip, and this was the technical basis of the minicomputer and the earliest microprocessors.

VM 1 Abbreviation of VIRTUAL MACHINE.
2 Abbreviation of VIRTUAL MEMORY.

VMEbus, VME (Versa Module Europa bus) A 32-bit backplane BUS which serves as both a system and expansion bus, accepting circuit boards of EUROCARD format. VME was introduced by Motorola and Philips in the mid-1980s and became popular for industrial and engineering applications, but was never adopted for personal computers. VME offers good support for multiprocessor operation, and is defined in an open standard IEEE 1014-1987.

VML (Vector Markup Language) An application of XML defined by the WORLD WIDE WEB CONSORTIUM for encoding diagrams and illustrations on web pages as VECTOR information. VML provides a very compact notation for describing shapes and groups of shapes as vector paths composed of straight lines and BEZIER CURVES, while additional markup information describes how such shapes should be displayed and edited. The resulting files may be much smaller than a BITMAPPED description of the same diagram, and they remain fully editable. VML files may also contain HTML constructs to describe any text content, and employ CSS to position the various elements on the page.

VML shape types, such as 'downarrow', are parameterized so that many different shapes can be generated from a single statement, as in this example:

```
<v:shape type="#downArrow" style=
'position: absolute; left: 77; top:
16; width: 64; height: 128' />
```

VMS (Virtual Memory System) The operating system of Digital Equipment Corporation's VAX mincomputer range, which was much admired for its excellent security features and its pioneering support for multiple processors through clustering (see under CLUSTERED SMP). Dave Cutler, its chief architect, later moved to Microsoft and incorporated much of his VMS experience into the design of the KERNEL of WINDOWS NT.

VNC Abbreviation of VIRTUAL NETWORK COMPUTING.

vocoder A device, either hardware or software, for compressing voice data in order to transmit it over a channel of limited bandwidth. It is used, for example, in many wireless and mobile phone applications. See also CODEC, ADAPTIVE PULSE CODE MODULATION.

VoD Abbreviation of VIDEO-ON-DEMAND.

voice activated Any device that responds to spoken commands. At it simplest, this might mean a tape recorder that records only when spoken into. At its most complex, it refers to computer applications that understand a large vocabulary of user commands.

voiceband The region of audio frequencies inhabited by the human voice. For the purposes of pre-digital telephony this was considered to be 300 to 3000 hertz.

voice control The use of spoken commands to operate a computer program. Currently the most sophisticated of such applications are voice-controlled WORD PROCESSORS, into which one can dictate text through a microphone, and use commands such as 'back' and 'delete' to edit and correct mistakes without recourse to a keyboard. Voice control is also deployed to control machinery in situations where the hands must be kept free or where a keyboard is inappropriate (such as military equipment or postal sorting depots) typically with a very restricted set of commands to avoid ambiguity (see LIMITED-VOCABULARY RECOGNITION).

voice grade line An ANALOGUE communications link designed primarily to carry VOICE-BAND signals.

voice interface A user interface based on spoken commands. See also VOICE CONTROL, VOICE ACTIVATED.

voicemail A system for recording and replaying speech messages via a telephone line or computer network. In telephone-based voicemail systems, each telephone number or extension has its own voicemail box. When that line is busy or not answered, callers will hear a recorded message from the owner like that on an ordinary answering machine, and will be offered options to record a message or be transferred to another extension or an operator. Computer-based voicemail systems store recorded messages as files on the HARD DISK, and these may be replayed and managed in a similar way to other types of message such as EMAILS and FAXES (see UNIFIED MESSAGING).

voice memo A short passage of recorded speech stored on a computer as an aid to memory, and which can be replayed via the computer's sound system. Word processing systems such as MICROSOFT WORD allow voice memos to be embedded as comments within a document.

voice message Recorded speech stored in digital form. Many MODEMS have a built-in voice messaging function that allows a PC to act as a telephone answering machine, and some communications programs (such as Lotus Notes and Microsoft Exchange) permit voice messages to be managed alongside faxes and emails in the same MAILBOX. It is also possible to embed voice messages into documents and spreadsheets. See also VOICE-MAIL, UNIFIED MESSAGING.

voicenet, voice-net A joking name for the public telephone system that is employed by habitués of the USENET.

voice-over-IP (VOIP) Also referred to as *Internet telephony*. The use of the Internet to make long-distance telephone calls. It is so-called because the voice data has to be digitized, compressed and then split up into packets that conform to the Internet's IP protocol. Voice-over-IP may be performed using a software PLUG-IN for a web browser running on a PC, and a microphone or handset attached to the PC's SOUND CARD.

The advantage of voice-over-IP is that Internet charging structures are not so dependent on duration or distance, so the longest calls incur considerable cost savings. The disadvantage is that when the Internet becomes congested very poor speech quality or loss of connection may be enountered.

voice recognition See SPEECH RECOGNITION.

voice server A network SERVER that is dedicated to receiving and storing VOICEMAIL messages.

VoIP Abbreviation of VOICE-OVER-IP.

volatile Any type of storage medium that is incapable of retaining its contents when its power supply is withdrawn. The most commonly encountered volatile storage medium is the DRAM used as the main memory in most computers, which loses its contents whenever the computer is switched off – hence any data that will be needed again must be copied onto a permanent MASS STORAGE device such as a HARD DISK before switching off. See also NON-VOLATILE

volt (V) The SI unit of electrical potential or ELECTROMOTIVE FORCE. It is defined as the POTENTIAL DIFFERENCE between two points that requires one joule of work to move a charge of one coulomb between the points.

volume A logical unit of disk storage made up from the space existing on one or more physical disks. Under operating systems such as MS-DOS, Windows, MacOS and Unix, the 'drives' that the user sees and may refer to by names such as C: and D: are volumes rather than physical drives. A volume may be made up of several drives in the same machine (see under RAID), or may be located on several different drives connected by a network (see under SPANNED VOLUME). See also DYNAMIC STORAGE, BASIC STORAGE, PARTITION, NETWORK FILE SYSTEM.

volume manufacture Full production, rather than PROTOTYPING or short-run production.

volume table of contents (VTOC) An alternative name for a disk DIRECTORY. A special file on a storage disk that contains a list of all the other files and the locations of their data. The term is used mostly in reference to older MAINFRAME disk drives, and to CD-ROMS. See also TABLE-OF-CONTENTS.

volumetric lighting A scheme for deriving the light intensities within a scene in 3D GRAPHICS by dividing up the space into small cubes called VOXELS and estimating the light flux through each one. The technique permits a more realistic rendering of light rays and beams than is possible by considering only surfaces. It is therefore supported by all the leading ANIMATION programs such as SOFTIMAGE and MAYA. See also RAY TRACING, RADIOSITY.

von Neumann, John Hungarian-American mathematician and logician, inventor of games theory and the CELLULAR AUTOMATON. A pioneer of computing whose contribution was such that the basic architecture underlying almost all modern computers is named after him. In 1945 von Neumann helped develop the logic for ENIAC, and in 1947 while working on its successor EDVAC he arrived at the concepts of the STORED-PROGRAM COMPUTER and the FETCH–EXECUTE CYCLE.

Voodoo graphics accelerator A popular 3D GRAPHICS ACCELERATOR card manufactured by 3Dfx.

voxel Short for volume element. The smallest distinguishable cubic region within a three-dimensional space, the position of which is specified by the X, Y and Z coordinates of its centre. A voxel is the analogue in 3D GRAPHICS of a PIXEL in 2D graphics (i.e. the smallest element from which an object representation may be composed. However, since they are not confined to the surface of objects, voxel values are not restricted to representing colours, and may equally encode other physical properties such as density or elasticity. The term is mostly used in modelling and medical imaging (for example in Computer Aided Tomography).

VP See VISUAL PROGRAMMING.

VPL See VISUAL PROGRAMMING LANGUAGE.

VPN Abbreviation of VIRTUAL PRIVATE NETWORK.

VR Abbreviation of VIRTUAL REALITY.

VRAM Abbreviation of VIDEO RAM.

VRML (Virtual Reality Modelling Language) A language used to describe 3D VIRTUAL REALITY scenes independently of any particular computer graphics system. In the same way that HTML text can be sent across the Internet to create a web page in a web browser, VRML text can be sent over the Internet to recreate a 3D scene in a suitably equipped browser. VRML originated in SILICON GRAPHICS INC.'s Open-Inventor graphics format, but is now an open web standard.

VRML describes the geometry and motion of objects in a scene by decomposing them into primitive solid shapes, and describing these with statements of the form:

```
Cube { width 45 height 12 depth 8}
```

V standards A series of PROTOCOLS for electronic devices that transmit data over the public telephone lines such as MODEMS and FAX machines, issued by the ITU over the last 30 years. Each successive V standard specified a transmission speed, a MODULATION scheme and sometimes an ERROR CORRECTION and COMPRESSION method. The principal V standards are:

V.21 300 bits per second (bps): public telephone modem
V.22 1200 bps: public telephone modem
V.22bis 2400 bps: public telephone modem
V.23 1200/75 or 1200/1200 bps: fax
V.26 2400 bps: private data line
V.27 4800 bps: LEASED LINE
V.27bis 4800 bps: equalized leased line
V.27ter 4800 bps: public telephone modem
V.32 9600 bps: public telephone modem
V.32bis 4800–14,400 bps: public telephone modem (rate adaptive)
V.34 28,800 bps: public telephone modem
V.90 56,000 bps: public telephone modem
V.110, V.120 ISDN terminal adapter (rate adaptive)

VT Abbreviation of VERTICAL TAB.

vt52 One of the earliest computer TERMINALS produced by DIGITAL EQUIPMENT CORPORATION and launched in 1978 for the PDP-8 MINICOMPUTER. Aimed at programming and text editing duties, the vt52 provided simple cursor control through a set of ESCAPE SEQUENCES, and is still supported as a TERMINAL EMULATOR type in most communications programs. See also VT100, VT220, CURSOR-ADDRESSABLE TERMINAL.

vt100 A computer TERMINAL produced by DIGITAL EQUIPMENT CORPORATION in the early 1980s. Its set of control codes became the basis of the standard ANSI TERMINAL and is supported by all terminal and PC manufacturers. See also TERMINAL EMULATOR, VT52, VT220, CURSOR-ADDRESSABLE TERMINAL.

vt220 The successor to DIGITAL EQUIPMENT CORPORATION's influential VT100 terminal. It offered extra features such as control over background colours and character attributes such as blinking and underlined text. See also ANSI TERMINAL, TERMINAL EMULATOR, CURSOR-ADDRESSABLE TERMINAL.

vtable Short for virtual function table, a table of pointers to method code maintained by an OBJECT-ORIENTED software system such as Microsoft's ACTIVEX.

VTOC Abbreviation of VOLUME TABLE OF CONTENTS.

VxD Abbreviation of VIRTUAL DEVICE DRIVER.

W

W3C, W3 Consortium See under WORLD WIDE
WEB CONSORTIUM

WABI See WINDOWS APPLICATION BINARY
INTERFACE

wafer A thin disk of pure
SILICON upon which many
INTEGRATED CIRCUITS are
constructed by a process
of LITHOGRAPHY. Each
wafer is cut with a dia-
mond saw from a salami-
shaped single crystal of silicon called a BOULE.
After all the many stages of lithography and
chemical processing, the wafer is sawn up into
individual chips or dies. The diameter of a
wafer is a crucial parameter in the economics
of chip manufacture, since it determines how
many chips can be made at one time, in what
is still a batch production process. Over the
last two decades, the largest diameter that can
be made has increased from 3 inches to 8
inches.

wafer fab See FAB.

wafer-scale integration The construction of
a whole computer system by fabricating various different INTEGRATED CIRCUITS on the
same WAFER and connecting them together
without cutting up the wafer. Once seen as
promising technology in the 1980s, it found-
ered because of yield problems, since a single
defective chip ruins the whole wafer.

WAIS (Wide Area Information Servers) A distributed information retrieval service that
runs over the Internet. WAIS servers maintain
a full-text index to all their documents, enabling fast and efficient keyword searches.
Many US government departments and agencies (such as NASA) store archives of documents and pictures in WAIS format. A special
feature of WAIS is its 'relevance feedback'
mechanism, which allows users to mark the
best matches, and then uses these to improve
future searches. WAIS may be accessed either
using dedicated client software, via GOPHER or
TELNET, or increasingly via WAIS search forms
embedded in WEB PAGES.

wait state A delay of one or more CLOCK
CYCLES deliberately added to the execution
time of a processor instruction to assist communication with a slower external device
such as a bank of RAM. The number and duration of wait states may be preset or controlled
dynamically via signals sent to a dedicated
processor pin. Memory that is fast enough to
keep up with the processor without wait
states is called *zero-wait-state memory*.

walk-through 1 A quality control procedure
that involves inspecting the code of a developing program, with its author explaining its
functions, line-by-line, to other programmers.
2 A VIRTUAL REALITY model of an architectural
or engineering design that enables viewers to
experience walking inside the proposed
layout.

wallet A small program, typically a plug-in for
a web browser, that is employed by many
micropayment (see MICROBILLING) schemes to
keep a record of the amount the user has
spent in online transactions. The wallet may
be periodically refilled with virtual money,
which is eventually charged to a real bank or
credit card account.

wallpaper An image, chosen by the user, that is displayed as a screen background in graphical operating systems (such as Microsoft Windows and Apple's MacOS), over which ICONS and other windows appear.

WAN (wide area network) A network that joins computers that are geographically widely separated – typically more than a kilometre apart in different buildings, towns, countries or continents. The Internet is a wide area network.

WAP Abbreviation of WIRELESS APPLICATION PROTOCOL.

warehouse See DATA WAREHOUSE.

warm boot The restarting of a computer's operating system without shutting off the power supply, in contrast to a COLD BOOT.

wastebasket An ICON that deletes any file that is dragged and dropped onto it. Under the original Apple MACINTOSH graphical interface it was called Trash, and other systems such as Windows have employed a wastebasket (*US* trash can) or RECYCLE BIN to create the same visual metaphor. The advantage of a wastebasket is that such deleted files can be undeleted at any point before the basket is emptied. See also UNDELETE.

watch Also called a *spy* or *spy-point*. A facility provided in most SYMBOLIC DEBUGGERS that enables the programmer to nominate particular variables, messages or events whose values will then be continuously displayed while the program is executed in SINGLE STEP mode. This allows the programmer to identify the exact point at which any error intervenes. See also BREAKPOINT, DEBUGGER, BUG.

watchdog A special subsystem that supports non-stop, unattended computer operation, and is often incorporated into computers that are to be used for EMBEDDED and REAL TIME control applications. It consists of a timer chip and a software process driven by its timing pulses that periodically interrogates the main program to see whether it still running. If the watchdog times out because the main program has HUNG, a hardware RESET is automatically performed to restart the system.

Watcom International A Canadian software vendor renowned for its C and C++ compilers and programming tools.

waterfall model An outdated model of the way that software development projects should proceed, which assumes a linear progression from SPECIFICATION through DESIGN and IMPLEMENTATION to final TESTING. The more recent SPIRAL MODELS stress an ITERATIVE development process in which repeated testing, redesign and reimplementation follow one another until an acceptable quality is achieved. See also LIFE-CYCLE, METHODOLOGY, CASE.

watt The SI unit of power, defined as the power dissipated by a current of one AMPERE flowing across a POTENTIAL DIFFERENCE of one VOLT. A watt is equivalent to 1.341×10^{-3} horsepower or one joule per second.

watt-hour The amount of energy delivered by a power of one WATT applied for one hour. It is equivalent to 3,600 joules.

WAV A popular file format for stored digitized sounds, developed by Microsoft and used by many Windows applications: so called because it uses .WAV as the FILENAME EXTENSION. WAV files are used by most WAVETABLE sound cards to load sound samples and as sound effects for games. Some MIDI SEQUENCERS allow WAVs to be incorporated into a MIDI performance.

wave A periodic variation or oscillation propagated through some material medium such as air or water, or an electromagnetic field in free space, which may be used to transmit energy or information from one place to another (see SIGNAL). The periodic behaviour of a wave is caused by a transfer of energy between two different modes of perturbation, for example between electrical and magnetic fields in a radio transmitter, between compression and rarefaction in a sound wave, and between vertical and horizontal displacements in a water wave. See also MODULATE.

wave file The popular name for WAV format audio files.

waveform The precise shape of a wave of some kind (electrical, sound, etc) when its varying property is plotted against time. If the wave has been MODULATED to carry a message, the waveform is a representation of this message. See AMPLITUDE MODULATION and FREQUENCY MODULATION, SIGNAL, WAVEFORM EDITOR.

waveform editor A type of program used to manipulate the contents of digitized sound recordings, such as those stored as WAV files. A typical waveform editor displays the sound sequence on the screen as a waveform (hence the name) that can be zoomed to the most appropriate magnification to isolate the section of interest. The user can visually select, cut and move sections of the waveform using the mouse, and then audition the results of each operation. The amplitude of selected portions of the wave may be altered in various ways (for example to fade out a sound), and special effects such as echo and reverberation may be applied.

The more sophisticated professional waveform editors support working on several sound sequences at once, cutting and mixing sections from each. Such programs often visually mimic the appearance of a recording studio mixing desk, as well as duplicating its operations.

waveguide A conductor used to convey ultra-high-frequency signals such as microwaves, radar and optical signals. Unlike simple wires, waveguides have an internal structure whose geometry is designed to confine and steer the signals by repeated reflection. For example, microwaves are often conducted through a hollow tube of rectangular cross-section.

wavelet A type of mathematical transform comparable to the FOURIER TRANSFORM in that it analyses a complex signal (e.g. a sound) into a set of simpler forms. However, where Fourier analysis transforms a signal into a collection of continuous sine waves of constant frequency and infinite duration, a wavelet transform converts it to a string of discrete, hump-like waveforms bounded in both frequency and duration: these are wavelets.

Real-world signals such as music or digital images are of finite duration and contain abrupt changes of frequency and rough edges, so the wavelet transform is more suited to processing them than the Fourier transform is, and can offer greater storage efficiency. A number of COMPRESSION algorithms based on wavelets are now in use.

wavetable synthesis A type of SOUND CARD in which the instruments that the synthesizer chip can imitate are not predefined, but may be loaded as data files into memory on the card, a popular example being Creative Technology's AWE32. By using suitable SAMPLING software, the user of such a card can even record their own new instrument sounds.

weakly typed See under TYPE CHECKING.

wearable computer A portable computer made small enough to be worn as jewellery or embedded into an article of clothing.

Web See under WORLD WIDE WEB.

web archive 1 A collection of documents or software made available remotely through a WEB SITE.
2 The name employed by Microsoft for a single file containing various different types of multimedia content encoded in MHTML format.

web authoring The activity of creating a WEB SITE by writing the HTML code that describes each page, assembling the text and images, and forming the HYPERLINKS to other pages. Web authoring is now typically performed using special software tools (such as FrontPage and Dreamweaver) that enable pages to be laid out interactively, rather like a restricted form of DESKTOP PUBLISHING.

web browser An application program whose purpose is to request and read pages from the WORLD WIDE WEB. The most widely used browsers are currently Microsoft's INTERNET EXPLORER and NETSCAPE NAVIGATOR.

The two main functions of a web browser are firstly to send out across the INTERNET a request for the page whose URL the user has typed into it, and secondly to interpret the HTML representation of the page that the remote WEB SERVER returns and display it on the user's computer screen. Most browsers also perform a number of additional functions, such as storing the URLs of frequently visited sites, and performing FTP file downloads. Most also accept PLUG-INS that enhance the browser so it can display special kinds of multimedia data such as animation, STREAM-ING video and audio or VOICE-OVER-IP telephone calls.

webcam Also called a *netcam*. A type of low-cost video camera that can be connected to a computer supporting a WEB SITE to provide online live video streams.

webcast 1 An alternative name for those PUSH technologies that involve sending selected World Wide Web content to customers over pre-defined channels, rather than waiting for the customers to request it.

2 A web access technology in which users send requests to the server over a land-based telephone connection as normal, but receive the returned pages via their satellite television set. Web data is inserted as a subchannel within a digital television signal and this allows for data rates of 250 kilobits per second to 2 megabits per second – much faster than the telephone BACK CHANNEL.

web clipping A technique for accessing the WORLD WIDE WEB from pocket computers, invented by 3COM CORPORATION for its PALM VII communicating pocket computer. Instead of providing a full WEB BROWSER to perform interactive web searches, in web clipping a query form is offered to the user to fill in, and the computer then connects briefly to the web and retrieves only the requested information.

WebCrawler One of the earliest SEARCH ENGINES on the WORLD WIDE WEB, so named because it 'crawls' around the web visiting sites in order to index their contents.

web form A form embedded in a WEB PAGE so that a reader of that page can fill in its fields with information (say to register for a service or to buy an article) and the entered data may then be passed to some other program running on the same WEB SERVER. Web forms can be written in HTML by using its Form, Input, Select, Option and Textarea tags. See also PERL SCRIPT, ASP, SERVER-SIDE.

webmaster The person who runs a WEB SITE.

WebObjects An APPLICATION FRAMEWORK, supplied with the NEXTSTEP operating system, that simplifies the writing of application programs that are connected to a WEB SERVER.

web page The basic unit of information published on the WORLD WIDE WEB. It consists of a document (perhaps including multimedia content such as images, video clips and sounds) that is encoded in HTML and stored on a computer running a WEB SERVER, so that it can be viewed remotely via the Internet using a WEB BROWSER. The Hypertext Transfer Protocol (HTTP) that lies at the heart of the web works by requesting a single web page at a time, so a new page is requested every time the user clicks on a LINK.

Beyond the limited formatting features supported by HTML (variable type sizes and colours, tables, etc) many more functions (such as database searches, calculations or complex graphical animations) can be embedded into web pages by creating links to external programs, using various methods including CGI scripts, JAVA applets and ACTIVEX objects.

web ring A group of WEB SITES that each contain LINKS to the next, in circular fashion, typically all dealing with the same subject.

web search An operation that locates occurrences of a particular text or image by using a SEARCH ENGINE to examine the contents of millions of WEB SITES.

web server A program that accepts requests from remote WEB BROWSERS and returns WEB PAGES that can be viewed in the browser – hence one of the crucial software components that enable the WORLD WIDE WEB to function. More properly called an HTTP server, such a server accepts HTTP protocol requests across a TCP/IP network, and returns documents formatted in HTML. Multiple web servers may run on the same computer so long as they use different PORT numbers.

The most widely used web server is the free, OPEN SOURCE program APACHE which runs under UNIX. There are also many commercially available web servers that offer special features for secure E-COMMERCE and other purposes. Most web servers support CGI, and Microsoft's INTERNET INFORMATION SERVER for example provides a second, more efficient binary interface called ISAPI. There is a growing tendency to build miniature web servers into electronic appliances (from laser printers and video cameras right down to light switches), to permit them to be controlled remotely from a web browser.

web service A type of distributed application that runs on a particular WEB SERVER, but which may be called from WEB PAGES on many other servers throughout the world. For example, a weather forecasting service might run on a meteorological bureau's server, but may be incorporated (usually for a fee) into millions of other company's sites merely by adding LINKS to it. The ability to create such web services forms a key part of Microsoft's .NET initiative and is supported in version 7 of VISUAL BASIC. See also SOAP, UDDI.

web site Any one of the virtual locations from which the WORLD WIDE WEB is constructed – a collection of related WEB PAGES with the same owner and stored on the same SERVER. More technically, a web site is a collection of documents encoded in HTML (Hypertext Markup Language), stored on a computer running a WEB SERVER program and connected to one another by HYPERTEXT LINKS. The URL of one (or more) of the pages is published, so that anyone can 'visit' (i.e. view) the site over the Internet by typing the URL into a WEB BROWSER running on their own computer (which may be anywhere in the world). See also HTTP.

Web TV A new class of entertainment medium that consists of a television set that can both receive normal programs and access the WORLD WIDE WEB. Eventually special programming content will permit web pages to overlay the television picture with additional information, for example to display a team line-up or statistics over a football match. These applications require a BROADBAND connection to the Web, either via CABLE, satellite or ADSL.

Web TV is also the name of the US company that is pioneering such technology, now owned by Microsoft.

well-behaved 1 Software that conforms to the interface standards for a particular operating system and employs the prescribed operating system services to access the hardware, rather than attempting to access it directly.

2 A mathematical function that exhibits only predictable, rather than chaotic or catastrophic, behaviour. See also NON-LINEAR.

well-formed Correctly created according to the rules of some syntax or grammar. For example, even though it does not exist, 020 7009 0000 is a well-formed UK telephone number, whereas 9090 is not. See also SYNTAX CHECKING, SYNTAX ERROR.

wetware Sardonic programmers' term for the human brain.

WFP Abbreviation of WINDOWS FILE PROTECTION.

WFW See WINDOWS FOR WORKGROUPS.

WGL4 (Windows Glyph List 4) A new pan-European CHARACTER SET containing 652 characters, created by Microsoft for the latest versions of Windows. WGL4 contains all the characters needed for Western, Central and Eastern European languages, including both the Cyrillic and Greek alphabet symbols. It incorporates the old CODE PAGES 1250 (Eastern), 1251 (Cyrillic), 1252 (ANSI), 1253 (Greek) and 1254 (Turkish), and employs the UNICODE character numberings for compatibility. See also ISO 8859.

What You See Is What You Get See WYSIWYG.

wheel mouse A variety of the MOUSE input device in which an extra thumb-wheel control is fitted between the mouse buttons. This is used to scroll documents up and down (particularly when reading web pages). See also INTELLIMOUSE.

Whetstone The first widely adopted benchmark for measuring a computer's FLOATING-POINT ARITHMETIC performance, developed by HJ Curnow and BA Wichman of the UK National Physical Laboratory in 1976 and named after a town in Leicestershire. See also DHRYSTONE, LINPACK.

whiteboard A type of computer display that allows several people to simultaneously view an assortment of graphical images and annotate them. Microsoft's NetMeeting VIDEO-CONFERENCING software contains such a facility. Some such systems employ an actual whiteboard (or an easel with a flipchart) that doubles as a GRAPHICS TABLET, so that anything written on it by the lecturer is duplicated on a computer screen, possibly at remote locations via a network.

White Book 1 A standards document issued in 1994 that redefines the format for the data CD-ROM disk to make it more fully compliant with the ISO 9660 logical data format. The White Book format enhances and replaces the earlier YELLOW BOOK standard. See also RED BOOK, GREEN BOOK, ORANGE BOOK.

2 Kernighan and Ritchie's definitive textbook *The C Programming Language* which is the final authority on matters of C syntax.

white pages An Internet DIRECTORY SERVICE for locating people by name, so called by analogy with the (white) US telephone directory. It consists of a database of individual's EMAIL address, telephone numbers and postal addresses.

white paper A technical document describing the workings of a technology, rather than a specific product.

whois An Internet DIRECTORY SERVICE that enables the real names of users on remote servers to be looked up. From the Unix command line the command 'whois -h bigserver.com jo' would return the real name of the user nicknamed 'jo' on the bigserver system, assuming that the issuer of the command has the necessary security permissions to be given access to this information. Whois can also return information about the resources (such as servers, subnetworks and domains) available at a site. See also WHITE PAGES, FINGER, PING.

Wide Area Information Servers See WAIS.

wide area network See WAN.

wideband Any signal channel that simultaneously carries a large number of different frequencies. See also BROADBAND.

Wide SCSI, Wide Ultra SCSI See under SCSI.

widget An all-purpose nonsense word used by engineers and programmers to describe any small device or gadget that defies easier description. The term is often employed to stand for whole classes of real objects in tutorial examples (particularly for DATABASES, where widget manufacturers abound). See also METASYNTACTIC VARIABLE.

The term is also widely used in discussion of GRAPHICAL USER INTERFACES, to describe visual controls such as scrollbars or buttons (possibly because it suggests a contraction of 'windows gadget'). It has, in fact, been adopted as the official name for the various visual components of the MOTIF graphical user interface for UNIX systems.

Wi-Fi The brand name (short for either wireless-fidelity or wide-fidelity) given to the IEEE 802.11b standard for wireless networking. Wi-Fi employs the ETHERNET protocols over short-range radio connections to create wireless LANs suitable for businesses and institutions located on a single site. It operates in the same 2.4 gigahertz (Industry, Science and Medicine) radio band as BLUETOOTH, but has a longer range (about 100 metres from each base station or 'access point', compared to Bluetooth's 10 metres). Some computer manufacturers, including Apple and Compaq, have begun to build Wi-Fi links into their equipment.

wildcard A special character or sequence of characters that matches any other character when performing text searches and comparisons. The term derives from card games like Poker, where a particular card such as the Joker may be deemed to stand for any card when making a hand.

Most operating systems support wildcard filenames when copying and deleting, and most WORD PROCESSORS offer them in their SEARCH-AND-REPLACE functions. A common convention, used in both MS-DOS and UNIX is to let ? stand for any single character and * stand for any sequence of characters, so that: ch?p matches chip, chop and chap, but not chit; and ch* matches chalk, cheese, chowder, but not clown.

See also REGULAR EXPRESSION, PATTERN MATCHING.

WIMP A whimsical term used to describe GRAPHICAL USER INTERFACES in the days when they were still a novelty. Short for Windows, Icons, Mouse, Pull-down menus.

Win 9x See WINDOWS 9x.

Win16 The 16-bit APPLICATION PROGRAMMING INTERFACE employed by all versions of Microsoft WINDOWS prior to WINDOWS 95. Programs written for Win16 require special treatment (see under THUNK), if they are to run under later 32-bit version of Windows.

Win32 An APPLICATION PROGRAMMING INTERFACE that is common to all the fully 32-bit and the hybrid 16/32-bit versions of the Microsoft WINDOWS operating system, including WINDOWS 95, WINDOWS 98, WINDOWS NT and WINDOWS 2000, and which therefore allows them all to run the same 32-bit programs. See also WIN32S.

Win32s A free extension released by Microsoft for 16-BIT version of WINDOWS to enable them to run 32-BIT programs.

Win 95 An abbreviation of WINDOWS 95.

Win 98 An abbreviation of WINDOWS 98.

WinBench A family of benchmarks, developed by the Ziff-Davis Publishing Corporation through its *PC Magazine* for PC systems running WINDOWS. WinBench tests all the major component subsystems of the PC: processor and RAM, HARD DISKS, CD-ROM, and GRAPHICS CARD full-motion video and 3D performance. The individual components of the suite deliver their results as WinMark scores. See also WINSTONE.

Winchester disk The IBM internal code name given to its miniature HARD DISK drive, developed in 1973. The name Winchester technology subsequently became attached to all such floating-head drives. It has been suggested the name derives from the Winchester 30/30 rifle because the drive either had two 30 megabyte platters or a 30 millisecond access time.

window A rectangular area on a computer display screen that behaves like a miniature display in its own right – that is, the text CURSOR will not move beyond its borders, and its contents may be SCROLLED independently of the rest of the screen. Several programs may run at the same time, each in its own window, and the user can switch between these instantly by clicking the mouse in the desired window. Most modern operating systems allow windows to overlap and to be dragged around to any desired position, so as to make best use of the limited screen space.

A window typically has a border that displays the name of the program running in it, along with several control BUTTONS that close, MINIMIZE (reduce to an ICON) or MAXIMIZE (zoom to fill the whole screen) the window. A window may be resized, normally by dragging on its borders or on special HANDLES at its corners using the MOUSE POINTER.

window border A thin region of screen surrounding the main area of a screen WINDOW, which may be dragged with the mouse pointer to resize the window. See also TITLE BAR.

window manager That section within a GRAPHICAL USER INTERFACE to control the opening, closing, sizing and placement of WINDOWS on the screen, and also their visual properties (such as the style of borders and control buttons). Some such interfaces, especially those based on the X WINDOW SYSTEM, permit the user to install alternative window managers to change the appearance of the interface without altering its functions. See also CONTROL, SCREEN FURNITURE, SKIN.

window RAM (WRAM) A fast variety of VIDEO RAM whose performance is enhanced by accelerated, aligned block fill and move operations, which speed up BIT BLOCK TRANSFER and similar operations.

Windows The most widely used computer OPERATING SYSTEM, published by MICROSOFT CORPORATION for IBM-compatible PCs. Windows employs a GRAPHICAL USER INTERFACE that enables the computer's user to work with multiple programs at the same time, each in its own screen WINDOW (hence the name). Windows provides basic utilities for file management and simple text editing, and in its later versions comes with support for connecting to a LAN and to the INTERNET. Windows imposes a set of user interface conventions that ensure that most applications, from whatever vendor, share a broadly similar LOOK-AND-FEEL (for example in the layout and naming of MENUS) that eases the task of learning a new program.

Windows version 1 was released in 1985, and consisted merely of a cosmetic user interface layered over the old text-based MS-DOS. Later versions added real enhancements, such as better memory management and MULTITASK-ING ability. During this process, Windows borrowed several features from the MACINTOSH user interface which provoked a partly successful law suit (though in fact Apple had itself borrowed many of these features from research done at Xerox PARC in the 1970s).

It was not until version 3.0 that Windows won over most PC users and became the best-selling operating system in the world. From WINDOWS 95 onwards it has progressively jettisoned the remains of the underlying MS-DOS and became a full operating system in its own right. The current version is WINDOWS 2000. See also WINDOWS NT, WINDOWS CE.

Windows 9x A generic term for any of the Microsoft operating systems WINDOWS 95 or WINDOWS 98 and their various versions.

Windows 95 A major revision of Microsoft Windows released in 1995 that greatly improved the operating system's use of memory, its multitasking and the user interface, and also eased the installation of new hardware devices. However, Windows 95 retained a significant amount of 16-bit code and did not completely dispense with the underlying use of MS-DOS to support its initial loading and its disk file system.

Windows 95 introduced a new task manager applet for killing errant processes and provided a separate 2 gigabyte address region for 32-bit applications, but it did not isolate this completely from 16-bit programs, which could still crash the system. It also failed to remedy a design flaw in earlier versions that permits programs to run out of system RESOURCES, even though plenty of main memory is available.

The new PLUG-AND-PLAY system ushered in by Windows 95 detects the presence of new EXPANSION CARDS and automatically loads drivers for them, which significantly simplifies the job of configuring a new PC, though the system does not work with many older ISA BUS cards. The new Windows 95 user interface significantly changed the LOOK-AND-FEEL of Windows (making it even more similar to Apple's MACINTOSH) by allowing icons to be placed directly onto the DESKTOP (instead of

confining them within windows), and by introducing SHORTCUTS and the START MENU as alternative means to launch programs. Windows 95 also provided more extensive networking features, including a built-in TCP/IP PROTOCOL STACK.

Internally Windows 95 remained a hybrid 16/32-bit system despite some superficial similarities to the fully-32-bit WINDOWS NT (see THUNK). See also WINDOWS 98.

Windows 98 A relatively minor revision to Microsoft's WINDOWS 95 operating system released in 1998. Its principal new features were the integration of the INTERNET EXPLORER web browser into the DESKTOP (see more under ACTIVE DESKTOP), and support for several important new hardware technologies including the USB fast serial port and AGP graphics adaptors. However Windows 98 was essentially built around the Windows 95 (rather than the WINDOWS NT) KERNEL and so remains a hybrid 16/32-bit operating system, retaining also Windows 95's vulnerability to being crashed by 16-bit applications or by running out of RESOURCES. Windows 98 does, however, introduce some enhancements to improve system stability (including the SYSTEM FILE CHECKER) and some efficiency improvements in the way that applications are loaded, cached and swapped to disk.

Microsoft had intended Windows 98 to be the last version of Windows to contain any 16-bit code, or to require the presence of MS-DOS. However, it has released two further versions called Windows 98 SE (Second Edition) and Windows 98 ME (Millenium Edition) which include only minor cosmetic enhancements. Windows 98 ME is still the operating system shipped with most consumer PCs, though it is intended that it will eventually be displaced by the fully 32-bit WINDOWS 2000.

Windows 2000 The latest version of Microsoft's Windows operating system, previously named WINDOWS NT version 5. Windows 2000 is a full 32-BIT operating system that contains many new features aimed at mobile and large-scale network server applications, including a fully distributed DIRECTORY SERVICE. Other features new to Windows 2000 include protection of key system files against being overwritten; an improved mechanism for installing applications, and better security provisions such as encryption at file or folder level.

Windows Application Binary Interface (WABI) A software interface written by SUN MICROSYSTEMS that enables many Microsoft WINDOWS programs to be run on UNIX systems by redirecting Windows library calls to the X WINDOW SYSTEM to provide equivalent graphical functions. Even computers using non-Intel compatible CPUs (such as the SPARC and POWERPC) can run Windows code under WABI, since it includes processor EMULATION for non-Intel instructions.

Windows CE An operating system created by Microsoft for use in hand-held computers, mobile telephones and in EMBEDDED SYSTEMS. It has some degree of compatibility with desktop Windows, but is built on an entirely different REAL TIME kernel. Windows CE is a full 32-BIT operating system, but is not capable of running most Windows programs in unmodified form. Special versions of the key MICROSOFT OFFICE applications including Pocket Word and Pocket Excel have been written for it. See also POCKET PC.

Windows File Protection (WFP) A security mechanism introduced in Windows 2000 under which the operating system runs a BACKGROUND TASK that continually checks the contents of one or more protected folders. If it detects an attempt to replace or modify a protected file, then the modified file (typically, a DLL) is immediately replaced with the correct version from a special CACHE maintained for this purpose. See also SYSTEM FILE CHECKER, DLL HELL.

Windows for Workgroups (WfW) A version of Microsoft's popular WINDOWS 3.1 that added support for NETWORKS, released in 1992.

Windows Internet Naming Service See WINS.

Windows Media Audio A streaming music data format launched by Microsoft in 1999. It claims to offer better reproduction quality and smaller file sizes than its popular rival MP3 format. See also REALAUDIO.

Windows messaging An alternative name for Microsoft's email system also called EXCHANGE.

Windows Metafile Format (WMF) A compact VECTOR GRAPHICS file format devised by Microsoft for use in early versions of Windows and now supported by most graphics, desktop publishing applications and web authoring programs. See also BMP/DIB.

Windows NT Standing for Windows New Technology, Microsoft's first full 32-BIT operating system. NT marked a radical break in the development of the WINDOWS operating system by finally dispensing with the underlying MS-DOS file system and providing a new one called NTFS, which offers more professional security, fault-tolerance and larger disk capacities. Windows NT is also more stable than previous versions of Windows, thanks to better memory protection in its MULTITASKING kernel. As a result it has found more use as a network client and server operating system than on single-user PCs, for which Windows 98 remains the most popular operating system.

The first NT version, 3.1 was introduced in 1993, and NT4 (4.0), the most popular version, in 1997. WINDOWS 2000 is in fact a renamed version 5 of Windows NT, and is intended eventually to reunite Microsoft's consumer and professional operating system product lines.

Windows Printing System A combined hardware and software system introduced by Microsoft for printing documents from Windows PCs. It dispenses with PAGE DESCRIPTION LANGUAGES such as PCL and POSTSCRIPT and employs the PC's own CPU to preprocess the data and send a rasterized image (see RASTERIZER) to the printer. The printing system communicates directly with the Windows GRAPHICAL DEVICE INTERFACE and hence is totally platform-dependent. As a result it both increases printing speed and yields nearly perfect WYSIWYG results, since there is no translation between different imaging models: the same commands that produce the screen display also produce the printed image (though their RESOLUTIONS may differ). The printing system establishes a two-way connection with the printer, enabling the printer status to be reported on the PC screen in real time via animated pop-up windows that show the paper moving through the printer, and can flag paper jams or out-of-paper errors.

For printer manufacturers, an attraction of the Windows Printing System is that it enables them to make cheaper laser printers that need less internal RAM and a less powerful processor, since most of the processing is done at the PC end. The disadvantage is that such printers cannot be used with computers running any other operating system. Also, the bidirectional reporting functions work only on a locally attached printer.

Windows Scripting Host (WSH) A Microsoft technology introduced for Windows NT4, and now built into WINDOWS 2000, that permits scripts written in various languages to gain direct access to the Windows APPLICATION PROGRAMMING INTERFACE. The WSH comes with support for scripting in Visual Basic Script (see VBSCRIPT) and JAVASCRIPT but it provides an interface via which other languages and their runtime systems can be added by third parties: Perl, Rexx, TCL and Python are already available by this route. See also SCRIPTING LANGUAGE, ACTIVE SERVER PAGES.

Windows SDK See under SOFTWARE DEVELOPERS KIT.

Windows sockets See WINSOCK.

WINE A SHAREWARE emulator that enables WINDOWS programs to be executed on UNIX systems.

Winframe A MULTIUSER application server based on the WINDOWS NT operating system, created by the US company CITRIX. Winframe permits multiple users to run NT applications on a single central server, using relatively low-powered terminals that need only display the application's user interface. They may therefore be non-Intel compatible computers (such as Apple MACINTOSHES or even hand-held or pocket computers) so long as there is a version of Citrix's CLIENT software available for them. See also Citrix ICA, TERMINAL SERVER.

Wingdings A FONT that consists solely of symbols and logos rather than alphabetic characters – examples being ☎☺⌨⌨➜ – which is supplied with Microsoft's Windows operating system.

WinMark The name given to the individual results produced by *PC Magazine*'s WINBENCH benchmark suite.

WINS (Windows Internet Naming Service) A service supplied by Microsoft's Windows 95, 98 and NT operating systems to resolve Internet-style HOSTNAMES into IP ADDRESSES, allowing NETBIOS-based Microsoft networking software to access servers across the Internet. See also DYNAMIC HOST CONFIGURATION PROTOCOL.

Winsock (Windows sockets) A network-independent interface between applications running under Microsoft Windows that is most commonly employed to interface Windows applications (such as web browsers) to the Internet. Winsock is modelled on the SOCKET concept introduced in Berkeley Unix (see BSD), and sits on top of a network-dependent component that supports some specific network PROTOCOL STACK, normally TCP/IP. See also PPP, SLIP, SECURE SOCKETS LAYER.

Winstone An application-based benchmark suite, created by Ziff Davis Publishing's *PC Magazine* for PCs running Windows. Winstone works by timing the running of various real-world application programs including Microsoft Word, Access, Excel and PowerPoint, Netscape Navigator, CorelDraw, Adobe Photoshop and Premiere. See also WINBENCH.

Wintel A contraction of 'Windows' and 'Intel', used as a shorthand to mean any computer that runs a version of the Microsoft WINDOWS operating system on an Intel 80x86 family (or compatible) processor: that is, a mainstream IBM-COMPATIBLE PC.

WinZip A widely used SHAREWARE file COMPRESSION program for Windows PCs that employs the popular ZIP FILE format. See also PKZIP.

wire Any thin metal strip used to conduct electric currents. It is also informally used to refer to the tracks on an INTEGRATED CIRCUIT chip or PRINTED CIRCUIT BOARD, and to NETWORK cabling.

Wired The most successful paper magazine devoted entirely to the INTERNET culture, launched in San Francisco in 1993.

wire-frame A representation of the surface of a 3D object in terms of lines alone – for example a mesh of joined triangles or other polygons. Once a wire-frame representation has been built it may be RENDERED to create a realistic 3D image, by applying to the face of each polygon SMOOTH SHADING, which takes account of the object's colour and the ambient lighting.

Wireless Application Protocol (WAP) A wireless communications standard developed jointly by ERICSSON, NOKIA, MOTOROLA and Phone.com that permits mobile phones and pocket computers to read email and web-based information. WAP is a high-level protocol that defines a format for documents to be sent to mobile devices, and is accompanied by an HTML-like MARKUP LANGUAGE called WML, which is adapted to the tiny displays available on such devices.

wireless communications Any means of communication in which the sender transmits a message using radiation that travels through free space, rather than there being a fixed conducting path to the receiver. The term is generally used of systems that employ electromagnetic radiation in the radio or infrared regions of the spectrum, though systems based on visible light or sound may, strictly speaking, be wireless too.

A distinction can be drawn between long-range wireless communications (which include broadcast radio and television and MOBILE PHONE systems) and short range systems that are used to connect local devices. For example, line-of-sight infrared links are employed to connect remote control handsets to televisions and hi-fis, mice and keyboards to desktop computers, and portable comput-

ers to printers. Radio links may be used, as in the BLUETOOTH system, to connect portable devices to a larger wired network via strategically-placed receiving nodes. See also WAP, GSM, WI-FI, CDMA, TDMA, WLAN, DSSS, FHSS.

Wireless Markup Language The language used to mark up documents to be sent to a mobile device via the WIRELESS APPLICATION PROTOCOL.

wire-wrap An early prototype of a hardware circuit design, made by mounting discrete electronic components onto a perforated tray called a BREADBOARD and connecting them together by wires wrapped around protruding metal pins (hence the name).

Wirth, Niklaus (b. 1934) Swiss professor of computer science, co-inventor of STRUCTURED PROGRAMMING and creator of the PASCAL, MODULA-2 and OBERON programming languages. Wirth is best known for his formula 'Algorithms + Data Structures = Programs'. His beneficial influence on the infant art of computer programming would be impossible to overestimate.

wish list A list of desired features to be added to a software product, submitted by users or testers.

wizard **1** A style of interactive user interface component that leads the user through a complex configuration process in a step-by-step fashion. A wizard may encourage the user, for example, to fill in a TEXT BOX or tick a CHECK BOX and then press the Next button to continue to the next step, or press the Back button to undo previous choices. Wizards were introduced by Microsoft as part of WINDOWS 95, but are now employed very widely.
2 One of the ranks adopted by players in multiuser role-playing games.
3 A talented expert in the use of a particular product, as in 'a Photoshop wizard' or 'C++ wizard'.

WK1 A FILENAME EXTENSION employed by LOTUS 1-2-3 SPREADSHEET files.

WLAN (Wireless LAN) A local area network (LAN) that uses radio waves instead of cables to connect workstations to the server. See also FHSS, DSSS, WI-FI.

WMA Abbreviation of WINDOWS MEDIA AUDIO.

WMF Abbreviation of WINDOWS METAFILE FORMAT.

WML Abbreviation of WIRELESS MARKUP LANGUAGE.

Wolfram Research, Inc. The US vendor of the SYMBOLIC MATHS program MATHEMATICA.

word A unit of data larger than a byte. It may be 16-bits or 32-bits in size depending on the WORD LENGTH of the processor in question. See also DOUBLEWORD, QUADWORD.

WordArt A graphical APPLET supplied with MICROSOFT WORD that enables its user to create fancy headlines by distorting, colouring and adding 3D effects to a short passage of text.

WordBasic A BASIC-based scripting language that was built into early versions of MICROSOFT WORD. It has been replaced (from Word 97 onwards) by VISUAL BASIC FOR APPLICATIONS which is now common to all the Microsoft Office applications.

Word for Windows See MICROSOFT WORD.

word length Also called *word size*. The size in bits of the largest data object that a particular computer can process in a single operation. Modern processor designs have made word length an ambiguous concept since they may contain different lengths of REGISTER for different purposes. However, word length is normally accepted as the width of the integer PIPELINE or REGISTER FILE, which may well differ from the width of any FLOATING-POINT UNIT (FPU) or external bus. For example, the Intel PENTIUM is considered a 32-bit processor, even though it employs an 80-bit FPU and a 64-bit memory bus.

WordMail The facility within MICROSOFT WORD to send EMAIL messages directly from the word processor. This is achieved via OLE integration between Word and the EXCHANGE mail program.

WordPerfect A WORD PROCESSOR originally written for MS-DOS PCs that was for some years the most popular writing tool among business users. However, its tardy and initially unsatisfactory transition to WINDOWS lead to it being displaced from this top placing

by MICROSOFT WORD. It is now owned by COREL and forms part of an OFFICE SUITE that has been ported to other operating systems, including LINUX.

word processing The preparation of documents using a WORD PROCESSOR.

word processor A program used to create, modify and print text-based documents. The word processor is the single most popular application for computers, and has almost completely replaced the typewriter in the production of business documents. A word processor enables a writer to easily alter all aspects of the text and layout of a document, in contrast to the typewriter, where a mistake often forces a complete retyping of the page. Current examples of popular word processing programs are MICROSOFT WORD, Lotus Word-Pro and Corel WORDPERFECT.

The basic function of a word processor is to allow words to be typed onto the MONITOR screen, to be manipulated in various ways, and then saved in a disk file and/or printed out on paper. All word processors support a similar set of basic text-editing functions: scrolling to view documents larger than the screen, automatic wrapping of lines when they reach the edge of the screen (or page), backspacing to replace a misstyped character, insertion of new text in the middle of existing text, selection of a whole passage to be deleted or moved, and automated searching that can find all occurrences of a particular word or phrase and replace it with another.

There is a fairly clear distinction between a TEXT EDITOR, which performs just these basic editing functions, and a word processor, which is further concerned with the appearance of the finished text. Word processors enable the use of different type faces (see FONT) and character styles such as bold, italic and underline, and allow fine control over the placement of text on the page, far beyond the simple carriage returns and tabs used by a text editor. Modern word processors can display these attributes on the screen, more or less as they will appear when printed (see WYSIWYG). To remember the attributes of each item of text, the word processor stores information about the attributes in the same file as the text itself and, since each brand of word processor employs a different storage format, this means that documents created by one word processor must be viewed in the same word processor, or else be converted before viewing them with a different one.

All word processors now support sophisticated document layouts, including section headings and different paragraph indentations, as well as footnotes and tables of contents. Style sheets define uniform typographical styles that can be applied to whole paragraphs, pages or documents using a few keystrokes. Word processors increasingly include support for illustrations to be viewed in place in the document, multi-column text (as on this dictionary page), and elaborate formatting of headlines, and permit such highly designed pages to be saved in HTML format for use as WEB PAGES.

Word processors also offer a range of facilities to assist in the writing of documents: automatic spelling and grammar checking, built-in thesauruses, automatic correction of common spelling mistakes, and AUTO COMPLETION (in which the program offers to complete partly-typed words by making a guess based on what has been typed previously).

word size See WORD LENGTH.

Wordstar The first truly mass-market word processing program, published by Micro-Pro for the CP/M operating system in 1979. Wordstar's numerous three-key command sequences were devilishly hard to remember, but were in fact cleverly chosen to assist fast touch typists, which won it many ardent supporters. Wordstar pioneered many features now taken for granted in word processors, such as FULL-SCREEN editing, CUT-AND-PASTE and MAIL MERGE. Wordstar was later ported across to MS-DOS, but it failed to prosper in the era of WINDOWS.

word-wrap, wordwrap, word wrap To cause lines of text to wrap around automatically onto a new line when the right MARGIN is reached, without the user having to press the RETURN KEY. A word wrap is the default mode of input for all modern word processors. Only whole words are moved onto the new line, unless a HYPHENATION feature is active.

The advantage of word wrap is that it avoids embedding CARRIAGE RETURN characters into the text (a so-called HARD RETURN). This enables each paragraph to be stored as a single line internally, so the software can re-wrap it at will if the margin settings are altered.

workaround A trick used to compensate for some BUG in a software system.

workbook The name given to a set of SPREADSHEETS stored in the same file in Microsoft EXCEL.

workflow The scheduling of the various stages of a production process so that jobs pass more or less smoothly from the input to a final output. For example, insurance claim forms might pass through an office, where many different people have to read them, alter them and sign them off.

The term 'workflow management' is used to describe a type of software system, and even a whole market segment, that offers support for such processes by keeping track of the individual jobs. Often workflow systems consist of various independent software products (such as WORD PROCESSORS, SPREADSHEETS and DATABASES) integrated by an EMAIL system and an overall workflow management framework. This framework may automate the process of moving jobs from one operator to another, using certain events (such as completing a form) to trigger a move to the next stage.

workgroup A group of computer users, connected by a local network or the Internet, who share and work on the same set of documents. A workgroup therefore requires facilities for MESSAGING between individuals, CONFERENCING for larger groups, shared file editing, VERSION CONTROL of documents, and possibly for REPLICATION and SYNCHRONIZATION of portions of some large database. See, for example, LOTUS NOTES and WINDOWS FOR WORKGROUPS. See also REPOSITORY, WORKFLOW, GROUP CALENDAR, DOCUMENT MANAGEMENT SYSTEM.

working parameter One of a set of values stored in some hardware or software device that determine its current mode of operation.

work-related upper limb disorder (WRULD) An alternative term for RSI.

worksheet The name given to an individual SPREADSHEET in Microsoft EXCEL.

workspace 1 The screen display of a computer or an individual program, containing a number of data files open in separate windows. Some programs permit the saving of the workspace when they are closed down, so that it may be restored at the next session with all the same files open in the same windows.

2 The area of memory allocated for the running of user programs under an INTERPRETED PROGRAMMING LANGUAGE such as BASIC or LISP.

workstation **1** The small computer that each individual user of a NETWORK has on their desk, and which stores some or all of its programs and data on a central SERVER shared with other users. Nowadays most workstations are ordinary personal computers, which may contain little or no local disk storage of their own, depending upon the policy of the particular company (see DISK-LESS WORKSTATION). Some network operating systems (such as WINDOWS NT and WINDOWS 2000) come in different versions for running on a workstation or a server. See also GRAPHICS WORKSTATION, DUMB TERMINAL, SMART TERMINAL.

2 A cubicle, desk, or specially designed piece of computer furniture at which a single person may work a computer.

World-Wide Wait A joking reference to the long delays experienced when accessing the WORLD WIDE WEB.

World Wide Web (WWW) A set of technology standards that enables the publishing of multimedia documents (which may contain text, images, sound and video), to be read by anyone with access to the INTERNET. Using WEB BROWSER software running on a personal computer or workstation, users may type the address of a WEB PAGE anywhere in the world and see it displayed on their own screens. The WWW was invented by the British physicist Tim BERNERS-LEE working at the High-Energy Physics laboratories of CERN in Geneva, Switzerland in the early 1990s. The Internet at that time was a text-based medium, and the WWW was developed to facilitate the sharing of scientific papers. The web was opened up to the public in 1991 with the release of the first free web browser, MOSAIC, which was developed at the National Center for Supercomputing Applications in the USA.

The revolutionary feature of the WWW is that it permits HYPERTEXT links to be embedded in each page of information – clicking such a link with the mouse causes an immediate jump to another page, which may be located anywhere on the web, i.e. anywhere in the world. It is this feature that gives the web its very apt name, and has encouraged the emergence of a world-wide subculture of enthusiasts who use the web as a medium for communication and for free and uncensored publishing. This same ease of navigation makes the WWW attractive as a conduit for commercial sales activity (E-COMMERCE), which may one day replace conventional retail outlets.

Thanks to its scientific origins, the World Wide Web is a free public service, maintained by the non-profit WORLD WIDE WEB CONSORTIUM (of which Berners-Lee remains director). However, since it runs over the Internet, an Internet address or an account with an ISP (which usually costs money) is required to use it.

The WWW depends for its operation on three main software components: the Hypertext Markup Language HTML that describes what a web page should look like; a web browser that can interpret HTML and display it on a computer screen; and the Hypertext Transfer Protocol HTTP that enables a browser to send requests for pages across the Internet and returns HTML descriptions to it. Pages on the WWW are identified by unique labels called Uniform Resource Locators or URLs that look like, for example, http://www.penguin.com.

The Web is currently a read-only medium, so visitors can read published pages but cannot edit or alter them. However web pages can be designed to receive input from visitors by presenting a WEB FORM using various SCRIPTING technologies.

As well as links to other web pages, web pages can link to any object whose location can be described by a URL, including files and other resources accessible via other Internet protocols such as FTP. See also WEB SITE, WEB BROWSER, WEB SERVER, WEB SERVICE.

World Wide Web Consortium (W3C) The non-profit organization set up to maintain and develop the technology standards on which the WORLD WIDE WEB is based, including the HTTP protocol and the HTML and XML markup languages. In recent years, the W3C has branched out into technical innovation in its own right, developing graphical standards such as the PNG bitmap graphics format, the SVG vector graphics format, and various formats for use in next-generation interactive television and telephone services. The W3C is based in Cambridge, Massachusetts and at www.w3.org on the Web.

worm A type of invasive computer program, similar to a VIRUS but designed to infect networks rather than just individual computers. A worm propagates copies of itself from one networked machine to another by gaining illicit access to the EMAIL or file copying system. The famous Internet Worm of 1998 infected 6000 key network servers and brought Internet traffic to a standstill.

wormhole routing A high-speed network routing method, in which messages that arrive at a NODE may continue their journey to the next node before their end has arrived. Hence the message is conceptually threaded through the node like a worm through an apple. Each node needs to read only a few bits from the message HEADER to determine in which direction to forward it.

worst case A concept widely used in engineering and programming, where the required capacity of some system is assessed against the most difficult, rather than the average, tasks that it will face.

WOW (Windows On Windows) A software emulator written by Insignia Solutions that enables 16-bit WINDOWS programs to be executed on a 32-bit WINDOWS NT system running on a non-Intel processor such as the DEC ALPHA.

Wozniak, Steve (b. 1950) Co-founder along with Steve JOBS of APPLE COMPUTER INC. He is a talented hardware designer whose elegant chip designs for the Apple II were widely admired among engineers. Fortune made, he later left the computer industry to promote free music festivals.

WP Abbreviation of WORD PROCESSING and of WORD PROCESSOR.

WRAM Abbreviation of WINDOW RAM.

wrap-around A (usually undesirable) condition where some quantity in a program exceeds the maximum that can be represented by a number of its size, and either returns to zero or to a negative quantity. For example if 255 is stored as an 8-bit quantity (11111111 binary) then adding one to it yields 0. The YEAR 2000 BUG is a related type of problem.

wrapper A layer of software that mediates between other programs and some valuable resource that is to be protected or rationed. The term is most often used to describe a trick used when integrating older LEGACY CODE into a new OBJECT-ORIENTED software project, by enclosing the old code within an object whose methods then call it to perform calculations. In OBJECT-RELATIONAL DATABASE MANAGEMENT SYSTEMS, wrappers may be used to bundle up collections of queries and STORED PROCEDURES into objects.

writable Capable of having its content altered, the opposite of read-only.

write To place data into some storage device. For example a computer's processor might write data to its RAM or to an external magnetic disk. The term is also used as a noun, short for *write operation*, as in '25 writes per second'. See also READ.

write-back cache A type of processor CACHE design in which data is written to main memory only when it needs to be removed from the cache to make room for more. The advantage is speed, as most writes take place without incurring the cost of a memory access. The disadvantage is that a system crash could cause loss of unwritten data in the cache. The alternative WRITE-THROUGH CACHE scheme writes to cache and main memory simultaneously, thus avoiding this risk.

write-behind See under DISK CACHE.

write buffer A small area of memory provided inside a computer's processor into which one or more data words that are to be written to external memory can be placed. This allows the PROCESSOR CORE to proceed without pausing for the external WRITE to complete. Write buffers that hold more than one word are organized as FIFO (First In–First Out) queues. In a processor (such as a simple microcontroller) that does not use a CACHE, such a buffer can reduce or eliminate the need for WAIT STATES. In a processor with a cache it can reduce delays caused by contention between memory reads and writes. See also WRITE-THROUGH CACHE, WRITE-BACK CACHE.

write-enabled Said of a disk or other storage medium that has been set to a state where its contents may be altered.

write-once Any type of MASS STORAGE medium that (unlike a read-only medium) allows the user to write data to it but which cannot be erased or altered once it has been written to. Write-once media are therefore most useful for creating permanent data ARCHIVES, the most popular current example being the optical CD-R disk.

write-only code Poorly documented or cryptic program code that cannot be understood by anyone but its author.

write-protect To set a file or disk in a state where its contents cannot be altered.

write-through cache A variety of processor CACHE design in which every data item written into the cache is also simultaneously written to the associated main memory location. The

advantage of this scheme is greater security against data loss in the event of a software crash. The cost lies in slower performance than the alternative WRITE-BACK CACHE, owing to the longer write operation.

WRT Online shorthand for With Regard (Respect) To.

WRULD Abbreviation of work-related upper limb disorder, an alternative term for RSI.

WSH Abbreviation of WINDOWS SCRIPTING HOST.

WWW Abbreviation of WORLD WIDE WEB.

WYSIWYG (What You See Is What You Get) A phrase coined to describe graphical WORD PROCESSORS that can display different fonts and styles on screen, so giving a more or less true impression of what the printed document will look like. Before WYSIWYG, word processors employed embedded CONTROL CODES, with the result that the on-screen text bore no resemblance to the final output.

X

X.25 The ITU standard protocol for PACKET SWITCHING data networks. Issued in 1976, X.25 was the first standard packet protocol for public networks, and has been widely implemented around the world, for example as SPRINTNET and BT's TYMNET.

X.25 is a low-level protocol, defining only layers 1 to 3 of the OSI REFERENCE MODEL model. It was designed in the era of analogue communications, and hence employs a robust ERROR CHECKING scheme implemented in software, which limits transmission speed to 56 kilobits per second or less. For this reason, it has now mostly been displaced by FRAME RELAY and ASYNCHRONOUS TRANSFER MODE.

X.75 See X STANDARDS.

X.121 See X STANDARDS.

X.400 The ITU standard protocol for exchanging EMAIL, more used in Europe and Canada than in the USA (where SMTP is the dominant standard). X.400 to SMTP GATEWAYS permit mail to flow from one system to the other.

X.400 addresses are longer (and even more cryptic) than Internet mail addresses. They are typically composed of an Administrative Management Domain name, a Private Management Domain name and the user's first and last names, as in ADMD:MCImail, PRMD:WidgetLAN, FN:Joe, SN:Bloggs. The intention is that such names should rarely be typed manually, as X.400 is intended to be supported by X.500 directory services.

X.500 The ITU standard protocol for accessing online DIRECTORY SERVICES, such as WHITE PAGES and WHOIS. X.500 supports distributed directories that can contain many kinds of data, including the EMAIL addresses of personnel, and network addresses of resources such as file archives, printers or servers. X.500 directories can synchronize themselves to propagate changes, and for efficiency may be replicated onto many different computers.

The X.500 standard was issued in 1988, but it is so complex that compliant commercial implementations have been slow to emerge. Microsoft's WINDOWS 2000 includes an X.500 directory service based on the LIGHTWEIGHT DIRECTORY ACCESS PROTOCOL, which was invented to provide a simpler solution.

XA Abbreviation of EXTENDED ARCHITECTURE.

Xanadu A project launched by Ted NELSON in 1965 to create the first HYPERTEXT system for global document publishing. It was later bought by AUTODESK INC. who tried to bring it to commercial fruition. Xanadu has many advanced features, including a built-in system for automatic royalty payments, but its complexity caused it to be overtaken by the much simpler, if less powerful, WORLD WIDE WEB.

XbaseY A 'template' according to which the names of the standards for different kinds of ETHERNET cabling are formed, where X stands for the speed of the Ethernet in megabits per second, base stands for baseband (rather than radio frequency) and Y denotes the type of cable employed. Y is either a number specifying the longest permitted cable run in hundreds of metres, or a letter code indicating a type of wiring: T denotes TWISTED-PAIR cable, TX denotes CATEGORY 5 cable, F denotes OPTICAL FIBRE, and VG denotes voice grade (i.e. CATEGORY 3 UTP) cable.

Hence 10BASE2 is a 10 megabits per second Ethernet whose maximum cable span is 185 metres, while 100BASETX is Fast Ethernet over Category 5 cable.

X client A program running under the X WINDOW SYSTEM whose user interface is displayed on a remote X TERMINAL.

X Consortium The group of companies that develops and licences the X WINDOW SYSTEM, its chief members including SUN MICROSYSTEMS, IBM, HEWLETT-PACKARD and COMPAQ.

xDSL A generic acronym used by telecommunications engineers to refer to all of the DIGITAL SUBSCRIBER LINE technologies: ADSL, HDSL, SDSL, VDSL, RADSL and others.

XENIX A version of the UNIX operating system for INTEL processors, originally developed by Microsoft but later sold to the SANTA CRUZ OPERATION and now incorporated into SCO UNIX.

Xeon The name given by INTEL to members of its PENTIUM II and III microprocessor families intended for server applications, which feature extra large LEVEL 2 CACHES up to 2 megabytes. The Pentium III Xeon also features the STREAMING SIMD EXTENSIONS for faster FLOATING-POINT performance.

xerography The use of dry powdered pigments to create images (from the Greek for 'dry writing') as employed in photocopiers and LASER PRINTERS. Finely powdered TONER is attracted to a drum coated with a SEMICONDUCTOR, which bears the desired image as a pattern of electrostatic charge. From the drum it is impressed onto a sheet of paper, and then fixed by passing through a heater that briefly melts it.

Xerox Corporation A US company founded on making photocopiers. It moved into computers and document processing by setting up one of the most influential research laboratories at Xerox PARC.

Xerox Dorado Possibly the first true personal computer, an advanced workstation created at Xerox PARC in 1981 and used as the test-bed for the influential SMALLTALK-80 programming language. The Dorado derived from a previous experimental Xerox workstation, the Alto, but differed from it in that it was MICRO-PROGRAMMABLE – which permitted the creation of special machine instructions to support efficient language implementation. The Dorado had a high-resolution graphical screen, a MOUSE and local HARD DISK storage, much like a modern PC. It was never on sale to the public, being manufactured in hundreds only for PARC researchers. See also XEROX STAR.

Xerox PARC See under PARC.

Xerox Star The first commercial computer to employ a GRAPHICAL USER INTERFACE, developed at Xerox PARC and launched in 1981. Designed as a workstation for corporate word processing, the Star was the first attempt to provide WYSIWYG printing. It featured a MOUSE, a high-resolution black-and-white graphical monitor with variable FONTS and an ICON-based user interface. The Star failed commercially because of its very high price and a general incomprehension of its abilities among both customers and Xerox management. However it was seeing a Star during a visit to PARC that prompted Steve JOBS to make the Apple LISA (and eventually the MACINTOSH). See also XEROX DORADO.

XGA (eXtended Graphics Array) The last of IBM's proprietary GRAPHICS ADAPTERS, introduced in 1990 as a replacement for the 8514/A adapter for professional graphics applications. With 1 megabyte of video memory, the XGA adapter supported resolutions up to 1024 ×768 in 256 colours (8 bits per pixel) and 640× 480 in 65,536 colours (16 bits per pixel). It is still supported as a resolution standard on many LAPTOP and NOTEBOOK computers, though desktop systems have moved on to higher resolutions. See also CGA, EGA, VGA, SUPER VGA.

x-height An indication of the height of the LOWER CASE letters in a line of text, taken as the height of the lower case letter x, measured in printer's POINTS. Characters with ASCENDERS and DESCENDERS therefore exceed the x-height.

Xilinx Inc. A US manufacture of FIELD-PROGRAMMABLE GATE ARRAY chips.

xlisp A subset of the COMMON LISP programming language that is available as FREEWARE for many personal computers.

XLL (Extensible Link Language) A language, still under development, that will be used to defined HYPERTEXT links from WEB PAGES written in XML. In HTML, an HREF link is an absolute address (see ABSOLUTE ADDRESSING) fixed into the code of a page, but XLL will support indirect links that do not break when their target moves to a new address. Other features will include different types of link, bi-directional links, links to multiple addresses, and the separation of links from their documents so that they can be managed separately.

XML (Extensible Markup Language) A document MARKUP LANGUAGE adopted by the WORLD WIDE WEB CONSORTIUM as a future standard that will eventually displace HTML as the language for writing WEB PAGES. XML is a simplified subset of SGML and, unlike HTML, it permits programmers to define new markup TAGS and their meanings for each particular kind of application. As in SGML, the grammar of such new XML tags may be defined in a separate HEADER FILE called a DOCUMENT TYPE DEFINITION, which is downloaded along with the page code and read by the browser. XML cannot be read by a standard HTML browser, and all the major web browsers are being enhanced to handle XML.

XML divorces presentation from structure by employing separate STYLE SHEETS, written in XSL. These describe the way a page should appear (e.g. its layout, fonts and colours), so the same information can be viewed or printed in radically different ways simply by swapping to a new style sheet. XML also fixes the 'broken link' problem caused by HTML's one-way, hard-coded hypertext links. Separate link definitions written in XLL can describe two-way links and indirect links that are not broken if their target moves to a new address.

XMM Abbreviation of EXTENDED MEMORY MANAGER.

XMODEM A FILE TRANSFER protocol that was very popular in the early days of personal computer communications, until it was displaced by the superior ZMODEM.

XMS Abbreviation of EXTENDED MEMORY SPECIFICATION.

XON/XOFF A software FLOW CONTROL protocol for SERIAL communications lines that employs the two characters XON (ASCII code 17) and XOFF (ASCII code 19) as commands to start and stop transmissions. See also HANDSHAKE.

X/Open An international consortium of UNIX software vendors, founded in 1984, whose purpose was to define a Common Applications Environment to assist the portability of applications between different versions of the Unix operating system. Its main publication was the X/Open Portability Guide or XPG. In 1994 Novell gave the international trademark 'Unix' (which it had bought from AT&T) to X/Open, and in 1996 X/Open merged with the OPEN SOFTWARE FOUNDATION to create The Open Group. See also POSIX, OPEN SYSTEMS.

XOR Exclusive OR. A BOOLEAN operator whose result is true only if one or the other, but not both, of its arguments are true. Its truth table is therefore:

A	B	A xor B
T	T	F
T	F	T
F	T	T
F	F	F

where T=true and F=false. The XOR operation is frequently employed in BITMAPPED graphics to reverse an image out of its background. See also OR, AND.

X protocol The protocol used to transmit screen images, mouse and keyboard events over a network or serial link between two computers running the X WINDOW SYSTEM. X protocol messages consist of lists of commands that draw primitive graphical objects such as lines and filled shapes. These are interpreted by the X SERVER running on the receiving machine to draw its own screen contents. See also INTELLIGENT CONSOLE ARCHITECTURE, DISPLAY POSTSCRIPT, HTML.

x-ray Electromagnetic radiation with a wavelength between 10^{-8} metres and 10^{-11} metres that is generated by bombarding matter with high-speed electrons. X-rays are highly penetrating and may be employed for photographing the interior structure of solid objects (as for example in medicine) and in some advanced types of semiconductor LITHOGRAPHY.

x-ray lithography The use of x-rays to illuminate the MASK representing an INTEGRATED CIRCUIT and project it onto a silicon WAFER. In principle, x-rays (with their shorter wavelengths) permit smaller FEATURE SIZES to be accurately reproduced than do visible or ULTRAVIOLET light. However, the extreme difficulty of generating and focusing x-rays, and of finding a mask material that is opaque to them, has so far prevented commercial adoption of the process.

xref An abbreviation for CROSS-REFERENCE that is also the name of a UNIX programmers' cross-referencing tool.

X server Under the X WINDOW SYSTEM, software that runs on a computer that is required to display the USER INTERFACE of a CLIENT program running on a remote machine. The job of the X server is to interpret a stream of X PROTOCOL commands and draw the remote program's screen contents on the local display. It is therefore highly hardware-dependent, and a different X server must be written for each type of X TERMINAL.

XSL (Extensible Style Language) The language used to specify STYLE SHEETS that define the appearance of XML documents. A web browser that understands XSL can change the presentation of a web page (for example to omit some elements, show them in a different order, or a different font) by merely swapping to a different style sheet without having to access the server again. XSL will permit layout styles that are not possible in HTML (such as rotated and multicolumn text). XSL is still in the process of being defined by the W3C. See also CASCADING STYLE SHEETS.

X standards A series of global standards for telecommunications issued by the ITU, whose names all take the form X.n. For example X.25 was the first standard for PACKET SWITCHING data networks; X.400 is a standard for electronic mail; X.75 is a standard for MODEMS. See also V STANDARDS.

XT bus Another name for the ISA BUS.

xterm A TERMINAL EMULATOR utility for the X WINDOW SYSTEM.

X terminal A computer that can be used to run programs on a remote SERVER under the X WINDOW SYSTEM by displaying the user interface of the remote program on its own screen. Any type of computer of sufficient power, and capable of displaying graphics, can be made into an X terminal by implementing an X SERVER program for it.

XVGA (eXtended Video Graphics Array) A graphics display standard derived from the specification of IBM's 8514/A card but popularized by other manufacturers of IBM-compatible GRAPHICS ADAPTERS. It supports 1024×768 pixels in 256 colours and is still to be found as a standard for LCD display on some low-cost laptop and notebook computers. See also VGA, XGA.

XVT A CROSS-PLATFORM development tool that enables the same program to be compiled to run under the Windows Macintosh, Unix and OS/2 USER INTERFACES.

X-Windows A double misspelling of the X WINDOW SYSTEM.

X Window System A distributed display technology for UNIX computers that allows users to interact with an APPLICATION PROGRAM from a computer other than the one that the program is running on. The X Window System provides a typical GRAPHICAL USER INTERFACE using a BITMAPPED display to create overlapping screen WINDOWS, POP-UP MENUS and selection via a MOUSE POINTER – but display and keyboard and mouse input may all take place on a REMOTE networked computer rather than the one that the application program is running on.

X Window System is a CLIENT/SERVER system, in which display and input become remote services provided to the application program. Hence the application is called an X client, while the software running on the display computer is called the X server. This nomenclature somewhat confusingly reverses the normal conventions, since the application (i.e. the X client) is usually running on a server while the X server runs on a workstation (ie. what is normally called a client).

A dedicated x PROTOCOL carries messages containing display instructions to the X server, and carries input events such as keypresses and mouse movements back to the X client. Rather than sending bulky BITMAPS over the network to create the screen display, X protocol sends compact drawing instructions that are executed by the X server soft-ware – a trade-off that reduces the required network BANDWIDTH by requiring considerable graphical processing power in the X server.

The X Window System was invented at MIT as part of project Athena to provide a campus-wide multimedia computer service to students, and its name reflects the fact that it superceded another remote windowing system called W Window. Its name is very commonly misspelled as X-Windows in many publications: it should be neither hyphenated nor pluralized.

Y

Y2K A computer trade abbreviation for Year 2000.

yacc Short for 'yet another compiler compiler'. A UNIX software tool that can generate a PARSER for a new programming language from a description of its SYNTAX written in yacc notation (a modified version of BACKUS-NAUR FORM).

Yahoo! One of the earliest and most popular web SEARCH ENGINES, which went on to become the first and most popular web PORTAL.

Year 2000 bug Often jargonized as Y2K bug. The inability of many computer systems, both hardware and software, to cope with a change of century. The most common cause was storing years as two-digit numbers, the transition from 99 to 00 thus being incorrectly interpreted as a rolling back of time. (This is not strictly speaking a bug but a short-sighted design decision, made in the early days of computing in order to economise on storage space). Other causes included the ill-advised placing of a presumed 'false' date of 9/9/99 to mark the end of some date-based data sequence, and the use of clock/calendar chips that had only a two digit register for year values.

Year 2000 compliant Software or hardware that is guaranteed not to incorrectly display dates after 1st January 2000.

Yellow Book The document published in 1983 by Sony and Philips that defines the physical data format for CD-ROM disks. See also ISO 9660, RED BOOK, GREEN BOOK, ORANGE BOOK, WHITE BOOK.

Yet Another... A humorous naming tradition among UNIX programmers for new versions of much-revised utilities, as in YACC (yet another compiler compiler).

YHM Online shorthand for You Have Mail. Used in group discussion forums such as NEWSGROUPS to initiate a private correspondence by email.

YMODEM A once-popular file transfer protocol (FTP) that displaced XMODEM and was itself overtaken by the now-preferred ZMODEM.

Yourdon method One of the earliest SOFTWARE ENGINEERING methodologies based on DATAFLOW diagrams, invented in the 1970's by Edward Yourdon. It has since spawned many variants such as Coad/Yourdon, Yourdon/Demarco, Yourdon/Constantine. See also METHODOLOGY.

Z

Z A specification language used to produce formal descriptions of computer systems, based on SET THEORY and first-order PREDICATE CALCULUS. Z was developed at Oxford University and used by IBM in developing CICS.

Z80 One of the most successful 8-bit microprocessors, released by the ZILOG Corporation in 1976. The Z80 was used in many personal computers of the early 1980s, including the ZX80 (see SINCLAIR COMPUTERS), which took its name from the chip. The Z80's popularity with computer designers derived from its instruction compatibility with the earlier INTEL CORPORATION 8080 (which enabled it to run the popular CP/M operating system) and the fact that it generated its own DRAM REFRESH signals (which made memory systems simpler and cheaper to design). Later, faster derivatives of the Z80 are still used today as EMBEDDED CONTROLLERS in toys and other small electrical appliances.

ZBR Abbreviation of ZONED-BIT RECORDING.

Z-buffer A hardware design used to accelerate 3D GRAPHICS systems by omitting the parts of an image that would not be visible from the current viewpoint. An extra memory bank called the Z-buffer stores the depth of the last PIXEL to be drawn at each screen location X,Y; before any pixel gets drawn, its depth coordinate Z is compared to the value currently in the Z-buffer and if greater (i.e. farther from the viewer), that pixel is ignored.

zero insertion force (ZIF) A type of socket for mounting large integrated circuits (typically microprocessors) that are packaged in PIN GRID ARRAYS. It consists of a grid of holes that only loosely fit the pins of the package – the chip is then locked into place by depressing a lever on the socket that moves a sliding shutter to grip all the pins tightly. The name reflects the fact that fitting such large chips into the older style of friction-gripped socket would have required too much force and would have damaged the pins.

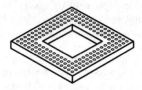

zero latency read A feature of HARD DISK drives, in which a read operation is begun as soon as *any* block of a requested TRACK passes under the head, rather than waiting for a particular block to come around. If a whole track has been requested, as is typically the case in systems that employ a DISK CACHE, this speeds access, though it cannot speed up the location of individual blocks.

zero-wait-state memory See under WAIT STATE.

ZIF Abbreviation of ZERO INSERTION FORCE.

Zilog A US semiconductor manufacturer whose 8-bit Z80 microprocessor dominated the personal computer industry for a while in the early 1980s, until displaced by the IBM-PC's Intel 8088. Zilog still makes variants of the Z80 in large quantities for use as low-cost EMBEDDED CONTROLLERS. See also CP/M.

zinc-air battery A battery technology that offers three times greater energy density by weight than the NICAD or NICKEL METAL HYDRIDE CELL, promising working times of 12 hours per charge in laptop computer applications. Problems over physical bulk and a limited number of recharge cycles have so far inhibited its general adoption.

zinc–carbon cell Originally named the Leclanché cell after its inventor, the oldest type of non-rechargeable battery, which employs its zinc outer casing as the CATHODE, with a central carbon rod as the ANODE immersed in an ammonium chloride paste electrolyte. Known as torch and radio batteries, zinc-carbon cells were the only low-cost disposable batteries available for most of the 20th century, until they were displaced by the ALKALINE CELL in the 1990s.

zine See E-ZINE.

zip disk The removable storage disk used in a ZIP DRIVE.

Zip drive A disk storage device, made by Iomega, that uses removable media. It is available for both internal and external mounting and in two versions with media capacities of 100 megabytes or 250 megabytes per diskette. The removable 3.5 inch Zip diskettes are enclosed in plastic casings, and employ BERNOULLI DRIVE technology. See also SUPER-FLOPPY.

zip file A file compressed by the popular SHAREWARE utility PKZIP, widely used on MS-DOS and Windows computers and originally developed by the US company PKWARE. The term is also used as a verb – 'to zip' means to compress one or more files into such a zip file either for archival purposes, or to speed their transfer over the Internet. Zip has became a *de facto* standard, and there are now many utilities from companies other than PKWare that can compress and expand zip files.

Zip files are compressed using a variant of the LZW COMPRESSION algorithm. See also WINZIP, TAR, STUFFIT, FILE COMPRESSION.

ZMODEM The most widely used file transfer protocol (FTP) outside of the Unix and Internet worlds – particularly popular with DIAL-UP services based on IBM-compatible PCs. ZMODEM's most attractive characteristics are its efficiency, and its ability to automatically restart where it left off after losing a connection – a feature that its Unix equivalent FTP

lacks, and which must be supplied by extra utilities.

zone **1** A categorization employed by Microsoft's INTERNET EXPLORER browser for AUTHENTICATION purposes. It divides the networked world into regions in ascending order of the level of security risk they pose: the Intranet Zone means a local network, while the Trusted, Restricted and Internet zones are for external sites. Explorer defaults to automatic log-on for the Intranet zone, but not for the Internet zone (the outside world).

2 A set of TRACKS on a HARD DISK. See more under ZONED-BIT RECORDING.

3 A logical subset of the NODES on an APPLE-TALK network.

zoned-bit recording (ZBR) A technique for increasing the storage capacity of HARD DISK drives by writing more SECTORS onto the longer outer tracks than on the inner tracks.

zoom The ability to enlarge a selected portion of a digital image or text, provided by most drawing and painting programs, and by some word processors and web browsers.

Zoomed Video (ZV) A video port, fitted to many LAPTOP and NOTEBOOK computers, that supports the input of full motion video streams (including MPEG 1 streams) from video cameras and TV tuners. The ZV port is based on a modification of the Type II PC CARD format, and is capable of transferring 27 megabytes per second, or 24-bit colour at 640×480 resolution at 30 frames per second.

Zoomer A type of hand-held computer made by Casio.

Zork An early text-based adventure game, written at MIT in the 1970s. It still retains a certain popularity.

ZV Abbreviation of ZOOMED VIDEO.

ZX80 See SINCLAIR COMPUTERS.

ZX81 See SINCLAIR COMPUTERS.

Zyxel A successful US manufacturer of network HUBS, ROUTERS and MODEMS.